Alcohol-induced mood disorder
Alcohol-induced anxiety disorder
Alcohol-induced sexual dysfunction
Alcohol-induced sleep disorder
Alcohol-related disorder NOS

## Amphetamine (or Amphetamine-Like)–Related Disorders

*Amphetamine Use Disorders*
Amphetamine dependence
Amphetamine abuse

*Amphetamine-Induced Disorders*
Amphetamine intoxication
Amphetamine withdrawal
Amphetamine intoxication delirium
Amphetamine-induced psychotic disorder
   With delusions
   With hallucinations
Amphetamine-induced mood disorder
Amphetamine-induced anxiety disorder
Amphetamine-induced sexual dysfunction
Amphetamine-induced sleep disorder
Amphetamine-related disorder NOS

## Caffeine-Related Disorders

*Caffeine-Induced Disorders*
Caffeine intoxication
Caffeine-induced anxiety disorder
Caffeine-induced sleep disorder
Caffeine-related disorder NOS

## Cannabis-Related Disorders

*Cannabis Use Disorders*
Cannabis dependence
Cannabis abuse

*Cannabis-Induced Disorders*
Cannabis intoxication
Cannabis intoxication delirium
Cannabis-induced psychotic disorder
   With delusions
   With hallucinations
Cannabis-induced anxiety disorder
Cannabis-related disorder NOS

## Cocaine-Related Disorders

*Cocaine Use Disorders*
Cocaine dependence
Cocaine abuse

*Cocaine-Induced Disorders*
Cocaine intoxication
Cocaine withdrawal
Cocaine intoxication delirium
Cocaine-induced psychotic disorder
   With delusions
   With hallucinations
Cocaine-induced mood disorder

Cocaine-induced anxiety disorder
Cocaine-induced sexual dysfunction
Cocaine-induced sleep disorder
Cocaine-related disorder NOS

## Hallucinogen-Related Disorders

*Hallucinogen Use Disorders*
Hallucinogen dependence
Hallucinogen abuse

*Hallucinogen-Induced Disorders*
Hallucinogen intoxication
Hallucinogen persisting perception disorder (flashbacks)
Hallucinogen intoxication delirium
Hallucinogen-induced psychotic disorder
   With delusions
   With hallucinations
Hallucinogen-induced mood disorder
Hallucinogen-induced anxiety disorder
Hallucinogen-related disorder NOS

## Inhalant-Related Disorders

*Inhalant Use Disorders*
Inhalant dependence
Inhalant abuse

*Inhalant-Induced Disorders*
Inhalant intoxication
Inhalant intoxication delirium
Inhalant-induced persisting dementia
Inhalant-induced psychotic disorder
   With delusions
   With hallucinations
Inhalant-induced mood disorder
Inhalant-induced anxiety disorder
Inhalant-related disorder NOS

## Nicotine-Related Disorders

*Nicotine Use Disorder*
Nicotine dependence

*Nicotine-Induced Disorder*
Nicotine withdrawal
Nicotine-related disorder NOS

## Opioid-Related Disorders

*Opioid Use Disorders*
Opiod dependence
Opiod abuse

*Opioid-Induced Disorders*
Opioid intoxication
Opioid withdrawal
Opioid intoxication delirium
Opioid-induced psychotic disorder
   With delusions
   With hallucinations
Opioid-induced mood disorder
Opioid-induced sexual dysfunction

Opioid-induced sleep disorder
Opioid-related disorder NOS

## Phencyclidine (or Phencyclidine-Like)–Related Disorders

*Phencyclidine Use Disorders*
Phencyclidine dependence
Phencyclidine abuse

*Phencyclidine-Induced Disorders*
Phencyclidine intoxication
Phencyclidine intoxication delirium
Phencyclidine-induced psychotic disorder
   With delusions
   With hallucinations
Phencyclidine-induced mood disorder
Phencyclidine-induced anxiety disorder
Phencyclidine-related disorder NOS

## Sedative-, Hypnotic-, or Anxiolytic-Related Disorders

*Sedative, Hypnotic, or Anxiolytic Use Disorders*
Sedative, hypnotic, or anxiolytic dependence
Sedative, hypnotic, or anxiolytic abuse

*Sedative-, Hypnotic-, or Anxiolytic-Induced Disorders*
Sedative, hypnotic, or anxiolytic intoxication
Sedative, hypnotic, or anxiolytic withdrawal
Sedative, hypnotic, or anxiolytic intoxication delirium
Sedative, hypnotic, or anxiolytic withdrawal delirium
Sedative-, hypnotic-, or anxiolytic-induced persisting dementia
Sedative-, hypnotic-, or anxiolytic-induced persisting amnestic disorder
Sedative-, hypnotic-, or anxiolytic-induced psychotic disorder
   With delusions
   With hallucinations
Sedative-, hypnotic-, or anxiolytic-induced mood disorder
Sedative-, hypnotic-, or anxiolytic-induced anxiety disorder
Sedative-, hypnotic-, or anxiolytic-induced sexual dysfunction
Sedative-, hypnotic-, or anxiolytic-induced sleep disorder
Sedative-, hypnotic-, or anxiolytic-related disorder NOS

*(continued on inside back cover)*

# Fundamentals
# of
# Abnormal
# Psychology

# Fundamentals
# of
# Abnormal
# Psychology

## Ronald J. Comer
Princeton University

**W. H. Freeman and Company**
New York

*To Greg and Jon,*
*with great love and pride*

**Library of Congress Cataloging-in-Publication Data**

Comer, Ronald J.
    Fundamentals of abnormal psychology / Ronald J. Comer.
      p.   cm.
    Includes bibliographical references and index
    ISBN 0-7167-2717-X
    1. Psychology, Pathological.    I. Title.
  RC454.C6343 1996
  616.89--dc20

                                       95-32648
                                         CIP

© 1996 by W. H. Freeman and Company

Printed in the United States of America

First printing 1995, RRD

# Contents in Brief

# Contents

## Chapter 15
## Disorders of Childhood and Old Age       *399*

## Chapter 16
## Personality Disorders       *431*

## Chapter 17
## Law, Society, and the Mental Health Profession       *459*

# *Preface*

*I* have been extremely gratified by the success of my textbook *Abnormal Psychology* over the past four years. Many professors and students have found it to be just the textbook they need, and they have praised its readability, rich clinical and research material, and striking art and photography. Along with this positive reaction, however, my publisher and I have received from another group of professors pleas that have gnawed at my obsessive mind. Although they too have liked the book a great deal, these professors have found it to be too long for the students at their particular schools, where the length of the semester, the students' general workload, or the educational goals of their course dictate a shorter book. A number of these professors suggested that I also write a second textbook similar in quality and tone to the first, but more moderate in length and level of detail. From these suggestions has grown a new textbook, *Fundamentals of Abnormal Psychology*.

I kept two goals in mind while writing *Fundamentals of Abnormal Psychology*: moderate length and scholastic integrity. I believe that the textbook delivers on both counts.

## Features and Strengths

1. **MODERATE IN LENGTH, SOLID IN CONTENT:** Even though *Fundamentals of Abnormal Psychology* is of moderate length, it offers balanced and probing coverage of its broad and dynamic subject. It expands and challenges students' thinking rather than short-changing or underestimating their intellectual capacity.

2. **NUMEROUS PEDAGOGICAL TOOLS:** A number of learning aids have been introduced throughout the book to help students effectively absorb the material. These include a *running glossary* at the bottom of the text pages; *critical-thinking questions* (under the rubric, "Consider This"); periodic *short summaries* within each chapter; *frequent tables* that summarize and compare information about the various disorders; and at the end of each chapter, a thorough "Chapter Review," lists of "Key Terms," and a "Quick Quiz."

3. **BALANCED COVERAGE:** The major psychological, biological, and sociocultural models are presented in a balanced and integrated way. This is not predominantly a psychodynamic or behavioral or biological or any other type of textbook. *Fundamentals of Abnormal Psychology* is a book about all these models.

4. **BROAD COVERAGE OF TREATMENT:** Complete discussions of treatment are presented throughout the book. In addition to presentations of treatment theories, techniques, and issues in the early introductory chapters, each of the pathology chapters includes a full discussion of relevant treatment approaches.

5. **RICH CASE MATERIAL:** Numerous actual clinical examples bring clinical, theoretical, and treatment considerations to life. Discussion of specific case studies is interwoven throughout.

6. **A FOCUS ON ETHNIC AND GENDER ISSUES:** Issues raised by ethnic and gender differences, as well as related problems of bias, are given constant consideration throughout the book.

7. **TOPICS OF SPECIAL INTEREST:** The book devotes full chapters to certain important subjects that are of special interest to college-age readers, such as eating disorders, suicide, and memory disorders. It also provides balanced assessments of controversial issues (for example, repressed memories of childhood abuse, and stalking) that are currently being spotlighted by the news media.

8. **READABILITY:** The book is written with a single voice, in clear and straightforward language. This, I believe, is the primary advantage of having a single author. Moreover, in writing the book, I have tried to

communicate my excitement, enthusiasm, and sense of discovery about abnormal psychology.

9. **A FOCUS ON CRITICAL THINKING:** The book provides tools for thinking critically about abnormal psychology. Readers acquire an ability to assess and question current beliefs and process new knowledge effectively. As noted earlier, each chapter includes a number of critical-thinking questions. Further, each pathology chapter ends with a "State of the Field" section that integrates the information and ideas coming from different theoretical fronts and provides a sense of perspective about where the clinical field is today, where it came from, and where it seems to be going.

10. **DSM-IV:** The clinical discussions in the textbook are organized around the field's new diagnostic system, DSM-IV. The definitions, diagnoses, and criteria set forth in DSM-IV are fully integrated into the book.

11. **COVERAGE OF ORGANICITY:** Disorders that were distinguished as organic mental disorders in past DSMs are integrated throughout the book, in keeping with the structure of the current DSM, particularly in the chapters on substance-related disorders (Chapter 11), memory disorders (Chapter 14), and disorders of childhood and aging (Chapter 15).

## Supplements

The kinds of supplemental materials that are proving so successful with my other textbook are available with this one as well. Each has been prepared to correspond in level, content, and format to *Fundamentals of Abnormal Psychology*. They are:

- The *Student Workbook* by Katherine M. Nicolai of Rockhurst College actively engages the student with the material in the textbook by means of a variety of intriguing and innovative exercises. Completing the exercises allows students to better organize and apply their studies and also provides them with a clear set of study notes.

- A comprehensive *Test Bank* written by Melvyn B. King of the State University of New York at Cortland and Debra E. Clark of the New Medico Rehabilitation Center of Cortland offers approximately 2,000 multiple-choice and fill-in questions. Each question is graded according to its difficulty, identified as either factual or applied, and keyed to the page in the textbook where the source information appears.

- Computerized versions of the *Test Bank* are available in both Macintosh and IBM formats.

- For the first time, a full-color *Overhead Transparency Set* is offered, consisting of 40 key figures from the textbook to aid during lecture presentations.

- I have prepared a special package of *Video Segments for Abnormal Psychology* designed to be integrated into lectures. This package consists of 50 video segments, each between 1 and 8 minutes in length, which illustrate or present clinical topics, pathologies, treatments, historical footage, laboratory experiments, clinical dilemmas, and more. They are taken from a variety of sources including clinical documentaries, special filmings at clinical sites, and client and therapist interviews. This package saves instructors potentially long searches for the right enriching and relevant example of footage for a lecture.

- Tying all these supplements together is the *Instructor's Manual and Video Guide,* which I and Fred W. Whitford of Montana State University have prepared. Included in this extensive supplement will be a comprehensive guide to the *Video Segments* with descriptions and topical listings for each segment and specific recommendations for their use with the textbook; strategies for using the *Student Workbook, Test Bank,* and *Overhead Transparency Set* images; and, in response to many requests, the precise DSM-IV criteria for the various psychological disorders discussed in the textbook. Additionally, instructors will find thorough chapter outlines and a large selection of teaching suggestions. The *Instructor's Resource Manual* has been designed to be valuable for first-time and veteran instructors alike.

- *Abnormal psychology newsletters* will be sent to adopters of the textbook on a regular basis between editions. Newsletters will update topics in the textbook, providing new information and research and new ideas for lecture topics, classroom demonstrations, and homework assignments.

## Acknowledgments

I am enormously grateful to the many people who have contributed to the writing and production of this textbook. Indeed, their efforts have meant much more to me than I can possibly express.

I particularly thank Marlene Comer (whose last name is more than a coincidence) for her never-ending, superb work on just about every aspect of the manuscript, from editorial judgments to typing. In addition, I am indebted to Linda Chamberlin, Marion Kowalewski, Arlene Kronewitter, Vera Sohl, Arlene Kerch, Elaine Bacsik, Bernie Van Uiter, Drew Cutler, Lorraine Garratt, Amy Harris, Greg Comer, and Jon Comer for their wonderful help.

Not to be forgotten are professors Joseph LoPiccolo, Dolores Gallagher-Thompson, and Larry Thompson, who contributed chapters to my other textbook on the subjects of sexual disorders and problems of aging. Guest chapters are not included in the current volume; however, as my citations indicate, the wisdom of these superb academicians certainly enhances my coverage of those topics in *Fundamentals of Abnormal Psychology*.

I also wish to thank my good friend, Professor Joseph Palladino, University of Southern Indiana, for writing most of the critical-thinking ("Consider This") questions throughout the textbook. The questions always raise provocative points and start the reader thinking about the implications of the material under study.

Throughout my work on this textbook, I have also received valuable feedback and ideas from a number of outstanding academicians and clinicians, who have reviewed portions of the manuscript: Otto Berliner, Alfred State College; Steve Collins, Rio Hondo Community College; John Conklin, Camosun College; Marjorie Hatch, Southern Methodist University; Mary Livingston, Louisiana Tech University; and Charles Spirrison, Mississippi State University. Their suggestions and insights have found their way into the textbook, and I am indebted to them. In the same vein, I wish to acknowledge and thank once again the individuals who served as reviewers of *Abnormal Psychology*. Their contributions remain integral to the accuracy and soundness of *Fundamentals of Abnormal Psychology*. They include Kent G. Bailey, Virginia Commonwealth University; Marna S. Barrett, Indiana University of Pennsylvania; Allan Berman, University of Rhode Island; Douglas Bernstein, University of Illinois; Kirk R. Blankstein, University of Toronto in Mississauga; Sarah Cirese, College of Marin; Victor B. Cline, University of Utah; S. Wayne Duncan, University of Washington (Seattle); Morris N. Eagle, York University; Alan Fridlund, University of California, Santa Barbara; Stan Friedman, Southwest Texas State University; Lawrence L. Galant, Gaston College, NC; David A. Hoffman, University of California, Santa Cruz; Bernard Kleinman, University of Missouri, Kansas City; Alan G. Krasnoff, University of Missouri, St. Louis; Robert D. Langston, University of Texas, Austin; Harvey R. Lerner, Kaiser-Pemanente Medical Group; Michael P. Levine, Kenyon College; Janet R. Matthews, Loyola University; Robert J. McCaffrey, State University of New York, Albany; Jeffery Scott Mio, Washington State University; Katherine M. Nico-

lai, Iowa State University; Paul A. Payne, University of Cincinnati; David V. Perkins, Ball State University; Norman Poppel, Middlesex County College; David E. Powley, University of Mobile; Max W. Rardin, University of Wyoming, Laramie; Leslie A. Rescorla, Bryn Mawr College; Vic Ryan, University of Colorado, Boulder; A. A. Sappington, University of Alabama, Birmingham; Roberta S. Sherman, Bloomington Center for Counseling and Human Development; David E. Silber, The George Washington University; Janet A Simons, Central Iowa Psychological Services; Jay R. Skidmore, Utah State University; Thomas A. Tutko, San Jose State University; Norris D. Vestre, Arizona State University; Joseph L. White, University of California, Irvine; and Amy C. Willis, Washington D.C. Veterans Administration Medical Center.

I am also indebted to the team of highly skilled professionals at W. H. Freeman and Company with whom I have worked so closely on this project. I particularly want to mention the book's brilliant developmental editor, Moira Lerner; extraordinary project editor, Diane Cimino Maass; gifted art director, Armen Kojoyian; insightful photo researcher, Travis Amos; and W. H. Freeman's visionary psychology editor, Susan Finnemore Brennan. I am not just being modest when I say that this book is as much theirs as it is mine. In addition, I would like to thank the book's production coordinator, Paul Rohloff; designer, Laura Ierardi; cover artist, Bruno Paciuli; assistant editor, Larry Marcus; and indexer, Bernice Soltysik, all of whom have performed superbly and contributed so much to this undertaking.

I also wish to thank Marie Schappert, vice-president of academic sales and marketing; John Britch, marketing manager; and all of Freeman's regional sales managers and sales representatives whose outstanding skills and enormous efforts have brought my textbooks to the attention of professors around the country.

Finally, I would like to thank and express my love to my family and, in particular, to Marlene, Greg, Jon, and Annie (bow-wow), whose day-in–day-out presence in my life sustains me and makes all things, including this book, possible. In case I forget to mention it sometimes, I feel very fortunate that they share their lives with me.

**Ron Comer**
*September 1995*

Table 6-1 *Anxiety Disorders Profile*

| | One-Year Prevalence | Female:Male Ratio | Typical Age of Onset | Prevalence among Close Relatives |
|---|---|---|---|---|
| Panic disorders | 2.3% | 5:2 | 15–35 years | Elevated |
| Obsessive-compulsive disorder | 2.0% | 1:1 | 4–25 years | Elevated |
| Acute and posttraumatic stress disorders | 0.5% | 1:1 | Variable | Unknown |

Sources: APA, 1994; Kessler et al., 1994; Regier et al., 1993; Eaton et al., 1991; Blazer et al., 1991; Davidson et al., 1991.

misdiagnosed as panic disorder and nothing else (Coplan et al., 1992; Agras, 1985).

A panic disorder is often accompanied by agoraphobia (fear of venturing into public places), a pattern that DSM-IV terms **panic disorder with agoraphobia.** In such cases, the agoraphobic pattern usually seems to emerge from the panic attacks (Barlow, 1988). After experiencing unpredictable and recurrent panic attacks, people become fearful of having one someplace where help is unavailable or escape difficult. Anne Watson was one such person:

> Ms. Watson reported that until the onset of her current problems two years ago, she had led a normal and happy life. At that time an uncle to whom she had been extremely close in her childhood died following a sudden unexpected heart attack. . . . Six months after his death she was returning home from work one evening when suddenly she felt that she couldn't catch her breath. Her heart began to pound, and she broke out into a cold sweat. Things began to seem unreal, her legs felt leaden, and she became sure she would die or faint before she reached home. She asked a passerby to help her get a taxi and went to a nearby hospital emergency room. The doctors there found her physical examination, blood count and chemistries, and electrocardiogram all completely normal. . . .

Four weeks later Ms. Watson had a second similar attack while preparing dinner at home. She made an appointment to see her family doctor, but again, all examinations were normal. She decided to put the episodes out of her mind and continue with her normal activities. Within the next several weeks, however, she had four attacks and noticed that she began to worry about when the next one would occur. . . .

She then found herself constantly thinking about her anxieties as attacks continued; she began to dread leaving the house alone for fear she would be stranded, helpless and alone, by an attack. She began to avoid going to movies, parties, and dinners with friends for fear she would have an attack and be embarrassed by her need to leave. When household chores necessitated driving, she waited until it was possible to take her children or a friend along for the ride. She also began walking the twenty blocks to her offi...

Obsessive-compulsive disorder 41.3%
Panic disorder 54.4%

PERCENTAGE OF AFFLICTED ADULTS RECEIVING TREATMENT EACH YEAR — MILLI...

Figure 6-1 *Who receives treatment for their anxiety disorders? More th... persons who have a panic disorder and more than 40 percent of those with... compulsive disorder in the United States receive professional treatment eac... 2.2 million people in all. (Adapted from Regier et al., 1993; Blazer et al., 1990.)*

---

*Although most people are terrified by the very thought of hang gliding above the clouds, some are stimulated by the experience and others are calmed by it. Such individual reactions represent differences in situation, or state, anxiety.*

known as the **sympathetic nervous system**) that quicken our heartbeat and produce the other changes that we experience as fear or anxiety. When a perceived danger passes, a second group of ANS nerve fibers, the **parasympathetic nervous system**, return our heartbeat and other body processes to normal. Together, these two parts of the ANS help regulate our fear and anxiety reactions and enable our body to maintain both the stability and the adaptability essential to life.

We all have our own level of ongoing anxiety. Some people are always relaxed, while others almost always feel some tension, even when no threat is apparent. A person's general level of anxiety is sometimes called **trait anxiety,** because it seems to be a trait or characteristic that the person brings to each event in life (Spielberger, 1985, 1966). People also differ in their sense of which situations are threatening. Walking through a forest, for example, may be fearsome for one person but relaxing for another. Such variations are called differences in **situation, or state, anxiety.** The fear and anxiety most of us have experienced, however, are quite different from the disproportionate, frequent, and enduring waves of tension and dread experienced by persons who suffer from an anxiety disorder.

*Summing Up*
*We all experience fear and anxiety in life, particularly in the face of stressors that we appraise as threatening. We each have different levels of ongoing anxiety, and we each find certain situations more threatening than others. Only some of us, however, experience an anxiety disorder.*

## Generalized Anxiety Disorder

> Bob Donaldson was a 22-year-old carpenter referred to the psychiatric outpatient department of a community hospital. . . . During the initial interview Bob was visibly distressed. He appeared tense, worried, and frightened. He sat on the edge of his chair, tapping his foot and fidgeting with a pencil on the psychiatrist's desk. He sighed frequently, took deep breaths between sentences, and periodically exhaled audibly and changed his position as he attempted to relate his story:
>
> BOB: It's been an awful month. I can't seem to do anything. I don't know whether I'm coming or going. I'm afraid I'm going crazy or something.

---

result, and the child may develop into an adult with an "anal character," prone to be stubborn, contrary, stingy, or overcontrolling.

*Consider This*
*In our society there are many people who fit the description of an oral or anal character, but are these styles necessarily the result of fixation at early stages of development? What other explanations can you suggest? Are there ways in which oral or anal traits may be constructive and beneficial?*

During the **phallic stage,** between the third and fourth years, the focus of sexual pleasure shifts to the genitals—the penis for boys and the clitoris for girls. Boys become attracted to their mother as a fully separate object, a sexual object, and see their father as a rival they would like to push aside. This pattern of desires is called the **Oedipus complex,** after Oedipus, a character in a Greek tragedy who unknowingly kills his father and marries his mother.

The phallic conflict for girls is somewhat different. During this stage, girls become aware that they do not have a penis—an organ that, according to Freud, they value and desire (so-called **penis envy**). They develop a sexual attraction for their father, rooted in the fantasy that by seducing him they can have a penis. This pattern of desires in girls is called the **Electra complex,** after Electra, a character in another Greek tragedy who conspired to kill her mother to avenge her father's death.

Both boys and girls fear that they will be punished for their phallic impulses, and so they repress these desires and identify with the parent of their own sex. Boys aspire to be like their fathers and girls to be like their mothers in every way. If children are punished too harshly for sexual behavior during this stage, or if they are subtly encouraged to pursue their desire for the parent of the opposite sex, they might later develop a sexual orientation different from the norm, fear sexual intimacy, be overly seductive, or have other difficulties in romantic relationships.

At 6 years of age children enter the **latency stage,** in which their sexual desires apparently subside and their libidinal energy is devoted to developing new interests, activities, and skills. They seek friends of the same sex,

oral stage, fail to grow beyond their oral needs, and display an "oral character" throughout their lives: extreme dependence or, by the same token, extreme mistrust, and perhaps habits such as pencil chewing, constant talking, or overindulgence in eating, smoking, and drinking.

During the second 18 months of life, the **anal stage,** the child's focus of pleasure shifts to the anus. Libidinal gratification comes from retaining and passing feces, and the child becomes very interested in this bodily function. If parental toilet-training techniques during this stage are too severe, an anal fixation may

*Freud believed that toilet training is a critical developmental experience. Those whose training is too harsh may become "fixated" at this stage and develop an "anal character."*

*Oedipus complex* In Freudian theory, the pattern of desires in which boys become attracted to their mother as a sexual object and see their father as a rival they would like to push aside.

*Electra complex* According to Freud, the pattern of desires all girls experience in which they develop a sexual attraction for their father, rooted in the fantasy that by seducing him they can have his penis.

---

Frequent *"profile" tables* compare and contrast key statistics for important groups of disorders.

Provocative *thought questions* challenge readers to apply their personal experiences to the ideas presented in the text.

Numerous examples from actual case studies bring discussions of symptoms and treatments to life.

*Brief summaries* recapitulate key ideas at the close of each major discussion.

Important *definitions* are repeated in a running glossary at the foot of the page.

# Mastering the Fundamentals

Chapters conclude with a *"State of the Field" section* that sums up what is known and what remains to be learned about a given category of disorders.

*...tnam veterans have helped many of their members overcome the anxiety, depression, sleep problems, and flashbacks that linger for years after the war.*

*End-of-chapter summaries* repeat the chapter's key ideas in outline form.

The findings of recent years have illustrated the explanatory and treatment potential of several models that previously seemed to have relatively little to offer these areas. In particular, the cognitive and biological models have emerged, along with the behavioral model, as major forces in the study and treatment of panic and obsessive-compulsive disorders.

The findings of recent years have also shown that concepts and techniques from various models may be combined to yield broader insights or more effective treatment. For example, the cognitive explanation of panic disorders builds on the biological notion that the disorders begin with unusual physiological sensations. Similarly, therapists often combine medications with cognitive techniques to treat panic disorders, with behavioral techniques to treat obsessive-compulsive disorder, and with psychodynamic, humanistic, behav-

how many children I had killed and was I guilty and depressed about it. He asked how it felt to kill people. He also kept on asking me about my brothers and sisters. But he never asked me about what my experiences were like in Vietnam. He never did. I saw him for treatment for about a month—about three visits, but I quit because we weren't getting anywhere. . . . He just kept on giving me more and more medications. I could've set up my own pharmacy. I needed someone to talk to about my problems, my real problems, not some bullshit about my childhood. I needed someone who wanted to help. The clinic later referred me to another shrink. . . . I guess she thought she was being honest with me, by telling me that she was not a veteran, was not in Vietnam, and did not know what was wrong with me. She also told me that she had no experience working with Vietnam veterans, and that I should go to the Veterans Administration for help. . . .

It was only in the last 3 years when my wife made an important phone call to a local Veterans Outreach Center that I started feeling I had hope, that something could be done for me. I received the help that I have always needed. Finally, I found it easier to hold a job and take care of my family. My nightmares are not as frightening or as frequent as they used to be. Things are better now; I am learning to trust people and give more to my wife and children.

(Brende & Parson, 1985, pp. 206–208)

### Summing Up
*People with acute and posttraumatic stress disorders react with a distinct pattern of anxiety and related symptoms long after the occurrence of a traumatic event. Childhood experiences, personal variables, and social support appear to help influence whether people develop one of these disorders. Clinicians have applied various treatments, including medications, exposure techniques, and supportive and humanistic therapy, particularly in the form of group therapy.*

### The State of the Field
## Panic, Obsessive-Compulsive, and Stress Disorders

Panic, obsessive-compulsive, and stress disorders—once known in clinical circles simply as the "other" anxiety disorders—have received intense study over the past decade, resulting in growing insights about them.

## Chapter Review

1. *Panic, Obsessive-Compulsive, and Stress Disorders:* A number of discoveries during the past ten years have shed new light on the causes of panic disorders, obsessive-compulsive disorder, and stress disorders. Promising treatments have been developed for each of them as well.
2. *Panic Disorder:* Sufferers of a *panic disorder* experience panic attacks frequently, unpredictably, and without apparent provocation.
   A. *Biological Perspective:* Biological theorists believe that abnormal *norepinephrine* activity in the *locus coeruleus* is a key factor in panic disorders. Biological therapists use certain antidepressant drugs to treat many people with panic disorders.
   B. *Cognitive Perspective:* The cognitive position is that panic-prone people become preoccupied with some of their bodily sensations and mental states and often misinterpret them as indicative of imminent catastrophe. Cognitive therapists teach patients that the physical sensations they experience are actually harmless.
3. *Obsessive-Compulsive Disorder:* People with an *obsessive-compulsive disorder* are beset by *obsessions*—repetitive and unwanted thoughts, ideas, impulses, or images that keep invading their consciousness and causing anxiety, or *compulsions*—repetitive and rigid actions that they feel compelled to perform to reduce anxiety.
   A. *Psychodynamic Perspective:* According to the psychodynamic view, obsessive-compulsive disor-

namic therapists use free association, therapist interpretation, and related techniques to try to help people overcome their disorder.
   B. *Behavioral Perspective:* Behaviorists suggest that compulsive behaviors often develop through chance associations and operant conditioning. The leading behavioral approach combines prolonged *in vivo exposure* with *response prevention*, the blocking of compulsive behaviors.
   C. *Cognitive Perspective:* Cognitive theorists suggest that obsessive-compulsive disorder grows from a normal human tendency to have unwanted and unpleasant thoughts—a tendency that some persons misinterpret as dangerous, reprehensible, and controllable. Their efforts to eliminate or avoid such thoughts inadvertently lead to the development of obsessions and compulsions. In a promising cognitive-behavioral approach, *habituation training,* therapists encourage clients to summon their obsessive thoughts to mind for a prolonged period, expecting that such prolonged exposure will cause the thoughts to lose their threatening meaning and generate less anxiety.
   D. *Biological Perspective:* Biological researchers have identified two biological factors that may

contribute to this disorder: low activity of the neurotransmitter *serotonin* and abnormal functioning in key regions of the brain, including the *caudate nuclei. Antidepressant* drugs that raise serotonin activity seem to be a useful form of treatment for this disorder.
4. *Stress Disorders:* People with *acute stress disorder* or *posttraumatic stress disorder* react with a distinct pattern of symptoms after a traumatic event, including reexperiencing the traumatic event, avoidance of related events, reduced responsiveness, and increased arousal, anxiety, and guilt. The symptoms of acute stress disorder begin soon after the trauma and last less than a month. Those of posttraumatic stress

## Key Terms

| | |
|---|---|
| panic disorder | locus coeruleus |
| obsessive-compulsive disorder | alprazolam |
| | anxiety sensitivity |
| acute stress disorder | biological challenge test |
| posttraumatic stress disorder | obsession |
| | compulsion |
| mitral valve prolapse | compulsive ritual |
| thyroid disease | cleaning compulsion |
| panic disorder with agoraphobia | checking compulsion |
| | isolation |
| norepinephrine | undoing |

| | |
|---|---|
| neutralizing | PET scan |
| habituation training | psychic numbing |
| covert-response prevention | dissociation |
| | victimization |
| serotonin | hardiness |
| clomipramine | rap group |
| fluoxetine | Veterans Outreach Center |

A list of *key terms* and a *brief quiz* at the end of each chapter test readers' recall of the chapter's fundamental concepts and facts.

## Quick Quiz

1. What biological factors contribute to the onset of panic disorders, and precisely what biological interventions are effective in the treatment of these disorders?
2. How do cognitive theorists explain and treat panic disorders?
3. What are biological challenge tests, and how are they used by researchers and by therapists?
4. Describe six different types of compulsions.
5. Which defense mechanisms do psychodynamic theorists believe are particularly common in obsessive-compulsive disorder?
6. How do normal thinking processes and "neutralizing" combine to yield obsessive-compulsive disorder, according to cognitive therapists? What kinds of research support has the cognitive explanation received?

7. Describe and compare the effectiveness of the behavioral approach (exposure and response prevention) and the biological approach (antidepressant medications) to obsessive-compulsive disorder.
8. What biological factors have been linked to obsessive-compulsive disorder?
9. Compare and contrast acute stress disorder and posttraumatic stress disorder.
10. What factors seem to bear upon who does and who does not develop a stress disorder after experiencing a traumatic event?
11. What treatment techniques have been used with people suffering from stress disorders?

# 1

# Abnormal Psychology Past and Present

## Topic Overview

Mental dysfunctioning is a loose term for the wide spectrum of problems that seem to have their roots in the human brain or mind. It crosses all boundaries—cultural, economic, emotional, and intellectual. It affects the famous and the obscure, the rich and the poor, the upright and the perverse. Politicians, actors, writers, and other public icons of the present and the past have struggled with mental dysfunctioning. It can bring great suffering, but it can also be the source of inspiration and energy.

Because they are so ubiquitous and so personal, mental problems capture the interest of us all. Hundreds of novels, plays, films, and television programs have, for example, explored what many people see as the dark side of human nature, and self-help books flood the market.

The field devoted to the scientific study of the abnormal behavior we find so fascinating is usually called *abnormal psychology*. As in the other sciences, workers in this field, called *clinical scientists,* gather information systematically so that they may describe, predict, explain, and exert some control over the phenomena they study. The knowledge that they acquire is then used by a wide variety of *clinical practitioners* to detect, assess, and treat abnormal patterns of functioning.

Although their general goals are similar to those of other scientific disciplines, clinical scientists and practitioners confront problems that make their work especially difficult. One of the most troubling problems is that psychological abnormality is extremely hard to define.

## Defining Psychological Abnormality

Miriam cries herself to sleep every night. She is certain that the future holds nothing but misery. Indeed, this is the only thing she does feel certain about. "I'm going to die and my daughters are going to die. We're doomed. The world is ugly. I detest every moment of this life." She has great trouble sleeping. She is afraid to close her eyes, afraid that she will never wake up, and what will happen to her daughters then? When she does drift off to sleep, her dreams are nightmares filled with blood, dismembered bodies, thunder, decay, death, destruction.

One morning Miriam has trouble getting out of bed. The thought of facing another day overwhelms

her. Again she wishes she were dead, and she wishes her daughters were dead. "We'd all be better off." She feels paralyzed by her depression and anxiety, too tired to move and too afraid to leave her house. She decides once again to stay home and to keep her daughters with her. She makes sure that all shades are drawn and that every conceivable entrance to the house is secured. She is afraid of the world and afraid of life. Every day is the same, filled with depression, fear, immobility, and withdrawal. Every day is a nightmare.

During the past year Brad has been hearing mysterious voices that tell him to quit his job, leave his family, and prepare for the coming invasion. These voices have brought tremendous confusion and emotional turmoil to Brad's life. He believes that they come from beings in distant parts of the universe who are somehow wired to him. Although it gives him a sense of purpose and specialness to be the chosen target of their communications, they also make him tense and anxious. He dreads the coming invasion. When he refuses an order, the voices insult and threaten him and turn his days into a waking nightmare.

Brad has put himself on a sparse diet to avoid the possibility that his enemies may be contaminating his food. He has found a quiet apartment far from his old haunts where he has laid in a good stock of arms and ammunition. His family and friends have tried to reach out to Brad, to understand his problems, and to dissuade him from his disturbing activities. Every day, however, he retreats further into his world of mysterious voices and imagined dangers.

Miriam and Brad are the kinds of people we think of when abnormal behavior is mentioned. Most of us would probably label their emotions, thoughts, and behavior as *psychologically abnormal,* or, alternatively, as *psychopathological, maladjusted, emotionally disturbed,* or *mentally ill.*

But *are* Miriam and Brad psychologically abnormal, and if so, why? What is it about their thoughts, emotions, and behavior that might lead us to this conclusion? Many definitions of abnormal mental functioning have been proposed over the years, but none of them has won universal acceptance. Still, most of the definitions do have common features, often called "the four D's": deviance, distress, dysfunction, and danger. Abnormal patterns of psychological functioning, then, are patterns that, in a given context, are *deviant*—that is, different, extreme, unusual, perhaps even bizarre; *distressful,* or unpleasant and upsetting to the individual; *dysfunctional,* or disruptive to the person's ability to conduct daily activities in a constructive manner; and possibly *dangerous.* This definition provides a useful starting point from which to explore the phenom-

---

*Abnormal psychology*   The scientific study of abnormal behavior in order to describe, predict, explain, and exert some control over abnormal patterns of functioning.

ena of psychological abnormality, although, as we shall see, it has significant limitations.

## Deviance

Abnormal mental functioning is functioning that is deviant, but deviant from what? Miriam's behavior, thoughts, and emotions are different from those that are considered normal in our place and time. We do not expect people to cry themselves to sleep every night nor to wish themselves dead. Similarly, Brad's obedience to voices that no one else can hear contradicts our expectation that normal people perceive only the material world accessible to everyone's five senses.

In short, abnormal behavior, thoughts, and emotions are those that violate a society's ideas about proper functioning. Each society establishes *norms*—explicit and implicit rules for appropriate conduct. Behavior that violates legal norms is called criminal. Behavior, thoughts, and emotions that violate norms of psychological functioning are called abnormal.

This focus on social values as a yardstick for measuring deviance suggests that judgments of abnormality vary from society to society. A society's norms emerge from its particular *culture*—its history, values, institutions, habits, skills, technology, and arts. Thus a society whose culture places great value on competition and assertiveness may accept aggressive behavior, whereas one that highly values courtesy, cooperation, and gentleness may consider aggressive behavior unacceptable and even abnormal. A society's values may also change over time, causing its views of what is psychologically abnormal to change as well. In Western society, for example, a woman's participation in the business or professional world was considered inappropriate and strange a hundred years ago, but today the same behavior is valued.

### Consider This

One way to measure deviance is to collect data on the frequency of a variety of behaviors. The ones that occur rarely can then be labeled "abnormal"; they are deviant. This approach may appear to be straightforward, but it is not without problems. What problems do *you* see with the approach of identifying abnormal behaviors based on their frequency of occurrence?

Judgments of abnormality depend on *specific circumstances* as well as on psychological norms. The description of Miriam, for example, might lead us to con-

*Along the Niger River, men of the Wodaabe tribe don elaborate makeup and costumes to attract women. In Western society, the same behavior would violate behavioral norms and probably be judged abnormal.*

clude that she is functioning abnormally. Certainly her unhappiness is more intense and pervasive than that of most of the people we encounter every day. Before you conclude that this woman is abnormal, however, consider that Miriam lives in Lebanon, a country pulled apart by years of combat. The happiness she once knew with her family vanished when her husband and son were killed. As year follows year with only temporary respites, Miriam has stopped expecting anything except more of the same.

In this light, Miriam's reactions do not seem inappropriate. If anything is abnormal here, it is her situation. Many things in our world elicit intense reactions—large-scale catastrophes and disasters, rape, child abuse, war, terminal illness, and chronic pain. Is there an "appropriate" way to react to such things? Should we ever call reactions to them abnormal?

## Distress

Even functioning that is considered unusual and inappropriate in a given context does not necessarily qualify as abnormal. According to many clinical theorists, one's behavior, ideas, or emotions usually have to cause one distress before they can be labeled abnormal. Consider the Ice Breakers, a group of people in Michigan who go swimming in lakes throughout the state every weekend from November through February. The colder the weather, the better they like it. One man, a member of the group for seventeen years, says he loves the challenge. Man against the elements. Mind versus body. A 37-year-old lawyer believes that

---

*Culture* A people's common history, values, institutions, habits, skills, technology, and arts.

*In Val d' Isère, France, these students bury themselves in snow up to their necks. Far from experiencing distress, they are engaging in a Japanese practice designed to open their hearts and enlarge their spirits, so diagnosticians are unlikely to judge them to be abnormal.*

the weekend shock is good for her health. "It cleanses me," she says. "It perks me up and gives me strength for the week ahead." Another avid Ice Breaker likes the special feelings the group brings to him. "When we get together, we know we've shared something special, something no one else understands. I can't even tell most of the people I know that I'm an Ice Breaker. They wouldn't want anything to do with me. A few people think I'm a space cadet."

Certainly these people are different from most of us, but they are enjoying themselves. Far from experiencing distress, they feel invigorated and challenged. Their absence of internal distress must cause us to hesitate before we conclude that these people are functioning abnormally.

Should we conclude, then, that feelings of distress must always be present before a person's functioning can be considered abnormal? Not necessarily. Some people who function abnormally may maintain a relatively positive frame of mind. Consider once again Brad, the young man who hears mysterious voices. Brad does experience severe distress over the coming invasion and the changes he feels forced to make in the way he lives. But what if he felt no such anxiety? What if he greatly enjoyed listening to the voices, felt honored to be chosen, and looked forward to the formidable task of saving the world? Shouldn't we still consider his functioning abnormal?

## Dysfunction

Abnormal behavior tends to interfere with daily functioning. It so upsets, distracts, or confuses its victims that they cannot care for themselves properly, participate in ordinary social relationships, or work effectively. Brad, for example, has quit his job, left his family, and prepared to withdraw from the productive and meaningful life he once led to an empty and isolated existence in a distant apartment.

Here again one's culture plays a role in the definition of abnormality. Our society holds that it is important to carry out certain expected daily activities in an effective, self-enhancing manner. Thus Brad's behavior is likely to be regarded as abnormal and undesirable, whereas that of the Ice Breakers, who continue to perform well at their jobs and maintain appropriate family and social relationships, would probably be considered unusual but not a sign of psychological abnormality.

## Danger

Perhaps the ultimate in psychological dysfunctioning is behavior that becomes dangerous to oneself or others. A pattern of functioning that is marked by carelessness, poor judgment, hostility, or misinterpretation can jeopardize one's own well-being and that of many other people. Brad, for example, seems to be endangering himself by his diet and others by his stockpile of arms and ammunition.

Although danger to oneself or others is usually cited as a criterion of abnormal psychological functioning, research suggests that it is more often the exception than the rule. Despite popular misconceptions, most people struggling with anxiety, depression, and even bizarre behavioral patterns pose no immediate danger to themselves or to anyone else.

## Difficulties in Defining Psychological Abnormality

Efforts to define psychological abnormality typically raise as many questions as they answer. The major difficulty is that the very concept of abnormality is relative, dependent on the norms and values of the society in question. Ultimately a society selects the general criteria for defining abnormality and then interprets them in order to judge the normality or abnormality of each particular case.

One clinical theorist, Thomas Szasz (1987, 1961), places such emphasis on society's role that he finds the whole concept of mental illness to be invalid. According to Szasz, the deviations that society calls abnormal are simply "problems in living," not signs of something inherently wrong within the person. Societies, he is convinced, invent the concept of mental illness to justify their efforts to control or change people whose unusual patterns of functioning threaten the social order.

Even if we assume that psychological abnormality is a valid concept and that such abnormalities are unhealthy, a society may have difficulty agreeing on a definition and applying it consistently. If a certain behavior—excessive consumption of alcohol among college students, say—is common in a society, the society may fail to recognize that the behavior is often a symptom of deviance, a source of distress, highly dysfunctional, and dangerous. Thousands of college students throughout the United States are so dependent on alcohol that it interferes greatly with their personal and academic functioning, causes them significant discomfort, places their health in jeopardy, and often endangers them and the people around them. Yet their problem often goes unnoticed, certainly undiagnosed, by college administrators, other students, and health professionals. Alcohol consumption is so much a part of the college subculture that it is easy to overlook drinking behavior that has become abnormal.

Conversely, a society may have trouble distinguishing an abnormality that requires intervention from an *eccentric* individuality that others have no right to interfere with. From time to time, we see or hear about people who behave in ways we consider strange, such as a man who lives alone and rarely talks to anyone. The man's behavior is deviant and may well be distressful and dysfunctional, yet his propensities are thought of by most professionals as eccentric rather than abnormal. When is an unusual pattern of behavior deviant, distressful, and dysfunctional *enough* to be considered abnormal? This question may be impossible to answer.

In short, while we may agree that abnormal patterns of functioning are those that are deviant, distressful, dysfunctional, and sometimes dangerous in a given context, we should always be aware of the ambiguity and subjectivity of this definition. We should also be aware that few of the current categories of abnormality are as clear-cut as they sometimes seem.

*Behavior considered disturbing during one period in history may be admired during another. When Owen Totten wore his suit of 5,600 buttons in 1946, his hoarding behavior, even more than his choice of attire, raised many eyebrows. Today, he might be an entrepreneur thriving in the business of collectibles.*

### Summing Up
*The field devoted to the scientific study of abnormal behavior is called abnormal psychology. Abnormal patterns of psychological functioning are generally considered to be those that are deviant, distressful, dysfunctional, and dangerous. The very concept of abnormality is relative, however, dependent on the norms and values of the society in question.*

## Past Views and Treatments

The current facts and figures on psychological abnormality are almost numbing. It is estimated that in any given year around 30 percent of the adults and at least 17 percent of the children and adolescents in the United States display serious mental disturbances and are in need of clinical treatment (Kessler et al., 1994;

Kazdin, 1993). It is estimated that at least thirteen of every hundred adults have a significant anxiety disorder, six suffer from profound depression, one is schizophrenic (loses touch with reality for an extended period of time), one experiences the brain deterioration of Alzheimer's disease, and close to ten abuse alcohol or other drugs. Add to these figures as many as 600,000 suicide attempts, 600,000 rapes, and 2.9 million cases of child abuse in this country each year, and it becomes apparent that abnormal psychological functioning is a major problem in our society. Beyond these disturbances, most people have difficulty coping at various points in their lives and experience high levels of tension, demoralization, or other forms of psychological discomfort.

Given such numbers, it is tempting to conclude that something about today's world—rapid technological change, for example, or a decline in religious, community, or other support systems—fosters emotional maladjustment. Although the special pressures of modern life probably do contribute to psychological dysfunctioning, they are hardly its primary cause. Indeed, every society, past and present, has contended with psychological abnormality.

Perhaps the proper place to begin our examination of abnormal behavior and treatment is in the past. If we look back, we may better understand such issues as the nature of psychological abnormality, which of its features remain constant in human societies and which vary from place to place and from time to time, how each society has struggled to understand and treat it, and how present-day ideas and treatments can often be traced to the past. A look backward makes it clear that progress in the understanding and treatment of mental disorders has hardly been a steady movement forward. Indeed, many of the inadequacies and controversies that characterize the clinical field today parallel those of the past. At the same time, looking back can help us to appreciate the full significance of the field's most recent developments and breakthroughs.

## Ancient Views and Treatments

Most of our knowledge of prehistoric societies has been acquired indirectly and is based on inferences made from archaeological discoveries. Historians scrutinize the unearthed bones, artwork, artifacts, and other remnants of ancient societies to find clues about those societies' customs, beliefs, and daily life. Their conclusions are at best tentative and always subject to revision in the face of new discoveries.

Thus our knowledge of how ancient societies viewed and treated people with mental disturbances is

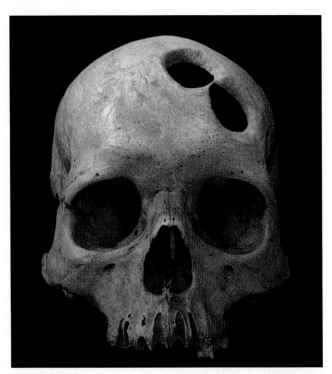

The skulls of some Stone Age people show evidence of trephination, possibly for the purpose of releasing evil spirits and thus remedying abnormal psychological functioning. Signs of bone regrowth around the two holes in this skull suggest that this patient survived two trephinations.

limited. Historians have concluded that prehistoric societies probably viewed abnormal behavior as the work of evil spirits. They believe that people in these early societies explained the phenomena around and within them as resulting from the actions of magical, sometimes sinister beings who shaped and controlled the world. In particular, these early people viewed the human body and mind as sites of battle between external forces, and they viewed behavior, both normal and abnormal, as the outcome of battles between good and evil spirits, positive forces and demons, or good and bad gods. Abnormal behavior was often interpreted as a victory by evil spirits, and the cure for such behavior was to force the spirits to leave the person's body.

This supernatural view of abnormality may have begun as far back as the Stone Age, a half-million years ago. Some skulls from that period recovered by archaeologists in Europe and South America show evidence of an operation called *trephination,* in which a stone instrument, or *trephine,* was used to cut away a circular section of the skull. Some historians have surmised that this operation was performed as a treatment for severe abnormal behavior—either hallucinatory expe-

---

*Trephination*  An ancient operation in which a stone instrument was used to cut away a circular section of the skull. It is believed to have been a Stone Age treatment for abnormal behavior.

riences, in which people saw or heard things not actually present, or melancholic reactions, characterized by extreme sadness and immobility—and that the purpose of opening the skull was to release the evil spirits that were supposedly causing the problem (Selling, 1940).

In recent years other historians have raised doubts about this interpretation of trephination, suggesting that the procedure may have been used to remove bone splinters or blood clots caused by stone weapons during tribal warfare (Maher & Maher, 1985). Whether or not Stone Age people actually believed that evil spirits caused abnormal behavior, archaeological findings from later societies clearly indicate that ancient people did eventually account for such behavior by reference to demonic possession. The early writings of the Egyptians, Chinese, and Hebrews, for example, attribute psychological deviance to the influences of evil spirits or demons. This view of abnormality is frequently expressed in the Bible, which describes, for example, how an evil spirit from the Lord affected King Saul and how David feigned madness in order to convince his enemies that he was inhabited by divine forces.

*Consider This*

The discovery of trephined human skulls is an intriguing anthropological enigma. The people who lived at the time the skulls were trephined did not leave written records to help us understand the primary purpose of trephining. How might investigators resolve the controversy about the purpose of trephining even without written records?

People of these early societies practiced *exorcism* as a common treatment for abnormality. The idea was to coax the evil spirits to leave or to make the person's body an uncomfortable place for the spirits to live. A *shaman,* or priest, might recite prayers, plead with the evil spirits, insult them, perform magic, make loud noises, or have the person drink noxious solutions. If these techniques failed, a more extreme form of exorcism, such as whipping or starvation, was employed.

## Greek and Roman Views and Treatments

Although demonological views concerning mental and physical illness were still widespread in the years when the Greek and Roman civilizations flourished (from 500 B.C. to A.D. 500), philosophers and physicians began to offer alternative explanations during this period. Hippocrates (460–377 B.C.), often called the father of modern medicine because of his teaching that illnesses had natural causes rather than metaphysical ones, saw abnormal behavior as a disease caused by internal medical problems rather than by conflicts between gods or spirits. Specifically, he believed that brain pathology was the culprit, and that it resulted—like all other forms of disease, in his view—from an

*Imbalances of the four humors were believed by Hippocrates to affect personality and cause mental disorders. In these depictions, (top) yellow bile drives a choleric husband to beat his wife; (bottom) black bile renders a man melancholic and sends him to bed.*

*Exorcism*   The practice in early societies of treating abnormality by coaxing evil spirits to leave the person's body.

## Box 1-1

# *The Moon and the Mind*

The once widespread belief in demonic possession as a cause of abnormal behavior has been replaced in developed countries by the assumption that biological, psychological, and sociocultural explanations can be found; yet some ancient theories still have a hold on us today. One is the persistent belief that the phases of the moon have a direct effect on personality and behavior.

Primitive societies believed that the moon had magical, mystical powers and that its changes predicted events of many kinds. The moon had the power to impregnate women, to make plants grow, and to drive people insane. Later societies also accepted the power of the moon to affect behavior, and they applied the terms "lunatic" and "lunacy" to the person and the behavior to capture their moonlike, or lunar, qualities. Today

many respected institutions and people actively support the idea that behavior is affected by the phases of the moon. The belief that bizarre behavior increases when the moon is full is so prevalent that a successful lunar newsletter services a number of hospitals and law enforcement officials, warning them to be wary on nights of a full moon (Gardner, 1984). Anecdotal evidence abounds: New York City

*Moonstruck maidens dance in the town square in this eighteenth-century French engraving.*

police officers note more violent and bizarre crimes during the full moon, and hospitals claim to experience an increase in births. One hospital has linked the full moon to the onset of ulcers and heart attacks. A Wall Street broker has for years used the schedule of the full moon as a guide in giving investment advice—successfully (Gardner, 1984).

Scientists, who generally rely on explanations other than the inherent mystical prowess of the moon, have advanced many theories to make sense of a lunar effect on human behavior. Some say that since the moon causes the tides of the oceans, it is reasonable to expect that it has a similar effect on the bodily fluids of human beings (whose composition is more than 80 percent water). The increase in births might therefore be explained by the force of the moon on the expectant mother's am-

imbalance of four fluids, or **humors,** that flowed through the body: *yellow bile, black bile, blood,* and *phlegm.* An excess of yellow bile, for example, caused mania (frenzied euphoria); an excess of black bile was the source of melancholia (unshakable sadness). Hippocrates' focus on internal causes for abnormal behavior was later shared and in some cases extended by the great Greek philosophers Plato (427–347 B.C.) and Aristotle (384–322 B.C.) and by influential Greek and Roman physicians.

These theories led Greek and Roman physicians to treat mental disorders with a mixture of medical and psychological techniques. Before resorting to such severe methods as bleeding patients or restraining them with mechanical devices, many Greek physicians first prescribed a warm and supportive atmosphere, music, massage, exercise, and baths. Roman physicians were

even more emphatic about the need to soothe and comfort patients who had mental disorders.

## Europe in the Middle Ages: Demonology Returns

That demonological views were dismissed by noted physicians and scholars during the Greco-Roman period was not enough to shake many people's belief in demons. Such views and practices never disappeared entirely (see Box 1-1), and with the decline of Rome they enjoyed a strong resurgence.

After the Roman Empire fell, a growing distrust of science spread throughout Europe. In the years from A.D. 500 to 1350, the period known as the Middle Ages, the power of the clergy increased greatly. The church rejected secular studies and scientific forms of investigation, and it controlled all education. Religious beliefs—themselves highly superstitious and demono-

---

*Humors*    From Greek and, later, medieval medical theory, four fluids thought to influence a person's health and temperament.

niotic fluid. Similar tidal and gravitational effects have been proposed to explain the increase in bizarre behavior in people who may already be viewed as emotionally disturbed. Aside from the abundant anecdotal evidence, a study of clams by the biologist Frank Brown is often cited to show the ubiquitous power of the moon over the behavior of creatures of the earth (Gardner, 1984). Brown reports moving a group of clams, which had been gathered in Connecticut, to a laboratory in the landlocked city of Evanston, Illinois. At first the clams opened up to receive food during the times of high tide in Connecticut, as they had done all of their lives. After two weeks, however, the clams adopted an eating pattern that followed what would have been the schedule of high tides in Evanston—if Evanston had actually had any tides.

This evidence may seem to be compelling, but any hypothesis devised to explain the alleged effects of the moon is only a tentative assumption; none has been substantiated. Some researchers, less moonstruck, have performed rigorous statistical analyses of the actual numbers of births, crimes, and incidents of bizarre behavior that occur during the full moon. They have found no evidence supporting the influence of the moon on any of a variety of scales of human behavior (Byrnes & Kelly, 1992; Kelly et al., 1990; Culver et al., 1988). In view of this lack of support for the popular lunacy theory, some scientists have suggested that we drop the entire question. Other researchers, unconvinced, claim that the lack of statistical evidence is not the problem—the problem has been the researchers' failure to look at the right variables, to use the appropriate measures, or to look at enough days both before and after the full moon. It has been suggested, for example, that studies of mental hospital admissions should take a lag time into account because the moon-induced behavior may not be identified or the individuals may not be processed until a week or more after the full moon (Cyr & Kalpin, 1988).

Most clinicians remain convinced that moon-induced abnormality is a myth, yet some people do exhibit strange behavior during the full moon, or report strange sensations or increased sexual desire. The simplest explanation for these phenomena is most likely the most accurate. Personal belief, superstition, and bias can be powerful motivators of behavior. For people who already exhibit abnormal behavior or are searching for an excuse or a cue to break with society's behavioral norms, the historical belief in the power of the moon provides a convenient outlet. One waives personal responsibility by attributing one's behavior to the moon. The cause of lunacy may lie far less in the heavens than in our minds.

logical at this time—came to dominate all aspects of life. Personal experience and conduct were generally interpreted in religious terms, often as a conflict between good and evil, God and the devil, and deviant behavior was seen as evidence of an association with Satan. Although some scientists and physicians still argued for medical explanations and treatments for mental dysfunctioning, their views carried little weight in this atmosphere of rigid religious doctrine.

The Middle Ages were centuries of great stress and anxiety, times of war, urban uprisings, and plagues. People blamed the devil for these hard times and feared him intensely; specifically, they feared being possessed by the devil. The incidence of abnormal behavior apparently increased dramatically during this stressful period. In addition, there were outbreaks of **mass madness,** in which large numbers of people apparently shared the same delusions and hallucinations. Two prevalent forms were tarantism and lycanthropy.

*Tarantism* (also known as *St. Vitus's dance*) occurred throughout Europe between A.D. 900 and 1800. Groups of people would suddenly start to jump around, dance, and go into convulsions (Sigerist, 1943). Some dressed oddly, others tore off their clothing. All were convinced that they had been bitten and possessed by a wolf spider, now called a tarantula, and they sought to cure their disorder by performing a dance called a "tarantella." The dance was thought to have originated in the town of Taranto in southern Italy; thus the name tarantism.

People with *lycanthropy* thought they were possessed by wolves or other animals. They acted wolflike and might imagine that fur was growing all over their

---

*Tarantism*   A phenomenon that occurred throughout Europe between A.D. 900 and 1800 in which groups of people would suddenly start to jump around, dance, and go into convulsions.

*Lycanthropy*   A condition in which a person believes himself or herself to be possessed by wolves or other animals.

*Exorcism, one of the earliest forms of treatment for mental disorders, was revived during the Middle Ages. In this detail from the fifteenth-century painting,* St. Catherine Exorcising a Possessed Woman, *the devil flees after being cast out of the woman's head by the saint.*

bodies. Stories of lycanthropes, more popularly known as **werewolves,** have been passed down to us and continue to capture the imagination of novelists, moviemakers, and their audiences.

Many earlier demonological treatments for psychological abnormality reemerged in the Middle Ages. Once again the key to a cure was to rid the person's body of the devil that possessed it, and techniques of exorcism were revived. Clergymen, who generally were in charge of treatment during this period, would plead, chant, or pray to the devil or evil spirits. They might also administer holy water or bitter-tasting concoctions, and if these techniques did not work, they might try to insult the devil and attack his pride (Satan's great weakness, they believed). These milder forms of exorcism were sometimes supplemented by torture in the form of starvation, whipping, scalding, or stretching.

As the Middle Ages drew to a close, demonology and its methods began to lose favor. Cities throughout Europe grew larger, and municipal authorities gained more power and increasingly took over the secular activities of the church. Among other responsibilities, they began to administer hospitals and direct the care of sick people, including the mentally ill. Medical views of psychological abnormality started to gain prominence once again, and many of those with mental disturbances were treated in medical hospitals, under municipal authority, rather than by the clergy. The Trinity Hospital in England, for example, was established to treat "madness" along with other kinds of illness, and to keep the mad "safe until they are restored to reason" (Alldridge, 1979, p. 322).

## The Renaissance and the Rise of Asylums

Demonological views of abnormality continued to decline in popularity during the first half of the period of flourishing cultural and scientific activity known as the Renaissance (approximately 1400–1700). During these years the German physician Johann Weyer (1515–1588) apparently became the first medical practitioner to specialize in mental illness. Believing that the mind was as susceptible to sickness as the body, Weyer is now considered the founder of the modern study of **psychopathology,** another term for mental dysfunctioning.

Care for many people with mental disorders continued to improve in this atmosphere. In England many mental patients were kept at home, and their families were given extra funds by the local parish. Across Europe a number of religious shrines became consecrated to the humane and loving treatment of the mentally ill. Perhaps the best-known such shrine was at Gheel in Belgium. Beginning in the fifteenth century, people with mental problems ranging from melancholia to hallucinations came from all over the world to

*Belief in demonological possession persisted into the Renaissance. For example, a great fear of witches swept Europe during the fifteenth and sixteenth centuries. At least some of those who were accused appear to have had mental disorders that caused them to act strangely (Zilboorg & Henry, 1941). In this illustration from a book by the French demonologist Pierre de Lancre, Satan takes the form of a five-horned goat (upper right) and presides over a witches' Sabbath.*

*London's Bethlehem Hospital, or Bedlam, was typical of insane asylums from the sixteenth to the nineteenth centuries. In William Hogarth's eighteenth-century work from A Rake's Progress, ladies and gentlemen of fashion come to marvel at the strange behavior of the inmates.*

In 1547, for example, the Bethlehem Hospital in London was given to the city by Henry VIII for the exclusive purpose of confining the mentally ill. Here patients, restrained in chains, cried out their despair for all to hear. The hospital actually became a popular tourist attraction; people were eager to pay to look at the howling and gibbering inmates. The hospital's name, pronounced "Bedlam" by the local people, has become synonymous with a chaotic uproar. Similarly, in the Lunatics' Tower in Vienna, mental patients were kept in narrow hallways by the outer walls, so that tourists outside could look up and see them.

Although some caregivers did attempt to provide "medical" cures during this period, such interventions tended to be misguided and unintentionally cruel. In the eighteenth century, no less a figure than Benjamin Rush (1745–1813), often called the father of American psychiatry, treated some mental patients by drawing blood from their bodies, a technique used to treat many bodily illnesses during that period. This treatment was meant to lower an excessively high level of blood in the brain, which Rush believed was causing the patient's abnormal behavior (Farina, 1976).

visit this shrine (actually established centuries earlier) for psychic healing. Local residents welcomed them into their homes, and many pilgrims stayed on to form the world's first "colony" of mental patients. This colony set the stage for many of today's community mental health and foster care programs, and Gheel continues to demonstrate that people with mental disorders can respond to loving care and respectful treatment (Aring, 1975, 1974). Many patients still live in foster homes there until they recover, interacting with and accepted by the town's other residents.

Unfortunately, the improvements in the care for the mentally ill began to fade by the mid-sixteenth century. Municipal authorities eventually discovered that only a small percentage of the severely mentally ill could be accommodated in private homes and community residences, and that medical hospitals were too few and too small. Officials in cities across the world converted hospitals and monasteries into *asylums,* institutions to which people with mental disorders could be sent. These institutions apparently began with the best of intentions—to provide care for the mentally ill. Once the asylums started to overflow with patients, however, they abandoned such goals and eventually became virtual prisons in which patients were held in filthy and degrading conditions and treated with unspeakable cruelty.

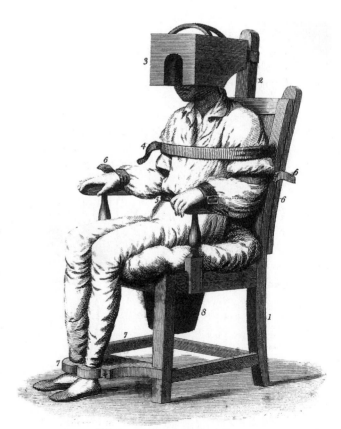

*Even Benjamin Rush, later called the father of American psychiatry, initially used crude treatment techniques, such as the "restraint chair," which reflected contemporary medical thought.*

---

*Asylum* An early type of mental institution. Initially established to provide care for people with mental disorders, most became virtual prisons in which patients endured degrading conditions.

# The Nineteenth Century: Reform and Moral Treatment

As 1800 approached, the treatment of people with mental disorders began to change for the better once again. Historians usually point to the Parisian asylum of La Bicêtre (for male patients) as the initial site of asylum reform. In 1793, during the French Revolution, Philippe Pinel (1745–1826) was named the chief physician there and began a series of reforms. He argued that the patients were sick people whose mental illnesses should be treated with support and kindness rather than with chains and beatings. He unchained them and gave them the liberty of the hospital grounds, replaced the dark dungeons with sunny, well-ventilated rooms, and offered patients support and advice.

Pinel's new approach proved remarkably successful. Many patients who had been locked away in darkness for decades were now enjoying fresh air and sunlight and being treated with dignity. Some improved significantly over a short period of time and were released. Pinel was later commissioned to reform another Parisian mental hospital, La Salpetrière (for female patients), and had excellent results there as well. Jean Esquirol (1772–1840), Pinel's student and successor, followed his teacher's lead and went on to help establish ten new mental hospitals that operated by the same principles.

During this same period an English Quaker named William Tuke (1732–1819) was bringing similar reforms to northern England. In 1796 he founded the York Retreat, a rural estate where about thirty mental patients were lodged as guests in quiet country houses and treated with a combination of rest, talk, prayer, and manual work.

## The Spread of Moral Treatment

The methodologies espoused by Pinel and Tuke, called *moral treatment* by their contemporaries because of their emphasis on moral guidance and on humane and respectful intervention, caught on throughout Europe and the United States. Increasingly, mental patients were perceived as potentially productive human beings whose mental functioning had broken down under overwhelming personal stresses. These unfortunate (rather than possessed) people were considered deserving of individualized care that included discussions of their problems, constructive activities, work, companionship, and quiet.

The person most responsible for the early spread of moral treatment in the United States was Benjamin Rush. As we have seen, Rush's earlier medical views were sometimes naive and harsh by today's standards, but he fully embraced the concept of moral treatment when he learned about it. As an eminent physician at Pennsylvania Hospital, he limited his practice and study to mental illness, and he developed numerous humane approaches to treatment. One of his innovations was to require the hospital to hire intelligent and sensitive attendants to work closely with patients, reading and talking to them and taking them on regular walks. He also suggested that it would be of therapeutic value for doctors to give small gifts to their patients now and then.

Rush was a most influential physician, but it was a Boston schoolteacher named Dorothea Dix (1802–1887) who was largely responsible for the passage of new laws in the United States that mandated more humane care for the mentally ill. In 1841 Dix had gone to teach Sunday school at a local prison and been shocked by the conditions she saw there. Her interest in prison conditions broadened to include the plight of poor and mentally ill people throughout the country. A powerful campaigner, Dix went from state

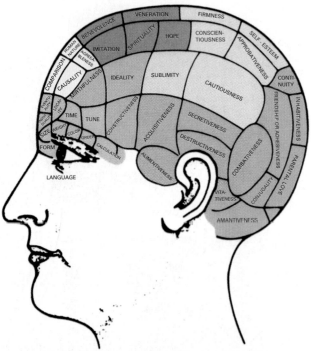

*Nineteenth-century efforts to understand abnormal behavior in less demonological terms were not always scientifically sound. In one popular hypothesis, called "phrenology," the brain was thought to consist of discernible portions, each responsible for some aspect of personality. Phrenologists tried to assess personality by feeling bumps and indentations on a person's head.*

---

*Moral treatment*   A nineteenth century approach to treating people with mental disorders, which emphasized moral guidance, humane and respectful intervention, and kindness.

*From 1841 to 1881 the Boston schoolteacher Dorothea Dix tirelessly campaigned for more humane forms of treatment in mental hospitals throughout the United States. Her efforts led to new laws providing for the establishment of public mental hospitals, supported and administered by the states.*

legislature to state legislature and to Congress speaking of the horrors she had observed and calling for reform.

Dix's campaign, which spanned the decades from 1841 until 1881, led to new laws and the appropriation of funds to improve the treatment of people with mental disorders. Each state was made responsible for developing effective public mental hospitals. Dix personally helped establish thirty-two of these *state hospitals,* all intended to offer moral treatment (Bickman & Dokecki, 1989).

For years the moral treatment movement improved the care of people with mental disorders. By the 1850s, a number of mental hospitals throughout Europe and North America reported that most of their patients were recovering and being released (Bockoven, 1963). Unfortunately, however, social changes at the end of the nineteenth century once again altered this promising situation for the worse.

## The Decline of Moral Treatment

As we have observed, the treatment of abnormality has followed a crooked path. Over and over again, relative progress has been followed by serious decline. Viewed

*State hospital* A public mental institution run by the state.

in this context, the decline of moral treatment in the late nineteenth century is disappointing but not surprising.

Several factors contributed to this decline (Bockoven, 1963). One was the reckless speed with which the moral treatment movement had advanced. As mental hospitals multiplied, severe money and staffing shortages developed, and in turn, recovery rates declined. Fewer and fewer patients left the hospitals each year, and admissions continued unabated; overcrowding became a major problem.

The basic assumptions of moral treatment also contributed to its downfall. The major one was that patients would begin to function normally if they were treated with dignity and if their physical needs were met. For some patients this was indeed the case. Others, however, needed more effective treatments than any that had yet been developed. Many of these people remained hospitalized till they died.

A further reason for the decline of moral treatment was the emergence of a new wave of prejudice against people with mental disorders. As more and more patients disappeared into the large, distant mental hospitals, the public once again came to view them as strange and dangerous and were less open-handed when it came to making donations or allocating government funds. Moreover, by the end of the nineteenth century, many of the patients entering public mental

*Overcrowding and limited funding led to the formation of crowded, often appalling, back wards in state hospitals across the United States during the early twentieth century.*

hospitals in the United States were impoverished for-eign immigrants, whom the public had little interest in helping.

By the early years of the twentieth century, the moral treatment movement had ground to a halt in both the United States and Europe. Public mental hos-pitals provided minimal custodial care and medical in-terventions that did not work and became more over-crowded and less effective every year. Long-term hospitalization became the norm once again.

This state of affairs was powerfully described in 1908 by Clifford Beers (1876–1943) in *A Mind That Found Itself,* an autobiographical account of his severe mental disturbance and of the "treatment" he received in three mental institutions. Beers revealed that he and other patients were repeatedly restrained, beaten, choked, and spat on in these places, all in the name of treatment. Unfortunately, although his moving account brought considerable attention to the terrible condi-tions in public mental hospitals, these institutions were not to improve significantly for forty more years.

## The Somatogenic Perspective

Another significant trend that began in the late nine-teenth century was a dramatic resurgence of the *somatogenic perspective,* the view that abnormal psy-chological functioning has physical causes. This per-spective had at least a 2,300-year history—remember Hippocrates' view that abnormal behavior resulted from brain pathology and an imbalance of humors, or bodily fluids—but it had never before been so widely accepted as it was at this time.

Two factors were responsible for this development. One was the work of Emil Kraepelin (1856–1926), a German researcher who was interested in the relation between abnormal psychological functioning and such physical factors as fatigue, and who had measured the effects of various drugs on abnormal behavior. In 1883 Kraepelin published an influential textbook expound-ing the view that physical factors are responsible for mental dysfunctioning. In addition, as we shall see in Chapter 2, he constructed the first system for classify-ing abnormal behavior.

The rise of the somatogenic perspective was also spurred by a series of biological and anatomical dis-coveries. One of the most important discoveries was that general paresis was caused by an organic disease, syphilis. *General paresis* is an irreversible, progressive

disorder with both physical and mental symptoms, in-cluding paralysis and delusions of grandeur. The or-ganic basis of the disorder had been suspected as early as the mid-nineteenth century, but concrete evidence did not emerge until decades later.

In 1897 Richard von Krafft-Ebing (1840–1902), a German neurologist, established a direct link between general paresis and syphilis. He inoculated paretic pa-tients with matter from syphilis sores and found that none of the patients developed symptoms of syphilis. Their immunity could have been caused only by an earlier case of syphilis, and since all paretic patients were immune to syphilis, Krafft-Ebing theorized that it was the cause of their general paresis.

The work of Kraepelin and the new understanding of general paresis led many researchers and practition-ers to suspect that organic factors were responsible for many mental disorders, perhaps all of them. Practi-tioners in mental hospitals proceded to develop nu-merous medical treatments for hospitalized mental pa-tients throughout the first half of the twentieth century, but most of the techniques—extraction of teeth, tonsillectomy, hydrotherapy (alternating hot and cold baths to soothe excited patients), insulin coma shock (a "therapeutic" convulsion induced by lower-ing a patient's blood sugar level with insulin), and lo-botomy (a surgical severing of certain nerve fibers in the brain)—proved ineffectual. Not until the middle of the century, when a number of effective medications were finally discovered, did the somatogenic perspec-tive truly begin to pay off for patients with mental disorders.

## The Psychogenic Perspective

Yet another important trend to unfold in the late nine-teenth century was the emergence of the *psychogenic perspective,* the view that the chief causes of abnormal functioning are psychological. This perspective, too, has a long history. However, the psychogenic perspec-tive did not command a significant following until the late nineteenth century, when studies of the technique of hypnotism demonstrated the potential of this line of inquiry.

*Hypnotism* is the inducing of a trancelike mental state in which a person becomes extremely sug-gestible. Its use as a means of treating psychological disorders actually dates back to 1778. In that year an Austrian physician named Friedrich Anton Mesmer

---

*Somatogenic perspective*    The view that abnormal psychological functioning has physical causes.

*General paresis*    An irreversible, progressive disorder with both physical and mental symptoms, including paralysis and delusions of grandeur.

---

*Psychogenic perspective*    The view that the chief causes of abnormal functioning are psychological.

*Hypnotism*    The inducing of a trancelike mental state in which a person becomes extremely suggestible.

*The nineteenth century's leading neurologist, Jean Charcot, gives a clinical lecture on hypnotism and hysterical disorders in Paris.*

(1734–1815) established a clinic in Paris where he employed an unusual treatment for patients with *hysterical disorders,* mysterious bodily ailments that had no apparent physical basis. Mesmer's patients would sit in a darkened room filled with music. In the center of the room, a tub held bottles of chemicals from which iron rods protruded. Suddenly Mesmer would appear in a flamboyant costume, withdraw the rods, and touch them to the troubled area of each patient's body. Surprisingly, a number of patients did seem to be helped by this treatment. Their pain, numbness, or paralysis disappeared.

Mesmer's treatment, called *mesmerism,* was so controversial that eventually he was banished from Paris. But few could deny that at least some patients did indeed improve after being mesmerized. Several scientists believed that Mesmer was inducing a trancelike state in his patients, and that this state caused their symptoms to disappear. In later years the technique was developed further and relabeled *neurohypnotism,* later shortened to *hypnotism* (from *hypnos,* the Greek word for sleep).

It was not until years after Mesmer died, however, that many researchers had the courage to investigate hypnotism and its effects on hysterical disorders. That a technique that enhanced the power of suggestion could alleviate hysterical ailments indicated to some scientists that hysterical disorders must be caused by the power of suggestion—that is, by the mind—in the first place. Two physicians, Hippolyte-

Marie Bernheim (1840–1919) and Ambroise-Auguste Liébault (1823–1904), practicing in the city of Nancy in France, finally provided support for this notion when they showed that hysterical disorders could actually be induced in otherwise normal subjects while they were under the influence of hypnosis. That is, the physicians were able to make normal people experience deafness, paralysis, blindness, or numbness by means of hypnotic suggestion—and they could remove these artificially induced symptoms by the same means. In short, they established that a mental process—hypnotic suggestion—could both cause and cure a physical dysfunction. Most leading scientists, including Jean Charcot, an eminent neurologist who had previously opposed this view, finally embraced the idea that hysterical disorders were largely psychological in origin.

Among those who studied the effects of hypnotism on hysterical disorders was a Viennese doctor named Josef Breuer (1842–1925). He discovered that his hypnotized patients sometimes awoke without their hysterical symptoms after speaking freely about past traumas under hypnosis. During the 1890s Breuer was joined in his work by another Viennese physician, Sigmund Freud (1856–1939). As we shall see in greater detail in Chapter 3, Freud's work eventually led him to develop the theory of *psychoanalysis,* which holds that many forms of abnormal and normal psychological functioning are psychogenic. He believed

---

*Hysterical disorder*　A disorder, without any organic basis, in which physical functioning is changed or lost.

*Psychoanalysis*　Either the theory or the treatment of abnormal mental functioning that emphasizes unconscious conflicts as the cause of mental dysfunctioning.

that conflict between powerful psychological processes operating at an unconscious level is the source of much abnormal psychological functioning. Freud also developed the *technique* of psychoanalysis, a form of discussion in which psychotherapists help troubled people acquire insight into their psychological conflicts. Such insight, he believed, would help the patients overcome their psychological problems. By the early twentieth century, psychoanalytic theory and treatment were widely accepted throughout the Western world.

Freud and his followers applied the psychoanalytic treatment approach primarily to patients with relatively modest mental disorders, problems of anxiety or depression that did not require hospitalization. These patients visited psychoanalytic therapists in their offices for sessions of approximately an hour and then went about their daily activities—a format of treatment now known as *outpatient therapy*.

The psychoanalytic approach had little effect on the treatment of severely disturbed patients in mental hospitals, where the somatogenic view and medical approaches continued to dominate. Psychoanalytic therapy requires levels of clarity, insight, and verbal skill beyond the capabilities of most such patients. Moreover, psychoanalysis often takes years to be effective, and the overcrowded and understaffed public mental hospitals could not accommodate such a leisurely pace.

> *Summing Up*
> The history of mental disorders provides many clues to the nature of psychological abnormality. Views have ranged from demonology to biological (somatogenic) perspectives to perspectives that considered the causes to be largely psychological. Likewise, treatments of the past have ranged from exorcism to insulin coma shock therapy, and from simply warehousing people with mental disorders to attempts at providing them with systematic psychological therapies.

# Current Trends

It would hardly be accurate to say that we now live in a period of widespread enlightenment or dependable treatment. Indeed, a recent survey found that 43 percent of respondents believe that people bring on mental disorders themselves and 35 percent consider them

to be caused by sinful behavior (Murray, 1993). Nevertheless, the past forty years have brought significant changes in the understanding and treatment of abnormal functioning. There are more theories and types of treatment, more research studies, more information, and, perhaps for these reasons, more disagreements about abnormal functioning today than at any time in the past. In some ways the study and treatment of mental disorders have come a long way, but in other respects, clinical scientists and practitioners are still struggling to make a difference. The current era of abnormal psychology can be said to have begun in the 1950s.

## Severe Disturbances and Their Treatment

In the 1950s researchers discovered a number of new *psychotropic medications*—drugs that primarily affect the brain and alleviate many symptoms of mental dysfunctioning. They included the first *antipsychotic drugs,* to correct grossly confused and distorted thinking; *antidepressant drugs,* to lift the mood of severely depressed people; and *antianxiety drugs,* to reduce tension and anxiety.

With the discovery and application of these drugs, many severely disturbed patients in mental hospitals—the same patients who had languished there for years—began to show signs of significant improvement. Hospital administrators, encouraged by the effectiveness of the drugs and pressured by a growing public outcry over the high cost of care and the terrible conditions in public mental hospitals, began to discharge patients almost immediately.

Since the discovery of these medications, mental health professionals in most of the developed nations of the world have followed a policy of *deinstitutionalization,* and hundreds of thousands of patients have been released from public mental hospitals. On any given day in 1955, close to 600,000 people were confined in public mental institutions across the United States. Today the daily patient population in the same hospitals is around 100,000 (Manderscheid & Sonnenschein, 1992) (see Figure 1-1).

In short, outpatient care has now become the primary mode of treatment for people with severe psychological disturbances as well as for those with more moderate problems. When severely impaired people do require institutionalization, the current practice is to provide them with short-term hospitalization and

---

*Psychotropic medications* Drugs that primarily affect the brain and alleviate many symptoms of mental dysfunctioning.

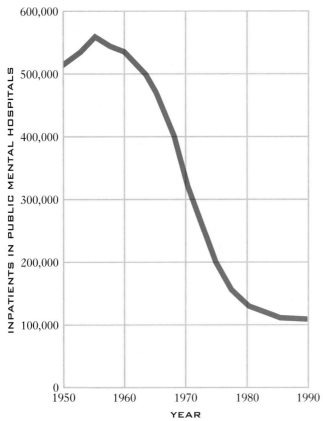

Figure 1-1   *The number of patients (100,000) now hospitalized in public mental hospitals in the United States is a small fraction of the number hospitalized in 1955. (Adapted from Manderscheid & Sonnenschein, 1992; Torrey, 1988.)*

then return them to the community. Ideally, they are then provided with outpatient psychotherapy and medication monitoring in community mental health centers. Other community programs such as supervised residences (halfway houses) and vocational rehabilitation centers may also be available.

This recent emphasis on community care for people with severe psychological disturbances, called the *community mental health approach,* will be discussed further in Chapters 4 and 13. The approach has been very helpful for many patients, but unfortunately too few community facilities and programs are available to address the needs of severely disturbed people in the United States. As a result, hundreds of thousands fail to make lasting recoveries, and are shuffled back and forth between the mental hospital and the community. After they are released from the hospital, they receive at best minimal care and often wind up living in de-

*Community mental health approach*   A sociocultural treatment approach emphasizing community care for people with psychological disturbances.

crepit rooming houses or on the streets. It is now estimated that 200,000 persons with severe psychological disturbances are, in fact, homeless on any given day (Manderscheid & Rosenstein, 1992), while another 50,000 are prison inmates (NIMH, 1992). Their virtual abandonment is truly a national disgrace.

## Less Severe Disturbances and Their Treatment

The treatment picture for people with less severe psychological disturbances has been more positive since the 1950s. Outpatient care has continued to be the preferred mode of treatment for these people, and the number and types of facilities that offer such care have expanded to meet the need.

Before the 1950s, almost all outpatient care took the form of *private psychotherapy,* an arrangement by which an individual directly paid a psychotherapist for counseling services. This tended to be an expensive form of treatment, available almost exclusively to the affluent. Since the 1950s, however, many medical health insurance plans have expanded coverage to include private psychotherapy, a trend that current government health-care reforms have pledged to continue, so that this service is now more widely available to people with more modest incomes (Levin, 1992). In addition, outpatient therapy has become increasingly available in a variety of relatively inexpensive settings—community mental health centers, crisis intervention centers, family service centers, and other social service agencies (Olfson et al., 1994). The new settings have spurred a dramatic increase in the number of persons seeking outpatient care for psychological problems.

The growth in the use of outpatient services by both severely disturbed and less disturbed persons is seen in Figure 1-2. In 1955 approximately 23 percent of people treated for psychological disturbances were treated as outpatients. Today that figure is about 94 percent.

Another change in outpatient care since the 1950s has been the development of specialized programs that focus exclusively on one kind of psychological problem. We now have, for example, suicide prevention centers, substance abuse programs, eating disorder programs, phobia clinics, and sexual dysfunction programs. Practitioners in these programs acquire the kind of expertise that can come only by concentrating one's efforts in a single area.

*Private psychotherapy*   An arrangement by which an individual directly pays a psychotherapist for counseling services.

**1950'S (1.7 MILLION CASES)**

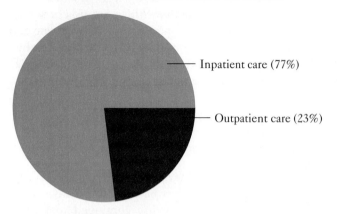

Inpatient care (77%)

Outpatient care (23%)

**TODAY (22 MILLION CASES)**

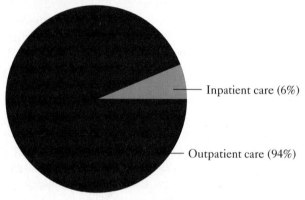

Inpatient care (6%)

Outpatient care (94%)

Figure 1-2   *The percentage of mental health patients who are treated on an outpatient basis has grown steadily since the 1950s. "Inpatient care" includes mental hospitals, general hospitals, and Veterans Administration hospitals. "Outpatient care" includes community mental health agencies, private therapists, day-care centers, and specialists in social and vocational rehabilitation. (Adapted from Regier et al., 1993; Narrow et al., 1993; Witkin et al., 1990; NIMH, 1983.)*

## Today's Perspectives and Professionals

One of the most significant developments in the understanding and treatment of abnormal psychological functioning has been the recent emergence of numerous, often competing theoretical perspectives. Before the 1950s, the *psychoanalytic* perspective, with its emphasis on unconscious conflicts as the cause of psychopathology, was dominant. Then the discovery of effective psychotropic drugs in the 1950s brought new stature to the somatogenic, or *biological,* view of abnormality. Other influential perspectives have also emerged since the 1950s, including the *behavioral, cognitive, humanistic-existential,* and *sociocultural* schools of thought, which explain and treat abnormality in very different ways. At present no single perspective dominates the clinical field as the psychoanalytic perspective once did.

In addition, a variety of professional practitioners now offer help to people with psychological problems—both those who warrant a clinical diagnosis and others who simply want to learn to cope better with the stresses in their lives (Murstein & Fontaine, 1993). This, too, represents a change from the situation of several decades ago. Before the 1950s, psychotherapy was the exclusive province of *psychiatrists,* physicians who had completed three to four additional years of training after medical school (a residency) in the treatment of abnormal mental functioning. After World War II, however, the demand for mental health services expanded more rapidly than the ranks of psychiatrists, so other professional groups stepped in to fill the need.

Prominent among those other groups are *clinical psychologists*—professionals who earn a doctorate in clinical psychology by completing four years of graduate training in abnormal functioning and its treatment and also complete a one-year internship at a mental hospital or mental health agency. Other important groups that provide psychotherapy and related services are *counseling psychologists, educational psychologists, psychiatric nurses, marriage therapists, family therapists,* and—the largest group—*psychiatric social workers.* Each of these specialties requires completion of its own graduate training program (Dial et al., 1992). Theoretically, each specialty conducts therapy in a distinctive way, but in reality there is considerable overlap in the ways practitioners of the various specialties work.

One final important development in the study and treatment of mental disorders since World War II has been a heightened appreciation of the need for effective research. As numerous theories and forms of treatment have been proposed, *clinical researchers,* professionals who systematically study psychological abnormality, have tried to single out the concepts that best explain and predict abnormal behavior, to determine which treatments are most effective, and to discover whether they should be modified and, if so, how. Today well-trained clinical researchers are conducting studies in academic institutions, laboratories, mental hospitals, mental health centers, and other clinical settings throughout the world. Their work has already yielded important discoveries and changed many of our ideas about abnormal psychological functioning.

*Summing Up*

*The past forty years have brought significant changes in the understanding and treatment of abnormal functioning. For example, the availability of psychotropic drugs has led to a policy of deinstitutionalization and a focus on outpatient treatment for those with serious mental disorders. There has also been a dramatic increase in treatment for patients suffering less severe psychological disturbances.*

*Today, a variety of perspectives characterize the field of abnormal psychology, and various professional groups offer help to people with psychological problems. At the same time, there is a heightened appreciation of the need for systematic research in the clinical field.*

# The Task of Clinical Researchers

Research is the key to accuracy and progress in all fields of study, and it is particularly important in abnormal psychology, because inaccurate beliefs about mental abnormality can cause or prolong enormous suffering. Unfortunately, although effective and rigorous research is essential for progress in this field, the nature of the issues under study makes such research particularly difficult. Researchers must figure out ways to measure such elusive concepts as unconscious motives, private thoughts, mood change, and human potential, while at the same time complying with the ethical standards that have been established to protect the rights of research subjects, both human and animal. Let us examine the leading methods used by today's researchers so that we may better understand the many studies and findings that will be referred to throughout this textbook.

Clinical researchers try to discover universal "laws" or principles of abnormal psychological functioning. Like researchers in other fields, they try to use the *scientific method* in their work—that is, they systematically acquire and evaluate information through observation to gain an understanding of the phenomena they are studying. They search for general, or *nomo-*

thetic, truths about the nature, causes, and treatments of abnormality ("nomothetic" is derived from the Greek *nomothetis,* "lawgiver"), often by identifying and studying the "average" behaviors and "typical" reactions of large numbers of people.

To formulate a nomothetic explanation of abnormal psychology, scientists in abnormal psychology, like scientists in all disciplines, attempt to identify and explain relationships between variables. Simply stated, a **variable** is any characteristic or event that can vary, whether from time to time, from place to place, or from person to person. Clinical researchers are particularly interested in such variables as childhood traumas and other life experiences, moods, levels of social and occupational functioning, and responses to treatment techniques. They seek to determine whether two or more such variables change together and whether a change in one variable causes a change in another. Will the death of a parent, for example, cause a child to become depressed? If so, will a given therapy reduce that depression?

To acquire valid information about abnormal behavior, clinical researchers depend primarily on three methods of investigation: the case study, the correlational method, and the experimental method. Each is best suited to certain circumstances and to answering certain questions. Collectively, they enable clinical scientists to formulate and test **hypotheses,** or hunches, that certain variables are related in certain ways, and to draw broad conclusions as to why.

*Over the years, researchers have increasingly protected the rights of human subjects. Although the rights of animal subjects are also of concern, these are less clear cut and more controversial, leading at times to heated debates between animal researchers and animal rights activists.*

---

*Nomothetic understanding*  In the context of abnormal psychology, a general understanding of the nature, causes, and treatments of abnormality.

*One of the most celebrated case studies in abnormal psychology is a study of identical quadruplets called the Genain sisters by researchers (after the Greek words for "dire birth"). All of the sisters developed schizophrenia in their 20s. This case study suggested that an interaction of biological and environmental factors may contribute to schizophrenia (Buchsbaum & Haier, 1987.)*

# The Case Study

A *case study* is a detailed and often interpretive description of one person. It describes the person's background, present circumstances, and symptoms. It may also describe the application and results of a particular treatment, and it may speculate about how the person's problems developed. For example, a well-known study of a case of multiple personality disorder, *The Three Faces of Eve,* provides a clinical account of a woman who displayed three alternating personalities, each having a distinct set of memories, preferences, and personal habits (Thigpen & Cleckley, 1957).

All clinicians take notes and keep records in the course of treating their patients, and many further organize such notes into a formal case study that is shared with other professionals. Faced with the task of helping someone, a clinician must first gather all relevant information and search through it for factors that may have brought about the person's problems. The clues provided by the case study may have direct implications for the person's treatment, but case studies also play nomothetic roles that go far beyond the individual clinical case (Smith, 1988).

## Contributions of the Case Study

Case studies often serve as a source of ideas about the reasons for abnormal behavior and, as such, "open the way for discoveries" (Bolgar, 1965). Indeed, Freud's theory of psychoanalysis was based mainly on the cases he saw in private practice. Second, a case study may provide tentative support for a theory. Freud used case studies in precisely this way, as preliminary evidence for the accuracy of his ideas. Conversely, case studies may serve to challenge theoretical assumptions (Kratochwill, 1992).

Case studies also may serve as a source of ideas for new therapeutic techniques or as examples of unique applications of existing techniques. The psychoanalytic principle that patients may derive therapeutic benefit from discussing their problems and underlying psychological issues, for example, has roots in the famous case of Anna O., described by Freud's collaborator, Josef Breuer.

And, finally, case studies may offer opportunities to study unusual problems that do not occur often enough to permit more general observations and comparisons (Lehman, 1991). Investigators of problems such as multiple personality disorder, amnesia, and gender identity disorder once relied exclusively on case studies for information about these problems.

## Limitations of the Case Study

Although case studies are useful in many ways, they have limitations. To begin with, they are reported by biased observers (Lehman, 1991). Therapists are participants in the healing process as well as observers of it, and they have a personal stake in the outcomes of their cases and the apparent success of their treatments.

A related problem is that most case studies do not provide objective evidence that a client's dysfunction has in fact been caused by the events that the therapist

---

*Case study* A detailed account of a person's life and psychological problems.

**Table 1-1**    *Relative Strengths and Weaknesses of Research Methods*

|  | Provides Individual Information | Provides General Information | Provides Causal Information | Statistical Analysis Is Possible | Replicable |
|---|---|---|---|---|---|
| Case study | Yes | No | No | No | No |
| Correlational method | No | Yes | No | Yes | Yes |
| Experimental method | No | Yes | Yes | Yes | Yes |

or client says are responsible. After all, the events they single out as significant are only a fraction of those that may have played a part in creating the person's predicament.

Finally, case studies provide little basis for generalization. Factors or treatment techniques that seem important in one case may be of no help at all in efforts to understand or treat others.

The limitations of the case study are largely addressed by two other methods of investigation: the *correlational method* and the *experimental method*. They do not offer the richness of detail that makes case studies such interesting reading, but they do help investigators draw broad conclusions about the occurrence and characteristics of abnormality in the population at large. Three characteristics of these methods enable clinical investigators to gain nomothetic insights. (1) Researchers observe many individuals to collect enough information, or **data,** on which to base a conclusion. (2) They apply careful procedures uniformly, so that other researchers can replicate their studies to see whether they consistently yield the same findings. (3) The results of studies conducted by these methods can be analyzed by statistical tests that help indicate whether broad conclusions are justified. Table 1-1 summarizes the strengths and weaknesses of case studies, correlational studies, and experiments.

## The Correlational Method

*Correlation* is the degree to which events or characteristics vary in conjunction with each other. The *correlational method* is a research procedure used to determine this "co-relationship" between variables. This method has, for example, been applied in various ways

to answer the question, "Is there a correlation between the amount of life stress people confront and the degree of depression they experience?" That is, as people repeatedly confront stressful events, are they increasingly likely to become depressed?

As one way of answering this question, researchers have collected life stress scores (for example, the number of threatening events experienced during a certain period of time) and depression scores (for example, scores on a survey that assesses a person's degree of depression). Typically, they have found that these variables increase or decrease together (Paykel & Cooper, 1992). That is, the greater a particular person's life stress score, the higher his or her score on a depression scale. Correlations of this kind are said to have a positive *direction,* and the correlation is referred to as a *positive correlation.*

Correlations can have a negative rather than a positive direction. In a *negative correlation,* as the value of one variable increases, the value of the other variable decreases. Researchers have found, for example, a negative correlation between depression and activity level. The greater one's depression, the lower one's number of activities.

The third possible conclusion of a correlational study is that two variables are *unrelated*, that there is no systematic relationship between them. As the measures of one variable increase, those of the other variable sometimes increase and sometimes decrease. Such a lack of relationship has been found between depression and intelligence, for example.

In addition to knowing the direction of a correlation, researchers need to know its *magnitude,* or strength. That is, how closely do the two variables correspond? Does one always vary as a direct reflection of the other, or is their relationship less precise? When two variables are found to vary together very closely in subject after subject, the correlation is said to be high or strong.

The direction and magnitude of a correlation is often calculated numerically and expressed by a statis-

*Correlation*  The degree to which events or characteristics vary in conjunction with each other.

*Correlational method*  A research procedure used to determine the extent to which events or characteristics vary together.

tical term called the *correlational coefficient*. The correlational coefficient can vary from $+1.00$, which conveys a perfect positive correlation, down to $-1.00$, which represents a perfect negative correlation between two variables. The sign of the coefficient ($+$ or $-$) signifies the direction of the correlation; the number represents its magnitude. The closer the coefficient is to .00, the weaker, or lower in magnitude, the correlation.

Because the behavior and reactions of every human being are subject to change and because many human responses can be measured only approximately, most correlations found in psychological research fall short of a perfect positive or negative correlation. One study of the correlation between recent life stress and depression had a sample of 68 adults and found a correlation of $+.53$ between the two variables (Miller et al., 1976). Although hardly perfect, a correlation of this magnitude with a sample of this size is considered large in psychological research.

## Statistical Analysis of Correlational Data

Once scientists determine the correlation between variables for a particular group of subjects, they must decide whether it accurately reflects a real correlation in the general population from which the subjects are drawn. Scientists can never know for certain that the correlation they find is truly characteristic of the larger population, but they can test their conclusions to some extent by doing a *statistical analysis* of their data. In essence, they apply principles of probability to their findings to learn how likely it is that those particular findings have occurred by chance. If the statistical analysis suggests that chance is a likely reason for the correlation they found in the sample, the researchers have no basis for drawing broader conclusions from that correlation. But if the statistical analysis indicates that chance is unlikely to account for the relationship they found, they call the correlation *statistically significant* and they conclude that their findings reflect a correlation that really exists in the general population.

> ### Consider This
> Although the size and significance of a correlation may seem impressive, it may have more than one interpretation. How would *you* interpret the sizable correlation between life events and depression? How would you decide which of various possible interpretations is the most accurate?

---

*Correlational coefficient*   A statistical expression of the direction and the magnitude of a correlation, ranging from $-1.00$ to $+1.00$.

## Strengths and Limitations of the Correlational Method

The correlational method has certain advantages over the case study. When researchers quantify their variables, observe numerous subjects, and apply statistical analyses, they are in a better position to generalize their findings to people beyond the ones they have studied. Researchers are also able to repeat correlational studies on new samples of subjects in order to support or clarify particular relationships, thus corroborating the results of a particular study.

On the other hand, although correlations give researchers evidence that allows them to predict the presence or absence of one variable based on the presence or absence of another, they do not *explain* the relationship between the variables. Looking at the positive correlation found in many life stress studies, we might be tempted to conclude that increases in recent life stress cause people to feel more depressed. Actually, however, the two variables may be correlated for any one of three reasons: (1) life stress may cause depression; (2) depressive functioning may cause persons to experience more life stress; or (3) depression and life stress may each be caused by a third variable, such as poverty. Questions about causality call for the use of the experimental method, described below.

## Special Forms of Correlational Research

Two kinds of correlational research that are used widely by clinical researchers—epidemiological studies and longitudinal studies—warrant special consideration. *Epidemiological studies* are investigations that determine the incidence and prevalence of a disorder in a given population (Weyerer & Hafner, 1992). *Incidence* is the number of new cases of a disorder that emerge in the population within a particular time interval; *prevalence* is the total number of cases (that is, the sum of existing and newly emerging cases) of the disorder in the population at any given time.

Over the past fifteen years, clinical researchers across the United States, under the sponsorship of the National Institutes of Mental Health, have worked on the most comprehensive epidemiological study ever

---

*Epidemiological study*   An investigation that determines the incidence and prevalence of a disorder in a given population.

*Incidence*   The number of new cases of a problem or disorder that occur in a population over a specific period of time.

*Prevalence*   The total number of cases of a problem or disorder occurring in a population over a specific period of time.

*Correlational studies of many pairs of twins have determined that a strong relationship exists between genetic factors and certain psychological disorders. A "concordance" rate represents the likelihood that if one twin has a disorder, the other will develop it. Identical twins (twins, like those pictured here, who have identical genes) have higher concordance rates for some psychopathologies than do fraternal twins (twins whose genetic makeup is not identical).*

conducted. In the Epidemiologic Catchment Area Study, they interviewed more than 20,000 people from five cities to determine the prevalence of numerous mental disorders in this country and the nature and availability of appropriate treatment programs (Regier et al., 1993). The data from this extraordinary study have been compared with figures from well-conducted epidemiological studies done in other countries around the world to see how rates of mental disorders and treatment programs vary from country to country (Weissman et al., 1992).

Collectively, these epidemiological studies have indicated various trends: women have a higher prevalence rate of anxiety disorders and depression than men, men have a higher rate of alcoholism than women, elderly people have a higher rate of suicide than younger people, African Americans have a higher rate of high blood pressure than white Americans, and persons from some non-Western countries (such as Taiwan) have a higher rate of mental disorders than people from Western countries (such as the United States). Findings of this sort help investigators identify groups and settings at risk for particular disorders and often lead them to suspect that something unique about the group or setting is helping to cause the disorder (Rogers & Holloway, 1990). Declining health in elderly people, for example, may make them more likely to commit suicide than younger people, or cul-

tural pressures or attitudes prevalent in one country may be responsible for a rate of mental dysfunctioning that differs from the rate found in another country. Yet, as in other forms of correlational research, such suspicions can be confirmed only by the experimental method.

*Longitudinal studies* (also called **high-risk** or **developmental studies**) are investigations in which the characteristics or behavior of the same subjects is observed on many occasions over a long period of time. In several well-known longitudinal studies (Parnas, 1988; Mednick, 1971), investigators observed the progress over the years of normally functioning children whose mothers or fathers manifested schizophrenia (that is, normal children who were considered to be at risk for schizophrenia). The researchers found, among other things, that the children of the parents with the most severe cases of schizophrenia were more likely to develop a psychological disorder and to commit crimes at later points in their development. Because longitudinal studies document the order of certain events, they provide stronger clues than conventional correlational studies about which events may be causes and which are likely to be consequences. But they still do not pinpoint causation. Are the psychological problems that certain high-risk children encounter later in their lives caused by a genetic factor inherited from their parents, by their parents' inadequate coping behaviors, by the loss of their parents to extended hospitalization, or by other factors? Again, experimental studies are necessary to answer these questions.

## The Experimental Method

An *experiment* is a research procedure in which a variable is manipulated and the manipulation's effect on another variable is observed. The manipulated variable is called the *independent variable,* and the variable being observed is called the *dependent variable.*

One of the questions that clinical scientists most frequently ask, for example, is "Does a particular therapy relieve the symptoms of a given disorder?"

---

*Longitudinal study* An investigation in which the characteristics or behavior of the same subjects is observed on many different occasions over a long period of time.

*Experiment* A research procedure in which a variable is manipulated and the effect of the manipulation is observed.

*Independent variable* The variable in an experiment that is manipulated to determine whether it has an effect on another variable.

*Dependent variable* The variable in an experiment that is expected to change as the independent variable is manipulated.

(Lambert & Bergin, 1994). Because this question is about a causal relationship, it can be answered only by an experiment. That is, experimenters must administer the therapy to subjects who are suffering from a disorder and then observe whether the subjects improve. The administration of the therapy is the *independent variable*, while the subjects' disorder is the *dependent variable*.

The investigators must then apply a statistical analysis to the data and determine how likely it is that the pattern and size of changes in the dependent variable are due to chance. As in correlational studies, if the statistical analysis shows this likelihood to be very low, the observed differences are considered to be *statistically significant*, and the experimenter may conclude with some confidence that they are due to the independent variable.

If the true or primary cause of a certain effect cannot be separated from a host of other possible causes, then an experiment gives us very little information. The major obstacles to isolating the true cause and thus carrying out an effective experiment are *confounds*—variables other than the independent variable that are also acting on the dependent variable. When there are confounds in an experiment, the experimenter cannot confidently attribute the results to the independent variable under investigation because it may actually be the confounding variables that are causing the observed changes (Geyer, 1992).

For example, situational variables such as the location of the particular therapy office (say, a quiet country setting) or a soothing color scheme in the office may have a positive effect on subjects in a therapy study. Or perhaps the subjects in a particular experiment are unusually motivated or have extraordinarily high expectations that the therapy will work, which thus accounts for their improvement. To minimize the influence of potential confounds, researchers incorporate three important features into their experiments—a control group, random assignment, and a blind design (Viken, 1992) (see Box 1-2).

## The Control Group

A *control group* is a group of subjects who are not exposed to the manipulation of the independent variable under investigation, but whose experience is otherwise similar to that of the *experimental group,* the subjects who *are* exposed to the independent variable. By comparing the two groups, an experimenter can better determine the effect of the manipulated variable. In ther-

*"Oh, not bad. The light comes on, I press the bar, they write me a check. How about you?*
(Drawing by Cheney; © 1993 The New Yorker Magazine, Inc.)

apy studies, for example, experimenters typically divide clients into two groups. The experimental group may come into an office and receive the therapy in question for an hour, while the control group may simply come into the office. If the experimenters find later that the clients in the experimental group improve more than clients in the control group, they may conclude that the therapy was effective in helping them above and beyond the effects of the office setting, time, and any other confounds. Experimenters must guard against confounds by trying to provide all subjects, both control and experimental, with experiences that are identical in every way except for the one critical item under investigation, the independent variable.

## Random Assignment

It is possible that systematic differences may exist between subjects in the experimental and control groups prior to a study. In a therapy study, for example, it may happen that an unintentional bias on the part of a research assistant has caused her to put the wealthier subjects into the experimental group and the poorer subjects into the control group. This difference, rather than therapy, could be the cause of greater improvement later found among the experimental subjects. To reduce the possibility that preexisting systematic differences are causing the differences observed between the groups in an experiment, experimenters typically use *random assignment*. This is the general term for any selection procedure that ensures that every subject

---

*Control group* In an experiment, a group of subjects who are not exposed to the independent variable.

*Random assignment* A selection procedure that ensures that subjects in an experiment are randomly placed either in the control group or in the experimental group.

## Box 1-2

# *Confounding the Experts: Stress and the Executive Monkey*

Every so often, an experiment yields results so compelling that the thinking of an entire generation is affected. But beware: an experiment that influences our view of the world may later prove to have serious flaws that have gone unnoticed. Even the best-intentioned and most painstaking researchers are only human. They do not always recognize every possible confound. Usually journal reviewers catch the mistake before the research is published; or if it is published, it does not become particularly influential and is lost in the crowd. If such an experiment passes journal review and is then seen as important, however, the consequences can be both embarrassing to the researcher and harmful to the discipline. Consider the "executive monkey study."

What happens if you take two monkeys, put them in separate wire cages, and then give them shocks every 20 seconds for 6 hours—shocks that one of the monkeys can terminate (for itself and the other monkey) by pressing a lever? The psychologist J. V. Brady predicted that the monkeys who did not have a lever to press would develop ulcers because they had no control over the shocks (Brady et al., 1958). In his experiment, exactly the opposite happened. In each of four pairs of monkeys, the "executive" monkey—the one who was able to stop the shocks—developed duodenal ulcers and died. The other monkey in each pair was not affected. This result ran counter to predictions offered by contemporary theories that the monkeys without control would suffer a

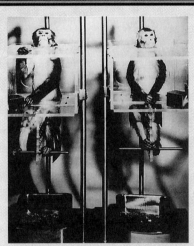

*The executive monkey (left) learns that it can prevent shocks by pressing a level with its hand. The control monkey (right) is given no control over the shocks and appears to lose interest in both the lever and its surroundings.*

greater number of problems than those in control of the shocks. Nevertheless, the research community and the public embraced the finding, partly because it supported the intuitive notion that people with high-level positions in business, people who make important decisions every day, were prone to get ulcers. For thirteen years Brady's results exerted great influence on psychological views about the relationship between environment and stress.

To "replicate" an experiment is to repeat it exactly as it was done the first time and get the same results. The executive monkey study could not be replicated. Investigators who attempted and failed, including Brady himself, looked carefully at the original procedure used and finally found a glaring

mistake. It turned out that Brady had failed to consider the importance of assigning his subjects at *random* to each of the conditions in the experiment. Prior to the experiment, he had pretested all eight monkeys by giving them shocks. The first four monkeys to press the lever were assigned to the "executive" condition. A later study found that animals with a higher response rate (animals that would press the lever first in Brady's pretest) were more likely to develop ulcers (Weiss, 1977). It appeared that their higher emotionality was responsible for both the response rate and the ulcers. In later executive monkey studies in which there was random assignment, the animals *without control* over the shocks suffered more than those with control. Brady's finding had been an artifact—a product of his own activity, not the monkeys'.

Brady was an outstanding researcher who had made an honest mistake. His result was the opposite of his expectations and surprised him as much as anyone else. Unfortunately, it also was generally accepted and cited for more than a dozen years. Nevertheless, the erroneous experiment has proved to be valuable: it spurred an enormous amount of research that has ultimately led to a more accurate understanding of stress and how it relates to health. It also taught the scientific community a great lesson. There is always the chance of inadvertent mistakes in research. The only way to minimize such mistakes is to train investigators as carefully as possible and to review critically each study that is announced.

in the experiment is as likely to be placed in one group as the other—from flipping a coin to picking names out of a hat. Boxes 1-2 and 1-3 show what can happen when assignment is not random.

## Blind Design

Finally, subjects may bias an experiment's results by trying to please or help the experimenter (Kazdin, 1994). In a therapy experiment, for example, subjects who receive treatment, knowing the purpose of the study and knowing which group they are in, might actually work harder consciously or unconsciously to feel better in order to fulfill the experimenter's expectations. If so, *subject bias* rather than therapy could be causing their improvement.

Experimenters may prevent the potential effects of subject bias in an experiment by not letting subjects know which group they are in. In a therapy study, for example, control subjects could undergo a procedure or receive a pill that looks or tastes like real therapy but has none of the ingredients of actual therapy. This "imitation" therapy is called *placebo therapy*. If the experimental (true therapy) subjects then improve more than the control (placebo therapy) subjects, experimenters may more confidently conclude that the true therapy is the cause of their improvement. This experimental strategy is called a *blind design* because subjects are blind as to which group they are in.

> ### Consider This
> When researchers study the effectiveness of drug therapies, they often administer a placebo (or sugar) pill to the control group. If the therapy under study is effective, the subjects who receive the real drug will generally improve more than those who receive the placebo drug. However, at least some subjects who receive placebo pills do, in fact, improve. Why might sugar pills or other kinds of placebo treatment help people to feel better?

Even when subject bias is addressed, an experiment may still be invalidated by the existence of *experimenter bias* (Margraf et al., 1991). That is, an experimenter may have expectations that are subtly transmitted to subjects and affect the outcome of the experiment. This confound source is referred to as the *Rosenthal effect*, after the psychologist who first helped clarify the effects of experimenter bias

(Rosenthal, 1966). Experimenters can eliminate the potential effects of their own bias by contriving to be blind themselves. In a drug therapy study, for example, an aide could make sure that the real drugs and placebo drugs look identical. The experimenter could then administer the drugs without knowing which subjects were receiving true medications and which were receiving false medications.

While the subjects or the experimenter may be kept blind in an experiment, it is best that *both* be blind (a *double-blind design*). In fact, most clinical experimenters now use double-blind designs to test the efficacy of antianxiety, antidepressant, and antipsychotic medications (Stonier, 1992). Many experimenters also arrange for a group of judges to assess the patients' improvement independently, and the judges, too, are blind to the group each patient is in—a *triple-blind design*.

# Variations in Experimental Design

For reasons of logistics and, more importantly, of ethics, clinical experimenters often settle for imperfect variations of optimal experimental designs to determine cause-and-effect relationships. The most common such variations are the quasi-experimental design, the natural experiment, the analogue experiment, and the single-subject experiment.

## Quasi-Experimental Design

*Quasi-experiments* are experiments in which investigators do not randomly assign subjects to control and experimental groups but instead make use of groups that already exist in the world at large (Kazdin, 1994). Some researchers refer to this research method as a *mixed design.* For example, because investigators of child abuse cannot inflict abuse on a randomly chosen group of children, they instead compare children who already have a history of abuse with children who do not. In such studies they may further use *matched control groups.* That is, they match the experimental subjects with control subjects who share several of the same potentially confounding variables with them, including age, sex, race, birth order, number of children in the family, socioeconomic status, and type of neighborhood (Kinard, 1982). That is, for every abused child in the experimental group, they choose an unabused child of the same age, sex, race, and so on to be included in the control group.

---

*Blind design*   An experimental design in which subjects, experimenters, or evaluators do not know which subjects are actually in the experimental condition.

*Quasi-experiment*   An experiment in which investigators do not randomly assign the subjects to control and experimental groups but instead make use of groups that already exist in the world at large.

Box 1-3

# *Gender, Race, and Age Bias in Research*

Sometimes mistakes are committed by an entire community of researchers. Blinded by certain biases about society, investigators may consistently err in their efforts to design appropriate studies. For example, for many years scientists in Western society have favored the use of young white men as subjects for research on human functioning (Stark-Adamek, 1992; Eichler et al., 1992). Only recently have researchers come to appreciate the extent to which some of science's broad conclusions about human functioning are, in fact, sometimes inaccurate generalizations drawn from this select sample of subjects. In short, the findings of studies that use only young white male subjects may not be relevant to persons of a different sex, race, or age. Such bias may, we are now learning, lead to some very serious misconceptions about the symptoms, causes, course, and treatment of various mental disorders.

A recent review of the leading studies on schizophrenia revealed that male subjects outnumbered female subjects by more than 2 to 1 (Wahl & Hunter, 1992), despite the fact that this serious disorder is as prevalent in women as in men. How can we be sure that the psychological and biological insights gleaned from these studies are valid for all persons with schizophrenia rather than just men with schizophrenia?

In a similar vein, many medications for mental disorders have been tested on groups made up largely of young, white, male subjects, and on that basis alone have been made available to all patients. Often, however, such medications have turned out to act differently, sometimes dangerously so, in elderly, female, or nonwhite populations (Wolfe et al., 1988), suggesting that many persons may be receiving the wrong dosages of medications that they might otherwise profit from.

The need to correct this kind of research bias is much more than a mere academic formality. It is tied closely to such important issues as scientific credibility, public health, and even sexism, racism, and ageism. Although recent reviews show that researchers are doing better each year—becoming more aware of gender, race, and age, and designing more appropriate studies—it is also clear that more improvement is needed (Sue et al., 1994; Gannon et al., 1992). The American Psychological Association and the Canadian Psychological Association have recently offered guidelines to help enlighten their members about the problem and its remedies (Stark-Adamek, 1992). They are aware that when research is biased in these ways, knowledge is limited, progress is stifled, and everyone loses.

## Natural Experiment

*Natural experiments* are those in which nature rather than an experimenter manipulates an independent variable, and the experimenter systematically observes the effects. This is the design that must be used for studying the psychological effects of unusual and unpredictable events, such as floods, earthquakes, plane crashes, and fires. Because the subjects in these studies are selected for the experimental group by an accident of fate rather than by conscious design, natural experiments are actually a kind of quasi-experiment.

## Analogue Experiment

Experimenters who use *analogue experiments* induce laboratory subjects to behave in ways they believe to parallel real-life abnormal behavior. They then conduct

experiments on this laboratory-created, analogous form of abnormality in the hope of shedding light on the real-life counterpart. For example, in a series of well-known studies, investigator Martin Seligman has produced depression-like symptoms in laboratory subjects by repeatedly exposing them to unpleasant experiences (shocks, loud noises, task failures) over which they have no control. In these "learned helplessness" studies, the subjects seem to give up, lose their initiative, and become sad. Experimenters may use animals or humans as subjects in analogue studies. It is important to recognize, however, that analogue experiments are enlightening only to the extent that the laboratory-induced condition is indeed analogous to the human abnormality in question (Vredenburg et al., 1993).

## Single-Subject Experiment

Sometimes scientists do not have the luxury of experimenting on numerous subjects. They may, for example, be investigating a disorder so rare that few subjects are available. Experimentation is still possible in

---

*Natural experiment* An experiment in which nature, rather than an experimenter, manipulates an independent variable and the experimenter systematically observes the effects.

*Analogue experiment* In the context of abnormal psychology, an investigation in which the experimenter induces laboratory subjects to behave in ways that resemble real-life abnormal behavior.

*The Great Flood of 1993 brought destruction and homelessness to thousands of people in America's Midwest, including this man on Front Street in Clarksville, Missouri. Natural experiments conducted in the aftermath of this and other natural catastrophes have found that many survivors experience lingering feelings of anxiety and depression.*

such cases in the form of **single-subject,** or **single-case, experimental designs** (Kazdin, 1994). In designs of this kind, the single subject is observed and measured before the manipulation of an independent variable. **Baseline data**—data gathered during the observation, or baseline, period—reveal what a subject's behavior is like in the absence of any manipulations or interventions, and thus establish a standard with which later changes may be compared. The experimenter next introduces the independent variable and observes the subject's behavior once again. Any changes in behavior are attributed to the effects of the independent variable. A common single-subject experimental design is the *ABAB.*

In an ABAB design, a subject's reactions are measured and compared not only during a baseline period (condition A) and after the introduction of the independent variable (condition B) but once again after the independent variable has been removed (condition A) and yet again after it has been reintroduced (condition B). If the subject's responses change back and forth systematically with changes in the independent variable, the experimenter may conclude that the independent variable is causing the shifting responses (Kratochwill, 1992). Essentially, in an ABAB design a subject is compared with him- or herself under different conditions rather than with control subjects. Subjects therefore serve as their own controls.

Clinicians are likely to resort to an ABAB design when they wish to determine the effectiveness of a particular form of therapy on a client but are unable to obtain other clients with similar problems for a prop-

erly controlled experiment. One therapist used this design to determine whether a behavioral reinforcement treatment program, such as we will be discussing in Chapter 3, was helping to reduce a retarded teenage boy's habit of disrupting his special education class with loud talk (Deitz, 1977). The reinforcement program consisted of rewarding the boy with extra teacher time whenever he managed to go 55 minutes without talking in class more than three times. When the student's level of talking was measured during a baseline period, it was found to consist of frequent verbal disruptions. Next the boy was given a series of teacher reinforcement sessions (the independent variable); as expected, his loud talk soon decreased dramatically. Then the reinforcement treatment was stopped, and the student's loud talk was found to increase once again. Apparently the independent variable had indeed been the cause of the improvement.

To be more confident about this conclusion, the therapist introduced the teacher reinforcement treatment yet again and found that once again the subject's behavior improved. This reintroduction of the independent variable helped rule out the possibility that some confounding factor (such as the onset of magnificent spring weather or a present from a relative) had actually been causing the boy's improvement.

*Chimpanzees and human beings share more than 90 percent of their genetic material, but the brains and bodies of the two species are enormously different, as are their perceptions and experiences. Thus abnormal-like behavior produced in animal analogue experiments may differ in key ways from the human abnormality under investigation.*

## The Limits of Clinical Investigation

We began this discussion of research by observing that clinical scientists look for general laws that will help them to understand, prevent, and treat psychological disorders. As we have seen, however, a variety of circumstances may impede their progress.

Each of the various investigative approaches addresses some of the problems inherent in studying human behavior, but no one approach overcomes them all. Thus it is best to view each method of investigation as one of a battery of approaches that collectively may shed considerable light on abnormal human functioning. When more than one of these methods has been used to investigate a certain disorder, it is important to ask whether all the results seem to point in the same direction. If they do, it is likely that clinical investigators are close to attaining a clear understanding of that disturbance or an effective treatment for it. Conversely, if the various methods seem to produce conflicting results, investigators must admit that their knowledge in that clinical area is still limited.

> ***Summing Up***
> *Clinical researchers use the scientific method to uncover nomothetic, or general, principles of abnormal psychological functioning. They depend primarily on three methods of investigation: the case study, the correlational method, and the experimental method. Each has certain strengths and weaknesses.*

# Chapter Review

1. **The Field:** The field devoted to the scientific study of abnormal behavior is called *abnormal psychology.* Its goals are to understand and to treat abnormal patterns of functioning.

2. **What Is Abnormality?** Abnormal patterns of psychological functioning are generally considered to be those that are *deviant, distressful, dysfunctional,* and *dangerous.* However, behavior must be considered in the context in which it occurs; behavior considered deviant in one set of circumstances may be the norm in another.

3. **Abnormality in Ancient Times:** The history of mental disorders, stretching back to the origins of humankind, provides any number of clues to the nature of psychological abnormality.

   A. **Prehistoric Societies:** There is evidence that Stone Age cultures used *trephination,* a primitive form of brain surgery, to treat abnormal behavior. People of early societies also sought to drive out evil spirits by *exorcism.*

   B. **Greeks and Romans:** Physicians of the Greek and Roman empires offered alternative explanations of mental illness. Hippocrates believed that abnormal behavior was due to an imbalance of bodily fluids, or *humors.* Treatment for mental disorders consisted of correcting diet and lifestyle.

4. **Abnormality during the Middle Ages and Renaissance:** In the Middle Ages, Europeans resurrected the demonological explanation of abnormal behavior and held that mental disorders were the work of the devil. As the Middle Ages drew to a close, medical explanations and treatments for psychological abnormality started to gain prominence.

   Care of people with mental disorders continued to improve during the Renaissance, highlighted by religious shrines dedicated to the humane treatment of such individuals. By the middle of the sixteenth century, however, persons with mental disorders were being warehoused in *asylums.*

5. **The Period of Moral Treatment:** Care of those with mental disorders started to improve again in the nineteenth century. Reformers Philippe Pinel and William Tuke viewed and treated such individuals as people suffering from an illness that required support and kindness. This *moral treatment* methodology also spread to the United States, where *state hospitals* were established to care for people with mental disorders.

   Unfortunately, moral treatment was costly and sometimes ineffective. As a result, the system disintegrated and mental hospitals reverted to warehouses where the inmates received minimal care.

6. **The Somatogenic and Psychogenic Views:** The late nineteenth century saw the return of the *somatogenic perspective,* the view that abnormal psychological functioning is rooted in physical causes. This change was precipitated in part by the work of Emil Kraepelin and the finding that general paresis was caused by the organic disease syphilis.

   The same period saw the emergence of the *psychogenic perspective,* the view that the chief causes of abnormal functioning are psychological. Sigmund Freud's *psychoanalytic approach* eventually gained wide acceptance and influenced future generations of researchers and practitioners.

7. **Recent Trends:** In the 1950s, researchers discovered a number of new *psychotropic drugs.* Their success

led to a policy of *deinstitutionalization,* under which hundreds of thousands of patients were released from public mental hospitals. In addition, *outpatient treatment* has become the primary approach for most persons with mental disorders.

Today a variety of perspectives and professionals characterize the field of abnormal psychology. Similarly, there are now many well-trained clinical researchers.

8. **The Task of Clinical Researchers:** Clinical researchers use the scientific method to uncover *nomothetic,* or general, principles of abnormal psychological functioning. They depend primarily on three methods of investigation.
   A. The *case study* is a detailed account of a person's life and psychological problems.
   B. The *correlational method* is a procedure for systematically observing the extent to which events

or characteristics vary together. This method allows researchers to draw broad conclusions about abnormality in the population at large.

Two widely used forms of the correlational method are *epidemiological studies,* which determine the incidence and prevalence of a disorder in a given population, and *longitudinal studies,* which observe the characteristics or behavior of the same subjects over a long period of time.

C. In the *experimental method,* researchers manipulate suspected causes to see whether expected effects will result. Clinical experimenters must often settle for imperfect variations of the optimal experimental design, including the *quasi-experimental design,* the *natural experiment,* the *analogue experiment,* and the *single-subject experiment.*

## Key Terms

| | | | |
|---|---|---|---|
| abnormal psychology | hypnotism | correlation | control group |
| culture | hysterical disorder | correlational method | random assignment |
| trephination | mesmerism | positive correlation | blind design |
| exorcism | psychoanalysis | negative correlation | experimenter bias |
| humors | outpatient therapy | correlational coefficient | Rosenthal effect |
| tarantism | psychotropic medication | statistical analysis | double-blind design |
| lycanthropy | community mental health | epidemiological study | triple-blind design |
| asylum | private psychotherapy | incidence | quasi-experiment |
| moral treatment | psychiatrist | prevalence | matched control group |
| state hospital | clinical psychologist | longitudinal study | natural experiment |
| somatogenic perspective | psychiatric social worker | experiment | analogue experiment |
| general paresis | nomothetic | independent variable | single-subject |
| psychogenic perspective | case study | dependent variable | experimental design |

## Quick Quiz

1. What four features commonly characterize abnormal psychological functioning?
2. Name three forms of past treatments that reflected a demonological view of abnormal behavior.
3. Cite examples of the somatogenic view of psychological abnormality from the time of Hippocrates, the Renaissance, the nineteenth century, and the recent past.
4. What factors brought on the fall of moral treatment?
5. How did hypnotism and the study of hysterical disorders contribute to the emergence of the psychogenic hypothesis?
6. How did Sigmund Freud come to develop the theory and technique of psychoanalysis?

7. Cite four major developments that have occurred since the 1950s in the treatment of people with mental disorders.
8. What are the advantages and disadvantages of the case study, correlational method, and experimental method?
9. What characteristics of the correlational and experimental methods enable researchers to gain nomothetic insights?
10. What safeguards do researchers incorporate into experiments in order to minimize the influence of potential confounds?
11. Describe four frequently used alternatives to the classic experimental design.

# 2

# Clinical Assessment, Diagnosis, and Treatment

## Topic Overview

*Clinical Assessment*
  Clinical Interviews
  Clinical Tests
  Clinical Observations

*Diagnosis*
  Classification Systems
  DSM-IV

*Treatment*
  Clients and Therapists
  Is Treatment Effective?

> Angela Savanti was 22 years old, lived at home with her mother, and was employed as a secretary in a large insurance company. She . . . had had passing periods of "the blues" before, but her present feelings of despondency were of much greater proportion. She was troubled by a severe depression and frequent crying spells, which had not lessened over the past two months. Angela found it hard to concentrate on her job, had great difficulty falling asleep at night, and had a poor appetite. . . . Her depression had begun after she and her boyfriend Jerry broke up two months previously.
>
> *(Leon, 1984, p. 109)*

Eventually Angela Savanti made an appointment with a therapist at a local counseling center. The first step the clinician took toward helping Angela was to learn as much as possible about her. Who is she, what is her life like, and what precisely are her symptoms? This information was expected to throw light on the causes and the probable course of her present dysfunction and help the clinician decide what kinds of treatment strategies would be likely to help her.

Whereas researchers in abnormal psychology seek primarily a nomothetic, or broad, understanding of abnormal functioning, clinical practitioners are interested in compiling **idiographic,** or individual, information about their clients. If practitioners are to help particular people, they must have full understanding of those people and know the nature and origins of their problems. This idiographic understanding of the client is arrived at through assessment and diagnosis.

# *Clinical Assessment*

**Assessment,** the collection and interpretation of relevant information about a subject, goes on at every stage and in every realm of life, from grade school to college admissions to the job market, and from shopping for groceries to voting for president. Clinical assessment techniques are used to determine how and why a person is behaving abnormally and how that person might be helped, as well as to evaluate clients after they have been in treatment for a while, to see what progress they are making and whether the treatment ought to be modified the leading techniques of clinical assessment are clinical interviews, tests, and observations.

---

*Idiographic understanding*  An understanding of the behavior of a particular individual.

*Assessment*  The process of collecting and interpreting relevant information about a client or subject.

Clinical assessment also plays an important role in research. When researchers want to know the causes of certain disorders or their responsiveness to various kinds of treatment, they have to be sure that the subjects they select are representative of people with those disorders.

## Clinical Interviews

Most of us feel instinctively that the best way to get to know people is to meet with them. In face-to-face interactions we can see other persons' reactions to our questions, observe as well as listen as they answer, watch them observing us, and generally get a sense of who they are. The *clinical interview* is a face-to-face encounter of this kind (Wiens, 1990). If a man says that the death of his mother saddened him but looks as happy as can be, the clinician may suspect that the man actually has conflicting emotions about this loss. Almost all practitioners use clinical interviews as part of the assessment process.

### Conducting the Interview

The interview is often the first contact between client and clinician. Clinicians usually seek detailed information about the person's current problems and feelings, current life situations and relationships, and personal history. They may also examine the person's expectations of therapy and motives for seeking it. The clinician working with Angela Savanti reported:

> Angela was dressed neatly when she appeared for her first interview. She was attractive, but her eyes were puffy and ringed with dark circles. She answered questions and related information about her life history in a slow, flat tone of voice, which had an impersonal quality to it. She sat stiffly in her chair with her hands in her lap, and moved very little throughout the entire interview.
>
> The client stated that the time period just before she and her boyfriend terminated their relationship had been one of extreme emotional turmoil. She was not sure whether she wanted to marry Jerry, and he began to demand that she decide either one way or the other. Mrs. Savanti did not seem to like Jerry and was very cold and aloof whenever he came to the house. Angela felt caught in the middle and unable to make a decision about her future. After several confrontations with Jerry over whether she would marry him or not, he told her he felt that she would never decide, so he was not going to see her anymore. . . .
>
> Angela stated that her childhood was a very unhappy period. Her father was seldom home, and when he was present, her parents fought constantly. . . . Angela recalled feeling very guilty

when Mr. Savanti left. . . . She revealed that whenever she thought of her father, she always felt that she had been responsible in some way for his leaving the family. Angela had never communicated this feeling to anyone, and her mother rarely mentioned his name.

Angela described her mother as the "long-suffering type" who said that she had sacrificed her life to make her children happy, and the only thing she ever got in return was grief and unhappiness. Angela related that her mother rarely smiled or laughed and did not converse very much with the girls. . . . When Angela and [her sister] Doreen began dating, Mrs. Savanti . . . commented on how tired she was because she had waited up for them. She would make disparaging remarks about the boys they had been with and about men in general. . . .

Angela revealed that she had often been troubled with depressed moods. During high school, if she got a lower grade in a subject than she had expected, her initial response was one of anger, followed by depression. She began to think that she was not smart enough to get good grades, and she blamed herself for studying too little. Angela also became despondent when she got into an argument with her mother or felt that she was being taken advantage of at work. . . .

The intensity and duration of the [mood change] that she experienced when she broke up with Jerry were much more severe. She was not sure why she was so depressed, but she began to feel it was an effort to walk around and go out to work. Talking with others became difficult. Angela found it hard to concentrate, and she began to forget things she was supposed to do. It took her a long time to fall asleep at night, and when she finally did fall asleep, she sometimes woke up in the midst of a bad dream. She felt constantly tired, and loud noises, including conversation or the television, bothered her. She preferred to lie in bed rather than be with anyone, and she often cried when alone.

*(Leon, 1984, pp. 110–115)*

Interviews can be either unstructured or structured. Although most clinical interviews have both structured and unstructured portions, many clinicians favor one kind over the other (Leon et al., 1989). In an **unstructured interview,** the clinician asks open-ended questions ("Would you tell me about yourself?"), follows interesting leads, and places few constraints on what the client can discuss. The lack of structure allows clinicians to focus on important topics that they could not anticipate before the interview. Also, it gives them a better appreciation of the issues that are important to the client.

"So, Mr. Fenton . . . Let's begin with your mother."

*In a structured interview, clinicians gather information by asking a set of standard questions irrespective of the client's particular symptoms. (The Far Side cartoon by Gary Larson is reprinted by permission of Chronicle Features, San Francisco, CA. All rights reserved.)*

In a **structured interview,** clinicians ask a series of prepared questions. Sometimes they use a published **interview schedule**—a standard set of questions or topics designed for use in all interviews (Shea, 1988). Structured formats enable clinicians to cover the same kinds of important issues in all their interviews and to compare the responses of one individual with those of others. Structured interviews often include a **mental status exam,** interview questions and observations that systematically cover areas of functioning such as the client's awareness of what is going on, orientation with regard to time and place, attention span, memory, judgment and insight, thought content and processes, mood, and appearance.

## Limitations of Clinical Interviews

Despite the value of the clinical interview as a source of information about a client, there are limits to what it can accomplish. One problem is that the information gathered during an interview is to some extent preselected by the client. Clients may try to present them-

*Unstructured interview* An interview format in which the clinician asks questions spontaneously, based on issues that emerge during the interview.

*Structured interview* An interview format in which the clinicians asks prepared questions.

## Box 2-1

# *Tests, Lies, and Videotape: The Public Misuse of Assessment*

In movies, criminals being grilled by the police reveal their guilt by sweating, shaking, cursing, or twitching. When they are hooked up to a *polygraph* (a lie detector), the needles bounce all over the paper. Such images have been with us since World War I, when some clinicians developed the theory that certain detectable physiological changes occur in people who are being deceptive (Marston, 1917).

The logic and design of a lie detector test are straightforward. A subject's respiration level, perspiration level, and heart rate are recorded while he or she answers questions. The clinician observes these physiological responses while the subject answers yes to control questions that are known to be true, such as "Are your parents both alive?", and then compares them to the physiological responses when the subject answers the test questions, such as "Did you commit this robbery?" If, as

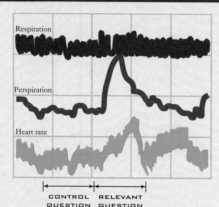

shown here, breathing, perspiration, and heart rate increase while the subject responds to the test questions, he or she may be judged to be lying (Raskin, 1982). The danger of relying on such tests, however, is that there is no compelling evidence that they work (Steinbrook, 1992).

Yet polygraph tests have enjoyed widespread popularity for many years despite an almost total lack of evidence that they are meaningful. Only recently has this

inconvenient fact reduced people's reliance on these tests and instigated responsible inquiries into their validity. In 1984 the U.S. Office of Technology Assessment concluded that the tests lacked validity (Saxe et al., 1985). Similarly, in 1986 the American Psychological Association concluded that polygraphs were inaccurate and, more fundamentally, that no physiological response pattern was associated with deception in the first place.

With the polygraph's popularity in decline, a rush began to develop a test to replace it, especially as a screening tool for employment. Businesses and governments were losing billions of dollars to theft, low productivity, and other dishonest behavior. This need stimulated development of so-called *integrity tests*, personality tests that seek to measure whether the test takers are generally honest or dishonest—and whether it is safe to hire them for a particular job.

---

selves in the best light or feel reluctant to introduce embarrassing topics.

Another problem is that some clients are simply unable to provide accurate information in an interview. For example, people who suffer from depression take an unduly negative view of themselves; some may describe themselves inaccurately as incompetent at their jobs, or inadequate as parents.

Yet another drawback is that interviewers may make subjective judgments that skew the information they gather. They usually rely too heavily on first impressions, for example, and give too much weight to unfavorable information about a client (Aiken, 1985; Meehl, 1960). The interviewers' biases, including gender and race biases, may also influence the way they interpret what a client says.

Finally, clients respond differently to different interviewers. Studies show that clients feel uncomfortable with clinicians who are cold and distant, and offer them less information than they do to clinicians who

are warm and supportive (Eisenthal et al., 1983). A clinician's race, sex, age, and appearance may also influence the client's responses (Paurohit et al., 1982).

In these circumstances, it is not surprising that different clinicians can obtain different answers and draw different conclusions even when they ask the same questions of the same person (Langwieler & Linden, 1993). Accordingly, some researchers believe that interviewing, a time-honored approach to assessment, should be discarded. This might be a reasonable suggestion if there were other, problem-free techniques to use instead. As we shall see, however, the two other methods of clinical assessment also have serious limitations.

## Clinical Tests

Tests are devices for gathering information about a few aspects of a person's psychological functioning, from which broader information about that person can be

More than forty of these written tests are now in use, supposedly revealing other broad characteristics such as dependability, deviance, social conformity, wayward impulses, and hostility to rules. However, here again research suggests that they have virtually no theoretical foundation, are easy to fake, are often interpreted by unqualified testers, and, most important, yield high rates of false accusations (Camara & Schneider, 1994).

Yet other psychological tests have also caused uproars. In Old Town, Maine, a police officer lost his job after refusing to take a penile plethysmograph test, meant to evaluate his sexual impulses. The officer had been accused of child sexual abuse. Although there was no substantiation, indictment, or conviction, the police department required that the officer see a sex-abuse therapist and undergo testing in order to retain his job.

A *penile plethysmograph test* consists of placing a rubber tube filled with mercury around a subject's penis and then showing him different stimuli, such as videotapes or slides of naked adults or children. When the subject becomes sexually aroused, the band stretches and the mercury acts as a conductor that transmits the results. Clinicians can chart the arousal on a computer program to determine whether a subject is more aroused by adults than by children, by males than by females, or by coerced rather than consensual sex.

Psychologists point out that although the test does accurately report sexual arousal, it has no predictive validity—it cannot predict whether or not an individual will act on those sexual feelings (Barker & Howell, 1992). Researchers also note that of all the people who may be sexually attracted to children, relatively few

would actually try to satisfy those desires. The test therefore cannot determine whether a person has committed a sexual offense or predict whether he is likely to do so in the future.

The officer from Maine brought a civil rights lawsuit against the city of Old Town, claiming that the government does not have the right to make such an intimate physical test a condition of employment. An employment arbitrator ordered that the officer be reinstated in the police force.

Lives can be changed dramatically when people are labeled, whether the label be "dishonest," "criminal," "depressive," or "sexually deviant." Those who administer psychophysiological, personality, or other kinds of tests have an obligation to consider the consequences carefully, particularly before they make any results, especially questionable results, public.

---

inferred (Aiken, 1994; Goldstein & Hersen, 1990). Clinicians use them to uncover subtle information that might not become apparent during an interview or observation and to determine how one person's functioning compares with that of others. More than 500 standard clinical tests are currently used throughout the United States.

## Characteristics of Tests

On the surface, it may appear relatively simple to design an effective test. Every month in magazines and newspapers we come across new tests that purport to reveal information about our selves, our relationships, our sex lives, our ability to succeed in business, and more. These tests can seem convincing, but they are often misleading. Most of them do not yield consistent or accurate information about our functioning or say anything meaningful about where we stand in comparison with others. If a test is to be useful, it must be *standardized* and have *reliability* and *validity* (see Box 2-1).

**Standardization** If a test score is to be meaningful, we must be able to compare it with the scores other people receive on the same test (Dahlstrom, 1993). We can do so if the test has gone through the process of *standardization;* that is, it has been administered to a group of subjects whose performance then serves as a common standard, or norm, against which any individual's score can be measured.

**Reliability** *Reliability* is a measure of the consistency of test results. A good test should always yield the same results in the same situation. Generally speaking, a good test is one that demonstrates various

---

*Standardization* The process in which a test is administered to a large group of subjects whose performance then serves as a common standard or norm.

*Reliability* A measure of the consistency of test or research results.

*"And the cloud that's just overhead and to your right—
what does that remind you of?"*
(Drawing by C. Barsotti; © 1990 The New Yorker Magazine, Inc.)

kinds of reliability, such as test-retest reliability, alternate-form reliability, internal reliability, and interrater reliability (Kline, 1993).

A test has high *test-retest reliability* if it yields the same results when it is given again to the same people. If, for example, a woman's responses on a particular test indicate that she is a heavy drinker, the test should produce the same result when she takes it again a week later. Of course, the second time people take a test, they may try to give the same answers they gave the first time around, thus inflating the apparent reliability of the test (Kline, 1993). To avoid this problem, test designers may devise an alternate test with the same kinds of items as the original test, give both forms of the test to trial subjects, and correlate their scores. A high correlation indicates high *alternate-form reliability.*

A test has high *internal reliability* when different parts of it yield the same results. To check for this kind of consistency, researchers may use the split-half method: they compare responses on odd-numbered test items with responses on even-numbered items. If the test is internally reliable, scores on the two halves of the test will be highly correlated.

Finally, a test shows high *interrater* (or *interjudge*) *reliability* if different evaluators independently agree on the scoring of the test. True-false and multiple-choice tests yield consistent scores no matter who evaluates them, but other tests require the evaluator to make a judgment, and three evaluators may come up with three different scores.

**Validity**   A test must also yield accurate, or valid, results. An instrument's *validity* is the accuracy with which it measures what it is supposed to be measuring (Kline, 1993).

Some tests appear to be valid because they seem to make sense. This sort of validity, called *face validity*, does not by itself establish a test's trustworthiness. A test should not be used unless it has successfully been subjected to other, more exacting measures of validity.

*Predictive validity* is a test's ability to predict a person's future characteristics or behavior. Let us say that a test is designed to gather information about the habits of the parents of elementary school children, their personal characteristics, and their attitudes toward smoking, and on that basis to identify the children who will take up cigarette smoking in junior high school. We could establish its predictive validity by administering the test to a group of elementary school students, waiting until they were in junior high

---

*Validity*   The accuracy of a test's or study's results; that is, the extent to which the test or study actually measures or shows what it claims to.

school, and then checking to see which children actually did become smokers.

*Concurrent validity* is the degree to which test scores agree with other available information. A test designed to measure students' anxiety, for example, should produce anxiety scores that agree with school counseling records and parents' reports.

A test displays high *content validity* if it assesses all important aspects of the behavior, skill, or quality it is designed to reveal. Consider *achievement tests,* designed to measure a student's ability in a particular school subject. A foreign-language achievement test would have low content validity if it tested only for vocabulary without paying attention to grammar, language usage, or comprehension.

Finally, tests should have high *construct validity;* that is, they should measure what they are intended to measure and not something else altogether (Cronbach & Meehl, 1955). Perhaps a high school student who does well on a chemistry achievement test is actually demonstrating skill at selecting multiple-choice answers rather than an exceptional knowledge of chemistry. In that case, the chemistry achievement test would be lacking in construct validity.

Before any test can be truly useful, it must meet the requirements of standardization, reliability, and validity. Unfortunately, as we shall see, more than a few clinical tests fall short on these essential characteristics, suggesting that at least some clinical assessments miss their intended mark (Shedler et al., 1993).

> ### Consider This
> How high would you grade the tests that you take in school? That is, how well do they fare on predictive, concurrent, and other forms of validity? How about the tests you read and take in magazines?

## Projective Tests

*Projective tests* require subjects to give interpretive answers to questions about relatively vague stimuli such as inkblots or ambiguous pictures, or to follow openended instructions such as "Draw a person." The assumption behind these tests is that when clues and instructions are so open to interpretation, subjects must "project" aspects of their own personality into the task. The most widely used projective tests are the *Rorschach test,* the *Thematic Apperception Test, sentence-completion tests,* and *drawings.*

---

*Projective test* A test that consists of unstructured or ambiguous material to which people are asked to respond.

**Figure 2-1** *An inkblot similar to those used in the Rorschach Test.*

**Rorschach Test** In 1911 Hermann Rorschach, a Swiss psychiatrist, experimented with the use of inkblots in psychiatric diagnosis. He made thousands of blots by dropping ink on paper, folding the paper in half, and then unfolding it to reveal a symmetrical but wholly accidental composition, such as the one shown in Figure 2-1. Rorschach found that everyone saw images in these blots and that the perceived image corresponded in important ways with the psychological condition of the viewer. People who received a diagnosis of schizophrenia, for example, tended to see images that differed radically from those that people with anxiety disorders saw.

Believing that inkblots might be a useful assessment tool, he selected ten and published them in 1921 with instructions for their use. This set of ten inkblots was called the *Rorschach Psychodynamic Inkblot Test.*

Clinicians administer the Rorschach, as it is commonly called, by presenting one inkblot card at a time to subjects and asking them what they see, what the inkblot seems to be, or what it reminds them of. The subjects are encouraged to give more than one response.

Clinicians evaluate a person's Rorschach responses on the basis of various criteria. In the early years, Rorschach testers paid greater attention to the themes, images, and fantasies evoked by the inkblots. Subjects who saw numerous water images, for example, were often thought to be grappling with alcoholism, whereas those who saw bizarre images might be suffering from schizophrenia. Testers now pay more attention to the *style* of subjects' responses: Do the subjects view the design as a whole or see specific details? Do they focus on the blots or on the white spaces between them? Do they use or ignore the shadings and colors in several of the cards?

**Thematic Apperception Test**   The *Thematic Apperception Test (TAT)* is a pictorial projective test developed by the psychologist Henry A. Murray (Murray, 1938; Morgan & Murray, 1935). The most common version of this test consists of thirty black-and-white pictures, each depicting people in a somewhat indeterminate situation. There is also a children's version of the test, known as the Children's Apperception Test, or CAT, which has pictures more evocative of the concerns of children (Bellak & Bellak, 1952).

People who take the TAT are shown one picture at a time and asked to make up a dramatic story about it stating what is happening in the picture, what led up to it, what the characters are feeling and thinking, and what the outcome of the situation will be.

Clinicians who use the TAT believe that people identify with one of the characters on each card. This character, called the *hero*, has certain needs and faces certain environmental demands. In their stories, people are thought to be expressing their own circumstances, needs, and emotions. For example, a female client seems to be identifying with the hero and revealing her own feelings in this story about the TAT picture shown in Figure 2-2, one of the few TAT pictures permitted for display in textbooks:

Figure 2-2   *A picture used in the Thematic Apperception Test.*

This is a woman who has been quite troubled by memories of a mother she was resentful toward. She has feelings of sorrow for the way she treated her mother, her memories of her mother plague her. These feelings seem to be increasing as she grows older and sees her children treating her the same way that she treated her mother.

*(Aiken, 1985, p. 372)*

Clinicians evaluate TAT responses by looking not only at the content of the stories but also at the style in which the person responds to the cards in general. Slow or delayed responses, for example, are thought to sometimes indicate depression; overcautiousness and preoccupation with details are thought to suggest obsessive thoughts and indecisiveness (Aiken, 1985).

**Sentence-Completion Test**   The sentence-completion test, first developed more than sixty years ago (Payne, 1928), consists of a series of unfinished sentences that people are asked to complete, such as, "I wish _____ ," or, "My father _____ ." The test is considered a good springboard for discussion and a quick and easy way to pinpoint topics to be explored.

**Drawings**   On the assumption that a drawing tells us something about its creator, clinicians often ask clients to draw human figures and talk about them. Evaluations of these drawings are based on the quality and shape of the drawing, solidity of the pencil line, location of the drawing on the paper, size of the figures, features of the figures, use of background, and comments made by the respondent during the drawing task.

The Draw-a-Person Test (DAP) is the most popular drawing test among clinicians (Machover, 1949). Subjects are first told to draw "a person"; that done, they are told to draw another person of the opposite sex. Theories about these drawings include the notion that a disproportionately large or small head may reflect problems in intellectual functioning, and that exaggerated eyes may indicate high levels of suspiciousness.

**The Value of Projective Tests**   Until the 1950s, projective tests were likely to be relied on as the primary indicator of a client's personality. In recent years, however, clinicians and researchers have treated these instruments more as sources of "supplementary" insights about their clients (Lerner & Lerner, 1988). One reason for this shift is that the tests have not typically demonstrated impressive levels of reliability and validity.

Reliability studies in which several clinicians have been asked to score the same person's projective test have usually found relatively low agreement (that is, low interrater reliability) among the clinicians' scores (Little & Shneidman, 1959). Similarly, research has challenged the projective tests' validity (Kline, 1993). Various researchers have given clinicians the responses of clinical subjects to projective tests and asked them to describe the personalities and feelings that the responses revealed (Golden, 1964; Sines, 1959). The descriptions have then been compared with descriptions of the same subjects provided by their psychotherapists or gathered from extensive case histories. The conclusions drawn from projective tests have repeatedly proved inaccurate.

Another validity problem is that projective tests are sometimes biased against ethnic minorities. For example, people are supposed to identify with the characters in the Thematic Apperception Test (TAT) when they make up stories about them, yet none of the figures depicted are members of ethnic minorities. In response to this problem, some clinicians have developed new versions of existing tests, such as the TAT with African American figures, or designed entirely new tests for use with a particular group, such as the Tell-Me-a-Story (TEMAS) for Hispanic persons (Constantino, et al., 1981).

## Personality Inventories

An alternative kind of test for understanding individual clients is simply to ask them to assess themselves by filling out inventories. One kind of inventory is the *personality inventory,* which asks respondents a wide range of questions about their behaviors, beliefs, and feelings. The typical personality inventory consists of a series of statements, and subjects are asked to indicate whether or not each statement applies to them. Clinicians then use the responses to draw broad conclusions about the person's personality traits and psychological functioning.

### Minnesota Multiphasic Personality Inventory The *Minnesota Multiphasic Personality Inventory (MMPI)* is by far the most widely used personality inventory (Colligan & Offord, 1992). Two versions of this test are available—the original test, published in 1945, and the MMPI-2, a 1989 revision. Currently the two versions are competing for the favor of clinicians (Clavelle, 1992).

The traditional MMPI consists of 550 self-statements—to be labeled "true," "false," or "cannot

<hr />

*Personality inventory* A test designed to measure broad personality characteristics, consisting of statements about behaviors, beliefs, and feelings that people are asked to evaluate as characteristic or uncharacteristic of them.

*Drawing tests are commonly used to assess the functioning of children. Two popular tests are the House-Tree-Person test, in which subjects draw a house, tree, and person, and the Kinetic Family Drawing test, in which subjects draw their household members engaged in some activity ("kinetic" means "active").*

say"—about numerous areas of personal functioning, including the respondent's physical concerns; mood; morale; attitudes toward religion, sex, and social activities; and possible symptoms of psychological dysfunction, such as phobias and hallucinations.

The items in the MMPI make up ten clinical scales:

*HS (Hypochondriasis)* Items that show abnormal concern with bodily functions ("I have chest pains several times a week").

*D (Depression)* Items showing extreme pessimism and hopelessness ("I often feel hopeless about the future").

*Hy (Conversion hysteria)* Items that suggest the use of physical or mental symptoms as a way of unconsciously avoiding difficult conflicts and responsibilities ("My heart frequently pounds so hard I can feel it").

*PD (Psychopathic deviate)* Items showing a repeated and flagrant disregard for social customs and an emotional shallowness ("My activities and interests are often criticized by others").

*Mf (Masculinity-Femininity)* Items differentiating between male and female respondents ("I like to arrange flowers").

*Pa (Paranoia)* Items showing abnormal suspiciousness and delusions of grandeur or persecution ("There are evil people trying to influence my mind").

*Pt (Psychasthenia)* Items that indicate obsessions, compulsions, abnormal fears, and guilt and indecisiveness ("I save nearly everything I buy, even after I have no use for it").

*Sc (Schizophrenia)* Items suggesting bizarre or unusual thoughts or behavior, including extreme withdrawal, delusions, or hallucinations ("Things around me do not seem real").

*Ma (Hypomania)* Items showing emotional excitement, overactivity, and flight of ideas ("At times I feel very 'high' or very 'low' for no apparent reason").

*Si (Social introversion)* Items showing shyness, little interest in people, and insecurity ("I am easily embarrassed").

Scores for each scale can range from 0 to 120. When people score above 70 on a particular scale, their functioning on the dimension measured by that scale is considered deviant. The pattern made when the scale scores are graphed, called the person's profile, is evaluated to determine that person's general personality style and underlying emotional needs (Graham, 1993; Meehl, 1951). The MMPI profile of J.A.K., a depressed 27-year-old man whose MMPI profile is shown in Figure 2-3, indicates that he is very depressed, feels anxious and threatened, and is socially withdrawn and prone to somatic complaints.

**Response Sets and the MMPI** Each person approaches an inventory such as the MMPI with a particular *response set,* a tendency to respond in fixed ways. Some people, for example, tend to respond affirmatively to statements irrespective of their content ("yea-sayers"). Others try to answer in ways that they believe are socially acceptable. Obviously, if people's answers are heavily influenced by their response set, their MMPI scores will be misleading. Thus, additional scales have been built into the MMPI to detect such influences.

The *L scale,* or *lie scale,* consists of items that test whether a person is responding truthfully. People who keep answering true to such items as "I smile at everyone I meet" and false to items like "I gossip a little at times" receive a high L score. Similarly, the MMPI includes items that measure whether a person is a careless test taker *(F scale)* and others that indicate whether persons are defensive test takers who keep trying to protect their own image in their responses *(K scale).* If the individual scores high on the L, F, or K

scale, clinicians may alter their MMPI conclusions or pronounce the test results invalid.

**MMPI-2** The new version of the MMPI tries to update and broaden the original while preserving those items and scoring techniques that so many clinicians are familiar with and find useful. The new inventory contains 567 items, many identical to those in the original, some rewritten to reflect contemporary language ("upset stomach," for instance, replaces "acid stomach"), and others that are totally new. In addition to the ten basic scales, which are the same as in the original, the MMPI-2 adds a number of new scales to measure such things as a vulnerability to eating disorders, a tendency to abuse drugs, and poor functioning at work.

Many clinicians have welcomed the MMPI-2 as a valuable improvement and appropriate update. Others, however, believe that the new test has significant flaws and may never be an adequate substitute for the original. One complaint is that the large body of research that has been conducted on the original MMPI may not be applicable to the MMPI-2. Researchers are now exploring such concerns, and any decision to shelve one of the versions awaits the outcome of their work.

**The Value of Personality Inventories** The MMPI and other personality inventories have several advantages over projective tests. They are paper-and-pencil tests that do not take much time to administer, and they are objectively and easily scored. In addition, they are usually standardized, so that one person's scores can be compared with many others'. Moreover, they usually display greater test-retest reliability than projective tests. For example, people who take the MMPI a second time after an interval of less than two weeks receive approximately the same scores (Graham, 1987, 1977).

Personality inventories also appear to have greater validity than projective tests, so that clinicians can assess respondents' personal characteristics more accurately (Graham & Lilly, 1984). All the same, they can hardly be considered *highly* valid test instruments (Kline, 1993). When clinicians use these tests alone, they have not consistently been able to judge a subject's personality accurately (Aiken, 1994; Shedler et al., 1993). One problem is the very nature of what the tests are trying to measure. The broad qualities and traits personality inventories purport to measure are not physical entities whose existence and strength can be verified directly.

Despite such limitations, the personality inventories continue to be very popular assessment tools. Studies

---

*Response set* A particular way of responding to questions or statements on a test, such as always selecting "true," regardless of the content of the questions.

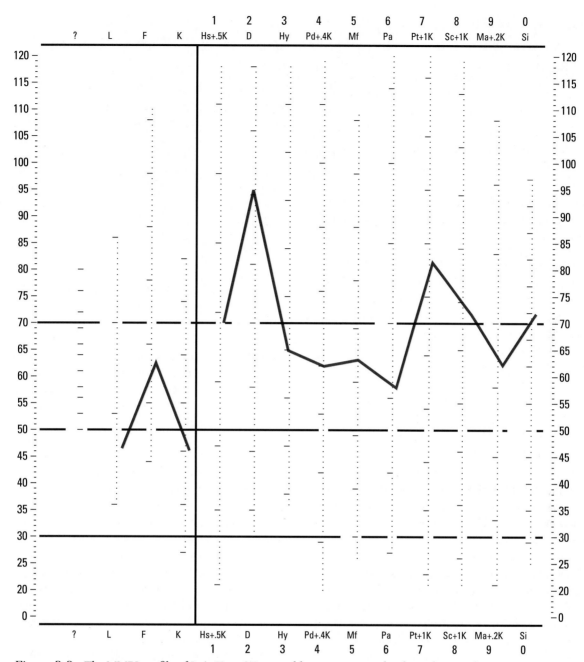

**Figure 2-3** *The MMPI profile of J. A. K., a 27-year-old man, suggests that he is depressed. He also appears to be anxious, prone to somatic complaints, indecisive, introverted, and insecure. (From Graham, 1977, p. 164.)*

indicate that when they are used along with interviews or other assessment tools, they can help clinicians draw clearer pictures of people's characteristics and disorders (Levitt, 1989).

## Response Inventories

Clinicians may also use self-report tests to collect detailed information about a person's responses in one specific area of functioning. There are, for example, *re-*

*sponse inventories* to measure affect (emotion), social skills, and cognitive processes.

*Affective inventories* measure the severity of such emotions as anxiety, depression, and anger. The most widely used affective inventory is the Fear Survey Schedule, shown in Table 2-1, in which people rate how intensely they fear various objects and situations

---

*Response inventories* Tests designed to measure a person's responses in one specific area of functioning, such as affect, social skills, or cognitive processes.

## Table 2-1    *Partial Fear Survey Schedule*

Indicate how much fear you experience when confronted with the following:

| | | | | | | | |
|---|---|---|---|---|---|---|---|
| 1. Sharp objects | None | Very little | A little | Some | Much | Very much | Terror |
| 2. Being a passenger in a car | None | Very little | A little | Some | Much | Very much | Terror |
| 3. Dead Bodies | None | Very little | A little | Some | Much | Very much | Terror |
| 4. Suffocating | None | Very little | A little | Some | Much | Very much | Terror |
| 5. Failing a test | None | Very little | A little | Some | Much | Very much | Terror |
| 6. Looking foolish | None | Very little | A little | Some | Much | Very much | Terror |
| 7. Being a passenger in an airplane | None | Very little | A little | Some | Much | Very much | Terror |
| 8. Worms | None | Very little | A little | Some | Much | Very much | Terror |
| 9. Arguing with parents | None | Very little | A little | Some | Much | Very much | Terror |
| 10. Rats and mice | None | Very little | A little | Some | Much | Very much | Terror |

*Source:* Geer, 1965.

(Lang, 1985; Geer, 1965). *Social skill inventories* ask respondents to indicate how they would react in a variety of social situations. Clinicians use these inventories to assess a person's social skills, deficits, and fears, and to determine the role these factors play in the person's disorder. *Cognition inventories* disclose the kinds of thoughts and assumptions that are typical of a client, and are used to uncover counterproductive thoughts and patterns of thinking that may be at the root of abnormal functioning (Burgess & Haaga, 1994).

Like personality inventories, the response inventories collect information directly from the subjects themselves, and so have a strong face validity and a seeming efficiency. As a consequence, both the number of these tests and the number of clinicians using them have increased steadily in the past two decades. At the same time, these narrow inventories have significant limitations (Shedler et al., 1993). First, unlike the personality inventories, they rarely contain questions to help determine whether people are being careless or inaccurate in their accounts. Second, relatively few of these inventories have been subjected to rigorous standardization, reliability, and validity procedures (Sanderman & Ormel, 1992). They are often improvised as the need for them arises, without being tested for accuracy and consistency.

## Psychophysiological Tests

More and more during the past decade clinicians have used tests that measure physiological responses (Stoyva & Budzynski, 1993). The interest in *psychophysiological measures* began when a number of

studies suggested that states of anxiety are regularly accompanied by physiological changes such as increases in heart rate, body temperature, blood pressure, electrical resistance in the skin (galvanic skin response), and muscle contraction and that measures of these psychophysiological changes were often more precise than interviews, projective tests, self-reports, and so on (Cook et al., 1988; Lang, 1985).

Psychophysiological tests also have been used in the assessment of medical problems, such as headaches and hypertension (high blood pressure), that are thought to relate to a person's psychological state. As we shall see in Chapter 5, clinical researchers have discovered that the physiological components of such problems can sometimes be treated by *biofeedback,* a technique in which the client is given systematic information about key physiological responses as they occur and thus learns gradually to control them (Norris & Fahrion, 1993; Stoyva & Budzynski, 1993). For example, when tension-headache sufferers are given detailed feedback about the levels of tension in their head muscles, many can learn to relax those muscles at will, and the frequency of their headaches declines.

The measuring of physiological changes has become integral to the assessment of many psychological disorders. Like other kinds of clinical tests, however, psychophysiological tests pose problems for clinicians.

*Psychophysiological test*   A test that measures physical responses (such as heart rate and muscle tension) as possible indicators of psychological problems.

*Biofeedback*   A treatment technique in which the client is given systematic information about key physiological responses as they occur and learns to control the responses voluntarily.

One is logistical. Most psychophysiological tests require expensive recording equipment that must be carefully maintained and expertly calibrated (Nelson, 1981).

A second problem is that psychophysiological measurements can be misleading because they are not always indicative of the person's usual state. The laboratory equipment itself—impressive, unusual, and sometimes frightening—may arouse a subject's nervous system and thus alter physiological readings. Moreover, physiological responses are often observed to change when they are measured repeatedly in a single session. Galvanic skin responses, for example, often decrease upon repeated testing (Montagu & Coles, 1966).

## Neuropsychological Tests

Some problems in personality or behavior are caused primarily by neurological damage in the brain or alterations in brain activity. Head injury, brain tumors, brain malfunctions, alcoholism, infections, and other diseases can all cause such organic impairment. If a psychological dysfunction is to be treated effectively, it is important to know whether it stems primarily from some physiological abnormality in the brain.

Neurological problems can sometimes be detected through brain surgery and biopsy; brain X rays; a *computerized axial tomogram (CAT scan)*, for which X rays of the brain are taken at different angles; an *electroencephalogram (EEG)*, a recording of electrical impulses in the brain gathered by wires attached to the scalp; a *positron emission tomogram (PET scan)*, a computer-produced motion picture of rates of metabolism throughout the brain; or *magnetic resonance imaging (MRI)*, a complex procedure that uses the magnetic property of certain atoms in the brain to create a detailed picture of the brain's structure.

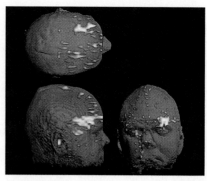

*An "echo-planar" MRI, a high-speed MRI, reveals the reaction of a patient with an obsessive-compulsive disorder to "an envelope soiled with illicit drugs."*

Subtle brain abnormalities, however, may escape these methods of detection. Clinicians have, therefore, developed less direct but sometimes more revealing *neuropsychological tests* that help identify neurological problems by measuring a person's cognitive, perceptual, and motor skills (Matarazzo, 1992). Because neurological damage is likely to affect visual perception, recent memory, and visual-motor coordination, neuropsychological tests usually focus on these areas of functioning.

The *Bender Visual-Motor Gestalt Test* (Bender, 1938), one of the most widely used neuropsychological tests, consists of nine cards, each displaying a simple design (see Figure 2-4). Test subjects look at the designs one at a time and copy each one on a piece of paper. Later they try to reproduce the designs from memory. By the age of 12, most people can remember and copy the designs accurately. Notable errors in the accuracy of the drawings are thought to reflect organic brain impairment.

Clinicians are able to distinguish organically impaired from nonorganically impaired people on the basis of this test in approximately 75 percent of cases (Heaton et al., 1978). Because there is such a wide variety of organic impairments, however, no single neuropsychological test can consistently identify the different kinds of neurological impairments (Goldstein, 1990). This is the major limitation of the Bender Gestalt Test, and of any other neuropsychological test.

*Electrodes pasted to a patient's scalp detect electrical impulses from the brain. The impulses are then amplified and converted into ink tracings on a roll of graph paper to produce an electroencephalogram (EEG). The EEG, used here to measure the brain waves of a 4-month-old being stimulated with toys, is only a gross indicator of the activity of the brain.*

*Neuropsychological test*  A test that detects brain impairment by measuring a person's cognitive, perceptual, and motor performances.

Original                                        Copy

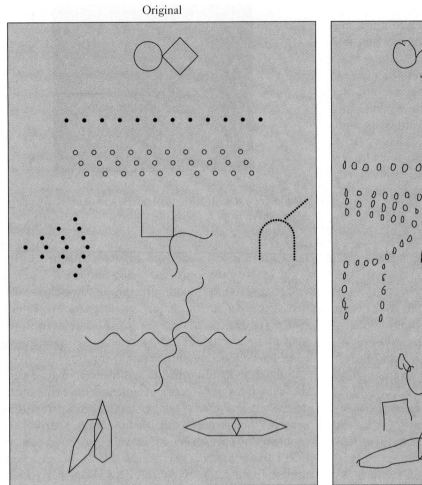
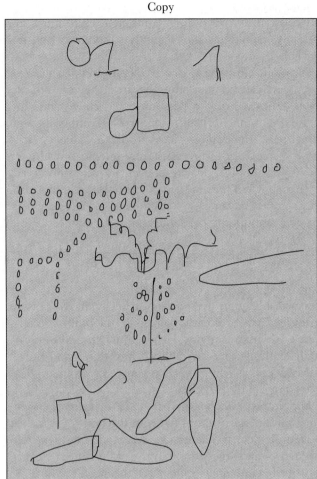

**Figure 2-4** *In the Bender Gestalt Test subjects copy each of nine designs on a piece of paper, then produce them again from memory. Sizable errors in a drawing (as in the one on the right, which was done by a person with brain damage) may reflect organic brain dysfunction of some kind. (Adapted from Lacks, 1984, p. 33.)*

At best it is a rough screening device for neurological impairment in general.

To achieve greater precision and accuracy in neurological assessment, clinicians frequently use a comprehensive series, or *battery,* of neuropsychological tests, each of which targets a specific neurological skill area. The Halstead-Reitan Neuropsychology Battery, a lengthy series of tests that measure sensorimotor, perceptual, and memory skills, and the shorter Luria-Nebraska Battery are highly regarded and widely used by today's clinicians (Reitan & Wolfson, 1985; Halstead, 1947).

## Intelligence Tests

There is little agreement about the precise nature of intelligence, although most educators and clinicians agree in a general way with an early definition of intelligence as "the capacity to judge well, to reason well,

and to comprehend well" (Binet & Simon, 1916, p. 192). Because intelligence is an inferred notion rather than a specific physical process or entity, it can be measured only indirectly. In 1905 the French psychologist Alfred Binet and his associate Theodore Simon produced an intelligence test consisting of a series of tasks that require people to use various verbal and nonverbal skills. The general score derived from this and subsequent intelligence tests is termed an *intelligence quotient,* or *IQ.*

Since Binet and Simon's first test, intelligence tests and studies of intelligence have been a major preoccupation of the educational and clinical fields. There are now many such tests. The intelligence tests most

*Intelligence test*  A test designed to measure a person's intellectual ability.

*Intelligence quotient (IQ)*  A general score derived from intelligence tests that is considered to represent a person's overall level of intelligence.

widely used today are the Wechsler Adult Intelligence Scale, the Wechsler Intelligence Scale for Children, and the Stanford-Binet Intelligence Scale. As we shall discuss in Chapter 15, information gathered from intelligence tests plays a large role in the diagnosis of mental retardation and can also be helpful in the diagnosis of other problems, such as neurological disorders.

Intelligence tests are among the most carefully constructed of all clinical tests. Large standardization samples have been used to calibrate the major ones, so that clinicians have a good idea of how each person's scores compare with the performance of the population at large. These tests have demonstrated very high reliability: people who take the same IQ test years apart receive approximately the same scores (Kline, 1993). Finally, the major IQ tests appear to have relatively high validity: children's IQ scores correlate fairly highly with their performance in school (Anastasi, 1982).

Nevertheless, intelligence tests have some significant shortcomings. Factors that have nothing to do with intelligence, such as low motivation and high anxiety, can greatly influence a person's performance (Frederiksen, 1993, 1986). In addition, IQ tests may contain culturally biased language, items, or tasks that place people from one background at an advantage over those from another (Helms, 1992; Puente, 1990). Similarly, members of certain minority groups may also have relatively little experience taking this kind of test or be uncomfortable with test examiners from a

majority ethnic background, and their performances may suffer accordingly.

## Integrating Test Data

Most clinical tests fall short on one or more of the three key criteria of standardization, reliability, and validity, so it is unwise to put too much faith in any one test. Clinicians usually administer a battery of tests to assess psychological functioning and use this collection of information primarily to clarify and supplement the information gathered in the clinical interview.

# Clinical Observations

In addition to interviewing and testing people, clinicians may follow specific strategies for observing their behavior. One such technique is the *naturalistic observation,* also called an *in vivo* (literally, "in the living") *observation,* in which clinicians observe clients in their everyday environments. Another is the *structured observation,* in which clinicians monitor people in artificial settings created in their offices or laboratories. They may also have clients observe themselves, a technique called *self-monitoring.*

## Naturalistic and Structured Observations

Most naturalistic clinical observations take place in homes, schools, institutions such as hospitals and prisons, and community settings. The observations have usually focused on parent-child, sibling-child, and teacher-child interactions, and fearful, aggressive, or disruptive behavior. Actually, most such observations

*The Wechsler Adult Intelligence Scale-Revised (WAIS-R) has 11 subtests, which cover areas such as factual information, memory, vocabulary, arithmetic, design, and eye-hand coordination.*

*Naturalistic observation*  A method for observing behavior in which clinicians or researchers observe clients or subjects in their everyday environments.

*Structured observation*  A method for observing behavior in which people are monitored in artificial settings created in clinicians' offices or in laboratories.

*Self-monitoring*  A technique for monitoring behavior in which clients observe themselves.

are made by *participant observers,* key persons in the client's environment, and reported to the clinician.

When naturalistic observation is impractical, clinicians may choose to observe some clients in a structured setting. Interactions between parents and their children, for example, may be observed in an office or laboratory on videotape or from behind a one-way mirror (Field, 1977).

Although it is helpful for a clinician actually to watch behavior that may be leading to a person's disturbances, these methods have several disadvantages as well. For one thing, clinical observations are not always reliable (Foster & Cone, 1986). It is quite possible for various clinicians who observe the same person to focus on different aspects of behavior, evaluate the person differently, and draw different conclusions.

Secondly, observers may make errors that also affect the validity of their observations (Foster & Cone, 1986). The observer may, for example, be unable to see all relevant behavior and events. Or the observer may experience *observer drift,* a steady deterioration in accuracy as a result of fatigue or of a gradual unintentional change in the criteria used when an observer judges behavior over a long period of time (O'Leary & Kent, 1973). Another possibility is *observer bias*—the observer's judgments are inappropriately influenced by information and expectations he or she already has about the client (Shuller & McNamara, 1980).

A third factor that often limits the validity of clinical observations is the subject's *reactivity*—his or her behavior is affected by the very presence of the observer (Harris & Lahey, 1982). If schoolchildren are aware that someone special is watching them, for example, they may alter their usual classroom behavior, perhaps in the hope of impressing the observer.

Finally, clinical observations may lack *cross-situational validity.* A child who behaves aggressively in school is not necessarily aggressive at home or with friends after school. Because behavior is often specific to particular situations, observations in one setting cannot always be applied to other settings (Simpson & Halpin, 1986).

## Self-Monitoring

In *self-monitoring,* people observe themselves and carefully record the frequency or circumstances of designated behaviors, feelings, or cognitions as they occur throughout the day (Bornstein et al., 1986). Self-monitoring offers several advantages. First, it may be the only way to observe behavior that occurs relatively infrequently. Second, it is useful for observing behavior that occurs so frequently that any other comprehensive observation of it would be impossible. In this regard, it has been employed to collect information about the nature and frequency of smoking, drinking, drug use, and feelings of anger and anxiety. Third, self-monitoring is the only way private thoughts or perceptions can be observed and counted.

Like all other clinical assessment procedures, however, self-monitoring has drawbacks. One is the question of its validity. Clients may not be motivated to record their observations accurately. Furthermore, there is often a powerful reactivity effect when clients try to monitor themselves. Smokers often smoke fewer cigarettes than usual when they are monitoring themselves (Kilmann et al., 1977), people with drug-related disorders take drugs less frequently (Hay et al., 1977), and teachers give more positive and fewer negative comments to their students (Nelson, 1977).

*Clinicians often view works of art as informal tests in which artists reveal their own conflicts and concerns. The sometimes bizarre cat portraits of early twentieth-century artist Louis Wain have, for example, been interpreted by some as reflections of the psychosis with which he struggled for many years.*

*Summing Up*

*Clinical practitioners are interested primarily in compiling idiographic, or individual, information about their clients. They seek this understanding of a client's problems through assessment and diagnosis.*

*Most assessment methods fall into three general categories: clinical interviews, tests, and observations. The interview may be either unstructured or structured. Types of tests include projective, personality, response, psychophysiological, neuropsychological, and intelligence tests. Types of observation include naturalistic observation, structured observation, and self-monitoring.*

# Diagnosis

After they have collected and interpreted the assessment information, clinicians attempt to form a *clinical picture*, an integrated picture of the various factors causing and sustaining the person's disturbed functioning. The clinician who worked with Angela Savanti offered the following clinical picture of her problem:

Angela was rarely reinforced for any of her accomplishments at school, but she gained her mother's negative attention for what Mrs. Savanti judged to be poor performance at school or at home. Mrs. Savanti repeatedly told her daughter that she was incompetent, and any mishaps that happened to her were her own fault. . . . When Mr. Savanti deserted the family, Angela's first response was that somehow she was responsible. From her mother's past behavior, Angela had learned to expect that in some way she would be blamed. At the time that Angela broke up with her boyfriend, she did not blame Jerry for his behavior, but interpreted this event as a failing solely on her part. As a result, her level of self-esteem was lowered still more. . . .

Angela's uncertainties intensified when she was deprived of the major source of gratification she had, her relationship with Jerry. Despite the fact that she was overwhelmed with doubts about whether to marry him or not, she had gained a great deal of pleasure through being with Jerry. Whatever feelings she had been able to express, she had shared with him and no one else. Angela labeled Jerry's termination of their relationship as proof that she was not worthy of another person's interest. She viewed her present unhappiness as likely to continue, and she attributed it to some failing on her part. As a result, she became quite depressed.

(Leon, 1984, pp. 123–125)

*Clinicians and historians often try to diagnose the psychological problems of famous people who are no longer alive. The turbulent and unhappy life of the artist Vincent van Gogh, who is shown here in a self-portrait, has at various times been attributed to a mood disorder, schizophrenia, Geschwind's syndrome (a personality disorder possibly that may be related to brain seizures), and Menière's syndrome (a disorder caused by an excessive buildup of fluid that exerts severe pressure on the inner ear).*

Clinicians also use assessment information to make a *diagnosis*—that is, to determine that a person's psychological problems constitute a particular disorder. Although clinicians can sometimes learn enough about a person from assessment information to develop ideas about the nature and causes of the person's problems, they need still other information to know the probable future course of the problem and what treatment strategies are likely to be helpful.

When clinicians decide that a person's pattern of dysfunction constitutes a particular disorder, they are saying that the pattern is basically the same as one that has been displayed by many other people, has been investigated in a variety of studies, and perhaps has responded to particular forms of treatment. If their diagnosis is correct, clinicians can fruitfully apply what is

*Diagnosis*  The process of determining whether a person's dysfunction constitutes a particular psychological disorder.

generally known about the disorder to the particular person they are trying to help.

## Classification Systems

The principle behind diagnosis is straightforward. When certain symptoms regularly occur together (a cluster of symptoms is called a *syndrome*) and follow a particular course, clinicians agree that those symptoms constitute a particular mental disorder. When people display this particular cluster and course of symptoms, diagnosticians assign them to that category. A comprehensive list of such categories, with a description of the symptoms characteristic of each and guidelines for assigning individuals to categories, is known as a *classification system.*

As we saw in Chapter 1, Emil Kraepelin developed the first influential classification system for abnormal behavior in 1883. The categories of disorders established by him have formed the foundation for the psychological part of the classification system now used by the World Health Organization, called the *International Classification of Diseases (ICD)*. Similarly, Kraepelin's work has been incorporated into the *Diagnostic and Statistical Manual of Mental Disorders (DSM)*, a classification system developed by the American Psychiatric Association.

The DSM, like the ICD, has been changed over time. The DSM was first published in 1952 (DSM-I) and has undergone major revisions in 1968 (DSM-II), 1980 (DSM-III), 1987 (DSM-III-R), and 1994 (DSM-IV). The current edition, DSM-IV, is by far the most widely used classification system in the United States today. The descriptions of mental disorders presented throughout this textbook adhere to the categories and distinctions in DSM-IV.

## DSM-IV

DSM-IV lists close to 300 mental disorders. Each entry describes the criteria for diagnosing the disorder, the essential clinical features of the disorder (features that are invariably present), and any associated features (features that are often but not invariably present), and gives information about specific age-, culture-, or gender-related features, prevalence and risk, course, complications, predisposing factors, and family patterns.

*Classification system* A comprehensive list of categories of mental dysfunctioning, including a description of the symptoms that characterize each category and guidelines for assigning people to the categories.

*DSM-IV (Diagnostic and Statistical Manual-IV)* The current edition of the classification system developed by the American Psychiatric Association.

The criteria in DSM-IV are more detailed and objective than those of the early DSMs.

When clinicians use DSM-IV to make a diagnosis, they must evaluate a client's condition on five separate *axes,* or branches of information. This requirement forces diagnosticians to review and use a broad range of observations and data. First, clinicians must decide whether the client is displaying one or more of the disorders from *Axis I,* an extensive list of florid clinical syndromes that typically cause significant impairment (see Table 2-2). Some of the more common disorders listed on Axis I are the anxiety disorders and mood disorders:

*Anxiety disorders* Anxiety is the predominant disturbance in this group of disorders. People with anxiety disorders may experience broad feelings of worry and anxiety (*generalized anxiety disorders)*, anxiety concerning a specific situation or object (*phobic disorders)*, or other forms of anxiety (*panic disorder, obsessive-compulsive disorders, acute stress disorder,* or *posttraumatic stress disorder)*.

*Mood disorders* Disorders in this group are marked by severe disturbances of mood that cause people to feel extremely and inappropriately sad or elated for extended periods of time. These disorders include *major depressive disorder* and *bipolar disorders*. In the latter, episodes of mania alternate with episodes of depression.

Next, diagnosticians must decide whether the client is displaying one of the disorders from *Axis II,* long-standing problems that are frequently overlooked in the presence of the disorders listed in Axis I. There are only two major categories of Axis II disorders:

*Mental retardation* People with this disorder display significant subaverage intellectual functioning by 18 years of age and concurrent deficits or impairment in adaptive functioning.

*Personality disorders* People with these disorders display an enduring pervasive, inflexible, and maladaptive pattern of inner experience and behavior that deviates markedly from the expectations of the individual's culture. One example is *antisocial personality disorder,* in which people display a pervasive pattern of disregard for and violation of the rights of others.

Although people usually receive a diagnosis from *either* Axis I or Axis II, they may receive diagnoses from both axes. Angela Savanti would first receive a diagnosis of *major depressive disorder,* an Axis I disorder (one of the mood disorders) because her pattern of dysfunction meets the DSM-IV criteria for this disorder. Let us suppose, in addition, that the diagnostician judged

**Table 2-2    *Axis I Disorders in DSM-IV***

*Disorders Usually First Diagnosed in Infancy, Childhood, and Adolescence*    Disorders in this group tend to emerge and sometimes dissipate before adult life. They include *pervasive developmental disorders* (such as *autism*); *learning disorders; attention-deficit hyperactivity disorder; conduct disorder;* and *separation anxiety disorder.*

*Delirium, Dementia, Amnestic, and Other Cognitive Disorders*    These disorders are dominated by impairment in cognitive functioning. They include *Alzheimer's disease* and *Huntington's disease.*

*Mental Disorders Due to a General Medical Condition*    These are mental disorders that are caused primarily by a general medical disorder. They include *mood disorder due to a general medical condition.*

*Substance-Related Disorders*    These disorders are brought about by the use of substances that affect the central nervous system, such as *alcohol use disorders, opioid use disorders, amphetamine use disorders, cocaine use disorders,* and *hallucinogen use disorders.*

*Schizophrenia and Other Psychotic Disorders*    In this group of disorders, functioning deteriorates until the patient reaches a state of *psychosis,* or loss of contact with reality.

*Mood Disorders*    Disorders in this group are marked by severe disturbances of mood that cause people to feel extremely and inappropriately sad or elated for extended periods of time. They include *major depressive disorder* and *bipolar disorders.*

*Anxiety Disorders*    Anxiety is the predominant disturbance in this group of disorders. They include *generalized anxiety disorder, phobic disorders, panic disorder, obsessive-compulsive disorder, acute stress disorder,* and *posttraumatic stress disorder.*

*Somatoform Disorders*    These disorders, marked by physical symptoms that apparently are caused primarily by psychological rather than physiological factors, include *pain disorders, conversion disorders, somatization disorder,* and *hypochondriasis.*

*Factitious Disorders*    People with these disorders intentionally produce or feign psychological or physical symptoms.

*Dissociative Disorders*    These disorders are characterized by changes in integrated functioning that are not due to clear physical causes. They include *dissociative amnesia; dissociative fugue;* and *dissociative identity disorder (multiple personality disorder).*

*Eating Disorders*    People with these disorders display abnormal patterns of eating that significantly impair their functioning. The disorders include *anorexia nervosa* and *bulimia nervosa.*

*Sexual Disorders and Gender Identity Disorder*    These disorders in sexual functioning, behavior, or preferences include *sexual dysfunctions, paraphilias,* and *gender identity disorder.*

*Sleep Disorders*    People with these disorders display chronic sleep problems. The disorders include *primary insomnia, primary hypersomnia, sleep terror disorder,* and *sleepwalking disorder.*

*Impulse-Control Disorders*    People with these disorders are chronically unable to resist impulses, drives, or temptations to perform certain acts that are harmful to them or to others. The disorders include *pathological gambling, kleptomania, pyromania,* and *intermittent explosive disorders.*

*Adjustment Disorders*    The primary feature of these disorders is a maladaptive reaction to a clear stressor such as divorce or business difficulties that occurs within three months after the onset of the stressor.

*Other Conditions That May Be a Focus of Clinical Attention*    This category consists of certain conditions or problems that are worth noting because they cause significant impairment, such as *relational problems, problems related to abuse or neglect, medication-induced movement disorders,* and *psychophysiological disorders.*

---

Angela to have also displayed a life history of chronic dependent behavior. In this case, she might also receive an Axis II diagnosis of *dependent personality disorder.*

The remaining axes of DSM-IV guide diagnosticians to report factors other than a client's symptoms that are potentially relevant to the understanding of the case. *Axis III* information is a listing of any relevant general medical condition the person is currently suffering from. *Axis IV* information is a listing of psychosocial or environmental problems the person is facing (for example, education or housing problems) that may affect the diagnosis, treatment, or course of the psychological disorder. And *Axis V* information is a *global assessment of functioning (GAF),* the diagnostician's rating (on a scale of 0 to 100) of the person's overall level of psychological, social, and occupational

functioning. If Angela Savanti had diabetes, for example, the clinician might include that under Axis III information. Angela's recent breakup with her boyfriend would be noted on Axis IV. And because she seemed moderately impaired at the time of diagnosis, Angela's functioning would probably be rated approximately 55 on Axis V in accordance with DSM-IV's Global Assessment of Functioning Scale. The complete diagnosis for Angela Savanti would then be:

Axis I: Major depressive disorder

Axis II: Dependent personality disorder

Axis III: Diabetes

Axis IV: Problem related to the social environment (termination of engagement)

Axis V: GAF = 55 (current)

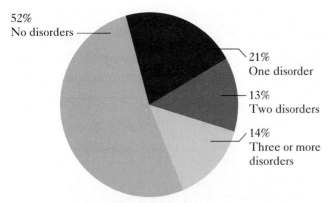

52%
No disorders

21%
One disorder

13%
Two disorders

14%
Three or more
disorders

Figure 2-5   *How many people in the United States qualify for a DSM diagnosis during their lives? Almost half, according to a recent survey. In some cases these individuals even experience two or more disorders simultaneously, an occurrence known as "comorbidity." (Adapted from Kessler et al., 1994.)*

Because several kinds of diagnostic information are used in DSM-IV, each defined by a different "axis," it is known as a *multiaxial system*. The diagnoses arrived at under this classification system are expected to be more informative and more carefully considered than those derived from the earliest DSMs (see Figure 2-5).

## Reliability and Validity in Classification

The value of a diagnostic classification system, like that of the various assessment methods, is judged by its reliability and validity. The *reliability* of a diagnosis means that different diagnosticians agree that a given pattern of observed behavior should be assigned to a given category. If different diagnosticians keep arriving at different diagnoses after observing the same behavior, then the classification system is not very reliable.

Early editions of the DSM were only moderately reliable. In the early 1960s, for example, four clinicians, each relying on DSM-I, independently interviewed and diagnosed 153 patients recently admitted to a mental hospital (Beck et al., 1962). Only 54 percent of these clinicians' diagnoses were in agreement. The more objective criteria provided by later editions of the DSM yielded somewhat more reliable diagnoses than their predecessors (DiNardo et al., 1993). Nevertheless, reliability studies rarely found more than 70 percent agreement among clinicians who used these editions (Kirk & Kutchins, 1992).

In order to maximize the reliability of DSM-IV, its framers first conducted comprehensive reviews of relevant research to pinpoint which categories from past DSMs were indeed producing low reliability (APA, 1994). Then, upon developing new diagnostic criteria

and categories for inclusion in DSM-IV, they conducted extensive field studies at more than 70 sites, with 6000 participating subjects, to make sure that the new criteria and categories were indeed reliable. As a result, it is expected that DSM-IV will have greater reliability than any of its predecessors (APA, 1994). Similar claims were made during the early years of the previous DSMs, though, so many clinicians suggest that we wait until DSM-IV is widely used and tested before making any assumptions about its reliability (Kirk & Kutchins, 1992).

The *validity* of a classification system refers to the accuracy of the information that a diagnostic category provides about the people assigned to that category and about their symptoms. Categories are of most use to clinicians when they demonstrate predictive and concurrent validity. A category has **predictive validity** when it helps predict future symptoms or events. A common symptom of major depressive disorder, for example, is insomnia or hypersomnia. When clinicians give Angela Savanti a diagnosis of major depression, they expect that she may eventually develop this symptom even if she does not manifest it now. Moreover, they expect her to respond to treatments that are effective for other depressed persons. The more often such predictions are accurate, the greater a given category's predictive validity.

Categories show **concurrent validity** when they give clinicians accurate information about "associated" features of a disorder, beyond the "essential" diagnostic symptoms. For example, DSM-IV reports that people who manifest major depressive disorder often also become excessively concerned about their physical health. If Angela Savanti and most other people who receive this diagnosis do indeed display this associated feature, the category is displaying a high degree of concurrent validity.

DSM-IV's framers have tried to maximize the validity of this newest version of the DSM by again conducting comprehensive reviews of the most recent literature and directing many field studies to the issue of validity. Thus, the new criteria and categories of DSM-IV are expected to have stronger validity than earlier editions of the DSM, but like DSM-IV's reliability, the validity of this newest edition has yet to be broadly tested (Clark et al., 1995) (see Box 2-2).

## Problems of Clinical Misinterpretation

Even with trustworthy assessment data and reliable and valid classification categories, clinicians will sometimes arrive at a wrong conclusion (Woody &

## Box 2-2

# *The Battle over Premenstrual Dysphoric Disorder*

Some categories of mental dysfunctioning are much more controversial than others. Clinicians and even the public wage intense battles over their usefulness and appropriateness whenever the DSM is revised. For example, after very long and heated discussions a decade ago, DSM-III dropped *homosexuality* as a category of mental dysfunctioning, citing a lack of evidence in support of such a category and concern about the continued social implications of calling this sexual preference abnormal.

Similarly, battles ensued in 1987 when many practitioners wanted to include the category *self-defeating* (or *masochistic*) *personality disorder* in the DSM to describe persons who display a pervasive pattern of undermining their own pleasurable experiences, being drawn to relationships or situations in which they suffer, and preventing others from helping them. Many critics feared this was a female-targeted category that would foster a harmful stereotype of women and would suggest that abused women were the cause of their damaging relationship rather than the victims of it. The framers of DSM-III-R ultimately agreed and did not enter it as an official category. Instead, they assigned it as a category "for further study." DSM-IV has dropped it altogether.

Perhaps the biggest controversy in the development of DSM-IV centered on the category *premenstrual dysphoric disorder (PMDD)*. After years of study, a DSM work group recommended in 1993 that this category be listed in the new

DSM as a type of depressive disorder. The category was to be applied when a woman is regularly impaired by at least 5 of 11 symptoms during the week prior to menses: sad or hopeless feelings; tense or anxious feelings; marked mood changes; frequent irritability or anger and increased interpersonal conflicts; decreased interest in usual activities; lack of concentration; lack of energy; changes in appetite; insomnia or sleepiness; a subjective feeling of being overwhelmed or out of control; and physical symptoms such as swollen breasts, headaches, muscle pain, "bloating" sensations, or weight gain.

The work group claimed that women with this severe pattern of symptoms do not respond well to treatments used for other kinds of depression, such as antidepressant drugs, and therefore that PMDD needed to be researched and treated as a separate category. If it were not included, they argued, many women who are severely impaired by these symptoms would be denied treatment, and their very real problems would not be fully investigated or, in turn, properly understood.

This recommendation set off an uproar. Many clinicians (including some dissenting members of the work group itself), several national organizations, interest groups, and the media voiced their concern that this diagnostic category would "pathologize" severe cases of *premenstrual syndrome,* or *PMS,* the premenstrual discomforts that are common and normal in many women (Chase, 1993; DeAngelis, 1993). The National Organization

of Women (NOW) argued that 42 percent of all women experience the vague and general symptoms of PMDD and could qualify for a diagnosis (Chase, 1993), although the DSM work group estimated that only 5 percent of women would meet the recommended criteria. NOW also argued that a diagnosis of PMDD would cause women's behavior in general to be attributed largely to hormonal changes (a stereotype that society is finally rejecting), placing a stigma on women and promoting discrimination in courtrooms, in the workplace, and during child custody hearings.

Opponents of the new category also argued that there was insufficient data to include it. In addition, they said, clinicians have paid far less attention to the possible relationships between male hormones and mental health.

The solution to this huge controversy was a compromise. The PMDD category has not been listed formally in DSM-IV, but clinicians can, on their own, specify it under the broad category of *depressive disorder not otherwise specified.* In addition, DSM-IV describes the pattern and its criteria in an appendix and suggests that it be studied more in the coming years. Whether this "shadow" status will lead to formal inclusion in DSM-V or to the category's quiet disappearance is anyone's guess at this point. Meanwhile, the issue of PMDD illustrates the many important factors—scientific, social, political, and personal—that come into play in the development of a diagnostic system.

---

Robertson, 1988). Numerous factors can adversely affect their thinking.

First, like all human beings, clinicians are flawed information processors. They often give too much

weight to the data they encounter first and too little to data they acquire later (Meehl, 1960). They may sometimes pay too much attention to certain sources of information, such as a parent's report about a child, and

**NORMAL**

**DOMINANT SYMPTOMATOLOGY:** Characterized by unimpaired occupational, social, and sexual functioning for a period of one year or more. During this time individuals are free of neurotic or psychotic symptoms, i.e., anxiety, depression, hallucinations, or delusional thinking. Judgment is good, self-esteem high. Age onset: birth. More commonly diagnosed in the early twentieth century, this condition is rarely seen today.

*As the list of mental disorders grows ever longer, some clinical observers believe that normal behavior is increasingly being viewed as the somewhat drab absence of abnormal functioning.*

too little to others, such as the child's point of view (McCoy, 1976). And, finally, their judgments can be distorted by any number of personal biases—gender, age, race, and socioeconomic status, to name just a few (Strakowski et al., 1995; Jenkins-Hall & Sacco, 1991). In a recent study, for example, white American therapists were asked to watch a videotaped clinical interview and then to evaluate either an African American or a white American woman who either was or was not depressed. Although the therapists rated the nondepressed African American woman much the same as the nondepressed white American woman, they rated the depressed African American woman with more negative adjectives and judged her to be less socially competent than the depressed white American woman.

Second, clinicians may bring various misconceptions about methodology to the decision-making process (Reisman, 1991). Many think, for example, that the more assessment techniques they use, the more accurate their interpretations will be—a belief that is not borne out by research (Kahneman & Tversky, 1973; Golden, 1964).

A third factor that can distort clinical interpretation is the clinicians' expectation that a person who consults them professionally must in fact have some disorder. Because they are looking for abnormal functioning, clinicians may overreact to any assessment data

that suggest abnormality, a phenomenon that has been called the "reading-in syndrome" (Phares, 1979).

## Dangers of Diagnosing and Labeling

Classification is intended to help clinicians understand, predict, and change abnormal behavior, but it can have some unfortunate and unintended consequences. Some theorists believe that diagnostic labels may be self-fulfilling prophecies (Rosenhan, 1973; Scheff, 1975). According to this notion, when persons are diagnosed as mentally disturbed, they may be viewed and treated in stereotyped ways, reacted to as sick or deficient, and expected to take on a sick role; they may in turn consider themselves sick and deficient and act in a corresponding manner.

Furthermore, our society attaches a stigma to abnormality, and as a result people labeled mentally ill may find it difficult to get a job, especially a position of responsibility, or to enter into social relationships. Similarly, once people receive a clinical diagnosis, it may stick to them for a long time. Clinicians, friends, relatives, and the people themselves may all continue to apply the label long after the disorder has disappeared.

Because of these problems, some clinicians would like to do away with the clinical field's reliance on diagnosis. Others disagree. Although they too recognize the limitations of classifying and labeling, they believe that the best remedy is to work toward increasing what is known about the various disorders and improving the means of diagnosing them (Akiskal, 1989). They hold that classification and diagnosis can yield valuable information that greatly advances the understanding and treatment of people in distress.

> *Summing Up*
> *Clinicians use assessment information to diagnose a psychological disorder. DSM-IV, the leading classification system in the United States, lists hundreds of disorders to choose from. Clinicians who use it to make a diagnosis must evaluate a client's condition on five axes. Clinicians do not always arrive at the correct conclusion, however. They often fall prey to biases, misconceptions, and expectations. Moreover, the labeling process may sometimes be damaging to the person being diagnosed.*

# Treatment

Over the course of ten months, Angela Savanti received extensive treatment for depression and related symptoms. She improved significantly during this time, as described in the following report.

> Angela's depression eased as she began to make progress in therapy. A few months before the termination of treatment, she and Jerry resumed dating. Angela discussed with Jerry her greater comfort in expressing her feelings and her hope that Jerry would also become more expressive with her. They discussed the reasons why Angela was ambivalent about getting married, and they began to talk again about the possibility of marriage. Jerry, however, was not making demands for a decision by a certain date, and Angela felt that she was not as frightened about marriage as she previously had been. . . .

Psychotherapy provided Angela with the opportunity to learn to express her feelings to the persons she was interacting with, and this was quite helpful to her. Most important, she was able to generalize from some of the learning experiences in therapy and modify her behavior in her renewed relationship with Jerry. Angela still had much progress to make in terms of changing the characteristic ways

she interacted with others, but she had already made a number of important steps in a potentially happier direction.

*(Leon, 1984, pp. 118–125)*

Clearly, by the conclusion of treatment Angela was a happier, more functional person than the woman who had first sought help ten months earlier. All sorts of factors may have contributed to her improvement. Friends and family members may have offered support or advice. A vacation may have lifted her spirits. Perhaps she changed her diet or started to exercise. Any or all of these things may have been useful to Angela, but they could not be considered *therapy*. That name is usually reserved for special, systematic methods for helping people overcome their psychological difficulties.

According to the clinical theorist Jerome Frank, all forms of therapy have three essential features:

1. A sufferer who seeks relief from the healer.
2. A trained, socially sanctioned healer.
3. A circumscribed, more or less structured series of contacts between the healer and the sufferer, through which the healer, often with the aid of a group, tries to produce certain changes in the sufferer's emotional state, attitudes, and behavior.

*(Frank, 1973, pp. 2–3)*

The healing process may be exercised primarily by *psychotherapy*—in Frank's words, "by words, acts, and rituals in which sufferer, healer, and—if there is one—group participate jointly," or by *biological therapy,* consisting of "physical and chemical procedures."

Each clinician tends to follow a particular system of therapy in his or her work. A *system of therapy* is a set of principles and techniques employed in accordance with a particular theory of causation and change. Today's leading systems are the psychoanalytic, behavioral, cognitive, humanistic, biological, and sociocultural systems that we shall be discussing in the next two chapters. Practitioners who follow one system of therapy tend to disagree strenuously with the philosophies and techniques of those who follow the other systems. Furthermore, each system of therapy may be applied in any of several *formats*—individual, group, family, or couple therapy. The number of systems and

---

*Psychotherapy* A treatment procedure in which sufferer and healer employ words, acts, and rituals as a means of overcoming psychological difficulties.

*Biological therapy* The use of physical and chemical procedures to help people overcome psychological difficulties.

*System of therapy* A set of treatment principles and techniques employed in accordance with a particular theory of causation and change.

*(Drawing by Shanahan; © 1992 The New Yorker Magazine, Inc.)*

formats of therapy and their variations seem to grow daily; altogether, there are as many as 400 forms of therapy practiced in the clinical field today (Karasu, 1992).

Clinicians also differ on such basic issues as what to call the person undergoing therapy. This person is called the *patient* by clinicians who view abnormality as an illness and therapy as a procedure that corrects the illness, and the *client* by clinicians who see abnormality as a maladaptive way of behaving or thinking and who see therapists as teachers of more functional behavior and thought. Because both terms are so common in the field, they will be used more or less interchangeably throughout this book.

> ### Consider This
> Some people who are in distress as a result of a psychological disorder seek the help of professionals; others turn to friends, relatives, or self-help groups. What characteristics differentiate the services provided by professionals from the help offered by self-help groups, relatives, or friends?

## Clients and Therapists

Nationwide surveys of adults have suggested that between 16 and 22 million people in this country receive therapy for psychological problems in the course of a year (Kessler et al., 1994; Narrow et al., 1993). This figure represents approximately 12 percent of the en-

tire adult population. It has become increasingly common for children to be treated for psychological problems, too (Kazdin, 1993).

The number and variety of problems for which treatments are available have increased during this century. When Freud and his colleagues first began to conduct therapy, most of their patients suffered from anxiety or depression. Anxiety and depression still dominate the therapy picture (almost half of today's clients in the United States suffer from these problems), but people with other kinds of disorders are also receiving therapy (Narrow et al., 1993). In fact, large numbers of people with milder psychological problems, sometimes called "problems in living," are also in therapy.

Other characteristics of clients have also changed over the years. Until the middle of this century, therapy was primarily a privilege of the wealthy, largely because of the high fees that outpatients were required to pay. However, with the recent expansion of medical insurance coverage and the emergence of publicly supported community mental health centers, people at all socioeconomic levels now receive both outpatient and inpatient therapy (Simons, 1989). Women used to outnumber men in therapy by two to one, partly because they were less reluctant than men to seek help (Lichtenstein, 1980). Lately, however, our society's attitudes and sex-role expectations have been changing, and men are becoming increasingly willing to enter therapy. Almost half of today's therapy patients are male (Manderscheid & Sonnenschein, 1992). In contrast, ethnic minority groups often differ considerably in the rates at which they utilize therapy services (see Box 2-3).

People enter therapy in a variety of ways. Many decide on their own to consult a therapist. Others may do so on the advice of a minister, physician, or other professional with whom they have discussed their difficulties. Still others are forced into treatment. Parents, spouses, teachers, and employers may virtually order people to seek treatment if they are causing disruptions or are in obvious distress; or judges may formally pronounce people mentally dysfunctional and dangerous and commit them to a mental hospital for treatment.

The length of time people spend in therapy varies with the nature of the problem and the approach the therapist takes. More than half of all clients visit their therapist fifteen times or fewer (Narrow et al., 1993; Knesper et al., 1985). At the other extreme, a small percentage of people continue in therapy for much of their lives. People with severe problems generally receive longer and more intense treatment than people with milder problems (Ware et al., 1984).

As we observed in Chapter 1, a variety of professionals conduct therapy today (see Figure 2-6). Whatever their profession, these therapists generally see the same kinds of patients (Knesper et al., 1985); that is, the majority of their clients are people with anxiety, depression, or relationship problems. At the same time, psychiatrists see a somewhat larger number of patients with schizophrenia and other severe disorders (16 percent of their cases) than do psychologists (5 percent) or social workers (7 percent). The providers of mental health services are concentrated in urban areas across the United States. In fact, there is a severe shortage of practitioners available to serve the needs of

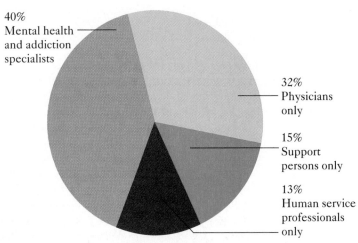

**Figure 2-6** *Where do people with psychological problems seek help? Approximately 40 percent of the Americans who receive treatment see mental health or drug addiction specialists. Another 32 percent see a physician only; 13 percent work exclusively with a human service professional, such as a religious counselor; and 15 percent discuss their problems only with support persons, such as a self-help group, family member, or friend. (Adapted from Regier et al., 1993.*

the 50 million people who live in the towns, farms, and countryside of rural America (Human & Wasem, 1991; Murray & Keller, 1991).

Therapy takes place in all sorts of settings, from public institutions to schools to private offices. As we observed in Chapter 1, most clients, even those who are severely disturbed, are treated as outpatients (Narrow et al., 1993); they live in the community and make regular visits to the therapist's office. Outpatients with higher incomes tend to be treated in private offices, while many of those with lower incomes are treated at publicly supported community mental health centers (Knesper et al., 1985). Whatever the patients' psychological problems, therapy sessions in community mental health centers tend to be shorter, less frequent, and fewer than those offered by private therapists (Knesper et al., 1985).

Most of the people who receive inpatient treatment, whether in privately funded or public institutions, such as state mental hospitals, have severe psychological problems. The private institutions usually offer better physical facilities, more trained staff members per patient, and more varied treatments (Redick et al., 1992). Personal wealth, more than any other factor, determines whether a patient is treated in a private or a public institution (Knesper et al., 1985).

Hospitalization now usually lasts weeks instead of months or years. When people develop severe psychological disorders, therapists now try to treat them first

*The oldest of the modern adult therapy formats is individual, or one-to-one, therapy in which the therapist meets alone with a client.*

## Box 2-3

# *Ethnic Minorities in the Mental Health System*

Researchers and clinicians have recently become interested in the different use rates, dropout rates, and experiences of persons from ethnic minority groups who are in need of mental health services. For example, while African Americans and Native Americans use these services as often as white Americans, other ethnic groups, such as Asian Americans and Hispanic Americans, make less use of those services (Flaskerud & Hu, 1992; Sue, 1991, 1977). Moreover, although African Americans in general make about the same use of mental health facilities as white Americans, African Americans who abuse drugs and alcohol are less likely to seek or complete treatment than white Americans, who abuse such substances (Booth et al., 1992; Longshore et al., 1992).

Several factors may lead to the underuse of mental health services by ethnic minority groups. Cultural beliefs, a language barrier, and lack of information about available services sometimes prevent minority individuals from seeking those services. People who need treatment for a mental disorder may be more stigmatized in some cultures than in others. Fur-

thermore, many members of minority groups simply do not trust the establishment, and rely instead on remedies traditional in their immediate social network. Some Hispanic persons, for example, practice spiritualism and believe that bad spirits can enter the body and cause mental disorders, and that good spirits can cure those disorders (Rogler et al., 1989). Since these beliefs are incompatible with Western beliefs about mental disorders and traditional therapy, these Hispanic persons may seek help not from therapists but from folk healers, family members, and friends.

Studies have also found that African Americans, Native Americans, Asian Americans, and Hispanic Americans all have higher therapy dropout rates than white Americans (Wierzbicki & Pekarik, 1993). This finding may be due in part to the fact that the dropout rate is higher among poorer clients, and ethnic minorities are overrepresented in lower-income groups. In addition, members of ethnic minority groups may terminate treatment because they do not feel that they are benefiting from therapy or because ethnic and cul-

tural differences keep them from experiencing rapport with their therapist (Sue, 1991).

Studies have also found that ethnic minority individuals may differ in the *type* of mental health facility where they are most likely to be treated. A study in California, for example, found that Hispanic American, Asian American, and African American adolescents were more likely to be treated in public hospitals, whereas white American adolescents were more likely to be treated in private mental hospitals (Mason & Gibbs, 1992). One explanation for this difference is that white American adolescents are more likely to have private insurance and thus to be able to afford treatment in private hospitals, while the ethnic minority adolescents are more likely to need public funding for their treatment, and thus to be placed in public facilities. Another consequence of the reliance on public funding by many ethnic minority adolescents is that they have shorter hospitalizations than privately insured white American adolescents, who can afford longer hospitalizations (Mason & Gibbs, 1992).

Some clinicians have recently

as outpatients. If this strategy proves ineffective, the patient may be admitted to a hospital for a short period so that the condition can be monitored, diagnosed, and stabilized. As soon as hospitalization has served this purpose, the patient is returned to the community. In theory, this may be a reasonable treatment plan; but, as we observed in Chapter 1, community treatment facilities have been so underfunded and understaffed over the years that they have not been able to meet the treatment needs of people with severe impairments, and hundreds of thousands of people have been condemned to an endless cycle of hospital discharges and readmissions.

## Is Treatment Effective?

Probably the most important question to ask about a particular treatment is whether it does what it is supposed to do—that is, whether it helps people cope with and overcome their psychological problems. On the surface, this may seem to be a simple question. In fact, it is one of the most difficult questions for clinical researchers to answer (Persons, 1991). Several problems must be addressed.

The first problem is how to define a "successful" treatment (Strupp, 1989). If, as her therapist suggests, Angela Savanti still has much progress to make after

developed a number of *culture-sensitive therapies,* approaches that are designed to address the unique issues and pressures faced by members of minority groups, especially when the issues contribute largely to the clients' emotional problems (Prochaska & Norcross, 1994; Watkins-Duncan, 1992). These approaches often include features such as (1) raising the consciousness of clients about the impact of the dominant culture and their own culture on their self-views and behaviors, (2) helping clients express suppressed anger and come to terms with their pain, and (3) helping clients make choices that work for them and achieve a bicultural identity and balance that feels right for them.

Researchers have also begun to intensify their investigations into the treatment of persons from ethnic minority groups. This body of research is very limited so far, but a few preliminary trends have emerged (Sue et al., 1994; Prochaska & Norcross, 1994):

1. Ethnic minority groups are generally underserved in the mental health field.

2. Clients from ethnic minority groups appear to improve as much as white American clients in some studies and less in other studies; in no comparative study, however, do they improve more than white American clients.

3. Clients from ethnic minority groups tend to prefer therapists who are ethnically similar to themselves, although this is but one of many characteristics preferred by such clients.

4. Some, but not all, studies suggest that having an ethnically similar therapist improves the outcome of treatment. This is certainly true in cases where the client's primary language is not English.

5. Certain features seem to increase the effectiveness of treatment for clients from ethnic minorities: heightened therapist sensitivity to cultural issues, inclusion of cultural morals and models in treatment (especially in therapies for children and adolescents), and pretherapy intervention programs in which clients from certain ethnic groups are initially introduced to what psychotherapy is and what to expect.

6. Reviews of research have often made the mistake of lumping together subjects from different ethnic minority groups and failing to consider the important differences between such groups. Similarly, research has only recently begun to consider the important individual differences that exist *within* each ethnic minority group.

This research makes clear the urgency of efforts to address ethnic minority issues in research and practice, to increase the number of ethnic minority clinicians and the availability of their services, and to increase the sensitivity of all health-care providers to the cultures and needs of ethnic minority populations. In cities where the needs of the various ethnic groups have been addressed, the numbers of persons in these groups who use mental health services have increased and the clients are more satisfied with the services they receive and are more likely to continue treatment (O'Sullivan et al., 1989; Rodriguez, 1986).

her ten-month course of therapy, should her recovery be considered successful? Different clinical researchers would answer this question differently. Because definitions of success vary from investigator to investigator, it is not always appropriate to combine the results from different treatment studies and use them to draw general conclusions (Kazdin, 1994).

The second problem is *how* to measure improvement. Should researchers give equal weight to the reports of clients, friends, relatives, therapists, and teachers? Should they use rating scales, inventories, checklists, therapy insights, behavior observations, or some other measure? The various measures of improvement correlate only moderately with one another (Lambert & Hill, 1994).

Perhaps the biggest problem is the range and complexity of the treatments currently in use. Clients differ in their problems, personal styles, and motivation for therapy; therapists differ in skill, experience, orientation, and personality; and therapies differ in theory, format, and setting. Because a client's progress in therapy is influenced by all these factors and more, results from a particular study will not always apply to other clients and therapists.

Despite such difficulties, the job of evaluating therapies must be done, and clinical researchers have

*Our culture is inundated with "treatments" that come in such forms as self-help books, radio and television call-in shows, and advice columns. One of the most famous practitioners in this tradition is "Dr. Ruth" Westheimer, who offers counseling and advice on sexual functioning.*

plowed ahead with it (Lambert & Bergin, 1994). Thousands of studies have been conducted to test the effectiveness of various treatments, and numerous reviewers have tried to assess those studies and draw overall conclusions. The studies fall into three categories: (1) those that ask whether therapy in general is effective, (2) those that ask whether a particular therapy is generally effective, and (3) those that ask whether particular therapies are effective for particular problems.

*Consider This*

The multitude of therapies and the wide variety of disorders make it difficult for researchers to evaluate therapy. What problems do you foresee in evaluating the effectiveness of therapy? What kinds of information about therapy would be most useful to potential clients as well as policy makers?

## Is Therapy Generally Effective?

Most studies suggest that therapy is often (though not always) more helpful than no treatment or than placebos (Lambert & Bergin, 1994). A broad review examined 375 controlled effectiveness studies, covering a total of almost 25,000 clients seen in a wide assortment of therapies (Smith et al., 1980; Smith & Glass, 1977). The findings from all 375 studies were com-

bined using a statistical technique called a ***meta-analysis*** (Schmidt, 1992). It rated the level of improvement in each treated person and in each untreated control subject and computed the average difference between those two groups. According to this meta-analysis, the average person who received treatment was better off than 75 percent of the untreated control subjects (see Figure 2-7). Still other meta-analyses have revealed a similar relationship between treatment and improvement (Lambert et al., 1993; Crits-Cristoph et al., 1991).

A number of clinicians have also concerned themselves with an important related question: Can therapy be harmful? In his book *My Analysis with Freud* the psychoanalyst Abraham Kardiner (1977) wrote, "Freud was always infuriated whenever I would say to him that you could not do harm with psychoanalysis. He said: 'When you say that, you also say it cannot do any good. Because if you cannot do any harm, how can you do good?'" A number of studies conducted since the 1950s agree with Freud that some patients actually seem to worsen because of therapy (Lambert & Bergin, 1994; Mays & Franks, 1985). The deterioration may take the form of a general worsening of symptoms or the development of new symptoms, including a sense of failure, guilt, low self-concept, or hopelessness over one's inability to profit from therapy (Lambert et al., 1986; Hadley & Strupp, 1976).

## Are Particular Therapies Effective?

Most of the studies that have considered the general effectiveness of therapy have lumped all therapies together and treated them all alike, a procedure that many researchers consider inappropriate. One critic suggested that such studies were operating under a *uniformity myth*—a false belief that all therapies are equivalent despite differences in the therapists' training, experience, theoretical orientations, and personalities (Kiesler, 1966).

An alternative approach has been to examine the effectiveness of particular therapies. Most such studies show each of the major systems and formats of therapy to be superior to no treatment or to placebo treatment. A number of studies have also compared particular therapies with one another, and have failed to find that one form of therapy consistently stands out over others (Luborsky et al., 1975).

This finding of similar overall success rates in various kinds of therapy has led to a ***rapprochement movement,*** an effort to delineate a set of "common thera-

---

*Rapprochement movement*  An effort to delineate a set of "common therapeutic strategies" that characterize the work of all effective therapists.

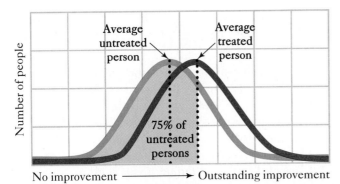

Figure 2-7 *Combining subjects and results from hundreds of studies, investigators have determined that the average person who receives psychotherapy experiences greater improvement than do 75 percent of all untreated people with similar problems. (Adapted from Lambert et al., 1993; Smith et al., 1980; Smith & Glass, 1977.)*

peutic strategies" that may characterize the work of all effective therapists irrespective of their particular orientation (Prochaska & Norcross, 1994; Beutler et al., 1994). A survey of highly successful therapists of various orientations suggests that most provide feedback to patients, help patients focus on their own thoughts and behavior, pay attention to the way therapist and patient are interacting, and try to promote self-mastery in their patients. In short, effective therapists often seem to practice more similarly than they preach (Korchin & Sands, 1983).

## Are Particular Therapies Effective for Particular Disorders?

Different people with different disorders may respond differently to the various therapeutic systems, formats, and settings (Zettle et al., 1992). As the influential clinical theorist Gordon Paul said some years back, the most appropriate question to ask regarding the effectiveness of therapy may be "*What* specific treatment, by *whom,* is most effective for *this* individual with *that* specific problem, and under *which* set of circumstances?" (Paul, 1967, p. 111).

This consideration has impelled a number of researchers to be as specific as possible in the design of therapy studies, investigating, for example, how effective particular therapies are at treating particular disorders (Kazdin, 1994; Beutler, 1991). These studies have often found sizable differences among the various therapies. As we shall see in the next chapter, for example, behavioral therapies appear to be the most effective of

all therapies in the treatment of phobic disorders (Emmelkamp, 1994), and drug therapy is the single most effective treatment for schizophrenia (Meltzer, 1992).

Studies have also revealed that some clinical problems may respond better to combined therapy approaches than to any one therapy alone (Beitman, 1993; Sander & Feldman, 1993). Drug therapy may be combined with certain forms of psychotherapy, for example, to treat depression. A combination of therapies also seems to be in order when a client is suffering from more than one psychological disorder (Clarkin & Kendall, 1992). In line with such combination approaches, it is becoming increasingly common for clients to be seen by two therapists—(1) a *psychopharmacologist,* or *pharmacotherapist,* a psychiatrist who only prescribes medications, and (2) a psychologist, social worker, or other therapist who conducts psychotherapy (Woodward et al., 1993).

Specific information on how particular therapies fare with particular disorders can help therapists and clients alike make better decisions about treatment (Beutler, 1991, 1979), and it can provide researchers with a better understanding of therapy processes and ultimately of abnormal functioning. Thus, the effectiveness of particular treatments is a question to which we shall keep returning as we examine the disorders they have been devised to combat.

### Summing Up

*Therapy is a systematic procedure for helping people overcome their psychological difficulties. There are numerous systems of therapy, and each system may be applied in any of several formats—individual, group, family, or couple therapy.*

*The critical question to be asked is whether the various treatments actually help people overcome their psychological problems. Studies indicate, first, that people in therapy are usually better off than people with similar problems who receive no treatment. Second, the various therapies do not appear to differ dramatically in their general effectiveness. Third, certain therapies or combinations of therapies appear to be more effective than others for certain disorders.*

---

*Psychopharmacologist*   A psychiatrist who primarily prescribes medications.

# Chapter Review

1. **The Practitioner's Task:** Clinical practitioners are interested primarily in compiling *idiographic,* or individual, information about their clients. They seek a full understanding of the specific nature and origins of a client's problems through *assessment,* or the gathering and interpreting of information about the person's problems, and *diagnosis,* or the process of determining whether the person's dysfunction constitutes a particular psychological disorder.

2. **Clinical Assessment:** Clinical assessment is carried out before, during, and after treatment. Most assessment methods fall into three general categories: clinical interviews, tests, and observations.

   A. **Clinical Interview:** A clinical interview permits the practitioner to interact with a person and generally get a sense of who he or she is. The clinician may conduct either an *unstructured* or *structured* interview.

   B. **Clinical Tests:** Clinical tests are devices that gather information about a few aspects of a person's psychological functioning from which broader information about that person can be inferred. They include *projective tests, personality inventories, response inventories, psychophysiological tests, neuropsychological tests,* and *intelligence tests.* To be useful a test must be *standardized, reliable,* and *valid.* Clinicians generally administer a *battery* of tests to assess psychological functioning.

   C. **Clinical Observations:** Two strategies for observing people's behavior are *naturalistic observation* and *structured observation.* Practitioners also employ the related procedure of *self-monitoring:* subjects observe themselves and carefully record designated behavior, feelings, or cognitions as they occur throughout the day.

3. **Diagnosis:** After collecting and interpreting the assessment information, clinicians form a *clinical picture* and reach a *diagnosis.* A *classification system* lists recognized disorders and describes the symptoms characteristic of each.

4. **DSM-IV:** The classification system developed by the American Psychiatric Association is the *Diagnostic and Statistical Manual of Mental Disorders (DSM).*

The most recent version of the manual, known as *DSM-IV,* lists close to 300 disorders. Clinicians who use it to make a diagnosis must evaluate a client's condition on five *axes,* or categories of information. Because DSM-IV is new, its reliability and validity have yet to receive broad clinical review.

5. **Clinical Misinterpretation:** Even with trustworthy assessment data and reliable and valid classification categories, clinicians will not always arrive at the correct conclusion. Many factors can mar their judgment. Clinicians are human and fall prey to various biases, misconceptions, and expectations.

6. **Dangers of Diagnosing:** Some people think that diagnosing a patient does more harm than good, because the labeling process and the prejudices that labels arouse may be damaging to the person being diagnosed.

7. **Therapy:** Therapy is a systematic procedure for helping people overcome their psychological difficulties. All forms of therapy have three things in common: a sufferer seeking relief, a trained healer, and a series of contacts between healer and sufferer. At the same time, therapies vary in their goals, methods, and ways of measuring success.

   As many as 400 distinct forms of therapy are being practiced today. A *system* of therapy is a set of principles and techniques employed in accordance with a particular theory of causation and change. The system may be applied in any of several *formats*—*individual, group, family,* and *couple therapy.*

8. **Is Therapy Effective?** The critical question to be asked about the various treatments is whether or not they actually help people cope with and overcome their psychological problems. Three general conclusions have been reached. First, most recent findings indicate that people in therapy are usually better off than people with similar problems who receive no treatment. Second, the various therapies do not appear to differ dramatically in their *general* effectiveness. Third, certain therapies do appear to be more effective than others for certain disorders, and often a particular combination of approaches is more effective than a single approach in the treatment of certain disorders.

# Key Terms

| | | | |
|---|---|---|---|
| idiographic | construct validity | neuropsychological test | diagnosis |
| assessment | projective test | CAT scan | syndrome |
| unstructured interview | Rorschach test | EEG | classification system |
| structured interview | Thematic Apperception | PET scan | ICD |
| interview schedule | Test (TAT) | MRI | DSM-IV |
| mental status exam | sentence completion test | Bender Gestalt Test | axes |
| standardization | Draw-a-Person Test | battery | psychotherapy |
| reliability | (DAP) | intelligence test | biological therapy |
| test-retest reliability | personality inventory | intelligence quotient (IQ) | patient |
| alternate-form reliability | MMPI | naturalistic observation | client |
| internal reliability | response set | structured observation | system of therapy |
| interrater reliability | response inventory | self-monitoring | therapy format |
| validity | affective inventory | participant observer | uniformity myth |
| face validity | social skill inventory | observer drift | rapprochement |
| predictive validity | cognition inventory | observer bias | movement |
| concurrent validity | psychophysiological test | reactivity | psychopharmacologist |
| content validity | biofeedback | clinical picture | pharmacotherapist |

# Quick Quiz

1. What are the relative strengths and weaknesses of structured and unstructured interviews as tools of assessment?
2. What forms of reliability and validity should clinical tests display?
3. List and describe today's leading projective tests.
4. What are the key features of the MMPI?
5. How do clinicians determine whether psychological problems are linked to neurological damage?
6. What are the relative strengths and weaknesses of projective tests, personality inventories, and other kinds of clinical tests?
7. Describe the ways in which clinicians may make observations of clients' behaviors.
8. What is the purpose of clinical diagnoses?
9. Describe the content and structure of DSM-IV.
10. What problems may accompany the use of classification systems and the process of clinical diagnosis?
11. What are the key features of therapy, who receives it, and who conducts it?
12. How effective is therapy according to recent studies?

# 3

# The Psychological Models of Abnormality

## Topic Overview

*The Psychodynamic Model*
Freud's Theory
Ego Theory, Self Theory, and Object Relations Theory
Psychodynamic Therapies

*The Behavioral Model*
Classical Conditioning
Operant Conditioning
Behavioral Therapies

*The Cognitive Model*
Maladaptive Assumptions
Specific Upsetting Thoughts
Illogical Thinking
Cognitive Therapies

*The Humanistic-Existential Model*
Rogers's Theory
Gestalt Theory
Existential Theories
Humanistic and Existential Therapies

Philip Berman, a 25-year-old single unemployed former copy editor for a large publishing house, . . . had been hospitalized after a suicide attempt in which he deeply gashed his wrist with a razor blade. He described [to the therapist] how he had sat on the bathroom floor and watched the blood drip into the bathtub for some time before he telephoned his father at work for help. He and his father went to the hospital emergency room to have the gash stitched, but he convinced himself and the hospital physician that he did not need hospitalization. The next day when his father suggested he needed help, he knocked his dinner to the floor and angrily stormed to his room. When he was calm again, he allowed his father to take him back to the hospital.

The immediate precipitant for his suicide attempt was that he had run into one of his former girlfriends with her new boyfriend. The patient stated that they had a drink together, but all the while he was with them he could not help thinking that "they were dying to run off and jump in bed." He experienced jealous rage, got up from the table, and walked out of the restaurant. He began to think about how he could "pay her back."

Mr. Berman had felt frequently depressed for brief periods during the previous several years. He was especially critical of himself for his limited social life and his inability to have managed to have sexual intercourse with a woman even once in his life. As he related this to the therapist, he lifted his eyes from the floor and with a sarcastic smirk said, "I'm a 25-year-old virgin. Go ahead, you can laugh now." He has had several girlfriends to date, whom he described as very attractive, but who he said had lost interest in him. On further questioning, however, it became apparent that Mr. Berman soon became very critical of them and demanded that they always meet his every need, often to their own detriment. The women then found the relationship very unrewarding and would soon find someone else.

During the past two years Mr. Berman had seen three psychiatrists briefly, one of whom had given him a drug, the name of which he could not remember, but that had precipitated some sort of unusual reaction for which he had to stay in a hospital overnight. Another gave him three treatments with electroconvulsive therapy (ECT) because he complained that he was suicidal. These had no effect on his mood but, according to him, caused significant memory loss. He saw the third psychiatrist for three months, but while in treatment he quit his job and could no longer afford the therapy. When asked why he quit, he said, "The bastards were going to fire me anyway." When asked whether he realized he would have to drop out of therapy when he quit his job, he said, "What makes you think I give a damn what happens to therapy?" Concerning his hospitalization, the patient said that "It was a dump," that the staff refused to listen to what he had to say or to respond to his needs, and that they, in fact, treated all the patients "sadistically." The referring doctor corroborated that Mr. Berman was a difficult patient who demanded that he be treated as special, and yet was hostile to most staff members throughout his stay. After one angry exchange with an aide, he left the hospital without leave, and subsequently signed out against medical advice.

Mr. Berman is one of two children of a middle-class family. His father is 55 years old and employed in a managerial position for an insurance company. He perceives his father as weak and ineffectual, completely dominated by the patient's overbearing and cruel mother. He states that he hates his mother with "a passion I can barely control." He claims that his mother used to call him names like "pervert" and "sissy" when he was growing up, and that in an argument she once "kicked me in the balls." Together, he sees his parents as rich, powerful, and selfish, and, in turn, thinks that they see him as lazy, irresponsible, and a behavior problem. When his parents called the therapist to discuss their son's treatment, they stated that his problem began with the birth of his younger brother, Arnold, when Philip was 10 years old. After Arnold's birth Philip apparently became an "ornery" child who cursed a lot and was difficult to discipline. Philip recalls this period only vaguely. He reports that his mother once was hospitalized for depression, but that now "she doesn't believe in psychiatry."

Mr. Berman had graduated from college with average grades. Since graduating he had worked at three different publishing houses, but at none of them for more than one year. He always found some justification for quitting. He usually sat around his house doing very little for two or three months after quitting a job, until his parents prodded him into getting a new one. He described innumerable interactions in his life with teachers, friends, and employers in which he felt offended or unfairly treated, . . . and frequent arguments that left him feeling bitter . . . and spent most of his time alone, "bored." He was unable to commit himself to any person, he held no strong convictions, and he felt no allegiance to any group.

The patient appeared as a very thin, bearded, and bespectacled young man with pale skin who maintained little eye contact with the therapist and who had an air of angry bitterness about him. Although he complained of depression, he denied other symptoms of the depressive syndrome. He seemed preoccupied with his rage at his parents, and seemed particularly invested in conveying a despicable image of himself. When treatment was discussed with Mr. Berman, the therapist recommended frequent contacts, two or three per week, feeling that Mr. Berman's potential for self-injury, if not suicide, was rather high. The judgment was based not so much on the severity of Mr. Berman's depression as on his apparent impulsivity, frequent rages, childish disregard for the consequences of his actions, and his pattern of trying to get other people to suffer by inflicting injury on himself. Mr. Berman willingly agreed to the frequent sessions, but not because of eagerness to get help. "Let's make it five sessions a week," he said. "It's about time my parents paid for all that they've done to me."

(Spitzer et al., 1983, pp. 59–61)

Philip is clearly a troubled person, but how did he come to be that way? How do we explain and correct his many problems? In confronting these questions, we must acknowledge their complexity. First, we must appreciate the wide range of complaints we are trying to understand: Philip's depression and anger, his social failures, his lack of employment, his distrust of those around him, and the problems within his family. Second, we must sort through all kinds of potential primary causes, internal and external, biological and interpersonal, past and present, and decide which is having the biggest impact on Philip's behavior.

Over the course of our lives, each of us has developed a perspective that helps us make sense of the things other people say and do. Such a perspective helps us to explain other people's behavior to our own satisfaction. In science, such perspectives are known as **paradigms** or **models**. Each is an explicit set of basic assumptions that gives structure to an area under study and sets forth guidelines for its investigation (Kuhn, 1962). The paradigm or model influences what the investigators observe, what questions they ask, what information they consider legitimate, and how they interpret this information (Lehman, 1991). To understand how a clinical scientist explains and treats a specific pattern of abnormal functioning, such as Philip's pattern of symptoms, we must appreciate the model that shapes his or her view of abnormal functioning.

Until recent times the models used by clinical scientists were usually monolithic and culturally determined; that is, a single model was paramount in a particular place and at a particular time, couched in the metaphors of the prevalent worldview. Recall the demonological model used to explain abnormal functioning during the Middle Ages. Practitioners of that period viewed each person as a battleground where the devil challenged God. Abnormal behavior signaled the devil's victory.

Medieval practitioners would have seen the devil's guiding hand in Philip Berman's efforts to commit sui-

cide, and they would have pointed to demonological possession as the ultimate explanation for Philip's feelings of depression, rage, jealousy, and hatred. Moreover, while they might have employed any of a variety of treatments to help Philip overcome his difficulties, from prayers to bitter drinks to whippings, all such treatments would have had the common purpose of driving a foreign spirit from his body. Anyone brazen enough to offer an explanation or treatment outside of the accepted demonological model would have been harshly criticized for failure to appreciate the fundamental issues at stake.

Whereas one model was dominant during the Middle Ages, a variety of models are being employed to explain and treat abnormal functioning today. This state of affairs has resulted from shifts in values and beliefs over the past half century and from improvements in the quality and quantity of clinical research. At one end of the spectrum is the *biological model*, which cites organic processes as the key to human behavior. At the other end is the *sociocultural model*, which scrutinizes the effect of society and culture on individual behavior. In between are four models that focus on more psychological dimensions of human functioning: the *psychodynamic model*, which looks at people's unconscious internal dynamics and conflicts; the *behavioral model*, which emphasizes ingrained behavior and the ways in which it is learned; the *cognitive model*, which concentrates on the process and content of the thinking that underlies behavior; and the *humanistic-existential model*, which stresses the role of values and choices in determining human individuality and fulfillment. We shall examine the psychological models in this chapter and explore the biological and sociocultural models in the next chapter.

Rooted as they are in different assumptions and concepts, the models are sometimes in conflict, and proponents of one perspective often scoff at the "naive" interpretations, investigations, and treatment efforts of the rest. At the same time, none of the models is complete in itself; each focuses primarily on one aspect of human functioning, and none is capable of explaining the entire spectrum of abnormality.

## Summing Up
*Scientists use paradigms, or models, to understand abnormal behavior. Each model in use today highlights a different dimension of human behavior and explains abnormality with reference to that dimension. The leading psychological models are the psychodynamic, behavioral, cognitive, and humanistic-existential models.*

---

*Model*   A set of logically connected assumptions and concepts that helps scientists explain and interpret observations.

**Table 3-1**   *Comparing the Psychological Models*

|  | *Psychodynamic* | *Behavioral* | *Cognitive* | *Humanistic* | *Existential* |
|---|---|---|---|---|---|
| Cause of dysfunction | Underlying conflicts | Maladaptive learned behaviors | Maladaptive thinking | Self-deceit | Avoidance of responsibility |
| Research support | Modest | Strong | Strong | Weak | Weak |
| Consumer designation | Patient | Client | Client | Patient or client | Patient or client |
| Therapist role | Interpreter | Teacher | Persuader | Observer | Collaborator |
| Key therapist technique | Free association and interpretation | Conditioning | Reasoning | Reflection | Varied |
| Therapy goal | Broad psychological change | Functional behaviors | Adaptive thinking | Self-actualization | Authentic life |

# The Psychodynamic Model

The oldest and most famous of the modern psychological models is the **psychodynamic model**. Psychodynamic theorists believe that a person's behavior, whether normal or abnormal, is determined to a large extent by underlying psychological forces of which the person is not consciously aware. These internal forces are considered *dynamic*—that is, they interact with one another; and their interaction gives shape to an individual's behavior, thoughts, and emotions. Abnormal behaviors or symptoms are viewed as the consequences of *conflicts* between these forces (see Table 3-1).

Thus, psychodynamic theorists would view Philip Berman as a person in conflict, a person whose underlying needs and motives are in a state of disharmony. They would want to explore his past experiences because, in their view, people's psychological conflicts are related to their early relationships and to traumatic experiences that occurred during their early years. Psychodynamic theories rest on the **deterministic** assumption that no symptom or behavior is "accidental." All behavior is determined by past experiences, particularly the experiences of childhood. Thus Philip's hatred for his mother, his recollections of her as cruel and overbearing, the weakness and ineffectuality of his father, and the birth of a younger brother when Philip was 10 may all be relevant issues.

The psychodynamic model was first formulated by the Viennese neurologist Sigmund Freud (1856–1939) at the turn of the century. After studying hypnosis under the famous neurologist Jean Charcot and collaborating with the eminent physician Josef Breuer on a number of case studies, Freud developed the theory of **psychoanalysis** in which he proposed that "unconscious" conflicts account for all forms of normal and abnormal psychological functioning. Freud also formulated a corresponding method of treatment, a conversational approach in which patients would explore their unconscious with a psychoanalyst and come to terms with the conflicts they discovered there. During the early 1900s, Freud and several of his colleagues in the Vienna Psychoanalytic Society—including Carl Gustav Jung (1875–1961) and Alfred Adler (1870–1937)—became the most influential clinical theorists in the Western world. Freud's twenty-four volumes on psychoanalytic theory and treatment are still widely studied today.

## Freudian Explanations of Normal and Abnormal Functioning

As Freud studied the lives and problems of his patients, he came to believe that three central forces shape or "constitute" the personality—instinctual needs, rational thinking, and moral standards. Freud called these three forces the id, ego, and superego and he believed them to be dynamic, or interactive, components whose jostling for expression molds the person's behavior, feelings, and thoughts.

---

*Psychoanalysis*   The theory or treatment of abnormal psychological functioning, first developed by Sigmund Freud, that emphasizes unconscious conflicts as the cause of psychopathology.

## The Id

Freud used the term *id* to denote the instinctual needs, drives, and impulses, which he believed are the primary motivators of human behavior. The id operates at the *unconscious* level, unavailable to immediate, cognizant awareness. It functions in accordance with the *pleasure principle;* that is, it always seeks gratification.

Freud also believed that all id instincts tend to be sexual, noting that from the very earliest stages of development a child's gratification has sexual dimensions, as much of its pleasure is derived from nursing, defecating, and masturbating. Freud created the concept of **libido** to represent the sexual energy that fuels not only the id but the other forces of personality as well.

## The Ego

During our early years we come to recognize that our environment will not meet every instinctual need. Our mother, for example, is not always available to provide nurturance at our bidding. Thus a part of the id becomes differentiated into a separate force called the *ego.* Like the id, the ego seeks gratification, but it does so in accordance with the *reality principle,* the knowledge we acquire through experience and from the people around us that it can be dangerous or unacceptable to express our id impulses outright. The ego, employing reason and deliberation, guides us to recognize when we can and cannot express those impulses without suffering negative consequences.

The ego also develops basic strategies, called *ego defense mechanisms,* to control unacceptable id impulses and avoid or reduce the anxiety they arouse. The most basic defense mechanism, *repression,* prevents unacceptable impulses from ever reaching consciousness. There are many other ego defense mechanisms, and each of us tends to favor some over others (see Box 3-1).

## The Superego

The *superego* grows from the ego, just as the ego grows out of the id. As we learn from our parents that many of our id impulses are unacceptable, we unconsciously incorporate, or *introject,* our parents' values. We identify with our parents and judge ourselves by their standards. When we uphold their values, we feel good; when we go against them, we feel guilty.

According to Freud, these three parts of the personality are often in conflict, so that we often seem impelled to act, think, and feel in contradictory ways. A healthy personality is one in which an effective working relationship, a stable and acceptable compromise, has been established among the three forces. If the id, ego, and superego are in excessive conflict, the person's behavior may show signs of dysfunction.

Freudians would therefore view Philip Berman as someone whose personality forces have a poor working relationship. His rational, constructive ego is unable to control his id impulses, which lead him repeatedly to act in impulsive and often dangerous ways—suicide gestures, jealous rages, job resignations, outbursts of temper, frequent arguments. At the same time, his superego seems to be poorly formulated and largely ineffective. Having had weak and ineffectual parental models, Philip never incorporated an effective set of values, a positive ego ideal that might have helped to channel and guide his id impulses.

## Developmental Stages

Freud proposed that the forces of personality are called to action throughout a person's psychological development, beginning in early infancy. At each developmental stage the child is confronted with events and pressures that challenge and perhaps threaten his or her habitual way of doing things. Such clashes require adjustments in the id, ego, and superego. If the adjustments are successful, they foster personal growth.

Under certain pressures, the id, ego, and superego may not mature properly or interact effectively, and the child becomes *fixated,* or entrapped, at an early stage of development. Then all subsequent development suffers, and the child may well be headed for abnormal functioning in the future. Because parents provide the primary environmental input during the early years of life, they are often seen as the cause of this improper development.

---

*Id* One of the three psychological forces proposed by Freud as central to shaping personality. The id is the source of instinctual needs, drives, and impulses.

*Ego* One of the three psychological forces proposed by Freud as central to shaping the personality. The ego operates in accordance with the reality principle, employing reason and deliberation.

*Ego defense mechanisms* According to psychoanalytic theory, strategies developed by the ego to control unacceptable id impulses and to avoid or reduce the anxiety they arouse.

*Superego* One of the three psychological forces proposed by Freud as central to shaping the personality. The superego embodies the values and ideals taught to us by our parents.

*Introjection* The unconscious incorporation of parental values that leads to the development of the superego in the child.

*Fixation* According to Freud, a condition in which the id, ego, and superego do not mature properly and are frozen at an early stage of development.

Freud distinguished most stages of normal development by the body area, or *erogenous zone,* that he considered representative of the child's sexual drives and conflicts at that time. He called these phases the oral, anal, phallic, latency, and genital stages.

The earliest developmental stage, embracing the first 18 months of life, is called the *oral stage* because the infant's main libidinal gratification comes from feeding and from the body parts involved in it—the mouth, lips, and tongue. The most significant threat to children during the oral stage is the possibility that the mother who feeds and comforts them will disappear. If mothers consistently fail to gratify the oral needs of their children, the children may become fixated at the oral stage, fail to grow beyond their oral needs, and display an "oral character" throughout their lives: extreme dependence or, by the same token, extreme mistrust, and perhaps habits such as pencil chewing, constant talking, or overindulgence in eating, smoking, and drinking.

During the second 18 months of life, the *anal stage,* the child's focus of pleasure shifts to the anus. Libidinal gratification comes from retaining and passing feces, and the child becomes very interested in this bodily function. If parental toilet-training techniques during this stage are too severe, an anal fixation may

*Freud believed that toilet training is a critical developmental experience. Those whose training is too harsh may become "fixated" at this stage and develop an "anal character."*

result, and the child may develop into an adult with an "anal character," prone to be stubborn, contrary, stingy, or overcontrolling.

> ### Consider This
>
> In our society there are many people who fit the description of an oral or anal character, but are these styles necessarily the result of fixation at early stages of development? What other explanations can you suggest? Are there ways in which oral or anal traits may be constructive and beneficial?

During the *phallic stage,* between the third and fourth years, the focus of sexual pleasure shifts to the genitals—the penis for boys and the clitoris for girls. Boys become attracted to their mother as a fully separate object, a sexual object, and see their father as a rival they would like to push aside. This pattern of desires is called the *Oedipus complex,* after Oedipus, a character in a Greek tragedy who unknowingly kills his father and marries his mother.

The phallic conflict for girls is somewhat different. During this stage, girls become aware that they do not have a penis—an organ that, according to Freud, they value and desire (so-called *penis envy*). They develop a sexual attraction for their father, rooted in the fantasy that by seducing him they can have a penis. This pattern of desires in girls is called the *Electra complex,* after Electra, a character in another Greek tragedy who conspired to kill her mother to avenge her father's death.

Both boys and girls fear that they will be punished for their phallic impulses, and so they repress these desires and identify with the parent of their own sex. Boys aspire to be like their fathers and girls to be like their mothers in every way. If children are punished too harshly for sexual behavior during this stage, or if they are subtly encouraged to pursue their desire for the parent of the opposite sex, they might later develop a sexual orientation different from the norm, fear sexual intimacy, be overly seductive, or have other difficulties in romantic relationships.

At 6 years of age children enter the *latency stage,* in which their sexual desires apparently subside and their libidinal energy is devoted to developing new interests, activities, and skills. They seek friends of the same sex,

*Oedipus complex* In Freudian theory, the pattern of desires in which boys become attracted to their mother as a sexual object and see their father as a rival they would like to push aside.

*Electra complex* According to Freud, the pattern of desires all girls experience in which they develop a sexual attraction for their father, rooted in the fantasy that by seducing him they can have his penis.

## Box 3-1

# The Defense Never Rests

Sigmund Freud claimed that the ego tries to defend itself from the anxiety arising out of the conflicts created by unacceptable desires. His daughter, Anna Freud (1895–1982), extended the concept of the ego defense mechanism beyond her father's reliance on repression as the key means for defense of the ego. Though repression is the cornerstone of the psychodynamic model of abnormality, it is but one of many methods by which the ego is thought to protect itself from anxiety. Some of these mechanisms are described below.

*Anna Freud, the last of Sigmund Freud's six children, studied psychoanalysis with her father and then opened a practice next door to his. (They shared a waiting room.) Through her work on defense mechanisms, other ego activities, and child development, she earned widespread professional recognition in her own right.*

**Repression** is the central focus of the psychoanalytic approach to therapy. All other defense mechanisms grow out of it. The person who engages in repression avoids anxiety by simply not allowing painful or dangerous thoughts to become conscious. Once thoughts have been repressed, other ego defense mechanisms may be employed to provide additional insulation.

*Example:* An executive's desire to run amok and attack his boss and colleagues at a board meeting is denied access to his awareness.

**Denial** is an extreme sort of self-protection. A person who denies reality simply refuses to acknowledge the existence of an external source of anxiety.

*Example:* You have a final exam in abnormal psychology tomorrow and you are entirely unprepared, but you tell yourself that it's not actually an important exam and that there's no good reason not to go to see a movie tonight.

**Fantasy** is the use of imaginary events to satisfy unacceptable, anxiety-producing desires that would otherwise go unfulfilled.

*Example:* Pulling into the parking lot at school, a student finds the space he was about to enter suddenly filled by an aggressive, unpleasant person in an expensive sports car. Instead of confronting the offender, the student later fantasizes about getting out of his car and beating the other man to a pulp in front of admiring onlookers, who laud him for his courage and righteousness.

**Projection** is the attributing of one's own unacceptable motives or desires to others. Rather than admit to having an anxiety-producing impulse, such as anger toward another person, the individual represses the feelings and sees the other person as being the angry one.

*Example:* The disturbed executive who repressed his destructive desires may project his anger onto his employer and claim that it is actually the boss, not he, who is hostile.

**Rationalization,** one of the most common defense mechanisms, is the construction of a socially acceptable reason for an action that actually reflects unworthy motives. Freud explained rationalization as an attempt to explain our behavior to ourselves and to others even though much of our behavior is

express dislike for the opposite sex, and are embarrassed by sexual displays. The broader process of socialization, of learning one's roles in family and society, takes place at this time.

At approximately the age of 12, with the onset of puberty and adolescence, the child's sexual urges emerge once again. Now, in what is termed the *genital stage,* sexual pleasure begins to be found in heterosexual relationships. During this stage, adolescents become increasingly capable of genuine affection and caring for others and in the normal course of events learn to participate fully in loving and altruistic relationships. The genital stage ends when sexual, social, and vocational maturity is achieved.

motivated by unconscious drives that are irrational and infantile.

*Example:* A student explains away poor grades one semester to her concerned parents by citing the importance of the "total experience" of going to college and claiming that an overemphasis on grades would reduce the overall goal of a well-rounded education. This rationalization may hide an underlying fear of failure and lack of self-esteem.

**Reaction formation** is the adoption of behavior that is the exact opposite of impulses that one is afraid to acknowledge.

*Example:* A man experiences homosexual feelings and responds by taking a strong antihomosexual stance in front of his colleagues.

**Displacement,** like projection, is a transferral of repressed desires and impulses. In this case one displaces one's hostility away from a dangerous object and onto a safer substitute.

*Example:* The student whose parking spot was taken may release his pent-up anger by going home and starting a fight with his girlfriend.

**Intellectualization** (isolation) is repression of the emotional component of a reaction in favor of a determinedly logical treatment of the problem at hand. Such an attitude is exemplified by Mr. Spock

of the Star Trek television and movie series, who believes that emotional responses interfere with the analysis of an event.

*Example:* A woman who has been raped gives a detached, methodical description of the effects that the ordeal is known to have on a victim.

**Undoing,** as the name suggests, is an attempt to atone for unacceptable desires or acts, frequently through ritualistic behavior.

*Example:* A woman who has aggressive feelings toward her husband ceremoniously dusts and repositions their wedding photograph every time such thoughts occur to her.

**Regression** is a retreat from an anxiety-producing conflict to a developmental stage at which no one is expected to behave maturely and responsibly.

*Example:* A boy who is unable to cope with the anger he feels toward an unfeeling and rejecting mother reverts to infantile behavior, ceasing to take care of his basic needs and soiling his clothes, for instance.

**Identification** is the opposite of projection. Rather than attribute one's thoughts or feelings to someone else, one tries to increase one's sense of self-worth by taking on the values and feelings of another person.

*Example:* In concentration camps during World War II, some prisoners adopted the behavior and attitudes of their oppressors, even to the point of harming other prisoners. By identifying with their captors, these prisoners were attempting to reduce their own fear.

**Overcompensation** is an attempt to cover up a personal weakness by focusing on another, more desirable trait.

*Example:* A very shy young woman overcompensates for her lack of social abilities and the problems that her awkwardness causes by spending many hours in the gym trying to perfect her physical condition.

**Sublimation** is the expression of sexual and aggressive energy in a way that is acceptable to society. This is a unique defense mechanism in that it can actually be quite constructive and beneficial to both the individual and the community. Freud saw love as sublimation at its best: it allows for the expression and gratification of sexual energy in a way that is socially acceptable.

*Example:* High achievers in our society—athletes, artists, surgeons, and other highly dedicated and skilled people—may be seen as reaching such high levels of accomplishment by directing otherwise potentially harmful energies into their work.

## Other Psychodynamic Explanations

Personal and professional differences between Freud and his colleagues led to a split in the Vienna Psychoanalytic Society early in this century. Carl Jung, Alfred Adler, and others left to develop new theories, many of which perpetuated Freud's basic belief that all human

functioning is shaped by dynamic (interacting) psychological forces, though they departed from his model in other respects. Accordingly, all such theories, including Freud's psychoanalytic theory, are referred to as *psychodynamic*. Three of today's most influential psychodynamic theories are ego theory, self theory, and object relations theory.

*The psychoanalytic notion of the "Electra complex" holds that 4-year-old girls repress threatening desires for their fathers and identify with their mothers, trying to emulate them by dressing, acting, and talking as their mothers do.*

***Ego psychologists*** believe that the ego is a more independent and powerful force than Freud recognized. They contend that the ego grows independently of the id and has autonomous, "conflict-free" functions in addition to its id-related responsibilities. The ego guides memory and perception and strives for mastery and competence independent of the id. Both the conflict-free and conflict-resolving activities of the ego must be considered if psychological functioning is to be explained properly.

Another modern movement in psychodynamic theory has focused on the role of the *self*—the unified personality that defines one's sense of identity—rather than on the various components of personality, such as the id, ego, and superego. In the theory of ***self psychology*** developed by Heinz Kohut (1913–1981), the self is conceptualized as an independent, integrating, and self-motivating force and the basic human motive is to preserve and enhance its wholeness (Kramer & Akhtar, 1994; Kohut, 1977).

In classical Freudian theory, *objects* (other people, and occasionally things) acquire their importance to the individual because they help to satisfy fundamental drives. Psychodynamic ***object relations theory,*** in contrast, proposes that objects (which are exclusively human in this theory) are important because people are motivated *primarily* by a need to establish relationships with others.

Object relations theorists focus on relationship issues as the central factors in personality development and in the emergence of psychopathology. They be-

lieve that children who have appropriate relationships with their parents progress effectively through several developmental stages, each characterized by processes of attachment and separation, the building and breaking of bonds (Settlage, 1994). In contrast, severe deficiencies in the child/caregiver relationship may result in fixation, abnormal development, and psychological problems.

## Psychodynamic Therapies

A variety of psychodynamic therapies are now being practiced, ranging from classical Freudian psychoanalysis to modern therapies based on object relations theory or self theory. All share the goals of helping clients to uncover past traumatic events and the inner conflicts that have resulted from them; to resolve, or settle, those conflicts; and to resume interrupted personal development (Arlow, 1989). Because awareness is the key to psychodynamic therapy, this system is considered an "insight therapy."

According to psychodynamic therapists, the process of gaining insight cannot be rushed or imposed. If therapists were simply to tell clients about their inner conflicts, the explanations would sound "off the wall" and the clients would not accept them. Thus therapists must subtly guide the therapeutic discussions so that the patients discover their underlying problems for themselves. To help them do so, psychodynamic therapists rely on such techniques as free association, therapist interpretation, catharsis, and working through.

### Free Association

In psychodynamic therapies the patient is responsible for initiating and leading each discussion. The therapist tells the patient to describe any thought, feeling, or image that comes to mind, even if it seems unimportant or irrelevant. This is the process known as *free association.* The therapist probes the patient's associations, expecting that they will eventually reveal unconscious events and unearth the dynamics underlying the individual's personality. Notice how free association helps the woman quoted below to discover threatening impulses and conflicts within her.

> PATIENT: So I started walking, and walking, and decided to go behind the museum and walk through Central Park. So I walked and went through a back field and felt very excited and wonderful. I saw a park

---

*Free association*    A psychodynamic technique in which the patient describes any thought, feeling, or image that comes to mind, even if it seems unimportant.

bench next to a clump of bushes and sat down. There was a rustle behind me and I got frightened. I thought of men concealing themselves in the bushes. I thought of the sex perverts I read about in Central Park. I wondered if there was someone behind me exposing himself. The idea is repulsive, but exciting too. I think of father now and feel excited. I think of an erect penis. This is connected with my father. There is something about this pushing in my mind. I don't know what it is, like on the border of my memory. (Pause)

THERAPIST: Mm-hmm. (Pause) On the border of your memory?

PATIENT: (The patient breathes rapidly and seems to be under great tension.) As a little girl, I slept with my father. I get a funny feeling. I get a funny feeling over my skin, tingly-like. It's a strange feeling, like a blindness, like not seeing something. My mind blurs and spreads over anything I look at. I've had this feeling off and on since I walked in the park. My mind seems to blank off like I can't think or absorb anything.

*(Wolberg, 1967, p. 662)*

## Therapist Interpretation

Although psychodynamic therapists allow the patient to generate the discussion, they are listening carefully, looking for clues, and drawing tentative conclusions. They share their interpretations with the patient when they think the patient is ready to hear them. The interpretation of three phenomena that occur during therapy is particularly important—resistance, transference, and dreams.

Patients demonstrate *resistance* when they encounter a block in their free associations or change the subject so as to avoid a potentially painful discussion. Through the entire course of therapy, the therapist remains on the lookout for resistance, which is usually unconscious, and may point it out to the patient and interpret it.

Psychodynamic therapists also believe that patients act and feel toward the therapist as they did toward important figures in their childhood, especially their parents and siblings. By interpreting this *transference* behavior, therapists may better understand how a patient unconsciously feels toward a parent or some other significant person in the patient's life. Consider

*Transference* According to psychodynamic theorists, a phenomenon that occurs during psychotherapy, in which patients act toward the therapist as they did or do toward important figures in their lives, particularly parents.

again the woman who walked in Central Park. As she continues talking, the therapist helps her to explore some transference issues:

PATIENT: I get so excited by what is happening here. I feel I'm being held back by needing to be nice. I'd like to blast loose sometimes, but I don't dare.

THERAPIST: Because you fear my reaction?

PATIENT: The worst thing would be that you wouldn't like me. You wouldn't speak to me friendly; you wouldn't smile; you'd feel you can't treat me and discharge me from treatment. But I know this isn't so, I know it.

THERAPIST: Where do you think these attitudes come from?

PATIENT: When I was nine years old, I read a lot about great men in history. I'd quote them and be dramatic. I'd want a sword at my side; I'd dress like an Indian. Mother would scold me. Don't frown, don't talk so much. Sit on your hands, over and over again. I did all kinds of things. I was a naughty child. She told me I'd be hurt. Then at fourteen I fell off a horse and broke my back. I had to be in bed. Mother then told me on the day I went riding not to, that I'd get hurt because the ground was frozen. I was a stubborn, self-willed child. Then I went against her will and suffered an accident that changed my life, a fractured back. Her attitude was, "I told you so." I was put in a cast and kept in bed for months.

*(Wolberg, 1967, p. 662)*

Finally, many psychodynamic therapists try to help patients interpret their *dreams*. Freud (1924) called dreams the "royal road to the unconscious." He believed that repression and other defense mechanisms operate less completely during sleep. Thus a patient's dreams, correctly interpreted, can reveal the person's unconscious instincts, needs, and wishes (see Box 3-2).

Freud defined two kinds of dream content, manifest and latent. *Manifest content* is the consciously remembered dream, *latent content* its symbolic meaning. To interpret a dream, therapists must translate its manifest content into its latent content. Psychodynamic therapists believe that some types of manifest content are universal and have much the same meaning in everybody's dreams. For example, a house's basement, downstairs, upstairs, attic, and front porch are often identified as symbols of anatomical parts of the body (Lichtenstein, 1980).

## Box 3-2

# Perchance to Dream

All people dream; so do dogs, and maybe even fish. But what purpose do dreams serve? Some claim that dreams reveal the future; others see them as inner journeys or alternate realities. The Greek philosopher Plato saw dreams as reflections of inner turmoil and wish fulfillment,

> . . . desires which are awake when the reasoning and taming and ruling power of the personality is asleep; the wild beast in our nature, gorged with meat and drink, starts up and walks about naked, and surfeits at his will. . . . In all of us, even in good men, there is such a latent wild beast nature, which peers out in sleep.
>
> (Phaedrus, c. 380 B.C.)

The Nightmare *by Johann Einrich Füssli.*

Psychodynamic therapists consider dreams to be highly revealing. Rather like Plato, Sigmund Freud (1900) contended that dreaming is a mechanism with which we express and attempt to fulfill the unsatisfied desires we spend our lives pursuing. His colleague Carl Jung (1909) also believed them to be expressions of the unconscious psyche. And another colleague, Alfred Adler, believed that dreams serve to prepare us for waking life by providing a medium for solving the problems we anticipate: they give us a setting in which to rehearse new behavior patterns or alert us to internal problems of which we have not been aware (Kramer, 1992). All of these theorists claimed that patients would benefit from interpreting their dreams in therapy and understanding the underlying needs, aspirations, and conflicts symbolized therein.

Biological theorists offer a different, though not entirely incompatible, view of dreams. In 1977, J. Allan Hobson and Robert McCarley proposed an *activation-synthesis model* of dreams. They claimed that during *REM sleep* (the stage of sleep characterized by rapid eye movement, or REM), memories are elicited by random signals from the brain stem—in evolutionary terms, a very old region of the brain. The brain's cortex, the seat of higher cognitive functioning, attempts to make sense of this random bombardment of electrical activity. The result is a dream, often irrational or weird, but the best fit given the variety of signals received by the cortex (Begley, 1989). Hobson later revised the theory to include the idea that the resulting dream, far from being arbitrary, is influenced by the dreamer's drives, fears, and ambitions.

More recently the neuroscientist Jonathan Winson of Rockefeller University contended that dreams are a "nightly record of a basic mammalian process: the means by which animals form strategies for survival and evaluate current experience in light of those strategies" (Winson, 1990). By recording electrical activity in the brains of sleeping and awake nonprimate mammals, Winson found that the brain waves of animals during dreaming were similar to their brain waves when they were engaged in survival activities. Thus Winson concluded that dreams are a means of reprocessing information necessary for an animal's survival. The information is "accessed again and integrated with past experience to provide an ongoing strategy for behavior" (Winson, 1990). In

## Catharsis

Insight must be an emotional as well as intellectual process. Psychodynamic therapists believe that patients must experience *catharsis,* a reliving of past repressed feelings, if they are to settle internal conflicts and overcome their problems. Only when catharsis accompanies intellectual insight is genuine progress achieved.

---

*Catharsis*   The reliving of past repressed feelings in order to settle internal conflicts and overcome problems.

essence, dreams rehash, reprocess, and reevaluate the day's activities, in preparation for the next day's fight for survival.

Surveys and studies of the content of human dreams have revealed some interesting patterns. For example, two thirds of people's dreams involve unpleasant material, such as aggression, threats, rejection, confusion, or an inability to communicate (Van de Castle, 1993). Commonly, a dreamer is pursued or in some way attacked by a threatening figure. Such chase dreams have often been taken to mean that the dreamers are running from internal fears or issues that they do not want to face, or from someone in their lives whom they do not trust.

Eighty percent of college students report having had dreams of falling. Such dreams are thought by some theorists to occur when our sense of security is threatened or when we are in fear of losing control. Many people say falling dreams are the first ones they can remember, although people can have them at any stage of life (Van de Castle, 1993; Cartwright & Lamberg, 1992).

In some studies, one third of subjects claim to have had dreams in which they have the ability to fly (Van de Castle, 1993); however, in a laboratory study, flying occurred in only one out of 635 dreams (Hennager, 1993; Snyder, 1970). These results are not necessarily contradictory; even if flying dreams occur infrequently, they may still occur at least once in the lives of many people. Dreams of flying tend to be associated with positive feelings. Freud considered them to be a symbol of sexual desire; others see them as an expression of freedom, like "being on top of the world" (Hennager, 1993; Jung, 1967; Adler, 1931, 1927).

Another common theme is public nudity. The incidence of such dreams appears to vary across cultures. One study found that 43 percent of American college-age subjects reported having them, compared to 18 percent of Japanese subjects (Vieira, 1993). Freud (1900) viewed dreams of nudity as an unconscious wish to exhibit oneself. Other theorists contend that people having these dreams may be afraid of being seen for who they really are (Van de Castle, 1993).

Dreams are also distinguished by gender. Some observers have said that the dreams of American women have more in common with the dreams of Aboriginal women than with those of American men (Kramer, 1989). In a landmark dream study in 1951, researcher Calvin Hall found that men dreamed twice as often about men as they did about women, whereas women dreamed about men and women in equal proportions. In addition, most male dreams took place in outdoor settings, while female dreams were more often set in the home or indoors. Men's sexual dreams were more likely to include women they did not know, whereas women dreamed more often about men they cared for. In 1980, Hall and his colleagues compared the dream content of college-aged men and women with the data he had recorded in 1950 and found no significant changes (Van de Castle, 1993). Other researchers are finding that dreams of men and women are becoming more androgynous, that the dreams of women now take place outdoors more than they did in the past, and that women are now as likely as men to behave aggressively in their dreams (Kramer, 1989).

Finally, the research on dreams has succeeded in putting a number of myths to rest (Walsh & Engelhardt, 1993):

*Myth #1: Some people never dream.* Actually, all human beings experience three to six periods of REM sleep each night, and dreaming probably occurs in every one.

*Myth #2: Dreams are experienced in black and white.* Laboratory studies show that everyone dreams in color.

*Myth #3: All the places in your dreams are places you have been.* Many people dream about places or things they have never seen. Some researchers believe these represent compilations of images or things that are familiar to us.

*Myth #4: If you die in your dreams, you will die in actuality.* There are people who have reported dying in their dreams, and, thank goodness, remain alive to tell about it.

## Working Through and Resolving a Problem

A single session of interpretation and catharsis will not change a person. For deep and lasting insight to be gained, the patient and therapist must examine the same issues over and over in the course of many sessions, each time with new and sharper clarity. This process is called **working through**. Because working through a disorder can take a long time, psychodynamic treatment is usually a long-term proposition, often lasting years.

### Short-Term Psychodynamic Therapies

In recent years, several therapists have developed a short version of psychodynamic therapy (Sifneos, 1992, 1987; Davanloo, 1980). In this approach, patients identify a single problem or issue—a *dynamic focus*—early in therapy, such as difficulty getting along with certain persons or a marital problem. The therapist helps the patient maintain attention on this focus throughout treatment and helps him or her work only on psychodynamic issues, such as an unresolved Oedipal conflict, that relate to the focus. It is expected that resolution of this focus will generalize to other important life situations.

From the beginning, the therapist tells the patient that therapy will last for a fixed number of sessions, usually fewer than thirty. The time limit requires that the therapist sometimes be bolder or more anxiety-provoking when making interpretations. Freud himself tried short-term therapy with some of his patients and judged it to be relatively effective "provided that one hits the right time at which to employ it."

## Assessing the Psychodynamic Model

Freud and his followers have had a most significant impact on the ways abnormal functioning is understood (Joseph, 1991). Their theories of personality and abnormality are eloquent and comprehensive.

Largely because of their groundwork, a wide range of theorists today look for answers and explanations outside the confines of biological processes.

Psychodynamic theorists have also helped us to understand that abnormal functioning may be rooted in the same processes that underlie normal functioning. Psychological conflict, for example, is a universal experience; it leads to abnormal functioning, the psychodynamic theorists say, only if the conflict becomes excessive.

Freud and his many followers have also had a most significant impact on the treatment of abnormal psychological functioning. They were the first practitioners to demonstrate the value of systematically applying theory and techniques to treatment. In addition, their systems of therapy were the first to underscore the potential of psychological, as opposed to biological, treatment and have served as a starting point for many other psychological treatments.

At the same time, the psychodynamic model has shortcomings and limitations. First, its concepts can be difficult to define and to research (Erdelyi, 1992, 1985). Because processes such as id drives, ego defenses, and fixation are abstract and supposedly operate at an unconscious level, it is often impossible to determine if they are occurring. Not surprisingly, then, psychodynamic explanations have received little research support, and psychodynamic theorists have been forced to rely largely on individual case studies to support their theories.

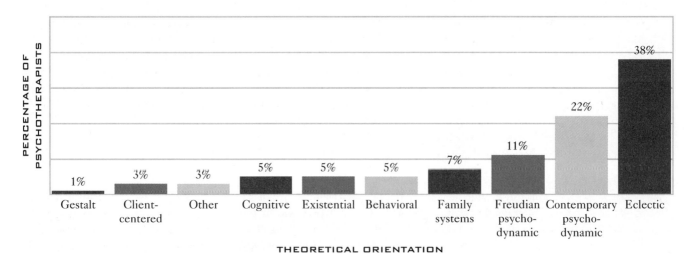

**Figure 3-1**    *Theoretical orientations of today's clinicians. In one survey, almost 40 percent of 818 psychologists, counselors, psychiatrists, and social workers labeled themselves as primarily "eclectic." The cross-professional percentages in this figure fail to reveal that psychologists and counselors are even more likely to follow a behavioral or cognitive model, psychiatrists a Freudian psychodynamic model or eclectic model, and social workers a family systems model. (Adapted from Prochaska & Norcross, 1994; Norcross, Strausser, & Missar, 1988; Norcross & Prochaska, 1986.)*

Similarly, systematic research has generally failed to support the effectiveness of psychodynamic therapies. For the first half of the twentieth century, the value of these approaches was supported principally by the case studies of enthusiastic psychodynamic clinicians and by uncontrolled research studies. Controlled investigations have been conducted only since the 1950s, and only a minority of these have found psychodynamic therapies to be more effective than no treatment or than placebo treatments (Prochaska & Norcross, 1994). It is worth noting, however, that some studies conducted on the newer short-term psychodynamic approaches suggest that these interventions are often quite helpful to certain patients (Messer et al., 1992; Crits-Christoph, 1992).

Critics also argue that, with the exception of the short-term approaches, psychodynamic treatment simply takes too long and costs too much money and hence is impractical for millions of troubled people (Simons, 1981). Psychodynamic therapists respond that the necessary steps of free association, therapist interpretation, catharsis, and working through cannot always be rushed if lasting change is to occur.

Partly in response to these problems, other psychological models have emerged over the past several decades. It is important to recognize, however, that despite the significant growth in popularity of alternative models, 11 percent of today's therapists continue to identify themselves principally as Freudian psychodynamic therapists (see Figure 3-1) and 22 percent as contemporary psychodynamic therapists (Prochaska & Norcross, 1994). And, interestingly, many practitioners of other models report that when they seek help for their own problems, psychodynamic therapy is their choice (Norcross & Prochaska, 1984).

*Summing Up*
*Supporters of the psychodynamic model believe that a person's behavior is determined by underlying interacting forces. Psychodynamic therapists help patients uncover past traumatic events and the inner conflicts that have resulted from those events.*

# The Behavioral Model

Like psychodynamic theorists, behavioral theorists hold a deterministic view of human functioning: they believe that our actions are determined largely by our experiences in life. The psychological dimensions on which behavioral theorists focus, however, are quite different from those the psychodynamic theorists favor. They concentrate on specific **behaviors,** the responses that an organism makes to the stimuli in its environment, and on the **principles of learning,** the processes by which behaviors change in response to the environment. In the behavioral view, people are the sum total of their learned behaviors—both external (going to work, say) and internal (having a feeling or thought).

Many learned behaviors are constructive and adaptive, helping people to cope and to lead happy, productive lives. However, abnormal and undesirable behaviors also can be learned. Behaviorists who try to explain Philip Berman's problems might view him as a man who has received improper training in life. He has learned behaviors that alienate and antagonize others, behaviors that repeatedly work against him. He does not know how to engage other people, express his emotions constructively, or enjoy himself.

Whereas the psychodynamic model had its origins in the clinical work of physicians, the behavioral model was conceived in laboratories run by psychologists who were conducting experiments on **conditioning,** a simple form of learning. In these experiments, the scientists manipulated stimuli and rewards and observed how the responses of experimental subjects were affected.

During the 1950s, many clinicians were growing disenchanted with what they viewed as the vagueness, slowness, and imprecision of the psychodynamic model. Looking for an alternative approach, some of them began to apply the principles of conditioning to the study and treatment of psychological problems (Wolpe, 1987). These efforts gave rise to the behavioral model of psychopathology. Three principles of conditioning have been applied to the clinical domain: classical conditioning, operant conditioning, and modeling.

## Classical Conditioning

*Classical conditioning* is a process of learning by *temporal association*. Theoretically, two events that repeatedly occur close together in time become fused in a person's mind, and before long the person responds in the same way to both events. If one event elicits a response of joy, the other brings joy as well; if one event brings feelings of relief, so does the other.

---

*Classical conditioning*     A process of learning by temporal association in which two events that repeatedly occur close together in time become fused in a person's mind and elicit the same response.

The early animal studies of Ivan Pavlov, the Russian physiologist who first demonstrated classical conditioning, illustrate this process. Pavlov placed a bowl of meat powder before a dog, eliciting the innate response that all dogs have to meat: they start to salivate (see Figure 3-2). Next Pavlov inserted an additional step: just before presenting the dog with meat powder, he sounded a metronome. After several such pairings of metronome tone and presentation of meat powder, Pavlov observed that the dog began to salivate as soon as it heard the metronome. The dog had learned to salivate in response to a sound.

In the vocabulary of classical conditioning, the meat in this demonstration is an **unconditioned stimulus (US)**; it elicits the **unconditioned response (UR)** of salivation (that is, a natural response the dog is born with). The sound of the metronome is a **conditioned stimulus (CS)**, a previously neutral stimulus that comes to be associated with meat in the dog's mind. As such, it too elicits a salivation response. When the salivation response is elicited by the conditioned stimulus rather than by the unconditioned stimulus, it is called a **conditioned response (CR)**.

### Before Conditioning

CS: Tone ➡️ No response

US: Meat ➡️ UR: Salivation

### After Conditioning

CS: Tone ➡️ CR: Salivation

US: Meat ➡️ UR: Salivation

If, after conditioning, the conditioned stimulus is repeatedly presented alone, without being paired with

Figure 3-2   *In Ivan Pavlov's experimental device, the dog's saliva was collected in a tube as it was secreted, and the amount was recorded on a revolving cylinder called a kymograph. The experimenter observed the dog through a one-way glass window.*

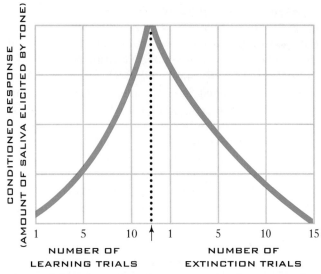

Figure 3-3   *Classical conditioning. During learning trials, a stimulus such as a loud tone is repeatedly paired with another stimulus such as meat. The dog learns to salivate in response to the tone, just as it naturally salivates whenever it sees meat. During extinction trials, the tone is no longer paired with the meat, and salivation in response to the tone eventually stops.*

the unconditioned stimulus, it will eventually stop eliciting the conditioned response. When Pavlov stopped pairing the metronome tone and meat powder, for example, the dog salivated less and less in response to the tone. The conditioned response was undergoing *extinction* (see Figure 3-3).

Classical conditioning accounts for many familiar behaviors. The amorous feelings a young man experiences when he smells his girlfriend's perfume, say, may represent a conditioned response. Initially this perfume may have had no emotional effect on him, but because the fragrance was present during several romantic encounters, it too came to elicit an amorous response.

## The Classical Conditioning of Abnormal Behavior

Abnormal behaviors, too, can be acquired by classical conditioning. Consider the situation of a young boy who is repeatedly frightened by a neighbor's large German shepherd dog. Whenever the child walks past the neighbor's front yard, the dog barks loudly and lunges at him, stopped only by a rope tied to the porch. In this unfortunate situation, the boy's parents are not surprised to discover that he develops a fear of

---

*Extinction*   The decrease in responding that occurs when an unconditioned stimulus is no longer paired with the conditioned stimulus or when a response is no longer rewarded.

dogs. They are mystified, however, by another intense fear the child displays, a fear of sand. They cannot understand why he cries whenever they take him to the beach, refuses to take a single step off the beach blanket, and screams in fear if sand even touches his skin.

Where did this fear of sand come from? The answer is found in the principle of classical conditioning. It turns out that a big sandbox is set up in the neighbor's front yard for the fearsome dog to play in. Every time the dog barks and lunges at the boy, the sandbox is there too. After repeated associations of this kind, the child comes to fear sand as much as he fears the dog. Through a simple process of conditioning, the child develops a fear response that may persist throughout his life. The child may be so successful at avoiding sand that he never learns how harmless it is.

## Treatments Based on Classical Conditioning

The goal of behavioral therapy is to identify the client's specific problem-causing behaviors and manipulate and replace them with more appropriate ones. The therapist's attitude toward the client is that of teacher rather than healer.

Classical conditioning treatments are intended to change clients' dysfunctional reactions to stimuli (Emmelkamp, 1994). *Systematic desensitization,* for example, is a process of teaching phobic clients, clients with specific, unreasonable fears, to react calmly instead of with intense fear to the objects or situations they dread (Wolpe, 1990, 1958). It is a step-by-step procedure that begins with teaching them the skill of deep muscle relaxation over the course of several sessions. Next, the clients construct a *fear hierarchy,* a list of feared objects or situations, starting with those that are minimally feared and ending with the ones that are most fearsome. The following hierarchy was developed by a man who was afraid of criticism, especially about his mental stability:

1. Friend on the street: "Hi, how are you?"
2. Friend on the street: "How are you feeling these days?"
3. Sister: "You've got to be careful so they don't put you in the hospital."
4. Wife: "You shouldn't drink beer while you are taking medicine."
5. Mother: "What's the matter, don't you feel good?"
6. Wife: "It's just you yourself, it's all in your head."
7. Service station attendant: "What are you shaking for?"

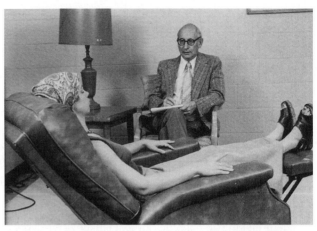

*Joseph Wolpe, the psychiatrist who developed the behavioral treatment of systematic desensitization, first teaches a client to relax, then guides her to confront feared objects or situations, real or imagined, while she remains relaxed.*

8. Neighbor borrows rake: "Is there something wrong with your leg? Your knees are shaking."
9. Friend on the job: "Is your blood pressure okay?"
10. Service station attendant: "You are pretty shaky, are you crazy or something?"

*(Marquis & Morgan, 1969, p. 28)*

Desensitization therapists next have clients either imagine or physically confront each item on the hierarchy while they are in a state of deep relaxation. In step-by-step pairings of feared items and relaxation, clients move up the hierarchy until at last they can relax in the presence of all the items.

As we shall see in Chapter 5, research has repeatedly found systematic desensitization and other classical conditioning techniques to reduce phobic reactions more effectively than placebo treatments or no treatment at all (Emmelkamp, 1994). These approaches have also been helpful in treating several other kinds of problems, including sexual dysfunctions, posttraumatic stress disorders, and asthma attacks (Emmelkamp, 1994).

In the diametrically opposite use of classical conditioning known as **aversion therapy,** therapists help clients to *acquire* anxiety responses to stimuli that the clients have been finding too attractive. This approach has been used with people who want to stop excessive smoking, for example (Blanchard, 1994). In repeated sessions, the clients may be given an electric shock, a nausea-producing drug, or some other noxious stimulus whenever they reach for a cigarette. After numerous pairings of this kind, the clients are expected to develop an unpleasant emotional reaction to cigarettes.

---

*Systematic desensitization*   A behavioral treatment in which phobic clients learn to react calmly instead of with intense fear to the objects or situations they dread.

---

*Aversion therapy*   A behavioral technique that helps clients acquire anxiety responses to stimuli that they have been finding too attractive.

Studies show, however, that the effects of this approach as a means of controlling smoking are usually short-lived.

Aversion therapy has also been applied to help eliminate such undesirable behavior as self-mutilation, sexual deviance, and alcoholism (Emmelkamp, 1994). In the following case, aversion therapy was used successfully with a man who felt repeated urges to make obscene phone calls.

> He was a married, 32-year-old police officer who made up to 20 obscene telephone calls a week to young women in his community. Therapy consisted of the client making an obscene call to a female listener in another office who was instructed to listen and answer questions in a passive but noncomplying manner. Two young, attractive women listeners were part of the treatment; they were instructed not to hang up first. After each telephone contact, the client and listener shared their feelings. This evoked a great deal of anxiety, shame, and embarrassment on the part of the client. The therapist also was present at each of the meetings. Under these circumstances the client experienced the telephone calls as extremely unpleasant. These feelings apparently generalized to the client's real-life situation. For nine months after the brief three-week treatment, the client reported no strong urges to make an obscene call and the authorities in the community were not notified of any such calls.
>
> *(Adapted from Boudewyns, Tanna, & Fleischman, 1975, pp. 704–707)*

# Operant Conditioning

In *operant conditioning,* humans and animals learn to behave in certain ways because they receive certain *reinforcements* from their environment whenever they do so. Behavior that leads to satisfying consequences, or rewards, is likely to be repeated, whereas behavior that leads to unsatisfying, or aversive, consequences, is unlikely to be repeated. This form of conditioning was first elucidated by the eminent psychologists Edward L. Thorndike and B. F. Skinner.

Using the principle of operant conditioning, experimenters have taught animal subjects a wide range of behaviors (see Figure 3-4), from pulling levers and turning wheels to navigating mazes and even playing Ping-Pong (Skinner, 1948). To teach complex behaviors, they typically employ *shaping*—a procedure in which successive approximations of the desired behavior are rewarded. Behaviorists believe that many human behaviors are learned by operant conditioning.

---

*Operant conditioning*    A process of learning in which behavior that leads to satisfying consequences, or rewards, is likely to be repeated.

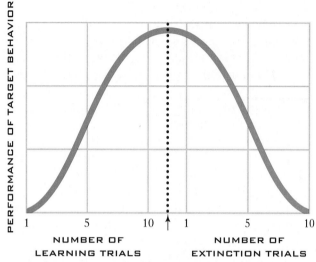

Figure 3-4   *Operant conditioning. During learning trials, a target behavior (such as lifting a paddle) is repeatedly rewarded, and the subject increasingly performs the target behavior. During extinction trials, the target behavior is no longer rewarded, and the subject steadily stops performing the target behavior.*

Children acquire manners by receiving praise, attention, or treats for desirable behaviors and censure for undesirable ones. Adults work at their jobs because they are paid when they do and fired when they do not.

## The Operant Conditioning of Abnormal Behavior

Behaviorists also claim that many abnormal behaviors develop as a result of rewards. Some people may learn to abuse alcohol and drugs because initially such behaviors brought feelings of calm, comfort, or pleasure (Conger, 1951). Others may exhibit bizarre, psychotic behaviors because they enjoy the attention they get when they do so.

Some of Philip Berman's maladaptive behaviors may have been acquired through operant conditioning. When he first became "ornery" at the age of 10, how did his parents react? Perhaps they unintentionally reinforced his rebellious behavior by giving him more attention; and rather than teaching him alternative ways to express his needs, perhaps they simply gave in and let him have his way.

## Treatments Based on Operant Conditioning

In operant conditioning treatments, therapists consistently provide rewards for appropriate behavior and withhold rewards for inappropriate behavior. This technique has been employed frequently, and often

*Pet owners have discovered that they can teach animals a wide assortment of tricks through shaping—rewarding successive approximations of a desired behavior.*

successfully, with people experiencing psychosis (Glynn, 1990). When these patients talk coherently and behave normally, they are rewarded with food, privileges, attention, or something else they value. Conversely, they receive no rewards when they speak bizarrely or display other psychotic behaviors.

In addition, parents, teachers, and therapists have successfully used operant conditioning techniques to change problem behaviors in children (such as repeated tantrums) and to teach skills to individuals with mental retardation (Kazdin, 1994; Schloss & Smith, 1994). Rewards in these cases have included meals, recreation time, and social rewards such as hugs and statements of approval.

As we shall see in Chapter 13, operant conditioning techniques typically work best in institutions or schools, where a person's behavior can be reinforced systematically throughout the day. Often a whole ward or classroom is converted into an operant conditioning arena. Such programs are referred to as *token economy*

*Token economy* A program in which a person's desirable behavior is reinforced systematically throughout the day by the awarding of tokens that can be exchanged for goods or privileges.

programs because in many of them desirable behavior is reinforced with tokens that can later be exchanged for food, privileges, or other rewards.

One token economy program was applied in a classroom where children were behaving disruptively and doing poorly at their studies (Ayllon & Roberts, 1974). The children earned tokens whenever they did well on daily reading tests or successfully performed other targeted behaviors. They could then exchange their tokens for a reward, such as extra recess time or seeing a movie. Under this system, reading accuracy increased from 40 to 85 percent, and the proportion of time spent in disruptive behavior decreased from 50 percent to 5 percent.

> **Consider This**
> Some clinicians and civil libertarians are concerned that the use of behavioral therapies, particularly aversion conditioning and token economies, in clinics, schools, and even business, could be misused or may sometimes violate a person's rights. How might this occur? Do you think such concerns are legitimate?

## Modeling

*Modeling* is a form of learning in which individuals acquire responses through *observation* and *imitation* (Bandura, 1977, 1976, 1969)—that is, by observing others (the *models*) and repeating their behaviors. Behaviors are especially likely to be imitated when the models are themselves being rewarded for the behaviors or when the models are important to the observer.

Behaviorists believe that many everyday human behaviors are learned through modeling. Children may acquire language, facial gestures, tastes in food, and the like by imitating the words, gestures, and eating behaviors of their parents. Similarly, adults may acquire interpersonal skills or vocational interests by imitating the behaviors and preferences of important people in their lives.

### The Modeling of Abnormal Behavior

This form of conditioning, too, can lead to abnormality. A famous study showed that aggressive behaviors could be acquired through modeling (Bandura et al., 1963). The experimenters had young children observe adult models acting aggressively toward a doll. Later, in the same setting, many of the children behaved in the same highly aggressive manner. Other children

*Modeling* A process of learning in which an individual acquires responses by observing and imitating others.

*"Homogamy," the possession of physical and psychological characteristics that are very similar to those of one's spouse, may be explained, in part, by modeling. That is, people may unknowingly imitate the gestures and behaviors of those with whom they spend most of their time until such gestures and behaviors are equally characteristic of them.*

some cases, therapists model new emotional responses for clients. For example, therapists have calmly handled snakes to show clients with snake phobias that it is possible to be relaxed in the presence of these animals (Bandura, 1977, 1971). After several modeling sessions, clients themselves are encouraged to interact with the snakes. As we shall see in Chapter 5, the modeling of emotion can be quite effective in the treatment of phobias.

Behavioral therapists have also used modeling in combination with other techniques to help people acquire or improve their social skills and assertiveness. In an approach called *social skills training,* for example, therapists point out the social deficits of clients and then role-play social situations with the clients. In some enactments the therapist may take the role of the client and demonstrate appropriate social behaviors; in others, the client may try out and rehearse the behaviors, always receiving feedback from the therapist. Ultimately the client practices the behaviors in real-life situations.

Using such techiques, therapists have successfully taught social and assertion skills to shy, passive, or socially isolated people, as well as to people who have a pattern of bursting out in rage or violence over perceived social slights (Emmelkamp, 1994). As we shall note in later chapters, the approach has also been used to improve the social skills of people who are depressed, alcoholic, or anxious (Cooney et al., 1991; Hersen et al., 1984).

who had not observed the adult models behaved much less aggressively.

Similarly, children of poorly functioning people may themselves develop maladaptive reactions because of their exposure to inadequate parental models. Certainly the selfish and demanding behaviors displayed by Philip Berman's mother could have served as the model for his own self-centered and hypercritical style. Just as his mother was repeatedly critical of others, Philip was critical of every person with whom he developed a close relationship. Similarly, the severe depressive symptoms exhibited by his mother, which led her to be hospitalized, could have been a model for Philip's own depression and discontent.

### Treatments Based on Modeling

Modeling therapy was first developed by the pioneering social learning theorist Albert Bandura (1977, 1969). The basic design is for therapists to demonstrate appropriate behaviors for clients, who, through a process of imitation and rehearsal, then acquire the ability to perform the behaviors in their own lives. In

## Assessing the Behavioral Model

The number of behavioral clinicians has grown steadily since the 1950s, and the behavioral model has become a powerful force in the clinical field. Various schools of behavioral thought have emerged over the years, and many treatment techniques have been developed. Approximately 5 percent of today's therapists report that their approach is primarily behavioral (Prochaska & Norcross, 1994).

Perhaps the most prominent reason that the behavioral model is so attractive is that behavioral explanations and treatments can be tested in the laboratory, whereas the psychodynamic theories generally cannot. The behaviorists' basic concepts—stimulus, response, and reinforcement—can be observed and measured. Even more important, the results of research have lent considerable support to the behavioral model

*Social skills training*   A therapeutic approach used by behavioral therapists to help people acquire or improve their social skills and assertiveness through the use of role playing and rehearsing of behaviors.

*Modeling may account for some forms of abnormal behavior. A well-known study by Albert Bandura and his colleagues (1963) demonstrated that children learned to abuse a doll by observing an adult model hit it. Children who had not been exposed to the adult model did not mistreat the doll.*

(Emmelkamp, 1994). Experimenters have successfully used the principles of conditioning to create a number of clinical symptoms in laboratory subjects, thus suggesting that mental disorders may indeed develop in this way.

Similarly, behavioral treatments have been effective for numerous problems seen in clinical practice, including specific fears, social deficits, and mental retardation (Emmelkamp, 1994; Bierman & Furman, 1984). Their effectiveness is all the more impressive in view of the relatively short duration and low overall cost of these therapies.

Research has also, however, revealed certain weaknesses in the behavioral model. For example, although behavioral researchers have induced specific symptoms in subjects, they have not established that such symptoms are ordinarily acquired in this way. There is still no indisputable evidence that the people with mental disorders in our society are largely victims of improper conditioning.

Similarly, behavioral therapies have limitations. First, the improvements they bring about do not always extend to the person's real life and do not necessarily last without further behavioral interventions (Stokes & Osnes, 1989). Second, as we shall observe in later chapters, behavioral therapies do not appear to be particularly effective with psychological disorders that are broad, such as generalized anxiety disorder (O'Leary & Wilson, 1987). Third, some people have raised ethical questions about the behavioral approaches (Kipnis, 1987). It troubles them, for example, that token economy programs and other operant conditioning techniques are imposed on many clients without their permission. In addition, they are concerned about the pain and discomfort that may be inflicted on clients in aversion therapy.

Finally, some critics hold that the behavioral perspective is too simplistic, that its concepts and principles fail to capture the complexity of human behavior.

In 1977 the behaviorist Albert Bandura, who had previously identified modeling as a key learning process, argued that in order to feel happy and function effectively people must develop a positive sense of *self-efficacy*, a belief that they can master and perform needed behaviors whenever necessary. Similarly, other behaviorists of the 1960s and 1970s recognized that human beings engage in *cognitive behaviors*, ways of thinking, anticipating, or perceiving, which were being largely ignored in behavioral theory and therapy. Accordingly, they developed *cognitive-behavioral theories* that took unseen cognitive behaviors into account (Meichenbaum, 1993; Goldiamond, 1965).

Cognitive-behavioral theorists bridge the behavioral model and cognitive model, the perspective that we shall be turning to next. On the one hand, their explanations are firmly entrenched in behavioral principles. They believe, for example, that cognitive processes are acquired and maintained by classical conditioning, operant conditioning, and modeling. On the other hand, cognitive-behavioral theorists share with other kinds of cognitive theorists a belief that the ability to think is the most important aspect of both normal and abnormal human functioning.

### Summing Up
*Theorists who espouse the behavioral model concentrate on a person's behaviors, which are held to develop in accordance with principles of learning. Three types of conditioning—classical conditioning, operant conditioning, and modeling—account for behavior, whether normal or dysfunctional. Behavioral therapists try to identify a client's problem-causing behaviors and replace them with more appropriate ones.*

*Self-efficacy*  The judgment that one can master and perform needed behaviors whenever necessary.

**"Stimulus, response! Stimulus, response! Don't you ever *think*?"**

*(The Far Side © FARWORKS, Inc. Reprinted with permission of Universal Press Syndicate. All rights reserved.)*

# *The Cognitive Model*

Philip Berman, like the rest of us, has *cognitive* abilities—special intellectual capacities to think, remember, and anticipate. These cognitive abilities serve him in all his activities and can help him accomplish a great deal in life. Yet they can also work against him. As he cognitively organizes and records his experiences, Philip may be developing false ideas or misinterpreting experiences in ways that lead to counterproductive decisions, maladaptive responses, and unnecessarily painful emotions.

According to the cognitive model, to understand human behavior, we must understand the content and process of human thought. What assumptions and attitudes color a person's perceptions? What thoughts run through that person's mind, and what conclusions do they lead to? When people display abnormal patterns of functioning, cognitive theorists assume that cognitive problems are to blame.

The cognitive model of abnormal psychology had its formal beginning in the early 1960s when two clinicians, Aaron Beck and Albert Ellis, proposed cognitive theories of abnormality (Beck, 1967; Ellis, 1962).

Building on earlier work in this area, these theorists claimed that cognitive processes are at the center of behavior, thought, and emotions, and that we can best understand abnormal functioning by looking to the cognitive realm. A number of theorists and therapists soon incorporated and expanded upon the ideas and techniques of Beck and Ellis.

## Cognitive Explanations of Abnormal Behavior

To cognitive theorists, we are all artists who are both reproducing and creating our worlds in our minds as we try to understand the events going on around us. If we are effective artists, our cognitive representations tend to be accurate (agreed upon by others) and useful (adaptive). If we are ineffective artists, however, we may create a cognitive inner world that is alien to others and painful and harmful to ourselves. Abnormal functioning can result from several kinds of cognitive problems: maladaptive assumptions or attitudes, specific upsetting thoughts, and illogical thinking processes.

### Maladaptive Assumptions

Albert Ellis (1991, 1989, 1962) proposes that each of us holds a unique set of assumptions about ourselves and our world. Unfortunately, some people's assumptions are largely irrational, guiding them to act and react in ways that are inappropriate and that prejudice their chances of happiness and success. Ellis calls these *basic irrational assumptions*.

Some people, for example, irrationally assume that they are abject failures if they are not loved or approved of by virtually every person they know. Such people constantly seek approval and repeatedly feel rejected. All their interactions and interpretations are affected by this assumption, so that an otherwise successful presentation in the classroom or boardroom can make them sad or anxious because one listener seems bored, or an evening with friends can leave them dissatisfied because the friends do not offer enough compliments.

According to Ellis (1962), other common irrational assumptions are these:

The idea that one should be thoroughly competent, adequate, and achieving in all possible respects if one is to consider oneself worthwhile.

*Basic irrational assumptions*   Inappropriate assumptions guiding the way in which one acts that prejudice a person's chances for happiness and success.

The idea that it is awful and catastrophic when things are not the way one would very much like them to be.

The idea that one should be dependent on others and need someone stronger than oneself on whom to rely.

The idea that there is invariably a right, precise, and perfect solution to human problems and that it is catastrophic if this perfect solution is not found.

Philip Berman often seems to hold the basic irrational assumption that his past history has inexorably determined his present behavior, and that something that once affected his life will have the same effect indefinitely. Philip believes he was victimized by his parents and that he is now doomed by his oppressive past. He seems to approach all new experiences and relationships with expectations of failure and disaster.

## Specific Upsetting Thoughts

Cognitive theorists believe that specific upsetting thoughts may also contribute to abnormal functioning. As we confront the myriad situations that arise in life, numerous thoughts come into our minds, some comforting, others upsetting. Aaron Beck has called these unbidden cognitions *automatic thoughts.* When a person's stream of automatic thoughts is overwhelmingly negative, Beck would expect that person to become depressed (Beck, 1993, 1991, 1976). Philip Berman has made it clear what fleeting thoughts and images keep popping into his mind as he interacts with others: "My old girlfriend wants to jump into bed with

*Aaron Beck proposes that many forms of abnormal behavior can be traced to cognitive factors, such as upsetting thoughts and illogical thinking.*

her date. . . . I'm a 25-year-old virgin. . . . The therapist wants to laugh at me. . . . My boss wants to fire me. . . . My parents think I'm lazy and irresponsible." Certainly such automatic thoughts are contributing to his pervasive feelings of despondency.

Similarly, the theorist Donald Meichenbaum (1993, 1986, 1977) suggests that people who suffer from anxiety have inadvertently learned to generate counterproductive *self-statements* (statements about themselves) during stressful situations and as a result react to any difficult situation with automatic fear and discomfort. When Philip Berman met his old girlfriend and her date, his mind may have been flooded with such self-statements as "Oh, no, I can't stand this. . . . I look like a fool. . . . I'm getting sick. . . . Why do these things always happen to me?" These statements may have fueled his anxiety and rage and prevented him from handling the encounter constructively.

> ### Consider This
> How might researchers study the occurrence and effects of self-statements? What evidence could they offer to demonstrate that self-statements are related to different forms of abnormal behavior? As you read this question, were you aware of any of your own self-statements?

## Illogical Thinking Processes

Cognitive theorists also point to illogical thinking processes to explain abnormal functioning. Beck (1993, 1991, 1967) has found that some people habitually think in illogical ways and keep drawing self-defeating and even pathological conclusions. As we shall observe in Chapter 7, Beck has identified a number of illogical thought processes characteristic of depression, including *selective perception,* seeing only the negative features of an event, and *overgeneralization,* drawing broad negative conclusions on the basis of a single insignificant event. One depressed student couldn't remember the date of Columbus's third voyage to America during a history class and, overgeneralizing, spent the rest of the day in despair over her invincible ignorance.

## Cognitive Therapies

According to cognitive theorists, people with psychological disorders can overcome their difficulties by developing new, more functional ways of thinking. Because different forms of abnormality may involve different kinds of cognitive dysfunctioning, cognitive therapists have developed a number of cognitive strategies.

## Ellis's Rational-Emotive Therapy

In line with his belief that irrational assumptions give rise to abnormal functioning, Albert Ellis has developed an approach called *rational-emotive therapy* (Ellis, 1991, 1976, 1962). Therapists help clients to discover the irrational assumptions that govern their emotional responses and to change those assumptions into constructive ways of viewing themselves and the world.

In his own practice, Ellis is a direct and active therapist who points out clients' irrational assumptions in a blunt, confrontational, and often humorous way, and then models the use of alternative assumptions. After criticizing a man's perfectionistic standards, for example, he might say, "So what if you did a lousy job on your project? It's important to realize that one lousy project simply means one lousy project, and no more than that!" Ellis also gives clients homework assignments requiring them to observe their assumptions as they operate in everyday life and to think of ways to test the assumptions' rationality.

A number of studies have found that rational-emotive therapy is often helpful to clients with various problems (Lyons & Woods, 1991; Ellis, 1989, 1973). As we shall observe in Chapter 5, anxious clients in particular who are treated with this therapy improve more than anxious clients who receive no treatment or placebo treatments.

## Beck's Cognitive Therapy

Aaron Beck has independently developed a system of therapy that is similar to Ellis's rational-emotive therapy. Called simply *cognitive therapy,* this approach has been most widely used in cases of depression (Beck, 1993, 1976, 1967). Cognitive therapists help clients to recognize the negative thoughts, biased interpretations, and errors in logic that pervade their thinking and, according to Beck, cause them to feel depressed. The therapists also guide clients to challenge their dysfunctional thoughts, try out new interpretations, and ultimately apply alternative ways of thinking in their daily lives. As we shall see in Chapter 7, depressed

---

*Rational-emotive therapy*    A therapeutic system developed by Albert Ellis that helps clients to discover the irrational assumptions governing their emotional responses and to change those assumptions into constructive ways of viewing the world and themselves.

*Cognitive therapy*    A therapeutic system developed by Aaron Beck which helps people recognize and change their faulty thinking processes.

people who are treated with Beck's approach improve significantly more than those who receive no treatment (Hollon & Beck, 1994; Young et al., 1993). In recent years Beck's cognitive therapy has also been successfully applied to panic disorders and other anxiety disorders (Beck, 1993).

Here a cognitive therapist guides a depressed 26-year-old graduate student to see the relationship between the way she interprets her experiences and the way she feels and to begin questioning the accuracy of her interpretations:

PATIENT:  I get depressed when things go wrong. Like when I fail a test.

THERAPIST:  How can failing a test make you depressed?

PATIENT:  Well, if I fail I'll never get into law school.

THERAPIST:  So failing the test means a lot to you. But if failing a test could drive people into clinical depression, wouldn't you expect everyone who failed the test to have a depression? . . . Did everyone who failed get depressed enough to require treatment?

PATIENT:  No, but it depends on how important the test was to the person.

THERAPIST:  Right, and who decides the importance?

PATIENT:  I do.

THERAPIST:  And so, what we have to examine is your way of viewing the test (or the way that you think about the test) and how it affects your chances of getting into law school. Do you agree?

PATIENT:  Right.

THERAPIST:  Do you agree that the way you interpret the results of the test will affect you? You might feel depressed, you might have trouble sleeping, not feel like eating, and you might even wonder if you should drop out of the course.

PATIENT:  I have been thinking that I wasn't going to make it. Yes, I agree.

THERAPIST:  Now what did failing mean?

PATIENT:  (Tearful) That I couldn't get into law school.

THERAPIST:  And what does that mean to you?

PATIENT:  That I'm just not smart enough.

*"Has it ever occurred to you just to say, 'Hey, I quit. I don't want to be a part of the food chain anymore'?"*

*Cognitive therapists try to help clients interpret life situations differently, expecting that such changes in thought will lead to more constructive reactions and choices. (Drawing by Ziegler; © 1992 The New Yorker Magazine, Inc.)*

THERAPIST: Anything else?

PATIENT: That I can never be happy.

THERAPIST: And how do these thoughts make you feel?

PATIENT: Very unhappy.

THERAPIST: So it is the meaning of failing a test that makes you very unhappy. In fact, believing that you can never be happy is a powerful factor in producing unhappiness. So, you get yourself into a trap—by definition, failure to get into law school equals "I can never be happy."

(Beck et al., 1979, pp. 145–146)

## Meichenbaum's Self-Instruction Training

The psychologist Donald Meichenbaum (1993, 1986, 1977, 1975) has developed a technique called *self-instruction training* to help people solve problems and cope with stress more effectively. Using a step-by-step procedure, therapists teach clients how to make helpful statements to themselves—positive *self-statements*—and how to apply them in difficult circum-

stances. The therapists begin by explaining and modeling effective self-statements; they then have clients practice and apply the statements in stressful situations.

Using this procedure, Meichenbaum has taught anxious clients to make the following kinds of self-statements as they try to cope with anxiety-arousing situations:

Just think about what you can do about it. That's better than getting anxious.

Just "psych" yourself up—you can meet this challenge.

One step at a time: you can handle the situation.

Relax; you're in control. Take a slow deep breath.

Don't try to eliminate fear totally; just keep it manageable.

(Meichenbaum, 1974)

In comparison with no treatment and placebo treatment, Meichenbaum's self-instruction training has been found helpful for people with impulsive disorders, social anxiety, test anxiety, pain, and problems with anger (Meichenbaum, 1993). On the other hand, it is not clear whether the cognitive problem-solving skills that are learned by this technique are retained for an extended period of time (Schlichter & Horan, 1981).

*Self-instruction training* A cognitive therapy that teaches people how to make helpful statements to themselves and how to apply such statements in difficult circumstances.

## Assessing the Cognitive Model

The cognitive model has had very broad appeal. In addition to the many behaviorists who have incorporated cognitive concepts into their theories about learning, a great many clinicians believe that thinking processes are much more than conditioned reactions. Cognitive theory, research, and treatment techniques have developed in so many interesting ways that the model is now viewed as distinct from the behavioral school that spawned it.

Approximately 5 percent of today's therapists identify their orientation as cognitive (Prochaska & Norcross, 1994). This overall percentage actually disguises a split in the clinical community: A full 10 percent of psychologists and other counselors employ cognitive therapy primarily, compared to only 1 percent of psychiatrists and 4 percent of social workers (Prochaska & Norcross, 1994; Norcross et al., 1993).

There are several reasons for this model's appeal. First, it focuses on the most singular of human processes, human thought. Many theorists from varied backgrounds find themselves drawn to a model that views human thought as the primary contributor to normal or abnormal behavior.

Cognitive theories also lend themselves to testing. Researchers have found evidence that people often do exhibit the assumptions, specific thoughts, and thinking processes that supposedly contribute to abnormal functioning, and have shown that these cognitive phenomena are indeed operating in many cases of pathology (Garber et al., 1993).

Yet another reason for the popularity of the cognitive model is the impressive performance of cognitive therapies thus far in research. These interventions have, for example, proved to be very effective for treating depression and sexual dysfunctioning and moderately effective for anxiety problems (Hollon & Beck, 1994; Carey et al., 1993).

Nevertheless, the cognitive model, too, has its drawbacks (Beck, 1991). First, although it is becoming clear that cognitive processes are involved in many forms of abnormality, their precise role has yet to be determined. The maladaptive cognitions seen in psychologically troubled people could well be a consequence rather than a cause of their difficulties. Certainly processes so central to human functioning must be highly vulnerable to disturbances of any kind.

Second, although cognitive therapies are clearly of help to people with various kinds of problems, they are far from a panacea. After an initial wave of enormous enthusiasm for these approaches, research findings have begun to raise important questions about their possible limitations. Is it enough to alter the cognitive features of a case of psychological dysfunctioning? Can such specific kinds of thought changes make a general and lasting difference in the way a person feels and behaves? These and related questions will probably receive more attention and analysis in the coming years.

Finally, like the other models, the cognitive model has been criticized for the narrowness of its scope. Although cognition is a very special human dimension, it is still but one part of human functioning. Are human beings not more than their thoughts—indeed, more than the sum total of their fleeting thoughts, emotions, and behaviors? For those who believe that they are, explanations of human functioning must at least sometimes embrace broader issues, such as how people approach life, what they get from it, and how they deal with the question of life's meaning. This is the contention of the humanistic-existential perspective.

*Summing Up*
*The cognitive model claims that we must understand the content and process of human thought to understand human behavior. When people display abnormal patterns of functioning, cognitive theorists point to cognitive problems. Cognitive therapists try to help people recognize and change their faulty ideas and thinking processes.*

# The Humanistic-Existential Model

Philip Berman is more than psychological conflicts, learned behaviors, and cognitions. Being human, he also has the ability to confront complex and challenging philosophical issues such as self-awareness, values, meaning, and choice, and to incorporate them into his life. And according to humanistic and existential theorists, Philip's problems can be understood only in the light of those issues. Humanistic and existential theorists are usually grouped together because of their common focus on the broader dimensions of human existence. At the same time, there are some important differences between them.

*Humanists,* the more optimistic of the two groups, believe that human beings are born with a natural inclination to be friendly, cooperative, and constructive,

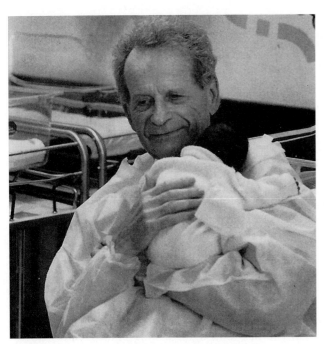

*Humanists suggest that self-actualized people show concern for the welfare of humanity, as does this volunteer who regularly cares for babies afflicted with AIDS. Self-actualized people are also thought to be highly creative, spontaneous, independent, and humorous.*

and are driven to *self-actualize*—that is, to fulfill this potential for goodness and growth. They will be able to do so, however, only if they can honestly appraise and accept their weaknesses as well as their strengths and establish a satisfying system of personal values to live by.

*Existentialists* agree that human beings must have an accurate awareness of themselves and live subjectively meaningful—they say "authentic"—lives in order to be psychologically well adjusted. These theorists do not believe, however, that people are naturally inclined to live constructively. They believe that from birth we have total freedom, either to face up to our existence and give meaning to our lives or to shrink from that responsibility. Those who choose to "hide" from responsibility and choice will view themselves as helpless and weak and may live empty, inauthentic, and dysfunctional lives as a consequence.

The humanistic and existential views of abnormality both date back to the 1940s. At that time Carl Rogers (1902–1987), often considered the pioneer of the humanistic perspective, developed client-centered therapy, a warm and supportive approach that contrasted sharply with the influential psychodynamic principles of the day. Moreover, he proposed a human-

*Self-actualization*    The humanistic process by which people fulfill their potential for goodness and growth.

istic theory of personality that deemphasized irrational instincts and conflicts and emphasized instead a special, positive potential inherent in human beings. About the same time, other humanistic theories developed by Abraham Maslow (1908–1970) and Fritz Perls (1893–1970) also received widespread attention.

The existential view of personality and abnormality came into prominence during this same period. It derived from the ideas of nineteenth century European existential philosophers who had held that human beings are constantly defining their existence through their actions and that the meaning of individual existence lies in such efforts at definition. In the late 1950s a book titled *Existence,* now considered a classic work on the clinical existential perspective, described all the major existential ideas and treatment approaches of the time and helped them gain widespread attention (May et al., 1958).

The humanistic and existential theories were extremely popular during the 1960s and 1970s, years of considerable soul-searching and social upheaval in Western society. Humanistic theories, which reaffirmed the human spirit, and existential theories, which challenged people to take charge of their lives, seemed to be a perfect remedy to the feelings of alienation and spiritual emptiness that had become common in the face of rapid technological and bureaucratic growth. Although the humanistic-existential model lost some of its popularity in the 1980s, it continues to influence the treatment techniques of many clinicians.

## Rogers's Humanistic Theory and Treatment

According to Carl Rogers (1987, 1961, 1951), the road to dysfunction begins in infancy. We all have a basic need to receive *positive regard* from the significant other people in our lives (primarily from our parents). Those who receive *unconditional* (nonjudgmental) *positive regard* early in life are likely to develop *unconditional self-regard*. That is, they come to recognize their worth as persons, even while recognizing that they are not perfect. They feel comfortable about themselves and are able to evaluate themselves in a clear-sighted way. Such people are in a good psychological position to actualize their inherently positive potential.

Unfortunately, some children are repeatedly made to feel that they are not worthy of positive regard. As a result, they acquire **conditions of worth**, standards that tell them they are lovable and acceptable only when they conform to the standards they have been exposed to, and they constantly judge themselves accordingly. In order to maintain positive self-regard, these people have to look at themselves in a very selective fashion, denying or distorting thoughts and actions that do not measure up to their conditions of worth.

The constant self-deception makes it impossible for these people to self-actualize. They have a distorted view of themselves and their experiences, and so they do not know what they are genuinely feeling or needing, or what values and goals would be meaningful for them. Moreover, they spend so much energy trying to protect their self-image that little is left to devote to self-actualizing. Problems in functioning are then inevitable.

Thus Carl Rogers might view Philip Berman as a man who has gone astray. Rather than striving to fulfill his positive human potential, he drifts from job to job, relationship to relationship, and outburst to outburst. In every interaction he is defending himself, trying to interpret events in ways he can live with. He always considers his problems to be someone else's fault, and he keeps presenting himself as a strong person who cares little about what other folks may think. Yet his constant efforts at self-defense and self-enhancement are only partially successful. His basic negative self-image and his assumption that others will think badly of him keep breaking through.

In Rogers' *client-centered therapy,* therapists try to create a supportive climate in which clients can look at themselves honestly and begin to accept what they discover themselves to be (Rogers, 1987, 1967, 1951). The therapist must display three important qualities throughout the therapy—unconditional positive regard for the client, accurate empathy, and genuineness.

Therapists show *unconditional positive regard* by conveying full and warm acceptance no matter what clients say, think, or feel (see Box 3-3). They show *accurate empathy* by accurately hearing what clients are saying and sensitively communicating it back to the clients. They neither interpret what clients are saying nor try to teach them; rather, they listen, and help their clients listen to themselves as well. Finally, therapists must convey *genuineness,* also referred to as *congruence,* to clients. Unless therapists' communications are honest and sincere, clients may perceive them as mechanical and false. The following interaction shows the therapist using all these qualities to move the client toward greater self-awareness:

---

*Client-centered therapy*    The therapeutic approach developed by Carl Rogers in which therapists try to help clients by being accepting, empathizing accurately, and conveying genuineness.

*Unconditional positive regard*    According to humanists, full, warm acceptance of a person regardless of what he or she says, thinks, or feels.

CLIENT: Yes, I know I shouldn't worry about it, but I do. Lots of things—money, people, clothes. In classes I feel that everyone's just waiting for a chance to jump on me. It's like they were breathing down my neck waiting for a chance to find something wrong. At school there were fellows like that waiting for me. I can't stand people laughing at me. I can't stand ridicule. That's why I'm afraid of kids. When I meet somebody I wonder what he's actually thinking of me. Then later on I wonder how I match up to what he's come to think of me.

THERAPIST: You feel that you're pretty responsive to the opinions of other people.

CLIENT: Yes, but it's things that shouldn't worry me.

THERAPIST: You feel that it's the sort of thing that shouldn't be upsetting, but they do get you pretty much worried anyway.

CLIENT: Just some of them. Most of those things do worry me because they're true. The ones I told you, that is. But there are lots of little things that aren't true. And time bothers me, too. That is, when I haven't anything to do. Things just seem to be piling up, piling up inside of me. When I haven't anything to do I roam around. I feel like—at home when I was at the theater and nobody would come in, I used to wear it off by socking the doors. It's a feeling that things were crowding up and they were going to burst.

THERAPIST: You feel that it's a sort of oppression with some frustration and that things are just unmanageable.

CLIENT: In a way, but some things just seem illogical. I'm afraid I'm not very clear here but that's the way it comes.

*"Why, you swine!"*

Criticizing a client's remarks, however subtly or carefully, is the worst thing a therapist can do, according to client-centered therapists. (Drawing by Richter; © 1952, 1980 The New Yorker Magazine, Inc.)

THERAPIST:  That's all right. You say just what you think.

*(Snyder, 1947, pp. 2–24)*

In such an atmosphere, clients can be expected increasingly to feel accepted by their therapist; they then may be able to look at themselves with honesty and acceptance—a process called *experiencing.* That is, they begin to value their own emotions, thoughts, and behaviors, and so are freed from the insecurities and doubts that prevented their self-actualization.

Client-centered therapy has not fared particularly well in research. Although people who receive this therapy do seem to improve more than control subjects in some studies (Greenberg et al., 1994; Stuhr & Meyer, 1991), they show no such superiority in many others (Rudolph et al., 1980; Dircks et al., 1980). All the same, Rogers' therapy has had a positive influence on clinical practice. It was the first major alternative to psychodynamic therapy, and as such it helped open up what had been a highly complacent field to new systems and formats. Second, Rogers helped open up the practice of psychotherapy to psychologists; it had previously been considered the province of psychiatrists. Third, Rogers' commitment to clinical research has strengthened the position of those who argue the importance of systematic research in the treatment domain (Rogers & Sanford, 1989; Sanford, 1987). Approximately 3 percent of today's therapists report that they employ the client-centered approach (Prochaska & Norcross, 1994).

## Gestalt Theory and Therapy

Gestalt theory and therapy is another humanistic approach, developed in the 1950s by a charismatic clinician named Frederick (Fritz) Perls (1893–1970). Like Rogers, Perls believed that people experience psychological difficulties when they are unaware of their needs or unwilling to accept or express them. Such individuals act only to protect themselves from perceived threats and do little to actualize their potential.

Thus gestalt therapists, like client-centered therapists, try to move clients toward self-recognition and self-acceptance (Yontef & Simkin, 1989). But unlike client-centered therapists, they try to achieve this goal by frustrating and challenging clients, using a variety of techniques, exercises, and games in treatment.

In the technique of *skillful frustration,* for example, gestalt therapists simply refuse to meet their clients' expectations or even their outright demands. This use of frustration is meant to help clients see how they try to manipulate other people into meeting their needs.

*Clients in gestalt therapy are guided to express their needs and feelings in their full intensity, through role playing, banging on pillows, and other exercises. In the typical gestalt therapy group, members help each other to "get in touch" with their needs and feelings.*

Perls (1973) describes his use of skillful frustration with a male client:

> The first six weeks of therapy—more than half the available time—were spent in frustrating him in his desperate attempts to manipulate me into telling him what to do. He was by turn plaintive, aggressive, mute, despairing. He tried every trick in the book. He threw the time barrier up to me over and over again, trying to make me responsible for his lack of progress. If I had yielded to his demands, undoubtedly he would have sabotaged my efforts, exasperated me, and remained exactly where he was.
>
> *(p. 109)*

Unlike psychodynamic therapists, who guide clients toward events and emotions in their past, gestalt therapists make it a practice to keep clients in the *here and now.* Clients have needs now, are camouflaging their needs now, and must observe them now. As clients talk about the events and people in their lives, the therapist may ask, "What are you feeling about that person now?" or "What are you doing now, as you speak?"

Another way gestalt therapists try to promote self-awareness is by instructing clients to *role-play*—that is, to act out various roles assigned by the therapist. Clients may be told to be another person, an object, or even a part of the body. They are instructed to talk as the other would talk and to feel what the other would feel. Role playing can become intense, as clients are encouraged to be uninhibited in feeling and expressing emotions. Many cry out, scream, or pound. Through this experience they gradually come to "own" (accept) feelings that were previously unknown to them.

*Role play*   A therapy technique in which clients are instructed to act out roles assigned to them by the therapist.

## Box 3-3

# *Animals: A Source of Unconditional Positive Regard*

For thousands of years humans have brought animals into the home to serve every purpose from protection to companionship. In recent years pets have even been looked upon as facilitators in human relationships and in the process of achieving psychological and emotional relief. Has "man's best friend" been elevated to the role of therapist?

It is widely believed that animals can provide solace, comfort, and friendship to a person in need of emotional support. The undying loyalty of the pet dog can supersede all human interactions in the eyes of a child who has been scolded for misbehaving or the elderly nursing home resident whose children no longer visit. Without judging and without condition our favorite pet provides love and companionship. From the humanistic perspective, these are qualities that help ensure a truly successful treatment outcome.

Physiological studies indicate that the presence of a dog can re-

duce heart rate and blood pressure in children—the same effect that was noted in children who were asked to read aloud from a book of poetry (Friedmann et al., 1983). Even the survival rates of heart patients have been linked to owner-

ship and interaction with a pet. Similar results have been suggested for elderly people who have little interaction with other human beings (Gammonley & Yates, 1991).

Studies have also indicated that animals can improve the emotions and behavior of persons with psychological problems. An approach known as *pet-facilitated therapy* (Corson & Corson, 1978) has, for example, been employed in helping children with emotional disturbances. A group of such children, all of whom had many problems in their relationships with peers and adults, participated in a program in which they lived and worked on a farm (Ross, 1983). Each child was given a special pet and was responsible for its care. After being involved in this program, the children showed improvement in their self-esteem and sense of control. Similar results have been reported in more formal therapeutic settings. Researchers reason that by making the situation feel less

---

Perls also developed a list of *rules* to ensure that clients will look at themselves more closely. For example, clients may not ask "why" questions. If they ask, "Why do you do that?" therapists make them change the question into a statement, such as "I hate it when you do that." Another rule is that clients must use "I" language rather than "it" language. They must say, "I am frightened," rather than "The situation is frightening."

Approximately 1 percent of clinicians describe themselves as gestalt therapists (Prochaska & Norcross, 1994). Because they believe that subjective experiences and self-awareness defy objective measurement, controlled research has rarely been conducted on the gestalt approach (Greenberg et al., 1994).

## Existential Theories and Treatments

Like humanists, existentialists believe that psychological dysfunctioning is caused by self-deception; but existentialists are talking about a kind of self-deception in which people hide from life's responsibilities and fail to recognize that it is up to them to give meaning to their lives and that they have the capacity and freedom to do so. According to existentialists, people start to hide from personal responsibility and choice when they become engulfed in the constant change, confusion, and emotional strain of present-day society, as well as in the particular stresses of their immediate environment. Overwhelmed by these pressures, many people look to others for guidance and authority, and conform excessively to social standards. Others may

threatening, pets serve as a bridge between therapist and child, allowing the child to feel safe with the therapist. Moreover, the pet is an attractive addition to the session that most likely helps maintain the child's interest and attention.

Researchers have also found that social interactions between people improve when a pet is around. Pets can facilitate staff-patient interactions and patient-visitor relations and promote stronger bonds between volunteers and residents of institutions (Savishinsky, 1992; Chinner & Dalziel, 1991). Pets have also been used in psychotherapy to improve the *interactions* between therapist and client.

One of the most exciting uses of pet therapy centers on the dramatic and heart-rending mental disorder of autism. As we shall observe in Chapter 15, the unusual set of behaviors in people afflicted with autism hinders their ability to form bonds and relate to other people. Therapy with these individuals is typically slow and laborious as practitioners try to reduce disrup-

tive behaviors and encourage the person to interact with others.

In one study, a dog was introduced into the individual treatment sessions of a number of children with autism (Redefer & Goodman, 1989). At first the children displayed typical autistic behaviors—hand posturing, making humming and clicking noises, jumping, continual spinning of objects, roaming. During a number of otherwise routine treatment sessions, the therapist interacted with the dog and encouraged the child to join in. In most cases, by the end of the session the child showed significantly fewer autistic behaviors, a decrease in self-absorption, and an increase in positive social behavior, such as joining the therapist in simple games, initiating activities, reaching for hugs, and imitating the therapist's actions.

The researchers conjectured that the presence of the dog and the interactions with it heightened the "affective and impulsive state of the children" so that they were better able to participate in and en-

joy social interactions. The success of this experiment was not attributed solely to the dog's presence, however; it was the orchestration by the therapist of the interaction between the children and the dog that facilitated the improvement. Pets are not a magical solution, but they may offer help in the treatment of some persons with autism.

Researchers are now looking to see whether pet-facilitated therapy can be applied to other populations as well. One program at a prison has found that inmates given the responsibility of caring for a pet show reductions in violent behavior (Moneymaker & Strimple, 1991).

Although evidence is scanty, both anecdotal and formal studies suggest that pets can and do influence our emotional and physical well-being. Particularly for people who are developing their sense of self or who suffer a psychological disorder that inhibits this development, pet therapy may prove instrumental. It is no wonder that pets occupy such an important and honored role in many societies.

build resentment toward society. Either way, they overlook their personal freedom of choice and avoid responsibility for their lives and decisions (May & Yalom, 1989). This abdication of responsibility and choice may offer a form of refuge, but at a cost. Such people are left with empty, inauthentic lives. Their prevailing emotions are anxiety, frustration, alienation, and depression.

Thus existentialists might view Philip Berman as a man who considers himself incompetent to resist the forces of society. He views his parents as "rich, powerful, and selfish," and he sees teachers, acquaintances, and employers as perpetrators of abuse and oppression. Overwhelmed, he fails to appreciate his choices in life and his capacity for finding meaning and direc-

tion. Quitting becomes a habit with him—he leaves job after job, ends every romantic relationship, flees difficult situations, and even tries suicide. For existentialists, Philip's problems are best summarized by the part of the case description that states, "He spent most of his time alone, 'bored.' He was unable to commit himself to any person, he held no strong convictions, and he felt no allegiance to any group."

In existential therapy, clients are encouraged to accept responsibility for their lives (and for their problems), to recognize their freedom to choose a different course, and to choose to live an authentic life, one full of meaning and values (May & Yalom, 1989). Like humanistic therapists, existential therapists emphasize the individual's subjective view of things (van den

*While imprisoned in Nazi concentration camps from 1942 to 1945, psychotherapist Viktor Frankl observed that the victims who found some spiritual meaning in their suffering were able to resist despair and to survive. He later developed "logotherapy" (from the Greek, "logos," for word or thought), an existential therapy that helps clients assign values and spiritual meaning to their existence. Frankl himself displays the positive attitude toward life and the sense of exploration that he espouses.*

Berg, 1971) and the here and now (May, 1987). For the most part, however, these therapists care more about the goals of therapy than the use of specific therapeutic techniques, and their methods and the length of treatment vary greatly from practitioner to practitioner (May & Yalom, 1989). Here an existential therapist uses a highly confrontational approach to try to help a patient accept responsibility for her choices both in therapy and in life:

PATIENT: I don't know why I keep coming here. All I do is tell you the same thing over and over. I'm not getting anywhere. . . .

DOCTOR: I'm getting tired of hearing the same thing over and over, too. [Doctor refusing to take responsibility for the progress of therapy and refusing to fulfill the patient's expectations that he cure her. . . . ]

PATIENT: Maybe I'll stop coming. [Patient threatening therapist; fighting to maintain role as therapist's object.]

DOCTOR: It's certainly your choice. [Therapist refusing to be intimidated; forcing patient-as-subject.]

PATIENT: What do you think I should do? [Attempt to seduce therapist into role of subject who objectifies patient.]

DOCTOR: What do you want to do? . . .

PATIENT: I want to get better. . . .

DOCTOR: I don't blame you. . . .

PATIENT: If you think I should stay, ok, I will. . . .

DOCTOR: You want me to tell you to stay? [Confrontation with patient's evasion of the decision and calling attention to how patient is construing the therapy.]

PATIENT: You know what's best; you're the doctor. [Patient's confirmation of how she is construing the therapy.]

DOCTOR: Do I act like a doctor?

(Keen, 1970, p. 200)

Existential therapists do not believe that experimental methods can adequately test the effectiveness of their treatment interventions (May & Yalom, 1989). They believe that research that reduces patients to test measures or scale scores serves only to dehumanize them. Not surprisingly, then, virtually no controlled research has been conducted on the effectiveness of existential therapy (Prochaska & Norcross, 1994). A lack of empirical data does not, however, represent evidence for ineffectiveness, and, indeed, surveys suggest that as many as 5 percent of today's therapists use an approach that is primarily existential (Prochaska & Norcross, 1994).

### Consider This

One of modern society's advances has been to see people with mental disorders as victims rather than as morally bad persons deserving of blame for their disorders. Does the existential model contradict this contemporary view? Might advocacy of this model result in a return to less sympathetic attitudes toward and harsher treatment of people with mental disorders? How might existentialists counter this claim?

*Emphasizing the need to accept responsibility, recognize one's choices, and live an authentic life, existential therapists guide clients to reject feelings of victimhood. (Calvin and Hobbes © 1993 Watterson. Reprinted with permission of Universal Press Syndicate. All rights reserved.)*

## Assessing the Humanistic-Existential Model

The humanistic-existential model appeals to many people in and out of the clinical field for several reasons. First, the model focuses on broad human issues rather than on a single aspect of psychological functioning. In recognizing the special features and challenges of human existence, humanistic and existential theorists tap into a dimension of psychological life that is typically missing from the other models (Fuller, 1982). Moreover, the factors that they say are essential to effective psychological functioning—self-acceptance, personal values, personal meaning, and personal choice—are undeniably lacking in many people with psychological disturbances.

The optimistic tone of the humanistic-existential model is also an attraction. Humanistic and existential theorists offer great hope when they assert that despite the often overwhelming pressures of modern society, we can make our own choices, determine our own destiny, and accomplish much.

Still another attractive feature of the humanistic-existential model is its emphasis on health rather than illness (Cowen, 1991). Unlike proponents of some of the other models who see individuals as patients with psychological illnesses, humanists and existentialists view them simply as people whose special potential has yet to be fulfilled. And although they acknowledge the impact of past events on present behavior, they do not hold a deterministic view of behavior. They believe our behavior can be influenced by our innate goodness and potential, and by our willingness to take responsibility, more than by any factor in our past.

Although appealing in these ways, the humanistic-existential focus on abstract issues of human fulfillment also gives rise to a significant problem: these issues are resistant to research. In fact, with the notable exception of Rogers, who spent years empirically testing his psychotherapeutic methods, humanists and existentialists tend to reject the experimental approaches that now dominate the field. They have tried to establish the merits of their views by appealing primarily to logic, introspection, and individual case histories.

A final problem is the model's heterogeneity. Theories and therapies called humanistic or existential are so numerous and so varied that it is almost misleading to lump them together into a single category. Still, this extremely varied group of theorists and practitioners does share a belief that human beings are self-determining and have an enormous potential for growth, and that self-exploration is the key to this growth.

*Summing Up*
*Humanists believe that people are driven to self-actualize, that is, to fulfill their potential for goodness and growth. Thus, humanistic therapists try to help clients look at themselves and their situations more accurately and acceptingly, so that they may actualize their full potential. Existentialists, in contrast, believe that all of us have total freedom either to face up to our existence and give meaning to our lives or to shrink from that responsibility. Thus, existential therapists encourage clients to accept responsibility for their lives and make constructive choices.*

# Chapter Review

1. *Models of Psychological Abnormality:* Scientists use paradigms to understand abnormal behavior. Each paradigm, or *model,* is a set of basic assumptions that influences what questions are asked, what information is considered legitimate, and how that information is interpreted.

2. *Psychodynamic Model:* Supporters of the psychodynamic model believe that a person's behavior, whether normal or abnormal, is determined by underlying psychological forces. They consider psychological conflicts to be rooted in early parent-child relationships and traumatic experiences .

   The psychodynamic model was formulated by Sigmund Freud, who developed a general theory of *psychoanalysis* as well as a treatment approach. Freud envisioned three dynamic forces—the *id, ego,* and *superego*—constituting the personality and interacting to mold thought, feeling, and behavior. Other psychodynamic theories are *ego theory, self theory,* and *object relations theory.*

   *Psychodynamic therapists* help patients uncover past traumatic events and the inner conflicts that have resulted from those events. They use a number of techniques such as *free association* and interpretations of psychological phenomena such as *resistance, transference,* and *dreams.*

3. *Behavioral Model:* Theorists who espouse the behavioral model concentrate on a person's behaviors, which are held to develop in accordance with the *principles of learning.* Three types of conditioning—*classical conditioning, operant conditioning,* and *modeling*—account for behavior, whether normal or dysfunctional.

   The goal of the *behavioral therapies* is to identify the client's problem-causing behaviors and replace them with more appropriate ones. Behavioral therapists use techniques that follow the principles of classical conditioning, operant conditioning, modeling, or a combination of these.

4. *Cognitive Model:* The cognitive model claims that we must understand the content and process of human thought to understand human behavior. When people display abnormal patterns of functioning, cognitive theorists point to cognitive problems, including *maladaptive assumptions, specific upsetting thoughts,* and *illogical thinking processes.*

   Cognitive therapists try to help people recognize and change their faulty ideas and thinking processes. Among the most widely used cognitive therapies are Ellis's *rational-emotive therapy,* Beck's *cognitive therapy,* and Meichenbaum's *self-instruction training.*

5. *Humanistic and Existential Model:* Proponents of the humanistic-existential model focus on the human ability to confront complex and challenging philosophical issues such as self-awareness, values, meaning, and choice, and to incorporate them into one's life.

   A. *Humanists* Humanists believe that people are driven to *self-actualize,* that is, to fulfill their potential for goodness and growth. When this drive is interfered with, abnormal behavior may result. One group of humanistic therapists, *client-centered therapists,* try to create a very supportive climate in which clients can look at themselves honestly and begin to accept what they discover themselves to be, thus opening the door to self-actualization. Another group, *gestalt therapists,* try to move clients to recognize and accept their needs through more active techniques such as *skillful frustration* and *role playing.*

   B. *Existentialists* Existentialists, in contrast, believe that all of us have total freedom either to face up to our existence and give meaning to our lives or to shrink from that responsibility. Abnormal behavior is seen as the result of a person's hiding from life's responsibilities. Existential therapists encourage clients to accept responsibility for their lives, to recognize their freedom to choose a different course, and to choose to live an authentic life.

# Key Terms

| | | | |
|---|---|---|---|
| model | psychoanalysis | libido | repression |
| psychodynamic model | unconscious | ego | superego |
| dynamic | id | reality principle | introjection |
| deterministic | pleasure principle | ego defense mechanism | fixation |

erogenous zone
oral stage
anal stage
phallic stage
Oedipus complex
penis envy
Electra complex
latency stage
genital stage
ego psychology
self psychology
object relations theory
free association
resistance
transference
dream
manifest content

latent content
catharsis
working through
behavioral model
behavior
principles of learning
conditioning
classical conditioning
unconditioned stimulus
unconditioned response
conditioned stimulus
conditioned response
extinction
systematic desensitization
fear hierarchy
aversion therapy
operant conditioning

reinforcement
shaping
token economy
modeling
social skills training
self-efficacy
cognitive-behavioral
  theories
cognitive model
basic irrational
  assumption
automatic thought
self-statement
rational-emotive therapy
cognitive therapy
self-instruction training
humanist

humanistic-existential
  model
self-actualization
existentialist
authentic life
positive regard
unconditional positive
  regard
unconditional self-regard
conditions of worth
client-centered therapy
accurate empathy
genuineness
congruence
experiencing
skillful frustration
role play

## Quick Quiz

1. For each of the following concepts, identify the model associated with it: (a) learned responses, (b) values, (c) responsibility, (d) underlying conflicts, (e) irrational assumptions, (f) illogical thinking.
2. For each of the following concepts, identify the treatment that utilizes it: (a) unconditional positive regard, (b) free association, (c) systematic reinforcement, (d) skillful frustration, (e) self-statements, (f) dream interpretation.
3. State the key theme of each of the four psychological models.
4. According to psychodynamic theorists what roles do the id, ego, and superego play in the development of both normal and abnormal behavior?
5. Describe the five stages of psychosexual development identified by Sigmund Freud. How might these stages contribute to adult functioning?

6. What are the key techniques used by psychodynamic therapists?
7. What are the three forms of conditioning according to behaviorists? How do they account for abnormal behaviors?
8. What are the leading techniques used by behavioral therapists?
9. Identify three forms of cognitive dysfunctioning that can lead to abnormal behavior.
10. Compare the cognitive approaches of Ellis, Beck, and Meichenbaum.
11. Compare Rogers' and Perls' humanistic theories and therapies. How, in turn, are they different from existential philosophies and approaches?

# 4

# The Biological and Sociocultural Models of Abnormality

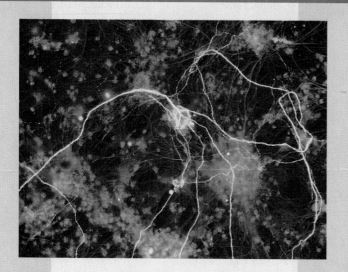

## Topic Overview

The models discussed in the last chapter hold that normal and abnormal mental functioning are rooted in psychological events such as a person's thoughts, memories, needs, and personal experiences. But surely these are not the only forces to which we answer in life. We are also biological beings, operating as a result of the physiological processes occurring throughout our bodies. In addition, we are social beings, influenced by the rules and structure of our society and by the behavior and opinions of its members. Thus, two other models of explanation and treatment for abnormal functioning—the *biological* and *sociocultural* models—have also gained prominence during this century. Although the proponents of these models favor principles and concepts of their own, their views and interventions are, as we shall see, often quite compatible with those of the psychological models.

# The Biological Model

Think back to the case of Philip Berman presented in the previous chapter. Philip is a biological being. His thoughts and feelings are the results of complex biochemical and bioelectrical processes throughout his brain and body. Biological theorists believe that a full understanding of his psychological functioning must include an understanding of the biological basis of his thoughts, emotions, and behavior. Not surprisingly, they believe that once this understanding is attained, the most effective interventions for Philip's problems will be biological ones.

As we saw in Chapter 1, the roots of the biological model of abnormal psychology actually stretch back thousands of years. However, the model's influence has been especially strong since the 1950s, when researchers produced several kinds of effective **psychotropic drugs,** drugs that have their dominant effect on emotions or thought processes and in some cases alleviate symptoms of mental dysfunctioning.

## Biological Explanations of Abnormal Behavior

Adopting a medical perspective, biological theorists view abnormal behavior as an illness brought about by malfunctioning parts of the organism. Specifically, they point to a malfunctioning brain as the primary cause of abnormal behavior (Gershon & Rieder, 1992). The brain comprises approximately 100 billion nerve cells, called **neurons,** and thousands of billions of support cells, called **glia** (Fischbach, 1992). Within the brain, large groups of neurons form anatomically distinct areas, or **brain regions.** Initially it is easier to read an anatomical map of the brain if one conceptualizes these regions as continents, countries, and states.

At the bottom of the brain is the "continent" known as the **hindbrain,** which is in turn composed of countrylike regions called the *medulla, pons,* and *cerebellum* (see Figure 4-1). In the middle of the brain is the "continent" called the **midbrain.** And at the top is the "continent" called the **forebrain,** which is composed of countrylike regions called the *cerebrum* (the two cerebral hemispheres), the *thalamus,* and the *hypothalamus,* each in turn made up of statelike regions. The cerebrum, for instance, consists of the *cortex* (see Figure 4-2), *corpus callosum, basal ganglia, hippocampus,* and *amygdala.* The neurons in each of these brain regions control important functions. For example, the hippocampus helps regulate emotions and memory, and the hypothalamus helps regulate hunger.

Biological theorists believe that mental disorders are linked to problems in brain-cell functioning. The problems may be *anatomical* (the size or shape of certain brain regions may be abnormal) or *biochemical* (the chemicals that enable neurons to operate may not work properly). Such difficulties may be the result of various factors, such as excessive stress, infections, tumors, inadequate blood supply, and physical injury (Haroutunian, 1991).

Biological researchers initially came to believe that most or all mental disorders have at least some physical basis largely as a result of insights gained from the study of the psychotropic medications (Gershon & Rieder, 1992). By studying where these drugs go and what they do in the brain, they learned much about the mental disorders they alleviate (Hollister & Csernansky, 1990). In recent years these researchers have added to their understanding of the physical underpinnings of abnormal behavior by using scanning techniques that enable them to take "photographs" of the living brain, such as *computerized axial tomography (CAT scanning), positron emission tomography (PET scanning),* and *magnetic resonance imaging (MRI).*

Using such strategies and tools, biological researchers have learned, for example, that mental disorders are often related to subtle dysfunctioning in the transmission of brain messages from neuron to neuron. Information spreads throughout the brain in the form of electrical impulses that travel from one neuron to one or more others. An impulse is received by a

---

*Psychotropic drugs*    Drugs that primarily affect the brain.

*Neuron*    A nerve cell.

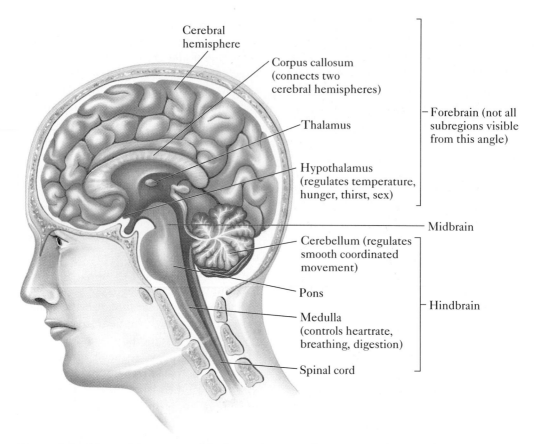

**Figure 4-1** *Many of the regions of the human brain can be seen in a side view of the brain sliced down the center. Each region, composed of numerous neurons, is responsible for certain functions.*

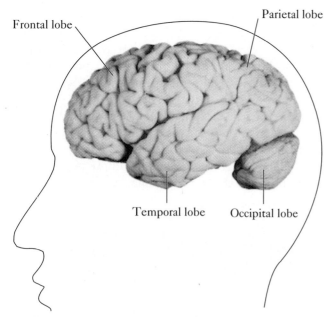

**Figure 4-2** *The cortex, the gray outer layer of the cerebrum, contains at least 70 percent of all neurons and is responsible for the highest levels of cognitive and perceptual analysis, including reasoning, speaking, reading, hearing, and seeing. Anatomists separate the cortex of each hemisphere into four regions called lobes.*

neuron's **dendrites,** extensions (or antennae) located at one end of the neuron; travels down the neuron's **axon,** a long fiber extending from the neuron body; and is transmitted to other neurons through the **nerve endings** which are located at the other end of the neuron (see Figure 4-3). An important question is how messages get from the nerve endings of one neuron to the dendrites of another neuron. After all, the neurons do not actually touch each other. A tiny space, called the **synapse,** separates one neuron from the next, and the message must somehow move across that space. When an electrical impulse reaches a neuron's ending, apparently the nerve ending is stimulated to release a chemical, called a **neurotransmitter,** that travels across the synaptic space to **receptors** (actually proteins) on the dendrites of the adjacent neurons. The neurotransmitter in turn leads the receiving neuron either to generate another electrical impulse ("firing" or "trigger-

*Synapse*    The tiny space between the nerve ending of one neuron and the dendrite of another.

*Neurotransmitter*    A chemical that, released by one neuron, crosses the synaptic space to be received at receptors on the dendrites of adjacent neurons.

*Receptor*    A site on a neuron that receives a neurotransmitter.

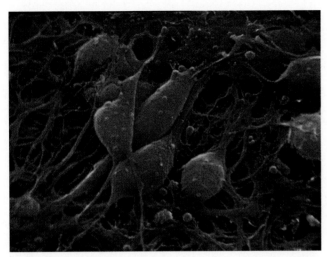

*State-of-the-art electron microscopes and color-enhancement techniques reveal the complex network of cell bodies, axons, and dendrites that make up the brain.*

ing") or to cease firing, depending on the neurotransmitter involved. Obviously, neurotransmitters play a key role in moving information through the brain (Kanof, 1991).

Researchers have so far identified dozens of neurotransmitters in the brain, and have learned that each neuron uses only certain kinds (Barondes, 1993). Neurological studies indicate that abnormalities in the activity of different neurotransmitters can help cause different mental disorders (Gershon & Rieder, 1992). Anxiety disorders, for example, have been linked to insufficient activity of the neurotransmitter *gamma aminobutyric acid (GABA),* schizophrenia to excessive activity of the neurotransmitter *dopamine,* and depression to low activity of the neurotransmitters *norepinephrine* and *serotonin.* Indeed, biological theorists would probably point to deficient norepinephrine and serotonin activity to account for Philip Berman's pattern of depression and rage.

Biological researchers also have examined the frequencies with which mental disorders occur among biological relatives. Some have, for example, conducted *risk studies* in which they survey the biological relatives of patients who have been diagnosed with a specific psychological abnormality to see how many and which of the relatives have the same disorder (Sameroff & Seifer, 1990). Many of these studies have demonstrated that the risk of developing severe depression increases directly with the closeness of one's biological relationship to someone with that disorder (Gottesman, 1991).

Given their orientation, practitioners of the biological model look for certain kinds of clues when they search for the cause of a particular person's abnormal

behavior. Does the family have a history of that behavior, and hence a possible genetic predisposition to it? (Philip Berman's case history mentions that his mother was once hospitalized for depression.) Does the disorder seem to be related to a past illness or accident, or to follow its own course, irrespective of situational

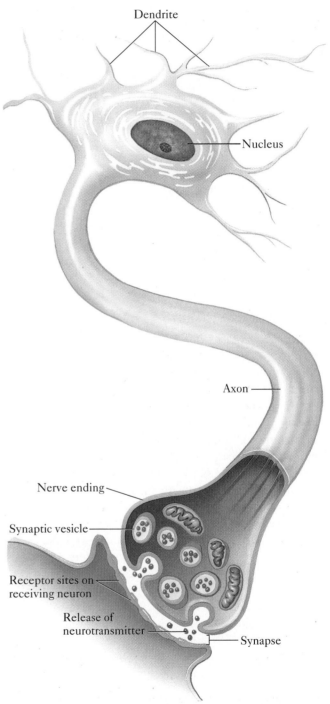

**Figure 4-3** *A typical neuron. A message travels down the neuron's axon to the nerve ending, where neurotransmitters carry the message across the synaptic space to a receiving neuron. (Adapted from Bloom, Lazerson, & Hofstadter, 1985, p. 35).*

changes? (Philip's depressed feelings were described as periodic; they seemed to come and go over the course of several years.) Is the behavior exacerbated by events that could be construed as having a physiological effect? (Philip was having a drink when he flew into a jealous rage at the restaurant.) Once these practitioners have pinpointed particular areas of presumed organic dysfunctioning, they are in a better position to choose a course of biological treatment (Apter, 1993).

### Consider This
Studies have found systematic biological differences between people who suffer from certain psychological disorders and those who do not. Does this "prove" that the disorders have biological causes? Might there be alternative explanations for the finding?

## Biological Therapies
The three principal kinds of biological interventions used today are drug therapy, electroconvulsive therapy, and psychosurgery. Drug therapy is by far the most common approach, whereas psychosurgery is relatively infrequent.

### Drug Therapy

As we observed earlier, in the 1950s researchers discovered several kinds of effective psychotropic drugs. These drugs have radically changed the outlook for a number of mental disorders and are now used widely, either as an adjunct or as the dominant form of therapy. Four major groups of psychotropic drugs are used in therapy: antianxiety, antidepressant, antibipolar, and antipsychotic drugs.

*Antianxiety drugs,* also called **minor tranquilizers** or **anxiolytics** (from "anxiety" and the Greek *lytikos,* "able to loosen or dissolve"), reduce tension and anxiety. Research clearly indicates that these drugs, which include *alprazolam* (trade name Xanax) and *diazepam* (trade name Valium), help reduce anxiety (Papp & Gorman, 1993). They have been overused and even misused, however, and, as we shall see in Chapter 5, they can induce physical dependence if they are taken in high dosages over an extended period of time (Murphy et al., 1984; Winokur et al., 1980).

*Antidepressant drugs* help lift the spirits of people who are depressed. Indeed, their very trade names of-

---

*Drug therapy*   The use of psychotropic drugs to alleviate the symptoms of mental disorders.

*Antianxiety drugs*   Psychotropic drugs that help reduce tension and anxiety.

*Antidepressant drugs*   Psychotropic drugs that lift the mood of people with depression.

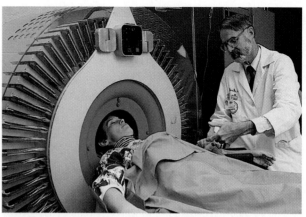

*Elaborate biological tests such as positron emission tomography (PET) help detect abnormalities that may be causing psychological problems.*

ten imply a significant elevation of mood (see Table 4-1). There are three kinds of antidepressants: the *MAO inhibitors,* the *tricyclics,* and the recently developed *second-generation antidepressants,* which include *fluoxetine hydrochloride* (Prozac). The drugs have an average success rate of 65 percent in cases of depression, but may cause uncomfortable (and in the case of MAO inhibitors, dangerous) side effects.

### Table 4-1   *The Name Game*

The trade names of psychotropic medications often seem to advertise the drug's intended effect.

| Trade Name | Linguistic Connotation |
| --- | --- |
| **Antianxiety** | |
| Halcion | Halcyon (pleasingly calm or peaceful) |
| Equanil | Equanimity |
| Unisom | Unified somnolence |
| Librium | Equilibrium (balance) |
| **Antidepressant** | |
| Flavil | To elevate |
| Sinequan | Sine qua non (the one essential thing) |
| Vivactil | Vivacious |
| Asendin | To ascend |
| Zoloft | Lofty |
| **Antipsychotic** | |
| Serentil | Serenity |
| Thorazine | Thor (powerful Norse god of thunder) |
| **Anti-Parkinsonian** | |
| Symmetrel | Symmetry |
| **Anti-Alzheimer's** | |
| Cognex | Cognizant |

*Antibipolar drugs* help stabilize the moods of persons with a bipolar mood disorder, a disorder marked by mood swings from mania to depression. As we shall see in greater detail in Chapter 7, the most effective antibipolar drug is *lithium,* a metallic element that occurs in nature as a mineral salt. This drug is helpful in more than 65 percent of cases of bipolar disorders (Prien, 1992). The dosage of lithium must be carefully monitored, however (Jefferson & Greist, 1989). Too high a concentration may dangerously alter the body's sodium level and even threaten the patient's life.

*Antipsychotic drugs* help alleviate the confusion, hallucinations, and delusions of psychosis, a loss of contact with reality. Common antipsychotic drugs are *chlorpromazine* (trade name Thorazine), *haloperidol* (Haldol), and *clozapine* (Clozaril). Research has repeatedly shown that antipsychotic drugs are more effective than any other single form of treatment for schizophrenia and related psychotic disorders (Klerman et al., 1994). The drugs are particularly effective when combined with appropriate community programs and adjunct psychotherapy. Unfortunately, the drugs may cause very serious undesired effects in many patients, particularly *extrapyramidal effects,* movement disorders such as severe shaking, bizarre-looking contractions of the face and body, and extreme restlessness.

## Consider This

The use of psychotropic medications to help people cope with problems or disorders is on the increase in our society. What might the enormous popularity of these drugs suggest about the needs, coping styles, and reinforcements of individuals today, about the pace of modern life, and about problem-solving in our technological society?

## Electroconvulsive Therapy

Another form of biological treatment used widely today, primarily on depressed patients, is *electroconvulsive therapy (ECT),* a technique first developed in the 1930s by two Italian physicians, Ugo Cerletti and Lucio Bini. Two electrodes are attached to a patient's forehead, and an electrical current of 65 to 140 volts is

---

*Antibipolar drugs*   Psychotropic drugs that help stabilize the moods of people suffering from bipolar mood disorder.

*Antipsychotic drugs*   Psychotropic drugs that help correct the grossly confused or distorted thinking characteristic of psychotic disorders.

*Electroconvulsive therapy (ECT)*   A form of biological treatment, used primarily on depressed patients, in which a brain seizure is triggered as an electric current passes through electrodes attached to the patient's forehead.

*Unfortunately, a clinician's choices about which psychotropic drugs to prescribe may be influenced not only by research literature but by a pharmaceutical company's promotional campaigns. Enticing ads for drugs fill the journals read by psychiatrists and other physicians.*

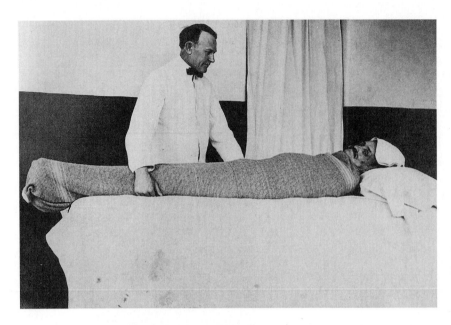

*Prior to the discovery of effective psychotropic drugs, clinicians in mental institutions used techniques such as the "wet pack," designed for calming excited patients.*

briefly passed through the brain. The current causes a brain seizure, or convulsion, that lasts up to a few minutes. After an average of seven to nine ECT sessions, spaced two or three days apart, many patients feel considerably less depressed.

ECT helps approximately 65 percent of depressed subjects to improve (Wechsler et al., 1965). Accordingly, the procedure is used on tens of thousands of depressed persons annually (Foderaero, 1993). Although administered less often today than it was in the past (see Box 4-1), ECT is still applied when people have a severe, particularly a psychotic, depressive episode that is unresponsive to other forms of treatment (Buchan et al., 1992).

### Psychosurgery

Brain surgery as a treatment for mental disorders is thought to have roots as far back as trephining, the prehistoric practice of chipping a hole in the skull of a person who behaved strangely. Modern forms of psychosurgery are derived from a technique first developed in the late 1930s by a Portuguese neuropsychiatrist, Antonio de Egas Moniz. In this procedure, known as a *lobotomy*, a surgeon cut the connections between the cortex of the brain's frontal lobes and the lower centers of the brain.

As we shall observe in Chapter 13, it became clear by the late 1950s that lobotomies were not so effective as many psychosurgeons had been claiming. Even more disturbing, many lobotomized patients later suf-

*Psychosurgery*   Brain surgery performed as a treatment for mental disorders.

*Lobotomy*   Psychosurgery that severs the connections between the cortex of the brain's frontal lobes and the lower centers of the brain.

fered terrible and irreversible effects—seizures, extreme listlessness, stupor, and in some cases death (Barahal, 1958). Thus, this procedure declined in popularity during the 1960s. Today's procedures are much more precise than the lobotomies of the past (Beck & Cowley, 1990). They produce fewer unwanted effects and are apparently beneficial in some cases of severe depression, anxiety, and obsessive-compulsive disorder. Even so, they are considered experimental and are used infrequently, usually only after a severe disorder has continued for years without responding to any other form of treatment (Goodman et al., 1992).

## Assessing the Biological Model

Today the biological model enjoys considerable prestige in the clinical field, and investigations into the biological underpinnings of abnormal functioning are proliferating. The model has many virtues. First, it serves to remind us that psychological processes, however complex and subtle, have biological causes worthy of examination and study. Second, thanks to sophisticated procedures developed over centuries of experimentation, research into the biological aspects of abnormal functioning often progresses rapidly, producing valuable new information in a relatively short time (see Table 4-2). Finally, biological treatments have often been known to afford significant help and relief for abnormal functioning after other interventions have failed.

At the same time, the biological model has characteristic limitations and problems. Some of its proponents seem to expect that all human behavior can be explained in biological terms and treated with biologi-

## Box 4-1

# ECT and the Law

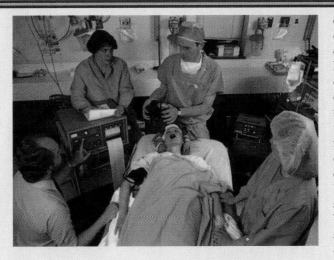

Since its introduction in the 1930s, electroconvulsive therapy has increasingly come under the scrutiny of courts and state legislatures throughout the United States. The primary reason: the clinical field has done a poor job of regulating the use of this powerful and frightening procedure. When self-regulation fails, the government and legal system typically step in.

During ECT's first decade, psychiatrists and clinical researchers were left on their own to apply, experiment with, and modify the procedure (Winslade, 1988). Although this work often yielded impressive results, it also elicited numerous complaints from patients and some clinicians (Rothman, 1985). In 1947 a psychiatric task force, the Group for the Advancement of Psychiatry, finally conducted an investigation into "shock therapy" and issued a critical report noting that ECT was being used indiscriminately and excessively, often for punitive rather than therapeutic purposes and for controlling difficult, dangerous, and uncooperative patients (GAP, 1947).

The next official report on ECT did not appear until 1978, more than thirty years later, when the American Psychiatric Association issued a task force report titled *Electroconvulsive Therapy*. This report endorsed the use of ECT for severe depression when drugs have failed, and made detailed recommendations for informing patients about ECT and obtaining their consent to the procedure (Winslade, 1988; Winslade et al., 1984). Subsequent psychiatric reports have continued to endorse this procedure as a treatment for people with severe depression (APA, 1993, 1990; Fink, 1992).

Legal regulation of ECT did not begin in earnest until the mid-1970s, when the California state legislature, responding to criticism from patients and former patients, passed a law restricting its use (Senter et al., 1984). All competent mental patients in California—both voluntary and involuntary—were granted the right to be informed about the nature of ECT and to consent to or refuse to undergo it. Many other states have since passed laws regulating ECT use. Some of these states, such as California and Texas, have strict regulations requiring concurring independent opinions from professionals that ECT is appropriate and necessary and mandating court hearings to determine whether involuntary patients are competent to consent to ECT. Other states have less restrictive laws that allow hospital superintendents to override a patient's right to refuse ECT simply by documenting that the procedure is being done for "good cause" (Senter et al., 1984).

Probably the most significant federal court decision regarding ECT has been *Wyatt* v. *Hardin*, which defined the legal standards for ECT treatments in Alabama, specifically forbidding some uses of ECT and establishing fourteen rules that severely restrict its practice (Winslade et al., 1984). This decision dictates, for example, that two psychiatrists (with the hospital director's concurrence) decide in each case that ECT is the most appropriate treatment, that a physical and neurological examination be conducted ten days before ECT, that anesthesia and muscle relaxants be used, that a psychiatrist and anesthesiologist be present during ECT, and that a single series of treatments be limited to twelve ECT sessions at most in a twelve-month period. In an effort to standardize the safe practice of ECT, the American Psychological Association and the National Institutes of Health have devised similar guidelines (APA, 1990, 1978; NIH, Consensus Conference, 1985).

Legal and judicial restrictions over the use of ECT have stirred heated debate in the clinical community. Many theorists believe that such protective measures are long overdue (Tenenbaum, 1983). Some would even like to make it harder for administrators to override a patient's refusal of ECT, and some would require that all patients be given a complete description of ECT's effects when their consent is obtained, including a clear statement about the risk of some permanent memory loss (Fink, 1992; Friedberg, 1975). Others believe that the laws and courts have gone too far, that such requirements as voluntary consent, professional board approval, and full disclosure often slow or prevent the therapeutic administration of ECT, leaving many patients unnecessarily depressed. Like the debate over the value and humaneness of ECT itself, this argument continues with no end in sight (Winslade, 1988; Taylor & Carroll, 1987).

**Table 4-2    Comparing the Biological and Sociocultural Models**

|  | Biological | Sociocultural |
|---|---|---|
| Cause of dysfunction | Biological malfunction | Family or social stress |
| Research support | Strong | Moderate |
| Consumer designation | Patient | Client |
| Therapist role | Doctor | Social facilitator |
| Key therapist technique | Biological intervention | Social intervention |
| Therapy goal | Biological repair | Effective family or social system |

cal methods. This narrow view can limit rather than enhance our understanding of abnormal functioning. Although biological processes certainly do affect our behavior, thoughts, and emotions, they are just as certainly affected by our behavior, thoughts, and emotions. When we perceive the negative events in our lives to be beyond our control, for example, the activity of norepinephrine or serotonin in our brains usually drops off, thus intensifying a depressive reaction. Our mental life is an interplay of biological and nonbiological factors, and it is important to explore that interplay rather than to focus exclusively on biological variables.

A second problem is that the evidence for biological explanations is often incomplete or inconclusive. Many neurological studies, for example, must be conducted on animals in whom apparent symptoms of depression, anxiety, or some other abnormality have been induced by drugs, surgery, or behavioral manipulation. Researchers can never be certain that these animals are experiencing the human disorder under investigation. Similarly, the human risk studies often cited in support of biological explanations are open to alternative interpretations. Evidence that close relatives are more likely to develop certain disorders than more distant relatives may simply mean, for example, that close relatives are more likely to have shared harmful "psychological" experiences early in their lives.

> **Summing Up**
> *Biological theorists believe that mental disorders are linked to either biochemical problems in the brain, such as abnormalities in neurotransmitter activity, or to anatomical problems in the brain. The biological treatments used to help people overcome psychological problems are drug therapy, electroconvulsive therapy, and, on rare occasions, psychosurgery.*

# The Sociocultural Model

Philip Berman is also a social being. He is surrounded by people and by institutions, he is a member of a family and a society, and he participates in social and professional relationships. Thus external social forces are always operating on Philip, setting rules and expectations that guide and at times pressure him, helping to shape his behavior, thoughts, and emotions as surely as any internal biological or psychological mechanism.

According to the sociocultural model of psychology, abnormal behavior is best understood in light of the social and cultural forces brought to bear on an individual. What are the norms and values of the society? What roles does the person play in the social environment? What kind of family structure is this person exposed to? And how do other people view and react to him or her?

The sociocultural view of abnormality derives its basic assumptions from the fields of *sociology,* the study of human relationships and social groups, and *anthropology,* the study of human cultures and institutions. Sociologists have proposed that societies themselves are capable of generating abnormal behavior in their members. Certain communities, for example, may be so disorganized that many of their members are forced to engage in odd behavior to adapt to the community's norms or standards.

Similarly, anthropologists have found that some patterns of abnormality vary from society to society, from culture to culture. For example, the disorder of "windigo," an intense fear of being turned into a cannibal by a flesh-eating monster, was found only among Algonquin Indian hunters, and "koro," a fear that one's penis will withdraw into the abdomen, was found only in Southeast Asia. Each of these abnormal patterns

*Sociology*    The study of human relationships and social groups.

*Anthropology*    The study of human cultures and institutions.

seemed uniquely tied to the society's particular history and culture (see Box 4-2).

For years, these sociological and anthropological notions influenced the study and treatment of abnormal psychology. Finally, in the 1950s, a new clinical model—the sociocultural model—emerged, marked by three key events. One was the publication in 1958 of a major study, *Social Class and Mental Illness,* by August Hollingshead and Frederick Redlich, which found that psychotic, aggressive, and rebellious behavior was much more common in the lower socioeconomic classes than in the upper classes. A second event was the development of family theory and therapy during the 1950s. A third factor in the emergence of the sociocultural model was the influential work of Thomas Szasz (1987, 1961), the outspoken psychiatrist who in the 1950s launched an attack against the mental health system, challenged the very concept of mental illness, and took the extreme position that mental disorders are the creations of society.

## Sociocultural Explanations of Abnormal Behavior

Because behavior is shaped by social forces, sociocultural theorists hold, we must examine the social context if we are to understand abnormal behavior in individual cases. Their explanations focus on family structure and communication, societal stress, and societal labels and reactions.

### Family Structure and Communication

According to *family systems theory,* the family is a *system* of interacting parts, the family members, who relate to one another in consistent ways and are governed by implicit rules unique to each family (Nichols, 1992; Minuchin, 1987). The parts interact in ways that enable the system to maintain itself and survive—a state known as *homeostasis.* Family systems theorists believe that the structure, rules, and communication patterns of some families actually force individual members to behave in a way that the society at large may define as abnormal. If the individual members were to behave normally, they would severely upset the family's boundaries, implicit rules, and homeostasis and actually increase their own and their family's turmoil. The responses by other family members would quickly extinguish such "normal" behavior.

*Family systems theory* An approach to human behavior that views the family as a system of interacting parts and proposes that members of a given family interact in consistent ways and operate by implicit rules.

Family systems theory portrays certain family systems as being particularly likely to produce abnormal functioning in individual family members (Becvar & Becvar, 1993; Nichols, 1992, 1984). Some families, for example, have a rigidly *enmeshed* structure in which the members are grossly overinvolved in each others' activities, thoughts, and feelings. Children from this kind of family may have great difficulty establishing autonomy in life. Conversely, some families display a structure of *disengagement,* which is characterized by overly rigid boundaries between the members. Children from these families may find it hard to function interdependently and may have difficulty giving or requesting support when needed. Problematic family patterns are often passed on from one generation to the next.

Philip Berman's angry and impulsive personal style might be interpreted as the product of a disturbed family structure. According to family systems theorists, the whole family—mother, father, Philip, and his brother Arnold—relate in such a way as to maintain Philip's behavior. Family theorists might be particularly interested in the conflict between Philip's mother and father and the imbalance between their parental roles. They might see Philip's behavior as both a reaction to and stimulus for his parents' behaviors, and consider his "ornery" behavior, like his mother's critical comments and his father's weakness and ineffectuality, as functioning to preserve the parents' troubled marriage and stabilize the family. With Philip acting out the role of the misbehaving child, or "scapegoat," his parents may have little need or time to question their own relationship. Family systems theorists would also seek to clarify issues such as the precise nature of Philip's relationship with each parent (Is he enmeshed with his mother and/or disengaged from his father?), the implicit rules governing the sibling relationship in the family, the power structure and relationship between the parents and Philip's brother, and the nature of parent-child relationships in previous generations of the family.

### Societal Stress

The unique characteristics of a given society may create special stresses that heighten the likelihood of abnormal functioning in its members. Studies have found relationships between rates of abnormal functioning and such factors as widespread social change, social class membership, ethnic and national background, race and sex, and cultural institutions and values. As a consequence, clinicians are becoming increasingly sensitive to the "hidden injuries" that result

## Box 4-2

# *Culture-Bound Abnormality*

Red Bear sits up wild-eyed, his body drenched in sweat, every muscle tensed. The horror of the dream is still with him; he is choked with fear. Fighting waves of nausea, he stares at his young wife lying asleep on the far side of the wigwam, illuminated by the dying embers.

His troubles began several days before, when he came back from a hunting expedition empty-handed. Ashamed of his failure, he fell prey to a deep, lingering depression. Others in the village, noticing a change in Red Bear, watched him nervously, afraid that he was becoming bewitched by a windigo. Red Bear was also frightened. The signs of windigo were all there: depression, lack of appetite, nausea, sleeplessness and, now, the dream. Indeed, there could be no mistake.

He had dreamed of the windigo—the monster with a heart of ice—and the dream sealed his doom. Coldness gripped his own heart. The ice monster had entered his body and possessed him. He himself had become a windigo, and he could do nothing to avert his fate.

Suddenly, the form of Red Bear's sleeping wife begins to change. He no longer sees a woman, but a deer. His eyes flame. Silently, he draws his knife from under the blanket and moves stealthily toward the motionless figure. Saliva drips from the corners of his mouth, and a terrible hunger twists his intestines. A powerful desire to eat raw flesh consumes him.

With the body of the "deer" at his feet, Red Bear raises the knife high, preparing to strike. Unexpectedly, the deer screams and twists away. But the knife flashes down, again and again. Too late, Red Bear's kinsmen rush into the wigwam. With cries of outrage and horror, they drag him outside into the cold night air and swiftly kill him.

> (*Lindholm & Lindholm, 1981,
> p. 52*)

Red Bear was suffering from *windigo,* a disorder once common among Algonquin Indian hunters who believed in a supernatural monster that ate human beings and also had the power to bewitch them and turn them into cannibals. Like Red Bear, a small number of afflicted hunters actually did kill and eat household members.

Windigo is one of the unusual mental disorders discovered around the world, each unique to a particular culture, each apparently growing from the particular pressures, history, institutions, and ideas of the culture (Lindholm & Lindholm, 1981; Kiev, 1972; Lehmann, 1967; Yap, 1951). Proponents of the sociocultural model cite disorders such as windigo as evidence that societies often help to produce abnormal behavior in their members. The following are other exotic disorders that have been reported:

*Susto,* a disorder found among members of Indian tribes in Central and South America and non-Indian natives of the Andean highlands of Peru, Bolivia, and Colombia, is most likely to occur in infants and young children. The symptoms are extreme anxiety, excitability, and depression, along with loss of weight, weakness, and rapid heartbeat. The culture holds that this disorder is caused by contact with supernatural beings or with frightening strangers, or by bad air from cemeteries and other supposedly dangerous places. Treatment includes rubbing certain plants and animals against the skin.

*Amok,* a disorder found in Malaya, the Philippines, Java, and some parts of Africa, is more likely to occur in men than in women. Those who are afflicted jump around violently, yell loudly, grab weapons, such as knives, and attack any people and objects they encounter. This behavior is usually preceded by an earlier stage in which the victim withdraws socially and suffers some loss of contact with reality. The periods of violent behavior are followed by depression and by amnesia concerning the outburst. Within the culture, amok is thought to be caused by stress, severe shortage of sleep, alcohol consumption, and extreme heat.

*Koro* is a pattern of anxiety found in Southeast Asia in which a man suddenly becomes intensely fearful that his penis will withdraw into his abdomen and that he will die as a result. Cultural lore holds that the disorder is caused by an imbalance of "yin" and "yang," two natural forces believed to be the fundamental components of life. Accepted forms of treatment include having the individual keep a firm hold on his penis until the fear passes, often with the assistance of family members or friends, and clamping the penis to a wooden box.

*Latah* is a disorder found in Malaya, usually among uneducated middle-aged or elderly women. Certain circumstances (hearing someone say "snake"; being tickled) trigger a fright reaction marked by repeating others' words and acts, using obscene words, and doing the opposite of what others ask.

from racism, sexism, and poverty, as well as from less obvious societal stressors such as urbanization and cultural change (Vega & Rumbaut, 1991).

**Social Change** When a society undergoes major change, the mental health of its members can be greatly affected. Societies undergoing rapid urbanization, for example, usually show a rise in the prevalence of mental disorders, although it is not known which features of urbanization—overcrowding, technological change, social isolation, and so forth—are most to blame (Ghubash et al., 1992). Similarly, a society in the throes of economic depression is likely to show a significant rise in rates of clinical depression and suicide (Hammer, 1993), which may be explained in part by an increase in unemployment and the resulting loss of self-esteem and personal security.

**Social Class** Studies have found that rates of psychological abnormality, especially severe psychological abnormality, are three times higher in the lower socioeconomic classes than in the higher ones (Dohrenwend et al., 1992; Eron & Peterson, 1982). Perhaps the special pressures of lower-class life help explain this relationship (Adler et al., 1994). The higher rates of crime, unemployment, overcrowding, and even homelessness, the inferior medical care, and the limited educational opportunities that often characterize lower-class life may place great stress on members of these groups. Of course, other factors could also be to blame. People who suffer from significant mental disturbances may be less effective at work, earn less money, and as a result drift downward to settle in a lower socioeconomic class.

**Ethnic, Religious, and National Background** Ethnic, religious, and national groups have distinctive traditions that may influence the kinds of abnormal functioning to which they are vulnerable. Alcoholism, for example, is more prevalent in groups that tolerate heavy drinking (Catholics, Irish, Western Europeans, Eastern Europeans) than in groups that frown on it (Jews, Protestants) (Barry, 1982).

**Racial and Sexual Prejudice** Prejudice and discrimination may also contribute to certain forms of abnormal functioning. Societies typically have "in-groups" and "out-groups," the latter composed of people who are deprived of many of the opportunities and comforts available to the former. The out-groups—whose members are often fewer than the in-group members and different from them in ethnicity, race, or gender—are sometimes called "minority groups" or "ethnic minorities." In the United States such terms typically refer to all nonwhite groups of Americans.

Women in Western society receive diagnoses of anxiety and depressive disorders at least twice as often as men (Wittchen et al., 1992). African Americans experience unusually high rates of certain anxiety disor-

*People in the lower socioeconomic classes have higher rates of psychological dysfunctioning than people in the middle and upper classes. Conditions of chronic poverty, such as experienced by the Irish "travelers," may contribute.*

*Some sociocultural theorists believe that intense social stressors may produce outbreaks of "mass madness" such as the Los Angeles riots of 1992. In a vicious cycle, the riots, which occurred against a backdrop of poverty, unemployment, and prejudice, produced further stress for members of the community, such as Joe and Joyce Wilson, who survey the damage to their business, "Pop's Restaurant."*

ders (Blazer et al., 1991; Eaton et al., 1991). Hispanic people, particularly young men, have higher rates of alcoholism than members of most other ethnic groups (Helzer et al., 1991). Native Americans display unusually high alcoholism and suicide rates (Kinzie et al., 1992). Although many factors may combine to produce these differences, racial and sexual prejudice and the struggles and the limitations they impose may contribute to pathological patterns of tension, unhappiness, low self-esteem, and escape (Sue, 1991).

**Cultural Institutions and Values**   Disorders such as windigo and koro are thought to grow out of the institutions and values of the cultures where they arise. So is *anorexia nervosa,* a disorder particularly prevalent among young women in Western society (Garner et al., 1991). As we will see in Chapter 10, people with this disorder intentionally deprive themselves of food and lose dangerous amounts of weight. Many theorists believe that the current emphasis on thinness as the female aesthetic ideal in Western culture is largely responsible for anorexia nervosa's high incidence there.

### Societal Labels and Reactions

Sociocultural theorists also believe that abnormal functioning is influenced greatly by the diagnostic labels given to troubled people and by the ways other people react to those labels (Szasz, 1987, 1963; Scheff, 1975). The theorists hold that when people violate the norms of their society, the society categorizes them as deviant and assigns them labels such as "mentally ill."

This label tends to stick to a person, condemning him or her to be viewed in stereotyped ways, reacted to as "crazy," and expected and subtly encouraged to be incapacitated. According to sociocultural theorists, the person gradually learns to accept and play the assigned role, functioning and behaving in an increasingly disturbed manner. Ultimately the label seems fully justified.

A famous and controversial study by the clinical investigator David Rosenhan (1973) supports this position. Eight normal people presented themselves at various mental hospitals, complaining that they had been hearing voices say the words "empty," "hollow," and "thud." On the basis of this complaint alone, each "pseudopatient" was diagnosed as schizophrenic and admitted to the hospital. According to the researchers, the events of the following weeks highlighted several issues. First, it was hard to get rid of the label. The length of hospitalization ranged from seven to fifty-two days, even though the pseudopatients behaved normally as soon as they were admitted to the hospital. Second, the schizophrenic label kept influencing the way staff viewed and dealt with the pseudopatients. A pseudopatient who paced the corridor out of boredom was, for example, said to be "nervous." Third, pseudopatients reported that the staff's reactions toward patients in general were often authoritarian, brief, and counterproductive. Overall, the pseudopatients came to feel powerless, depersonalized, and bored.

## Sociocultural Therapies

Clients often see therapists in *individual therapy,* the time-honored format in which the two meet alone for sessions that last from fifteen minutes to two hours, depending on such factors as the client's problem and the therapist's orientation. There are, however, several other formats and settings in which therapy may be conducted. Therapists may see a client with other clients who share similar problems, in *group therapy;* with family members, in *couple* and *family therapy;* or in the client's natural habitat, in *community treatment.* Therapists of any theoretical orientation can apply the explanations and concepts of their preferred models when working with clients in these broad formats. However, more and more of the practitioners who use such formats are embracing the sociocultural position that psychological problems emerge in a social setting and are best addressed in such a setting. Thus, a number of special sociocultural strategies have been developed for use specifically in group, family, couple, and community therapeutic formats.

## Group Therapy

At the turn of the century, a physician in Boston named Joseph Pratt brought patients with tuberculosis together in groups to teach them about their illness and encourage them to provide emotional support for each other. This appears to have been the first clinical application of group therapy (Rosenbaum & Berger, 1963). American and British clinicians continued to experiment with group processes over the next fifty years, but it was not until after World War II that group therapy became a popular format for treating people with psychological problems. At that time, a growing demand for psychological services forced therapists throughout the United States and Europe to look for alternatives to individual therapy. Many who tried the group format found it to be efficient, time-saving, and relatively inexpensive. They also found that group therapy was often as helpful as individual therapy.

Thousands of therapists now specialize in group therapy, and countless others conduct therapy groups as one aspect of their practice. A recent survey of 481 clinical psychologists, for example, revealed that almost a third of them practice group therapy to some degree (Norcross et al., 1993).

Typically, members of a therapy group meet together with a therapist and discuss the problems of one or more of the members. Groups are often created with particular client populations in mind; for example, there are groups for people with alcoholism, for those who are physically handicapped, and for people who are divorced, abused, or bereaved (Bednar & Kaul, 1994; DeAngelis, 1992). The group format has also been used for purposes that are educational rather than therapeutic, such as for "consciousness raising" and spiritual inspiration.

On the basis of his own work and on a number of investigations, the group therapy theorist Irvin Yalom (1985) suggests that successful forms of group therapy share certain "curative" features:

1. *Guidance:* they usually provide information and advice for members.
2. *Identification:* they provide models of appropriate behavior.
3. *Group cohesiveness:* they offer an atmosphere of solidarity in which members can learn to take risks and accept criticism.
4. *Universality:* members discover that other people have similar problems.
5. *Altruism:* members develop feelings of self-worth by helping others.
6. *Catharsis:* members develop more understanding of themselves and of others and learn to express their feelings.
7. *Skill building:* members acquire or improve social skills.

Because groups vary widely in type and conduct and in the characteristics of their leaders and members, and because group interactions can be complex, it has been difficult to assess their effectiveness (Bednar & Kaul, 1994). Moreover, many of the studies that have been done have not used proper research methodology (Sadock, 1989; Lubin, 1983). Thus only a modest number of conclusions can be drawn about therapy that takes this format.

Research does indicate that group therapy is of help to many clients, often as helpful as individual therapy (Bednar & Kaul, 1994; DeAngelis, 1992). It appears that candid feedback is usually useful for group members as long as a balance is struck between positive and negative feedback. Some people have been harmed by group therapy, but such occurrences are not frequent. Apparently, skilled group leaders are usually able to screen out those prospective members who need more individual attention or who would not be able to tolerate the demands of the group experience (Sadock, 1989).

Over the years, various specialized kinds of group therapy have been developed. Two of the most influential are psychodrama and self-help groups.

**Psychodrama**   In the 1920s Jacob Moreno, a Viennese psychiatrist and the first person to use the term "group psychotherapy," developed the therapy known as *psychodrama*, in which group members act out dramatic roles as if they were participating in an improvised play. The atmosphere of structured fantasy is expected to make the participants feel secure enough to express their feelings and thoughts, explore new behavior and attitudes, and empathize with the feelings and perspectives of others. Often the group members act on a stage and even in front of an audience. The acting is guided by the therapist, or "director," who also provides feedback about each participant's performance. The audience, too, may give useful feedback.

Although relatively few of today's therapists limit their groups' activities to psychodrama alone, many have incorporated its role-playing techniques and principles into their practice. As we saw earlier, many

---

*Group therapy*   A therapeutic approach in which a group of people with similar problems meet together with a therapist and discuss the problems or concerns of one or more of the members.

*Psychodrama*   A group therapy technique that calls for group members to act out dramatic roles as if they were participating in an improvised play in which they express their feelings and thoughts, explore new behaviors and attitudes, and empathize with the feelings and perspectives of others.

behavioral and humanistic therapists now use role playing to teach assertiveness and social skills and to facilitate interactions among members of their groups (Wood et al., 1981). Similarly, psychodrama's emphasis on spontaneity and empathy has become a part of most group therapies (Lubin, 1983).

**Self-Help Groups**    *Self-help groups* (or *mutual-help groups*) are made up of people who have similar problems and come together to help and support one another without the direct leadership of a professional clinician. These groups have become increasingly popular over the last two decades, and today there are about 500,000 such groups attended by 15 million people in the United States alone, addressing a wide assortment of issues, including alcoholism and other forms of drug abuse, compulsive gambling, bereavement, overeating, phobias, child abuse, medical illnesses, rape victimization, unemployment, and divorce (White & Madara, 1992).

Self-help groups are popular for several reasons. Some of the participants are looking for inexpensive and interesting alternatives to traditional kinds of treatment and find self-help groups in their search. Others have simply lost confidence in the ability of clinicians and social institutions to help with their particular problems (Silverman, 1992). Alcoholics Anonymous, the well-known network of self-help groups for people dependent on alcohol, was developed in 1934 in response to the general ineffectiveness of clinical treatments for alcoholism. Still others are drawn to self-help groups because they find them less threatening and less stigmatizing than therapy groups. Finally, the popularity of self-help groups may be related to the decline of the extended family and other traditional sources of emotional support in Western society (Bloch et al., 1982).

Self-help groups encourage more helping among members than therapy groups do (Silverman, 1992). Often new members are assigned to veteran members who take a special interest in them and help integrate them into the group. In addition, self-help groups encourage members to exchange information more than other groups do. People who are newly bereaved, for example, can obtain specific information from their self-help group about funeral arrangements and business matters, as well as about what feelings to expect and how to cope with them.

Many clinicians consider these groups a form of therapy despite the absence of a therapist-leader (Christensen & Jacobson, 1994). At the very least,

*Thousands of self-help groups around the world help people cope with a variety of problems.*

therapists usually view the groups as compatible with traditional forms of therapy. They often urge clients to participate in self-help groups as part of a broader treatment program for problems such as alcoholism, eating disorders, and victimization.

> *Consider This*
> Interest in self-help groups has grown in recent years. What might be the advantages and disadvantages of these groups compared to professional treatment?

## Family Therapy

Adhering to the sociocultural position that disturbances in social structure often cause disturbances in individual functioning, several clinicians in the 1950s developed *family therapy*—a format in which therapists meet with all members of a family, point out problematic behavior and interactions between the members, and help the whole family to change. Most family therapists meet with family members as a group, but some choose to see them separately. Either way, the family is viewed as the unit under treatment. Here is a typical interaction between family members and therapist:

> "I just don't understand. We have had a happy family all along until Tommy started acting up." Bob Davis was visibly exasperated. "You are supposed to be the family expert, Ms. Fargo, what do you think?"
> "We have tried so hard to be good parents to both of the children," Bob glanced at his wife, "but Tommy just doesn't respond anymore. I wish he was more like

*Self-help group*    A therapy group made up of people who have similar problems and come together to help and support one another without the direct leadership of a professional clinician.

*Family therapy*    A therapy format in which therapists meet with all members of a family, point out problematic behavior and interactions between the members, and help the whole family to change.

his little sister. She is so well behaved and is a joy to have around."

Tommy sat motionless in a chair gazing out the window. He was fourteen and a bit small for his age. He looked completely disinterested in the proceedings.

Sissy was eleven. She was sitting on the couch between her Mom and Dad with a smile on her face. Across from them sat Ms. Fargo, the family therapist.

Ms. Fargo spoke. "Could you be a little more specific about the changes you have seen in Tommy and when they came about?"

Mrs. Davis answered first. "Well, I guess it was about two years ago. Tommy started getting in fights at school. When we talked to him at home he said it was none of our business. He became moody and disobedient. He wouldn't do anything that we wanted him to. He began to act mean to his sister and even hit her."

"What about the fights at school?" Ms. Fargo asked.

This time it was Mr. Davis who spoke first. "Ginny was more worried about them than I was. I used to fight a lot when I was in school and I think it is normal. I had a lot of brothers and sisters in my family and I learned early that I had to fight for whatever I could; it's part of being a boy. But I was very respectful to my parents, especially my Dad. If I ever got out of line he would smack me one."

"Have you ever had to hit Tommy?" Ms. Fargo inquired softly.

"Sure, a couple of times, but it didn't seem to do any good."

All at once Tommy seemed to be paying attention, his eyes riveted on his father. "Yeah, he hit me a lot, for no reason at all!"

"Now, that's not true, Thomas." Mrs. Davis has a scolding expression on her face. "If you behaved yourself a little better you wouldn't get hit. Ms. Fargo, I can't say that I am in favor of the hitting, but I understand sometimes how frustrating it may be for Bob."

"You don't know how frustrating it is for me, honey." Bob seemed upset. "You don't have to work all day at the office and then come home to contend with all of this. Sometimes I feel like I don't even want to come home."

Ginny gave him a hard stare. "You think things at home are easy all day? I could use some support from you. You think all you have to do is earn the money and I will do everything else. Well, I am not about to do that anymore." . . .

There was a long tense silence.

"What about you, Sissy," Ms. Fargo looked at the little girl, "what do you think about what's happening at home?"

"I think Tommy is a bad boy. I wish he would stop hitting me. I liked him before when he was nice."

Tommy began to fidget and finally he got up from his chair and started to walk around the room.

"Sit down, son," Mr. Davis demanded in a firm voice.

Tommy ignored him.

"Sit down before I knock you down!" . . .

Ms. Fargo spoke thoughtfully. "I get the feeling that people in this family would like things to be different. Bob, I can see how frustrating it must be for you to work so hard and not be able to relax when you get home. And, Ginny, your job is not easy either. You have a lot to do at home and Bob can't be there to help because he has to earn a living. And you kids sound like you would like some things to be different too. It must be hard for you, Tommy, to be catching so much flack these days. I think this also makes it hard for you to have fun at home too, Sissy."

She looked at each person briefly and was sure to make eye contact. "There seems to be a lot going on. What I would like to do is talk with you together and then see the parents for a while and then maybe you kids alone, to hear your sides of the story. I think we are going to need to understand a lot of things to see why this is happening. . . . What I would like everyone to do is to think about how each of you, if you could, would change the other family members so that you would be happier in the family. I will want everyone to tell me that and I want you all to listen to what the others have to say."

*(Sheras & Worchel, 1979, pp. 108–110)*

Like group therapists, family therapists may ascribe to any of the major theoretical models (Gurman et al., 1986), but more and more of them are embracing the principles of *family systems theory*, the theory that holds that each family has its own implicit rules, relationship structure, and communication patterns that shape the behavior of the individual members. And, indeed, 7 percent of today's therapists identify themselves primarily as family systems therapists—13 percent of all social workers, 7 percent of psychologists and counselors, and 1 percent of psychiatrists (Prochaska & Norcross, 1994).

Family systems therapists argue that for one family member to change, the family system must be changed. In one family systems approach, *structural family therapy,* therapists pay particular attention to the family power structure, the role each member plays, and the alliances between family members (Minuchin, 1992, 1987, 1974). The goal of therapy is to build a new family structure in which a working balance, or *homeostasis,* is achieved without the need for any member to adopt a sick role.

In *conjoint family therapy* the therapist focuses primarily on communication in the family system, helping members recognize harmful patterns of communication, appreciate the impact of such patterns on other family members, and change the patterns (Satir, 1987, 1967, 1964). Here a therapist helps a mother, father, and son identify their communication difficulties:

THERAPIST: (To husband) I notice your brow is wrinkled, Ralph. Does that mean you are angry at this moment?

HUSBAND: I did not know that my brow was wrinkled.

THERAPIST: Sometimes a person looks or sounds in a way of which he is not aware. As far as you can tell, what were you thinking and feeling just now?

HUSBAND: I was thinking over what she [his wife] said.

THERAPIST: What thing that she said were you thinking about?

HUSBAND: When she said that when she was talking so loud, she wished I would tell her.

THERAPIST: What were you thinking about that?

HUSBAND: I never thought about telling her. I thought she would get mad.

THERAPIST: Ah, then maybe that wrinkle meant you were puzzled because your wife was hoping you would do something and you did not know she had this hope. Do you suppose that by your wrinkled brow you were signaling that you were puzzled?

HUSBAND: Yeh, I guess so.

THERAPIST: As far as you know, have you ever been in that same spot before, that is, where you were puzzled by something Alice said or did? . . .

WIFE: He never says anything.

THERAPIST: (Smiling, to Alice) Just a minute, Alice, let me hear what Ralph's idea is of what he does. Ralph, how do you think you have let Alice know when you are puzzled?

HUSBAND: I think she knows.

THERAPIST: Well, let's see. Suppose you ask Alice if she knows.

HUSBAND: This is silly.

THERAPIST: (Smiling) I suppose it might seem so in this situation, because Alice is right here and certainly

has heard what your question is. She knows what it is. I have the suspicion, though, that neither you nor Alice are very sure about what the other expects, and I think you have not developed ways to find out. Alice, let's go back to when I commented on Ralph's wrinkled brow. Did you happen to notice it, too?

WIFE: (Complaining) Yes, he always looks like that.

THERAPIST: What kind of message did you get from that wrinkled brow? . . .

WIFE: (Exasperated and tearfully) I don't know.

THERAPIST: Well, maybe the two of you have not yet worked out crystal-clear ways of giving your love and value messages to each other. Everyone needs crystal-clear ways of giving their value messages. (To son) What do you know, Jim, about how you give your value messages to your parents?

*(Satir, 1967, pp. 97–100)*

Research indicates that family therapies of various kinds are indeed useful for certain persons and problems (Alexander et al., 1994; Shadish et al., 1993). Studies have found that the overall improvement rate for cases treated in this format is between 50 and 65 percent, compared to 35 percent for those in placebo control groups (Gurman et al., 1986; Todd & Stanton, 1983). Some studies also clarify that the involvement of the father in family therapy substantially increases the likelihood of a successful outcome.

## Couple Therapy

In *couple therapy,* or *marital therapy,* the therapist works with two people who are in a long-term relationship, focusing again on the structure and communication patterns in their relationship. Often this format of therapy focuses on a husband and wife (see Figure 4-4), but the couple need not be married or even living together. Couple therapy is usually used when a relationship is unsatisfying or in conflict (Epstein et al., 1993). Also, a couple approach may be employed rather than family therapy when a child's psychological problems are traced to problems between the parents (Fauber & Long, 1992).

Certain complaints are particularly common among the people who enter couple therapy. The most common complaints by women include feeling unloved by their spouses (66 percent), constantly belittled (33 percent), and repeatedly criticized (33 percent) (Kelly,

---

*Couple therapy* A therapeutic approach in which the therapist works with two people who share a long-term relationship.

Figure 4-4   *Although the rate of marriage has remained the same in the United States since 1920, the divorce rate has almost tripled. Eleven of every 1,000 people get married each year, but 5 of every 1,000 get divorced. (U.S. Census Bureau, National Center for Health Statistics.)*

1982). Men complain of being neglected (53 percent) and unloved (37 percent) by their spouses and of sensing a longstanding incompatibility of one kind or another (39 percent). Approximately a third of both women and men also complain that they are sexually deprived and that their spouse is chronically angry or nasty.

A number of special couple therapies have been developed. In one widely used approach, *behavioral marital therapy,* therapists help spouses identify and change problem behaviors largely by teaching specific communication and problem-solving skills to the spouses (Cordova & Jacobson, 1993; Jacobson, 1989). Spouses may be instructed to follow such guidelines as these when they discuss their marital problems with each other:

Always begin with something positive when stating the problem.

Use specific behaviors to describe what is bothersome, rather than derogatory labels or overgeneralizations.

Admit one's own role in the development of the problem.

When deciding what actions to take to solve the problem, spouses are to:

Focus on solutions by brainstorming as many solutions as possible.

Focus on mutuality and compromise by considering solutions that involve change by both partners.

Offer to change something in one's own behavior.

In addition, some general guidelines for problem solving are to be followed:

Discuss only one problem at a time; that is, be aware of sidetracking.

Paraphrase what the partner has said and check out perceptions to what was said before responding to it.

(Margolin, 1983, pp. 265–266;
Jacobson & Margolin, 1979)

Recently, some practitioners of behavioral marital therapy have expanded the approach with a treatment

*Although most couples who are seen together in couple therapy are married, the approach is now available and helpful to unmarried heterosexual and gay couples as well.*

called *integrative behavioral couple therapy* (Cordova & Jacobson, 1993). In addition to skill-building techniques, this broader approach is designed to help partners accept marital behaviors that they cannot change and adopt the view that such behaviors are an understandable consequence of basic differences between them.

Research suggests that couples treated with behavioral marital therapy or integrative behavioral couple therapy do indeed develop more effective interpersonal skills and greater tolerance for one another, and feel more satisfied with their relationship than those who receive no treatment at all (Cordova & Jacobson, 1993; Jacobson & Addis, 1993). One review of relevant studies computed that 72 percent of troubled couples treated with these approaches show improvement (Hahlweg & Markman, 1988).

More generally, research suggests that couples treated by most forms of couple therapy show greater improvement in their relationships than couples with similar problems who fail to receive treatment, with no one form of couple therapy standing out as superior to other forms (Alexander et al., 1994). Nevertheless, only about 50 percent of treated couples are "happily married" at the end of couple therapy. Moreover, the few studies that have been conducted on the long-term effects of marital therapy suggest that as many as 38 percent of successfully treated couples may relapse within two to four years after therapy (Snyder et al., 1991). Couple approaches that help individuals gain insight into their marital problems seem to have a lower relapse rate (Snyder et al., 1991).

*"I've been a cow all my life, honey. Don't ask me to change now."*

In *"integrative behavioral couple therapy,"* partners are taught to accept their differences and problematic marital behaviors. (Drawing by Ziegler; © 1992 The New Yorker Magazine, Inc.)

## Community Treatment

The sociocultural view is also expressed in the *community mental health treatment* programs that operate in many locations. In 1963 President John Kennedy called for a "bold new approach" to the treatment of mental disorders—a community approach in which most people with psychological difficulties would receive mental health services from nearby community mental health centers and other publicly funded agencies. The assumption behind this approach was that people would respond better to treatment if they could remain in comfortable and familiar surroundings while trying to recover. Soon after Kennedy's proclamation, Congress passed the Community Mental Health Act, launching the *community mental health movement* across the United States.

A key aspect of the community movement is the principle of *prevention* (Price, 1988). The mandate to prevent, or at least minimize, mental disorders has instilled in clinicians an active (go after the client) attitude that contrasts with the passive (wait for the client) posture of traditional therapy (see Box 4-3). Community workers generally pursue three types of prevention: primary, secondary, and tertiary.

*Primary prevention* consists of efforts to improve community attitudes and policies, with the goal of preventing mental disorders altogether. Community workers may, for example, lobby for better community recreational programs or child-care facilities, consult with a local school board to help formulate a curriculum, or offer public workshops on stress reduction.

Community workers engaged in *secondary prevention* try to identify and treat mental disorders at their earliest stages of development and thus prevent the disorders from reaching more serious levels. Workers may, for instance, consult with schoolteachers, ministers, or police to help them recognize the early signs of psychological dysfunction and teach them how to help people find appropriate treatment (Zax & Cowen, 1976, 1969). Similarly, communities may offer hotlines or walk-in clinics that encourage individuals to make early treatment contacts and receive immediate help before their psychological problems get worse.

Community workers who practice *tertiary prevention* seek to prevent moderate or severe mental disorders from becoming long-term problems by providing appropriate and effective treatment when it is needed. Tertiary care has typically been provided for people with moderate psychological problems, such as anxiety disorders, through traditional therapy at commu-

---

*Community mental health treatment*   A therapy format in which therapists try to work with people in settings close to the clients' home, school, and work.

nity mental health centers across the country. Community programs have often failed, however, to provide the tertiary services needed for hundreds of thousands of severely disturbed persons—*day centers* (or *day hospitals*), treatment facilities that provide day-long activities and treatment; *halfway houses,* residential group homes where live-in staff offer support, guidance, and practical advice to residents; and *sheltered workshops,* protected and supervised workplaces that offer clients occupational training.

Why has the community mental health approach fallen short for so many people with severe disturbances? One of the major reasons is lack of funding. In 1981, when only 750 of the planned 2,000 community mental health centers were in place, virtually all federal funding was withdrawn and replaced with smaller financial grants to the states. As a result, the existing centers have been forced to focus much of their effort on financial survival (Humphreys & Rappaport, 1993).

Whether or not this trend will characterize community mental health for the remainder of the 1990s is unclear. It will depend partly on how health care is reformed (Kiesler, 1992) and also on how state legislatures decide to allocate the hundreds of millions of dollars saved by the continuing closing of large state hospitals. Mental health advocates continue to urge politicians to put those savings into community-based programs, but their advice may not be heeded. In the meantime, the enormous promise of community mental health and prevention programs remains unfulfilled for many in our society.

## Assessing the Sociocultural Model

The sociocultural model has added an important dimension to the understanding and treatment of abnormal functioning. Today most clinicians take family structure and social issues into account in their efforts to understand and address individual cases of mental disorder, factors that were largely overlooked just thirty years ago. Moreover, practitioners are by and large more sensitive to the negative impact of clinical labels. And, finally, as we have just observed, sociocultural treatment formats often succeed where more traditional approaches have failed.

At the same time, the sociocultural model, like other models, leaves some questions unanswered and

problems unresolved. To begin with, the studies done to date have failed to support certain key predictions of the sociocultural model (Gove, 1982). Although some forms of abnormality are indeed uniquely associated with certain societies, as the model predicts, other forms, particularly the most severe ones, appear to be universal, with a similar incidence and similar symptoms in a wide range of settings. Schizophrenia, for example, occurs throughout the world irrespective of a given country's values and pressures. Approximately 1 percent of people everywhere appear to exhibit this disorder's central symptoms of confusion, distorted ideas, and hallucinations; and every society considers these symptoms abnormal (Regier et al., 1993; Murphy, 1976).

Still another problem is that sociocultural research findings are often difficult to interpret. Studies that reveal a relationship between sociocultural factors and mental disorders may fail to establish that the former cause the latter. For example, a number of studies show a link between family conflict and schizophrenic disorders (Vaughan et al., 1992). Although this finding may indicate that family dysfunction helps cause schizophrenia, it is equally possible that the schizophrenic behavior of a family member disrupts normal family functioning and creates conflicts.

Perhaps the most serious limitation of the sociocultural model is its inability to predict psychopathology in specific individuals. If, say, the current emphasis on thinness in women is a major reason for the growing incidence of anorexia nervosa in Western nations, why do only a small fraction of the women in these countries manifest this disorder? Are still other factors necessary for the disorder to develop? In response to such criticisms, most clinicians choose to view sociocultural explanations as going hand in hand with biological or psychological explanations. They believe that sociocultural variables may set a climate favorable to the development of certain mental disorders, but that biological or psychological conditions or both must also be present for the mental disorders to unfold.

*Day center (day hospital)*    A treatment center that provides daylong therapeutic activities and care.

*Halfway house*    A group home that has a live-in staff to offer support, guidance, and practical advice to residents.

*Sheltered workshop*    A protected and supervised workplace that offers clients occupational training.

*Summing Up*
*Sociocultural theorists believe that mental disorders result largely from social and cultural forces brought to bear on the individual, including dysfunctional family relationships and communication, societal stress, and harmful labeling. The principles of the sociocultural model are put into practice in such therapy formats as group, family, couple, and community therapy.*

## Box 4-3

# *The Sociocultural Model in Action: Treating the Victims of Disaster*

In 1992, about 250,000 people were displaced by Hurricane Andrew, and thousands more were affected by it. For years the American Red Cross has provided food, shelter, and clothing when needed by survivors of disasters such as this, and the federal government has helped them find the financial resources for rebuilding their ruined homes and businesses. But until recently no organization addressed the psychological needs of disaster survivors, even though a very large number appear to require mental health services after large-scale disasters. Researchers estimate, for example, that survivors experience a 17 percent increase in mental disorders, and over half suffer from significant mental distress (Rubonis & Bickman, 1991; Roberts, 1990).

In 1991 the American Psychological Association, in collaboration with the American Red Cross, created the Disaster Relief Network to help provide the large numbers of mental health professionals needed after a disaster. The more than 1200 psychologists in the network volunteer to provide free emergency mental health services at disaster sites throughout the United States (APA, 1991). They

*In the aftermath of Hurricane Andrew, a mother must wash her newborn baby with water from a jug, while the family takes up residence in a tent.*

have been mobilized for such natural disasters as the Midwest's Great Flood of 1993, Hurricane Andrew in 1992, and the earthquakes in southern California, and such human-caused disasters as the Los Angeles riots, the Oklahoma City federal building and World Trade Center bombings, and business office shootings.

The Disaster Relief Network provides active short-term community intervention because traditional, longer-term mental health services are often not appropriate, and in any case are usually not available or are not sought after a disaster (Joyner & Swenson, 1993). Unfortunately, the emotional support that survivors may seek out and receive from friends and relatives often breaks down

within a few days or weeks. People soon get tired of hearing about the survivors' experiences and the stress of the disaster. Moreover, many survivors feel guilty about discussing their own losses if others' losses were greater, and so are reluctant to seek out professional help. Those who are unmarried and without children, for example, often feel they are supposed to be able to deal with their losses and anguish better than people who also have to care for children. And many survivors simply do not recognize their own emotional fragility immediately after a disaster (Michaelson, 1993). People who live in poverty are in particular need of community-level interventions. These survivors apparently have more psychological distress after disasters than survivors with higher incomes (Gibbs, 1989), they cannot afford private counseling, and they are also less likely to know where to go to seek counseling.

Since psychological needs cannot be addressed if basic survival needs are not met, the first aim of disaster mental health professionals arriving at a disaster site is to help survivors meet their basic needs as quickly as possible. Dur-

# *Relationships between the Models*

The models we have examined in the past two chapters vary widely in the dimensions of behavior, emotion, and thought they focus on; the assumptions and

concepts they employ; and the conclusions they reach. Each has proponents, many of whom not only hold their particular model to be the most enlightened but criticize the other models as misleading or even foolish (Marmor, 1987). Yet none of the models has proved consistently superior to the rest. Each helps us appreciate a critical dimension of human functioning,

ing the Great Flood of 1993, for example, mental health professionals worked in shelters and service centers and rode in Red Cross emergency vehicles to deliver food and water along with counseling services. Other counselors joined flood victims in piling sandbags to protect their homes from further damage. Counselors also used these early contacts with victims as an opportunity to determine which individuals were most in need of counseling. At this stage any counseling had to be brief, perhaps only 10 to 30 minutes with each person, often in a highly distracting environment—a shelter, a sandbag brigade, a line at a water truck.

Once mental health volunteers become involved in the community, they may intervene more actively to meet the psychological needs of the survivors. Psychologists and other mental health workers often use a four-stage approach, as the community workers did during the Great Flood of 1993 (Michaelson, 1993).

1. *Normalize people's responses to the disaster.* The counselors educate survivors about the symptoms they may experience, such as sleep disturbances, eating disturbances, and difficulty concentrating. Survivors of disasters may also suffer from irritation, sadness, grief, fear, anger, and resentment. Essentially, survivors are given per-

mission to experience these emotions and told that these are normal responses to a disaster.
2. *Diffuse anxiety, anger, and frustration.* To diffuse the anxiety, anger, and frustration that survivors often feel after a disaster, counselors help them talk about their experiences and their feelings about the event.
3. *Teach self-helping skills.* Community professionals educate and train survivors to develop such self-help skills as stress management. As part of this effort, they may hand out fliers on handling stress to survivors. The survivors can then put the fliers aside until they need the information.
4. *Provide referrals.* The workers eventually may refer survivors to other professionals and agencies that can provide long-term counseling. Some mental disorders may emerge within days; others, however, may not surface for months after the disaster. It is estimated that between 15 and 25 percent of survivors need more specialized assistance.

The mental health professionals counsel not only the survivors but relief workers, who can become overwhelmed by the traumas they witness. During the Los Angeles riots, for example, the primary responsibility of many counselors was to debrief Red Cross workers

(Youngstrom, 1992)—to help them vent and normalize their feelings and teach them about acute and posttraumatic stress disorders and how to identify victims who need further treatment. Many mental health professionals who live in the disaster area need counseling themselves, since they, too, are survivors. The dual role they are thrown into may make it difficult for them to deal with their own experiences.

To meet the needs of large numbers of disaster survivors, *paraprofessionals*—lay persons who receive training and supervision from professionals—may also be called upon. For example, graduate students at various schools in the Los Angeles area were enlisted to provide counseling for survivors of the riots. Some of them were actually more effective than professionals because they were more familiar with the afflicted community and shared the survivors' socioeconomic and minority status.

Clearly, community-level interventions are essential after large-scale disasters to provide psychological counseling to needy survivors who might not seek out mental health services. The Disaster Relief Network has helped address the enormous need for this type of counseling, and at the same time has demonstrated the application of the sociocultural theory at its best.

and each has important strengths as well as serious limitations.

In fact, while today's models may differ from one another in significant ways, their conclusions are often compatible (Friman et al., 1993). Certainly our understanding of a person's abnormal behavior is more complete if we appreciate the biological, psychological, *and*

sociocultural aspects of his or her problem rather than one of those aspects to the exclusion of the rest. Even the various psychological models can sometimes be compatible. In cases of sexual dysfunction, for example, psychodynamic causes (such as internal conflicts in childhood), behavioral causes (such as learning incorrect sexual techniques), and cognitive causes (such as misconceptions about sex) often seem to combine to produce the problem.

The models also demonstrate compatibility when each emphasizes a different kind of causal factor. When theorists talk about a disorder's cause, they are referring either to *predisposing factors,* events that occur long before the appearance of the disorder and set the stage for later difficulties; to *precipitating factors,* events that trigger the disorder; or to *maintaining factors,* events that keep the disorder going.

When each of several models focuses on a different kind of causal factor, their explanations may be far from contradictory. Clinicians are increasingly embracing **diathesis-stress** explanations of abnormal behavior—the view that a person must first have a biological, psychological, or sociocultural predisposition to a disorder and must then be subjected to an immediate form of stress to develop and maintain certain forms of abnormality. If we were to explore a case of depression, for instance, we might well find a neurotransmitter dysfunction as a predisposing factor, a major loss as a precipitating factor, and errors in logic as a maintaining factor.

As different kinds of disorders are presented throughout this textbook, we will look at how the proponents of today's models explain each disorder, how each model's practitioners treat people with the disorder, and how well the explanations and treatment approaches are supported by research. Moreover, we will observe both how the explanations and treatments differ *and* how they may build upon and illuminate each other.

## Chapter Review

1. *The Biological and Sociocultural Models:* Many theorists and practitioners focus primarily on biological or sociocultural factors to explain or treat abnormal behavior. Those with a biological bent look inward at the biological processes that accompany all human functioning. In contrast, sociocultural theorists look outward at the social rules, pressures, and related factors which impact on members of a society.

2. *Biological Explanations:* Biological theorists believe that psychological disorders are linked to anatomical or biochemical problems in the brain. Researchers have found that abnormalities in the activity of different *neurotransmitters*—chemicals released into the *synapse* between two *neurons*—are often connected with different psychological disorders.

3. *Biological Therapies: Biological therapies* comprise physical and chemical methods developed to help people overcome their psychological problems. The principal kinds of biological interventions are *drug therapy, electroconvulsive therapy,* and, on rare occasions, *psychosurgery.*

4. *Sociocultural Explanations:* Some sociocultural theorists focus on *family structure and communication;* they see the family as a system of interacting parts in which structure, rules, and patterns of communication may force family members to behave in abnormal ways. Others focus on *societal stress* and consider the unique characteristics of a given society that may create special problems for its members and heighten the likelihood of abnormal functioning. Still other theorists focus on *societal labels and reactions;* they hold that society categorizes certain people as "crazy" or "mentally ill," and that the label produces expectations that influence the way the person behaves and is treated.

5. *Sociocultural Therapies:* Sociocultural principles are on display in such therapy formats as group, family, couple, and community therapy. Some therapists continue to apply the explanations and concepts of other models when working with clients in these broad formats. However, increasingly, practitioners who use such formats are embracing a sociocultural view of abnormal functioning and are using special sociocultural strategies in their work.

   A. Research indicates that **group therapy** is of help to many clients. The feedback and support that group members experience is usually beneficial. Two specialized forms of group therapy are *psychodrama* and the *self-help groups.*

   B. *Family therapy* is a format in which therapists meet with all members of a family, point out problematic behavior and interactions, and work on helping the whole family to change. In *couple therapy,* the therapist works with two people who share a long-term relationship. An increasing body of research on the effectiveness of various family and couple therapies suggests that they are useful for some problems and under some circumstances.

   C. In *community treatment,* therapists try to work with persons in settings close to home, school, and work. Their goal is to either prevent mental disorders altogether by improving community attitudes and policies *(primary prevention)*, prevent disorders from reaching a more serious level by early identification and treatment in schools, church, or other community settings *(secondary prevention)*, or prevent moderate or severe disorders from becoming long-term problems by providing appropriate and effective treatment in traditional settings when needed *(tertiary prevention)*.

6. *Relationships between the Models:* The models vary widely yet they often provide compatible conclusions, suggesting that our understanding of a person's abnormal behavior is more complete if we appreciate the biological, psychological, *and* sociocultural aspects of his or her problem.

7. *The Diathesis-Stress Concept:* Clinicians are increasingly embracing *diathesis-stress* explanations of abnormal behavior—the view that people must first have a biological, psychological, or sociocultural predisposition to a disorder and must then be subjected to an immediate form of stress to develop and maintain certain forms of abnormality.

## Key Terms

psychotropic drug
neuron
glia
hindbrain
midbrain
forebrain
dendrite
axon
nerve ending
synapse
neurotransmitter
receptor
GABA
dopamine
norepinephrine
serotonin

risk study
drug therapy
antianxiety drug
minor tranquilizer
anxiolytic
antidepressant drug
MAO inhibitor
tricyclic
second-generation
    antidepressant
antibipolar drug
lithium
antipsychotic drug
extrapyramidal effect
electroconvulsive therapy
psychosurgery

lobotomy
sociology
anthropology
family systems theory
homeostasis
group therapy
psychodrama
self-help group
mutual-help group
family therapy
structural family therapy
conjoint family therapy
couple therapy
marital therapy
behavioral marital
    therapy

integrative behavioral
    couple therapy
community mental health
    treatment
community mental health
    movement
primary prevention
secondary prevention
tertiary prevention
day center
day hospital
halfway house
sheltered workshop
diathesis-stress
    explanation

## Quick Quiz

1. What are the key regions of the brain? How do brain messages travel from neuron to neuron?

2. What kinds of problems in brain-cell functioning have researchers linked to mental disorders?

3. What kinds of methods and events have led to our current understanding of the biological underpinnings of abnormal behavior?

4. Describe the different forms of biological treatment used in cases of abnormal psychological functioning.

5. What are the key principles and concepts of family systems theory?

6. What kinds of societal stress appear to be linked to abnormal functioning?

7. How do diagnostic labels themselves produce or maintain abnormal behavior, according to sociocultural theorists?

8. What curative features do various forms of successful group therapy seem to share?

9. Identify and describe some of the leading forms of family therapy and couple therapy.

10. In what ways do community mental health workers try to prevent mental disorders?

11. According to research, how effective are each of the sociocultural treatment approaches?

# 5

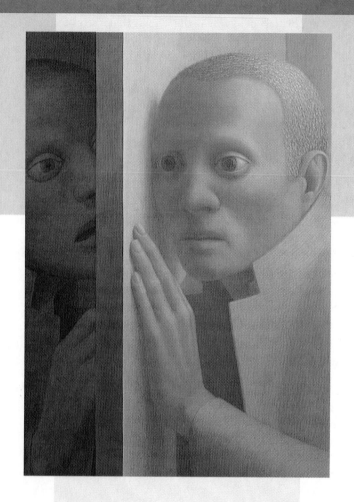

# Generalized Anxiety Disorder and Phobias

## Topic Overview

*Stress, Coping, and the Anxiety Response*

*Generalized Anxiety Disorder*

*Phobias*
Agoraphobia
Social Phobias
Specific Phobias

Think about a time when your breathing quickened, your muscles tensed, and your heart pounded with a sudden sense of dread. Was it when your car almost skidded off the road in the rain? When your professor announced a pop quiz? What about when the person you most cared about went out with someone else, or your boss suggested that your job performance ought to improve? Any time you confront what seems to be a serious threat to your well-being, you may react with the state of tension or alarm known as *fear*. Sometimes, though, you cannot pinpoint a specific cause for alarm, but still you feel tense and edgy, as if something unpleasant were going to happen. The ominous sense of being menaced by an unspecified threat is usually termed *anxiety,* and it has the same clinical features—the same acceleration of breathing, the muscular tension, perspiration, and so forth—as fear.

Although everyday experiences of fear and anxiety are not pleasant, they have an adaptive function: they prepare us for action—for "fight or flight"—when danger threatens. They may motivate us to drive more cautiously in a storm, keep up with our reading assignments, treat our date more sensitively, and work harder at our job. Unfortunately, some people suffer such continuous and disabling fear and anxiety that they cannot lead a normal life. Their discomfort is too severe or too frequent; it lasts too long; it is triggered too readily by what the sufferers themselves recognize as minimal, unspecified, or nonexistent threats. These people are said to have an *anxiety disorder.*

Anxiety disorders are the most common mental disorders in the United States. In any given year, between 15 and 17 percent of the adult population—23 million people—suffer from one or another of the six anxiety disorders identified by DSM-IV (Kessler et al., 1994; Regier et al., 1993; Davidson et al., 1991). Almost a third of these people receive treatment (Narrow et al., 1993). Collectively, the anxiety disorders are also society's most expensive mental disorders, costing an estimated total of $46.6 billion in 1990 alone, almost a third of all mental health costs (Rovner, 1993). Approximately $35 billion of that amount is attributable to indirect costs, such as the value of reduced or lost work productivity; the rest is accounted for by treatment fees.

People with *generalized anxiety disorder* experience general and persistent feelings of anxiety. People with *phobias* experience a persistent and irrational fear of a specific object, activity, or situation. People with *panic disorder* have recurrent attacks of terror. Those with *obsessive-compulsive disorder* are beset by recurrent and unwanted thoughts that cause anxiety or by the need to perform repetitive and ritualistic actions to reduce anxiety. People with *acute stress disorder* and *posttraumatic stress disorder* are tormented by fear and related symptoms well after a traumatic event (military combat, rape, torture) has ended. Typically a client will be assigned only one of these diagnoses at a time, but studies suggest that most people with a primary diagnosis of one anxiety disorder also meet the criteria for a secondary diagnosis of another anxiety disorder (Brown et al., 1993; Sanderson et al., 1990).

In this chapter, we shall cover generalized anxiety disorder and phobias, the most common anxiety disordes and the ones with the longest history of study. The other anxiety disorders—panic disorder, obsessive-compulsive disorder, and stress disorders—will be the subject of Chapter 6. It is only in recent years that these latter disorders have come to be understood and successfully treated.

# Stress, Coping, and the Anxiety Response

Before we examine any of the anxiety disorders, we need to take a closer look at the kinds of situations that normally cause us to feel threatened and the kinds of changes we experience in response to such situations. Actually, we feel some degree of threat, called a state of *stress,* whenever we are confronted with demands or opportunities that require us to change in some manner. A state of stress has two components: a *stressor,* the event that creates the demands, and a *stress response,* a person's idiosyncratic reactions to the demands.

The stressors of life may take the form of daily hassles, such as rush-hour traffic or the appearance of unexpected company; major life events or transitions, such as college graduation or marriage; chronic problems, such as poverty, poor health, or overcrowded living conditions; or traumatic events, such as catastrophic accidents, assaults, or military combat.

Our response to such stressors is influenced by how we *appraise* both the events and our capacity to react to them in an effective way (Lazarus & Folkman, 1984). People who sense that they have sufficient ability and resources to cope are more likely to respond constructively to stressors, take them in stride, and avoid having negative emotional, behavioral, and cognitive reactions to them.

---

*Stressor*    An event that creates a degree of threat by confronting a person with a demand or opportunity for change of some kind.

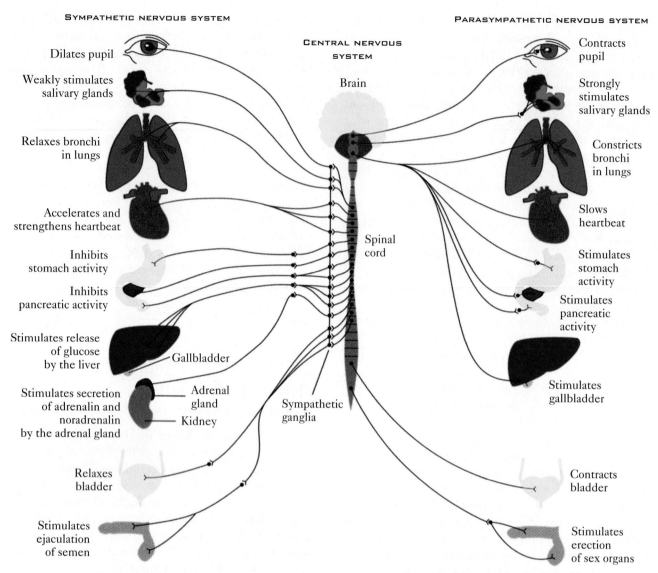

SYMPATHETIC NERVOUS SYSTEM                    CENTRAL NERVOUS SYSTEM                    PARASYMPATHETIC NERVOUS SYSTEM

Dilates pupil

Weakly stimulates salivary glands

Relaxes bronchi in lungs

Accelerates and strengthens heartbeat

Inhibits stomach activity

Inhibits pancreatic activity

Stimulates release of glucose by the liver

Stimulates secretion of adrenalin and noradrenalin by the adrenal gland

Relaxes bladder

Stimulates ejaculation of semen

Brain

Spinal cord

Gallbladder

Adrenal gland

Kidney

Sympathetic ganglia

Contracts pupil

Strongly stimulates salivary glands

Constricts bronchi in lungs

Slows heartbeat

Stimulates stomach activity

Stimulates pancreatic activity

Stimulates gallbladder

Contracts bladder

Stimulates erection of sex organs

**Figure 5-1**  *The autonomic nervous system (ANS) regulates the involuntary functions of the body. When the sympathetic division of the ANS is activated, it stimulates some organs and inhibits others. The result is a state of general arousal. In contrast, the parasympathetic division's stimulation and inhibition of various organs have an overall calming effect.*

One of the key human responses to a stressor we appraise as threatening is a sense of fear. Fear is actually a package of responses—physical, emotional, and cognitive. Physically, we perspire, our breathing quickens, our muscles tense, and our heart beats faster. We may turn pale and develop goose bumps, our lips may tremble, and we may feel nauseated. If the situation is extremely threatening, we may feel such emotions as horror, dread, and even panic. Fear can interfere with our ability to concentrate and distort our view of the world. We may exaggerate the harm that actually threatens us or remember things incorrectly after the threat has passed.

These features of the fear and anxiety response are generated by the action of the body's *autonomic nervous system (ANS)*, an extensive network of nerve fibers that connect the *central nervous system* (the brain and spinal cord) to all the other organs of the body. The ANS helps regulate the involuntary activities of these organs—breathing, heartbeat, blood pressure, perspiration, and the like (See Figure 5-1).

When our brain interprets a situation as dangerous, it excites a special group of ANS fibers (collectively

*Autonomic nervous system (ANS)*   The extensive network of nerve fibers that connect the central nervous system to all the other organs of the body.

*Although most people are terrified by the very thought of hang gliding above the clouds, some are stimulated by the experience and others are calmed by it. Such individual reactions represent differences in situation, or state, anxiety.*

known as the *sympathetic nervous system*) that quicken our heartbeat and produce the other changes that we experience as fear or anxiety. When a perceived danger passes, a second group of ANS nerve fibers, the *parasympathetic nervous system,* return our heartbeat and other body processes to normal. Together, these two parts of the ANS help regulate our fear and anxiety reactions and enable our body to maintain both the stability and the adaptability essential to life.

We all have our own level of ongoing anxiety. Some people are always relaxed, while others almost always feel some tension, even when no threat is apparent. A person's general level of anxiety is sometimes called *trait anxiety,* because it seems to be a trait or characteristic that the person brings to each event in life (Spielberger, 1985, 1966). People also differ in their sense of which situations are threatening. Walking through a forest, for example, may be fearsome for one person but relaxing for another. Such variations are called differences in *situation,* or *state, anxiety.* The fear and anxiety most of us have experienced, however, are quite different from the disproportionate, frequent, and enduring waves of tension and dread experienced by persons who suffer from an anxiety disorder.

*Summing Up*
*We all experience fear and anxiety in life, particularly in the face of stressors that we appraise as threatening. We each have different levels of ongoing anxiety, and we each find certain situations more threatening than others. Only some of us, however, experience an anxiety disorder.*

## Generalized Anxiety Disorder

Bob Donaldson was a 22-year-old carpenter referred to the psychiatric outpatient department of a community hospital. . . . During the initial interview Bob was visibly distressed. He appeared tense, worried, and frightened. He sat on the edge of his chair, tapping his foot and fidgeting with a pencil on the psychiatrist's desk. He sighed frequently, took deep breaths between sentences, and periodically exhaled audibly and changed his position as he attempted to relate his story:

> BOB: It's been an awful month. I can't seem to do anything. I don't know whether I'm coming or going. I'm afraid I'm going crazy or something.

DOCTOR: What makes you think that?

BOB: I can't concentrate. My boss tells me to do something and I start to do it, but before I've taken five steps I don't know what I started out to do. I get dizzy and I can feel my heart beating and everything looks like it's shimmering or far away from me or something—it's unbelievable.

DOCTOR: What thoughts come to mind when you're feeling like this?

BOB: I just think, "Oh, Christ, my heart is really beating, my head is swimming, my ears are ringing—I'm either going to die or go crazy."

DOCTOR: What happens then?

BOB: Well, it doesn't last more than a few seconds, I mean that intense feeling. I come back down to earth, but then I'm worrying what's the matter with me all the time, or checking my pulse to see how fast it's going, or feeling my palms to see if they're sweating.

DOCTOR: Can others see what you're going through?

BOB: You know, I doubt it. I hide it. I haven't been seeing my friends. . . . I'm not with them when I'm with them anyway—I'm just sitting there worrying. . . . So, anyway, I just go home and turn on the TV or pick up the sports page, but I can't really get into that either.

Bob went on to say that he had stopped playing softball because of fatigability and trouble concentrating. On several occasions during the past two weeks he was unable to go to work because he was "too nervous."

*(Spitzer et al., 1983, pp. 11–12)*

Bob suffers from many of the symptoms of a ***generalized anxiety disorder***. Like Bob, people with this disorder experience excessive anxiety and worry about numerous events or activities (see Box 5-1). Given the scope of their worries, their problem is often described as *free-floating anxiety*.

Generalized anxiety disorder is relatively common in our society. Surveys suggest that up to 3.8 percent of the United States population have the symptoms of this disorder in any given year (Kessler et al., 1994; Blazer et al., 1991), and around a quarter of these people seek treatment (see Figure 5-2). Although the disorder may emerge at any age, it most commonly first appears in childhood or adolescence. Women diagnosed with this disorder outnumber men 2 to 1.

Like Bob, people with a generalized anxiety disorder typically feel restless, keyed up, or on edge,

---

*Generalized anxiety disorder*   A disorder characterized by persistent and excessive feelings of anxiety and worry about numerous events and activities.

---

are easily fatigued, have difficulty concentrating, act irritable, experience muscle tension, and have sleep problems. The symptoms last at least six months (APA, 1994). Nevertheless, most people with this disorder are able, with some difficulty, to maintain adequate social relationships and occupational activities.

A variety of factors have been cited to explain the development of generalized anxiety disorder. We shall examine here the views and treatments offered by proponents of the sociocultural, psychodynamic, humanistic-existential, cognitive, and biological models. The behavioral perspective will be examined later when we turn our attention to phobias, because that model's approach to generalized anxiety disorder and phobias is essentially the same.

## The Sociocultural Perspective

According to sociocultural theorists, a generalized anxiety disorder is more likely to develop in people who are confronted with societal pressures and situations that pose real danger. Studies have found that people in highly threatening environments are indeed more likely to develop the general feelings of tension, anxiety, and fatigue, the exaggerated startle reactions, and the sleep disturbances that characterize this disorder (Baum & Fleming, 1993; Melick et al., 1982).

### Societal Changes

Stressful changes have occurred in our society over the past several decades. Older workers have felt increasingly threatened by the introduction of computer technology, parents by the increased media attention to child abuse and abduction, and travelers by the heightened incidence of terrorism. In addition, public concern about the dangers of nuclear energy has intensified. As sociocultural theorists might predict, these societal stresses have been accompanied by steady increases in the prevalence of generalized anxiety disorder throughout the United States.

A 1975 survey of the general population indicated that 2.5 percent of the population suffered from generalized anxiety disorder (Weissman et al., 1978). That rate has now increased to 3.8 percent (Regier et al., 1993; Blazer et al., 1991). Moreover, surveys indicate that the prevalence rate of generalized anxiety disorder is typically higher in urbanized countries that have greater numbers of stressful changes than in less urbanized countries (Compton et al., 1991). Similarly, prevalence studies across the world (Japan, Britain, Canada, Taiwan, Poland, India, France, Italy, Chile, Israel, and Nigeria) suggest that the prevalence of anx-

## Box 5-1

# *Fears, Shmears: The Odds Are Usually on Our Side*

People with anxiety disorders have an enormous range of fears. And millions without these disorders worry about possible disaster every day. Most of the feared events are *possible* but, thank goodness, *not probable*. What are the actual odds that commonly feared events will happen to us? This sample list shows the range of probability; it also makes it clear that the odds are usually heavily in our favor.

| | |
|---|---|
| One will undergo an IRS audit this year. | 1 in 100 |
| A city resident will be a victim of a violent crime. | 1 in 60 |
| A small-town resident will be a victim of a violent crime | 1 in 2,000 |
| One will be bumped off any given airline flight. | 1 in 4,000 |
| One will be struck by lightning. | 1 in 9,100 |
| One will be murdered this year. | 1 in 12,000 |

| | |
|---|---|
| One will be killed on one's next bus ride. | 1 in 500 million |
| One will be hit by a baseball at a major-league game. | 1 in 300,000 |
| One will drown in the tub this year. | 1 in 685,000 |
| One will be killed in an air crash. | 1 in 4.6 million |
| One's house will have a fire this year. | 1 in 200 |
| One will die in a fire this year. | 1 in 40,200 |
| One will die in a fall. | 1 in 200,000 |
| One's carton will contain a broken egg. | 1 in 10 |
| One will contract AIDS from a blood transfusion. | 1 in 100,000 |
| One will be attacked by a shark. | 1 in 4 million |
| One will receive a diagnosis of cancer this year. | 1 in 8,000 |

| | |
|---|---|
| A woman will develop breast cancer during her lifetime. | 1 in 9 |
| One will develop a brain tumor this year. | 1 in 25,000 |
| A piano player will eventually develop lower back pain. | 1 in 3 |
| One will be killed in one's next automobile outing. | 1 in 4 million |
| One will eventually die in an automobile accident. | 1 in 140 |
| Condom use will eventually fail to prevent pregnancy. | 1 in 10 |
| An IUD will eventually fail to prevent pregnancy. | 1 in 10 |
| Coitus interruptus will eventually fail to prevent pregnancy. | 1 in 5 |

*(Adapted from Krantz, 1992)*

iety symptoms often increases along with societal changes caused by war, political oppression, urbanization, modernization, and related national events (Compton et al., 1991).

### Consider This
It appears that culture can play a significant role in the development of generalized anxiety disorder. What kinds of societal changes or personal qualities might act to relieve the stresses of modern society, and thus reduce the likelihood of people developing this disorder?

## Poverty and Race

One of the most direct indicators of societal stress is poverty. People without sufficient means typically live in homes that are more rundown and communities with higher crime rates, have fewer educational and job opportunities and more job instability, and are at greater risk for health problems. As sociocultural theorists would predict, research indicates that poorer people have a higher rate of generalized anxiety disorder. In the United States, for example, the rate is twice as high among people with incomes of less than $10,000 a year as among those with higher incomes (Blazer et

*The stresses of living and working in a complex, highly technological society may also increase the prevalence of anxiety symptoms and disorders.*

al., 1991). Indeed, as job income decreases in this country, the rate of generalized anxiety disorder steadily increases.

Since race is closely related to income and job opportunity in the United States (Belle, 1990), it is not surprising that the prevalence rate of generalized anxiety disorder is also tied to race (see Figure 5-3). In any given year, approximately 6 percent of all African Americans suffer from this disorder, compared to 3.5 percent of white Americans. African American women, perhaps the most socially stressed group in this country (Bennett, 1987), have the highest rate of all (6.6 percent).

Even granting the broad influence of sociocultural factors, theorists still must explain why some people develop a generalized anxiety disorder and others do not. The psychodynamic, humanistic-existential, cognitive, and biological schools of thought have each tried to provide an explanation of this kind, along with corresponding treatments.

## The Psychodynamic Perspective

Sigmund Freud (1933, 1917) formulated the initial psychodynamic position on generalized anxiety disorder. To begin with, he proposed that all persons experience anxiety (1) when they are repeatedly prevented, by their parents or by circumstances, from expressing their id impulses *(neurotic anxiety)* or (2) when they are punished or threatened for expressing those impulses *(moral anxiety)*. In addition, as we saw in Chapter 3, Freud proposed that people try to control their neurotic and moral anxiety by employing ego defense mechanisms.

### Psychodynamic Explanations

According to Freud, a pattern of broad anxiety results when a person's defense mechanisms are overrun by his or her neurotic or moral anxiety. It may be that the person's level of anxiety is just too high. If, for example, a young boy is harshly spanked every time he cries for milk as an infant, messes his pants as a 2-year-old, and explores his genitals as a toddler, he may eventually come to believe that his various id impulses are extremely dangerous and may experience overwhelming anxiety whenever he has such impulses. Or perhaps the defense mechanisms are too weak or inadequate. Overprotected children, shielded by their parents from all frustrations and sources of anxiety, have little opportunity to develop effective defense mechanisms. Later, when they encounter the inevitable pressures of adult life, their defense mechanisms may be too weak to cope with the resulting anxieties. Many contemporary psychodynamic theorists differ with some of Freud's specific notions, but they too believe that generalized anxiety disorder can be traced to inadequacies in the early relationships between children and their parents.

To support the psychodynamic explanations of generalized anxiety disorder, researchers have tried to show that people with this disorder use defense mechanisms excessively. Evaluators who have looked for ev-

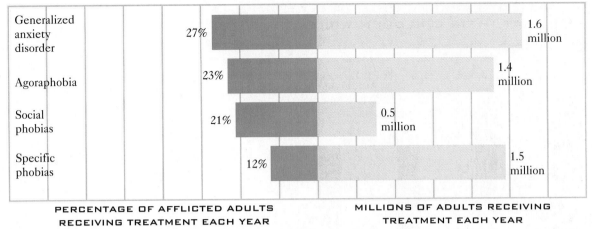

Figure 5-2    *Who receives treatment for their anxiety disorders? More than a quarter of all persons who have a generalized anxiety disorder in the United States receive professional treatment each year, but only about one-eighth of those with a specific phobia, a less disabling disorder, receive treatment. (Adapted from Regier et al., 1993; Blazer et al., 1991; Boyd et al., 1990.)*

idence of repression in the transcripts of early therapy sessions with anxious patients have found that when the patients are asked to discuss anxiety-arousing experiences, they do often react defensively by quickly forgetting what they were just talking about, changing the direction of the discussion, or denying negative feelings (Luborsky, 1973).

Several findings are also consistent with the psychodynamic claim that extreme punishment for early id impulses may lead to higher levels of anxiety at later points in life (Chiu, 1971). In many cultures where children are regularly punished and threatened, adults seem to have more fears and anxieties (Whiting et al., 1966). In addition, several studies have supported the psychodynamic position that extreme protectiveness by parents may also lead to heightened anxiety in their children (Jenkins, 1968).

Although these studies are consistent with the psychodynamic explanation of generalized anxiety disorder, they have been criticized on several grounds. First, some scientists question whether certain studies show what they claim to show. When people are reluctant to talk about upsetting events early in therapy, for example, they are not necessarily repressing those events. They may be consciously focusing on the positive aspects of their lives or be too embarrassed to share personal negative events until they develop trust in the therapist.

Second, even if people in such studies are exhibiting repression, it does not necessarily follow that people with generalized anxiety disorder are afraid of their id impulses or that defense mechanisms have broken down. Even strong proponents of the psychodynamic perspective acknowledge that it is very difficult to de-

velop research designs capable of testing the fundamental theoretical components of this model.

A final problem is that a number of research studies and clinical reports have actually contradicted the psychodynamic explanation. In one, sixteen people with generalized anxiety disorder were interviewed to obtain histories of their upbringing (Raskin et al., 1982). They reported relatively little of the disturbed childhood environments that psychodynamic therapists might expect for people with this disorder.

## Psychodynamic Therapies

As we observed in Chapter 3, psychodynamic therapists approach all psychological problems in a similar manner, using the techniques of free association and therapist interpretations of transference, resistance, and dreams to help patients work through and overcome their problems. Using such techniques, Freudian psychodynamic therapists try to help clients with generalized anxiety disorder become less afraid of their id impulses and more able to control them successfully. Other psychodynamic therapists such as object relations therapists focus more on helping anxious patients identify and resolve the anxiety-provoking childhood relationship problems that they seem to be repeating in adulthood (Zerbe, 1990; Diamond, 1987).

Controlled research has not consistently supported the effectiveness of psychodynamic approaches in cases of generalized anxiety disorder (Svartberg & Stiles, 1991; Prochaska, 1984). The bulk of evidence suggests that psychodynamic therapy is at best of modest help to people suffering from this disorder (Nemiah, 1984; Berk & Efran, 1983).

## PERCENTAGE OF PARENTS WHO WORRY "A LOT" THAT THEIR CHILDREN WILL:

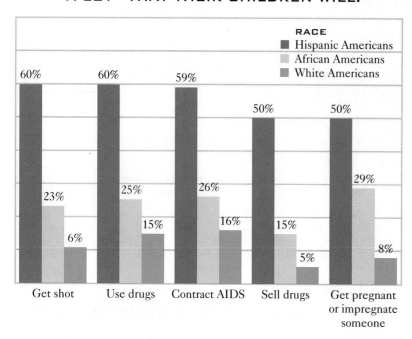

## PERCENTAGE OF PARENTS WHO WORRY "A LOT" THAT THEIR CHILDREN WILL:

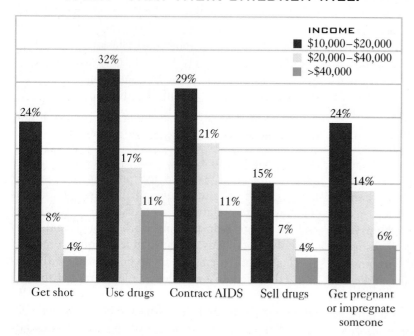

**Figure 5-3** *According to a survey of 1,738 parents in the United States, African Americans and Hispanic Americans are much more likely than white Americans to worry significantly about their children's safety, future, and survival. Similarly, parents with lower incomes are much more likely than wealthier parents to worry greatly about their children's welfare, irrespective of race, suggesting that the higher anxiety levels of racial minority groups may be largely a matter of living in poorer, more deprived, or more dangerous environments. (Adapted from National Commission on Children, 1991.)*

## The Humanistic and Existential Perspectives

Humanistic and existential theorists propose that a generalized anxiety disorder, like other mental disorders, arises when people stop looking at themselves honestly and acceptingly and instead deny and distort their true thoughts, emotions, and behavior. Their de-

fensive postures ultimately serve to make them extremely anxious and incapable of fulfilling their potential as human beings.

### Humanistic Explanations and Treatments

The humanistic position on why people develop a generalized anxiety disorder is best illustrated by Carl

Rogers' explanation. As we observed in Chapter 3, Rogers believed that some people develop a defensive way of functioning when as children they fail to receive **unconditional positive regard** from significant others and so become overly critical of themselves. They develop harsh self-standards—Rogers called them **conditions of worth**—which they try to meet by repeatedly distorting and denying their true experiences. Using such defensive techniques, these people succeed only partially in feeling good about themselves; threatening self-judgments persist in breaking through and causing intense anxiety. This foundation of anxiety sets the stage for a generalized anxiety disorder or some other form of mental dysfunctioning.

Practitioners of Rogers' treatment approach, **client-centered therapy,** try to show unconditional positive regard for their clients and to empathize with them, expecting that an atmosphere of genuine acceptance and caring will provide the security they need to recognize their true inner needs, thoughts, and emotions (Raskin & Rogers, 1989). The therapists' goal is to help clients "experience" themselves—that is, become completely trusting of their instincts and honest and comfortable with themselves. Their anxiety or other symptoms of psychological dysfunctioning will then subside. Here Rogers describes the progress made by a client with anxiety and related symptoms.

> She was unusually sensitive to the process she was experiencing in herself. To use some of her expressions, she was feeling pieces of a jigsaw puzzle, she was singing a song without words, she was creating a poem, she was learning a new way of experiencing herself which was like learning to read Braille. Therapy was an experiencing of herself, in all its aspects, in a safe relationship. At first it was her guilt and her concern over being responsible for the maladjustments of others. Then it was her hatred and bitterness toward life for having cheated and frustrated her in so many different areas, particularly the sexual, and then it was the experiencing of her own hurt, of the sorrow she felt for herself for having been so wounded. But along with these went the experiencing of self as having a capacity for wholeness, a self which was not possessively loving toward others but was "without hate," a self that cared about others. This last followed what was, for her, one of the deepest experiences in therapy . . .—the realization that the therapist cared, that it really mattered to him how therapy turned out for her, that he really valued her. She experienced the soundness of her basic directions. She gradually became aware of the fact that, though she had searched in every corner of herself, there was nothing fundamentally bad, but rather, at heart she was positive and sound. She realized that the values

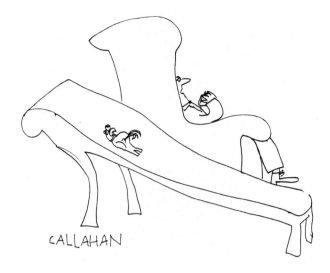

CALLAHAN

"DO YOU WANT A CRACKER, OR DO YOU NEED A CRACKER?"

*Both psychodynamic and humanistic therapists guide clients with generalized anxiety disorder (and other disorders as well) to uncover hidden feelings and needs, although they do so with different therapy goals in mind.*

> she deeply held were such as would set her at variance with her culture, but she accepted this calmly. . . .
>
> (Rogers, 1954, pp. 261–264)

In spite of this and other optimistic case reports, controlled studies have only sometimes found client-centered therapy more effective than placebo therapy or no therapy at all (Greenberg et al., 1994; Prochaska & Norcross, 1994). Moreover, researchers have found at best limited support for Rogers' explanation of generalized anxiety disorder and other forms of abnormal behavior. Nor have other humanistic theories and treatments for generalized anxiety disorder received much research support. Indeed, most humanistic theorists believe that traditional research methods cannot provide a fair test for their explanations and treatments, and thus they have not even tried to test their ideas empirically.

## Existential Explanations and Treatments

Existentialists believe that generalized anxiety disorder grows out of *existential anxiety,* a universal human fear of the limits and responsibilities of one's existence (Tillich, 1952). We experience existential anxiety, they say, because we know that life is finite and we fear the death that awaits us. We also know that our actions and choices may hurt others unintentionally. Finally, we suspect that our personal existence may ultimately lack meaning.

*Existential anxiety*   A universal pervasive fear of the limits and responsibilities of one's existence.

"Honestly now, Mr. Claus, how do
you expect others to believe in you
if you don't believe in yourself"

*The doubts and anxieties of people with anxiety disorders sometimes take the form of the "imposter phenomenon"—a persistent, gnawing feeling that one does not deserve one's success, that it is based on manipulating or fooling others rather than on competence (Clance & O'Toole, 1987). (RUBES by Leigh Rubin by permission of Leigh Rubin and Creators Syndicate.)*

According to existentialists, people can confront their existential anxiety head on by taking responsibility for their actions, making decisions, making their lives meaningful, and appreciating their own uniqueness, or they can shrink from this confrontation. Caught up in the change, confusion, and strain of modern civilization, some people choose to lead "inauthentic lives": they deny their fears, overlook their freedom of choice, avoid taking responsibility, and conform excessively to the guidelines imposed by society (May, 1967; Bugental, 1965). According to existentialists, such a lifestyle inevitably fails to reduce a person's existential anxiety, which continues to erupt in the form of generalized and other anxiety disorders.

Existential therapists use a variety of techniques, from supportive to confrontational, to help anxious clients take more responsibility and make them live more meaningfully. Like most humanists, however, ex-

istentialists believe that traditional research methods miss subtle, internal experiences by looking only at what can be observed and defined objectively. They resort instead to reason, introspection, and individual case examples as evidence for their views and approaches.

## The Cognitive Perspective

As we observed in Chapter 3, proponents of the cognitive model suggest that maladaptive ways of thinking are often the cause of psychological problems; thus, practitioners of the cognitive approach treat people by helping to change their thinking. Given that excessive worry is a defining characteristic of generalized anxiety disorder, it is not surprising that cognitive theorists have had much to say about the causes and treatments for this disorder in particular.

### Cognitive Explanations

The most prominent cognitive theories suggest that a generalized anxiety disorder is caused by *maladaptive assumptions*. As we saw in Chapter 3, for example, Albert Ellis believes that some people hold basic irrational assumptions that color their interpretations of events and lead to inappropriate emotional reactions (Ellis, 1984, 1962). According to Ellis, people with generalized anxiety disorders often hold the following assumptions:

"It is a dire necessity for an adult human being to be loved or approved of by virtually every significant other person in his community."

"It is awful and catastrophic when things are not the way one would very much like them to be."

"If something is or may be dangerous or fearsome one should be terribly concerned about it and should keep dwelling on the possibility of its occurring."

"One should be thoroughly competent, adequate, and achieving in all possible respects if one is to consider oneself worthwhile."

(Ellis, 1962)

When people with these basic assumptions are faced with a stressful event, such as an exam or a blind date, they are likely to interpret it as highly dangerous and threatening, to overreact, and to experience fear. As they apply the assumptions to more and more life events, they may begin to develop a generalized anxiety disorder.

In a similar cognitive theory, Aaron Beck holds that people with a generalized anxiety disorder constantly hold unrealistic silent assumptions that imply that

they are in imminent danger (Beck, 1991, 1976; Beck & Emery, 1985):

> "Any strange situation should be regarded as dangerous."
>
> "A situation or a person is unsafe until proven to be safe."
>
> "It is always best to assume the worst."
>
> "My security and safety depend on anticipating and preparing myself at all times for any possible danger."
>
> *(Beck & Emery, 1985, p. 63)*

According to Beck, such silent assumptions lead people to experience persistent anxiety-provoking images and thoughts, called *automatic thoughts.* In social situations, for example, they may think, "I'll make a fool of myself," "I won't know what to say," "People will laugh at me," and so on. Similarly, when they work on important tasks, they may be plagued by automatic thoughts such as "What if I fail?," "I won't have enough time," and "I'm falling behind."

Researchers have found that many people with generalized anxiety disorder do indeed hold dysfunctional assumptions, just as Ellis and Beck suggest (Himle et al., 1989; Hibbert, 1984). One study found that thirty-two subjects with this disorder held exaggerated notions concerning possible harmful events or consequences (Beck et al., 1974). Each subject reported upsetting assumptions, images, and automatic thoughts about at least one of the following danger areas: physical injury, illness, or death; mental illness; psychological impairment or loss of control; failure and inability to cope; and rejection, depreciation, and domination. Related studies have also found that people with generalized anxiety symptoms are more attentive to threatening cues than to other kinds of cues (Mathews et al., 1995; Mineka & Sutton, 1992).

## Cognitive Therapies

Two kinds of cognitive approaches are commonly used in cases of generalized anxiety disorder. In one, based on the theories of Ellis and Beck, therapists help clients change the maladaptive assumptions that are supposedly at the root of their disorders. In the other, therapists teach clients how to cope during stressful situations.

**Changing Maladaptive Assumptions** In Ellis's technique of *rational-emotive therapy,* which we first observed in Chapter 3, the practitioner's role is to point out the irrational assumptions held by clients, offer alternative (more realistic) assumptions, and assign homework that gives clients practice at challenging old assumptions and applying new ones. Therapists who use this approach help clients with generalized

*Automatic thoughts* According to Aaron Beck, unbidden cognitions that come into the mind, some comforting and some upsetting.

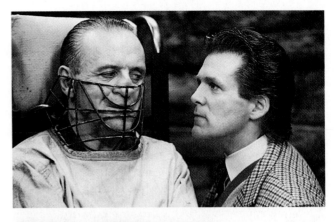

*Many people actually enjoy the feeling of fear as long as it occurs under controlled circumstances, such as when viewing the sinister Hannibal Lecter, a menacing Tyrannosaurus rex, or other movie villains.*

anxiety disorder pinpoint and change those assumptions that may be causing them to feel all-encompassing anxiety. Although controlled research has been limited, some studies do suggest that this approach brings about modest reductions in anxiety in such clients (Lipsky et al., 1980). The approach is illustrated in the following discussion between Ellis and an anxious client who fears failure and disapproval at work, especially over a testing procedure that she has developed for her company.

CLIENT: I'm so distraught these days that I can hardly concentrate on anything for more than a minute or two at a time. My mind just keeps wandering to that damn testing procedure I devised, and that they've put so much money into; and whether it's going to work well or be just a waste of all that time and money. I'm certainly sorry I ever thought of it in the first place! . . . And if they don't like this procedure, or it just doesn't work at all when it's all set up, I could easily lose my job. . . .

ELLIS: Point one is that you must admit that you *are* telling yourself something to start your worrying going, and you must begin to look, and I mean really *look,* for the specific nonsense with which you keep reindoctrinat-

ing yourself. . . . The false statement is: "If, because my testing procedure doesn't work and I am functioning inefficiently on my job, my co-workers do not want me or approve of me, then I shall be a worthless person". . . .

CLIENT: But if I want to do what my firm also wants me to do, and I am useless to them, aren't I also useless to me?

ELLIS: No—not unless you *think* you are. You are frustrated, of course, if you want to set up a good testing procedure and you can't. But need you be desperately unhappy because you are frustrated? And need you deem yourself completely unworthwhile because you can't do one of the main things you want to do in life?

CLIENT: No I guess not. . . . I must convince myself, then, that even though it would be highly *inconvenient* for me to have my associates disapprove of my work, and especially of this new testing procedure I've been devising, it won't be *terrible* if they do disapprove?

ELLIS: Exactly. You've got to see that the inconvenience and frustration of being disapproved or even fired from your job have nothing at all to do with your personal worth as a human being.

(Ellis, 1962, pp. 160–165)

Beck has developed a treatment for generalized anxiety disorder that is called, simply, **cognitive therapy** and is similar to the rational-emotive approach (Hollon & Beck, 1994). He starts by trying to alter the numerous automatic thoughts that he says arise from the maladaptive assumptions of anxiety-prone persons and bombard their thinking in situation after situation ("What if I fail?"; "Other things might get in the way"; "I'm falling behind."). In a procedure that is somewhat more systematic than Ellis's approach, the therapist helps the client recognize his or her automatic thoughts, observe the faulty logic and assumptions underlying them, and test the validity of the thoughts. As clients increasingly recognize the inaccuracy of their automatic thoughts and underlying assumptions, they are expected to become less prone to see danger where there is none.

Beck's cognitive treatment for generalized anxiety disorder is really an adaptation of his influential and very effective treatment for depression (which is discussed in Chapter 7). It has been applied to generalized anxiety disorder only in recent years, but researchers are beginning to find that it is often helpful to people with this disorder, reducing their anxiety to more tolerable levels (Hollon & Beck, 1994; Barlow et al., 1992).

**Teaching Clients to Cope**    Donald Meichenbaum (1993, 1975) has developed a cognitive technique for coping with stress called *self-instruction training,* or *stress inoculation training.* It is based on the belief that

during stressful situations, many people make statements to themselves ("self-statements"), similar to Beck's automatic thoughts, that heighten their anxiety. Therapists who practice self-instruction training teach clients to rid themselves of these negative self-statements ("Oh, no, everything is going wrong") and replace them with coping self-statements ("One step at a time; I can handle the situation").

Clients are taught coping self-statements that they can apply during the different stages of a stressful situation. First they learn to say things to themselves that prepare them for a stressful situation, for example, self-statements that might be employed prior to asking for a raise. They also learn self-statements that enable them to cope with stressful situations as they are occurring, the kind of self-statements that can help them when they are actually in the boss's office asking for a raise. Third, they learn self-statements that will help them through the very difficult moments when a situation seems to be going badly, as when the boss glares at them as they ask for more money. And finally, they learn to make reinforcing self-statements after they have coped effectively. Here are a few examples of these four kinds of self-statements:

### Preparing for a Stressor

What is it you have to do?

You can develop a plan to deal with it.

Just think about what you can do about it. That's better than getting anxious.

### Confronting and Handling a Stressor

Just psych yourself up—you can meet this challenge.

This tenseness can be an ally: a cue to cope.

Relax: you're in control. Take a slow deep breath.

### Coping with the Feeling of Being Overwhelmed

When fear comes, just pause.

Keep the focus on the present: what is it you have to do?

You should expect your fear to rise.

Don't try to eliminate fear totally: just keep it manageable.

### Reinforcing Self-Statements

It worked: you did it.

It wasn't as bad as you expected.

You made more out of your fear than it was worth.

Your damn ideas—that's the problem. When you control them, you control your fear.

(Meichenbaum, 1974)

Self-instruction training has proved to be of modest help in cases of generalized anxiety disorder (Sanchez-Canovas et al., 1991; Ramm et al., 1981) and somewhat more helpful to people who suffer from test-

taking anxiety or mild forms of anxiety (Meichenbaum, 1993, 1972). It has also been adapted with some success to help athletes compete better and people behave less impulsively, control anger, and control pain.

In view of the limited effectiveness of self-instruction training in treating generalized anxiety disorder, Meichenbaum (1972) himself has suggested that it should be used primarily to supplement other treatments. In fact, anxious people treated with a combination of self-instruction training and rational-emotive therapy have been seen to improve more than people treated by either approach alone (Glogower et al., 1978).

## The Biological Perspective

Biological theorists believe that generalized anxiety disorder is related to biological factors and that these factors must be corrected in order to help people with this disorder. For years these claims were supported primarily by family risk studies. If biological tendencies toward generalized anxiety disorder are inherited, people who are biologically related should have more similar probabilities of developing this disorder. Studies have indeed found that blood relatives of persons with a generalized anxiety disorder are more likely than nonrelatives to have the disorder too (Kendler et al., 1992; Carey & Gottesman, 1981). And the closer the relative (an identical twin, for example, as opposed to a fraternal twin or other sibling), the greater the likelihood that he or she will also have the anxiety disorder (Marks, 1986; Slater & Shields, 1969).

Of course, investigators cannot be fully confident in genetic and biological interpretations of these studies. The findings could also be suggesting that generalized anxiety disorder is caused by environmental experiences. Because relatives are likely to share aspects of the same environment, their shared disorders may be reflecting similarities in environment and upbringing rather than similarities in biological makeup. Indeed, the closer the relatives, the more similar their environmental experiences are likely to be.

In recent decades important discoveries by brain researchers have offered more compelling evidence that generalized anxiety disorder is indeed related to biological factors, in particular to biochemical dysfunctioning in the brain.

### A Biological Explanation

The first discovery that helped open the door to a biological understanding of generalized anxiety disorder was made in the 1950s, when researchers determined

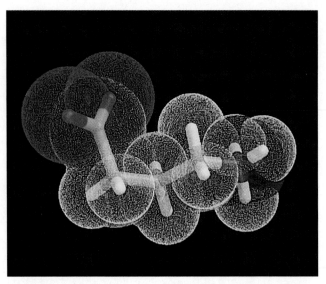

*A computer-drawn molecule of gamma aminobutyric acid (GABA), the neurotransmitter that carries an inhibitory message to neuron receptors.*

that *benzodiazepines*, the family of drugs that includes diazepam (Valium), alprazolam (Xanax), and chlordiazepoxide (Librium), provide relief from anxiety. No one understood, however, why they were effective.

It was not until the late 1970s that newly developed radioactive techniques enabled researchers to pinpoint the exact sites in the brain that are affected by benzodiazepines (Mohler & Okada, 1977; Squires & Braestrup, 1977). Apparently certain neurons have receptor molecules that receive the benzodiazepines, just as a lock receives a key. Particularly high concentrations of these receptors are located in brain areas known to be heavily involved in controlling emotional states. Investigators also soon discovered that these same receptors ordinarily receive *gamma aminobutyric acid (GABA)*, a common and important neurotransmitter in the brain (Haefely, 1990; Costa et al., 1978, 1975). As we saw in Chapter 4, neurotransmitters are chemicals that carry messages from one neuron to another. GABA carries inhibitory messages: when GABA is received at a neuroreceptor, it causes the neuron to stop firing.

Researchers have studied the possible role of GABA and GABA receptors in fear reactions (Barondes, 1993; Costa, 1985, 1983) and have pieced together the following scenario: In normal fear reactions, neurons throughout the brain fire more rapidly, trigger the firing of still more neurons, and create a general state of hyperexcitability throughout the brain and body; thus

*Benzodiazepines*   The most common group of antianxiety drugs, which includes Valium, Xanax, and Librium.

*GABA*   The neurotransmitter gamma aminobutyric acid, whose low activity has been linked to generalized anxiety disorder.

**Table 5-1** *Drugs That Reduce Anxiety*

| Class/ Generic Name | Trade Name | Usual Daily Dose (milligrams) | Absorption |
|---|---|---|---|
| *Benzodiazepines* | | | |
| Alprazolam | Xanax | 0.75–4.0 | Rapid |
| Chlordiazepoxide | Librium | 15–100 | Rapid |
| Clorazepate dipotassium | Tranxene | 15–60 | Very rapid |
| Clonazepam | Klonopin | 1–4 | Very rapid |
| Diazepam | Valium | 4–40 | Very rapid |
| Lorazepam | Ativan | 2–6 | Intermediate |
| Oxazepam | Serax | 30–120 | Slow |
| Triazolam | Halcion | 0.125–0.250 | Rapid |
| *Azaspirones* | | | |
| Buspirone | BuSpar | 15–60 | Slow |
| *Beta blockers* | | | |
| Propanolol | Inderal | 10–40 | Rapid |
| Atenolol | Tenormin | 50–100 | Rapid |

*Sources: Physician's Desk Reference, 1994; Shader & Greenblatt, 1993, p. 1399; Leaman, 1992, p. 236; Silver & Yudofsky, 1988, pp. 807–809.*

the increases in perspiration, breathing, and heartbeat. This state is experienced as fear or anxiety. After neuron firing continues for a while, it triggers a feedback system that reduces the level of excitability. Some neurons throughout the brain release the neurotransmitter GABA, which then binds to GABA receptors on receiving neurons and essentially instructs those neurons to stop firing. The state of excitability is thereby reduced, and the experience of fear or anxiety subsides.

Some researchers believe that a problem in this feedback system can cause fear or anxiety to go unchecked (Lloyd et al., 1992). In fact, when some investigators reduced the capacity of GABA to bind to GABA receptors, they found that animal subjects reacted with heightened anxiety (Costa, 1985; Mohler et al., 1981). This finding suggests that people with a generalized anxiety disorder may have ongoing problems in their anxiety feedback system. Perhaps their brain supplies of GABA are too low, they have too few GABA receptors, or their GABA receptors do not readily bind the neurotransmitters (Barondes, 1993).

This explanation of generalized anxiety disorder is promising, but it has certain problems. One is that much of the research on the biological regulation of anxiety has been done on laboratory animals. When researchers generate fear responses in animals, they are assuming that the animals are experiencing something that approximates human anxiety, but it is impossible to be certain. The animals may be experiencing a high level of arousal that is quite distinct from human anxiety.

In addition, biological theorists are faced with the problem of establishing a causal relationship. Although biological studies implicate physiological functioning in generalized anxiety disorder, they do not usually establish that the physiological events *cause* disorder. The biological responses of chronically anxious adults may be the result rather than the cause of their anxiety disorders. Perhaps chronic anxiety eventually leads to poorer GABA reception.

## Biological Treatments

The leading biological approach to treating anxiety disorders is to prescribe *antianxiety drugs.* Indeed, it would be hard to find someone in our society who is not familiar with the words "tranquilizer," "Valium," or the like. Another biological intervention is *biofeedback,* in which people learn to control underlying biological processes that may be contributing to their problems.

**Antianxiety Drugs**  Until the 1950s, medications called **barbiturates** were the major biological treatment for anxiety disorders (Lader, 1992). These drugs created serious problems, however. They made people very drowsy, too high a dose could lead to death, and those who took them over an extended period could become physically dependent on them. Then, a new kind of antianxiety medication named *meprobamate* (brand name Miltown) was developed. This drug was less dangerous and less addictive than barbiturates, but it still caused drowsiness, so researchers continued to search for more satisfactory antianxiety medications.

Finally, in the late 1950s, yet another group of antianxiety drugs called *benzodiazepines,* which includes *chlordiazepoxide* (Librium) and *diazepam* (Valium), was marketed (see Table 5-1). Still other benzodiazepine drugs were developed subsequently. Doctors and patients alike initially looked at benzodiazepines as miracle drugs (Lader, 1992) because the drugs seemed to reduce anxiety without making people exceptionally tired and at the same time appeared relatively nontoxic even in large dosages. Some benzodiazepines also gained wide use as sleeping medications (see Box 5-2).

Only years later did researchers begin to understand the reasons for the effectiveness of benzodiazepine drugs. As we noted earlier, investigators learned that there are specific neuron sites in the brain that receive benzodiazepines and that these receptor sites are the same ones that ordinarily receive GABA, the neurotransmitter that inhibits neuron firing, slows physical arousal, and reduces anxiety (Barondes, 1993). When benzodiazepines bind to these neuron receptor sites, they increase the ability of GABA to bind to them as well, and so apparently improve GABA's ability to slow neuron firing and reduce bodily arousal (Lloyd et al., 1992).

Benzodiazepines are prescribed for generalized anxiety disorder more than for any other kind of anxiety disorder. Controlled studies reveal that they do some-

## Box 5-2

# *The Dark Side of Halcion*

In 1982, when *Halcion* (generic name *triazolam*) was first approved by the Food and Drug Administration, it was heralded as the perfect sleeping pill. Unlike other benzodiazepines, which linger in the body and leave people somewhat groggy the next day, Halcion is metabolized in four to six hours. This gave Halcion such an advantage over other medications that within a few years it became the most commonly prescribed sleeping pill in the world. More than 7 million orders were filled by American pharmacists in 1990 alone.

Unfortunately, the other side to Halcion's quick removal from the body is a possible "rebound effect" of severe daytime anxiety. In addition, since its approval, users have increasingly reported numerous troubling undesired effects, such as confusion, memory loss, depression, agitation, and aggression, and many people have become physically dependent on the drug (Roache et al., 1993; Berlin et al., 1993).

In view of such reports, the FDA has recently conducted further reviews of the drug. In May 1992 the FDA advisory committee decided to let Halcion stay on the

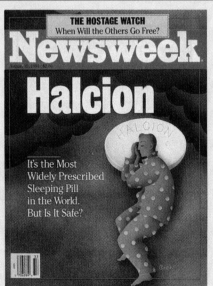

U.S. market, but it reduced the recommended maximum dose from 0.5 to 0.25 milligrams a day. In addition, the FDA committee recommended strengthening the package warnings about the possibility of rebound effects and hostile reactions. Currently the FDA is continuing to investigate the drug.

Meanwhile, public sentiment seems to have turned against the pharmaceutical company that makes Halcion. In some civil cases, the company has been assessed large financial damages when the drug appeared to play a role in the commission of a crime. In addition, the company's forthrightness in reporting results of early studies of Halcion has been questioned.

Today, five countries have banned the use of Halcion. In 1993, Great Britain permanently revoked the pharmaceutical company's license to market Halcion in the United Kingdom. Several other countries have lowered the maximum prescribed dosages allowed because the undesirable effects are more common at higher dosages.

The debate over Halcion has resulted in a sizable reduction in the number of prescriptions written for the drug. By 1994, Halcion's annual sales had dropped by half. The negative perception of Halcion has led many physicians to turn increasingly to other kinds of drugs to help their clients sleep. But until further research more precisely clarifies Halcion's unwanted effects, or until a safer and equally effective drug is found for relieving insomnia, Halcion is likely to remain on the market in the United States and many other countries, although with greater warnings and restrictions on its use.

times reduce the symptoms of this disorder (Leonard, 1992; Klein et al., 1985). However, in recent years, clinicians have begun to realize that the wide use of these drugs has been excessive and potentially dangerous (Lader, 1992). It has, for example, become clear that benzodiazepines alone are not a long-term solution for anxiety. When the medications are stopped, many clients' anxieties return as strong as ever (Rickels & Schweizer, 1990). In addition, it has become clear that people who take benzodiazepines in large dosages for an extended time can become physically dependent on them and can also develop significant undesired effects such as drowsiness, lack of coordination, and worse (Apter, 1993).

Several new kinds of antianxiety drugs have also been applied to generalized anxiety disorder (Roy-Byrne & Wingerson, 1992). One group of drugs, called *beta blockers,* bind to receptors in the brain called β-adrenergic receptors and in turn reduce specific physical symptoms of anxiety, such as palpitations and tremors. Another antianxiety drug, *buspirone,* a member of a group of drugs called *azaspirones,* binds to yet different receptors in the brain (Shah et al., 1991). While these new antianxiety drugs undergo further investigation, benzodiazepines continue to be the drugs most widely prescribed to curb broad anxiety symptoms (Shader & Greenblatt, 1993).

### Consider This
Drug therapies for the anxiety disorders have sometimes been helpful in the short run. However, there are problems associated with the use of these drug therapies. How might other forms of therapy be combined with drug therapies to reduce or even eliminate these associated problems?

**Biofeedback**    Another biological approach commonly used in cases of generalized anxiety disorder is *biofeedback,* a technique in which people are connected to a monitoring device that gives them continuous information about a physiological activity (such as heart rate or muscle tension) in their body. As we observed in Chapter 2, by following the therapist's instructions and attending to the signals from the monitor, they gradually learn to control the activity. With practice, a person can learn to control even seemingly involuntary physiological processes.

Biofeedback has been applied to a wide range of problems, including excessive feelings of anxiety (Stoyva & Budzynski, 1993). The most widely applied technique uses a device called an *electromyograph*

*Electromyograph* (EMG)   A device that provides feedback about the level of muscular tension in the body.

*(EMG),* which provides feedback about the level of muscular tension in the body so that clients can learn to reduce it (and, presumably, their anxiety) at will. Electrodes are attached to the client's muscles—usually the frontalis, or forehead, muscles—where they detect the minute electrical activity that accompanies muscle contraction (see Figure 5-4). The electric potentials coming from the muscles are then amplified and converted into an image, such as lines on a screen, or into a tone whose pitch and volume vary along with changes in muscle tension. Thus clients "see" or "hear" when their muscles are becoming more or less tense. After repeated trial and error, they become skilled at voluntarily reducing muscle tension and, theoretically, at reducing tension and anxiety in everyday stressful situations. Research indicates that EMG biofeedback training helps both normal and anxious subjects reduce their anxiety levels to a modest degree (Hurley & Meminger, 1992; Rice & Blanchard, 1982).

In the 1960s and 1970s, many people hailed biofeedback training as an approach that would change the face of clinical treatment. This early expectation has not been fulfilled. So far, biofeedback procedures have tended to be more cumbersome, less

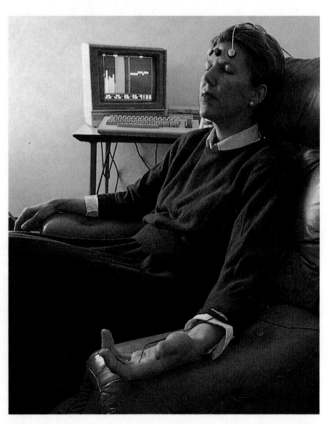

*The muscular tension experienced by this client is detected by electrodes attached to her body and displayed on the nearby monitor. Electromyograph biofeedback training has proved modestly helpful in reducing anxiety.*

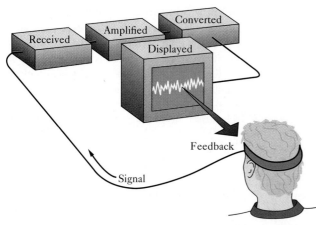

**Figure 5-4** *This biofeedback system is recording tension in the forehead muscle of a headache sufferer. The system receives, amplifies, converts, and displays information about the tension, allowing the client to "observe" it and to try to reduce his tension responses.*

efficient, and less productive than mental health clinicians had envisioned (Wittrock & Blanchard, 1992; Blanchard & Epstein, 1978). The techniques have played an important adjunct role in the treatment of some physical problems, including headaches, gastrointestinal disorders, seizure disorders, and such neuromuscular disorders as cerebral palsy (King, 1992; Whitehead, 1992), but they have played a limited role in the treatment of generalized anxiety disorder and other psychological problems.

*Summing Up*
*People with a generalized anxiety disorder experience excessive worry about numerous events or activities. Theorists from each of the leading models have proposed factors that may help cause this disorder, including an increase in societal pressures, inadequate defense mechanisms, a distorted view of the self, assumptions of harm, and GABA deficiencies. Correspondingly, many treatments for the disorder have been developed. Research has not yet produced strong supporting evidence for any of the explanations or treatment approaches, although the cognitive and biological perspectives show promise.*

# Phobias

A *phobia* (from the Greek for "fear") is a persistent and unreasonable fear of a particular object, activity, or situation. People with a phobia become fearful if they even think about the dreaded object or situation, but they usually remain comfortable and functional as long as they avoid the object or thoughts about it. Most are well aware that their fears are excessive and unreasonable. Many have no idea how their fears started.

We all have our areas of special fear, and it is normal for some things to upset us more than other things. To some extent, the objects and events we fear may be related to our stage of life. A survey of residents of a community in Burlington, Vermont, found that fears of crowds, death, injury, illness, and separation were more common among people in their 60s than in other age groups, whereas fears of snakes, heights, storms, enclosures, and social situations were much more prevalent among 20-year-olds (Agras et al., 1969) (see Figure 5-5).

How do these common fears differ from phobic disorders? How, for instance, does a "normal" fear of snakes differ from a snake phobia? DSM-IV indicates that the fear experienced in a phobic disorder is more intense and persistent, and the desire to avoid the object or situation is more compelling (APA, 1994). People with phobic disorders experience such distress that their fears often interfere dramatically with their personal, social, or occupational functioning.

Phobic disorders are common in our society. Surveys suggest that 10 to 11 percent of the adult population in the United States suffer from a phobia in any given year (Regier et al., 1993; Eaton et al., 1991). More than 14 percent develop a phobia at some point in their lives. These disorders are more than twice as common in women as in men.

*Consider This*
Ask a number of people what they fear and you will probably collect a long list of menacing objects and situations. Nevertheless, most people get along well every day and never seek treatment for their fears. Do these people's fears differ from phobias? Or are some people simply better able to work around their phobias than others are?

## Types of Phobias

DSM-IV distinguishes three categories of phobia: agoraphobia, social phobias, and specific phobias. *Agoraphobia* (from the Greek for "fear of the marketplace") is a fear of venturing into public places, especially when one is alone. *Social phobias* are fears of social

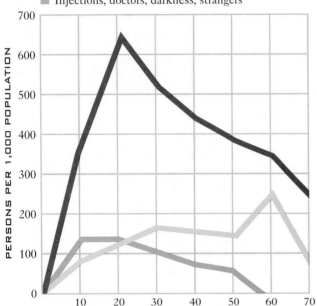

- ■ Snakes, heights, enclosed places, social situations
- ■ Crowds, death, injury, separation, illness
- ■ Injections, doctors, darkness, strangers

**Figure 5-5**  *Certain age groups are particularly likely to have certain fears. Close to 70 percent of all 20-year-olds surveyed in Burlington, Vermont—the highest rate of any age group—feared snakes and heights. On the other hand, 60-year-olds were more likely than others to be afraid of crowds and of death. (Adapted from Agras, Sylvester, & Oliveau, 1969, p. 153.)*

or performance situations in which embarrassment may occur. All other phobias are classified as *specific phobias.*

## Agoraphobia

The following report describes the disorder of **agoraphobia,** a pervasive and complex phobia that makes people avoid public places or situations in which escape might be difficult or help unavailable should they develop incapacitating or upsetting symptoms, such as dizziness, palpitations, diarrhea, or nausea (APA, 1994). In any given year approximately 4 percent of the adult population experience this problem, women twice as frequently as men (Kessler et al., 1994; Eaton et al., 1991). Almost a quarter of them receive treatment (Regier et al., 1993). People typically develop agoraphobia in their 20s or 30s.

*Agoraphobia*   A pervasive and complex phobia that makes people avoid public places or situations in which escape might be difficult or help unavailable should they develop incapacitating or upsetting symptoms, such as dizziness or palpitations.

For several months prior to her application for treatment Veronica had been unable to leave her home. . . . "It is as if something dreadful would happen to me if I did not immediately go home." Even after she would return to the house, she would feel shaken inside and unable to speak to anyone or do anything for an hour or so. However, as long as she remained in her own home or garden, she was able to carry on her routine life without much problem. . . . Because of this agoraphobia, she had been unable to return to her position as a mathematics teacher in the local high school after the summer vacation.

". . . [Veronica] stated that she had always been a somewhat shy person who generally preferred keeping to herself, but that up until approximately a year ago she had always been able to go to her job, shop, or go to church without any particular feelings of dread or uneasiness. It was difficult for her to recall the first time . . . but it seemed to her that the first major experience was approximately a year before, when she and her mother had been Christmas shopping. They were standing in the middle of a crowded department store when she suddenly felt the impulse to flee. She left her mother without an explanation and drove home as fast as she could. . . . After the Christmas vacation she seemed to recover for a while and was at least able to return to her classroom duties without any ill effect. During the ensuing several months she had several similar experiences, usually when she was off duty; but by late spring these fears were just as likely to occur in the classroom. . . . In thinking further about the occurrence of her phobia, it seemed to Veronica that there was actually no particular stress which might account for her fear. Often it seemed to come over her when she was momentarily relaxed, although always when she was in public.

(Goldstein & Palmer, 1975, pp. 163–164)

It is typical of people with agoraphobia to avoid entering crowded streets or stores, driving through tunnels or on bridges, traveling on public transportation, and using elevators. If they venture out of the house at all, it is usually only in the company of close relatives or friends.

In many cases the intensity of the agoraphobia fluctuates, as it did for Veronica. In severe cases, people become virtual prisoners in their own homes. Their social life dwindles, and they cannot hold a job. Persons with agoraphobia may also become depressed, sometimes as a result of the severe limitations that their phobia places on their lives.

Many people with agoraphobia are in fact actually prone to experience extreme and sudden explosions of fear, called *panic attacks,* when they enter public places. In such cases, the agoraphobic pattern is considered a type of panic disorder, specifically **panic dis-**

*George Tooker's painting* Subway *expresses the sense of threat, entrapment, and disorientation experienced by many people with agoraphobia when they enter public places.*

**order with agoraphobia,** because the disorder involves much more than an overblown fear of venturing away from home and developing upsetting symptoms. This disorder, which will be discussed in the next chapter's section on panic disorders, is thought to have different origins from the phobia under discussion here.

## Social Phobias

Many people have qualms about interacting with others or talking or performing in front of others. Such normal social fears are inconvenient, but the people who have them manage to function adequately, some at a very high level.

By contrast, people with a *social phobia* have severe, persistent, and irrational fears of social or performance situations in which embarrassment may occur. A social phobia may be specific, such as a fear of talking or performing in public, eating in public, using a public bathroom, or writing in front of others, or it may be a broader fear of social situations, such as a general fear of functioning inadequately or inappropriately when others are watching (Mannuzza et al., 1995).

Social phobias can be highly incapacitating (Stein et al., 1994). A person who is unable to interact with others or speak in public may fail to perform impor-

tant scholastic or professional responsibilities. One who cannot eat in public may reject dinner invitations and other social engagements. Since most people with these phobias keep their fears secret, their social reluctance is often misinterpreted as snobbery, disinterest, or stubborness.

Social phobias are apparently more common than agoraphobia (see Table 5-2). As much as 8 percent of the population—women somewhat more frequently than men—experience this problem in any given year (APA, 1994; Kessler et al., 1994). Around one-fifth of them seek treatment (Regier et al., 1993). The disorder often begins in late childhood or adolescence and may persist for many years, although its intensity may fluctuate over the years.

## Specific Phobias

A *specific phobia* is a persistent fear of a specific object or situation other than being in public places (agoraphobia) or in socially embarrassing situations (social phobia). When they are exposed to or anticipate being exposed to the dreaded object or situation, people with this disorder invariably experience immediate fear. Common specific phobias are intense fears of specific animals or insects, heights, enclosed spaces, and thun-

---

*Social phobia*    A severe and persistent fear of social or performance situations in which embarrassment may occur.

*Specific phobia*    A persistent fear of a specific object or situation (excluding social phobia and agoraphobia).

**Table 5-2** *Anxiety Disorders Profile*

| | One-Year Prevalence | Female : Male Ratio | Typical Age of Onset | Prevalence among Close Relatives |
|---|---|---|---|---|
| Agoraphobia without panic disorder | 2.8% | 2 : 1 | 20–40 years | Unknown |
| Social phobia | 8.0% | 3 : 2 | 10–20 years | Elevated |
| Specific phobia | 9.0% | 3 : 1 | Variable | Elevated |
| Generalized anxiety disorder | 3.8% | 2 : 1 | 0–20 years | Elevated |

Sources: APA, 1994 ; Kessler et al., 1994; Regier et al., 1993; Eaton et al., 1991; Blazer et al., 1991; Davidson et al., 1991.

derstorms. Many familiar and not-so-familiar specific phobias have been given names by clinicians (see Box 5-3). Here are a few firsthand descriptions (all in Melville, 1978):

### Spiders (Arachnophobia)

Seeing a spider makes me rigid with fear, hot, trembling and dizzy. I have occasionally vomited and once fainted in order to escape from the situation. These symptoms last three or four days after seeing a spider. Realistic pictures can cause the same effect, especially if I inadvertently place my hand on one.

(p. 44)

### Flying (Aerophobia)

We got on board, and then there was the take-off. There it was again, that horrible feeling as we gathered speed. It was creeping over me again, that old feeling of panic. I kept seeing everyone as puppets, all strapped to their seats with no control over their destinies, me included. Every time the plane did a variation of speed or route, my heart would leap and I would hurriedly ask what was happening. When the plane started to lose height, I was terrified that we were about to crash.

(p. 59)

### Thunderstorms (Tonitrophobia)

I have been afraid since my early twenties, but the last three years have been the worst. I have such a heartbeat that for hours after a storm my whole left side is painful. . . . I say I will stay in the room, but when it comes I am a jelly, reduced to nothing. I have a little cupboard and I go there, I press my eyes so hard I can't see for about an hour, and if I sit in the cupboard over an hour my husband has to straighten me up.

(p. 104)

Each year as many as 9 percent of the United States population have the symptoms of a specific phobia (APA, 1994; Kessler et al., 1994). Eleven percent develop a specific phobia sometime during their lives, and many people have more than one specific phobia at a time (Eaton et al., 1991). Women with this disorder outnumber men by at least 2 to 1.

The impact of a specific phobia on a person's life depends on what arouses the fear. Some things are easier to avoid than others. People whose phobias center on dogs, insects, or water will repeatedly encounter or expect to encounter the objects they dread. In contrast, people with snake phobias have a much easier time. The vast majority of people who have a simple phobia (almost 90 percent of them) do not seek treatment, concentrating instead on avoiding their objects of fear (Regier et al., 1993).

Specific phobias can develop at any time of life, although some, such as animal phobias, tend to begin during childhood and may disappear on their own before adulthood (APA, 1994). Phobias that do last into or begin during adulthood tend to hold on stubbornly and usually lessen only under treatment.

## Explanations of Phobias

Each of the models has offered explanations for specific phobias that are consistent with its concepts and principles. For years, Freud's psychodynamic explanation was the most influential. In recent years, however, behavioral explanations have received the most attention and support.

### Psychodynamic Explanations

Freud believed that phobias result when people make excessive use of the defense mechanisms of *repression* and *displacement* to control underlying anxiety. Such persons repeatedly push their anxiety-producing impulses deeper into unconsciousness (repression) and transfer their fears to neutral objects or situations (displacement) that are easier to cope with and control. Although the new objects of fear are often related to the threatening impulses, the phobic person is not aware of the relationship.

Consider Sigmund Freud's (1909) famous case study describing Little Hans, a 4-year-old child who seemed suddenly to have developed an excessive fear of horses. When Hans had previously expressed sexual feelings toward his mother by handling his penis and asking his mother to place her finger on it, she had threatened to cut off his penis and had stressed that his desires were totally improper. According to Freud, this threat so frightened Hans that he became unconsciously afraid that his father, too, would learn of his desires and castrate him. Hans *repressed* his sexual impulses and *displaced* his fears onto a neutral object—horses. According to Freud, Hans chose horses because he had come to associate the blinders worn by carriage horses and the black around their mouths with his father's eyeglasses and mustache.

Freud's explanation of phobias, like his explanation of generalized anxiety disorder, has received very limited research support over the years. Similarly, contemporary psychodynamic, humanistic, cognitive, and biological theorists have been unable to shed much light on why people develop phobias. In contrast, the explanations offered by *behavioral theorists* have received considerable research support and are today the most influential in the clinical field.

## Behavioral Explanations

Behaviorists believe that people with phobias first learn to fear certain objects, situations, or events through conditioning. Once the fears are acquired, the individuals keep avoiding the dreaded object or situation, so that the phobia becomes all the more entrenched.

**Learning to Fear and Avoid**  Behaviorists propose *classical conditioning* as a common way of acquiring fear reactions to objects or situations that are not inherently dangerous. Two events that occur close together in time become closely associated in a person's mind, and, as we saw in Chapter 3, the person then reacts similarly to both of them. If one event triggers a fear response, the other may also.

Over 70 years ago, a clinician described the case of a young woman who apparently acquired a phobic fear of running water through classical conditioning (Bagby, 1922). As a child of 7 she went on a picnic

with her mother and aunt, and ran off by herself into the woods after lunch. While she was climbing over some large rocks, her feet became deeply wedged between two of them, and the harder she tried to free herself, the more firmly trapped she became. No one heard her screams, and she became more and more terrified. In the terminology of behaviorists, the entrapment was eliciting a fear response.

Entrapment ➡️ Fear response

As she struggled to free her feet, the girl was also exposed to other stimuli. In particular, she heard a waterfall nearby. The sound of the running water became linked in her mind to her terrifying encounter with the rocks, and she developed a fear of running water as well.

Running water ➡️ Fear response

Eventually the aunt found the screaming child, freed her from the rocks, and gave her comfort and reassurance; but significant psychological damage had been done. From that day forward, the girl was terrified of running water. For years family members had to hold her down to bathe her. When she traveled on a train, friends had to cover the windows so that she would not have to look at any streams. The young woman had apparently acquired a phobia through classical conditioning.

In conditioning terms, the entrapment was an *unconditioned stimulus* (US) that understandably elicited an *unconditioned response* (UR) of fear. The running water represented a *conditioned stimulus* (CS), a formerly neutral stimulus that became associated with entrapment in the child's mind and came to elicit a fear reaction. The newly acquired fear was a *conditioned response* (CR).

CS: Running water ➡️ CR: Fear
US: Entrapment ➡️ UR: Fear

Another way of acquiring fear reactions is through *modeling;* that is, through observation and imitation (Bandura & Rosenthal, 1966). A person may observe that others are afraid of certain objects or events and develop fears of the same objects or events. Consider a young boy whose mother is afraid of illnesses, doctors, and hospitals. If she frequently expresses those fears, before long the boy himself may fear illnesses, doctors, and hospitals.

Why should one fear-provoking experience develop into a long-term phobia? Shouldn't the trapped girl, for example, later have seen that running water would bring her no harm? According to behaviorists, after acquiring a fear response, people try to avoid what they

## Box 5-3

# *Phobias, Familiar and Not So Familiar*

| | | | | | |
|---|---|---|---|---|---|
| Air | Aerophobia | Germs | Spermophobia | Rain | Ombrophobia |
| Animals | Zoophobia | Ghosts | Phasmophobia | Ridicule | Katagelophobia |
| Beards | Pogonophobia | God | Theophobia | Rivers | Potamophobia |
| Being afraid | Phobophobia | Graves | Taphophobia | Robbers | Harpaxophobia |
| Being dirty | Automysophobia | Heart disease | Cardiophobia | Russia or | Russophobia |
| Being stared at | Scopophobia | Heat | Thermophobia | things | |
| Blood | Hematophobia | Heights | Acrophobia | Russian | |
| Books | Bibliophobia | Home | Domatophobia | Satan | Satanophobia |
| Children | Pediophobia | Homosexuality | Homophobia | Shadows | Sciophobia |
| Choking | Pnigophobia | Horses | Hippophobia | Sharp objects | Belonophobia |
| Churches | Ecclesiaphobia | Human beings | Anthropophobia | Skin | Dermatophobia |
| Corpses | Necrophobia | Ice, frost | Cryophobia | Skin diseases | Dermatosio- |
| Crossing a | Gephyrophobia | Illness | Nosemaphobia | | phobia |
| bridge | | Imperfection | Atelophobia | Sleep | Hypnophobia |
| Crowds | Ochlophobia | Injections | Trypanophobia | Snakes | Ophidiophobia |
| Daylight | Phengophobia | Insects | Entomophobia | Snow | Chionophobia |
| Demons, devils | Demonophobia | Machinery | Mechanophobia | Speed | Tachophobia |
| Dogs | Cynophobia | Marriage | Gamophobia | Spiders | Arachnophobia |
| Dolls | Pediophobia | Meat | Carnophobia | Stings | Cnidophobia |
| Dreams | Oneirophobia | Men | Androphobia | Strangers | Xenophobia |
| Drugs | Pharmacophobia | Mice | Musophobia | Sun | Heliophobia |
| Empty rooms | Kenophobia | Mirrors | Eisoptrophobia | Surgery | Ergasiophobia |
| Enclosed space | Claustrophobia | Missiles | Ballistophobia | Swallowing | Phagophobia |
| England and | Anglophobia | Money | Chrometophobia | Teeth | Odontophobia |
| things | | Nakedness | Gymnophobia | Touching or | Haphephobia |
| English | | Night | Nyctophobia | being | |
| Eyes | Ommatophobia | Noise or loud | Phonophobia | touched | |
| Feces | Coprophobia | talking | | Travel | Hodophobia |
| Fire | Pyrophobia | Odors | Osmophobia | Trees | Dendrophobia |
| Flood | Antlophobia | Odors (body) | Osphresiophobia | Wasps | Spheksophobia |
| Flowers | Anthophobia | Physical love | Erotophobia | Water | Hydrophobia |
| Flying | Aerophobia | Pleasure | Hedonophobia | Wind | Anemophobia |
| Fog | Homichlophobia | Poison | Toxiphobia | Women | Gynophobia |
| Foreigners | Xenophobia | Poverty | Peniaphobia | Words | Logophobia |
| France and | Gallophobia | Pregnancy | Maieusiophobia | Worms | Helminthophobia |
| things | | Punishment | Poinephobia | Wounds, | Traumatophobia |
| French | | Railways | Siderodromo- | injury | |
| Fur | Doraphobia | | phobia | Writing | Graphophobia |

*(Melville, 1978, pp. 196–202)*

fear. Whenever they find themselves near a fearsome object, they quickly move away. They may also plan ahead to ensure that such encounters will not occur. Unfortunately, such avoidance also serves to preserve their fear responses (Miller, 1948; Mowrer, 1947, 1939). Phobic people do not get close to the dreaded objects often enough to learn that they are really quite harmless.

It is worth noting that behaviorists propose that specific learned fears may further blossom into a gen-

eralized anxiety disorder when a person acquires a large number of them. This development is presumed to come about through **stimulus generalization:** responses to one stimulus are also elicited by similar stimuli. The fear of running water acquired by the girl in the rocks could have generalized to such similar stimuli as milk being poured into a glass or even the

---

*Stimulus generalization* A phenomenon in which responses to one stimulus are also elicited by similar stimuli.

sound of bubbly music. If a person experiences a series of upsetting events, if each event produces one or more feared stimuli, and if the person's reactions to each of these stimuli generalize to yet other stimuli, that person may build up a large number of fears and eventually develop a generalized anxiety disorder.

**Evidence for the Behavioral Explanations**  Behavioral studies have indicated that fear reactions can indeed be acquired through conditioning. Some analogue experiments have found that animal and human subjects can be taught to fear objects through classical conditioning (Miller, 1948; Mowrer, 1947, 1939). In a famous report, psychologists John B. Watson and Rosalie Rayner (1920) described how they taught a baby boy called Little Albert to fear white rats. For weeks Albert was allowed to play with a white rat and appeared to enjoy doing so. One time when Albert reached for the rat, however, the experimenter struck a steel bar with a hammer, making a very loud noise that upset and frightened Albert. The next several times that Albert reached for the rat, the experimenter again made the loud noise. Albert acquired a fear and avoidance response to the rat. As Watson (1930) described it, "The instant the rat was shown, the baby began to cry . . . and began to crawl away so rapidly that he was caught with difficulty before he reached the edge of the mattress" (p. 161). According to some reports, Albert's fear of white rats also generalized to such objects as a rabbit, human hair, cotton, and even a Santa Claus mask.

Research has also supported the behavioral position that fears can be acquired through modeling. Psychologists Albert Bandura and Theodore Rosenthal (1966), for example, had human subjects observe a person apparently being shocked by electricity whenever a buzzer sounded. The victim was actually the experimenter's accomplice—in research terminology, a *confederate*—who pretended to experience pain by twitching, writhing, and yelling whenever the buzzer went on. After the unsuspecting subjects had observed several such episodes, they themselves underwent a fear reaction whenever they heard the buzzer. The process of acquiring fear reactions through modeling in this way is called *vicarious conditioning*.

Although these studies support behaviorists' explanations of phobias, other research has called those explanations into question (Marks, 1987). Several laboratory studies with adult subjects, for example, have attempted but failed to condition fear reactions (Hallam & Rachman, 1976). Similarly, clinical case reports and questionnaires do not universally support

*Vicarious conditioning*  The process of acquiring fear or other reactions through modeling.

*When people observe others (models) being afraid of or victimized by an object or situation, they themselves may develop a fear of the object. Alfred Hitchcock's film* The Birds *led to an increase in ornithophobia (fear of birds) during the 1960s.*

the theory that phobias result from specific incidents of classical conditioning or modeling. Although specific incidents have been cited in some cases (Ost, 1991), other cases suggest no clear origin (Marks, 1987; Keuthen, 1980). Thus, although researchers have found that these phobias can be acquired by classical conditioning or modeling, they have not established that the disorder is ordinarily acquired in this way.

**A Modified Behavioral Explanation**  Some phobias are much more common than others. Phobic reactions to animals, heights, and darkness are more common than phobic reactions to meat, grass, and houses. Behaviorists often account for this uneven distribution of fears by proposing that human beings, as a species, have a *predisposition* to develop certain fears (Ohman & Soares, 1993; Seligman, 1971). This idea is referred to as *preparedness,* because human beings, theoretically, are "prepared" to acquire some phobias and not others.

In a series of important tests of this notion, the psychologist Arne Ohman and his colleagues have conditioned different kinds of fears in two groups of human subjects (Ohman & Soares, 1993; Ohman et al., 1975). In one such study they showed all subjects slides of faces, houses, snakes, and spiders. One group received electric shocks whenever they observed the slides of faces and houses, while the other group was shocked during their observations of snakes and spiders. Using the subjects' galvanic skin responses (GSRs) as a mea-

*Preparedness*  A predisposition to acquire certain fears.

sure of fear, the experimenters found that both groups learned to fear the intended objects after repeated shock pairings, but then they noted an interesting distinction: after a short shock-free period, the subjects who had learned to fear faces and houses stopped registering high GSRs in the presence of those objects; but subjects who had learned to fear snakes and spiders continued to show high GSRs in response to them for a long while. One interpretation of this finding is that animals and insects are stronger candidates for human phobias than faces or houses.

Researchers do not know whether such human fear predispositions are imposed biologically or culturally. Proponents of a biological predisposition argue that the fear propensities have been transmitted genetically through the evolutionary process (Ohman, 1993). They suggest that the objects of common phobias represented real dangers to our ancestors and that the ancestors who more readily acquired a fear of animals and the like had a greater chance of surviving long enough to reproduce. Proponents of a cultural predisposition argue that experiences teach us early in life that certain objects are legitimate sources of fear, and this training predisposes many people to acquire corresponding phobias (Carr, 1979).

## Treatments for Phobias

Practitioners from each major school of thought have developed interventions for phobias, but behavioral approaches have predominated. Research has shown them to be highly effective and to fare better than other approaches in most head-to-head comparisons (Emmelkamp, 1994, 1982). Thus, our discussion will focus primarily on the leading behavioral interventions for, in turn, specific phobias, agoraphobia, and social phobias.

### Behavioral Treatments for Specific Phobias

Specific phobias were among the first anxiety disorders to be successfully treated in clinical practice. The major behavioral approaches to these phobias are *desensitization, flooding,* and *modeling*. Collectively, these approaches are called *exposure treatments,* because in all of them clients are exposed to the object or situation they dread.

**Systematic Desensitization**    Clients treated by *systematic desensitization,* a technique developed by Joseph Wolpe (1990, 1958), learn to relax while they are confronted with the objects or situations they fear. Since relaxation and fear are incompatible, the new relaxation response is thought to substitute for the fear response.

*Seeking to reduce the $1.5 billion a year lost to aerophobia, the fear of flying, the airline industry has offered desensitization programs for sufferers. USAir's Fearful Flyers Program begins with an instructor guiding would-be passengers in relaxation exercises.*

Desensitization therapists first teach clients to *relax* by releasing all the tension in their bodies on cue. Over the course of several sessions and homework assignments, clients learn to identify individual muscle groups, tense them, relax them, and ultimately relax the whole body. With continued practice, the clients are able to bring on a state of deep muscle relaxation at will.

During the early sessions of desensitization, therapists also help clients to make a *fear hierarchy,* a list of specific situations in which their phobia is aroused ranked in ascending order, from circumstances that evoke only a trace of fear to those that the clients consider extremely frightening (see Table 5-3).

Next the clients learn how to pair relaxation with their feared objects. While they are in a state of relaxation, the therapist has them confront the event at the bottom of their fear hierarchy. This may be an actual physical confrontation (a person who fears heights, for example, may stand on a chair or climb a stepladder)—in which case the process is called *in vivo desensitization*—or a confrontation that is imagined, with the client creating a mental image of the frightening event while the therapist describes it—in which case the process is called *covert desensitization.*

The clients move through the entire list, pairing their relaxation responses with each feared item in the hierarchy. Because the first item is only mildly frightening, it is usually only a short while before they are able to relax totally when they confront it. Over the course of several sessions, clients move up the ladder of their fears until they reach and overcome the one

*Fear hierarchy*    A list of the objects or situations that frighten a person, starting with those which are minimally feared and ending with those which are feared the most. Used in systematic desensitization.

**Table 5-3   *Sample "Fear of Flying" Hierarchy***

Read from the bottom up:

- The plane starts down the runway, and the motors get louder as the plane increases speed and suddenly lifts off.
- The plane encounters turbulence.
- The plane has taken off from the airport and banks as it changes direction. I am aware of the "tilt."
- The plane is descending to the runway for a landing. I feel the speed and see the ground getting closer.
- I am looking out the window and suddenly the plane enters clouds and I cannot see out the window.
- I notice the seat-belt signs light up, so I fasten my seat belt and I notice the sound of the motors starting.
- I am now inside the plane. I move in from the aisle and sit down in my assigned seat.
- I walk down the ramp leading to the plane and enter the door of the plane.
- I hear my flight number announced, and I proceed to the security checkpoint with my hand luggage.
- I am entering the terminal. I am carrying my bags and tickets.
- I am driving to the airport for my flight. I am aware of every plane I see.
- It is ten days before the trip, and I receive the tickets in the mail.
- I have called the travel agent and told him of my plans.
- A trip has been planned, and I have decided "out loud" to travel by plane.

*Sources:* Adapted from Martin & Pear, 1988, p. 380; Roscoe et al., 1980.

that frightens them most of all. At this point they can relax in the face of all items on the hierarchy.

### Consider This
Individuals who suffer from anxiety disorders might benefit if they could simply relax at will. What specific techniques or instructions might be used to teach people how to relax? Might relaxation training also be useful for other people as they try to cope with everyday situations? Which situations in particular?

**Flooding**   Another behavioral exposure treatment for specific phobias is *flooding,* or *implosive therapy* (Stampfl, 1975). Flooding therapists believe that clients will stop fearing things when they are exposed to them repeatedly and made to see that they are actually quite harmless. These therapists use no relaxation training and no graduated approach. The flooding procedures, like desensitization, can be either in vivo or imaginal.

When therapists guide clients in imagining the feared objects or situations, they often embellish and

*Flooding*   A treatment for phobias in which clients are exposed repeatedly and intensively to the feared object and made to see that it is actually quite harmless.

exaggerate the description so that the clients experience intense emotional arousal. In the case of a woman who had a phobic reaction to snakes, the therapist had her imagine the following scene, among others:

Close your eyes again. Picture the snake out in front of you, now make yourself pick it up. Reach down, pick it up, put it in your lap, feel it wiggling around in your lap, leave your hand on it, put your hand out and feel it wiggling around. Kind of explore its body with your fingers and hand. You don't like to do it, make yourself do it. Make yourself do it. Really grab onto the snake. Squeeze it a little bit, feel it. Feel it kind of start to wind around your hand. Let it. Leave your hand there, feel it touching your hand and winding around it, curling around your wrist.

*(Hogan, 1968, pp. 423–431)*

**Modeling**   The behavioral technique of *modeling,* or *vicarious conditioning,* has also been used to treat specific phobias (Bandura, 1977, 1971). In this procedure it is the therapist who confronts the feared object or situation while the fearful client observes. The therapist essentially acts as a model who demonstrates that the client's fear is groundless or highly exaggerated. It is expected that after several sessions clients will be able to approach the objects or situations with relative composure.

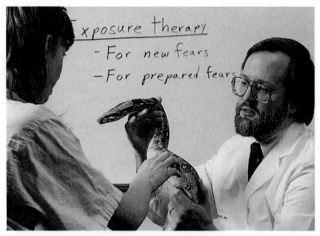

*In the behavioral exposure technique of participant modeling, a therapist treats a client with a snake phobia by first handling the snake himself, then encouraging the client to touch and handle the snake.*

The most effective modeling technique is *participant modeling,* or *guided participation.* Here the therapist and client first construct a fear hierarchy, just as they would in desensitization. Then, while the client observes, the therapist experiences the least feared item in the hierarchy. Eventually the client is encouraged to join in, and they move up the hierarchy until the client is able to confront the most feared object or situation on the list.

**The Effectiveness of Behavioral Treatments for Specific Phobias** Clinical researchers have repeatedly found that each of the behavioral exposure therapies for specific phobias is helpful (Emmelkamp, 1994). Moreover, in most cases once a phobia has been successfully treated by a behavioral method, new symptoms do not arise to replace it, as some psychodynamic theorists had predicted would occur.

The key to success with a behavioral approach appears to be *actual* contact with the feared object or situation (Emmelkamp, 1994; Arntz & Lavy, 1993). In vivo desensitization is more effective than covert desensitization, in vivo flooding more effective than imaginal flooding, and participant modeling more helpful than modeling that is strictly vicarious (Menzies & Clarke, 1993). When the exposure factor is kept constant, desensitization, flooding, and modeling appear to be equally effective treatments for specific phobias (Ritchie, 1992).

## Behavioral Treatments for Agoraphobia

As with specific phobias, behaviorists have led the way in the treatment of agoraphobia by developing a variety of in vivo exposure approaches (Emmelkamp,

1994; Gelder, 1991). These approaches do not always bring as much relief to sufferers as the highly successful treatments for specific phobias, but they do offer considerable relief to many people. Therapists typically help clients to venture farther and farther from their homes and to enter outside places gradually, one step at a time. The therapists use rewards, support, reasoning, and coaxing to get clients to confront the outside world. Figure 5-6 demonstrates the progress of an agoraphobic client treated by this approach.

Exposure therapy for people with agoraphobia often includes additional therapeutic features as well. In the *support group* approach, for example, a small number of people with agoraphobia go out together for exposure sessions that last for several hours. The group members support and encourage one another, and eventually coax one another to move away from the safety of the group and perform exposure tasks on their own. In *home-based self-help programs,* clinicians give clients and their families detailed instructions for carrying out exposure treatments themselves (Emmelkamp et al., 1992).

Between 60 and 80 percent of the agoraphobic clients who receive exposure treatment find it easier to enter public places, and the improvement persists for

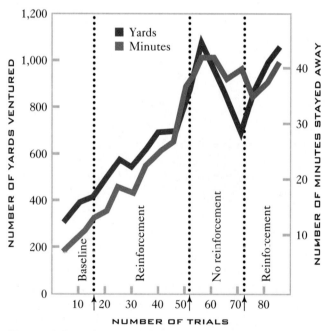

**Figure 5-6** *When an agoraphobic patient was increasingly reinforced for walking out of and staying away from the front door of the hospital, she ventured increasingly farther and stayed away longer. When reinforcements were then stopped, she initially ventured even farther and stayed away even longer ("extinction burst"), but then steadily decreased the distance and time spent away from the hospital. When reinforcements were reinstated, she again ventured farther and stayed away longer. (Adapted from Agras et al., 1968.)*

years after the beginning of treatment (Craske & Barlow, 1993; O'Sullivan & Marks, 1991). Unfortunately, these improvements are often partial rather than complete, and relapses may occur in as many as 50 percent of successfully treated clients, although these people readily recapture previous gains if they are treated again (O'Sullivan & Marks, 1991).

## Behavioral and Cognitive Treatments for Social Phobias

Clinicians have only recently begun to report consistent success in treating social phobias, persistent fears of social or performance situations in which embarrassment may occur. This recent progress is due in large part to the growing recognition that social phobias have two distinct components that may feed each other: (1) people with these phobias may have incapacitating social fears, and (2) they may lack skill at initiating conversations, communicating their needs, or addressing the needs of others. Armed with this insight, clinicians now treat social phobias by either trying to reduce social fears, providing social skills training, or both, depending on the client.

**Reducing Social Fears** Although some studies suggest that certain psychotropic medications, particularly beta blockers, may help reduce the social and performance fears of people with social phobias (Oberlander et al., 1994), clinicians have primarily used psychotherapeutic techniques to achieve this goal. In recent years, for example, behaviorists have effectively employed exposure techniques to reduce social fears (Mersch, 1995; Scholing & Emmelkamp, 1993). Here again the therapists guide, encourage, and persuade clients to expose themselves to dreaded social situations, and to remain in each until their fear subsides.

Group therapy often provides an ideal setting for these exposure treatments, enabling people to confront the social situations they fear head on in an atmosphere of support and concern (Hope & Heimberg, 1993). In one group, for example, a man who was afraid that his hands would tremble in the presence of others had to write on a blackboard in front of the group and serve tea to the other members (Emmelkamp, 1982).

Cognitive interventions have also been employed in the treatment of social fears. In the following discussion, Albert Ellis uses rational emotive therapy to help a client who fears that he will be rejected if he speaks up at gatherings. This discussion took place after the client had followed a homework assignment in which he was to observe his self-defeating thoughts and beliefs and force himself to say anything he had on his mind in social situations, no matter how stupid it might seem to him.

> After two weeks of this assignment, the patient came into his next session of therapy and reported: "I did what you told me to do. . . . [Every] time, just as you said, I found myself retreating from people, I said to myself: 'Now, even though you can't see it, there must be some sentences. What are they?' And I finally found them. And there were many of them! And they all seemed to say the same thing."
>
> "What thing?"
>
> "That I, uh, was going to be rejected. . . . [If] I related to them I was going to be rejected. And wouldn't that be perfectly awful if I was to be rejected. And there was no reason for me, uh, to take that, uh, sort of thing, and be rejected in that awful manner." . . .
>
> "And did you do the second part of the homework assignment?"
>
> "The forcing myself to speak up and express myself?"
>
> "Yes, that part."
>
> "That was worse. That was really hard. Much harder than I thought it would be. But I did it."
>
> "And—?"
>
> "Oh, not bad at all. I spoke up several times; more than I've ever done before. Some people were very surprised. Phyllis was very surprised, too. But I spoke up." . . .
>
> "And how did you feel after expressing yourself like that?"
>
> "Remarkable! I don't remember when I last felt this way. I felt, uh, just remarkable—good, that is. It was really something to feel! But it was so hard. I almost didn't make it. And a couple of other times during the week I had to force myself again. But I did. And I was glad!"
>
> *(Ellis, 1962, pp. 202–203)*

Numerous studies indicate that rational-emotive therapy and similar cognitive approaches help reduce social fears (Emmelkamp, 1994; Chambless & Gillis, 1993). Moreover, these reductions are still apparent in follow-up observations up to five years after treatment (Heimberg et al., 1991). At the same time, research also suggests that cognitive therapy, like exposure treatment, rarely enables clients to overcome social phobias fully. Although it does reduce social fear, it does not consistently help people perform effectively in the social realm (Gardner et al., 1980). This is where social skills training has come to the forefront.

**Social Skills Training** *Social skills training* combines several behavioral techniques in an effort to help people acquire needed social skills. Therapists usually model appropriate social behaviors for clients and encourage the clients to try them out. Typically clients role-play with the therapists, rehearsing their new social behaviors until they become proficient. Throughout the process, therapists provide candid feedback and reinforce (praise) the clients for effective social performances.

*Social skills training groups* and *assertiveness training groups* often help serve these functions. Members try out and rehearse new social behavior with or in front of other group members, such as looking people in the eye or speaking up. The group can provide a consensus on what is socially appropriate, and social reinforcement from group members is often more powerful than reinforcement from a therapist alone.

Studies have found that social skills training helps socially fearful people perform better in social situations (Emmelkamp, 1994; Mersch et al., 1991). It appears, however, that this form of treatment alone has only a limited effect on some clients, who often continue to experience uncomfortable levels of fear (Marks, 1987; Falloon et al., 1977).

Thus, while exposure treatment, cognitive therapy, and social skills training are each helpful in the treatment of social phobias, it appears that no single one of them is consistently able to bring about a complete change (Wlazlo et al., 1990). When the approaches are combined, however, the results have been most encouraging (Hope & Heimberg, 1993).

*Summing Up*

*A phobia is an excessive fear of a particular object, activity, or situation. The leading explanations and treatments for phobias come from the behavioral model. Behaviorists propose that these fears are the result of classical conditioning or modeling. They treat them with exposure techniques and, in the case of social phobias, social skills training.*

## The State of the Field
# Generalized Anxiety Disorder and Phobias

Generalized anxiety disorder and phobias are the two most common anxiety disorders and indeed two of the most common of all psychological disorders. Given their impact on so many people, it is no wonder that each has long been a focus of clinical theorizing, investigation, and treatment.

Unfortunately, despite years of work, generalized anxiety disorder continues to be rather poorly understood. The various models of psychopathology all have something to say about this disorder, but each explanation is weakened by its model's characteristic limitations. Similarly, the many treatments applied to this disorder have had at best modest success. Thus, although some promising findings are now emerging, much more must be accomplished in order for a broad understanding and effective interventions to be achieved.

In contrast, the many years of clinical theory and research have yielded considerable success and promise in the understanding and treatment of phobias. The behavioral perspective in particular has offered many insights into phobias, and behavioral interventions are often effective in treating specific phobias, agoraphobia, and (when used in combination with cognitive therapy) social phobias.

Perhaps the most promising trend that has begun to emerge with regard to these two anxiety disorders is the inclination of clinicians to combine concepts and treatments from various models in order to explain and address the disorders. For example, some clinicians now view social phobias as a consequence of both behavioral and cognitive factors, and many treat this disorder with a combination of exposure therapy, cognitive therapy, and social skills training. Similarly, cognitive or psychodynamic therapy has often been combined with antianxiety drugs or biofeedback in the treatment of generalized anxiety disorder.

The tendency to combine concepts and interventions from various models has been even more apparent with regard to the remaining anxiety disorders—panic disorders, obsessive-compulsive disorder, and stress disorders. These disorders once seemed to defy explanation and treatment, but the past 15 years have seen dramatic progress. Theorists and researchers have developed remarkable insights and therapeutic procedures that practitioners are now applying, often in combination, with increasing success. In the next chapter we shall turn to these other anxiety disorders and to the promising work being done to understand and treat them.

# Chapter Review

1. *Anxiety and Anxiety Disorders: Fear* is a state of tension or alarm. *Anxiety* is a broader reaction that occurs when our sense of threat is more diffuse or vague. People with anxiety disorders, collectively the most common mental disorders in the United States, experience ongoing fear and anxiety that prevent them from leading a normal life.

2. *Generalized Anxiety Disorder:* People with generalized anxiety disorder experience excessive anxiety and worry about numerous events or activities. Up to 3.8 percent of the United States population suffer from this disorder in any given year, women twice as often as men.

3. *Explanations and Treatments for Generalized Anxiety Disorder:* Proponents of the various models have focused on different factors and offered different explanations and treatments for generalized anxiety disorder. These explanations and treatments have received only limited research support to date, although recent cognitive and biological efforts seem to be promising.

   A. *Sociocultural Perspective:* According to the *sociocultural view,* increases in societal dangers and pressures may establish a climate in which generalized anxiety disorder is more likely to develop.

   B. *Psychodynamic Perspective:* Freud, the initial formulator of the *psychodynamic view,* said that a generalized anxiety disorder develops when defense mechanisms break down and function poorly. Psychodynamic therapists use free association, interpretation, and related psychodynamic techniques to help patients overcome this problem.

   C. *Humanistic and Existential Perspectives:* Carl Rogers, the leading *humanistic* theorist, believed that people with generalized anxiety disorder fail to receive *unconditional positive regard* from significant others during their childhood and so become overly critical of themselves. He employed *client-centered therapy* to help clients become more self-accepting and less anxious.

   *Existentialists* believe that generalized anxiety disorder results from the existential anxiety people experience because they know that life is finite and suspect that it may have no meaning. Existential therapists help anxious clients take more responsibility and live more meaningfully.

   D. *Cognitive Perspective: Cognitive* theorists believe that generalized anxiety disorder is caused by *maladaptive assumptions* that lead people to view most life situations as dangerous. Cognitive practitioners treat clients by helping them to change such assumptions and by teaching them how to cope during stressful situations.

   E. *Biological Perspective: Biological* theorists argue that generalized anxiety disorder results from deficient activity of the neurotransmitter GABA. The most common biological treatment is antianxiety drugs, particularly benzodiazepines. Biofeedback is also applied in many cases.

4. *Phobias:* A *phobia* is a persistent and unreasonable fear of a particular object, activity, or situation. As many as 11 percent of the adult population in the United States suffer from this disorder in any given year. There are three main categories of phobias. *Agoraphobia* is a fear of venturing into public places in which escape might be difficult or help unavailable should immobilizing or upsetting symptoms develop. A *social phobia* is a severe, persistent, and irrational fear of social or performance situations in which embarrassment may occur. All other phobias are called *specific phobias.*

5. *Behavioral Explanations and Treatments for Phobias*

   A. *Behavioral* explanations of phobias have been the most influential over the years. Behaviorists believe that phobias are learned from the environment through *classical conditioning* or *modeling* and then maintained because of avoidance behaviors.

   B. Behaviorists have treated *specific phobias* successfully by using *exposure techniques* in which clients confront their objects of fear. The exposure may be gradual and relaxed (desensitization), intense (flooding), or vicarious (modeling).

   C. Behaviorists have also used exposure techniques successfully to treat *agoraphobia.* Treatment often includes a support group or a home-based self-help program.

   D. Therapists typically distinguish two components of *social phobias:* social fears and lack of specific skills. They may try to reduce social fears by using exposure techniques, group therapy, and various cognitive interventions. They may improve social skills with *social skills training,* often offered in a group format. Often a combination of exposure techniques, cognitive therapy, and social skills training is used.

# Key Terms

| | | | |
|---|---|---|---|
| fear | conditions of worth | biofeedback | vicarious conditioning |
| anxiety | client-centered therapy | barbiturate | preparedness |
| generalized anxiety | existential anxiety | meprobamate | systematic desensitization |
|   disorder | maladaptive assumptions | electromyograph (EMG) | relaxation training |
| phobia | automatic thoughts | agoraphobia | fear hierarchy |
| stress | rational-emotive therapy | social phobia | in vivo desensitization |
| stressor | cognitive therapy | specific phobia | covert desensitization |
| autonomic nervous system | self-instruction training | repression | flooding |
| central nervous system | self-statements | displacement | implosive therapy |
| sympathetic nervous | benzodiazepine | classical conditioning | participant modeling |
|   system | diazepam | unconditioned stimulus | exposure therapy |
| free-floating anxiety | alprazolam | unconditioned response | home-based self-help |
| neurotic anxiety | chlordiazepoxide | conditioned stimulus |   exposure therapy |
| moral anxiety | gamma aminobutyric acid | conditioned response | social skills training |
| unconditional positive |   (GABA) | modeling | assertiveness training |
|   regard | antianxiety drug | stimulus generalization | |

# Quick Quiz

1. What factors determine how people react to stressors in life?
2. Describe the relationship between generalized anxiety disorder and sociocultural factors such as societal change and poverty and race.
3. What are the key notions in the psychodynamic, humanistic-existential, cognitive, and biological explanations of generalized anxiety disorder? How have these notions fared in research?
4. How effective have treatments been for generalized anxiety disorder? Compare the effectiveness of the leading treatment approaches.
5. Describe the biological explanations of anxiety and generalized anxiety disorder. What are the limitations and drawbacks of today's leading biological interventions for this disorder?
6. Distinguish and compare the three kinds of phobias.
7. How do behaviorists explain the onset and maintenance of phobias? What evidence exists for these explanations?
8. Describe the three behavioral exposure techniques used to treat specific phobias. How effective are they?
9. How do behaviorists treat agoraphobia? How successful is this approach?
10. What are the two different components of a social phobia, and how are each of them addressed in treatment?

# 6

# Panic, Obsessive-Compulsive, and Stress Disorders

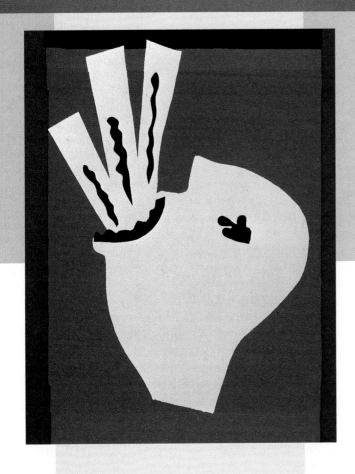

## Topic Overview

*Panic Disorders*
 Biological Perspective
 Cognitive Perspective

*Obsessive-Compulsive Disorder*
 Psychodynamic Perspective
 Behavioral Perspective
 Cognitive Perspective
 Biological Perspective

*Stress Disorders*
 Acute Stress Disorder
 Posttraumatic Stress Disorder

For most of this century, generalized anxiety disorder and phobias received much more attention from clinical practitioners and researchers than did the other anxiety disorders—panic, obsessive-compulsive, and stress disorders. The latter appeared to be less common, explanations for them more elusive, and treatments less effective. This situation has changed drastically in the past 10 years.

Recent studies have revealed that panic, obsessive-compulsive, and stress disorders are more common than previously believed, although they still seem to be less prevalent than generalized anxiety disorder and phobias. Moreover, researchers have uncovered very promising clues concerning the origins of these disorders, and therapists have developed treatments for them that are very helpful indeed. Accordingly, this is where investigators of anxiety disorders are now focusing much of their attention.

As with generalized anxiety disorder and phobias, anxiety plays a key role in panic, obsessive-compulsive, and stress disorders. As we noted in the previous chapter, people with *panic disorders* have recurrent attacks of terror. Those with *obsessive-compulsive disorder* are beset by recurrent and unwanted thoughts that cause anxiety or by the need to perform repetitive actions to reduce anxiety. And people with *acute stress disorder* and *posttraumatic stress disorder* are tormented by fear well after a traumatic event has ended.

# Panic Disorders

Sometimes an anxiety reaction accelerates into a smothering, nightmarish panic. When that happens to people, they lose control of their behavior, are practically unaware of what they are doing, and feel a sense of imminent doom. Anyone can react with panic if a situation is provocative enough. Some people, however, experience *panic attacks*—periodic, discrete bouts of panic that occur abruptly and reach a peak within ten minutes. Such attacks consist of at least four symptoms of panic, the most common of which are palpitations of the heart, tingling in the hands or feet, shortness of breath, sweating, hot and cold flashes, trembling, chest pains, choking sensations, faintness, dizziness, and a feeling of unreality (APA, 1994). Small wonder that during a panic attack many people fear they will die, go crazy, or lose control. Here a woman describes such an episode:

> I was inside a very busy shopping precinct and all of a sudden it happened: in a matter of seconds I was like a mad woman. It was like a nightmare, only I was

awake; everything went black and sweat poured out of me—my body, my hands and even my hair got wet through. All the blood seemed to drain out of me; I went as white as a ghost. I felt as if I were going to collapse; it was as if I had no control over my limbs; my back and legs were very weak and I felt as though it were impossible to move. It was as if I had been taken over by some stronger force. I saw all the people looking at me—just faces, no bodies, all merged into one. My heart started pounding in my head and in my ears; I thought my heart was going to stop. I could see black and yellow lights. I could hear the voices of the people but from a long way off. I could not think of anything except the way I was feeling and that now I had to get out and run quickly or I would die. I must escape and get into the fresh air.

> (*Hawkrigg, 1975*)

People suffering from any of the anxiety disorders may experience a panic attack when they confront one of the objects or situations they dread (APA, 1994). Some people, however, experience panic attacks without apparent provocation, and do so recurrently and unpredictably. They may receive a diagnosis of *panic disorder.*

According to DSM-IV, a diagnosis of panic disorder is warranted if after one or more unexpected panic attacks a person spends a month or more worrying persistently about having another attack, worrying about the implications or consequences of the attack (such as fear of going crazy or having a heart attack), or changing his or her behavior markedly in response to the attack.

In any given year, as many as 2.3 percent of adults in the United States suffer from a panic disorder (Kessler et al., 1994; Regier et al., 1993; Eaton et al., 1991). Around half of them receive treatment (Narrow et al., 1993) (see Figure 6-1). Most people develop the disorder between late adolescence and the mid-thirties, and the diagnosis is at least twice as common among women as among men (APA, 1994) (see Table 6-1).

Many other people experience panic attacks that are not severe or frequent enough to be diagnosed as a panic disorder (Eaton et al., 1994). In one survey, 43 percent of 534 Australian adolescents reported having experienced at least one panic attack (King et al., 1993).

Many people mistakenly believe that they have a general medical problem when they first experience panic attacks (Oakley-Browne, 1991). Conversely, certain medical problems, such as *mitral valve prolapse,* a cardiac malfunction marked by periodic episodes of heart palpitations, and *thyroid disease,* may initially be

---

*Panic disorder*   An anxiety disorder characterized by recurrent and unpredictable panic attacks that occur without apparent provocation.

## Table 6-1  *Anxiety Disorders Profile*

| | *One-Year Prevalence* | *Female:Male Ratio* | *Typical Age of Onset* | *Prevalence among Close Relatives* |
|---|---|---|---|---|
| Panic disorders | 2.3% | 5:2 | 15–35 years | Elevated |
| Obsessive-compulsive disorder | 2.0% | 1:1 | 4–25 years | Elevated |
| Acute and posttraumatic stress disorders | 0.5% | 1:1 | Variable | Unknown |

Sources: APA, 1994; Kessler et al., 1994; Regier et al., 1993; Eaton et al., 1991; Blazer et al., 1991; Davidson et al., 1991.

misdiagnosed as panic disorder and nothing else (Coplan et al., 1992; Agras, 1985).

A panic disorder is often accompanied by agoraphobia (fear of venturing into public places), a pattern that DSM-IV terms *panic disorder with agoraphobia.* In such cases, the agoraphobic pattern usually seems to emerge from the panic attacks (Barlow, 1988). After experiencing unpredictable and recurrent panic attacks, people become fearful of having one someplace where help is unavailable or escape difficult. Anne Watson was one such person:

Ms. Watson reported that until the onset of her current problems two years ago, she had led a normal and happy life. At that time an uncle to whom she had been extremely close in her childhood died following a sudden unexpected heart attack. . . . Six months after his death she was returning home from work one evening when suddenly she felt that she couldn't catch her breath. Her heart began to pound, and she broke out into a cold sweat. Things began to seem unreal, her legs felt leaden, and she became sure she would die or faint before she reached home. She asked a passerby to help her get a taxi and went to a nearby hospital emergency room. The doctors there found her physical examination, blood count and chemistries, and electrocardiogram all completely normal. . . .

Four weeks later Ms. Watson had a second similar attack while preparing dinner at home. She made an appointment to see her family doctor, but again, all examinations were normal. She decided to put the episodes out of her mind and continue with her normal activities. Within the next several weeks, however, she had four attacks and noticed that she began to worry about when the next one would occur. . . .

She then found herself constantly thinking about her anxieties as attacks continued; she began to dread leaving the house alone for fear she would be stranded, helpless and alone, by an attack. She began to avoid going to movies, parties, and dinners with friends for fear she would have an attack and be embarrassed by her need to leave. When household chores necessitated driving, she waited until it was possible to take her children or a friend along for the ride. She also began walking the twenty blocks to her office to avoid the possibility of being trapped in a subway car between stops when an attack occurred.

*(Spitzer et al., 1983, pp. 7–8)*

Biological theorists and therapists initially led the way in explaining and treating panic disorders. In recent years cognitive researchers and practitioners have built upon the insights gathered from biological research.

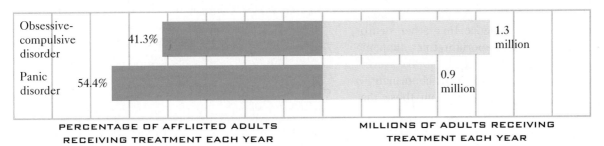

**Figure 6-1**  *Who receives treatment for their anxiety disorders? More than half of all persons who have a panic disorder and more than 40 percent of those with an obsessive-compulsive disorder in the United States receive professional treatment each year, a total of 2.2 million people in all. (Adapted from Regier et al., 1993; Blazer et al., 1991; Boyd et al., 1990.)*

## The Biological Perspective

Biological explanations and treatments for panic disorders had their beginning in the 1960s with the surprising discovery that people with these disorders were helped not by benzodiazepine drugs, the drugs effective in treating generalized anxiety disorder, but by certain *antidepressant drugs,* drugs that are usually used to alleviate the symptoms of depression (Klein, 1964; Klein & Fink, 1962).

### Biological Explanations

To understand the biology of panic disorders, researchers worked backward from their understanding of the effective antidepressant drugs. They knew that the drugs in question alter the activity of *norepinephrine,* a neurotransmitter that carries messages from neuron to neuron in the brain. If antidepressant drugs alter norepinephrine activity in such a way as to eliminate panic attacks, researchers wondered, might it be that panic disorders are caused in the first place by abnormal norepinephrine activity?

They have since gathered evidence that norepinephrine activity may in fact be irregular in people who experience panic attacks (Papp et al., 1992). For example, when the *locus coeruleus*—a brain area rich in neurons that use norepinephrine (see Figure 6-2)—is electrically stimulated in monkeys, the monkeys display a paniclike reaction. This finding suggests that panic reactions may be related to changes in norepinephrine activity in the locus coeruleus (Redmond, 1981, 1979, 1977). In another line of research, scientists have *induced* panic attacks in human beings by administering chemicals known to alter the activity of norepinephrine (Basoglu, 1992).

Although these studies seem to point to abnormal norepinephrine activity, particularly in the locus coeruleus, as a key cause of panic disorders (Papp et al., 1992; Gorman et al., 1990, 1989), the nature of this abnormal activity is still not fully understood. Moreover, there is some evidence that other neurotransmitters may also play important roles in panic disorders (Leonard, 1992; Kahn et al., 1988). Nevertheless, whatever the precise biological abnormalities may be, they appear to be different from those that cause generalized anxiety disorder.

---

*Norepinephrine*   A neurotransmitter whose abnormal activity is linked to depression and panic disorder.

*Locus coeruleus*   A small area in the brainstem that seems to be active in the regulation of emotions. It is rich in neurons that use norepinephrine.

### Drug Therapies

As we noted earlier, in 1962 the clinical investigators Donald Klein and Max Fink discovered that panic attacks could be prevented or at least made less frequent by antidepressant drugs, the medications used primarily to lift the spirits of people suffering from depression. Since then, studies across the world have repeatedly confirmed that certain antidepressant drugs bring relief to many people with panic disorders and that the drugs seem to be helpful whether or not the panic disorders are accompanied by depressive symptoms (Klerman et al., 1994).

It seems that the antidepressant drugs act to restore appropriate norepinephrine activity in people with a panic disorder, particularly in the locus coeruleus, and in doing so help to reduce the symptoms of the disorder. Recently *alprazolam* (Xanax), a benzodiazepine drug whose action is somewhat more powerful and different from that of the other benzodiazepine drugs, has also proved effective in the treatment of panic disorders (Rickels et al., 1993; Ballenger et al., 1988).

Altogether, studies conducted around the world indicate that these drugs bring at least some improvement to 80 percent of patients who have a panic disorder (Hirschfeld, 1992). Approximately 40 percent reach full recovery or improve markedly, and the improvements have been observed up to four years after the start of treatment. On the other hand, 20 percent of people with this disorder remain severely debilitated in spite of such treatment (Hirschfeld, 1992).

Clinicians have also found antidepressant drugs or alprazolam to be helpful in most cases of panic disorder with agoraphobia, cases in which the client's outbreaks of panic help produce a general fear of entering public places (Rickels et al., 1993). As the drugs eliminate or reduce the client's panic attacks, he or she becomes more confident that the attacks have ceased and less hesitant to approach public settings. For some clients with this disorder, however, a combination of antidepressant drugs and behavioral exposure treatments is more effective than either treatment alone (Nagy et al., 1993; Mavissakalian, 1993).

## The Cognitive Perspective

In recent years a number of cognitive theorists and practitioners have suggested that biological difficulties are but the first step in a chain leading to panic attacks and disorders (Ehlers, 1993; Craske & Barlow, 1993). They argue that full panic reactions are experienced only by people who misinterpret or overreact to internal, physiological events, and they have fo-

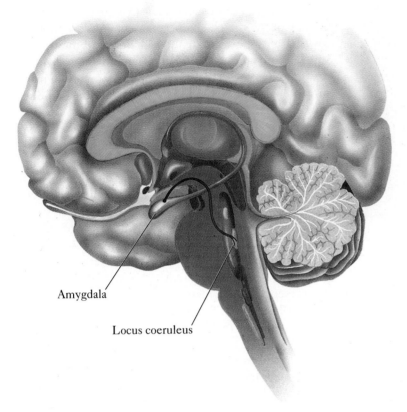

Amygdala

Locus coeruleus

**Figure 6-2** *The locus coeruleus, a small area in the brain stem, sends its major messages to the amygdala, a structure in the brain's limbic system that is known to trigger emotional reactions. The neurons of the locus coeruleus use norepinephrine, a neurotransmitter implicated in panic disorders and in depression.*

cused their theories and treatments primarily on such misinterpretations.

## The Cognitive Explanation

Cognitive theorists believe that panic-prone people may be highly sensitive to certain bodily sensations and misinterpret them as indicative of an imminent catastrophe. Rather than understanding the probable cause of their sensations as "something I ate" or "a fight with the boss," the panic-prone grow increasingly worried about losing control, fear the worst, lose all perspective, and rapidly deteriorate into panic. Expecting that their "dangerous" sensations may return at any time, they set themselves up for future misinterpretations and panic attacks.

Research suggests that panic-prone individuals have a high degree of *anxiety sensitivity:* they are preoccupied with their bodily sensations, lose their ability to assess them logically and knowledgeably, and interpret them as potentially harmful (Taylor, 1995). One study found that subjects who scored high on an anxiety sensitivity survey were five times more likely than other subjects to develop a panic disorder within three years after the survey (Maller & Reiss, 1992). Another study found that people with panic disorders are in-

deed more frightened by their bodily sensations than other people (Taylor et al., 1992).

According to cognitive theorists, such people tend to misinterpret several kinds of sensations. Many seem to "overbreathe," or hyperventilate, in stressful situations. Apparently the abnormal breathing makes them think they are in danger or even dying, so they panic (Rapee, 1995; Margraf, 1993). Other physical sensations that trigger misinterpretations in the panic-prone include euphoric excitement, fullness in the abdomen, acute anger, and sudden tearing in the eyes (Sokol-Kessler & Beck, 1987). One patient, on learning that her artwork had been accepted for exhibit at a gallery, became extremely excited, experienced "palpitations of the heart," misinterpreted them as a sign of a heart attack, and panicked.

In so-called *biological challenge tests,* researchers produce a hyperventilation reaction or other biological sensations in subjects by administering drugs or by instructing the subjects to breath, exercise, or think in certain ways. When such procedures are applied to people with a panic disorder, they do indeed experi-

*Biological challenge test* A procedure used to induce panic in subjects or clients by having them exercise vigorously or perform other physical tasks in the presence of a therapist or researcher.

*Almost anyone is capable of experiencing panic in the face of a clear and overwhelming threat that unfolds at breakneck speed. Uncontrollable crowds led to panic when a wall collapsed at the European Cup soccer finals in Brussels in 1985. Thousands of persons were injured and thirty-eight were killed.*

ence greater anxiety than people without this disorder, particularly when the panic-prone subjects believe that the hyperventilation or other bodily sensations are relatively dangerous or out of their control (Rapee, 1995).

Although the cognitive explanation of panic disorders is relatively new, it has already captured the attention of numerous panic theorists and has received considerable empirical support. As we have noted, research clearly indicates that the panic-prone may interpret bodily sensations in ways that are not at all common. Precisely how different their misinterpretations are and how they interact with biological factors are questions that need to be answered more fully in the coming years.

### Consider This

The cognitive explanation of panic disorders focuses on the statements that individuals make to themselves. What kinds of internal statements could lead to a panic disorder? Cognitive theorists also suggest that people prone to panic disorders are often poor interpreters of their bodily sensations. Why might some people be inaccurate interpreters of their sensations?

## Cognitive Therapies

Cognitive therapists try to correct the misinterpretations of body sensations that they believe are leading to a client's panic attacks. Aaron Beck (1988), for example, tries to teach patients that their physical sensations are harmless. Initially he briefs clients on the general nature of panic attacks, the actual causes of

their bodily sensations, and their tendency to misinterpret them. As the clients become convinced that such explanations are accurate interpretations of their physical sensations, they are able to remind themselves in real-life situations that the sensations are not signs of impending catastrophe, thus shorting out the panic sequence at an early point. Over the course of therapy, clients may also be taught to distract themselves from their sensations by, for example, starting a conversation with someone when the sensations occur.

Beck and other cognitive therapists also use biological challenge procedures to induce panic sequences during therapy sessions so that clients can develop and apply their new insights and skills under watchful supervision. In these procedures, clients whose attacks are ordinarily triggered by a rapid heart rate may be instructed to jump up and down for several minutes in the presence of the therapist or to run up a flight of stairs (Clark, 1993; Rapee, 1993). They can then practice interpreting their heightened heart rate appropriately and distracting themselves from dwelling on their sensations.

Research indicates that this and similar cognitive treatments for panic disorders are often quite helpful (Fava et al., 1995; Margraf et al., 1993). Recent studies conducted internationally revealed that 85 percent of subjects with panic disorders were panic free both immediately after receiving cognitive therapy and up to two years later, compared to 13 percent of control subjects who were on a waiting list or who received supportive therapy (Chambless & Gillis, 1993).

Head-to-head research comparisons show cognitive therapy to be at least as helpful as antidepressant drugs or alprazolam in the treatment of panic disorders, sometimes more so (Margraf et al., 1993; Brown et al., 1992). In view of the effectiveness of both cognitive and drug treatments for panic disorders, some clinicians have tried combining these treatments, but it is not yet clear that the addition of medication is more effective than cognitive therapy alone (Clum et al., 1993; Brown et al., 1992).

### Summing Up

*Sufferers of panic disorders experience panic attacks frequently, unpredictably, and without apparent provocation. Biological clinicians trace the disorder to abnormal norepinephrine activity in the locus coeruleus and treat it with certain antidepressant drugs or with alprazolam. Cognitive therapists, believing that panic-prone people misinterpret their bodily sensations, try to teach their clients that such sensations are actually harmless.*

# Obsessive-Compulsive Disorder

*Obsessions* are persistent thoughts, ideas, impulses, or images that seem to invade a person's consciousness. *Compulsions* are repetitive and rigid behaviors or mental acts that a person feels compelled to perform in order to prevent or reduce anxiety or distress. Minor obsessions and compulsions are familiar to almost everyone. We may find ourselves preoccupied with thoughts about an upcoming performance, date, examination, or vacation; worry that we forgot to turn off the stove or lock the door; or be haunted for days by the same song, melody, or poem. Similarly, we may feel better when we avoid stepping on cracks, turn away from black cats, follow a strict routine every morning, or arrange our closets in a carefully prescribed manner.

Minor obsessions and compulsions can play a helpful role in life. Distracting tunes or little rituals often calm us during times of stress. A man who repeatedly clicks his pen or taps his fingers during a test may be releasing tension and thus improving his performance. Many people find it comforting to repeat religious or cultural rituals, such as touching a mezuzah, sprinkling holy water, or fingering rosary beads.

According to DSM-IV, a diagnosis of *obsessive-compulsive disorder* is appropriate when a person's obsessions or compulsions feel excessive, unreasonable, intrusive, and inappropriate; are hard to dismiss; cause significant distress; are very time-consuming; or interfere with daily functions. Consider the obsessive-compulsive pattern displayed by Georgia, beginning with the concerns expressed by her husband.

You remember that old joke about getting up in the middle of the night to go to the john and coming back to the bedroom to find your wife has made the bed? It's no joke. Sometimes I think she never sleeps. I got up one night at 4 a.m. and there she was doing the laundry downstairs. Look at your ash tray! I haven't seen one that dirty in years! I'll tell you what it makes me feel like. If I forget to leave my dirty shoes outside the back door she gives me a look like I had just crapped in the middle of an operating room. I stay out of the house a lot and I'm about half-stoned when I do have to be home. She even made us get rid of the dog because she said he was always filthy. When we used to have people over for supper she would jitterbug around everybody till they couldn't digest their food. I hated to call them up and ask them over because I could always hear them hem and haw and make up excuses not to come over. Even the kids are walking down the street nervous about getting dirt on them. I'm going out of my mind but you can't talk to her. She just blows up and spends twice as much time cleaning things. We have guys in to wash the walls so often I think the house is going to fall down from being scrubbed all the time. About a week ago I had it up to here and told her I couldn't take it any more. I think the only reason she came to see you was because I told her I was going to take off and live in a pig pen just for laughs.

Georgia's obsessive concern with cleanliness forced her to take as many as three showers a day, one in the morning, one before supper, and one before going to bed, and on hot days the number of showers would rise in direct proportion to the temperature. . . .

Georgia was aware, in part, of the effect she was having on her family and friends, but she also knew that when she tried to alter her behavior she got so nervous that she felt she was losing her mind. She was frightened by the possibility that "I'm headed for the funny-farm." As she said,

I can't get to sleep unless I am sure everything in the house is in its proper place so that when I get up in the morning, the house is organized. I work like mad to set everything straight before I go to bed, but, when I get up in the morning, I can think of a thousand things that I ought to do. I know some of the things are ridiculous, but I feel better if I get them done, and I can't stand to know something needs doing and I haven't done it.

*(McNeil, 1967, pp. 26–28)*

Georgia's obsessive-compulsive disorder consisted of both obsessions (her repeated concerns about becoming dirty or disordered) and compulsions (her repeated cleaning rituals). In fact, her obsessive worries seemed to generate and fuel her cleaning compulsions. In most but not all cases of this disorder, people display both obsessions and compulsions.

Close to 2 percent of the population in the United States suffer from obsessive-compulsive disorder in any given year (APA, 1994; Regier et al., 1993). It is equally common in males and females and usually begins in childhood, adolescence, or the early 20s (APA, 1994; Flament, 1990). As with Georgia, the disorder

---

*Obsession*   A persistent thought, impulse, or mental image that is experienced repeatedly, feels intrusive, and causes anxiety.

*Compulsion*   A repetitive and rigid behavior or mental act that a person feels compelled to perform in order to prevent or reduce anxiety.

*Obsessive-compulsive disorder*   A disorder in which a person has recurrent and unwanted thoughts or a need to perform repetitive and ritualistic actions, and an experience of intense anxiety whenever these behaviors are suppressed.

typically persists for many years, and the symptoms and their severity fluctuate over time (Flament et al., 1991). Many people with an obsessive-compulsive disorder are also depressed (APA, 1994). Only around 41 percent of those with this disorder receive treatment each year (Regier et al., 1993; Narrow et al., 1993).

## Obsessions

Obsessions are not the same as excessive worries about real problems. They are thoughts that feel both intrusive ("ego dystonic") and foreign ("ego alien") to the people who experience them. Attempts to ignore or resist these thoughts may arouse even more anxiety, and before long they come back more strongly than ever. Like Georgia, people with obsessions are usually quite aware that their cognitions are excessive, inappropriate, and in fact products of their own mind, and many experience them as disgusting and torturous.

Clinicians have found it useful to distinguish various kinds of obsessions, although a single person may have several kinds. Obsessions often take the form of obsessive *wishes* (for example, repeated wishes that one's spouse would die), *impulses* (repeated urges to yell out obscene words at work or church), *images* (fleeting visions of forbidden sexual scenes), *ideas* (notions that germs are lurking everywhere), or *doubts* (concerns that one has made or will make wrong decisions). Here a clinician describes a 20-year-old college junior who experienced obsessive doubts.

He now spent hours each night "rehashing" the day's events, especially interactions with friends and teachers, endlessly making "right" in his mind any and all regrets. He likened the process to playing a videotape of each event over and over again in his mind, asking himself if he had behaved properly and telling himself that he had done his best, or had said the right thing every step of the way. He would do this while sitting at his desk, supposedly studying; and it was not unusual for him to look at the clock after such a period of rumination and note that, to his surprise, two or three hours had elapsed.

*(Spitzer et al., 1981, pp. 20–21)*

Certain basic themes permeate the thoughts of most people troubled by obsessive thinking (APA, 1994). The most common theme appears to be *dirt* or *contamination*. Other common ones are *violence* and *aggression*, *orderliness*, *religion*, and *sexuality* (Rachman & Hodgson, 1980; Akhtar et al., 1975).

## Compulsions

Although compulsive behaviors are technically under voluntary control, the people compelled to do them have little sense of choice in the matter. They believe something terrible, often unspecified, will happen if they do not act on their compulsion. Many, but not all, such people recognize at the same time that their behavior is excessive and unreasonable (Foa & Kozak, 1995).

Some people develop the act into a **compulsive ritual,** performed in a detailed and often elaborate manner. They must go through the ritual in exactly the same way every time, according to certain carefully observed rules. Failure to complete it properly will generate further anxiety and often call for the ritual to be repeated from the beginning.

Like obsessions, compulsions take various forms and center on a variety of themes. A *cleaning compulsion* is very common. Like Georgia, people with these compulsions feel compelled to keep cleaning themselves, their clothing, or their homes. The cleaning may follow ritualistic rules and be repeated dozens or hundreds of times a day. People with *checking compulsions* check the same things over and over, such as appliances, door locks, gas taps, ashtrays, or important papers. Another common compulsion is displayed by people who repeatedly seek *symmetry, order,* or *balance* in their actions and surroundings. They must place certain items (such as clothing, books, or foods) in perfect order in accordance with strict rules.

Ted is a 13-year-old referred to a Midwestern inpatient psychiatric research ward because of "senseless rituals and attention to minutiae." He can spend 3 hours centering the toilet paper roll on its holder or rearranging his bed and other objects in his room. When placing objects down, such as books or shoelaces after tying them, he picks them up and replaces them several times until they seem "straight." Although usually placid, he becomes abusive with family members who try to enter his room for fear they will move or break his objects. When he is at school, he worries that people may disturb his room. He sometimes has to be forced to interrupt his routine to attend meals. Last year he hid pieces of his clothing

---

*Compulsive ritual*    A detailed, often elaborate, set of actions that a person feels compelled to perform at frequent intervals, always in the identical manner.

*Cleaning compulsion*    A common compulsion in which people feel compelled to keep cleaning themselves, their clothing, and their homes.

*Checking compulsion*    A compulsion in which people feel compelled to check the same things over and over.

*People who yield to compulsions, such as the compulsion to avoid stepping on cracks, typically believe that something terrible will happen if they don't act on them. (The Far Side © FARWORKS Inc. Reprinted with permission of Universal Press Syndicate. All rights reserved.)*

around the house because they wouldn't lie straight in his drawers. Moreover, he often repeats to himself, "This is perfect; you are perfect."

*(Spitzer et al., 1983, p. 15)*

Still other common compulsions involve *touching* (repeatedly touching or avoiding touching certain items), *verbal rituals* (repeating expressions or chants), or *counting* (consistently counting the things one sees throughout the day). The two famous men described in Box 6-1 exhibited a number of the compulsions commonly seen in people with obsessive-compulsive disorder.

## Relationship between Obsessions and Compulsions

Although some people with an obsessive-compulsive disorder experience obsessions only or compulsions only, most of them experience both (Jenike, 1992). In fact, as we noted earlier, their compulsive acts are often a response to their obsessive thoughts.

One investigation found that in 61 percent of the cases reviewed, a subject's compulsions seemed to represent a *yielding* to obsessive doubts, ideas, or urges (Akhtar et al., 1975). A man who keeps doubting that his house is secure may yield to that obsessive doubt by repeatedly checking locks and gas jets. Or a man who obsessively fears contamination may yield to that fear by performing cleaning rituals. In 6 percent of the cases reviewed, the compulsions seemed to serve to *control* obsessions. Here a teenager describes how she tried to control her obsessive fears of contamination by performing counting and verbal rituals:

PATIENT: If I heard the word, like, something that had to do with germs or disease, it would be considered something bad, and so I had things that would go through my mind that were sort of like "cross that out and it'll make it okay" to hear that word.

INTERVIEWER: What sort of things?

PATIENT: Like numbers or words that seemed to be sort of like a protector.

INTERVIEWER: What numbers and what words were they?

PATIENT: It started out to be the number 3 and multiples of 3 and then words like "soap and water," something like that; and then the multiples of 3 got really high, and they'd end up to be 124 or something like that. It got real bad then. . . .

*(Spitzer et al., 1981, p. 137)*

Many people with obsessive-compulsive disorder worry that they will act out their obsessions. A man with obsessive images of mutilated loved ones may worry that he is but a step away from committing murder; or a woman with obsessive urges to yell out in church may worry that she will one day give in to them and embarrass herself. Most of these concerns are unfounded. Although many obsessions lead to compulsive acts—particularly to cleaning and checking compulsions—they do not usually lead to acts of violence, immorality, or the like.

Obsessive-compulsive disorder was once among the least understood of the psychological disorders. In recent years, however, researchers, particularly in the biological realm, have begun to learn more about it. The most influential explanations and treatments come from the psychodynamic, behavioral, cognitive, and biological models.

## Box 6-1

# Samuel Johnson and Howard Hughes: Famous Case Studies in Obsessive-Compulsive Behavior

Samuel Johnson, famous during his lifetime for his *Dictionary of the English Language* and his celebrated series of *Rambler* essays, was born to a struggling bookseller in Lichfield, England, in 1709. Johnson's courageous personality, prolific works, and philosophical commentaries on English life continue to fascinate biographers and scholars today. However, his letters and the detailed descriptions of his friend and famed biographer, James Boswell, also show him to have been prone to depression, obsessive-compulsive behavior, and hypochondriasis.

Contemporaries described him as a "noisy beehive of crackpot mannerisms" (Davis, 1989; Malamud, 1979), muttering to himself, keeping count as he walked, touching posts anxiously, and ritually gesticulating with his hands and feet before crossing a threshold (Davis, 1989).

He had another particularity, of which none of his friends ever ventured to ask an explanation. It appeared to me some superstitious habit, which he had contracted early, and from which he had never called upon his reason to disentangle him. This was his anxious care to go out or in at a door or passage by a certain number of steps from a certain point, or at least so as that either his right or his left foot (I am not certain which) should constantly make the first actual movement when he came close to the door or passage. . . . It is requisite to mention, that while talking or even musing as he sat in his chair, he commonly held his head to one side towards his right shoulder, and shook it in a tremendous manner, moving his body backwards and forwards, and rubbing his left knee in the same direction, with the palm of his hand. In the intervals of articulating he made various sounds with his mouth, sometimes as if ruminating, or what is called chewing the cud, sometimes giving a half whistle, sometimes making his tongue play backwards from the roof of his mouth, as if clucking like a hen, and sometimes protruding it against his upper gums in front as if pronouncing quickly under his breath, too, too, too: all this accompanied sometimes with a thoughtful look, but more frequently with a smile.

(*Boswell, 1933, pp. 301–302*)

It is interesting, however, that despite his notable oddities, Johnson was able to make an enormous success of his professional life. In the words of William Blake, "though he looked like a mad hatter, [he] inspired men to reason and courage. He had learned from life" (Davis, 1989; Malamud 1979).

Howard Hughes was born on December 24, 1905, and died on April 5, 1976, aboard a private jet bound for a hospital in Houston, Texas. Hughes's career is legendary. After inheriting a company that made drill bits used in drilling for oil, he went on to become a successful movie producer and record-setting flyer, to build the world's largest flying boat, and to found an international airline, TWA.

Hughes's personal habits are also legendary. He vanished from view in 1951 and lived his last twenty-five years in isolation, dominated by obsessive fears of contamination and the compulsion to carry out bizarre cleaning rituals. James Phelan, an investigative reporter, wrote a biography of Hughes, gathering his information from Hughes's closest aides. As the following excerpts show, Howard Hughes, one of the richest and most powerful men in the world, was at the same time a sad figure imprisoned by his obsessive-compulsive disorder:

Stewart [a barber] was admitted by a man who introduced himself as

## The Psychodynamic Perspective

Psychodynamic theorists believe that the familiar battle between anxiety-provoking id impulses and anxiety-reducing defense mechanisms is played out very explicitly in an obsessive-compulsive disorder rather than at an unconscious level. The id impulses usually take the form of obsessive thoughts, and the ego defenses appear as counterthoughts or compulsive actions. This process is at work when a woman keeps having images of family members horribly injured and counters those thoughts with repeated safety checks throughout the house, or when a man repeatedly has forbidden sexual thoughts and distances himself from them by constantly washing or meticulously avoiding sexual content in conversations.

### Psychodynamic Explanations

According to psychodynamic theorists, three ego defense mechanisms are particularly common in obsessive-compulsive disorder: isolation, undoing, and reaction formation. People who resort to *isolation* isolate

---

*Isolation*    An ego defense mechanism in which people unconsciously isolate and disown undesirable and unwanted thoughts, experiencing them as foreign intrusions.

John Holmes. Holmes gave Stewart detailed instructions. He was to scrub up, doctor-style, in the bathroom before beginning the hair cutting. Then he was to put on a pair of rubber surgical gloves. He was to have no foreign objects, such as pencils or pens, on his person. And, finally, he was not to speak to the man whose hair he would cut. . . .

Finally Holmes said, "Okay, Mr. Hughes will see you now," and took him into the bedroom. What he found stunned him.

"I found a skinny, bare-assed naked man sitting on an unmade three-quarter bed. His hair hung about a foot down his back. His beard was straggly and down to his chest. I tried not to act surprised, as if I was used to meeting naked billionaires sitting on unmade beds.

"I started to put my case with the barber tools on a chair. Hughes shouted, 'No, no! Not on the chair!'

Hughes turned to Holmes and said, "Get some insulation for our friend to put his equipment on."

*When Howard Hughes was flying around the world setting records, starting an international airline, and running several businesses at once, no one suspected that he would one day become a near-helpless prisoner of phobias and an obsessive-compulsive disorder.*

Holmes got a roll of paper towels and laid out a layer on a nearby sideboard. The sideboard was already covered with a sheet, and so was the other furniture in the bedroom. . . .

Barbering Hughes took three hours. There was a series of special procedures, which Hughes outlined in detail. Stewart was to use one set of combs and scissors to cut his beard, but a different set to cut his hair. Before Stewart began, Hughes ordered a series of wide-mouthed jars filled with isopropyl alcohol. When Stewart used a comb he was to dip it into the alcohol before using it again, to "sterilize" it. After using a comb a few times, he was to discard it and proceed with a new comb.

While Stewart was trimming his hair on either side of his head, Hughes carefully folded his ears down tight "so none of that hair will get in me."

Stewart trimmed his beard to a short, neat Vandyke and gave his hair a tapered cut well above the collar line.

When he finished, Hughes thanked him and Holmes escorted him out. A few days later an emissary came down to Huntington Park and gave Stewart an envelope. In it was $1000. . . .

*(Phelan, 1976, pp. 27–28, 44–46, 82)*

and disown undesirable and unwanted thoughts, and experience them as foreign intrusions. People who engage in **undoing** perform acts that implicitly cancel out their undesirable impulses. People who wash their hands repeatedly or conduct elaborate symmetry rituals may be symbolically undoing their unacceptable id impulses. People who develop a *reaction formation* take on lifestyles that directly oppose their unaccept-able impulses. One person may live a life of compulsive kindness and total devotion to others to counteract unacceptable aggressive impulses. Another may lead a life of total celibacy to counteract obsessive sexual impulses.

Sigmund Freud believed that during the anal stage of development (occurring at about 2 years of age) some children experience intense rage and shame that fuel the id-ego battle and set the stage for obsessive-compulsive functioning. He theorized that during this period in their lives, children are deriving their psychosexual pleasure from their bowel movements, while at the same time their parents are trying to toilet

---

*Undoing* An ego defense mechanism in which a person unconsciously attempts to atone for an unacceptable desire or act by another act.

*Reaction formation* An ego defense mechanism in which a repressed desire is instead expressed by taking on an opposite lifestyle.

train them and teach them to delay their anal gratification. If parents are premature or too harsh in their toilet training, the children may experience rage and develop *aggressive id impulses,* antisocial impulses that repeatedly seek expression. They may soil their clothes all the more and become generally destructive, messy, or stubborn.

If parents then handle this aggressiveness by further pressuring and embarrassing the child, the child may also feel shameful, guilty, and dirty. The aggressive impulses will now be countered by the child's strong desire to control them; the child who wants to soil will also have a competing desire to retain. This intense conflict between the id and ego may continue throughout life and eventually blossom into an obsessive-compulsive disorder.

In accord with Freud's explanation, there is evidence that many people who develop an obsessive-compulsive disorder have rigid and demanding parents; however, most of these studies have been poorly designed (Fitz, 1990). Moreover, this disorder also occurs in people whose family backgrounds are very different from the kind Freud anticipated.

Not all psychodynamic theorists agree with Freud's explanation of obsessive-compulsive disorder. A number of ego psychologists, for example, believe that the aggressive impulses experienced by people with this disorder reflect a need to overcome feelings of vulnerability or insecurity rather than poor toilet-training experiences (Salzman, 1968; Erikson, 1963). Even these theorists, however, agree with Freud that people with this disorder have intense, aggressive impulses, along with a competing need to control those impulses.

### Psychodynamic Therapies

Psychodynamic therapies try to help patients with obsessive-compulsive disorder uncover and overcome their underlying conflicts and defenses, using — once again — the techniques of free association and therapist interpretation. Research has, however, offered little evidence that a traditional psychodynamic approach is of much help to people with this disorder (Salzman, 1980).

In fact, there is some suspicion that psychodynamic therapy may actually add to the difficulties of patients with obsessive-compulsive disorder (Salzman, 1980). Free association and interpretation may inadvertently play into the tendency of obsessive-compulsive persons to ruminate and overinterpret (Noonan, 1971). Thus some psychodynamic therapists now prefer to employ *short-term psychodynamic therapies* with obsessive-compulsive clients, therapies that, as we observed in Chapter 3 (see p. 74), are more direct and action-based than the classical techniques. In one approach, the therapist directly advises obsessive-compulsive clients that their compulsions are defense mechanisms and urges them to stop acting compulsively (Salzman, 1985, 1980).

## The Behavioral Perspective

Behaviorists have concentrated on compulsions rather than obsessions in explaining and treating this disorder. Although the behavioral explanation itself has received at best limited support, behavioral treatments for compulsive behaviors have been highly successful and have helped change the once gloomy treatment picture for this disorder.

### The Behavioral Explanation

According to behaviorists, people initially happen upon their compulsions quite randomly. In an anxiety-provoking situation, they happen to wash their hands, dress a certain way, or carry out a particular sequence of actions, and when the threat lifts, they link the improvement to those coincidental activities. They may believe that their actions brought them good luck or actually changed the situation, and may perform the same actions again the next time they find themselves in similar straits.

Repeated chance associations of this kind increase the likelihood that such people will associate certain acts with a reduction of anxiety and continue to perform those acts to alleviate anxiety. Indeed, the acts may become their primary method of avoiding or reducing anxiety. This explanation has nothing to say, however, about why some people go on to develop compulsions and others do not. Certainly everyone experiences some chance associations, yet relatively few become compulsive.

Experiments by clinical researcher Stanley Rachman and his associates are consistent with the behavioral explanation of compulsions. In one experiment, twelve persons who had compulsive hand-washing rituals were placed in contact with objects that they considered contaminated (Hodgson & Rachman, 1972). As behaviorists would predict, the hand-washing rituals of these subjects seemed to lower their anxiety. Similarly, a study of persons with compulsive checking rituals found that subjects' anxiety levels dropped significantly after they completed their checking rituals (Roper et al., 1973). Of course, although such studies suggest that compulsions may now be rewarded by a reduction in anxiety, they do not address the origins of the behaviors.

## Behavioral Therapy: Exposure and Response Prevention

In the mid-1960s V. Meyer (1966) treated two patients with a chronic obsessive-compulsive disorder by instructing the hospital staff to supervise them around the clock and prevent them from performing their compulsive acts. The patients' compulsive behavior improved significantly, and the improvement was still apparent after fourteen months. In the 1970s Stanley Rachman and his colleagues dropped the staff-supervision feature of this procedure and simply instructed clients to try to restrain themselves from performing compulsive acts (Rachman, 1985; Rachman & Hodgson, 1980).

In Rachman's *exposure and response-prevention procedure,* clients were repeatedly exposed to objects or situations that typically elicited anxiety, obsessive fears, and compulsive behaviors, but were instructed to refrain from performing any of the behaviors they might feel compelled to perform. Because clients found this very difficult to do, the therapists often went first. As the clients watched, the therapists interacted with the objects without performing any compulsive actions, and then they encouraged the clients to do the same.

Rachman's procedure has since been employed by many behavioral therapists. Some therapists believe that after several therapy sessions, clients can and should carry out *self-help* procedures in their own homes (Emmelkamp, 1994; Mehta, 1990). The following exposure and response-prevention homework assignments were among those given over the course of therapy to a woman with a cleaning compulsion:

Do not mop the floor of your bathroom for a week. After this, clean it within three minutes, using an ordinary mop. Use this mop for other chores as well without cleaning it.

Buy a fluffy mohair sweater and wear it for a week. When taking it off at night do not remove the bits of fluff. Do not clean your house for a week.

You, your husband, and children all have to keep shoes on. Do not clean the house for a week.

Drop a cookie on the contaminated floor, pick the cookie up and eat it.

Leave the sheets and blankets on the floor and then put them on the beds. Do not change these for a week.

(Emmelkamp, 1982, pp. 299–300)

Eventually therapists help such clients to determine a reasonable schedule and procedure for cleaning themselves and their houses and to institute more normal cleaning policies.

It has been found that between 60 and 90 percent of obsessive-compulsive clients who are treated with this type of technique, in either individual or group therapy, improve considerably (Fals-Stewart et al., 1993; Riggs & Foa, 1993). Improvements include a decrease in the frequency of compulsive acts and in consequent experiences of anxiety (see Figure 6-3), a reduction in obsessive thinking, and better family, social, and work adjustments. Such improvements continue to be observed years later (Marks & Swinson, 1992; O'Sullivan et al., 1991).

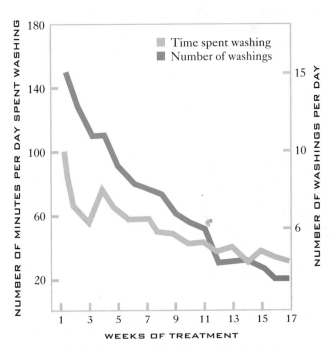

**Figure 6-3** *When treated for his compulsive cleaning rituals by exposure and response prevention, a client showed a steady decline in the frequency of his daily washings and in the total amount of time he spent at them. (Adapted from Rachman, Hodgson, & Marzillier, 1970, p. 390.)*

---

*Exposure and response prevention* A treatment for obsessive-compulsive disorder in which clients are exposed to anxiety-arousing thoughts or situations and then prevented from performing their compulsive acts.

At the same time, relatively few clients who receive this treatment overcome all their symptoms, and as many as one-quarter of them apparently fail to improve at all (Marks & Swinson, 1992; Greist, 1990). Another limitation of this approach is that it does relatively little to help people who have obsessions but no compulsions (Jenike, 1992). After all, the way this intervention "reaches" obsessions is by blocking the resulting compulsive acts.

The effectiveness of the exposure and response-prevention technique suggests once again to many behaviorists that people with obsessive-compulsive disorder are like the superstitious man in the old joke who keeps snapping his fingers to keep elephants away. When someone points out, "But there aren't any elephants around here," the man replies, "See? It works!" One review concludes, "With hindsight, it is possible to see that the obsessional individual has been snapping his fingers, and unless he stops (response prevention) and takes a look around at the same time (exposure), he isn't going to learn much of value about elephants" (Berk & Efran, 1983, p. 546).

---

### Consider This

Behaviorists use exposure and response prevention to treat obsessive-compulsive disorder. Can you think of instances in your own life where you instinctively tried a simpler version of this approach in order to stop reacting or stop behaving in certain ways? Were your efforts successful? What does this suggest about the need for systematic and, perhaps, supervised applications of the technique?

---

## The Cognitive Perspective

In recent years, cognitive theorists have developed a promising explanation and several treatments for obsessive-compulsive disorder. Because their theory and intervention techniques also make use of a number of behavioral principles, many observers prefer to describe the approach as cognitive-behavioral.

### The Cognitive Explanation

The cognitive explanation of obsessive-compulsive disorder begins with the premise that everyone has repetitive, unwanted, unpleasant, and intrusive thoughts, such as thoughts of harming others, engaging in unacceptable sexual acts, or being contaminated by germs (Rachman, 1993; Salkovskis, 1989, 1985; Clark, 1989). Whereas most people regard normal and universal thoughts of this kind as meaningless and dismiss or ignore them with ease, those who develop an obsessive-compulsive disorder typically believe themselves responsible and reprehensible for having such terrible thoughts, and worry that the thoughts will lead to harmful acts or consequences.

These people find the intrusive thoughts so repulsive and stressful that they try to eliminate or avoid them by *neutralizing*—thinking or behaving in ways calculated to put matters right internally, to make amends for the unacceptable thoughts. They may use such neutralizing techniques as requesting special reassurance from others, deliberately thinking "good" thoughts, cleaning their hands, or checking for possible sources of danger.

When such a neutralizing strategy brings a temporary reduction in discomfort, it becomes reinforced; thus it is likely to be employed again in the future. Eventually the neutralizing thought or act is employed so often that it becomes, by definition, an obsession or compulsion. At the same time, the fact that the neutralizing strategy is effective confirms to the individual that the initial intrusive thought was indeed reprehensible or dangerous and in need of elimination. The intrusive thought now feels even more distressing and worrisome; as a result it begins to occur so frequently that it too becomes an obsession.

One of the key questions raised by this cognitive explanation is why some people (those who go on to develop an obsessive-compulsive disorder) find universal and normal thoughts so disturbing to begin with. Research has indicated that people who are depressed have more numerous and more intense unwanted thoughts than other persons (Clark & Purdon, 1993; Conway et al., 1991); people with exceptionally high standards of conduct and morality find their unwanted thoughts more unacceptable than other persons (Rachman, 1993; Rachman & Hodgson, 1980); people who believe that their thoughts are potentially harmful and who feel responsible for them are particularly likely to be disturbed by them (Purdon & Clark, 1995; Salkovskis 1989, 1985); and people who mistakenly believe that they can and should have perfect control over all of their thoughts are likely to be disturbed by their unwanted thoughts (Clark & Purdon, 1993; Rachman, 1993).

Research has also supported other aspects of this cognitive theory. Some investigators have found that people with obsessive-compulsive disorder have more

---

*Neutralizing* A person's attempt to eliminate unwanted, intrusive thoughts by thinking or behaving in ways that put matters right internally or that make amends for unacceptable thoughts.

intrusive thoughts than other people (Clark, 1992). In addition, studies have confirmed that people who develop obsessive-compulsive disorder resort, at least sometimes, to more elaborate neutralizing strategies than other people do in efforts to suppress their unwanted thoughts (Freeston et al., 1992), and that such neutralizing strategies do temporarily reduce the discomfort they feel (Roper et al., 1973).

## Cognitive Therapies

Several approaches that combine cognitive and behavioral techniques have been used to treat people with obsessive-compulsive disorder. In one, called *habituation training,* therapists try to *evoke* a client's obsessive thoughts again and again, with the expectation that such intensified *exposure* to the thoughts will eventually cause them to lose their threatening meaning, to generate less anxiety, and so to trigger fewer new obsessive thoughts or compulsive acts (Salkovskis & Westbrook, 1989; Rachman & Hodgson, 1980).

In one version of habituation training, clients are simply instructed to summon the obsessive thought or image to mind and then to hold it for a prolonged period. In another version, clients spend up to an hour once or twice a day listening to their own voices on tape repeating their obsessional thoughts again and again.

For clients who experience obsessions only, habituation training is often the entire plan of treatment (Rachman & Hodgson, 1980); however, for other clients, cognitive therapists may further employ *covert-response prevention.* The clients are taught to prevent or distract themselves from carrying out any other obsessive thoughts or compulsive actions that may emerge during habituation training. Over the course of repeated sessions, clients' obsessions and/or compulsions are expected to decrease. The bulk of support for this approach has come from promising case studies rather than empirical investigations (Ladouceur et al., 1995; Hollon & Beck, 1994).

# The Biological Perspective

Partly because obsessive-compulsive disorder was so difficult to explain in the past, researchers repeatedly have tried to identify hidden biological factors that might contribute to the disorder (Jenike, 1992). Their efforts have been rewarded in recent years. Correspondingly, promising biological interventions for the disorder have emerged.

## Biological Explanations

Two intersecting lines of biological research now offer great promise in explaining the biology of obsessive-compulsive disorder. One points to abnormally low activity of the neurotransmitter serotonin in people with the disorder, the other to abnormal functioning in key regions of their brains.

*Serotonin,* like GABA and norepinephrine, is a brain chemical that carries messages from neuron to neuron. It first became implicated in obsessive-compulsive disorder when clinical researchers discovered unexpectedly that obsessive and compulsive symptoms were reduced by the antidepressant drugs *clomipramine* and *fluoxetine* (brand names Anafranil and Prozac) (Klerman et al., 1994; Rapoport, 1991, 1989). Since these drugs seem to increase serotonin activity while reducing obsessive and compulsive symptoms, some researchers have concluded that the disorder is associated with low serotonin activity (Altemus et al., 1993). In fact, the only antidepressant drugs that alleviate obsessive-compulsive disorder are those that increase serotonin activity; antidepressants that primarily affect other neurotransmitters have no effect on this disorder (Jenike, 1992).

Another line of research links obsessive-compulsive disorder to abnormal functioning in the *orbital region* of the frontal cortex (a brain area just above each eye) and the *caudate nuclei* (parts of the basal ganglia, which lie under the cerebral cortex). These parts of the brain set up a circuit that controls the conversion of sensory input into cognitions and actions (see Figure 6-4). The circuit begins in the orbital region, where impulses involving bodily excretion, sexuality, violence, and other primitive activities normally arise. Nerve fibers then carry these impulses down into the caudate nuclei for possible translation into action. These nuclei serve as a filter that allows only the most powerful impulses to reach the *thalamus,* the next stop on the circuit. If the thalamus receives the impulses,

---

*Habituation training* A therapeutic technique in which a therapist tries to evoke a client's obsessive thoughts again and again with the expectation that the thoughts will eventually lose their threatening meaning and generate less anxiety.

*Serotonin* A neurotransmitter whose abnormal activity is linked to depression, eating disorders, and obsessive-compulsive disorder.

*Clomipramine* An antidepressant drug (brand name Anafranil) that has also proven useful in treating obsessive-compulsive disorder.

*Caudate nuclei* Structures of the basal ganglia that participate in the conversion of sensory input into cognitions and actions.

Basal ganglia

Putamen and
globus pallidus

Caudate
nucleus

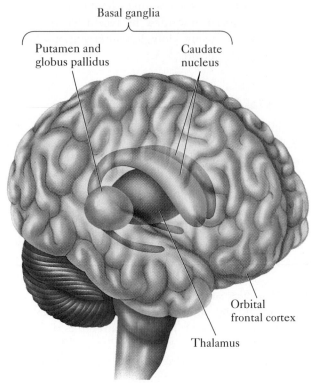

Orbital
frontal cortex

Thalamus

**Figure 6-4**  *A three-dimensional view of the human brain (with parts shown as they would look if the overlying cerebral cortex were transparent) clarifies the locations of the orbital frontal cortex and the basal ganglia (including the caudate nucleus)—areas that appear to be too active in people with obsessive-compulsive disorder. (Adapted from Rapoport, 1989, p. 85.)*

the person is driven to think further about them. Many biological theorists now believe that either the orbital region or the caudate nuclei of some people function too actively, leading to a constant breakthrough of troublesome thoughts and actions (Baxter et al., 1992; Swedo et al., 1992). Consistent with this theory, studies using *positron emission tomography (PET scans)*, which show the brain in action, have revealed that the caudate nuclei and the orbital regions of obsessive-compulsive patients are more active than those of control subjects (Baxter et al., 1990).

These two sets of findings, one tying obsessive-compulsive disorder to low serotonin activity and the other to some kind of heightened functioning in the orbital region and the caudate nuclei, may themselves be linked. It turns out that the neurotransmitter serotonin plays a very active role in the operation of these brain areas, so low serotonin activity might well be expected to disrupt their proper functioning. Many researchers now believe that such abnormalities set up some kind of biological predisposition for the development of this disorder (Rapoport, 1991, 1989).

## Biological Therapies

As we saw above, researchers have learned that antidepressant drugs that raise serotonin activity, particularly clomipramine, are a useful form of treatment for obsessive-compulsive disorder (see Figure 6-5). According to several studies, these drugs bring improvement to between 50 and 80 percent of subjects with obsessive-compulsive disorder, whereas placebo drugs bring improvement to as few as 5 percent of similar subjects (Greist et al., 1995; Orloff et al., 1994; Jenike, 1992). The obsessions and compulsions of people who take these antidepressant drugs do not usually disappear totally, but they are reduced an average of almost 50 percent within eight weeks of treatment (DeVeaugh-Geiss et al., 1992; Greist, 1990). People whose improvement is based on these drugs alone, however, tend to relapse if the medication is discontinued (Michelson & Marchione, 1991).

Obviously, the treatment picture for obsessive-compulsive disorder, like that for panic disorders, has improved over the past decade (Zetin, 1990). Once a very stubborn problem, unresponsive to all forms of treatment, obsessive-compulsive disorder now appears to be helped by several interventions, particularly exposure and response-prevention treatment and antidepressant drugs, either separately or in combination (Riggs & Foa, 1993). Moreover, a startling recent research finding suggests that both the behavioral and biological interventions may ultimately have the same effect on the brain: a group of subjects who responded to a behavioral exposure and response-prevention approach and a group of subjects who responded to antidepressant drug treatment both showed a marked reduction in activity in the caudate nucleus (Baxter et al., 1992). This is the first time that behavior therapy for a mental disorder has been so directly tied to an observable change in brain function.

*Summing Up*
*People with an obsessive-compulsive disorder are beset by obsessions or compulsions or, more commonly, both. Theorists from each of the models have offered explanations for the disorder, with the biological and cognitive views gathering the most research support. Today's leading treatments are the behavioral approach (exposure and response prevention) and the biological approach (serotonin-enhancing antidepressant drugs).*

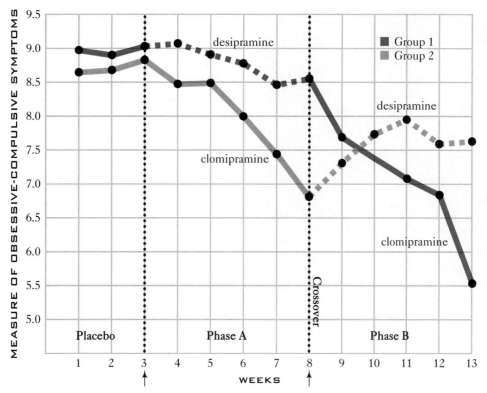

**Figure 6-5**   *A "crossover study" demonstrates that obsessive-compulsive disorder is improved only by antidepressants that increase serotonin activity, not by those that increase norepinephrine activity. The obsessive-compulsive symptoms of all patients in the study stayed the same while the patients were on placebo drugs for the initial three weeks. Then, in phase A, the symptoms of patients who were given the serotonin enhancer clomipramine for five weeks decreased significantly, while the symptoms of the patients given desipramine, a norepinephrine enhancer, stayed the same. Next, in phase B, when clomipramine patients were switched (crossed over) to five weeks on desipramine, their symptoms returned; by contrast, when desipramine patients were switched to five weeks of clomipramine, their symptoms decreased significantly. (Rapoport, 1989.)*

## Stress Disorders

Mark remembers his first "firefight" and encountering the VC [Viet Cong] for the first time. He lost all bladder and bowel control—in a matter of a few minutes. In his own words, "I was scared and literally shitless; I pissed all over myself, and shit all over myself too. Man, all hell broke loose. I tell you, I was so scared, I thought I would never make it out alive. I was convinced of that. Charlie had us pinned down and [was] hitting the shit out of us for hours. We had to call in the napalm and the bombing." During the first fight, Mark, an infantryman, experienced gruesome sights and strange sounds in battle. He witnessed headless bodies. "One guy said to me, 'Hey, Mark, new greenhorn boy, you saw that head go flying off that gook's shoulder. Isn't that something?' " Within 2 weeks Mark saw the head of a running comrade blown off his shoulders, the headless body moving for a few feet before falling to the ground.

Mark, nauseous and vomiting for a long time, couldn't see himself surviving much longer: "I couldn't get that sight out of my head; it just kept on coming back to me in my dreams, nightmares. Like clockwork, I'd see R's head flying, and his headless body falling to the ground. I knew the guy. He was very good to me when I first got to the unit. Nobody else seemed to give a damn about me; he broke me in. It's like I would see his head and body, you know, man, wow!" Mark often found himself crying during his first weeks of combat. "I wanted to go home. I was so lonely, helpless, and really scared. But I knew I could not go home until my year was up."

*(Brende & Parson, 1985, pp. 23–24)*

Mark's reaction to these combat experiences is normal and understandable. During or immediately after an unusual and traumatic situation, many people become highly anxious and depressed. For some, however, anxiety and depression persist well after the situation is over. These people may be suffering from *acute*

*The symptoms of posttraumatic stress disorder appear after combat (or after another traumatic event), often when the individual is safely back home. The pain displayed by tens of thousands of veterans at the unveiling of the Vietnam War Memorial in Washington, D.C., more than a decade after the war ended, revealed that the war and its psychological effects were far from over for many people.*

**stress disorder** or **posttraumatic stress disorder,** distinct patterns that arise in reaction to a psychologically traumatic event (APA, 1994). The event usually involves actual or threatened serious injury or threatened death to the person or to a family member or friend. Unlike other anxiety disorders, which typically are triggered by objects or situations that most people would not find threatening, situations that cause acute stress disorder or posttraumatic stress disorder—combat, rape, an earthquake, an airplane crash—would be traumatic for anyone.

According to DSM-IV, if the anxiety-linked symptoms begin within four weeks of the traumatic event and last for less than a month, the pattern is diagnosed as *acute stress disorder* (APA, 1994). If the symptoms continue longer than a month, a diagnosis of *posttraumatic stress disorder* is appropriate. The symptoms of a posttraumatic stress disorder may begin either shortly after the traumatic event or months or years afterward. Aside from the differences in onset and duration, these two anxiety disorders are almost identical, and include the following symptoms:

*Acute stress disorder*   An anxiety disorder in which fear and related symptoms are experienced soon after a traumatic event and last less than a month.

*Posttraumatic stress disorder*   An anxiety disorder in which fear and related symptoms continue to be experienced long after a traumatic event.

1. *Reexperiencing the traumatic event.* The person may have recurring recollections, dreams, or nightmares about the event. A few relive the event so vividly in their minds that they think they are back in the traumatic situation.
2. *Avoidance.* The person will usually avoid activities or situations that are reminiscent of the traumatic event, and will try to avoid thoughts, feelings, or conversations associated with it.
3. *Reduced responsiveness.* Reduced responsiveness to the external world, often called "psychic numbing" or "emotional anesthesia," may begin during or soon after the traumatic event. The person feels detached or estranged from other people or loses interest in activities enjoyed previously. The ability to experience such intimate emotions as tenderness and sexuality is often impaired. Reduced responsiveness is particularly prominent in acute stress disorder, where it may further include signs of *dissociation*, or emotional separation: dazedness, loss of memory, derealization (feeling that the environment is unreal or strange), or depersonalization (feeling that one's thoughts or body are unreal or foreign).
4. *Increased arousal, anxiety, and guilt.* People with these disorders may experience hyperalertness, an exaggerated startle response, sleep disturbances, or other signs of increased arousal, and may also have trouble concentrating or remembering things. They may feel extreme guilt because they survived the traumatic event while others did not. Some also feel guilty about what they may have had to do to survive.

We can see these symptoms in the recollections of Vietnam combat veterans years after they returned home:

*Alan:* I can't get the memories out of my mind! The images come flooding back in vivid detail, triggered by the most inconsequential things, like a door slamming or the smell of stir-fried pork. Last night I went to bed, was having a good sleep for a change. Then in the early morning a storm-front passed through and there was a bolt of crackling thunder. I awoke instantly, frozen in fear. I am right back in Vietnam, in the middle of the monsoon season at my guard post. I am sure I'll get hit in the next volley and convinced I will die. My hands are freezing, yet sweat pours from my entire body. I feel each hair on the back of my neck standing on end. I can't catch my breath and my heart is pounding. I smell a damp sulfur smell.

(Davis, 1992)

*Ron:* You get tired of being shot at again, over and over and over again. How many times do I gotta get blown up. I'm tired of seeing bullets hit me. I'm tired of seeing my friends get shot at. I'm tired. . . . I grew up and died right there [at the scene of battle]. And the last ten years have just been a space. I've just occupied space, just space. I've accomplished nothing. Nothing but occupied space.

*("The War Within," 1985)*

*Lucas:* [My wife] said that I wasn't the loving guy she used to know and love, that something horrible must have happened to me over there to change me so completely. . . . She said that the look in my eyes was the look of a deeply terrorized person, with a long-distance stare, looking off into the beyond—not into the present with her at this time. She also mentioned that my frightened look and pallid complexion, my uptight way of sitting, talking, walking, you name it, my aloofness, and all that, made her too uncomfortable for us to continue our relationship. . . . Finally, as time went on, I realized that so many people couldn't be wrong about me. The change in me began to seem deep to me—deeper than I would ever have imagined to be the case.

*(Brende & Parson, 1985, pp. 46–47)*

An acute or posttraumatic stress disorder can occur at any age, even in childhood, and can impair one's personal, family, social, or occupational functioning (Jordan et al., 1992). Clinical surveys show that approximately 0.5 percent of the total population experience one of these disorders in any given year; at least 1.3 percent will suffer from one of them within their lifetime (Davidson et al., 1991). As many as 15 percent of all people experience some of the symptoms of these disorders.

> ### Consider This
> Acute and posttraumatic stress disorders result from exposure to very traumatic events. What types of events in modern society might be likely to trigger these disorders? Do you think the vivid images seen daily on television, movies, rock videos, and the like would make people more vulnerable to developing such disorders or less likely to do so?

## Stress Disorders Caused by Combat

For years clinicians have recognized that many soldiers develop symptoms of severe anxiety and depression *during* combat (Oei et al., 1990). The pattern of symptoms was called "nostalgia" during the American Civil War and was considered to be the result of extended absence from home (Bourne, 1970). The syndrome was called "shell shock" during World War I because it was thought to result from minute brain hemorrhages or concussions caused by explosions during battle. During World War II and the Korean War, it was referred to as "combat fatigue" (Figley, 1978). Not until after the Vietnam War, however, did clinicians come to recognize that a great many soldiers, perhaps as many as 29 percent, also experience serious psychological symptoms *after* combat. This percentage is even higher, as high as 80 percent, for soldiers who were prisoners of war (Sutker et al., 1993).

In the first years after the Vietnam War, the psychological problems of combat veterans were generally overlooked, perhaps in part because of the nation's desire to put reminders of this unpopular war behind it. By the late 1970s, however, it had become apparent to staff members in veterans' hospitals throughout the United States that many Vietnam combat veterans were still experiencing war-related psychological problems that had been delayed in onset or previously ignored (Williams, 1983).

We now know that as many as 29 percent of all persons, male or female, who served in Vietnam subsequently suffered an acute or posttraumatic stress disorder, while another 22 percent suffered from at least some of the symptoms of these disorders (Weiss et al., 1992). In fact, 10 percent of the veterans of this war still experience significant posttraumatic stress symptoms. Veterans of more recent wars report similar symptoms. In a study of a group of Persian Gulf War combat veterans, over a third reported six months later that they were experiencing nightmares and drinking more than before (Labbate & Snow, 1992).

## Stress Disorders Caused by Other Traumas

Acute and posttraumatic stress disorders may also follow *natural and accidental disasters* such as earthquakes, floods, tornados, fires, airplane crashes, and serious car accidents. One study found that 10 percent of victims of serious traffic accidents qualified for a diagnosis of posttraumatic stress disorder within six months of their accident (Brom et al., 1993).

Stress reactions have, for example, been found among the survivors of Hurricane Andrew, the 1992 storm that ravaged Florida and other parts of the southeastern United States, destroying hundreds of thousands of homes, automobiles, and other personal belongings, wreaking havoc on the natural environment, and leaving millions impoverished (Gelman & Katel, 1993; Treaster, 1992). By a month after the storm, the number of calls received by the Domestic Violence Hotline in Miami and the number of spouses

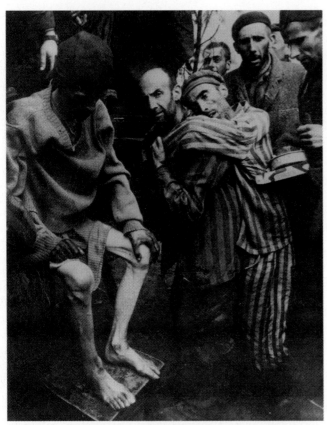

*Many survivors of Nazi concentration camps faced a long road back to psychological health. Because knowledge of posttraumatic stress disorder was nonexistent until recent years, most survivors had to find their way back without professional help.*

applying for police protection had doubled. Moreover, hundreds of mental health professionals who went door to door shortly after the storm seeking to help victims throughout Florida reported seeing an extraordinary number of acute and posttraumatic stress symptoms, including edginess, sleep difficulties, spontaneous crying, flashbacks, depression, disorientation, and even short-term memory loss. By six months after the storm it was clear that many elementary school–age children were also victims of posttraumatic stress disorder, their symptoms ranging from disruptive behavior in school to failing grades and problems with sleep.

Acute and posttraumatic stress disorders may also follow incidents of *victimization*. Lingering stress symptoms have been observed in survivors of Nazi concentration camps years after their liberation (Kuch & Cox, 1992; Eitinger, 1973, 1969, 1964). Indeed, a recent retrospective study of 124 Holocaust survivors found that 46 percent eventually fully met the diagnostic criteria for posttraumatic stress disorder (Kuch & Cox, 1992).

A common form of victimization in our society is sexual assault and rape. A Senate Judiciary Committee report (1991) stated that more than 100,000 rapes are reported to police annually, and it is believed that these reports represent only a small portion of the actual number of such incidents (Koss, 1993). Some recent national surveys, which ask more detailed and explicit questions than earlier ones and help subjects answer more honestly, suggest that more than 600,000 women may be raped each year (Youngstrom, 1992). One study found that 94 percent of rape victims qualified for a diagnosis of acute stress disorder when they were observed an average of twelve days after their assault (Rothbaum et al., 1992). Even years after their attack, both female and male rape victims have been found to experience severe stress symptoms—fearfulness and anxiety, suspiciousness, depression, guilt, self-blame, high startle responses, reliving the assault, nightmares, and other sleep disturbances (Steketee & Foa, 1987). Such symptoms are apparent in the following case description:

Mary Billings is a 33-year-old divorced nurse, referred to the Victim Clinic at Bedford Psychiatric Hospital for counseling by her supervisory head nurse. Mary had been raped two months ago. The assailant gained entry to her apartment while she was sleeping, and she awoke to find him on top of her. He was armed with a knife and threatened to kill her and her child (who was asleep in the next room) if she did not submit to his demands. He forced her to undress and repeatedly raped her vaginally over a period of 1 hour. He then admonished her that if she told anyone or reported the incident to the police he would return and assault her child.

After he left, she called her boyfriend, who came to her apartment right away. He helped her contact the Sex Crimes Unit of the Police Department, which is currently investigating the case. He then took her to a local hospital for a physical examination and collection of evidence for the police (traces of sperm, pubic hair samples, fingernail scrapings). She was given antibiotics as prophylaxis against venereal disease. Mary then returned home with a girlfriend who spent the remainder of the night with her.

Over the next few weeks Mary continued to be afraid of being alone and had her girlfriend move in with her. She became preoccupied with thoughts of what had happened to her and the possibility that it could happen again. Mary was frightened that the rapist might return to her apartment and therefore had additional locks installed on both the door and the windows. She was so upset and had such difficulty concentrating that she decided she could not yet return to work. When she did return to work several weeks later, she was still clearly upset, and her

*Many people eventually overcome the effects of traumatic stress. During a reunion, these concentration camp survivors proudly display their tattooed camp identification numbers as symbols of their triumph over their psychological wounds.*

supervisor suggested that she might be helped by counseling.

During the clinic interview, Mary was coherent and spoke quite rationally in a hushed voice. She reported recurrent and intrusive thoughts about the sexual assault, to the extent that her concentration was impaired and she had difficulty doing chores such as making meals for herself and her daughter. She felt she was not able to be effective at work, still felt afraid to leave her home, to answer her phone, and had little interest in contacting friends or relatives.

The range of Mary's affect was constricted. She talked in the same tone of voice whether discussing the assault or less emotionally charged topics, such as her work history. She was easily startled by an unexpected noise. She also was unable to fall asleep because she kept thinking about the assault. She had no desire to eat, and when she did attempt it, she felt nauseated. Mary was repelled by the thought of sex and stated that she did not want to have sex for a long time, although she was willing to be held and comforted by her boyfriend.

*(Spitzer et al., 1983, pp. 20–21)*

## Explanations of Stress Disorders

There is an obvious cause-and-effect relationship between an extraordinary trauma and the subsequent onset of an acute or posttraumatic stress disorder. The stressful event alone, however, is not a complete explanation. Although everyone who experiences an unusual trauma is certainly affected by it, only some people develop one of these disorders. Researchers do not yet understand why some people do and others do not develop them, but they have called three factors to our attention: the survivor's childhood experiences, personality, and social support system (Schnurr et al., 1993).

A recent wave of studies has uncovered *childhood events* that seem to leave some people vulnerable to developing acute and posttraumatic stress disorders in response to later traumatic experiences. People whose childhoods have been characterized by poverty, whose parents separated or divorced before their child was 10, whose family members suffered from mental disorders, or who experienced assault, abuse, or catastrophe at an early age appear more likely to develop stress disorders in the face of later trauma than people without such childhood experiences (Bremner et al., 1993; Kolb, 1992; Davidson et al., 1991).

Other studies suggest that people with certain *personality profiles or attitudes* are more likely to develop these disorders (Clark et al., 1994). It has been found, for example, that rape victims who had psychological problems before they were raped or were struggling with stressful life situations (Sales et al., 1984) and war veterans who had poor relationships before they went into combat run a greater risk of developing lingering stress reactions after their traumatic experiences (Chemtob et al., 1990). Similarly, people who generally view life's aversive events as beyond their control develop more severe stress symptoms after criminal assaults than people who feel more control over aversive events (Kushner et al., 1992). These findings are reminiscent of another: that many people respond to stress with a set of positive attitudes, collectively called **hardiness,** that enable them to carry on their lives with a sense of fortitude, control, and commitment (Kobasa, 1990, 1987, 1979).

Lastly, it has been found that people whose *support systems* are weak after a traumatic event are more likely to develop an extended disorder (Perry et al., 1992). Rape victims who feel loved, cared for, and accepted by a group of friends or relatives and who are treated with dignity and respect by agents of the criminal justice system are more likely to recover successfully from their sexual assault. In contrast, clinical reports suggest that weak social support systems have contributed to the development of posttraumatic stress disorder in some Vietnam veterans (Figley & Leventman, 1990). This man's return home was, sadly, not at all unusual:

Next morning my sisters went to school as usual, while my brother went to college. Everything seemed the same to them, real routine, you know. I didn't feel "routine." I felt out of it. I felt nervous, tense, jittery, even shaky. I wasn't able to fall asleep, so I got up at 10:00 a.m. I was home alone. So I walked down to the package store and bought me some liquor to help me out—you know, with the nervousness, and my anger about everything. . . .

Then, like out of nowhere, six guys showed up on the scene; I knew most of them. They wanted to know about the "good dope" in Vietnam. They didn't seem interested in me as a person. They had heard of the Thai red, the opium, and all that stuff. They asked me about the Vietnamese whores; and how many times I caught the clap [gonorrhea].

They also wanted to know what it was like having sex with Vietnamese women. One of them yelled out, "How many babies you've burned, man? How many young children don't have their fathers because of guys like you? Yeah, you killers, man; you heard me." Before I knew what had happened the cops were there. I had beaten four guys up severely; three had to be taken to the hospital. I seemed to have lost my head totally. I didn't want to hurt anybody. I had done a lot of killing in the 'Nam; I just wanted to be left alone, now. . . . I came back to my room, and began really drinking. I just kept thinking to myself that the streets of Cholon, Saigon, Nha Trang, and other cities and villages in Vietnam were probably safer for me than back in the United States.

(Brende & Parson, 1985, pp. 49–50)

It is important to keep in mind that the events that trigger acute and posttraumatic stress disorders can sometimes be so extreme and traumatic that they override such factors as a positive childhood, hardy personality, and supportive social context. A follow-up study of 253 Vietnam prisoners of war found that five years after their release, 23 percent warranted a clinical diagnosis, though all had been effective Air Force officers and had been evaluated as well adjusted before their imprisonment (Ursano et al., 1981). Moreover, it was the men who had been imprisoned longest and treated most harshly who had the highest percentage of such diagnoses. Childhood, personal, and social variables notwithstanding, it is, as a survivor of trauma

*Millions reacted to the San Francisco earthquake of 1989 with dread and panic, but some laid-back individuals thrived on all the excitement. Their "hardy" personality styles may have helped to protect them from the development of stress disorders.*

once said, "hard to be a survivor" (Kolff & Doan, 1985, p. 45).

## Treatments for Stress Disorders

The relatively recent identification of acute and post-traumatic stress disorders as specific diagnostic categories has spurred the development of numerous treatment programs for the psychologically troubled survivors of traumatic events (Marmar et al., 1993; McFarlane, 1991). Although the specific features of these treatment programs vary from trauma to trauma, all the programs share basic goals: they try to help survivors reduce or overcome their lingering symptoms, gain perspective on their traumatic experiences, and return to constructive living (see Box 6-2). Treatment programs for war veterans who suffer from posttraumatic stress disorder demonstrate how these issues may be addressed.

Therapists have used a combination of techniques to alleviate the posttraumatic symptoms of veterans. Antianxiety drugs have reduced the tension, hyperalertness, and exaggerated startle responses that many veterans experience (Marmar et al., 1993; Braun et al., 1990). In addition, antidepressant medications have sometimes lessened nightmares, flashbacks, intrusive recollections, and feelings of depression (Marmar et al., 1993; Nagy et al., 1993).

Behavioral exposure techniques have also been employed (Brown et al., 1992; Mueser et al., 1991). For example, flooding along with relaxation training helped rid a 31-year-old veteran of his frightening combat flashbacks and nightmares (Fairbank & Keane, 1982). The therapist and client first singled out combat scenes that the veteran had been reexperiencing frequently. The therapist then helped the client to imagine one of these scenes in great detail and urged him to retain the image until his anxiety subsided. After each of these flooding exercises, the therapist switched to positive imagery and led the client through relaxation exercises. In response to this treatment, the man's flashbacks and nightmares diminished.

Although symptomatic relief of this kind is useful, most clinicians believe that veterans with posttraumatic stress disorder cannot fully recover until they also develop insight and perspective in regard to their combat experiences and the impact those experiences continue to have on them (Marmar et al., 1993; Weiss & Marmar, 1993). Sometimes clinicians help clients to bring out deep-seated feelings, accept what they have

done and experienced, become less judgmental of themselves, and learn to trust others once again.

Attempts at expressing feelings and developing insight are often undertaken in group therapy, or "rap groups," in which veterans meet to share experiences and give mutual emotional support. In an atmosphere of group trust, social support, and common experience, many individuals find it easier to recall events and confront feelings they have been trying to avoid for a number of years (Sipprelle, 1992; Rozynko & Dondershine, 1991).

One of the major issues dealt with in rap groups is guilt—guilt about things the members may have done to survive or about the very fact that they did survive while close friends died. Once the veterans are finally able to talk candidly about their combat experiences and guilt feelings, they may start to recover from them and gauge their responsibility for past actions more accurately. Another important issue addressed in rap groups is the rage that many veterans feel. Many veterans of the Vietnam War, for example, are intensely angry that they had to fight for a questionable cause, face unbearable conditions and tensions in Vietnam, and deal with an accusing society upon their return.

Rap groups originated in 1971, when an organization called Vietnam Veterans Against the War decided that there was a pressing need for a forum in which veterans could discuss their experiences with other veterans and together heal their psychological wounds (Lifton, 1973). Today more than 150 small counseling centers (Veteran Outreach Centers) across the country, as well as numerous treatment programs in Veterans Administration hospitals, specialize in rap groups (Brende & Parson, 1985). In addition, these agencies offer individual therapy, counseling for the spouses and children of troubled veterans, family therapy, and assistance in securing employment, education, and benefits (Blank, 1982).

Because most Veteran Outreach Centers have existed only a relatively short time, research into their effectiveness is just beginning (Funari et al., 1991). So far, clinical reports and empirical studies suggest that they offer an important, sometimes life-saving treatment opportunity. Julius's search for help upon his return from Vietnam was, unfortunately, an ordeal that many veterans of that war have shared:

> When I got back from the 'Nam, I knew I needed psychotherapy or something like that. I just knew that if I didn't get help I was going to kill myself or somebody else. . . . I went to see this doctor; he barely looked at me. I felt he "saw me coming" and knew all about my sickness. I was the "sicky" to him. He just kept on asking me all that bullshit about

---

*Rap group*   A group that meets to help participants converse about and explore problematic issues in an atmosphere of mutual support.

*Rap groups for Vietnam veterans have helped many of their members overcome the anxiety, depression, sleep problems, and flashbacks that linger for years after the war.*

how many children I had killed and was I guilty and depressed about it. He asked how it felt to kill people. He also kept on asking me about my brothers and sisters. But he never asked me about what my experiences were like in Vietnam. He never did. I saw him for treatment for about a month—about three visits, but I quit because we weren't getting anywhere. . . . He just kept on giving me more and more medications. I could've set up my own pharmacy. I needed someone to talk to about my problems, my real problems, not some bullshit about my childhood. I needed someone who wanted to help. The clinic later referred me to another shrink. . . . I guess she thought she was being honest with me, by telling me that she was not a veteran, was not in Vietnam, and did not know what was wrong with me. She also told me that she had no experience working with Vietnam veterans, and that I should go to the Veterans Administration for help. . . .

It was only in the last 3 years when my wife made an important phone call to a local Veterans Outreach Center that I started feeling I had hope, that something could be done for me. I received the help that I have always needed. Finally, I found it easier to hold a job and take care of my family. My nightmares are not as frightening or as frequent as they used to be. Things are better now; I am learning to trust people and give more to my wife and children.

*(Brende & Parson, 1985, pp. 206–208)*

*Summing Up*
*People with acute and posttraumatic stress disorders react with a distinct pattern of anxiety and related symptoms long after the occurrence of a traumatic event. Childhood experiences, personal variables, and social support appear to help influence whether people develop one of these disorders. Clinicians have applied various treatments, including medications, exposure techniques, and supportive and humanistic therapy, particularly in the form of group therapy.*

## The State of the Field
## *Panic, Obsessive-Compulsive, and Stress Disorders*

Panic, obsessive-compulsive, and stress disorders—once known in clinical circles simply as the "other" anxiety disorders—have received intense study over the past decade, resulting in growing insights about them.

Box 6-2

# *Preparing Victims for Rape's Aftermath*
## *Mary Koss and Mary Harvey*

Victims as well as significant others can benefit from some discussion of the usual symptomatic responses to rape, the psychological impact of rape, and the length of time required to feel recovered. Such information may prevent more serious problems from developing by making the expectations of involved others more realistic and by encouraging the victim to feel justified to seek help. The information that could be shared with victims and their families might be similar to the following comments. . . .

Rape is a trauma just like a major disaster such as a tornado or a bad car accident.

## *Physical Symptoms*

Because of the shock that these events cause to your systems, some physical problems usually develop afterwards. You may experience symptoms you usually associate with extreme fear, such as pounding heart, shortness of breath, or dizziness. You may find your appetite or sleeping is changed as when you're worried about a major traumatic event like a court appearance or are under a lot of pressure at work.

You may notice problems with sex that you've rarely experienced before. Often this is a signal that you're not ready to resume your former activities so quickly. It's perfectly okay to substitute other forms of feeling close and [to avoid] intercourse until you feel ready.

Even though these physical symptoms are typical, they will still upset you. Seek a doctor's care but be sure to tell him or her of your recent rape so that they can treat you properly.

## *Feelings*

Nearly everyone experiences some psychological problems after a rape. Particularly upsetting are nightmares, flashbacks of the experience, and the feeling that you need to talk about your experience over and over again until everyone around you is fed up. These are normal psychological processes that operate after a major trauma. Their purpose is to gradually wear down the frightening impact of an experience. They will eventually help you put the experience behind you.

Even if you don't have any problems now, it's not unusual for some to crop up six months or a year from now. The problems that are most common are fears that you never had before or were never that pronounced, feeling bad about yourself and about life in general, conflicts in your intimate relationships, and problems getting back to your former enjoyment of sex.

You may find that the rape has affected your whole family. Don't be surprised if you develop negative feelings about someone that are stronger or different than you've ever had before. Try to talk your feelings over and be specific about what the other person can do to help you feel better. Family members may feel pretty impatient that it is taking you so long to get on top of things.

## *Availability of Services*

You may find that although your enjoyment of life is less, you can live with your symptoms and cope. However, there may come a time when you feel that the toll is too great and you need relief. Or, you may notice that your important relationships are suffering or deteriorating. A number of people are available to help you at this point. I'm going to give you a sheet listing some of them so that you'll know who to call.

Besides counselors who could see you privately if you wanted, it is possible to become a member of a group made up of women who have been raped. It can often help to feel less crazy and alone if you know other people who share your experience and know what it's like.

## *Length of Recovery*

It usually takes over a year to feel fully recovered from rape, to be able to think of your assault without crying, and to feel the same level of health you enjoyed previously. Going through a court process or anything else that reminds you of the assault may make you feel temporarily worse after you thought you were finally getting on top of things. It's not unusual for there to be ups and downs on the way to recovery.

If it's okay with you, I'd like to call you at home in a few days and see how you're doing. Then, or at a later time, I'd be glad to see you again or help you make an appointment with a counselor.

*(Koss & Harvey, 1987, pp. 109–110)*

The findings of recent years have illustrated the explanatory and treatment potential of several models that previously seemed to have relatively little to offer in these areas. In particular, the cognitive and biological models have emerged, along with the behavioral model, as major forces in the study and treatment of panic and obsessive-compulsive disorders.

The findings of recent years have also shown that concepts and techniques from various models may be combined to yield broader insights or more effective treatment. For example, the cognitive explanation of panic disorders builds on the biological notion that the disorders begin with unusual physiological sensations. Similarly, therapists often combine medications with cognitive techniques to treat panic disorders, with behavioral techniques to treat obsessive-compulsive disorder, and with psychodynamic, humanistic, behav-ioral, or cognitive interventions to treat stress disorders. For the millions of people who suffer from these anxiety disorders, such insights and interventions are most positive and momentous developments.

Several important tasks lie ahead for those who theorize about, research, and treat the anxiety disorders that we have reviewed in this chapter and the last. They must demonstrate conclusively that the factors and variables they consider crucial are indeed significant in the development or continuance of these disorders; they must distinguish causal factors from maintaining ones; and lastly, they must further determine how the variables emphasized in the different models interact with one another. Only when such tasks are accomplished will clinicians at last have a full understanding of these disorders and their prevention and treatment.

# Chapter Review

1. *Panic, Obsessive-Compulsive, and Stress Disorders:* A number of discoveries during the past ten years have shed new light on the causes of panic disorders, obsessive-compulsive disorder, and stress disorders. Promising treatments have been developed for each of them as well.

2. *Panic Disorder:* Sufferers of a *panic disorder* experience panic attacks frequently, unpredictably, and without apparent provocation.

   A. *Biological Perspective:* Biological theorists believe that abnormal *norepinephrine* activity in the *locus coeruleus* is a key factor in panic disorders. Biological therapists use certain antidepressant drugs to treat many people with panic disorders.

   B. *Cognitive Perspective:* The cognitive position is that panic-prone people become preoccupied with some of their bodily sensations and mental states and often misinterpret them as indicative of imminent catastrophe. Cognitive therapists teach patients that the physical sensations they experience are actually harmless.

3. *Obsessive-Compulsive Disorder:* People with an *obsessive-compulsive disorder* are beset by *obsessions*—repetitive and unwanted thoughts, ideas, impulses, or images that keep invading their consciousness and causing anxiety, or *compulsions*—repetitive and rigid actions that they feel compelled to perform to reduce anxiety.

   A. *Psychodynamic Perspective:* According to the *psychodynamic view,* obsessive-compulsive disor-der arises out of a battle between id impulses, which appear as obsessive thoughts, and ego defense mechanisms, which take the form of counterthoughts or compulsive actions. Psychodynamic therapists use free association, therapist interpretation, and related techniques to try to help people overcome their disorder.

   B. *Behavioral Perspective:* Behaviorists suggest that compulsive behaviors often develop through chance associations and operant conditioning. The leading behavioral approach combines prolonged in vivo *exposure* with *response prevention,* the blocking of compulsive behaviors.

   C. *Cognitive Perspective: Cognitive* theorists suggest that obsessive-compulsive disorder grows from a normal human tendency to have unwanted and unpleasant thoughts—a tendency that some persons misinterpret as dangerous, reprehensible, and controllable. Their efforts to eliminate or avoid such thoughts inadvertently lead to the development of obsessions and compulsions. In a promising cognitive-behavioral approach, *habituation training,* therapists encourage clients to summon their obsessive thoughts to mind for a prolonged period, expecting that such prolonged exposure will cause the thoughts to lose their threatening meaning and generate less anxiety.

   D. *Biological Perspective: Biological* researchers have identified two biological factors that may contribute to this disorder: low activity of the neurotransmitter *serotonin* and abnormal functioning in key regions of the brain, including the *caudate nuclei. Antidepressant drugs* that raise serotonin activity seem to be a useful form of treatment for this disorder.

4. *Stress Disorders:* People with *acute stress disorder* or *posttraumatic stress disorder* react with a distinct pattern of symptoms after a traumatic event, including reexperiencing the traumatic event, avoidance of related events, reduced responsiveness, and increased arousal, anxiety, and guilt. The symptoms of acute stress disorder begin soon after the trauma and last less than a month. Those of posttraumatic stress disorder may begin at any time (even years) after the trauma, and may last for months or years.

A. *Key Factors:* In attempting to explain why some people develop acute or posttraumatic stress disorder and others do not, researchers have focused on childhood experiences, personal variables, and social support.

B. *Treatments:* Techniques used for symptomatic relief of the stress disorders include medications and exposure techniques. Most clinicians also use supportive and humanistic therapy, including group therapy, to help sufferers develop insight and perspective regarding their continuing symptoms.

## Key Terms

| | | | |
|---|---|---|---|
| panic disorder | locus coeruleus | reaction formation | orbital region |
| obsessive-compulsive disorder | alprazolam | aggressive id impulses | caudate nuclei |
| acute stress disorder | anxiety sensitivity | exposure and response prevention | basal ganglia |
| posttraumatic stress disorder | biological challenge test | neutralizing | thalamus |
| mitral valve prolapse | obsession | habituation training | PET scan |
| thyroid disease | compulsion | covert-response prevention | psychic numbing |
| panic disorder with agoraphobia | compulsive ritual | serotonin | dissociation |
| norepinephrine | cleaning compulsion | clomipramine | victimization |
| | checking compulsion | fluoxetine | hardiness |
| | isolation | | rap group |
| | undoing | | Veterans Outreach Center |

## Quick Quiz

1. What biological factors contribute to the onset of panic disorders, and precisely what biological interventions are effective in the treatment of these disorders?

2. How do cognitive theorists explain and treat panic disorders?

3. What are biological challenge tests, and how are they used by researchers and by therapists?

4. Describe six different types of compulsions.

5. Which defense mechanisms do psychodynamic theorists believe are particularly common in obsessive-compulsive disorder?

6. How do normal thinking processes and "neutralizing" combine to yield obsessive-compulsive disorder, according to cognitive therapists? What kinds of research support has the cognitive explanation received?

7. Describe and compare the effectiveness of the behavioral approach (exposure and response prevention) and the biological approach (antidepressant medications) to obsessive-compulsive disorder.

8. What biological factors have been linked to obsessive-compulsive disorder?

9. Compare and contrast acute stress disorder and posttraumatic stress disorder.

10. What factors seem to bear upon who does and who does not develop a stress disorder after experiencing a traumatic event?

11. What treatment techniques have been used with people suffering from stress disorders?

# 7

# Mood Disorders

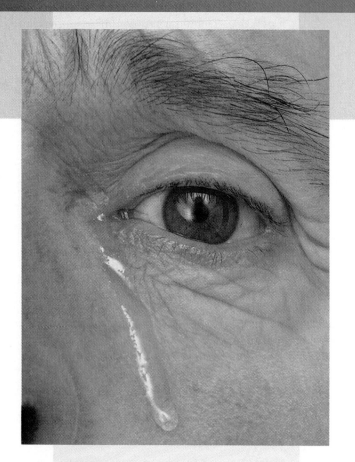

## Topic Overview

### Unipolar Patterns of Depression
  Clinical Picture of Depression
  Diagnosing Unipolar Depression
  Explanations and Treatments

### Bipolar Disorders
  Clinical Picture of Mania
  Diagnosing Bipolar Disorders
  Explanations and Treatments

ost people's moods are transient. Their feelings of elation or sadness are understandable responses to daily events and change readily without affecting the overall tenor of their lives. The moods of people with mood disorders, in contrast, tend to last a long time, color all of their interactions with the world, and disrupt their normal functioning. Virtually all of such people's actions are dictated by their powerful moods.

Depression and mania are the dominating emotions in mood disorders. *Depression* is a low, sad state in which life seems bleak and its challenges overwhelming. *Mania,* the extreme opposite of depression, is a state of breathless euphoria, or at least frenzied energy, in which people have an exaggerated belief that the world is theirs for the taking. Most people with a mood disorder suffer exclusively from depression, a pattern often called *unipolar depression.* They have no history of mania and return to a normal or nearly normal mood state when their depression lifts. Others undergo periods of mania that alternate with periods of depression, a pattern called *bipolar disorder.*

Mood disorders have always captured people's interest, in part because so many prominent people have suffered from them. The Bible speaks of the severe depressions of Nebuchadnezzar, Saul, and Moses. Queen Victoria of England and Abraham Lincoln seem to have experienced recurring depressions. Similarly, depression and sometimes mania have plagued such artists as George Frideric Handel, Ernest Hemingway, Virginia Woolf, and Sylvia Plath (Andreasen, 1980). The plight of these famous figures has been shared by millions, and the economic consequences (costs of treatment, hospitalization, work loss, and so on) amount to $44 billion each year (MIT, 1993). The human suffering these disorders cause is incalculable.

*Abraham Lincoln was one of many leaders who suffered from episodes of depression. In 1841 he wrote to a friend, "I am now the most miserable man living. If what I feel were equally distributed to the whole human family, there would be not one cheerful face on earth."*

term confuses a normal mood with a dysfunctional clinical syndrome. All of us experience dejection from time to time; only an unfortunate minority experience unipolar depression.

## Unipolar Patterns of Depression

Because so much psychological terminology has entered the popular vernacular over the last thirty years, people more dejected and unhappy than usual often say they are "depressed." In most cases, what they are describing is a perfectly normal mood swing, a response perhaps to sad events, understandable fatigue, or unhappy thoughts. Unfortunately, this use of the

*Depression*   A low, sad state in which life seems bleak and its challenges overwhelming.

*Unipolar depression*   Depression without a history of mania and followed, upon recovery, by a normal or nearly normal mood.

### Consider This
Almost every day we experience ups and downs in our mood. Although we might label the "down" mood as depression, it is not the same as clinical depression. How might mental health professionals distinguish the everyday "blues" from clinical depression?

### The Prevalence of Unipolar Depression

Surveys suggest that between 5 and 10 percent of adults in the United States suffer from a severe unipolar pattern of depression in any given year (see Table

**Table 7-1**   *Mood Disorders Profile*

| | *One-Year Prevalence* | *Female:Male Ratio* | *Typical Age of Initial Onset* | *Prevalence among Close Relatives* | *Most Effective Treatment* | *Percent Improved by Treatment* |
|---|---|---|---|---|---|---|
| Major depressive disorder | 5–10% | 2:1 | 24–29 years | Elevated | Cognitive, interpersonal, biological | 60% |
| Dysthymic disorder | 2.5–5.4% | Between 3:2 and 2:1 | 10–25 years | Elevated | Behavioral, cognitive, interpersonal, or biological | 60% |
| Bipolar I disorder | 0.7% | 1:1 | 15–44 years | Elevated | Biological | 65% |
| Bipolar II disorder | 0.5% | 1:1 | 15–44 years | Elevated | Biological | 65% |
| Cyclothymic disorder | 0.4% | 1:1 | 15–25 years | Elevated | Psychotherapy or biological | 65% |

*Sources:* APA, 1994; Kessler et al., 1994; Regier et al., 1993; Weissman et al., 1991.

7-1), with half of them receiving treatment (Kessler et al., 1994; Regier et al., 1993). Another 3 to 5 percent of adults suffer from mild forms of the disorder. The prevalence rates are similar in Canada, England, and many other countries. In fact, it is estimated that as many as 17 percent of all adults in the world experience an episode of severe unipolar depression at some point in their lives. A worldwide research project further suggests that the risk of experiencing severe depression has steadily increased with each successive generation since 1915 (Weissman et al., 1992; Klerman & Weissman, 1989).

In almost all industrialized countries, women are at least twice as likely as men to experience severe episodes of unipolar depression (Weissman et al., 1991; Klerman & Weissman, 1989) (see Box 7-1). As many as 26 percent of women may have such an episode at some time in their lives, compared with 12 percent of men (APA, 1993). Among children, the prevalence of unipolar depression is similar for girls and boys. All of these rates are similar across all socioeconomic classes.

Relatively few differences in prevalence have been found between ethnic groups. White Americans between the ages of 30 and 64 have a somewhat higher rate than African Americans in that age range, but the rates for younger and older adults are the same in both populations (Weissman et al., 1991).

Episodes of severe unipolar depression may begin at any age. Approximately two-thirds of severely depressed people recover within six months, some without treatment (APA, 1994; Keller, 1988). Having been depressed once, however, a person has an increased risk of becoming depressed again (Goldberg et al., 1995).

## The Clinical Picture of Depression

Some depressed people manage to function after a fashion, but their depression robs them of effectiveness and pleasure, as we see in the case of Derek:

Derek has probably suffered from depression all of his adult life but was unaware of it for many years. Derek called himself a night person, claiming that he could not think clearly until after noon even though he was often awake by 4:00 A.M. He tried to schedule his work as editorial writer for a small town newspaper so that it was compatible with his depressed mood at the beginning of the day. Therefore, he scheduled meetings for the mornings; talking with people got him moving. He saved writing and decision making for later in the day.

Derek had always been a thoughtful person and was often preoccupied. His family and colleagues grew used to his apparent inattention and absentmindedness. He often failed to answer people when they spoke to him. Sometimes they were surprised to hear his slow, soft-spoken reply 20 or 30 seconds later. His wife tried to be patient when it took him 20 seconds to respond to "Do you want coffee or tea tonight?" Derek's private thoughts were rarely cheerful and self-confident. He felt that his marriage was a mere business partnership. He provided the money, and she provided a home and children. Derek and his wife rarely expressed affection for each other. Occasionally, he had images of his own violent death in a bicycle crash, in a plane crash, or in a murder by an unidentified assailant.

Derek felt that he was constantly on the edge of job failure. He was disappointed that his editorials had not attracted the attention of larger papers. He was certain that several of the younger people on the paper had better ideas and wrote more skillfully than he did. He scolded himself for a bad editorial that he had written ten years earlier. Although that particular piece had not been up to his usual standards, everyone else on the paper had forgotten it a week after it appeared. But ten years later, Derek was still ruminating over that one editorial. . . .

Derek attributed his inability to enjoy himself and his methodical, passionless marriage to his severe Anglo-Saxon Protestant upbringing. He had been brought up to do the "right thing," not to enjoy himself. Raucous merrymaking was only for the irresponsible. Even a game of Go Fish had to be played in secret when he was a child.

Derek brushed off his morning confusion as a lack of quick intelligence. He had no way to know that it was a symptom of depression. He never realized that his death images might be suicidal thinking. People do not talk about such things. For all Derek knew, everyone had similar thoughts.

*(Lickey & Gordon, 1991, pp. 183–185)*

As this case description indicates, depression has many symptoms other than sadness, and the symptoms often reinforce one another. Moreover, depression can be somewhat differently expressed in different people. The symptoms associated with depression span five areas of functioning: the emotional, motivational, behavioral, cognitive, and somatic.

## Emotional Symptoms

Most people who are depressed feel intensely sad and dejected. They describe themselves as feeling "miserable," "empty," and "humiliated." They report getting little pleasure from anything, and they tend to lose their sense of humor. Some depressed people also experience anxiety, anger, or agitation. This sea of misery may find expression in crying spells.

## Motivational Symptoms

Depressed people usually lose the desire to participate in their accustomed activities. Almost all report a lack of drive, initiative, and spontaneity, and they may have to force themselves to go to work, converse with friends, eat meals, or have sex (Buchwald & Rudick-Davis, 1993). One individual recalls, "I didn't want to do anything—just wanted to stay put and be let alone" (Kraines & Thetford, 1972, p. 20).

Suicide represents the ultimate escape from life's activities and pressures. As we shall observe in Chapter 12, many depressed people become indifferent to life or wish to die; others wish that they could kill themselves, and some actually try. It has been estimated that between 7 and 15 percent of people who suffer from depression commit suicide (Coryell & Winokur, 1992).

## Behavioral Symptoms

The activity of depressed people usually decreases dramatically. They do less and are less productive. They spend more time alone and may stay in bed for long periods. One man recalls, "I'd awaken early, but I'd just lie there—what was the use of getting up to a miserable day?" (Kraines & Thetford, 1972, p. 21). Depressed people may also move and even speak more slowly, with seeming reluctance and lack of energy (Parker et al., 1993).

## Cognitive Symptoms

Depressed people hold decidedly negative views of themselves. They consider themselves inadequate, undesirable, inferior, perhaps evil. They blame themselves for nearly every negative event, even things that have nothing to do with them, and they rarely credit themselves for positive achievements.

Another cognitive symptom of depression is a negative view of the future. Depressed people are usually convinced that nothing will ever improve and they feel

*Some people in the midst of a depression mask it by smiling and looking happy most of the time. Movie star Marilyn Monroe was such an individual.*

## Box 7-1

# *Depressing News for Women*

More women than men are diagnosed with major unipolar depression. More women report being mildly depressed. The inescapable conclusion is that women are at least twice as likely as men to suffer from unipolar depression (Pajer, 1995). Depressing news, indeed. This apparent gender difference has generated much theorizing and investigation. One theorist, the psychologist Susan Nolen-Hoeksema (1990, 1987), has reviewed five possible explanations.

1. *The artifact hypothesis.*
   Women and men are equally prone to depression, but gender differences arise because studies fail to detect depression in men. One reason could be that men find it less socially acceptable to report feeling depressed or to seek treatment. Alternatively, depressed women may display emotional symptoms, such as sadness and crying, that are easily diagnosed, while depressed men may mask these symptoms. It has been suggested that depressed men turn to drink and are diagnosed as alcoholic.

*Edvard Munch's painting* Melancholy (Laura) *was inspired by his sister's bouts of severe depression.*

In fact, the gender difference in alcoholism—men outnumber women 2 to 1—is complementary to the gender difference in depression; moreover, many persons with alcoholism show other symptoms of depression (Davidson, 1995). The artifact hypothesis, however, lacks consistent research support (Fennig et al., 1994).

2. *The X-linkage hypothesis.* De-

---

helpless to control or change any aspect of their lives (Metalsky et al., 1993). They expect the worst and hence are likely to procrastinate. This sense of hopelessness and helplessness also makes depressed people especially vulnerable to suicidal thinking.

People with depression frequently complain that their intellectual ability is deteriorating (Willner, 1984). They feel confused, unable to remember things, easily distracted by outside noises, and unable to solve even small problems. Time crawls for them, yet they feel that they cannot get anything done (Hawkins et al., 1988). Overall, these difficulties are often imagined rather than real.

## Somatic Symptoms

Depression is often accompanied by such physical ailments as headaches, indigestion, constipation, dizzy spells, unpleasant sensations in the chest, and generalized pain. In fact, many depressions are initially misdiagnosed as medical problems (Kirmayer et al., 1993). Disturbances in appetite and sleep are particularly common, as are complaints of constant tiredness that is not relieved even when rest and sleep are increased. Depressed people usually get less sleep overall than others and awaken more frequently during the night. At the other end of the spectrum, however, are the appression is caused by a dominant mutation on the X chromosome. Since women are genotypically XX, they run a greater risk of inheriting the gene than men, who are genotypically XY. The hypothesis is supported by the finding that depression is correlated with other X-chromosome abnormalities, such as color blindness. Family pedigree studies, however, have contradicted it. If depression were an X-chromosome disorder, a depressed father would always transmit it to his daughters but not to his sons; yet studies indicate that more father-son than father-daughter pairs are diagnosed with unipolar depression.

3. *Classical psychoanalytic explanations.* At the Oedipal stage of psychological development a girl realizes that she lacks a penis and believes herself to have been castrated by her mother; she feels both hostility toward her mother and a sense of her own inferiority. She also identifies with her mother. With this background, women's relationships with men are motivated by a desire to possess a phallus in symbolic form. They suffer low self-esteem as a result of their lifelong penis envy, are more vulnerable to loss, and thus are more prone to develop depression. This view, which supplements the explanation offered by Freud and Abraham, lacks empirical support and has been widely criticized as being chauvinistic.

4. *A sociocultural explanation.* The quality of women's roles in society makes them more vulnerable to depression. On the one hand, as the housewife role has become increasingly devalued and less rewarding, women in this role may become depressed because they have limited sources of gratification (Gove & Tudor, 1973). On the other hand, working women may be prone to depression because they bear the double burden of housework and a job outside the home.

5. *The learned helplessness explanation.* Women are more vulnerable to depression because they are more likely to feel they have little control over their lives. Studies have shown that women are more prone to laboratory learned helplessness effects than men. One found that female college students who were exposed to a helplessness-inducing set of insoluble anagrams later performed other tasks much more poorly than their male counterparts (Le Unes et al., 1980). Nolen-Hoeksema notes, however, that a stringent test of this explanation for depression remains to be carried out.

The artifact hypothesis implies that more effort should be made to identify and treat depression in men. The biological and classical psychoanalytic explanations say that therapeutic resources could be fruitfully focused on women themselves. The sociocultural and learned helplessness explanations suggest that it is society itself that requires "treatment," or restructuring. No explanation of the gender difference in depression has gained unequivocal support, leaving this difference one of the most talked about, but least understood, phenomena in the clinical field.

proximately 9 percent of depressed people who sleep excessively (Ballenger, 1988).

## Diagnosing Unipolar Patterns of Depression

DSM-IV describes several different patterns of unipolar depression. People are experiencing a *major depressive disorder* when their depression is significantly disabling, lasts for two weeks or more, is characterized by at least five symptoms of depression, and is not caused by such factors as drugs or a general medical condition. In a small percentage of cases, such episodes of depression may include psychotic symptoms, that is, the person loses contact with reality, experiencing *delusions*—bizarre ideas without foundation—or *hallucinations*—perceptions of things that are not actually present (APA, 1994). A depressed man with psychotic symptoms may imagine, for example, that he "can't eat because my intestines are deteriorating and will soon stop working," or he may believe that he sees his dead wife.

A major depressive disorder is further described as *recurrent* if it has been preceded by previous depressive episodes; *seasonal* if it fluctuates with seasonal

*Major depressive disorder*   A severe pattern of unipolar depression that is significantly disabling and is not caused by such factors as drugs or a general medical condition.

*Children whose mothers are depressed are at greater risk of later experiencing depression than are children of nondepressed mothers (Cummings & Davies, 1994).*

changes (for example, if the depression tends to recur each winter); or *postpartum* if it occurs within four weeks of giving birth.

People who display a more chronic but less disabling pattern of unipolar depression may receive a diagnosis of *dysthymic disorder* (the term is Greek for "despondency"). Here depressed mood and only two or three other symptoms of depression are typically present, and the depression persists for at least two years (or at least one year in children and adolescents). Periods of normal mood, lasting only days or weeks, may occasionally interrupt the depressed mood.

## Recent Life Events and Unipolar Depression

Clinicians have noted that episodes of unipolar depression often seem to be triggered by stressful events. Correspondingly, the British psychiatric researcher Eugene Paykel and his colleagues have found that depressed people as a group experience a greater number of stressful life events just before the onset of their dis-

*Dysthymic disorder*  A mood disorder that is similar to but more chronic and less disabling than a major depressive disorder.

order than do nondepressed people during the same period of time (Paykel & Cooper, 1992). Stressful life events also appear to precede other psychological disorders, but depressed people report significantly more such events than anybody else.

Researchers have found that people whose lives are generally difficult and isolated and who lack social support seem more likely than others to become depressed when stresses multiply (Paykel & Cooper, 1992). In fact, people who are separated or divorced, as well as those living in nursing homes or prisons, are much more likely than others to be depressed (Weissman et al., 1991) (see Figure 7-1).

Some clinicians consider it important to distinguish a *reactive* (or *exogenous*) *depression,* which follows clear-cut precipitating events, from an *endogenous depression,* which unfolds without apparent antecedents and seems to be caused by internal factors. But how does one know whether a depression is reactive or not? Even if stressful events have occurred before the onset of depression, clinicians cannot be certain that the depression is reactive. The events could be a minor factor only or even a pure coincidence. Conversely, even when a depression seems to emerge in the absence of stressful events, clinicians cannot be sure that it is endogenous. Perhaps a subtle stressor has escaped notice.

The current leading explanations and treatments for unipolar depression fall into two major categories. Some clinicians focus on the situational components of the disorder, while others concentrate on the possible role of internal, or biological, factors. In line with the growing recognition that these components are often hard to separate and that unipolar depression may involve *both* situational and biological causes, it is probably best to view each of these approaches as offering a partial rather than a comprehensive account of who develops unipolar depression and why.

*Summing Up*
*People with mood disorders have moods that disrupt their normal functioning. The victims of unipolar depression, the most common pattern of mood disorder, suffer exclusively from depression. The symptoms of depression span five areas of functioning: emotional, motivational, behavioral, cognitive, and somatic. Some unipolar depressions seem to be triggered by stressful life events, and are called reactive (exogenous); others are assumed to be caused by internal factors, and are called endogenous. This distinction is often difficult to make, however.*

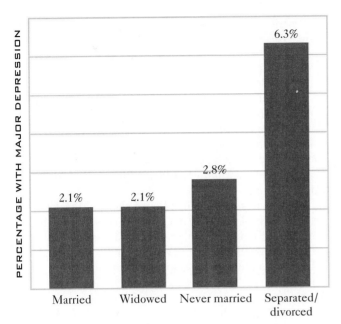

**Figure 7-1**  *The one-year prevalence rates of major depressive disorder make it clear that marital status is linked to major depression. Currently separated or divorced people are three times as likely to be depressed as people who currently are married. It may be that the stress of undergoing divorce precipitates depression, that depression puts intolerable stress on some marriages, or that marital problems lead to both depression and divorce. (Adapted from Weissman et al., 1991.)*

## The Psychodynamic Perspective

Sigmund Freud and his student Karl Abraham developed the initial psychodynamic explanation and treatment for unipolar depression (Freud, 1917; Abraham, 1916, 1911). Although many of today's psychodynamic theorists have rejected or altered some of their principles, they continue to embrace the notion that dependence and loss play major roles in the onset of this disorder.

### Psychodynamic Explanations

The starting point for Freud and Abraham was the similarity they noticed between clinical depression and the grief reactions of people who lose loved ones. Constant weeping, loss of appetite, difficulty sleeping, inability to find pleasure in life, and general withdrawal are common features of both mourning and depression (Stroebe et al., 1992).

According to Freud and Abraham, a series of unconscious processes is set in motion when a loved one dies or is lost in some other way. At first, unable to accept the loss, mourners regress to the oral stage of development, the period when infants are so dependent

that they cannot distinguish themselves from their parents. By regressing to this stage the mourners fuse their own identity with that of the person they have lost, symbolically regaining the lost person in the process. In other words, they *introject* the loved one and then experience all their feelings toward the loved one as feelings about themselves.

For most mourners, this unconscious process is temporary and lasts only for the period of mourning. For some, however, the grief reaction worsens. They feel empty, continue to avoid social relationships, and become more preoccupied with their sense of loss. Introjected feelings of anger toward the loved one for departing, or perhaps over unresolved conflicts from the past, cause these people to experience self-hatred, which leads to a negative mood, self-blame, and further withdrawal. In effect, these people become depressed.

Freud and Abraham believed that two kinds of people are particularly prone to introjection and depression in the face of loss: those whose parents failed to meet their nurturance needs during the oral stage of infancy and those whose parents gratified those needs excessively. People of either kind may spend their lives desperately seeking love and approval from others and devoting themselves to others. Such people are likely to experience a greater sense of loss when a loved one dies and greater anger toward the loved one for having departed.

Of course, many people become depressed without losing a loved one. To explain why, Freud invoked the concept of *imagined,* or *symbolic, loss.* A man who loses his job, for example, may unconsciously interpret the experience as the loss of his wife, believing that she will no longer want him if he is unsuccessful at work.

As we noted earlier, this theory's influence on current psychodynamic thinking remains very strong (APA, 1993; Coccaro, 1991). For example, *object relations theorists,* the psychodynamic theorists who emphasize *relationships,* propose that depression results when people's relationships leave them feeling unsafe and insecure, and that people whose parents pushed them toward either excessive dependence or excessive self-reliance are more likely to become depressed when they later confront complications or losses in their relationships (Horner, 1991; Kernberg, 1976).

In the following case report of a depressed middle-aged woman, the therapist's description emphasizes

---

*Symbolic loss*  According to Freudian theory, the loss of a valued object (for example, a loss of employment) which is unconsciously interpreted as the loss of a loved one.

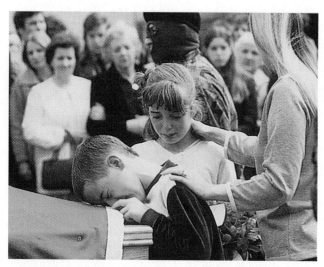

*Psychodynamic theorists believe that depression is caused by the real or imagined loss of a loved one. Research has found that people who lose their parents as children have an increased likelihood of experiencing depression as adults.*

the psychodynamic concepts of dependence, loss of a loved one, symbolic loss, and introjection:

Mrs. Marie Carls was in her middle fifties when she came for the first interview. . . . The patient had always felt very attached to her mother. As a matter of fact, they used to call her "Stamp" because she stuck to her mother as a stamp to a letter. She always tried to placate her volcanic mother, to please her in every possible way. The mother, however, did not fulfill her maternal role very well. . . .

After marriage [to Julius], she continued her pattern of submission and compliance. Before her marriage she had difficulty in complying with a volcanic mother, and after her marriage she almost automatically assumed a submissive role. . . .

Several months after beginning treatment, the patient reported a dream. Ignatius and she had decided not to see each other again. She would have to leave him forever. I asked who Ignatius was, because I had not heard the name until then. The patient replied almost with surprise, "But the first time I came to see you, I told you that in the past I had an infatuation." She then told me that when she was thirty years old. . . . the patient and her husband invited Ignatius, who was single, to come and live with them. Ignatius and the patient soon discovered that they had an attraction for each other. They both tried to fight that feeling; but when Julius had to go to another city for a few days, the so-called infatuation became much more than that. There were a few physical contacts. . . . There was an intense spiritual affinity. Ignatius understood her: he spoke her language, liked what she liked, and gave her the feeling of being alive. Ignatius suggested that they elope, but she did not take him

seriously. A few months later everybody had to leave the city. Nothing was done to maintain contact. Two years later, approximately a year after the end of the war, Marie heard that Ignatius had married. She felt terribly alone and despondent. . . .

Her suffering had become more acute as she realized that old age was approaching and she had lost all her chances. Ignatius remained as the memory of lost opportunities . . . . Her life of compliance and obedience had not permitted her to reach her goal. An Ignatius existed in the world, but she had lost him forever.

For many years she had hoped she could make up for the loss of Ignatius, but now she could no longer do so. She could no longer scream, "Long live life!" She would rather think, "Down with life without Ignatius, a life which has lost its meaning."

When she became aware of these ideas, she felt even more depressed . . . . She felt that everything she had built in her life was false or based on a false premise.

*(Arieti & Bemporad, 1978, pp. 275–284)*

**Investigating the Psychodynamic Explanations** Studies by psychodynamic researchers have generally supported the psychodynamic ideas that depression is often triggered by a major loss and that people who experience early losses and early dependent relationships are more vulnerable to losses later in life (APA, 1993). In a famous study of 123 infants who were placed in a nursery after being separated from their mothers, René Spitz (1946, 1945) found that 19 of the infants became very weepy and sad upon separation, withdrew from their surroundings, ignored others, and lay passively in their cots. Later studies confirmed that separation from one's mother before the age of 6 years often brings about a reaction of this kind, a pattern called *anaclitic depression* (Bowlby, 1980, 1969). Studies of infant monkeys who are separated from their mothers have noted a similar pattern of apparent despair (Harlow & Harlow, 1965).

Still other research suggests that losses suffered early in life may also set the stage for depression during adulthood. For instance, a depression scale was administered to 1,250 medical patients during visits to their family physicians, and the patients whose fathers had died during their childhood were found to average higher scores of depression (Barnes & Prosen, 1985).

A related body of research also supports the psychodynamic proposition that people whose childhood needs were improperly addressed are the ones most

---

*Anaclitic depression*   A pattern of behavior that includes sadness, withdrawal, weight loss, and trouble sleeping and that is associated with separation from one's mother before the age of 6 years.

*Researcher Harry Harlow and his colleagues found that infant monkeys reacted with apparent despair to separation from their mothers. Even monkeys raised with surrogate mothers—wire cylinders wrapped with foam rubber and covered with terry cloth—formed an attachment to them.*

likely to become depressed after experiencing loss (Parker, 1992). When, for example, depressed subjects filled out a scale called the *Parental Bonding Instrument,* which indicates how much care and protection individuals feel they received as children, many reported that their parents had displayed a child-rearing style identified as "affectionless control," consisting of a mixture of low care and high protection.

**Evaluating Psychodynamic Research** These various studies offer some support for the psychodynamic view of depression, but it is important to be aware of their limitations. First, although the findings indicate that losses and inadequate parenting *sometimes* precipitate depression, they do not establish that such factors are *typically* responsible for the disorder. Indeed, it is estimated that less than 10 percent of all people who experience major losses in life actually become depressed (Paykel & Cooper, 1992; Paykel, 1982).

A second problem with the psychodynamic evidence is that many of the findings are inconsistent. For example, though many studies find evidence of a relationship between childhood loss and later depression, others do not (Parker, 1992; Owen et al., 1986).

A final drawback to this research is that important components of the psychodynamic explanation of depression are nearly impossible to test. Because such processes as symbolic loss and introjection are said to operate at an unconscious level, it is difficult for researchers to determine if and when they are occurring.

## Psychodynamic Therapy

Psychodynamic therapists use the same basic procedures with depressed clients that they use with others: they encourage the client to associate freely during therapy; suggest interpretations of the client's associations, dreams, and displays of resistance and transference; and help the client reexperience and reevaluate past events and feelings. Free association helped one patient recall the early experiences of loss that, according to his therapist, had set the stage for his depression:

> Among his earliest memories, possibly the earliest of all, was the recollection of being wheeled in his baby cart under the elevated train structure and left there alone. Another memory that recurred vividly during the analysis was of an operation around the age of five. He was anesthetized and his mother left him with the doctor. He recalled how he had kicked and screamed, raging at her for leaving him.
>
> *(Lorand, 1968, pp. 325–326)*

Despite some successful case reports, researchers have found long-term psychodynamic therapies to be helpful only occasionally in cases of unipolar depression (APA, 1993). Two features of the approach have been cited to explain its limited effectiveness. First, depressed clients may be too passive and feel too fatigued to participate fully in therapy discussions and to exercise the subtle insight that psychodynamic therapy requires. Second, clients may become discouraged and end treatment too early when this long-term approach is unable to provide the quick relief that they desperately seek. Short-term psychodynamic approaches have shown somewhat greater promise, although research has been limited and results modest (APA, 1993; Svartberg & Stiles, 1991).

*Consider This*

What other characteristics of depressed individuals might create difficulties for psychodynamic therapists? What kinds of interactions might psychodynamic therapists expect to occur in therapy with these persons?

## The Behavioral Perspective

Behaviorists believe that unipolar depression results from significant changes in the rewards and punishments people receive in their lives, and they treat people with this disorder by trying to reestablish more favorable reinforcement patterns. Clinical theorist Peter Lewinsohn has offered the leading behavioral explanation and treatment (Lewinsohn et al., 1990, 1984).

### The Behavioral Explanation

Lewinsohn suggests that for some people the rewards that ordinarily reinforce positive behaviors start to dwindle, and they respond by performing fewer and fewer positive behaviors and develop a depressed style of functioning. The rewards of campus life, for example, may disappear for a young woman when she graduates from college and takes a job in the business world; or an aging baseball player may lose the reinforcements of high salary and adulation when his athletic skills deteriorate. Although many people manage to greet such changes with a sense of perspective and fill their lives with other forms of gratification, some become disheartened and perform fewer constructive behaviors. As their activity level drops, their positive reinforcements decrease even more, and the decline in reinforcements leads to even fewer positive behaviors. In this manner, a person may spiral toward depression.

Researchers have found that a person's number of reinforcements is indeed often related to the presence or absence of depression. Not only did the depressed subjects in one study report a lower number of positive reinforcements, as measured on a "Pleasant Events Schedule," than the nondepressed subjects over a thirty-day period, but when their reinforcements increased, the mood of these depressed subjects improved as well (Lewinsohn et al., 1979).

Lewinsohn and other behaviorists believe that *social* reinforcements are particularly important (Peterson, 1993; Lewinsohn et al., 1984). Studies have indicated that depressed subjects tend to experience fewer positive social reinforcements than nondepressed subjects, and that as their mood improves, their positive social reinforcements increase as well. Although depressed people may be the victims of social circumstances, it is also possible that their flat behaviors and dark mood are partly responsible for the decreases in their social reinforcements (Segrin & Abramson, 1994).

### Behavioral Therapy

Lewinsohn has developed a behavioral treatment for unipolar depression in which therapists reintroduce clients to pleasurable events and activities, systematically reinforce nondepressive behavior, and help clients improve their social skills.

First, guided by a client's responses on a Pleasant Events Schedule and an Activity Schedule (see Table 7-2), a therapist selects activities that the client considers pleasurable, such as going shopping or taking photographs, and encourages the client to set up a weekly schedule for engaging in them. Studies have shown that reintroducing selected activities in this way leads to increased participation in the activities and to a better mood (Teri & Lewinsohn, 1986; Lewinsohn & Graf, 1973).

Second, to combat negative depressive behavior such as complaining, crying, and self-deprecation— behavior that serves to keep people and opportunities for positive reinforcement at a distance—therapists may use a *contingency management* approach. That is, they systematically ignore a client's depressive behavior while giving attention and other rewards to constructive statements and behavior.

Finally, Lewinsohn and other behavioral therapists may teach or at least reteach depressed people to exercise effective social skills. In one group therapy program, called *personal effectiveness training*, group members work with one another to improve "expressive" behaviors such as eye contact, facial expression, tone of voice, and posture (King et al., 1974).

Research has found that Lewinsohn's behavioral techniques are of little help when only one of them is applied. However, treatment programs that combine several of these techniques do appear to reduce depressive symptoms, particularly if the depression is mild or moderate (Lewinsohn et al., 1990, 1984). Such programs appear to be especially effective when the treatments are systematically offered in group format along with lectures, classroom activities, homework assignments, and an explanatory guidebook (Teri & Lewinsohn, 1986; Lewinsohn et al., 1984, 1982).

## The Cognitive Perspective

Cognitive theorists believe that unipolar depression is primarily a cognitive disorder and that people with this problem repeatedly perceive the world and interpret events in counterproductive ways that lead to a depressed mood. Correspondingly, they contend that treatment must focus primarily on thinking processes

---

*Contingency management*    A behavioral approach to combat negative, depressive behavior in which the therapist systematically ignores a client's depressive behavior while giving attention and positive reinforcement to constructive statements and behavior.

## Table 7-2  *Sample Items in a Behavioral Activity Schedule*

Make check mark(s) within the parentheses to correspond to the activities of this day. Only activities that were at least a little pleasant should be checked.

| Activity | Frequency Check |
|---|---|
| 1. Buying things for myself | ( ) |
| 2. Going to lectures or hearing speakers | ( ) |
| 3. Saying something clearly | ( ) |
| 4. Watching TV | ( ) |
| 5. Thinking about something good in the future | ( ) |
| 6. Laughing | |
| 7. Having lunch with friends or associates | ( ) |
| 8. Having a frank and open conversation | ( ) |
| 9. Working on my job | ( ) |
| 10. Being helped | ( ) |
| 11. Wearing informal clothes | ( ) |
| 12. Being with friends | ( ) |
| 13. Reading essays or technical, academic, or professional literature | ( ) |
| 14. Just sitting and thinking | ( ) |
| 15. Social drinking | ( ) |
| 16. Seeing good things happen to my family or friends | ( ) |
| 17. Having a lively talk | ( ) |

*Source:* Lewinsohn et al., 1976, p. 117.

rather than mood. Two cognitive explanations of unipolar depression have received enormous attention—Seligman's theory of learned helplessness and Beck's theory of maladaptive thinking.

## The Learned Helplessness Explanation

Feelings of helplessness emerge repeatedly in this account of a young woman's depression:

Mary was 25 years old and had just begun her senior year in college. . . . Asked to recount how her life had been going recently, Mary began to weep. Sobbing, she said that for the last year or so she felt she was losing control of her life. Because of a gradual deterioration in her vision, she was now forced to wear glasses all day. "The glasses make me look terrible," she said, and "I don't look people in the eye much any more." Also, to her dismay, Mary had gained 20 pounds in the past year. She viewed herself as overweight and unattractive. At times she was convinced that with enough money to buy contact lenses and enough time to exercise she could cast off her depression; at other times she believed nothing would help. . . .

Mary saw her life deteriorating in other spheres, as well. She felt overwhelmed by schoolwork and, for the first time in her life, was on academic probation. . . . In addition to her dissatisfaction with her appearance and her fears about her academic future, Mary complained of a lack of friends. Her social network consisted solely of her boyfriend, with whom she was living. Although there were times she experienced this relationship as almost unbearably frustrating, she felt helpless to change it and was pessimistic about its permanence. . . .

*(Spitzer et al., 1983, pp. 122–123)*

Mary feels that she is "losing control of her life." Often she believes that she can do nothing to change what she considers to be her unattractive appearance and feels helpless to change her frustrating relationship with her boyfriend. According to psychologist Martin Seligman (1992, 1975), such feelings of helplessness are at the *center* of Mary's depression. Since the mid-1960s, Seligman has been developing the **learned helplessness** theory of depression, which holds that people become depressed as a result of thinking (1) that they no longer have control over the reinforcements in their lives and (2) that they themselves are responsible for this helpless state.

Seligman's theory first began to take shape when he and his colleagues were conducting conditioning studies with laboratory dogs, trying to teach them to escape and then avoid shocks. They placed each dog in a **shuttle box**, a box partitioned by a barrier over which the animal could jump to reach the other side (see Figure 7-2). Then they dimmed the lights as a warning signal and seconds later administered shocks to the dog. The shocks continued until the dog learned to escape them by jumping over the barrier.

Some of the dogs had been allowed to rest the day before ("naive" dogs); others had spent the previous day strapped into an apparatus called a hammock, in which they received inescapable shocks at random intervals. What fascinated Seligman was how these two groups then differed in their reactions to the shocks in the shuttle box. The naive dogs quickly learned to jump over the barrier in the shuttle box and escape the shocks. However, the dogs who had previously been

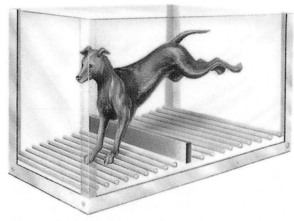

**Figure 7-2** *Experimental animals learn to escape or avoid shocks that are administered in one compartment of a shuttle box by jumping to the other (safe) compartment.*

given inescapable shock failed to learn anything in the shuttle box. After a flurry of activity, they simply "lay down and quietly whined."

Seligman concluded that the dogs who had previously received random inescapable shocks had learned that they had no control over aversive reinforcements (shocks) in their lives. That is, they had learned that they were helpless to do anything to change negative situations. Thus, even when these dogs were later placed in a new situation where they could in fact control their fate, they continued to believe that they had no control. They continued to act helpless and failed to learn to escape painful shock by jumping to the safe side of the shuttle box.

In subsequent experiments, Seligman and other investigators demonstrated that such helplessness effects can be generated in various animal species and under a variety of conditions (Hiroto & Seligman, 1975). Believing that the effects of learned helplessness greatly resemble the symptoms of human depression, he proposed that humans in fact become depressed after developing the implicit belief that they have no control over reinforcements in their lives.

### Investigating the Learned Helplessness Explanation

Consistent with Seligman's theory, many laboratory studies have found that both human and animal subjects who undergo helplessness training display reactions similar to depressive symptoms. When human subjects are given random aversive reinforcements, for example, they later score higher on a depressive mood survey than do subjects who are allowed control over their reinforcements (Miller & Seligman, 1975); and just as depressed people often show reductions in

overt aggressive behavior, helplessness-trained subjects withdraw more and compete less in laboratory games (Kurlander et al., 1974). Similarly, animals subjected to inescapable shock eat little and lose weight, and they lose interest in sexual and social activities—common symptoms of human depression (Lindner, 1968). Finally, uncontrollable aversive events result in lower activity of the brain neurotransmitter norepinephrine in rats, a depletion that has also been noted in the brains of people with unipolar depression, as we shall see (Hughes et al., 1984).

### Learned Helplessness Theory and Attributions

During the past 15 years, the learned helplessness explanation of depression has been further refined. According to the revised theory, when people perceive events to be beyond their control, they implicitly ask themselves why (Abramson et al., 1989, 1978). If they attribute their present lack of control to some *internal* cause that is both *global* and *stable* ("I am inadequate at *everything* and I *always* will be"), they may well feel helpless to prevent future negative outcomes and bereft of hope that anything positive will occur, and they may experience unipolar depression (see Table 7-3). If they make other kinds of attributions, that reaction is unlikely. The *attribution* factor helps explain why some people react helplessly and become depressed when they experience losses of control while others do not (Metalsky et al., 1993).

Consider, for example, a college student whose girlfriend breaks up with him. If he attributes this loss of control over a key source of gratification to an internal cause that is both global and stable—"It's my fault [internal], I ruin everything I touch [global], and I always will [stable]"—he then has reason to expect future losses of control and may therefore experience an enduring sense of helplessness. According to the learned helplessness view, he is a prime candidate for depression.

If the internal cause to which the student pointed were more *specific* ("The way I've behaved the past couple of weeks blew this relationship") and *unstable* ("I don't know what got into me—I don't usually act like that"), he would not be so likely to anticipate future losses of control. Similarly, if the student were to attribute the breakup to *external* causes ("She never did know what she wanted"), he would be less likely to expect future losses of control, and would probably not experience helplessness and depression.

---

*Attribution* An explanation of things we see going on around us which points to particular causes.

Table 7-3    *Internal and External Attributions*

| Event: "I failed my psych test today" | | | |
|---|---|---|---|
| Internal | | External | |
| Stable | Unstable | Stable | Unstable |
| **Global** "I have a problem with test anxiety." | "Getting into an argument with my roommate threw my whole day off." | "Written tests are an unfair way to assess knowledge." | "No one does well on tests that are given the day after vacation." |
| **Specific** "I just have no grasp of psychology." | "I got upset and froze when I couldn't answer the first two questions." | "Everyone knows that this professor enjoys giving unfair tests." | "This professor didn't put much thought into the test because of the pressure of her book deadline." |

Since the helplessness theory was revised, hundreds of studies have tested and supported the relationship between styles of attribution, helplessness, and depressive functioning in both children and adult subjects (Peterson et al., 1992; Nolen-Hoeksema et al., 1992). In one study, a group of moderately depressed adults were asked to fill out an Attributional Style Questionnaire before and after successful therapy. Before therapy, their high levels of depression were accompanied by attribution styles that were highly internal, stable, and global. At the end of therapy and again one year later, their depression levels were lower and their attribution styles were significantly less internal, stable, and global (Seligman et al., 1988).

**Evaluating the Learned Helplessness Research** Although the helplessness model of unipolar depression is a promising and widely applied theory, it poses some problems. First, laboratory-induced helplessness does not parallel depression in every respect. Uncontrollable shocks administered in the laboratory, for example, invariably produce heightened anxiety along with the helplessness effects, but human depression is not always accompanied by anxiety.

A second problem is that much of the research on learned helplessness relies on animal subjects. While the animals' passivity, social withdrawal, and other reactions seem to correspond to the symptoms of human depression, it is impossible to know whether they are true reflections of the same psychological phenomena.

Finally, the attributional aspect of the helplessness theory has raised important questions. What about the many dogs and rats who learn helplessness? Are they *attributing* their lack of control to internal, global, and stable causes? Can animals make attributions, even implicitly? Or is this an area where animal and human helplessness part company?

## The Maladaptive Thinking Explanation

Aaron Beck's (1991, 1967) research and clinical observations have led him to propose that depressed people are so filled with negative thoughts about themselves, their situations, and the future that all aspects of their functioning are affected dramatically. According to Beck, *maladaptive attitudes,* the *cognitive triad, errors in thinking,* and *automatic thoughts* combine to produce this pervasive negativity and lead to unipolar depression.

**Maladaptive Attitudes** Beck believes that children's attitudes toward themselves and the world are based on their own experiences, their family relationships, and the judgments of the people around them. Unfortunately, some children develop negative attitudes, such as "My general worth is tied to every task I perform" and "If I fail, others will feel repelled by me." Many failures are inevitable in a full, active life, so such attitudes are inaccurate and self-defeating. The negative attitudes become templates, or schemas, against which the child evaluates every experience (Young et al., 1993; Beck et al., 1990).

**The Cognitive Triad** The negative cognitive schemas that develop during childhood may lie dormant for years, as long as life proceeds smoothly, without major disturbances or disappointments. But at any time a traumatic situation—particularly one reminiscent of early failure or loss—can trigger an extended round of pervasive negative thinking. According to Beck, such negative thinking typically takes three forms and is therefore termed the *cognitive triad:* the individuals repeatedly interpret (1) *their experiences,*

*Cognitive triad*   The three forms of negative thinking, encompassing one's view of one's experiences, one's view of oneself, and one's view of the future, that theorist Aaron Beck says lead people to feel depressed.

(2) *themselves,* and (3) *their futures* in negative ways that lead them to feel depressed. That is, depressed people may interpret their experiences as burdens, obstacles, or traumas that repeatedly defeat, deprive, or disparage them. They may view themselves as deficient, undesirable, worthless, and inadequate. And they may regularly see the future as bleak, sure to be a never-ending series of hardships, miseries, frustrations, and failures. Some features of the cognitive triad are at work in the thinking of the following depressed person:

> I can't bear it. I can't stand the humiliating fact that I'm the only woman in the world who can't take care of her family, take her place as a real wife and mother, and be respected in her community. When I speak to my young son Billy, I know I can't let him down, but I feel so ill-equipped to take care of him; that's what frightens me. I don't know what to do or where to turn; the whole thing is too overwhelming. . . . I must be a laughing stock. It's more than I can do to go out and meet people and have the fact pointed up to me so clearly.
>
> *(Fieve, 1975)*

**Errors in Thinking**   According to Beck, depressed people habitually employ errors of logic, forms of distorted thinking that help build and maintain the cognitive triad. In one common error of logic, they draw *arbitrary inferences*—negative conclusions based on little or even contrary evidence. For example, a man walking through the park passes a woman who is looking at nearby trees and flowers, and he concludes, "She's avoiding looking at me."

Similarly, depressed people often *minimize* the significance of positive experiences or *magnify* that of negative ones. A college student receives an A on a difficult English exam, for example, but concludes that the grade reflects the professor's generosity rather than her own ability (minimization). Later in the week, the same student must miss an English class and is convinced that she will be unable to keep pace the rest of the semester (magnification).

**Automatic Thoughts**   Depressed people experience the cognitive triad in the form of negative *automatic thoughts,* a steady train of unpleasant thoughts that repeatedly remind them of their assumed inadequacy and the hopelessness of their situation. In the course of only a few hours, depressed people may be visited by hundreds of such thoughts: "I'm worthless. . . . I let everyone down. . . . Everyone hates me. . . . My responsibilities are overwhelming. . . . I've failed as a parent. . . . I'm stupid. . . . Everything is difficult for me. . . . Things will never change."

### Investigating the Maladaptive Thinking Explanation

Beck's cognitive view of unipolar depression has received considerable research support. Several studies have confirmed that depressed people tend to hold such maladaptive attitudes as "People will probably think less of me if I make a mistake" (Garber et al., 1993). Moreover, the number of maladaptive attitudes correlate strongly with the degree of depression, suggesting that the more of these attitudes one holds, the more depressed one tends to be.

Other research has supported Beck's idea that depressed people exhibit the cognitive triad (Cole & Turner, 1993). In various studies, depressed subjects recalled unpleasant experiences more readily than positive ones; rated themselves and their performances lower than nondepressed subjects did, even when they had performed just as well; and tended to select pessimistic statements in storytelling tests, such as "I expect my plans will fail" and "I feel like I'll never meet anyone who's interested in me."

Beck's association of depression with errors in logic has also received support. In one study, female subjects were asked to read paragraphs about women in difficult situations and then to answer multiple-choice questions about them. The women who were depressed chose a significantly greater number of responses reflecting errors in logic (such as arbitrary inference, magnification, and minimization) than the nondepressed women did (Hammen & Krantz, 1976).

Finally, research has supported Beck's claim that depressed people repeatedly experience negative automatic thoughts (Garber et al., 1993). In one study, hospitalized depressed patients scored significantly higher on an Automatic Thought Questionnaire than other kinds of patients did, and in another nondepressed subjects who were manipulated into reading negative automatic thought-like statements about themselves became increasingly depressed (Ross et al., 1986; Strickland et al., 1975).

This body of research clearly indicates that negative cognitions are associated with depressive functioning, but it fails to establish that cognitive dysfunctioning represents the cause and core of unipolar depression. Most investigations leave open the possibility that a central mood problem leads to cognitive difficulties, which then take a further toll on mood, motivation, behavior, and physiology.

### Cognitive Therapy

Beck has developed the leading cognitive treatment for unipolar depression. This approach, which grows from his explanation of depression, helps clients recognize and change their dysfunctional cognitive processes,

Drawings by Charles Shultz. © 1956 United Feature Syndicate, Inc.

*Charlie Brown's feelings of depression are caused by errors of logic, such as arbitrary inference.*

thus improving both their mood and their behavior (Beck, 1993, 1985, 1967). The treatment, which usually requires twelve to twenty sessions, is similar to Albert Ellis's rational-emotive therapy (discussed in Chapters 3 and 5) but is tailored more to the specific cognitive errors found in depression. The approach includes four successive phases of treatment.

### Phase 1: Increasing Activities and Elevating Mood
Therapists set the stage for cognitive therapy by encouraging clients to become more active and confident, spending time during each session preparing a detailed schedule of hourly activities for the coming week (see Figure 7-3). As clients become more active from week to week, their mood is expected to improve. Obviously, this aspect of treatment is similar to Lewinsohn's behavioral approach. Beck, however, believes that the increases in activity produced by this approach will not by themselves lead a person out of depressive functioning; cognitive interventions must follow.

### Phase 2: Examining and Invalidating Automatic Thoughts
Once clients are somewhat active again and feeling some relief from their depression, cognitive therapists help educate them about their unrelenting negative automatic thoughts, assigning "homework" in which the client must recognize and record the thoughts as they occur. In session after session, therapist and client engage in a form of collaborative empiricism in which they test the objective reality behind the thoughts and often conclude that they are groundless.

### Phase 3: Identifying Distorted Thinking and Negative Biases
As clients begin to recognize the fallacies in their automatic thoughts, cognitive therapists show them how illogical thinking processes may be contributing to these thoughts. The therapists also guide them to recognize that almost all their interpretations of events have a negative bias and to change their biased style of interpretation.

### Phase 4: Altering Primary Attitudes
In the final phase of therapy, therapists help clients to change their primary attitudes, the central beliefs that have predisposed them to depression in the first place. As part of the change process, therapists often encourage clients to *test* their attitudes, as in the following therapy discussion:

> *THERAPIST:* On what do you base this belief that you can't be happy without a man?
>
> *PATIENT:* I was really depressed for a year and a half when I didn't have a man.
>
> *THERAPIST:* Is there another reason why you were depressed?
>
> *PATIENT:* As we discussed, I was looking at everything in a distorted way. But I still don't know if I could be happy if no one was interested in me.
>
> *THERAPIST:* I don't know either. Is there a way we could find out?
>
> *PATIENT:* Well, as an experiment, I could not go out on dates for a while and see how I feel.
>
> *THERAPIST:* I think that's a good idea. Although it has its flaws, the experimental method is still the best way currently available to discover the facts. You're fortunate in being able to run this type of experiment. Now, for the first time in your adult life you aren't attached to a man. If you find you can be happy without a man, this will greatly strengthen you and also make your future relationships all the better.
>
> (Beck et al., 1979, pp. 253–254)

### Effectiveness of Cognitive Therapy
Over the past few decades, literally hundreds of studies have concluded that mildly to severely depressed people who receive cognitive therapy improve significantly more than those who receive placebo treatments or no treatments at all (Hollon & Beck, 1994; Pace & Dixon, 1993). Approximately 50 to 60 percent of clients treated with this approach show a total elimination of depressive symptoms. In view of this strong research

|       | Monday | Tuesday | Wednesday | Thursday | Fr |
|-------|--------|---------|-----------|----------|----|
| 9–10  |        | Go to grocery store | Go to museum | Get ready to go out | |
| 10–11 |        | Go to grocery store | Go to museum | Drive to Doctor's appointment | |
| 11–12 | Doctor's appointment | Call friend | Go to museum | Doctor's appointment | |
| 12–1  | Lunch | Lunch | Lunch at museum | | |
| 1–2   | Drive home | Clean front room | Drive home | | |
| 2–3   | Read novel | Clean front room | Washing | | |
| 3–4   | Clean bedroom | Read novel | Washing | | |
| 4–5   | Watch TV | Watch TV | Watch TV | | |
| 5–6   | Fix dinner | Fix dinner | Fix dinner | | |
| 6–7   | Eat with family | Eat with Family | Eat with family | | |
| 7–8   | Clean kitchen | Clean kitchen | Clean kitchen | | |
| 8–12  | Watch TV, read novel, sleep | Call sister, watch TV, read novel, sleep | Work on rug, read novel, sleep | | |

**Figure 7-3**   *In the early stages of cognitive therapy for depression, the client and therapist prepare an activity schedule such as this. Activities as simple as watching television or calling a friend are specified. (Adapted from Beck et al., 1979, p. 122.)*

support, increasing numbers of therapists have been employing this approach (Hollon et al., 1993).

### Consider This
Friends and family members try, with limited success, to convince depressed people that their gloom-and-doom view of things is wrong. How does the very successful cognitive approach to unipolar depression differ from such efforts at friendly persuasion?

## The Sociocultural Perspective

Sociocultural theorists propose that depression can often be traced to the broader social structure in which people live and the roles they are required to play. As we observed in Box 7-1, for example, one sociocultural theory holds that the quality of women's roles in society makes women particularly vulnerable to depression.

Another sociocultural theory, **interpersonal theory**, holds that unpolar depression is often the result of social pressures that overwhelm and disable a person. According to this theory, any of four interpersonal

problem areas may lead to depression—interpersonal loss, interpersonal role dispute, interpersonal role transition, or interpersonal deficits. Proponents of this perspective hold that these problem areas can best be addressed by **interpersonal psychotherapy (IPT)**, an approach developed by clinical researchers Gerald Klerman and Myrna Weissman in the 1980s. IPT borrows certain concepts and techniques from the psychodynamic, humanistic, and behavioral perspectives, but these are used primarily to clarify and address the social context (Klerman & Weissman, 1992).

First, depressed persons may, as psychodynamic theorists suggest, be experiencing a grief reaction over **interpersonal loss,** the loss of a significant loved one. In such cases, IPT therapists encourage clients to explore their relationship with the lost person and express angry feelings toward the departed. As clients formulate new ways of remembering the lost person, they are also expected to develop new relationships to "fill the empty space."

Second, depressed people often find themselves in the midst of an **interpersonal role dispute**. Role disputes occur when two people have different expectations about their relationship and about the role each should play. Such disputes may lead to smoldering resentments and to depressed feelings. IPT therapists help clients to explore any role disputes in their relationships and to develop strategies for solving their role disputes.

Depressed people may also be experiencing an **interpersonal role transition**, brought about by significant life changes such as divorce or the birth of a child. In particular, they may feel unable to cope with the role change that accompanies the life change. In such cases, IPT therapists help clients review and evaluate their old roles, explore the opportunities offered by the new roles, and develop the social support system and skills the new roles require.

The fourth interpersonal problem area that may accompany depression is the existence of **interpersonal deficits**, such as extreme shyness, insensitivity to others' needs, and social awkwardness. According to Klerman and Weissman, many depressed people have experienced severely disrupted relationships as children and have failed to establish intimate relationships as adults. IPT therapists may help such clients to recognize their deficits and teach them social skills and assertiveness in order to improve their social effective-

*Interpersonal psychotherapy (IPT)*   A treatment for unipolar patterns of depression. It is based on the premise that because depression occurs in an interpersonal context, clarifying and renegotiating that context is important to a person's recovery.

ness. In the following therapy discussion, the therapist encourages the client to recognize the effect his demeanor has on others.

CLIENT: *(After a long pause with eyes downcast, a sad facial expression, and slumped posture)* People always make fun of me. I guess I'm just the type of guy who really was meant to be a loner, damn it. *(Deep sigh)*

THERAPIST: Could you do that again for me?

CLIENT: What?

THERAPIST: The sigh, only a bit deeper.

CLIENT: Why? *(Pause)* Okay, but I don't see what . . . okay. *(Client sighs again and smiles)*

THERAPIST: Well, that time you smiled, but mostly when you sigh and look so sad I get the feeling that I better leave you alone in your misery, that I should walk on eggshells and not get too chummy or I might hurt you even more.

CLIENT: *(A bit of anger in his voice)* Well, excuse me! I was only trying to tell you how I felt.

THERAPIST: I know you felt miserable, but I also got the message that you wanted to keep me at a distance, that I had no way to reach you.

CLIENT: *(Slowly)* I feel like a loner, I feel that even you don't care about me—making fun of me.

THERAPIST: I wonder if other folks need to pass this test, too?

*(Young & Beier, 1984, p. 270)*

Several comprehensive studies indicate that IPT and related interpersonal approaches are effective treatments for mild to severe cases of unipolar depression (Elkin, 1994; Klerman & Weissman, 1992). These studies have found that symptoms almost totally disappear in 50 to 60 percent of depressed clients who received IPT treatment, a success rate similar to that achieved by cognitive therapy. On the basis of such findings, IPT is frequently used for depressed clients, particularly those who are struggling with psychosocial conflicts or who are in the midst of negotiating a transition in their career or social role (APA, 1993).

## The Biological Perspective

During the past several decades, compelling evidence has emerged that biological abnormalities also contribute to the development of unipolar depression (Siever et al., 1991). In addition, some highly effective biological treatments for this disorder have been developed. The role of biological factors is implied by genetic studies and more directly supported by investigations that tie unipolar patterns of depression to biochemical dysfunction.

### Genetic Explanations

Many theorists believe that some people *inherit* a predisposition to develop unipolar depression. Support for this genetic view has come primarily from family pedigree studies, twin studies, and adoption studies.

Researchers who conduct *family pedigree studies* select people with unipolar depression and examine their close relatives to see whether depression afflicts other members of the family. If a predisposition to unipolar depression is inherited, relatives should have a higher rate of depression than the population at large. And researchers have found that as many as 20 percent of those relatives are depressed, compared to 5 to 10 percent of the general population (Harrington et al., 1993).

*Among the things that happy people have in common are spiritual faith, social involvement, productive work that is linked to self-esteem, satisfying sleep, and a satisfying love relationship (Tice, 1990; Erber, 1990; Diener, 1984). It is not always clear, however, whether these are the causes or the effects of their happiness.*

In addition, if a predisposition to unipolar depression is inherited, one would also expect more cases of depression among the close relatives of depressed people than among their distant relatives. *Twin studies* have found rates consistent with this expectation (Nurnberger & Gershon, 1992, 1984). A Danish study determined that when an identical twin has unipolar depression, there is a 43 percent chance that the other twin will have the same disorder, whereas when a fraternal twin has unipolar depression, the other twin has only a 20 percent chance of developing the disorder (Bertelsen et al., 1977).

Finally, *adoption studies* have implicated a genetic factor, at least in *severe* cases of unipolar depression. A study of the families of adopted persons who had been hospitalized for unipolar depression in Denmark determined that the biological parents of these severely depressed adoptees had a higher incidence of severe depression (but not mild depression) than did the biological parents of a control group of nondepressed adoptees (Wender et al., 1986).

## Biochemical Explanations

As we have seen, neurotransmitters are the brain chemicals that carry messages from one nerve cell, or neuron, to another. *Norepinephrine* and *serotonin* are two neurotransmitters whose reduced activity has been strongly implicated in unipolar patterns of depression (see Figure 7-4).

In the 1950s, several pieces of evidence pointed to low norepinephrine and low serotonin activity in the brain as possible factors in depression. First, medical researchers discovered that certain drugs used to treat high blood pressure may cause depression in some people (Amsterdam et al., 1980; Ayd, 1956). Further research indicated that some of these blood pressure medications lowered norepinephrine supplies and others lowered serotonin, thus suggesting to researchers that depression may be related to low activity of norepinephrine or serotonin in the brain.

A second piece of evidence emerged from the discovery of effective antidepressant drugs. Although these medications were initially discovered by accident, researchers soon learned that the compounds act to increase either norepinephrine or serotonin activity. The possibility that this was the means by which the antidepressants alleviate depression again fitted in with the idea that depression is related to low activity of norepinephrine or serotonin.

Over the past two decades an enormous amount of research has been devoted to sorting out the contributions of norepinephrine and serotonin to unipolar depression. It appears that low activity by *either* neuro-transmitter can lead to depression (Yazici et al., 1993; Baldessarini, 1983). Moreover, it may be that a unipolar depression which is linked to low norepinephrine is qualitatively different from a unipolar depression linked to low serotonin. Investigator Marie Asberg and her colleagues (1976) found, for example, that depressed subjects whose serotonin was low were more apathetic and suicidal than depressed subjects with normal serotonin levels.

The neurotransmitter theories of depression have deservedly generated much enthusiasm, but research in this area has important limitations. First, the research has consisted to a large degree of analogue studies that create depressionlike symptoms in laboratory

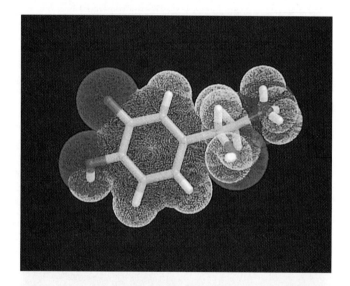

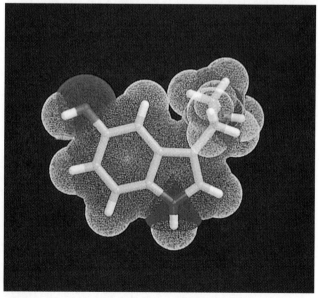

Figure 7-4   *Computer-drawn molecules of the neurotransmitters norepinephrine (top) and serotonin (bottom). Low activity of these neurotransmitters has repeatedly been implicated in unipolar depression.*

animals. Researchers cannot be certain that these symptoms do in fact reflect the quality and substance of the human disorder (Overstreet, 1993). Second, until recent years, the limitations of technology required most biological studies on human depression to measure brain chemical activity indirectly, and as a result investigators could never be quite certain of the actual biochemical events (Katz et al., 1993). Studies using newer technology, such as the PET and MRI, should address such concerns in the coming years. And, finally, some studies have raised the possibility that biological factors other than norepinephrine and serotonin may also play a central role in at least some forms of unipolar depression (see Box 7-2).

## Biological Treatments

Two very different biological treatments are widely used in the treatment of unipolar depression—electroconvulsive therapy and antidepressant drugs. The latter approach is applied much more often than the former, but electroconvulsive therapy continues to be relatively popular because of its speed of action and its effectiveness in severe cases that are resistant to other forms of treatment.

**Electroconvulsive Therapy** One of the most controversial forms of treatment for depression is *electroconvulsive therapy,* or *ECT* (Fink, 1992). In an ECT procedure, two electrodes are attached to the patient's head, and an electrical current of 65 to 140 volts is sent through the brain for half a second or less. In *bilateral ECT* one electrode is applied to each side of the forehead, and the current passes through the brain's frontal lobes. A method used increasingly in recent years is *unilateral ECT,* in which the electrodes are placed so that the current passes through only one side of the brain.

The electrical current causes a *convulsion,* or brain seizure, that lasts from 25 seconds to a few minutes. The convulsion itself, not any attendant pain, appears to be the key to ECT's effectiveness (Ottosson, 1985, 1960; Weiner, 1984). A typical program of ECT for depressed persons consists of six to nine treatments administered over two to four weeks (Lerer et al., 1995).

The discovery that electric shock can be therapeutic for people with depression was made by accident. In the 1930s, clinical researchers mistakenly came to believe that convulsions could cure schizophrenia and other forms of psychosis, and they searched for ways to induce convulsions in patients with schizophrenia. Early techniques in which patients were given the drug *metrazol,* a derivative of camphor, or large doses of insulin (*insulin coma therapy*) proved highly dangerous, sometimes even lethal.

Finally, the Italian psychiatrist Ugo Cerletti discovered that he could induce seizures relatively safely in patients by applying electric currents to their heads, much as he had observed on a visit to a slaughter house, where butchers clamped the heads of hogs with metallic tongs to stun the animals before slaughtering them (Cerletti & Bini, 1938). ECT soon became popular and was applied to a wide range of psychological problems, as new techniques so often are. Its effectiveness with depressive disorders in particular became quite apparent.

In the early years of ECT, fractures and dislocations of the jaw and shoulder sometimes resulted, either from the ECT convulsion itself or from excessive restraint by nurses and attendants (Kiloh, 1982). Practitioners avoid this problem today by giving patients *muscle relaxants* so that restraint is unnecessary and there is no undesirable tension in the body. Similarly, short-term *anesthetics* (barbiturates) are used to put patients to sleep during the procedure, thus reducing their terror and any consequent trauma (Fink, 1992). As a result of these changes, ECT is medically more complex than it used to be, but also less dangerous and somewhat less frightening (Fink, 1992; Hamilton, 1986).

Patients who receive ECT, primarily bilateral ECT, typically have difficulty remembering the period of

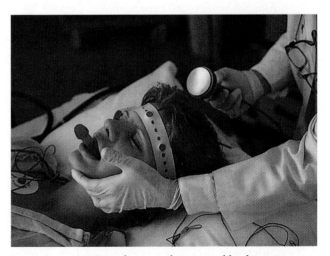

*Patients given ECT today are administered barbiturate drugs to help them sleep, muscle relaxants to prevent convulsive jerks of the body and broken bones, oxygen to guard against brain damage, and, often, unilateral, rather than bilateral, applications of electricity in order to reduce memory loss.*

*Electroconvulsive therapy (ECT)* A controversial biological treatment for unipolar depression in which electrodes attached to a patient's head send an electric current through the brain, causing a convulsion.

## Box 7-2

# Bringing Depression to Light

Endocrine glands are located throughout the body, working along with the nervous system to regulate such vital activities as growth, reproduction, sexual activity, heart rate, body temperature, energy, and responses to stress. Under various conditions, the glands release hormones, chemicals which in turn propel body organs into action. This entire endocrine system is run by the *hypothalamus,* the brain area often called the "brain of the brain."

Secretions of the hormone *melatonin* appear to be particularly important in depression (Lam et al., 1990). This hormone, nicknamed "the Dracula hormone," is secreted by the brain's *pineal gland* when our surroundings are dark, but not when they are light. The role of melatonin in human biology is not entirely understood, but in animals it seems to help regulate hibernation, activity levels, and reproductive cycles. As nights grow longer during the fall and winter, animals secrete more and more melatonin, which has the effect of slowing them down and preparing them for an extended seasonal rest. When daytime hours lengthen in the spring and summer, melatonin secretions decrease, raising energy

levels and setting the stage for reproduction. Although human activity levels and reproduction cycles do not appear to be so closely tied to light and dark, our pineal glands nevertheless carry on the tradition of secreting greater amounts of melatonin during the dark nights of winter than during the short nights of summer.

Some theorists believe that because of our heightened melatonin secretions, humans slow down, have less energy, and need more rest in the wintertime, much as hibernating animals do. Most people manage to adjust to these internal changes, but some people may be so sensitive to winter's heightened melatonin secretions that they find it almost impossible to carry on with business as usual. Their seasonal slowdown takes the form of depression, but a depression characterized by symptoms that are quite consistent with animal hibernation—a large appetite, a craving for carbohydrates, weight gain, oversleeping, and fatigue (Gupta, 1988). This seasonal pattern, often called *seasonal affective disorder,* or *SAD,* is now described in the DSM (Rosenthal & Blehar, 1989). Researchers believe that these people are also sometimes extremely

sensitive to the drop in melatonin secretions that occurs during the longer days of summer. Some of them, in fact, become overenergized and overactive and display a hypomanic or manic pattern every summer (Faedda et al., 1993).

Research suggests that the *suprachiasmatic nuclei (SCN),* a small cluster of neurons in the hypothalamus connected to the pineal gland and to the eyes, may be an important regulator for the body's general schedule of hormonal releases and for melatonin releases in particular (Rietvald, 1992). When light enters the eyes, the "light" message is carried to the SCN. This message is then carried by the neurotransmitter norepinephrine to the pineal gland, which reacts by stopping its manufacture of melatonin. If the pineal gland were to fail to receive this "light" message, it would keep producing melatonin. Depressed people may have an abnormality in the SCN or in some other link in this chain, leading to inappropriate secretions of melatonin, to a broad disruption of the body's hormonal rhythms (called "circadian rhythms"), and, in turn, to depressive symptoms (Anderson et al., 1992).

---

time just before their ECT treatments, but much of this memory loss usually clears up after about a month (APA, 1993; Squire & Slater, 1983). Some may also experience gaps in more distant memory, and this form of amnesia can be permanent (Squire, 1977). Understandably, the relatively small number of people who suffer significant permanent memory losses are often left embittered.

Research indicates that ECT is an effective treatment for unipolar depression, although the precise reason for its effectiveness remains unclear. In most studies that compare depressed patients receiving ECT

with those receiving placebos, the ECT patients improve significantly more than the placebo patients (APA, 1993; Wechsler et al., 1965). Overall, these studies suggest that between 60 and 70 percent of ECT patients improve. The procedure seems to be particularly effective in severe cases characterized by delusions (Buchan et al., 1992).

Although research has repeatedly established the effectiveness of ECT, and although ECT techniques have improved markedly, the use of this procedure has generally declined since the 1950s. Apparently more than 100,000 patients underwent ECT each year during the

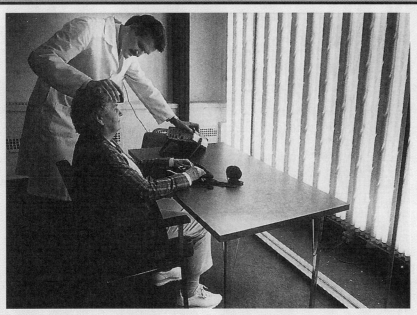

*Various techniques have been developed to provide SAD patients with extra amounts of light on short winter days.*

sunlight is available each day. The effectiveness of this form of "treatment" has yet to be investigated scientifically.

In view of the impracticalities of light therapy, clinicians have searched actively for alternative ways to alter melatonin levels. One promising possibility is **melatonin pills.** Researchers are beginning to demonstrate that it is not really the *amount* of melatonin secreted that causes depression for SAD-prone people but the *timing* of these secretions. Ill-timed melatonin secretions over the 24-hour period may disrupt the body's hormonal rhythms and so leave the person vulnerable to depression. A team of researchers headed by Alfred Lewy (1992) believe that SAD may eventually be better treated by a dose of melatonin given in pill form at key times of the day than by hours of phototherapy. If these pills do indeed turn out to be a useful treatment for seasonal affective disorders, we may have reached a major turning point in effectively and efficiently addressing the suffering of people with this roller-coaster problem.

If in fact darkness *is* the problem in SAD, the answer may be light. An effective treatment for SAD turns out to be light therapy, or **phototherapy,** exposure to extra synthetic light throughout the winter. When seasonally depressed patients sit under intense light for several hours every winter day, their depression can be reduced or eliminated (Avery et al., 1993).

Of course, there is another, more enjoyable way to get more light—take a winter vacation in a sunny place. Some theorists go so far as to suggest that people with wintertime blues, and certainly those with SAD, should spend a week or two just before winter begins in a location approximately 3 to 4 degrees north or south of the equator, where 70 percent more

---

1940s and 1950s. Today as few as 30,000 to 50,000 per year are believed to receive it (Foderaero, 1993). Several factors have contributed to ECT's decline, including the frightening nature of the procedure and the attractive medical alternative offered by antidepressant drugs.

**Antidepressant Drugs**    In the 1950s, two kinds of drugs were discovered that seemed to alleviate depressive symptoms: *MAO (monoamine oxidase) inhibitors* and *tricyclics.* These antidepressant drugs have recently been joined by a third group, the so-called sec-

ond-generation antidepressants. Before the discovery of these medications, the only drugs that brought any relief for depression were amphetamines. Amphetamines stimulated some depressed people to greater activity, but they did not result in greater joy.

The effectiveness of *MAO inhibitors* as a treatment for unipolar depression was discovered accidentally when physicians first noted that *iproniazid,* a drug being tested on patients with tuberculosis, had an inter-

---

*MAO inhibitor*    An antidepressant drug that inhibits the action of the enzyme monoamine oxidase.

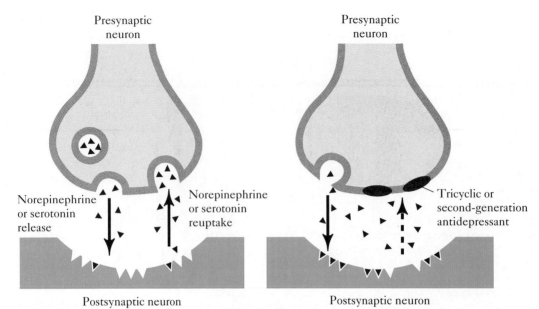

Presynaptic neuron

Presynaptic neuron

Norepinephrine or serotonin release

Norepinephrine or serotonin reuptake

Tricyclic or second-generation antidepressant

Postsynaptic neuron

Postsynaptic neuron

**Figure 7-5**  *(Left) When a neuron releases norepinephrine or serotonin from its endings, a pumplike reuptake mechanism immediately begins to recapture some of the neurotransmitter molecules before they are received by the postsynaptic (receptor) neuron. (Right) Tricyclic and second-generation antidepressant drugs block this reuptake process, enabling more norepinephrine or serotonin to reach, and thus fire, the postsynaptic (receptor) neuron. (Adapted from Snyder, 1986, p. 106.)*

esting effect on many such patients: it seemed to make them happier. It was found to have the same effect on depressed patients (Kline, 1958; Loomer et al., 1957). Researchers were later able to create similar drugs, such as *phenelzine* (trade name Nardil), that were less toxic than iproniazid but equally powerful in fighting depression. What these drugs all had in common biochemically was that they slowed the body's production of the enzyme *monoamine oxidase (MAO)*. Thus they were called *MAO inhibitors*. Research has indicated that approximately half of the mild to severely depressed patients who take MAO inhibitors are helped by them (Davis, 1980; Davis et al., 1967).

During the past few decades, scientists have learned how MAO inhibitors operate on the brain and how they alleviate depression. Apparently, when the enzyme MAO interacts chemically with molecules of norepinephrine, it breaks down the neurotransmitter. MAO inhibitors block MAO from carrying out this destructive activity and thereby stop the destruction of norepinephrine. The result is a heightened level of norepinephrine activity, causing depressive symptoms to disappear.

As clinicians have gained experience with the MAO inhibitors, they have learned that the liver and intestine of people who take this drug can no longer perform the critical task of destroying *tyramine,* a chemical contained in many common foods that raises blood pressure dangerously if too much of it accumulates (Davidson, 1992). Thus, people who take MAO inhibitors cannot eat cheeses, bananas, certain wines, and other foods that contain tyramine. These restrictions, along with other dangers associated with MAO inhibitors, have reduced clinicians' enthusiasm for these medications (Montgomery et al., 1993).

The discovery of *tricyclics* in the 1950s was also accidental. Researchers were looking for a new drug to combat schizophrenia and came upon a drug called *imipramine* (Kuhn, 1958). Imipramine did not turn out to be an effective treatment for schizophrenia, but doctors soon discovered that it did relieve unipolar depression in many people. Imipramine (Tofranil) and related drugs became known as *tricyclic antidepressants* because they all share a three-ring molecular structure.

Research has repeatedly demonstrated the effectiveness of tricyclics for treating unipolar patterns of depression. In hundreds of studies, mildly to severely depressed patients taking tricyclics have within a month or so improved significantly more than similar patients taking placebos (Montgomery et al., 1993; APA, 1993). Numerous case reports have also described the successful impact of these drugs. The case of Derek, whom we met earlier, is typical of the glowing reviews tricyclics often receive:

*Tricyclic drug*  An antidepressant drug such as imipramine that has three rings in its molecular structure.

Derek might have continued living his battleship-gray life had it not been for the local college. One winter Derek signed up for an evening course called "The Use and Abuse of Psychoactive Drugs" because he wanted to be able to provide accurate background information in future newspaper articles on drug use among high school and college students. The course covered psychiatric as well as recreational drugs. When the professor listed the symptoms of affective mood disorders on the blackboard, Derek had a flash of recognition. Perhaps he suffered from depression with melancholia.

Derek then consulted with a psychiatrist, who confirmed his suspicion and prescribed imipramine. A week later, Derek was sleeping until his alarm went off. Two weeks later, at 9:00 a.m. he was writing his column and making difficult decisions about editorials on sensitive topics. He started writing some feature stories on drugs just because he was interested in the subject. Writing was more fun than it had been in years. His images of his own violent death disappeared. His wife found him more responsive. He conversed with her enthusiastically and answered her questions without the long delays that had so tried her patience.

*(Lickey & Gordon, 1991, p. 185)*

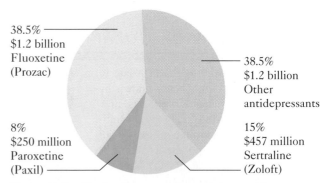

**ANTIDEPRESSANT SALES**

38.5%
$1.2 billion
Fluoxetine
(Prozac)

38.5%
$1.2 billion
Other
antidepressants

8%
$250 million
Paroxetine
(Paxil)

15%
$457 million
Sertraline
(Zoloft)

**Figure 7-6** *The leading second-generation antidepressant drugs are Prozac, Zoloft, and Paxil. They accounted for more than 60 percent of antidepressant drug sales in 1993. (Adapted from Cowley, 1994.)*

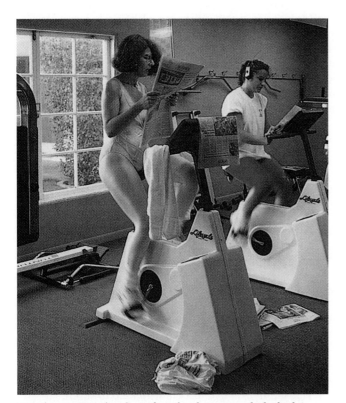

*Regular exercise has been found to be positively linked to one's level of happiness, and exercise may help prevent or reduce feelings of depression (Diener, 1984).*

Many researchers have concluded that tricyclics alleviate depression by acting on neurotransmitter "reuptake" mechanisms (Goodwin, 1992; McNeal & Cimbolic, 1986). We saw earlier that a message is carried from a sending neuron to a receiving neuron by means of a neurotransmitter released from the nerve ending of the sending neuron. However, there is a complication in this process. While the nerve ending is releasing a neurotransmitter, a pumplike mechanism in the same nerve ending is trying to recapture it. The purpose of this mechanism is to prevent the neurotransmitter from remaining in the synapse too long and repeatedly stimulating the receiving neuron. Among depressed people, this pumplike reuptake mechanism may be too successful, causing too great a reduction of norepinephrine or serotonin activity and hence of neural firing, and resulting in a clinical picture of depression. Studies have indicated that tricyclics act to block this reuptake process (see Figure 7-5), thus increasing neurotransmitter activity (Goodwin, 1992; Iversen, 1965).

Today tricyclics are prescribed more often than MAO inhibitors, primarily for two reasons. First, they are less dangerous than MAO inhibitors and they do not necessitate dietary restrictions (Montgomery et al., 1993). Second, patients taking tricyclics typically show higher rates of improvement than those taking MAO inhibitors (Swonger & Constantine, 1983). On the other hand, some patients respond better to the MAO inhibitors (Goodwin, 1993; McGrath et al., 1993).

The third category of antidepressant drugs, discovered over the past several years, are known as *second-generation antidepressants* (see Figure 7-6). Some of these new drugs (including *fluoxetine,* or Prozac) have

## Box 7-3

# Flying with Prozac

First approved by the FDA late in 1987, *fluoxetine*, better known by its trade name Prozac, has now been prescribed for over 11 million people throughout the world. Its enormous popularity is attributable to two factors. (1) As a second-generation antidepressant, it has fewer undesired effects than MAO inhibitors and tricyclics, so that many depressed people are able to tolerate and benefit from an antidepressant drug for the first time in their lives. (2) Prozac also appears to be an effective treatment for other problems, such as eating disorders and obsessive-compulsive disorder.

Prozac's enormous popularity among prescribing psychiatrists and physicians as well as the public at large has itself caused considerable concern in the clinical community and in the media. Many people believe that it is being glamorized and overused, and that possible dangers in taking the drug have been largely ignored. The first major professional attack on Prozac came in 1990 from the psychiatrist Martin Teicher and several colleagues at Harvard

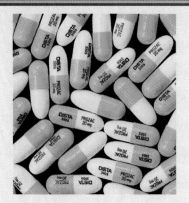

Medical School, who reported six cases in which patients who had previously been free of serious suicidal thoughts developed intense and violent suicidal tendencies after taking Prozac for two to seven weeks. This report hit the field and public like a tornado. It stirred an intense debate among clinicians regarding the proper role of the drug and seemed to inspire some patients to sue the drug's manufacturer for damages as a result of similar undesirable effects.

A clear link between Prozac and intensified suicidal thinking was not subsequently established by

empirical research (Ashleigh & Fesler, 1992), but the negative publicity led to at least a slight decline in Prozac's popularity and acceptance and loosened its grip on the antidepressant drug marketplace as the 1990s progressed. Tricyclic antidepressants regained some of their lost popularity among physicians, and other second-generation antidepressants, including sertraline (Zoloft) and paroxetine (Paxil), were soon being prescribed in numbers beyond their manufacturers' expectations.

The hype surrounding Prozac had begun to die down when the publication of Dr. Peter Kramer's book *Listening to Prozac* (1993) reignited America's interest in it. Kramer, a Rhode Island psychiatrist and a professor at Brown University, described case studies in which Prozac not only alleviated the symptoms of clinical depression but actually had a transforming effect on some of his patients' personalities. Some patients were completely unaffected by the drug, but some, with long histories of social masochism, low self-esteem, and a despondent outlook on life,

been labeled *selective serotonin reuptake inhibitors (SSRIs)*, as they are thought to alter serotonin activity specifically, without affecting other neurotransmitters or biochemical processes (Singh & Lucki, 1993). Although these drugs do not appear to be any more effective than tricyclics (APA, 1993; Workman & Short, 1993), their sales have zoomed (see Box 7-3). Prescribing clinicians often prefer them because they have not been implicated in as many deaths due to overdose as the tricyclics have (Barondes, 1994) and because some of the undesired side effects associated with the tricyclics, such as dry mouth, constipation, impaired vision, and weight gain, are avoided entirely with the newer drugs (McElroy et al., 1995; APA, 1993).

*Selective serotonin reuptake inhibitors (SSRIs)*   A group of second-generation antidepressant drugs (including fluoxetine, paroxetine, and sertraline) that are thought to alter serotonin activity specifically, without affecting other neurotransmitters or biochemical processes.

### Summing Up
*The psychodynamic, behavioral, cognitive, sociocultural, and biological perspectives have all contributed explanations and treatments for unipolar depression. The cognitive explanations, which point to learned helplessness and maladaptive thinking, and the biological explanations, which emphasize low norepinephrine and low serotonin activity, have received the most research support. Studies also indicate that cognitive, interpersonal, and biological approaches are the most effective treatments for unipolar depression; each is of considerable help to people with mild to severe levels of depression.*

were, according to Kramer, able to adopt new patterns of interacting with the world.

> Within weeks of starting Prozac, Tess settled into a satisfying dating routine. I'd never seen a patient's social life reshaped so rapidly and dramatically. Low self-worth and poor interpersonal skills—the usual causes of social awkwardness—are so deeply ingrained and difficult to influence that ordinarily change comes gradually, if ever. But Tess blossomed all at once.

Although Dr. Kramer reports twinges of uneasiness about prescribing Prozac to his patients for extended periods of time, he, like a growing number of clinicians, believes he would be withholding the bounties of science from them if he did not. Kramer suggests that the authentic self is revealed only as the depressive mask is removed. If Tess no longer feels like her "self" when she goes off the medication, and decides to continue taking the drug indefinitely, who is he to claim she should be naturally unhappy?

Kramer's enthusiasm and the public's enthusiastic response to his book have once again alarmed many clinicians. Some are concerned that Kramer is overstating Prozac's effectiveness. They argue that the drug is no more effective than most other antidepressants (although it apparently has fewer undesired effects) and that it hardly changes personality. As one person said after taking Prozac for depression, "I have my ability to not snap at people back, my energy back . . . [but] I don't feel like Superman, and I still can't stand parties" (Toufexis, 1993). Others worry that extended Prozac therapy may rob people of the adaptive aspects of despair, interfering with their realistic connection to external events and their ability to withstand the natural emotional reactions when those events are unpleasant. Finally, some professionals worry that Prozac will do away with the human vulnerabilities that people need in order to create and to grow.

Kramer's response is that by increasing some people's resilience, Prozac enables them to participate more fully in life. He finds the chemical's success both exciting and, at the same time, unnerving, as it usurps what heretofore has been considered the realm of the psychotherapist. In many cases he has found a combination of psychotherapy and drug therapy to be the most effective treatment, and he believes that these patients would not have done so well on drugs alone. Nevertheless, he observes that some of his patients "harbored a kernel of vulnerability that the psychotherapy did not touch" but that responded to drug intervention.

Vulnerability, anxiety, guilt, sadness . . . are these essential parts of what it means to be a human being? Dr. Peter Kramer says perhaps they are not. Conceding that the moral implications of Prozac are complex, he argues that its discovery will be as impossible to ignore as Freud's discovery of the unconscious. At the very least, the discovery and advocacy of this drug are proving to be just as controversial.

# Bipolar Disorders

People with bipolar disorders experience both the lows of depression and the highs of mania. Many describe their life as an emotional roller-coaster, as they shift back and forth between extreme moods. This roller-coaster ride and its impact on relatives and friends is dramatically seen in the following description:

> In his early school years he had been a remarkable student and had shown a gift for watercolor and oils. Later he had studied art in Paris and married an English girl he had met there. Eventually they had settled in London.

**Bipolar disorder** A disorder marked by alternating or intermixed periods of mania and depression.

Ten years later, when he was thirty-four years old, he had persuaded his wife and only son to accompany him to Honolulu, where, he assured them, he would be considered famous. He felt he would be able to sell his paintings at many times the prices he could get in London. According to his wife, he had been in an accelerated state, but at that time the family had left, unsuspecting, believing with the patient in their imminent good fortune. When they arrived they found almost no one in the art world that he was supposed to know. There were no connections for sales and deals in Hawaii that he had anticipated. Settling down, the patient began to behave more peculiarly than ever. After enduring several months of the patient's exhilaration, overactivity, weight loss, constant talking, and unbelievably little sleep, the young wife and child began to fear for his sanity. None of his plans materialized. After five months in the Pacific, with finances growing thin, the patient's overactivity subsided and he fell into a depression. During that period he refused to move, paint, or leave the house. He lost twenty pounds, became utterly dependent on his wife, and insisted on seeing none of the friends he had accumulated in his manic state. His despondency became so severe that several doctors came to the house and advised psychiatric hospitalization. He quickly agreed and received twelve electroshock treatments, which relieved his depressed state. Soon afterward he began to paint again and to sell his work modestly. Recognition began to come from galleries and critics in the Far East. Several reviews acclaimed his work as exceptionally brilliant.

This was the beginning of the lifelong career of his moodswing. In 1952, while still in Honolulu, he once again became severely depressed. . . . Four years later he returned to London in a high. When this manic period subsided and he surveyed the wreckage of his life, an eight-month interval of normal mood followed, after which he again switched into a profound depression.

*(Fieve, 1975, pp. 64–65)*

## The Clinical Picture of Mania

In contrast to the unrelieved gloom of depression, a person in a state of mania is governed by a dramatic and inappropriate elevation of mood. The symptoms of mania encompass the same areas of functioning—emotional, motivational, behavioral, cognitive, and physical—as those of depression, but mania affects those areas in an almost diametrically opposite way (see Table 7-4).

Mania is characterized by active, expansive *emotions* that seem to be looking for an outlet. The mood of euphoric joy and well-being is out of all proportion to the actual happenings in the person's life. One person with mania explained, "I feel no sense of restriction or censorship whatsoever. I am afraid of nothing and no one" (Fieve, 1975, p. 68). Not every person with mania is a picture of happiness, however. Some can also become irritable and angry—especially when others get in the way of their ambitions, activities, and plans.

In the *motivational* realm, people with mania seem to want constant excitement, involvement, and companionship. They enthusiastically seek out new friends and old, new interests and old, and have little awareness that their social style is overwhelming, domineering, and excessive.

The *behavior* of people with mania is usually very active. They move quickly, as though there were not enough time to do everything they want to do. They may talk rapidly and loudly, their conversations filled

*Mania*   A state or episode of euphoria, frenzied activity, or related characteristics.

**Table 7-4   *Manifestations of Mania and Depression***

| Mania | Depression |
|---|---|
| *Emotional* | |
| Elation | Depressed mood |
| Liking for self | Dislike of self |
| Increased mirth response | Loss of mirth response |
| *Cognitive* | |
| Positive self-image | Negative self-image |
| Positive expectations | Negative expectations |
| Tendency to blame others | Tendency to blame self |
| Denial of problems | Exaggeration of problems |
| Arbitrary decision making | Indecisiveness |
| *Motivational* | |
| Driven and impulsive behavior | Paralysis of the will |
| Action-oriented wishes | Wishes for escape |
| Drive for independence | Increased wishes for dependency |
| Desire for self-enhancement | Desire for death |
| *Behavioral* | |
| Hyperactivity | Inertia/agitation |
| Productivity | Lack of productivity |
| Loudness | Quietness |
| *Physical* | |
| Indefatigability | Easy fatigability |
| Increased libido | Loss of libido |
| Insomnia | Insomnia |

*Source:* Beck, 1967, p. 91.

with jokes and efforts to be clever or, conversely, with complaints and hostile tirades. Flamboyance is another characteristic of manic functioning: dressing in flashy clothes, giving large sums of money to strangers, getting involved in dangerous activities. Several of these qualities are evident in the monologue delivered by Joe to the two policemen who escorted him to a mental hospital:

You look like a couple of bright, alert, hardworking, clean-cut, energetic go-getters and I could use you in my organization! I need guys that are loyal and enthusiastic about the great opportunities life offers on this planet! It's yours for the taking! Too many people pass opportunity by without hearing it knock because they don't know how to grasp the moment and strike while the iron is hot! You've got to grab it when it comes up for air, pick up the ball and run! You've got to be decisive! decisive! decisive! No shilly-shallying! Sweat! Yeah, sweat with a goal! Push, push, push, and you can push over a mountain! Two mountains, maybe. It's not luck! Hell, if it wasn't for bad luck I wouldn't have any luck at all! Be there firstest with the mostest! My guts and your blood! That's the system! I know, you know, he, she or it knows it's the only way to travel! Get 'em off balance, baby, and the rest is leverage! Use your head and save your heels! What's this deal? Who are these guys? Have you got a telephone and a secretary I can have instanter if not sooner? What I need is office space and the old LDO [long-distance operator].

*(McNeil, 1967, p. 147)*

In the *cognitive* realm, people with mania usually display poor judgment and planning, as if they feel too good or move too rapidly to consider consequences or possible pitfalls. Filled with optimism, they rarely listen when others try to slow them down, interrupt their buying sprees, or prevent them from investing money unwisely. They may also hold an inflated opinion of themselves, and sometimes their self-esteem approaches grandiosity (Silverstone & Hunt, 1992). During acute episodes of mania, some have trouble remaining coherent or in touch with reality.

Finally, in the *physical* realm, people with mania feel remarkably energetic. They typically get little sleep, yet feel and act wide awake (Silverstone & Hunt, 1992). Even if they miss a night or two of sleep, their energy level seems very high.

## Diagnosing Bipolar Disorders

DSM-IV considers people to be experiencing a full *manic episode* when they display for at least one week an abnormally elevated, expansive, or irritable mood, along with at least three other symptoms of mania. Such episodes may vary from moderate to extreme in severity and may include such psychotic features as delusions or hallucinations. When the symptoms of mania are less severe (causing no marked impairment) and shorter in duration (at least four days) than those of a manic episode, the person is said to be experiencing a *hypomanic episode* (APA, 1994).

DSM-IV distinguishes two general kinds of *bipolar disorders*—bipolar I and bipolar II disorders. People

*Echoing Shakespeare's observation that "the lunatic, the lover, and the poet are all compact," researchers Frederick Goodwin and Kay Jamison (1990) claim that some of our most famous poets, including Sylvia Plath, have experienced bipolar disorders. Plath committed suicide in 1963 at the age of 31.*

with *bipolar I disorder* experience full manic episodes and major depressive episodes. Most of them experience an *alternation* of the episodes; some, however, have *mixed episodes* that consist of both manic and depressive symptoms within the same day. In *bipolar II disorder,* hypomanic—that is, mildly manic—episodes alternate with major depressive episodes over the course of time. Only individuals who have never had a full manic episode receive this diagnosis. In the absence of treatment, manic and depressive episodes tend to recur for people with either type of bipolar disorder (Goldberg et al., 1995; APA, 1994).

Surveys conducted around the world indicate that between 0.4 and 1.3 percent of all adults suffer from a bipolar I or II disorder in any given year (Kessler et al., 1994; Regier et al., 1993). The disorders are equally common in women and men, and usually begin between the ages of 15 and 44 years (Smith & Weissman, 1992). Research also suggests that the disorders are distributed equally among all socioeconomic classes and ethnic groups (APA, 1994; Weissman et al., 1991).

When individuals experience numerous periods of *hypomanic* symptoms and *mild* depressive symptoms, DSM-IV assigns a diagnosis of *cyclothymic disorder.* The milder symptoms of this form of bipolar disorder

*Bipolar I disorder*    A type of bipolar disorder in which a person experiences full manic and major depressive episodes.

*Bipolar II disorder*    A type of bipolar disorder in which a person experiences mildly manic (hypomanic) episodes and major depressive episodes.

*Cyclothymic disorder*    A disorder characterized by numerous periods of hypomanic symptoms and mild depressive symptoms.

continue for two or more years at a time, interrupted occasionally by normal moods that last for only days or weeks. This disorder, like the bipolar I and bipolar II disorders, usually begins in adolescence or early adulthood and is equally common among women and men. At least 0.4 percent of the population develops cyclothymic disorder (APA, 1994).

> ## Summing Up
>
> *In bipolar disorders, episodes of mania alternate or intermix with episodes of depression. Like the symptoms of depression, those of mania encompass five areas of functioning, from emotional to physical. Those who experience full manic episodes and major depressive episodes receive a diagnosis of bipolar I disorder. People who experience hypomanic episodes and major depressive episodes receive a diagnosis of bipolar II disorder. And those whose mood swings consist of mild depressive and hypomanic episodes receive a diagnosis of cyclothymic disorder.*

## Explanations of Bipolar Disorders

Throughout the first half of this century, the study of bipolar disorders made little progress. Various models were proposed to explain bipolar mood swings, but research did not support their validity. However, some promising clues from the biological realm have led to a new understanding of bipolar disorders in recent years. These biological insights come from research into *neurotransmitter activity, sodium ion activity,* and *genetic factors.*

### Neurotransmitters

When researchers first proposed that 2 low level of norepinephrine activity leads to depression, they also argued that overactivity of norepinephrine is related to mania (Schildkraut, 1965). Research has offered some support for this claim. One study, for example, found the norepinephrine levels of patients with mania to be significantly higher than those of depressed or control subjects (Post et al., 1980, 1978).

The belief that mania is related to high norepinephrine activity has also been supported by research on the action of the drug *lithium*. As we shall see shortly, lithium is by far the most effective treatment for bipolar disorders. Researchers have found that one of lithium's actions is to reduce norepinephrine activity at key sites in the brain (Bunney & Garland, 1984). If lithium reduces manic symptoms while reducing nor-

epinephrine activity, it may be that mania itself is related to high norepinephrine activity in the first place.

Because serotonin activity often parallels norepinephrine's in relation to depression, theorists expected that 2 high activity level of serotonin would also be related to manic functioning, but no such correspondence has shown up. Instead, research has indicated that mania, like depression, is often associated with a *low* level of serotonin activity (Price, 1990). Somehow, depression and mania both seem to be related to low levels of serotonin activity.

### Sodium Ion Activity

On both sides of the cell membrane of every neuron are positively charged *sodium ions* that play a critical role in sending incoming messages down the axon to

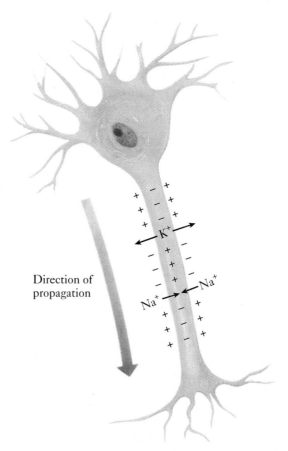

**Figure 7-7**   *Neurons relay messages in the form of electrical impulses that begin in the cell body and travel down the axon toward the nerve endings. As an impulse travels along the axon, sodium ions ($Na^+$), which had been resting on the outside of the neuron's membrane, flow to the inside, causing the impulse to spread down the axon. As sodium flows in, potassium ions ($K^+$) flow out, thus helping the membrane's electrical balance to return to its resting state, ready for the arrival of a new impulse. (Adapted from Snyder, 1986, p. 7.)*

the nerve endings (see Figure 7-7). When the neuron is at rest, most of the sodium ions sit on the outer side of the membrane; when the neuron is stimulated by an incoming message at its receptor site, however, the sodium ions from the outer side of the membrane travel across to the inner side, thus starting a wave of electrochemical activity that continues down the length of the axon and results in the "firing" of the neuron. This activity is followed by a flow of *potassium ions* from the inside to the outside of the neuron, thus helping the neuron to return to its original resting state.

If brain messages are to be transmitted properly, the sodium ions must travel properly back and forth between the outside and the inside of the neural membrane. Some theorists believe that improper transport of these ions may cause neurons to fire too easily, resulting in mania, or to be too resistant to firing, resulting in depression (Kato et al., 1993). Not surprisingly, then, researchers have found clear indications of defective sodium ion transportation at certain neuron membranes in the brains of people with bipolar disorders (Kato et al., 1993; Meltzer, 1991).

## Genetic Factors

Many theorists have argued that people inherit a predisposition to develop the biological abnormalities underlying bipolar disorders (Siever et al., 1991; Blehar et al., 1988). *Family pedigree studies* have provided strong evidence that this is so. Close relatives of people with a bipolar disorder have been found to have a 4 to 25 percent likelihood of developing the same or a related mood disorder, compared to the 1 percent prevalence rate in the general population (APA, 1994; Nurnberger & Gershon, 1992). Moreover, the more similar the genetic makeup of two people, the more similar their tendency to develop a bipolar disorder.

Researchers have also conducted *genetic linkage studies* to identify possible patterns in the inheritance of bipolar disorders. They select extended families that have exhibited high rates of the disorder over several generations, observe the pattern of distribution of the disorder among family members, and determine whether it closely follows the distribution pattern of genetically transmitted family traits, such as color blindness, red hair, or a particular medical syndrome.

After studying the records of Israeli, Belgian, Italian, and Old Order Amish families that had shown high rates of bipolar disorder across several generations, researchers seemed for a while to have linked bipolar disorders to genes on the x chromosome and chromosome 11 (Baron et al., 1987; Mendlewicz et al., 1987; Egeland et al., 1987, 1984). However, recent failures to replicate these findings have raised questions about their validity (Nurnberger & Gershon, 1992; Kelsoe et al., 1989).

## Treatments for Bipolar Disorders

Until recently, people with bipolar disorders were usually destined to spend their lives on an emotional roller coaster. Psychotherapists of varying orientations reported almost no success (Lickey & Gordon, 1991), and biological therapists found antidepressant drugs and ECT to be of little help (Prien et al., 1974).

### Lithium Therapy

The drug *lithium* has so dramatically changed this gloomy picture that many people view the silvery-white element—found in various simple mineral salts throughout the natural world—as a true miracle drug. Lithium's effectiveness in the treatment of bipolar symptoms was first discovered in 1949 by an Australian psychiatrist, John Cade. It was not until 1970, however, that the U.S. Food and Drug Administration approved it for use in bipolar disorders.

Determining the correct lithium dosage for a given patient is a delicate process. Too low a dose will have little or no effect on the bipolar mood swings, but too high a dose of lithium can result in lithium intoxication (literally, lithium poisoning), which can cause nausea, vomiting, sluggishness, tremors, seizures, sodium imbalance, kidney dysfunction, and even death (Abou-Saleh, 1992). Once the correct dose is achieved, however, lithium may produce a noticeable change within five to fourteen days. Some patients respond better to drugs such as *carbamazepine* (Tegretol) or *valproic acid* (Depake) that have also been discovered to have therapeutic effects in bipolar disorders.

**Effectiveness of Lithium**  All manner of research has attested to lithium's effectiveness in treating manic episodes (Klerman et al., 1994; Bunney & Garland, 1984). In numerous studies, lithium has been found to be much more effective than placebos. Improvement rates of patients with mania range upward from 60 percent. Another frequent finding is that patients with recurrent mania undergo fewer new episodes as long as they are taking lithium (Prien, 1992; Suppes et al., 1991). Accordingly, today's clinicians often recommend that patients continue lithium treatments even after their manic episodes subside (Abou-Saleh, 1992).

---

*Lithium*  A metallic element that occurs in nature as a mineral salt and is the most effective antibipolar drug.

Research indicates that lithium also alleviates the depressive episodes of bipolar disorders. Moreover, maintenance doses of lithium apparently decrease the risk of future depressive episodes, just as they often seem to prevent the recurrence of manic episodes (Klerman et al., 1994; Abou-Saleh, 1992).

**Lithium's Mode of Operation**    Researchers do not really understand how lithium operates. Some suspect that it alters synaptic activity in neurons, though not in the same way as antidepressant drugs. Recent research indicates that the firing of a neuron actually consists of several phases that unfold at lightning speed. After a neurotransmitter binds to a receptor site on the receiving neuron, a series of chemical changes in the receiving neuron set the stage for firing. These changes are often called *second messengers* because they intervene between the reception of the original message and the actual firing of the neuron (Snyder, 1986).

The second-messenger events cause the neuron's ions (which sit along the neural membrane) to cross the neuron's membrane, resulting in a change in the electrical charge of the neuron, the transmission of the message down the cell's axon, and the firing of the neuron. Whereas antidepressant drugs affect the initial reception of neurotransmitters by neurons, lithium appears to affect the second-messenger systems in certain neurons and in so doing may correct the neural abnormalities that lead to bipolar disorders (Goodwin & Jamison, 1990).

Alternatively, it may be that lithium effectively treats bipolar functioning by directly altering sodium ion activity in neurons (Swonger & Constantine, 1983). Several studies indicate that lithium ions often substitute, although imperfectly, for sodium ions, the ions that sit along each neural membrane (Baer et al., 1971), and others suggest that lithium directly alters the transport mechanisms that move sodium ions back and forth across the neural membrane as the neuron is firing (Goodwin & Jamison, 1990).

## Adjunctive Psychotherapy

Clinicians rarely treat bipolar patients with psychotherapy alone (Klerman et al., 1994). At the same time, clinicians have learned that lithium therapy alone is not always sufficient either. Thirty percent or more of patients with bipolar disorders may not respond to lithium, may not receive the proper dosage, or may relapse while taking it (Solomon et al., 1995; Abou-Saleh, 1992).

*sSecond messengers*   Chemical compound changes within the neuron that are responsible for the cell's response to a neurotransmitter.

*In recent years actress Patty Duke has written about her roller-coaster life with bipolar disorder.*

In view of these problems, many clinicians now advocate individual, group, or family therapy as an adjunct to lithium treatment (Graves, 1993; Wulsin et al., 1988). Most often, therapists use these formats to stress the need for the proper management of medications, establish supportive family and social relationships, educate patients and families about bipolar disorders, and help patients solve the special problems caused by their disorder (APA, 1993; Van Gent & Zwart, 1991; Goodwin & Jamison, 1990).

### Consider This
If bipolar disorders are largely biological in origin, why do so many people with this disorder need more than just an antibipolar drug as treatment? What issues of lifestyle, family and social relationships, and other areas of functioning might need to be addressed in adjunctive psychotherapy?

Few controlled studies have tested the effectiveness of psychotherapy as an adjunct to drug therapy for patients with severe bipolar disorders, but a growing number of clinical reports suggest that its use leads to less hospitalization, better social functioning, and higher employment rates for clients (Clarkin et al., 1990; Miklowitz et al., 1988).

### Summing Up
*Bipolar disorders have been related to high norepinephrine activity, to the improper transportation of sodium ions back and forth between the outside and the inside of the nerve cell's membrane, and to genetic factors. Lithium, often given in combination with psychotherapy, is the most effective treatment for bipolar disorders.*

## The State of the Field
### *Mood Disorders*

Because of the research gains of the past twenty-five years, mood disorders are now being diagnosed and distinguished with greater precision, with more knowledge about their breadth and course, and with greater awareness of possible contributing factors.

Researchers have identified several factors that are closely tied to unipolar patterns of depression, including a reduction in positive reinforcements, a perception of helplessness, negative ways of thinking, interpersonal problems, biological abnormalities, and, in some cases, life stresses such as the loss of a loved one. Precisely how these factors relate to unipolar depression is not yet clear. Any of several relationships are possible:

1. One of these factors may indeed be the key cause of unipolar depression.
2. Any of the leading factors may be capable of initiating unipolar depression. Some people may, for example, begin with low serotonin activity, which could predispose them to react helplessly in stressful situations, interpret events negatively, and enjoy fewer pleasures in life. Others may begin by experiencing a severe loss that sets off helplessness reactions, low serotonin activity, and reductions in positive reinforcements.
3. An interaction between two or more factors may be necessary to produce unipolar depression. Perhaps people will become depressed only if they have low levels of serotonin activity, feel helpless to control their reinforcements, *and* repeatedly blame themselves for negative events.
4. The various factors may play different roles in unipolar depression. Some may cause the disorder, some may result from it, and some may help maintain it.

Also during the past twenty-five years, unipolar depression has become one of the most treatable of all mental disorders. Indeed, it may respond to any of several approaches. Researchers have uncovered the following trends:

1. Cognitive, interpersonal, and biological therapies are each highly effective treatments for unipolar depression, from mild to severe (Elkin, 1994; Hollon et al., 1992). Each approach brings significant improvement to around 60 percent of clients in treatment.
2. Behavioral therapy is more helpful than no treatment but less effective than cognitive, interpersonal, or biological therapy. Also, behavioral therapy is less helpful to those who are severely depressed than those with mild or moderate levels of depression (Emmelkamp, 1994).
3. Psychodynamic therapies are less effective in treating all levels of unipolar depression than these other therapies (Svartberg & Stiles, 1991).
4. A combination of psychotherapy (usually cognitive or interpersonal) and drug therapy is modestly more helpful to depressed people than either treatment alone (Klerman et al., 1994).

Clinicians and researchers have also learned much about the causes of and treatments for bipolar disorders during the past twenty-five years. But, unlike unipolar depression, bipolar disorders appear to be best explained by and treated with one kind of variable—biological. The evidence suggests that biological abnormalities, perhaps inherited and perhaps precipitated by life stress, cause bipolar disorders. Moreover, the choice of treatment for these disorders is narrow and simple—lithium (or a similar drug), perhaps combined with psychotherapy.

There is no question that the present situation holds great promise both for people with unipolar depression and for those with bipolar disorders. On the other hand, the sobering fact remains that as many as 40 percent of people with a mood disorder do not improve under treatment and must suffer their mania or depression until it runs its course. For these individuals and for those close to them, it is imperative that clinical scientists uncover further pieces of the puzzle called mood disorders and develop even better ways to predict, prevent, and treat them.

## *Chapter Review*

1. *Mood Disorders:* People with mood disorders have moods that tend to last for months or years, dominate their interactions with the world, and disrupt their normal functioning.

2. *Unipolar Depression:* Victims of unipolar depression, the most common pattern of mood disorder, suffer exclusively from depression. Women are more likely than men to experience unipolar

depression. The symptoms of depression span five areas of functioning: emotional, motivational, behavioral, cognitive, and physical. Depressed people are also at greater risk for suicidal behavior.

A. **Psychodynamic Perspective:** According to the psychodynamic view, people who experience real or imagined losses may *introject* feelings for the lost object and may come to feel self-hatred and depression. Psychodynamic therapists try to help clients with unipolar depression become aware of and work through their losses and excessive dependence on others.

B. **The Behavioral Perspective:** The behavioral view says that when people experience a significant reduction in their positive reinforcements, they are more likely to develop a depressive style of functioning. Behavioral therapists reintroduce clients to events and activities that the clients once found pleasurable, systematically reinforce nondepressive behaviors, and teach effective interpersonal skills.

C. **The Cognitive Perspective:** The leading cognitive explanations for unipolar depression are the learned helplessness explanation and the maladaptive thinking explanation.

(1) **Learned Helplessness:** According to the *learned helplessness* theory, people become depressed when they perceive a loss of control over the reinforcements in their lives and when they attribute their loss of control to causes that are internal, global, and stable.

(2) **Maladaptive Thinking:** According to Beck's maladaptive thinking explanation, *maladaptive attitudes,* the *cognitive triad, errors in thinking,* and *automatic thoughts* help generate unipolar depression.

(3) **Cognitive Therapy:** Cognitive treatment for depression helps clients increase their activities, invalidate their automatic thoughts, identify their distorted thinking and negative biases, and change their broad maladaptive attitudes.

D. **The Sociocultural Perspective:** Interpersonal psychotherapy (IPT) is based on the assumption that depressive functioning stems primarily from interpersonal problem areas. In particular, clients may be experiencing an *interpersonal loss, interpersonal role dispute, interpersonal role transition,* or *interpersonal deficits.* IPT therapists try to help clients to develop insight into such problems, change them, and learn skills to protect themselves in the future.

E. **The Biological Perspective:** According to the biological view, deficiencies in two chemical neurotransmitters, *norepinephrine* and *serotonin,* may cause depression. These deficiencies may be linked to genetic factors.

(1) **Electroconvulsive Therapy:** Electroconvulsive therapy (ECT) is a controversial treatment, although it is an effective and fast-acting intervention for unipolar depression.

(2) **Antidepressants:** There are three kinds of antidepressant drugs. *MAO inhibitors* block the destruction of norepinephrine. Those who take this medication must avoid eating foods with tyramine. *Tricyclics* block neurotransmitter reuptake mechanisms, thereby increasing the activity of norepinephrine and serotonin. The *second-generation antidepressants* selectively increase the activity of serotonin.

F. **Comparison of the Perspectives:** The cognitive and biological explanations for unipolar depression have received the most research support. In treatment, the cognitive, interpersonal, and biological therapies appear to be the most successful for mild to severe depression. Combinations of psychotherapy and drug therapy tend to be modestly more helpful than any one approach alone.

3. **Bipolar Disorders:** In bipolar disorders, episodes of mania alternate or intermix with episodes of depression.

A. **Mania** is a state of dramatic, inappropriate, or disproportionate elevation in mood. Five areas are again affected: emotional, motivational, behavioral, cognitive, and physical. Manic episodes almost always indicate a bipolar disorder, one in which depressive episodes also occur.

B. Bipolar disorders are much less common than unipolar depression, afflict women and men equally, and tend to recur if they are not treated. They may take the form of *bipolar I* disorder, *bipolar II* disorder, or *cyclothymic disorder.*

C. **Explanations of Bipolar Disorder:** Mania has been related to high norepinephrine activity. Moreover, bipolar disorders have been linked to improper transportation of sodium ions back and forth between the outside and the inside of the nerve cell's membrane. Some *genetic studies* have suggested that people may inherit a predisposition to the biological abnormalities underlying bipolar disorders.

D. **Treatment for Bipolar Disorders:** Lithium has proved to be effective in alleviating and preventing both the manic and the depressive episodes of bipolar disorders. Researchers suspect that lithium may reduce bipolar symptoms by affecting *second messenger* systems in key neurons throughout the brain. Alternatively, lithium may interact directly with sodium ions in certain neurons. In recent years it has become clear that patients may fare better when the drug is supplemented by psychotherapy.

## Key Terms

| | | | |
|---|---|---|---|
| depression | contingency management | norepinephrine | second-generation |
| mania | arbitrary inference | serotonin | antidepressant |
| unipolar depression | minimization | electroconvulsive therapy | serotonin reuptake |
| bipolar disorder | magnification | (ECT) | inhibitor (SSRI) |
| major depressive disorder | learned helplessness | bilateral ECT | fluoxetine (Prozac) |
| delusion | attribution | unilateral ECT | manic episode |
| hallucination | cognitive triad | convulsion | hypomanic episode |
| dysthymic disorder | automatic thoughts | metrazol | bipolar I disorder |
| reactive (exogenous) | interpersonal | insulin coma therapy | bipolar II disorder |
| depression | psychotherapy (IPT) | antidepressant drug | cyclothymic disorder |
| endogenous depression | interpersonal role dispute | MAO inhibitor | genetic linkage study |
| symbolic loss | interpersonal role | tyramine | lithium |
| anaclitic depression | transition | tricyclic | second messenger |

## Quick Quiz

1. What are the key symptoms of depression and mania?
2. What is the difference between unipolar depression and bipolar disorder?
3. Describe the epidemiological differences (prevalence, gender, age, ethnicity) exhibited by the various mood disorders.
4. Describe Freud and Abraham's psychodynamic theory of depression and the evidence for it.
5. How do behaviorists describe the role of reinforcement in depression?
6. How might laboratory-induced learned helplessness be related to human depression?

7. What kinds of maladaptive thinking are thought to lead to mood problems?
8. How do interpersonal psychotherapists account for and treat unipolar depression?
9. Describe the role of the neurotransmitters norepinephrine and serotonin in unipolar depression.
10. What roles do biological and genetic factors seem to play to bipolar disorders?
11. Discuss the leading treatments for unipolar depression and bipolar disorders. How effective are these various approaches?

# 8

# Psychological Factors and Physical Disorders

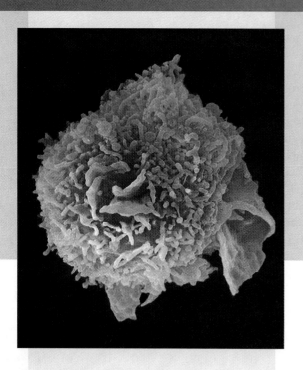

## Topic Overview

*Factitious Disorders*

*Somatoform Disorders*
Conversion Disorder
Somatization Disorder
Pain Disorder
Hypochondriasis
Body Dysmorphic Disorder

*Psychophysiological Disorders*
"Traditional" Psychophysiological Disorders
"New" Psychophysiological Disorders
Psychoneuroimmunology

*Psychological Treatments for Physical Disorders*

Throughout this text we have repeatedly encountered mental disorders that have physical causes. Abnormal neurotransmitter activity, for example, contributes to the development of generalized anxiety disorder, panic disorders, and unipolar patterns of depression. Today's clinicians also recognize that somatic, or bodily, illnesses can have psychological causes. In fact, this idea is not new at all. It can be traced back to the fourth century B.C., when Socrates said, "You should not treat body without soul" (Fiester, 1986; Gentry & Matarazzo, 1981).

Despite its ancient roots, the idea that psychological factors may contribute to physical illnesses held little appeal before the twentieth century. The seventeenth-century French philosopher René Descartes went so far as to claim that the mind, or soul, was a separate entity from the body, totally unable to affect physical matter or somatic processes. His position, called **mind-body dualism,** dominated medical theory for the next 200 years.

During the past 100 years, however, medicine has moved steadily toward an interactive view of physical illness. Clinical research and observations have persuaded medical scientists that many physical illnesses are **psychogenic**—brought on by such psychological factors as worry, family stress, and unconscious needs. Some of these physical illnesses, those that are today called *factitious disorders* and *somatoform disorders,* are thought to be caused exclusively by psychological factors. Others, called *psychophysiological disorders,* are believed to result from an interaction of organic and psychological factors.

# Factitious Disorders

People who become physically sick usually go to a physician. Sometimes, however, an illness defies medical assessment, and physicians may suspect some causes other than the physical factors they have been seeking. They may conclude, for instance, that the patient is *malingering*—intentionally feigning illness to achieve some external gains, such as financial compensation.

Alternatively, physicians may suspect that the patient is manifesting a *factitious disorder,* more precisely, a *factitious disorder with predominantly physical signs and symptoms.* People with this disorder intentionally produce or feign physical symptoms, but, unlike malingerers, their motivation for assuming the sick role is the role itself (APA, 1994). They have no external incentives for developing the symptoms.

> A 29-year-old female laboratory technician was admitted to the medical service via the emergency room because of bloody urine. The patient said that she was being treated for lupus erythematosus by a physician in a different city. She also mentioned that she had had Von Willebrand's disease (a rare hereditary blood disorder) as a child. On the third day of her hospitalization, a medical student mentioned to the resident that she had seen this patient several weeks before at a different hospital in the area, where the patient had been admitted for the same problem. A search of the patient's belongings revealed a cache of anticoagulant medication. When confronted with this information she refused to discuss the matter and hurriedly signed out of the hospital against medical advice.
>
> *(Spitzer et al., 1981, p. 33)*

The physical symptoms of a factitious disorder of this kind may be a total fabrication, self-inflicted, or an exaggeration of a preexisting physical condition (APA, 1994). People with the disorder usually describe their medical history dramatically, but become vague when pressed for details. Their knowledge of medical terminology and hospital routine is often extensive. Many eagerly undergo painful testing or treatment, even surgery. If physicians confront them with evidence that their symptoms are factitious, they typically deny the charges and rapidly discharge themselves from the hospital; they are quite likely to enter another hospital the same day.

**Munchausen syndrome** is the chronic form of this disorder. Like Baron Munchausen, an eighteenth-century cavalry officer who journeyed from tavern to tavern in Europe telling fantastical tales about his supposed adventures, people with this syndrome travel from hospital to hospital reciting their symptoms, gaining admission, and receiving treatment (Zuger, 1993). In a related but apparently rare form of factitious disorder, **Munchausen syndrome by proxy,** parents fabricate or induce physical illnesses in their children in order to get attention from physicians (McQuiston, 1993). When these children are removed from their parents and placed in the care of others, their symptoms disappear.

Although clinical researchers have yet to determine the prevalence of factitious disorder, they believe the

---

*Psychogenic illness*  An illness caused primarily by psychological factors such as worry, family stress, and unconscious needs.

*Factitious disorder*  An illness with no identifiable physical cause, in which the patient is believed to be intentionally producing or feigning symptoms in order to assume a sick role.

*Munchausen syndrome*  A factitious disorder in which a person travels from hospital to hospital reciting symptoms, gaining admission, and receiving treatment.

**Table 8-1    *Disorders That Have Physical Symptoms***

| Disorder | Voluntary Control of Symptoms? | Symptoms Linked to Psychological Factor? | An Apparent Goal? |
|---|---|---|---|
| Malingering | Yes | Maybe | Yes |
| Factitious disorder | Yes | Yes | No* |
| Somatoform disorder | No | Yes | Maybe |
| Psychophysiological disorder | No | Yes | Maybe |
| Physical illness | No | Maybe | No |

* Except for medical attention.

*Source:* Adapted from Hyler & Spitzer, 1978.

syndrome to be more common among men than among women (APA, 1994). Cases usually begin during early adulthood and often develop into a pattern that greatly impairs the person's ability to hold a steady job, maintain family ties, or form enduring social relationships. The disorder seems to be most common among people who (1) received extensive medical treatment and hospitalization as children for a true physical disorder, (2) carry a grudge against the medical profession, (3) have worked as a nurse, laboratory technician, or medical paraprofessional, (4) had a significant relationship with a physician in the past, or (5) have underlying dependent, exploitive, or self-defeating personality traits (APA, 1994).

The precise causes of factitious disorders are not really understood. These disorders have received little systematic study, and clinicians have not been able to develop standard effective treatments for them. Some success has been reported in individual cases with the use of a flexible, multidisciplinary treatment team (Schwarz et al., 1993; Parker, 1993).

## *Somatoform Disorders*

When a physical illness eludes medical assessment, physicians may alternatively suspect that the patient has a *somatoform disorder.* Such patients have physical complaints that are again rooted exclusively in psycho-

logical causes. However, in contrast to people with factitious disorders, patients with somatoform disorders experience no sense of willing their symptoms or having control over them (see Table 8-1). Indeed, they rarely believe that the problems are anything but organic.

Some somatoform disorders, known as **hysterical disorders,** involve an actual loss or change of physical functioning. People with a *conversion disorder,* for instance, develop dramatic physical symptoms or deficits affecting voluntary motor or sensory functioning; those with a *somatization disorder* experience multiple physical symptoms; and those with a *pain disorder* experience pain that is not predominantly attributable to a medical cause.

In another group of somatoform disorders, the **preoccupation disorders,** physical functioning is at most minimally lost or changed, but people with these disorders become preoccupied with the notion that something is wrong with them physically. Those who experience *hypochondriasis* mistakenly and repeatedly fear that fluctuations in their physical functioning indicate a serious disease. Those with a *body dysmorphic disorder* worry excessively that some aspect of their physical appearance is defective.

## Hysterical Somatoform Disorders

Hysterical disorders, the somatoform disorders that involve altered or lost physical functioning, are often difficult to distinguish from problems with a medical base. The symptoms of these disorders take many forms and typically have a major impact on patients' lives.

---

*Somatoform disorder*  A physical illness or ailment that is primarily explained by psychological causes, in which the patient experiences no sense of willing the symptoms or having control over them.

## Conversion Disorder

A *conversion disorder* is characterized by one or more physical symptoms or deficits affecting voluntary motor or sensory function that are actually expressions of a psychological problem, such as a conflict or need: the psychological problem is converted to a physical symptom. The symptoms often suggest a neurological dysfunction, such as paralysis, seizures, blindness, loss of feeling, or loss of speech, and are thus often called "pseudoneurological" (APA, 1994). One woman developed a conversion symptom of dizziness in apparent response to her unhappy marriage:

A 46-year-old married housewife . . . . described being overcome with feelings of extreme dizziness, accompanied by slight nausea, four or five nights a week. During these attacks, the room around her would take on a "shimmering" appearance, and she would have the feeling that she was "floating" and unable to keep her balance. Inexplicably, the attacks almost always occurred at about 4:00 P.M. She usually had to lie down on the couch and often did not feel better until 7:00 or 8:00 P.M. After recovering, she generally spent the rest of the evening watching TV; and more often than not, she would fall asleep in the living room, not going to bed in the bedroom until 2:00 or 3:00 in the morning.

The patient had been pronounced physically fit by her internist, a neurologist, and an ear, nose, and throat specialist on more than one occasion. Hypoglycemia had been ruled out by glucose tolerance tests.

When asked about her marriage, the patient described her husband as a tyrant, frequently demanding and verbally abusive of her and their four children. She admitted that she dreaded his arrival home from work each day, knowing that he would comment that the house was a mess and the dinner, if prepared, not to his liking. Recently, since the onset of her attacks, when she was unable to make dinner he and the four kids would go to McDonald's or the local pizza parlor. After that, he would settle in to watch a ballgame in the bedroom, and their conversation was minimal. In spite of their troubles, the patient claimed that she loved her husband and needed him very much.

*(Spitzer et al., 1981, pp. 92–93)*

Most conversion disorders emerge between late childhood and young adulthood; they are diagnosed at least twice as often in women as in men (APA, 1994; Tomasson et al., 1991). They usually appear suddenly, at times of extreme psychological stress, and last a matter of weeks. Conversion disorders are thought to be quite rare, occurring in at most 3 out of every 1000 persons (APA, 1994).

> *Consider This*
> A conversion disorder is typically thought of as a physical disorder that does not have physical causes. But is it possible for people to be deprived of vision, feeling in their limbs, or other bodily functions without some physical factors playing a significant role? Would an alternative definition be preferable? What are the implications of this idea for explaining and treating these disorders?

## Somatization Disorder

Sheila baffled a variety of medical specialists with the wide range of her symptoms:

Sheila reported having abdominal pain since age 17, necessitating exploratory surgery that yielded no specific diagnosis. She had several pregnancies, each with severe nausea, vomiting, and abdominal pain; she ultimately had a hysterectomy for a "tipped uterus." Since age 40 she had experienced dizziness and "blackouts," which she eventually was told might be multiple sclerosis or a brain tumor. She continued to be bedridden for extended periods of time, with weakness, blurred vision, and difficulty urinating. At age 43 she was worked up for a hiatal hernia because of complaints of bloating and intolerance of a variety of foods. She also had additional hospitalizations for neurological, hypertensive, and renal workups, all of which failed to reveal a definitive diagnosis.

*(Spitzer et al., 1981, pp. 185, 260)*

When we read the case description of Sheila, we are struck by the sheer quantity and range of medical problems she experienced. People who have numerous physical ailments without an organic basis, and whose difficulties continue or recur for several years, are likely to receive a diagnosis of *somatization disorder*. This pattern, first described by Pierre Briquet in 1859, is also known as *Briquet's syndrome*. To receive a diagnosis of somatization disorder, the person's multiple ailments must include pain symptoms, gastrointestinal symptoms (such as nausea or diarrhea), a sexual symptom (such as erectile or menstrual difficulties), and a pseudoneurologic symptom (such as double vision or paralysis).

Patients with a somatization disorder usually go from doctor to doctor in search of relief (APA, 1994).

---

*Conversion disorder*  A somatoform disorder characterized by one or more physical symptoms or deficits affecting voluntary motor or sensory function.

*Somatization disorder*  A somatoform disorder characterized by recurring, numerous physical ailments without a primary organic basis.

They often describe their many symptoms in dramatic terms. Most also feel anxious and depressed.

Between 0.2 and 2.0 percent of all women in the United States are believed to experience a somatization disorder in any given year, compared to less than 0.2 percent of all men (APA, 1994; Regier et al., 1993). The disorder often runs in families; 10 to 20 percent of the close female relatives of women with the disorder also develop it. It usually begins between adolescence and young adulthood with no identifiable precipitating event (APA, 1994).

A somatization disorder lasts considerably longer than a conversion disorder, typically for many years. The symptoms may fluctuate over time but rarely disappear completely without psychotherapy (APA, 1994). Two-thirds of the people diagnosed with this disorder in the United States in any given year receive treatment from a medical or mental health professional (Regier et al., 1993).

## Pain Disorder

When people experience severe or prolonged pain and psychological factors play a significant role in the onset, severity, exacerbation, or maintenance of the pain, they may receive a diagnosis of *pain disorder* (APA, 1994). The psychological factors at work may be the exclusive cause of the pain, or may join with an actual medical problem to cause the pain. The pain may occur in any part of the body. Patients with conversion or somatization disorders may also experience pain without a dominant medical cause, but in a pain disorder the pain is the central symptom.

Researchers have not been able to determine the precise prevalence of pain disorders, but they appear to be relatively common, and women seem to experience them more often than men. The disorder may begin at any age and in some cases continues for years (APA, 1994). Laura, a 36-year-old woman with sarcoidosis, reported pains that far exceeded the usual symptoms of that tubercular disease.

LAURA: Before the operation I would have little joint pains, nothing that really bothered me that much. After the operation I was having severe pains in my chest and in my ribs, and those were the type of problems I'd been having after the operation, that I didn't have before. . . . I'd go to an emergency room at night, 11:00, 12:00, 1:00 or so. I'd take the medicine, and the next day it stopped hurting, and I'd go back again. In the meantime this is when I went to the other doctors, to complain about the same thing, to find out what was wrong; and they could never find out what was wrong with me either. . . .

DOCTOR: With these symptoms on and off over the years, has that interfered with the way you've lived your life?

LAURA: Yes. At certain points when I go out or my husband and I go out, we have to leave early because I start hurting. . . . A lot of times I just won't do things because my chest is hurting for one reason or another. . . . Two months ago when the doctor checked me and another doctor looked at the x-rays, he said he didn't see any signs of the sarcoid then and that they were doing a study now, on blood and various things, to see if it was connected to sarcoid. . . .

(Green, 1985, pp. 60–63)

## Identifying Hysterical Symptoms

In an effort to distinguish hysterical somatoform disorders from "true" medical problems, diagnosticians rely on several distinctions:

**Neurological and Anatomical Inconsistencies** The symptoms of some hysterical disorders do not usually correspond to what medical scientists know about the anatomical distribution of nerves and the way the nervous system works (APA, 1994). Some patients, for example, display a conversion symptom called "glove anesthesia," numbness that begins abruptly at the wrist and extends with uniform intensity throughout the hand to the fingertips. As Figure 8-1 shows, such clearly defined and equally distributed numbness is not characteristic of neurological damage. Even the newly recognized neurological disease *carpal tunnel syndrome,* which is characterized by numbness, tingling, and pain in the hand, does not typically involve a uniform distribution of symptoms throughout the hand.

**Unexpected Course of Development** Hysterical disorders do not necessarily lead to the same physical consequences as corresponding medical problems (Levy, 1985). When paraplegia (paralysis from the waist down) is caused by damage to the spinal cord, for example, the leg muscles may atrophy, or waste away, unless the patient receives proper physical therapy and exercise. People whose paralysis is a conversion disorder do not ordinarily experience such atrophy; presumably they use their muscles to some degree, without being aware that they are doing so.

**Selective Symptomatology** The physical symptoms of hysterical disorders may operate selectively or inconsistently. People with conversion blindness, for example, have fewer accidents than people who are organically blind, an indication that they have at least some vision even if they are unaware of it.

---

*Pain disorder* A somatoform disorder characterized by severe and prolonged pain, with psychological factors playing a significant role in the onset, severity, exacerbation, or maintenance of the pain.

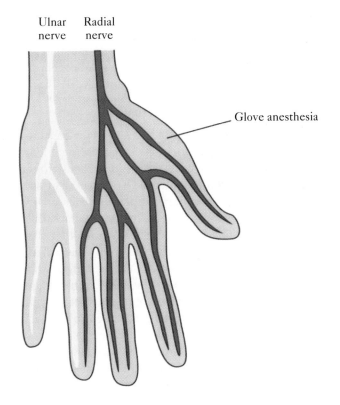

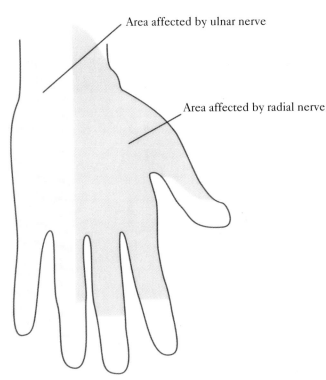

**Figure 8-1**  *In the conversion symptom called "glove anesthesia," the entire hand extending to the wrist becomes numb. Actual physical damage to the ulnar nerve, in contrast, causes anesthesia in the ring finger and little finger and beyond the wrist partway up the arm; and damage to the radial nerve causes insensitivity only in parts of the ring, middle, and index fingers and the thumb and partway up the arm. (Adapted from Gray, 1959.)*

# Preoccupation Somatoform Disorders

People who have *hypochondriasis* and *body dysmorphic disorder,* both characterized as **preoccupation somatoform disorders,** misinterpret physical symptoms as signs of serious physical problems. Friends, relatives, and physicians may try to dissuade them from this notion, but usually without success. Although often these kinds of somatoform disorders cause considerable distress, they do not affect a person's social or occupational functioning so profoundly as hysterical disorders do (APA, 1994).

## Hypochondriasis

People who suffer from **hypochondriasis** unrealistically and fearfully interpret bodily signs or symptoms as signs of a serious illness. Often the reported ailments are merely normal fluctuations in physical functioning, such as occasional coughing, sores, or sweating. Despite repeated diagnostic tests, patients with hypochondriasis are not reassured. Some patients actually recognize that their concern is excessive; others do not (APA, 1994).

Hypochondriasis can present a picture very similar to that of a somatization disorder. Each typically involves numerous physical symptoms and frequent visits to doctors, and each causes patients great concern. Diagnosticians try to distinguish between the two on the basis of the following criteria: if the anxiety level is significant and the bodily symptoms are relatively minor, a diagnosis of hypochondriasis is in order; if the bodily symptoms are more significant and overshadow the patient's anxiety, they probably indicate a somatization disorder.

Although hypochondriasis can begin at any age, it emerges most commonly in early adulthood. Some patients eventually overcome their preoccupation, but for most the symptoms wax and wane over the years. Like pain disorders, hypochondriasis is reportedly very familiar to physicians, but its exact prevalence is unknown. Men and women are equally likely to receive this diagnosis (APA, 1994).

## Body Dysmorphic Disorder

People who experience a **body dysmorphic disorder,** also known as **dysmorphophobia,** become preoccupied with some imagined or exaggerated defect in their ap-

*Hypochondriasis*  A somatoform disorder in which people mistakenly and incessantly fear that minor fluctuations in their physical functioning indicate a serious disease.

*Body dysmorphic disorder (dysmorphophobia)*  A somatoform disorder marked by excessive worry that some aspect of one's physical appearance is defective.

pearance. Most commonly they worry about facial flaws such as wrinkles, spots on the skin, excessive facial hair, swelling of the face, or a misshapen nose, mouth, jaw, or eyebrow (APA, 1994). Some worry about the appearance of their feet, hands, breasts, penis, or another body part. Others are concerned about bad odors coming from sweat, the breath, the genitals, or the rectum (Marks, 1987). Some people are distressed by several body features. Here we see a case of body dysmorphic disorder that centers on body odor:

> A woman of 35 had for 16 years been worried that her sweat smelled terrible. The fear began just before her marriage when she was sharing a bed with a close friend who said that someone at work smelled badly, and the patient felt that the remark was directed at her. For fear that she smelled, for 5 years she had not gone out anywhere except when accompanied by her husband or mother. She had not spoken to her neighbors for 3 years because she thought she had overheard them speak about her to some friends. She avoided cinemas, dances, shops, cafes, and private homes. . . . Television commercials about deodorants made her very anxious. She refused to attend the local church because it was small and the local congregants might comment on her. The family had to travel to a church 8 miles away in which the congregants were strangers; there they sat or stood apart from the others. . . . She used vast quantities of deodorant and always bathed and changed her clothes before going out, up to 4 times daily.

> *(Marks, 1987, p. 371)*

It is common for people in our society to be somewhat concerned about their appearance (see Figure 8-2). Adolescents and young adults in particular often worry about such things as acne. The concerns of people with a body dysmorphic disorder, however, are extreme and disruptive. Sufferers may even have difficulty looking others in the eye, convinced that their flaws are on display. They may also go to great lengths to conceal the "defect"—always wearing sunglasses to hide the shape of their supposedly misshapen eyes, for example, or even seeking plastic surgery to correct the problem. One study found that 30 percent of subjects with the disorder were housebound, and 17 percent had attempted suicide (Phillips et al., 1993). Most cases begin during adolescence and persist for an extended period. Often, however, they are not diagnosed for many years because individuals with the disorder are reluctant to reveal their concerns. Researchers have

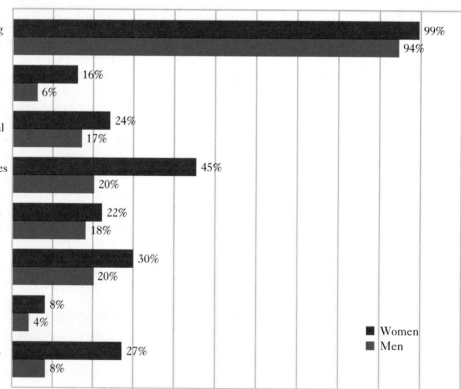

**Figure 8-2**  *"Mirror mirror on the wall. . . " People with body dysmorphic disorder are not the only ones who have concerns about their appearance. Indeed, it is estimated that 1.5 million Americans undergo "aesthetic surgery" each year. Surveys find that in our society, surprisingly high percentages of people regularly think about and try to change the way they look. (Kimball, 1993; Poretz & Sinrod, 1991; Weiss, 1991; Simmon, 1990.)*

not yet determined the prevalence of this disorder, but preliminary reports suggest that it may be equally common among men and women (APA, 1994).

## Views on Somatoform Disorders

Most theorists explain the preoccupation somatoform disorders—hypochondriasis and body dysmorphic disorders—the same way they explain certain anxiety disorders (discussed in Chapters 5 and 6). Behaviorists, for example, believe that the disproportionate fears displayed by people with these disorders have been acquired earlier in life through classical conditioning or modeling. The hysterical somatoform disorders, however—conversion, somatization, and pain disorders—are considered to be unique and to require special explanations (Kirmayer et al., 1994).

The ancient Greeks believed that hysterical disorders were experienced only by women and came about when the uterus of a sexually ungratified woman wandered throughout her body in search of fulfillment, producing a physical symptom wherever it lodged. (Our word "hysteria" comes from the Greek word for uterus, *hustera*.) Hippocrates suggested marriage as the most effective treatment for hysterical disorders. Today's explanations are more sophisticated, but as we shall see, none has received much research support, and the disorders are still poorly understood (Kirmayer et al., 1994). The leading explanations come from the psychodynamic, cognitive, and behavioral models.

### The Psychodynamic Explanation

As we noted in Chapter 1, Freud's theory of psychoanalysis actually began with his efforts to account for hysterical symptoms. After studying hypnosis in Paris, Freud became interested in the work of an older physician, Joseph Breuer (1842–1925), who had successfully used hypnosis to treat the woman he called Anna O. Although critics have since questioned whether Anna's ailments were entirely hysterical and whether

Breuer's hypnotic treatment was as helpful to her as he claimed (Ellenberger, 1972), at the time it seemed to confirm the idea that hysterical ailments could be treated effectively by hypnosis.

Partly because hysterical disorders seemed to respond to hypnosis, Freud (1894) came to believe that these ailments represented a conversion of underlying emotional conflicts into physical symptoms. Observing that most of his patients with these disorders were women, he proposed that the underlying conflicts developed during a girl's phallic stage (ages 3 through 5), when he believed girls develop an *Electra complex:* they experience strong sexual feelings for their father, but out of deference to their mother and to cultural taboos, they repress their sexual feelings and adopt a socially approved abhorrence of such desires.

Freud believed that if a child's parents overreact to her sexual feelings, the Electra conflict will go unresolved and the child may reexperience sexual anxiety throughout her life. Whenever events trigger sexual

*Historians have identified Bertha Pappenheim, a wealthy Viennese woman, as the subject of Josef Breuer's famous case of "Anna O," in which a patient with hysterical symptoms was said to be cured by hypnosis.*

feelings, she may experience an overwhelming unconscious need to hide them from both herself and the world. Freud concluded that some women hide such reemerging sexual feelings by unconsciously converting them into physical symptoms.

Most of today's psychodynamic theorists have modified Freud's explanation of hysterical disorders (Kriechman, 1987). They continue to believe, however, that the disorders reflect (1) an unconscious conflict of some kind that arouses anxiety and (2) a conversion of this anxiety into "more tolerable" physical symptoms that symbolize the underlying conflict.

Psychodynamic theories have distinguished two mechanisms at work in hysterical somatoform disorders—primary gain and secondary gain (Colbach, 1987). People are said to be achieving *primary gain* when their hysterical symptoms keep their internal conflicts out of awareness. People are said to be achieving *secondary gain* when their hysterical symptoms also enable them to avoid unpleasant activities or to receive kindness or sympathy from others. Both forms of gain help to lock in their symptoms. According to psychodynamic theorists, primary gains initiate hysterical symptoms; secondary gains are by-products of the symptoms. Although such psychodynamic notions are widely accepted, they have received little research support.

### The Cognitive Explanation

A number of theorists propose that hysterical disorders are forms of *communication*: through them people manage to express emotions that they cannot express otherwise (Lipowski, 1987). Like their psychodynamic colleagues, these theorists hold that the emotions of patients with hysterical disorders are being converted into physical symptoms. They suggest, however, that the purpose of the conversion is not to "defend" against anxiety but to communicate some distressing emotion—anger, fear, depression, guilt, jealousy—in a "physical language of bodily symptoms" that is familiar to the patient and therefore comfortable (Fry, 1993; Barsky & Klerman, 1983).

According to this view, people who have difficulty acknowledging their emotions or expressing them to others are candidates for a hysterical disorder, especially when they are in the midst of a difficult interpersonal situation. Similarly, those who learn the language of physical dysfunction through firsthand experience

*"He didn't really die of anything. He was a hypochondriac."*
*(Drawing by Geo. Price; ©1970 The New Yorker Magazine, Inc.)*

with a genuine physical malady either in themselves or in a relative or friend may then adopt hysterical symptoms as a form of communication (Woodruff et al., 1973). In support of this last notion, hysterical disorders often emerge after people have had similar medical problems or after close relatives or friends have experienced such maladies (Levy, 1985).

### The Behavioral Explanation

Behavioral theorists propose that the physical symptoms of hysterical disorders bring the sufferer rewards. Perhaps the symptoms keep the sufferer out of a difficult work situation or relationship, or elicit attention that is otherwise withheld (Mullins et al., 1992; Ullmann & Krasner, 1975). According to behaviorists, such reinforcements operantly condition people into assuming the role of a physically impaired person.

The behavioral focus on rewards is similar to the psychodynamic notion that many people with hysterical disorders attain secondary gains from their physical symptoms. The key difference between the two positions is that psychodynamic theorists view such gains as indeed secondary—that is, as a feature that develops only after underlying dynamic conflicts produce the disorder. Behaviorists view the gains (or rewards) as the primary factor in the development of the disorder.

Like the psychodynamic and cognitive explanations, the behavioral view of hysterical disorders has received little research support. Even clinical case reports only occasionally support this position. In many cases the pain and upset that accompany the disorders seem to outweigh any rewards the symptoms may bring.

---

*Primary gain* In psychodynamic theory, the gain achieved by hysterical symptoms of keeping internal conflicts out of awareness.

*Secondary gain* In psychodynamic theory, the gain achieved by hysterical symptoms of eliciting kindness or sympathy from others or of providing an excuse to avoid unpleasant activities.

## Treatments for Somatoform Disorders

People with somatoform disorders usually seek psychotherapy only as a last resort. They fully believe that their problems are somatic and initially reject all suggestions by physicians to the contrary. Eventually, however, many patients do try psychotherapy for their problems.

Those with preoccupation somatoform disorders typically receive the kinds of treatment that are applied to phobic and obsessive-compulsive disorders, particularly *exposure and response-prevention interventions* (discussed in Chapter 6). The effectiveness of these approaches for preoccupation somatoform disorders, however, has yet to be determined.

People with hysterical somatoform disorders typically receive interventions that stress either *insight, suggestion, reinforcement,* or *confrontation.* The most commonly applied insight approach has been psychodynamic therapy, which helps patients bring their anxiety-arousing conflicts into consciousness so they can work through them, theoretically eliminating the need to convert anxiety into physical symptoms. Approaches that employ suggestion include telling patients persuasively that their physical symptoms will soon disappear (Bird, 1979) or suggesting the same thing to them under hypnosis (Ballinger, 1987). Therapists who take a reinforcement approach try to arrange the removal of rewards for a client's "sick" behavior and an increase in positive rewards for non-symptomatic behaviors (Mullins et al., 1992). Finally, therapists who take a confrontational approach straightforwardly tell patients that their symptoms are without an organic foundation, hoping to force them out of the sick role (Brady & Lind, 1961).

Researchers have been unable to determine the effects of these various forms of psychotherapy on hysterical disorders (Ballinger, 1987). Case studies suggest, however, that conversion disorders and pain disorders respond better to psychotherapy than do somatization disorders, and that approaches that rely on insight, suggestion, and reinforcement bring more lasting improvement than the confrontation strategy.

One thing that makes the study and treatment of hysterical disorders difficult is the ever-present possibility that a diagnosis of hysteria may be a misdiagnosis, that the problem under examination may actually have an organic base. Although organic causes must be ruled out before a diagnosis of somatoform disorder is reached, the tools of medical science are too imprecise to eliminate organic factors completely (APA, 1994; Merskey, 1986). Some of the medical problems most difficult for doctors to diagnose are those involving vague, multiple, and confusing symptoms and these

problems have often been initially misdiagnosed as somatoform disorders. Thus it is now recommended that clinicians employ an integrated, multidisciplinary approach when they assess and treat people with the symptoms of these disorders (Woodbury et al., 1992; Wherry et al., 1991).

> *Summing Up*
> *Psychological factors may contribute to physical illnesses. Some physical illnesses appear to be caused largely or totally by psychological factors and may be diagnosed as malingering, a factitious disorder, or a somatoform disorder. The somatoform disorders, in which sufferers fully believe that their illnesses are organic, may involve an actual loss or alteration of physical functioning (conversion disorder, somatization disorder, and pain disorder) or a preoccupation with the notion that something is wrong physically (hypochondriasis and body dysmorphic disorder). Clinicians do not have a clear understanding of these disorders, nor have they developed treatments that are clearly effective.*

# *Psychophysiological Disorders*

Earlier in this century clinicians identified a group of physical illnesses that seemed to result from an interaction of psychological and physical factors (Dunbar, 1948; Bott, 1928). These illnesses differed from somatoform disorders in that *both* psychological and physical factors played significant causal roles and the illnesses themselves brought about actual medical damage. Whereas early versions of the DSM labeled these illnesses *psychosomatic* or *psychophysiological disorders,* DSM-IV uses the label *psychological factors affecting medical condition* and further clarifies that the factors at work may be *psychological symptoms, personality traits, coping styles,* or another such factor. We shall use the more familiar and less cumbersome term "psychophysiological" in discussing them.

At first clinicians believed that only a limited number of illnesses were psychophysiological. In recent years, however, researchers have learned that many kinds of physical illnesses—including bacterial and viral infections—may be caused by an interaction of psychological and physical factors. Let us focus first on the "traditional" psychophysiological disorders, and then on the newer members of this category.

*Psychophysiological (psychosomatic) disorders* Illnesses believed to result from an interaction of organic and psychological factors.

# "Traditional" Psychophysiological Disorders

During the first seventy years of this century, clinicians identified several disorders that they believed were psychophysiological. The best known and most prevalent were ulcers, asthma, chronic headaches, hypertension, and coronary heart disease.

*Ulcers* are lesions, or holes, that form in the wall of the stomach (gastric ulcers) or of the duodenum (peptic ulcers), resulting in burning sensations or pain in the stomach, occasional vomiting, and stomach bleeding. This disorder is experienced by 5 to 10 percent of all persons in the United States and is responsible for more than 6,000 deaths each year (Suter, 1986). Ulcers are apparently caused by an interaction of psychological factors, such as environmental stress, intense feelings of anger or anxiety, or a dependent personality, and physiological factors, such as excessive secretions of the gastric juices or a weak lining of the stomach or duodenum (Tennant, 1988; Fiester, 1986; Weiner et al., 1957).

*Asthma* causes the body's airways (the trachea and bronchi) to constrict periodically, so that it is hard for air to pass to and from the lungs. The resulting symptoms are shortness of breath, wheezing, coughing, and a terrifying choking sensation. Approximately 15 million people in the United States suffer from asthma. Most victims are under 15 years of age at the time of the first attack (DeAngelis, 1994). Approximately 70 percent of all cases appear to be caused by an interaction of such psychological factors as anxiety, heightened dependency needs, environmental stress, and troubled family relationships and such physiological factors as allergies to specific substances, a slow-acting sympathetic nervous system, and a weakness of the respiratory system traceable to respiratory infections or biological inheritance (Creer, 1994; Young, 1994; Rees, 1964).

*Chronic headaches* are frequent intense aches of the head or neck that are not caused exclusively by a physical disorder. There are two types. *Muscle contraction headaches* (also called *tension headaches*) bring pain at the back or front of the head or at the back of the neck. These headaches occur when the muscles surrounding the skull contract, constricting the blood vessels. Approximately 40 million Americans suffer

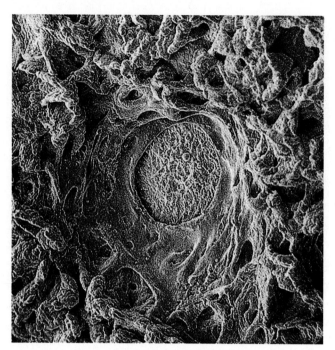

*An ulcer in the stomach lining of a rat. Such open sores can occur in the mucous lining of the duodenum as well.*

from these headaches. *Migraine headaches* are extremely severe and often immobilizing aches located on one side of the head, often preceded by a warning sensation called an *aura,* and sometimes accompanied by dizziness, nausea, or vomiting. Migraine headaches develop in two phases: (1) blood vessels in the brain constrict, so that the flow of blood to parts of the brain is reduced, and (2) the same blood vessels later dilate, so that blood flows through them rapidly, stimulating numerous neuron endings and causing pain. Migraines are suffered by about 12 million people in the United States. Research suggests that chronic headaches are caused by an interaction of psychological factors, such as environmental stress, general feelings of helplessness, feelings of hostility, compulsiveness, or a passive or depressive personality style, and such physiological factors as serotonin dysfunction, vascular weakness, or musculoskeletal deficiencies (Mathew, 1990; Raskin et al., 1987; Levor et al., 1986).

*Hypertension* is a state of chronic high blood pressure. That is, the blood pumped through the body's arteries by the heart produces too much pressure against the artery walls. It is estimated that 40 million people in the United States have hypertension, tens of thousands die directly from it annually, and millions more perish because of illnesses brought on by this condi-

---

*Ulcer*  A lesion or hole that forms in the wall of the stomach or of the duodenum.

*Asthma*  A medical problem marked by constricting of the trachea and bronchi, which results in shortness of breath, wheezing, coughing, and a choking sensation.

*Muscle contraction headache*  A chronic headache caused by the contraction of muscles surrounding the skull.

---

*Migraine headache*  An extremely severe headache that occurs on one side of the head, often preceded by a warning sensation and sometimes accompanied by dizziness, nausea, or vomiting.

*Hypertension*  Chronic high blood pressure.

*Children who suffer from asthma may use an aerochamber, or inhaler, to help them inhale helpful medications. The child pumps the medication into the device's plastic tube, then inhales it.*

tion (Johnson et al., 1992). Only 5 to 10 percent of all cases of hypertension are caused exclusively by physiological abnormalities; the vast majority are brought about by a combination of psychological and physiological factors and are often designated *essential hypertension* (Johnson et al., 1992). Some of the leading psychological causes of essential hypertension are constant environmental danger, chronic feelings of anger or its inhibition, and an unexpressed need for power (Johnston, 1992; McClelland, 1985). Leading physiological causes include a diet high in salt and dysfunctional *baroreceptors*—sensitive nerves in the blood vessels responsible for signaling the brain that blood pressure is becoming too high (Julius, 1992; Schwartz, 1977).

*Coronary heart disease* is caused by a blocking of the *coronary arteries*—the blood vessels that surround the heart and are responsible for providing oxygen to the heart muscle. The term actually refers to any of several specific problems, including *myocardial infarction* (a "heart attack") and blockages of coronary arteries. Together such problems are the leading causes of death in men over the age of 35 and of women over 40 in the United States, accounting for close to 800,000 deaths each year (Blanchard, 1994; Matarazzo, 1984). More than half of all cases of coronary heart disease are related to an interaction of such psychological factors as job stress and the so-called

---

*Coronary heart disease* Illness of the heart caused by a blocking of the coronary arteries.

*Type A personality style* A personality pattern characterized by hostility, cynicism, drivenness, impatience, competitiveness, and ambition.

---

*Type A personality style* (high levels of hostility, impatience, frustration, and competitiveness, and constant striving for control and success) and such physiological factors as a high level of serum cholesterol, obesity, hypertension, the effects of smoking, and lack of exercise (Johnston, 1992; Friedman & Rosenman, 1974, 1959).

## The Disregulation Explanation of Traditional Psychophysiological Disorders

By definition, psychophysiological disorders are caused by an interaction of psychological and physical factors. But how do these factors combine to produce a given illness? Gary Schwartz, a leading researcher, has proposed the *disregulation model* to account for this phenomenon (see Figure 8-3). Schwartz suggests that our brain and body ordinarily establish **negative feedback loops** that guarantee a smooth, self-regulating operation of the body (Schwartz, 1982, 1977). The brain receives information about external events from the environment, processes this information, and then stimulates body organs into action. Mechanisms in the organs then provide critical negative feedback, telling the brain that its stimulation has been sufficient and should now stop.

This process can be seen in the blood pressure feedback loop (Julius, 1992; Egan, 1992). In one part of this loop the brain receives the information that a danger exists in the environment, such as nearby lightning or cars speeding by. In the next part of the loop, the brain processes this information and alerts the nervous system to elevate the blood pressure. And in a later part of the loop, baroreceptors, the pressure-sensitive cells in the body's blood vessels, alert the nervous system when the blood pressure rises too high, and the nervous system then lowers the blood pressure. In short, the various parts of the feedback loop work together to help maintain the blood pressure at an appropriate level.

According to Schwartz, if one part of a loop falters, the body will enter a state of disregulation rather than effective self-regulation, problems will occur throughout the loop, and a psychophysiological disorder may ultimately develop. Hypertension, for example, may result from problems in any part of the blood pressure feedback loop. Should information from the environment be excessive (as when one is faced with continuous job stress or extended unemployment), should the processing of information be faulty (as when one keeps misinterpreting or overreacting to everyday

---

*Disregulation model* A theory that explains psychophysiological disorders as breakdowns in the body's negative feedback loops, resulting in an interruption of the body's smooth, self-regulating operation.

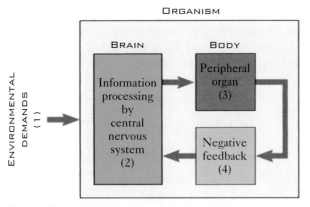

Figure 8-3 *Schwartz's disregulation model states that in the normal process of regulation (1) the organism receives environmental pressure; the brain (2) processes information about this pressure and (3) stimulates body organs into action; and (4) the organs then provide negative feedback to the brain stating that the stimulation has been sufficient and should cease. (Adapted from Schwartz, 1977.)*

events), should a peripheral organ malfunction (as when the aorta narrows abnormally), or should a feedback mechanism fail (as when baroreceptors fail to inform the brain that blood pressure is rising too high), inaccurate information will be fed to the next part of the loop and relayed to the next, until every part in the loop has been stimulated to raise the blood pressure.

## Factors That Contribute to Psychophysiological Disorders

Over the years, theorists have suggested a variety of factors that may contribute to psychophysiological disorders. As suggested by Schwartz's disregulation model, these factors may include *extraordinary environmental stress, dysfunctional psychological reactions* (maladaptive ways of processing information), or *dysfunctional physiological reactions* (improper operation of body organs or feedback mechanisms).

**Environmental Pressures** Sometimes the psychological demands placed on people are so intense or long-lasting that they lead to disregulation and set the stage for psychophysiological disorders. Such environmental stresses may be of various kinds. Wars and natural disasters, for example, can have a broad negative effect on a whole population. After the 1979 nuclear accident at Three Mile Island, people who lived near the nuclear plant were found to experience an unusually large number of psychophysiological disorders (not radiation-linked illnesses), and they continued to do so for years (Schneiderman & Baum, 1992; Baum et al., 1983). Alternatively, stress may be generated by ongoing, seemingly unvarying circumstances that produce persistent feelings of tension, such as living in a

crime-ridden neighborhood or working in an unsatisfying job. Thus, hypertension is twice as common among African Americans as among white Americans (Johnson et al., 1992). Although physiological factors may help account for this difference, some theorists propose that it is also linked to the dangerous environments in which so many African Americans live and to the unsatisfying jobs at which so many must work (Anderson et al., 1992). Finally, stress may come from unpleasant personal events, such as a severe illness, a death in the family, or divorce. Losing one's job and extended unemployment have both been tied to hypertension (Johnson et al., 1992; Kasl & Cobb, 1970).

**Psychological Reactions** Certain needs, attitudes, emotions, and coping styles may increase a person's chances of developing psychophysiological disorders (Friedman & Booth-Kewley, 1987). Such factors cause some people to overreact repeatedly to stressors, thus setting the stage for psychophysiological dysfunctioning. Recently, for example, researchers have found that men with a "repressive" coping style (discomfort expressing anger and hostility) tend to experience a rise in blood pressure in response to mental stress tests (Vogele & Steptoe, 1993; Lai & Linden, 1992). Increased rates of asthma have also been found among those with a repressive coping style (DeAngelis, 1992).

Similarly, broad personality styles have been linked to certain psychophysiological disorders. In the most famous example of this kind, two cardiologists, Meyer Friedman and Raymond Rosenman (1959), introduced the concept of the Type A personality, mentioned above. People with this personality style are consistently hostile, cynical, driven, impatient, competitive, and ambitious, interacting with the world in a way that, according to Friedman and Rosenman, produces continual stress and often leads to coronary heart disease. People with a Type B personality style, by contrast, are thought to be more relaxed, less aggressive, and less concerned about time, and so less likely to experience cardiovascular deterioration.

The link between Type A personality style and coronary heart disease has been supported by numerous studies (Rosenman, 1990; Williams, 1989). In one well-known investigation of more than 3,000 subjects, Friedman and Rosenman (1974) separated healthy men in their 40s and 50s into Type A and Type B categories and then followed the health of the men over the next eight years. They found that when physiological factors such as cholesterol level were controlled for, more than twice as many Type A men developed coronary heart disease. Later studies found a similar relationship among women (Haynes et al., 1980). Recent studies have found a weaker link between this person-

*A currency dealer shouts orders during trading at the Paris Stock Exchange. The stresses of working in high-pressure environments apparently increase one's risk of developing a medical illness, including coronary heart disease.*

ality style and heart disease than earlier ones; however, it appears that some of the characteristics associated with the Type A style, particularly hostility, are indeed related to heart disease (Ironson et al., 1992; Mendes de Leon, 1992).

**Physiological Reactions**   We saw in Chapter 5 that when the brain stimulates body organs into action, it does so through the operation of the *autonomic nervous system (ANS)*, consisting of the many nerve fibers that connect the central nervous system to the body's organs. If we see a frightening animal, for example, a group of ANS fibers identified as the *sympathetic nervous system* increases its activity and prepares us for action by causing our heart to beat quickly, our respiration to speed up, and the like. As the danger passes, another group of ANS fibers known as the *parasympathetic nervous system* becomes more active in the reverse direction, slowing our heartbeat, respiration, and other bodily functions. Essentially, it calms down our functioning. These two subparts of the ANS are constantly working and complementing each other, helping our bodies to operate smoothly and stably (Selye, 1976, 1974; Cannon, 1927).

Because the ANS is at the center of stress reactions, defects in its operation are believed to contribute to the development of psychophysiological disorders (Stanford & Salmon, 1993; Friedman & Booth-Kewley, 1987). If, for example, one's ANS is stimulated too easily, it may keep overreacting to situations that most people find only mildly stressful, so that certain organs eventually become damaged. A psychophysiological disorder may then develop.

The ANS is not the only point of connection between stress and bodily reactions. Another is the *pituitary-adrenal endocrine system,* which when stimulated at times of stress causes the pituitary gland to secrete hormones that affect functioning throughout the body. If this system malfunctions, body organs may be overworked and damaged, and again a psychophysiological disorder may develop.

Local biological dysfunction also may contribute to psychophysiological disorders. People may, for example, have *local somatic weaknesses*—particular organs that are either defective or prone to dysfunction under stress (Rees, 1964). Those with a "weak" gastrointestinal system may be candidates for an ulcer. Those with a "weak" respiratory system may develop asthma.

Finally, organ dysfunction may also be caused by *individual biological reactions* to stress. Some people, for example, perspire in response to stress, others develop stomachaches, and still others experience a faster heartbeat or a rise in blood pressure. Although such variations are perfectly normal, the repeated activation of a "favored" system may wear it down and ultimately result in a psychophysiological disorder.

Clearly, then, psychophysiological disorders have strong ties to environmental stress, psychological reactions, and biological functions. The interaction of such factors was once considered an unusual occurrence that could *occasionally* lead to these particular disorders. As the years have passed, however, more and more illnesses have been added to the list of traditional psychophysiological disorders.

*Summing Up*
*Psychophysiological disorders are those in which both psychological and physiological factors interact to cause a medical problem. Clinicians have used a disregulation model to explain these disorders. Traditionally, only a limited number of disorders were thought to be psychophysiological, including ulcers, asthma, chronic headaches, hypertension, and coronary heart disease.*

## "New" Psychophysiological Disorders

For years physicians and clinicians believed that psychological stress could impair physical health only in the form of traditional psychophysiological disorders, but researchers have recently discovered that stress may contribute to other medical illnesses, particularly to viral and bacterial infections (see Box 8-1). This discovery came after numerous studies suggested a link between stress and susceptibility to illness in general.

## Box 8-1

### *Psychological Factors in Physical Illness: Has the Pendulum Swung Too Far?*
*Benjamin Blech*

(*This essay originally appeared in Newsweek, September 19, 1988.*)

It started with a terrible backache. That's when I realized how pervasive the new-age mentality has become. When I read that Shirley MacLaine, its leading practitioner, had convinced her devotees that people create their own reality—"You are God," she said—I assumed she meant nothing more by it than inspirational motivation. After all, isn't that what parents and preachers have been saying all along? Do your best. Aim high. Onward and upward. Every day in every way. . . .

Then I discovered the flip side of MacLaine's argument: if I'm sick, it must be my fault. If my life is a mess, I've failed to fulfill my potential. Real life isn't always perfect. Extrapolate from that to such realities as poverty and pestilence and you have what I view as a contemporary madness: for every misfortune in life, we seem too ready to blame the victim.

But first let me tell you what happened when my back went bad. Remember when sciatica could elicit at least a murmur of sympathy? Well, not anymore. Friends are now Freudians; everyone is "into" psychology. And when I shared the news that I have a herniated disc, all-knowing laymen looked at me and repeatedly asked: "Why are you letting stress get to you that much? Why are you doing this to yourself?"

Believe it or not, wear and tear, age and time, can actually cause damage to bodily parts and functions. Yet in these psychologically sophisticated times, the insight that illness is affected by the mind has so overwhelmed us that we often forget that it is also physical.

Some years ago Norman Cousins caused a considerable stir in medical circles when he attributed his recovery from a critical arthritic illness to extended exposure to humor. His conclusion deserved widespread circulation.

Laughter is good medicine. Feelings can foster health. Attitude may mean the difference between life and death. But—and here is the crucial cautionary that's often lost in the upbeat literature of our day—disease is still a cruel killer. Cancer victims who truly want to live do nevertheless die. Wishing doesn't necessarily alter dreadful conditions. Yet those who suffer with courage are now stigmatized for failing to recover—even viewed as if they were committing suicide.

I cannot forget the pain of my best friend in the weeks before he died. Sam faced his imminent demise with dignity. He was able to bear almost everything but he could not forgive himself for his illness. He had been led to believe by the apostles of new ageism, friends who embraced this cultural perspective, that he had failed. Failed, because if he had really wanted to, the purveyors of these Mary Poppins–style miracles assured him, he would certainly re-

---

Let us look first at how this link was established and then at the area of study known as *psychoneuroimmunology*, a new discipline that further ties stress and illness to the body's *immune system*.

## Stress and Susceptibility to Illness

In 1967 Thomas Holmes and Richard Rahe developed the Social Adjustment Rating Scale (see Table 8-2), a scale that assigned numerical values to the life stresses that most people experience at some time in their lives. On the basis of answers given by a large sample of subjects, the most stressful event on this scale was determined to be the death of a spouse, which receives a score of 100 *life change units* (*LCUs*). Lower on the scale is retirement (45 LCUs), and still lower is a minor violation of the law (11 LCUs). Even positive

events, such as an outstanding personal achievement, are somewhat stressful (28 LCUs). This scale gave researchers a yardstick for measuring the total amount of stress a person has experienced over a period of time.

The researchers then proceeded to examine the relationship between life stress (as measured in LCUs) and the onset of illness. They found that the total LCU scores of sick people during the year before they fell ill were much higher than those of healthy people (Holmes & Rahe, 1989, 1967). A particularly telling cutoff point was a score of 300 LCUs. If someone's life changes totaled more than 300 LCUs over the course of a year, that person was particularly likely to develop a serious health problem, in many cases a viral or bacterial infection.

In one study, Rahe (1968) divided 2,500 naval personnel into a high-risk group (the 30 percent with the

cover. Failed because if he would only try a bit harder he would rid himself of the poisons that were destroying his body. Failed because as a husband and father, his will to live should have overpowered and overcome everything.

Hope is a wonderful tonic, but I fear that these days exhortation has overcome compassion. The result is a kind of indifference and unwillingness to face the fact that some misfortunes will always persist, in spite of our best efforts:

People can be poor not because they didn't try hard enough to pull themselves out of their ghettos but because society really stacked the deck against them so that they literally didn't have a chance.

People can be uneducated because the teachers were not there, because the help which should have been given was not offered, because the "system" failed to work.

People can require welfare and food stamps because, in the words of President Kennedy, life is not fair and there are times when tragedy strikes uninvited and unexpected, even unavoidably.

People can be hungry not because they don't want to work but because the world turns its back on those with unproductive skills and then calls them parasites.

People can even be sick and really need a medical doctor, not a holistic health healer.

Carlyle was of course quite correct when he said, "The greatest of faults is to be conscious of none." Self-awareness demands recognition of personal failings. But it seems we have allowed the pendulum to swing too far. From the blind extreme of "It's always their fault" to the delusionary and self-destructive "It's always my fault," we have veered from truth in equal measure.

Ironically, our obsession with self-incrimination is a product of those very movements which promised peace of mind through an emphasis on personal accountability. Of course in the spirit of est we must "take responsibility for our lives." But must we take as our identities the scripts that all too often are simply handed us?

If I slip on a banana peel that somebody else carelessly left on the ground, I can curse my bad luck and get on with my life. But if I drop the peel myself and was stupid enough to slip on it too, then I will never forgive myself.

Perhaps the time has come for us to call an amnesty in the war on ourselves. No matter what the comic-strip character Pogo may have said, there are times when we have met the enemy—and it isn't us.

When I was a small boy, I loved the story of the little engine that kept telling itself it could and it did. Growing up has taught me that there are times when it can't and maturity demands awareness not only of our abilities, but also of our limits.

highest LCU scores over the previous six months) and a low-risk group (the 30 percent with the lowest LCU scores), and he kept track of the subsequent health changes of the two groups when they went to sea. Twice as many high-risk as low-risk subjects developed illnesses during their first month at sea; in addition, the high-risk group continued to develop more illnesses each month for the next five months.

Since Holmes and Rahe's pioneering work, stresses of various kinds have been tied to a wide range of diseases and physical conditions, from trench mouth and upper respiratory infection to cancer (Cooper & Faragher, 1991; Kiecolt-Glaser et al., 1991). The greater the life stress, the greater the likelihood of illness.

One shortcoming of the Social Adjustment Rating Scale is that it may not accurately measure the life stress of specific populations. In their development of the scale, Holmes and Rahe (1967) used a sample composed predominantly of white Americans. Less than 5 percent of the subjects were African American. But since their ongoing life experiences often differ in significant ways, might not African Americans and white Americans differ in their stress reactions to various kinds of life events? One study indicates that indeed they do (Komaroff et al., 1989, 1986). Both white and African Americans rank the death of a spouse as the most stressful life event, but African Americans experience greater stress from such events as a major personal injury or illness, a major change in work responsibilities, and a major change in living conditions than white Americans do. Such differences probably reflect the differences in the impact and meaning of such events in the lives of persons of the two groups.

Similarly, college students often face stressors that are different from those listed in the Social Adjustment Rating Scale (Crandall et al., 1992). Instead of having marital difficulties, being fired at work, or applying for a job, a college student may have trouble with a roommate, fail a class, or apply to graduate school. When researchers developed special scales to measure life events more accurately in this population (see Table 8-2), they found the expected correlations between stressful events and illness (Crandall et al., 1992).

### Consider This

The Social Adjustment Rating Scale has been subjected to a number of criticisms. One criticism focuses on the scale's assigning specific numbers to each major life event. Why might these numbers fail to provide a good index of the amount of stress the event actually causes for a particular individual?

## Psychoneuroimmunology

How is a stressful event translated into a viral or bacterial infection? Researchers have increasingly focused on our body's immune system as the key to this relationship and have developed a new area of study called **psychoneuroimmunology** to examine the links between stress, the immune system, and health.

The body's **immune system** is a complex network of cells that helps protect people from **antigens**—foreign invaders, such as bacteria and viruses, that stimulate an immune response—and from cancer cells. Among the most important cells in the system are billions of **lymphocytes,** white blood cells that are manufactured in the lymph system and circulate throughout the bloodstream. Upon stimulation by antigens, lymphocytes spring into action to help the body overcome the invaders.

One group of lymphocytes, called **helper T-cells,** identify antigens and then multiply and trigger the production of still other kinds of immune cells. Another group, **killer T-cells,** destroy body cells that have already been infected by viruses, thus helping to stop the spread of a viral infection. A third group of lym-

*These killer T-cells surround a larger cancer cell and destroy it, thus helping to prevent the spread of cancer.*

phocytes, **B-cells,** produce **antibodies,** or immunoglobulins, protein molecules that bind to a specific antigen, mark it for destruction, and prevent it from causing infection.

Researchers suspect that stress can interfere with the activity of lymphocytes and other cells of the immune system, slowing them down and thus increasing a person's susceptibility to viral and bacterial infections (Ader et al., 1991). This notion has been supported by numerous studies.

When laboratory animals are subjected to stressors of various kinds, their lymphocytes and antibodies reproduce more slowly than normal and destroy antigens less effectively (Maier et al., 1994; Hibma & Griffin, 1994). In one study, the immunological functioning of infant monkeys was reduced for up to two months after they had been separated from their mothers for a single day (Coe et al., 1987).

Similarly, a relationship has also been found between human stress, such as divorce, caregiving, and bereavement, and poor immunologic functioning (Maier et al., 1994; Kiecolt-Glaser & Glaser, 1992). In

---

*Psychoneuroimmunology*  The study of the connections between stress, the body's immune system, and illness.

*Immune system*  The sum of complex bodily systems that detect and destroy antigens.

*Antigen*  A foreign invader, such as a bacterium or virus, that stimulates an immune response.

*Lymphocytes*  White blood cells that are manufactured in the lymph system and circulate throughout the bloodstream, helping the body overcome antigens.

*Antibodies*  Bodily chemicals, produced by certain lymphocytes, that seek out and help destroy antigens.

## Table 8-2    *Most Stressful Life Events*

### Adults: "Social Adjustment Rating Scale" *

| | |
|---|---|
| 1. Death of spouse | 12. Pregnancy |
| 2. Divorce | 13. Sex difficulties |
| 3. Marital separation | 14. Gain of new family member |
| 4. Jail term | 15. Business readjustment |
| 5. Death of close family member | 16. Change in financial state |
| 6. Personal injury or illness | 17. Death of close friend |
| 7. Marriage | 18. Change to different line of work |
| 8. Fired at work | 19. Change in number of arguments with spouse |
| 9. Marital reconciliation | 20. Mortgage over $10,000 |
| 10. Retirement | 21. Foreclosure of mortgage or loan |
| 11. Change in health of family member | 22. Change in responsibilities at work |

### Students: "Undergraduate Stress Questionnaire" †

| | |
|---|---|
| 1. Death (family member or friend) | 12. Went into a test unprepared |
| 2. Had a lot of tests | 13. Lost something (especially wallet) |
| 3. It's finals week | 14. Death of a pet |
| 4. Applying to graduate school | 15. Did worse than expected on test |
| 5. Victim of a crime | 16. Had an interview |
| 6. Assignments in all classes due the same day | 17. Had projects, research papers due |
| 7. Breaking up with boy-/girlfriend | 18. Did badly on a test |
| 8. Found out boy-/girlfriend cheated on you | 19. Parents getting divorce |
| 9. Lots of deadlines to meet | 20. Dependent on other people |
| 10. Property stolen | 21. Having roommate conflicts |
| 11. You have a hard upcoming week | 22. Car/bike broke down, flat tire, etc. |

* Full scale has 43 items.
† Full scale has 83 items.
*Source:* Holmes & Rahe, 1967; Crandall et al., 1992.

a landmark study, R. W. Bartrop and his colleagues (1977) in New South Wales, Australia, compared the immune systems of twenty-six people whose spouses had died eight weeks earlier with those of twenty-six matched controls whose spouses had not died. Blood samples revealed that lymphocyte functioning was significantly lower in the bereaved subjects than in the control subjects.

These studies seem to be telling a remarkable story. The subjects have all been healthy individuals who happened to experience unusual levels of stress. During the stressful periods, they remained healthy on the surface, but their experiences were apparently slowing their immune systems so that they became susceptible to illness. If stress affects our body's capacity to fight off illness in this way, we can see why researchers have repeatedly found a relationship between life stress and medical illnesses of various kinds (see Box 8-2).

Researchers are now working to understand exactly *how* stress alters the immune system, and several have come to focus once again on the autonomic nervous system. As we saw earlier, stress leads to increased activity by the sympathetic nervous system. Studies suggest that this increased autonomic arousal is accompanied by the release of the neurotransmitters *norepinephrine* and *epinephrine* throughout the brain and body. Beyond supporting the activity of the sympathetic nervous system, these chemicals apparently help slow down the functioning of the immune system (Felten, 1993; Bellinger et al., 1992).

## Box 8-2

# *The Psychological Effects of HIV and AIDS*

The *human immunodeficiency virus (HIV)* is a parasite that leads to the death of its host cell. This virus infects T-4 helper lymphocytes, cells in the immune system that normally protect the body from disease (Batchelor, 1988). The lymphocytes in turn, transport the killer deep into the immune system. In many cases, HIV develops into *acquired immune deficiency syndrome (AIDS)*, a serious dismantling of the immune system. The progression from HIV infection to AIDS may take weeks, months, or even years (Kiecolt-Glaser & Glaser, 1988), and very little is known about how and why it occurs.

Most AIDS victims do not die of AIDS per se but instead succumb to infections that would not typically survive in the body if the immune system were not disabled. And because extreme stress, mental dysfunctioning, and environ-

mental pressures can adversely affect the general ability of the immune system to ward off illness, researchers have suspected that there may be a deadly interplay be-

tween the effect of suffering from HIV or AIDS on a person's mental health and the effect of that declining mental health on his or her physical well-being. For many years, the psychological suffering of people who are HIV-positive and people with AIDS was overlooked, but now it is an issue receiving serious attention from researchers and health-care workers alike.

Psychological disorders associated with HIV may be caused by factors that are either primarily organic or primarily psychological. The HIV may invade the brain, for example, causing *AIDS dementia complex (ADC)*, a disease that is characterized by a general decrement in cognitive functioning—that is, it takes longer to think or remember (Maj et al., 1994). In a vicious and fatal cycle, the patient's psychological well-being diminishes, causing

---

### Consider This

In the past, physicians failed to recognize that psychological factors often contribute to physical illness. Some observers now fear that today there may be too much emphasis on such factors. What problems might result from an overemphasis on the role of psychological factors in physical illness or from a simplistic application of the mind-body perspective?

Do stressful events inevitably slow the functioning of the immune system and lead to medical problems? Apparently not. It seems that various factors can influ-

ence the relationship between stress and the immune system, including perceptions of control, personality and mood, and social support.

## Perceptions of Control and Immune System Functioning

Researchers have found that perceptions of control may influence our vulnerability to immune system dysfunctioning. One study examined the immune reactions of rats who were being subjected to the stress of electric shock (Maier et al., 1985). The rats in the control group were repeatedly shocked in their cages but could learn to turn off the shocks by turning a

the immune system to weaken further. In severe cases, ADC can also result in deep lethargy, manic-depressive symptoms, and psychosis. Not a great deal is known about ADC, but some researchers believe that it may affect as many as 90 percent of AIDS sufferers and that it may be one of the earliest symptoms to develop (Price et al., 1988). Unfortunately, clinicians' unfamiliarity with ADC may interfere with its early detection.

Although not all HIV sufferers will develop ADC, almost all are subjected to a more subtle but equally destructive array of environmental stressors that lead to psychological problems and weaken their ability to fight disease. Society does not provide AIDS sufferers with a supportive environment in which to wage their war. Instead it attaches considerable stigma to the disease and to the people who contract it.

Surveys show that a large part of the population continues to view AIDS as a punishment being visited on a subset of the populace, primarily gay men and intravenous drug users (Herek & Glunt, 1988). The public disclosures of several famous people who contracted AIDS through means other than

homosexual contact or intravenous drug use encouraged AIDS activists to believe that this view would change. When, for example, Magic Johnson told the world he had HIV, many activists hoped that with him as a spokesperson, the treatment of other sufferers would improve. However, even this admired athlete lost lucrative endorsement contracts and found other professional players unwilling to face him on the court for fear of contracting AIDS. Clearly, even Magic Johnson was not safe from the repercussions of the public's angst over AIDS.

Because of such attitudes, patients with AIDS may face discrimination and even harassment, along with a decline in services that most of us take for granted, such as health insurance and police protection (Tross & Hirsch, 1988). Surveys show that these attitudes continue despite experts' proclamations that incidental contact with AIDS sufferers does not lead to infection (Herek & Capitanio, 1993). Prejudice and misunderstanding continue. Moreover, major social changes face the victims of AIDS, some of whom must also contend with the loss of friends through social pressure.

This kind of stress can lead to apathy, depression, preoccupation with the illness, anxiety-related disorders, and other such problems, all of which can directly affect the ability of the immune system to fight off the disease (Fleishman & Fogel, 1994). Once again, a vicious and fatal cycle of events.

Some people with HIV infection or AIDS have benefited from psychotherapy. In addition, certain drugs, such as *AZT* and *zidoduvine,* have been developed that may help fight ADC and other HIV-related diseases of the brain (Portegies et al., 1993). However, to fully address the psychological problems and disorders associated with HIV, we must learn to give the patient with AIDS what is available to all other sufferers of a terminal illness—compassion and hope. We can do so only by educating the public, and this is proving extraordinarily difficult to do. Millions of dollars have been spent to educate both youngsters and adults about AIDS (Jacobs, 1993), yet deeply felt prejudices continue to deprive patients with AIDS of an environment that might help their recovery rather than one that accelerates their death.

wheel in the cage. A second group of rats, the experimental group, were also shocked in their cages and could also turn a wheel in the cage, but their wheel-turning had no effect on the shocks; the shocks were delivered at random, whether the rats turned the wheel or not.

The experimenters then injected antigens into the bodies of the rats to see how their lymphocytes would react. The lymphocytes of the control rats multiplied just as they would under unstressful conditions. In the experimental rats, who had had no control over being shocked, lymphocytes multiplied more slowly than usual. In short, stress per se did not cause immunologic dysfunctioning; that occurred only when the

stress was accompanied by a perceived lack of control. Correspondingly, it appears that uncontrollable life change in humans is more closely linked to the onset of illness than controllable life change (Roll & Theorell, 1987).

## Personality and Mood and Immune System Functioning

Several theorists have proposed that people who generally respond to life stress with optimism, constructive coping strategies, and resilience may experience better immune system functioning and be better pre-

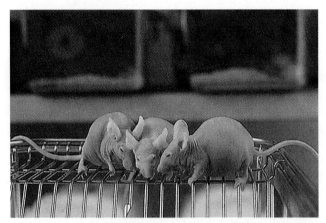

*Laboratory animals are widely used in research on the immune system. The destruction of the immune systems of these mice, which has caused their hair to fall out, enables researchers to produce and investigate various invasive cells and viruses.*

pared to fight off illness. As we observed in Chapter 6, some researchers have identified a "hardy" personality style, represented by people who welcome challenge and are willing to commit themselves and take control in their daily encounters (Maddi, 1990; Kobasa, 1990, 1987, 1979). According to various studies, people with a hardy personality are less likely than others to become ill after stressful events (Kobasa, 1984, 1982).

In a related line of research, the psychologist David McClelland and his associates have identified a personality style called the *inhibited power motive style* (McClelland, 1993, 1985). People who display this personality style are thought to have a strong need for power (the desire for prestige or influence over others) but have been taught to satisfy this need for power in indirect ways—by serving other people or worthy causes, for example, or by upholding high principles. People with inhibited power motives seem to be more likely than others to develop physical illnesses, particularly upper respiratory infections, in the face of academic and other power-related stresses (McClelland, 1993; Jemmott, 1987).

Numerous studies have also pointed out a correlation between certain personality characteristics and the prognosis of cancer patients (Anderson et al., 1994; Schulz, 1994; Levy & Roberts, 1992). These studies found that cancer patients who displayed a helpless coping style and who could not readily express their feelings, particularly anger, had a worse prognosis than patients who did express their emotions.

Lastly, research has also linked mood to immune system functioning. People whose mood is unhappy and depressed, even if they are not clinically de-

pressed, tend to have poorer immune system functioning (Perkins et al., 1991). It is not clear, however, whether depression causes poorer immune system functioning or whether poor immune functioning and its resultant viral infections help cause depression (Amsterdam & Hernz, 1993).

## Social Support and Immune System Functioning

Numerous studies have found that people who have few social supports and feel lonely have poorer immune functioning in the face of stress than people who do not feel lonely. In one such study, medical students were given the UCLA Loneliness Scale and then divided into "high" and "low" loneliness groups (Kiecolt-Glaser et al., 1984). The high-loneliness group showed lower lymphocyte responses during a final exam period. Similarly, a study of heart disease patients found that those who did not have anyone to talk to were three times more likely to die than those who did (Turkington, 1992; Williams et al., 1992).

Other studies have found that social support and affiliation actually help protect people from stress, poor immune system functioning, and subsequent medical illness (Cohen et al., 1992; Kiecolt-Glaser et al., 1991). Some studies have suggested, for example, that patients with certain forms of cancer who receive social support in their personal lives or supportive therapy often have a better prognosis than patients without such supports (Fawzy et al., 1995; Levy & Roberts, 1992).

The work of psychoneuroimmunologists suggests once again that the study of abnormal psychology must extend to behavior and illnesses that once seemed far removed from the clinical domain. Just as abnormal physical functioning may contribute to abnormal mental functioning, mental dysfunctioning may lead to physical problems of various kinds. At the same time, even an enlightened perspective such as this can be overstated and can lead to new misunderstandings about illness, as we were reminded in Box 8-1.

*Summing Up*
*Recently many "new" psychophysiological disorders, including viral and bacterial infections, have been added to the list. Stress can apparently slow down the immune system's functioning, leaving people more susceptible to various illnesses. The actual impact of stress on the immune system, however, is further affected by a person's perception of control, personality and mood, and social support.*

# Psychological Treatments for Physical Disorders

As clinicians have become more aware that psychological factors often contribute to physical disorders, they have increasingly used psychological interventions to help treat such disorders (Lehrer et al., 1993). The most common of these interventions have been relaxation training, biofeedback training, meditation, hypnosis, cognitive interventions, and insight therapy. The field of treatment that combines psychological and physical interventions to treat or prevent medical problems is known as *behavioral medicine* (Blanchard, 1994).

## Relaxation Training

As we saw in Chapter 5, people can be taught to relax their muscles at will, a process that also reduces feelings of anxiety. Clinicians believe that *relaxation training* can be of particular help in preventing or treating illnesses that are related to stress and heightened activity of the autonomic nervous system (Schneiderman & Baum, 1992).

Relaxation training, often in combination with medication, has been extensively used in the treatment of high blood pressure (Lehrer et al., 1993; Agras, 1984, 1974). Moreover, research has indicated that its positive effect persists for a year or more (Johnston, 1992). Relaxation training has also been of some help in treating headaches, insomnia, asthma, the undesired effects of cancer treatments, and Raynaud's disease, a disorder of the vascular system characterized by throbbing, aching, and pain (Bernstein & Carlson, 1993; Lehrer et al., 1993).

*Clinicians are always developing new techniques to help people relax. A climber dangles from Alaska's Mount Barrile to demonstrate the use of "Tranquilite" sleep goggles, which are supposed to induce relaxation with blue light and a soothing "pink sound."*

## Biofeedback Training

As we observed in Chapter 5, patients given *biofeedback training* are connected to machinery that gives them continuous data about their involuntary body activities. This information enables them gradually to gain control over those activities. Moderately helpful in the treatment of anxiety disorders, the procedure has also been applied to a growing number of physical disorders.

In one study, for example, electromyograph (EMG) feedback was used to treat sixteen patients who were experiencing facial pain caused in part by tension in their jaw muscles (Dohrmann & Laskin, 1978). In an

EMG procedure, electrodes are attached to a client's muscles so that the electrical activity that accompanies muscular contractions may be detected and converted into a tone for subjects to hear (see pp. 136–137). Changes in the pitch and volume of the tone indicate changes in muscle tension. After "listening" to EMG feedback repeatedly, experimental subjects learned how to relax their jaw muscles at will and later reported a decrease in facial pain. In contrast, control subjects showed little improvement in muscle tension or pain.

EMG feedback has also been used successfully in the treatment of tension headaches and muscular disabilities caused by strokes or accidents (Blanchard, 1994; Phillips, 1991). Other forms of biofeedback have been moderately helpful in the treatment of heart beat irregularities, asthma, migraine headaches, high blood

*Behavioral medicine* A field of study and treatment that combines psychological and physical concepts and interventions to better understand, treat, or prevent medical problems.

pressure, stuttering, pain from burns, and Raynaud's disease (Lehrer et al., 1993; Webster, 1991).

## Meditation

Although meditation has been practiced since ancient times, Western health-care professionals have only recently become aware of its effectiveness in relieving many forms of physical distress (Carrington, 1993). *Meditation* is a technique of turning one's concentration inward, achieving a slightly altered state of consciousness, and temporarily ignoring all stressors. In the most common approach, meditators go to a quiet place, assume a comfortable posture, utter or think a particular sound (called a *mantra*) to help focus their attention, and allow their minds to turn away from all ordinary thoughts and concerns (Carrington, 1993, 1978). Meditation is typically practiced in private for approximately 15 minutes twice a day. Many people who follow a regular schedule of meditation report feeling more peaceful, engaged, and creative; interacting more effectively with other people; and enjoying life more (Carrington, 1993, 1978; Schneider et al., 1992).

Meditation has been used to help manage pain in cancer patients (Goleman & Gurin, 1993) and to help treat high blood pressure, cardiovascular problems, asthma, the skin disorder psoriasis, diabetes, and even viral infections (Carrington, 1993, 1978; Shapiro, 1982). It has also been useful in relieving the stress-related problem of insomnia (Woolfolk et al., 1976) (see Box 8-3).

## Hypnosis

As we observed in Chapter 1, subjects who undergo *hypnosis* are guided by a hypnotist into a sleeplike, suggestible state during which they can be directed to act in unusual ways, to experience unusual sensations, to remember seemingly forgotten events, or to forget remembered events. With training some people are able to induce their own hypnotic state (*self-hypnosis*). Hypnosis is now used to supplement psychotherapy, to help conduct research, and to help treat many physical conditions (Barber, 1993, 1984).

Hypnosis is effectively used to control pain during surgical procedures (Evans & Stanley, 1991). One patient was reported to have undergone dental implant surgery under hypnotic suggestion (Gheorghiu & Orleanu, 1982): After a hypnotic state was induced, the dentist suggested to the patient that he was in a pleasant and relaxed setting listening to a friend de-

scribe his own success at undergoing similar dental surgery under hypnosis. The dentist then proceeded to perform a successful 25-minute operation.

Although only some people are able to undergo surgery when hypnotic procedures alone are used to control pain, hypnosis combined with chemical anesthesia is apparently beneficial to many patients (Wadden & Anderton, 1982). Given its effectiveness in reducing pain, hypnosis is also used frequently in the treatment of pain disorders. Hypnotic procedures have also been successfully applied to help combat such problems as skin diseases, asthma, insomnia, high blood pressure, warts, and other forms of infection (Barber, 1993; Agras, 1984).

## Cognitive Interventions

People with physical ailments have sometimes been taught new attitudes, or cognitive responses, toward their ailments as part of treatment. In particular, *self-instruction training,* also known as *stress inoculation training,* has helped patients to cope with chronic and severe pain reactions and disorders, including pain from burns, arthritis, surgical procedures, headaches, ulcers, multiple sclerosis, and cancer treatment (Meichenbaum, 1993, 1977, 1975). As we saw in Chapter 5, self-instruction therapists systematically teach clients to rid themselves of private negative statements ("Oh, no, I can't take this pain") and to re-

*"Dr. Birnes believes in the holistic approach."*

---

*Meditation* A technique of turning one's concentration inward and achieving a seemingly altered state of consciousness.

place them with private coping statements ("When pain comes, just pause; keep focusing on what you have to do").

## Insight Therapy

If stress and anxiety often contribute to physical problems, insight psychotherapy designed to reduce general levels of anxiety should help alleviate them (House et al., 1988; Varis, 1987). Thus, physicians often recommend insight psychotherapy to patients as an adjunct to medical treatment. Some recent research suggests that the discussion of past traumas may indeed have beneficial effects on one's health (Lutgendorf et al., 1994; Francis & Pennebaker, 1992). Moreover, a few studies have indicated that asthmatic children who receive individual or family therapy often adjust better to their life situations, experience less panic during asthma attacks, have fewer and milder attacks, and miss fewer days of school (Alexander, 1981). Beyond this small group of studies, however, the effectiveness of insight therapy in the medical domain has not been investigated systematically (Agras, 1984).

## Combination Approaches

A number of studies have found that the various psychological interventions for physical problems often are equal in effectiveness (Lehrer et al., 1993; Agras, 1984). Relaxation and biofeedback training, for example, are equally helpful (and more helpful than placebos) in the treatment of high blood pressure, headaches, asthma, and Raynaud's disease.

Psychological interventions are often of greatest help when they are combined both with other such treatments and with medical treatment (Lehrer et al., 1993; Lazarus, 1990; Maddi, 1990). In one study, for example, ulcer patients who were given relaxation, self-instruction, and assertiveness training along with medical interventions were found to be less uncomfortable, have fewer symptoms, be less anxious, and have a better long-term outcome than patients who received medication only (Brooks & Richardson, 1980). Similarly, studies have suggested that a combination of medical treatment, medical counseling, relaxation training, and cognitive therapy may lead to more personality and health improvements in Type A heart attack victims than does any one of these approaches alone (Johnston, 1992; Roskies et al., 1986; Friedman et al., 1984).

Clearly, the treatment picture for physical illnesses has been changing. Medical interventions continue to predominate, but the use of psychological techniques as adjuncts is clearly on the rise. Today's scientists and practitioners are traveling a course far removed from the path of mind-body dualism that once dominated medical thinking.

> ### Summing Up
> *Behavioral medicine combines psychological with physical interventions to treat or prevent medical problems. Psychological interventions such as relaxation training, biofeedback training, meditation, hypnosis, cognitive techniques, and insight therapy are increasingly being included in the treatment of various medical problems.*

## The State of the Field
## *Psychological Factors and Physical Disorders*

In recent years few subjects have wooed the attention of psychologists and clinical researchers more persuasively than the role of psychological processes in physical disorders. Once considered to be outside the field of abnormal psychology, these disorders are being seen increasingly as problems that fall squarely within its boundaries. Indeed, many clinicians now believe that psychological factors can contribute in some degree to the onset of virtually all physical ailments.

The number of studies devoted to the relationship between psychological dysfunction and physical illness has increased steadily during the past thirty years, and our knowledge of this topic has grown substantially. What researchers once saw as a vague tie between stress and physical illness is now understood more precisely as a complicated set of interrelationships involving such factors as individual psychological reactions to stress, dysfunction of the autonomic nervous system, activation of neurotransmitters, and suppression of the immune system.

Similarly, insights into treatment techniques have been accumulating rapidly in this area. Psychological approaches such as relaxation training and cognitive therapy are being applied increasingly in cases of physical impairment, usually in combination with traditional medical interventions. Although such approaches have yielded only modest results so far, clinicians are becoming convinced that psychological interventions will eventually play highly important roles in the treatment of many physical ailments.

Box 8-3

# Sleep and Sleep Disorders

Sleep is crucial to health and well-being. Without it people behave oddly and have strange experiences. Studies have found that sleep deprivation for 100 hours or more leads to hallucinations, paranoia, and bizarre behavior. When people who have gone without sleep attempt simple tasks, they find that their cognitive and motor functioning have deteriorated.

Physiological recordings indicate that when people remain awake for over 200 hours they frequently experience periods of "microsleep" lasting two to three seconds. It appears that the body refuses to be entirely deprived of sleep for extended periods. The odd effects of sleep deprivation are completely eliminated once a person is allowed a period of recovery sleep.

To study these phenomena, researchers bring people into the laboratory and record their activities as they sleep. One of the most important discoveries is that a person's eyes move rapidly during certain periods of the night (Aserinsky & Kleitman, 1953). This *rapid eye movement (REM)* occurs during approximately 25 percent of the time a person is asleep. The rest of the time, eye movements are either slow and regular or nonexistent.

Research on eye movement and brain activity has clarified that people normally cycle through five different stages during every hour and a half of sleep. Stages 1 through 4 are generally referred to as non-REM (NREM) to distinguish them from the unique activity of REM sleep (stage 5). As we

cycle through the five stages of sleep several times over the course of a night, we typically experience four to six periods of REM sleep. REM sleep is often called "paradoxical sleep" because it resembles both deep sleep and wakefulness. Although there are small movements and muscle twitches during REM sleep, the body is immobilized—essentially paralyzed. At the same time, the eyes are moving back and forth at a high rate. Blood flow to the brain increases, and the brain wave activity is almost identical to that of a waking and alert person. Eighty percent of the subjects who are awakened from REM sleep and asked about their experiences report that they were dreaming.

When we are deprived of enough sleep or if the normal sleep cycle is disrupted, we suffer. DSM-IV distinguishes the *dyssomnias,* sleep disorders involving disturbances in the amount, quality, or timing of sleep, from the *parasomnias,* disorders involving abnormal events that occur during sleep (APA, 1994). Some sleep disorders occur independent of other disorders; others occur in conjunction with a psychological or medical disorder, either as a result of the disorder itself or as an effect of drugs used to treat it.

## Dyssomnias

*Insomnia,* a disorder of initiating and maintaining sleep, is the most common dyssomnia. Over the course of each year between 30 and 40 percent of all adults experience difficulty falling and staying asleep, but only some of them qualify for a diagnosis of *primary insomnia,* in which this problem is their predominant complaint, lasts at least one month, and causes significant distress or impairment (APA, 1994). People with chronic insomnia are subject to periods of sleepiness or microsleep during the day, and their ability to function is often impaired. The causes of insomnia fall into five general categories:

1. *Biological factors.* Some researchers suggest that a biological predisposition to be a very light sleeper or to have an overactive arousal system may interfere with sleep (Hopson, 1986). In addition, some medical disorders can contribute to insomnia.

2. *Psychological disorders.* Many mental disorders, including depression and schizophrenia, are accompanied by difficulties in initiating and maintaining sleep.

3. *Lifestyle.* Sleeping late on weekends, sleeping in a room that is too hot or too cold, exercising just before going to sleep, ingesting too much caffeine, and other such habits may cause insomnia.

4. *Efforts to fall asleep.* People who experience difficulty in falling asleep may try virtually anything, including bedtime rituals, to do so. Unfortunately,

their behaviors may actually become a stimulus for not sleeping. Preparing for bed, thinking about sleeping, even counting sheep may condition the person to stay awake.

5. *Substance misuse.* Many people believe that alcohol and other drugs will help them fall asleep; however, sleeping pills and alcohol often have the opposite effect, leading to shallow sleep and abnormal REM periods (Murtagh & Greenwood, 1995).

A less common group of dyssomnias are disorders in which sleep or sleepiness are excessive or out of control. These include primary hypersomnia, narcolepsy, breathing-related sleep disorder, and circadian rhythm sleep disorder.

The predominant problem of the person with *primary hypersomnia* is excessive sleepiness for at least a month. The disorder may take the form of prolonged sleep episodes or daytime sleep episodes that occur almost daily (APA, 1994).

*Narcolepsy,* a disorder characterized by more than three months of irresistible attacks of REM sleep during waking hours, afflicts more than 200,000 people in the United States. The person's REM sleep is often brought on by strong emotion. Sufferers may find themselves suddenly experiencing REM sleep in the midst of an argument or during an exciting part of a football game.

*Breathing-related sleep disorder* is a dyssomnia in which sleep is frequently disrupted by a breathing disorder, causing excessive sleepiness or insomnia. The person with *sleep apnea,* the most common breathing disorder to cause this problem, found among 1 to 10 percent of the adult population (APA, 1994), actually stops breathing for up to 30 or more seconds while asleep. Sleep apnea is found predominantly in overweight men and is accompanied by heavy snoring. Hundreds of episodes may occur each night. During an episode, the trachea is partially or fully blocked and the diaphragm is unable to propel air out of the lungs, causing the heartbeat to slow and the brain to be deprived of oxygen. At the end of an episode, the person awakens very briefly and begins to breathe normally. Sufferers are often unaware of their disorder, but many report the extreme sleepiness during the day.

People with *circadian rhythm sleep disorder* experience excessive sleepiness or insomnia as a result of persistent or recurrent sleep disruptions brought about by a mismatch between the predominating sleep-wake schedule in their environment and their own circadian (daily) sleep-wake pattern. This dyssomnia may appear as a persistent pattern of falling asleep late and awakening late, a pattern of jet lag after repeated travel, or a pattern induced by night-shift work or frequent changes in work shifts.

## Parasomnias

*Nightmare disorder* is the most common of the parasomnias. Periodically during REM sleep, most people experience nightmares, or frightening dreams that awaken them, but their nightmares are usually infrequent and short-lived and do not affect normal functioning. In some cases, chronic nightmares persist and cause great distress and must be treated with psychotherapy or mild drug therapy. Such nightmares often increase when the people are under stress.

People with *sleep terror disorder*, another parasomnia, awaken suddenly during the first third of the night, screaming out in extreme fear and agitation. They are in a state of panic, are often incoherent, and have a heart rate to match. Generally the sufferer does not remember the episode the next morning. Sleep terrors most often appear in children between ages 4 and 12 years, and disappear on their own during adolescence. Approximately 1 to 6 percent of children experience them at some time (APA, 1994).

People with a *sleepwalking disorder* repeatedly leave their beds while asleep and walk around, without being conscious of the episode or remembering it later. The episodes usually occur in the first third of the night, and generally consist of sitting up, getting out of bed, and walking around, apparently with a specific purpose. People who are awakened while sleepwalking are confused for several moments. If allowed to continue sleepwalking, they eventually return to bed. Most people who sleepwalk manage to avoid obstacles, climb stairs, and perform complex activities, always in a seemingly emotionless and unresponsive state. Accidents do occur, however: tripping, bumping into objects, and even falling out of windows have all been reported. Approximately 1 to 5 percent of all children have this disorder at some time. As many as 30 percent of children have isolated episodes. The causes of sleepwalking are unknown, and it generally disappears by age 15 (APA, 1994).

Sleep and sleep disorders have caught the public interest in the last decade, and sleep research laboratories are now found in many major cities. Because sleep is so crucial in our lives, it is important to understand its underlying mechanisms. The sleep studies have implications not only for the treatment of sleep disorders and related psychological problems but for every human activity and endeavor.

The accumulating gains in this area are exciting less for their acknowledgment of psychological factors as causes of physical illness than for their emphasis on the interrelationship of the brain and the rest of the body. We have observed repeatedly that mental disorders are best understood and treated when both psychological and biological factors are taken into consideration. We now know that medical problems are also best explained by a focus on the way these factors interact.

## Chapter Review

1. **Somatic Illness and Psychological Factors:** Today's clinicians recognize that somatic, or bodily, illnesses can have psychological causes. Before the twentieth century, medical theory was dominated by *mind-body dualism,* or the belief that the mind and body were totally separate entities.

2. **Factitious Disorder:** Patients with a factitious disorder fake physical disorders in order to assume the role of a person with an illness.

3. **Somatoform Disorders:** Patients with a somatoform disorder have physical complaints whose causes are almost exclusively psychological. Unlike people with a factitious disorder, these sufferers believe that their illnesses are organic.

    A. **Hysterical Somatoform Disorders:** Hysterical somatoform disorders involve the actual loss or alteration of physical functioning. They include *conversion disorder, somatization disorder* (or *Briquet's syndrome*), and *pain disorder.*

    B. **Preoccupation Somatoform Disorders:** People with preoccupation somatoform disorders are preoccupied with the notion that something is wrong with them physically. In this category are *hypochondriasis,* which is characterized by unrealistic and fearful misinterpretations of bodily symptoms as signs of serious somatic diseases; and *body dysmorphic disorder,* characterized by intense concern that some aspect of one's physical appearance is defective.

    C. **Explanations for Somatoform Disorders:** Theorists explain preoccupation somatoform disorders much as they do specific phobias or panic disorders. Hysterical somatoform disorders, however, are viewed as unique disorders that are still poorly understood.

    D. **Treatments for Somatoform Disorders:** Therapy for preoccupation somatoform disorders includes exposure and response prevention and other treatments from the realm of anxiety disorders. Interventions for hysterical somatoform disorders emphasize either insight, suggestion, reinforcement, or confrontation.

4. **Psychophysiological Disorders:** Psychophysiological disorders are those in which both psychological and physiological factors interact to cause a medical problem. These disorders have been explained by the *disregulation model,* which proposes that our brain and body ordinarily establish *negative feedback loops* that guarantee a smooth operation of the body. When this system fails to regulate itself properly, psychophysiological problems may result.

    A. **Traditional Psychophysiological Disorders:** For years, clinical researchers singled out a limited number of physical illnesses as psychophysiological. These "traditional" psychophysiological disorders include *ulcers, asthma, chronic headaches, hypertension,* and *coronary heart disease.*

    B. **New Psychophysiological Disorders:** Recently many "new" psychophysiological disorders have been identified. Viral and bacterial infections and other health problems have been linked to high levels of stress. Scientists view the body's *immune system* as a key to the relationship between stress and such physical illnesses and have developed a new area of study called *psychoneuroimmunology.*

        (1) **The Immune System:** The body's immune system consists of *lymphocytes* and other cells which fight off *antigens*—bacteria, viruses, and other foreign invaders.

        (2) **Stress and the Immune System:** Stress can slow down lymphocyte activity, thereby interfering with the immune system's ability to protect against illness during times of stress.

        (3) **Other Factors and Immune System Vulnerability:** Other factors that seem to affect immune functioning include an individual's perception of control over life changes, personality and mood, and social support.

5. **Treatments for Physical Disorders:** *Behavioral medicine* combines psychological and physical interventions to treat or prevent medical problems. Psychological interventions such as relaxation training, biofeedback training, meditation, hypnosis, cognitive techniques, and insight therapy are increasingly being included in the treatment of various medical problems.

# Key Terms

mind-body dualism
psychogenic
malingering
factitious disorder
Munchausen syndrome
Munchausen syndrome
    by proxy
somatoform disorder
hysterical disorder
preoccupation disorder
conversion disorder
somatization disorder
Briquet's syndrome
pain disorder
glove anesthesia
hypochondriasis
body dysmorphic
    disorder

dysmorphophobia
Electra complex
primary gain
secondary gain
exposure and response-
    prevention
psychosomatic
psychophysiological
ulcer
asthma
chronic headache
muscle contraction
    headache
tension headache
aura migraine
    headache
hypertension
essential hypertension

coronary heart disease
coronary artery
myocardial infarction
disregulation
negative feedback loop
Type A personality style
Type B personality style
autonomic nervous system
    (ANS)
sympathetic nervous
    system
parasympathetic nervous
    system
pituitary-adrenal
    endocrine system
Social Adjustment Rating
    Scale
life change units

psychoneuroimmunology
immune system
antigen
lymphocyte
helper T-cell
killer T-cell
B-cell
antibody
"hardy" personality style
inhibited power motive
UCLA Loneliness Scale
behavioral medicine
relaxation training
biofeedback training
meditation
mantra
hypnosis
self-instruction training

# Quick Quiz

1. How do factitious disorders differ from somatoform disorders?

2. What are the symptoms of each of the hysterical somatoform disorders? How do diagnosticians distinguish hysterical disorders from "real" medical problems?

3. List the central features of each of the preoccupation somatoform disorders.

4. What are the leading explanations and treatments for the somatoform disorders? How well does research support them?

5. What are the key causes of ulcers, asthma, headaches, hypertension, and coronary heart disease?

6. What kinds of environmental, psychological, and biological factors appear to contribute to psychophysiological disorders?

7. What kinds of relationships have been found between life stress and physical illnesses? What scale has helped researchers to investigate this relationship?

8. Describe the relationship between stress, the immune system, and physical illness. Explain the specific roles played by lymphocytes.

9. Discuss how immune system functioning may be affected by a person's perceptions of control, personality and mood, and social support.

10. What psychological treatments have been used to help treat physical illnesses? To which specific illnesses have each of these treatments been applied? How effective are such approaches?

# 9

# Sexual Disorders and Gender Identity Disorder

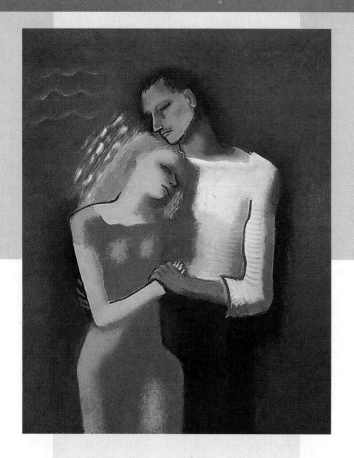

## Topic Overview

Few areas of functioning are of more interest to human beings than sexual behavior. Because sexual feelings are so much a part of our development and daily functioning, because sexual activity is so tied to the satisfaction of our basic needs, and because sexual performance is so linked to our self-esteem, sexual behavior is a major focus of both private thoughts and public discussions. Correspondingly, abnormal sexual behavior is of more interest to most people than almost all other forms of abnormal functioning. Most people are fascinated by the sexual problems of others and worry about the normality of their own sexuality.

There are two kinds of sexual disorders: sexual dysfunctions and paraphilias. People with *sexual dysfunctions* are unable to function normally in some area of the human sexual response cycle. They may not be able to become sexually aroused, for example, or to achieve orgasm. People with *paraphilias* experience recurrent and intense sexual urges or fantasies in response to sexual objects or situations that society deems inappropriate, and they may behave inappropriately as well. They may, for example, be aroused by sexual activity with a child or by exposure of their genitals to strangers, and may act on those urges. In addition to these sexual disorders, there is *gender identity disorder,* a sex-related disorder in which people persistently feel that they have been assigned to the wrong sex and in fact identify with the other gender.

## Sexual Dysfunctions

*Sexual dysfunctions* are disorders that make it difficult or impossible for an individual to have or enjoy coitus. The dysfunctions are typically very distressing to those who experience them, and often lead to sexual frustration, guilt about failure, loss of self-esteem, and interpersonal problems with the sex partner. Sexual dysfunctioning will be described here in the context of heterosexual couples in long-term relationships, because this is the context in which the majority of cases are seen in therapy. Both male and female homosexual couples are subject to the same dysfunctions, however, and therapists use the same basic techniques when they treat these couples (LoPiccolo, 1995).

The sexual response cycle consists of four phases: the desire, excitement, orgasm, and resolution phases (see Figure 9-1). Sexual dysfunctions typically affect

*Sexual dysfunction*  A disorder in which a person is unable to function normally in some area of the human sexual response cycle.

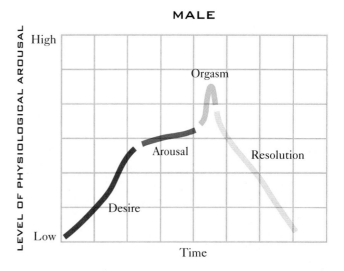

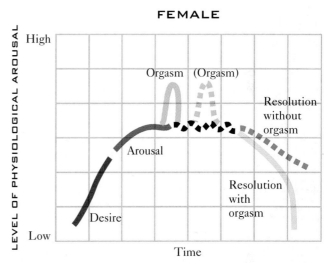

**Figure 9-1**  *Researchers have found a similar sequence of phases in the normal sexual response cycle of both males and females. Sometimes, however, women do not experience orgasm, which leads to a somewhat different resolution phase. And sometimes women experience two or more orgasms in succession before the resolution phase. (Adapted from Masters & Johnson, 1970, 1966; Kaplan, 1974.)*

one or more of the first three phases of the cycle. The resolution phase consists simply of the relaxation and decline in arousal that follow orgasm, and there are no sexual dysfunctions associated with it.

Some individuals have struggled with their sexual dysfunction their whole lives (labeled **lifelong type** in DSM-IV); in other cases the dysfunction was preceded by normal sexual functioning (*acquired type*). Similarly, in some cases the dysfunction is present during all sexual situations (*generalized type*); in others it is tied to particular situations (*situational type*) (APA, 1994).

# Disorders of the Desire Phase

The *desire phase* of the sexual response cycle consists of feeling an urge to have sex, having sexual fantasies or daydreams, and feeling sexually attracted to others. Two dysfunctions—*hypoactive sexual desire disorder* and *sexual aversion disorder*—are associated with the desire phase.

*Hypoactive sexual desire disorder* is characterized by a lack of interest in sex, and, as a result, a low level of sexual activity. When a person with hypoactive sexual desire does have sex, however, he or she often functions normally and may even enjoy the experience.

Some degree of hypoactive sexual desire is found in 20 to 35 percent of the general population of women (LoPiccolo, 1995); and in spite of the cultural stereotype that portrays all men as wanting all the sex they can get, it is found in about 15 percent of men as well (LoPiccolo, 1995; Spector & Carey, 1990). In fact, the number of men seeking therapy for this problem has increased markedly during the past decade or so (LoPiccolo & Friedman, 1988).

Precise figures on hypoactive sexual desire are elusive, however. DSM-IV defines this dysfunction as "deficient or absent sexual fantasies and desire for sexual activity," but it does not specify what a "deficient" level is. Age, number of years married, education, social class, ethnic background, and a number of other factors can all influence the frequency of sex. Moreover, frequency of sexual intercourse does not necessarily indicate level of desire. Table 9-1 shows the results of a survey of ninety-three happily married couples who were asked to report both the actual and the desired frequency of their sexual encounters. Their responses reveal a wide range of desired frequency and suggest that anything between once a day and twice a week is typical. Based on such results, it has been suggested that the diagnosis of hypoactive sexual desire disorder is not warranted unless a patient desires sex less frequently than once every two weeks (LoPiccolo & Friedman, 1988).

> ## Consider This
> Some theorists suggest that recent increases in the number of men receiving treatment for hypoactive sexual desire disorder may be linked to the impact of the women's movement. What factors might account for this relationship?

People with a *sexual aversion disorder* find sex actively unpleasant, often reporting feelings such as revulsion, disgust, anxiety, and fear. Aversion to sex seems to be quite rare in men and somewhat more common in women. Precise prevalence rates are, however, not available.

A person's sex drive is determined by a combination of biological and psychological factors, any of which may play a part in reducing sexual desire. Most cases of low sexual desire are attributable primarily to sociocultural and psychological factors, but certain biological conditions can also lower a person's sex drive significantly (Kresin, 1993).

## Biological Causes

A number of hormones help to produce the emotions and physiological changes involved in sexual desire and activity, and abnormalities in their levels can be a cause of low sex drive (Kresin, 1993; Segraves, 1988). For example, low levels of the male sex hormone *testosterone* can result in low sexual desire. Similarly, high levels of the hormone *prolactin* may interfere with sex drive in both men and women. And either high or low levels of the female sex hormone *estrogen* can result in low sex drive. Low sex drive has, for example, been linked to the high levels of estrogen contained in certain oral contraceptives and to insufficient levels of estrogen produced by post-menopausal women or by women who have recently given birth. It appears, however, that abnormal hormone levels are the cause of only a very small percentage of cases of hypoactive sexual desire disorder (Kresin, 1993; LoPiccolo & Friedman, 1988).

A number of drugs, both prescription and illicit, may also suppress sex drive (Nitenson & Cole, 1993; Buffum, 1992). These include medications for certain medical disorders, pain-reducing medications, some psychotropic drugs, and illicit drugs such as cocaine, marijuana, amphetamines, and heroin. Similarly, although low levels of alcohol may enhance sex drive by lowering psychological inhibitions, high levels will cause sexual feelings to diminish (Roehrich & Kinder, 1991). It is interesting that, while any number of drugs are known to suppress sex drive, centuries of searching have failed to find a true *aphrodisiac,* a substance that increases sex drive (Bancroft, 1989).

Not surprisingly, chronic physical illness can also suppress sex drive (Kresin, 1993; Bullard, 1988). A low sex drive can be the direct result of an illness, an

---

*Hypoactive sexual desire disorder*    A disorder characterized by a lack of interest in sex and hence a low level of sexual activity.

*Sexual aversion disorder*    A disorder characterized by an aversion to and active avoidance of genital sexual contact with a sexual partner.

Table 9-1    *Desired vs. Actual Frequency of Sexual Intercourse for Males and Females in 93 Happily Married Couples\**

| Frequency | Percentage Reporting as "Desired" | | Percentage Reporting as "Actual" | |
|---|---|---|---|---|
| | Males | Females | Males | Females |
| More than once a day | 12.2% | 3.3% | 2.2% | 1.1% |
| Once a day | 28.9 | 19.8 | 2.2 | 1.1 |
| 3–4 times a week | 42.4 | 50.6 | 35.6 | 39.6 |
| Twice a week | 12.2 | 16.5 | 30.0 | 24.2 |
| Once a week | 4.4 | 9.9 | 15.6 | 20.9 |
| Once every 2 weeks | 0 | 0 | 8.9 | 8.8 |
| Once a month | 0 | 0 | 2.2 | 2.2 |
| Less than once a month | 0 | 0 | 3.3 | 0 |
| Not at all | 0 | 0 | 0 | 0 |

\*Mean age, 34 for men, 32 for women; married mean of 9 years; mean number of children, 2.6; mean family income, $33,000.
*Source:* LoPiccolo & Friedman, 1988.

effect of medication, or the result of the stress, pain, or depression that may accompany a chronic illness.

## Sociocultural and Psychological Causes

A variety of sociocultural factors may contribute to hypoactive sexual desire and sexual aversion. For example, situational pressures such as divorce, a death in the family, job stress, or having a baby often lead to hypoactive sexual desire (Letourneau & O'Donohue, 1993; Kaplan, 1979).

Relationship problems are another sociocultural factor that may contribute to hypoactive sexual desire and sexual aversion. Simply being in an unhappy, conflicted relationship may suppress sex drive or make sex unpleasant. Similarly, people who feel powerless in their relationships and very dominated by their partner can lose sexual interest. Even in generally happy relationships, if one partner is a very unskilled, unenthusiastic lover, the other can begin to lose interest in sex. And sometimes partners in a relationship differ in their needs for closeness and "personal space." The one who needs more personal space may develop hypoactive sexual desire as a way of creating the necessary distance (LoPiccolo, 1995).

Contradictory cultural standards can also set the stage for hypoactive sexual desire and sexual aversion. For example, some men, having adopted our culture's double standard concerning the sexuality of women, are unable to feel sexual desire for a woman they love

and respect. They may lose sexual interest when their wife has their first child, as they cannot see a mother as a sexually exciting woman. More generally, because our society defines sexual attractiveness in terms of youth, many aging men and women lose interest in sex as their self-esteem and attraction to their partner diminish with age (LoPiccolo, 1995).

Psychological factors such as personal beliefs and fears about sex may also contribute to hypoactive sexual desire and sexual aversion. Cognitive theorists have noted that certain attitudes or fears are commonly held by people with these problems (LoPiccolo, 1995). Some have extreme antisexual religious beliefs, often the result of being raised in a strict religious culture. Others have an exaggeratedly hardworking and serious approach to life and think of sex as frivolous or self-indulgent. Some people with low sexual desire or with sexual aversion are afraid of losing control over their sexual urges and therefore suppress them completely. And still others have a fear of pregnancy.

Certain psychological disorders may also contribute to hypoactive sexual desire. Even a mild level of depression, for example, sometimes causes low sexual desire. In addition, some people with obsessive-compulsive characteristics find contact with another person's body fluids and odors to be unpleasant and aversive (LoPiccolo, 1995).

While any of these factors can lead to either hypoactive sexual desire or sexual aversion, the trauma of having been molested or assaulted is espe-

**BIZARRO**

*Psychological factors such as one's attitudes toward sex and nudity play major roles in human sexuality and can contribute to the development of sexual dysfunctions. (The "Bizarro" cartoon by Dan Piraro is reprinted by permission of Chronicle Features, San Francisco, CA. All rights reserved.)*

cially likely to result in sexual aversion (Browne & Finklehor, 1986). Research has indicated that sexual aversion is very common in victims of sexual abuse and persists for years, even decades, afterward (Jackson et al., 1990; Becker, 1989). In extreme cases, such individuals may experience vivid flashbacks during sexual activity, and visual memories of the assault overwhelm them.

## Disorders of the Excitement Phase

The *excitement phase* of the sexual response cycle is marked by a sense of sexual pleasure and general physical arousal; increases in heart rate, muscle tension, blood pressure, and respiration; and changes in the pelvic region. Blood pooling in the pelvis leads to erection of the penis in men and to swelling of the clitoris and labia and the production of vaginal lubrication in women. Dysfunctions affecting this phase are *female sexual arousal disorder* (once referred to as *frigidity*) and *male erectile disorder* (once called *impotence*).

### Female Sexual Arousal Disorder

Women with a sexual arousal disorder are repeatedly unable to attain or maintain sexual excitement, including adequate lubrication or genital swelling, during sexual activity (APA, 1994). Understandably, many also experience an orgasmic disorder (see pp. 248–249) or other sexual dysfunction along with this disorder. Studies have varied widely in their estimates of the prevalence of this disorder, ranging from 10 to 50 percent of women (LoPiccolo, 1995).

Because lack of sexual arousal is so often tied to orgasmic dysfunctioning, and because researchers usually study and explain these two problems together, we shall further examine the causes of the two disorders together in the section on female orgasmic disorder.

> ### Consider This
> The prevalence rates for sexual behavior are typically based on surveys of the general population. However, many people feel that sex is a private matter and refuse to participate in such surveys, and those who do comply tend to be more liberal, sexually experienced, and unconventional than the norm. What problems might this biased sample produce for researchers of sexual dysfunctioning?

### Male Erectile Disorder

Men with an erectile disorder experience a persistent inability to attain or maintain an adequate erection during sexual activity (APA, 1994). This problem occurs in about 8 to 10 percent of the general male population. Because of their association with several diseases that afflict older adults, erectile problems are most often seen in men over the age of 50 (Bancroft, 1989). The prevalence of erectile failure is 7 percent at age 40, 18 percent at age 60, 27 percent at age 70, and 76 percent at age 80 (Weizman & Hart, 1987).

Erectile problems are often caused by a combination of factors, as suggested by the following case history:

*Female sexual arousal disorder*    A female dysfunction characterized by a persistent inability to attain or maintain sexual excitement, including adequate lubrication or genital swelling, during sexual activity.

*Male erectile disorder*    A male dysfunction characterized by a persistent or recurrent inability to attain an erection or to maintain an erection during sexual activity.

Robert, a 57-year-old man, . . . had not had a problem with erections until six months earlier, when [he and his wife] attempted to have sex after an evening out, during which he had had several drinks. They attributed his failure to get an erection to his being "a little drunk," but he found himself worrying over the next few days that he was perhaps becoming impotent. When they next attempted intercourse, he found himself unable to get involved in what they were doing because he was so intent on watching himself to see if he would get an erection. Once again he did not, and they were both very upset. His failure to get an erection continued over the next few months. Robert's wife was very upset and sexually frustrated, accusing him of having an affair, or of no longer finding her attractive. Robert wondered if he was getting too old, or if his medication for high blood pressure, which he had been taking for about a year, might be interfering with erection. Robert was a heavy smoker and was overweight—two factors that contributed to his high blood pressure. When they came for sex therapy, they had not attempted any sexual activity for over two months.

*(LoPiccolo, 1995, p. 492)*

Many cases of male erectile disorder—perhaps the majority—involve some partial organic impairment of the erection response that then makes the man more vulnerable to the psychological factors that inhibit erection (LoPiccolo, 1985). A recent study found that only 10 of 63 cases of this disorder were caused by purely psychological factors, and only 5 were the result of organic impairment alone (LoPiccolo, 1991).

**Biological Causes**    The same hormonal abnormalities that can cause hypoactive sexual desire can also produce erectile problems. Again, however, these abnormal levels of testosterone, estrogen, prolactin, or thyroid hormones are found in only a small percentage of cases (Morales et al., 1991).

Vascular abnormalities are much more common biological causes of male erectile disorder. Since an erection occurs when the chambers in the penis fill with blood, conditions that reduce blood flow into the penis may be responsible, including heart disease and clogging of the arteries (Huws, 1991). Similarly, leakage of blood out of the penile chambers through holes or tears can also cause erectile failure, as can disease or damage to the nervous system from conditions such as diabetes, spinal cord injuries, or kidney failure, or treatment with an artificial kidney machine. As with hypoactive sexual desire, medications for a variety of ailments may also interfere with erection (Tanagho et al., 1988; Morrissette et al., 1993).

A number of medical procedures have been developed for identifying organic causes of an erectile disor-

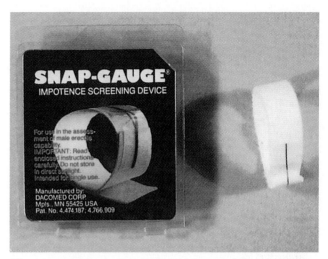

*The snap-gauge, worn around the penis at night, is a fabric band with three plastic filaments. If the filaments are broken in the morning, the man has experienced normal erections during REM sleep.*

der, including ultrasound recording and blood tests. Evaluation of **nocturnal penile tumescence (NPT)**, or erections during sleep, is very useful in assessing neurological causes (Schiavi et al., 1993). Men typically have erections during **rapid eye movement (REM) sleep**, the phase of sleep that corresponds with dreaming (see p. 236). A healthy man will have two to five REM periods each night, with perhaps two to three hours of penile erections (see Figure 9-2). Abnormal or absent nightly erections usually indicate some organic basis for erectile failure (Mohr & Beutler, 1990). As a rough screening device, a patient may be instructed to fasten a simple "snap gauge" band around his penis before going to sleep and then check the next morning. A broken band indicates that penile erection has occurred during the night. An unbroken band indicates a lack of nightly erections and suggests that the patient's general erectile difficulties may have an organic basis (Mohr & Beutler, 1990).

**Sociocultural and Psychological Causes**    Any of the sociocultural or psychological causes of hypoactive sexual desire, such as marital conflict or fear of closeness, can also interfere with arousal and lead to an erectile disorder. Some such issues, however, seem to be particularly associated with erectile disorders. In the sociocultural realm, for example, men who have lost their jobs and are under financial stress often develop erectile problems (Morokoff & Gillilland, 1993).

In addition, clinicians have noted two sexual-interaction patterns that often contribute to an erectile disorder (LoPiccolo, 1991). In one, the wife provides inadequate physical stimulation to her aging husband,

---

*Nocturnal penile tumescence (NPT)*    Erections during sleep.

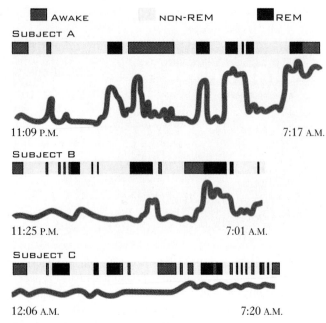

Figure 9-2   *Measurements of erections during sleep help reveal the sources of erectile problems. Subject A, a man without erectile problems, has normal erections during REM sleep. Subject B, a man with erectile failure problems, has some erections during REM sleep, suggesting that his dysfunctioning is not entirely organic. Subject C's male erectile disorder is related to organic problems, an interpretation supported by his lack of erections during REM sleep. (Adapted from Bancroft, 1985.)*

who, as a normal part of aging, now requires more intense, direct, and lengthy physical stimulation of the penis for erection to occur. In the second pattern, a couple believes that only intercourse can give the wife an orgasm. This idea increases the pressure on the man to have an erection and makes him more vulnerable to erectile failure. If the wife reaches orgasm manually or orally, she does not depend on his erection for her sexual gratification, and his performance pressure is reduced.

One of the most influential psychological explanations for erectile problems is a cognitive theory developed by the pioneering sex researchers William Masters and Virginia Johnson (1970). This explanation, which highlights the mechanisms of *performance anxiety* and the *spectator role,* has also received considerable research support (Barlow, 1986). Once a man begins to experience erectile problems, for whatever initial reason, he becomes fearful about failing to have an erection and worries during each sexual encounter. Instead of relaxing and enjoying the sensations of sex-

*Performance anxiety*   The fear of performing inadequately and a consequent tension experienced during sex.

*Spectator role*   A state of mind that some people experience during sex, focusing on their sexual performance to such an extent that their performance and their enjoyment are impeded.

ual pleasure, he remains somewhat distanced from the activity, watching himself and focusing on the goal of reaching erection. Instead of being an aroused participant, he becomes a self-evaluative spectator. Whatever the initial reason for the erectile problem, the resulting anxious, self-evaluative spectator role becomes the reason for the ongoing problem. In this self-perpetuating vicious cycle, the original cause of the erectile difficulty becomes less important than the continuing fear of failure.

> **Consider This**
> Some theorists cite performance anxiety and the spectator role as contributing factors in certain sexual dysfunctions. Are there other important areas of dysfunctioning in life that might also be explained by performance anxiety and the spectator role?

## Disorders of the Orgasm Phase

During the *orgasm phase* of the sexual response cycle, an individual's sexual pleasure peaks, and sexual tension is released as the muscles in the pelvic region contract rhythmically (see Figures 9-3 and 9-4). In men, semen is ejaculated, and in women the outer third of the vaginal wall contracts. Dysfunctions of this phase of the sexual response cycle are premature ejaculation, male orgasmic disorder, and female orgasmic disorder.

### Premature Ejaculation

Eddie's experience is typical of many men with premature ejaculation:

> Eddie, a 20-year-old student, sought treatment after his girlfriend ended their relationship because his premature ejaculation left her sexually frustrated. Eddie had had only one previous sexual relationship, during his senior year in high school. With two friends he would drive to a neighboring town and find a certain prostitute. After picking her up, they would drive to a deserted area and take turns having sex with her, while the others waited outside the car. Both the prostitute and his friends urged him to hurry up because they feared discovery by the police, and besides, in the winter it was cold. When Eddie began his sexual relationship with his girlfriend, his entire sexual history consisted of this rapid intercourse, with virtually no foreplay. He found caressing his girlfriend's breasts and genitals and her touching of his penis to be so arousing that he sometimes ejaculated before complete entry of the penis, or after at most only a minute or so of intercourse.
>
> *(LoPiccolo, 1995, p. 495)*

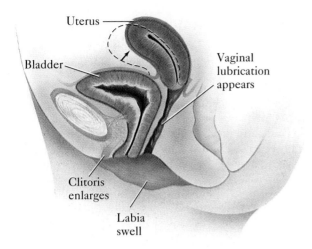

DESIRE

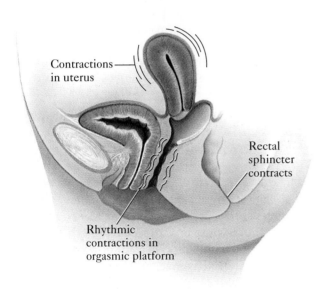

ORGASM

Figure 9-3   *Changes in the female sexual anatomy during the desire and the orgasm phases of the sexual response cycle. (Adapted from Hyde, 1990, p. 200.)*

In the dysfunction of **premature ejaculation,** a man reaches orgasm and ejaculates with minimal sexual stimulation before, on, or shortly after penetration and before he wishes it (APA, 1994). The rates of premature ejaculation found in surveys of the general population have varied between 10 and 38 percent, probably because definitions of the problem vary (LoPiccolo, 1995; Hunt, 1974; Kinsey et al., 1948). It appears that the typical duration of intercourse in our society has increased dramatically over the past several decades, increasing in turn the distress of men who

suffer from premature ejaculation, typically men under the age of 30 (Bancroft, 1989).

**Explanations of Premature Ejaculation**   Behavioral explanations of premature ejaculation have received the most compelling research support. As in the case of Eddie, this dysfunction seems to be typical of young, sexually inexperienced men who simply have not learned to slow down, modulate their arousal, and prolong the pleasurable process of making love. In fact, premature ejaculation is a normal experience for young men having their first sexual encounters. With continued sexual experience, most acquire greater control over their sexual responses. Men who have sex only infrequently are also prone to ejaculate prematurely (LoPiccolo, 1985).

Clinicians have also suggested that premature ejaculation may in addition be related to heightened anxiety, rapid masturbation experiences during adolescence (trying to avoid being "caught" by parents), or inaccurate perceptions of one's own sexual arousal. However, none of these theories has received clear research support (Strassberg et al., 1990, 1987; Heiman et al., 1986).

## Male Orgasmic Disorder

In *male orgasmic disorder,* a man repeatedly is unable to reach orgasm or is delayed significantly in reaching orgasm following normal sexual excitement. The disorder, also referred to as *inhibited male orgasm, inhibited ejaculation, ejaculatory incompetence,* or *retarded ejaculation* by sex therapists, is relatively uncommon, occurring in 1 to 3 percent of the population (Dekker, 1993).

**Explanations of Male Orgasmic Disorder**   A number of biological factors can inhibit ejaculation. A low testosterone level, certain neurological diseases, and some head injuries can interfere (LoPiccolo, 1995, 1985). Drugs that inhibit arousal of the sympathetic nervous system, such as alcohol, certain medications for high blood pressure, some antidepressants, and many antianxiety and antipsychotic medications can also inhibit ejaculation (Bancroft, 1989). For example, the widely prescribed antidepressant *fluoxetine,* or Prozac, appears to inhibit ejaculation to some degree in 15 to 25 percent of men who take it (Norden, 1994; Nitenson & Cole, 1993; Buffum, 1992).

A leading psychological cause of male orgasmic disorder appears to be performance anxiety and the spec-

---

*Premature ejaculation*   A dysfunction in which a man reaches orgasm and ejaculates before, on, or shortly after penetration and before he wishes it.

*Male orgasmic disorder*   A male dysfunction characterized by a repeated absence of or very long delay in reaching orgasm following normal sexual excitement.

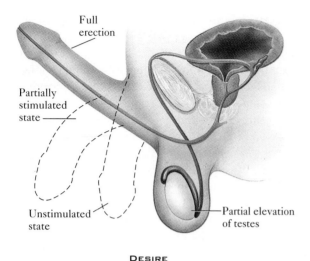

Full erection

Partially stimulated state

Unstimulated state

Partial elevation of testes

DESIRE

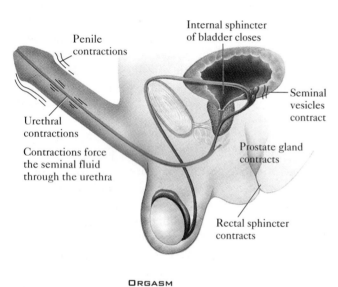

Penile contractions

Internal sphincter of bladder closes

Seminal vesicles contract

Urethral contractions

Contractions force the seminal fluid through the urethra

Prostate gland contracts

Rectal sphincter contracts

ORGASM

Figure 9-4    *Changes in the male sexual anatomy during the desire and the orgasm phases of the sexual response cycle. (Adapted from Hyde, 1990, p. 199.)*

tator role, the cognitive factors also involved in erectile disorder. Once a man begins to focus on reaching orgasm, he stops being an aroused participant in his sexual activity and instead becomes a sexually unaroused, self-critical, and fearful observer (LoPiccolo, 1995). A few studies also suggest that men who do not ejaculate have generally high levels of anxiety and hostility, but this relationship has not been found consistently in other research (Dekker, 1993).

Finally, inhibited ejaculation may also grow from hypoactive sexual desire (LoPiccolo & Friedman, 1988). A man who engages in sex primarily because of pressure from his partner, without any real desire for sex, simply may not get aroused enough to reach orgasm.

## Female Orgasmic Disorder

Stephanie and Bill, married for three years, came for sex therapy because of her total lack of orgasm.

> Stephanie had never had an orgasm in any way, but because of Bill's concern, she had been faking orgasm during intercourse until recently. Finally she told him the truth, and they sought therapy together. Stephanie had been raised by a strictly religious family. She could not recall ever seeing her parents kiss or show physical affection for each other. She was severely punished on one occasion when her mother found her looking at her own genitals, at about age 7. Stephanie received no sex education from her parents, and when she began to menstruate, her mother told her only that this meant that she could become pregnant, so she mustn't ever kiss a boy or let a boy touch her. Her mother restricted her dating severely, with repeated warnings that "boys only want one thing." While her parents were rather critical and demanding of her (asking her why she got one B among otherwise straight A's on her report card, for example), they were loving parents and their approval was very important to her.
>
> (LoPiccolo, 1995, p. 496)

In *female orgasmic disorder,* also called **inhibited female orgasm,** a woman repeatedly fails to experience an orgasm or repeatedly experiences a very delayed orgasm following normal sexual excitement (APA, 1994). Studies indicate 10 to 15 percent of women today have never had an orgasm, either when alone or during intercourse, and another 10 to 15 percent only rarely experience orgasm (LoPiccolo, 1995). Research also suggests that around 50 percent of women experience orgasm in intercourse at least fairly regularly (LoPiccolo & Stock, 1987).

Most clinicians agree that orgasm during intercourse per se is not critical to normal sexual functioning, provided a woman can reach orgasm with her partner during direct stimulation of the clitoris, for example, through caressing by her partner (LoPiccolo, 1995). Evidence suggests that women who have "clitoral" orgasms are entirely normal and healthy (Stock, 1993; LoPiccolo & Stock, 1987).

Sigmund Freud (1905) began the controversy about what constitutes sexual health for women when he proposed that orgasms in response to vaginal stimulation are more mature and healthy than those emerging from stimulation of the clitoris. Modern sex therapists are, however, virtually unanimous in rejecting Freud's ideas about clitoral and vaginal orgasms. Scientists now know that in comparison with the clitoris, the

*Female orgasmic disorder*    A female dysfunction characterized by a repeated absence of or very long delay in reaching orgasm following normal sexual excitement.

vagina is poorly supplied with nerve endings (Kinsey et al., 1953). The clitoris and penis both develop from the same structure in the embryo, so expecting a woman to lose clitoral sensitivity makes as much sense as expecting a man's sexual focus somehow to switch from his penis to his scrotum (LoPiccolo, 1995). Masters and Johnson (1966) have shown that there actually is no difference between a "clitoral" and a "vaginal" orgasm. When orgasm occurs during vaginal intercourse, it does so primarily because of indirect stimulation of the clitoris.

As we observed earlier, female orgasmic disorders typically are linked to female arousal disorders, and the two are investigated, explained, and treated together (APA, 1994). Once again, biological, sociocultural, and psychological factors have been cited in these disorders.

**Biological Causes** A number of physiological conditions can affect a woman's arousal and orgasm. One example is diabetes, which can damage the nervous system in ways that interfere with arousal, vaginal lubrication, and orgasm. Similarly, lack of orgasm has sometimes been linked to multiple sclerosis and other neurological diseases, to the same medications and drugs that inhibit ejaculation in men, and to postmenopausal changes in skin sensitivity and in the structure of the clitoris and the vaginal walls (Morokoff, 1993, 1988). Several theories have also linked female orgasm to the size or location of the clitoris, the strength of the pelvic muscles, and similar factors, but research has failed to support these ideas (Stock, 1993; LoPiccolo & Stock, 1987).

**Sociocultural and Psychological Causes** For years, many clinicians have embraced the sociocultural belief that female arousal and orgasmic disorders are largely the result of society's recurrent message to women that they should suppress and deny their sexuality. In support of this position, most inorgasmic women in treatment report that they, like Stephanie, were raised in a sexually restrictive manner, suggesting that factors such as religious upbringing, punishment for childhood masturbation, lack of preparedness for the onset of menstruation, restrictions placed on adolescent dating, and being told that "nice girls don't" may indeed help cause orgasmic dysfunctioning (Masters & Johnson, 1970).

Research has also demonstrated, however, that this kind of history is just as common among women without a sexual arousal or orgasmic disorder (LoPiccolo & Stock, 1987; Morokoff, 1978). Moreover, negative cultural messages about female sexuality have been declining in recent years, while the prevalence of

female arousal and orgasmic disorders remains stable. Thus, clinicians are still left with the question of why some women and not others develop sexual arousal and orgasmic dysfunctions. A number of studies have tied the problems to several specific kinds of events, traumas, or relationships.

First, it appears that the various factors listed earlier as causes of hypoactive sexual desire and sexual aversion may also contribute to female arousal and orgasmic disorders. For example, 50 to 75 percent of women molested as children or raped as adults have arousal and orgasmic dysfunctions (Browne & Finklehor, 1986).

Second, as psychodynamic theorists might predict, memories of childhood traumas and relationships have sometimes been associated with female arousal and orgasmic problems. In one large study, memories of an unhappy childhood or loss of a parent during childhood were sometimes associated with lack of orgasm in adulthood (Raboch & Raboch, 1992). In another, childhood memories of a positive relationship with one's mother, affection between parents, the mother's positive personality qualities, and the mother's expression of positive emotions were all shown to be related to functional orgasm (Heiman et al., 1986).

Third, research has linked orgasmic behavior to the quality of a woman's intimate relationships. In one study, the likelihood of reaching orgasm was tied to the degree of emotional involvement and the length of the relationship at the time of each subject's first experiences of coitus, the pleasure she obtained during that experience, her current attraction to her partner's body, and marital happiness (Heiman et al., 1986). Interestingly, the same study found that use of sexual fantasies during sex with the current partner was much more common in orgasmic than in nonorgasmic women.

## Sexual Pain Disorders

Two sexual dysfunctions do not fit neatly into a specific phase of the sexual response cycle. These are the sexual pain disorders, *vaginismus* and *dyspareunia,* in which sexual activity causes extreme physical dysfunctioning or discomfort.

### Vaginismus

In **vaginismus,** involuntary contractions of the muscles around the outer third of the vagina prevent entry of the penis. Severe cases can result in "unconsummated marriage," which means that a couple has never been

---

*Vaginismus* A condition marked by involuntary contractions of the muscles around the outer third of the vagina, preventing entry of the penis.

able to have intercourse. Little data is available on the prevalence of this disorder. While perhaps 20 percent of women occasionally experience pain during intercourse, vaginismus probably occurs in less than 1 percent of the population (LoPiccolo, 1995).

**Explanations of Vaginismus**    Most clinicians agree with the cognitive-behavioral view that vaginismus is a conditioned fear response, set off by anticipation that vaginal penetration will be painful and damaging. A variety of factors can apparently set the stage for this fear, including anxiety and ignorance about sexual intercourse, exaggerated stories about how painful and bloody the first occasion of intercourse is for women, trauma caused by an unskilled lover who forces his penis into the vagina before the woman is aroused and lubricated, and, of course, the trauma of childhood sexual abuse or adult rape (LoPiccolo, 1995).

Some women experience painful intercourse because of an infection of the vagina or urinary tract or a gynecological disease such as herpes simplex, or after menopause. As a result, they may develop a "rational" vaginismus: the insertion of the penis will indeed cause them pain unless they receive medical treatment for these conditions (LoPiccolo, 1995).

Most women who have vaginismus also experience other sexual dysfunctions, but this is not always the case. Some enjoy sex, have a high sex drive, and reach orgasm through clitoral stimulation. Their negative emotions are specific to a fear of vaginal penetration.

## Dyspareunia

In *dyspareunia* (from Latin words meaning "painful mating"), the person experiences severe pain in the genitals during sexual activity. Dyspareunia occasionally occurs in men, but it is much more common in women. Precise prevalence rates are not known, however.

**Explanations of Dyspareunia**    Dyspareunia in women usually has a physical cause, the most common being injury during childbirth to the vagina, cervix, uterus, or pelvic ligaments (Sarrel & Sarrel, 1989). Similarly, the scar left by an episiotomy (a cut often made to enlarge the vaginal entrance and ease delivery) can be a source of pain. Other reported causes have included the penis hitting remnants of the hymen; vaginal infection; wiry pubic hair abrading the labia during intercourse; pelvic diseases; tumors; cysts; and allergic reactions to the chemicals in vaginal douches, contraceptive creams, the rubber in condoms or diaphragms, or the protein in male semen

*Most middle-aged and elderly women and men remain capable of sexual performance and orgasms, although the speed and intensity of their sexual response may lessen somewhat.*

(LoPiccolo & Stock, 1987). Women who suffer from organically caused dyspareunia typically enjoy sex and get aroused, but find their sex life severely hindered by the pain that accompanies what used to be a positive event.

Dyspareunia that is caused entirely by psychological factors is rare, and in fact most such diagnoses represent a mistake by a gynecologist or therapist (LoPiccolo & Stock, 1987). Those cases that are truly psychogenic are actually, in general, the direct result of a lack of sexual arousal. That is, penetration into an unaroused, unlubricated vagina is painful.

### Summing Up

*Sexual dysfunctions typically affect one or more phases of the sexual response cycle. Hypoactive sexual desire disorder and sexual aversion disorder affect the desire phase; female sexual arousal disorder and male erectile disorder are disorders of the excitement phase; and premature ejaculation, male orgasmic disorder, and female orgasmic disorder are problems of the orgasm phase. Most of these disorders may be caused by a combination of sociocultural, psychological, and biological factors, although premature ejaculation is usually attributable entirely to sociocultural and psychological factors.*

*There are also two sexual pain disorders: vaginismus and dyspareunia. Dyspareunia usually occurs in women and in most cases has a primary physical cause.*

---

*Dyspareunia*    A disorder in which a person experiences severe pain in the genitals during sexual activity.

## Treatments for Sexual Dysfunctions

The last twenty years have brought significant changes in the treatment of sexual dysfunctions. For the first half of this century, the major approach was long-term Freudian psychoanalysis, on the assumption that sexual dysfunctioning was caused by failure to progress through the psychosexual stages of childhood development. This approach, an attempt to bring about broad personality changes, was generally unsuccessful (Bergler, 1951).

In the 1950s and 1960s, behavioral therapists offered alternative treatments for sexual dysfunctions. Usually, they tried to reduce the anxieties that they believed were causing sexual dysfunctions, using procedures such as relaxation and systematic desensitization (Lazarus, 1965; Wolpe, 1958). Those approaches were moderately successful but failed to work for clients whose sexual dysfunction was characterized by misinformation, negative attitudes, and lack of effective sexual technique.

*The extensive research, theories, and clinical reports of William Masters and Virginia Johnson have dramatically changed the way clinicians understand and treat sexual functioning and dysfunctioning.*

A revolution in the treatment of sexual dysfunctions occurred with the publication of Masters and Johnson's book *Human Sexual Inadequacy* in 1970. Their treatment, known as "sex therapy," has evolved into a complex approach combining cognitive, behavioral, communication skill–building, and related techniques. Modern sex therapy is short term, directive in nature, and focused on specific sexual problems. It typically lasts fifteen to twenty sessions. The eminent sex therapist and researcher Joseph LoPiccolo (1995) has summarized six components of modern sex therapy:

1. *Assessment and conceptualization of the problem.* Patients initially receive a medical examination and are interviewed concerning their "sex history." The emphasis during the interview is on understanding past life events and, in particular, current factors that are causing the dysfunction.
2. *Education about sexuality.* Many patients who suffer from sexual dysfunctions know very little about the anatomy, physiology, and technique of sexual activity. Sex therapists supplement their patients' knowledge through discussions, instructional books and videotapes, and educational films.
3. *Changing problematic attitudes, cognitions, and beliefs.* Therapists help patients to examine and change the false beliefs about sexuality that may be preventing their sexual arousal and pleasure. Some widespread myths about male and female sex roles are listed in Box 9-1.
4. *Elimination of performance anxiety and the spectator role.* Therapists teach couples **sensate focus** and **nondemand pleasuring**, "petting" exercises in which they explore and caress each other's bodies at home, without demands to have intercourse or reach orgasm. Initially, couples are told to refrain from intercourse or genital caressing at home and instructed that sexual activity is to be restricted to kissing, hugging, and sensual massage of various body parts, not including breasts or genitals. Over successive weeks, their sexual repertoire is gradually rebuilt, with a constant emphasis on enjoying the experience of sensual pleasure and not striving for results.
5. *Increasing communication and the effectiveness of sexual technique.* Couples are told to use their sensate focus sessions at home to try sexual positions in which the person being caressed can guide the other's hands and regulate the speed, pressure, and location of the caressing. Couples are also taught to

*Sensate focus* A treatment for sexual disorders that instructs couples to take the focus away from orgasm or intercourse and instead spend time concentrating on mutual massage, kissing, and hugging.

give verbal instructions in a nonthreatening, informative manner ("It feels better over here, with a little less pressure"), rather than a threatening uninformative manner ("The way you're touching me doesn't turn me on").

6. *Changing destructive lifestyles and interactions.* Therapists suggest that couples rearrange their priorities, and have their sexual interactions and sensate focus sessions at times when they are relaxed, not when tired or under time pressure. Similarly, if the couple's general relationship is lacking or in conflict, the therapist will try to help them improve the relationship.

In addition to these widely applicable approaches, therapists have developed specific techniques for treating each particular kind of sexual dysfunction.

## Hypoactive Sexual Desire and Sexual Aversion

Therapists often use a combination of techniques to help clients overcome low sexual desire or sexual aversion (LoPiccolo & Friedman, 1988). In one of these techniques, called **affectual awareness,** patients visualize sexual scenes in an effort to uncover feelings of anxiety, vulnerability, and other negative emotions about sex. In another, patients receive cognitive self-instruction training and learn to generate "coping statements" that help them change such negative emotions. A typical statement might be, "I can allow myself to enjoy sex; it doesn't mean I'll lose control."

Therapists may also use several behavioral approaches to help heighten patients' sex drive. They may, for example, have patients keep a "desire diary" in which they record sexual thoughts and feelings, read books and view films with erotic content, and develop sexual fantasies. Pleasurable shared activities, such as dancing and walking together, are also encouraged, to help strengthen feelings of sensual enjoyment and sexual attraction.

For sexual aversion resulting from sexual assault or childhood molestation, additional procedures may include encouraging the patient to remember, talk, and think about the assault until such memories are no longer traumatic. Or the patient may be instructed to write mock letters to or have a mock dialogue with the molester, in order to finally express the feelings of rage and powerlessness the assault created.

Such programs have been helpful to both women and men with hypoactive sexual desire and sexual aversion disorders. Studies find that most clients treated with a combination of these techniques eventually have intercourse more than once a week (Schover & LoPiccolo, 1982).

*"When I touch him he rolls into a ball."*

## Male Erectile Disorder

Treatment for an erectile disorder includes special techniques to help reduce a man's performance anxiety and increase his stimulation. The couple is typically instructed to add the **tease technique** to their non-demand sensate focus sessions at home; if the man gets an erection in response to his partner's caressing, they stop until he loses it. This exercise teaches the couple that erections occur naturally in response to stimulation, as long as they focus on his enjoyment rather than his performance. Other exercises show them that he does not have to have a rigid penis to accomplish entry and that there are many ways for him to help his partner achieve orgasm (LoPiccolo, 1995).

When major physical problems underlie a man's erectile disorder, a physical intervention is often needed. A common approach is surgical implantation of a **penile prosthesis,** which produces an artificial erection. This device consists of a semirigid rod made of rubber and wire. This approach is expensive, but over 25,000 are installed each year in the United States (LoPiccolo, 1991). A less expensive, nonsurgical approach to erectile disorder is the use of a **vacuum erection device (VED),** consisting of a hollow cylinder that is placed over the penis. The man uses a hand pump to pump air out of the cylinder, thus drawing blood into his penis and producing an erection (Aloni et al., 1992; Turner et al., 1991). Finally, for some kinds of organically caused erectile disorders, the injection of drugs to dilate the arteries in the penis may be useful (Wagner & Kaplan, 1993).

---

*Penile prosthesis*    A surgical implant consisting of a semirigid rod made of rubber and wire that produces an artificial erection.

*Vacuum erection device (VED)*    A nonsurgical device that can be used to produce an erection. It consists of a hollow cylinder that is placed over the penis and connected to a hand pump.

## Male Orgasmic Disorder

Like treatment for an erectile disorder, sex therapy for male orgasmic disorder includes techniques to help reduce performance anxiety and ensure adequate stimulation. Often, for example, the couple is instructed that during sex the penis is to be caressed manually until the man is aroused, but that stimulation is to stop whenever he feels he might be close to having an orgasm. This paradoxical instruction helps reduce anxiety about performance and allows the man to enjoy the sexual pleasure provided by the caressing.

When the male orgasmic disorder is caused by organic factors such as undesired effects of a medication or neurological damage or injury, treatment may include medical approaches such as a drug to increase arousal of the sympathetic nervous system (Murphy & Lipshultz, 1988).

> ### Consider This
> A key technique in sex therapy is to have a couple explore and caress each other's bodies (sensate focus) while refraining from orgasm or intercourse. Why might people become more aroused during sexual caressing if they are prohibited from reaching orgasm or having intercourse?

## Premature Ejaculation

Premature ejaculation has been treated with enormous success by direct behavioral retraining procedures (Masters & Johnson, 1970; Semans, 1956). In the *stop-start,* or *pause,* procedure, the penis is manually stimulated until the man is fairly highly aroused. The couple then pause until his arousal subsides, and then the stimulation is resumed. This sequence is repeated several times before stimulation is carried through to ejaculation, so the man ultimately experiences much more total time of stimulation than he has ever experienced before and learns to have a higher threshold for ejaculation (LoPiccolo, 1995). The couple then progress to putting the penis in the vagina, making sure to withdraw it and to pause whenever the man becomes too highly aroused. Typically, the couple is able to enjoy prolonged intercourse without any need for pauses after two or three months of treatment (LoPiccolo, 1995).

## Female Arousal and Orgasm Dysfunctions

Specific treatment techniques for female arousal and orgasmic dysfunctions include self-exploration, body awareness, and directed masturbation training (Heiman & LoPiccolo, 1988). These procedures are especially useful for women with generalized and lifelong lack of orgasm.

In *directed masturbation training,* a woman is taught in a step-by-step manner how to masturbate effectively and, eventually, how to reach orgasm during sexual interactions. The training includes the use of diagrams and reading material, self-stimulation, erotic material and fantasies, role playing, sensate focus with one's partner, and sexual positioning that allows stimulation of the clitoris during intercourse.

This training program has been found to be very effective: Over 90 percent of women learn to have an orgasm during masturbation, about 80 percent during caressing by their partner, and about 30 percent during intercourse (Heiman & LoPiccolo, 1988). It can be administered in group or individual therapy or through a self-help book and instructional videotape (LoPiccolo, 1990).

As we saw earlier, a lack of orgasm during intercourse is not necessarily a sexual dysfunction, provided the woman enjoys intercourse and can reach orgasm when her partner caresses her. For this reason, straightforward reassurance about their normality may be the most effective approach for women whose only concern is situational lack of orgasm during intercourse (LoPiccolo, 1995).

## Vaginismus

Treatment for vaginismus takes place on two fronts. First, women may practice contracting and relaxing the muscle that surrounds the vagina, until they have acquired voluntary control over their vaginal muscles. Second, they may receive gradual behavioral exposure treatment to help them overcome their fear of penetration, beginning by inserting increasingly large dilators in their vagina at home and at their own pace, and ending with the insertion of the partner's penis. Over 90 percent of the women treated for vaginismus eventually have pain-free intercourse (Beck, 1993; LoPiccolo, 1990).

## Dyspareunia

When a case of dyspareunia has a known, physical cause, such as the presence of scars or lesions, a couple may be taught intercourse positions that avoid putting pressure on the injured area. When the pain results from an arousal problem instead, treatment consists of general sex therapy and the specific procedures used to treat female arousal and orgasmic problems (Quevillon, 1993). Of course, many cases of dyspareunia are actually caused by undiagnosed physical problems, making a gynecological exam by an expert in this area essential (Reid & Lininger, 1993).

## Box 9-1

# Sex-Role Myths

### Myths of Male Sexuality

1. *Men should not have certain emotions.* Men believe they are supposed to be strong, aggressive, competitive, unemotional, and in control. All of these emotions interfere with the tenderness, closeness, sensuality, openness, and emotional expressiveness that contribute to good sex.

2. *In sex, it's performance that counts.* Men take a goal-oriented approach to sex, equating erections and orgasm with success, and are unable to relax and enjoy sex as a pleasurable process rather than as an end to be achieved.

3. *The man must take charge and orchestrate sex.* Men who think this way do not let the woman guide them to do what she likes to have done to her. This attitude also leads a man to focus on what he is doing to the woman, rather than learning to receive pleasure from what she does to him.

4. *A man always wants and is always ready to have sex.* This myth pressures men to try to have sex in situations or relationships in which they are not emotionally comfortable, with predictably unpleasant results.

5. *All physical contact must lead to sex.* This notion prevents men from simply enjoying kissing, hugging, cuddling, and caressing, as they see these activities as only a prelude to "the real thing."

6. *Sex equals intercourse.* This myth is especially destructive to men with erectile problems. If a man and his partner can derive sexual pleasure and orgasm from manual or oral genital caressing, any performance anxiety that might interfere with erection will be greatly reduced.

7. *Sex requires an erection.* This is a corollary to myth #6. The truth is that the penis is not the only sexual part of the man's body, and couples can have very pleasurable sex without an erection.

8. *Good sex is a linear progression of increasing excitement terminated only by orgasm.* Acceptance of this myth eliminates the pleasure of leisurely, playful sex, which may include breaks to talk, rest, and enjoy each other fully as people rather than as just genital organs.

9. *Sex should be natural and spontaneous.* This myth prevents couples from teaching each other what they like during sex. For today's typical couple, with both partners working, sharing child-rearing responsibilities, and living high-stress lives, it is often necessary to make very nonspontaneous plans for sex, designating a time when both are likely to be relaxed, not exhausted, and capable of responding sexually.

10. *In this enlightened age, myths 1–9 no longer have any influence on us.* While the sexual liberalization of the past thirty years has eliminated some sexual inhibitions, it has caused us to worry much more about being good enough at sex and to strive to emulate the supersexual role models in current literature, films, and music.

(LoPiccolo, 1995; Zilbergeld, 1978)

### Myths of Female Sexuality

1. *Sex is only for women under 30.* Many women don't reach their

### Summing Up

*Contemporary sex therapy combines a variety of cognitive, behavioral, communication skill-building, and related techniques. The treatment program may include a careful assessment, patient education, attitude changes, sensate focus exercises to help eliminate performance anxiety and the spectator role, improvements in communication and sexual technique, and couple therapy. In addition, specific techniques have been developed for each of the sexual dysfunctions.*

# Paraphilias

**Paraphilias** are disorders characterized by recurrent and intense sexual urges, fantasies, or behaviors involving either nonhuman objects, children, nonconsenting adults, or experiences of suffering or humiliation. According to DSM-IV, the diagnosis should be applied only when the urges, fantasies, or behaviors last at least six months and cause great distress or impairment in social, occupational, or other important

*Paraphilias* Disorders characterized by recurrent and intense sexual urges, fantasies, or behaviors involving either nonhuman objects, children, nonconsenting adults, or experiences of suffering or humiliation.

peak of sexual responsiveness until their mid-30s, and there is no real decline thereafter.

2. *Normal women have an orgasm every time they have sex.* Even for easily orgasmic women, the average rate of orgasm per sexual experience is 70 to 80 percent.

3. *All women can have multiple orgasms.* Research indicates that 20 percent of women are multiply orgasmic. There is no relationship between sexual adjustment or satisfaction and the number of orgasms a woman has each time she has sex.

4. *Pregnancy and delivery reduce women's sexual responsiveness.* While discomfort during the last months of pregnancy and just after delivery can temporarily inhibit sex, the increased blood supply to the pelvis that develops during pregnancy can actually increase sexual responsiveness.

5. *A woman's sex life ends with menopause.* While vaginal dryness can interfere with enjoyment of intercourse in some postmenopausal women who do not receive estrogen therapy, many women, freed from concerns about contraception and pregnancy, experience increased sexual arousal and interest after menopause.

6. *There are different kinds of orgasm related to a woman's personality. Vaginal orgasms are more feminine and mature than clitoral orgasm.* An orgasm is an orgasm, not a personality trait.

7. *A sexually responsive woman can always be turned on by her partner.* Fatigue, anger, worry, and many other emotions suppress sexuality in even the most responsive women.

8. *Nice women aren't aroused by erotic books or films.* Research indicates that women are just as aroused by erotica as men are.

9. *You are frigid if you don't like the more exotic forms of sex.* Many very sexual women aren't interested in oral or anal sex, sex toys such as vibrators, or group sex.

10. *If you can't have an orgasm quickly and easily, there's something wrong with you.* The threshold for orgasm varies naturally among women. Just as some women can run faster than others, some have orgasm more rapidly.

11. *Feminine women don't initiate sex or become wild and unrestrained during sex.* This is a holdover of the Victorian double standard.

12. *Double jeopardy: you're frigid if you don't have sexual fantasies and a wanton woman if you do.* Many, but not all, sexually responsive women do have sexual fantasies.

13. *Contraception is a woman's responsibility, and she's just making up excuses if she says contraceptive issues are inhibiting her sexually.* Many highly sexual women find their sexual enjoyment interfered with by contraceptive technology. Many couples who feel their families are complete find vasectomy to be a good solution.

(LoPiccolo, 1995; Heiman & LoPiccolo, 1988)

areas of functioning (APA, 1994). Many people with a paraphilia can become aroused only when a paraphiliac stimulus is present, acted out, or fantasized about. Other people seem to need the paraphiliac stimulus only occasionally, as during times of stress. People with one kind of paraphilia often display others as well (Abel & Osborn, 1992).

Actually, relatively few people receive a formal diagnosis of paraphilia, but the large market in paraphiliac pornography and other items leads clinicians to suspect that the disorders may be quite prevalent (APA, 1994). People whose paraphilias involve children or nonconsenting adults often wind up in legal trouble and come to the attention of professionals in that way. Those who do receive a diagnosis are almost always men. Theorists have proposed various explanations for paraphilias and applied various treatments to them (Stein et al., 1992; Fedoroff, 1992). Overall, however, research has revealed relatively little about the causes of and possible treatments for most of these disorders (APA, 1994).

## Fetishism

The key feature of *fetishism* is recurrent and intense sexual urges, fantasies, or behaviors that involve the

---

*Fetishism* A paraphilia consisting of recurrent and intense sexual urges, fantasies, or behaviors that involve the use of a nonliving object, often to the exclusion of all other stimuli.

use of a nonliving object, often to the exclusion of all other stimuli. Usually the disorder begins in adolescence (APA, 1994). Almost anything can be a fetish object; women's underwear, shoes, and boots are particularly common (APA, 1994; Raphling, 1989). Some people with fetishism commit petty theft for the purpose of collecting as many of the objects of their desire as possible. The objects may be touched, smelled, worn, or used in some other way while the person masturbates, or the individual may ask the partner to wear the object when they have sex. In the nineteenth century, Richard von Krafft-Ebing ([1886] 1975) described one such case:

> A lady told Dr. Gemy that in the bridal night and in the night following her husband contented himself with kissing her, and running his fingers through the wealth of her tresses. He then fell asleep. In the third night Mr. X produced an immense wig, with enormously long hair, and begged his wife to put it on. As soon as she had done so he richly compensated her for his neglected marital duties. In the morning he showed again extreme tenderness, whilst he caressed the wig. When Mrs. X removed the wig she lost at once all charm for her husband. . . . The result of this marriage was, after five years, two children and a collection of 72 wigs.

Researchers have not been able to pinpoint the causes of fetishism. Psychodynamic theorists have proposed that fetishes are defense mechanisms to help the person avoid the anxiety associated with normal sexual contact. Their efforts to translate this explanation into an effective psychodynamic treatment, however, have met with relatively little success (LoPiccolo, 1992).

Behaviorists have proposed that fetishes are acquired through classical conditioning. In one behavioral study, male subjects were shown a series of slides of nude women interspersed with slides of boots (Rachman, 1966). After numerous trials, the subjects became aroused by the boot photos alone. If early sexual experiences similarly occur in conjunction with a particular object, the stage may be set for development of a fetish.

Behaviorists have sometimes treated fetishism with *aversion therapy* (Kilmann et al., 1982). In one study, an electric shock was administered to the arms or legs of subjects with fetishes while they imagined their objects of desire (Marks & Gelder, 1967). After two weeks of therapy all subjects in the study showed at least some improvement. In another aversion technique, *covert sensitization,* persons with fetishism are guided to imagine the pleasurable but unwanted object and repeatedly to pair this image with an imagined

aversive stimulus, until the object of erotic pleasure is no longer desired.

Another behavioral treatment for fetishism is *masturbatory satiation* (Quinsey & Earls, 1990; Marshall & Lippens, 1977). In this method, the client masturbates to orgasm while fantasizing aloud about a sexually appropriate object, then switches to fantasizing in detail about fetishistic objects while masturbating and continues to elaborate on the fetishistic fantasy for an hour. The procedure is meant to produce a feeling of boredom, which in turn becomes associated with the fetishistic object.

Yet another behavioral approach to fetishism, also used for other paraphilias, is *orgasmic reorientation,* which conditions clients to new, more appropriate sources of erotic stimulation: they are shown conventional stimuli while they are responding to other unconventional objects. For example, a man with a shoe fetish may be instructed to obtain an erection from pictures of shoes and then to begin masturbating to a picture of a nude adult. If he starts to lose the erection, he must return to the pictures of shoes until he is masturbating effectively, then change back to the picture of the nude adult. All focus should be on the conventional stimulus when orgasm becomes imminent.

## Transvestic Fetishism

*Transvestic fetishism,* also known as *transvestism* or *cross-dressing,* is characterized by recurrent and intense sexual urges, fantasies, or behaviors that involve dressing in clothes of the opposite sex. The typical person with transvestism, almost always a heterosexual male, begins cross-dressing in childhood or adolescence (APA, 1994). He is the picture of characteristic masculinity in everyday life, and cross-dresses only in relative privacy. A small percentage of such men cross-dress to visit bars or social clubs. Some wear a single item of women's apparel, such as underwear or hosiery, under their masculine clothes. Others wear makeup and dress fully as women. Many married men with transvestism involve their wives in their cross-dressing behavior (Kolodny et al., 1979). A number report high

---

*Masturbatory satiation*   A behavioral treatment in which a client masturbates for a prolonged period of time while fantasizing in detail about a paraphiliac object. The procedure is expected to produce a feeling of boredom that in turn becomes associated with the object.

*Orgasmic reorientation*   A procedure for treating certain paraphilias by conditioning clients to respond to new, more appropriate sources of erotic stimulation.

*Transvestic fetishism*   A paraphilia consisting of recurrent and intense sexual urges, fantasies, or behaviors that involve dressing in clothes of the opposite sex.

*"Crossroads" is a self-help group for men with transvestic fetishism, a recurrent need to dress in women's clothing as a means to achieve sexual arousal.*

levels of marital discord, which is often independent of the cross-dressing behavior (Wise et al., 1991). Transvestic fetishism is often confused with transsexualism, but, as we shall observe shortly, the two are entirely separate disorders.

The development of transvestic fetishism sometimes seems consistent with the behavioral principles of operant conditioning. Several case studies describe individuals who were reinforced for cross-dressing as children, openly encouraged and supported by parents or other adults for this behavior. In one case, for example, a woman was delighted to discover that her young nephew enjoyed dressing in girls' clothes; she had al-

*The big "secret" in the popular 1992 movie* The Crying Game *was that the sultry and alluring character Dil is a man with transsexualism. More than a cross dresser, Dil felt as if he had been assigned to the wrong sex and he wanted to be a woman in every possible way.*

ways wanted a niece, and she proceeded to buy him dresses and jewelry and sometimes dressed him as a girl and took him out shopping.

## Exhibitionism

A person with *exhibitionism* has recurrent sexually arousing urges to expose or fantasies of exposing his genitals to another person, almost always a member of the opposite sex, and may carry out the fantasies or urges (APA, 1994; Abel, 1989). Further sexual activity with the other person is not usually attempted or desired. What is often desired, however, is a reaction of shock or surprise. Sometimes a so-called flasher will frequent a particular neighborhood, or exhibit at particular hours. Urges to expose themselves typically intensify when people with this disorder have free time or are under significant stress (Abel, 1989).

Generally, the disorder begins before age 18, and most such individuals are males (APA, 1994). Persons with exhibitionism are immature in their approaches to the opposite sex and have difficulty in interpersonal relationships. Over half are married, but their sexual relationships with their wives are typically not satisfactory (Blair & Lanyon, 1981; Mohr et al., 1964). Many have doubts or fears about their masculinity, and some apparently have a strong bond to a possessive mother.

Treatment is the same as for other paraphilias, including aversion therapy and masturbatory satiation, possibly combined with orgasmic reorientation, social skills training, or psychodynamic therapy (LoPicolo, 1992; McNally & Lukach, 1991). One unusual, apparently successful version of aversion therapy pairs the unpleasant smell of valeric acid with images of self-exposure (Maletzky, 1980). Clinicians have also reported some success with hypnotherapy (Polk, 1983; Epstein, 1983).

## Voyeurism

A person who engages in *voyeurism* has recurrent and intense sexual desires to observe unsuspecting people in secret as they undress or to spy on couples engaged in intercourse, and may carry out these desires. The risk of being discovered often adds to the person's excitement. The individual generally does not seek to have sex with the person being spied on (APA, 1994).

*Exhibitionism*  A paraphilia in which persons have recurrent sexually arousing urges to expose or fantasies about exposing their genitals to another person, and may act upon those urges or fantasies.

*Voyeurism*  A paraphilia in which a person has recurrent and intense sexual desires to observe unsuspecting people in secret as they undress or to spy on couples engaged in intercourse, and may act upon these desires.

People with voyeurism may masturbate either during the act or when thinking about it afterward. The vulnerability of the people being observed and the probability that they would feel humiliated if they found out are often part of the individual's enjoyment. Voyeurism usually begins before the age of 15 and tends to be chronic (APA, 1994).

Elements of both exhibitionism and voyeurism can play a role in normal sexuality, but if so they are engaged in with the consent or understanding of the partner. The clinical disorder of voyeurism is marked by the repeated invasion of another person's privacy. Some people with voyeurism are unable to have normal sexual interplay; others, however, maintain normal sexual relationships apart from their voyeurism.

Many clinicians believe that people with voyeurism are seeking by their actions to exercise power over others, possibly because they feel inadequate or are sexually or socially inhibited. Psychodynamic theorists have explained voyeurism as an attempt to reduce castration anxiety, originally generated by the sight of an adult's genitals. Theoretically, those with voyeurism are repeating the behavior that produced the original fright, so they can be reassured that there is nothing to fear (Fenichel, 1945). Behaviorists explain the disorder as a learned behavior that can be traced to a chance and secret observation of a sexually arousing scene. If such observations are repeated on several occasions in conjunction with masturbation, a voyeuristic pattern may develop.

## Frotteurism

A person who exhibits *frotteurism* has recurrent and intense sexual urges or fantasies about touching and rubbing against a nonconsenting person, and may act on these urges or fantasies. Frottage (from French *frotter*, to rub) is usually committed in a crowded place, such as a subway or a busy sidewalk (APA, 1994). The person, almost always a male, may rub his genitals against the victim's thighs or buttocks or fondle her genitalia or breasts with his hands. Typically he fantasizes during the act that he is having a caring relationship with the victim (APA, 1994).

Frotteurism usually begins in adolescence or earlier, often after the person observes others committing an act of frottage. After the person reaches the age of 25, the acts gradually decrease and often disappear (APA, 1994).

## Pedophilia

A person who is subject to *pedophilia,* literally "love of children," has recurrent and intense sexual urges or fantasies about watching, touching, or engaging in sexual acts with prepubescent children, usually those 13 years old or younger, and may carry out these urges or fantasies. Some persons with this disorder are satisfied by child pornography; others are driven to watching, fondling, or engaging in sexual intercourse with children (Barnard et al., 1989). Some persons with pedophilia are attracted only to children *(exclusive type);* others are attracted to adults as well *(nonexclusive type)* (APA, 1994).

One study found that 4 percent of pedophilia victims are 3 years old or younger, 18 percent are 4 to 7 years old, and 40 percent are 8 to 11 (Mohr et al., 1964). In addition, studies suggest that the victim usually knows the molester and that 15 to 30 percent of sexual molestation cases are incestuous (Gebhard et al., 1965; Mohr et al., 1964). Both boys and girls can be pedophilia victims, but there is some evidence that three-quarters of them are girls (Koss & Heslet, 1992).

People with pedophilia usually develop their disorder during adolescence. Many were themselves sexually abused as children (McCormack et al., 1992). It is not unusual for them to be married and to have sexual difficulties or other frustrations in life that lead them to seek an arena in which they can be masters. Alcohol abuse is another factor that figures prominently in many cases (Rada, 1976).

Some clinicians suggest that immaturity is often the primary cause of this disorder (Groth & Birnbaum, 1978). Social and sexual skills may be underdeveloped, so that the person feels intense anxiety at the very thought of a normal sexual relationship. Some persons with pedophilia also display faulty thinking, such as "It's all right to have sex with children as long as they agree" (Abel et al., 1984).

Most offenders with pedophilia are imprisoned or forced into treatment if they are caught. After all, they are committing child sexual abuse when they approach a child. Treatments include those already mentioned for other paraphilias, such as aversion therapy, masturbatory satiation, and orgasmic reorientation (LoPiccolo, 1992; Enright, 1989).

There is also a cognitive-behavioral treatment for pedophilia: *relapse-prevention training.* Modeled after the relapse-prevention programs used, as we shall see,

---

*Frotteurism*    A paraphilia consisting of recurrent and intense sexual urges, fantasies, or behaviors that involve touching and rubbing against a nonconsenting person.

---

*Pedophilia*    A paraphilia in which a person has recurrent and intense sexual urges or fantasies about watching, touching, or engaging in sexual acts with prepubescent children, and may carry out these urges or fantasies.

in the treatment of substance dependence, this approach helps clients to identify the problematic situations that typically trigger their pedophilic fantasies and actions (such as depressed mood or distorted thinking) and to develop strategies to avoid or cope more effectively with those situations, thus preventing the pedophilic behavior (LoPiccolo, 1992; Pithers, 1990). One study of 147 people with pedophilia found only a 4 percent relapse rate over a five-year period among offenders who received this treatment (Pithers & Cumming, 1989). Relapse-prevention training has also been applied in cases involving other paraphilias.

## Sexual Masochism

*Sexual masochism* is a pattern characterized by recurrent and intense sexual urges, fantasies, or behaviors that involve being humiliated, beaten, bound, or otherwise made to suffer. Although many people have fantasies (while they masturbate or have intercourse) of being forced into sexual acts against their will, only those who are markedly distressed or impaired by the fantasies would receive this diagnosis (APA, 1994; Reik, 1989). Many people with the disorder act on the masochistic urges by themselves, perhaps binding, sticking pins into, or even mutilating themselves. Others have their sexual partners restrain, tie up, blindfold, spank, paddle, whip, beat, electrically shock, "pin and pierce," or humiliate them (APA, 1994).

In one form of sexual masochism, *hypoxyphilia,* people strangle or smother themselves, or ask their partner to do this, in order to enhance their sexual pleasure. There have, in fact, been a growing number of clinical reports of *autoerotic asphyxia,* in which individuals, usually males and as young as 10 years old, inadvertently die by hanging, suffocating, or strangling themselves while masturbating. There is some debate as to whether this practice should be characterized as sexual masochism, but it is commonly accompanied by other acts of bondage (Blanchard & Hucker, 1991).

Most masochistic sexual fantasies begin in childhood. The person does not act out the urges until later, usually by early adulthood. The disorder typically continues over the course of many years. The masochistic

acts of some people remain at the same level of severity during that time; others keep increasing the potential dangerousness of their acts over time or show an increase during times of particular stress (APA, 1994).

In many cases the pattern of sexual masochism seems to have developed through classical conditioning. One case study tells of a teenage boy with a broken arm who was caressed and held close by an attractive nurse as the physician set his fracture without anesthesia (Gebhard, 1965). He experienced a powerful combination of pain and sexual arousal that may have been the cause of his later masochistic urges and acts.

## Sexual Sadism

*Sexual sadism* is a pattern characterized by recurrent and intense sexual urges, fantasies, or behaviors that involve inflicting physical or psychological suffering on others, such as by dominating, restraining, blindfolding, cutting, strangling, mutilating, or even killing the victim. The label is derived from the name of the Marquis de Sade (1740–1814), who inflicted severe cruelty on other people in order to satisfy his sexual desires. People who fantasize about sadism typically imagine that they have total control over a sexual victim who is terrified by the prospect of the sadistic act. Many carry out sadistic acts with a consenting partner, often a person with sexual masochism. Some act out their urges on nonconsenting victims. In all cases, the real or fantasized victim's suffering is the key to arousal.

Fantasies of sexual sadism, like those of sexual masochism, may appear as early as childhood, and sadistic acts, when they occur, develop by early adulthood. The pattern, usually found in males, is chronic (APA, 1994). The acts sometimes stay at the same level of cruelty, but more often they increase in severity over the years. Obviously, people with severe forms of the disorder may be highly dangerous to others (Dietz et al., 1990).

The pattern has been associated with a variety of causes. Behaviorists suggest that classical conditioning often plays a role in its development. While inflicting pain, perhaps unintentional, on an animal or person, an adolescent may feel intense emotions and sometimes sexual arousal. The association between inflicting pain and being aroused sexually sets the stage for a pattern of sexual sadism. Behaviorists also propose

---

*Sexual masochism*   A paraphilia characterized by repeated and intense sexual urges, fantasies, or behaviors that involve being humiliated, beaten, bound, or otherwise made to suffer.

*Hypoxyphilia*   A pattern in which people strangle or smother themselves, or ask their partner to strangle or smother them, to enhance their sexual pleasure.

*Autoerotic asphyxia*   A fatal lack of oxygen that people may inadvertently self-induce while hanging, suffocating, or strangling themselves during masturbation.

---

*Sexual sadism*   A paraphilia characterized by recurrent and intense sexual urges, fantasies, or behaviors that involve inflicting physical or psychological suffering on others.

*People with sexual masochism and those with sexual sadism often achieve satisfaction with each other. Although many such relationships stay within safe bounds and are often portrayed with humor in photos, novels, and movies, they can cross the line and result in severe physical or psychological damage.*

that many cases result from modeling, when adolescents observe others achieving sexual satisfaction by inflicting pain. The ubiquitous sexual magazines, books, and videotapes in our society make such models readily available. Indeed, one broad review of pornographic magazines and books determined that close to one quarter of these materials contained an act of paraphilia, and sadomasochism was overwhelmingly the most common type of paraphilia depicted (Lebegue, 1991).

Psychodynamic and cognitive theorists have suggested that people with sexual sadism may have underlying feelings of sexual inadequacy or insecurity and that they inflict pain in order to achieve a sense of power, which in turn increases their sexual arousal. Alternatively, some biological investigations have found signs of possible abnormal functioning in the endocrine systems of persons with sadism (Langevin

et al., 1988). However, none of these explanations has been systematically investigated or consistently supported by research (Breslow, 1989).

Sexual sadism has been treated by aversion therapy. The public's view of and perhaps distaste for this procedure have been influenced by the description of treatment given to a cruel and sadistic character in Anthony Burgess's novel (later a movie) *A Clockwork Orange:* simultaneous presentation of sadistic images and electrical shocks. It is not clear that aversion therapy is consistently helpful in sexual sadism. Relapse-prevention training, used in some criminal cases, seems somewhat effective (Vaillant & Antonowicz, 1992; Pithers & Cumming, 1989).

## Societal Norms and Sexual Labels

The definitions of the various paraphilias, like those of sexual dysfunctions, are closely tied to the norms of the particular society in which they occur rather than to fixed diagnostic criteria (Brown, 1983). It could be argued that except when people are hurt by them, many paraphiliac behaviors are not disorders at all. Especially in light of the stigma associated with sexual disorders and the self-revulsion that many people experience when they believe they have such a disorder, we need to be very careful about applying such labels to others or to ourselves.

Keep in mind that homosexuality was for years considered a paraphilia by clinical professionals and that this judgment was used to justify laws and even police actions against homosexual persons. Only when the gay rights movement helped change society's understanding of and attitudes toward homosexuality did clinicians stop considering it a disorder. In the meantime, the clinical field had inadvertently contributed to the persecution, anxiety, and humiliation of millions of people because of personal sexual behavior that differed from the conventional norms (see Box 9-2).

*Summing Up*
*Paraphilias are disorders characterized by intense and recurrent sexual urges, fantasies, or behaviors involving either nonhuman objects, children, nonconsenting adults, or experiences of suffering or humiliation. Research has not yet fully clarified their causes or how to treat them effectively.*

*Feeling like a woman trapped in a man's body, the English writer James Morris (left)*
*underwent sex-reassignment surgery, described in his 1974 autobiography* Conundrum.
*Today Jan Morris (right) is a successful author and seems comfortable with her change of*
*gender.*

# Gender Identity Disorder

One of the most fascinating disorders related to sexuality is *gender identity disorder,* or *transsexualism,* a disorder in which people persistently feel that a vast mistake has been made—they have been assigned to the wrong sex. Such persons are preoccupied with getting rid of their primary and secondary sex characteristics (many of them find their own genitals repugnant) and acquiring the characteristics of the other sex. Men with the disorder outnumber women by more than 3 to 1 (APA, 1994).

People with gender identity disorder usually feel uncomfortable wearing the clothes of their own sex and dress instead in clothes of the opposite sex. They are not, however, manifesting transvestism. People who display that paraphilia cross-dress in order to become sexually aroused; people with transsexualism have much deeper reasons for cross-dressing, reasons of sexual identity. In addition to cross-dressing, individuals with transsexualism often engage in activities that are traditionally associated with the other sex.

Sometimes gender identity disorder occurs in children (APA, 1994). Like adults with this disorder, they too feel extremely uncomfortable about their assigned sex and thoroughly wish to be a member of the opposite sex. In addition to a strong preference for cross-dressing, these children markedly prefer to play cross-sex roles in make-believe play, to participate in the stereotypical games of the other sex, and to play with children of the other sex. Their discomfort and preferences are much more extreme than that often observed in children as they develop.

This childhood pattern usually disappears by adolescence or adulthood, but in some cases it develops into adult transsexualism. Thus many adults with transsexualism have had a childhood gender identity disorder (Tsoi, 1992), but most children with a gender identity disorder do not develop adult transsexualism. Moreover, a number of adult persons with transsexualism do not develop any symptoms until mid-adulthood.

Various psychological theories have been proposed to explain gender identity disorder, but research in this area has been limited and generally weak. Some clinicians suspect that the disorder has largely biological causes (Orlebeke et al., 1992); but most studies have failed to find consistent biological differences between persons with and persons without transsexualism.

Many adults with transsexualism enter psychotherapy. A number also receive hormone treatments to alter their sexual characteristics. The hormone prescribed for men with this disorder is the female sex

*Gender identity disorder*    A disorder in which a person persistently feels extremely uncomfortable about his or her assigned sex and strongly wishes to be a member of the opposite sex.

## Box 9-2

# Homosexuality and Society

Homosexuality has always existed in all cultures. It is not new, nor is the controversy that surrounds it. Most cultures do not openly advocate homosexuality, but historically few have condemned it so fiercely as Western culture has since the Victorian era.

Before 1973, the DSM listed homosexuality as a sexual disorder. Protests by gay activist groups and many psychotherapists eventually led to its elimination from the manual as a sexual disorder per se, but the DSM did retain a category called *ego dystonic homosexuality*—the experience of extreme distress over one's homosexual preference. Recent editions of the DSM have dropped even this category, and the issue of homosexuality is no longer mentioned. Most clinicians now accept homosexuality as a variant of normal sexual behavior and not a disorder.

Despite the growing acceptance of homosexuality by clinicians, many people in Western society continue to foster antihomosexual attitudes and to propagate myths about the lifestyles of homosexual persons. The research data show that homosexual persons do *not* suffer from gender confusion; they are *not* more prone to psychopathology than others; and there is *not* an identifiable "homosexual personality."

To cope with the stress, discrimination, and even danger they encounter, many homosexual people have chosen to live on streets or in neighborhoods that are predominantly homosexual. Certain bars or restaurants serve as gathering places where gay persons exchange information and socialize. Organizations exist to support and lobby for issues affecting homosexual people, demanding equal treatment under the law and in society

(Freiberg, 1994). This battle is being fought constantly.

One of the key issues affecting support for homosexual rights has been the debate over whether homosexual persons choose their lifestyle or whether it is a natural part of their physiological and psychological make-up. This debate is fueled by findings from the scientific community. Recent research has suggested that sometimes homosexuality is not simply a lifestyle choice but linked to a physiological predisposition (LeVay & Hamer, 1994), supporting the claim from some segments

---

hormone estrogen. It causes breast development, loss of body and facial hair, and change in the distribution of body fat. Similar treatments with the male sex hormone testosterone are given to women with transsexualism.

Drug therapy and psychotherapy are sufficient to enable many persons with transsexualism to lead a satisfactory existence in the gender role that they believe represents their true identity. For others, however, this is not enough, and their dissatisfaction leads them to undergo one of the most controversial practices in medicine: *sex-change surgery.*

The first sex-change operation actually took place in 1931, but the procedure did not gain acceptance among practitioners working on this problem until

1952, when an operation converted an ex-soldier named George Jorgensen into a woman, renamed Christine Jorgensen. This transformation made headlines around the world and sparked the interest of people everywhere.

By 1980, sex-reassignment surgery was routine in at least forty medical centers in the Western Hemisphere (Arndt, 1991). This surgery is preceded by one to two years of hormone therapy, after which the operation itself involves, for men, amputation of the penis, creation of an artificial vagina, and face-altering plastic surgery. For women, surgery may include bilateral mastectomy and hysterectomy. The procedure for creating a functioning penis, called *phalloplasty,* is not yet perfected and not recommended; however,

of the gay community that homosexuality is a naturally occurring phenomenon.

Some recent studies, for example, have suggested that homosexuality sometimes has a genetic component. Several studies of both male and female homosexual individuals have found genetic markers indicating that homosexuality may sometimes be passed on by the mother's genes (Hamer et al., 1993). Similarly, two studies found that in pairs of identical twins (who share an identical genetic makeup) in which one twin was homosexual, more than 50 percent of the other twins were also homosexual. The number dropped to less than 20 percent when the siblings were fraternal twins or non-twins and to under 10 percent when the children were adopted and biologically unrelated (Bailey et al., 1993). Although environmental factors also appear to have a major impact on homosexuality—otherwise all persons with a homosexual identical twin would be homosexual as well—genetics may sometimes play a key role.

The homosexual community takes the position that since sexual preference is the only behavioral variable that consistently distinguishes homosexual from heterosexual couples, gay couples should be accorded the same rights as heterosexual ones. Thus, today marriages are sometimes performed for same-sex couples. Moreover, homosexual couples are increasingly demanding access to housing reserved for couples only and to health insurance "spouse" coverage, and recent court cases are supporting such rights. These issues affect the day-to-day lives of homosexual couples in the same way that they affect heterosexual couples.

In the early 1990s many issues regarding acceptance of homosexuality came to a head in the United States. Media coverage exposed numerous episodes of gay-bashing in which homosexual men were beaten, even killed. The practice of "outing," in which public figures who have not made their homosexuality known are exposed by gay activists, increased. And President Clinton reviewed the military's policy regarding homosexuality, an action that stirred a national debate.

One of the most important issues to emerge during the debate on homosexuality and the military was whether Americans—those in the armed services specifically, but throughout the country as well—could overcome prejudice against homosexuality. Despite the high emotions this issue evokes, reviews of relevant literature suggest that, through education and exposure, people can learn to accept and work with others who are different from them (Herek & Capitanio, 1993).

Obviously, homosexuality continues to be a lifestyle that many people adopt, whether through choice, environment, genetics, or psychosocial development. Now that clinical concerns about homosexuality have been put aside, one of the key remaining issues is how society will deal with a significant proportion of its population that typically does not differ from the rest in any way other than sexual preference. So far, Western society cannot claim to have dealt very effectively or fairly with this question, but at least a trend toward understanding and equality seems to be emerging.

doctors have developed a silicone prosthesis that gives the patient the appearance of having male genitals (Hage & Bouman, 1992). Approximately 1,000 sex-change operations are performed each year in the United States. Studies in some European countries suggest that 1 out of every 30,000 men and 1 out of every 100,000 women seek sex-change surgery (APA, 1994).

Clinicians have heatedly debated the legitimacy of surgery as a treatment for gender identity disorder. Some consider it a humane solution. Others argue that transsexual surgery is a "drastic nonsolution" for a purely psychological problem, akin to lobotomy (Restak, 1979). Research has not yet been able to settle the matter. The long-term psychological outcome of surgical sex reassignment is not well established. Without any form of treatment, gender identity disorder among adults is usually chronic, but some cases of spontaneous recovery have reportedly occurred.

*Summing Up*
*People with gender identity disorder persistently feel that they have been assigned to the wrong sex. The causes of the disorder are not well understood. Drug (hormone) therapy and psychotherapy have been used to treat the disorder. The appropriateness of sex-change surgery has been hotly debated.*

## The State of the Field
## *Sexual Disorders and Gender Identity Disorder*

Because there is so much public interest in and discussion about sexual disorders, it sometimes appears as if much is known about these problems; such is not the case. Clinical theorists and practitioners have only recently begun to understand the nature and origins of sexual dysfunctions and to develop effective treatments for them. Moreover, they have made only limited progress in explaining and treating paraphilias, the other group of sexual disorders, or the sex-related gender identity disorder.

Yet this picture is changing rapidly, at least in the realm of sexual dysfunctions. In 1970 William Masters and Virginia Johnson published their research on human sexual functioning and dysfunctioning and began a veritable revolution in the clinical field that continues today. Over the past two decades, sexual functioning has been one of the most broadly investigated subjects in clinical research, with systematic studies providing enlightening and useful information about the nature and causes of various sexual dysfunctions.

Correspondingly, clinicians have developed very helpful treatments for people with sexual dysfunctions—people previously doomed to a lifetime of sexual frustration and distress. Today sex therapy is typically a complex program with multiple components tailored to the particular problems and personality of an individual and couple. The breadth of current research and therapy programs suggests that our understanding and treatment of sexual dysfunctions will continue to improve in the coming years.

One of the most important insights to emerge from all this work is the need for proper education about sexual dysfunctions. Popular myths and judgments still abound in this area, often contributing directly to a person's sexual difficulties. Sex therapists have come to recognize that even a modest amount of education about sexual dysfunctioning can help the people who come to them for treatment.

In fact, most people, not just those who seek treatment, can benefit from a more accurate understanding of sexual functioning. Public education about sexual functioning—through books, television and radio, school programs, group presentations, and the like—has become a new focus in recent years and appears to be as important as private treatment in improving the general well-being of the population. It is to be hoped that this too will continue and increase in the coming years.

## *Chapter Review*

1. *Sexual Dysfunctions:* Sexual dysfunctions are disorders that make it difficult or impossible for a person to have or enjoy coitus.
2. *The Desire Phase:* Disorders of the desire phase of the sexual response cycle are *hypoactive sexual desire disorder,* a lack of interest in sex and a corresponding low level of sexual activity, and *sexual aversion disorder,* a persistent revulsion to and active avoidance of sexual activity with a partner.
   A. *Biological causes* cited in hypoactive sexual desire and sexual aversion include abnormal hormone levels, certain drugs, and some chronic illnesses.
   B. *Sociocultural and psychological causes* include situational pressures, relationship problems, fears, and the trauma of having been sexually molested or assaulted.
3. *The Excitement Phase:* Disorders of the excitement phase of the sexual response cycle are *female sexual arousal disorder,* a persistent inability to attain or maintain adequate lubrication or genital swelling during sexual activity, and *male erectile disorder,* a persistent inability to attain or maintain an erection during sexual activity.
   A. *Biological causes* cited in male erectile disorder include abnormal hormone levels, vascular abnormalities, medical conditions, and certain medications.
   B. *Sociocultural and psychological causes* of male erectile disorder include situational pressures such as job loss, relationship problems, and, in particular, *performance anxiety* and the *spectator role.*
4. *The Orgasm Phase:* Disorders of the orgasm phase of the sexual response cycle are *premature ejaculation, male orgasmic disorder,* and *female orgasmic disorder.*
   A. Premature ejaculation, recurrently reaching orgasm and ejaculating before or shortly after penetration, has been related to behavioral causes, such as inappropriate early learning and inexperience.
   B. Male orgasmic disorder, a repeated absence of or long delay in reaching orgasm, has been related

to biological causes such as low testosterone levels, neurological diseases, head injuries, and certain drugs; and to psychological causes such as performance anxiety and the spectator role. The dysfunction may also grow from hypoactive sexual desire.

C. Female orgasmic disorder, a repeated absence of or long delay in reaching orgasm, has been tied to biological causes such as certain medical diseases, some drugs, and several postmenopausal changes; and to sociocultural and psychological causes such as society's mixed messages about female sexuality, the trauma of sexual molestation or assault, childhood traumas, and relationship problems. Most clinicians agree that orgasm during intercourse is not critical to normal sexual functioning, provided a woman can reach orgasm with her partner during direct stimulation of the clitoris.

5. *Sexual Pain Disorders:* In *vaginismus,* involuntary contractions of the muscles around the outer third of the vagina prevent entry of the penis. In *dyspareunia,* the person experiences severe pain in the genitals during sexual activity. Dyspareunia usually occurs in women and typically has a physical cause such as injury during childbirth.

6. *Sex Therapy:* In the 1970s the work of William Masters and Virginia Johnson led to the development of sex therapy. Its major components are careful assessment, education, attitude changes, sensate focus exercises to help eliminate performance anxiety and the spectator role, improvements in communication and sexual technique, and couple therapy. Specific techniques are also applied for each of the sexual dysfunctions.

7. *Paraphilias:* Paraphilias are characterized by recurrent and intense sexual urges, fantasies, or behaviors involving either nonhuman objects, children, nonconsenting adults, or experiences of suffering or humiliation. The diagnosis is applied only when the urges, fantasies, or behaviors last at least six months and cause great distress or impairment.

A. These problems are found primarily in men.

B. The paraphilias are *fetishism, transvestic fetishism* (transvestism), *exhibitionism, voyeurism, frotteurism, pedophilia, sexual masochism,* and *sexual sadism.*

8. *Gender Identity Disorder:* People who manifest a *gender identity disorder,* or *transsexualism,* persistently feel that they have been assigned to the wrong sex and are preoccupied with acquiring the physical characteristics of the other sex. Males outnumber females with this disorder by approximately 3 to 1.

A. The causes of gender identity disorder are not well understood.

B. Hormone treatments and psychotherapy have been used in many cases of this disorder. Sex change operations have also been applied in a number of cases, but the appropriateness of surgery as a form of "treatment" has been hotly debated.

## Key Terms

| | | | |
|---|---|---|---|
| sexual dysfunction | male erectile disorder | sex therapy | transvestic fetishism |
| sexual response cycle | nocturnal penile | sensate focus | transvestism |
| desire | tumescence | nondemand pleasuring | cross-dressing |
| excitement | REM | affectual awareness | exhibitionism |
| orgasm | snap gauge | tease technique | voyeurism |
| resolution | performance anxiety | penile prosthesis | frotteurism |
| lifelong type | spectator role | vacuum erection device | pedophilia |
| acquired type | premature ejaculation | (VED) | relapse-prevention |
| generalized type | male orgasmic disorder | stop-start technique | training |
| situational type | inhibited male orgasm | pause technique | sexual masochism |
| hypoactive sexual desire | inhibited ejaculation | directed masturbation | hypoxyphilia |
| sexual aversion disorder | ejaculatory incompetence | training | autoerotic asphyxia |
| testosterone | retarded ejaculation | paraphilia | sexual sadism |
| prolactin | female orgasmic disorder | fetishism | gender identity disorder |
| estrogen | inhibited female orgasm | aversion therapy | transsexualism |
| aphrodisiac | vaginismus | covert sensitization | sex-change surgery |
| female sexual arousal | "rational" vaginismus | masturbatory satiation | phalloplasty |
| disorder | dyspareunia | orgasmic reorientation | |

# *Quick Quiz*

1. What sexual dysfunctions are associated with the desire phase of the sexual response cycle? How prevalent are they, and what factors help cause them?

2. What are the symptoms and prevalence rates of female sexual arousal disorder and male erectile disorder? What phase of the sexual response cycle are they associated with?

3. What are the possible causes of male erectile disorder?

4. Which sexual dysfunctions seem to involve the mechanisms of performance anxiety and the spectator role?

5. What are the symptoms, prevalence rates, and primary causes of premature ejaculation, male orgasmic disorder, and female orgasmic disorder? Which phase of the sexual response cycle are they associated with?

6. Identify, describe, and explain the sexual pain disorders.

7. What are the major components of modern sex therapy? What specific techniques are further used to treat specific sexual dysfunctions?

8. List, describe, and explain the leading paraphilias.

9. Describe the treatment techniques of aversion therapy, masturbatory satiation, orgasmic reorientation, and relapse-prevention training. Which paraphilias have they been used to treat, and how successful are they?

10. Distinguish transvestism from transsexualism (gender identity disorder).

11. What are the leading treatments for gender identity disorder?

# 10

# Eating Disorders

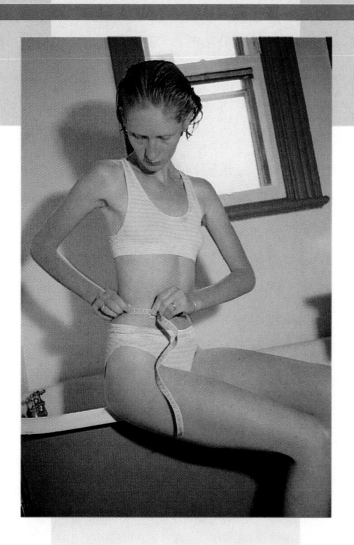

*B*ecause contemporary Western society equates thinness with health and beauty, most of us are as preoccupied with the quantity of the food we eat as we are with its taste and nutritional value. One need only count the articles about dieting in magazines and newspapers to be convinced that thinness has become a national obsession (see Figure 10-1). Perhaps it is not coincidental that during the past two decades we have also witnessed an increase in two dramatic eating disorders at whose core is a morbid fear of gaining weight. Sufferers of **anorexia nervosa** relentlessly pursue extreme thinness and lose so much weight that they may starve themselves to death. People with **bulimia nervosa** go on frequent eating binges during which they uncontrollably consume large quantities of food, then force themselves to vomit or take other strong steps to keep from gaining weight.

Lately, the news media have published so many reports about these disorders that we may safely assume the public finds them interesting. Certainly one reason for this surge in public interest is the frightening medical consequences that can result from anorexic or bulimic behavior. Another widespread concern about these disorders is their disproportionate prevalence among adolescent girls and young women.

Up until the past decade, anorexia nervosa and bulimia nervosa were viewed as distinct disorders that had different characteristics and causes and required different forms of treatment. Today, however, clinicians and researchers have come to understand that often the similarities between the two disorders are as important as the differences between them (APA, 1994).

## Anorexia Nervosa

Janet Caldwell, 14 years old and in the eighth grade, displays many characteristic symptoms of anorexia nervosa: she refuses to maintain more than 85 percent of her normal body weight, intensely fears becoming overweight, has a disturbed view of her weight and shape, and has stopped menstruating (APA, 1994).

> Janet Caldwell was . . . five feet, two inches tall and weighed 62 pounds. . . . Janet began dieting at the age of 12 when she weighed 115 pounds and was chided by her family and friends for being "pudgy." She continued to restrict her food intake over a two-year period, and as she grew thinner, her parents

*Perhaps the most publicized victim of anorexia nervosa during the past decade was Karen Carpenter, the young singer who developed this disorder at the height of her career and died of related medical problems.*

became increasingly more concerned about her eating behavior. . . .

Janet . . . felt that her weight problem began at the time of puberty. She said that her family and friends had supported her efforts to achieve a ten-pound weight loss when she first began dieting at age 12. Janet did not go on any special kind of diet. Instead, she restricted her food intake at meals, generally cut down on carbohydrates and protein intake, tended to eat a lot of salads, and completely stopped snacking between meals. At first, she was quite pleased with her progressive weight reduction, and she was able to ignore her feelings of hunger by remembering the weight loss goal she had set for herself. However, each time she lost the number of pounds she had set for her goal she decided to lose just a few more pounds. Therefore she continued to set new weight goals for herself. In this manner, her weight dropped from 115 pounds to 88 pounds during the first year of her weight loss regimen.

Janet felt that, in her second year of dieting, her

*Anorexia nervosa* A disorder characterized by the relentless pursuit of extreme thinness and by an extreme loss of weight.

*Bulimia nervosa* A disorder characterized by frequent eating binges that are followed by forced vomiting or other extreme compensatory behaviors to avoid gaining weight.

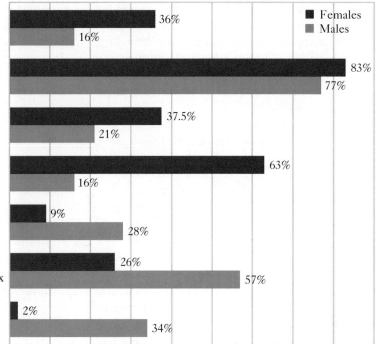

Pay attention to the calories of every meal — Females 36%, Males 16%

Underweight people who like their appearance — Females 83%, Males 77%

Adults trying to lose weight — Females 37.5%, Males 21%

Adolescents trying to lose weight — Females 63%, Males 16%

Adolescents trying to gain weight — Females 9%, Males 28%

Users of the "personals" who look for "very attractive" persons of the opposite sex — Females 26%, Males 57%

Users of the "personals" who look for "thin" persons of the opposite sex — Females 2%, Males 34%

**Figure 10-1** *Surveys reveal that females and males in our society are held, both by themselves and by members of the opposite sex, to very different standards of appearance and worth. (Adapted from Weiss, 1991; Calorie Control Council national survey, 1991; Smith et al., 1990; Britton, 1988; Rosen & Gross, 1987; Cash et al., 1986.)*

weight loss had continued beyond her control. . . . She became convinced that there was something inside of her that would not let her gain weight. . . . Janet commented that although there had been occasions over the past few years when she had been fairly "down" or unhappy, she still felt driven to keep on dieting. As a result, she frequently went for walks, ran errands for her family, and spent a great deal of time cleaning her room and keeping it in a meticulously neat and unaltered arrangement.

When Janet's weight loss continued beyond the first year, her parents insisted that she see their family physician, and Mrs. Caldwell accompanied Janet to her appointment. Their family practitioner was quite alarmed at Janet's appearance and prescribed a high-calorie diet. Janet . . . said that she often responded to her parents' entreaties that she eat by telling them that she indeed had eaten but they had not seen her do so. She often listed foods that she said she had consumed which in fact she had flushed down the toilet. She estimated that she only was eating about 300 calories a day.

Mrs. Caldwell indicated that Janet appeared quiet and withdrawn, in contrast to her generally active and cheerful disposition, at the time she began dieting. . . . Janet became very critical of her girlfriends, and Mrs. Caldwell felt that Janet behaved in an argumentative and stubborn manner with them. . . . In general, Janet seemed less spontaneous and talked less with her family and others than she

had during any previous period that her parents could recall.

*(Leon, 1984, pp. 179–184)*

Like Janet, at least half of the people with anorexia nervosa reduce their weight by restricting their intake of food, a pattern called *restricting type anorexia nervosa.* At first, people with this kind of anorexia tend to cut out sweets and fattening snacks, then increasingly cut out other foods (Simon et al., 1993). Eventually, they take little pleasure in eating and often show almost no variability in diet. Others with this disorder lose weight by forcing themselves to vomit after meals or by abusing laxatives or diuretics, and they may even engage in eating binges, a pattern called *binge-eating/ purging type anorexia nervosa,* which we shall discuss in more detail when we examine bulimia nervosa (APA, 1994).

Approximately 90 to 95 percent of all cases of anorexia nervosa occur in females, and although the disorder can appear at any age, the peak age of onset is between 14 and 18 years (APA, 1994). As many as 1 percent of adolescent and young adult females develop the disorder, and many more display at least some of its symptoms. Moreover, anorexia nervosa seems to be on the increase (APA, 1994; Nielsen, 1990).

Typically the disorder begins after a person who is slightly overweight or of normal weight decides to "just lose a few pounds" and follows a stressful event such as separation of the parents, a move away from home, or an experience of personal failure (APA, 1994; Patton et al., 1990). Although most victims recover, between 2 and 10 percent of them become so seriously ill that they die, usually of medical problems brought about by starvation.

> ### Consider This
> Many, perhaps most, women in Western society feel as if they are dieting, or between diets, their entire adult lives. Is it possible to be a woman in this society and not struggle with at least some issues of eating and appearance? Who is responsible for perpetuating the societal standards and pressures that affect so many women?

*Becoming thin* is life's central goal for persons with anorexia nervosa, but fear is at the root of their preoccupation. They are afraid of becoming obese, of giving in to their growing desire to eat, and more generally of losing control over the size and shape of their body.

Despite their focus on thinness and the severe restrictions they may place on their food intake, people with this disorder are *preoccupied with food*. They may spend considerable time thinking and even reading about food and planning their limited meals (King et al., 1991). Many report that their dreams are filled with images of food and eating (Frayn, 1991; Levitan, 1981).

This preoccupation with food may in fact be the *result* of food deprivation rather than its cause (Yates, 1989; Andersen, 1986). In a famous "starvation study," conducted in the late 1940s, thirty-six normal-weight conscientious objectors were put on a semistarvation diet for six months (Keys et al., 1950). Like people with anorexia nervosa, the volunteers became preoccupied with food and eating. They spent hours each day planning their small meals, talked about food more than any other topic, studied cookbooks and recipes, mixed food in odd combinations, and dawdled over their meals. Many also had vivid dreams about food.

Persons with anorexia nervosa also exhibit *cognitive dysfunctions* of various kinds. For example, they usually have a low opinion of their body shape and consider themselves unattractive (Heilbrun & Witt, 1990). In addition, they are likely to overestimate their actual proportions. A 23-year-old anorexic woman said:

> I look in a full-length mirror at least four or five times daily and I really cannot see myself as too thin. Sometimes after several days of strict dieting, I feel that my shape is tolerable, but most of the time, odd as it may seem, I look in the mirror and believe that I am too fat.
>
> *(Bruch, 1973)*

The tendency to overestimate body size has been tested in the laboratory (Williamson et al., 1993). In a popular assessment technique, subjects are asked to look at a photograph of themselves through an apparatus with an adjustable lens and to manipulate the lens until the image it shows depicts their actual body size. The image can be made to vary from 20 percent thinner to 20 percent larger than actual appearance as the lens is adjusted. In one study, more than half of the anorexic subjects were found to overestimate their body size, stopping the lens when the image was larger than they actually were. The majority of control subjects, in contrast, underestimated their body size (Garner et al., 1976).

Another cognitive feature of anorexia nervosa is the development of maladaptive attitudes and misperceptions (Wertheim & Poulakis, 1992). People with the disorder often hold such beliefs as "I must be perfect in every way"; "I will become a better person if I deprive myself"; and "I can avoid guilt by not eating."

People with anorexia nervosa also display several *psychological* and *mood problems*. Again, studies of normal subjects placed on semistarvation diets have reported similar problems, suggesting that some such features may be the result of starvation (Keys et al., 1950; Schiele & Brozek, 1948). People with the disorder tend to be at least mildly depressed, have low self-esteem, and show symptoms of anxiety. Some are also

*Thirty-six male subjects who were put on a semistarvation diet for six months developed many of the psychological symptoms seen in anorexia nervosa (Keys et al., 1950).*

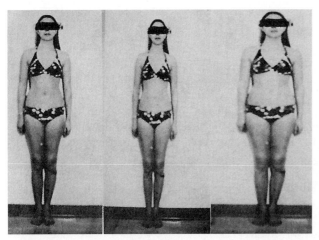

*Subjects who look at photographs of themselves through an anamorphic lens adjust the lens until they see what they believe is their actual image. A subject may change her actual image (left) from 20 percent thinner (middle) to 20 percent larger (right). Most subjects with anorexia nervosa overestimate their body size.*

troubled by sleep disturbances such as insomnia (APA, 1994).

Anorexia nervosa is often accompanied by obsessive-compulsive patterns of behavior (APA, 1994; Vitousek & Manke, 1994). It is common for the person to set herself rigid rules for food preparation or to cut her food into specific shapes. Even broader obsessive-compulsive patterns are common. In one study anorexic patients and obsessive-compulsive patients earned equally high scores for obsessiveness and compulsiveness (Solyom et al., 1982).

Finally, the starvation habits of anorexia nervosa cause a range of *medical problems* (Sharp & Freeman, 1993; Salisbury & Mitchell, 1991). *Amenorrhea,* the absence of menstrual cycles, has already been mentioned. Other consequences include lowered body temperature, low blood pressure, body swelling, reduced bone mineral density, and slow heart rate. Metabolic and electrolyte imbalances also may occur, and can lead to death by cardiac arrest, congestive heart failure, or circulatory collapse.

The severe nutritional deficiencies of anorexia may also cause skin to become rough, dry, and cracked; nails to become brittle; and hands and feet to be cold and blue. Some people lose hair from their scalp, and some grow lanugo (the fine, silky hair that covers some newborns) on their trunk, extremities, and face.

As Michael Levine, a leading theorist on eating disorders, says "Although self-destruction is not the motive, the end result of the battle with starvation is the tightening of a noose" (1987, p.48).

*Amenorrhea*     The absence of menstrual cycles.

# Bulimia Nervosa

A married woman with bulimia nervosa describes her morning:

Today I am going to be really good and that means eating certain predetermined portions of food and not taking one more bite than I think I am allowed. I am very careful to see that I don't take more than Doug does. I judge by his body. I can feel the tension building. I wish Doug would hurry up and leave so I can get going!

As soon as he shuts the door, I try to get involved with one of the myriad of responsibilities on the list. I hate them all! I just want to crawl into a hole. I don't want to do anything. I'd rather eat. I am alone, I am nervous, I am no good, I always do everything wrong anyway, I am not in control, I can't make it through the day, I just know it. It has been the same for so long.

I remember the starchy cereal I ate for breakfast. I am into the bathroom and onto the scale. It measures the same, BUT I DON'T WANT TO STAY THE SAME! I want to be thinner! I look in the mirror, I think my thighs are ugly and deformed looking. I see a lumpy, clumsy, pear-shaped wimp. There is always something wrong with what I see. I feel frustrated trapped in this body and I don't know what to do about it.

I float to the refrigerator knowing exactly what is there. I begin with last night's brownies. I always begin with the sweets. At first I try to make it look like nothing is missing, but my appetite is huge and I resolve to make another batch of brownies. I know there is half of a bag of cookies in the bathroom, thrown out the night before, and I polish them off immediately. I take some milk so my vomiting will be smoother. I like the full feeling I get after downing a big glass. I get out six pieces of bread and toast one side in the broiler, turn them over and load them with patties of butter and put them under the broiler again till they are bubbling. I take all six pieces on a plate to the television and go back for a bowl of cereal and a banana to have along with them. Before the last toast is finished, I am already preparing the next batch of six more pieces. Maybe another brownie or five, and a couple of large bowlfuls of ice cream, yogurt or cottage cheese. My stomach is stretched into a huge ball below my ribcage. I know I'll have to go into the bathroom soon, but I want to postpone it. I am in never-never land. I am waiting, feeling the pressure, pacing the floor in and out of the rooms. Time is passing. Time is passing. It is getting to be time.

I wander aimlessly through each of the rooms again tidying, making the whole house neat and put back together. I finally make the turn into the bathroom. I brace my feet, pull my hair back and stick my finger down my throat, stroking twice, and get up a huge pile

## Box 10-1

# *Obesity: To Lose or Not to Lose*

By medical standards, as many as 24 percent of middle-aged adults in the United States are *obese*, significantly over the weight that is typical of people of their height (National Center for Health Statistics, 1988). Being overweight is not a mental disorder, nor in most cases is it the result of abnormal psychological processes. Nevertheless, this problem causes great anguish to the many people who have it.

Our society's reaction to obesity is one of the main reasons for their anguish. The media, people on the streets, and even health professionals often treat obesity as shameful. Indeed, obese people are often the unrecognized victims of discrimination in gaining admissions to college, jobs, promotions, and satisfaction in their personal relationships (Rothblum, 1992; Stunkard & Wadden, 1992).

Mounting evidence indicates that obesity results from multiple physiological, social, and other factors and that the overweight person is not to be sneered at as weak and out of control. First, genetic and biological factors seem to play

a role. Researchers have found that the biological children of obese parents are more likely to be obese than children whose biological parents are not obese, whether or not the people who raise those children are obese (Stunkard et al., 1986). Moreover, researchers have recently identified a gene that seems to be linked to obesity (Hallaas et al., 1995). Still other research has indicated that there may be a link between the neurotransmitter serotonin and obesity—deficits of serotonin in the brain may increase one's craving for carbohydrates and predispose some people to overeat and become obese (Logue, 1991).

Environment also plays a key causal role in obesity. Studies have shown that people tend to eat more when they are in the company of others, particularly if the other people are eating (Logue, 1991). It has also been found consistently that people of lower socioeconomic environments are more likely to be obese than people of higher socioeconomic backgrounds (Ernst & Harlan, 1991).

Despite such findings, societal

pressures continue to push people to see their obesity as a disgrace and weight loss as the sole solution to their problems. Perhaps the primary reason for society's disdain for obese people lies in the web of myths that surround them. One such myth, that overweight people lack character or have personality defects, is, as we have seen, quite inaccurate. So, apparently, are three perceptions that have permeated our society for many years: (1) overweight people are significantly endangering their health; (2) dieting is the best way to lose weight; and (3) weight loss is the appropriate central goal of people who are overweight.

### *Health Risk?*

Contrary to popular belief, people with mild obesity do not appear to be at greater risk of coronary disease or cancer or any other disease. There is no hard evidence linking modest obesity to early death, and in fact quite the opposite may be true—being underweight puts a person at some health risk (Andres et al., 1993; Robertson, 1992).

of food. Three times, four and another pile of food. I can see everything come back. I am glad to see those brownies because they are SO fattening. The rhythm of the emptying is broken and my head is beginning to hurt. I stand up feeling dizzy, empty and weak. The whole episode has taken about an hour.

                                                                *(Hall, 1980, pp. 5–6)*

Sufferers of bulimia nervosa—a disorder also known as *binge-purge syndrome*—habitually engage in episodes of uncontrollable overeating ("binges") such as the one recalled by this woman, who later recovered and wrote about her experience. In addition, according to DSM-IV, they repeatedly perform inappropriate *compensatory* behaviors, such as self-induced vomiting, misuse of laxatives, fasting, or excessive ex-

ercise. Moreover, their evaluations of themselves are unduly influenced by their body shape and weight (APA, 1994).

Clinicians have also observed that many people seem to display a pattern of binge eating without any accompanying compensatory behaviors, often called *binge-eating disorder*. However, this category is not officially listed in DSM-IV.

Many adolescents and young adults go on occasional eating binges or experiment with self-induced vomiting or laxatives after they hear about people doing these things from their friends or from the media (Rand & Kuldau, 1991). Only some of them, however, satisfy the DSM-IV criteria for a diagnosis of bulimia

---

*Binge*   An episode of uncontrollable eating during which a person consumes a very large quantity of food.

*Binge-eating disorder*   A type of eating disorder in which a person displays a pattern of binge eating without any accompanying compensatory behaviors.

### Dieting Works?

There are scores of diets. There is little evidence, however, that any diet yet devised can ensure long-term weight loss (Wilson, 1994). While most studies look only at the weight that obese people have lost during the first year, any examination of long-term effects generally shows a net gain in the person's weight and certainly not a significant loss (Cogan & Rothblum, 1992; Kramer et al., 1989). This rebound effect is common among people who go on very low-calorie diets, which, in addition to failing to keep weight off, frequently are nutritionally deficient and physically dangerous (Wadden et al., 1988).

One reason that dieting fails to achieve long-term weight loss is that the dieter is engaged in a losing battle against his or her own *weight set point,* the weight level that a particular body is organized to maintain. In response to weight loss below the set point, a dieter's body increasingly stores energy in its fat cells rather than in its lean muscle mass. The person is thus likely to start gaining weight again, now more in the form of fat than before the dieting (Dulloo & Girardier, 1990). Furthermore, the body's metabolic rate (the rate at which it uses energy) decreases in the course of dieting and remains depressed after dieting stops. These physiological changes are compounded by the fact that many people with obesity already have lower metabolic rates and two to three times the number of fat cells that thin people have.

Most low-calorie dieters shift from weight loss to weight gain, then to loss again, and so on. In the end this yo-yo pattern may itself be a health risk, increasing the likelihood of high blood pressure and cardiovascular disease (Brownell & Rodin, 1995, 1994; Lissner et al., 1991). In cases of extreme obesity, where weight loss is desired and clearly advisable, it appears that establishing a realistic, attainable goal rather than an unrealistic ideal is most likely to lead to long-term weight loss and prevent a yo-yo pattern of dieting (Brownell & O'Neil, 1993; Brownell & Wadden, 1992).

### Lower Body Weight Is the Proper Goal?

Some researchers contend that emphasis should shift away from weight loss and toward improving general health and attitudes. Obesity has often been linked to poor self-concept and distorted body image (Rosen et al., 1995). If the psychological health of overweight people can be improved and if they and others can be educated about the myths and truths regarding obesity, perhaps everyone will be better off.

A growing number of researchers are beginning to conclude that obesity should often be left alone, at least so far as weight loss is concerned; at the very least, weight loss should involve more modest and realistic goals. It is certainly desirable to intervene against the biological, environmental, and societal factors that may push a person toward obesity, but many researchers now counsel that maintaining good physical and psychological health is the most reasonable and useful goal, whatever one's weight may be.

---

nervosa. Surveys suggest that between 1 and 6 percent of adolescent and young adult females develop the full syndrome (APA, 1994; Bennett et al., 1991).

Like anorexia nervosa, bulimia nervosa usually occurs in females (again, 90 to 95 percent of the cases), begins in adolescence or young adulthood (most often between 15 and 19 years of age), and arises after a period of intense dieting (APA, 1994; Patton et al., 1990). It often lasts for several years, with intermittent letup.

The weight of people with bulimia nervosa usually stays within a normal range, although it may fluctuate noticeably within that range (APA, 1994). Some people with this pattern, however, become significantly underweight and may qualify for a diagnosis of anorexia nervosa instead. Still other bulimic individuals become overweight, largely as a result of their binge eating (APA, 1994; Mitchell et al., 1990). Most overweight people, however, are not bulimic (see Box 10-1).

*Binge eating* is the central feature of bulimia nervosa. A binge occurs over a discrete period of time, such as an hour, during which the person consumes an amount of food that is considerably larger than most people would eat during a similar period of time under similar circumstances (APA, 1994). As in the example described above, binges are usually carried out in secret or as inconspicuously as possible. Although the term "bulimia" comes from the Greek *bous limos,* meaning "cattle hunger," the food ingested during a binge is hardly tasted or thought about.

Binges usually begin with feelings of unbearable tension (Johnson et al., 1995; Lingswiler et al., 1989). The individual feels irritable, removed from the scene,

*Members of "Overeaters Anonymous," a worldwide network of support groups for people with various eating problems, acknowledge that they use food self-destructively and learn to treat their bodies with greater respect.*

and powerless to control an overwhelming need to eat "forbidden" foods (Levine, 1987). During the binge, the person usually feels unable to stop eating. A binge typically ends within an hour or two. Although the binge itself may be experienced as pleasurable in the sense that it relieves the unbearable tension, it is followed by feelings of extreme self-reproach, guilt, and depression, and a fear of gaining weight and being discovered (APA, 1994; Mizes & Arbitell, 1991).

After a binge, people with bulimia nervosa try to compensate for and undo its effects. Many resort to vomiting. Actually, vomiting fails to prevent the absorption of at least one-third of the calories consumed during a binge. And ironically, repeated vomiting disrupts the body's satiety mechanisms, making people even hungrier and leading to more frequent and intense binges (Wooley & Wooley, 1985). Similarly, the compensatory use of laxatives or diuretics fails almost completely to undo the caloric effects of binging (Garner et al., 1985).

Vomiting and other kinds of compensatory behavior may quickly relieve the uncomfortable physical feelings of fullness or temporarily reduce the feelings of anxiety, self-disgust, and lack of control attached to binge eating (French et al., 1993), so that over time a cycle evolves in which purging allows more binging and binging necessitates more purging. The cycle eventually makes persons with bulimia nervosa feel generally powerless, useless, and disgusted with themselves. Most recognize fully that they have an eating disorder, but their anxiety over gaining weight prevents them from interrupting the cycle.

The woman from the earlier example recalls how the pattern of binging, purging, and self-disgust took hold while she was an adolescent in boarding school:

Every bite that went into my mouth was a naughty and selfish indulgence, and I became more and more disgusted with myself. . . .

The first time I stuck my fingers down my throat was during the last week of school. I saw a girl come out of the bathroom with her face all red and her eyes puffy. She had always talked about her weight and how she should be dieting even though her body was really shapely. I knew instantly what she had just done and I had to try it. . . .

I began with breakfasts which were served buffet-style on the main floor of the dorm. I learned which foods I could eat that would come back up easily. When I woke in the morning, I had to make the decision whether to stuff myself for half an hour and throw up before class, or whether to try and make it through the whole day without overeating. . . . I always thought people noticed when I took huge portions at mealtimes, but I figured they assumed that because I was an athlete, I burned it off. . . . Once a binge was under way, I did not stop until my stomach looked pregnant and I felt like I could not swallow one more time.

That year was the first of my nine years of obsessive eating and throwing up. . . . I didn't want to tell anyone what I was doing, and I didn't want to stop. . . . [Though] being in love or other distractions occasionally lessened the cravings, I always returned to the food.

*(Hall, 1980, pp. 9–12)*

As noted before, a bulimic pattern typically begins during or after a period of intense dieting in which the individual has tried to address a mild or moderate weight problem (APA, 1994). Research has found that normal subjects placed on very deficient diets also develop a tendency to binge. Some of the subjects in the conscientious objector study, for example, later engaged in binging when they were allowed to return to regular eating, and a number of them continued to be hungry even after large meals (Keys et al., 1950). Thus the intense dieting that typically precedes the onset of bulimia nervosa may itself predispose some people to the disorder.

## Bulimia Nervosa vs. Anorexia Nervosa

Bulimia nervosa is similar to anorexia nervosa in many ways. Both disorders typically unfold after a period of intense dieting by people who are fearful of becoming obese, driven to become thin, preoccupied with food, weight, and appearance, and grappling with feelings of depression, anxiety, and the need to be perfect. Both groups of people believe that they weigh too much and look too heavy, regardless of their actual weight or appearance, and feel dominated by conflicts about what, when, and how much to eat. Both disorders are often associated with disturbed attitudes toward eating.

Yet bulimia nervosa also differs from anorexia nervosa in important ways (see Table 10-1). People with bulimia nervosa are much more likely to recognize that their behavior is pathological. They also tend to be more interested in pleasing others and to care more about being attractive to others and having intimate relationships (Striegel-Moore et al., 1993; Muuss, 1986). Correspondingly, they are typically more sexually experienced and active than people with anorexia nervosa.

People with bulimia nervosa display fewer of the obsessive qualities that enable people with restricting type anorexia nervosa to regulate their caloric intake so rigidly (Andersen, 1985). At the same time, sufferers of bulimia nervosa demonstrate several disturbed characteristics of their own. They may have long histories of mood swings, have enormous difficulty controlling their impulses, and are more likely than the general population to abuse alcohol and other drugs (APA, 1994; Higuchi et al., 1993). More than one-third of people with bulimia nervosa display the characteristics of a personality disorder, a pattern we shall examine more closely in Chapter 16 (APA, 1994; Pendleton et al., 1991).

Finally, the medical complications of bulimia nervosa differ from those of anorexia nervosa. Only half of women with bulimia nervosa are amenorrheic or have very irregular menstrual periods, compared to almost all of those with anorexia nervosa. Moreover, the daily repeated vomiting of many bulimic people washes their teeth and gums in hydrochloric acid, leading in some cases to serious dental problems (APA, 1994; Philipp et al., 1991). People who vomit regularly or have chronic diarrhea may also develop a dangerous potassium deficiency called *hypokalemia* (Mitchell et al., 1991, 1990).

**Table 10-1    *Anorexia Nervosa vs. Bulimia Nervosa***

| *Restricting Type Anorexia Nervosa* | *Bulimia Nervosa* |
| --- | --- |
| Refusal to maintain a minimum body weight for healthy functioning | Underweight, normal weight, near normal weight, or overweight |
| Hunger and disorder denied; often proud of weight management and more satisfied with body | Intense hunger experienced and binge-purge considered abnormal; greater body dissatisfaction |
| Less antisocial behavior | Greater tendency to antisocial behavior and alcohol abuse |
| Amenorrhea of at least 3 months' duration common | Irregular menstrual periods common; amenorrhea uncommon unless body weight is low |
| Mistrust of others, particularly professionals | More trusting of people who wish to help |
| Tend to be obsessional | Tend to be dramatic |
| Greater self-control, but emotionally overcontrolled with problems experiencing and expressing feelings | More impulsivity and emotional instability |
| More likely to be sexually immature and inexperienced | More sexually experienced and sexually active |
| Females are more likely to reject traditional feminine role | Females are more likely to embrace traditional feminine role |
| Age of onset often around 14–18 | Age of onset around 15–19 |
| Greater tendency for maximum pre-disorder weight to be near normal for age | Greater tendency for maximum pre-disorder weight to be slightly greater than normal |
| Lesser familial predisposition to obesity | Greater familial predisposition to obesity |
| Greater tendency toward pre-disorder compliance with parents | Greater tendency toward pre-disorder conflict with parents |
| Tendency to deny family conflict | Tendency to perceive intense family conflict |

*Sources:* APA, 1994; Levine, 1987; Andersen, 1985; Garner et al., 1985; Neuman & Halvorson, 1983.

*Summing Up*
Anorexia nervosa and bulimia nervosa are
particularly common among adolescent and young
adult females. Both disorders are typically preceded
by intense dieting and are marked by a drive toward
thinness, preoccupation with food and weight,
cognitive misperceptions, psychological problems,
and medical problems. People with bulimia nervosa
tend to be more concerned than people with
anorexia nervosa about being attractive to others,
are more likely to display a personality disorder,
and often have greater mood swings and more
substance abuse problems.

# Explanations of Eating Disorders

In recent years theorists and researchers have applied a
**multidimensional risk perspective** to explain the eating
disorders, a view that identifies several key factors that
place a person at risk for the disorders (Martin, 1990;
Garfinkel & Garner, 1982). Presumably the more of
these factors that are present, the greater a person's
risk of developing such a disorder. Some of the leading
factors identified to date are sociocultural pressures,
family environment, ego deficiencies and cognitive disturbances, mood disorders, and biological factors.

## Sociocultural Pressures

Many theorists believe that Western society's current
emphasis on thinness has contributed to the recent increases in eating disorders. Western standards of female attractiveness have changed throughout history
and now favor a slender figure.

The shift to a thinner female frame has been steady
since the 1950s. One investigation collected data on
the height, weight, and age of contestants in the Miss
America Pageant from 1959 through 1978 (Garner et
al., 1980). After controlling for height differences, the
investigators found an average decline of 0.28 pounds
per year among the contestants and 0.37 pounds per
year among winners. These same researchers examined
data on all *Playboy* magazine centerfold models over

*Multidimensional risk perspective*   A theory about the causes of a
disorder that identifies several different kinds of risk factors which
combine to help cause the disorder.

*"Seated Bather," by Pierre Auguste Renoir (1841–1919),
like other works of art, shows that the aesthetically ideal
woman of the past was considerably larger than today's
ideal.*

*Mannequins were once made extra thin to show the lines
of the clothing for sale to best advantage. Today the shape
of the ideal woman is indistinguishable from that of a
mannequin.*

the same twenty-year span and found that the average weight, bust, and hip measurements of these women decreased significantly throughout that period. A more recent study of Miss America contestants and *Playboy* magazine centerfolds indicates that each of these trends has continued into the 1990s (Wiseman et al., 1992).

Because thinness is especially valued and rewarded in the subcultures of fashion models, actors, dancers, and certain kinds of athletes, members of these groups are likely to be particularly concerned about their weight (Silverstein et al., 1986). As sociocultural theorists would predict, studies find that these people are more vulnerable than others to eating disorders (Prussin & Harvey, 1991).

> ### Consider This
> The most successful of today's fashion models, often referred to as "supermodels," are afforded a celebrity status that did not exist in previous years. Why do you think the fame and status of models has risen in this way? Do you see a possible relationship between their popularity and the rising prevalence of eating disorders?

Subcultural differences may also help explain the striking gender gap for eating disorders. Our society's emphasis on appearance has been aimed at women much more than men during most of our history (Rolls et al., 1991). Some theorists believe that this double standard of attractiveness has left women much more concerned about being thin, much more inclined to diet, and much more vulnerable to eating disorders (Rand & Kuldau, 1991). It is interesting to note that an increased emphasis on male thinness and dieting in recent years has been accompanied by an apparent increase in the number of eating disorders among males (Seligmann et al., 1994; Striegel-Moore et al., 1986) (see Box 10-2).

Western society not only glorifies thinness; it creates a climate of prejudice and hostility against overweight people. Cruel comments and jokes about obesity are standard fare on television shows and in movies, books, and magazines, whereas similar slurs based on ethnicity, race, and gender are considered unacceptable. Research indicates that the prejudice against people with obesity is deep-rooted (Brownell & O'Neil, 1993; Wooley & Wooley, 1982, 1979). In one study prospective parents were shown a picture of a chubby child and one of a medium-weight and rated the former as less friendly, energetic, intelligent, and desirable than the latter. In another study, preschool children, given a choice between a chubby and a thin rag doll, chose the thin one, although they could not say why.

Some clinicians argue that physicians, insurance companies, and health organizations such as the American Heart Association may also contribute to society's bias against obesity by their overstated warnings about the dangers of being overweight (Robertson, 1992; Wooley & Wooley, 1982). Although extreme obesity is indeed unhealthy, mild obesity is apparently not. Similarly, despite the claims of many psychologists, researchers have not found overweight people to be more disturbed psychologically than persons of normal weight (Garner et al., 1985). Nevertheless, such claims help establish a climate in which people seek thinness and fear weight gain (see Figure 10-2).

## Family Environment

As a primary transmitter of societal values, the family often plays a critical role in the development of eating disorders. Research suggests that as many as half of the families of people with eating disorders have a long history of emphasizing thinness, physical appearance, and dieting (Thelen & Cormier, 1995; Strober, 1992). Families may also set the stage for eating disorders by establishing abnormal and confusing family interactions and forms of communication throughout a child's upbringing (Lundholm & Waters, 1991).

The influential family theorist Salvador Minuchin believes that what he calls an *enmeshed family pattern* often leads to eating disorders (Minuchin et al., 1978). In an enmeshed system, family members are overinvolved with each other's affairs and overconcerned about each other's welfare. On the positive side, enmeshed families can be affectionate and loyal. On the negative side, they can be clinging and foster dependency. There is little room in them for individuality and autonomy.

Minuchin argues that adolescence poses a special problem for these families. The adolescent child's normal push for independence threatens to disrupt the family facade of harmony and closeness. In contrast, the child's disorder enables the family to maintain its illusion of living in harmony. A sick child needs her family, and family members can rally round and protect her. Case studies and empirical studies have sometimes, but not consistently, lent support to such family systems explanations (Axtell & Newlon, 1993; Gowers et al., 1985).

---

*Enmeshed family pattern*   A family system in which members are overinvolved with each other's affairs and overconcerned about each other's welfare.

## PERCENTAGE DISSATISFIED WITH THEIR:

**1972**                                                                    **1987**

| | | |
|---|---|---|
| 25% | Overall body | 38% Females |
| 15% | | 34% Males |
| 48% | Weight | 55% |
| 35% | | 41% |
| 13% | Height | 17% |
| 13% | | 20% |
| 26% | Breast/Chest | 32% |
| 18% | | 28% |
| 50% | Abdomen | 51% |
| 36% | | 50% |
| 49% | Hips and upper thighs | 50% |
| 12% | | 21% |

Figure 10-2    *According to surveys on body image conducted in the early 1970s and late 1980s, people in our society are more dissatisfied with their bodies now than they were a generation ago. Women are still more dissatisfied than men, but today's men are more dissatisfied with their bodies than the men of a generation past. (Adapted from Rodin, 1992, p. 57.)*

# Ego Deficiencies and Cognitive Disturbances

Hilde Bruch, a pioneer in the study and treatment of eating disorders, developed an influential theory that incorporates both psychodynamic and cognitive notions (Bruch, 1986, 1981, 1962). She argued that disturbed mother-child interactions lead to serious *ego deficiencies* in the child (including a poor sense of autonomy and control) and to severe *perceptual and other cognitive disturbances* that jointly produce disordered eating patterns.

According to Bruch (1974, 1973), parents may respond to their young children either effectively or ineffectively. *Effective parents* provide discriminating attention to their children's biological and emotional needs, giving them food when they are crying from hunger and comfort when they are crying out of fear. *Ineffective parents,* by contrast, fail to attend to their children's internal needs and instead arbitrarily decide when their children are hungry, cold, or tired, without correctly interpreting the children's actual condition. They may feed the children at times of anxiety rather than hunger, or comfort them at times of tiredness rather than anxiety. Children who are subjected to this kind of parenting may grow up confused and may be

unable to differentiate between their own internal needs, not knowing when they are hungry or satiated and unable to identify their own emotions or levels of fatigue.

Unable to rely on internal standards, these children turn instead to external guides, such as their parents, and seem to be "model children." But they fail to develop genuine self-reliance and "experience themselves as not being in control of their behavior, needs, and impulses, as not owning their own bodies" (Bruch, 1973, p. 55).

As adolescence approaches, these children are under increasing pressure to establish autonomy but feel unable to do so (Strauss & Ryan, 1987). To overcome their sense of helplessness, they seek extreme control over their body size and shape and over their eating habits. Helen, an 18-year-old, describes her experience:

There is a peculiar contradiction—everybody thinks you're doing so well and everybody thinks you're great, but your real problem is that you think that you are not good enough. You are afraid of not living up to what you think you are expected to do. You have one great fear, namely that of being ordinary, or average, or common—just not good enough. This peculiar dieting begins with such anxiety. You want to prove that you have control, that you can do it. The peculiar part of it is that it makes you feel good about yourself, makes you feel "I can accomplish something." It makes you feel "I can do something nobody else can do."

(*Bruch, 1978, p. 128*)

Clinical reports and research have provided some support for Bruch's theory. Clinicians have repeatedly observed that the parents of adolescents with eating disorders tend to define their children's needs for them rather than allow them to define their own needs (Steiner et al., 1991; Bruch, 1973).

Research has also supported Bruch's proposition that people with eating disorders perceive and distinguish internal cues inaccurately, including cues of hunger and emotion. When, for example, bulimic persons are anxious or upset, they mistakenly think they are also hungry, and they respond as they might respond to hunger—by eating (Rebert et al., 1991).

Finally, research has supported Bruch's argument that people with eating disorders rely excessively on the opinions, wishes, and views of others. Studies reveal, for example, that they are more likely than others to worry about how other people view them, to seek approval, to be conforming, and to feel relatively little control over their lives (Vitousek & Manke, 1994; Striegel-Moore et al., 1993).

*Hilde Bruch, a pioneer in the study of eating disorders, called attention to the prevalence of these disorders and the role of low self-esteem and lack of autonomy.*

## Mood Disorders

Earlier we noted that many people with eating disorders, particularly those with bulimia nervosa, experience symptoms of depression, such as sadness, low self-esteem, pessimism, and errors in logic (Ledoux et al., 1993). This finding has led some theorists to conclude that mood disorders predispose some people to eating disorders (Hsu et al., 1992).

Their claim is supported by four kinds of evidence. First, many more people with an eating disorder qualify for a clinical diagnosis of major depression than do people in the general population (Brewerton et al., 1995). Second, the close relatives of people with eating disorders apparently have a much higher rate of mood disorders than do close relatives of people without such disorders (APA, 1994; Johnson & Maddi, 1986). Third, persons with eating disorders, particularly bulimia nervosa, often display low activity of the neurotransmitter serotonin, similar to the serotonin depletions found in depressed people (Goldbloom et al., 1990; Wilcox, 1990). Fourth, persons with eating disorders are often helped significantly by some of the same antidepressant drugs that alleviate depression (Mitchell & deZwaan, 1993).

Although such findings are consistent with the notion that depression helps cause eating disorders, alternative explanations are also possible. It is possible, for example, that the pressure and pain of having an eating disorder help cause the mood disorder (Silverstone, 1990). Whatever the correct interpretation, it is clear that many people grappling with eating disorders also suffer from depression.

### *Consider This*
Research suggests that many people with bulimia nervosa also suffer from depression. It may be that bulimia nervosa helps cause depression or that depression helps cause bulimia nervosa. It may also be that each of the disorders is caused by a common third variable. What sociocultural, family, or biological factors might lead to both an eating disorder and depression?

## Biological Factors

Over the past decade, researchers have tried to determine whether biological factors help cause eating disorders. One influential theory has argued that people with bulimia nervosa have a heightened physiological need for carbohydrates, thus accounting for a strong preference for carbohydrates during binges (Wurtman

## Box 10-2

# The Gender Gap in Eating Disorders

Only 5 to 10 percent of all cases of eating disorders occur in males. Although the reasons for this striking gender difference are not entirely clear, several explanations have been proposed. One is that men and women are subject to different sociocultural pressures. For example, a survey of college men found that the majority selected "muscular, strong and broad shoulders" to describe the ideal male body, and "thin, slim, slightly underweight" to describe the ideal female body (Kearney-Cooke & Steichen-Asch, 1990). Of course, although the emphasis on a muscular, strong, and athletic body as the ideal male body may decrease the likelihood of eating disorders in men, it may create other problems such as steroid abuse or excessive weight-lifting to increase muscular size and strength (Mickalide, 1990).

A second reason for the different rates of eating disorders among men and women may be the different methods of weight loss used by the two groups. According to some clinical observations, men may be more likely to use exercise to lose weight, while women diet more often (Mickalide, 1990). Dieting is the precipitant to most cases of eating disorders.

Finally, eating disorders among men may be underdiagnosed. Some men do not want to admit that they have a traditionally "female problem" and may try to hide their disorder. In addition, clinicians may be less able to identify eating disorders in men because of different clinical manifestations. For example, amenorrhea, an obvious symptom of anorexia nervosa in females, is not an available indicator among men with this disorder. It is much more difficult to test for male reproductive problems, such as low levels of testosterone (Andersen, 1990).

How do men who do develop eating disorders compare to women with these problems? Some of them apparently grapple with similar issues. A number, for example, report that they aspire to a "lean, toned, thin" shape similar to the ideal female body, rather than a strong, muscular shape with broad shoulders typical of the male ideal body (Kearney-Cooke & Steichen-Asch, 1990).

In some cases, however, the precipitants of eating disorders are apparently different for men and women. For example, there are some indications that men with these disorders usually are overweight when they first start trying to lose weight (Andersen, 1990; Edwin & Andersen, 1990). In one study, men with eating disorders reported having been teased about their bodies and picked less for athletic teams during adolescence than men without eating disorders (Kearney-Cooke & Steichen-Asch, 1990). In contrast, women with eating disorders usually feel overweight when they begin dieting but may not actually be overweight according to objective measures (Edwin & Andersen, 1990).

---

& Wurtman, 1984, 1982; Wurtman, 1983). However, consistent evidence either for or against this notion has not yet emerged.

More recently, biological researchers have focused on the **hypothalamus,** a part of the brain that helps maintain various bodily functions, and the concept of *weight set point* to help explain eating disorders. Researchers have located two separate centers in the hypothalamus that control eating (Grossman, 1990; Bray et al., 1980). One, the *lateral hypothalamus,* or *LH,* produces hunger in persons and animals when it is activated. The other hypothalamus center, the **ventromedial hypothalamus,** or *VMH,* depresses hunger when it is activated.

It is now believed that the LH and VMH work together to help set up a "weight thermostat" in the body that predisposes individuals to keep their body at a particular weight level, called their **weight set point** (Garner et al., 1985; Keesey & Corbett, 1983). When a person's weight falls below his or her particular set point, the LH is activated and seeks to restore the lost weight by producing hunger. It also decreases the body's **metabolic rate,** that is, the rate at which the body expends energy. When a person's weight rises above his or her set point, the VMH is activated, and it seeks to remove the excess weight by depressing hunger and increasing the body's metabolic rate.

In short, a person's weight set point reflects the range of body weight that is normal for that individual in accordance with such influences as genetic inheri-

---

*Lateral hypothalamus (LH)*    The region of the hypothalamus that, when activated, produces hunger.

*Ventromedial hypothalamus (VMH)*    The region of the hypothalamus that, when activated, depresses hunger.

*Weight set point*    The weight level that a person is predisposed to maintain, set up by a "weight thermostat" that is governed, in part, by the lateral and ventromedial hypothalamus.

One group of men who suffer from particularly high rates of eating disturbances are athletes. Their problems are precipitated not by a cultural requirement to be thin but rather by the requirements and pressures of certain sports (Thompson & Sherman, 1993). The highest rates of eating disturbances have been found among jockeys, wrestlers, distance runners, body builders, and swimmers. One study of male jockeys, for example, found that they used such methods as restricting their food intake, abusing laxatives and diuretics, and inducing vomiting to lose weight (King & Mezey, 1987). Jockeys commonly spent up to four hours before a race in a sauna, shedding up to seven pounds of weight at a time. Similarly, male wrestlers in high school and college commonly restrict their food intake for up to three days before a match in order to "make weight," often losing between 2 and 12 percent of their body weight. One method that is particularly common in this group is practicing or running in several layers of warm or rubber clothing in order to lose up to five pounds of water weight shortly before weighing in for a match (Thompson & Sherman, 1993).

Whereas most women with eating disorders are obsessed with thinness at all times, wrestlers and jockeys are usually preoccupied with weight reduction only during the season, and indeed most wrestlers return to their normal weight once the season is over. After "making weight," many wrestlers go on eating and drinking binges in order to gain strength and hydrate themselves for the upcoming match, only to return to a weight-loss strategy after the match to get prepared for the next weigh-in. This eating cycle of weight loss and regain each match and each season has an adverse effect on the body, altering its metabolic activity and hindering future efforts at weight control (Steen et al., 1988). In addition, the weight reduction of male athletes has been found to have an adverse effect on their health (Mickalide, 1990).

Another difference that has been found between male athletes with eating problems and women with eating disorders is that male athletes tend to make accurate estimates of their body size (Enns et al., 1987). Finally, it is worth noting that recent research further suggests that female athletes with eating disorders display many of the same characteristics as male athletes with these disorders (Prussin & Harvey, 1991).

As the number of males with eating disturbances increases, researchers are becoming more interested in understanding both the similarities and differences between men and women with such disturbances (Andersen, 1992). All eating disturbances are capable of producing physical and psychological damage. Thus, they must all be well researched and addressed in future investigations and clinical work.

tance, early eating practices, and the body's need to maintain internal equilibrium (Levine, 1987). If weight falls significantly below a person's set point, the hypothalamus will act to alter thinking, biological functioning, and behavior in an effort to restore weight to the set point (Polivy & Herman, 1985; Wooley & Wooley, 1985).

According to weight set point theory, when people pursue a strict diet, their weight eventually moves below their weight set point and their brain begins compensatory activities. The psychological symptoms that result from starvation, such as preoccupation with food and desire to binge, are manifestations of the hypothalamus's efforts to reestablish the weight set point. In another compensatory move, the hypothalamus sets in motion bodily changes that make it harder and harder to lose weight however little one eats, as well as likelier and likelier to gain weight whenever one does eat (Spalter et al., 1993).

Once the brain and body begin acting to raise weight to the set point, dieters enter a battle of sorts against their compensatory activities. Some people are apparently "successful" in this battle, manage to shut down and control their eating almost completely, and move toward restricting type anorexia nervosa. For others, the battle spirals toward the binge-purge pattern found in binge eating/purging type anorexia nervosa or bulimia nervosa (Johnson & Maddi, 1986).

According to the multidimensional risk perspective, these biological factors and the various factors discussed on the preceding pages intersect in some people and together encourage eating disorders to unfold (Gleaves et al., 1993; Garner & Garfinkel, 1980). It is not necessary to display all of the associated characteristics or to be exposed to all of the influences to develop anorexia nervosa or bulimia nervosa. At the same time, researchers have yet to clarify precisely how the various factors interact, why only some

*The repeated electrical stimulation of a rodent's lateral hypothalamus by researchers can lead to extreme overeating and weight gain.*

vulnerable persons develop eating disorders, and why some people develop bulimia nervosa instead of anorexia nervosa or vice versa (Levine, 1987; Garfinkel & Garner, 1982).

---

### Summing Up

*Theorists usually apply a multidimensional risk perspective to explain the eating disorders. Individuals may be more likely to develop the disorders if they experience some (though not necessarily all) of the following factors: sociocultural pressures to be thin, a maladaptive family environment, poor parenting that leads to a poor sense of autonomy and to perceptual disturbances, a mood disorder, and hypothalamic reactions to dieting.*

---

# Treatments for Eating Disorders

Today's treatments for eating disorders have two dimensions. First, they seek to correct as quickly as possible the pathological eating pattern that is endangering the client's health. Second, therapists try to address the broader psychological and situational factors that led to and now maintain the dysfunctional eating pattern. In addition, family and friends can play an important role in helping to correct the disorder (Sherman & Thompson, 1990) (see Box 10-3).

## Treatments for Anorexia Nervosa

The immediate aim of treatment for anorexia nervosa is to help the individuals regain their lost weight, recover from malnourishment, and reestablish normal eating habits. Therapists must then help them to make psychological changes that enable them to maintain their immediate gains.

### Weight Restoration and Resumption of Eating

A variety of methods are used to help patients with anorexia nervosa gain weight quickly and restore them to health in a matter of weeks (Powers et al., 1991). In the past the methods were almost always applied in a hospital, but now they are increasingly being offered in outpatient settings (Kennedy et al., 1992).

In life-threatening cases, clinicians may provide nourishment directly by forcing *tube and intravenous feedings* on patients. Unfortunately, such feedings often breed a patient's distrust and set up a power struggle (Zerbe, 1993; Tiller et al., 1993). Another approach, used in many cases, is *antidepressant drug therapy* (Kaye et al., 1991; Gwirtsman et al., 1990). Yet another weight restoration intervention involves the use of *operant conditioning* approach is often included in weight restoration programs (Halmi, 1985; Martin, 1985). Patients are given positive reinforcement when they eat properly or gain weight and no reinforcement when they eat improperly or fail to gain weight. However, the impact of this approach has proved limited (Halmi, 1985).

In recent years, *supportive nursing care*, combined with a high calorie diet, has become the most popular weight-restoration technique (Andersen, 1986; Garfinkel & Garner, 1982). In this approach, well-trained nurses gradually increase a patient's diet over the course of several weeks to between 2,500 and 3,500 calories a day. The nurses educate patients about the program, give them progress reports, provide encouragement, and help them recognize that their weight gain is proceeding in a controlled manner and that they will not go overboard into obesity. Studies suggest that patients on nursing care programs usually gain the necessary weight in a period of eight to twelve weeks (Garfinkel & Garner, 1982; Russell, 1981).

## Box 10-3

# *How Family and Friends Can Help*
### *Michael Levine*

1. Write down specific instances of the person's problematic behavior or attitudes, and encourage other friends and family members to do the same. [Later therapy discussions will then be more precise.]

2. Educate yourself and other family members about eating disorders, and about the nearest resources offering professional and expert treatment.

3. Get support and advice from people you trust—clergy, social workers, friends, family physicians. Don't isolate yourself from people who care about you and who can help. Attend a support group.

4. Arrange for family and friends to speak confidentially with the person about the specifics and consequences of his or her disordered eating and weight-management practices. Try to remain calm, caring, and non-judgmental. Avoid giving simplistic suggestions about nutrition or self-control.

5. Communicate directly to the person the seriousness of your concern, your conviction that treatment is necessary, and your willingness to provide emotional, financial, and other practical support.

6. Exercise responsibility, authority, and authoritative wisdom in obtaining treatment for (a) minors with eating disorders and (b) anyone who is suicidal, very sick, or out of control.

7. Reaffirm the importance of yourself and your other family members. Don't allow your life to be disrupted by emotional upheaval—arguments, threats, blame, guilt, bribes, resentment—concerning issues of food, weight, and eating.

8. Sustain the person's sense of importance and dignity by encouraging decision-making and personal responsibility. Don't be manipulated into shielding the person from the consequences of the disorder,

including separation from you.

9. Be patient: Recovery is a long process because treatment must address the physical, psychological, behavioral, social, and cultural dimensions of complex disorders.

10. Love your relative or friend for himself or herself, not for appearance, health, body weight, or achievement. Encourage healthy feelings and interests, and avoid talking about appearance, eating habits, and weight.

11. Remember that families [by themselves] neither cause nor cure eating disorders, but they can make a major contribution to recovery and future development. Dwelling on guilt or causes is counterproductive.

12. Remember that compassion is "bearing with" a person in distress, not suffering unduly because of their injustices or unwillingness to get help.

*(Levine, 1988)*

## Broader Psychological Changes

Clinical researchers have found that people with anorexia nervosa must address their underlying emotional problems and alter their maladaptive thinking patterns if they are to experience lasting improvement (Tobin & Johnson, 1991; Garfinkel, 1985). Therapists typically offer a mixture of therapy and education to achieve this goal, using individual, group, and family therapy formats (Ehle, 1992; Crisp et al., 1991).

One focus of psychological treatment is to help patients with anorexia nervosa *recognize their need for autonomy and independence* and *exercise control in more appropriate ways* (Bruch, 1986, 1962). Another is to help them *recognize and trust their internal sensations and feelings* (Bruch, 1973). In the following exchange, a therapist tries to help a 15-year-old client identify and share her feelings:

PATIENT: I don't talk about my feelings; I never did.

THERAPIST: Do you think I'll respond like others?

PATIENT: What do you mean?

THERAPIST: I think you may be afraid that I won't pay close attention to what you feel inside, or that I'll tell you not to feel the way you do—that it's foolish to feel frightened, to feel fat, to doubt yourself, considering how well you do in school, how you're appreciated by teachers, how pretty you are.

PATIENT: *(Looking somewhat tense and agitated)* Well, I was always told to be polite and respect other people, just like a stupid, faceless doll *(Affecting a vacant, doll-like pose)*.

THERAPIST: Do I give you the impression that it would be disrespectful for you to share your feelings, whatever they may be?

PATIENT:  Not really; I don't know.

THERAPIST:  I can't, and won't, tell you that this is easy for you to do. . . . But I can promise you that you are free to speak your mind, and that I won't turn away.

(*Strober & Yager, 1985, pp. 368–369*)

Another focus of treatment is to help people with this eating disorder *change their misconceptions and attitudes* about eating and weight. Using Beck's cognitive approach, therapists may guide clients to focus on, challenge, and change maladaptive assumptions, such as "I must always be perfect" or "My weight and shape determine my value" (Wilson & Fairburn, 1993; Garner & Bemis, 1985, 1982).

Therapists may also educate clients with anorexia nervosa about the body distortions typical of their disorder and train them to recognize that their own assessments of their size are incorrect (Garner & Bemis, 1982). Such education often paves the way for more accurate body perceptions.

Finally, *family therapy* is often used in cases of anorexia nervosa (Dare & Eisler, 1992; Vanderlinden & Vandereycken, 1991). As in other family therapy situations, the therapist meets with the family as a whole, points out dysfunctional family patterns, and helps the members make appropriate changes. In particular, family therapists may try to help the person with anorexia nervosa separate her feelings and needs from those of other family members.

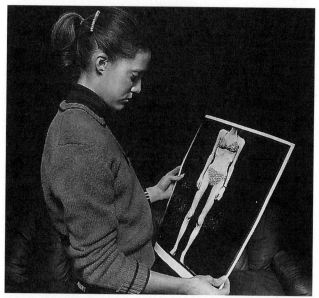

*After two years of treatment, this 16-year-old patient with anorexia nervosa gained back 25 pounds. Looking at pictures of other persons with the disorder helped her to recognize that body distortions are typical of this disorder.*

MOTHER:  I think I know what [Susan] is going through: all the doubt and insecurity of growing up and establishing her own identity. (*Turning to the patient, with tears*) If you just place trust in yourself, with the support of those around you who care, everything will turn out for the better.

THERAPIST:  Are you making yourself available to her? Should she turn to you, rely on you for guidance and emotional support?

MOTHER:  Well, that's what parents are for.

THERAPIST:  (*Turning to patient*) What do you think?

SUSAN:  (*To mother*) I can't keep depending on you, Mom, or everyone else. That's what I've been doing, and it gave me anorexia. . . .

THERAPIST:  Do you think your mom would prefer that there be no secrets between her and the kids—an open door, so to speak?

OLDER SISTER:  Sometimes I do.

THERAPIST:  (*To patient and younger sister*) How about you two?

SUSAN:  Yeah. Sometimes it's like whatever I feel, she has to feel.

YOUNGER SISTER:  Yeah.

(*Strober & Yager, 1985, pp. 381–382*)

Studies suggest that the combining of these various approaches is indeed often helpful to people with anorexia nervosa (Tobin & Johnson, 1991; Garfinkel & Garner, 1982). Such programs are now offered in mental health facilities and hospitals across the United States and Canada. Inasmuch as several pathways may lead to anorexia nervosa, it makes sense that the most effective form of intervention would be a treatment program that is varied and tailored to the unique needs of the patient.

## The Aftermath of Anorexia Nervosa

The development of multiple treatment approaches to anorexia nervosa has greatly improved the outlook for people with this disorder in recent years. Nevertheless, many of them still face significant obstacles on the road to recovery. Although the course and outcome of anorexia nervosa are highly variable, certain trends have emerged in numerous follow-up studies:

1. Weight is often quickly restored once treatment begins, but complete psychological and physical recovery may take several years. Altogether, approximately 75 percent of patients continue to show improvement when they are examined sev-

eral years or more after their initial recovery (APA, 1994; Andersen et al., 1985; Garfinkel & Garner, 1982).

2. The death rate from anorexia nervosa seems to be declining. Earlier diagnosis and safer and faster weight-restoration techniques may account for this trend. Deaths are usually caused by starvation, suicide, or electrolyte imbalance (APA, 1994; Andersen et al., 1985; Tolstrup et al., 1985).

3. Most females with anorexia nervosa menstruate again when they regain their weight. Others remain amenorrheic at least for a while (Crisp, 1981).

4. Typically, recovery is not a smooth process (Murray, 1986). At least 15 percent of patients have recurrences of anorexic behavior while they are recovering. These recurrences are usually precipitated by new stresses, such as marriage, pregnancy, or a major relocation (Sohlberg & Norring, 1992; Hsu et al., 1979).

5. Even years later, many persons continue to express concerns about their weight and appearance. Some continue to restrict their diets to some degree, experience anxiety when they eat with other people, or hold some distorted ideas about food, eating, and weight (Clinton & McKinlay, 1986).

6. At follow-up, around half of patients with anorexia nervosa continue to experience some emotional problems—particularly depression, social anxiety, and obsessiveness. Such problems are particularly common in those who have not succeeded in attaining a normal weight (Hsu et al., 1992).

7. Family problems persist for approximately half of patients with anorexia nervosa (Hsu, 1980).

8. Most patients with anorexia nervosa are performing effectively at their jobs at follow-up (Theander, 1970).

9. Those who recover go on to marry or have intimate relationships at rates comparable to those of nonanorexic populations (Hsu et al., 1979; Theander, 1970).

10. The more weight patients lose and the longer they have the problem before treatment, the poorer their recovery rate (Burns & Crisp, 1985). Some people with anorexia nervosa appear to recover without formal treatment of any kind.

11. Young adolescents seem to have a better recovery rate than older patients (APA, 1994). Females have a better recovery rate than males.

12. Those who display psychological, behavioral, or sexual problems before the development of anorexia nervosa tend to have a poorer recovery rate than those without such premorbid problems (Burns & Crisp, 1985).

# Treatments for Bulimia Nervosa

Treatment programs tailored to the particular features of bulimia nervosa have been developed only in recent years, but they have already had a meteoric rise in popularity. Most of these programs are offered in eating-disorder clinics, and all share the immediate goal of reducing and eliminating binge-purge patterns and normalizing eating habits and the broader goal of addressing the underlying causes of bulimic patterns. The programs emphasize education as much as therapy. Many programs combine several treatment strategies, including individual insight therapy, group therapy, behavioral therapy, and antidepressant drug therapy (Fahy et al., 1993; Fichter, 1990).

## Individual Insight Therapy

Psychodynamic and cognitive approaches have been the most common forms of individual insight therapy for clients with bulimia nervosa (Fichter, 1990). Psychodynamic therapists use free association and interpretive techniques to help these clients uncover and resolve their frustrating tensions, lack of self-trust, need for control, and feelings of powerlessness (Lerner, 1986; Yager, 1985). Only a few research studies have been conducted to test the effectiveness of this approach, but these studies are supportive (Garner et al., 1993; Yager, 1985).

Cognitive therapists try to help people with bulimia nervosa discuss and alter their maladaptive attitudes toward food, eating, weight, and shape (such as those listed in Table 10-2), thus eliminating the kinds of thinking that raise anxiety and lead to binging (Wilson & Pike, 1993; Garner et al., 1993). The therapists typically teach clients to identify and evaluate the dysfunctional thoughts that regularly precede their urge to binge—"I have no self-control," "I might as well give up," "I look fat,"—and guide them to draw more appropriate conclusions. The therapists may also guide clients to recognize, question, and eventually change their perfectionistic standards, sense of helplessness, and low self-concept. Researchers have found cognitive therapy to be relatively effective in cases of bulimia nervosa (Leitenberg et al., 1993; Wilson & Fairburn, 1993). Approaches that mix cognitive and psychodynamic techniques also appear to be helpful (Yager, 1985).

## Group Therapy

Most bulimia nervosa programs now include group therapy to give sufferers an opportunity to share their thoughts, concerns, and experiences with one another (Franko, 1993; Rathner et al., 1993). Here they learn that their disorder is not unique or shameful, and they receive support and understanding from the other members, along with candid feedback and insights (Asner, 1990). They can also work directly on underlying fears of displeasing others or being criticized. In one new group therapy technique, the *group meal,* clients plan and eat a meal together with the therapist, all the while discussing their thoughts and feelings as they occur (Franko, 1993). Research suggests that group therapy is helpful in as many as 75 percent of bulimia nervosa cases, particularly when it is combined with individual insight therapy (Wilfley et al., 1993; Mitchell et al., 1985).

### Behavioral Therapy

Behavioral techniques are often employed in cases of bulimia nervosa along with individual insight therapy or group therapy (Nutzinger & deZwaan, 1990; Long

& Cordle, 1982). Clients with this disorder may, for example, be asked to monitor and keep diaries of their eating behavior, their fluctuations of hunger and satiety, and their other feelings and experiences (Saunders, 1985; Greenberg & Marks, 1982). This strategy helps them to observe their eating patterns more objectively and to recognize the emotional triggers of their disorder.

Behaviorists are increasingly using the technique of *exposure and response prevention* to help break the binge-purge cycle (Gray & Hoage, 1990). As we saw in Chapter 6, this approach consists of exposing people to situations that would ordinarily raise anxiety and then preventing them from performing their usual compulsive acts, until the clients learn that the situations are actually quite harmless and their compulsive acts unnecessary. Viewing bulimic vomiting as a compulsive act that reduces fears about eating, behavioral therapists may have clients with bulimia nervosa eat

---

**Table 10-2    *Sample Items from the Eating Disorder Inventory II***

For each item, decide if the item is true about you ALWAYS (A), USUALLY (U), OFTEN (O), SOMETIMES (S), RARELY (R), or NEVER (N). Circle the letter that corresponds to your rating.

| | | | | | | |
|---|---|---|---|---|---|---|
| A | U | O | S | R | N | I think that my stomach is too big. |
| A | U | O | S | R | N | I eat when I am upset. |
| A | U | O | S | R | N | I stuff myself with food. |
| A | U | O | S | R | N | I think about dieting. |
| A | U | O | S | R | N | I think that my thighs are too large. |
| A | U | O | S | R | N | I feel ineffective as a person. |
| A | U | O | S | R | N | I feel extremely guilty after overeating. |
| A | U | O | S | R | N | I am terrified of gaining weight. |
| A | U | O | S | R | N | I get confused about what emotion I am feeling. |
| A | U | O | S | R | N | I feel inadequate. |
| A | U | O | S | R | N | I have gone on eating binges where I felt that I could not stop. |
| A | U | O | S | R | N | As a child, I tried very hard to avoid disappointing my parents and teachers. |
| A | U | O | S | R | N | I have trouble expressing my emotions to others. |
| A | U | O | S | R | N | I get confused as to whether or not I am hungry. |
| A | U | O | S | R | N | I have a low opinion of myself. |
| A | U | O | S | R | N | I think my hips are too big. |
| A | U | O | S | R | N | If I gain a pound, I worry that I will keep gaining. |
| A | U | O | S | R | N | I have the thought of trying to vomit in order to lose weight. |
| A | U | O | S | R | N | I think my buttocks are too large. |
| A | U | O | S | R | N | I eat or drink in secrecy. |
| A | U | O | S | R | N | I would like to be in total control of my bodily urges. |

*Source:* Garner, Olmsted, & Polivy, 1991, 1984.

*The emphasis on appearance and thinness begins early in life in our society, particularly for females. These preschool participants in a beauty contest are learning the kind of aesthetic standards by which they will be judged throughout their lives.*

particular kinds and amounts of food and then prevent them from vomiting (Rosen & Leitenberg, 1985, 1982). Studies have found that eating-related anxieties often decrease over the course of this treatment and that binge eating and vomiting decrease substantially (Wilson et al., 1986; Johnson et al., 1984).

## Antidepressant Medications

During the past decade, antidepressant drugs have often been added to the treatment package for bulimia nervosa. Studies indicate that these medications can indeed be helpful, especially in combination with other forms of therapy (Goldbloom & Olmsted, 1993; Mitchell & deZwaan, 1993). As in the treatment of anorexia nervosa, these drugs appear to be particularly effective for those who display depression and obsessive-compulsiveness as part of their problem (Yager, 1985).

## The Aftermath of Bulimia Nervosa

Left untreated, bulimia nervosa usually lasts for years, sometimes improving temporarily but then emerging again (APA, 1994). As with anorexia nervosa, relapses are usually precipitated by a new life stress, such as an impending examination, job change, illness, marriage, or divorce (Abraham & Llewellyn-Jones, 1984).

Approximately 40 percent of clients with bulimia nervosa show an outstanding response to treatment: they stop their binges and purging and stabilize their eating habits and weight (Fairburn et al., 1986; Pope et al., 1983). Another 40 percent show a moderate response—decreased binge eating and purging. The remaining 20 percent show no improvement in their eating patterns.

Relapse is a problem even among clients who respond successfully to treatment. One study found that close to one-third of recovered clients relapsed within two years of treatment (Olmsted et al., 1994). Relapse was more likely among persons who had vomited more frequently while bulimic and those who maintained a high degree of interpersonal distrust even at the end of treatment.

### Consider This

Relapse is a problem for some people who recover from bulimia nervosa. Why might people remain vulnerable even after recovery? How might they and therapists reduce the chances of relapse?

Research also suggests that treatment helps many people with bulimia nervosa make significant and lasting improvements in their psychological and social functioning (Yager et al., 1995; Herzog et al., 1990). Follow-up studies find former patients to be less depressed than they were at the time they were diagnosed (Brotman et al., 1988; Fairburn et al., 1986). Follow-up studies have also indicated that approximately one-third of former patients interact more healthily at home, at work, *and* in social settings; another third interact effectively in only two of these areas (Hsu & Holder, 1986).

---

### Summing Up

*Treatment for anorexia nervosa involves quickly increasing caloric intake and restoring weight, as well as more generally addressing broad underlying issues. Treatment for bulimia nervosa involves eliminating the binge-purge pattern, as well as addressing broad underlying issues. Treatment for either disorder is often successful, but relapses may occur, and eating-related anxieties and problems may linger for some people.*

---

## The State of the Field
## *Eating Disorders*

The prevalence of eating disorders has increased in Western society during the past two decades, and public and clinical interest has risen right along with it. Thus, researchers have been studying anorexia nervosa and bulimia nervosa with great fervor.

They have learned that the two disorders are similar in many important ways. They have uncovered the unusually significant role played by sociocultural pressures in the development of these disorders, and the critical influences of dieting, starvation, and biological factors in precipitating and maintaining them. They have also determined that the disorders are brought about by a host of intersecting factors, which can best be corrected by multidimensional intervention programs.

At the same time, many questions are still unanswered, and every new discovery forces clinicians to adjust their theories and treatment programs. Indeed, bulimia nervosa was not even formally identified as a clinical disorder until the 1980s, and recently researchers have learned that people with bulimia nervosa sometimes feel strangely positive toward their symptoms. A recovered patient said, for example, "I still miss my bulimia as I would an old friend who has died" (Cauwels, 1983, p. 173). Obviously, when such feelings are fully understood and addressed, treatment programs will become even more effective.

While clinicians and researchers strive for more answers about anorexia nervosa and bulimia nervosa and greater effectiveness in treating them, the clients themselves have begun to take an active role in providing intervention. A number of patient-initiated national organizations now provide information, education, and support to people with eating disorders and to their families through a national telephone hotline, professional referrals, printed information and newsletters, and workshops, seminars, and conferences. These organizations include the National Anorexic Aid Society, American Anorexia and Bulimia Association, National Association of Anorexia Nervosa and Associated Disorders, and Anorexia Nervosa and Related Eating Disorders, Inc.

The very existence of such organizations helps counter the isolation and shame felt by people with eating disorders. They also help countless sufferers recognize that they are hardly alone or powerless against the eating disorder that seems to have taken control of their life.

---

## *Chapter Review*

1. **Eating Disorders:** Eating disorders have increased dramatically since thinness has become a national obsession.

2. **Anorexia Nervosa:** Victims of *anorexia nervosa* relentlessly pursue extreme thinness and lose dangerous amounts of weight.
   A. Anorexia nervosa most often appears between the ages of 14 and 18; over 90 percent of its victims are female; and it strikes as many as 1 percent of adolescent and young adult females.
   B. Five central features of anorexia nervosa are a drive for thinness, preoccupation with food, cognitive disturbances, psychological and mood problems, and medical problems, including *amenorrhea*.

3. **Bulimia Nervosa:** Sufferers of *bulimia nervosa* go on frequent eating binges, then compensate by such means as forcing themselves to vomit or taking laxatives to keep from gaining weight.
   A. Bulimia nervosa, also known as the *binge-purge syndrome*, usually appears in females between the ages of 15 and 19 years and is displayed by between 1 and 6 percent of them. Over 90 percent of its victims are female. These young women generally maintain their body weight within the normal range.
   B. The binges of persons with bulimia nervosa often occur in response to growing tension. The binge episodes are followed, in turn, by feelings of guilt and self-reproach.

C. Purging behavior is initially reinforced by the immediate relief it brings from uncomfortable feelings of fullness or by temporary reduction of the feelings of anxiety, self-disgust, and loss of control attached to binge eating. Over time, however, people often feel increasingly disgusted with themselves, depressed, and guilty.

4. *Explanations of Eating Disorders:* Today's theorists usually apply a *multidimensional risk perspective* to explain eating disorders, and identify several key factors that place a person at risk for an eating disorder: society's emphasis on thinness, family environment, ego deficiencies (including a poor sense of autonomy) and cognitive disturbances, mood disorders, and biological factors (including hypothalamic reactions to excessive dieting).

5. *Treatments for Anorexia Nervosa:* The first step is to increase caloric intake and restore the person's weight quickly, using a strategy such as *supportive nursing care.* The second step is to address the underlying psychological problems, so that improvement may be lasting, by employing a mixture of individual, group, and family therapies.

A. Lasting recovery from anorexia nervosa is experienced by 75 percent of its victims.

B. Some of those who recover experience relapses, many continue to have concerns about their weight and appearance, and half continue to experience some emotional or family problems.

6. *Treatments for Bulimia Nervosa:* Treatments for bulimia nervosa focus on eliminating the binge-purge pattern and addressing the underlying causes of the disorder. Often several treatment strategies are combined, including individual insight therapy, group therapy, behavioral therapy, and antidepressant medications.

A. Left untreated, bulimia nervosa may last for years. Approximately 40 percent of clients show an outstanding response to treatment, another 40 percent a moderate response.

B. In one study, almost a third of recovered clients relapsed within two years.

## Key Terms

anorexia nervosa
bulimia nervosa
restricting type anorexia nervosa
binge-eating/purging type anorexia nervosa

amenorrhea
binge-purge syndrome
compensatory behavior
binge-eating disorder
binge
hypokalemia

multidimensional risk perspective
enmeshed family pattern
hypothalamus
weight set point
lateral hypothalamus (LH)

ventromedial hypothalamus (VMH)
tube and intravenous feeding
supportive nursing care
family therapy

## Quick Quiz

1. What are the symptoms and main features of anorexia nervosa?

2. What are the symptoms and main features of bulimia nervosa?

3. How are people with restricting type anorexia nervosa similar to those with bulimia nervosa? How are they different?

4. What evidence suggests that sociocultural pressures and factors may set the stage for eating disorders?

5. According to Hilde Bruch, how might parents' failure to attend appropriately to their baby's internal needs and emotions be contributing to the later development of an eating disorder?

6. How might a person's hypothalamus and weight set point contribute to the development of an eating disorder?

7. Theorists usually apply a multidimensional risk perspective to explain the eating disorders. What does this mean?

8. When clinicians treat people with anorexia nervosa, what are their initial and long-term goals, and what approaches do they use to accomplish them?

9. How well do people with anorexia nervosa recover from their disorder? What factors affect a person's recovery? What risks and problems linger after recovery?

10. What are the key goals and approaches used in the treatment of bulimia nervosa? How successful are they? What factors affect a person's recovery? What are the risks of relapse?

# 11

# Substance-Related Disorders

## Topic Overview

*Depressants*
Alcohol
Sedative-Hypnotic Drugs
Opioids

*Stimulants*
Cocaine
Amphetamines

*Hallucinogens*

*Cannabis*

*Combinations of Substances*

*Explanations of Substance-Related Disorders*

*Treatments for Substance-Related Disorders*

There is probably no substance on earth that has not been ingested by human beings somewhere, at some time. Curious and adventuresome, we have learned that a vast variety of substances are edible and nutritious when they are prepared in certain ways, and we have developed a long list of acceptable foods and delicacies. Humans have likewise stumbled upon substances that have interesting effects on the brain and the rest of the body. Many such substances have proved beneficial to health or healing and have gained use as medicines. Some have been found to have calming or stimulating effects and are used to enhance social and recreational experiences.

Unfortunately, many of the substances that humans have come across are capable of harming the body or adversely affecting behavior or mood. Indeed, the compulsive misuse of these substances has become one of society's most disabling problems. Technically, the term "drug" applies to any substance other than food that changes our bodily or mental functioning. Henceforth in this chapter, the words "drug" and "substance" will be used interchangeably with that connotation.

Drug misuse may lead to various kinds of abnormal functioning. First, ingestion of a drug may cause temporary changes in behavior, emotion, or thought. An excessive amount of alcohol, for example, may lead to a state of **intoxication** (literally, "poisoning"), a temporary syndrome in which a person exhibits impaired judgment, mood changes, irritability, slurred speech, and loss of coordination. Drugs such as LSD may produce a distinct form of intoxication, sometimes called **hallucinosis,** a state of perceptual distortions and hallucinations.

The regular use of some substances can also lead to longer-term patterns of maladaptive behavior and to changes in the body's response to the substance. People who regularly ingest a given substance may develop a pattern of **substance abuse,** in which they rely on the drug excessively and chronically and, as a result, seriously damage their family and social relationships, perform unreliably at work, and create physical hazards for themselves or others. People who display **substance dependence,** a more advanced substance-related disorder that is known popularly as *addiction,* further develop a *physical* dependence on a drug in ad-

dition to a pattern of abusing it—that is, they develop a *tolerance* for the drug or experience *withdrawal* symptoms if they suddenly stop taking it, or both.

*Tolerance* is a condition in which a person needs increasing doses of the substance in order to keep obtaining the desired effect. Similarly, long-term regular use may lead to **withdrawal,** a condition in which people experience unpleasant and at times dangerous symptoms—for example, cramps, anxiety attacks, sweating, nausea—when they suddenly stop taking or reduce their dosage of the drug. Withdrawal symptoms can begin within hours of the last dose and tend to intensify over several days before they subside. Surveys suggest that over the course of a year, between 9.5 and 11.3 percent of all adults in the United States, more than 15 million people, display a substance-related disorder, but only 20 percent of them receive treatment for it (Kessler et al., 1994; Regier et al., 1993).

Some potentially harmful drugs, such as antianxiety drugs and barbiturates, require a physician's prescription for legal use. Others, such as alcohol and the nicotine found in cigarettes, are legally available to all adults (see Box 11-1). Still others, such as heroin, are illegal under any circumstance. Nearly 13 percent of all people in the United States currently use marijuana, cocaine, heroin, or some other illegal substance (NIDA, 1993). Twenty-seven percent of high school seniors have used an illicit drug within the past year (Johnston et al., 1993).

The drugs that currently are arousing the most concern among the general public fall into four categories: substances that act to *depress* the central nervous system, such as alcohol and opioids; *stimulants* of the central nervous system, such as cocaine and amphetamines; *hallucinogens,* such as LSD, which cause illusions, hallucinations, and other powerful changes in sensory perception; and *cannabis* substances, such as marijuana, which cause a mixture of hallucinogenic, depressant, and stimulant effects.

# Depressants

**Depressants** are substances that slow the activity of the central nervous system and in sufficient doses cause a

---

*Intoxication*    A temporary drug-induced state in which a person exhibits symptoms such as impaired judgment, mood changes, irritability, slurred speech, and loss of coordination.

*Substance abuse*    A pattern of behavior in which a person relies on a drug excessively and chronically, allowing it to occupy a central position in his or her life.

*Substance dependence*    A pattern of behavior in which a person relies on a drug excessively and builds a tolerance to it or experiences withdrawal symptoms when he or she abstains from it, or both.

*Tolerance*    The adjustment the body makes to the habitual presence of certain drugs so that larger and larger doses are required to achieve the initial effect.

*Withdrawal*    Unpleasant, sometimes dangerous reactions that may occur when people who use a drug chronically suddenly stop taking or reduce their dosage of the drug.

*Depressant*    A substance that slows the activity of the central nervous system and in sufficient dosages causes a reduction of tension and inhibitions.

## Box 11-1

# *Other Substances, Other Problems*

The substances described in this chapter have received enormous attention from clinicians, largely because of the broad social problems tied to their misuse. But there are a number of other substances that researchers are increasingly discovering to be problematic and dangerous. Among the leading ones cited in DSM-IV are nicotine, caffeine, phencyclidine (PCP), and inhalants.

### Nicotine

The physiological effects and dangers of smoking tobacco are well documented. More than 410,000 people die each year in the United States as a result of it (Farley, 1994; Report of the Surgeon General, 1990, 1988). Smoking is directly associated with high blood pressure, coronary heart disease, lung disease, cancer, stroke, and other deadly medical problems.

Approximately a quarter of Americans over the age of 12 are regular smokers (NIDA, 1992). Indeed, 17 percent of all high school seniors smoke regularly (Johnston et al., 1993). Most adult smokers know that smoking is unhealthy and would rather not do it. So why do they continue to smoke? Because, as the surgeon general declared in 1988, nicotine, the active substance in tobacco and a *stimulant* of the central nervous system, is highly addictive.

Inhaling a puff of cigarette smoke delivers a dose of nicotine to the brain faster than it could be delivered by injection into the bloodstream, and it is believed to bind directly to receptors in the brain, which soon becomes dependent on it. When regular smokers

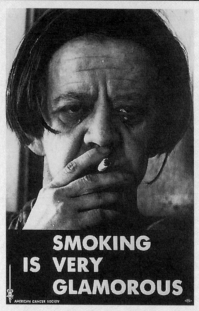

**SMOKING IS VERY GLAMOROUS**

AMERICAN CANCER SOCIETY

*An American Cancer Society antismoking poster.*

abstain, they experience withdrawal symptoms—irritability, increased appetite, sleep disturbances, cognitive difficulties, and a powerful desire to smoke. Smokers also develop a tolerance for nicotine and must increase the amount they ingest in order to achieve the same psychological and physiological results and to avoid withdrawal.

The currently available treatments for smoking are not particularly effective (Nides et al., 1995). Most people who do stop smoking after receiving treatment start smoking again within one year (Hall et al., 1985). Behavioral and biological approaches have been the most successful, especially when used in combination. In the behavioral *aversive conditioning* approach called *rapid smoking*, the smoker sits in a closed room and puffs quickly on a cigarette, as of-

ten as once every six seconds, until he or she begins to feel ill and cannot take another puff. The feelings of illness become associated with smoking, and the smoker experiences an aversive reaction to cigarettes (Baker & Brandon, 1988).

A common drug intervention for smoking is the use of *nicotine gum*, which contains a high level of nicotine that is released as the smoker chews. In theory, people who ingest nicotine by chewing no longer need to smoke, and the reinforcing effects of smoking are removed.

A similar biological approach is the *nicotine patch*. This small adhesive strip is attached to the skin throughout the day. Its nicotine content is supposedly absorbed through the skin, leaving the smoker with less need to smoke. Some people report that the patch helps them abstain from or cut down on cigarette smoking, but research has yet to establish its efficacy (Goldstein, 1994).

The more one smokes, the harder it is to quit. On the positive side, however, former smokers' risk for disease and death decreases steadily the longer they abstain from smoking (Goldstein, 1994; Jaffe, 1985). For those who are able to take the long view, this assurance may be a powerful motivator. In the meantime, more than 1,000 people die of smoking-related diseases each day.

### Caffeine

Caffeine is the world's most widely consumed stimulant drug (Chou, 1992). Seventy-five percent of the total amount consumed is taken in the form of coffee; the rest is consumed in tea, cola, and chocolate, as well as in numerous prescription and over-the-counter medications, such as Excedrin (Chou, 1992; Johnson-Greene et al., 1988).

Research has revealed that 99 percent of the caffeine one ingests is absorbed in the body and that it reaches its peak concentration within an hour, penetrating all body membranes and being distributed evenly to all body tissues (Julien, 1988). Like other stimulant drugs, caffeine produces a release of the neurotransmitters dopamine, serotonin, and norepinephrine in the brain (Benowitz, 1990), and thus increases vigilance and arousal and general motor activity and reduces fatigue. At the same time, however, it disrupts the performance of complex motor tasks and may interfere with both the duration and quality of sleep (Chou, 1992; Jacobson & Thurman-Lacey, 1992). Caffeine also produces biological changes throughout the body. Heart rate decreases with moderate amounts of consumption, respiration increases, blood pressure rises, and more gastric acid is secreted by the stomach (Shi et al., 1993).

More than 250 milligrams of caffeine (two to three cups of brewed coffee) can produce caffeine intoxication, which may include such symptoms as restlessness, nervousness, stomach disturbances, twitching, and increased heart rate (APA, 1994). Caffeine intoxication may also produce the symptoms of an anxiety disorder or sleep disorder in some people (APA, 1994).

Although DSM-IV does not include the category *caffeine depen-dence*, research is increasingly linking caffeine to a withdrawal syndrome in some persons. A recent study by Kenneth Silverman and his colleagues (1992) demonstrated that the abrupt cessation of caffeine intake by people who consume low to moderate amounts of it daily (the equivalent of two and a half cups of coffee or seven cans of cola) can cause significant withdrawal symptoms.

The widespread and casual use of caffeine has spurred much debate about its effects on health, and as public awareness of possible health risks has increased, researchers have observed a decline in caffeine consumption (Chou, 1992).

## Phencyclidine (PCP)

The drug *phencyclidine (PCP)*, also known as *angel dust,* was first developed as an anesthetic in the 1950s and became a street drug in the 1960s. PCP can be smoked or taken orally or intravenously. Its use, at least among teenagers, has declined in recent years (APA, 1994).

Some people consider PCP to be a hallucinogen, but DSM-IV categorizes it separately because it has psychological effects beyond those produced by hallucinogens. At low doses, users of PCP feel dizzy, nauseous, and weak. Their eyeballs shake noticeably, other body parts may move uncontrollably, their blood pressure rises, and their heart may beat rapidly. At higher doses, their thinking may become disorganized, they have a distorted body image and distorted sensory perceptions (including hallucinations), and they feel depersonal-ized and unreal. Many become upset and violent and behave bizarrely. Intoxication is often so severe as to require hospitalization. Indeed, PCP is the cause of numerous substance-related emergency room visits and deaths (APA, 1994). Some users develop a pattern of abuse. Tolerance and withdrawal responses have not, however, been clearly shown in humans (APA, 1994).

## Inhalants

Individuals can become intoxicated by inhaling large amounts of the *hydrocarbon* chemical compounds found in gasoline, glue, paint thinners, spray paints, and related products. The symptoms of these forms of intoxication are belligerence, assaultiveness, apathy, and impaired judgment, as well as dizziness, shaking eyeballs and other tremors, poor coordination, slurred speech, and related effects. A small percentage of users develop a broader pattern of abuse or dependence (APA, 1994).

## " . . . and More"

There are many other drugs that are also known to create short-term and long-term problems for users, drugs that do not belong to any of the categories listed in DSM-IV. Clinicians are increasingly recognizing, for example, that *anabolic steroids; nitrate inhalants,* or poppers; *nitrous oxide,* or laughing gas; *catnip;* and *over-the-counter* and *prescription drugs* such as cortisol and antihistamines can cause significant impairment, may in some cases lead to abuse or dependence, and are often dangerous. Clearly, the list continues to grow.

**Table 11-1**    *Relationships between Sex, Weight, Oral Alcohol Consumption, and Blood Alcohol Level*

| Absolute Alcohol (ounces) | Beverage Intake* | Blood Alcohol Level (percent) | | | | | |
|---|---|---|---|---|---|---|---|
| | | Female (100 lb) | Male (100 lb) | Female (150 lb) | Male (150 lb) | Female (200 lb) | Male (200 lb) |
| ½ | 1 oz spirits† 1 glass wine 1 can beer | 0.045 | 0.037 | 0.03 | 0.025 | 0.022 | 0.019 |
| 1 | 2 oz spirits 2 glasses wine 2 cans beer | 0.090 | 0.075 | 0.06 | 0.050 | 0.045 | 0.037 |
| 2 | 4 oz spirits 4 glasses wine 4 cans beer | 0.180 | 0.150 | 0.12 | 0.100 | 0.090 | 0.070 |
| 3 | 6 oz spirits 6 glasses wine 6 cans beer | 0.270 | 0.220 | 0.18 | 0.150 | 0.130 | 0.110 |
| 4 | 8 oz spirits 8 glasses wine 8 cans beer | 0.360 | 0.300 | 0.24 | 0.200 | 0.180 | 0.150 |
| 5 | 10 oz spirits 10 glasses wine 10 cans beer | 0.450 | 0.370 | 0.30 | 0.250 | 0.220 | 0.180 |

*In 1 hour.
†100-proof spirits.
*Source:* Ray & Ksir, 1993, p. 194.

reduction of tension and inhibitions and impair judgment, motor activity, and concentration. The three most widely used groups of depressants are *alcohol, sedative-hypnotics,* and *opioids.*

## Alcohol

Two-thirds of the people in the United States drink alcohol-containing beverages, at least from time to time. Indeed, alcohol is by far the most popular drug in the United States, and purchases of beer, wine, and liquor add up to tens of billions of dollars each year. More than 5 percent of all adults are heavy drinkers, consuming at least five drinks on at least five occasions during the past month (NIDA, 1993). Male heavy drinkers outnumber female heavy drinkers by more than 3 to 1 (NIDA, 1993).

All alcoholic beverages contain **ethyl alcohol.** This chemical compound is rapidly absorbed into the blood through the lining of the stomach and the intestine, and immediately begins to take effect. The ethyl alcohol is carried in the bloodstream to the central nervous system (CNS), where it acts to depress, or slow, its functioning. At first it depresses the centers of the CNS that control judgment and inhibition, and people become less constrained, more talkative, and often more friendly. As their inner control breaks down, they may feel relaxed, safe, self-confident, and happy. Alcohol's depression of these regions of the CNS also impairs fine motor skills, increases sensitivity to light, and causes the small blood vessels of the skin to dilate, so that the face and neck become flushed and the person feels warm.

As more alcohol is ingested, it eventually depresses other areas in the CNS and causes changes that are even more problematic. People become still less restrained and more confused. Their ability to make rational judgments declines, their speech becomes less guarded and less coherent, and their memory falters (Goldstein, 1994). Many become loud, boisterous, and aggressive, their emotions exaggerated and unstable; mildly amusing remarks or situations may strike them as hilarious.

Motor impairment also becomes more pronounced as drinking continues, and reaction times slow. People at this stage are unsteady when they stand or walk and clumsy in performing even simple activities. They may

*Alcohol*   Any beverage containing ethyl alcohol, including beer, wine, and liquor.

drop things, bump into doors and furniture, and misjudge distances. Their vision becomes blurred, particularly peripheral vision, and they have trouble distinguishing between different intensities of light. Hearing is affected, too. As a result of such impairments, people who have drunk too much alcohol have great difficulty driving or solving simple problems.

The extent of the effect of ethyl alcohol on body chemistry is determined by its concentration in the blood. Thus a given amount of alcohol will have less effect on a larger person than on a smaller one (see Table 11-1 and Figure 11-1), because the larger person has a greater volume of blood. Other factors may also influence the concentration of ethyl alcohol in the blood. For example, women become more affected than men at an equal dose of alcohol, since women have significantly less of the stomach enzyme *alcohol dehydrogenase,* which breaks down alcohol in the stomach before it enters the blood (NIAAA, 1992).

Levels of impairment are also closely related to the concentration of ethyl alcohol in the blood. By the time the alcohol constitutes 0.09 percent of the blood volume, a drinker crosses the line into intoxication. As the concentration of alcohol in the bloodstream further increases, the drinker becomes even more intoxicated and impaired. If the level goes as high as 0.55 percent, death will probably result. Most people, however, lose consciousness before they can drink enough to reach this level.

The effects of alcohol decline only as the alcohol concentration in the blood declines. Most of the alcohol is broken down, or *metabolized,* by the liver into carbon dioxide and water, which can be exhaled and excreted. Different people's livers conduct this process at somewhat different speeds; thus rates of "sobering up" vary. Despite a popular misconception, neither drinking black coffee, splashing cold water on the face, nor "getting hold of oneself" can speed the process up. Only time and metabolism can make a person sober.

Many people develop a long-term pattern of alcohol abuse or alcohol dependence—patterns collectively known as *alcoholism.* Surveys indicate that over a one-year period, between 7.4 and 9.7 percent of all adults in the United States abuse or are dependent on alcohol (Kessler et al., 1994; Regier et al., 1993). Between 13 and 23 percent of the adult population will display one of these patterns at some time in their lives, with men outnumbering women by as much as 5 to 1 (APA, 1994; Helzer et al., 1991).

The prevalence rate of alcoholism in a given year is 7 percent for both African Americans and white Americans and 9 percent for Hispanic persons (APA, 1994; Helzer et al., 1991). The men in these ethnic groups, however, show strikingly different age patterns in their rates of alcoholism. For white and Hispanic American men, the rate of alcoholism is highest—over 18 percent—during young adulthood. For African American men, the rate is highest—15 percent—during middle age.

## Alcohol Abuse and Dependence

People who abuse alcohol regularly drink excessive amounts of alcohol and rely on it to enable them to do things that would otherwise make them anxious. Eventually, the excessive drinking interferes with their socializing or with their cognitive ability and work performance. They may have frequent arguments with family members or friends, miss work repeatedly, and even lose their jobs.

People who abuse alcohol typically follow one or another of three broad drinking patterns: drinking large amounts of alcohol every day; drinking to excess only on weekends or evenings; or going on periodic binges of heavy drinking that can last weeks or months.

For many people, the pattern of alcoholism further includes physical dependence. As they use alcohol repeatedly, their body builds up a tolerance for it and they need to drink increasing amounts in order to feel any effects. They also experience withdrawal responses

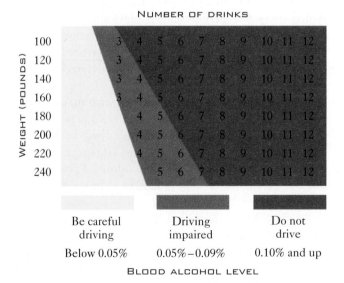

**Figure 11-1** *Counting a 12-ounce glass of beer as one drink, clinicians estimate that a 100-pound person will reach a state's legal limit for drunk driving, a blood alcohol level of 0.08 to 0.10 percent, after ingesting just three drinks. The ability to drive is somewhat impaired even when the blood alcohol level is below the legal limit. (Adapted from Frances & Franklin, 1988.)*

*Alcoholism* A pattern of behavior in which a person repeatedly abuses or develops a dependence on alcohol.

when they abstain from alcohol. When they try to stop drinking, within hours their hands, tongue, and eyelids begin to shake noticeably. They feel weak and nauseous. They sweat and vomit. Their heart beats rapidly and their blood pressure rises. They may also become anxious, depressed, unable to sleep, or irritable.

A small percentage of people who are alcohol dependent also experience a particularly dramatic withdrawal reaction within three days after they stop or reduce drinking: *alcohol withdrawal delirium,* or *delirium tremens ("the DT's").* Delirium is a state of abundant mental confusion and clouded consciousness. Persons in the throes of delirium tremens may have terrifying visual hallucinations: they believe they are seeing small frightening animals or objects moving about rapidly, perhaps pursuing them or crawling on them. Here is Mark Twain's classic description of Huckleberry Finn's alcoholic father:

> I don't know how long I was asleep, but . . . there was an awful scream and I was up. There was Pap looking wild, and skipping around every which way and yelling about snakes. He said they was crawling up on his legs; and then he would give a jump and scream, and say one had bit him on the cheek—but I couldn't see no snakes. He started and run round . . . hollering "Take him off! he's biting me on the neck!" I never see a man look so wild in the eyes. Pretty soon he was all fagged out, and fell down panting; then he rolled over . . . kicking things every which way, and striking and grabbing at the air with his hands, and screaming . . . there was devils a-hold of him. He wore out by and by. . . . He says . . .
> "Tramp-tramp-tramp: that's the dead; tramp-tramp-tramp; they're coming after me; but I won't go. Oh, they're here; don't touch me . . . they're cold; let go. . . ."
> Then he went down on all fours and crawled off, begging them to let him alone. . . .
>
> *(Twain, 1885)*

Some people who experience delirium tremens also have seizures and lose consciousness and are vulnerable to strokes and other life-threatening problems. Like most other alcohol withdrawal symptoms, the DT's usually run their course in two to three days.

## Personal and Social Impact of Alcohol and Alcoholism

Though legal, alcohol is actually one of society's most dangerous drugs. Alcoholism destroys millions of families, social relationships, and careers (Steinglass et al.,

1985). Medical treatment, lost productivity, and potential losses due to premature deaths from alcoholism have been estimated to cost society as much as $116 billion annually (NIAAA, 1991). It is also a factor in more than a third of all suicides, homicides, assaults, rapes, and accidental deaths, including close to half of all fatal automobile accidents in the United States (Painter, 1992). Altogether, intoxicated drivers are responsible for 23,000 deaths each year—an average of one alcohol-related death every 23 minutes (OSAP, 1991). Similarly, intoxicated pedestrians are 4 times more likely than sober pedestrians to be hit by a car (Painter, 1992).

Alcoholism has serious effects on the individual's family as well as on society at large. The millions of people who are children of persons with alcoholism are likely to have grown up in a dysfunctional family environment characterized by higher than average levels of disharmony, sexual abuse, and physical abuse (Mathew et al., 1993; Velleman & Orford, 1993). Indeed, fathers and mothers who abuse their children are respectively 10 and 3 times more likely than other parents to abuse alcohol (Painter, 1992).

Children of persons with alcoholism may be at increased risk for a variety of problems. Anxiety, depression, phobias, and substance abuse are the disorders most commonly reported by adults with alcoholic parents, and elevated levels of conduct disorder and attention-deficit hyperactivity disorder (disorders that we shall observe in Chapter 15) may occur in children living in alcoholic homes. Some investigators have suggested that some people with parents who abuse alcohol also display problematic patterns ranging from poor communication skills to low self-esteem and increased likelihood of marital instability (Greenfield et al., 1993).

Alcohol abuse and dependence are also major problems among the young. Approximately 3.4 percent of today's high school seniors report that they drink every day (Johnston et al., 1993). Around 10 percent of surveyed elementary school children admit to some alcohol use (Johnston et al., 1993; Hutchinson & Little, 1985).

Chronic and excessive alcohol consumption can also seriously damage one's physical health. It can, for example, cause serious, often fatal, damage to the liver. An excessive intake of alcohol overworks the liver, and if that excessive alcohol intake continues for years, a person may develop an irreversible condition, called *cirrhosis,* in which the liver becomes scarred, forms fibrous tissue, and begins to change its anatomy and

---

*Delirium tremens (DT's)*   A dramatic withdrawal reaction experienced by some people who are alcohol-dependent. It consists of mental confusion, clouded consciousness, and terrifying visual hallucinations.

*Cirrhosis*   An irreversible condition, often caused by excessive drinking, in which the liver becomes scarred and begins to change in anatomy and functioning.

functioning. Cirrhosis is the seventh most frequent cause of death in the United States, accounting for around 28,000 deaths each year (Ray & Ksir, 1993; ADAMHA, 1987); and a high percentage of these cases are the result of chronic alcohol use.

Alcohol abuse and dependence may also cause other medical problems, including heart problems and impaired immune system responses. The latter may increase susceptibility to cancer and to bacterial infections and speed the onset of AIDS after infection (NIAAA, 1992). In addition, chronic excessive drinking poses major problems in nutrition. Alcohol satiates people and lowers their intake of other foods, but has no food value itself. As a result, chronic drinkers are likely to become malnourished, their bodies weak, tired, and highly vulnerable to disease.

The vitamin and mineral deficiencies of alcoholic persons may also cause certain mental disorders. An alcohol-related deficiency of vitamin B (thiamine), for example, may lead to *Korsakoff's syndrome* (also called *alcohol-induced persisting amnestic disorder*), a neurological disease marked by extreme confusion, memory impairment, and other neurological symptoms (Kopelman, 1995). People with Korsakoff's syndrome cannot remember the past or learn new information, and may make up for their memory losses by *confabulating*—spontaneously reciting made-up events to fill in the gaps.

Finally, it is now clear that women who drink during pregnancy are placing the health of their fetuses at risk. Heavy drinking early in pregnancy often leads to a miscarriage. Moreover, alcohol use during pregnancy may lead to babies born with *fetal alcohol syndrome,* a pattern of abnormalities that can include mental retardation, hyperactivity, head and face deformities, heart defects and other organ malfunctions, and retarded growth (Goldstein, 1994; Ray & Ksir, 1993). Babies of women who drink heavily throughout their pregnancy are at greatest risk for developing these symptoms. At the same time, however, even relatively low levels of drinking by a pregnant woman apparently place her baby at some risk. It has been estimated that in the overall population, fewer than 3 out of every 1000 births are characterized by the fetal alcohol syndrome. The rate increases to as many as 29 out of every 1000 births among women who are problem drinkers (Ray & Ksir, 1993).

---

*Korsakoff's syndrome*    An alcohol-related disorder marked by extreme confusion, memory impairment, and other neurological symptoms.

*Confabulation*    A spontaneous fabrication to fill in a gap in one's memory. Characteristic of people suffering from Korsakoff's syndrome.

*Fetal alcohol syndrome*    A cluster of problems in a child, including low birth weight, irregularities in the head and face, and intellectual deficits, caused by excessive alcohol intake by its mother during pregnancy.

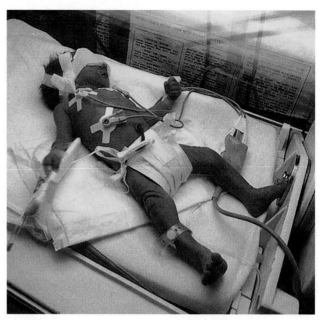

*A woman who uses drugs, including alcohol, during pregnancy risks harming her fetus. More than 50,000 babies are born with alcohol-related problems in the United States each year. Many of these babies suffer from "fetal alcohol syndrome."*

### Consider This

Drugs must be approved for distribution by the Food and Drug Administration. What factors do you think the FDA might take into consideration now if alcohol, caffeine, and nicotine were being submitted for approval by the FDA for the first time?

## Sedative-Hypnotic Drugs

*Sedative-hypnotic drugs* produce feelings of relaxation and drowsiness. At relatively low dosages, they have a calming or sedative effect. At higher ones, they are sleep inducers, or hypnotics. The two most widely used—and abused—kinds of sedative-hypnotics are antianxiety drugs and barbiturates.

### Antianxiety Drugs

As we saw in Chapter 5, *benzodiazepines,* the antianxiety drugs discovered in the 1950s, are now the most popular sedative-hypnotic drugs available. These drugs, which include Valium, Xanax, Halcion, and Librium, can relieve anxiety without making people as drowsy as other kinds of sedative-hypnotics. They

---

*Sedative-hypnotic drug*    A drug used in low doses to reduce anxiety and in higher doses to help people sleep.

## Table 11-2    Risks and Consequences of Drug Misuse

| | Intoxication Potential | Dependency Potential | Risk of Organ Damage or Death | Risk of Severe Social or Economic Consequences | Risk of Severe or Long-Lasting Mental and Behavioral Change |
|---|---|---|---|---|---|
| Opioids | High | High | Low | High | Low to moderate |
| Sedative-hypnotics: Barbiturates | Moderate | Moderate to high | Moderate to high | Moderate to high | Low |
| Benzodiazepines | Moderate | Low | Low | Low | Low |
| Stimulants (cocaine, amphetamines) | High | High | Moderate | Low to moderate | Moderate to high |
| Alcohol | High | Moderate | High | High | High |
| Cannabis | High | Low to moderate | Low | Low to moderate | Low |
| Mixed drug classes | High | High | High | High | High |

*Source:* APA, 1994; Gold, 1986, p. 28.

have less impact on the brain's respiratory center than barbiturates do, they are less likely than those drugs to depress respiratory functioning and cause death by overdose.

When benzodiazepines first appeared, they seemed so safe and effective that physicians prescribed them quite readily, and their use proliferated in our society. Eventually, clinicians learned that the drugs can in fact cause intoxication in high dosages and lead to a pattern of abuse or dependence (see Table 11-2). It is now estimated that more than 1 percent of the adult population in the United States abuse or become physically dependent on antianxiety drugs at some point in their lives (APA, 1994).

### Barbiturates

First discovered in Germany more than 100 years ago, *barbiturates* were widely prescribed by physicians throughout the first half of this century to combat anxiety and to help people sleep (Cooper, 1977). Despite the emergence of the safer benzodiazepines, some physicians still prescribe them, especially for sleep problems. Investigators have become aware that many dangers attend the use of barbiturates, not the least of which is their potential for abuse and dependence. Several thousand deaths a year are caused by acciden-

*Barbiturates*   Addictive sedative-hypnotic drugs used to reduce anxiety or to help persons fall asleep.

tal or suicidal overdoses of these drugs. A number of other sedative-hypnotic drugs, including **methaqualone** (trade name Quaalude), act upon the brain in barbiturate-like ways and can lead to similar forms of abuse or dependence.

Barbiturates are usually taken in pill or capsule form. In low doses they reduce a person's level of excitement in the same way that benzodiazepines do, by increasing the synaptic activity of the inhibitory neurotransmitter GABA (see pp. 134–136) (Vellucci, 1989). At higher doses, they depress the *reticular formation,* the body's arousal center, which is responsible for keeping people awake, thus causing the person to get sleepy. At still higher doses, barbiturates depress spinal reflexes and muscles and are often used as surgical anesthetics. At too high a level, they cause respiratory failure and low blood pressure, and can lead to coma and even death.

Barbiturates are actually more like alcohol than like benzodiazepines in their action on the brain and the rest of the body. In fact, before the development of barbiturates, alcohol and its derivatives were used widely as sedative-hypnotic drugs. People can get intoxicated from large doses of barbiturates, just as they do from alcohol.

Repeated excessive use of barbiturates can lead to abuse. A person may spend much of the day intoxicated, and social and occupational functioning may be disrupted by quarrels and poor job performance. Excessive use can also lead to dependence. Tolerance for barbiturates increases very rapidly; increasing amounts become necessary to calm people down or help them to sleep. Moreover, abstaining from the drug may cause withdrawal symptoms that are similar to those seen in alcoholism, such as nausea, anxiety, and sleep problems. In extreme cases, the withdrawal reaction may resemble delirium tremens (here called *barbiturate withdrawal delirium*). Barbiturate withdrawal is one of the most dangerous forms of drug withdrawal, as some addicted persons experience convulsions when they abstain from the drug.

One of the great dangers of barbiturate dependence is that the lethal dose of the drug remains the same even while the body is building up a tolerance for its other effects (Gold, 1986). In a common and tragic scenario, once the initial barbiturate dose prescribed by a physician stops working, a person decides independently to keep increasing it every few weeks. Eventually the person ingests a dose that may very well prove fatal.

## Opioids

*Opioids* include opium and the drugs derived from it, such as heroin, morphine, and codeine. A natural substance from the sap of the opium poppy seed, *opium* itself has been in use for thousands of years. In the past it was used widely in the treatment of medical disorders because of its ability to reduce both physical and emotional pain. Physicians eventually discovered, however, that the drug was physically addictive.

In 1804 a new substance, *morphine,* was derived from opium. It, too, was an effective pain reliever, even more effective than opium. Believing that morphine was free of opium's addictive properties, physicians began to use it widely, particularly in the United States during the Civil War. Unfortunately, as eventually became clear, repeated administrations of morphine could also lead to addiction. In fact, morphine addiction became known as "soldiers' disease."

In 1898 morphine was converted into yet another new pain reliever, *heroin.* For several years heroin was viewed as a wonder drug and was used as a cough medicine and for other medicinal purposes. Eventually, however, physicians recognized that heroin is even more addictive than the other opioids. By 1917 the U.S. Congress concluded that all drugs derived from opium were addictive and passed a law making opioids illegal except for medical purposes.

*Opioid* Opium or any of the drugs derived from opium, including morphine, heroin, and codeine.

*Heroin* A highly addictive substance derived from opium.

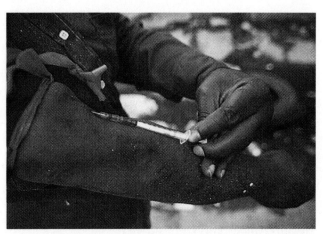
*Opioids may be taken by mouth, inhaled (snorted), injected just beneath the surface of the skin, or, as here, injected intravenously. Those who share needles to inject themselves run the risk of developing AIDS or hepatitis.*

New derivatives of opium have been discovered, and synthetic (laboratory-blended) opioids such as *methadone* have also been developed. All these various opioid drugs are known collectively as *narcotics.* Each has its own potency, speed of action, and tolerance level. Morphine and codeine have become the primary medical narcotics, usually prescribed to relieve pain. Heroin has remained illegal in the United States under all circumstances.

Narcotics may be smoked, inhaled ("snorted"), injected by needle just beneath the skin ("skin popped"), or injected directly into the bloodstream ("mainlined"). An injection quickly brings on a *rush,* a spasm of warmth and ecstasy that is sometimes compared with orgasm. The brief spasm is followed by several hours of a pleasant feeling called a *high* or *nod.* During a high, the drug user feels relaxed and euphoric, and even unconcerned about food, sex, or other bodily needs.

Heroin and other opioids create these effects by depressing the central nervous system, particularly the centers that generate emotion. The drugs are received at brain receptor sites that ordinarily receive *endorphins,* neurotransmitters that help relieve pain and reduce emotional tension (Snyder, 1991, 1986). When neurons at these receptor sites receive opioids, they fire and produce pleasurable and calming feelings just as they would do if they were receiving endorphins. In addition to pain relief, sedation, and mood changes, opioids cause nausea, constriction of the pupils of the eyes ("pinpoint pupils"), and constipation, bodily reactions that can also be brought about by a heightened release of endorphins in the brain.

*Endorphins* Neurotransmitters that help relieve pain and reduce emotional tension. They are sometimes referred to as the body's own opioids.

*Consider This*

Although alcohol, antianxiety drugs, and codeine clearly have biological effects, some of their initial effects (such as making us more comfortable in social situations, calming us, or relieving pain) may result from our shared expectations about what they will do for us. How might researchers design studies that can separate the biological effects of these substances from effects based on social expectations?

## Heroin Abuse and Dependence

Chronic users of heroin fall into patterns of abuse and dependence similar to those shown by chronic users of the less powerful opioids. It takes only a few weeks of repeated heroin use for people to be caught in a pattern of abuse: the drug becomes the center of their lives, and social and occupational functioning deteriorate significantly. Most abusers also develop a dependence on heroin, quickly building up a tolerance for it and experiencing withdrawal symptoms when they abstain. The withdrawal symptoms initially are anxiety, restlessness, perspiration, and rapid breathing, and eventually include severe twitching, constant aches, painful cramps, fever, acute vomiting and diarrhea, loss of appetite, high blood pressure, dehydration, and weight loss of up to 15 pounds. The withdrawal distress usually peaks by the third day, then gradually subsides and disappears by the eighth day.

Eventually people dependent on heroin need the drug just to maintain normal functioning and to avoid the distress of withdrawal, and they must continually increase their doses in order to achieve that state. The temporary high becomes less intense and less important (Goldstein, 1994). They may organize their lives around plans for getting their next dose. Many turn to criminal activities, such as theft or prostitution, to support their expensive "habit."

## Dangers of Heroin

The most direct danger of heroin abuse is an overdose, which depresses the respiratory center in the brain, virtually paralyzing it and in many cases causing death. Death is particularly likely during sleep, when a person is unable to fight the effect by consciously working at breathing. Each year, approximately 1 percent of the untreated persons dependent on heroin and other opioids die under the drug's influence, usually from an overdose (APA, 1994).

Users run risks aside from the effects of the drug itself. Often, profit-minded pushers mix heroin with a cheaper drug, such as a barbiturate or LSD, or even a deadly substance such as cyanide or battery acid. Addicted persons who use dirty needles and other unsterile equipment when they inject heroin are vulnerable to AIDS, hepatitis, and skin abscesses. In some areas of the United States the HIV infection rate among persons dependent on heroin is reported to be as high as 60 percent (APA, 1994).

Surveys suggest that close to 1 percent of the adult population become physically dependent upon heroin or other opioids at some time in their lives (APA, 1994). The number of addicted persons took its sharpest turn upward during the 1960s and 1970s, but there are apparently still more than 400,000 addicted persons in the United States (Elias, 1993; Gold, 1986).

*The more things change, the more they stay the same. Opium users used to get high at opium dens, such as this 1926 den in New York City's Chinatown. Today many crack users gather at "crack houses" to drug themselves into near oblivion.*

*Summing Up*
*Depressants are substances that slow the activity of the central nervous system. Some of the best known depressants are alcohol, whose active ingredient, ethyl alcohol, is rapidly absorbed into the blood upon ingestion and carried to the central nervous system; sedative-hypnotic drugs, including benzodiazepines and barbiturates, each of which increases the activity of the neurotransmitter GABA (barbiturates also affect the reticular formation); and opioids, which are received at neurons that ordinarily receive the neurotransmitters known as endorphins. Each of these drugs can lead to intoxication, a pattern of abuse or dependence, and various dangers.*

# Stimulants

**Stimulants** are substances that act to increase the activity of the central nervous system, resulting in increased blood pressure and heart rate and in an intensification of behavior, thought processes, and alertness. Two of the best-known and most troublesome stimulants are cocaine and amphetamines, whose effects on the brain are virtually indistinguishable (Snyder, 1986). When users report different effects from the two, it is because they have ingested different amounts of the drugs. Two of the most commonly used stimulants are caffeine and nicotine.

## Cocaine

**Cocaine**—the central active ingredient of the coca plant, found in South America—is the most powerful natural stimulant now known. The drug was first isolated from the plant in 1865. South American natives, however, have chewed the leaves of the plant since prehistoric times for the energy and alertness the drug content provides. Processed cocaine is an odorless, white, fluffy powder. For recreational use, it is most often inhaled ("snorted") so that it is absorbed through the mucous membrane of the nose. Some users prefer the more powerful effects of injecting cocaine intravenously or smoking cocaine "base" in a pipe or cigarette.

---

*Stimulant*   A substance that increases the activity of the central nervous system.

*Cocaine*   An addictive stimulant derived from the coca plant. It is the most powerful natural stimulant known.

For years the prevailing opinion of cocaine was that aside from causing intoxication and occasional temporary psychosis, it posed few significant problems (see Box 11-2). Only in recent years have researchers recognized its potential for harm and developed a clearer understanding of how cocaine produces its effects. This insight has been triggered by a dramatic increase in the drug's popularity and in problems related to its use. In the early 1960s an estimated 10,000 persons in the United States had tried cocaine; today more than 23 million have tried it (NIDA, 1993). Close to 2 million people are currently using cocaine at least once a month, most of them teenagers or young adults (NIDA, 1993).

Cocaine brings on a euphoric rush of well-being and confidence. Given a high enough dose, this rush can be almost orgasmic, like that produced by heroin. Initially cocaine makes its users feel excited, energetic, talkative, and even euphoric. As more is taken, it also produces a faster pulse, higher blood pressure, faster and deeper breathing, and further arousal and wakefulness. Cocaine apparently produces these effects by stimulating the release of the neurotransmitters dopamine and norepinephrine from neurons throughout the brain; supplies of these neurotransmitters at receiving neurons become excessive, and the CNS is overstimulated (Kleber & Gawin, 1987).

If a very high dose of cocaine is taken, the stimulation of the CNS will further result in poor muscle coordination, grandiosity, declining judgment, anger, aggression, anxiety, compulsive behavior, and confusion—all symptoms of *cocaine intoxication*. Some people experience hallucinations or delusions or both, a condition known as *cocaine-induced psychotic disorder* (Yudofsky et al., 1993).

> A young man described how, after free-basing, he went to his closet to get his clothes, but his suit asked him, "What do you want?" Afraid, he walked toward the door, which told him, "Get back!" Retreating, he then heard the sofa say, "If you sit on me, I'll kick your ass." With a sense of impending doom, intense anxiety, and momentary panic, the young man ran to the hospital where he received help.
>
> *(Allen, 1985, pp. 19–20)*

As the symptoms caused by cocaine subside, the user often experiences a depression-like letdown, popularly called "crashing," which may be accompanied by headaches, dizziness, and fainting. For occasional users, the effects of cocaine usually disappear within twenty-four hours. Those who have taken an excessive dose, however, may sink into stupor, deep sleep, or, in some cases, coma.

## Box 11-2

# "A Big Wild Man Who Has Cocaine in His Body"

Sigmund Freud's contributions to the understanding and treatment of mental disorders are second to none. Yet Freud, like so many people before and after him, was played for a fool by a drug—in his case, cocaine. Freud fell into the familiar trap of wishful thinking, prematurely concluding that cocaine was free of danger, largely because he enjoyed it and wanted it to be safe. His colossal misjudgment almost brought down his career before it had really begun.

In 1884 Freud's reputation as an effective neurologist and skillful researcher of neuroanatomy was growing. Having read about the stimulating effects of coca leaves on Peruvian Indians and about the isolation of pure cocaine, he wondered whether the substance might be an effective treatment for nervous exhaustion, and he proceeded to test it on himself. He quickly experienced a powerful reaction—euphoria, energy, alertness, strength, and disinterest in food.

He seemed more than a little smitten with cocaine when he wrote to his fiancée, "Woe to you my princess when I come. I will kiss you quite red and feed you until you are plump. And if you are forward, you shall see who is stronger, a gentle little girl who doesn't eat enough or a big wild man who has cocaine in his body" (Freud, 1885).

Freud proceeded to study the effects of cocaine on numerous subjects and soon proclaimed to the medical community of Western Europe:

> Cocaine brings about an exhilaration and lasting euphoria. . . . You perceive an increase of self-control and possess more vitality and capacity for work. . . . Long intensive mental or physical work is performed without any fatigue. . . . This result is enjoyed without any of the unpleasant after effects that follow exhilaration brought about by alcohol.
>
> *(Freud, 1885)*

Freud received a very rude awakening after he recommended to a close friend, Erst Fleischl von Marxow, that he take cocaine in order to relieve him of his addiction to morphine. Fleischl injected himself with increasingly higher doses of cocaine until finally he reached a point at which he became a victim of cocaine-induced psychosis.

The plight of his friend was more than a personal tragedy for Freud. Soon reports of cocaine psychosis from all over Europe led to severe criticism of Freud by the Continent's most eminent medical authorities and dealt a heavy blow to his reputation. It was not at all clear that he would be able to continue successfully in his medical career. But then he became interested in hypnosis and began to develop the theories and techniques of psychoanalysis, and this time his provocative and daring ideas served him and the clinical field very well indeed.

## Cocaine Abuse and Dependence

An extended period of cocaine use may lead to a pattern of abuse in which the person is intoxicated throughout the day and functions poorly in social and occupational spheres. A physical dependence may also develop, so that more cocaine is needed to achieve the desired effects and abstinence results in significant feelings of depression, fatigue, sleep problems, irritability, and anxiety (APA, 1994; Washton, 1987). These withdrawal symptoms may last for weeks or even months.

Despite the pleasurable, reinforcing properties of cocaine, in the past cocaine abuse and dependence were limited by the high cost of processed cocaine and by the fact that it was usually snorted—a means of ingestion that is limited by the constriction of nasal blood vessels and that has less powerful effects than either injection or smoking. Since 1984, however, newer, more powerful, and sometimes cheaper forms of cocaine have gained favor among users and have produced an enormous increase in abuse and dependence. Currently one user in five falls into a pattern of abuse or dependence. Many people use the technique of *free-basing,* in which the pure cocaine basic alkaloid is chemically separated or "freed" from processed cocaine, vaporized by heat from a flame, and inhaled with a pipe. And millions more use crack, a powerful, ready-to-smoke free-base cocaine.

*Crack* is cocaine that has been boiled down into crystalline balls. It is smoked with a special crack pipe. This form of cocaine makes a crackling sound when it is smoked, hence the name. Crack is sold in small quantities at a typical cost of between $10 and $20. Some cities have seen veritable crack epidemics among people who previously could not have afforded cocaine. Approximately 1.5 percent of high school

---

*Free-base*   A technique for ingesting cocaine in which the pure cocaine basic alkaloid is chemically separated from processed cocaine, vaporized by heat from a flame, and inhaled with a pipe.

*Crack*   A powerful, ready-to-smoke free-base cocaine.

seniors report using crack within the past year (Johnston et al., 1993). Although this rate represents a sizable drop from past rates, the crack epidemic is still very disturbing, particularly because of the unusual degree of violent crime and risky sex-for-drugs exchanges reported in the crack-using population (Balshem et al., 1992). The crack epidemic is also problematic in that it is concentrated in poor urban areas (OSAP, 1991).

## Dangers of Cocaine

Cocaine poses serious dangers. Aside from its effects on mental and emotional functioning, cocaine turns out to be highly dangerous to one's physical well-being. Its widespread use in increasingly powerful forms has caused the annual number of cocaine-related emergency room incidents in the United States to explode to more than 100,000, twenty-five times the number a decade ago (NIDA, 1993) (see Figure 11-2). The most obvious danger of cocaine use comes from

overdose. Excessive doses have a strong effect on the respiratory center of the brain, at first stimulating it and then depressing it, possibly to the point of respiratory failure and death.

Cocaine can also create significant, even fatal, heart problems. The heart beats rapidly and irregularly under the drug's influence and at the same time must work harder to pump blood through cocaine-constricted blood vessels. For some people, this strain on the heart causes a brain seizure that brings breathing or heart functioning to a sudden halt. These effects may be more common in people who have taken a high dose of cocaine and who have a history of cocaine abuse, but they also occur in casual cocaine users (Gold, 1986). Such was the case with Len Bias, the well-known college basketball player who died of these effects a few years back, apparently after ingesting only a moderate amount of cocaine.

The effects of prenatal cocaine exposure on future generations are also cause for serious concern (Scherling, 1994). Pregnant women who use cocaine

**DRUG-RELATED DEATHS**

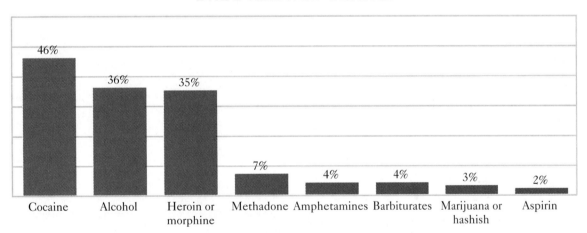

**DRUG-RELATED EMERGENCY ROOM VISITS**

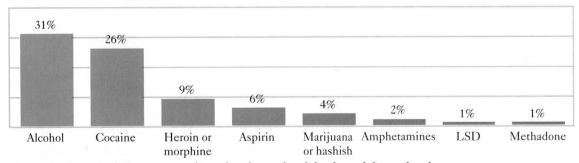

**Figure 11-2** *Which drugs are implicated in drug-related deaths and drug-related emergency room visits? In 1991 cocaine was cited by medical examiners in 46 percent of all drug-related deaths, while alcohol was cited in 36 percent and opioids in 35 percent. Alcohol was responsible for 31 percent of all drug-related emergency room visits, while cocaine was responsible for 26 percent and opioids for 9 percent. Percentages add up to more than 100 because more than one drug was cited in some cases. (NIDA, 1992.)*

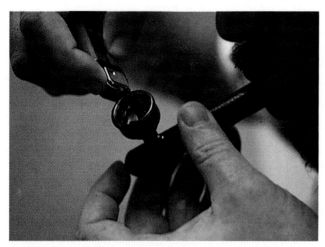

*Crack, a powerful form of free-base cocaine, is produced by boiling cocaine down into crystalline balls and is smoked with a special crack pipe.*

run the risk of having a baby with *fetal cocaine syndrome,* a highly damaging syndrome which is characterized by altered immune system function, learning deficits, decreased activity in the brain's dopamine system, and abnormal thyroid size (Adler, 1992).

## Amphetamines

The *amphetamines* are stimulant drugs that are manufactured in the laboratory. Some common ones are amphetamine (Benzedrine), dextroamphetamine (Dexedrine), and methamphetamine (Methedrine). First synthesized in the 1930s for use in the treatment of asthma, these drugs soon became popular among people trying to lose weight; athletes seeking an extra burst of energy; soldiers, truck drivers, and pilots trying to stay awake; and students studying for exams throughout the night. Today they are prescribed much more sparingly by medical practitioners. The drugs are far too dangerous to be used so casually.

Amphetamines are most often taken in pill or capsule form, although some people inject the drug intravenously for a quicker, more powerful impact. Others ingest the drug in such forms as "ice" and "crank," counterparts of free-base cocaine and crack, respectively.

Like cocaine, amphetamines increase energy and alertness and reduce appetite in low doses, produce intoxication and psychosis in high doses, and cause an emotional letdown as they leave the person's body. Also like cocaine, amphetamines stimulate the CNS by increasing the release of the neurotransmitters

---

*Amphetamine    A stimulant drug that is manufactured in the laboratory.*

dopamine and norepinephrine from neurons throughout the brain (Goldstein, 1994).

Tolerance to amphetamines builds so quickly that it is easy to become ensnared in a pattern of amphetamine dependence. People who start using amphetamines to reduce their appetite and weight may soon find they are as hungry as ever, and increase their amphetamine dosage in response. Similarly, athletes who use amphetamines to increase their energy may find before long that larger and larger amounts of the drug are needed. So-called speed freaks who pop pills all day for days at a time have built a tolerance so high that they now take as much as 200 times their initial amphetamine dose. When persons who chronically abuse amphetamines stop taking the drug, they enter the state of deep depression and extended sleep that also characterizes withdrawal from cocaine.

*Summing Up*
*Stimulants are substances that act to increase the activity of the central nervous system. Cocaine and the amphetamines (laboratory-produced stimulants) apparently stimulate the release of the neurotransmitters dopamine and norepinephrine. These drugs may cause intoxication, temporary psychosis, and patterns of abuse or dependence. In excessive doses, they may lead to respiratory failure. Cocaine has been found to cause fatal heart dysfunctioning and brain seizures, even in mild dosages.*

# *Hallucinogens*

*Hallucinogens* are substances that cause powerful changes primarily in sensory perception, including intensification of perceptions and the inducement of illusions and hallucinations. The drugs, also called *psychedelic drugs,* produce sensations so novel that they are sometimes called "trips." The trips may be exciting or frightening, enhancing or dangerous, depending on how a person's mind interacts with the drugs.

The hallucinogens include LSD (lysergic acid diethylamide), mescaline, psilocybin, MDMA ("ecstasy"), DMT, and morning-glory seeds (Strassman, 1995). Many of these substances come from plants or animals; others are laboratory-produced rearrangements of natural psychedelics.

---

*Hallucinogen    A substance that primarily causes powerful changes in sensory perception, including intensification of perceptions and the inducement of illusions and hallucinations.*

*Psychedelic art seemed all-pervasive in the 1960s. Displayed on advertisements, clothing, and book covers, it was inspired by the kinds of images and sensations that are produced by psychedelic drugs such as LSD.*

**LSD,** one of the most famous and most powerful hallucinogens, was derived in 1938 by the Swiss chemist Albert Hoffman from a group of naturally occurring drugs called *ergot alkaloids.* During the 1960s, a decade of social rebellion and experimentation, millions of people turned to LSD as a means of expanding their experience.

Within two hours of being swallowed, LSD brings on a state of *hallucinogen intoxication,* sometimes called *hallucinosis,* marked by a general intensification of perceptions, particularly visual perceptions, along with maladaptive psychological changes and physical symptoms. People may focus on minutiae—the pores of the skin, for example, or individual blades of grass. Colors may seem enhanced or take on a shade of purple. Illusions may be experienced in which objects seem distorted, and inanimate objects may appear to move, breathe, or change shape. A person under the influence of LSD may also hallucinate, seeing people, objects, or geometric forms that are not actually present.

Intoxication symptoms involving the other senses may include hearing sounds more clearly, feeling tingling or numbness in the limbs, or experiencing distorted sensations of hot and cold. Some people have been badly burned after touching flames that felt cool to them under the influence of LSD. LSD may also cause the senses to cross, an effect called *synesthesia.* Colors, for example, may be "heard" or "felt."

LSD can also cause emotional changes, ranging from euphoria to anxiety or depression. The percep-

tion of time may slow down dramatically. Long-forgotten thoughts and feelings may resurface. Physical symptoms can include dilation of the pupils, sweating, palpitations, blurred vision, tremors, and loss of coordination. All these effects take place while the user is fully awake and alert, and wear off in about six hours.

It seems that LSD produces these symptoms by preventing certain brain neurons from releasing the neurotransmitter serotonin (Jacobs, 1994, 1984). These neurons are ordinarily involved in the brain's transmission of visual information and (as we observed in Chapter 7) emotional experiences; thus LSD's interference produces a range of visual and emotional symptoms.

Although people develop minimal tolerance and do not experience withdrawal when they stop using LSD, it poses distinct dangers for both one-time and long-term users. First, LSD is so remarkably potent that any dose, no matter how small, is likely to elicit powerful perceptual, emotional, and behavioral reactions. Sometimes these powerful reactions to LSD are extremely unpleasant, an experience described in the drug vernacular as a "bad trip":

> A 21-year-old woman was admitted to the hospital along with her lover. He had had a number of LSD experiences and had convinced her to take it to make her less constrained sexually. About half an hour after ingestion of approximately 200 microgm., she noticed that the bricks in the wall began to go in and out and that light affected her strangely. She became frightened when she realized that she was unable to distinguish her body from the chair she was sitting on or from her lover's body. Her fear became more marked after she thought that she would not get back into herself. At the time of admission she was hyperactive and laughed inappropriately. Her stream of talk was illogical and affect labile. Two days later, this reaction had ceased.
>
> *(Frosch, Robbins, & Stern, 1965)*

Reports of LSD users who injure themselves or commit suicide or murder usually involve a severe reaction of this kind.

Another danger is the extended impact that LSD has on some people. Some, for example, develop a psychotic, mood, or anxiety disorder. About a quarter of users experience lingering effects called a *hallucinogen persisting perception disorder,* or simply, *flashbacks,* sensory and emotional changes that recur long after the LSD has left the body (APA, 1994). Flashbacks may occur days or even months after the last LSD experience. They may become less severe and disappear

---

*LSD*  A hallucinogenic drug derived from ergot alkaloids.

*Synesthesia*  A crossing over of sensory perceptions, caused by LSD.

*Flashback*  The recurrence of LSD-induced sensory and emotional changes long after the drug has left the body.

within several months. Some persons, however, report flashbacks five years or longer after taking LSD. Flashbacks are entirely unpredictable. A one-time LSD user may have multiple flashbacks, or a regular user with no history of flashbacks may suddenly start to experience them.

# Cannabis

*Cannabis sativa,* a hemp plant, grows in warm climates throughout the world. Its main active ingredient, *tetrahydrocannabinol (THC),* is found in the resin exuded by its leaves and flowering tops. The drugs produced from varieties of hemp are collectively called *cannabis.* The most powerful of them is *hashish;* drugs of intermediate strength include *ganja;* and the weaker ones include the best-known form of cannabis, *marijuana,* a mixture of the crushed leaves and flowering tops.

Although cannabis contains several hundred active compounds, THC appears to be the ingredient most responsible for its effects. The greater the THC content, the more powerful the cannabis: hashish contains a high portion, while marijuana's is relatively low.

Cannabis is smoked. At low doses it typically produces feelings of inner joy and relaxation and may lead people to become either contemplative or talkative. Some smokers, however, feel anxious, suspicious, apprehensive, or irritated, especially if they have been in a bad mood or are smoking in an upsetting environment. Many smokers report sharpened perceptions and great preoccupation with the intensified sounds and sights around them. Time seems to slow down, and distances and sizes seem greater than they actually are. This overall state of *cannabis intoxication* is known more commonly as a "high" or as being "stoned."

The physical changes induced by cannabis include reddening of the eyes, a fast heartbeat, an increase in blood pressure and appetite, dryness in the mouth, dizziness, and nausea. Some people become drowsy and may even fall asleep.

In high doses, cannabis produces visual distortions, alterations of body image, and hallucinations (Mathew

---

*Cannabis drugs*    Drugs produced from the different varieties of the hemp plant Cannabis sativa. They cause a mixture of hallucinogenic, depressant, and stimulant effects.

*Tetrahydrocannabinol (THC)*    The main active ingredient of cannabis substances.

*Marijuana*    One of the cannabis drugs, derived from the leaves and flowering tops of the hemp plant Cannabis sativa.

et al., 1993). Smokers may become confused or impulsive; some panic and fear that they are losing their minds. Some smokers develop delusions that other people are trying to hurt them. Most of the effects of cannabis last for three to six hours. The changes in mood, however, may continue for a longer time (Chait et al., 1985).

## Marijuana Abuse and Dependence

Until the early 1970s, the use of the weak form of cannabis, marijuana, rarely led to a pattern of abuse or dependence. Today, however, many people, including large numbers of high school students, are caught in a pattern of marijuana abuse—getting high on marijuana every day and finding their social and occupational or academic lives significantly affected by their heavy use of it (see Figure 11-3). Many chronic users also become physically dependent on marijuana. They develop a tolerance for it and may experience flulike withdrawal symptoms when they try to stop smoking, including hot flashes, runny nose, and diarrhea (Ray & Ksir, 1993).

Why have patterns of marijuana abuse and dependence emerged in the last two decades? Mainly because the drug has changed. The marijuana available in the United States today is two to ten times more powerful than that used in the early 1970s. The THC content of today's marijuana is as much as 10 to 15 percent, compared to 1 to 5 percent in the late 1960s (APA, 1994). Apparently marijuana is now cultivated in locations—both foreign and domestic—where a hot and dry climate produces higher THC content (Weisheit, 1990) (see Box 11-3).

## Dangers of Marijuana

As the strength and use of marijuana have increased, researchers have discovered that smoking this substance may pose significant problems and dangers. It occasionally elicits panic reactions similar to the ones caused by hallucinogens (Ray & Ksir, 1993). Typically the panic reaction ends in three to six hours, along with marijuana's other effects.

Marijuana also interferes with the performance of complex sensorimotor tasks, thus impairing a person's ability to drive. Small wonder that studies have implicated marijuana in numerous automobile accidents (Petersen, 1984). Similarly, marijuana appears to interfere with cognitive functioning (Hooker & Jones, 1987). People on a marijuana high often fail to remember information, especially recently acquired information, no matter how hard they try to concentrate.

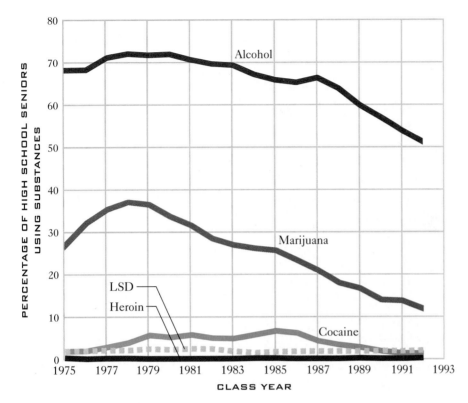

Figure 11-3   *The overall percentage of high school seniors who admitted to using drugs illicitly at least once within 30 days of being surveyed rose in the 1970s and then declined in the 1980s and 1990s. The rate of marijuana use has generally been falling since 1978, cocaine use since 1985, and alcohol use since 1980, while heroin and LSD use have each remained relatively stable. (Johnston et al., 1993.)*

Evidence has mounted that chronic marijuana smoking may also lead to long-term problems. It may, for example, contribute to lung disease. Studies have indicated that marijuana smoking reduces one's ability to expel air from the lungs even more than tobacco smoking does. One marijuana cigarette is equivalent to at least sixteen tobacco cigarettes in this regard. In addition, research indicates that marijuana smoke contains significantly more tar and benzopyrene than tobacco smoke. Both of these substances have been linked to cancer (Ray & Ksir, 1993).

Another concern is the effect of chronic marijuana smoking on human reproduction. Studies since the late 1970s have discovered lower sperm counts and reduced spermatozoa activity in men who are chronic smokers of marijuana, and irregular and abnormal ovulation has been found among women (Nahas, 1984; Hembree et al., 1979).

Finally, research has suggested that THC slows down the functioning of the immune system (Hollister, 1986). Although this suppression is mild and temporary and marijuana smokers have not displayed higher rates of infection, some researchers suspect that the effect may have longer-term implications.

Efforts to educate the public about the changing nature and impact of regular marijuana use appear to be paying off: 2 percent of today's high school seniors smoke marijuana on a daily basis, down from 11 per-

cent in 1978 (Johnston et al., 1993). Moreover, close to 80 percent of today's high school seniors believe that regular marijuana smoking poses a serious risk, more than double the percentage in 1978. Still other surveys show both junior high and senior high school students reporting little peer pressure to smoke marijuana; indeed, almost 90 percent of them believe that their friends would disapprove if they were to smoke it regularly (Johnston et al., 1993).

## *Combinations of Substances*

When different drugs are in the body at the same time, they may potentiate, or enhance, each other's effects. The combined impact, called a **synergistic effect,** is often greater than the sum of the effects of each drug taken alone: a small dose of one drug mixed with a small dose of another can produce an enormous change in body chemistry.

One kind of synergistic effect occurs when two or more drugs have *similar actions.* For instance, alcohol, antianxiety drugs, barbiturates, and opioids—all depressants of the central nervous system—may pro-

---

*Synergistic effect*   In pharmacology, an enhancement of effects that occurs when more than one drug is acting on the body at the same time.

## Box 11-3

# *Cannabis and Society*

For centuries cannabis played a respected role in the field of medicine. It was recommended as a surgical anesthetic by Chinese physicians 2,000 years ago and was used in other lands to treat cholera, malaria, coughs, insomnia, and rheumatism. In the mid-nineteenth century, Western European physicians used it to treat neuralgia, menstrual pain, and migraine.

Cannabis entered the United States in the early twentieth century, mainly in the form of marijuana. The U.S. drug company Parke-Davis became a leading importer of marijuana and distributed it for medical purposes.

Early in the century, however, the positive view of cannabis began to change. For one thing, more effective medicines replaced it, and physicians used cannabis less and less. Second, cannabis soon acquired some notoriety as a recreational drug and its illegal distribution became a law enforcement problem. Authorities associated marijuana with alcohol and other

*Marijuana is made from the leaves of the hemp plant* Cannabis sativa. *The plant is an annual herb, reaches a height of between 3 and 15 feet, and is grown in a wide range of altitudes, climates, and soils.*

disreputable drugs, assumed it was highly dangerous, and communicated this "fact" to the public. In

1937, when the "killer weed" was outlawed, the following magazine report was typical:

> In Los Angeles, Calif., a youth was walking along a downtown street after inhaling a marijuana cigarette. For many addicts, merely a portion of a "reefer" is enough to induce intoxication. Suddenly, for no reason, he decided that someone had threatened to kill him and that his life at that very moment was in danger. Wildly he looked about him. The only person in sight was an aged bootblack. Drug-crazed nerve centers conjured the innocent old shoe-shiner into a destroying monster. Mad with fright, the addict hurried to his room and got a gun. He killed the old man, and then, later, babbled his grief over what had been wanton, uncontrolled murder. . . .
>     That's marijuana!
> (Anslinger & Cooper, 1937, p. 153)

Marijuana was not finished, however. The substance resurfaced with renewed vigor in the 1960s. It seemed to fit right in with that decade's disillusionment, protest, and self-exploration. Young people

duce a severe depression of the CNS when mixed (Miller & Gold, 1990). Combining them, even in small doses, can sometimes lead to extreme intoxication, coma, and even death.

Many tragedies have been caused by synergistic effects of this kind. A young man may drink just a few alcoholic beverages at a party, for example, and shortly afterward take a normal dose of barbiturates or some other sedative-hypnotic drug to help him fall asleep. He believes he has acted with restraint and good judgment—yet he may never wake up.

A different kind of synergistic effect results when drugs have *opposite (antagonistic) actions.* Stimulant drugs, for example, interfere with the liver's usual disposal of barbiturates and alcohol. Thus people who combine barbiturates or alcohol with cocaine or amphetamines may build up toxic, even lethal, levels of

the depressant drugs in their systems. Students who take amphetamines to help them study late into the night and then take barbiturates to help them fall asleep are unwittingly placing themselves in serious danger.

Each year tens of thousands of people are admitted to hospitals with a multiple drug emergency, and several thousand of them die (NIDA, 1992). Sometimes the cause is carelessness or ignorance. Often, however, the person uses a combination of drugs precisely because he or she enjoys the synergistic effects. This kind of multiple drug use, or *polysubstance use,* appears to be on the rise—so much so that *polysubstance-related disorders* are becoming as common as

---

*Polysubstance-related disorder*   A long-term pattern of maladaptive behavior centered around the abuse of or dependence on a combination of drugs.

in particular discovered the pleasures of getting high, and smoking marijuana became a popular form of recreation. Many people saw marijuana as a symbol of the government's low credibility: the drug was hardly the killer weed the government claimed it to be, and the harsh legal punishments for smoking it seemed unreasonable.

In the 1970s marijuana use continued to expand throughout the United States. By the end of the decade 16 million people reported using it at least once, 11 percent of the population identified themselves as recent users, and 11 percent of high school seniors said they smoked marijuana every day (NIDA, 1982).

These rates declined considerably during the 1980s. The marijuana that was imported to the United States became more powerful and dangerous than the earlier form, and people stopped using it so often and so casually. At the same time, marijuana and other kinds of cannabis returned to their roots, so to speak, and once again

found respect as a form of medical treatment.

In the 1980s cannabis researchers developed precise techniques for measuring and controlling THC content and for extracting pure THC from cannabis. They also developed synthetic forms of THC. These newly acquired abilities opened the door to new medical applications for cannabis (Ray & Ksir, 1993). Cannabis became helpful in treating glaucoma, a severe eye disease in which fluid from the eyeball is obstructed from flowing properly. Oral THC combats glaucoma by lowering the pressure of fluid in the eye. Cannabis was also found to help patients with asthma, by causing the bronchi to dilate. And because THC helps prevent nausea and vomiting, it gained use among cancer patients whose chemotherapy elicited such reactions (Plasse et al., 1991; Gunby, 1981). Similarly, some studies have suggested that THC might help improve the appetites of AIDS patients (Plasse et al., 1991).

In light of all this, the National Organization for the Reform of Marijuana Laws (NORML) has campaigned for the medical legalization of marijuana cigarettes. In particular, the organization has argued that doses of THC are more controllable in marijuana cigarettes than in THC pill form. In the late 1980s the Drug Enforcement Administration (DEA) considered classifying marijuana as a medically useful drug that can be prescribed by physicians. In 1992, however, the DEA finally decided against this, and the Food and Drug Administration even stopped reviewing requests for the "compassionate use" of marijuana cigarettes (Karel, 1992). They held that prescriptions of pure THC, which are available in a capsule, serve all needed medical functions. Thus, although 36 states now have laws which allow physicians to prescribe marijuana cigarettes, such actions have been approved in only a handful of cases over the years (Karel, 1992).

individual substance–related disorders (Miller et al., 1990; Weisheit, 1990). Teenagers and young adults seem particularly likely to use drugs in combination (Wright, 1985). A look in on a group therapy session for individuals who use crack reveals that several of the group members have used numerous substances in addition to crack:

Okay. Now, can you give me a list of all the drugs you've used? Gary?

GARY: Pot. Coke. Crack. Mescaline. Acid. Speed. Crystal meth. Smack. Base dust. Sometimes alcohol.

DENNIS: Alcohol. Pot. Coke. Mescaline. LSD. Amyl nitrate. Speed and Valium.

DAVY: Coke. Crack. Reefer. Alcohol. Acid. Mescaline. Mushrooms. Ecstasy. Speed. Smack.

RICH: Alcohol. Pot. Ludes [Quaaludes]. Valium. Speed. Ups [amphetamines]. Downs [barbiturates]. Acid. Mescaline. Crack. Base. Dust. That's about it.

CAROL: Alcohol. Pot. Cocaine. Mescaline. Valium. Crack.
(Chatlos, 1987, pp. 30–31)

Some famous people have been the victims of polysubstance use. Elvis Presley's delicate balancing act of stimulant and depressant abuse eventually caused his demise. Janis Joplin's propensity for mixing wine and heroin was ultimately fatal. And John Belushi's and River Phoenix's liking for the combined effect of cocaine and opioids ("speedballs") also ended in tragedy. Obviously, whether it is intentional or accidental, mixing drugs is a hazardous undertaking.

*Polysubstance use, particularly a mixture of cocaine and opioids, eventually proved fatal for comedian John Belushi, who often made jokes about the use of drugs on "Saturday Night Live," and actor River Phoenix, who was a practicing vegetarian and an environmentalist. Their deaths were separated by years, at locations only blocks apart, from biological causes that were identical.*

### Summing Up

*Hallucinogens, such as LSD, are substances that cause powerful changes in sensory perception, including intensification of perceptions, illusions, and hallucinations. LSD, which apparently prevents the release of the neurotransmitter serotonin, also may cause flashbacks.*

*Cannabis substances, such as marijuana, cause a mixture of hallucinogenic, depressant, and stimulant effects. Today's marijuana has a much higher THC content than past versions, leading to greater problems and dangers.*

*Polysubstance-related disorders are becoming as common as individual substance-related disorders and leading to an increasing number of problems.*

## Explanations of Substance-Related Disorders

Clinicians have proposed a number of theories to explain why people abuse or become dependent on various substances. As we shall see, however, none has gained unqualified research support (Peele, 1989). Indeed, excessive and chronic drug use is increasingly being viewed as a consequence of a combination of psychological, biological, and sociocultural factors.

## The Psychodynamic Explanation

Psychodynamic theorists believe that people who ultimately abuse substances have inordinate dependency needs traceable to their early years (Shedler & Block, 1990; Abadi, 1984). They theorize that when parents fail to satisfy a child's need for nurturance, the child is likely to go through life in a dependent manner—relying too much on others for support, help, and comfort—in an effort to find the nurturance he or she did not receive as a child. If this search for external sources of support includes experimentation with a drug, such a person is likely to develop a dependent relationship with the substance.

Some psychodynamic theorists also believe that certain people develop a "substance abuse personality" that makes them particularly vulnerable to drugs. To support this notion, researchers have obtained profiles of subjects from interviews and personality tests, and have found that people who abuse drugs tend to be more dependent, antisocial, impulsive, and depressive than other people (Shedler & Block, 1990; Grinspoon & Bakalar, 1986).

But do such personality styles actually cause drug abuse? A longitudinal study measured the characteristics of a large group of nonalcoholic young men and then kept track of each man's development (Jones, 1971, 1968). The profiles of those men who later developed alcohol problems in middle age were compared with the profiles of those who did not. The men who developed alcohol problems had been more impulsive as adolescents and continued to be so in middle age, suggesting that impulsive men are indeed more prone to develop alcohol problems.

A major problem with these studies is that a suspiciously wide range of personality traits has been linked to drug abuse; in fact, different studies point to different "key" traits. Inasmuch as some people with a drug addiction are apparently dependent, others impulsive, and still others antisocial, researchers have been unable to conclude that any one personality trait or cluster of traits stands out as a factor in substance abuse and dependence (Rozin & Stoess, 1993).

## Behavioral Explanations

According to *reinforcement* theorists, the temporary reduction of tension, raising of spirits, or sense of well-being produced by a drug has a reinforcing effect and increases the likelihood that the user will seek this reaction again, especially under stress (Clark & Sayette, 1993). In support of this theory, studies have found that both human and animal subjects do in fact drink more alcohol when they are under stress (Young & Herling, 1986). One group of experimenters had individuals work on a difficult anagram task while another person unfairly criticized and belittled them (Marlatt et al., 1975). These subjects were then asked to participate in an "alcohol taste task": their job was supposedly to compare and rate various alcoholic beverages. The harassed subjects drank significantly more alcohol during the taste task than did control subjects who had not been criticized.

In a manner of speaking, the reinforcement theorists are arguing that many people take drugs to medicate themselves when they feel tense and upset. If so, one would expect elevated rates of drug abuse among people with high levels of anxiety, depression, or anger. This expectation has in fact been supported by research (King et al., 1993; Bukstein et al., 1992). Similarly, studies have found a higher than usual rate of drug abuse among persons with posttraumatic stress disorder, eating disorders, or histories of being abused (Yama et al., 1993; Higuchi et al., 1993).

Of course, even if a drug does initially reward the user with a reduction in tension, the picture seems to change later when the person takes the drug excessively and chronically. As we saw earlier, many people become increasingly anxious and depressed over time as they take more and more drugs. Why, then, do they keep ingesting them?

Some behaviorists use Richard Solomon's **opponent-process theory** to answer this question. Solomon (1980) holds that the brain is structured in such a way

that pleasurable emotions, such as drug-induced euphoria, inevitably lead to opponent processes—negative aftereffects—that leave the person feeling worse than usual. People who continue to use pleasure-giving drugs inevitably develop opponent aftereffects, such as cravings for more of the drug, withdrawal responses, and an increasing need for the drug. According to Solomon, the opponent processes eventually dominate the pleasure-giving processes, and avoidance of the negative aftereffects replaces pursuit of pleasure as the individual's primary motivation for taking drugs. Although a highly regarded theory, the opponent-process explanation has not received systematic research support (Peele, 1989).

Still other behaviorists have proposed that *classical conditioning* may also contribute to certain aspects of drug abuse and dependence (Ehrman et al., 1992). They hold that objects, such as the sight of a hypodermic needle, present at the time drugs are taken may act as conditioned stimuli and come to elicit some of the same pleasure brought on by the drugs themselves. In a similar manner, objects that are present during withdrawal distress may sometimes elicit withdrawal-like symptoms. One individual who had formerly been dependent on heroin for example, experienced nausea and some other withdrawal symptoms when he returned to the neighborhood where he had gone through withdrawal in the past—a reaction that led him to start taking heroin again (O'Brien et al., 1975).

## Biological Explanations

In recent years, researchers have come to suspect that many cases of drug misuse may be related to biological factors. Their suspicions have been bolstered by two areas of research—genetic predispositions and biochemical processes.

### Genetic Predispositions

For years, animal researchers have conducted animal-breeding experiments that implicate genetic factors in the development of drug dependence (Azar, 1995; Goldstein, 1994; George, 1990). In one line of research, for example, investigators have selected animals who prefer alcohol to other beverages, mated them to one another, and found that their offspring display the same preference.

Similarly, research with human twins has suggested that people may inherit a predisposition to substance

*Opponent-process theory*    An explanation for drug abuse and dependence based on the interplay of pleasurable emotions that initially come from ingesting the drug and inevitable negative aftereffects that leave a person feeling worse than usual.

abuse and dependence (Kendler et al., 1994, 1992; (Goodwin, 1984). In one study, for example, an alcohol-abuse concordance rate of 54 percent was found in a group of genetically identical twins; that is, in 54 percent of the cases in which one identical twin abused alcohol, the other twin also abused alcohol. In contrast, a group of fraternal twins had a concordance rate of only 28 percent (Kaij, 1960). Of course, as we have observed, such findings do not rule out other interpretations. For one thing, parents may act more similarly toward identical twins than toward fraternal twins.

A stronger indicator that there may be a genetic factor in drug abuse and dependence has come from adoption studies. A number of studies have examined the alcoholism rates of people who were adopted shortly after birth (Cadoret et al., 1995; Goodwin et al., 1973). Typically in these studies one group of adoptees have had biological parents who were alcoholic, while another group's biological parents were not. By adulthood, those with alcoholic biological parents have displayed significantly higher rates of alcohol abuse than those with nonalcoholic biological parents, suggesting once again that a predisposition to develop alcoholism may be inherited.

Even more direct evidence that a genetic factor may be at play in drug misuse has recently been provided by the "gene mapping" techniques that we discussed in Chapter 7. Using this new technology, investigators have found links between abnormal genes and substance-related disorders. One set of studies has found that an abnormal form of the so-called D2 receptor gene is present in the majority of subjects with alcohol

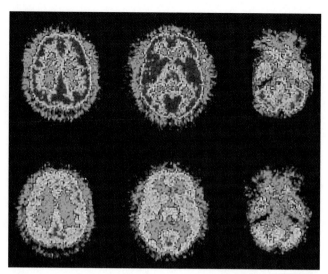

*Although cocaine and amphetamines stimulate the central nervous system, they decrease activity in some areas of the brain. The PET scans of a cocaine user (bottom row) reveal a drop in activity—indicated by the color blue—in some brain regions. PET scans of a nonuser (top row) reveal a high level of activity—indicated by the color red—in the same areas.*

dependence and in half of subjects with cocaine dependence, but in less than 20 percent of nondependent subjects (Blum & Noble, 1993; Blum et al., 1991).

## Biochemical Processes

After years of research, investigators have arrived at a general biochemical understanding of drug tolerance and withdrawal symptoms. It appears that the excessive and chronic ingestion of a particular kind of drug causes the brain to reduce its production of the particular neurotransmitter that would ordinarily act to sedate, alleviate pain, lift mood, or increase alertness (Goldstein, 1994). Because the drug acts to produce such a reaction, the presence of the neurotransmitter is less necessary. As the drug intake is increased, the body's production of the corresponding neurotransmitter decreases, leaving the person in need of more and more of the drug to achieve its initial effects. In short, the person builds tolerance for the drug. Moreover, as people become increasingly reliant on a drug rather than on their own neurotransmitter, they must continue to ingest the drug in order to feel reasonably calm, comfortable, happy, or alert. If they suddenly stop taking the drug, for a while they will have a deficient supply of the chemicals needed for feeling well; they will in fact feel terrible. That is, they will experience uncomfortable withdrawal symptoms until the brain resumes its normal production and release of the necessary neurotransmitter.

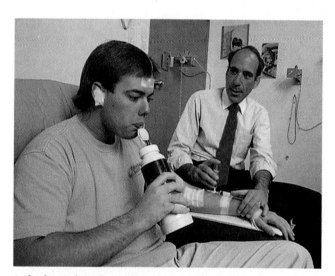

*In biological studies subjects ingest alcohol or other substances in the laboratory while researchers systematically observe the effects of those substances on brain and body functioning.*

Thus, a chronic use of opioids eventually reduces the brain's own production of endorphins, and a chronic use of cocaine or amphetamines lowers the brain's own production of dopamine and norepinephrine, leaving people with inadequate supplies of these neurotransmitters when they stop taking the drugs (Snyder, 1991, 1977). In addition, the recent discovery of *anandamide,* the body's own THC, suggests that excessive use of marijuana may reduce natural anandamide production, altering regulation of mood, pain, memory, and movement (Fackelmann, 1993).

Of course, even if biological factors do predispose some people to develop or maintain drug problems, most people with such predispositions never fall into the trap of drug abuse or dependence. Why do some and not others develop these grossly dysfunctional problems? This is where the psychological theories (discussed earlier) and the sociocultural theories have been enlightening.

## Sociocultural Explanations

Sociocultural theorists propose that the people most likely to develop a pattern of substance abuse or dependence are people living in socioeconomic circumstances that create an atmosphere of stress. Consistent with this claim, studies have found that geographical regions with higher levels of unemployment have higher rates of alcoholism (Linsky et al., 1985). Similarly, lower socioeconomic classes have higher substance abuse rates than other classes (Smith et al., 1993; Beauvais, 1992).

Sociocultural theorists also propose that drug abuse is more likely to emerge in families that value, or at least tolerate, drug taking. Researchers have, in fact, found that problem drinking is more common among teenagers whose parents and peers drink, as well as among teenagers whose family environment is stressful and unsupportive (Carey, 1993; Chassin et al., 1993). Moreover, lower rates of alcohol abuse have been found among Jews and Protestants, groups in which drinking is acceptable only so long as it remains within clearly defined boundaries (Calahan et al., 1969; McCord & McCord, 1960), whereas alcoholism rates are somewhat higher among the Irish and Eastern Europeans, who do not make as clear a distinction (Vaillant & Milofsky, 1982).

Findings of these kinds are consistent with the sociocultural view of substance abuse and dependence, but as we noted earlier, they are subject to nonsociocultural interpretations as well. In fact, as we have seen, none of the models has provided undisputed evidence to support its position on substance-related disorders, and certainly none by itself has been able to account for all aspects of dysfunctional drug use (Peele, 1989). Thus, at present, drug misuse remains a complex phenomenon that is far from being fully understood.

### Consider This
Different ethnic, religious, and national groups exhibit different rates of alcohol abuse. What social factors might help explain this observation? Can we be certain that biological factors are not involved?

# Treatments for Substance-Related Disorders

A wide variety of treatments have been applied to substance-related disorders, sometimes with great success, more often with only moderate effectiveness (Prochaska et al., 1992). The treatments may be applied on either an outpatient or an inpatient basis. Although the use of inpatient treatment for these disorders seems to be on the rise, research does not suggest that this more expensive format is consistently more effective than outpatient treatment (McKay et al., 1995; Miller & Hester, 1986).

Most of the approaches fall into one of several groups: insight, behavioral, cognitive-behavioral, biological, and sociocultural therapies. Although the various forms of intervention are presented separately below, most therapists actually use them in combination with each other.

*Some cultures encourage alcohol use more than others, thus increasing the risk of alcoholism. These men are participating in Germany's 16-day "Oktoberfest," during which bartenders serve 5 million liters of beer to thousands of revelers.*

## Insight Therapies

Insight therapists try to help people with substance-related disorders become aware of and address the psychological factors that contribute to their pattern of drug use (Jungman, 1985). Psychodynamic therapists, for example, first help clients uncover and resolve their underlying conflicts and then try to help them change their substance-related styles of living (Levinson, 1985). Client-centered therapists guide clients to accept the feelings and thoughts that, according to their theory, they have hidden from themselves while turning to drugs.

Although these approaches are often applied to substance-related disorders, research has not found them to be highly effective when offered by themselves (Meyer et al., 1989; Miller & Hester, 1980). They tend to be of greater help when they are combined with other approaches in a multidimensional treatment program (Galanter, 1993; Weidman, 1985).

## Behavioral Therapies

A widely used behavioral treatment for substance-related disorders is *aversion therapy,* the approach based on the principles of classical conditioning. Here individuals are repeatedly presented with an unpleasant stimulus (for example, an electric shock) at the same time that they are taking a drug. After repeated pairings, the individuals are expected to start reacting negatively to the substance itself and to lose their craving for it.

Aversion therapy has been applied to alcohol abuse and dependence more than to other substance-use disorders (Callner, 1975). In one technique, drinking behavior is paired with drug-induced nausea and vomiting (Elkins, 1991). Another (*covert sensitization*) requires people with alcoholism to imagine extremely upsetting, repulsive, or frightening scenes while they are drinking (Emmelkamp, 1994; Cautela, 1967). The supposition is that the pairing of these imagined scenes with liquor will elicit negative responses to liquor itself.

Another behavioral approach focuses on teaching *alternative behaviors* to drug taking. This approach, too, has been applied to alcohol abuse and dependence more than to other substance-related disorders. Problem drinkers may be taught to use relaxation, meditation, or biofeedback instead of alcohol to reduce their tensions (Rohsenow et al., 1985). Some are also taught assertiveness or social skills to help them both express their anger more directly and withstand social pressures to drink (Van Hasselt et al., 1993; Chaney et al., 1978). Similarly, leisure education programs teach substance abusers positive "fun" alternatives to taking drugs (Aguilar & Munson, 1992).

Most behavioral treatments for substance abuse and dependence have had at most limited success (Meyer et al., 1989). One of the major problems with these approaches is that they can be successful only when subjects are sufficiently motivated to continue with them despite their unpleasantness or demands. In fact, behavioral treatments generally work best in combination with cognitive approaches (Washton & Stone-Washton, 1990).

## Cognitive-Behavioral Therapies

Two leading treatments combine cognitive and behavioral techniques to help people gain control over their drinking behavior. In one, *behavioral self-control training (BSCT),* therapists first instruct clients to monitor their own drinking behavior (Miller et al., 1992; Miller, 1983). When clients record the times, locations, emotions, bodily changes, and other circumstances that accompany their drinking, they become more sensitive to the cues they associate with excessive drinking. They are then taught to set appropriate limits on their drinking, to recognize when the limits are being approached, to control their rate of drinking (perhaps by spacing their drinks or by sipping them rather than gulping), and to apply relaxation responses and other coping behaviors in situations that would otherwise elicit drinking. Approximately 70 percent of the clients who complete this program have been assessed as showing some improvement (Miller & Hester, 1980). The program appears to be more effective in cases where individuals are younger and not physically dependent on alcohol (Miller et al., 1992; Meyer et al., 1989).

In a similar approach, *relapse-prevention training,* heavy drinkers do many of the same tasks as in BSCT (Kivlaham et al., 1990; Marlatt & Gordon, 1985, 1980) and are further taught to plan ahead of time how much drinking is appropriate, what they will consume, and under what circumstances. Research indicates that this approach sometimes reduces the frequency of intoxication (Hollon & Beck, 1994; Annis et al., 1989). Like BSCT, it is apparently more effective for those who abuse alcohol than those who are physically dependent on alcohol (Meyer et al., 1989). It has also been adapted, with some success, to the treatment of cocaine abuse (Carrol et al., 1991).

## Biological Treatments

Biological techniques play a variety of roles in the treatment of substance-related disorders. They may be directed at helping people withdraw from substances, abstain from them, or simply maintain their existing substance use without further escalation. Research suggests that these approaches alone rarely lead to long-term improvement but can sometimes be a helpful component of broader treatment programs (Kleber et al., 1985).

## Detoxification

*Detoxification* is systematic and medically supervised withdrawal from a drug (Wartenberg et al., 1990). Many detoxification programs are set up in hospitals or clinics, as drug users often seem more motivated to persevere through withdrawal in those settings. Inpatient detoxification programs of this kind may also offer individual and group therapy, a "full-service" institutional approach that has become increasingly popular in recent years.

One detoxification strategy is to administer small doses of other kinds of drugs during withdrawal from the abused drug. When two drugs act on the brain similarly, users may build up tolerance to one drug while taking the other, a phenomenon called *cross-tolerance*. Correspondingly, the symptoms of withdrawal from one of the drugs may be partly reduced by taking the other drug. Some clinicians, for example, try to reduce the alcohol-withdrawal reaction of delirium tremens by administering antianxiety drugs, along with vitamins and electrolytes, during alcohol withdrawal.

Detoxification programs have proved effective in helping motivated people to withdraw from drugs. For people who fail to pursue psychotherapy after withdrawal, however, relapse rates tend to be high (Pickens & Fletcher, 1991).

## Antagonist Drugs

After successful withdrawal from a drug, the next challenge is to avoid a recurrence of drug abuse or dependence. In one biological technique, people are given *antagonist drugs,* drugs that block or change the effects of the addictive drug. *Disulfiram (Antabuse),* for example, is often given to people who are trying to refrain from drinking alcohol (Ray & Ksir, 1993). By itself this drug is believed to have relatively few negative effects; but a person who drinks alcohol while taking disulfiram will experience intense nausea, vomiting, blushing, faster heart rate, dizziness, and perhaps

fainting. Disulfiram has proved helpful but again only with people who are highly motivated (Meyer et al., 1989). After all, they can stop taking the disulfiram and return to alcohol at any time.

*Narcotic antagonists,* such as naloxone and naltrexone, are sometimes used with people who are dependent on opioids. These drugs attach to opioid receptor sites throughout the brain and make it impossible for the opioid to have its usual euphoric effect. Theoretically, without the rush or high, continued drug use becomes pointless. Although narcotic antagonists have been helpful in emergencies to rescue people from an overdose of opioids, they are usually considered too dangerous for treatment of opioid dependence. The antagonists must be administered very carefully because of their ability to throw persons with an addiction into severe withdrawal reactions (Goldstein, 1994; Kleber et al., 1985). Surprisingly, some recent studies have found that narcotic antagonists may also have some therapeutic value in alcohol and cocaine dependence (Goldstein, 1994; Volpicelli et al., 1992; O'Malley et al., 1992).

## Drug Maintenance Therapy

A drug-related lifestyle may be a greater problem than the drug's direct effects. Much of the damage caused by heroin addiction, for example, comes from overdoses, unsterile needles, harmful contaminants, and an accompanying life of crime. Thus clinicians were initially very enthusiastic when *methadone maintenance programs* were developed in the 1960s to treat heroin addiction (Dole & Nyswander, 1967, 1965). In these programs, clients with an addiction are given the synthetic opioid methadone as a substitute for heroin. Although the clients then become dependent on methadone, their new addiction is maintained under legal and safe medical supervision. The programs' creators believed methadone to be preferable to heroin because it can be taken orally, thus eliminating the dangers of needles, and it needs to be taken only once a day.

The initial methadone programs appeared to be very effective and led to the establishment of numerous such programs throughout the United States, Canada, and England (Payte, 1989). However, these programs became less popular during the 1980s, largely because of the addictiveness and dangers of methadone itself

*Detoxification* Systematic and medically supervised withdrawal from a drug.

*Cross-tolerance* Tolerance for a drug one has never taken, as a result of using another, similar drug.

*Narcotic antagonist* A substance that attaches to opioid receptors in the brain and, in turn, counteracts the effects of opioids.

*Methadone maintenance program* An approach to treating heroin dependence in which clients are given legally and medically supervised doses of a substitute drug, methadone, with which to satisfy their need for heroin.

(Peachey & Franklin, 1985). Many clinicians came to believe that substituting one addiction for another is not an acceptable "solution" for drug dependence, and many addicted persons found that methadone addiction creates an additional drug problem that simply complicates the original one, leaving them with a far from drug-free existence. In fact, methadone is harder to withdraw from than heroin.

> ### Consider This
>
> Inasmuch as the major dangers of heroin come from overdose, unsterilized needles, and criminal lifestyle, society has periodically tried legal, medically supervised use of heroin (in Great Britain) or of a heroin-substitute (in the United States) to combat the heroin problem. Generally, such approaches have had limited effectiveness. Why?

Despite such concerns, interest in methadone maintenance and other medically supervised treatments has increased once again in recent years as a result of the rapid spread of the HIV virus among intravenous drug abusers and their sex partners and children. Indeed, over a quarter of AIDS cases are directly associated with intravenous drug abuse (Brown, 1993; Batki, 1988).

## Sociocultural Treatments

As we have observed, sociocultural theorists believe that psychological problems emerge in a social setting and are best treated in a social context. Three kinds of sociocultural approaches have been applied to substance-related disorders: (1) self-help programs, in which persons with addictions help each other; (2) culture-sensitive programs; and (3) community prevention programs.

### Self-Help and Residential Treatment Programs

Many persons who abuse drugs have organized among themselves to help one another recover without professional assistance. The drug self-help movement dates back to 1935, when two alcoholic men from Ohio met to discuss alternative treatment possibilities. The first discussion led to others and to the eventual formation of a self-help group for persons with alcoholism. The members discussed alcohol-related problems, traded ideas, and provided support. The organization became known as *Alcoholics Anonymous (AA)*.

Today AA has more than 2 million members in 89,000 groups across the United States and nearly 100

*Alcoholics Anonymous (AA)*   A self-help organization that provides support and guidance for persons with alcohol abuse or dependence.

At "Via Avanta," a residential treatment center in Los Angeles, a therapist leads a parenting session for women dependent on opioids. Individuals live and work in such centers while treated for their substance dependence.

other countries (AA World Services, 1994). It provides peer support therapy with moral and spiritual features to help people overcome alcoholism. Different members apparently find different aspects of AA helpful. For some it is the peer support and identification; for others it is the spiritual dimension. Meetings take place regularly, and members are available to help each other 24 hours a day.

By establishing guidelines for living, the organization helps members abstain "one day at a time," urging them to accept as "fact" the idea that they are powerless over alcohol and that they must stop drinking entirely and permanently if they are to live normal lives (see Box 11-4). A related self-help organization is AlAnon, which offers support groups for people who live with and care about alcoholic persons. Self-help programs, such as Narcotics Anonymous and Cocaine Anonymous, have also been developed for other substance-related disorders.

Many self-help programs, such as Daytop Village and Phoenix House, have expanded into *residential treatment centers*, or *therapeutic communities*, where people formerly dependent on drugs live, work, and socialize in a drug-free environment while undergoing individual, group, and family therapies and making a transition back to community life.

The actual success of the self-help and residential treatment programs has been difficult to determine (Ray & Ksir, 1993; Meyer et al., 1989). The evidence that keeps them going comes in the form of individual testimonials. Many tens of thousands of people have revealed that they are members of these programs and credit them with turning their lives around.

*Residential treatment center*   A place where people formerly dependent on drugs live, work, and socialize in a drug-free environment.

## Box 11-4

# *Moderation or Abstinence?*

Is total abstinence the only cure for drug abuse and dependence, or can people with substance-related disorders learn to keep drug use under better control? This issue has been debated for years, especially when the drug in question is alcohol (Sleek, 1995).

As we have seen in the chapter, some cognitive-behavioral theorists believe that people can continue to drink in moderation if they learn to set more appropriate drinking limits. These advocates of controlled drinking argue that a goal of strict abstinence may in fact encourage people to abandon self-control entirely if they should have a single drink (Peele, 1989; Heather et al., 1982). Those who view alcoholism as a disease, in contrast, take the AA position of "Once an alcoholic, always an alcoholic," and hold that relapse is almost inevitable when people with alcoholism believe that they can safely take one drink (Pendery et al., 1982). They hold that this misguided belief will sooner or later open the door to alcohol once

again and lead back to uncontrollable drinking.

Feelings about this issue are so strong that the people on one side have at times challenged the motives and integrity of those on the other (Sobell & Sobell, 1984, 1976, 1973; Pendery et al., 1982). Research indicates, however, that both controlled drinking and abstinence may be viable treatment goals, depending on the individual's personality and on the nature of the particular drinking problem. Studies suggest, for example, that total abstinence is a more appropriate goal for people who have been dependent on alcohol for a long time, while controlled drinking can be helpful to younger abusive drinkers, who may, in fact, need to be taught a nonabusive form of drinking (Peele, 1992; Nathan, 1986; Marlatt, 1985; Miller, 1983, 1982). Studies also suggest that abstinence is more appropriate for people who believe (1) that they are alcoholic and (2) that abstinence is the only answer for them (Rosenberg,

1993). These people are more likely to relapse after having just one drink. The results of these studies may apply to other drug disorders as well.

It is important to keep in mind that, generally speaking, both abstinence and controlled drinking are extremely difficult for persons with alcoholism to achieve (Watson, 1987). Although treatment may help them to improve for a while, follow-up studies indicate high relapse rates. A study that followed the progress of 110 individuals found that thirty years after treatment, 20 percent had become moderate drinkers, 34 percent had become abstinent, and the rest continued to display significant drinking problems (Vaillant, 1983). Other alcoholism findings are even gloomier (Peele, 1989; Emrick & Hansen, 1983).

Such statistics serve as a harsh reminder that substance abuse and dependence continue to be among our society's most durable and disabling problems.

## Culture-Sensitive Programs

Many persons who abuse substances live in a poverty-stricken and violence-prone environment (NIDA, 1990). A growing number of today's treatment programs try to be sensitive to the special sociocultural pressures and problems faced by drug abusers who are poor, homeless, or members of ethnic minority groups (Deitch & Solit, 1993; Wallace, 1993). Sensitivity to each patient's unique challenges can be the best defense against the environmental and social stresses that can lead to relapse.

Similarly, therapists have become more aware that significant gender issues are often tied to substance-related disorders (Lisansky-Gomberg, 1993). Treatment of women who abuse substances may be complicated by numerous gender-specific issues, including the impact of sexual abuse, the stresses of raising children, and the fear of criminal prosecution for abusing drugs

during pregnancy (Chiavaroli, 1992; Roper, 1992; Wallen, 1992). Seventy percent of women with substance-related disorders have experienced sexual abuse before age 16 according to some investigations, (Arbiter, 1991; Worth, 1991). Thus, many women with such disorders feel more comfortable seeking help at gender-sensitive programs that focus on empowerment and education and that allow children to live with their recovering mothers (Copeland & Hall, 1992; DeAngelis, 1992).

## Community Prevention Programs

In recent years, drug prevention efforts have spread throughout society. Programs are now being conducted in schools, workplaces, activity centers, and many other community settings. Prevention programs may focus on the *individual* (for example, by providing education about undesirable drug effects), on the *family* (by teaching parenting skills and improving family functioning), on the *peer group* (by changing peer norms or teaching resistance to peer pressure), on the *school* (by establishing firm enforcement of drug policies), or on the *community* at large (by public service announcements such as the "Just say no" campaign). The most effective prevention efforts combine several such areas of focus to create a comprehensive and cooperative program that provides a consistent message about drug abuse in all areas of individuals' lives (NIDA, 1991). Some prevention programs have even been developed for preschool children (Oyemade, 1989).

> ### Summing Up
> *Substance-related disorders are increasingly being viewed as resulting from multiple contributing factors: psychological, biological, and sociocultural. Explanations have emphasized substance-abuse personalities, self-medication, opponent-processes, genetic factors, biochemical processes, and societal pressures. Similarly, treatment approaches have combined insight, behavioral, cognitive, biological, and sociocultural therapies. Thus far, such approaches have had moderate success at best.*

## The State of the Field
## *Substance-Related Disorders*

In some respects the story of drug misuse is the same today as for many years past. Substance use is still rampant and creates some of society's most prevalent psychological disorders and debilitating problems. New drugs keep emerging, and the public continues to go through periods of naiveté regarding their use, believing for a time that the drugs are "safe" and gradually learning that they pose significant dangers. And treatments for substance-related disorders continue to have only limited effect.

Yet there are some important new wrinkles in this familiar tale. Researchers have begun to develop a clearer understanding of the way many drugs act on the body and of the biological reasons for drug tolerance and withdrawal symptoms. In the treatment sphere, self-help groups and rehabilitation programs are flourishing. Preventive education to make people aware of the seduction of drugs and the dangers of drug misuse is also on the upswing and seems to be making a dent in the public's drug behavior, especially among teenagers, whose use of drugs has declined somewhat in recent years. And clinicians have discovered drug antagonists that seem to hold promise as future forms of biological intervention.

These developments are encouraging. Meanwhile, however, enormous quantities of drugs are being distributed and used. New drugs and drug combinations are discovered almost daily. And with them come new problems, new questions, and requirements for new research and new interventions. Thus despite their efforts, clinical practitioners and investigators have found it difficult to make a sizable change for the better. As drugs proliferate, perhaps the most valuable lesson to be learned from clinical research and from our society's drug-taking history is an old one: There is no free lunch. High psychological and biological costs are attached to the pleasures associated with many of these substances. Not all the costs are yet known, but costs do inevitably seem to emerge.

## *Chapter Review*

1. *Substance Misuse:* The term "drug" applies to any substance other than food that changes our bodily and mental functioning. Substance, or drug, misuse may lead to temporary changes in behavior, emotion, or thought, such as *intoxication*. Chronic excessive use can lead to either *substance abuse*, a pattern in which people rely heavily on a drug and structure their lives around it, or *substance dependence*, in which they show the symptoms of substance abuse plus physical dependence on the drug (often called *addiction*). People who become physically dependent on a drug develop a *tolerance* to it or experience unpleasant *withdrawal symptoms* when they abstain from it, or both.

2. *Depressants:* Depressants are drugs that slow the activity of the central nervous system. Each of the major ones can lead to assorted problems and dangers.
   A. *Alcohol:* Alcoholic beverages contain *ethyl alcohol*, which is carried to the central nervous system (CNS), depressing its function and leading

to impairment of fine motor skills and other physiological effects. *Intoxication* occurs when the concentration of alcohol in the bloodstream reaches 0.09 percent. Excessive use may lead to a pattern of abuse or dependence, also called *alcoholism*, as well as to health impairment and intoxication-related accidents and crises.

B. *Sedative-Hypnotic Drugs:* The sedative-hypnotic drugs, which produce feelings of relaxation and drowsiness, include *benzodiazepines (antianxiety drugs)* and *barbiturates,* the latter being the more dangerous. Both benzodiazepines and barbiturates increase the activity of the neurotransmitter GABA. Barbiturates also affect the reticular formation. Chronic and excessive benzodiazepine use may lead to a pattern of abuse or dependence. Barbiturate misuse often leads to particularly severe withdrawal symptoms.

C. *Opioids:* Opioids include *opium* and drugs derived from it, such as *heroin, morphine, codeine,* and various synthetic opioids. They all reduce tension and pain and cause other bodily reactions. Opioids operate by binding to neurons that ordinarily receive *endorphins.* Chronic and excessive use of opioids can lead to abuse or dependence. Dependence on the more powerful opioids, such as heroin, develops particularly rapidly.

3. *Stimulants:* Stimulants are substances that act to increase the activity of the central nervous system. They may lead to intoxication, abuse, and dependence, including a withdrawal pattern marked by depression, fatigue, and irritability. *Cocaine* produces a euphoric effect by stimulating the release of dopamine and norepinephrine in the brain. *Amphetamines,* stimulant drugs manufactured in the laboratory, operate in much the same manner.

4. *Hallucinogens:* Hallucinogens, such as LSD, are substances that cause powerful changes primarily in sensory perception, including intensification of perceptions and the inducement of illusions and hallucinations. LSD apparently causes such effects by disturbing the release of the neurotransmitter serotonin. LSD is extremely potent, and ingestion of the drug may lead to a "bad trip" or to *flashbacks.*

5. *Cannabis:* Cannabis sativa is a hemp plant whose main ingredient is *tetrahydrocannabinol (THC).* The most popular, and weakest, form of cannabis, *marijuana,* is more powerful today than it was in years past. It can cause intoxication, and regular use can lead to patterns of abuse and dependence.

6. *Polysubstance-Related Disorders:* Many people take more than one drug at a time, and the drugs interact with each other. When different drugs enhance each other's effects, they have a combined impact known as a *synergistic effect.* The use of two or more drugs at the same time—*polysubstance use*—has become increasingly common. Similarly, *polysubstance-related disorders* have also become a significant problem.

7. *Explanations for Substance-Related Disorders:* A variety of explanations for substance abuse and dependence have been put forward, but none has gained unqualified research support.

A. The *psychodynamic view* proposes that people who turn to substance abuse have inordinate dependency needs traceable to the oral stage of life.

B. The leading *behavioral view* proposes that drug use is initially reinforced because it reduces tension and raises spirits.

C. The *biological view* is supported by studies of twins and adoptees which suggest that people may inherit a predisposition to substance dependence. Biological researchers have further learned that drug tolerance and withdrawal symptoms may be related to the brain's reduced production of particular neurotransmitters during excessive and chronic drug use.

D. The *sociocultural view* proposes that the people most likely to develop a pattern of drug abuse are those living in socioeconomic conditions conducive to stress or whose families value or tolerate drug taking.

8. *Treatments for Substance-Related Disorders:* Treatments for substance abuse and dependence vary as widely as explanations for its cause. Often several approaches are combined.

A. *Insight therapies* try to help clients become aware of and address the psychological factors that contribute to their pattern of drug use.

B. A common *behavioral technique* is *aversion therapy,* in which an unpleasant stimulus is paired with the drug that the person is taking.

C. *Cognitive and behavioral techniques* have been combined in such forms as *behavioral self-control training (BSCT)* and *relapse-prevention training.*

D. *Biological treatments* include *detoxification, antagonist drugs,* and *drug maintenance therapy.*

E. *Sociocultural therapies* treat substance-related disorders in a social context. The leading approaches are *self-help groups,* such as Alcoholics Anonymous; *culture-sensitive treatments;* and *community prevention programs.*

## Key Terms

| | | | |
|---|---|---|---|
| intoxication | fetal alcohol syndrome | amphetamine | opponent-process theory |
| hallucinosis | benzodiazepine | hallucinogen | BSCT |
| substance abuse | barbiturate | psychedelic | relapse-prevention |
| substance dependence | methaqualone | LSD | training |
| addiction | GABA | ergot alkaloid | detoxification |
| tolerance | heroin | synesthesia | antagonist drug |
| withdrawal | morphine | flashback | disulfiram (Antabuse) |
| depressant | codeine | Cannabis sativa | narcotic antagonist |
| alcohol | rush | THC | methadone maintenance |
| sedative-hypnotic | high | cannabis | self-help program |
| opioid | endorphin | hashish | Alcoholics Anonymous |
| ethyl alcohol | stimulant | ganja | (AA) |
| alcohol dehydrogenase | caffeine | marijuana | Narcotics Anonymous |
| metabolize | nicotine | synergistic effect | Cocaine Anonymous |
| alcoholism | cocaine | polysubstance-related | residential treatment |
| delirium tremens | snort | disorder | center |
| cirrhosis | free-base | substance-abuse | therapeutic community |
| Korsakoff's syndrome | crack | personality | culture-sensitive program |
| confabulate | fetal cocaine syndrome | reinforcement | community prevention |

## Quick Quiz

1. How does alcohol act upon the brain and body? What are the problems and dangers of alcohol misuse?
2. Describe the features and problems of the misuse of the sedative-hypnotic drugs benzodiazepines and barbiturates.
3. Compare the various opioids (opium, heroin, morphine, and codeine). How do they act psychologically and biologically? What problems may emerge from their use, particularly from the use of heroin?
4. List and compare four kinds of stimulant drugs and describe the problems caused by each of them. How do cocaine and amphetamines act biologically?
5. Why has cocaine use become a major problem in recent years?
6. What are the short-term and long-term effects of hallucinogens, particularly LSD? How does LSD act biologically?
7. What are the effects of marijuana and other cannabis substances? What is their key ingredient?
8. Why is marijuana a bigger danger today than it was 25 years ago, and what are its dangers?
9. What special problems does polysubstance use pose?
10. Describe the leading explanations for substance-related disorders. How well supported are these explanations?
11. What are the leading treatments for substance-related disorders? How effective are these approaches?

# 12

# Suicide

## Topic Overview

*What Is Suicide?*

*Precipitating Factors in Suicide*
Stressful Events and Situations
Mood and Thought Changes
Alcohol Use
Mental Disorders
Modeling: The Contagion of Suicide

*Explanations of Suicide*

*Suicide in Different Age Groups*

*Treatment and Suicide*
Treatment after a Suicide Attempt
Suicide Prevention

*T*he animal world is filled with seemingly self-destructive behavior. Worker bees lose their stingers and die after attacking intrusive mammals. Salmon die after the exhausting swim upstream to spawn. Lemmings are said to rush to the sea and drown. In each of these cases a creature's behavior leads to its death, but it would be inaccurate to say the animal or insect wants to die or is trying to die. If anything, its actions are in the service of life. They are instinctual responses that help the species to survive in the long run. Only in the human act of suicide do beings knowingly end their own lives.

Suicide has been observed throughout history. It has been recorded among the ancient Chinese, Greeks, and Romans. King Saul's suicide is reported in the Old Testament. And in more recent times, suicides by such famous people as Ernest Hemingway, Marilyn Monroe, and rock star Kurt Cobain have both shocked and fascinated society.

Today suicide ranks among the top ten causes of death in Western society. According to the World Health Organization, approximately 120,000 deaths by suicide occur each year. More than 30,000 suicides are committed annually in the United States alone, by almost 13 of every 100,000 inhabitants, accounting for around 2 percent of all deaths in the nation (McIntosh, 1991; National Center for Health Statistics, 1988).

It is also estimated that each year more than 2 million other persons throughout the world—600,000 in the United States—make unsuccessful attempts to kill themselves; these people are called *parasuicides* (McIntosh, 1991). These numbing statistics come to life in the following statement:

> Before you finish reading this page, someone in the United States will try to kill himself. At least 60 Americans will have taken their own lives by this time tomorrow. . . . Many of those who attempted will try again, a number with lethal success.
> *(Shneidman & Mandelkorn, 1983)*

Actually, it is difficult to obtain accurate figures on suicide. Many investigators believe that the estimates are low (Smith, 1991; Shneidman, 1981). Because suicide is an enormously stigmatizing act in our society, relatives and friends may refuse to acknowledge that loved ones have taken their own lives. Moreover, it can be difficult for coroners to distinguish suicides from accidental drug overdoses, automobile crashes, drownings, and the like (Jacobs & Klein, 1993).

Despite the prevalence and long history of suicide, people have traditionally been misinformed about its symptoms and causes. A decade ago, when researchers administered a suicide fact test to several hundred un-

*The suicide of Nirvana's Kurt Cobain in 1994 shocked millions of young rock fans throughout the world and led many to experience profound grief and confusion. In Seattle, Cobain's home town, a candlelight vigil was attended by about 5,000 people, including these two fans.*

dergraduates, the average score was only 59 percent correct (McIntosh et al., 1985). Fortunately, the recent scores on a similar test by students in both Canada and the United States have been higher (Leenaars & Lester, 1992) (see Table 12-1). This heightened awareness probably reflects the fact that the study of suicide has become a major focus of the clinical field, and our insights are improving.

# What Is Suicide?

Not every self-inflicted death is a suicide. A man who crashes his car into a tree after falling asleep at the steering wheel is hardly trying to kill himself. Thus Edwin Shneidman (1993, 1981, 1963), one of the most influential writers on this topic, defines *suicide* as an intentioned death—a self-inflicted death in which one makes an intentional, direct, and conscious effort to end one's life.

Intentioned deaths may take various forms. Consider the following three imaginary instances. Although all of these people intended to die, their precise motives, the personal issues involved, and their suicidal actions differed greatly.

> *Dave:* Dave was a successful man. By the age of 50 he had risen to the vice presidency of a small but profitable office machine firm. He and his family lived in an upper-middle-class neighborhood, had a spacious house, and enjoyed a comfortable life.

---

*Suicide*    A self-inflicted death in which the person acts intentionally, directly, and consciously.

In August of his fiftieth year, everything changed. Dave was fired. Just like that, after many years of loyal and effective service.

Dave was shocked. The experience of rejection, loss, and emptiness was overwhelming. He looked for another position, but found only low-paying jobs for which he was overqualified. Each day as he looked for work Dave became more depressed, anxious, and desperate. He kept sinking, withdrawing from others, and entering a state of hopelessness.

Six months after losing his job, Dave began to consider ending his life. The pain was too great, the humiliation unending. He hated the present and dreaded the future. Throughout February he went back and forth. On some days he was sure he wanted to die. On other days, an enjoyable evening or uplifting conversation might change his mind temporarily. On a Monday late in February he heard about a job possibility and the anticipation of the next day's interview seemed to lift his spirits. But at Tuesday's interview, things did not go well. It was clear to him that he would not be offered the job. He went home, took a recently purchased gun from his locked desk drawer, and shot himself.

*Billy:* Billy never truly recovered from his mother's death. He was only 7 years old and unprepared for a loss of such magnitude. His father sent him to live with his grandparents for a time, to a new school with new kids and a new way of life. In Billy's mind, all these changes were for the worse. He missed the joy and laughter of the past. He missed his home, his father, and his friends. Most of all he missed his mother.

He did not really understand her death. His father said that she was in heaven now, at peace, happy. Billy's unhappiness and loneliness continued day after day, and he began to put things together in his own way. He believed that he would be happy again if he could join his mother. These thoughts seemed so right to him; they brought him comfort and hope. One evening, shortly after saying good night to his grandparents, Billy climbed out of bed, went up the stairs to the roof of their apartment house, and jumped to his death.

*Margaret:* Margaret and Bob had been going together for a year. It was Margaret's first serious relationship; it was her whole life. Thus when Bob told Margaret that he no longer loved her and was leaving her for someone else, Margaret was shocked and shaken.

As the weeks went by, Margaret was filled with two competing feelings—depression and anger. Several times she called Bob, begged him to reconsider, and pleaded for a chance to win him back. At the same time, she felt hatred toward Bob.

Margaret's friends became more and more worried about her. At first they understood her pain, sympathized with it, and assumed it would soon subside. But as time went on, her depression and anger actually intensified. Then Margaret began to act strangely. She started drinking heavily and casually mixing her drinks with all kinds of pills. She constantly seemed to flirt with danger.

One night Margaret went into her bathroom, reached for a bottle of sleeping pills, and swallowed a handful of them. She wanted to make her pain go away and she wanted Bob to know just how much pain he had caused her. When she began to feel drowsy, she decided to call her close friend Cindy. She was not sure why she was calling, perhaps to say good-bye, to explain her actions, or to make sure that Bob was told; or perhaps to be talked out of it. Cindy pleaded with Margaret, pointed out the irrationality of her actions, and tried to motivate her to live. Margaret was trying to listen, but she became less and less coherent. Cindy hung up the phone and quickly called Margaret's neighbor and the police. When reached by her neighbor, Margaret was already in a coma. Seven hours later, while her friends and family waited for news in the hospital lounge, Margaret died.

While Margaret seemed ambivalent about her death, Dave was clear in his wish to die. And whereas Billy viewed death as a trip to heaven, Dave saw it as an end to his existence. Such differences can be important in assessing, understanding, and treating suicidal clients. Accordingly, Shneidman has distinguished four kinds of people who intentionally end their lives: the *death seeker, death initiator, death ignorer,* and *death darer.*

**Death seekers** have a clear intention of ending their lives at the time they attempt suicide. This singleness of purpose is usually of short duration. It can change to ambivalence the very next hour or day. Dave, the middle-aged executive, was a death seeker. Granted, he had many misgivings about suicide and was ambivalent about it for weeks, but on Tuesday he was a death seeker—clear in his desire to die and acting in a manner that virtually guaranteed a fatal outcome.

Although **death initiators** also clearly intend to end their lives, they act out of a conviction that the process of death is already under way and that they are simply hastening the process. As we shall see later, many suicides among the elderly and sick fall into this category. The robust novelist Ernest Hemingway, for example, developed grave concerns about his failing body—concerns that some observers believe were at the center of his suicide.

**Death ignorers** do not believe that their self-inflicted death will mean the end of their existence. They believe they are trading their present life for a better or happier existence. Many child suicides, like Billy, fall into this category.

**Table 12-1    *Facts on Suicide Quiz (revised)***

*Circle the answer you feel is most correct for each question. "T" (true), "F" (false), or "?" (don't know)*

T  F  ?  1.  People who talk about suicide rarely commit suicide. [73%]*

T  F  ?  2.  The tendency toward suicide is not genetically (i.e., biologically) inherited and passed on from one generation to another. [46%]

T  F  ?  3.  The suicidal person neither wants to die nor is fully intent on dying. [38%]

T  F  ?  4.  If assessed by a psychiatrist, everyone who commits suicide would be diagnosed as depressed. [57%]

T  F  ?  5.  If you ask someone directly "Do you feel like killing yourself?" it will likely lead that person to make a suicide attempt. [95%]

T  F  ?  6.  A suicidal person will always be suicidal and entertain thoughts of suicide. [76%]

T  F  ?  7.  Suicide rarely happens without warning. [63%]

T  F  ?  8.  A person who commits suicide is mentally ill. [70%]

T  F  ?  9.  A time of high suicide risk in depression is at the time when the person begins to improve. [47%]

T  F  ?  10.  Nothing can be done to stop people from making the attempt once they have made up their minds to kill themselves. [92%]

T  F  ?  11.  Motives and causes of suicide are readily established. [58%]

T  F  ?  12.  A person who has made a past suicide attempt is more likely to attempt suicide again than someone who has never attempted. [80%]

T  F  ?  13.  Suicide is among the top 10 causes of death in the U.S. [83%]

T  F  ?  14.  Most people who attempt suicide fail to kill themselves. [74%]

T  F  ?  15.  Those who attempt suicide do so only to manipulate others and attract attention to themselves. [64%]

T  F  ?  16.  Oppressive weather (e.g., rain) has been found to be very closely related to suicidal behavior. [26%]

T  F  ?  17.  There is a strong correlation between alcoholism and suicide. [68%]

T  F  ?  18.  Suicide seems unrelated to moon phases. [49%]

19.  What percentage of suicides leaves a suicide note? [40%]
    a. 15–25%        b. 40–50%        c. 65–75%

20.  Suicide rates for the U.S. as a whole are _____ for the young. [8%]
    a. lower than        b. higher than        c. the same as

*Source*: Hubbard & McIntosh, 1992, p. 164.

* *Note*: The percentages in brackets following each question refer to the proportion of 331 undergraduates enrolled in general psychology who correctly answered the item.

***Death darers*** are ambivalent in their intent to die even at the moment of their attempt, and they show this ambivalence in the act itself. The person who plays Russian roulette—that is, pulls the trigger of a revolver randomly loaded with one bullet—is a death darer. So is the person who walks along the ledge of a tall building. Margaret might be considered a death darer. Although her unhappiness and anger were pronounced, she was not sure that she wanted to die. Even while taking pills, she called her friend, reported her actions, and listened to her friend's pleas.

When individuals play *indirect, covert, partial,* or *unconscious* roles in their own deaths, Shneidman classifies them in a suicide-like category called ***subintentional death*** (Shneidman, 1993, 1981). Seriously ill people who consistently mismanage their medicines may belong in this category. Although their deaths may represent a form of suicide, the full nature of their actions is unclear. In this chapter the term "suicide" refers only to deaths in which the victims intentionally, directly, and consciously end their own lives.

## The Study of Suicide

Suicide researchers are faced with a major problem: their subjects are no longer alive. How can investiga-

*A sky surfer tries to ride the perfect cloud over Sweden. Are thrill seekers daredevils searching for new highs, as many claim, or are some of them actually death darers?*

*Subintentional death*    A death in which the victim plays an indirect, covert, partial, or unconscious causal role.

## Table 12-1   *(continued)*

21. With respect to sex differences in suicide attempts: [65%]
    a. Males and females attempt at similar levels.
    b. Females attempt more often than males.
    c. Males attempt more often than females.
22. Suicide rates among the young are_____ those for the old. [7%]
    a. lower than      b. higher than      c. the same as
23. Men kill themselves in numbers _____ those for women. [67%]
    a. similar to      b. higher than      c. lower than
24. Suicide rates for the young since the 1950s have: [97%]
    a. increased      b. decreased      c. changed little
25. The most common method employed to kill oneself in the U.S. is: [28%]
    a. hanging      b. firearms      c. drugs and poison
26. The season of highest suicide risk is: [11%]
    a. winter      b. fall      c. spring
27. The day of the week on which most suicides occur is: [60%]
    a. Monday      b. Wednesday      c. Saturday
28. Suicide rates for non-whites are _____ those for Whites. [35%]
    a. higher than      b. similar to      c. lower than
29. Which marital status category has the lowest rates of suicide? [59%]
    a. married      b. widowed      c. single, never married

30. The ethnic/racial group with the highest suicide rate is: [15%]
    a. Whites      b. Blacks      c. Native Americans
31. The risk of death by suicide for a person who has attempted suicide in the past is _____ that for someone who has never attempted. [80%]
    a. lower than      b. similar to      c. higher than
32. Compared to other Western nations, the U.S. suicide rate is: [21%]
    a. among the highest      b. moderate      c. among the lowest
33. The most common method in attempted suicide is: [63%]
    a. firearms      b. drugs and poisons      c. cutting one's wrists
34. On the average, when young people make suicide attempts, they are _____ to die compared to elderly persons. [41%]
    a. less likely      b. just as likely      c. more likely
35. As a cause of death, suicide ranks _____ for the young when compared to the nation as a whole. [86%]
    a. the same      b. higher      c. lower
36. The region of the U.S. with the highest suicide rates is: [36%]
    a. east      b. midwest      c. west

*Answer key: true* items—2, 3, 7, 9, 12, 13, 14, 17, and 18; *false* items—1, 4, 5, 6, 8, 10, 11, 15, and 16. Items for which the correct answer is "a": 19, 22, 24, 27, 29, and 34. Items for which the correct answer is "b": 21, 23, 25, 32, 33, and 35. Items for which the correct answer is "c": 20, 26, 28, 30, 31, and 36.

tors draw accurate conclusions about people who are no longer available to answer questions about their actions? Two major research strategies have been used, each with its limitations.

One strategy is *retrospective analysis,* a kind of psychological autopsy in which clinicians and researchers piece together data from the person's past (Jacobs & Klein, 1993). Relatives, friends, or therapists may remember conversations and behavior that shed light on a subsequent suicide. Retrospective data may also be provided by the suicide notes that some victims leave behind (see Box 12-1). Unfortunately, these sources of information are not always available. Less than a quarter of all suicide victims have been in psychotherapy (Fleer & Pasewark, 1982), and less than a third leave notes (Black, 1993; Leenaars, 1992, 1989).

Because of these limitations, many researchers also use the strategy of *studying people who survive their suicide attempts* and equating them with those who commit fatal suicides. Of course, people who survive suicide may differ in important ways from those who actually do kill themselves (Lester, 1994; Maris, 1992). Many of them may not want to die, for example. Nevertheless, suicide researchers have found it useful and informative to study survivors of suicide, and we shall consider those who attempt suicide and those who commit suicide as more or less alike.

## Patterns and Statistics

Suicide rates vary from country to country. Hungary, Germany, Austria, and Denmark, have very high rates, more than 27 suicides annually per 100,000 persons; conversely, Egypt, Mexico, Greece, and Spain have relatively low rates, fewer than 5 per 100,000. The United States and Canada fall in between, each with a suicide rate of between 12 and 13 per 100,000 persons (Diekstra, 1990, 1989; WHO, 1988).

One factor often cited to account for these national differences is religious affiliation and beliefs (Shneidman, 1987). Countries that are predominantly Catholic, Jewish, or Muslim, for example, tend to have lower suicide rates than predominantly Protestant or

*Retrospective analysis*   A kind of psychological autopsy in which clinicians and researchers piece together data about a person's suicide from the person's past.

## Box 12-1

# Suicide Notes

Dear Bill:

I am sorry for causing you so much trouble. I really didn't want to and if you would have told me at the first time the truth probably both of us would be very happy now. Bill I am sorry but I can't take the life any more, I don't think there is any goodness in the world. I love you very very much and I want you to be as happy in your life as I wanted to make you. Tell your parents I am very sorry and please if you can do it don't ever let my parents know what happened.

Please, don't hate me Bill, I love you.

Mary
(Leenaars, 1991)

A suicide often passes undetected or remains shrouded in mystery because the only person who could tell us the truth has been lost to the world. At the same time, an estimated 12 to 34 percent of people who commit suicide leave notes (Black, 1995, 1993; Leenaars, 1992, 1989).

Each suicide note is a personal document, unique to the writer and the circumstances (Leenaars, 1989). Some are barely a single sentence, others run several pages. People who leave notes clearly wish to make a statement to those they leave behind (Leenaars, 1989), whether the message be "a cry for help, an epitaph, or a last will and testament" (Frederick, 1969, p. 17). Most suicide notes are addressed to specific individuals.

Suicide notes elicit varied reactions from survivors (Leenaars, 1989). A note can clarify the cause of death, thus saving relatives the ordeal of a lengthy legal inquiry. Friends and relatives may also find that it eases their grief to know the person's reasons for committing suicide (Chynoweth, 1977). Yet some suicide notes add to the guilt and negative emotions that survivors commonly experience.

Several aspects of suicide notes have been of particular interest to researchers: the grammatical structure of the note; the type and frequency of words used; the conscious and unconscious content; emotional, cognitive, and motivational themes; and even the handwriting (Leenaars, 1989).

Of course, a written note is only a fragment of the writer's experiences, perceptions, thoughts, and emotions and provides only a partial picture. Suicide notes are "not the royal road to an easy understanding of suicidal phenomena" (Shneidman, 1973, p. 380). In conjunction with other sources, however, the study of suicide notes may be a fruitful avenue of research.

Buddhist countries. Perhaps the first three religions, with their relatively strict proscriptions against suicide and heavy integration of members into church and communal life, help to deter people from committing suicide. Yet there are exceptions to this tentative rule. Austria, for example, a predominantly Roman Catholic country, has one of the highest suicide rates in the world.

In fact, research is beginning to suggest that it may not be religious *doctrine* that helps prevent suicide but rather the degree of an individual's *devoutness*. Irrespective of their particular persuasion, very religious people may be less likely to commit suicide (Holmes, 1985; Martin, 1984). Similarly, it seems that people who hold a greater reverence for life are less prone to contemplate or attempt self-destruction (Lee, 1985).

### Consider This
Suicide rates vary widely from country to country. What factors in addition to religion might help account for these differences?

The suicide rates of men and women also differ (see Figure 12-1b). Women attempt three times as many suicides as men, yet men succeed at more than three times the rate of women (McIntosh, 1991; Stillion, 1985). Almost 21 of every 100,000 men in the United States kill themselves each year; the suicide rate for women, which has been increasing in recent years, is less than 6 per 100,000 (NCHS, 1988).

One reason for these differing rates appears to be the different methods used by men and women (Kushner, 1985). Men tend to use more violent methods, such as shooting, stabbing, or hanging themselves, whereas women use less violent methods, such as drug overdose. Indeed, firearms account for close to two-thirds of the male suicides in the United States, compared to 40 percent of the female suicides (McIntosh, 1992; NCHS, 1990).

Suicide is also related to marital status. Married people, especially those with children, have a relatively low suicide rate; the single and widowed have higher rates; and divorced people have the highest rate of all (NCHS, 1988). One study compared ninety persons who committed suicide with ninety psychologically troubled patients matched for age, gender, and schooling who had never attempted suicide (Roy, 1982). Only 16 percent of the suicide subjects were married or cohabiting at the time of the suicide, compared to 30 percent of the control subjects. Similarly, an analysis conducted in Canada over three decades has revealed a strong positive correlation between national divorce rates and suicide rates (Trovato, 1987).

Finally, in the United States at least, suicide rates seem to differ markedly by race (see Figure 12-1*c*). The suicide rate of white Americans, 14 per 100,000 persons, is twice as high as that of African Americans and members of other racial groups (McIntosh, 1991; NCHS, 1988). The major exception to this pattern is the very high suicide rate of Native Americans (Berlin, 1987). Their overall suicide rate is twice the national average. Although the extreme poverty of many Native Americans may account in part for such trends, studies reveal that such factors as alcohol use, modeling, and availability of firearms may also be involved (Young, 1991; Bagley, 1991).

It is worth noting that some of the statistics on suicide have been called into question by researchers in recent years. One analysis suggests that the actual rate of suicide may be 15 percent higher for African Americans and 6 percent higher for women than usually reported (Phillips and Ruth, 1993). Individuals from these groups, more often than other persons, use methods of suicide that can be mistaken for accidental causes of death, for example, poisoning, drug overdose, single car crashes, and pedestrian deaths.

> *Summing Up*
> More than 120,000 suicides are committed each year worldwide. A person who attempts suicide may be a death seeker, death initiator, death ignorer, or death darer. Suicide rates vary by country and religious beliefs, gender, marital status, and race.

# Precipitating Factors in Suicide

Suicidal acts often are tied to contemporaneous events or conditions. Though these factors may not fully account for suicide, they do serve to precipitate it. Common kinds of precipitating factors are stressful events and situations, mood and thought changes, alcohol and other drug use, mental disorders, and modeling events.

## Stressful Events and Situations

Researchers have repeatedly counted more undesirable events in the recent lives of suicide attempters than in those of other subjects (Heikkinen et al., 1992; Paykel, 1991). In one study, suicide attempters reported twice as many stressful events in the year before their attempt as nonsuicidal depressed patients or nondepressed mental patients (Cohen-Sandler et al., 1982).

One of the most common kinds of recent stress in cases of suicide is loss of a loved one by death, divorce, breakup, or rejection (Heikkinen et al., 1992; Paykel, 1991). Another is loss of a job (Heikkinen et al., 1992; Snyder, 1992). Indeed, the unemployment rate and the suicide rate in the United States rose and fell together from 1940 to 1984 (Yang et al., 1992), and the rate of suicide among U.S. farmers tends to rise during a declining farm economy (Ragland & Berman, 1991).

People may also attempt suicide in response to long-term rather than recent stress. Four long-term stresses are commonly implicated—serious illness, abusive environment, occupational stress, and role conflict (see Table 12-2).

### Serious Illness

As we noted earlier, a painful or disabling illness is at the center of many suicide attempts (Lester, 1992; Allebeck & Bolund, 1991). People with such problems may come to feel that their death is unavoidable and imminent, or that the suffering and problems caused by their illness are more than they can endure. An analysis of the medical records of eighty-eight cancer patients who had died by suicide in Sweden revealed

*Hundreds of people wait in line when job openings are announced at a new hotel in Chicago. Research indicates that national suicide rates often climb during periods of increased unemployment.*

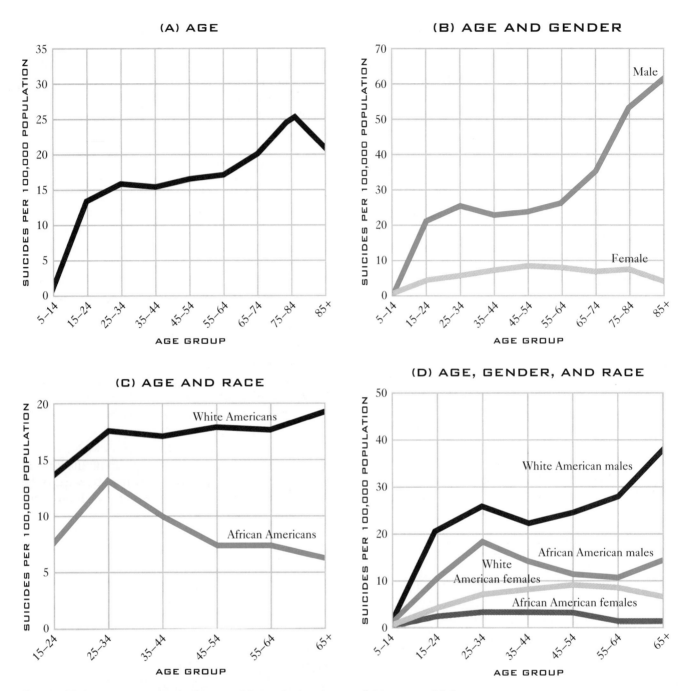

**Figure 12-1**  *Current U.S. suicide rates: (a) People over the age of 65 are more likely to commit suicide than those in any other age group; (b) males commit suicide at higher rates than females of corresponding ages; (c) white Americans commit suicide at higher rates than African Americans of corresponding ages; (d) elderly white American men have the highest risk of suicide. (Adapted from McIntosh, 1991, pp. 62–63; U.S. Bureau of the Census, 1990.)*

that nearly two-thirds were in an advanced or terminal phase of the disease and had severe symptoms (Bolund, 1985). Although illness-linked suicides have long been recorded in human history, they have become more prevalent and controversial in recent years (see Box 12-2).

## Abusive Environment

Victims of an abusive or repressive environment from which they have little or no hope of escape sometimes commit suicide. Some prisoners of war, inmates of concentration camps, abused spouses, abused children, and prison inmates have attempted to end their lives (Shaunesey et al., 1993; Counts, 1990). Like those who have serious illnesses, these people may have felt that they could endure no more suffering and believed that there was no hope for improvement in their condition.

## Occupational Stress

Some jobs create ongoing feelings of tension or dissatisfaction that can precipitate suicide attempts. Research has often found particularly high suicide rates among psychiatrists and psychologists, physicians, dentists, lawyers, and unskilled laborers (Holmes & Rich, 1990). Of course, these correlational data do not establish that occupational pressures are in fact pushing the suicide rate up. There are alternative interpretations. Unskilled workers may be responding to financial insecurity rather than job stress when they attempt suicide. Similarly, rather than reacting to the emotional strain of their work, suicidal psychiatrists and psychologists may have long-standing emotional problems that stimulated their career interest in the first place (Johnson, 1991).

## Role Conflict

Another long-term stress linked to suicide is role conflict. Everyone occupies a variety of roles in life—spouse, employee, parent, and colleague, to name a few possibilities. These roles may conflict and cause considerable stress. In recent years researchers have found that women who hold jobs outside of the home often experience role conflicts—conflicts between their family demands and job requirements, for example, or between their social needs and vocational goals—and that these conflicts may be reflected in a higher suicide rate (Stack, 1987; Stillion, 1985). Women in professional positions, such as physicians, appear to experience the most role conflict, and they display the highest suicide rate of women in the workforce (Stefansson & Wicks, 1991; Stillion, 1985).

# Mood and Thought Changes

Many suicide attempts are preceded by a shift in mood and thought. Although these shifts may not be severe enough to warrant a diagnosis of a mental disorder, they typically represent a significant change from the person's past mood or point of view.

The mood change most often linked to suicide is an increase in sadness (McGuire, 1982; Tishler et al., 1981). Also common are heightened feelings of anxiety, anger, or shame (Pine, 1981). Indeed, some have argued that psychological pain, or "psychache," is what suicidal people seek to escape (Shneidman, 1993).

In the cognitive realm, many people on the verge of suicide have become preoccupied with their problems,

---

**Table 12-2   *Common Predictors of Suicide***

1. Depressive disorder and certain other mental disorders
2. Alcoholism and other forms of substance abuse
3. Suicide ideation, talk, preparation; certain religious ideas
4. Prior suicide attempts
5. Lethal methods
6. Isolation, living alone, loss of support
7. Hopelessness, cognitive rigidity
8. Being an older white male
9. Modeling, suicide in the family, genetics
10. Economic or work problems; certain occupations
11. Marital problems, family pathology
12. Stress and stressful events
13. Anger, aggression, irritability
14. Physical illness
15. Repetition and comorbidity of factors 1–14

*Source:* Adapted from Maris, 1992.

## Box 12-2

# *The Right to Commit Suicide*

In the fall of 1989, a Michigan doctor, Jack Kevorkian, built a "suicide device." A person using it could . . . change a saline solution being fed intravenously into the arm to one containing chemicals that would bring unconsciousness and a swift death. The following June, under the doctor's supervision, Mrs. J. Adkins took her life. She left a note explaining: "This is a decision taken in a normal state of mind and is fully considered. I have Alzheimer's disease and I do not want to let it progress any further. I do not want to put my family or myself through the agony of this terrible disease." Mrs. Adkins believed that she had a right to choose death and that her choice was rational . . . Dr. Kevorkian believed that the "device" could be valuable in assisting persons with compelling grounds for suicide. Michigan authorities, however, promptly prohibited further use of the device.

*(Adapted from Belkin, 1990; Malcolm, 1990)*

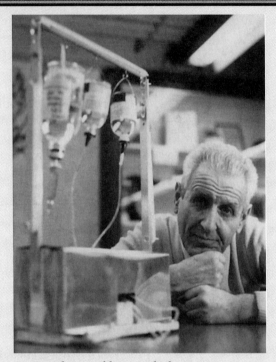

*Dr. Kevorkian and his suicide device.*

Dr. Kevorkian's continuing court battles have been covered widely in the news throughout the 1990s and have brought into public consciousness the issue of a person's right to commit suicide and soci-

ety's right to intervene (West, 1993).

The way a society views suicide depends greatly on its perceptions of life and death (Battin, 1993). The people of classical Greece valued physical and mental well-being in life and dignity in death; therefore, individuals with sufficient cause, such as a grave illness or mental anguish, had legal recourse to suicide (Humphry & Wickett, 1986).

In contrast, American attitudes toward suicide reflect a tradition that has long discouraged such acts (Siegel, 1988). A "sanctity of life" morality has prevailed, according to which all human existence is valued and should be protected (Eser, 1981). Today we speak of "committing" suicide as though it were a criminal act (Barrington, 1980), and we allow the state to use force and involuntary commitment to prevent it (Grisez & Boyle, 1979). Nevertheless,

---

lose perspective, and see suicide as an effective solution to their difficulties (Shneidman, 1993, 1987). They develop a sense of *hopelessness*—a pessimistic belief that their present circumstances, problems, and negative mood will not change (Klingman & Hochdorf, 1993; Ellis & Ratliff, 1986). Some clinicians believe that a feeling of hopelessness is the single most sensitive indicator of suicidal intent, and they take special care to look for signs of hopelessness when they assess the risk of suicide (Weishaar & Beck, 1992; Holden et al., 1985).

Another cognitive feature of people who attempt suicide is *dichotomous thinking,* viewing problems and solutions in rigid either/or terms (Shneidman, 1993, 1987). In the following statement a woman who survived her jump from a building describes her dichotomous thinking at the time of the jump.

> I was so desperate. I felt, my God, I couldn't face this thing. Everything was like a terrible whirlpool of confusion. And I thought to myself: There's only one thing to do. I just have to lose consciousness. That's the only way to get away from it. The only way to lose consciousness, I thought, was to jump off something good and high. . . .
>
> *(Shneidman, 1987, p. 56)*

## Alcohol and Other Drug Use

Studies indicate that at least 20 percent of the people who commit suicide drink alcohol just before the act (Hirschfeld & Davidson, 1988). Autopsies reveal that about one-fourth of these people are legally intoxicated at the time of death (Flavin et al., 1990). Such statistics suggest to many clinical researchers that alco-

times and attitudes are changing, and the idea of a "right to suicide" and "rational suicide" is receiving increasing support in our society.

Common law traditionally affirms a person's right to self-determination (Miesel, 1989), and some people argue that this right extends to the "liberty right" to end one's life (Battin, 1982; Siegel, 1988). Most proponents would restrict this right to situations in which the act of suicide is "rational," and believe that suicide should be prevented in "irrational" cases, including cases that are motivated by mental disorders such as depression (Weir, 1992; Battin, 1982, 1980). One clinical theorist argues that persons who seek the assistance of mental health professionals or prevention centers clearly desire and require help (Motto, 1980).

Public support for a right to suicide seems strongest in instances of terminal illness (Siegel, 1988). Polls suggest that about half of the population believe that terminally ill persons should be free to take their lives or to seek a physician's assistance to do so (Malcolm, 1990; Siegel, 1988). Now a legally competent person can write a "living will," declaring in advance the treatment that would be desired or refused in the event of terminal illness (Humphry & Wickett, 1986).

Even in cases of severe illness, however, the suicidal person's thinking may be affected by psychological disorders or stress. The fact is that a great many people face extremely difficult circumstances in which suicide might seem rational but very few of them actually choose this option. AIDS and cancer patients who commit suicide, for example, are a very small minority of those populations (Malcolm, 1990). Rather than being a natural response to the negative impact of illness, suicide in the face of terminal disease may instead be indicative of clinical depression, anxiety, deficiencies in coping skills, or distress in reaction to the emotional withdrawal of family members. Perhaps the suicidal terminally ill would benefit more from treatment and support that help them come to terms with their situation than from being given the "right" to die.

In addition, it has been argued that the right to suicide could be gravely abused. Although it is upheld as the ultimate freedom, a right to suicide might trap some people in an "obligation to suicide." An elderly person, for example, might feel unjustified in expecting relatives to support and care for him or her when suicide is a socially approved alternative (Sherlock, 1983).

Finally, a slippery-slope view predicts that if suicide is accepted as rational, it might be all too easy for society to slip into accepting practices such as forced euthanasia and infanticide (Annas, 1993; Battin, 1982).

How are these conflicts to be resolved? The future holds great challenges for those who seek to understand, treat, and prevent suicide, but the questions of whether and when we should stand back and do nothing pose just as great a challenge. Whatever one's stand on this issue, it is a matter of life and death.

---

hol consumption often contributes to suicidal behavior (Wasserman, 1992; Schuckit & Schuckit, 1991). Research suggests that the use of other kinds of drugs may have a similar tie to suicide, particularly in teenagers and young adults (Garrison et al., 1993; Marzuk et al., 1992). We shall return to this point later.

### Consider This
Investigators have linked many cases of suicide to the use of alcohol or other drugs. How might substance use contribute to suicidal thoughts or actions? Might the relationship between suicide and substance use be explained in other ways?

## Mental Disorders

As we noted earlier, people who attempt suicide do not necessarily have a mental disorder. Although they are troubled, unhappy, or anxious, their feelings may not add up to any disorder defined in DSM-IV. On the other hand, around half of all suicide attempters do display a mental disorder (Brent et al., 1993; Beaumont & Hetzel, 1992).

The mental disorders linked most strongly to suicide are *mood disorders* (unipolar and bipolar depression), *schizophrenia,* and *substance-related disorders* (particularly alcoholism). Research suggests that approximately 10 to 15 percent of people with each of these disorders try to kill themselves (Black & Winokur, 1990). People who are both depressed and dependent on alcohol seem to be particularly likely to try to kill themselves (Cornelius et al., 1995). *Panic disorders* too have been linked to suicide, but in most cases the disorder occurs in conjunction with one of the other conditions (Norton et al., 1993; Lepine et al., 1993).

In Chapter 7 we observed that most people with a major depressive disorder experience suicidal thoughts as part of their syndrome. Those whose disorder includes a strong sense of hopelessness seem most likely to attempt suicide (Fawcett et al., 1987). Even when depressed people are showing improvement in mood, they may remain high suicide risks. In fact, among those who are severely depressed, the risk of suicide may actually increase as their mood improves and they have more energy to act on their suicidal wishes.

In many cases of suicide after alcohol use the individuals actually have a long history of abusing alcohol or some other substance (Merrill et al., 1992). The basis for the link between substance-related disorders and suicide is not clear. It may be that the tragic lifestyle resulting from the long-term use of alcohol or other drugs or the sense of being hopelessly trapped by a drug leads to suicidal thinking. Alternatively, both substance abuse and suicidal thinking may be caused by a third factor—by psychological pain, for instance, or desperation (Frances & Franklin, 1988).

In Chapter 13 we shall examine schizophrenia, a disorder often marked by hearing voices that are not actually present (hallucinations) and holding bizarre beliefs (delusions). There is a popular notion that suicides by persons with schizophrenia must be in response to imagined voices commanding self-destruction or to a delusion that suicide is a grand and noble gesture. However, most suicides by persons with this disorder actually reflect feelings of demoralization (Haas et al., 1993). They tend to be committed by relatively young and unemployed people with schizophrenia who have experienced relapses over several years and now believe that the disorder will forever disrupt their lives (Drake et al., 1984).

## Modeling: The Contagion of Suicide

It is not unusual for people to try to commit suicide after observing or reading about a suicide (Phillips et al., 1992; Phillips, 1983). Perhaps these people have been struggling with major problems and the other person's suicide seems to reveal a possible solution; or they have been contemplating suicide and the other person's suicide seems to give them permission or finally persuades them to act. Whatever the specific mechanism may be in such cases, one suicidal act apparently serves as a model for another.

*Severely depressed about his progressive illness, Ernest Hemingway shot and killed himself in 1961.*

Three kinds of models in particular seem to trigger suicides: suicides by celebrities, highly publicized suicides, and suicides by co-workers or colleagues.

### Celebrities

In an analysis of suicide data spanning 1948 to 1983, researcher Steven Stack (1987) found that suicides by entertainers and political figures in the United States are regularly followed by unusual increases in the number of suicides across the nation. In 1994, for example, a depressed 28-year-old fan mourned the suicide of Nirvana's Kurt Cobain at a large outdoor Seattle candlelight vigil, then went home and, like Cobain, killed himself with a shotgun.

### Highly Publicized Cases

The news media often focus on a particular suicide because of its unusual nature or special implications. Such highly publicized accounts may trigger suicides that are similar in method or circumstance (Ishii, 1991). In England, for example, a widely publicized suicide by self-immolation was followed within one year by eighty-two other suicides in which the victims set themselves on fire (Ashton & Donnan, 1981).

The frightening impact of well-publicized suicides has led some clinicians to call for a code of practice that the news media should follow in reporting such deaths (Motto, 1967), and in recent times the media have tried to act responsibly. When, for example, thousands of young people called radio and television stations in the hours following Kurt Cobain's suicide, distraught, worried, and in some cases suicidal, some of the stations responded by posting "hot-line" numbers for suicide prevention centers, presenting interviews with suicide experts, and offering counseling services and advice directly to callers.

---

*Consider This*
What precautions or actions should the media and the arts take in their presentations of famous cases of suicide? Has there been an unintended glorification by media persons, artists, or fans of Kurt Cobain's suicide since the time of his death? Why has this happened?

---

### Co-workers and Colleagues

Suicides in a school, workplace, or small community often receive word-of-mouth publicity that may trigger suicide attempts by others in the setting. A suicide by a recruit at a U.S. Navy training school, for example, was followed by another completed and an attempted suicide at the school within a two-week period. To head off what threatened to become a suicide epidemic, the school initiated a program of staff education on suicide and group therapy sessions for recruits who had been close to the suicide victims (Grigg, 1988).

# *Explanations of Suicide*

Although numerous situations may precipitate suicide, most people who encounter such situations never try to kill themselves. In an effort to explain why some people are more prone to suicide than others, theorists have proposed still broader explanations for self-destructive action. The leading theories come from the psychodynamic, biological, and sociocultural perspectives. Unfortunately, as we shall see, these explanations have received limited empirical support, and in fact they fail to address all kinds of suicidal acts. Thus it would be inaccurate to conclude that the clinical field currently has a satisfactory understanding of suicide.

## The Psychodynamic Explanation

Many psychodynamic theorists believe that suicide results from depression and self-directed anger. This theory was first stated by Wilhelm Stekel at a meeting in Vienna in 1910, when he proclaimed that "no one kills himself who has not wanted to kill another or at least wished the death of another" (Shneidman, 1979).

As we saw in Chapter 7, Freud (1917) and Abraham (1916, 1911) proposed that when people experience the real or symbolic loss of a loved one, they come to "introject" the lost person; that is, they unconsciously incorporate the person into their own identity and feel toward themselves as they had felt toward the other. For a short while, negative feelings toward the loved one are experienced as self-hatred. Extreme anger toward the lost loved one may turn into unrelenting anger against oneself, and finally into a broad depressive reaction. Suicide is a further expression of this self-hatred. The following description of a suicidal patient demonstrates how such dynamics may operate:

> A 27-year-old conscientious and responsible woman took a knife to her wrists to punish herself for being tyrannical, unreliable, self-centered, and abusive. She was perplexed and frightened by this uncharacteristic self-destructive episode and was enormously relieved when her therapist pointed out that her invective described her recently deceased father much better than it did herself.
>
> *(Gill, 1982, p. 15)*

Late in his career, Freud further explained suicide by proposing that human beings have a basic "death instinct," which he called *Thanatos*, that functions in opposition to their "life instinct." According to Freud, while most people learn to redirect their death instinct and aim it toward others, suicidal people, caught in a web of self-anger, direct the instinct squarely upon themselves (Freud, 1955).

Consistent with Freud's view of suicide, a number of researchers have found a relationship between childhood losses (for example, a parent's death or the divorce of one's parents) and later suicidal behaviors (Paykel, 1991). In contrast, research has failed to establish that suicidal people are in fact dominated by intense feelings of anger. Although hostility is an important component in some suicides, several studies find that other emotional states are even more common (Linehan & Nielsen, 1981; Shneidman, 1979).

By the end of his career, Freud expressed dissatisfaction with his theory of suicide. Other psychodynamic theorists have modified his ideas over the years, yet themes of loss and self-directed aggression usually remain at the center of their explanations (Kincel, 1981; Furst & Ostow, 1979).

## The Biological Explanation

Until the 1970s the belief that biological factors contribute to suicidal behavior was based primarily on family pedigree studies. Researchers repeatedly found higher rates of suicidal behavior among the parents and close relatives of suicidal people than among those of nonsuicidal people, suggesting to some observers that genetic, and so biological, factors were at work (Roy, 1992).

Studies of twins also were consistent with this view of suicide. A study of twins born in Denmark between 1870 and 1920, for example, located nineteen identical pairs and fifty-eight fraternal pairs in which at least one of the twins had committed suicide (Juel-Nielsen & Videbech, 1970). In four of the identical pairs the other twin also committed suicide (21 percent), while there were no cases in which the other twin among the fraternal pairs committed suicide.

In the past few years laboratory research has provided more direct support for a biological view of suicide. People who commit suicide are often found to have lower activity of the neurotransmitter serotonin (Nordstrom & Asberg, 1992; Roy, 1992). In a series of studies, researchers have measured subjects' levels of *5-hydroxyindoleactic acid (5-HIAA)*, a chemical that is a metabolite, or by-product, of brain serotonin. One study found that depressed patients with particularly low levels of 5-HIAA (and presumably low activity of serotonin) were more likely to attempt suicide than depressed patients with relatively higher 5-HIAA levels (Asberg et al., 1976). Other studies have found that suicide attempters with low 5-HIAA levels were ten times more likely to make a repeat attempt and succeed than were suicide attempters with high 5-HIAA levels (Roy, 1992).

At first glance, these studies may appear to tell us little that is new. After all, as we discussed in Chapter 7, depression is itself related to low serotonin activity. Inasmuch as many depressed people attempt suicide, we would certainly expect many suicidal people to have low serotonin activity. On the other hand, there is evidence of low serotonin activity even among suicidal subjects who have had no history of depression (Van Praag, 1983; Brown et al., 1982). That is, low serotonin activity seems to also have a role in suicide outside of depression.

How, then, might low serotonin activity act to increase the likelihood of suicidal behavior? One possibility is that low serotonin helps cause aggressive behavior. It has been found, for example, that highly aggressive men have significantly lower 5-HIAA levels than less aggressive men (Brown et al., 1992, 1979) and that low serotonin levels often characterize those who commit aggressive acts such as arson and murder (Bourgeois, 1991). Such findings suggest to many theorists that low serotonin activity produces aggressive feelings and impulsive behavior (Bourgeois, 1991; Stanley et al., 1986). In people who are clinically depressed, low serotonin activity may produce aggressive and impulsive tendencies that leave them particularly vulnerable to suicidal thinking and action. Even in the absence of a depressive disorder, however, people with low serotonin activity may develop highly aggressive feelings and be dangerous to themselves or others.

## The Sociocultural Explanation

Just before the turn of the century, Emile Durkheim ([1897] 1951), a sociologist, developed the first comprehensive theory of suicidal behavior. Today this theory continues to be influential.

According to Durkheim, the probability of suicide is determined by how embedded a person is in such social institutions as the family, the church, and the community. The more a person belongs, the lower the risk of suicide. Conversely, people who are removed from or have poor relationships with society are at greater risk of killing themselves. He defined three categories of suicide based on the individual's relationship with society.

*Egoistic suicides* are committed by people over whom society has little or no control. These people are not concerned with the norms or rules of society, nor are they integrated into the social fabric. According to Durkheim, this kind of suicide is more likely in people who are isolated, alienated, and nonreligious. The larger the number of such people living in a society, the higher that society's suicide rate.

*Altruistic suicides,* in contrast, are committed by people who are so well integrated into the social structure that they intentionally sacrifice their lives for the well-being of society. Soldiers who threw themselves on top of a live grenade to save others, Japanese kamikaze pilots who gave their lives in air attacks, and Buddhist monks and nuns who protested the Vietnam

---

*5-Hydroxyindoleactic acid (5-HIAA)*     A component of cerebrospinal fluid that is a metabolite, or by-product, of brain serotonin.

*Egoistic suicide*     Suicide committed by people over whom society has little or no control, people who are not concerned with the norms or rules of society.

*Altruistic suicide*     Suicide committed by people who intentionally sacrifice their lives for the well-being of society.

*According to Emile Durkheim, people who intentionally sacrifice their lives for others are committing altruistic suicide. Betsy Smith, a heart transplant recipient who knew that she would probably die if she did not terminate her pregnancy, elected to have the baby and died giving birth.*

War by setting themselves on fire—all were committing altruistic suicide. According to Durkheim, societies that encourage altruistic deaths (as Far Eastern societies do) are likely to have higher suicide rates.

*Anomic suicides,* the third category proposed by Durkheim, are committed by people whose social environment fails to provide stable structures, such as family and church, to support and give meaning to life. Such a societal state, called *anomie* (literally, "without law"), leaves individuals without a sense of belonging and brings about what Durkheim called a heightened "inclination for suicide." In a sense, anomic suicide is the act of a person who has been let down by a disorganized, inadequate, often decaying, society.

Durkheim argued that when societies go through periods of anomie, their suicide rates increase accord-

*Anomic suicide*  Suicide committed by individuals whose social environment fails to provide stability, thus leaving them without a sense of belonging.

ingly. Historical research supports this claim. Periods of economic depression and social disintegration bring about relative anomie in a country, and national suicide rates tend to increase during such times (Yang et al., 1992; Lester, 1991). Similarly, periods of population change and increased immigration tend to bring about a state of anomie, and such increases are also reflected in higher suicide rates (Stack, 1981).

A profound change in an individual's immediate surroundings, rather than general societal deficiencies, can also lead to anomic suicide. People who suddenly inherit a great sum of money, for example, may go through a period of anomie as their relationships with social, economic, and occupational structures are upset or changed. Thus Durkheim predicted that societies with greater opportunities for change in individual wealth or status would have higher suicide rates, and this prediction, too, is supported by research (Lester, 1985).

Durkheim's theory of suicide highlights the potential importance of societal factors, a dimension sometimes overlooked by clinicians. On the other hand, his theory by itself is unable to explain why some individuals who experience anomie commit suicide yet the majority do not. Durkheim himself concluded that the final explanation probably involves an interaction between societal and individual factors.

**Summing Up**
*Suicide is commonly precipitated by factors such as recent stress, long-term stress, mood and thought changes, alcohol and other drug use, mental disorders, and modeling effects. Psychodynamic theorists explain suicide as self-directed anger. Biological theorists relate it to low serotonin activity. And sociocultural theorists believe that certain relationships with society may leave some individuals more prone to suicide.*

# Suicide in Different Age Groups

The likelihood of committing suicide generally increases with age, although people of all ages may try to kill themselves. Recently, particular attention has been focused on self-destruction in three age groups—children, adolescents, and the elderly.

## Children

Although suicide is relatively infrequent among children, it has been increasing rapidly during the past several decades. Approximately 250 children under 15 years of age in the United States now commit suicide each year, a rate increase of nearly 800 percent since 1950 (NCHS, 1993). Moreover, it has been estimated that as many as 12,000 children may be hospitalized in the United States each year for deliberately self-destructive acts, such as stabbing, cutting, burning, overdosing, or jumping from high places (NIMH, 1986).

One study of suicide attempts by children revealed that the majority had taken an overdose of drugs and made their attempt at home, half were living with only one parent, and a quarter had attempted suicide before (Kienhorst et al., 1987). Other studies have linked child suicides to the recent or anticipated loss of a loved one, family stress and parental unemployment, abuse by parents, and a clinical level of depression (Asarnow, 1992; Fasko & Fasko, 1991).

Most people find it hard to believe that children fully comprehend the implications of a suicidal act. They argue that by virtue of their cognitive limitations, children who attempt suicide fall into Shneidman's category of "death ignorers," like Billy, who sought to join his mother in heaven (Fasko & Fasko, 1991). However, many child suicides are in fact based on a clear understanding of death and on a clear wish to die (Carlson et al., 1994; Pfeffer, 1993, 1986).

Suicidal thinking among even normal children is apparently more common than most people once believed. Clinical interviews with schoolchildren have revealed that between 6 and 26 percent have contemplated suicide (Jacobsen et al., 1994; Kashani et al., 1989). It is not clear whether suicidal thinking by young children is a new phenomenon or was previously undetected.

## Adolescents

Dear Mom, Dad, and everyone else,

I'm sorry for what I've done, but I loved you all and I always will, for eternity. Please, please, please don't blame it on yourselves. It was all my fault and not yours or anyone else's. If I didn't do this now, I would have done it later anyway. We all die some day, I just died sooner.

Love,

John

*(Berman, 1986)*

The suicide of John, age 17, was not an unusual occurrence. Over 2,000 teenagers, or 11 of every 100,000, commit suicide in the United States each year, making it the third leading cause of death in this age group, and as many as 250,000 teenagers may make attempts (NCHS, 1991; U.S. Bureau of the Census, 1990). Moreover, in a 1991 poll, a full third of teenagers surveyed said they had considered suicide, and 15 percent said they had thought about it seriously. Many school counselors have identified the danger of adolescent suicide as a major problem in their schools and have requested guidelines for dealing with suicidal behavior in their students (Coder et al., 1991).

About half of teenagers' suicides have been linked to clinical depression, low self-esteem, and feelings of hopelessness (Harter & Marold, 1994; Kashden et al., 1993; Robbins & Alessi, 1985), but many teenagers who try to kill themselves also appear to struggle with anger and impulsivity (Kashden et al., 1993; Hoberman & Garfinkel, 1988). Many adolescents who attempt suicide experience long-term stresses such as missing or poor parental relationships, family conflict, inadequate peer relationships, and social isolation (Adams et al., 1994; D'Attilio et al., 1992). Their actions also seem to be triggered by immediate stresses, such as unemployment, discord, or financial setbacks in the family, or difficulties with a boyfriend or girlfriend (de Wilde et al., 1992; Pfeffer, 1990, 1988).

Stress at school seems to be a particularly common problem in teenagers who attempt suicide (Brent et al., 1988). Some have difficulty keeping up at school, while others may be high achievers who feel pressured to be perfect and to stay at the top of the class (Leroux, 1986; Delisle, 1986).

Some theorists believe that adolescent life itself produces a climate conducive to suicidal action (Harter & Marold, 1994; Maris, 1986). Adolescence is a period of rapid growth and development, and in our society it is often marked by conflicts, depressed feelings, tensions, and difficulties at home and school. Adolescents also tend to react to events more sensitively, angrily, dramatically, and impulsively than people in other age groups, so that the likelihood of suicidal actions during times of stress is increased. Finally, the suggestibility of adolescents and their eagerness to imitate others, including others who attempt suicide, may help set the stage for suicidal action.

It is important to note that far more teenagers attempt suicide than actually kill themselves. The unusually large number of incomplete attempts by teenagers may mean that they are more often ambivalent than older persons who make such attempts. While some do indeed wish to die, many may simply want to make others understand how desperate they are, get help, or teach others a lesson (Hawton, 1986; Hawton et al., 1982). Up to 40 percent of attempters go on to make more suicide attempts, and up to 14 percent eventually die by suicide (Spirito et al., 1989; Diekstra, 1989).

The suicide rate for adolescents is not only high but increasing. Indeed, like the suicide rate for young adults, it has tripled since 1953 (Harter & Marold, 1994; McIntosh, 1991). Several theories have been proposed to explain this increase. First, as the number and proportion of adolescents and young adults in the general population keeps rising, the competition for jobs, college positions, and academic and athletic honors keeps intensifying in this age group, leading perhaps to shattered dreams and frustrated ambitions (Holinger and Offer, 1991). Still other explanations point to weakening ties in the nuclear family, which may provoke feelings of alienation and rejection in many of today's young people, and to the increased availability of drugs and pressure to use them among teenagers and young adults (Schuckit & Schuckit, 1991; Peck, 1982).

Finally, some theorists explain the rising suicide rate of teenagers and young adults by pointing to the mass media coverage of suicide attempts by people in this age range (Myatt & Greenblatt, 1993; Gould & Shaffer, 1986). The detailed descriptions of such attempts that the media and arts have provided in recent years may serve as models for young people who are contemplating suicide. Within days of the highly publicized suicides of four adolescents in a garage in Bergenfield, New Jersey, in 1987, dozens of teenagers across the United States took similar actions (at least twelve of them fatal)—two in the same garage just one week later.

## The Elderly

Statistics indicate that in Western society elderly persons are more likely to commit suicide than people in any other age group (see Figures 12-1*a* and 12-2). More than 21 of every 100,000 persons over the age of 65 in the United States commit suicide (McIntosh, 1992). Elderly persons committed over 19 percent of all suicides in the United States during the 1980s, yet account for only 12 percent of the total population (McIntosh, 1992).

Many factors contribute to the high suicide rate among the elderly (Richman, 1991). As people grow older, all too often they become ill, lose close friends and relatives, lose control over their lives, and lose sta-

*The intense training and testing characteristic of Japan's educational system produce high levels of stress in many students. This may be a factor in the very high suicide rate found among older teenagers in Japan (Hawton, 1986). The students in this classroom are participating in summer "juku," a camp where they receive remedial help, extra lessons, and exam practice 11 hours a day.*

tus in our society. Such experiences may result in feelings of hopelessness, loneliness, depression, or inevitability among aged persons, and so increase the likelihood that they will attempt suicide (Osgood, 1987; Kirsling, 1986). In one study 44 percent of elderly people who committed suicide gave some indication that their act was prompted by the fear of being placed in a nursing home (Loebel et al., 1991). Similarly, those who have lost a spouse display a much higher suicide rate (Nieto et al., 1992; McIntosh, 1992).

Elderly persons are typically more resolute than younger persons in their decision to die, so their success rate is much higher (Turkington, 1987). Apparently one of every four elderly persons who attempts suicide succeeds (McIntosh, 1987). Compounded with these statistics is the finding that clinical depression once again appears to play an important role in at least 50 percent of suicides in this age group (Lyness et al., 1992), suggesting that more elderly persons should be receiving treatment for their depressive disorders than is typically the case (Simon, 1987).

### Consider This
Often people view the suicide of an elderly person as less tragic than that of a young person. Why might they think this way, and is their reasoning valid?

The suicide rate among elderly people in the United States is lower in some minority groups. Although Native Americans have the highest overall suicide rate, for example, the rate among elderly Native Americans is quite low (McIntosh & Santos, 1982). Similarly, the suicide rate among elderly African Americans is only one-third the rate of elderly white Americans.

Why are suicide rates for the elderly particularly low in some minority groups? The respect afforded elderly Native Americans may help account for their low rate (McIntosh & Santos, 1982). The aged are held in high esteem by Native Americans and looked to for the wisdom and experience they have acquired over the years. This heightened status is quite different from the loss of status often experienced by elderly white Americans (Butler, 1975).

The low suicide rate among elderly African Americans has been explained in different terms. One theory is that because of the pressures African Americans live under, "only the strongest survive" (Seiden, 1981). Those who reach an advanced age have overcome significant adversity and often feel proud of what they have accomplished. Advancement to old age is not in itself a form of success for white Americans, and leaves them with a different attitude toward life and age. Another explanation suggests that aged African Americans have successfully overcome the rage that characterizes many suicides in younger African Americans.

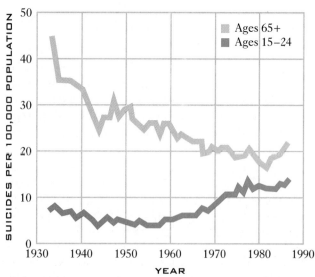

Figure 12-2   *Until recent years, the suicide rate of elderly people had been declining for at least a half-century, while that of young adults was increasing. Still, older people continue to be at higher risk for suicide. (Adapted from McIntosh, 1991, 1987; Buda & Tsuang, 1990. U.S. Bureau of the Census, 1968, 1947.)*

*Summing Up*
*Suicide by children is infrequent but on the rise. Suicide by adolescents is also increasing and has been related to the increased number of adolescents, weakening family ties, drug availability, and the effects of media coverage. Attempted suicides greatly outnumber actual suicides among adolescents. Elderly people are more likely to commit suicide than people in any other age group, a phenomenon that has been related to various kinds of loss and resultant feelings of hopelessness, loneliness, depression, and inevitability.*

# Treatment and Suicide

Treatment of people who are suicidal falls into two major categories: *treatment after suicide has been attempted* and *suicide prevention*. Treatment may also be given to relatives and friends, whose feelings of bereavement, guilt, and anger after a suicide fatality or attempt can be intense (Farberow, 1993, 1991), but the discussion here will be limited to the treatment afforded suicidal people themselves.

## Treatment after a Suicide Attempt

After a suicide attempt, most victims' primary need is medical care. Some are left with severe injuries, brain damage, or other medical problems. Once the physical damage is reversed or at least stabilized, psychotherapy may begin.

Unfortunately, even after trying to kill themselves, most suicidal people fail to receive systematic therapy. In a random survey of several hundred teenagers, 9 percent were found to have made at least one suicide attempt, and of those only half had been given subsequent psychological treatment (Harkavy & Asnis, 1985). Another study found that 46 percent of people treated for attempted suicide in a Helsinki general hospital were not given even a psychological consultation (Suokas & Lonnqvist, 1991).

When therapy is provided, it may be on an outpatient or inpatient basis (Deering et al., 1991). The goal of therapy is to keep the clients alive, help them achieve a nonsuicidal state of mind, and eventually guide them to develop more constructive ways of handling stress and solving problems (Shneidman, 1993; Möller, 1990). Various therapy systems and formats have been employed (Rotheram-Borus et al., 1994;

*Elderly people are held in high esteem in many traditional cultures because of the large store of knowledge they have accumulated. Perhaps not so coincidentally, suicides among the elderly seem to be less common in these cultures than in those of many modern industrialized societies.*

Berman & Jobes, 1991), but relatively little research has compared the effectiveness of the different approaches.

## Suicide Prevention

During the past thirty years, emphasis has shifted from suicide treatment to suicide prevention (Cantor, 1991; Maltsberger, 1991). In some respects this change is most appropriate: the last opportunity to keep many potential suicide victims alive comes before the first attempt.

The emphasis on suicide prevention began in earnest during the mid-1950s with the development of *suicide prevention programs.* The first such program in the United States was the Los Angeles Suicide Prevention Center; the first in England was called the Samaritans. There are now more than 200 independent, locally funded suicide prevention centers in the United States and over 100 in England, and the numbers are still growing (Lester, 1989; Roberts, 1979). In addition, many mental health centers, hospital emergency rooms, pastoral counseling centers, and poison control centers now include suicide prevention programs among their services.

There are also more than 1,000 *suicide hotlines,* 24-hour-a-day telephone services, in the United States

*Suicide prevention programs* Programs that try to identify people who are at the point of killing themselves and to help such people perceive their situation more accurately, make better decisions, act more constructively, and overcome their crisis.

(Garland et al., 1989). Callers reach a counselor, typically a trained *paraprofessional,* a person without a formal degree in a counseling profession who provides services under the supervision of a mental health professional.

Suicide prevention programs and hotlines define suicidal people as people *in crisis*—that is, under great stress, unable to cope, feeling threatened or hurt, and interpreting their situations as unchangeable. Accordingly, these programs engage in *crisis intervention:* they try to help suicidal people perceive their situations more accurately, make better decisions, act more constructively, and overcome their crisis. Because crises can occur at any time, the programs advertise their hotlines and may also welcome clients to walk in without appointments.

Although specific features vary from center to center, the general approach used by the Los Angeles Suicide Prevention Center reflects the goals and techniques of many such organizations (Lester, 1989; Shneidman & Farberow, 1968). During the initial contact, the counselor has several tasks: establishing a positive relationship with the caller, understanding and clarifying the problem, assessing the caller's suicide potential, assessing and mobilizing the caller's resources, and formulating a plan for overcoming the crisis (Shneidman & Farberow, 1968).

### Establishing a Positive Relationship

Counselors try to set a positive and comfortable tone for discussion. They convey the message that they are trustworthy, listening, understanding, interested, nonjudgmental, and available.

### Understanding and Clarifying the Problem

Counselors first try to understand the full scope of the caller's crisis, then help the person see the crisis in clear and constructive terms. In particular, counselors try to help callers identify the central issues and the transient nature of their crises and recognize the alternatives to suicidal action.

### Assessing Suicide Potential

Crisis workers at the Los Angeles Suicide Prevention Center fill out a questionnaire, often called a "lethality scale," to estimate the caller's potential for suicide. It helps them to determine the degree of stress the caller is under, relevant personality characteristics, how detailed the suicide plan is, the severity of symptoms, and the coping resources available to the caller.

### Assessing and Mobilizing the Caller's Resources

Although they may view themselves as ineffectual and helpless, people who are suicidal usually have

*The apparent 1993 mass suicide by dozens of the Branch Davidian religious sect at their Waco, Texas, compound produced a giant fireball that the nation, watching on television, will not soon forget. Group suicides are not well understood by clinicians.*

many strengths and resources, including relatives and friends. It is the counselor's job to recognize, point out, and activate those resources.

### Formulating a Plan

Together the crisis worker and caller formulate a plan of action. In essence, they are agreeing on a way out of the crisis, a constructive alternative to suicidal action. Most plans include a series of follow-up counseling sessions over the next few days or weeks, either in person at the center or by phone.

Each plan also usually requires that the caller take certain actions in his or her personal life. Counselors usually negotiate a "no suicide" contract with the caller—a promise not to attempt suicide, or at least a promise to reestablish contact if the caller again contemplates suicide. If callers are in the midst of a suicide attempt, counselors will also try to ascertain their whereabouts and get medical help to them immediately.

Although crisis intervention appears to be sufficient treatment for some suicidal people (Hawton, 1986), longer-term therapy is needed for most of them (Farberow, 1974). If the crisis intervention program does not offer this kind of therapy, the counselors will refer the individuals elsewhere.

As the suicide prevention movement spread during the 1960s, many clinicians concluded that crisis intervention techniques should also be applied to problems other than suicide. Crisis intervention has emerged during the past three decades as a respected form of treatment for such wide-ranging problems as teenage confusion, drug and alcohol abuse, rape victimization, and spouse abuse (Lester, 1989; Bloom, 1984).

## The Effectiveness of Suicide Prevention

It has been difficult for researchers to assess the effectiveness of suicide prevention programs (Eddy et al., 1987; Bloom, 1984). There are many kinds of programs, each with its own procedures and serving populations that vary in number, age, economic stability, and environmental pressures.

Do suicide prevention programs reduce the number of suicides in a community? Clinical researchers do not know (Lester, 1989; Auerbach & Kilmann, 1977). Studies comparing local suicide rates before and after the establishment of community prevention programs have yielded very different findings (Miller et al., 1984; Dashef, 1984; Barraclough et al., 1977).

Do suicidal people contact prevention programs? Apparently only a small percentage do. Moreover, the typical caller to an urban prevention program appears to be young, African American, and female, whereas the greatest number of suicides are committed by elderly white men (Lester, 1989, 1972).

At the same time, prevention programs do seem to be helpful in averting suicide for those high-risk people who do call. The clinical researchers Norman Farberow and Robert Litman (1970) identified 8,000 high-risk individuals who contacted the Los Angeles Suicide Prevention Center. Approximately 2 percent of these callers later committed suicide, compared to the 6 percent suicide rate usually found in similar high-risk groups.

One implication of such findings is that suicide prevention programs need to be more visible to and approachable by people who are harboring thoughts of suicide. The growing number of advertisements and announcements in newspapers and on television, radio, and billboards attest to a movement in this direction.

Shneidman (1987) has called for broader and more effective public education about suicide as the ultimate form of prevention. And at least some suicide education programs—most of them concentrating on teachers and students—have begun to emerge (Klingman & Hochdorf, 1993; Sandoval et al., 1987). Most clinicians agree with Shneidman when he states:

> The primary prevention of suicide lies in education. The route is through teaching one another and . . . the public that suicide can happen to anyone, that there are verbal and behavioral clues that can be looked for . . . , and that help is available. . . .
>
> In the last analysis, the prevention of suicide is everybody's business.
>
> *(Shneidman, 1985, p. 238)*

> *Summing Up*
> *Treatment following a suicide attempt seeks to help the individual achieve a nonsuicidal state of mind and develop more constructive ways of handling stress. Suicide prevention programs define suicidal people as people in crisis and apply crisis intervention techniques. The reach and impact of suicide prevention programs are not entirely clear, but effective programs for educating the public are beginning to emerge.*

# The State of the Field
## *Suicide*

Once a mysterious and hidden problem, hardly acknowledged by the public and barely investigated by researchers, suicide is today in the limelight. The public's curiosity about this problem is growing, and researchers are actively pursuing information about it. During the past two decades in particular, investigators have learned a great deal about the motives, states of mind, and environmental conditions tied to suicide. They have also made impressive progress in identifying its most common precipitants and risk factors.

Perhaps most promising of all, clinicians and educators have begun to enlist the public in the fight against this problem. They now believe that suicide rates can be reduced only if people recognize the enormous scope of the problem and learn how to identify and respond to suicide risks. They are calling for broader public education about suicide, programs aimed at both young and old.

This is a promising beginning, but only a beginning. Critical questions remain to be answered. First, when all is said and done, clinicians do not yet fully comprehend why some people kill themselves while others under similar circumstances manage to find alternative ways of addressing their problems. Psychodynamic, biological, and sociocultural explanations of suicide have received only limited research support and have been unable to predict specific attempts at suicide. Second, clinicians have yet to develop undisputably successful interventions for treating suicidal people.

It is reasonable to expect that the clinical field's current commitment to investigate, publicize, and overcome the problem of suicide will lead to a better understanding of suicide and to more successful interventions. Clearly such goals are of importance to everyone. Although suicide itself is typically a lonely and desperate act, the implications and impact of such acts are very broad indeed.

# *Chapter Review*

1. *Definition of Suicide:* Suicide is a self-inflicted death in which one makes an *intentional, direct,* and *conscious* effort to end one's life.
   A. Edwin Shneidman has distinguished four kinds of people who intentionally end their lives: the *death seeker,* the *death initiator,* the *death ignorer,* and the *death darer.*
   B. Shneidman has also distinguished a suicide-like category called *subintentional death,* in which people play indirect, covert, partial, or unconscious roles in their own deaths.
2. *Research Strategies:* The two major research strategies used in the study of suicide are *retrospective analysis,* a kind of psychological autopsy, and the study of people who survive suicide attempts, on the assumption that they are similar to those who commit fatal suicides. Each strategy has limitations.
3. *Patterns and Statistics:* Suicide rates vary from country to country. One reason seems to be cultural differences in religious affiliation, beliefs, or degree of devoutness. Suicide rates also differ according to race, sex, and marital status.
4. *Precipitating Factors:* Many suicidal acts are tied to contemporaneous events or conditions. Common precipitating factors are *stressful events and situations, mood and thought changes, alcohol and other drug use, mental disorders,* and *events that inspire modeling.*
5. *Explanations of Suicide:* The leading explanations come from the psychodynamic, biological, and sociocultural models. Each has received only limited research support.
   A. *Psychodynamic* theorists believe that suicide usually results from a state of depression and a process of self-directed anger.
   B. The *biological* view of suicide has focused on the finding that people who commit suicide often have lower activity of the neurotransmitter *serotonin.*
   C. Emile Durkheim's *sociocultural* theory defined

three categories of suicide based on the person's relationship with society: *egoistic suicides, altruistic suicides,* and *anomic suicides.*

6. *Age and Suicide:* Different age groups have a different likelihood of committing suicide.

   A. *Children:* Suicide is relatively infrequent among children, although it has been increasing rapidly in that group during the past several decades.

   B. *Adolescents:* Suicide by adolescents is increasing. Suicide attempts by this age group are extremely high in number. The rising suicide rate among adolescents and young adults may be related to the growing number and proportion of adolescents and young adults in the general population, the weakening of ties in the nuclear family, the increased availability and use of drugs among the young, and the broad media coverage attending suicide attempts by the young.

   C. *The Elderly:* In Western society the elderly are more likely to commit suicide than people in any other age group. Losses of health, friends, control, and status may produce feelings of hopelessness, loneliness, depression, or inevitability in this age group.

7. *Treatment and Suicide:* Treatment may follow a suicide attempt or may seek to prevent suicide.

   A. The goal of therapy after an attempted suicide is to help the client achieve a nonsuicidal state of mind and develop more constructive ways of handling stress and solving problems.

   B. Over the past thirty years, emphasis has shifted from suicide treatment to suicide prevention. *Suicide prevention programs* include 24-hour-a-day "suicide hotlines" and walk-in centers staffed largely by *paraprofessionals* who follow a *crisis intervention model.* Most suicidal people also need longer-term therapy. *Suicide education programs* for the public are also beginning to appear.

## Key Terms

| | | | |
|---|---|---|---|
| parasuicide | retrospective analysis | Thanatos | suicide prevention |
| suicide | hopelessness | serotonin | program |
| death seeker | dichotomous thinking | 5-hydroxyindoleactic acid | suicide hotline |
| death initiator | mood disorder | (5-HIAA) | paraprofessional |
| death ignorer | schizophrenia | egoistic suicide | crisis intervention |
| death darer | substance-related disorder | altruisic suicide | lethality scale |
| subintentional death | introjection | anomic suicide | suicide education |

## Quick Quiz

1. Define *suicide* and *subintentional death.*
2. Describe four different kinds of suicide.
3. What techniques do researchers use to study suicide?
4. How do statistics on suicide vary according to country, religion, gender, marital status, and race?
5. What kinds of immediate and long-term stresses have been linked to suicide?
6. What other factors have also been linked to suicide?
7. How do psychodynamic, biological, and sociocultural theorists explain suicide, and how well supported are their theories?
8. Compare the risk, rate, and causes of suicide among children, adolescents, and elderly persons.
9. How do theorists explain the increase in suicide attempts by adolescents and young adults?
10. Describe the nature and goals of treatment given to people after they have attempted suicide. How many people receive such treatments?
11. Describe the philosophy and format of suicide prevention programs. What procedures are employed by counselors in these programs? How effective are the programs?

# 13

# Schizophrenia

## Topic Overview

*The Clinical Picture of Schizophrenia*

*Explanations for Schizophrenia*
   Sociocultural Explanations
   Psychological Explanations
   Biological Explanations

*Treatments for Schizophrenia*
   Institutional Care
   Antipsychotic Drugs
   Psychotherapy
   The Community Approach

*P*sychosis is a condition characterized by loss of contact with reality. Often sufferers' capacity to perceive, process, and respond to environmental stimuli becomes so impaired and distorted that they may be unable to achieve even marginal adaptive functioning. Individuals in a state of psychosis may have hallucinations (false sensory perceptions) or delusions (false beliefs) or may withdraw into a private world.

Psychosis may result from various causes. As we noted in Chapter 11, taking LSD or abusing amphetamines or cocaine may produce psychosis. Similarly, brain injuries or brain diseases may cause psychotic disorders. Most commonly, psychosis appears in the form of *schizophrenia,* a disorder in which personal, social, and occupational functioning that had previously been adaptive deteriorates into a welter of distorted perceptions, disturbed thought processes, deviant emotional states, and motor abnormalities.

Approximately one of every 100 people on earth meets the DSM-IV criteria for schizophrenia (APA, 1994; Regier et al., 1993). More than 2 million people currently living in the United States have been or will be diagnosed as suffering from the disorder (Keith et al., 1991). Some 200,000 to 400,000 new cases are reported each year (Regier et al., 1993).

The financial cost of schizophrenia is enormous— estimated at tens of billions of dollars annually, including the costs of hospitalization, lost wages, and disability benefits. The catastrophic impact of this disorder on families represents an even greater emotional cost. Moreover, schizophrenia is associated with increased risk for suicide and for physical illness (Bruce et al., 1994; McGlashan, 1988).

Although it appears in all socioeconomic groups, schizophrenia is more likely to be found in people of the lower socioeconomic classes (see Figure 13-1). Some researchers believe that the stress of poverty is itself a cause of schizophrenia (Dohrenwend et al., 1992). Although this may indeed be part of the reason for the correlation, other factors have been cited as well. Schizophrenia may actually cause a person to migrate from a higher to a lower socioeconomic class (Munk & Mortensen, 1992). Victims of schizophrenia may be less able to maintain previous income levels after they become impaired. Similarly, those born into lower socioeconomic classes may find an upward economic climb interrupted by the onset of this disorder.

Equal numbers of men and women receive a diagnosis of schizophrenia (APA, 1994). Almost 3 percent of all divorced or separated persons suffer from this

*Schizophrenia*   A psychotic disorder in which personal, social, and occupational functioning that were previously adaptive deteriorate as a result of distorted perceptions, disturbed thought processes, deviant emotional states, and motor abnormalities.

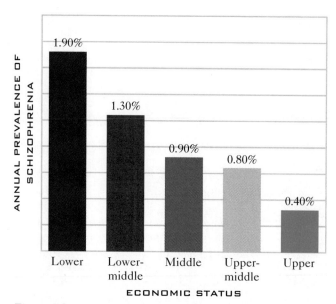

Figure 13-1   *According to recent surveys, poor people in the United States are much more likely than wealthy people to experience schizophrenia. (Adapted from Keith et al., 1991.)*

disorder over the course of their lives, compared to 1 percent of married people and 2 percent of people who remain single (Keith et al., 1991). As with socioeconomic class, however, it is not clear whether divorce increases one's risk of developing schizophrenia, or schizophrenia increases marital discord, or both.

Approximately 2.1 percent of African Americans suffer from this disorder over the course of their lives, compared to 1.4 percent of white Americans (Keith et al., 1991). This racial difference may be linked to the fact that African Americans are more likely to be poor and to experience marital separation. When researchers control for the factors of socioeconomic class and marital status, the prevalence rates of schizophrenia are equal for the two races.

Schizophrenia has been with us throughout history; it is the condition commonly described by the word "madness" (Cutting, 1985). Even the Bible speaks of King Saul's mad rages and terrors and of David's efforts to feign madness in order to escape his enemies. People today, like those of past times, show great interest in the disorder, reading books and flocking to movies and plays that examine schizophrenia.

## The Clinical Picture of Schizophrenia

Among people who are diagnosed as schizophrenic, there is considerable variation in symptoms, in the apparent cause and course of the disorder, and in responsiveness to treatment (APA, 1994). To illustrate the variety of forms schizophrenia may take, let us consider three people who were diagnosed as suffering from it. The cases are taken from the files of Silvano Arieti (1974), a prominent theorist on schizophrenia.

### Ann, 26 Years Old

Ann graduated from high school and from a school for commercial art. . . . At the age of 18 she began going out with Henry. . . . They became engaged shortly thereafter and went out together frequently until their marriage. . . .

Married life was considered a boring routine by both Ann and Henry. There was very little conversation between them. . . . Ann's disappointment in Henry increased. They had nothing in common; she was artistically inclined, whereas he had only an ordinary, conventional outlook toward life. It was at this time that she started to go dancing and then met Charles. Her interest in him increased, but she knew that she was married and that a divorce was not compatible with the precepts of the Catholic church. Her conflict grew and put her in a state of great agitation. . . .

. . . One evening she came home from dancing and told her mother that she was going to give up her husband Henry, marry Charles, go to Brazil with him, and have twenty babies. She was talking very fast and saying many things, several of which were incomprehensible. At the same time she also told her mother that she was seeing the Virgin Mary in visions. She then went to her mother-in-law and told her to take back her son Henry, because he was too immature. The following day Ann went to work and tried to get the entire office down on their knees with her to recite the rosary. A few days later, her mother took her to a priest, whom she "told off" in no uncertain terms. She finally spit at him. A psychiatrist was consulted, and he recommended hospitalization.

(Arieti, 1974, pp. 173–177)

### Richard, 23 Years Old

Richard remembered [the] period . . . after his discharge from the army . . . as one of the worst in his life. . . .

Approximately two years after his return to civilian life, Richard left his job because he became overwhelmed by . . . feelings of lack of confidence in himself, and he refused to go look for another one. He stayed home most of the day. His mother would nag him that he was too lazy and unwilling to do anything. He became slower and slower in dressing and undressing and taking care of himself. When he went out of the house, he felt compelled "to give interpretations" to everything he looked at. He did not know what to do outside the house, where to go, where to turn. If he saw a red light at a crossing, he would interpret it as a message that he should not go in that direction. If he saw an arrow, he would follow the arrow interpreting it as a sign sent by God that he should go in that direction. Feeling lost and horrified, he would go home and stay there, afraid to go out because going out meant making decisions or choices that he felt unable to make. He reached the point where he stayed home most of the time. . . . He gradually became worse, was completely motionless, and had to be hospitalized. . . .

Being undecided, he felt blocked, and often would remain mute and motionless, like a statue, even for days.

(Arieti, 1974, pp. 153–155)

### Laura, 40 Years Old

Laura's desire was to . . . leave home [in Austria] as soon as possible. She became a professional dancer at the age of 20. . . . and was booked for vaudeville theaters in many European countries. . . .

It was during one of her tours in Germany that Laura met her husband. . . . They were married and went to live in a small provincial town in France where the husband's business was. . . . She spent a year in that town and was very unhappy. . . . Finally . . . Laura and her husband decided to immigrate to the United States. . . .

They had no children, and Laura . . . showed interest in pets. She had a dog to whom she was very devoted. The dog became sick and partially paralyzed, and veterinarians felt that there was no hope of recovery. . . . Finally [her husband] broached the problem to his wife, asking her "Should the dog be destroyed or not?" From that time on Laura became restless, agitated, and depressed. . . .

. . . Later Laura started to complain about the neighbors. A woman who lived on the floor beneath them was knocking on the wall to irritate her. According to the husband, this woman had really knocked on the wall a few times; he had heard the noises. However, Laura became more and more concerned about it. She would wake up in the middle of the night under the impression that she was hearing noises from the apartment downstairs. She would become upset and angry at the neighbors. . . . Later she became more disturbed. She started to feel that the neighbors were now recording everything she said; maybe they had hidden wires in the apartment. She started to feel "funny" sensations. There were many strange things happening, which she did not know how to explain; people were looking at her in a funny way in the street; in the butcher shop, the butcher had purposely served her last, although she was in the middle of the line. During the next few days she felt that people were planning to harm either her or her husband. . . .

(Arieti, 1974, pp. 165–168)

# Symptoms of Schizophrenia

Ann, Richard, and Laura each regressed from a normal level of functioning to become significantly ineffective in dealing with the world. Each demonstrate some of the symptoms associated with schizophrenia. In recent years, clinicians have grouped the symptoms of schizophrenia into three categories—*positive symptoms,* so named because they seem to represent "pathological excess," bizarre additions to a normal repertoire of behavior; *negative symptoms,* symptoms that seem to reflect "pathological deficits," characteristics that are lacking; and *psychomotor symptoms.*

## Positive Symptoms

The positive symptoms of schizophrenia include delusions, disorganized thinking and speech, heightened perceptions and hallucinations, and inappropriate affect.

**Delusions**   Many people with schizophrenia develop *delusions,* ideas that they believe fervently but that have no basis in fact and are often absurd. Some hold a single delusion that dominates their life and behavior, while others have many delusions.

*Delusions of persecution* are the most common delusions in schizophrenia (APA, 1994). People with this kind of delusion believe that they are being plotted or discriminated against, spied on, slandered, threatened, attacked, or deliberately victimized. Laura believed that her neighbors were trying to irritate her and that other people were planning to harm her and her husband.

Other delusions found in schizophrenia include *delusions of reference,* in which a person attaches special and personal significance to the actions of others, or to various objects or events (Richard, for example, interpreted arrows on street signs as indicators of the direction he should take); *delusions of grandeur,* in which persons believe themselves to be great inventors, religious saviors, or other specially empowered persons; and *delusions of control,* beliefs that one's impulses, feelings, thoughts, and actions are being controlled by other people.

*No it's not "the King." But millions of Americans believe that Elvis Presley is still alive, leading to numerous Elvis sightings at Seven-Eleven stores around the country and an army of Elvis impersonators. Clinicians stop short of calling such beliefs delusions, however, noting that the Elvis loyalists do not hold onto their beliefs with a high degree of conviction. Most can be persuaded that Elvis has indeed "left the building."*

**Disorganized Thinking and Speech**   People with schizophrenia often display *positive formal thought disorders,* peculiar excesses of verbal expression that can cause the sufferer great disorganization and confusion and make communication with others extremely difficult.

People who display *loose associations,* or *derailment,* the most common formal thought disorder, rapidly shift from one topic to another, making inconsequential and incoherent statements and apparently believing them to make sense. For example, one man, asked about his itchy arms, responded:

---

*Positive symptoms*   Symptoms of schizophrenia that seem to represent pathological excesses or bizarre additions to a normal repertoire of behavior. They include delusions, hallucinations, disorganized thinking and speech, and inappropriate affect.

*Negative symptoms*   Symptoms of schizophrenia that seem to reflect pathological deficits or characteristics that are lacking—flat affect, poverty of speech, and loss of volition.

*Delusion*   A blatantly false belief firmly held despite evidence to the contrary.

*Formal thought disorder*   A disturbance in the production and organization of thought.

*Loose associations (derailment)*   A common thought disorder of schizophrenia, characterized by rapid shifts from one topic of conversation to another.

The problem is insects. My brother used to collect insects. He's now a man 5 foot 10 inches. You know, 10 is my favorite number. I also like to dance, draw, and watch television.

Some people with schizophrenia display a formal thought disorder called *neologisms,* made-up words that have meaning only to the person using them. Others may display the formal thought disorder of *perseveration,* that is, repeating their words and statements again and again. And some use *clang,* or rhyme, as a guide to formulating thoughts and statements. When asked how she was feeling, one person with schizophrenia replied, "Well, hell, it's well to tell." Another described the weather as "So hot, you know it runs on a cot."

It may be that some degree of disorganized speech or thinking appears long before a full pattern of schizophrenic symptoms unfolds (Bilder et al., 1992; Harvey, 1991). A number of researchers have conducted **high-risk studies** to investigate schizophrenia, studies in which people hypothesized to be at great risk for developing the disorder (such as people whose parents have schizophrenia) are followed throughout their childhood. These studies have indicated that high-risk people who later develop schizophrenia show significantly more disordered thinking at the age of 15 than similar high-risk subjects who do not later develop schizophrenia (Parnas et al., 1989, 1982).

**Heightened Perceptions and Hallucinations** Many people with schizophrenia feel that their senses are being *flooded* by all the sights and sounds that surround them, so that it is almost impossible for them to attend to anything important (APA, 1994; Perry & Braff, 1994).

Everything seems to grip my attention. . . . I am speaking to you just now, but I can hear noises going on next door and in the corridor. I find it difficult to shut these out, and it makes it more difficult for me to concentrate on what I am saying to you.
(*McGhie and Chapman, 1961*)

Related studies of high-risk subjects suggest that such attention problems may also develop years before a full schizophrenic pattern unfolds (Cornblatt & Keilp, 1994).

*Hallucinations,* perceptions that occur in the absence of corresponding external stimuli, are the most severe perceptual disturbance found in cases of schizophrenia. In *auditory* hallucinations, by far the most common kind in schizophrenia (APA, 1994; Mueser et al., 1990), people hear sounds and voices that seem to come from outside their heads. Often the voices talk directly to the hallucinator, perhaps giving commands or warning of dangers. In other cases, they are experienced as being overheard.

The voices . . . were mostly heard in my head, though I often heard them in the air, or in different parts of the room. Every voice was different, and each beautiful, and generally, speaking or singing in a different tone and measure, and resembling those of relations or friends. There appeared to be many in my head, I should say upwards of fourteen. I divide them, as they styled themselves, or one another, into voices of contrition and voices of joy and honour.
(*"Perceval's Narrative" in Bateson, 1974*)

Hallucinations can also involve the other senses. *Tactile* hallucinations may take the form of tingling, burning, or electrical-shock sensations, or the feeling of insects crawling over one's body or just beneath the skin. *Somatic* hallucinations convey the sensation that something is happening inside the body, such as an organ shifting position or a snake crawling inside one's stomach. *Visual* hallucinations run the gamut from vague perceptions of colors or clouds to distinct visions of people or objects that are not there. People with *gustatory* hallucinations regularly find that their food or drink tastes strange, and people with *olfactory* hallucinations smell odors that no one else does, being haunted, for example, by the smell of poison, smoke, or decay.

Hallucinations and delusional ideas often go hand in hand. A woman who hears voices issuing commands, for example, may have the delusion that the commands are being placed in her head by someone else. Similarly, a man with delusions of persecution may hallucinate the smell of poison in his bedroom or the taste of poison in his coffee.

**Inappropriate Affect** Many people with schizophrenia display *inappropriate affect,* emotions that are unsuited to the situation. They may, for example, smile inappropriately when making a somber statement or on being told terrible news, or become upset in situations that should make them happy. They may also undergo inappropriate shifts in mood. During a tender conversation with his wife, for example, a man with schizophrenia suddenly started yelling obscenities at her and complaining about her inadequacies. Often the inappropriate affect arises in response to other features of the disorder, such as to the words of an auditory hallucination.

---

*Hallucination* The experiencing of imagined sights, sounds, or other sensory experiences as if they were real.

*Inappropriate affect* A symptom of schizophrenia in which a person expresses emotions that are unsuited to the situation.

*The renowned ballet artist Vaslav Nijinsky, performing here in Schéhérazade, developed severe schizophrenia and spent the last years of his life in a mental institution.*

## Negative Symptoms

The negative symptoms of schizophrenia include poverty of speech, blunted and flat affect, loss of volition, and social withdrawal.

**Poverty of Speech**    People with schizophrenia often display *alogia,* a decrease in speech or speech content, characterized by absent or empty replies. Some people with alogia may think and say very little, particularly when their thoughts become *blocked.*

> I may be thinking quite clearly and telling someone something and suddenly I get stuck. You have seen me do this and you may think I am just lost for words or that I have gone into a trance, but that is not what happens. What happens is that I suddenly stick on a

word or an idea in my head and I just can't move past it. It seems to fill my mind and there's no room for anything else.

> (McGhie & Chapman, 1961)

Other persons with alogia may actually say quite a bit but still manage to convey little meaning, reflecting what is termed *poverty of content.*

**Blunted and Flat Affect**    Many people with schizophrenia have a ***blunted affect***—they manifest less anger, sadness, joy, or other feelings than most people—and some show almost no emotions at all, a condition known as *flat affect.* The faces of these persons are typically immobile, their eye contact is poor, and their voices are monotonous. One young man with schizophrenia told his father, "I wish I could wake up feeling really bad—it would be better than feeling nothing" (Wechsler, 1972, p. 17).

**Loss of Volition**    As people with schizophrenia struggle to function in a grossly distorted world, many display *avolition,* or apathy, feeling drained of energy and interest in normal goals, and unable to initiate or complete a course of action. This problem is particularly common in people who have had the disorder for many years, as if they have been worn down by it. Similarly, the individuals may display *ambivalence,* or having conflicted feelings about most things. For example, Richard, whose case was described earlier in the chapter, was overwhelmed by his ambivalence and related indecisiveness and seemed to lose his ability to act.

**Social Withdrawal**    People with schizophrenia often withdraw emotionally and socially from their environment and become totally preoccupied with their own ideas and fantasies. They may distance themselves from other people and avoid talking to them. Because their ideas are illogical and distorted, this withdrawal serves to distance them still further from reality.

## Psychomotor Symptoms

Loss of spontaneity in movement and the development of odd grimaces, gestures, and mannerisms are also symptoms of schizophrenia (APA, 1994). Such movements tend to be repetitive and often seem to be purposeful, like a ritualistic or magical act.

Sometimes the psychomotor symptoms of schizo-

---

*Alogia*    A symptom in schizophrenia, characterized by a decrease in speech or speech content.

*Flat affect*    A symptom of schizophrenia in which the person shows almost no emotions at all.

*Avolition*    A symptom in schizophrenia, characterized by apathy and an inability to initiate or complete a course of action.

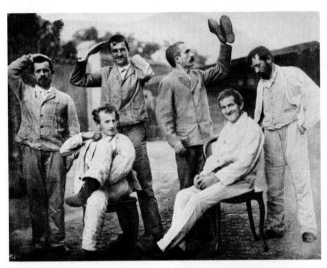
*Each of these patients with schizophrenia, photographed at the turn of the century, displays features of catatonia.*

phrenia take extreme forms, collectively called *catatonia*. People in a *catatonic stupor* become totally unaware of and unresponsive to their environment, remaining motionless and silent for long stretches of time. Recall how Richard would lie motionless and mute in bed for days. Some people show *catatonic rigidity,* maintaining a rigid, upright posture for hours and resisting efforts to be moved. Others exhibit *catatonic posturing,* assuming awkward, bizarre positions for long periods of time. They may spend hours holding their arms out at a 90-degree angle or balancing in a squatting position. Some also display *waxy flexibility,* indefinitely maintaining postures into which they have been placed by someone else. If a nurse raises a patient's arm or tilts the patient's head, for example, the individual will remain in that position until moved again.

People who display *catatonic excitement,* a different form of catatonia, move excitedly, sometimes with wild waving of arms and legs. When such patients are extremely hyperactive and uncontrolled, they pose a danger to themselves and others.

## The Course of Schizophrenia

Schizophrenia usually emerges between the victim's late teens and mid-30s (APA, 1994). Although the course of this disorder varies widely from person to person (APA, 1994), many patients seem to go through three phases: prodromal, active, and residual.

During the *prodromal phase,* schizophrenic symptoms are not yet prominent, but the person begins to deteriorate from previous levels of functioning. During

the *active phase,* schizophrenic symptoms become pronounced. In some instances this phase is triggered by stress in the person's life. For Ann, the confused and disoriented woman we read about earlier, the immediate precipitant was falling in love with a man she met dancing. Finally, the *residual phase* is marked by a return to the prodromal level of functioning. The striking symptoms of the active phase recede, but many individuals remain in a general state of decline.

Although as many as a third of patients with schizophrenia may recover completely, the majority continue indefinitely to show at least some residual impairment (Strange, 1992). Recovery from schizophrenia is more complete and more likely in subjects who functioned quite adequately before the disorder appeared (had good *premorbid* functioning), or when the disorder was precipitated by stressful events, was abrupt in onset (short prodromal phase), or developed during middle age (APA, 1994).

## Diagnosing Schizophrenia

DSM-IV calls for a diagnosis of schizophrenia when a person shows continuous signs of the disorder for six months or more (APA, 1994). For at least one month of this pattern, the person must display an active phase of schizophrenia that includes two or more major symptoms. In addition, the person must have deteriorated from a previous level of functioning in such areas as work, social relations, and self-care. People whose symptoms vary somewhat from these criteria may be suffering from a different psychotic disorder (see Box 13-1).

Emil Kraepelin, writing in 1896, distinguished three patterns of schizophrenia, hebephrenic, catatonic, and paranoid schizophrenic. The writers of DSM-IV continue to find his categories descriptive of patients' behavior and have labeled the various types of schizophrenia disorganized (hebephrenic), catatonic, paranoid, undifferentiated, and residual.

### Disorganized Type

The central symptoms of *disorganized schizophrenia* are confusion, incoherence, and flat or inappropriate affect. Formal thought disturbances and perceptual problems make for difficult communication, which leads in turn to extreme social withdrawal. Grimaces and odd mannerisms are common. "Silliness" is also a common feature; some patients giggle constantly without apparent reason. This is why the pattern was first

*Catatonia* A pattern of extreme psychomotor symptoms found in some forms of schizophrenia, that may include catatonic stupor, rigidity, or posturing.

*Disorganized schizophrenia* A type of schizophrenia characterized primarily by confusion, incoherence, and flat or inappropriate affect.

## Box 13-1

# *An Array of Psychotic Disorders*

Although schizophrenia is indeed the most common kind of psychosis, it is but one of several. When, for example, the symptoms of psychosis last less than a month (as opposed to six months or more in schizophrenia), a diagnosis of *brief psychotic disorder* may be called for. When they last from one to five months, persons may receive a diagnosis of *schizophreniform disorder*. If the psychotic symptoms are caused by a medical illness, the appropriate diagnosis is *psychotic disorder due to a general medical condition*. In addition to these, DSM-IV distinguishes the following psychotic disorders.

*In one or two of every 1,000 births, a mother suffers "postpartum psychosis," marked by hallucinations, severe depression, and, perhaps, impulses to kill herself or her child or both. This pattern, found in some cases of brief psychotic disorder or other psychotic disorders, is different from the much more common "postpartum depression without psychotic features."*

### Delusional Disorder

People who have at least one month of persistent delusions that are not bizarre and not part of a larger schizophrenic pattern may receive a diagnosis of *delusional disorder*. Aside from their delusions, they do not act in a particularly odd way and rarely show prominent hallucinations.

Persecutory, jealous, grandiose, and *somatic* delusions are common in people who have this disorder. Lately public attention has been drawn to *erotomanic* delusions.

People with these delusions believe, without any basis whatsoever, that they are loved by another person, who may be a casual acquaintance or even a complete stranger.

### Schizoaffective Disorder

Sometimes people display prominent symptoms of both schizophrenia and a mood disorder. In such cases, they may receive a diagnosis of *schizoaffective disorder*. To receive this diagnosis, however, the individual must, during the course of the disorder, also have at least one episode of psychotic symptoms only.

### Shared Psychotic Disorder

A person who embraces the delusions held by another individual may qualify for a diagnosis of *shared psychotic disorder*. Such individuals usually have a close relationship with a dominant person, such as a parent or sibling, whose psychotic thinking they come to share. When the disorder is found in a two-person relationship, as it usually is, it is often known as *folie à deux*. Sometimes the disorder occurs in a whole family or group.

### Substance-Induced Psychotic Disorder

If prominent hallucinations or delusions are caused by the direct physiological effects of a substance, the person is said to be suffering from a *substance-induced psychotic disorder*. The substance may be an abused drug, such as alcohol, hallucinogens, or cocaine, and the disorder may occur in association with either intoxication or withdrawal from the substance, depending on the substance. The symptoms may also be caused by a medication or by a toxin such as nerve gas, carbon monoxide, carbon dioxide, fuel, or paint.

---

called "hebephrenic," after Hebe, the Greek goddess of youth, who according to Greek mythology often acted like a clown to make the other gods laugh. Not surprisingly, people with disorganized schizophrenia are typically unable to take adequate care of themselves, to maintain social relationships, or to hold a job.

## Catatonic Type

The central feature of *catatonic schizophrenia* is a psychomotor disturbance of some sort. Some of the peo-

*Catatonic schizophrenia*    A type of schizophrenia characterized primarily by a severe psychomotor disturbance.

ple in this category spend their time in a catatonic stupor, mute and unresponsive; others are seized with catatonic excitement, waving their arms and acting in an uncontrolled manner; in still other cases, the extremes of stupor and excitement alternate. Richard, the unemployed young man who became mute and statuelike, would receive a diagnosis of this type of schizophrenia.

## Paranoid Type

The most prominent symptom of *paranoid schizophrenia* is an organized system of delusions and auditory hallucinations that often guide the person's life. Laura would receive this diagnosis. She believed that her neighbors and people on the street were out to get her (delusions of persecution). And she heard noises from the apartment downstairs (auditory hallucinations) and experienced "funny sensations" that further supported her beliefs.

## Undifferentiated Type

When people with schizophrenia do not fall neatly into one category, the disorder is classified as *undifferentiated type.* Over the years, this vague diagnosis has been particularly abused, and a range of schizophrenic and nonschizophrenic patterns have probably been incorrectly assigned to it.

## Residual Type

When the symptoms of schizophrenia lessen in intensity and number yet remain with the patient in a residual form, the diagnosis is usually changed to *residual type* of schizophrenia. People with this type of schizophrenia may continue to display blunted or inappropriate emotional reactions, social withdrawal, eccentric behavior, and some illogical thinking.

## Other Categorizations of Schizophrenia

Although DSM-IV favors the distinctions described above, a distinction between so-called Type I and Type II schizophrenia has also gained prominence in recent years (Crow, 1985, 1982, 1980). The label *Type I schizophrenia* is applied to cases dominated by positive symptoms, such as delusions, hallucinations, and positive formal thought disorders. Cases of *Type II schizophrenia* are those characterized by negative symptoms, such as flat affect, poverty of speech, and loss of volition (see Table 13-1).

Many researchers have found this distinction to be more useful than other kinds of distinctions in predicting the course and prognosis of the disorder. As we shall see shortly, Type I patients generally have a better premorbid adjustment, greater likelihood of improvement, and better responsiveness to traditional antipsychotic drugs than do Type II patients (Cuesta et al., 1994; Fenton & McGlashan, 1994). Moreover, the positive symptoms of Type I schizophrenia seem to be closely linked to biochemical abnormalities in the brain, while the negative symptoms of Type II schizophrenia have been tied to structural abnormalities in the brain (Ananth et al., 1991; Weinberger & Kleinman, 1986).

> ### Summing Up
> *One out of every 100 people worldwide meets the DSM-IV criteria for schizophrenia. The positive symptoms of schizophrenia include delusions, disorganized thinking, hallucinations, and inappropriate affect. The negative symptoms include poverty of speech, flat affect, loss of volition, and social withdrawal. The disorder may also be marked by psychomotor symptoms.*
>
> *DSM-IV distinguishes five patterns of the disorder: the disorganized type, catatonic type, paranoid type, undifferentiated type, and residual type. In addition, clinicians are increasingly attending to the distinction between Type I and Type II schizophrenia.*

# Explanations of Schizophrenia

As with many other kinds of psychological disorders, sociocultural, psychological, and biological theorists have each tried to explain schizophrenia. Only the biological explanations have received compelling research support. Nevertheless, many theorists contend that an interaction of factors contributes to schizophrenia—for example, that people with a biological predisposition to develop it may do so in response to certain societal factors and in the face of key psychological stressors (Yank et al., 1993; Cutting, 1985).

---

*Paranoid schizophrenia*   A type of schizophrenia characterized primarily by an organized system of delusions and hallucinations.

*Type I schizophrenia*   Schizophrenia that is dominated by positive symptoms, such as delusions, hallucinations, and positive formal thought disorders.

*Type II schizophrenia*   Schizophrenia that is dominated by negative symptoms, such as flat affect, poverty of speech, and loss of volition.

Table 13-1    *Type I vs. Type II Schizophrenia*

|  | Type I | Type II |
|---|---|---|
| Symptoms | Positive symptoms:<br>　Delusions<br>　Hallucinations<br>　Inappropriate affect<br>　Positive formal thought<br>　　disorders | Negative symptoms:<br>　Avolition<br>　Social withdrawal<br>　Blunted and flat affect<br>　Alogia |
| Premorbid adjustment | Relatively good | Relatively poor |
| Responsiveness to traditional antipsychotic drugs | Good | Poor |
| Outcome of disorder | Fair | Poor |
| Biological features | Abnormal neurotransmitter activity | Abnormal brain structures |

*Source:* Adapted from Crow, 1985, 1982, 1980.

## Sociocultural Explanations

Sociocultural theorists contend that persons with mental disorders are victims of larger social forces. Correspondingly, they have proposed that schizophrenia is the result of two different kinds of factors, *social labeling* and *family dysfunctioning*.

### Social Labeling

In the following passage, a man with schizophrenia discusses the power that labeling has had on his life.

> When I was six years old . . . my somewhat befuddled mother took me to the University of Washington to be examined by psychiatrists in order to find out what was wrong with me. These psychiatrists told my mother: "We don't know exactly what is wrong with your son, but whatever it is, it is very serious. We recommend that you have him committed immediately or else he will be completely psychotic within less than a year." My mother did not have me committed since she realized that such a course of action would be extremely damaging to me. But after that ominous prophecy my parents began to view and treat me as if I were either insane or at least in the process of becoming that way. Once, when my mother caught me playing with some vile muck I had mixed up—I was seven at the time—she gravely told me, "they have people put away in mental institutions for doing things like that." Fear was written all over my mother's face as she told me this. . . . The slightest odd behavior on my part was enough to send my parents into paroxysms of apprehension. My parents' apprehensions in turn made me fear that I was going insane. . . . My fate had been sealed not by my

genes, but by the attitudes, beliefs, and expectations of my parents. . . . I find it extremely difficult to condemn my parents for behaving as if I were going insane when the psychiatric authorities told them that this was an absolute certainty.

> *(Modrow, 1992, pp. 1–2)*

Many sociocultural theorists believe that the features of schizophrenia may be caused by the diagnosis itself (Modrow, 1992; Szasz, 1987, 1963; Scheff, 1966). They propose that the label "schizophrenia" is assigned by society to people who deviate from certain behavioral norms. Justified or not, once the label is assigned, it becomes a self-fulfilling prophecy that promotes the development of many schizophrenic symptoms. Like the man quoted above, people who are called schizophrenic are viewed and reacted to as "crazy" and expected and encouraged to display a schizophrenic style of behavior. Increasingly, they accept their assigned role and learn to play it convincingly.

At one level, this theory constitutes a general warning about the dangers of diagnostic labeling. Perhaps the most influential demonstration of these dangers has been offered in the famous Rosenhan (1973) study, which we first encountered in Chapter 4 (see p. 108). When eight normal people presented themselves at various mental hospitals complaining that they had been hearing voices utter the words "empty," "hollow," and "thud," they were readily diagnosed as schizophrenic and hospitalized. Although the pseudopatients then dropped all symptoms and proceeded to behave normally, they had great difficulty getting rid of the label.

The pseudopatients reported that staff members spent limited time interacting with them or with other patients, usually responded curtly to patients' questions, were frequently authoritarian in manner, and often treated patients as though they were invisible. The pseudopatients described feeling powerless, depersonalized, and bored, and often behaved in a listless and apathetic manner. Clearly, being labeled schizophrenic can lead to a range of individual reactions and behaviors.

> ### Consider This
> Rosenhan's pseudopatient study is one of the most controversial in the clinical field. What kinds of ethical, legal, and therapeutic concerns might be raised by this study?

Some theorists go so far as to assert that schizophrenia is largely the *creation* of society and that as a product of norms and expectations, the disorder can be expected to vary from society to society as norms and expectations vary. In short, symptoms that Western society calls schizophrenic should be different from the schizophrenic symptoms defined by other countries and cultures.

This prediction of variability has not, however, been borne out by research (Smith, 1982). In fact, most societies have a label that approximates the Western category of schizophrenia, and the behavior implied by this label tends to be remarkably the same from society to society. The anthropologist Jane Murphy (1976), for example, studied two non-Western societies—the

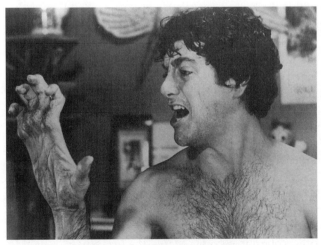

*People with lycanthropy, the delusion of being an animal, were once labeled by society as werewolves, rather than as persons suffering from schizophrenia or another psychotic disorder, and they were "treated" accordingly. This delusion has inspired storytellers for centuries, including the makers of the film* An American Werewolf in London.

Yupik-speaking Eskimos on an island in the Bering Sea and the Egba Yorubas of rural, tropical Nigeria—and found that each had a disorder whose name loosely translated into English as "insanity," and each disorder had symptoms (hallucinations, delusions, disorientation) that are remarkably similar to those of the Western disorder of schizophrenia.

## Family Dysfunctioning

Family theorists have argued for years that certain patterns of family interactions and communication help lead to schizophrenia. The leading family theories have pointed to so-called schizophrenogenic mothers and double-bind communications.

**The Schizophrenogenic Mother** The noted clinician Frieda Fromm-Reichmann (1948) used the term *schizophrenogenic mother* (schizophrenia-causing mother) to describe the mothers of individuals with schizophrenia, saying that such mothers are cold, domineering, and impervious to their children's needs. According to Fromm-Reichmann, they appear to be self-sacrificing but are actually using their children to address their own needs. At once overprotective and rejecting, they confuse their children and set the stage for schizophrenic functioning.

Although this notion has appealed to many clinicians, years of research have challenged its validity. The majority of people with schizophrenia do *not* appear to have had mothers who fit the schizophrenogenic description.

**Double-Bind Communications** One of the best-known family theories is the *double-bind hypothesis* (Bateson, 1978; Bateson et al., 1956), which maintains that some parents repeatedly communicate pairs of messages that are mutually contradictory, thus placing their children in double-bind situations: the children cannot avoid displeasing their parents; nothing they do is right. Double-bind messages arise from a contradiction between a verbal communication and the accompanying nonverbal communication. If one person says to another, "I'm glad to see you," yet frowns and avoids eye contact, the two aspects of the message are incongruent.

According to this theory, a child who is repeatedly exposed to double-bind situations may adopt a *special*

---

*Schizophrenogenic mother* A type of mother—supposedly cold, domineering, and impervious to the needs of others—that was once thought to cause schizophrenia in the child.

*Double-bind hypothesis* A family systems theory that says some parents help cause schizophrenic symptoms in their children by repeatedly engaging in communications with them that carry simultaneous contradictory messages.

*life strategy* for coping with the environment. Unfortunately, some such strategies can lead to schizophrenic symptoms. One strategy, for example, might be always to ignore verbal communications and respond only to nonverbal communications; that is, always be suspicious of what a person is saying, wonder about its true meaning, look for clues in the person's gestures or tones, and respond accordingly. People who increasingly respond to messages in this way may be on their way to manifesting symptoms of paranoid schizophrenia. Like the schizophrenogenic-mother theory, the double-bind hypothesis has been popular in the clinical field since its inception (Cronen et al., 1983), but investigations into the theory have been few and in fact unsupportive (Ringuette & Kennedy, 1966).

**The Status of Family Theories**   So far no single family explanation of schizophrenia has received impressive research support. At the same time, it has been found that schizophrenia, like other mental disorders, is often triggered by stressful family situations, including emotional instability of some kind in a parent (Leff & Vaughn, 1976). Moreover, some studies suggest that the parents of persons with schizophrenia tend to (1) *display more conflict,* (2) *have greater difficulty communicating with one another,* and (3) *be more critical of and overinvolved with their children* than other parents (Miklowitz, 1994; Faloon & Liberman, 1983).

Certainly these trends suggest that negative family experiences may contribute to schizophrenia (Mavreas et al., 1992). However, it is also possible that individuals with schizophrenia themselves disrupt family life and help cause the family problems that clinicians and researchers continue to observe (Asarnow & Horton, 1990).

# Psychological Explanations

The leading psychological explanations of schizophrenia have come from the psychodynamic, behavioral, existential, and cognitive perspectives. As with the sociocultural explanations, they have each received at best limited research support.

## A Psychodynamic Explanation

Freud (1924, 1915) believed that the development of schizophrenia involves a two-part psychological process: (1) *regression* to a pre-ego stage and (2) efforts to *restore* ego control. He proposed that when their external world is particularly harsh or withholding (for example, when their parents are consistently cold or

unnurturing), those who develop schizophrenia regress to the earliest point in their development, to a state of *primary narcissism,* in which only their own needs are felt. This near-total regression leads to self-indulgent symptoms such as neologisms, loose associations, and delusions of grandeur.

Freud also believed that upon regressing to this infantile state, these people start trying to reestablish contact with reality. Their efforts give rise to yet other schizophrenic symptoms. Auditory hallucinations, for example, may represent an unconscious attempt to substitute for a lost sense of reality.

Freud's position has been retained by many psychodynamic theorists throughout the twentieth century (Blatt & Wild, 1976; Fenichel, 1945), but it has received virtually no research support. More contemporary psychodynamic theorists tend to include both biological and psychodynamic notions in their explanations (Pollack, 1989).

---

*Consider This*

The family and psychodynamic explanations of schizophrenia reflect a long-standing tradition in the clinical field and in society of pointing to parents as key causes of mental disorders, even in cases where compelling evidence is lacking. Why are parents and family life pointed to so readily, why are these explanations so resistant to change, and how might clinicians better determine the role of these factors in cases of schizophrenia?

---

## A Behavioral Explanation

Behaviorists point primarily to *operant conditioning* to explain schizophrenia (Liberman, 1982; Ullmann & Krasner, 1975). They propose that most people are taught by their family and social environment to attend to social cues—for example, to other people's smiles, frowns, and comments. When they respond to these stimuli in a socially acceptable way, they are better able to satisfy their emotional needs and to achieve their goals. Some people, however, do not receive such reinforcements. Unusual circumstances may prevent their encountering social cues, or important figures in their lives may be socially inadequate and unable to provide proper reinforcements. Either way, these people stop attending to social cues and focus instead on other, often irrelevant, cues—the brightness of light in a room, a bird flying above, or the *sound* of a word rather than its meaning. As they attend more and more to such inappropriate signals, their responses become increasingly bizarre. Such responses in turn elicit heightened attention or other types of reinforcement from the environment, thus increasing the likelihood that they will be repeated.

Support for the behavioral position has been circumstantial. As we shall see later, in the discussion of treatment, researchers have found that patients with schizophrenia are often capable of learning appropriate verbal responses and social behaviors if their bizarre responses are consistently ignored by hospital personnel while normal responses are reinforced with cigarettes, food, attention, or other rewards (Belcher, 1988; Foxx et al., 1988). The fact that verbal and social responses can be successfully changed by such reinforcements suggests to some theorists that schizophrenic behaviors may be acquired through operant conditioning in the first place. As we know, however, an effective treatment for a disorder does not necessarily imply the cause of the disorder.

## An Existential Explanation

R. D. Laing (1967, 1964, 1959) combined key components of the family explanations of schizophrenia with the existential principles that were his hallmark, and formulated the most controversial view of schizophre-

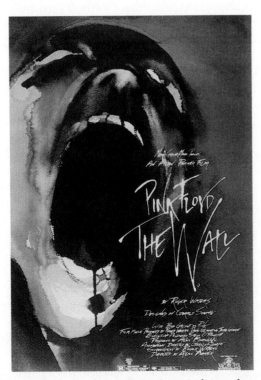

*"Is there anybody out there?" R. D. Laing's theory that schizophrenia is an extended inward search undertaken by some persons in order to cure themselves of confusion and unhappiness caused by their family and society has been romanticized in all the arts. It is, for example, the central theme of Pink Floyd's hugely popular album and movie, The Wall.*

nia in the clinical field. Laing believed that schizophrenia is actually a constructive process in which people try to cure themselves of the confusion and unhappiness caused by their social and family environment.

Laing contended that after receiving a lifetime of paradoxical communications and demands, some people undertake an inner search for a sense of strength and purpose. They withdraw from others and attend increasingly to their own inner cues as they try to recover their wholeness as human beings. Laing argued that these people would emerge stronger and less confused if they were simply allowed to continue this inner search. Instead, society and its clinicians tell them that they are sick. Yielding to society's expectations, the individuals assume the role of patient, submitting to efforts at treatment that actually serve to produce further schizophrenic symptoms. In attempting to cure these people, society dooms them to suspension in an inner world.

It is easy to understand why Laing's theory is so controversial. Most theorists reject his notion that schizophrenia is a constructive process. They see it as a problem that brings extensive suffering and no benefit. For the most part research has not resolved the controversy over Laing's existential explanation (Howells & Guirguis, 1985). Laing's ideas do not lend themselves to empirical research (Hirsch & Leff, 1975), and existentialists who embrace his view have little confidence in traditional research approaches.

## A Cognitive Explanation

A leading cognitive explanation of schizophrenia begins with a supposition (based on recent biological research) that biological factors of some kind cause strange sensory experiences for people with schizophrenia. It then states that further features of the disorder emerge as a result of the individuals' attempts to understand and explain their unusual experiences.

When first confronted by voices, visions, or other sensations, these people turn to friends and relatives to help them understand what is happening, only to have the existence of their new sensory experiences denied. Eventually they may come to believe that their friends and relatives are trying to hide the truth from them, may reject all feedback from others, and may develop beliefs (delusions) that they are being manipulated or persecuted (Garety, 1991; Maher, 1974).

Researchers have systematically documented that people with schizophrenia do indeed have special sensory and perceptual problems. As noted earlier, for example, many persons with this disorder experience hallucinations, and most have trouble keeping their attention focused on things, both in real life and in the laboratory (Elkins & Cromwell, 1994; APA, 1994). But researchers have yet to provide clear, direct support for the notion that sensory difficulties of this kind *lead* to delusions.

This cognitive explanation of schizophrenia explicitly acknowledges the role of biological factors in that disorder and tries to understand how psychological processes may interact with those factors. Such interactionist perspectives are being adopted increasingly by today's psychodynamic, behavioral, and family theorists. Let us now turn to the biological factors that so many different kinds of theorists are impressed by.

## Biological Explanations

What is arguably the most enlightening research on schizophrenia during the past few decades has come from the biological realm. This research has underscored the key role of genetic and biological factors in the development of schizophrenia and has opened the door to important changes in its treatment.

### Genetic Factors

Genetic researchers believe that some people inherit a biological predisposition to schizophrenia and, in accordance with a diathesis-stress model, come to develop the disorder when they are confronted by extreme stress, usually during late adolescence or early

adulthood (Gottesman, 1991). The genetic viewpoint has been supported by studies of (1) relatives of people with schizophrenia, (2) twins with schizophrenia, (3) people with schizophrenia who are adopted, and (4) chromosomal mapping.

**Studies of Relatives** Studies have found repeatedly that schizophrenia is more common among relatives of people with schizophrenia than among relatives of people who do not have schizophrenia (Kendler et al., 1994, 1993; Parnas et al., 1993). Moreover, the more closely related the relatives are to the person with schizophrenia, the greater their likelihood of developing the disorder (see Figure 13-2).

**Twin Studies** As we have noted previously, if both members of a pair of twins have a particular trait, they are said to be *concordant* for that trait. If genetic factors are at work in schizophrenia, identical twins (who share identical genes) should have a higher concordance rate for schizophrenia than fraternal twins (who share only some genes). This expectation has been supported repeatedly by research (APA, 1994; Gottesman, 1991). Studies have found that if one identical twin develops schizophrenia, there is a 40 to 60 percent chance that the other twin will do so as well. If one fraternal twin has schizophrenia, in contrast, the other twin has approximately a 17 percent chance of developing the disorder.

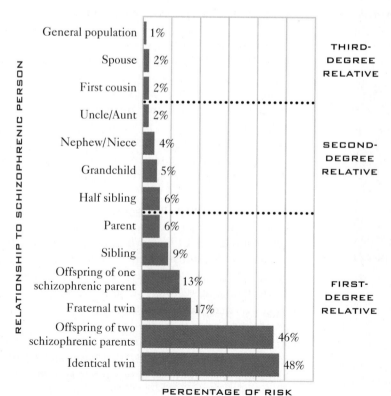

Figure 13-2  *People who are biologically related to people with schizophrenia have a heightened risk of developing the disorder during their lifetime. The closer the biological relationship, the greater the risk of developing the disorder. (Adapted from Gottesman, 1991, p. 96.)*

**Adoption Studies**    Adoption studies look at adults with schizophrenia who were adopted as infants and determine whether their present behavior is more similar to that of their biological relatives or to that of their adoptive relatives. Because the adults with schizophrenia in these studies were reared apart from their biological relatives, similar schizophrenic symptoms in those relatives would indicate genetic influences. Repeatedly, it has been found that the biological relatives of adoptees with schizophrenia are more likely to display schizophrenic symptoms than their adoptive relatives are (APA, 1994; Gottesman, 1991; Kety, 1988, 1974).

**Chromosomal Mapping**    As with bipolar disorders (see Chapter 7), researchers have conducted *chromosomal mapping* research to identify more precisely the possible genetic factors in schizophrenia. In this strategy, they select large families in which schizophrenia is unusually common, take blood and DNA samples from all members of the families, and then compare the gene segments from schizophrenic family members with the gene segments from nonschizophrenic members. Applying this procedure to families from Iceland and England, Hugh Gurling and his colleagues (1989) found that a particular area on chromosome 5 of family members with schizophrenia had a different appearance from the same area on chromosome 5 of family members without schizophrenia. The researchers concluded that an abnormal gene or cluster of genes in this area of chromosome 5 establishes a predisposition in at least some cases of schizophrenia.

Although this research is promising, major problems remain to be solved (Holzman & Matthysse, 1990). Researchers have yet to isolate the gene or cluster of genes on chromosome 5 that may contribute to schizophrenia. In addition, studies of families in Sweden and Italy have found no consistent discrepancy on chromosome 5 (Macciardi et al., 1992; Kennedy et al., 1988). And still other studies have recently identified possible gene defects on chromosomes 9, 10, 11, 18, and 19 that may predispose individuals to develop schizophrenia (Bassett, 1992; Garofalo et al., 1992).

## Biochemical Factors

How might genetic factors lead to the development of schizophrenia? Biological research has pointed to two kinds of biological abnormalities, each of which could conceivably be inherited: biochemical abnormalities and abnormal brain structure. Let us first review the case for biochemical abnormalities.

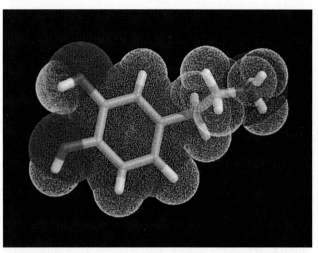

*A computer-drawn molecule of dopamine. Excessive activity of this neurotransmitter has been linked to schizophrenia and to amphetamine and cocaine psychosis, while low dopamine activity has been related to Parkinson's disease.*

Research conducted over the past two decades has suggested that in persons with schizophrenia, the neurons that use the neurotransmitter *dopamine* fire too often and transmit too many messages, thus producing the symptoms of the disorder. The chain of events leading to this *dopamine hypothesis* began with the accidental discovery of *antipsychotic medications,* drugs that help remove the symptoms of schizophrenia.

As we shall see in the treatment section, the first group of antipsychotic medications, the *phenothiazines,* were discovered in the 1950s by researchers who were looking for effective antihistamine drugs to combat allergies. Although phenothiazines failed as antihistamines, their effectiveness in reducing schizophrenic symptoms eventually became apparent, and clinicians began prescribing them for most people with schizophrenia.

Researchers soon learned that these drugs also produce a very troublesome effect, muscular tremors identical to those seen in Parkinson's disease. When patients with schizophrenia were given an antipsychotic drug, most seemed to develop some form of Parkinsonian symptoms.

This undesired effect of antipsychotic drugs gave researchers their first important clue to the biology of schizophrenia. Medical scientists already knew that people with Parkinson's disease have abnormally low levels of the neurotransmitter dopamine in some areas of the brain and that insufficient dopamine is the reason for their uncontrollable shaking.

*Dopamine hypothesis*    The theory that schizophrenia results from excessive firing of neurons that use the neurotransmitter dopamine.

*Phenothiazines*    A group of antihistamine drugs that became the first group of effective antipsychotic medications.

Scientists put these pieces of information together and came up with a pair of important hypotheses. If antipsychotic drugs generate Parkinsonian symptoms while alleviating schizophrenia, perhaps they operate by reducing dopamine activity. And if lowering dopamine activity alleviates the symptoms of schizophrenia, perhaps schizophrenia is related to excessive dopamine activity in the first place.

### Establishing the Dopamine-Schizophrenia Link

Since the 1960s, research has both supported and enlarged upon the dopamine hypothesis. It has been found, for example, that some people with Parkinson's disease develop schizophrenic symptoms if they take too much *L-dopa*, a drug used to raise dopamine levels and reduce tremors in patients with Parkinson's disease (Davis et al., 1988). Presumably the L-dopa raises their dopamine activity to schizophrenia-inducing levels.

Support for the dopamine hypothesis has also come from research on amphetamines, drugs that, as we saw in Chapter 11, stimulate the central nervous system. Researchers first noticed during the 1970s that people who take high doses of amphetamines over an extended period of time may develop *amphetamine psychosis*, a syndrome that closely mimics schizophrenia and includes hallucinations and motor hyperactivity. They later found that antipsychotic drugs can correct amphetamine psychosis, just as they are able to alleviate the symptoms of schizophrenia, and furthermore, that even small doses of amphetamines exacerbate the symptoms of schizophrenia (Janowsky & Davis, 1976; Janowsky et al., 1973). Researchers eventually traced these relationships to dopamine activity (Snyder, 1976). They found that amphetamines increase dopamine activity in the brain, thus inducing or exacerbating schizophrenic symptoms.

Such findings have led researchers to believe that messages from dopamine-sending neurons to receptors on dopamine-receiving neurons, particularly to a subgroup of dopamine receptors called *D-2 receptors*, are transmitted too readily or too often in people with schizophrenia. This theory has an intuitive appeal because dopamine-receiving neurons have been found to play an active role in guiding and sustaining attention (Cohen et al., 1988). People whose attention mechanisms are grossly impaired might well be expected to suffer from the abnormalities of attention, perception, and thought that characterize schizophrenia.

Why might the dopamine synapses of people with schizophrenia be overactive? One possibility is that the dopamine-sending neurons of these individuals produce and store too much dopamine (Seidman, 1990; Carlsson, 1978). Another is that people with schizo-

phrenia have a larger than usual number of dopamine receptors, particularly D-2 receptors (Sedvall, 1990; Seidman, 1990). Remember that when dopamine carries a message to a receiving neuron, it binds to receptors on the membrane of the neuron. Inasmuch as more receptors with lead to more firing, the numerous dopamine receptors of people with schizophrenia may ensure greater synaptic activity and overtransmission of dopamine messages (Strange, 1992).

### Questioning the Dopamine Hypothesis

Although these studies are helping to unravel the biology of schizophrenia, their results may not be so clear-cut as they first appear. To begin with, the dopamine hypothesis and its focus on D-2 receptors may be overstated (Meltzer, 1992, 1987). The biggest challenge to this hypothesis has come from the discovery of a new group of effective antipsychotic drugs, referred to as *atypical antipsychotics*, which operate at both D-2 receptors *and* another group of receptors, called *D-1 receptors* (Gerlach & Hansen, 1992). This finding suggests to some researchers that D-2 receptors may be less important in schizophrenia and D-1 receptors more so than the dopamine hypothesis currently holds.

Even more challenging for the dopamine hypothesis is the finding that the atypical drugs also operate at receptors for the neurotransmitter *serotonin*. This finding has led some researchers to believe that excessive serotonin functioning may also play a key role in schizophrenia (Kane & Freeman, 1994).

Finally, in yet another challenge to the traditional dopamine hypothesis, a number of theorists are beginning to assert that excessive dopamine activity contributes only to Type I schizophrenia (Ragin et al., 1989; Crow, 1985). As we saw earlier, cases of Type I schizophrenia are those characterized by positive symptoms such as delusions and hallucinations, whereas Type II cases are marked by negative symptoms such as flat affect and loss of volition. Research has increasingly linked Type II schizophrenia to a totally different kind of biological abnormality—abnormal brain structure.

## Abnormal Brain Structure

During the past decade, researchers have linked schizophrenia, particularly Type II schizophrenia, to specific abnormalities in brain structure (Strange, 1992; Buchsbaum & Haier, 1987). This development has

*Atypical antipsychotic drugs*   A new group of antipsychotic drugs that have a different mechanism of action than the traditional drugs.

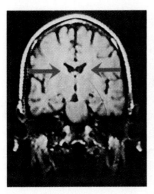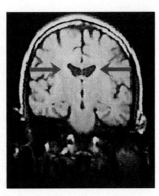

*In a study of fifteen pairs of identical twins in which one of each pair was diagnosed with schizophrenia, magnetic resonance imaging (MRI) revealed that the brain of the twin with schizophrenia (right) almost always had larger ventricles—butterfly-shaped spaces filled with fluid and located between the lobes—than the other (left).*

been made possible by improvements in autopsy tissue analyses and by the development of the computerized technologies (such as computerized axial tomography, positron emission tomography, and magnetic resonance imaging) that can produce pictures of brain structure and brain activity without harming the brain in the process (see p. 43).

Using these technologies, researchers have consistently found that many people with schizophrenia have *enlarged ventricles*—the brain cavities that contain cerebrospinal fluid—particularly on the left side of their brain (Cannon & Marco, 1994; Weinberger & Kleinman, 1986). Moreover, patients with enlarged ventricles tend to display more negative and fewer positive symptoms of schizophrenia, a poorer premorbid social adjustment, greater cognitive disturbances, and poorer responses to traditional antipsychotic drugs (Bornstein et al., 1992; Klausner et al., 1992).

Other kinds of structural abnormalities, quite possibly related to enlarged ventricles, have also been found in the brains and skulls of patients with Type II schizophrenia. Some studies suggest that these people have smaller frontal lobes, cerebrums, and craniums than people without schizophrenia (Raine et al., 1992; Suddath et al., 1990) and, perhaps most important, a reduced blood flow in their brains (Buchsbaum & Haier, 1987).

What might cause the ventricle enlargements, blood flow problems, or other structural abnormalities that seem to accompany many cases of schizophrenia? Various studies have collected evidence that such abnormalities may be caused by genetic factors, birth complications, immune reactions, or toxins (DeLisi et al., 1992, 1986; Andreasen et al., 1986). And, in a recent popular theory, several researchers suggest that the brain abnormalities may be the result of pre-birth ex-

posure to viruses. They hypothesize that the viruses enter the fetus's brain during pregnancy and remain latent until puberty or young adulthood, when they are reactivated by hormonal changes or another viral infection, thus causing schizophrenic symptoms (Torrey et al., 1993; Torrey, 1991).

Although investigators are only beginning to understand the precise nature and meaning of brain structure abnormalities, this research has already indicated that the biological underpinnings of schizophrenia are more complex than anyone had imagined. Together the biochemical and brain structure findings are shedding light on the mysteries of schizophrenia. At the same time, it is important to recognize that many people who manifest these biochemical and structural abnormalities never develop schizophrenia. Why not? Possibly, as we noted earlier, because biological factors merely set the stage for schizophrenia, while key sociocultural and psychological factors must be present for the disorder to unfold.

*Summing Up*
*Sociocultural theorists relate schizophrenia to the impact of labeling and to certain patterns of family dysfunctioning. Traditional psychodynamic theorists explain the disorder as a regression to a pre-ego state followed by efforts to restore ego control. Behaviorists use operant principles to explain schizophrenia, existentialists see it as a curative trip inward, and cognitive theorists believe that it is the outcome of efforts to make sense of strange sensory experiences. The leading biological explanations tie Type I schizophrenia to high activity of dopamine and Type II schizophrenia to enlarged ventricles and other abnormalities in brain structure. Only the biological explanations have received wide research support.*

# Treatments for Schizophrenia

For years, efforts at treating schizophrenia brought only frustration. Lara Jefferson, a young woman with schizophrenia, wrote of her treatment experience in the 1940s:

> They call us insane—and in reality they are as inconsistent as we are, as flighty and changeable. This one in particular. One day he derides and ridicules me unmercifully; the next he talks to me sadly and this

morning his eyes misted over with tears as he told me of the fate ahead. Damn him and all of his wisdom! . . . I have tried to follow his suggestions but have not learned to think a bit differently. It was all wasted effort. Where has it got me?

(*Jefferson, 1948*)

For much of human history, patients with schizophrenia, like this woman, were considered hopeless. The disorder is still extremely difficult to treat, but clinicians are much more successful today than they were in the past. Much of the credit goes to the recently discovered antipsychotic drugs, which help many people with schizophrenia think rationally enough to engage in therapeutic programs that previously had a limited effect at best. A look at how treatment has progressed over the years will help us understand the nature and implications of today's approaches to this debilitating disorder.

## Past Institutional Care

For more than half of this century, society's response to schizophrenia was *institutionalization*, usually in a public facility. Because patients with this disorder failed to respond to traditional therapies, the principal goals of these establishments were restraint and custodial care (provision of food, shelter, and clothing). Patients rarely saw therapists and were largely neglected. Many were abused.

The move toward institutionalization actually began in 1793, when the French physician Philippe Pinel "unchained the insane" from virtual imprisonment at La Bicêtre asylum and began the practice of "moral treatment" (as we saw in Chapter 1). For the first time in centuries, patients with severe disturbances were viewed as human beings who should be cared for with sympathy and kindness. Pinel's ideas spread throughout Europe and the United States, and led to the creation of large mental hospitals rather than asylums to care for people with mental disorders (Goshen, 1967).

These new mental hospitals were to be havens from the stresses of daily life and offer a healthful psychological environment in which patients could work closely with therapists (Grob, 1966). States throughout the United States were required to establish public mental institutions, *state hospitals*, to supplement the private ones.

Eventually, however, the state hospital system developed serious problems. Wards became increasingly overcrowded, admissions kept rising, and state funding was unable to keep up with the increasing need for professional therapists. Between 1845 and 1955 the number of state hospitals and mental patients rose steadily while the quality of care declined. During this period, close to 300 state hospitals were established in the United States. The number of hospitalized patients on any given day rose from 2,000 in 1845 to nearly 600,000 in 1955.

*Francisco de Goya's early nineteenth century painting* The Madhouse, *depicting a typical mental hospital of his day, is strikingly similar to the portrayal in Ken Kesey's 1950s novel (later a play and film),* One Flew Over the Cuckoo's Nest.

The priorities of the public mental hospitals changed during those 110 years. In the face of overcrowding and understaffing, the emphasis shifted from humanitarian care to order-keeping and efficiency. In a throwback to the asylum period, disruptive patients were physically restrained, isolated, and punished; individual attention diminished. Chronic patients were transferred to chronic wards, or "back wards" (Bloom, 1984).

These back wards were in fact human warehouses that were filled with an aura of hopelessness. Staff members often relied on mechanical restraints such as straitjackets and handcuffs to deal with difficult patients. More "advanced" forms of intervention included medically debilitating approaches such as the lobotomy (see Box 13-2). Most of the patients on these wards suffered from schizophrenia (Hafner & an der Heiden, 1988).

## Improved Institutional Care

In the 1950s, clinicians developed two institutional interventions, *milieu therapy* and the *token economy program*—the former based primarily on humanistic principles and the latter on behavioral principles—that finally offered some hope to patients who had been languishing in institutions for years (Bloom, 1984). These approaches were particularly helpful in addressing the personal-care and self-image problems exacerbated by institutionalization. They were soon adopted by many institutions and are now standard features of institutional care.

### Milieu Therapy

The premise of **milieu therapy** is that the social milieu of institutions must change if patients are to make clinical progress, and that an institutional climate conducive to self-respect, individual responsibility, and meaningful activity must be established.

The pioneer of this approach was Maxwell Jones, a London psychiatrist who in 1953 converted a psychiatric ward of patients with various disorders into a **therapeutic community**. Patients were treated as persons capable of running their own lives and making their own decisions. They participated in institutional planning and government, attending community meetings where they worked with staff members to estab-

lish rules and determine sanctions. The atmosphere was one of mutual respect, interdependence, support, and openness. Patients were involved in a variety of constructive activities, including special projects, semipermanent jobs, occupational therapy, recreation, and community government. In short, their daily schedule resembled life outside the hospital.

Milieu-style programs have since been developed in institutions throughout the Western world. The programs have varied from setting to setting, but at a minimum staff members try to facilitate interactions (especially group interactions) between patients and staff, keep patients active, and establish higher expectations of what patients should be able to accomplish. Although research has been limited, it does appear that patients with schizophrenia in some milieu hospital programs have improved and left the hospital at higher rates than patients in custodial programs (Paul & Lentz, 1977). On the other hand, many of these patients remain impaired and must live in sheltered settings after their release.

Despite its limitations, milieu therapy continues to be practiced in many institutions, often as a helpful adjunct to other approaches (Ciompi et al., 1992). It has also had an impact on community treatment programs. We shall see later that programs established at halfway houses to ease individuals with schizophrenia back into community residential life often incorporate resident self-government, work schedules, and other features of milieu therapy.

### The Token Economy

In the 1950s behaviorists discovered that the systematic application of operant techniques could help change the dysfunctional patterns of patients hospitalized with schizophrenia (Ayllon, 1963; Ayllon & Michael, 1959). Programs that apply such techniques were given the name *token economy programs*.

In token economy programs, patients are rewarded whenever they behave acceptably according to an established set of criteria and are not rewarded when they behave unacceptably. The immediate rewards for acceptable behavior are often tokens that can later be used to purchase specific items or privileges; thus the name "token economy."

The acceptable behaviors that are typically targeted in such programs include caring for oneself (making one's bed, dressing oneself, and the like), working in a vocational program, speaking normally, abiding by ward rules, and exercising self-control. Earned tokens

---

*Milieu therapy* A humanistic approach to institutional treatment based on the premise that institutions can help patients recover by creating a climate conducive to self-respect, individual responsibility, and meaningful activity.

*Token economy* A behavioral program in which a person's desirable behaviors are reinforced systematically throughout the day by the awarding of tokens that can be exchanged for goods or privileges.

## Box 13-2

# *Lobotomy: How Could It Happen?*

In 1949 the *New York Times* reported on a medical procedure that appeared to offer hope to an enormous number of sufferers of severe mental disorders, people for whom it seemed no future was possible outside of very overcrowded state mental institutions:

Hypochondriacs no longer thought they were going to die, would-be suicides found life acceptable, sufferers from persecution complex forgot the machinations of imaginary conspirators. Prefrontal lobotomy, as the operation is called, was made possible by the localization of fears, hates, and instincts [in the prefrontal cortex of the brain]. It is fitting, then, that the Nobel Prize in medicine should be shared by Hess and Moniz. Surgeons now think no more of operations on the brain than they do of removing an appendix.

We now know that the lobotomy was hardly the miracle treatment

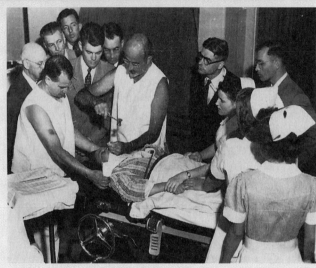

*Neuropsychiatrist Walter Freeman performs a lobotomy in 1949 by inserting a needle through a patient's eye socket into the brain.*

suggested in this report. In fact, far from "curing" people with mental disorders, the procedure left thousands upon thousands withdrawn, excessively subdued, and even stuporous. Yet, in the twenty-five years after the introduction of the lobotomy by the Portuguese neuropsychiatrist Egas Moniz in 1935, clinicians around the world considered psychosurgery to be an effective way to treat people suffer-

ing from schizophrenia and other severe mental disorders.

Moniz's particular lobotomy procedure, called a *prefrontal leukotomy*, consisted of drilling two holes in either side of the skull and inserting an instrument resembling an icepick into the brain tissue to cut or destroy nerve fibers. Moniz's theory was based on his belief that serious mental disorders were caused by "fixed thoughts" that interfered with mental functioning. The abnormal thought patterns could be altered, he believed, if the appropriate nerve pathways in the brain were cut.

In examining the factors that contributed to the widespread acceptance of the lobotomy in the 1940s and 1950s, the neuroscientist Elliot Valenstein (1986) considers one of the most important factors to have been the extreme overcrowding in mental hospitals at the time. This crowding was

can typically be exchanged for rewards such as food, cigarettes, hospital privileges, and entertainment. To keep widening a patient's repertoire of appropriate behaviors, clinicians must periodically introduce new target behaviors and reinforcements.

Research suggests that token economies do help change schizophrenic patterns and related inappropriate behaviors (Emmelkamp, 1994; Belcher, 1988). In one of the most successful such programs, Gordon Paul and R. L. Lentz (1977) applied operant principles to twenty-eight chronic patients with schizophrenia whose dysfunctional behaviors included mutism, repeated screaming, incontinence, smearing feces on walls, and physical assault. The program addressed every aspect of the patients' lives.

Most patients improved significantly under this program. By the end of the program, four and a half years later, 98 percent of the subjects had been released, usually to shelter care facilities. In comparison, patients treated in a milieu program made fewer gains and had a lower release rate (71 percent). Given such success, it is no wonder that token economy programs are used in many hospital settings (Emmelkamp, 1994).

Despite the effectiveness of many token economy programs, clinicians have often voiced ethical and legal concerns about them. In order for such programs to be effective, administrators need to control the important reinforcements in a patient's life, including, theoretically, basic reinforcements such as food, a com-

making it difficult to maintain decent standards in the hospitals, a problem being exacerbated by the multitude of returning World War II veterans who required treatment for emotional problems.

Valenstein also points to the personalities of the inventors and advocates of psychosurgery as important factors. Although he does not deny the fact that Moniz and his American counterpart, Walter Freeman, were gifted and dedicated physicians, Valenstein also calls attention to their desire for professional status. Just three months after seeing how the destruction of the prefrontal brain lobes in monkeys and chimpanzees had sedated them, Moniz performed the first prefrontal leukotomy on a human being.

Today it is hard to believe that respected physicians and scientists around the world would condone, much less applaud, this kind of impulsive experimentation on human beings. Moniz's prestige and capacity for diplomacy were so great, however, and the field of neurology was so small, that his work received relatively little criticism. Furthermore, for many peo-

ple, this "cure" seemed to offer an economic and social relief that was just too desirable to resist (Swayze, 1995).

In the 1940s Walter Freeman and his surgical partner, James Watts, developed a second kind of psychosurgery called the *transorbital lobotomy,* in which the surgeon inserted a needle into the brain through the eye socket and rotated it in order to destroy the brain tissue.

Physicians may have been misled by the initial outcome studies of lobotomy, which were methodologically flawed and offered no placebo comparison groups (Swayze, 1995; Valenstein, 1986). Apparently they were also captivated by glowing written reports of postoperative patient responses to lobotomy. By the 1950's, however, studies revealed that in addition to having a fatality rate of 1.5 to 6 percent, lobotomy resulted in objectionable physical consequences such as brain seizures, huge weight gain, loss of motor coordination, partial paralysis, incontinence, endocrine problems, and extreme intellectual and emotional unresponsiveness.

In the 1950s, concern also developed that psychosurgery might be used to control the perpetrators of violent crimes, and lobotomy became a civil rights issue as well. Furthermore, with the discovery of antipsychotic drugs, the lobotomy began to look like an expensive, complicated, and inhumane way of treating mental disorders. By 1960 the number of lobotomies being performed had been drastically reduced.

Today psychosurgery of any kind is rare. It is, in fact, considered experimental and used only as a last resort in the most severe cases of obsessive-compulsive disorder and depression (Goodman et al., 1992; Greist, 1992). Psychosurgical procedures have also been greatly refined, and hardly resemble the blind and brutal lobotomies of forty and fifty years ago. Yet despite such improvements, many professionals believe that any kind of surgery aimed specifically at destroying brain tissue is unethical, and argue that even a limited use of psychosurgery keeps alive one of the clinical field's most shameful and ill-advised efforts at cure.

---

fortable bed, and the like. But aren't there some items in life to which all human beings are entitled? A number of important court decisions have now affirmed that patients have certain basic rights that clinicians cannot violate, irrespective of the positive goals of a treatment program, including the right of free access to food, storage space, and furniture, as well as freedom of movement (Emmelkamp, 1994).

Some clinicians have also questioned the quality of the improvement achieved under token economy programs. Are behaviorists altering a patient's schizophrenic thoughts and perceptions in such programs or simply improving the patient's ability to mimic normal behavior? This issue is illustrated in the case of a middle-aged man with schizophrenia named John, who

had the delusion that he was the United States government. Whenever he spoke to others, he spoke as the government. "We are happy to see you. . . . We need people like you in our service. . . . We are carrying out our activities in John's body." When John's hospital ward was converted into a token economy, the staff members targeted his delusional statements, requiring him to identify himself properly to earn tokens.

After a few months on the token economy program, John stopped presenting himself as the government. When asked his name, he would say, "John." Although staff members were understandably pleased by his improvement, John himself had a different view of the situation. In a private discussion he said:

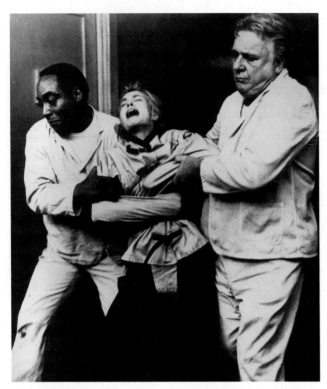

*For much of this century, state hospitals across the United States largely relied on mechanical restraints as a method of controlling patients. Patients were often tied to their beds or put in restraints such as the straitjacket (depicted in the film biography* Frances*).*

> We're tired of it. Every damn time we want a cigarette, we have to go through their bullshit. "What's your name? . . . Who wants the cigarette? . . . Where is the government?" Today, we were desperate for a smoke and went to Simpson, the damn nurse, and she made us do her bidding. "Tell me your name if you want a cigarette. What's your name?" Of course, we said, "John." We needed the cigarettes. If we told her the truth, no cigarettes. But we don't have time for this nonsense. We've got business to do. . . . And these people keep playing their games.
>
> *(Comer, 1973)*

Critics of the behavioral approach would argue that John was still delusional and therefore as "schizophrenic" as before. Behaviorists, however, would defend John's progress, arguing that he had improved by learning to keep his delusion to himself and at the very least had improved in his judgments about the consequences of his behavior. They also might see this as an important step toward changing his private thinking.

Token economy programs are no longer as popular as they once were (Glynn, 1990), but they are still employed in many mental hospitals, usually along with medication, and in some community residences as well. The token economy approach has also been ap-

plied with some success to other clinical problems, including mental retardation, delinquency, and hyperactivity, as well as in other fields, such as education and business.

## Antipsychotic Drugs

Milieu therapy and token economy programs helped to improve the gloomy prognosis for schizophrenia, but it was the discovery of antipsychotic drugs in the 1950s that truly revolutionized its treatment (Breslin, 1992; Weinberger, 1991). These drugs eliminate many symptoms of this disorder and today are almost always a part of treatment.

As we observed earlier, the discovery of antipsychotic medications dates back to the discovery of **antihistamine drugs,** drugs developed to combat allergies. The French surgeon Henri Laborit soon discovered that one group of antihistamines, **phenothiazines,** were also useful adjuncts to surgical anesthesia. They helped to calm patients before surgery, while allowing them to remain awake. Laborit and others experimented with several phenothiazine antihistamines and became most impressed with one called *chlorpromazine.*

Laborit suspected that chlorpromazine might also have a calming effect on persons with mental disorders. The psychiatrists Jean Delay and Pierre Deniker (1952) soon tested the drug on six psychotic patients and reported a sharp reduction in their symptoms. In 1954, chlorpromazine went on the market in the United States as an antipsychotic medication under the trade name Thorazine.

Since the discovery of the phenothiazines, other kinds of antipsychotic drugs have been developed. Collectively they are known as **neuroleptic drugs,** because they often produce effects similar to the symptoms of neurological diseases. As we saw earlier, these drugs apparently reduce schizophrenic symptoms by binding to receptors in the brain that usually receive the neurotransmitter dopamine, blocking dopamine from binding there, and thus reducing excessive activity of the neurotransmitter (Strange, 1992; Davis et al., 1988).

### The Effectiveness of Antipsychotic Drugs

Research has repeatedly shown that antipsychotic drugs reduce schizophrenic symptoms in around two-thirds of patients (Strange, 1992; Davis et al., 1988). Moreover, they emerge as the single most effective in-

---

*Chlorpromazine* A phenothiazine drug commonly used for treating schizophrenia. Marketed as Thorazine.

tervention for schizophrenia in direct comparisons with other forms of treatment such as psychodynamic therapy, milieu therapy, and electroconvulsive therapy (May et al., 1981; May & Tuma, 1964). Research has also indicated that schizophrenic symptoms return for some patients if they stop taking antipsychotic drugs too soon (Davis et al., 1993).

Recent research has indicated that antipsychotic drugs alleviate the *positive symptoms* of schizophrenia, such as hallucinations and delusions, more completely, or at least more quickly, than the *negative symptoms,* such as flat affect, poverty of speech, and loss of volition (Leff, 1992; Breier et al., 1991). Correspondingly, people dominated by positive symptoms (Type I schizophrenia) display generally higher recovery rates from schizophrenia, while those with negative symptoms (Type II schizophrenia) are less affected by drug treatment and have a poorer prognosis (Lindstrom et al., 1992; Pogue-Geile, 1989).

Antipsychotic drugs have now achieved widespread acceptance in the treatment of schizophrenia. Patients often dislike the powerful impact of these drugs, and some refuse to take them; but like Edward Snow, a writer who overcame schizophrenia, many are greatly helped by the medications.

> In my case it was necessary to come to terms with a specified drug program. I am a legalized addict. My dose: 100 milligrams of Thorazine and 60 milligrams of Stelazine daily. I don't feel this dope at all, but I have been told it is strong enough to flatten a normal person. It keeps me—as the doctors agree—sane and in good spirits. Without the brain candy, as I call it, I would go—zoom—right back into the bin. I've made the institution scene enough already to be familiar with what it's like and to know I don't want to go back.
> (*Snow, 1976*)

## Unwanted Effects of Antipsychotic Drugs

Unfortunately, in addition to their impact on schizophrenic symptoms, antipsychotic drugs sometimes produce disturbing movement abnormalities that may affect appearance and functioning (Pickar et al., 1991) (see Figure 13-3). These effects are called *extrapyramidal effects* because they appear to be caused by the drugs' impact on the extrapyramidal areas of the brain, areas that regulate motor activity. The effects include *Parkinsonian and related symptoms, neuroleptic malignant syndrome,* and *tardive dyskinesia.*

*Extrapyramidal effects*    Unwanted movements, such as severe shaking, bizarre-looking contractions of the face and body, and extreme restlessness, sometimes induced by traditional antipsychotic drugs, resulting from the effect of the drugs on the extrapyramidal areas of the brain.

**Parkinsonian and Related Symptoms**    As we saw earlier, antipsychotic drugs often produce effects that resemble the symptoms of the neurological disorder Parkinson's disease (Strange, 1992). Patients may experience such severe and continuous muscle tremors and muscle rigidity that they shake, move very slowly, shuffle their feet, and show little facial expression. Related undesired effects are *dystonia,* characterized by involuntary muscle contractions that cause bizarre and uncontrollable movements of the face, neck, tongue, and back; and *akathisia,* marked by a very high degree of restlessness, agitation, and discomfort in the limbs.

In most cases these unwanted effects can be reversed by prescribing an anti-Parkinsonian drug along with the antipsychotic drug. Alternatively, clinicians may reduce the dose of the antipsychotic drug or stop it altogether.

**Neuroleptic Malignant Syndrome**    In a small percentage of cases antipsychotic drugs produce *neuroleptic malignant syndrome,* a severe, potentially fatal reaction marked by muscle rigidity, fever, altered consciousness, and dysfunctions of the autonomic nervous system (Hermesh et al., 1992; Singh, 1981). The syndrome is treated by the immediate stoppage of antipsychotic drugs, along with interventions to reduce its various symptoms (Velamoor et al., 1994; Levenson, 1985).

**Tardive Dyskinesia**    *Tardive dyskinesia* means "late-appearing movement disorder." Whereas many of the other undesirable drug effects appear within days or

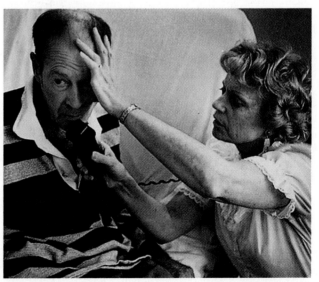

*This man has a severe case of Parkinson's disease, and his muscle tremors prevent him from shaving himself. Antipsychotic drugs often produce similar Parkinsonian symptoms.*

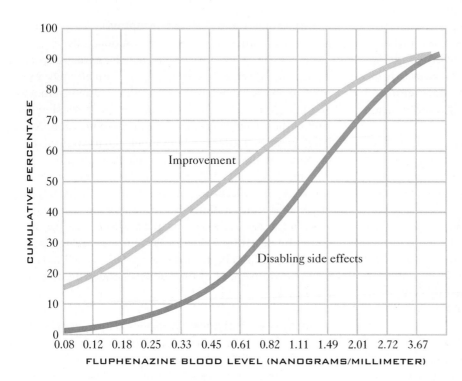

Figure 13-3    *The reactions of patients with schizophrenia to the traditional antipsychotic drug fluphenazine (Prolixin) demonstrate the close relationship between drug dosage, patient improvement, and serious unwanted drug effects. As blood levels of the drug increase, so do patient improvement and disabling unwanted drug effects. At higher levels of the drug, the benefits-risk trade-off becomes highly arguable. (Adapted from Barondes, 1993, p. 162.)*

weeks, tardive dyskinesia usually does not unfold until a person has taken antipsychotic drugs for more than a year. It consists of involuntary writhing or ticlike movements of the tongue, mouth, face, or whole body, and may include involuntary chewing, sucking, and lip smacking and jerky, purposeless movements of the arms, legs, or entire body.

Although most cases of tardive dyskinesia are mild and involve a single symptom such as tongue flicking, some are severe and include such features as irregular breathing and grotesque contortions of the face and body. It is believed that between 20 and 30 percent of the people who take antipsychotic drugs for an extended period of time develop tardive dyskinesia to some degree (APA, 1994; Strange, 1992). Apparently, people over 55 years of age are particularly vulnerable.

Tardive dyskinesia can be difficult, sometimes impossible, to eliminate. If it is discovered early and the antipsychotic drugs are stopped immediately, it will usually disappear (APA, 1994; Pickar et al., 1991). Early detection, however, is elusive. Some of the symptoms are so similar to schizophrenic symptoms that clinicians may overlook them, continue antipsychotic drug therapy, and inadvertently create a more serious case of tardive dyskinesia. The longer patients continue taking antipsychotic drugs, the less likely it is that their tardive dyskinesia will disappear when the antipsychotic drugs are finally stopped.

**Current Prescription Practices**    Clinicians are now wiser and more careful in their prescription practices

than they were in past years. In the past, when a patient did not respond to a neuroleptic drug, clinicians would keep increasing the dose (Kane, 1992); today they typically stop the neuroleptic drug in such cases (Simhandl & Meszaros, 1992). Similarly, today's clinicians try to prescribe the lowest effective dose of antipsychotic drugs for each patient and to reduce or halt medication weeks or months after the patient reestablishes nonpsychotic functioning (Kane, 1990, 1987). Unfortunately, however, as we noted earlier, some patients, particularly chronic patients, cannot hold their own without medications (Remington et al., 1993).

*Consider This*

In the early years of antipsychotic drug use, clinicians often kept raising dosages for hospitalized patients who failed to respond to the drugs, until many such patients seemed to be "walking zombies." Why might clinicians have continued this medication strategy, even in cases where the drugs failed to reduce symptoms? Might there be less than admirable reasons for these hospital prescription practices?

## New Antipsychotic Drugs

In recent years research has yielded several new antipsychotic drugs that may be given to patients who do not respond to, cannot tolerate, or are endangered by the traditional drugs. The most effective and widely used of these new drugs is *clozapine*, trade name

Clozaril (Buckley et al., 1994; Meltzer, 1991). Clozapine is considered an *atypical* antipsychotic drug because its biological impact differs from that of traditional antipsychotic medications. It has been found to be significantly more effective than the traditional drugs, helping approximately 80 to 85 percent of persons with schizophrenia, including those with negative symptoms (Breier et al., 1994; Kane, 1992).

Another major benefit of clozapine is that it causes few extrapyramidal symptoms, apparently because it does not block as many dopamine receptors as traditional neuroleptic drugs (Chengappa et al., 1994; Gerlach & Hansen, 1992). More important, few, if any, cases of tardive dyskinesia have been attributed to clozapine, even after prolonged treatment (Meltzer, 1993; Safferman et al., 1991). In addition, tardive dyskinesia and other extrapyramidal symptoms are often reduced when patients with schizophrenia are switched to clozapine (Clozapine Study Group, 1993; Levin et al., 1992).

Yet clozapine has some serious problems of its own (Banov et al., 1993). People who use this drug have a 1 to 2 percent risk of developing *agranulocytosis,* a life-threatening drop in white blood cells (granulocytes). Patients who take clozapine need frequent blood tests so that this unwanted effect can be detected early and the drug stopped. Because clozapine can induce agranulocytosis, it has been approved by the FDA only for patients who do not improve with traditional neuroleptic drugs.

# Psychotherapy

Before the discovery of antipsychotic drugs, psychotherapy was not really a viable option as a treatment for schizophrenia. Most patients with schizophrenia were simply too far removed from reality to profit from therapy.

Today, however, psychotherapy is successfully employed in many cases of schizophrenia, thanks to the discovery and effectiveness of antipsychotic drugs. By helping to relieve thought and perceptual disturbances, the drugs enable people with schizophrenia to play an active role in the therapeutic process, think more clearly about themselves and their relationships, and make changes in their behavior (Boker, 1992). The most helpful forms of psychotherapy include insight therapy, social therapy, and family therapy.

## Insight Therapy

A variety of insight therapies are now applied to schizophrenia (Wasylenki, 1992; Ernst, 1985). Studies suggest that insight therapists who are more experienced with schizophrenia have greater success, often regardless of their particular orientation (Karon, 1988, 1985; Lamb, 1982). According to one study, therapists who are successful with patients with schizophrenia tend to take a more active role than less successful therapists, setting limits, expressing opinions, challenging patients' statements, and providing guidance (Whitehorn & Betz, 1975). At the same time, the issue of gaining a patient's trust is a major part of such therapy.

## Social Therapy

Many clinicians make practical advice and life adjustment a central focus of treatment for people with schizophrenia. They direct therapy toward such issues as problem solving, decision making, development of social skills, and medication self-management (Liberman & Corrigan, 1993; Wixted et al., 1988). Therapists may also help their clients find work, financial assistance, and proper housing. Research has clarified that this kind of intervention, labeled *social therapy,* or *sociotherapy,* helps keep patients out of the hospital, especially those who are also taking antipsychotic medications (Hogarty et al., 1986, 1974).

## Family Therapy

Between 25 and 40 percent of community residents who are recovering from schizophrenia live with their families (Torrey et al., 1988; Lamb & Goertzel, 1977). Such unions create special pressures for both the patients and the family members.

Patients who are recovering from schizophrenia are greatly affected by the behavior and reactions of family members, even if family dysfunction was not a factor in the onset of the patients' disorder (Kreisman et al., 1988). It has been found, for example, that persons with schizophrenia who have positive perceptions of their relatives have better treatment outcomes (Lebell et al., 1993). Similarly, released patients whose relatives have high levels of *expressed emotion*—that is, high levels of criticism, emotional overinvolvement, and hostility—often have a higher relapse rate than those who return to cooler, less emotional relatives (Mavreas et al., 1992; Vaughan et al., 1992).

Family members, for their part, are often greatly affected by the behavior of a relative with schizophrenia living at home. Investigators found many family members to be greatly disturbed by the social withdrawal and unusual behaviors of relatives with schizophrenia (Creer & Wing, 1974). One family member complained, "In the evening you go into the sitting room and it's in darkness. You turn on the light and there he is just sitting there, staring in front of him."

To address such family issues, clinicians now commonly include family therapy in the treatment of schizophrenia (Domenici & Griffin-Francell, 1993; Goldstein, 1991, 1987). Family therapy provides family members with guidance, training, practical advice, education about schizophrenia (*psychoeducation*), and emotional support and empathy. It helps family members become more realistic in their expectations, more tolerant, less guilt-ridden, and more willing to try new patterns of interaction and communication. Over the course of treatment, family therapists also try to help the individual with schizophrenia cope with the pressures of family life, make better use of family resources, and avoid problematic interactions.

Family therapy often succeeds in improving communication and reducing tensions within the family. As such, it helps relapse rates to go down, particularly when combined with drug therapy (Zastowny et al., 1992; Mueser & Glynn, 1990).

Finally, the families of persons with schizophrenia may also need outside social support to be of most help to their troubled relatives (Perlick et al., 1992), and a number of *family support groups* and *family psychoeducational programs* have been organized (Hyde & Goldman, 1992). In such programs, family members come together with others in the same situation, share their thoughts and emotions, receive support, and learn about schizophrenia. Although research has yet to determine the usefulness of these groups, such approaches are becoming increasingly common.

# The Community Approach

Partly in response to the deplorable conditions in public mental institutions, Congress passed a bill called the Community Mental Health Act in 1963. According to this act, mental patients were to receive a range of mental health services—outpatient therapy, inpatient treatment, emergency care, preventive care, and aftercare—right in their communities rather than far from home. The act was intended to address a variety of psychological disorders, but patients with schizophrenia, especially those who had been institutionalized for years, were targeted and affected more than most. The government was ordering that these patients be released and treated in the community. Other countries around the world put similar community care programs into action shortly thereafter (Torrey, 1988; Hafner & an der Heiden, 1988).

Thus began three decades of *deinstitutionalization,* an exodus of hundreds of thousands of schizophrenic and other chronic mental patients from state institutions into the community. On a given day in 1955 close to 600,000 patients were living in state institu-

tions; today around 100,000 patients reside there (Manderscheid & Sonnenschein, 1992).

During these decades of deinstitutionalization, clinicians have learned that patients recovering from schizophrenia can profit greatly from community-based programs. Unfortunately, the quality and funding of community care for patients with schizophrenia have at the same time been grossly inadequate throughout the United States, leading to a "revolving door" syndrome in which patients are repeatedly released to the community, readmitted to an institution within months, released again, admitted yet again, and so on (Geller, 1992).

## Effective Community Care

Community residents recovering from schizophrenia need medication, psychotherapy, help in handling daily pressures and responsibilities, guidance in making decisions, training in social skills, residential supervision, and vocational counseling and training. According to research, patients whose communities systematically address these needs make greater progress than patients living in other communities (Hogarty, 1993). Some of the key elements in effective community care programs are coordination of patient services, short-term hospitalization, partial hospitalization, halfway houses, and occupational training.

**Coordinated Services**   The government commission whose work led to the Community Mental Health Act originally proposed that the cornerstone of community care should be a *community mental health center,* a treatment facility that would provide medication, psychotherapy, and inpatient emergency care to people with severe disorders. In addition, the community mental health center was to coordinate the patient services offered by other community agencies. When community mental health centers do in fact provide these services for patients with schizophrenia, the patients often make steady and significant progress (Madianos & Madianou, 1992). Coordination of services is particularly important for patients who have a dual diagnosis of schizophrenia and substance abuse, the so-called *mentally ill chemical abusers (MICAs)* (see Box 13-3).

**Short-Term Hospitalization**   When people develop schizophrenic symptoms, today's clinicians first try to treat them on an outpatient basis, usually administering antipsychotic medication and perhaps psychotherapy. If these interventions prove inadequate, short-term hospitalization that lasts a few weeks, rather than months or years, may be tried (Davis et al., 1988). As soon as the patients are stabilized, they are released for a program of posthospitalization care and treatment, or *aftercare,* out in the community (Sederer, 1992; Lamb, 1988).

**Partial Hospitalization** For people whose needs fall somewhere between full hospitalization and outpatient therapy sessions, some communities offer partial hospitalization at *day centers* or *day hospitals* (Kennedy, 1992; Hoge et al., 1988). These centers provide daily activities and specific treatment programs for patients, and programs to help them improve their social skills. Several studies suggest that patients recovering from schizophrenia in day centers often do better than those in programs that provide extended hospitalization or traditional outpatient therapy (Creed et al., 1989; Herz et al., 1971).

**Halfway Houses** *Halfway houses* are residences for people who do not require hospitalization but cannot live either alone or with their families. These residences, typically large houses in areas where housing is inexpensive, usually shelter between one and two dozen people. Although outside mental health professionals may be available to residents, the live-in staff usually consists of *paraprofessionals*—lay people who have received some training in providing emotional support and practical guidance about matters of daily living. The halfway houses are usually run with a milieu therapy philosophy that emphasizes support and resident responsibility. Various patient populations reside in such houses; patients with schizophrenia are among the most common.

Research indicates that halfway houses help many people recovering from schizophrenia adjust to community life and avoid rehospitalization (Simpson et al., 1989; Caton, 1982). In the following passage, a woman describes how living in such a residence (after ten hospitalizations in twelve years) contributed to her recovery from schizophrenia:

> The halfway house changed my life. First of all, I discovered that some of the staff members had once been clients in the program! That one single fact offered me hope. For the first time, I saw proof that a program could help someone, that it was possible to regain control over one's life and become independent. The house was democratically run; all residents had one vote and the staff members, outnumbered 5 to 22, could not make rules or even discharge a client from the program without majority sentiment. There was a house bill of rights that was strictly observed by all. We helped one another and gave support. When residents were in a crisis, no staff member hustled them off or increased their medication to calm them

down. Residents could cry, be comforted and hugged until a solution could be found, or until they accepted that it was okay to feel bad. . . . Choices were real, and failure and success were accepted equally.
>
> (Lovejoy, 1982, pp. 605–609)

**Occupational Training** Regular employment enables people to support themselves, exercise independence, gain self-respect, and learn to work with others. It also helps bring companionship and order to a person's daily life. For these reasons, occupational training and placement are important aspects of community treatment for people with schizophrenia (Leshner et al., 1992).

Many people with this disorder may, for example, receive occupational training in a *sheltered workshop,* a protected and supervised workplace for employees who are not ready for competitive or complicated jobs. For some the sheltered workshop becomes a permanent workplace. For others it is an important step toward better-paying and more complex outside employment or a return to their previous job or its equivalent.

Unfortunately, in the United States vocational rehabilitation is not consistently available to people with chronic schizophrenia or other severe mental disorders. One study found that only 25 percent of such people are employed, less than 10 percent outside of sheltered workplaces (Mulkern & Manderscheid, 1989).

## Inadequacies in Community Treatment

As we have observed, effective community programs clearly can help patients with schizophrenia recover. Unfortunately, however, less than half of all people with schizophrenia receive appropriate community

*Sheltered workshops, such as the one at New York City's Fountain House, provide job training and jobs and teach independence, self-respect, and social skills.*

## Box 13-3

# "Mentally Ill Chemical Abusers": A Challenge for Treatment

A state appeals court yesterday ordered Larry Hogue, who has for years frightened residents of Manhattan's Upper West Side with his bizarre behavior, to remain in a state mental hospital until a hearing next week. . . . Before he was arrested, Mr. Hogue had attacked passers-by and cars in the area around West 96th Street and Amsterdam Avenue. . . . Mr. Hogue has been arrested 30 times and served at least six terms in prison, ranging from five days to a year, according to law-enforcement records. He now faces charges of criminal mischief for scraping the paint off a car last August.

(New York Times, February 9, 1993)

Larry Hogue, nicknamed the "Wild Man of West 96th Street" by

*The case of Larry Hogue, the so-called "Wild Man of West 96th Street," has helped bring the plight of MICAs to public attention.*

his neighbors, is a *mentally ill chemical abuser (MICA)*, an individual who suffers from both a mental disorder (in his case schizophrenia) and a substance-related disorder. Between 20 and 50 percent of all people who suffer from chronic mental disorders may be MICAs (Polcin, 1992).

MICAs tend to be young and male. They often have lower-than-

average levels of social functioning and school achievement and increased levels of poverty, acting-out behavior, emergency room visits, and encounters with the criminal justice system (Bartels et al., 1993; O'Hare, 1992). MICAs commonly experience greater distress and have poorer treatment outcomes than non-substance-abusing patients with mental disorders (Carey et al., 1991).

The relationship between substance abuse and mental dysfunctioning is complex. A mental disorder may precede substance abuse, and the drug may be a form of self-medication or the result of impaired judgment (Polcin, 1992). Conversely, substance abuse may cause or exacerbate psychopathology. Cocaine, for example, exacerbates the symptoms of psychosis

---

mental health services (Von Korff et al., 1985). Two factors are primarily responsible: poor coordination of services and shortage of services.

**Poor Coordination of Services**   Often there is no communication among the various agencies in a community (Leshner et al., 1992). The advice that a patient receives in a day center may differ from that dispensed at the community mental health center; similarly, there could be an opening at a nearby halfway house and the therapist at the community mental health center might not even know about it. In addition, community agencies often cannot even provide patients with continuing contacts with the same staff members.

Poor communication between state hospitals and the state's various community mental health centers is also a barrier to good mental health care (McShane & Redoutey, 1987). In many cases, community agencies

are not even informed when patients are discharged from the hospital. Moreover, institutional care is so expensive today that hospitals often feel pressured to release patients before a discharge plan has been completed.

**Shortage of Services**   The number of community programs in existence for people with schizophrenia falls decidedly short of the number needed. Although there are now close to 800 community mental health centers in the United States, it is estimated that nearly three times that many are necessary. There is also a severe shortage of halfway houses and sheltered workshops.

Perhaps even more disturbing, in many areas the community mental health centers that do exist fail to provide adequate services for the people with schizophrenia whom they purport to treat. Often the centers devote their efforts to providing outpatient services for

and can cause schizophrenia to intensify quickly (Shaner et al., 1993). A third and perhaps the most compelling theory is that substance abuse and mental disorders interact to create a unique problem that is, so to speak, greater than the sum of its parts (Robertson, 1992). The course and outcome of one problem can be significantly influenced by the presence of the other disorder.

Treatment of MICAs has been undermined by the tendency of substance abuse to be underdiagnosed. Unrecognized substance abuse may lead to the misdiagnosis of mental disorders or the misunderstanding of the course and prognosis of a disorder (Shaner et al., 1993).

The treatment of MICAs is further complicated by the specialized nature of many mental health and substance abuse treatment facilities. Such facilities are often de-

signed and funded to treat primarily one disorder or the other, and few are either equipped or willing to treat both. As a result, it is not uncommon for MICA patients to be rejected as inappropriate for treatment in both substance abuse and mental health programs. Many MICAs fall through the cracks in this way and find themselves in jail or in homeless shelters for want of the treatment they sought in vain (Polcin, 1992).

The ideal MICA treatment program appears to be a safe and supportive therapeutic environment that adopts both mental health and substance abuse treatment techniques and takes into account the unique effects of both problems (Fals & Schafer, 1992; Carey, 1989). One particularly promising development is the recent establishment of self-help groups for MICAs living in the community.

The problem of falling through

the cracks is perhaps most poignant in the case of homeless MICAs. Researchers estimate that 10 to 20 percent of homeless persons may be MICAs (Drake et al., 1991). Homeless MICAs typically are homeless longer than other homeless persons and are more likely to experience extremely harsh conditions (such as living on the winter streets rather than in a homeless shelter), to be jailed, to grant sexual favors for food or money, and to be victimized. Thus, it has been suggested that treatment programs for homeless MICAs should seek to build trust, provide practical assistance, and include intensive case management with a commitment to long-term care (Drake et al., 1991). In short, treatment programs must be tailored to MICAs' unique combination of problems, rather than expecting them to adapt to traditional forms of treatment.

people with less disabling problems, such as anxiety and depressive disorders or problems in social adjustment. In some areas only a fraction of the patients treated by community mental health centers suffer from schizophrenia (Rosenstein et al., 1990, 1989; Torrey, 1988).

Why is there such a shortage of services for people with schizophrenia? First, most mental health professionals simply prefer to work with people whose problems are less severe and less chronic than schizophrenia (Harding et al., 1992). Second, community residents often object to the presence of community programs for recovering mental patients in their neighborhoods (Leshner et al., 1992). The third, and perhaps primary, reason for shortages in community care is economic. On the one hand, more public funds are allocated for people with mental disorders now than in the past (Redick et al., 1992; Torrey, 1988). On the other hand, relatively little of

this new money is going to community programs for the severely disturbed. Much of it still goes to state hospitals or to monthly subsistence payments such as social security disability income, subsidies for people with mental disturbances in nursing homes and general hospitals, and community services for people who are less disturbed.

### Consequences of Inadequate Community Treatment

What happens to persons with schizophrenia whose communities do not provide necessary services and whose families cannot afford private treatment? As we observed earlier, a large number receive no treatment at all; many others spend a short time in a state hospital and are then discharged prematurely, often without benefit of adequate follow-up treatment (Regier et al., 1993; Torrey et al., 1988).

As we observed earlier, many patients with schizophrenia return to their families, under whose care they may receive medication, perhaps emotional and financial support, but little else in the way of treatment. Between 5 and 11 percent enter an alternative institution such as a nursing home or rest home, where they receive only custodial care and medication (Smyer, 1989; Torrey et al., 1988).

As many as 35 percent are placed in single-room-occupancy hotels, boarding homes, or rooming houses, typically found in run-down inner-city neighborhoods (Torrey et al., 1988). In many such settings the persons live in a small room under conditions that are substandard and unsafe, surviving on government disability payments (Barker et al., 1992) and spending their days wandering through neighborhood streets. It is often said that these persons with schizophrenia are now being dumped and warehoused in the community, just as patients were once warehoused in institutions.

Finally, and perhaps saddest of all, a great number of people with schizophrenia have become homeless (Opler et al., 1994; Leshner et al., 1992). Many such persons are released hospital patients. Others are young adults who have not even received hospitalization in the first place. There are between 350,000 and 1 million street people in the United States. As many as one-third of them have a severe mental disorder, commonly schizophrenia (DeAngelis, 1994; Manderscheid & Rosenstein, 1992). An estimated 50,000 of them wind up in prisons when their pathology leads them to break the law (Glancy & Regehr, 1992; Leshner et al., 1992). The "lucky" ones find beds in public shelters. Certainly deinstitutionalization

*It is estimated that more than 100,000 of the homeless people in the United States suffer from schizophrenia or another severe mental disorder.*

and the community mental health movement have failed these people. Small wonder that many of them report feeling *relieved* when and if they return to hospital life: they no longer have to search fruitlessly to find housing, food, or treatment in the community (Drake & Wallach, 1992).

> *Consider This*
>
> Over the years, people with schizophrenia have been the victims of many treatment horrors, including confinement in asylums and back wards, lobotomies, misuse of antipsychotic drugs, and homelessness. Is there something about the features of this disorder or the way in which individuals with this disorder are viewed by others that has caused, allowed, or perpetuated such mistreatment?

## The Promise of Community Treatment

Despite these very serious problems, the demonstrated success and potential of proper community care for people recovering from schizophrenia continue to capture the interest of both clinicians and many government officials, who press for further development of community services. In recent years, for example, the federal government has created the Task Force on Homelessness and Severe Mental Illness, whose job is to find more effective ways for the federal government, states, and local organizations to meet the needs of people with mental disorders, with an emphasis on the needs of the homeless among them (Leshner et al., 1992). In 1992 the task force proposed such major initiatives as low-cost, stable housing for homeless people with mental disorders.

Another important development has been the formation of *national interest groups* that are successfully promoting community treatment for people with schizophrenia and other chronic problems (Rosenstein et al., 1989). One, the National Alliance for the Mentally Ill, now has more than 140,000 members in 1100 chapters (NAMI, 1994). Made up of family members of people with severe mental disorders, this group has become a powerful lobbying force in many state legislatures and has pressured community centers to provide treatment for persons with schizophrenia.

Today community care is a major aspect of treatment for patients recovering from schizophrenia in countries throughout the world (Liberman, 1994; Perris, 1988). Some countries, learning from the problems of deinstitutionalization in the United States, have managed to introduce their community programs in a better organized, less disruptive, and more successful manner. Clearly, both in the United States and abroad, wide-ranging and coordinated community treatment is viewed as an important part of the solution to the problem of schizophrenia.

*Summing Up*
*Antipsychotic drugs are now the most effective of all treatments for schizophrenia. Prior to their discovery, the only therapies that offered hope to patients with schizophrenia languishing in institutions were milieu therapy and token economy programs. The drugs help clear confused thinking and open the door to successful forms of psychotherapy, including insight, social, and family therapies. Research has shown that well-planned community treatment programs can play a major part in improving the lot of people with schizophrenia, but the promise of these programs has not been fulfilled, largely because of poor coordination and shortage of community services. Thus, many people with schizophrenia now live in one-room boarding homes, on the streets, or in prisons.*

## The State of the Field
## *Schizophrenia*

Schizophrenia, one of our species' most bizarre and frightening disorders, has been studied intensively throughout this century. Only since the discovery of antipsychotic drugs in the 1950s, however, have clinicians gained significant insight into its causes, particularly its biological causes.

Most clinical theorists now agree that schizophrenia is probably caused by a combination of factors. Many believe, for example, that genetic and biological factors establish a predisposition to develop the disorder, that psychological factors such as personal stress help bring the disorder to fruition, and that other psychological and sociocultural factors such as social labeling help maintain and exacerbate the symptoms.

Similarly, after years of frustration and failure in efforts to treat schizophrenia, clinicians finally have an arsenal of weapons with which to fight it—medication, institutional programs, psychotherapy, and community programs. These approaches can be combined to meet the specific needs of each individual.

Such approaches have greatly improved the chances that a person with schizophrenia will return to functional living, and today a large number of persons with this disorder are responding reasonably well to treatment. Today, even with the current inadequacies in community programs, up to 30 percent of persons with schizophrenia are believed to recover completely and permanently. Another 30 percent return to relatively independent lives, although their occupational and social functioning may continue to fall short of earlier levels.

Clinical practitioners have progressed considerably in developing effective treatment programs for schizophrenia, yet they still have far to go. It is intolerable that the majority of people with schizophrenia receive few or none of the effective community interventions that have been developed over the past three decades, worse still that tens of thousands have become homeless vagrants deserted by society. Although many factors have contributed to this state of affairs, neglect by clinical practitioners has certainly played a big role. It is now the task of these professionals, prodded by the newly developed interest groups and task forces, to address the needs of *all* people with schizophrenia.

## *Chapter Review*

1. *Schizophrenia:* Approximately 1 percent of the world's population suffers from schizophrenia.
2. *Symptoms:* The symptoms associated with schizophrenia fall into three groupings: *positive symptoms, negative symptoms,* and *psychomotor symptoms.*
   A. The leading positive symptoms in schizophrenia are *delusions, disorganized thinking and speech, hallucinations* and other disturbances in perception and attention, and *inappropriate affect.*
   B. Negative symptoms include *poverty of speech, blunted* and *flat affect, loss of volition,* and *social withdrawal.*
   C. The disturbances in psychomotor behavior are collectively called *catatonia.*
3. *Course of Schizophrenia:* Schizophrenia usually emerges during late adolescence or early adulthood and tends to progress through three phases, *prodromal, active,* and *residual.*
4. *Categories of Schizophrenia:* Patients may be placed in five categories of schizophrenia, according to DSM-IV criteria: *disorganized type, catatonic type, paranoid type, undifferentiated type,* and *residual type.* In addition, clinicians have distinguished between *Type I schizophrenia* and *Type II schizophrenia.*

5. *Explanations:* An interaction of sociocultural, biological, and psychological factors seems to contribute to schizophrenia.

  A. *Sociocultural Explanations:* One sociocultural view holds that society expects persons who are labeled as having schizophrenia to behave in certain ways, and these expectations help promote the further development of symptoms. The other sociocultural view points to family dysfunctioning as a cause of schizophrenia.

  B. *Psychological Explanations:* Several psychological explanations have been proposed for schizophrenia.

    (1) *Psychodynamic View:* Traditional psychodynamic theorists believe that schizophrenia involves *regression* to a pre-ego state of *primary narcissism* and efforts to reestablish ego control.

    (2) *Behavioral View:* Behaviorists theorize that people with schizophrenia fail to attend to relevant social cues and as a result develop bizarre responses to the environment.

    (3) *Existential View:* R. D. Laing's existential theory states that schizophrenia is actually a constructive process by which people search inward to try to cure themselves of the confusion and unhappiness caused by their environment.

    (4) *Cognitive View:* Cognitive theorists contend that when people with schizophrenia try to explain biologically induced hallucinations or other strange sensations, they develop delusional thinking.

  C. *Biological Explanations:* The biological explanations point to genetic, biochemical, and anatomical factors.

    (1) *Genetic Factors:* The genetic view is supported by studies of relatives, twins, adoptees, and chromosomal mapping.

    (2) *Biochemical Factors:* The predominant biochemical explanation focuses on an unusually high level of activity in neurons that use the neurotransmitter *dopamine.*

    (3) *Brain Structure:* Modern brain-imaging techniques have detected *abnormal brain structures* in people with schizophrenia, including enlarged ventricles and unusual variations in blood flow in certain parts of the brain.

6. *Treatments:* Today's treatments for schizophrenia are more successful than those of the past.

  A. *Institutional Care:* For more than half of this century the main treatment for schizophrenia was *institutionalization* in overcrowded hospitals and custodial care. In the 1950s, clinicians developed two in-hospital interventions—*milieu therapy* and the *token economy program*—that were somewhat helpful. They are now standard features of institutional care.

  B. *Antipsychotic Drugs:* The discovery of antipsychotic drugs, or *neuroleptic drugs,* in the 1950s revolutionized the treatment of schizophrenia. Theorists believe that the drugs operate by reducing excessive dopamine activity in the brain.

    (1) *Unwanted Effects:* Unfortunately, traditional antipsychotic drugs can also produce dramatic unwanted effects, particularly *extrapyramidal effects,* movement abnormalities that may affect appearance and functioning. These include *Parkinsonian symptoms, dystonia, akathisia, neuroleptic malignant syndrome,* and *tardive dyskinesia.*

    (2) *Atypical Antipsychotic Drugs:* Some *atypical* antipsychotic drugs (such as *clozapine*) that seem to be more effective and to cause fewer or no extrapyramidal effects have recently become available.

  C. *Psychotherapy:* Today, psychotherapy is often employed successfully in conjunction with antipsychotic drugs. The most helpful forms include insight therapy, social therapy, and family therapy.

  D. *Community Approaches:* Recently a community approach has been applied to the treatment of schizophrenia.

    (1) *Deinstitutionalization:* A policy of deinstitutionalization has produced a mass exodus of hundreds of thousands of patients with schizophrenia or other severe problems from state institutions into the community.

    (2) *Elements of Community Care:* Among the key elements of effective programs are coordination of patient services by a *community mental health center, short-term hospitalization* (followed by *aftercare*), *day centers, halfway houses,* and *occupational training.*

    (3) *Inadequacies of Community Care:* Unfortunately, the quality of and funding for community care for persons with schizophrenia has been grossly inadequate throughout the United States, resulting in a "revolving door" syndrome. Nevertheless, the potential of proper community care continues to capture the interest of clinicians, government officials, and national interest groups.

# Key Terms

schizophrenia
positive symptom
negative symptom
psychomotor symptom
delusion
formal thought disorder
loose association
derailment
neologism
perseverating
clang
hallucination
inappropriate affect
alogia
poverty of content
blunted affect
flat affect
avolition
ambivalence
catatonia

waxy flexibility
prodromal phase
active phase
residual phase
disorganized
    schizophrenia
catatonic schizophrenia
paranoid schizophrenia
undifferentiated
    schizophrenia
residual schizophrenia
Type I schizophrenia
Type II schizophrenia
regression
operant conditioning
schizophrenogenic mother
double-bind hypothesis
concordance
chromosomal mapping
dopamine hypothesis

antipsychotic medication
phenothiazine
L-dopa
amphetamine psychosis
atypical antipsychotic
clozapine
D-2 receptor
enlarged ventricle
institutionalization
state hospital
milieu therapy
token economy program
antihistamine drug
chlorpromazine
neuroleptic drug
extrapyramidal effect
Parkinsonian symptom
dystonia
akathisia
tardive dyskinesia

neuroleptic malignant
    syndrome
agranulocytosis
social therapy
sociotherapy
expressed emotion
psychoeducation
community mental health
deinstitutionalization
community mental health
    center
aftercare
day center
day hospital
halfway house
paraprofessional
sheltered workshop
national interest group
National Alliance for the
    Mentally Ill

# Quick Quiz

1. What is schizophrenia and how prevalent is it? What is its relationship to socioeconomic class, gender, and race?

2. What are the positive, negative, and psychomotor symptoms of schizophrenia?

3. What are the most common kinds of delusions, hallucinations, and formal thought disorders in schizophrenia?

4. What are the five types of schizophrenia distinguished by DSM-IV? What are the differences between Type I and Type II schizophrenia?

5. What are the key features of the social-labeling, family, psychodynamic, behavioral, existential, and cognitive explanations of schizophrenia?

6. Describe the dopamine and brain-structure explanations of schizophrenia and discuss how they have been supported in research. What is the genetic explanation of schizophrenia, and how has it been supported in research?

7. Describe institutional care for people with schizophrenia over the course of this century. How effective are the token economy and milieu treatment programs?

8. How do antipsychotic drugs operate on the brain, and how effective are they in the treatment of schizophrenia? What are the unwanted effects of these drugs?

9. What kinds of psychotherapy seem to help people with schizophrenia?

10. What is deinstitutionalization? What are the elements of community care that seem critical for helping people with schizophrenia?

11. Why has the community mental health approach often been inadequate for people with schizophrenia, and what are the results of this inadequacy?

*14*

# Disorders of Memory and Other Cognitive Functions

## Topic Overview

*Dissociative Disorders*
Dissociative Amnesia
Dissociative Fugue
Dissociative Identity Disorder (Multiple Personality Disorder)

*Organic Disorders Affecting Memory and Other Cognitive Functions*
Amnestic Disorders
Dementias

*O*ur memory links our past, present, and future. The recollection of past experiences, although not always precisely accurate, helps us make sense of and react to present events and guides us in making decisions about the future. We recognize our friends and relatives, teachers and employers, and respond to them in appropriate and consistent ways. Without a memory we would always be starting over; with it, life has progression and continuity.

People sometimes experience a significant alteration in their memory. Through interruptions in learning new information or recalling old information, memory is disrupted. Sometimes the alterations in memory lack a clear physical cause, and are, by tradition, called *dissociative disorders*. In other cases, the physical causes are quite clear, and the memory disorder is called *organic*.

The dissociative disorders include *dissociative amnesia, dissociative fugue,* and *dissociative identity disorder (multiple personality disorder)*. Organic memory disorders include *amnestic disorders* and *dementias*. Organic memory disorders are caused by medical diseases and conditions, substance misuse, injury, or other problems that impinge on the physical functioning of the brain.

# Dissociative Disorders

**Dissociative disorders** are disorders characterized by significant alterations in integrated functioning that are not due to clear physical causes. Typically, one part of the person's memory is dissociated, or separated, from another. Several memorable books and movies have dealt with these disorders. Two of the best known are *The Three Faces of Eve* and *Sybil*. The topic is so intriguing that the majority of television drama series seem to include at least one case of dissociative functioning each season, creating the impression that the disorders are very common. Many clinicians, however, believe that they are quite rare.

The dissociative disorders that have received the most attention are dissociative amnesia, dissociative fugue, and multiple personality disorder. **Depersonalization disorder,** a disorder in which people have persistent feelings of being detached from their mental processes or body, is also listed as a dissociative disorder in DSM-IV. Because this disorder does not actually involve clear alterations in memory, however, we shall not include it in the present discussion.

*Dissociative disorders*  Disorders characterized by significant alterations in integrated functioning that are not due to clear physical causes.

## Dissociative Amnesia

People with **dissociative amnesia** are suddenly unable to recall important information about their lives, usually information of a traumatic or stressful nature (APA, 1994). The loss of memory is much more extensive than normal forgetting and cannot be attributed to an organic disorder. Very often the episode of amnesia is directly precipitated by a specific upsetting event (Classen et al., 1993).

> Brian was spending the day sailing with his wife, Helen. The water was rough but well within what they considered safe limits. They were having a wonderful time and really didn't notice that the sky was getting darker, the wind blowing harder, and the sailboat becoming more difficult to control. After a few hours of sailing, they found themselves far from shore in the middle of a powerful and dangerous storm.
>
> The storm intensified very quickly. Brian had trouble controlling the sailboat amidst the high winds and wild waves. He and Helen tried to put on the safety jackets they had neglected to wear earlier, but the boat turned over before they were finished. Brian, the better swimmer of the two, was able to swim back to the overturned sailboat, grab the side, and hold on for dear life, but Helen simply could not overcome the rough waves and reach the boat. As Brian watched in horror and disbelief, his wife disappeared from view.
>
> After a time, the storm began to lose its strength. Brian managed to restore the sailboat to its proper position and sail back to shore. Finally he reached safety, but the personal consequences of this storm were just beginning. The next days were filled with pain and further horror: the Coast Guard finding Helen's body . . . discussions with authorities . . . breaking the news to Helen's parents . . . funeral plans . . . the funeral itself . . . conversations with friends . . . self-blame . . . grief . . . and more— the start of a nightmare that wouldn't end.

There are several kinds of dissociative amnesia, including *localized, selective, generalized,* and *continuous*. Let us imagine, for example, that on the day after the funeral Brian awakens and cannot recall any of the events of the past difficult days, beginning with the boating tragedy. He remembers everything that occurred before the accident and can now recall everything from the morning after the funeral forward, but the intervening days remain a total blank. In this case, Brian would be suffering from **localized amnesia,** the most common type of dissociative amnesia. Here a person forgets all events that occurred over a limited period of time, beginning almost always with an event that was very disturbing.

*Dissociative amnesia*  A dissociative disorder characterized by an inability to recall important personal events and information.

People with *selective amnesia,* the second most common form of dissociative amnesia, remember some, but not all, events occurring over the circumscribed period of time. Brian may remember his conversations with friends and breaking the news to his in-laws, for example, but have no recollection of making funeral plans or of the funeral itself.

The forgotten or partially forgotten period is called the *amnestic episode.* During an amnestic episode, people sometimes act puzzled and confused and may even wander about aimlessly. They are already experiencing memory difficulties, but seem to be unaware of them.

In some cases the forgetting extends back to a time before the traumatic period. Brian may awaken after the funeral and find that, in addition to the preceding few days, he cannot remember other events in his past life. In this case, he is experiencing *generalized amnesia.* In extreme cases, people with this form of amnesia do not even remember who they are and fail to recognize relatives and friends.

In *continuous amnesia,* forgetting continues into the present, and new and ongoing experiences fail to be retained. Brian's loss of memory, for example, may extend indefinitely into his life after the accident. He may remember what happened before the tragedy but keep forgetting events that occur since then. He is caught in a prolonged amnestic episode. This kind of forgetting is rare in cases of dissociative amnesia, but as we shall see later, it is often seen in cases of organic amnesia.

All of these forms of dissociative amnesia are similar in that the amnesia disrupts *episodic memory* primarily—a person's autobiographical memory of personal experiences and other highly personal material. *Semantic memory*—memory for abstract, encyclopedic, or categorical information—remains largely intact. Most people with dissociative amnesia are as likely as anyone else to know the name of the president of the United States, for example, and how to write, read, drive a car, and so on.

Many cases of dissociative amnesia occur during wartime and in natural disasters, when people's health and safety may be significantly threatened (APA, 1994; Kihlstrom et al., 1993). Combat veterans, for example, often report memory gaps of hours or days, and sometimes forget personal information, such as their name and address (Bremner et al., 1993). In fact, many clinicians consider dissociative amnesia or the other dissociative disorders to be a kind of posttraumatic stress

disorder. Recently, many cases of dissociative amnesia linked to child sexual abuse have also been reported to clinicians (see Box 14-1).

Dissociative amnesia may also arise under more ordinary circumstances. The sudden loss of a loved one through rejection, abandonment, or death can lead to it (Loewenstein, 1991). In other cases, guilt over behavior that a person considers immoral or sinful (such as an extramarital affair) may precipitate the disorder.

The personal impact of dissociative amnesia depends on the extent and importance of what is forgotten. Obviously, an amnestic episode of two years is more disabling than one of two hours. Similarly, an amnestic episode during which a person undergoes major life changes causes more difficulties than one that is largely uneventful.

## Dissociative Fugue

When a loss of memory takes on the added dimension of actual physical flight, it is labeled a *dissociative fugue.* People with this disorder forget their personal identity and at least some details of their past life and flee to an entirely different location. Some establish a new identity (APA, 1994).

In some cases, the individuals travel only a short distance, their new identity is not a complete one, and they have few social contacts (APA, 1994). Their fugue is brief—a matter of hours or days—and ends suddenly.

In other cases, however, the fugue is quite extensive. Such persons establish a new identity, adopt a new name, engage in complex social interactions, and even pursue a new line of work. In their new identity they may have personal characteristics they never displayed before. Usually they are more outgoing and less inhibited (APA, 1994). Fugues of this kind usually last longer than a few hours, and the distance traveled is more than a few miles.

On January 17, 1887, [the Rev. Ansel Bourne, of Greene, R.I.] drew 551 dollars from a bank in Providence with which to pay for a certain lot of land in Greene, paid certain bills, and got into a Pawtucket horsecar. This is the last incident which he remembers. He did not return home that day, and nothing was heard of him for two months. He was published in the papers as missing, and foul play being suspected, the police sought in vain his whereabouts. On the morning of March 14th, however, at Norristown, Pennsylvania, a man calling himself

*Episodic memory*   A person's autobiographical memory of personal experiences and other highly personal material.

*Semantic memory*   A person's memory for abstract, encyclopedic, or categorical information.

*Dissociative fugue*   A dissociative disorder in which a person travels to a new location and may assume a new identity, simultaneously forgetting his or her past.

A. I. Brown who had rented a small shop six weeks previously, stocked it with stationery, confectionery, fruit and small articles, and carried on his quiet trade without seeming to any one unnatural or eccentric, woke up in a fright and called in the people of the house to tell him where he was. He said that his name was Ansel Bourne, that he was entirely ignorant of Norristown, that he knew nothing of shop-keeping, and that the last thing he remembered—it seemed only yesterday—was drawing the money from the bank, etc. in Providence. . . . He was very weak, having lost apparently over twenty pounds of flesh during his escapade, and had such a horror of the idea of the candy-store that he refused to set foot in it again.

*(James, 1890, pp. 391–393)*

Approximately 0.2 percent of the population experiences dissociative fugue. Like dissociative amnesia, a fugue usually follows a severely stressful event, such as a wartime experience or a natural disaster, though it also can be triggered by personal stress, such as financial or legal difficulties or episodes of depression (APA, 1994; Kihlstrom et al., 1993). Some adolescent runaways are suspected to be in a state of fugue (Loewenstein, 1991). Fugues are also similar to dissociative amnesia in that primarily episodic memories from the past are impaired, while semantic knowledge remains intact (Kihlstrom et al., 1993).

Fugues tend to end abruptly. In some cases, as with the Reverend Bourne, the person "awakens" in an unfamiliar place, surrounded by strangers, and wonders how he or she got there. In other cases the lack of personal history may arouse curiosity or suspicion, a traffic accident or legal difficulty may lead police to discover the false identity, or friends may search for and find the missing person (Kihlstrom et al., 1993). When these people are found, it may be necessary to ask them extensive questions about the details of their lives, repeatedly remind them who they are, and even involve them in psychotherapy before they recover their memories.

Most people who experience a fugue regain most or all of their memories and never have a recurrence. Since fugues are usually brief and totally reversible, impairment and aftereffects are usually minimal (Keller & Shaywitz, 1986). People who have been away for months or years, however, often do have trouble adjusting to family, social, or occupational changes that have occurred during their flight. Moreover, some people commit illegal or violent acts in their fugue state and later must face the consequences of those acts.

*In 1980 a Florida park ranger found a woman naked and starving in a shallow grave. Unaware of her identity, she was hospitalized as "Jane Doe." Five months later, the woman was recognized on* Good Morning, America *by Irene Tomiczek (right) as her 34-year-old daughter, Cheryl Ann, who had been missing for seven years. With the help of treatment and reunion with her family, Cheryl Ann's fugue began to lift.*

## Dissociative Identity Disorder (Multiple Personality Disorder)

Multiple personality disorder is as dramatic as it is disabling, as we see in the case of Eric:

Dazed and bruised from a beating, Eric, 29, was discovered wandering around a Daytona Beach shopping mall on Feb. 9. . . . Transferred six weeks later to Daytona Beach's Human Resources Center, Eric began talking to doctors in two voices: the infantile rhythms of "young Eric," a dim and frightened child, and the measured tones of "older Eric," who told a tale of terror and child abuse. According to "older Eric," after his immigrant German parents died, a harsh stepfather and his mistress took Eric from his native South Carolina to a drug dealers' hideout in a Florida swamp. Eric said he was raped by several gang members and watched his stepfather murder two men.

One day in late March an alarmed counselor watched Eric's face twist into a violent snarl. Eric let loose an unearthly growl and spat out a stream of obscenities. "It sounded like something out of *The Exorcist*," says Malcolm Graham, the psychologist who directs the case at the center. "It was the most intense thing I've ever seen in a patient." That disclosure of a new personality, who insolently demanded to be called Mark, was the first indication that Graham had been dealing with a rare and serious emotional disorder: true multiple personality. . . .

Eric's other manifestations emerged over the next weeks: quiet, middle-aged Dwight; the hysterically blind and mute Jeffrey; Michael, an arrogant jock; the

Box 14-1

# Repressed Childhood Memories vs. False Memory Syndrome

In recent years, a unique type of dissociative amnesia has attracted enormous public attention. Reports of *repressed childhood memory*, in which adults recover buried memories of sexual and physical abuse from their childhood, have increased dramatically since the late 1980s.

A woman may claim, for example, that her father sexually molested her repeatedly between the ages of five and seven. Or a young man may remember that a family friend made sexual advances toward him on several occasions when he was very young. Often such individuals are in treatment for disorders such as an eating disorder or depression, and over the course of therapy, their repressed memories begin to surface. The traumatic events that have been repressed may be seen as responsible for various disorders from which the individuals now suffer.

Although some of these cases revolve around a single traumatic experience, many others involve repeated abuse over a number of years. In some of the most severe and bizarre cases, victims have reported memories of participating in bloody Satanic rituals that included forced sexual encounters and human sacrifices. Their recollections of abuse can be compelling and vivid and reflect great conviction.

Once people recall childhood sexual traumas, many confront their abusers. Some have even brought criminal charges and others civil charges. In fact, at least nineteen states have recently revised their laws to allow charges to be brought even after the statute of limitations has run out (Horn, 1993). Hundreds of such cases are now in the courts. Willingness by juries to decide in favor of the apparent victims indicates a growing acceptance of the notions of re-pressed and recovered memories.

Society has become deeply divided on this issue. Some people believe that recovered memories are as they appear—horrific memories of abuse that have been buried in the deep recesses of a person's mind, only to resurface years later in a safer climate. Others believe that the memories are in fact a very serious and damaging form of "illusory" childhood memory—images and stories falsely constructed or embraced by confused and suggestible persons. In fact, an organization called the False Memory Syndrome Foundation has been founded in Philadelphia to assist those claiming to be falsely charged with the abuse.

The claim that recovered memories are actually distorted or false has itself been gaining status in the courts. Recently, for example, a man who was publicly accused by his 23-year-old daughter of having sexually abused her when she was a child brought suit against her therapists, claiming that their treatment techniques had induced false memories in his daughter and thus deprived him of his reputation, job, marriage, and family. He won the suit and was granted a large financial judgment by the jury.

The clinical community is just as deeply divided on this issue, with some clinicians convinced that many of these cases are legitimate examples of repression and at least as many arguing forcefully against this view. The proponents of the repressed memory position point out that child sexual abuse is an enormous problem, victimizing at least 200,000 to 300,000 children in the United States each year (Horn, 1993; AAPC, 1992). Few experiences bring more horror or shame, are kept more private, or have a more lingering impact (Nash et al., 1993; Briere, 1992), making victims prime candidates for a reaction of dissociative amnesia. Some studies even suggest that more than 18 percent of sexual abuse victims have difficulty recalling at least some aspects of their trauma (Horn, 1993). Thus, the proponents argue, it is reasonable to expect that some children may totally repress their painful sexual abuse traumas until therapy discussions or life events later trigger their memories.

Proponents further point out that the notion of hidden memory is hardly foreign to the clinical field. The defense mechanism of repression has been at the center of psychodynamic explanations and treatments for years. Moreover, they assert, the DSM-IV category of dissociative amnesia represents a formal acknowledgement of the phenomenon.

The opponents to the repressed memory perspective have responded to each of these points. They agree that child sexual abuse is indeed an enormous problem, but, they claim, it is one that most victims remember all too well rather than forget. Systematic research has not found many cases in which such events are completely wiped from one's memory. One study, for example, observed teenagers who had been sexually abused and found no evidence of repression over a 10-year period (Loftus, 1993).

Opponents also question how accurate recalled sexual traumas are likely to be. Not only are adult memories of childhood events typically illusory, but memories of events that happen to us as adults are also fallible. Studies have shown, for example, that eyewitness accounts of crimes or other salient experiences may change over time or be influenced by various factors such as suggestions by other people or differing accounts of the events (Loftus, 1993). Even for highly memorable events such as the explosion of the space shuttle *Challenger,* people give inaccurate accounts of where they were or who told them of the event, although they seem certain of their recollections. In short, the opponents argue, the public's ready acceptance of so-called recovered memories is probably unwarranted.

*Early childhood memories appear to be important to the development and maintenance of our present sense of self. However, research suggests that their accuracy may be influenced by the reminiscences of family members, dream content, television and movie plots, and our present self-image.*

Opponents of the repressed memory position further point out that Sigmund Freud himself disagreed with the interpretations now being applied in these cases. Granted Freud did initially believe that many of his patients had been sexually abused as children, and that their repressed memories of those events had caused them to develop psychological problems. But, over the years, Freud changed his mind and came to believe that the patient memories which came to light in treatment actually represented repressed fantasies and desires rather than true recollections. The motives behind Freud's theoretical shift have been hotly debated in the clinical field, but the fact remains that his views can hardly be cited as support for the repressed childhood memory position.

If the recovery of childhood memories is not what it appears to be, what is it? A powerful case of suggestibility, according to the opponents. They hold that therapists themselves have been greatly influenced by both the clinical and public attention surrounding this diagnosis and some are prone to

accept it despite a lack of evidence (Frankel, 1993). With certain clients, these therapists may actively seek indicators that early sexual abuse occurred and may conduct therapy correspondingly, implicitly or explicitly encouraging the clients to find repressed memories (Ganaway, 1989). Many such therapists even use a variety of *memory recovery techniques* to help clients uncover such memories, including hypnosis, guided imagery, certain drugs, journal writing, dream interpretation, and interpreting body symptoms such as a dry mouth (Lindsay & Read, 1994). It may be that clients often oblige and unwittingly form illusory memories of abuse.

Several factors may contribute to the creation of false memories by clients: suggestions by a respected authority figure, long delays between the purported events and the surfacing of the memory, the plausibility of the events, and repetitive therapy discussions of the alleged abusive events (Loftus et al., 1993; Belli et al., 1992). In short, recovered memories may actually be *iatrogenic*—unintention-

ally created by the therapist.

Of course, repressed memories of child sexual abuse do not surface only in clinical settings. Many alleged victims come forward on their own. They report flashbacks revealing sexual abuse and they then seek therapy. These self-revelations are on the increase. Some clinical theorists attribute them to the large number of popular books, articles, and television shows that take a strong stand in support of recovering repressed memories (Loftus, 1993). Several such books offer readers lists of criteria for diagnosing repression of sexual abuse memories: long lists of symptoms that, in some cases, are actually rather common and not clinical in nature or that have not been reliably correlated with instances of sexual abuse (Tavris, 1993). When readers meet a number of these criteria, they may begin a search for repressed memories.

It is important to recognize that the heated debate over the phenomenon of repressed childhood memories does not in any way diminish the enormity of the problem of child sexual abuse. In fact, both proponents and opponents alike are greatly concerned that this controversy may be taken by the public to mean that clinicians have doubts about the scope of the problem of child sexual abuse. In a controversy filled with the potential for sad outcomes, that would be the most unfortunate result of all.

coquettish Tian, whom Eric considered a whore; and argumentative Phillip, the lawyer. "Phillip was always asking about Eric's rights," says Graham. "He was kind of obnoxious. Actually, Phillip was a pain."

To Graham's astonishment, Eric gradually unfurled 27 different personalities, including three females. . . . They ranged in age from a fetus to a sordid old man who kept trying to persuade Eric to fight as a mercenary in Haiti. In one therapy session, reports Graham, Eric shifted personality nine times in an hour.

(Time, *October 25, 1982, p. 70*)

A person with *multiple personality disorder* displays two or more distinct personalities, often called *subpersonalities,* each with a unique set of memories, behaviors, thoughts, and emotions. At any given time, one of the subpersonalities dominates the person's consciousness and interactions with the environment. Usually one subpersonality, the *primary,* or *host, personality,* appears more often than the others.

The transition from one subpersonality to another is usually sudden and often dramatic (APA, 1994; Dell & Eisenhower, 1990). Eric, for example, twisted his face, growled, and yelled obscenities while changing personalities. Transitions are usually triggered by a stressful event (APA, 1994), although hypnotic suggestion can also bring about the change (Smith, 1993; Brende & Rinsley, 1981).

Most clinicians consider multiple personality disorder to be a rare disorder, but recent reports suggest that it may be more common than it was once thought to be (APA, 1994; Kluft, 1991). Most cases are first diagnosed in late adolescence or young adulthood, but the symptoms usually begin to develop in early childhood after episodes of abuse, typically before the age of 5 (Sachs, 1986). Indeed, studies suggest that as many as 97 percent of these patients have been physically, often sexually, abused during their early years (Ross et al., 1991, 1990, 1989; Dell & Eisenhower, 1990). The disorder is diagnosed in women between three and nine times as often as it is in men (APA, 1994).

One of the cinema's best-known fictional sufferers of multiple personality disorder, Norman Bates, is horrified to discover his mother (actually his subpersonality) has stabbed a woman to death in the shower.

## The Subpersonalities

The subpersonalities relate to one another in ways that vary from case to case. Generally, there are three kinds of relationships: mutually amnesic, mutually cognizant, and one-way amnesic.

In *mutually amnesic* relationships, the subpersonalities have no awareness of one another (Ellenberger, 1970). Conversely, in *mutually cognizant* patterns, each subpersonality is well aware of the rest. They may hear one another's voices and even talk among themselves.

However, the most common pattern is the *one-way amnesic* relationship: some subpersonalities are aware of others, but the awareness is not reciprocated. Those that are aware are called *co-conscious subpersonalities.* They are "quiet observers" that watch the actions and thoughts of the other subpersonalities but do not interact with them. Sometimes, while another subpersonality is dominating consciousness, they make themselves known through such indirect means as auditory hallucinations (for example, a voice giving commands) or "automatic writing" (the conscious personality finds itself writing down words over which it experiences no control).

> ### Consider This
> Women are much more likely to receive a diagnosis of multiple personality disorder than men. What might be some reasons for this difference?

---

*Multiple personality disorder*    A dissociative disorder in which a person displays two or more distinct personalities that repeatedly take control of the person's behavior.

*Subpersonalities*    The distinct personalities found in individuals suffering from multiple personality disorder, each with a unique set of memories, behaviors, thoughts, and emotions.

Investigators used to believe that cases of multiple personality disorder usually involved two or three subpersonalities. Studies now suggest, however, that the average number of subpersonalities per patient is much higher—15 for women and 8 for men (APA, 1994; Ross et al., 1989). In fact, there have been cases in which 100 or more subpersonalities were observed. In a number of cases, the subpersonalities may emerge in groups of two or three at a time.

In the famous case of "Eve White," the woman made famous in the book and movie *The Three Faces of Eve*, a woman had three personalities—Eve White, Eve Black, and Jane (Thigpen & Cleckley, 1957). Eve White, the primary personality, was colorless, quiet, and serious; Eve Black was carefree, mischievous, and uninhibited; and Jane was mature and intelligent. According to the book, these three subpersonalities eventually merged into Evelyn, a stable and enduring personality who represented an integration of the other three.

It turned out, however, that this was not the end of Eve's dissociation. Twenty years later, in the mid-1970s, she identified herself in an autobiography. Now named Chris Sizemore, she described her pre- and posttherapy life more fully and said that altogether twenty-two subpersonalities had emerged, including nine subpersonalities after Evelyn! Usually they emerged in groups of three. Apparently the authors of *The Three Faces of Eve* had worked with her during the ascendancy of one such group, and never knew about her previous and subsequent subpersonalities. This woman has now overcome her disorder and achieved a single, stable identity for nearly twenty years (Sizemore & Huber, 1988).

*Chris Sizemore, the subject of the book and film* The Three Faces of Eve, *is now an accomplished author, artist, and mental health spokesperson. The variety of her portraits reflects the many subpersonalities Sizemore once displayed.*

As in Chris Sizemore's case, the subpersonalities often differ dramatically in their respective personalities. Thus, it seems strangely appropriate that they often have their own names. The subpersonalities may also differ in vital statistics, abilities and preferences, and even physiological responses (Alpher, 1992; Dell & Eisenhower, 1990).

**Vital Statistics**  The subpersonalities may differ in features as basic as age, sex, race, and family history (Coons et al., 1988), as in the famous case of Sybil Dorsett. Sybil's multiple personality disorder has been described in fictional form, but the novel is based on an actual case, and both the therapist and the patient have attested to its accuracy (Schreiber, 1973). Sybil manifested seventeen subpersonalities, all with different identifying features. They included adults, a teenager, and a baby named Ruthie; and while most of her personalities were female, two were male, named Mike and Sid.

Sybil's subpersonalities had distinct physical images of themselves and of each other. The subpersonality named Vicky, for example, saw herself as an attractive blonde, while another, Peggy Lou, was described as a pixie with a pug nose. Mary was plump with dark hair, and Vanessa was a tall redhead with a willowy figure. Mike's olive skin and brown eyes stood in contrast to Sid's fair skin and blue eyes.

**Abilities and Preferences**  Although semantic memory is not affected in dissociative amnesia or fugue, it can often be disrupted in multiple personality disorder. It is not uncommon for the different subpersonalities to have different abilities: one may be able to drive, speak a foreign language, or play a musical instrument, while the others cannot (Coons et al., 1988). Chris Sizemore ("Eve") pointed out, "If I had learned to sew as one personality and then tried to sew as another, I couldn't do it. Driving a car was the same. Some of my personalities couldn't drive" (1975, p. 4). Handwriting styles can also differ among subpersonalities (Coons, 1980). In addition, they usually have different tastes in food, friends, music, and literature.

**Physiological Activity**  Researchers have discovered that subpersonalities may also display actual physiological differences, as in autonomic nervous system activity, blood pressure levels, and menstrual cycles (Putnam et al., 1990). One study investigated the brain activities of different subpersonalities by measuring their *evoked potentials*—that is, the brain response patterns recorded on an electroencephalograph under

*Evoked potentials*  The brain response patterns recorded on an electroencephalograph while a subject performs a task.

varying conditions, such as while subjects observe a flashing light (Putnam, 1984). When an evoked potential test was administered to four subpersonalities of each of ten people with multiple personality disorder, it showed that the brain activity patterns of the subpersonalities differed greatly within each individual. This was a dramatic finding. The brain pattern in response to a specific stimulus is usually stable and unique to a given individual. The subpersonalities of these subjects showed the kinds of variations usually found in totally different people.

*Consider This*

In many cases of multiple personality disorder, one subpersonality may engage in criminal activity without the awareness of the other subpersonalities. What should be the punishment or treatment in such cases? How should the individual's needs be balanced against the needs of society?

## The Prevalence of Multiple Personality Disorder

As we noted earlier, multiple personality disorder has traditionally been thought of as a rare disorder. Some researchers have even argued that multiple personality disorder is not a legitimate diagnosis and suggest that many cases are actually *iatrogenic,* that is, unintentionally caused by practitioners. They believe that therapists create this disorder by subtly suggesting the existence of alternate personalities during therapy or by eliciting the personalities while patients are under hypnosis. In addition, they believe that a therapist who is looking for multiple personalities may reinforce these patterns by becoming more interested in a patient when he or she displays symptoms of dissociation (Merskey, 1992; Fahy, 1988).

On the one hand, these arguments seem to be supported by the fact that many cases of multiple personality disorder do initially come to the attention of a therapist while the client is being treated for a less serious problem (Allison, 1978). On the other hand, in many other cases people seek treatment only after having experienced losses of time throughout their lives or having displayed subpersonalities that other people have observed (Putnam, 1988, 1985; Schacter, 1989).

In recent years, the number of people diagnosed with multiple personality disorder has been increasing. Thousands of cases have been identified in the United States and Canada alone (Kluft, 1994; Ross et al.,

1989). Although the disorder is still relatively rare, the prevalence rate appears to have risen dramatically.

What accounts for this recent increase in the number of cases reported? At least two factors seem to be involved. First, belief in the authenticity of this disorder is growing, and willingness to diagnose it has increased accordingly (French, 1987). A second factor may be recent changes in diagnostic biases and criteria. From 1910 to 1978, schizophrenia was one of the most popular diagnoses in the clinical field (Rosenbaum, 1980). The diagnosis was readily and incorrectly applied to a wide range of unusual and mysterious patterns of abnormality, including, perhaps, multiple personality disorder. Under the stricter criteria of recent editions of the DSM, diagnosticians have applied the label of schizophrenia with greater accuracy, allowing multiple personality cases to be recognized and assessed more readily (Kluft, 1994; French, 1987). In addition, several diagnostic scales and tests have been developed in recent years to help identify multiple personality disorder and distinguish it from schizophrenia and other disorders (Allen & Smith, 1993; Steinberg, 1993).

Despite such changes in professional perceptions, diagnostic practices, and assessment tools, many clinicians remain reluctant to make this diagnosis (Saxe et al., 1993; McElroy, 1992). In fact, people suffering from this disorder still receive an average of four different diagnoses, such as schizophrenia and depression, and average nearly seven years of contact with health services before a diagnosis of multiple personality disorder is finally made (Putnam et al., 1986).

*Summing Up*
*People with dissociative disorders experience significant alterations in integrated functioning that are not due to clear physical causes Typically, one part of the person's memory is dissociated, or separated, from another. In dissociative amnesia, people are suddenly unable to recall important personal information or past events in their lives. Those with dissociative fugue not only lose their memory but flee to a different location and may establish a new identity. People with multiple personality disorder display two or more distinct subpersonalities which differ from one another in a number of ways.*

## Explanations of Dissociative Disorders

Relatively few researchers have investigated the origins of the dissociative disorders, although a variety of the-

---

*Iatrogenic disorder*    A disorder that is unintentionally caused by a practitioner.

*People with dissociative disorders are able to "get away from it all," including themselves, by totally forgetting many of their actions, thoughts, and experiences.*

ories have been offered to explain them. Proponents of older perspectives especially, such as the psychodynamic and behavioral viewpoints, have gathered little systematic data. On the other hand, newer theories that combine cognitive, behavioral, and biological principles and highlight such factors as state-dependent learning and self-hypnosis have begun to capture the enthusiasm of clinical scientists (Doan & Bryson, 1994).

## The Psychodynamic Explanation

Psychodynamic theorists believe that dissociative disorders represent an extreme use of *repression*, the most fundamental defense mechanism: people ward off anxiety by unconsciously preventing painful memories, thoughts, or impulses from reaching awareness. Everyone uses repression to a degree, but those people diagnosed as having dissociative disorders are thought to repress their memories excessively and dysfunctionally (Terr, 1988).

Dissociative amnesia and fugue are each seen as representing a single episode of massive repression in which a person unconsciously blocks the memory of an extremely upsetting event to avoid the pain of confronting it (Putnam, 1985). Repression may be the person's only means of protecting himself or herself from overwhelming anxiety.

In contrast, multiple personality disorder is held to reflect a lifetime of excessive repression that was origi-

nally triggered by extremely traumatic childhood experiences, particularly experiences of abuse (Reis, 1993). According to psychodynamic theorists, children who are exposed to such traumas may come to fear the dangerous world they live in and take to flight symbolically by regularly pretending to be another person who is safely looking on from afar.

Abused children may also become afraid of the impulses that they believe are leading to their excessive punishments. They may strive to be "good" and "proper" all of the time and keep repressing the impulses they consider "bad" and "dangerous." Whenever "bad" thoughts or impulses do break through, such children may feel bound to disown and deny them, and may unconsciously assign all unacceptable thoughts, impulses, and emotions to other personalities.

Most of the support for the psychodynamic position is drawn from case histories. Such brutal childhood experiences as beatings, cuttings, burnings with cigarettes, imprisonment in closets, rape, and extensive verbal abuse have often been reported in cases of multiple personality disorder. On the other hand, the backgrounds of some individuals with multiple personality disorder do not seem to be markedly deviant (Bliss, 1980). Moreover, child abuse appears to be far more prevalent than multiple personality disorder. Why, then, do only a small fraction of abused children develop this form of dysfunctioning?

## The Behavioral Explanation

Behaviorists believe that dissociation is a response acquired through operant conditioning. People who experience a horrifying event may later find temporary relief when their minds drift to other subjects. For some, this momentary forgetting, leading to a reduction in anxiety, increases the likelihood of future forgetting. In short, they are reinforced for the act of forgetting and learn—without being aware that they are learning—that forgetting lets them avoid or escape anxiety.

Thus, like psychodynamic theorists, behaviorists see dissociation as escape behavior of which the individual is unaware. But they believe that a subtle reinforcement process rather than a hardworking unconscious is what is keeping the individual unaware.

Like proponents of the psychodynamic explanation, proponents of the behavioral view have been forced to rely largely on case histories for support. While such descriptions do typically support this view, however, they are often equally consistent with other kinds of explanations as well, offering no evidence that one explanation is superior to the other.

In addition, the behavioral explanation fails to explain precisely how temporary distractions from painful memories grow into acquired responses or why more people do not develop dissociative disorders. Nor has it yet described how reinforcement can account for the complicated interrelationships of subpersonalities found in multiple personality disorder.

## State-Dependent Learning

It is sometimes the case that what people learn when they are in a particular state or situation they tend to remember best when they are returned to that same state or situation. Something learned under the influence of alcohol, for example, may be recalled better under the influence of alcohol than in an alcohol-free condition (Overton, 1966). Similarly, people given a learning task to do while they smoke cigarettes may later recall the learned material better when they are smoking.

This association between state and recall is called *state-dependent learning*. It was initially observed in experimental animals that were administered certain drugs, taught to perform certain tasks, and later tested on those tasks under various conditions. Researchers repeatedly found that the animals' subsequent test performances were better in corresponding drug states than in drug-free states (Spear, 1973; Overton, 1966, 1964).

Research with human subjects later showed that state-dependent learning could be associated with psychological states as well as physiological ones. One study found mood to be influential (see Figure 14-1): material learned during a happy mood was recalled best when the subject was again in a happy mood, and sad-state learning was recalled best during sad states (Bower, 1981).

One way of interpreting the phenomenon of state-dependent learning is to see it as an indication that *arousal levels* are an important part of memory processes. That is, a particular level of arousal will have a set of remembered events, thoughts, and skills attached to it. When a situation elicits that particular level of arousal, the person is more likely to recall the memories associated with it.

For most people, state-dependent learning is a relative phenomenon. They can recall past events across a range of arousal states, but will remember each better in some states than in others. Perhaps some people—those prone to develop dissociative disorders—have state-to-memory links that are extremely rigid and narrow. Their thoughts, memories, and skills may be tied

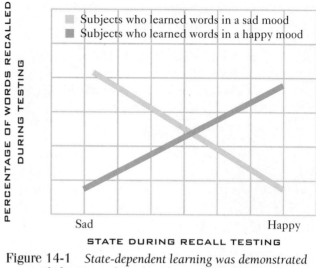

**Figure 14-1**  *State-dependent learning was demonstrated in a study by Bower (1981). Subjects who learned a list of words while in a hypnotically induced happy state remembered the words better if they were also in a happy mood when tested later than if they were in a sad mood. Conversely, subjects who learned the words when in a sad mood recalled them better if they were sad during testing than if they were happy.*

*exclusively* to particular states of arousal. They recall past events only when they experience arousal states almost identical to the states in which the memory was acquired. When such people are calm, for example, they may forget the events that occurred during an anxiety-filled trauma. Similarly, in multiple personality disorder, different arousal levels may elicit different clusters of memories, thoughts, and abilities—that is, different subpersonalities (Putnam, 1992).

Efforts to tie state-dependent learning to dissociative disorders keep running into a major problem: theorists do not yet agree about the nature of the contribution of state to memory. Many believe that arousal is not more important than any other cues that also help to jog a person's memory (for example, objects, smells, and sounds). They argue that the notion of state-dependent learning has little new to say about memory itself and less still about the active forgetting involved in dissociative disorders.

## Self-Hypnosis

As we first noted in Chapter 1, the word "hypnosis" describes the deliberate induction of a sleeplike state in which a person shows a very high degree of suggestibility. While in this state, the person can behave, perceive, and think in ways that would ordinarily seem impossible (Fromm & Nash, 1992).

Hypnosis can help people remember events that occurred and were forgotten years ago, a capability of

---

*State-dependent learning*   Learning that is closely linked to a person's state of arousal when the learning first occurred.

which many psychotherapists make frequent use. Conversely, it can also make people forget facts, events, and even their personal identity—a phenomenon that is called *hypnotic amnesia* (Spanos & Coe, 1992).

Most investigations of hypnotic amnesia follow similar formats. Subjects are asked to study a word list or other material until they are able to repeat it correctly. Under hypnosis, they are then instructed to forget the material until they receive a cancellation signal (such as the snap of a finger), at which time they will suddenly recall the learned material once again. Repeatedly these experiments have shown the subjects' memories to be severely impaired during the period of hypnotically suggested amnesia and then restored after the cancellation signal is given (Coe, 1989).

The parallels between hypnotic amnesia and dissociative disorders are striking (Bliss, 1980). Both are conditions in which people forget certain material for a period of time yet later recall it to mind. In both, the people forget without any insight into why they are

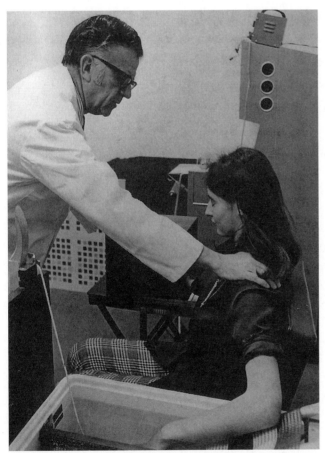

*Researcher Ernest Hilgard hypnotizes subjects into experiencing tepid water as painfully cold or ice water as comfortably warm. Work by researchers on hypnotic amnesia has suggested to many clinicians that dissociative disorders are a form of self-hypnosis.*

forgetting or any awareness that something has been forgotten. Finally, in both situations, events are more readily forgotten than basic knowledge.

These parallels have led some theorists to conclude that dissociative disorders may represent a form of self-hypnosis: people actively induce themselves to forget unpleasant events (Bliss, 1985, 1980; Hilgard, 1977). Dissociative amnesia, for example, may occur in people who, consciously or unconsciously, go so far as to hypnotize themselves into forgetting horrifying experiences that have recently occurred in their lives. If the self-induced amnesia extends to all memories of a person's past and identity, that person may undergo a dissociative fugue.

Self-hypnosis can also be used to explain multiple personality disorder. On the basis of several investigations, some theorists believe that multiple personality disorder often begins between the ages of 4 and 6, a time when children are generally very suggestible and excellent hypnotic subjects (Kluft, 1987; Bliss, 1985, 1980). These theorists argue that some abused or otherwise traumatized children manage to escape their threatening world by self-hypnosis, mentally separating themselves from their body and its surroundings and fulfilling their wish to become some other person or persons.

There are two schools of thought about the nature of hypnosis, each with distinct implications for dissociative disorders. Some theorists see hypnosis as a *special process* or *trance,* an out-of-the-ordinary kind of functioning (Hilgard, 1992, 1987, 1977). Other theorists believe that hypnotic behaviors, and hypnotic amnesia in particular, can be explained by *common social and cognitive processes* such as high motivation, attention, attributions, role enactments, and expectation (Spanos & Coe, 1992). According to them, hypnotic phenomena consist simply of motivated people performing tasks that are asked of them. Yet, because of their strong belief in hypnosis, they fail to recognize their own contributions.

Special-process theorists contend that people with dissociative disorders place themselves in internal trances during which their conscious functioning is significantly altered. In contrast, common-process theorists hold that people with dissociative disorders provide themselves (or are provided by others) with powerful suggestions to forget and to imagine, and implicitly use social and cognitive principles to follow those suggestions.

Whether hypnosis involves special or common processes, hypnosis research effectively demonstrates the power and potential of our normal thought processes, while rendering the idea of dissociative disorders somewhat less remarkable.

# Treatments for Dissociative Amnesia and Fugue

As we saw earlier, cases of dissociative amnesia and fugue often end spontaneously and lead to complete recovery. Sometimes, however, they linger and require treatment (Lyon, 1985). Several different interventions have been applied to these disorders, each reportedly with some degree of success.

*Psychodynamic therapy,* for example, is commonly applied to both disorders (Loewenstein, 1991). Therapists guide patients to free-associate and search their unconscious in the hope of bringing the forgotten experiences back to the level of consciousness. Actually, the focus of psychodynamic therapy is very much in harmony with the treatment needs of people with dissociative disorders. After all, people with dissociative amnesia and fugue need to recover lost memories, and psychodynamic therapists generally strive to uncover memories—as well as other psychological entities—that have been repressed. Thus many theorists, including some who do not espouse the psychodynamic perspective ordinarily, believe that psychodynamic therapy may be a particularly appropriate and effective approach for these disorders.

Another common treatment for dissociative amnesia and fugue is **hypnotic therapy,** or **hypnotherapy.** Therapists hypnotize patients and then try to guide them to recall the forgotten events (MacHovek, 1981; Bliss, 1980). If, as some theorists argue, dissociative amnesia and fugue involve self-hypnosis, then hypnotherapy too may be a highly relevant intervention for them. It has been applied both alone and in combination with other approaches.

> ### Consider This
> Hypnosis is often used by therapists to help *uncover* hidden memories, motives, needs, and the like. But hypnotic therapists can also use this suggestive technique to *create* desires, emotions, and behaviors. How can hypnotists know when they are uncovering a person's state of mind as opposed to creating it?

Sometimes intravenous injections of **sodium amobarbital** (Amytal) or **sodium pentobarbital** (Pentothal) are used to help patients regain lost memories (Ruedrich et al., 1985). The nickname "truth serum" is sometimes applied to these drugs, but the actual key to their impact is their capacity for sedating people

and lowering their inhibitions, thus helping them to recall forgotten events (Kluft, 1988; Perry & Jacobs, 1982). Unfortunately, these drugs often fail to work. Even when they do help people recall past events, individuals quickly forget what they have said and experienced under the drug's influence. For these reasons, the drugs tend to be used in conjunction with other treatment approaches, if they are used at all.

# Treatments for Multiple Personality Disorder

Unlike the victims of dissociative amnesia and fugue, people with multiple personality disorder rarely recover spontaneously. Therapists usually try to help people with this more chronic disorder to (1) recognize the full breadth of their disorder, (2) recover the gaps in their memory, and (3) integrate their subpersonalities into one (Kluft, 1994, 1992, 1983; Bliss, 1985, 1980).

## Recognizing the Disorder

Once a diagnosis of multiple personality disorder is made, therapists typically try to form a therapeutic alliance both with the primary personality and with each of the subpersonalities (Kluft, 1992). In general, these alliances are not easily achieved, owing to the history of abuse and mistrust of others.

Multiple personality patients are typically slow to recognize the full scope and nature of their disorder. The notion of having more than one personality may seem as strange to them as it does to everyone else. Thus, educating patients about their disorder is a key to beginning treatment (Allen, 1993).

Some therapists actually introduce the subpersonalities to one another under hypnosis (Ross & Gahan, 1988; Sakheim et al., 1988). Many have also found that group therapy helps to educate patients and reduce feelings of isolation (Buchele, 1993; Becker & Comstock, 1992). Family therapy is often used as an adjunct to individual therapy to help educate spouses and children about the disorder and to gather helpful information about the patient (Porter et al., 1993).

## Recovering Memories

To help these patients recover the missing pieces of their past, therapists use many of the approaches applied to the other dissociative disorders, including psychodynamic therapy, hypnotherapy, and sodium amobarbital (Smith, 1993; Kluft, 1991, 1985). These techniques work slowly for multiple personality pa-

---

*Hypnotic therapy (hypnotherapy)*    A treatment in which the patient undergoes hypnosis and is then guided to recall forgotten events or perform other therapeutic activities.

tients, as some subpersonalities may continually deny experiences that the others recall (Lyon, 1992). Indeed, it is not uncommon for patients to become self-destructive and violent during the memory-recovery phase of therapy (Kelly, 1993; Lamberti & Cummings, 1992).

## Integrating the Subpersonalities

The final goal of therapy is to help the person gain access to and merge the different subpersonalities. *Integration* is a continuous process that occurs throughout treatment until patients achieve continuous ownership of their behaviors, emotions, sensations, and knowledge. *Fusion* is the final merging of two or more subpersonalities. Many patients are reluctant to pursue this final treatment goal (Kluft, 1991, 1988). The subpersonalities themselves are likely to distrust the idea and to view integration as a form of death. Therapists have used a range of approaches to help integrate the personalities, including psychodynamic, supportive, cognitive, and drug therapies (Fichtner et al., 1990; Caddy, 1985).

In Sybil's case, the progress toward full integration was slow and halting and required eleven years of therapy (Schreiber, 1973):

*1957*

Integration? Far from it. As the past flooded back, there was all the more reason to regress into the other selves, defenses against the past. [p. 270]

*1962*

"Am I going to die?" each of the selves asked Dr. Wilbur. For some of the selves integration seemed synonymous with death. The doctor's assurances that, although one with Sybil, the individual selves would not cease to be seemed at best only partly convincing. [p. 316]

*1965*

Sybil's attitude toward these selves . . . had completely changed, from initial denial to hostility to acceptance—even to love. Having learned to love these parts of herself, she had in effect replaced self-derogation with self-love. This replacement was an important measure of her integration and restoration. . . . [p. 337]

Once the subpersonalities are integrated, further therapy is necessary to solidify the integrated personality and to provide the social and coping skills that will prevent subsequent dissociations (Fink, 1992). In case reports, some therapists report high success rates (Wilbur, 1984; Kluft, 1984), but others find that most patients continue to resist full and final integration. The relatively small number of reported cases has prevented researchers from gathering a large enough sample for assessing the effectiveness of the various approaches.

*Summing Up*
*Various factors have been cited to explain dissociative disorders, including extreme repression (the psychodynamic explanation) and operant conditioning (the behavioral view). Recent theories contend that the disorders may be related to state-dependent learning or to self-hypnosis. Therapists have used psychodynamic, hypnotic, and drug interventions to treat dissociative disorders. Therapists try to help those with multiple personality disorder recognize their disorder, recover memories, and integrate their subpersonalities.*

# Organic Disorders Affecting Memory and Other Cognitive Functions

Changes in memory can also have clearly organic causes such as brain injury, medical conditions, and substance misuse. Organic memory disorders fall into two categories—*amnestic disorders*, which primarily affect memory, and *dementias*, which affect both memory and other cognitive functions. Before discussing these disorders, let us consider what is presently known about the operation and biology of memory.

## Memory Systems

In essence, there are two human memory systems, and they work together to help us learn and recall. *Short-term memory* collects new information. *Long-term memory* is the repository of all the information that we have stored over the years—information that first made its way through the short-term memory system. The information held in short-term memory must be transformed, or consolidated, into long-term memory if we are to retain it. This transformation usually occurs in slow progressive steps. When short-term information becomes part of our long-term memory, it is said to have been *encoded*. Remembering such infor-

*Short-term memory*   The memory system that collects new information.

*Long-term memory*   The memory system that contains all the information that we have stored over the years.

mation involves *retrieval,* going into one's long-term memory to bring it out.

Information in long-term memory can be classified as either procedural or declarative. *Procedural memories* are learned skills we perform without needing to think about them, such as cutting with scissors or knowing how to solve a math problem. *Declarative memory* consists of information that is directly accessible to consciousness, such as names, dates, and other facts that have been learned. Declarative memory is far more disrupted than procedural memory in most organic disorders.

> ### Consider This
> Most people have had odd memory experiences such as forgetting why they are doing something, arriving at a destination without remembering any details of the drive there, forgetting an important appointment or occasion, having trouble remembering the name of a person or where they know someone from, or forgetting an event everyone else seems to remember. What kinds of memory difficulties might be occurring in each of these cases?

## The Anatomy of Memory

Memory functions—and memories themselves—have been difficult to locate. Researchers have searched for the specific place in the brain where the *content* of memory is stored, but their work has led to the conclusion that no such well-defined storehouse exists. What has emerged is the view that memory is a *process* rather than a place, involving activity and changes in cells throughout the brain; when the memory process is invoked, a memory is activated and comes forth.

Nevertheless, the study of organic memory disorders has led researchers to identify brain structures that appear to be particularly important in short-term and long-term memory processes. Two brain regions that have been implicated in the encoding and retrieving of memories are the *temporal lobes* (including the *hippocampus* and *amygdala,* key structures that are embedded under the lobes) and the *diencephalon* (including the *mammillary bodies, thalamus,* and *hypothalamus*) (see Figure 14-2). These brain areas seem to be involved in the transformation of short-term memory into long-term memory (Searleman & Herrmann, 1994). Many cases of organic memory loss involve damage to the areas.

---

*Temporal lobes*    Major regions in the cortex of each hemisphere of the brain that play a key role in memory, among other functions.

*Diencephalon*    A brain structure located below the cerebral cortex, consisting of the mammillary bodies, thalamus, and hypothalamus. It plays a key role in memory, among other functions.

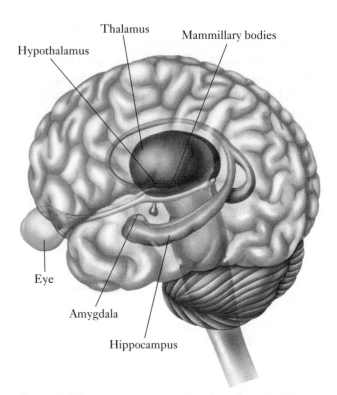

**Figure 14-2**    *Brain structures that play a major role in memory are the hippocampus, amygdala, mammillary bodies, thalamus, and hypothalamus. Dysfunctioning in these structures may produce a memory disorder. (Adapted from Bloom et al., 1988, p. 247.)*

One fact that has intrigued researchers (Squire et al., 1993) is that damage to memory-related brain structures appears to affect declarative knowledge (recall of conscious information) far more than procedural knowledge (recall of automatic-type skills). One explanation is that the temporal lobes and diencephalon, which have evolved more recently than other structures of the brain, are more closely related to the higher cognitive functions unique to humans. Automatic, unconscious processes, including those that execute motor tasks, may be controlled by older brain structures. As a result, when the temporal lobes and the diencephalon are injured, procedural knowledge is less likely to be disrupted.

## The Biochemistry of Memory

Beyond identifying and understanding the structures within the brain that are involved in memory processes, researchers would like to understand how the cells of the brain create and store memories. Although no one has yet found the "engram," or *memory trace*—the exact physical changes in the brain that account for a memory—many relevant discoveries have been made.

One of the most exciting of these findings is the role that *long-term potentiation (LTP)* may play in memory formation (Huang et al., 1992; Bliss & Gardner, 1973). Careful studies have shown that repeated electrical stimulation of nerve cells in some areas of the brain can lead to a significant increase in the likelihood that the cells will respond—and respond strongly—to future stimulation. This effect can last quite a long time (hence the name long-term potentiation) and may be a key mechanism in the formation of memories. As when many sleds are ridden down a snowy slope, creating a groove that later sledders easily find, LTP may serve to create a groove that corresponds to the process of making a memory, so that one can easily retrieve that memory later by following the same path. Of course, long-term potentiation does not in itself explain memory formation at the cellular level. Complicated chemical processes must also occur (Baraban, 1993; Lynch & Baudry, 1984).

With this picture of the systems, anatomy, and biochemistry of memory in mind, we now turn to the organic disorders that affect memory—the amnestic disorders and dementias.

# Amnestic Disorders

*Retrograde amnesia* is a lack of memory of events that occurred before the event that caused a person's amnesia. *Anterograde amnesia* is an ongoing inability to recall new information that is acquired after the event. As we noted earlier, people with a dissociative amnesia disorder often suffer from retrograde amnesia and rarely suffer from anterograde amnesia. The story for *amnestic disorders,* organic disorders in which memory impairment is the primary symptom, is quite different. Here people *sometimes* suffer from retrograde amnesia, depending on the particular disorder, but they *always* exhibit anterograde amnesia (see Table 14-1).

In severe forms of anterograde amnesia, people newly met are almost immediately forgotten, and problems solved one day must be tackled again the next. Patients may not remember any of the changes that have taken place since the time of an organic trauma. A middle-aged patient, for example, may continue to believe that Gerald Ford is president in 1995, more than twenty years after suffering his or her trauma. The sufferer of anterograde amnesia may retain all other cognitive skills, including verbal skills and problem-solving abilities. IQ is not changed.

In anterograde amnesia, it is as though information from short-term memory can no longer cross over into long-term memory. Thus, it is not surprising that the anterograde amnesias observed in amnestic disorders are often the result of damage to the brain's temporal lobes or diencephalon, the areas particularly responsible for transferring short-term memory into long-term memory.

## Korsakoff's Syndrome

As we observed in Chapter 11, approximately 5 percent of people with chronic alcoholism develop the severe amnestic disorder known as *Korsakoff's syndrome.* Excessive drinking, combined with a lack of proper diet, lead to a deficiency of the vitamin *thiamine.* The effect on portions of the diencephalon, among other areas, is dramatic.

Patients with Korsakoff's syndrome experience severe anterograde amnesia: they keep forgetting newly learned facts and information, although their general knowledge and intelligence remain intact (Butters & Cermak, 1980). Their memory deficit applies primarily to declarative knowledge; they are still able to incorporate new procedural knowledge, such as the way to solve a particular kind of puzzle, and they also maintain their language skills (Verfaellie et al., 1990). This may explain why Korsakoff's patients often *confabulate:* using their general intellectual skills and language skills, they create elaborate stories and lies to compensate for the memories they keep losing.

In addition to profound anterograde amnesia, patients with Korsakoff's syndrome experience some retrograde amnesia. They have particular difficulty remembering events from the years immediately preceding the onset of the syndrome, as opposed to events further back in the past (Albert et al., 1979). This problem may be due to damage of yet other brain areas, or it may in fact be due to the person's heavy drinking during those hard-to-remember years (which would have interfered with encoding at that time) and not to retrieval problems after onset of the disorder.

The effect of Korsakoff's syndrome on personality can also be profound. Before the onset of Korsakoff's syndrome, individuals may be aggressive, boisterous people; after the disorder has progressed, they often become more passive and unimposing.

---

*Long-term potentiation (LTP)*    A neuron's increased likelihood of responding strongly to future stimulation once it has been stimulated initially.

*Retrograde amnesia*    A lack of memory about events that occurred before the event that caused amnesia.

*Anterograde amnesia*    The inability to remember new information that is acquired after the event that caused amnesia.

*Amnestic disorders*    Organically caused disorders in which the primary symptom is memory impairment.

**Table 14-1** *Comparison of Memory Disorders*

| | Anterograde (continuous) Amnesia | Retrograde (localized, selective, and generalized) Amnesia | Declarative Memory Loss | Procedural Memory Loss | Organic Causes |
|---|---|---|---|---|---|
| Dissociative amnesia | Sometimes | Yes | Yes | Sometimes | No |
| Dissociative fugue | Sometimes | Yes | Yes | Sometimes | No |
| Multiple personality disorder | Yes | Yes | Yes | Yes | No |
| Amnestic disorders | Yes | Sometimes | Yes | Sometimes | Yes |
| Dementias | Yes | Yes | Yes | Yes | Yes |

## Head Trauma and Brain Surgery

Both head injuries and brain surgery are capable of causing amnestic disorders. Either may destroy memory-related brain structures or cut the connections between memory-related areas of the brain.

Second only to the popularity of emotional trauma as a cause of amnesia in television shows and movies, bumps on the head are portrayed as a quick and easy way to lose one's memory. In fact, *mild* head trauma, such as a concussion that does not result in coma or a period of unconsciousness, usually leaves a person with only minimal memory dysfunction, which disappears within days or at most months (Levin et al., 1987; McLean et al., 1983).

Almost half of the cases of *severe* head trauma, in contrast, do result in some permanent learning and memory problems, both anterograde and retrograde, partly the results of damage to the temporal lobes. The memories that do return often come back in a haphazard manner, but older ones typically return first (Searlemen & Herrmann, 1994).

Surgical lesions create much more specific memory problems. The most famous case of memory loss as a result of brain surgery belongs to H.M., a man whose identity has been more or less protected for decades (Ogden & Corkin, 1991; Corkin, 1984, 1968; Milner, 1971). H.M. suffered from severe epilepsy, a disorder that created seizures in his temporal lobes. To alleviate his symptoms, doctors removed parts of his temporal lobes, along with the amygdala and hippocampus. At that time the role of those brain regions in the formation of memories was not known. (Today temporal lobe surgery is generally restricted to *either* the right or left side of the brain.) H.M. has experienced severe an-

terograde amnesia ever since the surgery. He keeps failing to recognize anyone he has met since the 1953 operation.

## Other Amnestic Disorders

Other forms of physical trauma can also damage memory-related regions of the brain. These include *vascular disease,* which affects the flow of blood to the brain; *heart attacks,* which interrupt the flow of oxygen to the brain; and certain *infectious diseases.* Each may cause memory problems that vary from each other in character and severity.

# Dementias

*Dementias,* syndromes also associated with significant loss in memory, are sometimes difficult to distinguish from the amnestic disorders; the trademark of a dementia, however, is that at least one other cognitive function, such as abstract thinking or judgment, is also impaired (APA, 1994; Albert & Lafleche, 1991).

Dementias may be categorized according to any number of characteristics. One of the most useful distinctions is that between *cortical* and *subcortical dementias*; that is, dementias arising in the cortex and those that arise elsewhere in the brain.

## Cortical Dementias

In addition to memory impairment, some of the prominent problems that characterize the cortical de-

*Dementias* Organically caused syndromes marked by impairments of memory and at least one other cognitive function.

*Because of their long-term memory problems, people with very advanced cases of Alzheimer's disease are often unable to recognize even close relatives or friends. In addition, their short-term memory deficits may prevent them from completing simple tasks such as painting a picture.*

mentias are *aphasia,* difficulty in finding words to communicate with; personality changes such as inappropriate behavior and lack of foresight; and progressive deterioration. *Alzheimer's disease,* the most common cortical dementia, afflicts up to 4 percent of the elderly population in the United States, although it sometimes also occurs in middle-aged persons (APA, 1994). The prevalence of Alzheimer's disease doubles every five years in people over 60 (Cummings, 1993). A more complete discussion of the causes and treatments of this disease appears in Chapter 15, but we will briefly consider its effect on memory here.

The most common initial symptom of Alzheimer's disease is anterograde amnesia (Searleman & Herrmann, 1994). A person may start missing appointments, for example. Similarly, people with Alzheimer's disease have difficulty on tests requiring immediate

*Aphasia*   A common symptom in some kinds of dementia, characterized by difficulties in using or understanding language (for example, difficulty producing the names of objects and individuals).

*Alzheimer's disease*   The most common form of dementia, sometimes occurring before old age.

recall of new information (APA, 1994; Morris & Baddeley, 1988).

Memory for events from their past is also impaired; early in the disease memories from youth may be more easily recalled than more recent events (Beatty et al., 1988), but in more advanced cases, patients lose virtually all knowledge of the past. Eventually they cannot recognize the faces of even close relatives.

Once again, procedural memory frequently remains intact for some time, so that even patients with fairly advanced Alzheimer's disease can still learn to perform new motor tasks (Bondi & Kaszniak, 1991). Eventually, however, their cognitive abilities become so severely impaired that they are fully dependent on other people.

Other cortical dementias include Pick's disease and Creutzfeldt-Jakob disease. *Pick's disease* affects the frontal and temporal lobes and usually strikes people between the ages of 50 and 60 years. *Creutzfeldt-Jakob disease,* a pattern of dementia caused by a virus, typically occurs between 40 and 60 years of age (APA, 1994).

## Subcortical Dementias

Disorders that affect subcortical brain structures create a distinctive set of memory problems, along with severe movement problems. Here, the memory impairment is primarily the inability to retrieve information from long-term storage (retrograde amnesia), although retaining new information (anterograde amnesia) may also be a major problem (Cummings & Benson, 1984). The speech disorder aphasia, common in the cortical dementias, is not present in the subcortical dementias, but these disorders do often create debilitating personality changes.

*Huntington's disease,* an inherited progressive degenerative disease of cognition, emotion, and movement, is usually diagnosed in the victim's late 30s or early 40s but often begins much earlier (APA, 1994). It has a dramatic effect on personality and brings on depression, instability, and anxiety. Patients with Huntington's disease show severe retrograde amnesia early on and also suffer from impairments in learning procedural skills, such as new motor tasks (Butters et al., 1990). Memory problems get worse as the disease progresses. Children of people with Huntington's disease have a 50 percent chance of developing it.

*Parkinson's disease,* a slowly progressive neurological condition marked by tremors, rigidity, and un-

*Huntington's disease*   An inherited progressive degenerative disease of cognition, emotion, and movement.

*Parkinson's disease*   A slowly progressive neurological condition marked by tremors, rigidity, unsteadiness, and in many cases dementia.

## Box 14-2

# *"You Are the Music, While the Music Lasts"*
*Clayton S. Collins*

(*Excerpted by permission from* Profiles, *the magazine of Continental Airlines, February 1994.*)

Oliver Sacks danced to the Dead. For three solid hours. At 60. And with "two broken knees."

The Oxford-educated neurologist . . . explains (as only he would) . . . "in a tonic and dynamic sense they were quite overwhelming. And though I had effusions for a month after, it was worth it."

The power of music—not just to get an aging physician with classical tastes up and rocking, but also to "bring back" individuals rendered motionless and mute by neurological damage and disorders—is what's driving Sacks these days. The . . . best-selling author (*Migraine, A Leg to Stand On, The Man Who Mistook His Wife for a Hat, Seeing Voices* and *Awakenings*—which was made into a 1990 film starring Robin Williams) is working on another case-study book, one that deals in part with the role of music as a stimulus to minds that have thrown up stiff sensory barriers, leaving thousands of victims of stroke, tumors, Parkinson's disease, Tourette's syndrome, Alzheimer's and a wide range of less-publicized ailments alone, debilitated and disoriented.

*Over the years, neurologist Oliver Sacks has used treatment techniques that range from the medication L-dopa to the music of the Grateful Dead.*

"One sees how robust music is neurologically," Sacks says. "You can lose all sorts of particular powers but you don't tend to lose music and identity." . . .

Speaking in his distinctive stammer before a gathering of 1,400 music therapists in Toronto, Sacks . . . recalls all in one breath that the poet Novalis said, "Every disease is a musical disorder. Every cure is a musical solu-

tion," basking bemusedly in the appreciative gasps before admitting, "I've never known exactly what it means." . . .

Much of what he has encountered, particularly in working with patients at Beth Abraham Hospital, Bronx, N.Y., . . . relates to music.

"One saw patients who couldn't take a single step, who couldn't walk, but who could dance," he says. "There were patients who couldn't speak, but who could sing. The power of music in these patients was instantaneous . . . from a frozen Parkinsonian state to a freely flowing, moving, speaking state."

Sacks remembers a woman with Parkinson's who would sit perfectly still until "activated" by the music of Chopin, which she loved and knew by heart. She didn't have to hear a tune played. "It was sometimes sufficient to give her an opus number," Sacks says. "You would just say 'Opus 49,' and the F-minor 'Fantasy' would start playing in her mind. And she could move."

Music is certainly cultural, acknowledges the doctor, but it is basically biological. "One listens to music with one's muscles," he says. . . . "The 'tonic' [the key] is mostly brain-stem, an arousal response." The "dynamic," how loud or forcefully the music is played,

steadiness, causes dementia in 20 to 60 percent of cases, particularly among older people or those with advanced cases (APA, 1994; Weingartner et al., 1984). Patients with Parkinson's disease primarily have problems retrieving long-term memory. They also have difficulty learning new information, such as lists of words, and learning procedural skills, such as a new motor task (Harrington et al., 1990).

## Treatments for Amnestic Disorders and Dementias

Treating amnestic disorders and dementias is a frustrating and difficult challenge (see Box 14-2). Because these disorders affect a variety of brain structures and involve many neurochemical processes, no single approach or set of approaches is helpful in all cases, and

registers in the basal ganglia. And the "mnemonic" aspect of songs speaks to the unique memories of individuals: from tribal chant to blare of bagpipes to Bizet. The cliché about music's universality, he says, has merit.

"Deeply demented people respond to music, babies respond to music, fetuses probably respond to music. Various animals respond to music," Sacks says. "There is something about the animal nervous system . . . which seems to respond to music all the way down.

"I don't know how it is with invertebrates. I think it's a desperately needed experiment," the grin widens, "to see how squids and cuttlefish respond." . . .

"I think the notion of music as being a prosthesis in a way, for neurological dysfunctions, is very fundamental," Sacks says, citing the case of a patient with damage to the frontal lobes of his brain.

"When he sings, one almost has the strange feeling that [music] has given him his frontal lobes back, given him back, temporally, some function that has been lost on an organic basis," Sacks says, adding a quote from T.S. Eliot: "You are the music, while the music lasts."

The effects of music therapy may not always last. Sacks will take what he can get. "To organize a disorganized person for a minute

is miraculous. And for half an hour, more so." . . .

The key, says Sacks, is for patients to "learn to be well" again. Music can restore to them, he says, the identity that predates the illness. "There's a health to music, a life to music." . . . Music's been healing for thousands of years, Sacks says. "It's just being looked at now more systematically and with these special populations."

So if the Grateful Dead moved Sacks to dance, it had been in the name of research. Seeking a clinical application, Sacks returned to Beth Abraham the next day and "kidnapped" one of his patients. "Greg" was an amnesiac with a brain tumor and no coherent memories of life since about 1969—but an encyclopedic memory of the years that came before, and a real love of Grateful Dead tunes.

Sacks took Greg to that night's performance. "In the first half of the concert they were doing early music, and Greg was enchanted by everything," Sacks recalls. "I mean, he was not an amnesiac. He was completely oriented and organized and with it." Between sets Sacks went backstage and introduced Greg to band member Micky Hart, who was impressed with Greg's knowledge of the group but quite surprised when Greg asked after Pigpen. When told the former band member had died 20 years

before, "Greg was very upset," Sacks recalls. "And then 30 seconds later he asked 'How's Pigpen?'"

During the second half, the band played its newer songs. And Greg's world began to fall apart. "He was bewildered and enthralled and frightened. Because the music for him—and this is an extremely musical man, who understands the idiom of the Grateful Dead—was both familiar and unfamiliar. . . . He said 'This is like the music of the future.'"

Sacks tried to keep the new memories fresh. But the next day, Greg had no memory of the concert. It seemed as if all had been lost. "But—and this is strange—when one played some of the new music, which he had heard for the first time at the concert, he could sing along with it and remember it."

It is an encouraging development. . . . Children have been found to learn quickly lessons that are embedded in song. Sacks, the one-time quiet researcher, is invigorated by the possibilities. He wonders whether music could carry such information, to give his patient back a missing part of his life. To give Greg "some sense of what's been happening in the last 20 years, where he has no autobiography of his own."

That would have Sacks dancing in the aisles.

in fact, reliable, effective treatments do not yet exist. Fortunately, recent research on the genetic, biochemical, and anatomical causes of such disorders has provided hope that these diseases may be either better treated or prevented in the years to come.

The most important step in treating people with these disorders is to identify as clearly as possible the type and cause of the disorder, since the disorders of-

ten require different interventions. Thus, clinicians are careful to take a complete history of the patient, employ extensive neuropsychological testing to identify the patient's specific cognitive impairments, and employ brain imaging techniques to identify any clear, obvious cause of the disorder (see pp. 43–44).

Most of the research in this area has been directed at the dementias. As we shall see in Chapter 15, certain drugs are becoming available for treatment of the best known and most common dementias, particularly Alzheimer's disease, although these drugs seem to be of rather limited value thus far. Similarly, behavioral and cognitive interventions for dementias are as yet of limited value.

On the other hand, behavioral and cognitive approaches have been of some use in treating people with amnestic disorders whose amnesia is caused by head injury. These patients have successfully been taught special methods for remembering new information; in some cases the teachers have been computers (Schacter et al., 1990).

Rather than being discouraged by the lack of effective treatments for organic disorders of memory and other cognitive functions, researchers are now anticipating a period of significant advances in the understanding, treatment, and prevention of these disorders. The complexity of brain structures and biochemical processes underlying cognition can be overwhelming, but this decade is expected to see a number of significant breakthroughs.

---

### Summing Up

*Organic disorders that cause alterations in memory fall into two categories: the amnestic disorders, which primarily affect memory, and the dementias, which affect both memory and other cognitive functions. These disorders may be characterized by problems in short-term memory or long-term memory, or a combination of the two. Often they involve abnormalities in key structures of the brain, such as the temporal lobes (including the hippocampus and amygdala which are embedded under them) and the diencephalon (including the mammillary bodies, thalamus, and hypothalamus). Both drug therapies and behavioral therapies have been used with these disorders, but thus far their effectiveness has been limited.*

---

## The State of the Field
## *Disorders of Memory and Other Cognitive Functions*

Periodically a phenomenon will capture the public's interest but be scoffed at by scientists. Dissociative disorders suffered this fate for many years. On the one hand, the public's interest in this group of disorders has been almost insatiable over the years, as indicated by the popularity of books, magazine articles, movies, and television shows on the subject. On the other hand, until recently, investigations into dissociative amnesia and fugue were limited, and multiple personality disorder failed to stir the interest of empirical researchers. This skepticism and lack of attention on the part of scientists has changed greatly during the past decade. The growing number of reported cases of dissociative disorders, particularly of multiple personality disorder, has increasingly convinced many researchers that the patterns do in fact exist and often lead to significant dysfunctioning.

The last ten years have seen a veritable explosion of research designed to help clinicians recognize, understand, and treat the dissociative disorders. This research has suggested that the disorders may be more common than anyone previously believed and may in fact be rooted in processes, such as state-dependent learning and self-hypnosis, that are well known to clinical scientists from other contexts. This new wave of research enthusiasm will probably lead to improved understanding and treatment of these disorders in the coming years.

Some clinicians now worry that the interest and belief in dissociative disorders may be swinging too far in the other direction (Kelley & Kodman, 1987). They believe, for example, that at least some of the legal accusations and defenses based on dissociative disorders are contrived or inaccurate and that many current diagnoses have more to do with the increasing popularity of the disorder than with a careful assessment of symptoms. Such possibilities serve to underscore even further the importance of continued investigations into all aspects of these disorders.

Less controversial but equally intriguing are the disorders of memory that have organic causes. The enormous complexity of the brain and its functions makes it extremely difficult to understand, diagnose, or treat the range of amnestic disorders and dementias that have been identified. However, exciting new research on the biochemical and anatomical factors that affect these disorders has captured both the clinical and the public's attention.

A common thread in the study of the dissociative disorders and the organic disorders of memory is the inherent fascination that memory holds for us. This feature of human functioning is so central to each person's continuing sense of self that research in this realm is of fundamental importance to every person's well-being. As such, it is likely that investigations into the nature of memory and memory disorders will continue to expand in the coming years.

# Chapter Review

1. *Memory:* Memory plays a central role in our functioning by linking us to the past, present, and future.

2. *Dissociative Disorders:* People with dissociative disorders experience significant alterations in integrated functioning that are not due to clear physical causes. Typically, one part of the person's memory is dissociated, or separated, from another.

   A. People with *dissociative amnesia* are suddenly unable to recall important personal information or past events in their lives. There are four kinds of dissociative amnesia: localized, selective, generalized, and continuous.

   B. People with *dissociative fugue* not only lose their memory of their personal identity but flee to a different location and may establish a new identity.

   C. *Multiple personality disorder* is a rare, dramatic disorder in which a person displays two or more distinct subpersonalities.

      (1) A *primary* personality appears more often than the others, but transitions to the other subpersonalities may occur frequently and suddenly.

      (2) Most people with multiple personality disorder have been abused as children.

      (3) The subpersonalities often have complex relationships with one another and usually differ from one another in *personality characteristics, vital statistics, abilities and preferences,* and even *physiological responses.*

      (4) The number of people diagnosed with multiple personality disorder has increased in recent years.

3. *Explanations for Dissociative Disorders:* A number of factors have been cited to help explain dissociative disorders, including extreme repression, oper-

ant conditioning, state-dependent learning, and self-hypnosis.

4. *Treatments for Dissociative Disorders:* Dissociative amnesia and fugue may end spontaneously or may require treatment. Multiple personality disorder typically requires treatment for recovery to occur.

   A. Common interventions to help patients recover their lost memories are psychodynamic therapy, hypnotic therapy, and sodium amobarbital or sodium pentobarbital.

   B. Therapists usually try to guide people with multiple personality disorder to recognize the full scope and nature of their disorder, recover the gaps in their memories, and integrate their subpersonalities into one.

5. *Organic Disorders:* Amnestic disorders and dementias are organic disorders that cause problems in memory.

   A. These disorders may be characterized by problems in *short-term memory, long-term memory,* or both.

   B. Often the disorders involve abnormalities in key brain structures such as the *temporal lobes* (including the *hippocampus* and *amygdala* embedded under them) and the *diencephalon* (including the *mammillary bodies, thalamus,* and *hypothalamus*).

   C. *Amnestic disorders* are organic disorders that primarily affect memory. They include *Korsakoff's syndrome* and disorders caused by head trauma and brain surgery.

   D. *Dementias* are syndromes that affect both memory and other cognitive functions. They include *Alzheimer's disease, Huntington's disease,* and *Parkinson's disease.*

   E. *Treatment:* Both drug and behavioral therapies have been applied to organic memory disorders with limited success.

# Key Terms

| | | | |
|---|---|---|---|
| memory | selective amnesia | mutually amnesic | state-dependent learning |
| dissociative disorders | amnestic episode | mutually cognizant | hypnosis |
| dissociative amnesia | generalized amnesia | one-way amnesic | hypnotic amnesia |
| dissociative fugue | continuous amnesia | co-conscious | self-hypnosis |
| multiple personality | episodic memory | subpersonalities | special process |
| disorder | semantic memory | evoked potential | common process |
| depersonalization disorder | subpersonality | iatrogenic disorder | hypnotic therapy |
| localized amnesia | primary personality | repression | hypnotherapy |

| | | | |
|---|---|---|---|
| sodium amobarbital | temporal lobes | amnestic disorders | head trauma |
| sodium pentobarbital | hippocampus | dementias | brain surgery |
| integration | amygdala | Alzheimer's disease | aphasia |
| fusion | diencephalon | retrograde amnesia | Pick's disease |
| short-term memory | mammillary bodies | anterograde amnesia | Creutzfeldt-Jakob |
| long-term memory | thalamus | Korsakoff's syndrome | disease |
| procedural memory | hypothalamus | thiamine | Huntington's disease |
| declarative memory | long-term potentiation | confabulate | Parkinson's disease |

## Quick Quiz

1. List and describe the four different dissociative disorders.
2. What are four kinds of dissociative amnesia?
3. What are the different kinds of relationships that the subpersonalities may have in multiple personality disorder?
4. Describe the psychodynamic and behavioral explanations of dissociative disorders. How well are they supported by research?
5. How might the phenomenon of state-dependent learning help explain dissociative disorders?
6. Discuss the parallels between hypnotic amnesia and dissociative disorders. What is the self-hypnosis explanation of dissociative disorders?

7. What approaches have been used to treat dissociative disorders? What are the key features of treatment for multiple personality disorder?
8. What brain areas have been implicated in memory and in organic disorders of memory? Define short-term and long-term memory, procedural and declarative memory, and long-term potentiation.
9. Define amnestic disorders and discuss two such disorders.
10. What is dementia? What are the symptoms and features of Alzheimer's disease, Huntington's disease, and Parkinson's disease?

# 15

# Disorders of Childhood and Old Age

## Topic Overview

Most psychological disorders can occur at any time in life. Some, however, are particularly likely to emerge during a particular age, such as during childhood, or, at the other end of the spectrum, during old age. Some such disorders seem to be caused by the special pressures of the particular stage of life in which they emerge, others by unique traumatic experiences, and still others by biological abnormalities. Some of the disorders subside or can be corrected during the stage of their onset, others continue throughout the individual's life, and still others (particularly some of the childhood disorders) evolve into other kinds of disorders. In this chapter we shall examine some of the more common disorders that emerge during childhood or old age.

# Disorders of Childhood and Adolescence

People often think of childhood as a carefree time. However, it can also be a frightening and upsetting time during which one is regularly confronting new people, situations, and obstacles. In fact, most children experience at least some emotional problems in the normal course of development (see Box 15-1). Worrying, for example, is a common problem among children (King, 1993). Surveys suggest that almost half of all children have multiple fears (see Figure 15-1). Nor is adolescence necessarily an upbeat period. The physical and sexual changes, social and academic pressures, personal doubts, and temptations that characterize this time of transition leave many teenagers anxious, confused, and depressed (Petersen et al., 1993).

Beyond these common psychological difficulties, around a fifth of all children and adolescents in the United States experience a diagnosable mental disorder (Kazdin, 1994; Zill & Schoenborn, 1990). Boys with these disorders outnumber girls, although adult psychological disorders are usually more prevalent among women than among men.

## Consider This
Although boys with psychological disorders outnumber girls, adult women with such disorders outnumber adult men. Some theorists believe that this lifespan shift in prevalence rates reflects the special pressures placed on women in Western society. What kinds of factors might be operating here? Could there be other explanations for the shift in gender prevalence rates that occurs between childhood and adulthood?

# Childhood Anxiety Disorders

The anxiety disorders experienced by children and adolescents parallel those of adults, and include, for example, disorders such as specific phobias, social phobia, or generalized anxiety disorder (APA, 1994). One form of anxiety in children, *separation anxiety disorder,* is different enough from the adult anxiety disorders to be listed as a separate category in DSM-IV. Carrie, a 9-year-old girl suffering from this disorder, was referred to a local mental health center by her school counselor.

About 2 months ago Carrie seemed to become excessively anxious while at school for no apparent reason. She initially reported feeling sick to her stomach and later became quite concerned over being unable to get her breath. She stated that she was too nervous to stay at school and that she wanted her mother to come get her and take her home. . . . The counselor indicated that a similar incident occurred the next day with Carrie ending up going home again. She had not returned to school since. . . .

At the time of the intake evaluation the mother indicated that she felt Carrie was just too nervous to go to school. She stated that she had encouraged her daughter to go to school on numerous occasions but that she seemed afraid to go and appeared to feel bad, so she had not forced her. . . . When asked if Carrie went places by herself, the mother stated that Carrie didn't like to do that and that the two of them typically did most everything together. The mother went on to note that Carrie really seemed to want to have her (the mother) around all the time and tended to become upset whenever the two of them were separated.

*(Schwartz & Johnson, 1985, p. 188)*

Children with a separation anxiety disorder experience excessive anxiety, often panic, whenever they are separated from home or a parent. They have great trouble traveling independently away from home, and often refuse to visit friends' houses, go on errands, or attend camp or school. Many cannot even stay alone in a room, and cling to their parent around the house. The children may fear that they will get lost when they are separated or that their parent will meet with an accident or illness (APA, 1994).

It has been estimated that about 4 percent of children and adolescents experience this disorder. In many cases it is precipitated by a life stress such as the death

---

*Separation anxiety disorder*   A childhood disorder characterized by excessive anxiety, even panic, whenever the child is separated from home or a parent.

**PERCENTAGE OF CHILDREN WHO WORRY
"A LOT" THAT :**

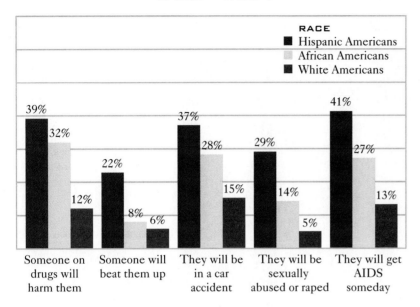

**PERCENTAGE OF CHILDREN WHO WORRY
"A LOT" THAT :**

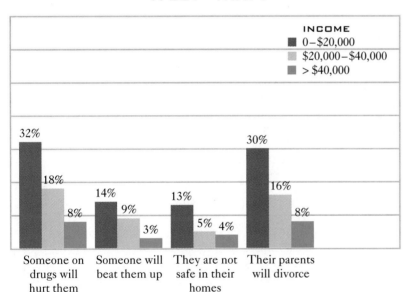

Figure 15-1 *According to a survey of over 900 children and adolescents, Hispanic American and African American children are much more likely than white American children to "worry a lot" about their safety and survival. Similarly, poorer children are more likely to worry about their welfare than wealthier children, irrespective of race, suggesting that the higher anxiety levels of children of racial minorities may be largely a matter of living in poorer, more deprived, or dangerous environments. (Adapted from National Commission on Children, 1991.)*

of a parent or pet, moving, or a change of schools. Surveys suggest that it is somewhat more common among girls than boys (APA, 1994) (see Table 15-1).

As in Carrie's case, a separation anxiety disorder sometimes takes the form of a *school phobia,* or *school refusal,* a common problem in which children experience extreme anxiety about attending school and often stay home for an extended period of time. Many cases of school phobia, however, involve factors other than separation, such as social fears, anxiety about academic performance, depression, and fears of specific objects or persons at school.

Although childhood anxiety disorders are generally explained in much the same way as adult anxiety disorders (discussed in Chapters 5 and 6), some features unique to childhood have also been cited as an important backdrop to these disorders. For example, since children have had fewer past experiences than adults, many aspects of their world are new and scary to them. Many are frightened by common developmental changes, such as a mother's return to work or the beginning of school, or by special traumas, such as moving to a new residence or becoming seriously ill (Tweed et al., 1989).

Box 15-1

# The Etiology and Treatment of Childhood
## Jordan W. Smoller

*This "clinical review" of the "disorder" called childhood originally appeared in Glen C. Ellenbogen [Ed.], Oral Sadism and the Vegetarian Personality. New York: Brunner/Mazel, 1986.*

Childhood is a syndrome that has only recently begun to receive serious attention from clinicians. The syndrome itself, however, is not at all recent. As early as the eighth century, the Persian historian Kidnom made reference to "short, noisy creatures," who may well have been what we now call "children." The treatment of children, however, was unknown until this century, when so-called child psychologists and child psychiatrists became common. Despite this history of clinical neglect, it has been estimated that well over half of all Americans alive today have experienced childhood directly (Seuss, 1983). In fact, the actual numbers are probably much higher, since these data are based on self-reports which may be subject to social desirability biases and retrospective distortion.

Clinicians are still in disagreement about the significant clinical features of childhood, but the proposed DSM-IV will almost certainly include the following core features:

1. Congenital onset
2. Dwarfism
3. Emotional lability and immaturity
4. Knowledge deficits
5. Legume anorexia

**Congenital Onset**  In one of the few existing literature reviews on childhood, Temple-Black (1982) has noted that childhood is almost always present at birth, although it may go undetected for years or even remain subclinical indefinitely. This observation has led some investigators to speculate on a biological contribution to childhood. As one psychologist has put it, "we may soon be in a position to distinguish organic childhood from functional childhood" (Rogers, 1979).

**Dwarfism**  This is certainly the most familiar clinical marker of childhood. It is widely known that children are physically short relative to the population at large. Indeed, common clinical wisdom suggests that the treatment of the so-called small child (or "tot") is particularly difficult. These children are known to exhibit infantile behavior and display a startling lack of insight (Tom & Jerry, 1967).

**Emotional Lability and Immaturity**  This aspect of childhood is often the only basis for a clinician's diagnosis. As a result, many otherwise normal adults are misdiagnosed as children and must suffer the unnecessary social stigma of being labeled a "child" by professionals and friends alike.

**Knowledge Deficits**  While many children have IQs within or even above the norm, almost all will manifest knowledge deficits. Anyone who has known a real child has experienced the frustration of trying to discuss any topic that requires some general knowledge.

**Legume Anorexia**  This last identifying feature is perhaps the most unexpected. Folk wisdom is supported by empirical observation—children will rarely eat their vegetables (see Popeye, 1957, for review).

## Causes of Childhood

Now that we know what it is, what can we say about the causes of childhood? Recent years have seen a flurry of theory and speculation from a number of perspectives. Some of the most prominent are reviewed below.

### Sociological Model

Emile Durkind was perhaps the first to speculate about sociological causes of childhood. He points out two key observations about children: (1) the vast majority of children are unemployed, and (2) children represent one of the least educated segments of our society. In fact, it has been estimated that less than 20 percent of children have had more than a fourth-grade education. . . . One promising rehabilitation program (Spanky & Alfalfa, 1978) has trained victims of severe childhood to sell lemonade.

### Biological Model

The observation that childhood is usually present from birth has led some to speculate on a biological contribution. An early investigation by Flintstone and Jetson (1939) indicated that childhood runs in families. Their survey of over 8,000 American families revealed that over half contained more than one child. Further investigation revealed that even most nonchild family members had experienced childhood at some point. . . .

## Psychological Models

A considerable number of psychologically based theories of the development of childhood exist. They are too numerous to review here. Among the more familiar models are Seligman's "learned childishness" model. According to this model, individuals who are treated like children eventually give up and become children. As a counterpoint to such theories, some experts have claimed that childhood does not really exist. Szasz (1980) has called "childhood" an expedient label. In seeking conformity, we handicap those whom we find unruly or too short to deal with by labeling them "children."

## *Treatment of Childhood*

Efforts to treat childhood are as old as the syndrome itself. Only in modern times, however, have humane and systematic treatment protocols been applied.

The overwhelming number of children has made government intervention inevitable. The nineteenth century saw the institution of what remains the largest single program for the treatment of childhood—so-called public schools. Under this colossal program, individuals are placed into treatment groups on the basis of the severity of their condition. For example, those most severely afflicted may be placed in a "kindergarten" program. Patients at this level are typically short, unruly, emotionally immature, and intellectually deficient.

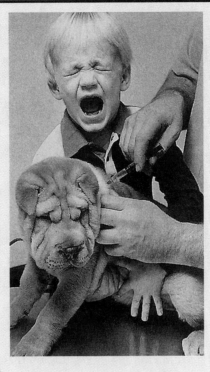

Unfortunately, the "school" system has been largely ineffective. Not only is the program a massive tax burden, but it has failed even to slow down the rising incidence of childhood.

Faced with this failure and the growing epidemic of childhood, mental health professionals are devoting increasing attention to the treatment of childhood. . . . The following case (taken from Gumbie & Pokey, 1957) is typical.

Billy J., age 8, was brought to treatment by his parents. Billy's affliction was painfully obvious. He stood only 4′3″ high and weighed a scant 70 pounds, despite the fact that he ate voraciously. Billy presented a variety of troubling symptoms. His voice was noticeably high for a man. He displayed legume anorexia and, according to his parents, often refused to bathe. His intellectual functioning was also below normal—he had little general knowledge and could barely write a structured sentence. Social skills were also deficient. He often spoke inappropriately and exhibited "whining behavior." His sexual experience

was nonexistent. Indeed, Billy considered women "icky." . . .

After years of this kind of frustration, startling new evidence has come to light which suggests that the prognosis in cases of childhood may not be all gloom. . . . Moe, Larrie, and Kirly (1974) began a large-scale longitudinal study. These investigators studied two groups. The first group comprised 34 children currently engaged in a long-term conventional treatment program. The second was a group of 42 children receiving no treatment. . . .

The results . . . of a careful 10-year follow-up were startling. . . . Shemp (1984) found subjects improved. Indeed, in most cases, the subjects appeared to be symptom-free. Moe et al. report a spontaneous remission rate of 95 percent, a finding that is certain to revolutionize the clinical approach to childhood.

These recent results suggest that the prognosis for victims of childhood may not be so bad as we have feared. We must not, however, become too complacent. Despite its apparently high spontaneous remission rate, childhood remains one of the most serious and rapidly growing disorders facing mental health professionals today. And beyond the psychological pain it brings, childhood has recently been linked to a number of physical disorders. Twenty years ago, Howdi, Doodi, and Beauzeau (1965) demonstrated a sixfold increased risk of chickenpox, measles, and mumps among children as compared with normal controls. Later, Barbie and Kenn (1971) linked childhood to an elevated risk of accidents—compared with normal adults, victims of childhood were much more likely to scrape their knees, lose their teeth, and fall off their bikes.

Clearly, much more research is needed before we can give any real hope to the millions of victims wracked by this insidious disorder.

**Table 15-1    Comparison of Childhood Disorders**

| Disorder | Usual Age of Identification | Prevalence Rate among All Children | Gender with Higher Rate | Elevated Family History | Recovery by Adulthood |
|---|---|---|---|---|---|
| Separation anxiety disorder | Before 12 years | 4 percent | Females | Yes | Often |
| Conduct disorder | Before 12 years | 8 percent | Males | Yes | Often |
| ADHD | Before 12 years | 5 percent | Males | Yes | Often |
| Enuresis | 5–8 years | 5 percent | Males | Yes | Usually |
| Encopresis | After 4 years | 1 percent | Males | Unclear | Always |
| Learning disorders | 6–9 years | 5 percent | Males | Yes | Often |
| Autism | 0–3 years | 0.05 percent | Males | Yes | Sometimes |
| Mental retardation | Before 10 years | 1 percent | Males | Unclear | Sometimes |

Furthermore, children are often presented by their culture with dark notions that may frighten them and set the stage for anxiety disorders. Today's children, for example, are repeatedly warned, both at home and at school, about the dangers of kidnapping and of drugs. Similarly, they are often bombarded by violent and scary images from television shows, movies, and news programs. Investigators have even noted that many of our time-honored fairy tales and nursery rhymes contain frightening images that upset many children.

A variety of approaches, including psychodynamic, behavioral, and family therapies, have been used to treat anxiety disorders in children, often with success (Kazdin, 1994; Kendall et al., 1991, 1989). Because children have a limited capacity for analyzing and reflecting on their feelings and motives, many therapists, particularly psychodynamic therapists, use **play therapy**. They have the children express their conflicts and feelings indirectly by playing with toys, drawing, and making up stories. The therapists then interpret these activities and, through continued play and fantasy, try to help the children develop relevant insights, resolve conflicts, and alter their emotions and behavior.

## Childhood Depression

Like adults, children may experience a depressive disorder. Bobby is one such child:

> In observing Bobby in the playroom it was obvious that his activity level was well below that expected for a child of 10. He showed a lack of interest in the toys that were available to him, and the interviewer was unable to get him interested in any play activity for more than a few minutes. In questioning him about home and school, Bobby indicated that he didn't like school because he didn't have any friends, and he wasn't good at playing games like baseball and soccer like the other kids were, stating "I'm not really very good at anything." . . . When asked what he would wish for if he could have any three wishes granted he indicated, "I would wish that I was the type of boy my

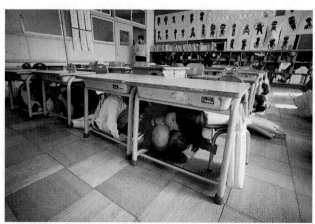

*Childhood anxieties can be caused by society's repeated warnings of possible catastrophes. These school children in Japan dive for cover during an earthquake drill.*

*Play therapy*    An approach to treating childhood disorders that helps children express their conflicts and feelings indirectly by drawing, playing with toys, and making up stories.

mother and father want, I would wish that I could have friends, and I would wish that I wouldn't feel sad so much."

In speaking with the parents, the mother reported that she and her husband had become increasingly concerned about their son during the past year. She indicated that he always seemed to look sad and cried a lot for no apparent reason and that he appeared to have lost interest in most of the things that he used to enjoy doing. The mother confirmed Bobby's statements that he had no friends, indicating that he had become more and more of a loner during the past 6 to 9 months. She stated that his schoolwork had also suffered in that he is unable to concentrate on school assignments and seems to have "just lost interest."

*(Schwartz & Johnson, 1985, p. 214)*

Studies suggest that approximately 2 percent of children under 17 years of age experience a major depressive disorder (Kazdin, 1994). The rate may be 7 percent among adolescents alone (Petersen et al., 1993, 1991). There appears to be no difference in the rates of depression in boys and girls before the age of 11, but by the age of 16, girls are twice as likely as boys to be depressed (Angold & Rutter, 1992; Kazdin, 1990).

Explanations of childhood depression are similar to those offered for adult depression. Theorists have pointed, for example, to such factors as loss, learned helplessness, negative cognitive bias, and low norepinephrine activity to account for the disorder (Petersen et al., 1993). Moreover, like adult depression, childhood depression often seems to be precipitated by a negative life event, major change, rejection, or ongoing abuse. Research also indicates that childhood depres-

sion often responds well to cognitive-behavioral therapy, social skills training, and family therapy (Kazdin, 1994, 1989; Stark et al., 1991).

## Disruptive Behavior Disorders

It is common for children to flout social rules or misbehave. Some children, however, display patterns of negativity, hostility, and defiance that are more frequent, intense, and disruptive than the norm, and they are considered to have either an oppositional defiant disorder or conduct disorder.

Children with *oppositional defiant disorder* argue repeatedly with adults, lose their temper, and feel great anger and resentment. They frequently defy adult rules and requests, annoy others, and blame others for their own mistakes and problems. The disorder is more common in boys than in girls before puberty, but equally common among boys and girls after puberty. Its prevalence is between 2 and 16 percent according to various studies (APA, 1994).

Children with *conduct disorder,* a more severe pattern, go further and repeatedly violate the basic rights of others. They are often aggressive and may in fact be physically cruel to people or animals, deliberately destroy others' property, lie and cheat, skip school, or run away from home. Many steal from, threaten, or harm their victims, committing such crimes as shoplifting, breaking into houses or cars, mugging, and armed robbery. As they get older their physical violence may extend to rape, assault, or in rare cases homicide (APA, 1994).

Conduct disorders usually, but not always, begin before age 16. Children with a mild conduct disorder may improve over time, but in severe cases the disorder often continues into adulthood and may lead to the development of an antisocial personality disorder, a disorder which we shall examine in the next chapter. Six to sixteen percent of boys and 2 to 9 percent of girls display conduct disorders (APA, 1994).

Many children with conduct disorders are suspended from school, placed in foster homes, or incarcerated. When children between the ages of 8 and 18 break the law, the legal system often labels them *juvenile delinquents.* More than half of the juveniles who are arrested each year are *recidivists,* that is, they have records of previous arrests. Many more males commit

*Childhood anxiety or depression may be the result of developmental traumas, such as the increasingly common experience of having to share a parent's affection with a new stepparent. The face of this boy after his mother's remarriage says it all.*

*Oppositional defiant disorder*   A childhood disorder in which children argue repeatedly with adults, lose their temper, and swear, feeling great anger and resentment.

*Conduct disorder*   A childhood disorder in which the child repeatedly violates the basic rights of others, displaying aggression and sometimes destroying others' property, lying, cheating, or running away from home.

*Aggressive behavior in 2-year-olds is considered quite normal. It is expected to become significantly less frequent and less intense as a child grows older. If it does not, the child may be displaying an oppositional defiant disorder or conduct disorder.*

juvenile crime than females, although rates for females are on the increase. Arrests of adolescents for serious crimes have at least tripled during the past twenty years, and the Department of Justice (1994) reported recently that the juvenile crime rate jumped almost 50 percent just between 1988 and 1992.

A variety of factors have been cited as causes of conduct disorders, including genetic and biological factors, drug abuse, and poverty (Linz et al., 1990). However, *family dysfunction* has been pointed to most often. Conduct disorders often emerge in an atmosphere of family conflict and hostility (Dadds et al., 1992; Whittaker & Bry, 1992). Children whose parents reject them, leave them, or fail to provide them with consistent discipline and supervision are apparently more likely than others to lie, steal, or run away (APA, 1994; Frick et al., 1992). Similarly, children whose parents are themselves antisocial or have alcohol or other kinds of substance dependence, mood disorders, or schizophrenia are more likely to display a conduct disorder (APA, 1994; Moore & Arthur, 1983).

Generally, treatments for conduct disorders have been more effective with children under 13 years of age than with those over 13, as disruptive behavior patterns become more tenacious with age (Loeber, 1991; McMahon & Wells, 1989). The most effective approaches appear to be *family interventions* in which (1) parents are taught more effective ways to deal with their children (for example, consistently to reward appropriate behaviors) or (2) parents and children meet together in behavior-oriented family therapy (Long et al., 1994; Bank et al., 1991). Residential programs in the community, interventions at school, and skill-

training techniques (training the child to cope with anger) have also had some success. And recently drug therapy has been tried to help control aggressive outbursts in these children (Kemph et al., 1993).

Many clinicians claim that the greatest promise for conduct disorders lies in *prevention* programs that begin in early childhood. Preventive measures that have been used include increasing training opportunities for young people, increasing recreational facilities, alleviating the conditions of poverty, and improving parents' child-rearing skills. All interventions work better when they educate and involve the family (Zigler et al., 1992).

## Attention-Deficit Hyperactivity Disorder

Children who display an *attention-deficit hyperactivity disorder* (ADHD) attend very poorly to tasks or behave overactively and impulsively, or both. An ADHD pattern often appears before the child starts school, as in the case of Steven, a child who displays poor attention, as well as overactivity and impulsiveness.

Steven's mother cannot remember a time when her son was not into something or in trouble. As a baby he was incredibly active, so active in fact that he nearly rocked his crib apart. All the bolts and screws became loose and had to be tightened periodically. Steven was also always into forbidden places, going through the medicine cabinet or under the kitchen sink. He once swallowed some washing detergent and had to be taken to the emergency room. As a matter of fact, Steven had many more accidents and was more clumsy than his older brother and younger sister. . . . He always seemed to be moving fast. . . .

. . . Since his entry into school, his life has been miserable and so has the teacher's. Steven does not seem capable of attending to assigned tasks and following instructions. He would rather be talking to a neighbor or wandering around the room without the teacher's permission. When he is seated and the teacher is keeping an eye on him to make sure that he works, Steven's body still seems to be in motion. He is either tapping his pencil, fidgeting, or staring out the window and daydreaming. Steven hates kindergarten and has few long-term friends; indeed, school rules and demands appear to be impossible challenges for him. The effects of this mismatch are now showing in Steven's schoolwork and attitude. He has fallen behind academically and has real difficulty mastering new concepts; he no longer follows directions from the teacher and has started to talk back.

*(Gelfand et al., 1982, p. 256)*

*Attention-deficit hyperactivity disorder (ADHD)*    A disorder characterized by the inability to focus attention or by overactive and impulsive behavior, or both.

The symptoms of ADHD often feed into one another. A child who has trouble focusing attention may be pulled into action in several directions at once. Similarly, a constantly moving child is likely to have difficulty attending to tasks or exercising careful judgment. Often one of these areas of disturbance is much more prominent than the other.

About half of the children with ADHD also experience learning or communication problems, many perform poorly in school, and about 80 percent misbehave, often quite seriously (Bird et al., 1993). Moreover, the disorder is common among children with mood and anxiety disorders (APA, 1994).

As many as 5 percent of schoolchildren appear to display ADHD, around 80 percent of them boys. The disorder spans all cultures (APA, 1994). Many children show a lessening of symptoms as they move into late adolescence, but, as Figure 15-2 indicates, in a number of cases some forms of learning, perceptual, and behavioral problems remain (APA, 1994; Mannuzza et al., 1993). ADHD continues into adulthood for about a third of affected individuals (Lie, 1992).

Research has not pointed to clear causes of ADHD. Various theorists have suggested biological factors (indeed, the disorder was once referred to as **minimal brain damage**), high levels of stress, and family dysfunctioning (Giedd et al., 1994; Cunningham et al., 1988). However, these notions have failed to receive consistent support (Anastopoulos & Barkley, 1992). Thus, today's clinicians generally view ADHD as a disorder with multiple and interacting causes. In addition, as sociocultural theorists point out, ADHD symptoms and a diagnosis of ADHD may create still further difficulties and generate additional symptoms in the child. That is, children with hyperactivity are often viewed more negatively than other children by their peers, their parents, and the children themselves (King & Young, 1981; Arnold, 1973).

There is considerable disagreement about the most effective treatment for ADHD. The most common approach has been stimulant drugs, such as **methylphenidate (Ritalin)**. These drugs sometimes have a quieting effect on children with ADHD and increase their ability to solve complex problems, perform academically, and control aggressive behavior (Hinshaw, 1991; Douglas et al., 1988). However, many clinicians have concern over the possible long-term effects of taking these drugs (Greenhill, 1992).

Behaviorists have treated ADHD primarily by teaching parents and teachers how to systematically reinforce the children for paying attention or behaving appropriately at home or school. Such operant conditioning treatments have been relatively successful, especially in combination with drug therapy (Du Paul & Barkley, 1993).

## Elimination Disorders

Children with elimination disorders repeatedly urinate or pass feces in their clothes, in bed, or on the floor, after an age at which they are expected to control these bodily functions. If the symptoms are caused by a general medical condition, the children are not considered to have such a disorder.

### Enuresis

**Enuresis** is involuntary (or in some cases intentional) bed-wetting or wetting of one's clothes. It typically occurs at night or, less commonly, during the day, or both. The prevalence of enuresis decreases with age. Seven percent of boys and 3 percent of girls who are 5 years old experience this disorder. In contrast, 3 percent of boys and 2 percent of girls who are 10 years old experience it. At age 18 years, the pattern is found among 1 percent of males and somewhat fewer females (APA, 1994).

Children who have been dry for a time may start to wet again as an apparent response to stress such as hospitalization, the birth of a sibling, and entrance into school. Whatever the precipitants, it is important

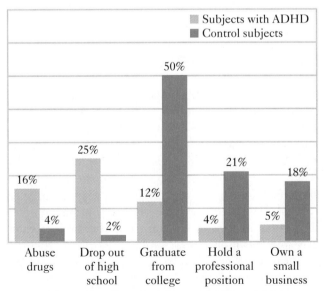

**Figure 15-2** *ADHD is a problem with a continuing impact for many individuals. In a recent study of 103 boys with ADHD and 100 control subjects, those with ADHD were more likely to abuse drugs as teenagers and less likely to earn a degree, hold a professional position, or own a small business. (Adapted from Mannuzza et al., 1993.)*

*Enuresis* A childhood disorder characterized by repeated bed-wetting or wetting of one's clothes.

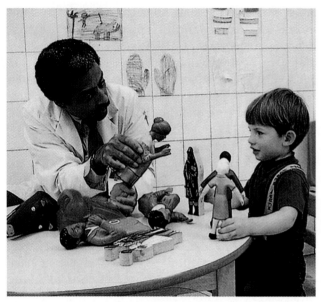

*Therapists may use play therapy to assess the functioning of children and to help them express their feelings and thoughts and understand themselves and others.*

to keep in mind that the point at which it is no longer considered "normal" to wet one's bed or pants varies from society to society.

As with other childhood disorders, various explanations of enuresis have been suggested, but none has received clear support. Psychodynamic theorists explain it as a symptom of more general conflicts (Olmos de Paz, 1990); family theorists attribute it to disturbed family interactions; behaviorists view it as poorly coordinated toilet training; and some biological theorists point to a delayed development of the physical structure of the urinary system (Erickson, 1992).

Most cases of enuresis eventually correct themselves even without treatment; however, therapy is often applied to accelerate this process. Treatments for enuresis based on behavioral principles have enjoyed much success (Friman & Warzak, 1990; Whelan & Houts, 1990). In a widely used classical conditioning approach, a bell and a battery are wired to a pad consisting of two metallic foil sheets, and the entire apparatus is placed under the child at bedtime (Howe & Walker, 1992; Mowrer & Mowrer, 1938). A single drop of urine acts as an electrolyte that sets off the bell. The child is awakened immediately after he or she starts to wet. Thus the bell (unconditioned stimulus) paired with the sensation of a full bladder (conditioned stimulus) produces the response of waking. Eventually, a full bladder alone awakens the child. Certain cognitive therapies and antidepressant drug therapies have also had some success (Fritz et al., 1994; Ronen et al., 1992).

## Encopresis

*Encopresis,* or repeated defecating into inappropriate places, such as clothing or the floor, is less common than enuresis and less well researched. This problem most often occurs during the day (Levine, 1975). Like enuresis, it may be a continuation of infancy behavior or regressive in nature. The problem, which is usually involuntary, starts after the age of 4. It affects about 1 percent of 5-year-olds, a rate that drops to near zero by adulthood. It is more common in boys than in girls (APA, 1994).

Some cases of encopresis are related to constipation and fecal impaction in the child. In other cases it has been related to inadequate, inconsistent toilet training or to stress (APA, 1994). Often it is accompanied by enuresis. Encopresis typically causes intense social problems, shame, and embarrassment. Children who suffer from it may try to conceal their condition from others and to avoid situations, such as camp or school, in which they might become embarrassed (APA, 1994; Ross, 1981).

The most common and successful treatments for encopresis are behavioral, medical, and combinations of the two (Ronen, 1993; Thapar et al., 1992). Family therapy has also been helpful (Wells & Hinkle, 1990).

# Disorders of Learning, Communication, and Coordination

More than 15 percent of children display highly inadequate development and functioning in learning, communication, or coordination (APA, 1994). Such disorders lead to impaired performance in school and daily living, and typically are more common in boys than in girls.

One group of problems are the *learning disorders,* in which children's reading, arithmetic, or written expression skills are well below their intellectual capacity and cause academic and personal dysfunctioning. Another group are the *communication disorders,* in which children either stutter, cannot make appropriate speech sounds, have great difficulty using language to express themselves, or have severe problems comprehending or expressing language. Finally, *developmental coordination disorder* is a problem in which children perform motor-coordinated activities at a level well below others of their age.

Studies have linked these disorders to such factors as genetic defects, birth injuries, lead poisoning, inappropriate diet, sensory dysfunction, and poor teaching

---

*Encopresis*   A childhood disorder characterized by repeated defecating into inappropriate places.

(Erickson, 1992; Gelfand et al., 1982). However, research support for these tentative explanations has been quite limited, and the precise causes of the disorders remain unclear.

Some of these disorders respond to special interventions such as reading therapy or speech therapy. In many cases, the disorder disappears before adulthood, even without any treatment. In some cases, the problem continues.

The classification of these problems as mental disorders is highly controversial. Many clinicians view them as primarily educational or social problems, appropriately addressed within the school or home. The framers of recent editions of the DSM have reasoned, however, that the dysfunctioning caused by the disorders and their frequent association with other psychological problems justify their special clinical classifications. Of special concern are studies that have found an increased risk of depression and even suicide in adolescents with such problems, particularly the learning disorders (Huntington & Bender, 1993).

*Summing Up*
*Children typically experience at least some emotional and behavioral problems in the normal course of development. Many, however, display clinical disorders. These children may suffer from adult-like disorders such as social phobia, generalized anxiety disorder, or depression, or they may experience disorders identified more closely with childhood, such as separation anxiety disorder, oppositional defiant disorder, conduct disorder, attention-deficit hyperactivity disorder, enuresis, encopresis, or disorders of learning, communication, and coordination. Some of these disorders, such as enuresis and encopresis, disappear or greatly improve as the individual ages, particularly with treatment interventions. Others, such as severe conduct disorders, may linger into adulthood, sometimes in an altered form.*

# Long-Term Disorders That Begin in Childhood

As noted earlier, most childhood disorders either subside during the stage of their onset or evolve into disorders of a somewhat different kind as the person ages. However, two of the disorders that emerge during childhood typically continue unchanged throughout a person's entire life. These disorders—autistic disorder and mental retardation—are our next subjects of discussion.

## Autistic Disorder

A little boy named Mark presents a typical picture of autistic disorder:

In retrospect [Susan, Mark's mother] can recall some things that appeared odd to her. For example, she remembers that . . . Mark never seemed to anticipate being picked up when she approached. In addition, despite Mark's attachment to a pacifier (he would complain if it were mislaid), he showed little interest in toys. In fact, Mark seemed to lack interest in anything. He rarely pointed to things and seemed oblivious to sounds. . . . Mark spent much of his time repetitively tapping on tables, seeming to be lost in his own world.

After his second birthday, Mark's behavior began to trouble his parents. . . . Mark, they said, would "look through" people or past them, but rarely at them. He could say a few words but didn't seem to understand speech. In fact, he did not even respond to his own name. Mark's time was occupied examining familiar objects, which he would hold in front of his eyes while he twisted and turned them. Particularly troublesome were Mark's odd movements—he would jump, flap his arms, twist his hands and fingers, and perform all sorts of facial grimaces, particularly when he was excited—and what Robert [Mark's father] described as Mark's rigidity. Mark would line things up in rows and scream if they were disturbed. He insisted on keeping objects in their place and would become upset whenever Susan attempted to rearrange the living room furniture. . . .

Slowly, beginning at age five, Mark began to improve. . . . The pronoun in the sentence was inappropriate and the sentence took the form of a question he had been asked previously, but the meaning was clear.

*(Wing, 1966)*

Mark was manifesting an *autistic disorder*, also called *autism*, a disorder first identified by the American psychiatrist Leo Kanner in 1943. Children with this disorder are extremely unresponsive to others, show poor communication skills, have limited skill at imaginative play, and often behave in a highly restricted and repetitive manner. The symptoms appear very early in life, before 3 years of age. Several other disorders are similar to autism, each differing in

*Autism*  A pervasive developmental disorder characterized by extreme unresponsiveness to others, poor communication skills, limited skill at imaginative play, and highly restricted and repetitive behavior.

time of onset or symptomology, but most clinicians use the term "autism" to refer to all of the disorders, and we shall do the same.

Autism affects only 2 to 5 of every 10,000 children (APA, 1994). Approximately 80 percent of children with autism are boys. Two in three remain severely impaired into adulthood and are unable to lead independent lives (APA, 1994).

**Unresponsiveness**    Aloofness, lack of responsiveness, and lack of interest in other people have long formed the cornerstone of the diagnosis of autism (Volkmar et al., 1993). Like Mark, children with autism typically do not reach for their parents during infancy, and may arch their backs when they are held. And, like Mark, they often fail to recognize or acknowledge those around them.

**Language and Communication Deficits**    Approximately half of all children with autism fail to speak or develop language skills (Dawson & Castelloe, 1992; Rutter, 1966). Those who do talk may show peculiarities in their speech. One of the most common speech problems is *echolalia,* the exact echoing or parroting of phrases spoken by others. The children repeat words with the same accent or inflection, but without comprehension. Some even repeat a sentence hours or days after they have heard it.

Children with autism may also display other speech oddities, such as *pronominal reversal,* or confusion of pronouns—the use of "you" instead of "I." When Mark was hungry, he would say, "Do you want dinner?" The children may also have difficulty naming objects, using abstract speech, using speech spontaneously, or fully understanding it.

**Limited Imaginative Play and Restricted Behavior**
Children with autism often have extreme difficulty playing in a varied, spontaneous way or imitating others in their play. Typically they become very upset at minor changes in objects or persons, or in their routine. Many also display ritualistic and repetitive behaviors. Mark, for example, would line things up, and would scream if they were disturbed. Kanner (1943) labeled this characteristic a *perseveration of sameness.*

Many children with autism become strongly attached to particular objects, such as plastic lids, rubber bands, buttons, or water. They may collect these things, carry them, or play with them constantly. Some are fascinated by movement, and may observe spinning objects, such as fans or records, for hours.

The motor movements of children with autism may also be unusual. Mark would jump, flap his arms, twist his hands and fingers, and grimace. In addition to such *self-stimulatory behaviors,* some children perform *self-injurious behaviors,* such as repeatedly lunging or banging their heads against walls, pulling their hair, or biting parts of their body.

These behaviors and limitations seem to reflect a highly disturbed and contradictory pattern of perceptual reactions (Wing, 1976; Wing & Wing, 1971). Sometimes the children appear *overstimulated* by sights and sounds and try to block them out, while at other times they seem to be *understimulated* and to perform self-stimulatory actions in compensation. They may, for example, fail to react to loud noises yet turn around when they hear soda being poured.

## Explanations of Autism

A variety of explanations have been offered for autism, including perceptual-cognitive, biological, and family and environmental views. Although each has received some support, none is without limitations and problems.

**Perceptual-Cognitive Views**    According to some theorists, children with autism have primary perceptual or cognitive disturbances that make normal communication, relationships, and interactions impossible (Baron-Cohen, 1991, 1989; Goodman & Ashby, 1990). One of the oldest such explanations holds that the children have a fundamental impairment in their ability to *comprehend sounds* (Klin, 1993; Rutter, 1971, 1968). Theoretically, they hear sounds but cannot make sense of them as other children can. This inability hinders their understanding of the world around them and makes them asocial. In support of this theory, several studies have found that children with autism do not respond appropriately to sounds, sometimes react to a sound as if they hear more than one, and sometimes remember meaningful speech no better than meaningless gibberish (Klin, 1993).

**Biological Views**    Because autism unfolds so early in life—often appearing at birth—many theorists believe that it must be the result of genetic and biological factors rather than environmental factors. Several lines of research implicate genetic and biological factors, but clear explanations of this kind have not yet emerged.

Examinations of the relatives of children with autism support the possibility of a genetic factor in this disorder (Folstein & Rutter, 1988). For example, the prevalence of autism among the siblings of persons

---

*Echolalia*    A symptom of autism or schizophrenia in which a person responds to being spoken to by repeating the other person's words.

with autism is between 1 and 2 per 100 (Rutter & Bartak, 1971), a rate fifty times higher than the general population's. In addition, certain chromosomal abnormalities have been discovered in 10 to 12 percent of persons with this disorder (Sudhalter et al., 1990).

Some studies suggest a link between autism and *prenatal difficulties or birth complications* (Rimland, 1992; Goodman, 1990). The chances of a child's developing the disorder are higher when the mother had rubella (German measles) during pregnancy, was exposed to toxic chemicals before or during pregnancy, or had labor or delivery complications while giving birth.

Research also suggests that *neurological dysfunction* may be involved in autism. Several studies find that children with autism have a higher number of neurological problems than other children (Gillberg et al., 1990). And some researchers have found differences between the electroencephalograms (EEGs) of children with and children without autism (APA, 1994; Dawson & Castelloe, 1992).

Many researchers now believe that autism can have multiple biological causes (Gillberg, 1992). It may be that any of the biological factors (genetic, prenatal, birth, and postnatal) may eventually lead to a common problem in the brain—a "final common pathway," such as a brain stem disturbance or neurotransmitter abnormalities, that produces autistic patterns of behavior (Martineau et al., 1992; Yuwiler et al., 1992).

**Family and Environmental Views** Over the years, many theories of autism have implicated the family and environment as a cause. These theories have focused largely on the characteristics of parents and early stress.

When he first identified autism, Kanner (1954, 1943) argued that particular *personality characteristics of the parents* of autistic children contribute to the disorder. He saw these parents as very intelligent people, yet obsessive and cold—"refrigerator parents." Although such claims have had enormous influence on the public's impression of these parents and on the self-image of the parents themselves, research has totally failed to support a picture of rigid, cold, rejecting, or disturbed parents (Roazen, 1992).

Some clinicians have suspected that unusual *environmental stress* helps cause autism. They have proposed that events that occur very early in life traumatize the children, stifle their development, and lead them into lives of near-total withdrawal. Once again, however, research has not supported this notion. Researchers who have compared children with and children without autism have found no differences in the incidence of parental death, divorce, separation, financial problems, or environmental deficits (Cox et al., 1975).

## Treatments for Autism

Although no treatment now known totally reverses the autistic pattern, it is possible to help many persons with this disorder attain more effective functioning and contact with the world. Treatments that have proved helpful are behavioral interventions, communication training, parent training, and community integration.

**Behavioral Therapy** Behavioral approaches have been applied to autism for more than thirty years. The approaches teach the children new, appropriate behaviors, including speech, social skills, classroom skills, and self-help skills, and reduce negative, dysfunctional ones. Most often, the therapists employ *modeling* techniques, in which they try to induce the children to imitate behaviors that they are demonstrating, and *operant conditioning* techniques, in which they reinforce the children for performing desired behaviors. For successful learning to occur, the desired behaviors often must be *shaped*—broken down and learned step by step—and the reinforcements must be explicit and consistent (Lovaas, 1987; Harris & Milch, 1981).

A recent long-term study (McEachin et al., 1993; Lovaas, 1987) compared the progress of nineteen children with autism who received intensive behavioral intervention with that of nineteen control subjects with autism. The treatment began when the children were 3 years old and continued until they were 7. By the age

*Behaviorists have had considerable success teaching many children with autism to speak. The therapist systematically models how to position the mouth and how to make appropriate sounds, and then rewards the child's accurate imitations.*

of 7, the experimental group required less specialized treatment in school (many of them entered regular classrooms) and had higher IQs than the control group. These gains were still evident in the children at 11 to 19 years of age. In light of such findings, many clinicians now consider early behavioral programs to be the preferred treatment for autism (Waters, 1990).

To eliminate self-injurious behaviors, such as head-banging or biting oneself, from the repertoire of children with autism, some behavioral programs use punishments, or "aversives," ranging from restraint to electric shock. Such procedures have understandably concerned many people and stirred debate (Gerhardt et al., 1991).

### Consider This

Should self-injurious behaviors be at a certain level of severity before punishments, or aversives, are allowed? Who do you believe should make the judgments about whether to use punishments in given cases? Is there a legitimate analogy between punishment as a treatment for autism and painful treatments for certain medical conditions?

Many therapies for children with autism, particularly the behavioral therapies, are conducted in a school setting. The children attend special classes, often at special schools, where education and therapy are pursued simultaneously. Specially trained teachers help the children improve their skills, behaviors, and interactions with the world. Many clinicians suggest that higher-functioning children with autism should be integrated into normal classrooms with nonautistic peers (Simpson & Sasso, 1992; Tomchek et al., 1992).

**Communication Training**    Despite intensive behavioral treatment aimed at teaching children with autism to talk, 50 percent remain speechless. As a result, many therapists also turn to nonvocal modes of communication, including *sign language* and *simultaneous communication,* a method combining sign language and speech. Other therapists advocate the use of *augmentative communication systems,* such as communication boards or computers that use pictures, symbols, letters, or written words to represent objects or needs. A child may point to a picture of a fork to represent "I am hungry," for example, or point to a radio for "I want music."

*Augmentative communication system*    A method for teaching individuals with autism, mental retardation, or cerebral palsy to communicate by pointing to pictures, symbols, letters, or words on a communication board or computer.

**Parent Training**    Treatment programs now typically try to involve parents. Behavioral programs, for example, include parent-training components to help parents learn and apply behavioral techniques at home (Love et al., 1990). Individual therapy and support groups to help parents address their own feelings and needs also are becoming increasingly available. In addition, a number of parent associations and lobbies are providing emotional support and practical help.

**Community Integration**    Educational and home programs are increasingly focusing on teaching self-help, self-management, living, social, and work skills to children with autism as early as possible, so that these individuals will be better able to live and function in their communities (Stahmer & Schreibman, 1992). In addition, carefully run *group homes* and *sheltered workshops* are increasingly being established for adolescents and young adults with autism (Van Bourgondien & Schopler, 1990). These and other community-based programs help integrate the individuals into the community (Pfeiffer & Nelson, 1992). Such efforts demonstrate the field's awareness that their special needs usually continue throughout their lives.

## Mental Retardation

Ed Murphy, aged 26, can tell you what it's like to be diagnosed as retarded:

What is retardation? It's hard to say. I guess it's having problems thinking. Some people think that you can tell if a person is retarded by looking at them. If you think that way you don't give people the benefit of the doubt. You judge a person by how they look or how they talk or what the tests show, but you can never really tell what is inside the person.

*(Bogdan & Taylor, 1976, p. 51)*

For much of his life Ed was labeled mentally retarded and was educated and cared for in special institutions. During his adult years, his clinicians came to suspect that Ed's intellect in fact surpassed that ordinarily implied by this term. Nevertheless, Ed did live the childhood and adolescence of a person labeled retarded, and his statement illustrates the kinds of difficulties often confronted by persons with mental retardation.

Persons with mental retardation are those who are significantly below average in intelligence and adaptive ability. The term has been applied to a broad and varied population, including children in institutional wards who rock vacantly back and forth, young people who work daily in special job programs, and men and

*In facilitated communication, one of the newest augmentative communication systems, a facilitator gently supports the hand of a person with autism while he or she points to or strikes letters on an alphabet board or computer keyboard. Recent studies suggest, however, that in many cases facilitators unintentionally influence the person's choice of letters, thus calling into question communications produced by this method.*

women who raise and support their families by working at undemanding jobs (APA, 1994). Approximately one of every 100 persons receives a diagnosis of mental retardation (APA, 1994). Approximately three-fifths of them are male. As we shall see, the vast majority are considered *mildly* retarded.

Echoing the criteria set forth by the American Association on Mental Retardation (AAMR) in 1992, DSM-IV holds that **mental retardation** should be diagnosed when people manifest significantly subaverage general *intellectual functioning* (an IQ of 70 or below) and at the same time display *deficient adaptive behavior* in such areas as communication, self-care, home living, interpersonal skill, self-direction, work, leisure, health, or safety (APA, 1994). DSM-IV further requires that the persons develop these symptoms before the age of 18. Although these criteria may seem straightforward, they are in fact hard to apply.

## Intelligence

As we observed in Chapter 2, clinicians rely on intelligence tests to measure intellectual functioning. These tests consist of questions or tasks chosen to represent different dimensions of intelligence, such as knowledge, reasoning, and judgment. An *intelligence quotient (IQ)* score derived from the individual's test performance theoretically indicates the person's overall intellectual capacity.

Many theorists have questioned whether IQ tests are valid—that is, whether they measure and predict

*Mental retardation* A disorder diagnosed when people manifest significantly subaverage general intellectual functioning and deficient adaptive behavior.

what they are supposed to measure and predict. Correlations between IQ and school performance range from .40 to .75, indicating that many children with lower IQs do, as one might expect, perform poorly in school, while many of those with higher IQs perform better (Smith & Smith, 1986; Anastasi, 1982). At the same time, these correlations also suggest that the relation-

*Studies suggest that IQ scores and school performances of children from poor neighborhoods can be improved by enriching their daily environments at a young age through programs like "Head Start" (shown above), thus revealing the powerful effect of the environment on IQ scores and intellectual performance.*

ship is far from perfect, and educators frequently find a particular child's school performance to be at odds with his or her IQ.

Another validity problem is that intelligence tests appear to be socioculturally biased, as we first noted in Chapter 2 (Helms, 1992; Puente, 1990). Children reared in middle- and upper-socioeconomic-level households tend to have an advantage in the tests because they are regularly exposed to the kinds of vocabulary, exercises, and challenges that the tests measure. The tests rarely reflect the "street sense" needed for survival by persons who live in poor, crime-ridden areas—a kind of know-how that certainly seems to require intellectual skills. Similarly, members of cultural minorities often appear to be at a disadvantage in taking these tests.

Such concerns have direct implications for the diagnosis of mental retardation (Wilson, 1992; Heflinger et al., 1987). It may be that some persons receive this diagnosis primarily because of cultural differences, discomfort in the testing situation, or the bias of a tester.

## Adaptive Functioning

Diagnosticians cannot rely solely on a cutoff IQ score of 70 to determine whether a person suffers from mental retardation, because some people with low IQ's are quite capable of managing their lives and functioning independently.

Brian comes from a lower-income family. He always has functioned adequately at home and in his community. He dresses and feeds himself and even takes care of himself each day until his mother returns home from work. He also plays well with his friends. At school, however, Brian refuses to participate or do his homework. He seems ineffective, at times lost, in the classroom. Referred to a school psychologist by his teacher, he received an IQ score of 60.

Jeffrey comes from an upper-middle-class home. He was always slow to develop, and sat up, stood, and talked late. During his infancy and toddler years, he was put in a special stimulation program and given special help and attention at home. Still Jeffrey has trouble dressing himself today and cannot be left alone in the backyard lest he hurt himself or wander off into the street. Schoolwork is very difficult for him. The teacher must work slowly and provide individual instruction for him. Tested at age 6, Jeffrey received an IQ score of 60.

Brian seems well *adapted* to his environment outside of school. Jeffrey's limitations are more pervasive. His low IQ score is complemented by poor adaptive

behaviors at home and elsewhere. A diagnosis of mental retardation may be more appropriate for Jeffrey than for Brian.

Various scales have been developed to assess adaptive behavior (Leland, 1991; Britton & Eaves, 1986). However, here again, some persons function better than the scales predict, while others fall short. Thus clinicians themselves must observe and judge the adaptive functioning of every individual, paying attention both to the person's background and to community standards. Unfortunately, this is often a subjective process.

## Characteristics of Individuals with Mental Retardation

Although there are some striking exceptions, the most consistent difference between people with and without mental retardation is that persons with mental retardation learn more slowly (Kail, 1992; Hale & Borkowski, 1991). Other areas of difference include attention, short-term memory, and language (Chamberlain, 1985; Yabe et al., 1985). These latter difficulties are particularly characteristic of institutionalized persons with retardation, and clinicians suspect that the unstimulating environment and infrequent adult-child interactions in most institutions contribute to such cognitive problems.

Following the tradition of educators and clinicians, DSM-IV distinguishes four levels of mental retardation: *mild* (IQ 50–70), *moderate* (IQ 35–49), *severe* (IQ 20–34), and *profound* (IQ below 20). For its part, the AAMR (1992) prefers to distinguish the different kinds of mental retardation on the basis of the level of support the person needs—"intermittent," "limited," "extensive," or "pervasive"—rather than use the DSM's IQ-based distinctions.

## Mild Retardation

Approximately 85 percent of all persons with mental retardation fall into the category of *mild retardation* (IQ 50–70) (APA, 1994). They are sometimes called "educably retarded" because they can benefit from an academic education and can support themselves during adulthood (APA, 1994). Still, they typically need assistance when they are under unusual social or economic stress. Their jobs tend to be unskilled or semiskilled.

Mild mental retardation is not usually detected until a child enters school, at which time school evaluators assign the label. Interestingly, the intellectual performance of individuals in this category often seems to improve with age; some even seem to leave the label behind them when they leave school and go on to function adequately in the community.

Research has linked mild mental retardation primarily to environmental factors, particularly environmental understimulation, inadequate parent-child interactions, and insufficient early learning experiences. These relationships have emerged in studies comparing deprived and enriched environments (see Figure 15-3). In fact, community projects in which workers go into the homes of young children with mild mental retardation and help enrich the environments often produce greatly improved functioning (Marfo & Kysela, 1985).

Although environmental factors seem to play the primary causal role in mild mental retardation, at least some biological factors also seem to be operating. Studies suggest, for example, that a mother's moderate drinking, drug use, or malnutrition during pregnancy may impair her child's intellectual potential (Stein et al., 1972; Harrell et al., 1955). Similarly, malnourishment during childhood increases the risk of a person developing mild mental retardation (Davison & Dobbing, 1966), although this effect is at least partly

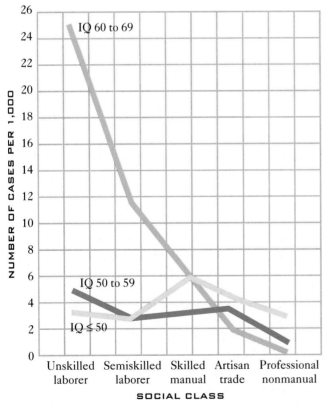

**Figure 15-3**  *The prevalence of mild mental retardation is much higher in the lower socioeconomic classes than in the upper classes. In contrast, more-impaired forms of mental retardation are evenly distributed. (Adapted from Popper, 1988; Birch et al., 1970.)*

reversible with early intervention (Winick et al., 1975).

## Moderate, Severe, and Profound Retardation

Approximately 10 percent of persons with mental retardation function at a level of *moderate retardation* (IQ 35–49). They can learn to care for themselves and can profit from vocational training, and many can work in unskilled or semiskilled jobs, usually under supervision. Most persons with moderate retardation adapt well to supervised life in the community (APA, 1994).

Approximately 4 percent of people with mental retardation are *severely retarded* (IQ 20–34). They usually require careful supervision, profit somewhat from vocational training, and can perform only basic vocational tasks in structured and sheltered settings. Their understanding of communication is usually better than their speech. Most adapt well to life in the community, in group homes or community nursing homes, or with their families (APA, 1994).

Around 1 percent of all people with mental retardation are *profoundly retarded* (IQ below 20). With training they acquire basic skills such as walking, some talking, and feeding themselves. They require a highly structured environment with close supervision and help and an individual relationship with a caregiver in order to develop to the fullest (APA, 1994).

The primary causes of moderate, severe, and profound retardation are biological, although people who function at these levels are also enormously affected by their environment. The leading biological causes are chromosomal and metabolic disorders, prenatal conditions, birth complications, and postnatal diseases and injuries.

**Chromosomal Causes**  *Down syndrome,* named after Langdon Down, the British physician who first identified it, is the most common of the chromosomal disorders leading to mental retardation (Evans & Hamerton, 1985). Fewer than 1 of every 1000 live births results in Down syndrome, but this incidence increases considerably when the mother's age is over 35.

Individuals with Down syndrome have a distinct appearance, with a small head, flat face, slanted eyes, high cheekbones, and, in some cases, a protruding tongue. They may also articulate poorly and be difficult to understand (Mahoney et al., 1981). They are often demonstratively affectionate with family mem-

*Down syndrome*  A form of mental retardation related to an abnormality in the twenty-first chromosome.

*Until the 1970s, clinicians were pessimistic about the potential of children with Down syndrome. Today these children are viewed as individuals who can learn and accomplish many things in their lives.*

bers, but more generally display the usual range of individual personality characteristics (Carr, 1994).

Several types of chromosomal abnormalities may cause Down syndrome, but the most common type by far is *trisomy 21,* in which the individual has three free-floating twenty-first chromosomes instead of two (Pueschel & Thuline, 1991). Most people with Down syndrome range in IQ from 35 to 55. The aging process appears to occur more quickly in people with Down syndrome, and most even show some signs of dementia as they approach 40 (Carr 1994; Burt et al., 1992). Studies suggest that Down syndrome and early dementia may occur together because the genes that produce each of these disorders are located close to each other on chromosome 21 (Tanzi et al., 1989).

*Fragile X syndrome* is the second most common chromosomal cause of mental retardation (Zigler & Hodapp, 1991). Children born with a fragile X chromosome (one with a genetic abnormality) generally have moderate to severe degrees of intellectual dysfunctioning, language impairments, and, in some cases, behavioral problems (McEvoy, 1992). The condition is more common in males.

**Metabolic Causes**   Metabolic disorders that affect intelligence and development are typically caused by the pairing of two defective *recessive genes,* one from each parent. Although one such gene would have no influence if it were paired with a normal dominant gene, its pairing with another defective gene leads to disturbed chemical production in the child and thus to disturbed metabolic processes.

The most common retardation-causing metabolic disorder is *phenylketonuria (PKU),* which strikes 1 of

every 17,000 children. Babies with PKU appear normal at birth but soon develop the overt symptoms of the disorder. Infants can now be screened for PKU, and if started on a special diet before three months of age, they may develop normal intelligence.

*Tay-Sachs disease,* another metabolic disorder resulting from a pairing of recessive genes, is characterized by progressive mental deterioration and loss of visual and motor functioning over the course of two to four years, followed by death. One of every 30 persons of Eastern European Jewish ancestry carries the recessive gene responsible for this disorder, so that 1 of every 900 Jewish couples is at risk for having a child with Tay-Sachs disease.

**Prenatal Causes**   As a fetus develops, significant physical problems in the pregnant mother can endanger the child's prospects for a normal life (Menke et al., 1991). When a pregnant woman has too little iodine in her diet, for example, her child may develop *cretinism,* characterized by a defective thyroid gland in the baby, slow development, mental retardation, and a dwarflike appearance. The disorder is rare today because the salt in most diets now contains iodine. Also, any infant born with this disorder may quickly be given thyroid extract to bring about a relatively normal development.

Other prenatal problems may also cause mental retardation. As we discussed in Chapter 11, children whose mothers abuse alcohol during pregnancy may be born with *fetal alcohol syndrome,* a cluster of very serious problems that includes intellectual deficiencies (Phelps & Grabowski, 1993). In addition, certain maternal infections during pregnancy may cause some childhood abnormalities including mental retardation.

**Birth-Related Causes**   Birth complications can also lead to mental retardation. A prolonged period without oxygen *(anoxia)* during or after delivery can cause brain damage and retardation in a baby (Erickson, 1992). Similarly, although premature birth does not necessarily pose problems for children, researchers have found that a very low birth weight (less than 3.5 pounds) resulting from prematurity may cause some degree of mental retardation (Largo et al., 1989).

**Childhood Causes**   After birth, particularly up to age 6, certain injuries and accidents can lead to mental retardation. Poisonings, serious head injuries caused by accident or abuse, excessive exposure to X rays, and excessive use of certain drugs pose special dangers in this regard. For example, *lead poisoning,* associated with eating lead-based paints and with inhaling high levels of automobile fumes, can interfere with cellular metabolism and cause retardation in children (Berney, 1993). Similarly, certain infections can lead to mental retardation, such as childhood cases of *meningitis* and *encephalitis* (Scola, 1991).

In some cases, hereditary, prenatal, birth, and childhood factors in combination cause moderate, severe, or profound mental retardation. For example, both *microcephaly,* characterized by a small, unusually shaped head, and *hydrocephalus,* characterized by an increase in cerebrospinal fluid and resultant head enlargement, are the result of multiple contributing factors.

## Interventions for People with Mental Retardation

The quality of life experienced by persons with mental retardation is influenced by several factors: (1) where they live, (2) the educational and treatment programs they participate in, and (3) the growth opportunities offered by their family and community.

**Residential Alternatives**   Until recent decades, parents of children with mental retardation would send them to live in public institutions—*state schools*—as early as possible. Unfortunately, in practice these overcrowded institutions provided custodial care only, and the people who lived in them were neglected, often abused, and isolated from society.

The 1960s and 1970s saw an increase in public awareness of these conditions, and as part of the broader *deinstitutionalization* movement (see p. 368), large numbers of people with retardation were released from the state schools (Beyer, 1991). Many had to make the transition to community life without special guidance, even without adequate residential placement. Like deinstitutionalized persons with schizophrenia, they were virtually dumped into the community. Not surprisingly, many failed to adjust and had to be institutionalized once again.

Fortunately, deinstitutionalization was not the mental health field's only reaction to inadequate institutional care for people with mental retardation. A series of institutional reforms have been introduced since the 1960s, such as the establishment of numerous small institutions that encourage self-sufficiency, devote more staff time to patient care, and offer educational and medical services.

Moreover, many institutions and community residences have offered *normalization programs,* programs first started in Denmark and Sweden, which provide the residents with living conditions and activities that closely resemble those enjoyed in the mainstream of society. Persons in such programs have the benefit of flexible routines, normal developmental experiences,

*As many as 10 percent of persons with autism and 0.06 percent of those with mental retardation are* **savants,** *mentally handicapped individuals with some spectacular ability or area of expertise. In the 1988 film* Rain Man, *Raymond is a man with autism whose disorder is complemented by extraordinary skills, such as being able to memorize all the numbers in a telephone book and to keep track of all cards in a blackjack game.*

opportunities to make their own decisions, the right to develop a sexual identity, and normal economic freedoms (Baldwin, 1985). A growing number of group homes, halfway houses, small local branches of larger institutions, and independent residences, applying the principles of normalization, are now available to persons with mental retardation.

Today the vast majority of children with mental retardation live at home rather than in an institution, at least until they are ready to enter a community residence (Erickson, 1992). As they approach adulthood and as their parents age, the family home becomes a less desirable setting for some of them (Krauss et al., 1992) and a community residence may become an appropriate alternative. Most persons with mental retardation, including virtually all with mild mental retardation, now live their adult lives either in the family home or in a community residence (Jacobson & Schwartz, 1991; Repp et al., 1986). Wherever the individual may live, the family remains important as a source of social support, guidance, and advocacy (Blacher & Baker, 1994).

**Educational Programs**   As we observed before, early intervention programs seem to offer great promise. Thus, some educational programs for children with mental retardation are begun during the child's first few years of life.

One of the greatest debates in the field of education centers on the correct educational environment for persons with mental retardation. Some educators favor special classes while others advocate mainstreaming

(Gottlieb et al., 1991). In the *special education* approach, children with mental retardation are grouped only with other retarded children and given a specially designed curriculum. In the *mainstreaming* approach, children with mental retardation are placed in regular classes with nonretarded students. Researchers have not been able to determine whether one of these approaches is superior to the other (Gottlieb, 1981). Perhaps mainstreaming is better for some children, special classes for others.

> ### Consider This
>
> Advocates of special classes for persons with mental retardation believe that such classes help the individuals to experience feelings of success and receive needed special attention, while proponents of mainstreaming argue that this format offers more normal educational experiences, reduces stigmatization, and facilitates interactions between children with and children without mental retardation. What might be the merits and flaws of each of these positions?

*Operant learning principles* are regularly applied in the education of children with mental retardation, especially to help teach them self-help skills, proper verbal responding, social responses, and academic tasks (Erickson, 1992; Matson & Gorman-Smith, 1986). Teachers break learning tasks down into small steps and give positive reinforcement as each small step is accomplished. In addition, many institutions, schools, and private homes have instituted *token economy programs*—the operant learning programs that have also been used with institutionalized patients suffering from schizophrenia.

**Therapy**   Like all other people, those with mental retardation often experience emotional and behavioral problems. Estimates are that 10 percent of people with mental retardation have another diagnosable mental disorder in addition to their retardation (Grizenko et al., 1991) Moreover, they may experience low self-esteem, interpersonal difficulties, and difficulty in adjusting to community life (Lubetsky, 1986; Reiss, 1985).

These problems have been addressed with some degree of effectiveness by both individual and group therapies (Hurley & Hurley, 1986). In addition, large numbers of persons with mental retardation are given psychotropic medications (Aman & Singh, 1991).

Many clinicians suggest, however, that too often the medications are used simply to keep persons with mental retardation docile (Erickson, 1992).

**Opportunities for Personal, Social, and Occupational Growth**   Feelings of self-efficacy and competence are important aspects of personal growth, and people with mental retardation can achieve them if they are allowed by their communities to grow and to make their own choices in life without undue pressure (Wehmeyer, 1992). Denmark and Sweden, the originators of the normalization movement, have led the way in this area as well, developing youth clubs that encourage persons with mental retardation to take risks and function independently.

Socializing, sex, and marriage are sometimes difficult issues for persons with mental retardation and their families. The Association for Retarded Citizens now provides guidance in these matters, and several *dating skills programs* have been developed by clinicians (Valenti-Hein et al., 1994). It appears that with proper training and experience, people with mental retardation can usually learn to use contraceptives, carry out responsible family planning, and in many cases rear children effectively (Dowdney & Skuse, 1993; Bakken et al., 1993).

Some states have laws restricting marriage for persons with mental retardation. These laws are rarely enforced, however, and in fact between a quarter and half of all mildly retarded persons eventually marry (Grinspoon et al., 1986). Contrary to popular stereotypes, the marriages can be very successful. Moreover, while

*The interpersonal and sexual needs of persons with mental retardation are normal, and many demonstrate considerable ability to express intimacy.*

---

*Mainstreaming*   An approach to educating children with mental retardation in which they are placed in regular classes with children who are not mentally retarded.

## Box 15-2

# Aging: Suddenly I'm the Adult?
*Richard Cohen*

*(This essay originally appeared in Psychology Today, May 1987.)*

Several years ago, my family gathered on Cape Cod for a weekend. My parents were there, my sister and her daughter, too, two cousins, and, of course, my wife, my son and me. We ate at one of those restaurants where the menu is scrawled on a blackboard held by a chummy waiter and had a wonderful time. With dinner concluded, the waiter set the check down in the middle of the table. That's when it happened. My father did not reach for the check.

In fact, my father did nothing. Conversation continued. Finally, it dawned on me. Me! I was supposed to pick up the check. After all these years, after hundreds of restaurant meals with my parents, after a lifetime of thinking of my father as the one with the bucks, it had all changed. I reached for the check and whipped out my American Express card. My view of myself was suddenly altered. With

a stroke of a pen, I was suddenly an adult.

Some people mark off their life in years, others in events. I am one of the latter, and I think of some events as rites of passage. I did not become a young man at a particular year, like 13, but when a kid strolled into the store where I worked and called me "mister," I turned around to see whom he was calling. He repeated it several times—"Mister, mister"—looking straight at me. The realization hit like a punch: Me! He was talking to me. I was suddenly a mister.

There have been other milestones. The cops of my youth always seemed to be big, even huge, and of course they were older than I was. Then one day they were neither. In fact, some of them were kids—short kids at that. Another milestone.

The day comes when suddenly you realize that all the football players in the game you're watching are younger than you. Instead of being big men, they are merely

big kids. With that milestone goes the fantasy that someday, maybe, you too could be a player—maybe not a football player but certainly a baseball player. I had a good eye as a kid—not much power, but a keen eye—and I always thought I could play the game. One day I realized that I couldn't. Without having ever reached the hill, I was over it.

For some people, the most momentous milestone is the death of a parent. This happened recently to a friend of mine. With the burial of his father came the realization that he had moved up a notch. Of course, he had known all along that this would happen, but until the funeral, the knowledge seemed theoretical at best. As long as one of your parents is alive, you stay in some way a kid. At the very least, there remains at least one person whose love is unconditional.

For women, a milestone is reached when they can no longer have children. The loss of a life, the inability to create one—they

---

### Consider This

Clinical theorists suggest that aging need not inevitably lead to depression, anxiety, or certain other psychological problems. What kinds of attitudes, preparations, and activities might help an individual to greet old age with a sense of contentment, peace of mind, and even pleasure?

---

Such stresses need not necessarily result in psychological dysfunction in an elderly person (Lewinsohn et al., 1990). Indeed, some older persons use situations of this kind to learn more about themselves and to grow as people. For others, however, the stresses of old age do lead to psychological problems. Studies indicate that as many as 50 percent of elderly people would benefit from mental health services (MacDonald & Schnur, 1987), yet fewer than 20 percent actually receive such help.

The psychological problems of elderly persons may be divided into two groups. One group consists of disorders found among persons of all ages but often closely connected to the process of aging when they occur in elderly persons. These include depression, anxiety disorders, substance abuse, and delirium. The other group consists of disorders that are almost always identified with old age, such as Alzheimer's disease and other forms of dementia.

## Depression, Anxiety, Substance Abuse, and Delirium in Later Life

*Depression,* the most common mental health problem in old age, is experienced by as many as 20 percent of elderly persons (Koenig & Blazer, 1992; Blazer, 1990). Those who have recently experienced a trauma such as

some persons with mental retardation may be incapable of raising children, many are quite able to raise children, either on their own or with special help and community services (Bakken et al., 1993; Keltner, 1992).

Finally, adults with mental retardation need the personal and financial rewards that come from holding a job (AAMR, 1992). Many work in **sheltered workshops,** where the pace and type of work are tailored to their skills and where supervision is available. After training in these workshops, persons with mild or moderate retardation may move out into the regular workforce. However, the sheltered workshop tends to be the highest level of employment that persons with severe and profound mental retardation can achieve.

Although training programs for persons with mental retardation have improved greatly over the past twenty-five years, much remains to be accomplished. Indeed, it is estimated that the majority of these persons fail to receive the full range of educational and vocational training services from which they could profit (Tyor & Bell, 1984).

*Summing Up*
*Persons with an autistic disorder are extremely unresponsive to others, communicate poorly, show limited skill at imaginative play, and behave in a restricted and repetitive manner. This disorder is not fully understood, but persons who suffer from it often make significant improvements in educational and treatment programs that feature behavioral techniques, communication training, parent training and therapy, and community integration.*

*People with mental retardation are significantly below average in intelligence and adaptive ability. Mild retardation, by far the most common form, appears to be caused primarily by environmental factors. Moderate, severe, and profound retardation are caused primarily by biological factors. Persons with mental retardation are educated in either special classes or regular classes (mainstreaming) and often are taught skills by means of operant conditioning principles. Those who are given opportunities for personal, social, and occupational growth appear to make the most progress.*

# Disorders of Later Life

Thus far in this chapter, we have seen that many psychological disorders have their onset during childhood. At the other end of the spectrum, a number of

disorders develop as old age approaches or advances As with childhood disorders, some of the disorders c later life seem to be caused primarily by pressures tha are particularly likely to appear at that time of life, oth ers by unique traumatic experiences, and still other by biological abnormalities.

"Old age" is arbitrarily defined in our society as r ferring to the years past age 65. In 1989, 31 millic people in the United States were over 65 (see Figu 15-4). This figure reflects a tenfold increase in t older population since 1900. Older women outnumb older men by a ratio of 3 to 2.

As people age, they experience many physical a psychological changes (see Box 15-2). They beco more prone to illness and injury than when they w younger and are more likely to experience cert kinds of psychological stress, such as the stress of nificant loss, from loss of loved ones to loss of empl ment, homes, or possessions (Gallagher-Thompsor Thompson, 1995).

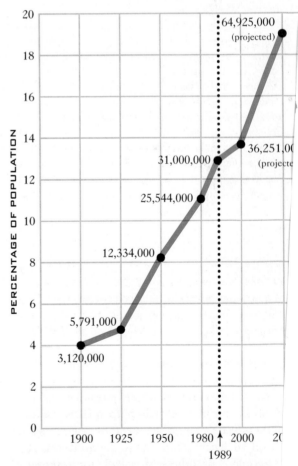

**Figure 15-4** *The population of people aged 65 and in the United States has been climbing throughout th twentieth century. The percentage of elderly people i population was 4 percent in 1900 and is expected to percent in 2030. (AARP, 1990; U.S. Bureau of the Ce 1988.)*

are variations on the same theme. For a childless woman who could control everything in life but the clock, this milestone is a cruel one indeed.

I count other, less serious milestones—like being audited by the Internal Revenue Service. As the auditor caught mistake after mistake, I sat there pretending that really knowing about taxes was for adults. I, of course, was still a kid. The auditor was buying none of it. I was a taxpayer, an adult. She all but said, Go to jail.

There have been others. I remember the day when I had a ferocious argument with my son and realized that I could no longer bully him. He was too big and the days when I could just pick him up and take him to his room/isolation cell were over. I needed to persuade, reason. He was suddenly, rapidly, older. The conclusion was inescapable: So was I.

One day you go to your friends' weddings. One day you celebrate the birth of their kids. One day you see one of their kids driving, and one day those kids have kids of their own. One day you meet at parties and then at weddings and then at funerals. It all happens in one day. Take my word for it.

I never thought I would fall asleep in front of the television set as my father did, and as my friends' fathers did, too. I remember my parents and their friends talking about insomnia and they sounded like members of a different species. Not able to sleep? How ridiculous. Once it was all I did. Once it was what I did best.

I never thought that I would eat a food that did not agree with me. Now I meet them all the time. I thought I would never go to the beach and not swim. I spent all of August at the beach and never once went into the ocean. I never thought I would appreciate opera, but now the pathos, the schmaltz and, especially, the combination of voice and music appeal to me. The deaths of Mimi and Tosca move me, and they die in my home as often as I can manage it.

I never thought I would prefer to stay home instead of going to a party, but now I find myself passing parties up. I used to think that people who watched birds were weird, but this summer I found myself watching them, and maybe I'll get a book on the subject. I yearn for a religious conviction I never thought I'd want, exult in my heritage anyway, feel close to ancestors long gone and echo my father in arguments with my son. I still lose.

One day I made a good toast. One day I handled a headwaiter. One day I bought a house. One day—what a day!—I became a father, and not too long after that I picked up the check for my own. I thought then and there it was a rite of passage for me. Not until I got older did I realize that it was one for him, too. Another milestone.

the loss of their spouse and those with serious physical illnesses have the highest rate of depression (Philpott, 1990). The prevalence of depression is higher in older women than in older men (Fernandez et al., 1995).

Like younger depressed patients, older persons who are depressed may be helped by a number of treatments, including cognitive therapy, antidepressant medications, or a combination of the two (Gantz et al., 1991). At the same time, it is sometimes difficult to use antidepressant drugs effectively and safely with older persons because the body breaks them down differently in later life than in the earlier years (Blazer, 1990).

*Anxiety* is also found in many elderly persons. Surveys indicate that generalized anxiety disorder is particularly common, experienced by about 7 percent of older people (Flint, 1994; Bliwise et al., 1987). Anxiety disorders may, however, be underreported by the elderly. Some may attribute the physical symptoms of anxiety, such as heart palpitations and sweating, to medical conditions (Blazer et al., 1991).

Older adults with anxiety disorders have often been treated with some form of psychotherapy (McCarthy et al., 1991). Some also receive antianxiety medications, particularly benzodiazepines, although those with obsessive-compulsive disorder have, like their younger counterparts, been increasingly treated with certain antidepressant drugs (Jenike, 1991). Again, however, these drugs must be used cautiously with people over 60 because their bodies respond to them quite differently than do the bodies of younger adults (Pomara et al., 1991).

Alcohol and other forms of *substance abuse* represent another problem for many older persons, although the prevalence of these disorders actually appears to decline after age 60. Surveys suggest that 3 to 5 percent of older persons, particularly men, experience alcohol-related disorders in any given year

*Clinical theorists point out that old age is more than a loss of youth or a march toward death. Elderly persons are filled with a mixture of past memories, present needs, and future goals, all of which must be addressed if they are to achieve fulfillment and psychological peace.*

(Helzer et al., 1991; Maddox, 1988). Researchers often distinguish older problem drinkers who have experienced significant alcohol-related problems for many years, often since their 20s or 30s, from those who do not start the pattern until their 50s or 60s. The latter individuals typically begin their abusive drinking as a reaction to the negative events and pressures of growing older, such as the death of a spouse or retirement. Alcohol abuse in an elderly person is treated in many of the same ways as alcohol abuse in someone younger (see pp. 313–318), utilizing, for example, such approaches as detoxification, Antabuse, Alcoholics Anonymous (AA), and cognitive behavioral therapy (Schiff, 1988).

Another leading form of substance abuse in the elderly is the unintentional or, less commonly, intentional misuse of prescription drugs, particularly in combination with alcohol (Gottheil, 1987). Surveys reveal that older persons receive twice as many prescriptions as younger persons and that a quarter of them take three or more drugs daily (Lipton, 1988). Clearly, the risk of confusing or missing medications under such circumstances is profound (Salzman, 1995). Clinicians, physicians, and pharmacists are increasingly learning to educate patients about their medications, clarify medication directions, simplify medication regimens, and instruct older persons to monitor the undesired effects of medications (Gallagher-Thompson & Thompson, 1995).

Finally, a number of elderly persons experience

*delirium,* a clouding of consciousness in which a person's awareness of the environment becomes less clear so that he or she has great difficulty concentrating, focusing attention, and maintaining a straightforward stream of thought (APA, 1994). The person may be disoriented to time, thinking that it is morning during the middle of the night; or disoriented to place, believing himself or herself to be home when actually in a hospital room. A state of delirium typically develops over a short period of time, usually hours or days. It may result in misinterpretations, illusions, and, on occasion, hallucinations.

This state of massive confusion may occur in people of any age, including children, but it is most common in elderly persons. It is seen in around 10 percent of elderly persons when they enter a hospital to be treated for a general medical condition (APA, 1994). Another 10 to 15 percent develop delirium during their stay in the hospital.

A number of factors may cause the syndrome of delirium, including medical conditions such as fever, infection, nutritional imbalances, head injuries, and certain neurological disorders. Intoxication by certain substances, such as illicit or prescription drugs, may also produce it. In addition, delirium may be induced by stress, such as that caused by surgery. Partly because older persons experience so many of the medical conditions, drug overdoses, and stresses which may precipitate delirium, they are more likely than persons of other ages to experience it.

If a diagnostician correctly identifies a case of delirium, the syndrome can often be readily reversed, for example, by treating the problematic infection or injury or changing the patient's drug prescription. Unfortunately, an accurate diagnosis is often elusive. One study conducted on a medical ward found that only one of 15 consecutive cases of delirium was detected by the admitting doctor (Cameron et al., 1987). Incorrect diagnoses of this kind contribute to a relatively high mortality rate for older people with delirium; over one third of patients have died from conditions related to delirium in some medical settings (Rabins & Folstein, 1982).

## Dementia

Fear that we are losing our mental abilities occasionally strikes all of us, perhaps after we have rushed out the door without our keys, when we meet a familiar person and cannot remember her name, or when in the middle of a critical test our mind seems to go

---

*Delirium* A rapidly developing clouded state of consciousness in which a person experiences great difficulty concentrating, focusing attention, and maintaining a straightforward stream of thought.

*A key to feeling vital and upbeat, whether old or young, is to be active, committed, and interested in one's surroundings. Charlotte Stinger, 79, a student at the Academy of Ballet, has been studying dance for 28 years.*

blank (Gallagher-Thompson & Thompson, 1995). At such times, we may well believe that we are experiencing the first stages of **dementia,** the highly disruptive syndrome that, as we discussed in Chapter 14, is marked by severe memory impairment and other cognitive disturbances, such as deficits in abstract thinking, judgment, or language (APA, 1994).

Minor memory lapses are a common and normal feature of aging. Typically, as people progress through middle age, memory difficulties and lapses of attention increase, and they may occur with regularity by the age of 60 or 70. Unfortunately, however, some people do experience the broad, severe, and excessive intellectual changes of dementia:

Harry appeared to be in perfect health at age 58, except that for a few days he had had a nasty flu. He worked in the municipal water treatment plant of a small city, and it was at work that the first overt signs of Harry's mental illness appeared. While responding to a minor emergency, he became confused about the correct order in which to pull the levers that controlled the flow of fluids. As a result, several thousand gallons of raw sewage were discharged into a river. Harry had been an efficient and diligent worker, so after puzzled questioning, his error was attributed to the flu and overlooked.

Several weeks later, Harry came home with a baking dish his wife had asked him to buy, having forgotten that he had brought home the identical dish two nights before. Later that week, on two successive nights, he went to pick up his daughter at her job in a restaurant, apparently forgetting that she had changed shifts and was now working days. A month after that, he quite uncharacteristically argued with a clerk at the phone company; he was trying to pay a bill that he had already paid three days before. . . .

Months passed and Harry's wife was beside herself. She could see that his problem was worsening. Not only had she been unable to get effective help, but Harry himself was becoming resentful and sometimes suspicious of her attempts. He now insisted there was nothing wrong with him, and she would catch him narrowly watching her every movement. From time to time he accused her of having the police watch him, and he would draw all the blinds in the house. Once he ripped the telephone out of the wall, convinced it was "spying." Sometimes he became angry—sudden little storms without apparent cause. . . . More difficult for his wife was Harry's repetitiveness in conversation: He often repeated stories from the past and sometimes repeated isolated phrases and sentences from more recent exchanges. There was no context and little continuity to his choice of subjects. He might recite the same story or instruction several times a day. His work was also a great cause of deep concern. . . .

Two years after Harry had first allowed the sewage to escape, he was clearly a changed man. Most of the time he seemed preoccupied; he usually had a vacant smile on his face, and what little he said was so vague that it lacked meaning. He had entirely given up his main interests (golf and woodworking), and he became careless about his person. More and more, for example, he slept in his clothes. Gradually his wife took over getting him up, toileted, and dressed each morning.

One day the county supervisor stopped by to tell his wife that Harry just could not work any longer. . . . He was just too much of a burden on his co-workers. Harry himself still insisted that nothing was wrong, but by now no one tried to explain things to him. He had long since stopped reading. His days were spent sitting vacantly in front of the television, but he couldn't describe any of the programs he had watched.

Harry's condition continued to worsen slowly. When his wife's school was in session, his daughter would stay with him some days, and neighbors were able to offer some help. But occasionally he would still manage to wander away. On those occasions he greeted everyone he met—old friends and strangers alike—with "Hi, it's so nice." That was the extent of his conversation, although he might repeat "nice, nice, nice" over and over again. . . . When Harry left a coffee pot on a unit of the electric stove until it melted, his wife, desperate for help, took him to see another doctor. Again Harry was found to be in good health. This time the doctor ordered a *CAT scan* . . . a sophisticated X-ray examination that made a visual image of Harry's brain, which, it revealed, had actually shrunk in size. The doctor said that Harry had "Pick-Alzheimer disease" and that there was no known cause and no effective treatment. . . .

Because Harry was a veteran . . . [he qualified for] hospitalization in a regional veterans' hospital about 400 miles away from his home. . . . Desperate, five years after the accident at work, [his wife] accepted with gratitude [this] hospitalization. . . .

At the hospital the nursing staff sat Harry up in a chair each day and, aided by volunteers, made sure he ate enough. Still, he lost weight and became weaker. He would weep when his wife came to see him, but he did not talk, and he gave no other sign that he recognized her. After a year, even the weeping stopped. Harry's wife could no longer bear to visit. Harry lived on until just after his sixty-fifth birthday, when he choked on a piece of bread, developed pneumonia as a consequence, and soon died.

(*Heston, 1992, pp. 87–90*).

The occurrence of dementia is closely related to age. Among people 65 years of age, its prevalence ranges from 2 to 4 percent. There is a gradual increase over the next ten years of the life span to a range of 10 to 15 percent, and a jump to 30 percent for all people over the age of 80 (Gallagher-Thompson & Thompson, 1995).

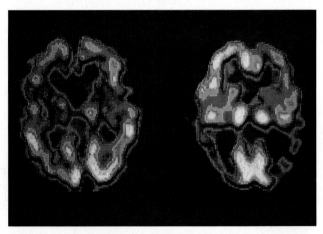

*A PET scan of the brain of an Alzheimer's disease sufferer (right) indicates diminished blood flow and degeneration of brain tissue; a PET scan of a normal subject's brain appears at the left.*

Like delirium, the syndrome of massive confusion for which it is often mistaken and with which it may co-occur, dementia sometimes has an underlying cause that is reversible. Some elderly persons, for example, may be suffering from metabolic or nutritional disorders that can be corrected. For others, improvement in sensory functions such as vision and hearing can lead to a substantial improvement in cognitive performance (Gallagher-Thompson & Thompson, 1995). Unfortunately, however, most cases of dementia are caused by neurological problems, such as Alzheimer's disease and stroke, that are difficult, if not impossible, to address.

## Alzheimer's Disease

As we note in Chapter 14, *Alzheimer's disease,* named after Alois Alzheimer, the German physician who first identified it in 1907, is the most common form of dementia, accounting for at least 50 percent of cases (Bliwise et al., 1987). This gradually progressive degenerative process sometimes appears in middle age (*early onset),* but most often it occurs after the age of 65 (*late onset),* with its prevalence increasing markedly among people in their late 70s and early 80s (APA, 1994). Some studies have reported higher rates of this disease in women, but this finding may be due simply to the fact that women live longer than men (Gallagher-Thompson & Thompson, 1995).

In most cases, Alzheimer's disease can be diagnosed with certainty only by studies after death that identify specific structural changes within the brain tissue (see Figure 15-5). The most notable of these changes are the excessive formation of *neurofibrillary tangles* and *senile plaques* in the brain.

*Neurofibrillary tangles* are twisted protein fibers found *within* the cells of the hippocampus and other brain structures vital to memory and learning. All people form tangles as they age, but people with Alzheimer's disease form an extraordinary number of them (Selkoe, 1992). *Senile plaques* are sphere-shaped deposits of a small molecule known as the *beta-amyloid protein* that form in the spaces *between* neurons, usually along the membranes of neurons located in the hippocampus, cerebral cortex, and some other brain regions, as well as in some blood vessels in these brain areas. As with tangles, the formation of plaques is a

*Alzheimer's disease*   The most common form of dementia, usually occurring during old age, marked by excessive formation of neurofibrillary tangles and senile plaques in the brain.

*Neurofibrillary tangles*   Twisted protein fibers found within certain brain cells of people with Alzheimer's disease, interfering with memory and learning.

*Senile plaques*   Sphere-shaped deposits of beta-amyloid protein that form excessively in the spaces between certain neurons in people with Alzheimer's disease.

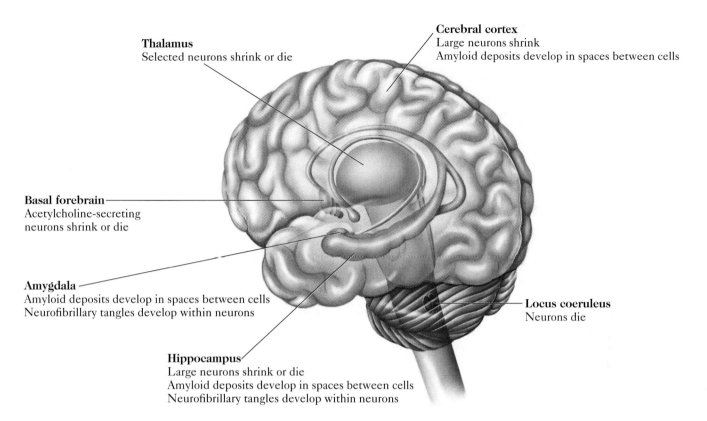

**Thalamus**
Selected neurons shrink or die

**Cerebral cortex**
Large neurons shrink
Amyloid deposits develop in spaces between cells

**Basal forebrain**
Acetylcholine-secreting
neurons shrink or die

**Amygdala**
Amyloid deposits develop in spaces between cells
Neurofibrillary tangles develop within neurons

**Locus coeruleus**
Neurons die

**Hippocampus**
Large neurons shrink or die
Amyloid deposits develop in spaces between cells
Neurofibrillary tangles develop within neurons

Figure 15-5  *The aging brain. In old age, our brains undergo structural changes that affect memory, learning, and reasoning to some degree. These same changes occur to an excessive degree in people with Alzheimer's disease. (Selkoe, 1992, p. 136.)*

normal part of aging, but it is dramatically increased in people with Alzheimer's disease (Selkoe, 1992). There is speculation that such plaques may interfere with exchanges between cells, which in turn leads to cell breakdown or death.

The course of Alzheimer's disease ranges from two to as many as fifteen years. Dysfunction progresses over time, usually beginning with mild memory problems and lapses of attention. These symptoms keep increasing in frequency and severity until at some point it becomes clear that the individual is having difficulty in completing complicated tasks or is forgetting important appointments. Eventually, the individual also has difficulty with simple tasks and may undergo noticeable changes in personality. For example, a person may become uncharacteristically aggressive or amorous.

Although people with Alzheimer's disease initially may deny that they have a problem, they soon become anxious or depressed about their impaired thinking. As the dementia progresses still further, however, they show less and less concern about or acknowledgment of their limitations. During the late stages of the disorder, they withdraw socially, become more disoriented as to time and place, wander frequently, and show extremely poor judgment (Gallagher-Thompson &

Thompson, 1995). They become more and more agitated at night and take frequent naps during the day. This phase can last from two to five years, with the individuals requiring constant care and supervision (Mace & Rabins, 1991).

Alzheimer's victims usually remain in fairly good health until the later stages of the disease. As their mental facilities decline, however, their activity level tends to drop off markedly. Eventually, they spend much of their time just sitting or lying in bed, and they increasingly develop physical ailments and serious illnesses, such as pneumonia, some of which can result in death (Gallagher-Thompson & Thompson, 1995).

## Other Forms of Dementia

As we observed in Chapter 14, several other disorders may also produce dementia. The symptoms of *vascular dementia,* or *multi-infarct dementia,* the second most common type of dementia in the elderly, are due to a cerebrovascular accident, or stroke, that causes a loss of blood flow to certain areas of the brain, which in

*Vascular dementia*   A form of dementia caused by a cerebrovascular accident, or stroke, that restricts the blood flow to certain areas of the brain.

turn damages specific areas of the brain. In vascular dementia, the brain damage is more localized than in Alzheimer's disease, and thus the loss of cognitive function is less broad. The symptoms develop abruptly rather than gradually, and behavioral changes occur in a stepwise rather than gradual fashion (Gallagher-Thompson & Thompson, 1995).

*Pick's disease,* a rare disease that affects the frontal and temporal lobes, is difficult to differentiate from Alzheimer's disease clinically, but the distinction becomes clear at autopsy. *Creutzfeldt-Jakob disease* is a rare progressive dementia that is caused by a slow-acting virus, but once it appears, it has a rapid course. It often includes spasmodic movements. *Huntington's disease,* which usually has its onset during the middle years, typically starts with a movement disorder, which is accompanied increasingly by dementia. The gene carrying this inherited disease has been located on chromosome 4. And finally, *Parkinson's disease,* the age-related disorder of the central nervous system that is marked by severe disturbances in psychomotor control and coordination, is often accompanied by dementia, particularly in the later stages.

## Explanations of Alzheimer's Disease

Alzheimer's disease has received considerable attention from researchers in recent years. Although theories abound, investigators still have only limited information about its causes.

**Neurotransmitter Explanations**    At least two common neurotransmitters, acetylcholine and L-glutamate, are depleted in the brains of Alzheimer victims. The neurotransmitter *acetylcholine* plays a key role in high-level cognitive processes such as learning, memory, and abstract thinking. The neurotransmitter *L-glutamate* is important in the transmission of impulses from the cortex to the hippocampus, the part of the brain that, as we observed in Chapter 14, is essential for the transformation of new information into long-term memory.

**Genetic Explanations**    Years of research have supported the notion that dementia may have a genetic basis. Investigators have found, for example, high rates of certain dementias in some families (Matsuyama et al., 1985). Because of such data, many clinicians now distinguish *familial* Alzheimer's disease from *sporadic* Alzheimer's disease, in which a family history of brain disease is not clearly in evidence (Gallagher-Thompson & Thompson, 1995).

As we noted earlier, an association between Alzheimer's disease and Down syndrome has led re-

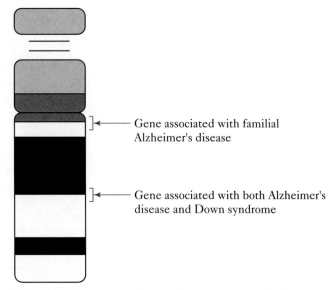

**Figure 15-6**    *A gene abnormality located toward the top of chromosome 21 is commonly found in patients with a familial form of Alzheimer's disease. In addition, scientists have located a gene lower on the chromosome which contributes to both Alzheimer's disease and Down syndrome. (Adapted from Tanzi, 1991; Tanzi et al., 1989.)*

searchers to propose that some genes on chromosome 21 may contribute to Alzheimer's disease (Tanzi, 1991) (see Figure 15-6). One line of research has identified a particular gene on chromosome 21 whose mutated form may lead to greater plaque accumulations in certain areas of the brain, in turn increasing the chances of developing early-onset familial Alzheimer's disease (Mullan et al., 1992; Murrell et al., 1991).

Yet other genetic studies have linked certain kinds of Alzheimer's disease to defects on chromosome 14 (Sherrington et al., 1995; Schellenberg et al., 1992) and chromosome 19 (Pericak-Vance et al., 1991). All of these discoveries are promising, but the majority of persons with Alzheimer's disease do not have clear family histories of inherited brain dysfunction. Thus, scientists still do not know the extent to which genetic mutations may influence the development of this disease in the population as a whole (Gallagher-Thompson & Thompson, 1995).

**Other Explanations**    Theorists have also pointed to other possible causes of Alzheimer's disease. Some scientists are looking for a slow-acting infectious agent that may help cause the disease (Prusiner, 1991). Others believe the immune systems of people who develop the disease may be impaired (Roberts et al., 1991). High concentrations of aluminum in the brains of some Alzheimer's victims have led some investigators to look for heavy metals or other toxic substances in the brains of Alzheimer's patients. Still other researchers have cited elevated levels of zinc in the brain as a possible factor in this disease.

## Treatments for Alzheimer's Disease

The first step in treating a person suspected of having Alzheimer's disease is to make as accurate a diagnosis as possible, based on a thorough examination, detailed medical history, and laboratory tests. If the person is suffering from a different form of dementia, a different course of treatment may be called for.

Once a diagnosis of Alzheimer's disease is made, various therapies may be employed, but unfortunately none of them are very helpful. *Drug therapies* are largely experimental and have produced modest improvements at best. One drug, *tacrine hydrochloride* (trade name Cognex), prevents the breakdown of acetylcholine, the neurotransmitter that is in low supply in people with the disease. Some patients who take high doses of this drug show slight improvements in short-term memory and reasoning ability, as well as in their use of language and their coping ability (Davis et al., 1992; Farlow et al., 1992).

Some *behavioral interventions* have been applied in cases of Alzheimer's disease. Typically, behaviorists identify specific everyday actions performed by the Alzheimer's victim that are stressful for the family, such as wandering at night, being incontinent, and demanding frequent attention, or deficient behaviors such as inadequate self-care (Fisher & Carstensen, 1990). They then teach family members how and when to apply reinforcement in order to help shape positive behaviors, using a combination of role-playing techniques, modeling, and in-home practice (Pinkston & Linsk, 1984). Similarly, behavioral principles and techniques are often taught to staff members in long-term care facilities and nursing homes.

Caregiving may take a very heavy toll, both psychological and physical, on the close relatives of Alzheimer's victims (Gallagher-Thompson & Thompson, 1995). In fact, one of the most frequent reasons for the institutionalization of victims is that overwhelmed caregivers can no longer cope with the demands of caring for an Alzheimer's victim at home (Colerick & George, 1986). To help reduce caretakers' feelings of depression, frustration, and anger, clinicians have emphasized the need for planned and regular time-out (Berman et al., 1987), offered psychoeducational programs about Alzheimer's disease, provided psychotherapy for distressed family members, and de-

*When long-term-care institutions offer programs that are stimulating, such as this exercise class for people with Alzheimer's disease, allow patients to control their lives, and involve family members and friends, elderly residents are generally happier and show relatively better cognitive functioning.*

veloped caretaker support groups (Gallagher et al., 1991).

> ### *Summing Up*
> *Depression, anxiety, substance abuse, delirium, and dementia are common problems in later life. Dementia appears most often in the form of Alzheimer's disease. This disease, marked by excessive formation of neurofibrillary tangles and senile plaques, is not well understood, although investigators have implicated a number of genetic and biological factors. Drugs and pyschological interventions have had a limited impact. Clinicians now also try to address the psychological needs of caretakers.*

## The State of the Field
# Disorders of Childhood and Old Age

Early in this century, children and elderly persons were largely ignored by researchers. All of that has changed in recent decades, and today the mental health of children and elderly persons is a major focus of both researchers and clinicians.

Numerous studies now concentrate exclusively on the problems of children. Many problems that begin primarily in childhood have been identified, and clinicians have proposed various explanations and devel-

---

*Tacrine hydrochloride*    A drug that is sometimes used to help treat Alzheimer's disease. It prevents the breakdown of the neurotransmitter acetylcholine.

oped special interventions for them. At the same time, clinicians have come to recognize that some degree of dysfunction and pain is a normal part of human development and that overlabeling or overreacting to many childhood difficulties may create extra problems for children and their families.

In recent years clinicians and researchers have also increasingly recognized the relative powerlessness of children, and have enlisted the aid of government agencies to protect the rights and safety of this population and to draw attention to such problems as child abuse and neglect, child sexual abuse, child malnourishment, and the fetal alcohol syndrome. In addition, as we shall see in Chapter 17, clinicians have helped to determine the psychological impact of such problems and developed interventions designed to prevent and treat them.

In a similar manner, the psychological problems of elderly persons have increasingly caught the attention of the clinical field. Some of the problems—depression, anxiety, alcoholism—are common in all age groups, but their emergence in old age is often the result of the special stresses of later life. Other problems—such as dementia, delirium, and the abuse of prescription drugs—are disproportionately common in the elderly population.

This increased focus on the problems of elderly persons has occurred for a variety of reasons. First, the number of people who are elderly in our society is steadily increasing, so that the needs of this age group are becoming more and more visible. Second, as the elderly population grows larger, greater caretaking pressures are being placed upon their adult children, and these people have lobbied for more clinical help. Third, as the number of elderly persons in our society rises, young and middle-aged adults are increasingly recognizing that the problems of old age await them as well. And fourth, as the number of elderly people grows, the number of aging-related psychological disorders continues to grow too.

As the study and treatment of elderly persons advance in the coming years, clinical investigations will certainly learn much more about the problems that confront this age group. In addition, the special concerns of caretakers for elderly persons with problems will probably be better appreciated and addressed. And it is hoped that more humane and comforting solutions for the residential needs of aged persons will be developed.

The study and treatment of children and elderly persons with psychological problems may have been relatively slow getting started, but they are now moving rapidly, and developments in these areas of abnormal psychology are likely to continue at an impressive pace. As the tongue-in-cheek box on the "disorder" called childhood implies, childhood and old age have been around for a long time; now that clinicians have discovered them, they are unlikely to underestimate the complexity of their special issues or the extent of their importance ever again.

## Chapter Review

1. *Disorders of Childhood and Old Age:* Some problems are particularly likely to emerge during a particular age, such as during childhood or old age.

2. *Disorders of Childhood:* Emotional and behavioral problems are common aspects of childhood and adolescence, but a fifth of all children and adolescents in the United States actually warrant a diagnosis of a clinical disorder.

   A. *Anxiety disorders* among children include adult-like disorders such as social phobia and generalized anxiety disorder, as well as the unique childhood pattern of *separation anxiety disorder,* which is characterized by excessive anxiety, often panic, whenever a child is separated from home or a parent.

   B. *Depression* is found among 2 percent of all children under 17 years of age, and among 7 percent of adolescents alone.

   C. Some children exceed the normal periodic breaking of rules, act very aggressively, and display one of the *disruptive behavior disorders.*

      (1) Children who display an *oppositional defiant disorder* argue repeatedly with adults, lose their temper, and suffer feelings of great anger and resentment.

      (2) Those with a *conduct disorder,* a more severe pattern of behavior, repeatedly violate the basic rights of others. These children often are violent and cruel, and may lie, cheat, steal, or run away.

   D. Children who display *attention-deficit hyperactivity disorder (ADHD)* attend poorly to tasks or act impulsively and move around excessively, or both.

   E. Children with *elimination disorders*—*enuresis* and *encopresis*—repeatedly urinate or pass feces in inappropriate places, respectively, during the day or at night while sleeping or both. The behavioral *bell-and-battery* technique is an effective treatment for enuresis.

F. Highly inadequate functioning in learning, communication, or coordination, is displayed by more than 15 percent of children, leading to such diagnoses as *learning disorders, communication disorders,* and *developmental coordination disorder.*

3. *Autism:* People with autism, a long-term disorder that begins in childhood, are unresponsive to others, have significant language and communication deficits, have very limited skill at imaginative play, and exhibit highly restricted and repetitive behavior. Interventions for autism seek to help the children adapt to their environment through such approaches as behavioral treatments, communication training, training for parents, and community integration.

4. *Mental Retardation.* People with **mental retardation,** another long-term disorder that begins in childhood, are significantly below average in intelligence (as measured on intelligence tests) and adaptive ability. Approximately 1 out of every 100 persons receives this diagnosis.

A. *Mild retardation,* by far the most common level of mental retardation, has been linked primarily to environmental factors.

B. *Moderate, severe, and profound mental retardation* are caused primarily by biological factors, although individuals who function at these levels of retardation are also enormously affected by their environment. The leading biological causes are *chromosomal disorders, metabolic disorders,* disorders related to *prenatal problems,* disorders related to *birth complications,* and *childhood disease and injuries.*

C. In recent decades education and treatment for people with mental retardation has focused on *normalization programs* that offer conditions of everyday life in community settings or institutions.

(1) One of the most intense debates in the field of education centers on whether individuals with mental retardation profit more from *special classes* or *mainstreaming.*

(2) In general, the use of *operant learning principles* has been successful in educating individuals with mental retardation. Those who also experience emotional or behavioral problems sometimes receive insight, behavioral, or drug therapy.

(3) To help enhance opportunities for growth by persons with mental retardation, increasing numbers of programs are offering training in such areas as socializing, sex, marriage, parenting, and vocational skills.

5. *Disorders of Later Life:* As many as 50 percent of elderly people would benefit from mental health services. Their problems are often linked to the losses, changes, and other stresses that they are facing.

A. *Depression* is experienced by as many as 20 percent of older adults.

B. Approximately 7 percent of elderly people suffer from *generalized anxiety disorder.*

C. Between 3 and 5 percent of the older adult population exhibit *alcohol-related problems* in any given year. The *misuse of prescription drugs* is also a significant problem among elderly persons.

D. Older people are more likely than people of other age groups to experience *delirium,* a rapidly developing clouding of consciousness in which a person's awareness of the environment becomes less clear and he or she has great difficulty concentrating, focusing attention, and maintaining a straightforward stream of thought. The syndrome may be caused by factors that are often quite reversible with proper identification and treatment.

E. *Dementia,* a syndrome characterized by severe memory impairment and other cognitive disturbances, becomes increasingly prevalent in older age groups. *Alzheimer's disease* is the most common form of dementia among the elderly. It is characterized by structural changes in the brain, particularly an excessive number of *neurofibrillary tangles* and *senile plaques.*

(1) A number of possible causes for Alzheimer's disease have been suggested, including *depletions of the neurotransmitters acetylcholine* and *L-glutamate, gene defects, slow-acting infectious agents, immune system dysfunctioning,* and heavy metals and other *toxic substances* in the brain.

(2) Although there is no medical cure for Alzheimer's disease, the drug *tacrine hydrochloride* (trade name Cognex) is sometimes used to help produce limited improvements in certain areas of cognitive functioning. In addition, behavioral therapies are used to teach family members how to encourage and reward specific behaviors. Programs to address the needs of caretakers are also increasing.

# Key Terms

| | | | |
|---|---|---|---|
| separation anxiety disorder | developmental coordination disorder | trisomy 21 | dementia |
| school phobia | autism | fragile X syndrome | Alzheimer's disease |
| school refusal | echolalia | phenylketonuria (PKU) | neurofibrillary tangle |
| play therapy | perseveration of sameness | Tay-Sachs disease | senile plaque |
| oppositional defiant disorder | self-stimulatory behavior | cretinism | beta-amyloid protein |
| conduct disorder | self-injurious behavior | fetal alcohol syndrome | vascular dementia |
| juvenile delinquent | sign language | anoxia | multi-infarct dementia |
| recidivist | simultaneous communication | lead poisoning | Pick's disease |
| attention-deficit hyperactivity disorder (ADHD) | augmentative communication system | microcephaly | Creutzfeldt-Jakob |
| | | hydrocephalus | Huntington's disease |
| | | state school | Parkinson's disease |
| methylphenidate (Ritalin) | mental retardation | normalization program | L-glutamate |
| enuresis | mild retardation | deinstitutionalization | acetylcholine |
| encopresis | moderate retardation | special education | familial Alzheimer's disease |
| learning disorder | severe retardation | mainstreaming | sporadic Alzheimer's disease |
| communication disorder | profound retardation | token economy program | |
| | Down syndrome | sheltered workshop | tacrine hydrochloride |
| | | delirium | |

# Quick Quiz

1. How do anxiety disorders and depression in childhood compare to adult versions of these disorders? What are separation anxiety disorder and school phobia?

2. What are the prevalence rates and gender ratios for the various childhood disorders?

3. Distinguish oppositional defiant disorders from conduct disorders. What factors help cause conduct disorders, and how are these disorders treated?

4. What are the symptoms of attention-deficit hyperactivity disorder? What are the current treatments for this disorder and how effective are they?

5. What are enuresis and encopresis?

6. What are the various disorders of learning, communication, and coordination, and what kinds of problems do they pose for children?

7. What are the symptoms and possible causes of autism?

8. What are the overall goals of treatment for autism, and which interventions have been most helpful for individuals with this disorder?

9. Describe the different levels of mental retardation and discuss their primary causes.

10. What kinds of residences, educational programs, intervention programs, and community programs are helpful to persons with mental retardation?

11. What kinds of psychological problems are common in elderly people?

12. What symptoms and biological changes characterize Alzheimer's disease and other forms of dementia? How effective are the treatments for Alzheimer's disease?

# 16

# Personality Disorders

## Topic Overview

*"Odd" Personality Disorders*
Paranoid Personality Disorder
Schizoid Personality Disorder
Schizotypal Personality Disorder

*"Dramatic" Personality Disorders*
Antisocial Personality Disorder
Borderline Personality Disorder
Histrionic Personality Disorder
Narcissistic Personality Disorder

*"Anxious" Personality Disorders*
Avoidant Personality Disorder
Dependent Personality Disorder
Obsessive-Compulsive Personality Disorder

*Categorizing the Personality Disorders*

*T*he word "personality" refers to the unique and enduring pattern of inner experience and outward behavior that is characteristic of a given individual: most people tend to react and behave in their own relatively predictable ways. At the same time, most of us also maintain a certain adaptive flexibility. Our personalities are not static. We learn from past experiences and try out different responses in our efforts to cope effectively. This learning and adapting is something that people who suffer from a personality disorder are frequently unable to do.

A *personality disorder* is a pervasive, enduring, and inflexible pattern of inner experience and behavior that deviates markedly from the expectations of a person's culture and leads to distress or impairment (APA, 1994). The narrow range of experiences and responses displayed by people with these disorders often leads to psychological pain and social or occupational difficulty. The disorders typically begin, or at least become recognizable, in adolescence or early adulthood, although in some cases they start during childhood (APA, 1994).

The personality disorders and the distress they produce make for lifelong ordeals, although the disorders differ in the extent to which they disrupt a person's life. Whether mild or severe, however, they tend to affect every facet of a person's being. And they are among the most difficult psychological disorders to treat. The prevalence of personality disorders among adults has been estimated at between 4 and 15 percent (APA, 1994; Zimmerman & Coryell, 1989).

As we saw in Chapter 2, DSM-IV distinguishes between Axis I disorders—vivid disorders that may emerge and end at various points in the life cycle—and Axis II disorders—disorders of long standing that usually begin before adulthood and persist in stable form into adult life. The personality disorders are Axis II disorders. Unlike most of the clinical syndromes of Axis I, personality disorders are not usually marked by periods of significant improvement and do not vary greatly in intensity or improve over time. Often, a person with a personality disorder suffers from an acute (Axis I) form of mental disorder as well (Flick et al., 1993).

DSM-IV distinguishes ten personality disorders and groups them in three clusters (APA, 1994). One cluster, characterized by odd behavior, consists of the *paranoid, schizoid,* and *schizotypal* personality disorders. A second cluster, characterized by dramatic behavior, consists of the *antisocial, borderline, histrionic,* and *narcissistic* personality disorders. The final cluster,

*Personality disorder* A pervasive, enduring, and inflexible pattern of inner experience and outward behavior that deviates markedly from the expectations of one's culture and leads to distress or impairment.

characterized by anxious behavior, consists of the *avoidant, dependent,* and *obsessive-compulsive* personality disorders (see Table 16-1).

As we examine these personality disorders, it will become evident that the symptoms of one disorder often overlap with those of another, thus making it difficult to distinguish them (Zimmerman, 1994). Even diagnosticians have difficulty of this kind, and in many cases they assign more than one personality disorder category to an individual (Dolan et al., 1995). In addition, clinicians often disagree as to the correct diagnosis for a given person with a personality disorder.

An important precaution to observe when one is learning about the personality disorders is to avoid the trap of overapplying any category to oneself or to the people one knows. It is all too easy to catch glimpses of ourselves or of our acquaintances in the descriptions of the various personality disorders (Widiger & Costa, 1994; Maher & Maher, 1994), but in the vast majority of cases, such interpretations are unwarranted. We all display personality traits; that is part of being human. And many of these traits inevitably resemble those that are characteristic of personality disorders. However, only rarely are they so inflexible, maladaptive, and distressful that they can be considered disorders.

> ### Consider This
> While it is common for people to mistakenly apply diagnoses of mental disorders to themselves, relatives, or acquaintances, this is particularly the case with regard to personality disorders. Why do you think these disorders are particularly subject to such efforts at amateur psychology?

# "Odd" Personality Disorders

The cluster of "odd" personality disorders consists of the paranoid, schizoid, and schizotypal personality disorders. People with these disorders typically display the kinds of odd or eccentric behaviors seen in the Axis I disorder schizophrenia (for example, extreme suspiciousness, social withdrawal, and cognitive and perceptual peculiarities). Such behaviors have the effect of leaving the person rather alone and isolated. Some clinicians believe that these personality disorders, along with several other schizophrenia-like syndromes, are indeed related to schizophrenia and call them *schizophrenia-spectrum disorders* (Siever, 1992).

As we shall see, clinicians have carefully delineated the symptoms of these odd personality disorders over

**Table 16-1**  *Comparison of Personality Disorders*

| | DSM-IV Cluster | Similar Disorders on Axis I | Responsiveness to Treatment |
|---|---|---|---|
| Paranoid | Odd | Schizophrenia <br> Delusional disorder | Modest |
| Schizoid | Odd | Schizophrenia <br> Delusional disorder | Modest |
| Schizotypal | Odd | Schizophrenia <br> Delusional disorder | Modest |
| Antisocial | Dramatic | Conduct disorder | Poor |
| Borderline | Dramatic | Mood disorders | Modest |
| Histrionic | Dramatic | Somatoform disorders <br> Mood disorders | Modest |
| Narcissistic | Dramatic | Cyclothymic disorder <br> (mild bipolar disorder) | Poor |
| Avoidant | Anxious | Social phobia | Moderate |
| Dependent | Anxious | Separation anxiety disorder <br> Dysthymic disorder <br> (mild depressive disorder) | Moderate |
| Obsessive-compulsive | Anxious | Obsessive-compulsive anxiety disorder | Moderate |

the years, yet the causes of the disorders have received relatively little systematic investigation and are not well understood. Nor have clinicians been very successful in treating persons with these personality disorders, although a variety of approaches have been tried. In fact, people with these disorders rarely seek treatment (Fabrega et al., 1991).

## Paranoid Personality Disorder

People with *paranoid personality disorder* display a pattern of pervasive distrust and suspiciousness of others (APA, 1994). Because people with this disorder suspect everyone of intending them harm, they shun close relationships. Their trust in their own ideas and abilities can be excessive, though, as we see in the case of Charles.

> Charles, an only child of poorly educated parents, had been recognized as a "child genius" in early school years. He received a Ph.D. degree at 24, and subsequently held several responsible positions as a research physicist. . . .
>
> His haughty arrogance and narcissism often resulted in conflicts with his superiors; it was felt that he spent too much time working on his own

---
*Paranoid personality disorder*   A personality disorder characterized by a pattern of pervasive distrust and suspiciousness of others.

"harebrained" schemes and not enough on company projects. Charles . . . began to feel . . . that both his superiors and his subordinates were "making fun of him" and not taking him seriously. To remedy this attack upon his status, Charles began to work on a scheme that would "revolutionize the industry". . . . After several months . . . he presented his plans to the company president. Brilliant though it was, the plan overlooked certain obvious simple facts of logic and economy.

> Upon learning of its rejection, Charles withdrew to his home where he became obsessed with "new ideas," proposing them in intricate schematics and formulas to a number of government officials and industrialists.
>
> *(Millon, 1969, pp. 329–330)*

Ever vigilant, cautious, and quick to react to perceived threats, people with a paranoid personality disorder continually expect to be the target of some trickery or exploitation, and they find "hidden" meanings everywhere, usually of a belittling or threatening nature (see Figure 16-1). In one study in which subjects were asked to role play, subjects with paranoia were more likely than controls without paranoia to interpret the ambiguous actions of others as reflecting hostile intentions, and to choose anger as the appropriate role-play response (Turkat et al., 1990).

People with paranoid personality disorder approach relationships with skepticism and guardedness. Quick

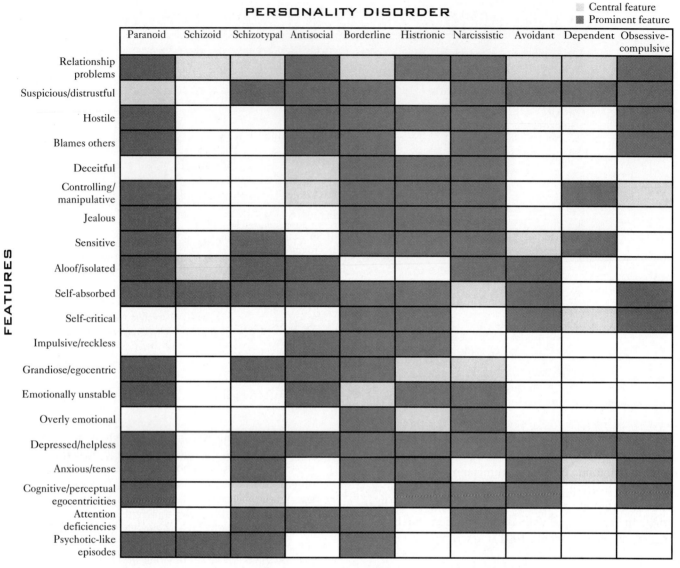

**Figure 16-1**   *Prominent and central features of DSM-IV's ten personality disorders. The symptoms of the various disorders often overlap significantly, leading to frequent misdiagnoses or to multiple diagnoses for a given client.*

to challenge the loyalty or trustworthiness of acquaintances, they remain cold and distant, reluctant to confide in others for fear of being hurt. Such unwarranted suspicions are exemplified by the classic paranoid husband who with no justification continually questions the fidelity of his wife. The suspiciousness of people with paranoid personality disorder, unlike that of persons with a paranoid type of schizophrenia or a delusional disorder, is not usually of a delusional nature, however: their ideas are not so bizarre or so firmly believed that they constitute a clear departure from reality.

People with a paranoid personality disorder are critical of weakness and fault in others, particularly in work-related situations, but they view themselves as blameless and consequently are hypersensitive to criticism. Argumentative and rigid, they are unable to recognize their mistakes, often blaming others for the things that go wrong in their own lives or even for their general unhappiness (Vaillant, 1994). They persistently bear grudges. Between 0.5 and 2.5 percent of the adult population, and apparently more men than women, are believed to manifest a paranoid personality disorder (APA, 1994).

## Explanations of Paranoid Personality Disorder

The causes of paranoid personality disorder, like those of most other personality disorders, have received little empirical investigation. Psychodynamic theories, the most prominent explanations for this disorder, trace it to early interactions with demanding and rejecting parents. (Indeed, psychodynamic explanations for almost all of the personality disorders begin with the proposition that people with these disorders have experienced rejection or lack of love when young.) According to one psychodynamic view, repeated mistreatment and the absence of consistent parental love during infancy and childhood cause some individuals to view their environment as hostile. They become overly vigilant to danger and to negative reactions from others, resulting in a broad and basic distrust of other people (Manschreck, 1985; Cameron, 1974). Children with such unfortunate roots are also considered likely to develop feelings of excessive hostility and rage, project those feelings onto others, and thus feel even more persecuted and attacked.

The possibility of a genetic factor influencing the development of paranoid personality disorder has also been proposed. A study of self-reported suspiciousness in several thousand pairs of twins in Australia found that if one twin was excessively suspicious, the other had an increased likelihood of also being suspicious (Kendler et al., 1987). As with other such studies, however, these findings alone cannot tell us whether it is genetic factors or common experiences that lead both twins to be overly suspicious.

## Treatments for Paranoid Personality Disorder

People with paranoid personality disorder do not typically see themselves as needing help, and so few come to therapy willingly. Moreover, once in therapy, they tend to distrust their therapist and resist treatment (Sparr et al., 1986). Thus, it is not surprising that therapy for paranoid personality disorder, like that for most other personality disorders, moves slowly and yields limited gains (Quality Assurance Project, 1990).

Object relations therapists, the psychodynamic therapists who give center stage to relationships, try to see through the patient's defensive anger and work on what they view as his or her deep wish for a satisfying relationship (Auchincloss & Weiss, 1992). Cognitive therapists try to help clients with paranoid personality disorder control their anxiety, improve their skills at solving interpersonal problems, develop more realistic perceptions of others' behaviors and intentions, and increase their awareness of other people's perspectives (Beck & Freeman, 1990). Drug therapy is generally ineffective (Block & Pristach, 1992).

# Schizoid Personality Disorder

People with schizoid personality disorder, like those with paranoid personality disorder, do not have close ties with others. The reason they avoid social contact, however, is not that they suspect other people's motives but that they genuinely prefer to be alone.

> Roy was a successful sanitation engineer. . . . ; his job called for considerable foresight and independent judgment but little supervisory responsibility. In general, he was appraised as an undistinguished but competent and reliable employee. There were few demands of an interpersonal nature made of him, and he was viewed by most of his colleagues as reticent and shy and by others as cold and aloof.
>
> Difficulties centered about his relationship with his wife. At her urging they sought marital counseling for, as she put it, "he is unwilling to join in family activities, he fails to take an interest in the children, he lacks affection and is disinterested in sex."
>
> The pattern of social indifference, flatness of affect and personal isolation which characterized much of Roy's behavior was of little consequence to those with whom a deeper or more intimate relationship was not called for; with his immediate family, however, these traits took their toll.
>
> *(Millon, 1969, p. 224)*

People with *schizoid personality disorder* display a pattern of detachment from social relationships and a restricted range of emotional expression (APA, 1994). Other people often view them as "loners." They are uninterested in initiating or maintaining acquaintanceships, take little interest in having sexual relationships, and even seem indifferent to their families.

People with this pattern typically seek out occupations that require little or no contact with others. When necessary, they can form stable, if distant, work relationships, but they prefer to keep to themselves, often working alone over the course of the day. They usually live by themselves as well and avoid socializing. As a result, their social skills tend to be relatively limited.

The restricted interactions of people with schizoid personality disorder reflect an equally restricted range of emotion and expression. They are self-absorbed and generally unaffected by praise or criticism. They rarely show their feelings, expressing neither joy nor anger. They seem to have no need for attention or acceptance, are typically viewed as cold, humorless, or dull, and generally succeed in being ignored.

---

*Schizoid personality disorder*    A personality disorder in which a person displays a pattern of detachment from social relationships and a restricted range of emotional expression.

*People with schizoid and avoidant personality disorders often spend much of their time alone. The former are indifferent to social relationships and truly want to be alone, whereas the latter yearn for, but fear, social relationships.*

The prevalence of schizoid personality disorder is not known (APA, 1994). Slightly more men than women are believed to have the disorder, and men may be more impaired by it (APA, 1994).

## Explanations of Schizoid Personality Disorder

Many psychodynamic theorists, particularly object relations theorists, believe that the extreme social withdrawal of people with a schizoid personality disorder is a defensive reaction to an unsatisfied basic need for human contact (Carstairs, 1992; Horner, 1991, 1975). The parents of people with this disorder, like those of persons with paranoid personality disorder, are seen as having been unaccepting, underprotective, rejecting, and in some cases, even abusive. Rather than reacting with a sense of distrust (as those with paranoid symptoms do), these individuals suffer an inability to give or receive love, and they develop a defensive coping strategy of shunning all relationships. Proponents of self theory, another psychodynamic theory, believe that faulty early parent-child interactions produce a "self-disorder" in schizoid people, one marked by a lack of self-esteem and self-confidence (Gabbard, 1990).

Cognitive theorists propose that people with schizoid personality disorder suffer from several cognitive deficits, including a poverty of thought and an inability to scan the environment effectively and arrive at accurate perceptions (Beck & Freeman, 1990). Unable to interpret subtle emotional cues from others, they are unlikely to respond to emotion-evoking stimuli. As this idea of cognitive deficits might predict, children with schizoid personality disorder have been found to

suffer more developmental delays in language, education, and motor functioning than control subjects, despite a similar level of intelligence in the two groups (Wolff, 1991).

## Treatments for Schizoid Personality Disorder

With their lack of emotion and their disengagement from interpersonal contact, people with schizoid personality disorder have little interest in initiating treatment. Those who enter therapy usually do so because of some other disorder, such as alcoholism. They often distance themselves from their therapist and seem not to care about their treatment (Siever, 1981). Thus, therapy gains tend to be limited for these persons as well.

Cognitive therapists have sometimes produced specific, limited improvements by helping clients with schizoid personality disorder become more aware of and experience more positive emotions. They may, for example, present the clients with a list of emotions to think about, or have them record interesting or pleasurable experiences (Beck & Freeman, 1990). Behavioral therapists have sometimes had success teaching social skills to these clients (Beck & Freeman, 1990). Group therapy is apparently useful when it provides a contained, safe setting for social contact (Vaillant & Perry, 1985), although some persons with this disorder feel stifled by any pressure to speak and to share more of themselves with other members (Gabbard, 1990). Drug therapy has offered little help (Liebowitz et al., 1986).

# Schizotypal Personality Disorder

The schizotypal personality disorder is so severe that those who suffer from it are greatly handicapped in all interactions with other people, as we see in the case of Harold:

> Harold was the fourth of seven children. . . . "Duckie," as Harold was known, had always been a withdrawn, frightened and "stupid" youngster. The nickname "Duckie" represented a peculiar waddle in his walk; it was used by others as a term of derogation and ridicule. Harold rarely played with his sibs or neighborhood children; he was teased unmercifully because of his "walk" and his fear of pranksters. . . . Harold was a favorite neighborhood scapegoat; he was intimidated even by the most innocuous glance in his direction. . . .
>
> Harold's family was surprised when he performed well in the first few years of schooling. He began to falter, however, upon entrance to junior high school. At about the age of 14, his schoolwork became

extremely poor, he refused to go to classes and he complained of a variety of vague, physical pains. By age 15 he had totally withdrawn from school, remaining home in the basement room that he shared with two younger brothers. Everyone in his family began to speak of him as "being touched." He thought about "funny religious things that didn't make sense"; he also began to draw "strange things" and talk to himself. When he was 16, he once ran out of the house screaming "I'm gone, I'm gone, I'm gone . . . ," saying that his "body went to heaven" and that he had to run outside to recover it; rather interestingly, this event occurred shortly after his father had been committed by the courts to a state mental hospital. By age 17, Harold was ruminating all day, often talking aloud in a meaningless jargon; he refused to come to the family table for meals.

*(Millon, 1969, pp. 347–348)*

People with **schizotypal personality disorder** display a pattern of interpersonal deficits marked by acute discomfort in close relationships, cognitive or perceptual distortions, and behavioral eccentricities (APA, 1994). They tend to seek isolation, experience considerable anxiety in the presence of others, and typically have few if any close friends outside of their immediate families. Not surprisingly, many feel intensely lonely.

It is the nature and extent of their cognitive distortions and behavioral eccentricities that distinguish these people from those with paranoid and schizoid personality disorders. Like people with paranoid personality disorder, for example, they are very suspicious about the motives of others, but they further demonstrate many peculiarities of thought. They may, for example, have *ideas of reference*, believing that unrelated events pertain to them in some important way. They may also have unusual perceptual experiences, including bodily *illusions*, such as sensing an external "force" or presence. Some see themselves as having special extrasensory abilities, and some believe that they have magical control over others.

Schizotypal persons may also display eccentric behavior, such as repeatedly arranging labels on cans, organizing closets, or wearing a peculiar assortment of clothing and accessories. In addition, the emotions of these individuals may be either inappropriate or flat, humorless, and bland.

People with schizotypal personality disorder often have great difficulty keeping their attention focused (Lenzenwerger et al., 1991). This problem may partially explain one of their most distinctive characteris-

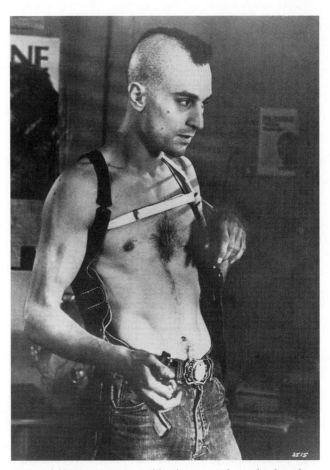

*Some of film's most memorable characters have displayed personality disorders. Travis Bickle, of* Taxi Driver *fame, seemed to manifest the symptoms of schizotypal personality disorder, including social discomfort and a reduced capacity for interpersonal relationships, as well as self-referential interpretations of various events, cognitive distortions, a highly suspicious nature, grandiosity, emotional flatness, and transient psychotic episodes.*

tics—*digressive speech*. They typically converse in a vague manner, making statements that are inappropriately elaborate. It is often difficult to follow their train of thought. Thus, in one study, more loose associations and related speech problems were found among children with this disorder than in control subjects (Caplan et al., 1990). Although these symptoms are obviously similar to those of people with schizophrenia, they rarely are as extreme and they do not represent a complete break from reality.

Perhaps because of their perceptual distortions and magical thinking, some persons with schizotypal disorder demonstrate significant creative ability (Schuldberg et al., 1988). However, the general tendency of people with this disorder is to drift aimlessly, hold undemanding jobs, and lead an idle, ineffectual life (Millon, 1990). It has been estimated that as many as 3 percent of all persons—though slightly more

---

*Schizotypal personality disorder*   A personality disorder in which a person displays a pattern of interpersonal deficits marked by acute discomfort in close relationships, cognitive or perceptual distortions, and behavioral eccentricities.

males than females—have a schizotypal personality disorder (APA, 1994).

## Explanations of Schizotypal Personality Disorder

Because the symptoms of schizotypal personality disorder and schizophrenia are often so similar, researchers have tried to show that some of the factors that explain schizophrenia can also help explain schizotypal personality disorder. Lately, many of these efforts have met with some success.

As in the case of schizophrenia, the development of schizotypal symptoms has been linked to poor family communication and to psychological disorders in parents (Asarnow et al., 1991; Nagy & Szatmari, 1986). Research has also suggested that defects in attention may contribute significantly to schizotypal personality disorder, just as they apparently do to schizophrenia (Weston & Siever, 1993; Siever & Davis, 1991). And, finally, recent research has begun to link schizotypal personality disorder to some of the same biological factors tied to schizophrenia, such as high activity of the neurotransmitter dopamine and enlarged brain ventricles (Weston & Siever, 1993; Siever et al., 1990; Rotter et al., 1991). There are also some indications that these biological factors may have a genetic base (Carey & DiLalla, 1994; Kendler et al., 1991).

## Treatments for Schizotypal Personality Disorder

As in cases of paranoid and schizoid personality disorder, the limited capacity for interaction displayed by persons with schizotypal personality disorder makes therapy difficult (Stone, 1989; McGlashan, 1986). Helping clients "reconnect" with the world and establish personal boundaries is often the central therapeutic task, irrespective of the therapist's theoretical orientation. To this end, therapists may set explicit limits, require punctuality, and distinguish clearly between the patient's views and those of the therapist (Stone, 1989). Other therapy goals are to prevent further social isolation, ease loneliness, avoid overstimulation, and develop self-awareness of personal feelings (Quality Assurance Project, 1990; Walsh, 1990).

Cognitive therapists further try to teach schizotypal clients to evaluate their unusual thoughts or perceptions objectively and to disregard inappropriate thoughts and refrain from acting on them (Beck & Freeman, 1990). On occasion, specific behavioral methods such as elocution lessons, social skills training, and tips on appropriate dress and manners have helped the individuals learn to fit in and feel less alienated around others (Liebowitz et al., 1986). And fi-

nally, antipsychotic drugs in low doses apparently help some patients, usually by reducing some of their thought disorders (Weston & Siever, 1993; Perry et al., 1990). Patients with this disorder may be particularly sensitive to the harmful effects of medication, however, so the dosage must be monitored closely.

*Summing Up*
*The "odd" personality disorders are marked by the kinds of strange symptoms often seen in schizophrenia, particularly distrust and suspiciousness, in paranoid personality disorder; detachment and restricted emotions, in schizoid personality disorder; and cognitive and perceptual distortions, in schizotypal personality disorder. The current explanations for these disorders have received limited research support, and highly successful treatments for them have yet to be developed.*

# "Dramatic" Personality Disorders

The cluster of "dramatic" personality disorders includes the antisocial, borderline, histrionic, and narcissistic personality disorders. People with these problems display behaviors that are highly dramatic, emotional, or erratic, making it almost impossible for them to have reciprocal or normal relationships. (Box 16-1 describes several other disorders that are also marked by erratic and impulsive actions).

As a group, these personality disorders are more commonly diagnosed than the others (Fabrega et al., 1991). Once again clinical theorists (particularly psychodynamic theorists) have offered numerous explanations for the disorders, but with the possible exception of antisocial personality disorder, research has shed little light on the causes and factors at work. Indeed, only antisocial personality disorder has received much empirical attention over the years, probably because it creates so many problems for society. Recently, however, borderline personality disorder has begun to receive considerable research attention as well (Linehan & Kehrer, 1993).

## Antisocial Personality Disorder

Robert Hare (1993), one of the world's leading researchers of antisocial personality disorder, recalls an early professional encounter with Ray, a prison inmate who displayed this disorder:

In the early 1960s, I found myself employed as the sole psychologist at the British Columbia Penitentiary. . . . I wasn't in my office for more than an hour when my first "client" arrived. He was a tall, slim, dark-haired man in his thirties. The air around him seemed to buzz, and the eye contact he made with me was so direct and intense that I wondered if I had ever really looked anybody in the eye before. That stare was unrelenting—he didn't indulge in the brief glances away that most people use to soften the force of their gaze.

Without waiting for an introduction, the inmate—I'll call him Ray—opened the conversation: "Hey, Doc, how's it going? Look, I've got a problem. I need your help. I'd really like to talk to you about this."

Eager to begin work as a genuine psychotherapist, I asked him to tell me about it. In response, he pulled out a knife and waved it in front of my nose, all the while smiling and maintaining that intense eye contact.

Once he determined that I wasn't going to push the button, he explained that he intended to use the knife not on me but on another inmate who had been making overtures to his "protégé," a prison term for the more passive member of a homosexual pairing. Just why he was telling me this was not immediately clear, but I soon suspected that he was checking me out, trying to determine what sort of a prison employee I was. . . .

From that first meeting on, Ray managed to make my eight-month stint at the prison miserable. His constant demands on my time and his attempts to manipulate me into doing things for him were unending. On one occasion, he convinced me that he would make a good cook. . . . and I supported his request for a transfer from the machine shop (where he had apparently made the knife). What I didn't consider was that the kitchen was a source of sugar, potatoes, fruit, and other ingredients that could be turned into alcohol. Several months after I had recommended the transfer, there was a mighty eruption below the floorboards directly under the warden's table. When the commotion died down, we found an elaborate system for distilling alcohol below the floor. Something had gone wrong and one of the pots had exploded. There was nothing unusual about the presence of a still in a maximum-security prison, but the audacity of placing one under the warden's seat shook up a lot of people. When it was discovered that Ray was the brains behind the bootleg operation, he spent some time in solitary confinement.

Once out of "the hole," Ray appeared in my office as if nothing had happened and asked for a transfer from the kitchen to the auto shop—he really felt he had a knack, he saw the need to prepare himself for the outside world, if he only had the time to practice he could have his own body shop on the outside. . . . I was still feeling the sting of having arranged the first transfer, but eventually he wore me down.

Soon afterward I decided to leave the prison to pursue a Ph.D. in psychology, and about a month before I left Ray almost persuaded me to ask my father, a roofing contractor, to offer him a job as part of an application for parole.

Ray had an incredible ability to con not just me but everybody. He could talk, and lie, with a smoothness and a directness that sometimes momentarily disarmed even the most experienced and cynical of the prison staff. When I met him he had a long criminal record behind him (and, as it turned out, ahead of him); about half his adult life had been spent in prison, and many of his crimes had been violent. Yet he convinced me, and others more experienced than I, of his readiness to reform, that his interest in crime had been completely overshadowed by a driving passion in—well, cooking, mechanics, you name it. He lied endlessly, lazily, about everything, and it disturbed him not a whit whenever I pointed out something in his file that contradicted one of his lies. He would simply change the subject and spin off in a different direction. Finally convinced that he might not make the perfect job candidate in my father's firm, I turned down Ray's request—and was shaken by his nastiness at my refusal.

Before I left the prison for the university, I took advantage of the prison policy of letting staff have their cars repaired in the institution's auto shop—where Ray still worked, thanks (he would have said no thanks) to me. The car received a beautiful paint job and the motor and drive-train were reconditioned.

With all our possessions on top of the car and our baby in a plywood bed in the backseat, my wife and I headed for Ontario. The first problems appeared soon after we left Vancouver, when the motor seemed a bit rough. Later, when we encountered some moderate inclines, the radiator boiled over. A garage mechanic discovered ball bearings in the carburetor's float chamber; he also pointed out where one of the hoses to the radiator had clearly been tampered with. These problems were repaired easily enough, but the next one, which arose while we were going down a long hill, was more serious. The brake pedal became very spongy and then simply dropped to the floor—no brakes, and it was a long hill. Fortunately, we made it to a service station, where we found that the brake line had been cut so that a slow leak would occur. Perhaps it was a coincidence that Ray was working in the auto shop when the car was being tuned up, but I had no doubt that the prison "telegraph" had informed him of the owner of the car.

*(Hare, 1993)*

Often referred to as "psychopaths" or "sociopaths," persons with *antisocial personality disorder* display a pervasive pattern of disregard for and violation of

---

*Antisocial personality disorder*   A personality disorder characterized by a pervasive pattern of disregard for and violation of other people's right.

## Box 16-1

# *Disorders of Impulse Control Rather than Personality*

Impulsivity is a symptom of numerous psychological disorders, including antisocial and borderline personality disorders, bipolar disorders, substance-related disorders, schizophrenia, and certain paraphilias. DSM-IV also distinguishes several other disorders of which impulsivity is the central disabling feature. People with one of these *impulse-control disorders* fail to resist an impulse, drive, or temptation to perform acts that are harmful to themselves or others (APA, 1994). Usually they experience increasing tension or arousal before the act and pleasure or relief while they are performing it. Some, but not all, feel regret, self-reproach, or guilt afterward. These disorders often cause enormous distress to the sufferer and the community.

The disorders of impulse control identified by DSM-IV include pyromania, kleptomania, and pathological gambling. Although these problems arouse much curiosity and are portrayed in numerous movies and television programs, they have in fact received relatively little research attention.

*Pyromania* is the deliberate and repeated setting of fires to achieve intense pleasure or relief from tension. The fires are not set for monetary or any other apparent gain. This poorly understood disorder, which is much more common among men than women, is thought to be related to a variety

of factors, including poor parental relationships, individual temperament, poor social skills, and possible biochemical predispositions (APA, 1994; Soltys, 1992; Lowenstein, 1989).

Research in this area has been hampered by the difficulty of distinguishing instances of pyromania from those of arson, the setting of fires for revenge or gain or because of a psychotic delusion (Puri et al., 1995). The inability of researchers to find more than a few cases of pyromania (APA, 1994; Koson & Dvoskin, 1982) suggests that the criteria for diagnosis, or perhaps the diagnostic category itself, may not be very useful.

The story is similar with respect to *kleptomania,* recurrent failure to resist the impulse to steal. People with this disorder, which is much more common in women, do not steal for gain. In fact, they often have more than enough money to pay for the articles they steal. Nor do they steal out of anger or revenge, or in response to a delusion or hallucination. Apparently it is the tension before the act and the sense of relief afterward that drive their behavior. The pattern may involve either brief episodes that occur sporadically, longer episodes that take place periodically, or a chronic, fluctuating course (APA, 1994).

Little research has been done on kleptomania. What is known has

been drawn largely from case studies of shoplifting and stealing; yet fewer than 5 percent of shoplifters have this disorder. Most clinicians consider it to be rare, and some question its usefulness as a clinical category (APA, 1994), but others believe it to be more prevalent, especially among persons who also suffer from mood or eating disorders (Goldman, 1992; McElroy et al., 1991; Gerlinghoff & Backmund, 1987).

The most common of the impulse disorders is *pathological gambling,* persistent and recurrent maladaptive gambling behavior that disrupts personal, family, or vocational pursuits (APA, 1994). It is estimated that between 1 and 3 percent of adults, and many adolescents as well, may suffer from it (APA, 1994; Winters et al., 1993). Clinicians are careful to distinguish pathological from social gambling, for unlike pyromania and kleptomania, this behavior occurs in mild forms that are not only legal but socially approved.

Pathological gambling is defined less by the amount of time or money spent in gambling than by the addictive nature of the behavior. People who manifest pathological gambling are unable to walk away from a wager and are restless and irritable if gambling is denied them. Repeated losses of money lead to more gambling in an effort to win the money back, and the

other people's rights (APA, 1994). Outside of substance-related disorders, this is the disorder most closely linked to adult criminal behavior, both minor and major. Most persons with the disorder have displayed some patterns of antisocial misbehavior before they were 15, including truancy, running away from home, initiation of physical fights, physical cruelty to animals or people, deliberate destruction of property, and frequent lying and stealing.

Like Ray, people with antisocial personality disorder are repeatedly deceitful. Many are unable to work consistently at a job; they have frequent absences and are likely to abandon their jobs altogether (Bland et al., 1988). Usually these individuals are also irresponsible with money, frequently failing to honor financial obligations. They are impulsive, taking action without planning ahead or considering the consequences. They may be irritable and aggressive, and frequently initiate

gambling continues even in the face of financial, social, and health problems. Four progressive phases characterize the course of many cases: winning, losing, desperation, and hopelessness (Rosenthal, 1992).

Pathological gambling differs from the other impulse-control disorders in one very important way. Because this disorder is more prevalent than the others and because the behavior resembles alcoholism, a great deal of attention has been directed toward its treatment. Treatments that combine approaches and that help build an individual's coping skills tend to be more effective than any one approach alone (McCormick, 1994;

Schwarz & Lindner, 1992). People with pathological gambling who join self-help support groups, such as Gambler's Anonymous, a network patterned after Alcoholics Anonymous, seem to have a higher recovery rate, perhaps in part because they have admitted that they have a problem and are seeking to conquer it.

Recently there has been some controversy over the adoption of a disease model of pathological gambling. Editorials in various newspapers ask whether the "medicalization" of gambling too easily excuses irresponsible or illegal behavior (Vatz & Weinberg, 1993), and express dismay at the public approval of famous persons who

have admitted to powerlessness over gambling impulses. However, several recent studies suggest that a neurochemical factor may in fact be related to pathological gambling and some of the other impulse-control disorders (Stein et al., 1993; McElroy et al., 1992; Moreno et al., 1991), and some case studies report effective treatment for this disorder when cognitive or behavioral approaches are applied (Bujold et al., 1994; Hollander et al., 1992).

DSM-IV also distinguishes two other impulse-control disorders. People with *intermittent explosive disorder,* a rare disorder more common in men than in women, have periodic aggressive outbursts in which they seriously assault people and destroy property. Their aggressiveness is grossly disproportionate to any provocation. People with *trichotillomania* repeatedly pull out hair from various parts of their bodies (particularly the scalp, eyebrows, and eyelashes), with resultant noticeable hair loss. Many clinicians believe that this disorder, which apparently is more common among women, is a compulsion and should be classified as an obsessive-compulsive anxiety disorder (McElroy et al., 1994). Because it often occurs without accompanying obsessions and without rigid rules, however, DSM-IV contends that it warrants its own category.

physical fights (Vaillant, 1994). Many drift from place to place. Reckless and egocentric, they have little regard for their own safety or for that of others, even for their children. Many also have difficulty maintaining an enduring attachment to another person (Gacono & Meloy, 1992).

People with antisocial personality disorder are very skillful at achieving personal profit through the manipulation of other people. The pain, loss, or damage they

cause seldom distresses them, so they are commonly perceived as lacking moral conscience. They glibly rationalize their actions by characterizing their victims as weak and deserving of being conned or stolen from.

Surveys indicate that between 1.5 and 3.5 percent of the adult population manifest an antisocial personality disorder (Kessler et al., 1994; Regier et al., 1993). The disorder is as much as three times more common

*Charles Manson, who directed his followers to kill nine people in 1969, fits many of the criteria of an antisocial personality disorder, including disregard for and violation of others' rights, impulsivity, disregard for truth, and lack of remorse.*

*Consider This*

Antisocial personality disorder is one of the clinical field's most controversial categories. Some people argue that it is simply a pseudoclinical name for "con" persons and various other kinds of criminals, and indeed the perpetrators of many crimes have been called "antisocial," "sociopathic," or "psychopathic." Others believe it to be a serious psychological disorder that the field needs to understand better and treat more effectively. What arguments might each side use to defend its position?

among men than among women (APA, 1994), and white Americans are somewhat more likely than African Americans to receive the diagnosis (Robins et al., 1991).

Because people with this disorder are often arrested, many researchers have looked for patterns of antisocial functioning in prison populations (Parker, 1991). Among male urban jail detainees, an antisocial personality pattern has been found to be a strong predictor of past violent arrests (Abram & Teplin, 1990).

Studies and clinical observations also indicate a higher rate of alcoholism among persons with antisocial personality disorder than the rest of the population (Sher & Trull, 1994; Lewis & Bucholz, 1991). Similarly, other substance-related disorders are also very common among people with the disorder (Sher & Trull, 1994; Kosten, 1988). The precise nature of this relationship is elusive however. On the one hand, early intoxication and substance abuse may loosen behavioral inhibitions and thus contribute to the development of antisocial personality disorder (Kaminer, 1991). On the other hand, perhaps an antisocial personality disorder can make a person vulnerable to substance abuse (Bukstein et al., 1989). Alternatively, antisocial personality disorder and substance abuse may share common causes, such as a deep-seated need to take risks (Sher & Trull, 1994). Interestingly, drug users with antisocial personality disorder specifically cite the recreational aspects of drug use as reasons for initiating and maintaining it (Mirin & Weiss, 1991).

## Explanations of Antisocial Personality Disorder

Explanations of antisocial personality disorder come primarily from the psychodynamic, behavioral, cognitive, and biological models. Psychodynamic theorists propose that this disorder, like many of the other personality disorders, begins with an absence of parental love during infancy, which leads to the child's lacking basic trust in others (Gabbard, 1990). Those who develop an antisocial personality disorder respond to such early inadequacies by becoming emotionally detached from all relationships, and attempt to bond with others only through the use of power and destructiveness.

Consistent with the psychodynamic explanation, researchers have found that people with this disorder are more likely than others to have experienced childhood stress, particularly in forms such as family poverty, family violence, and parental conflict or divorce (Luntz & Widom, 1994; Farrington, 1991). Many have also grown up with parents who themselves had an antisocial personality disorder (Lahey et al., 1988), a developmental experience which could certainly undermine one's trust in others.

Some behavioral theorists have suggested that antisocial symptoms may be acquired through modeling, and they too point to the heightened rate of antisocial personality disorder among parents of people with this disorder as possible evidence for their explanation (Lahey et al., 1988). Other behaviorists have suggested that some parents may unwittingly teach antisocial behavior in the home by, for example, reinforcing a child's aggressive behavior (Patterson, 1986, 1982).

Some cognitive theorists have suggested that people with this disorder hold a philosophy of life that trivializes the importance of other persons' needs (Levenson, 1992). These theorists believe that such a philosophy may be far more pervasive in our society than most people recognize. A number further propose that peo-

*Some clinicians believe that the hatred, prejudice, and violence displayed by members of supremacist groups are manifestations of antisocial personality disorder. Every country has citizens who fervently wish to violate the rights of others, from the so-called "skin heads" in the United States (above) to the neo-Nazis in Germany (below).*

ple with this disorder have genuine difficulty keeping another point of view in mind along with their own (Kagan, 1986).

Finally, research indicates that antisocial personality disorder may be linked to a number of biological variables, and twin and adoption investigations suggest that this link may be due to genetic factors (Dahl, 1993; McGuffin & Thapar, 1992). For example, the autonomic nervous systems of persons with this disorder seem to act more slowly than those of other persons, as indicated by a number of neurological tests (Raine, 1989; Bloomingdale & Bloomingdale, 1989). The continual search for excitement by persons with antisocial personality disorder and their disregard for caution may actually represent attempts to increase their own central nervous system activity. As Box 16-2 indicates, researchers have increasingly been closing in on the way biological factors may intersect with behavioral and cognitive factors to bring about some of the symptoms of the disorder.

## Treatments for Antisocial Personality Disorder

Approximately a quarter of all people with antisocial personality disorder receive treatment for it (Regier et al., 1993), yet no known specific intervention appears to be effective. Most of those in therapy act on an ultimatum from an employer, their school, or the law, or come to the attention of therapists when they also develop another disorder (Fulwiler & Pope, 1987). Not surprisingly, in one study 70 percent of patients with this disorder left treatment prematurely (Gabbard & Coyne, 1987).

A major difficulty in treating these individuals is their absence of conscience and their lack of motivation to change (Widiger et al., 1992). A milieu, therapeutic community approach has been applied in some hospitals and prisons in recent years, on the theory that a structured environment that emphasizes responsibility toward others may be helpful for at least some patients with antisocial personality disorder (Reid & Burke, 1989; Salama, 1988). In addition, challenging and rigorous wilderness programs that emphasize individual and group commitment have been employed increasingly in recent years, and have produced some improvements in the self-confidence, self-esteem, and interpersonal focus of persons with this disorder (Reid & Burke, 1989).

## Borderline Personality Disorder

The pervasive instability that characterizes the lives of people with a borderline personality disorder inevitably affects their relationships, as in the case of Helen.

> Helen [lost her ability to function] over several years . . . following persistent quarrels with her exasperated husband, a man she married in her teens. . . . For brief periods, Helen sought to regain her husband's affections, but these efforts were for naught, and she became bitterly resentful, guilt-ridden and self-deprecating. Her erratic mood swings not only increased feelings of psychic disharmony, but further upset efforts to gain her husband's attention and support. As she persisted in vacillating between gloomy despondency, accusatory attacks and clinging behaviors, more of her sources of support were withdrawn, thereby intensifying [her] separation anxieties. . . . The next step, that of a regression to invalidism, was especially easy for her since it was consistent with her lifelong pattern of passive-dependence. Along with it, however, came discomforting feelings of estrangement and the collapse of all self-controls, as evidenced in her ultimate infantile-like behaviors and the total disorganization of her cognitive processes.
>
> (Millon, 1969, pp. 360–361)

## Box 16-2

# A Lesson Not Learned

Personality disorders have received less systematic investigation than most other mental disorders. The one exception is antisocial personality disorder, or sociopathy. In one enlightening line of investigation spanning four decades, researchers have built study upon study in an effort to understand why persons with this disorder often seem incapable of learning from experience or weighing possible consequences before they act.

This line of empirical inquiry began in 1957, when the researcher David Lykken hypothesized that people with sociopathy may experience less anxiety than other people and thus may lack an ingredient that is essential for learning a number of important behaviors. He argued that people ordinarily learn socially appropriate behaviors in order to avoid or reduce the anxiety brought on by others' disapproval. People with sociopathy, however, cannot learn from feelings of anxiety, because they do not experience those feelings.

In a clever study, Lykken (1957) tested the relationship between anxiety and learning in people with antisocial personality disorder. In the first part of the study, Lykken asked whether subjects with sociopathy experience the same anxiety as normal subjects in response to real-life situations. He constructed a questionnaire in which subjects read thirty-three pairs of activities and were asked which of each pair they would rather do. Both items in each pair described an unpleasant event, but the events differed in the amount of anxiety they provoked. One activity was unpleasant because it was tedious ("cleaning out a cesspool"), the other because it provoked anxiety ("standing on a ledge on the 25th floor"). Lykken reasoned that if subjects with sociopathy were not deterred by anxiety, they would be more likely than the normal subjects to choose the anxiety-producing alternative over the tedious alternative. This was in fact the case. Lykken's findings suggested that people with sociopathy do experience less anxiety than other people.

Next Lykken examined the precise role that anxiety plays in learning for subjects with and subjects without sociopathy. He had subjects try to learn a mental maze that consisted of twenty choice points or steps. At each choice point, the subject was required to press one correct switch out of four choices in order to move to the next step. Subjects were instructed to get through the maze with as few errors as possible. The learning of the twenty correct responses was the *manifest* task. But embedded in this task was an avoidance-learning *latent* task. One of the three incorrect responses at each choice point was paired with an electric shock. That is, when subjects made this incorrect response, they were shocked. Lykken reasoned that in addition to learning correct responses (the manifest task), subjects would learn to avoid shocked incorrect responses (the latent task) and would eventually err only on unshocked responses. Lykken found that subjects with sociopathy learned the manifest task as well as normal subjects, but failed to learn the anxiety-motivated avoidance task —that is, the frequency of their shocked errors did not decrease. In short, when learning depended on anxiety, they failed to learn.

Next Lykken placed all of his subjects in a classical conditioning experiment in which an unconditioned stimulus (an electric shock) was paired with a conditioned stimulus (the sound of a buzzer) to condition an anxiety response (heightened galvanic skin response) to the sound of the buzzer alone. Lykken was unable to condition an anxiety response in the subjects with sociopathy. Taken together, these findings support the idea that people with an antisocial personality disorder are devoid of

---

People with **borderline personality disorder** display a pervasive pattern of instability in interpersonal relationships, self-image, and mood, along with marked impulsivity (APA, 1994). Individuals so labeled experience major shifts in mood, swinging in and out of intense depressive, anxious, and irritable states that last anywhere from a few hours to a few days. They are prone to bouts of anger and hostility (Gardner et al., 1991), sometimes resulting in physical aggression and violent behavior. Just as often, however, their anger is directed inward and expressed through impulsive, self-damaging acts that can be severe enough to cause significant bodily harm.

Many of the patients in mental health emergency rooms are borderline individuals who have engaged in self-mutilation (Bongar et al., 1990; Margo & Newman, 1989). Their self-destructive activities may range from alcohol and substance abuse to delinquency, un-

*Borderline personality disorder*  A personality disorder in which an individual displays a pervasive pattern of instability in interpersonal relationships, self-image, and mood, and marked impulsivity.

the normal anxiety needed to learn certain behaviors.

Are people with sociopathy ever capable of learning avoidance responses? Apparently yes. Some years later the investigator Frank Schmauk (1970) used Lykken's maze-learning problem and found that subjects with sociopathy did in fact learn to make the avoidance response when failure to do so resulted in a loss of money rather than a shock. This finding suggested to Schmauk that the *type* of punishment was a critical factor in teaching avoidance responses to people with sociopathy.

But the story did not end there. In recent years several researchers have suggested that it is not the type but the *salience* of the punishment that is critical in learning avoidance responses. They claim that in Schmauk's experiment, the loss of money was very salient because the subjects could see the money being taken away in front of them. The shock was not salient because it was a latent punishment that the subjects did not know they could avoid. The researchers found that when subjects with sociopathy were forced to focus their attention on punishments, even little punishments, they performed as well on avoidance learning tasks as subjects without sociopathy (Newman & Kosson, 1986).

Still more recent research has suggested that the learning problems of persons with sociopathy are also related to the difficulty they have *delaying* responses (Newman et al., 1992, 1987). In one experiment, subjects played a card game for financial gain in which the probability of punishment (losing 5 cents) increased by 10 percent after each turn, until punishment occurred 100 percent of the time. Therefore, subjects who stopped playing the game the earliest won the most money. When the subjects were allowed to take each turn immediately, those with sociopathy kept choosing to take more turns and lost more money than those without sociopathy. But when the subjects were forced to wait 5 seconds after each turn, subjects with sociopathy did not take more turns than those without sociopathy.

Altogether, these findings suggest that persons with sociopathy can be influenced by anxiety and can learn avoidance tasks if they are forced to pay attention to the risks involved in a given task, if they are forced to delay responses, or if the punishments involved in a task are made more salient (Newman et al., 1987; Newman & Kosson, 1986).

Why should people with antisocial personality disorder experience anxiety less readily than other people? Biological researchers have picked up the ball here and tried to locate a biological cause for the reactions of these individuals. In a series of studies they have found that subjects with sociopathy often respond to warnings or expectations of stress with physiological responses that collectively indicate low brain and bodily arousal (Patrick et al., 1993, 1990; Hare, 1978). Such low arousal may lead people with sociopathy to "tune out" threatening or emotional situations. Consequently, emotional situations may have less impact on them than on people without sociopathy, and failure to learn anxiety-motivated avoidance responses is inevitable (Ellis, 1987; Hare, 1978).

It could also be argued that chronic underarousal should lead persons with sociopathy to engage in sensation-seeking behavior. Indeed, they may be drawn to antisocial activity precisely because it meets their need for excitement. In support of this idea, researchers have found that antisocial personality disorder is often related to sensation-seeking behavior (Hesselbrock & Hesselbrock, 1992; Zuckerman, 1978; Blackstein, 1975). Simply put, people with this personality pattern generally take risks and seek thrills.

safe sex, irresponsible spending, reckless driving, and bloodletting or other forms of self-mutilation (Nace, 1992; Farrugia, 1992). Suicidal threats and actions are also common (APA, 1994; Paris, 1990). Many borderline individuals seem to engage in acts of self-destructiveness as a means of dealing with chronic feelings of emptiness, boredom, and confusion about their identity.

As a result of their poorly grounded and distorted sense of self, people with borderline personality disorder frequently seek to identify with others, but their social behavior is often as confused and impulsive as their self-image and mood. They form intense, conflict-ridden relationships in which their feelings are not necessarily reciprocated (Modestin & Villiger, 1989). Fearing abandonment (realistically or not), they have difficulty maintaining appropriate interpersonal boundaries (Melges & Swartz, 1989). They quickly become enraged when others fail to meet their expectations; yet they remain intensely attached to their relationships, paralyzed by their fear of being left alone. In the face of possible desertion, they frequently

*The unforgettable Alex Forrest, in the film* Fatal Attraction, *relentlessly pursued a married man with whom she'd had a relationship. Her symptoms of extreme instability and impulsiveness are reminiscent of a borderline personality disorder.*

resort to manipulative behaviors such as self-mutilation or suicidal gestures to prevent the other person from leaving the relationship.

The prevalence of borderline personality disorder has been estimated at 2 percent of the general population. Around 75 percent of the patients who receive this diagnosis are women (APA, 1994). The course of borderline personality disorder varies from person to person. In the most common pattern, however, the individual's degree of instability, impairment, and risk of suicide peak during young adulthood, then gradually wane with advancing age (APA, 1994).

## Explanations of Borderline Personality Disorder

The fear of abandonment that tortures so many people with borderline personality disorder has caused theorists and researchers once again to examine parental relationships as a possible source of this pathology. Psychodynamic theorists, particularly object relations theorists, suggest that the road to this pattern, as to other personality disorders, begins with a relationship problem between children and unaccepting parents (Kernberg, 1984; Mahler, 1979, 1974). In the case of borderline individuals, this lack of acceptance leads to a loss of self-esteem, heightened dependence on the parents, and a lower capacity for coping with separations (Richman & Sokolove, 1992; Arnow & Harrison, 1991).

Consistent with this view, researchers have found that the infancies of many people with borderline personality disorder were marked by such problems as parental neglect and rejection, grossly inappropriate parental behavior, and multiple mother and father substitutes (Ludolph et al., 1990; Paris et al., 1988). In addition, their childhoods have often been disrupted by parent divorce or death (Plakun, 1991). Some studies have further found a heightened prevalence of childhood physical and sexual abuse, including incest, among people with this disorder (Beitchman et al., 1992; Marcus, 1989).

Some features of borderline personality disorder have been linked to biological abnormalities. For example, borderline persons who are particularly impulsive, as demonstrated by a suicide attempt or aggression against others, have low brain-serotonin activity (Weston & Siever, 1993; Coccaro & Kavoussi, 1991). People with this disorder also experience sleep abnormalities similar to those of depressed persons (Weston & Siever, 1993; Siever & Davis, 1991). And the transient psychotic symptoms of some borderline individuals have been linked to abnormalities in dopamine activity (Coccaro & Kavoussi, 1991).

Finally, some sociocultural theorists suggest that cases of borderline personality disorder are particularly likely to emerge when a culture changes too rapidly and loses its cohesiveness (Paris, 1991). Indeed, there has been an apparent increase in the prevalence of this disorder in recent years, a phenomenon that some theorists attribute to the changing structure of society and of the family, and to a dearth of compelling social causes (Segal, 1988; Millon, 1987).

## Treatments for Borderline Personality Disorder

The dependency and anger of patients with borderline personality disorder makes treatment extremely difficult (Horton, 1992; Greenberg, 1989). Moreover, attempts to persuade these clients to look closely at their own mental state and at the viewpoints of others often fall flat initially (Fonagy, 1991). Nevertheless, it appears that long-term psychotherapy can eventually be effective and lead to improvement for some patients (Koenigsberg, 1993; Linehan & Kehrer, 1993).

Psychodynamic therapy has been successful in some cases, particularly when it focuses on such issues as the borderline patient's fundamental relationship disturbance, self-identity problems, and pervasive loneliness and emptiness (Michels, 1992; Egan, 1988). In a number of cases, cognitive or behavioral strategies have been combined with a psychodynamic approach (Katz & Levendusky, 1990). For example, the therapist may model alternative interpretations and reactions to situations in order to improve the patient's awareness of other people's perspectives (Westen, 1991).

The use of a group format has also sometimes proved effective in treating borderline patients (Leszcz, 1992; O'Leary et al., 1991). It offers an opportunity for them to form close attachments to several persons rather than investing all of their emotions and hopes in but one or two "chosen" relationships.

Finally, antidepressant, antibipolar, and antipsychotic drugs have been of some help in calming the emotional and aggressive storms of people with this disorder and slowing down their impulsivity (Weston & Siever, 1993; Siever & Davis, 1991). A combination of drug therapy and psychotherapy has also been helpful in some cases (Koenigsberg, 1993). However, the use of drugs on an outpatient basis in the treatment of this disorder is controversial, given these clients' higher risk for attempting suicide.

## Histrionic Personality Disorder

A histrionic personality disorder can complicate life considerably, as we see in the case of Suzanne:

Suzanne, an attractive and vivacious woman, sought therapy in the hope that she might prevent the disintegration of her third marriage. The problem she faced was a recurrent one, her tendency to become "bored" with her husband and increasingly interested in going out with other men. She was on the brink of "another affair" and decided that before "giving way to her impulses again" she had "better stop and take a good look" at herself. . . .

Suzanne was quite popular during her adolescent years. . . . Rather than going on to college, Suzanne attended art school where she met and married a fellow student—a "handsome, wealthy ne'er-do-well." Both she and her husband began "sleeping around" by the end of the first year, and she "wasn't certain" that her husband was the father of her daughter. A divorce took place several months after the birth of this child.

Soon thereafter she met and married a man in his forties who gave both Suzanne and her daughter a "comfortable home, and scads of attention and love." It was a "good life" for the four years that the marriage lasted. . . . In the third year of this marriage she became attracted to a young man, a fellow dancing student. The affair was brief, but was followed by a quick succession of several others. . . . The marriage was terminated after a stormy court settlement.

Suzanne "knocked about" on her own for the next two years until she met her present husband, a talented writer who "knew the scoop" about her past. . . . She had no inclination to venture afield for the next three years. She enjoyed the titillation of "playing games" with other men, but she remained loyal to her husband, even though he was away on reportorial assignments for periods of one or two months. The last trip, however, brought forth the "old urge" to start an affair. It was at this point that she sought therapy.

*(Millon, 1969, p. 251)*

People with **histrionic personality disorder**, once called **hysterical personality disorder**, display a pattern of excessive emotionality and attention seeking (APA, 1994). Indeed, they are typically described as "emotionally charged." Their moods are exaggerated and may shift rapidly. Irrational or angry outbursts are common.

People with this disorder are continually "on stage," using theatrical gestures and mannerisms and the most grandiose language to describe ordinary everyday events. They continually adapt themselves in order to attract and impress an audience, changing their surface characteristics, opinions, and beliefs from situation to situation and lacking a core sense of who they really are. Their speech is actually rather scanty in detail and substance, and they are likely to pursue the latest fads in their efforts to be admired.

Histrionic individuals require the constant presence of others to witness their emotionality and to validate their being and their mood states. Approval and praise are their lifeline. They do not tolerate delays in gratification well. Vain, self-indulgent, egocentric, and demanding, they overreact to any minor event that gets in the way of their insatiable quest for attention. Some make suicide attempts, purely as manipulative gestures (Guillard & Guillard, 1987).

People with this disorder may draw attention to themselves in various ways. An exaggerated display of physical illness and weakness is common (Morrison, 1989). So are inappropriate provocative behavior and sexual seduction. Most people with the disorder obsess over how they look and how others will perceive them, often wearing bright, eye-catching clothes.

Histrionic people are also likely to exaggerate the intensity of their relationships. For instance, they may consider themselves to be the intimate confidants of people who actually see them as casual acquaintances. They also tend to gravitate toward inappropriate romantic partners, people who may be exciting but who do not treat them well.

Until recently, histrionic personality disorder was believed to be more common in women than in men (Reich, 1987). Profiles of the "hysterical wife" have

---

**Histrionic personality disorder**   A personality disorder in which an individual displays a pattern of excessive emotionality and attention seeking. Once called *hysterical personality disorder.*

long been discussed in the psychological literature (Char, 1985). Several studies, however, have uncovered gender bias in past efforts to diagnose persons with this disorder. More recent epidemiological studies suggest that 2 to 3 percent of adults have this personality disorder, with males and females equally affected (APA, 1994; Nestadt et al., 1990).

## Explanations of Histrionic Personality Disorder

In view of psychodynamic clinicians' historical interest in hysteria, it is no surprise to find a great many psychodynamic theories of histrionic personality disorder in the literature. Most of the theories take the position that as children histrionic persons typically experienced unhealthy relationships with either one or both of their parents—often portrayed as cold and controlling—which left them feeling unloved, fearful of abandonment, and extraordinarily needful of nurturance from others (Gunderson, 1988). To defend against their deep-seated fears of loss, the individuals behave in an overly emotional manner and invent crises that encourage other people to act protectively toward them (Kuriansky, 1988).

A number of cognitive explanations have focused on the deficient cognitive functioning of people with a histrionic personality disorder, such as their vague speech and extreme suggestibility. According to these theories, as histrionic persons become increasingly self-involved and emotional, they have little room left for factual knowledge or intellectual curiosity. Increasingly they rely on hunches rather than on detailed memories (Hollender, 1988). Other cognitive theorists propose that histrionic persons have an underlying assumption that they are helpless to care for themselves, a belief that drives them constantly to seek out others who will meet their needs (Beck & Freeman, 1990).

Finally, sociocultural theorists have suggested that the development of histrionic personality disorder may have roots in society's norms and expectations. They point out that until recent years, our society encouraged girls to hold on to their dependency needs as they grew up, thus favoring the development of childishness in women and fostering the histrionic lifestyle (Hollender, 1988). Indeed, the vain, self-dramatizing, and selfish histrionic person may be viewed as a caricature of femininity as our culture once defined it (Beck & Freeman, 1990).

## Treatments for Histrionic Personality Disorder

People with histrionic personality disorder, unlike those with most other personality disorders, often seek out treatment. Working with them can be very difficult, however, as they commonly bring their unreasonable demands, tantrums, and seductiveness into the therapy session (Gabbard, 1990). A variety of approaches have been tried with this population, particularly psychodynamic approaches, cognitive therapies, and group therapies (Winston & Pollack, 1991; Quality Assurance Project, 1990). Clinical case reports suggest that each is helpful on occasion.

Irrespective of the therapist's orientation, the central goals in treatment are to help individuals with this disorder recognize their excessive dependency (Chodoff, 1989), find an inner source of satisfaction, and achieve a more independent way of life. To achieve such goals, therapists typically must strike an effective balance between providing support and maintaining strict professional boundaries (Gabbard, 1990; Liebowitz et al., 1986).

# Narcissistic Personality Disorder

The narcissistic personality disorder can be seen in the case of 30-year-old Steven, an artist who is married and has one child:

Steven came to the attention of a therapist when his wife insisted that they seek marital counseling. According to her, Steve was "selfish, ungiving and preoccupied with his work." Everything at home had to "revolve about him, his comfort, moods and desires, no one else's." She claimed that he contributed nothing to the marriage, except a rather meager income. He shirked all "normal" responsibilities and kept "throwing chores in her lap," and she was "getting fed up with being the chief cook and bottlewasher, tired of being his mother and sleep-in maid."

On the positive side, Steven's wife felt that he was basically a "gentle and good-natured guy with talent and intelligence." But this wasn't enough. She wanted a husband, someone with whom she could share things. In contrast, he wanted, according to her, "a mother, not a wife"; he didn't want "to grow up, he didn't know how to give affection, only to take it when he felt like it, nothing more, nothing less."

Steve presented a picture of an affable, self-satisfied and somewhat disdainful young man. He was employed as a commercial artist, but looked forward to his evenings and weekends when he could turn his attention to serious painting. He claimed that he had to devote all of his spare time and energies to "fulfill himself," to achieve expression in his creative work. . . .

His relationships with his present co-workers and social acquaintances were pleasant and satisfying, but he did admit that most people viewed him as a "bit

GARFIELD                                                            By Jim Davis

*The self-absorption of people with a narcissistic personality pattern is apparent even when they pretend to be interested in others.*

self-centered, cold and snobbish." He recognized that he did not know how to share his thoughts and feelings with others, that he was much more interested in himself than in them and that perhaps he always had "preferred the pleasure" of his own company to that of others.

*(Millon, 1969, pp. 261–262)*

People with **narcissistic personality disorder** display a chronic and pervasive pattern of grandiosity, need for admiration, and lack of empathy (APA, 1994). The Greek myth has it that Narcissus died enraptured by the beauty of his own reflection in a pool, pining away while longing to possess his own image. His name has come to be synonymous with extreme self-involvement, and indeed people with narcissistic personality disorder have a grandiose sense of self-importance. They exaggerate their achievements and talents, expecting others to recognize them as superior and often appearing arrogant and haughty.

Preoccupied with fantasies of unlimited success, power, or beauty, people with this disorder require the constant attention and admiration of those around them, although they are very choosy about the people and institutions they will associate closely with. Despite their charm and the favorable first impression they may make, people with this disorder are rarely able to maintain a stable, long-term relationship.

With their boastful and pretentious manner, narcissistic persons are seldom receptive to the feelings of others. Like Steven, they show a general lack of empathy, an inability or unwillingness to recognize and

identify with others' thoughts and needs. Often, they are envious of other people. Many take advantage of others to achieve their own ends.

Some narcissistic individuals react to criticism or frustration with bouts of rage, shame, or humiliation (Gramzow & Tangney, 1992). Yet others may react with cold indifference (Messer, 1985). Cycles of zest alternating with disappointment are common (Svrakic, 1990).

Less than 1 percent of adults are estimated to manifest a narcissistic personality disorder (APA, 1994). Between 50 and 75 percent of them are male (APA, 1994; Bourgeois et al., 1993). Narcissistic-type behaviors and thoughts are common and normal among teenagers; they do not usually lead to adult narcissism (APA, 1994).

## Explanations of Narcissistic Personality Disorder

Again, psychodynamic theorists more than others have theorized about the causes of narcissistic personality disorder, and again they begin with the proposition that the disorder may arise when cold and rejecting parents interact with their infants in an unloving and unaccepting manner, causing the children to feel unsatisfied, rejected, unworthy, and wary of the world. Some of these children spend their lives defending against these feelings by telling themselves that they are actually perfect and desirable and by seeking admiration from others (Vaillant, 1994). Object relations theorists, psychodynamic theorists who place particular emphasis on early relationships, further propose that the early negative treatment interrupts a critical process of attachment between children and their parents, causing the children to develop a grandiose self-

*Narcissistic personality disorder* A personality disorder characterized by a chronic and pervasive pattern of grandiosity, need for admiration, and lack of empathy.

image that helps them maintain illusions of self-sufficiency and freedom from dependence (Siomopoulos, 1988). In support of these psychodynamic theories, research has found that abused children, children of divorce, and children whose mother or father has died or who have been given up for adoption are at greater risk for the development of narcissistic personality disorder (Kernberg, 1989).

Other theorists, particularly those who espouse the behavioral and cognitive models, have argued that persons often develop narcissistic personality disorder as a result of being treated too *positively* rather than too negatively in early life. These theorists hold that individuals may acquire a narcissistic posture when their "admiring or doting parents" favor or even idealize them and teach them repeatedly to "overvalue their self worth" (Millon, 1987). In support of this idea, firstborn and only children, whose parents often do view and treat them as having special talents or intelligence, have been found to score higher on measures of narcissism than other children (Curtis & Cowell, 1993).

Finally, many sociocultural theorists link individual cases of narcissistic personality disorder to general "eras of narcissism" in society (Cooper & Ronningstam, 1992; Cooper, 1981). They suggest that periodic societal breakdowns in family structure and social and political ideals may produce generations of youth who are characterized by self-centeredness, a short attention span, and a materialistic outlook. Western cultures in particular, which encourage self-expression and individualism, are seen as more likely to foster such generational narcissism.

### Consider This
Some people believe that the past fifteen years have witnessed an increase in narcissistic behavior and thinking in Western society. What features and movements of Western society during this span of time (for example, child-rearing philosophies, advertising campaigns, sports trends, book topics, and television) may be contributing to a rise in narcissistic functioning?

### Treatments for Narcissistic Personality Disorder

People with narcissistic personality disorder, like those with most other personality disorders, only occasionally respond well to treatment. In fact, this disorder has been characterized as one of the most difficult conditions to treat (Lawrence, 1987). Narcissistic persons are likely to approach therapy with a sense of entitlement and may attempt to manipulate the therapist into supporting their sense of grandiosity.

Psychodynamic therapists seek to help narcissistic persons uncover their basic insecurities and defenses, either through a traditional approach of gentle interpretation (Spitzer, 1990; Masterson, 1990) or an approach that combines confrontation and interpretation (Kernberg, 1989). Cognitive therapists address the specific ways in which narcissistic clients think. The therapists may, for example, try to guide the clients' focus onto other people's opinions, increase their ability to empathize, and change their all-or-nothing categorizations (Beck & Freeman, 1990). Again, however, all such approaches seem to meet with little success.

### Summing Up
The "dramatic" personality disorders are marked by highly dramatic, emotional, or erratic symptoms. These powerful symptoms include disregard for and violation of others' rights, in antisocial personality disorder; emotional and interpersonal instability, in borderline personality disorder; excessive emotionality and attention seeking, in histrionic personality disorder; and self-centeredness and grandiosity, in narcissistic personality disorder. With the possible exception of antisocial personality disorder, research has not yet succeeded in clarifying the causes of the dramatic personality disorders. Current treatments have but a limited impact on them, particularly on the antisocial and narcissistic personality disorders.

# "Anxious" Personality Disorders

The "anxious" cluster of personality disorders includes the avoidant, dependent, and obsessive-compulsive personality disorders. People with these disorders typically display anxious and fearful behavior. Many symptoms of these disorders are similar to those characteristic of the Axis I anxiety and depressive disorders, but direct links have not been established (Weston & Siever, 1993). As with most of the other personality disorders, numerous explanations have been proposed for the anxious personality disorders, but empirical support for them is very limited. Treatments for these disorders appear to be modestly to moderately helpful, a significant improvement over the efficacy of interventions for most of the other personality disorders.

# Avoidant Personality Disorder

People with an avoidant personality disorder are so fearful of being rejected that they give no one an opportunity to reject them—or to accept them either.

> James was a bookkeeper for nine years. . . . He spoke of himself as a shy, fearful and quiet boy ever since early childhood. . . .
>
> James was characterized by his supervisor as a loner, a peculiar young man who did his work quietly and efficiently. They noted that he ate alone in the company cafeteria and never joined in coffee breaks or in the "horsing around" at the office. . . .
>
> As far as his social life was concerned, James had neither dated nor gone to a party in five years. . . . He now spent his free time reading, watching TV, daydreaming and fixing things around the house.
>
> James experienced great distress when new employees were assigned to his office section. Some 40 people worked regularly in this office and job turnover resulted in replacement of four or five people a year. . . . In recent months, a clique formed in his office. Although James very much wanted to be a member of this "in-group," he feared attempting to join them because "he had nothing to offer them" and thought he would be rejected. In a short period of time, he, along with two or three others, became the object of jokes and taunting by the leaders of the clique. After a few weeks of "being kidded," he began to miss work, failed to complete his accounts on time, found himself unsure of what he was doing and made a disproportionate number of errors. . . .
>
> (Millon, 1969, pp. 231–232)

People with *avoidant personality disorder* display a chronic and pervasive pattern of inhibition in social situations, feelings of inadequacy, and extreme sensitivity to negative evaluation (APA, 1994). Not surprisingly, they strenuously avoid occasions or activities that involve interpersonal contact. At the center of their social withdrawal lies not so much a low level of social skill as a dread of criticism, disapproval, or rejection.

In social situations, the manner of these persons is timid and hesitant; they are afraid of saying something foolish or inappropriate or of embarrassing themselves by blushing, crying, or nervousness, and are sensitive to social deprecation. Even in intimate relationships they act and express themselves with restraint, afraid of being shamed or ridiculed.

Individuals with this disorder believe themselves to be personally unappealing or inferior to others. They tend to exaggerate the potential difficulties of new situations, so they seldom take risks or engage in new activities. They usually have few or no close friends, though they actually yearn for intimate relationships, and frequently feel empty, depressed, and lonely. As a substitute, many take refuge in an inner world of fantasy and imagination (Millon, 1990).

Avoidant personality disorder is similar to social phobias (see p. 139), and often people with one of these disorders also experience the other (Holt et al., 1992; Schneier et al., 1991). However, there is an important difference between the two. People with social phobias primarily fear social *circumstances* rather than the close social *relationships* of concern to avoidant persons (Turner et al., 1986). Avoidant personality disorder is also common among people with a chronic depressive disorder (Alnaes & Torgersen, 1989).

Between 0.5 and 1.0 percent of adults have an avoidant personality disorder, men as frequently as women. Many children and teenagers may also be painfully shy and display avoidant behaviors, but this is usually just a normal part of their development.

## Explanations of Avoidant Personality Disorder

Theorists often assume that the avoidant personality disorder is caused by the same kinds of factors as other anxiety-related disorders—particulary, biochemical abnormalities, learned fears, or upsetting thought processes. However, direct ties have yet to receive much empirical study (Weston & Siever, 1993). In the meantime, explanations offered by psychodynamic and cognitive theorists have received the most clinical attention.

Psychodynamic theorists trace the pervasive shame experienced by people with avoidant personality disorder to childhood experiences such as early bowel and bladder accidents and accompanying parental reprimands or ridicule (Gabbard, 1990). It is thought that the people who develop this disorder have internalized their parents' reprimands and ridicule and now experience severe self-deprecation and a sense of unlovability (Liebowitz et al., 1986). Similarly, several cognitive theorists have suggested that strong criticisms and rejections in early childhood have led avoidant persons to assume that other people are generally negative and critical, to expect and fear rejection, to misinterpret people's reactions, and to discount positive feedback. In support of these theories, one study of patients with avoidant personality disorder revealed childhoods marked by unencouraging home climates and few

---

*Avoidant personality disorder* A personality disorder in which an individual displays a chronic and pervasive pattern of inhibition in social situations, feelings of inadequacy, and extreme sensitivity to negative evaluation.

*As the technology of film animation has become more complex over time, so have the personality problems of animated characters. (above) Troubled characters of the past were usually defined by a single undesirable personality trait, as demonstrated by Snow White's friend "Grumpy," second from left. (below) Today's characters have clusters of self-defeating traits. Beavis and Butt-head, for example, display poor control of impulses, disregard for others' rights, disturbed relationships, emotional and cognitive shallowness, and, in the case of Beavis, submissive and clinging behavior.*

demonstrations of parental love and pride (Arbel & Stravynski, 1991).

### Treatments for Avoidant Personality Disorder

Clients with avoidant personality disorder come to therapy in the hope of finding acceptance and affection. Typically, however, they distrust the therapist's sincerity and fear rejection in the therapeutic relationship, making trust building an important feature of treatment (Gabbard, 1990).

Therapists tend to treat people with avoidant personality disorder much as they treat persons with so-

cial phobias and other anxiety disorders. That is, psychodynamic therapists help the patients uncover the origins of their symptoms and work through the unconscious forces that are operating (Hurt et al., 1991). Behavioral therapists provide social skills training and exposure treatment, requiring avoidant clients to gradually increase their social contacts (Hurt et al., 1991; Quality Assurance Project, 1991). Cognitive therapists have had some success helping avoidant clients change their distressing beliefs and thoughts, increase their tolerance for emotional discomfort, and build up their self-image (Beck & Freeman, 1990; Alden, 1989). And antianxiety and antidepressant drugs have sometimes been useful in reducing the social anxiety and discomfort of avoidant persons, although the symptoms frequently return when medication is stopped (Liebowitz et al., 1991; Mattick & Newman, 1991). Research also suggests that group therapy formats help many people with avoidant personality disorder by providing a useful practice ground (Azima, 1993; Renneberg et al., 1990).

## Dependent Personality Disorder

People with dependent personality disorder are so reliant on others that they typically have difficulty making both big and small decisions for themselves. Mr. G. is a case in point.

Mr. G.'s. . . . place of employment for the past 15 years had recently closed and he had been without work for several weeks. He appeared less dejected about the loss of his job than about his wife's increasing displeasure with his decision to "stay at home until something came up." She thought he "must be sick" and insisted that he see a doctor. . . .

Mr. G. was born in Europe, the oldest child and only son of a family of six children. . . . His mother kept a careful watch over him, prevented him from engaging in undue exertions and limited his responsibilities; in effect, she precluded his developing many of the ordinary physical skills and competencies that most youngsters learn in the course of growth. . . .

A marriage was arranged by his parents. His wife was a sturdy woman who worked as a seamstress, took care of his home, and bore . . . four children. Mr. G. performed a variety of odds-and-ends jobs in his father's tailoring shop. His mother saw to it, however, that he did no "hard or dirty work," just helping about and "overlooking" the other employees. As a consequence, Mr. G. learned none of the skills of the tailoring trade. . . .

During the ensuing years, he obtained employment at a garment factory owned by his brothers-in-law.

Again he served as a helper, not as a skilled workman. Although he bore the brunt of essentially good-humored teasing by his co-workers throughout these years, he maintained a friendly and helpful attitude, pleasing them by getting sandwiches, coffee and cigarettes at their beck and call.

*(Millon, 1969, p. 242)*

People with *dependent personality disorder* display a pattern of submissive and clinging behavior, fears of separation, and a pervasive need to be taken care of (APA, 1994). It is normal and healthy to be dependent on others to some extent, but those with dependent personality disorder typically rely on others for continual advice and reassurance about all everyday matters and decisions, as well as for countering profound feelings of personal inadequacy and helplessness. Afraid of being unable to care for themselves, they go to great lengths to avoid being alone, clinging to close friends or relatives with an intensity and level of neediness uncharacteristic of most "healthy" relationships. In extreme cases, they are unable to tolerate any physical separation from their spouse or partner (Liebowitz et al., 1986).

Individuals with dependent personality disorder differ from people with avoidant personality disorder in that they experience difficulty with separation rather than with the initiation of relationships. They feel completely helpless and devastated when close relationships end and quickly seek out another relationship to fill the void and to provide care and support. Many continue to hold onto relationships even with partners who physically or psychologically abuse them.

People with dependent personality disorder tend to be submissive. Lacking confidence in their ability and judgment, they allow important decisions to be made for them and seldom disagree with others, no matter what the facts may be. People with this disorder typically depend on a parent or spouse to decide where to live, what job to have, and which neighbors to befriend (APA, 1994). As a result of their profound fear of rejection, these individuals are oversensitive to criticism and disapproval. Skillful social conformists, they adapt themselves to fit others' desires and expectations, and often volunteer for unpleasant or even demeaning tasks to win their approval.

People with dependent personality disorder often experience distress, loneliness, depression, self-criticism, and low self-esteem (Overholser, 1992) and

*Dependent personality disorder* A personality disorder characterized by a pattern of submissive and clinging behavior, fears of separation, and a pervasive need to be taken care of.

are at high risk for full depressive disorders and phobias and other anxiety disorders (APA, 1994). Their separation anxiety and their feelings of helplessness when they anticipate abandonment may leave them particularly susceptible to suicidal thoughts (Kiev, 1989).

It is not known how prevalent dependent personality disorder is in the general population. For years clinicians believed that more women than men manifested this pattern (Overholser, 1992), but recent research suggests that the disorder is as common in men as in women (APA, 1994; Reich, 1990).

## Explanations of Dependent Personality Disorder

For years psychodynamic theorists have proposed that many of the same dynamics that result in depression (see pp. 185–187) are at work in dependent personality disorder. Freudian theorists, for example, have suggested that a fixation at the oral stage of psychosexual development may set the stage for lifelong nurturance needs and a dependent personality disorder (Greenberg & Bornstein, 1988). Other psychodynamic theorists have suggested that the parents of dependent persons were overinvolved and overprotective and in turn inadvertently heightened their child's feelings of dependency, insecurity, and anxiety over separation (Main, 1989).

Behaviorists have taken a similar position. They have proposed that parents of persons with this disorder unintentionally rewarded clinging and loyal behavior by their child while punishing (perhaps through withdrawal of love) independent actions. Alternatively, some parents may have modeled their own dependent behavior for their children.

And cognitive theorists have proposed that a key problem for persons with dependent personality disorder is that they hold broad maladaptive beliefs that (1) they are inadequate and helpless to deal with the world and (2) they must find another person to provide protection before they can cope (Beck & Freeman, 1990). These persons may also engage in dichotomous thinking: "If one is to be dependent, one must be completely helpless," or "If one is to be independent, one must be alone," which guide them to avoid any efforts at autonomy.

## Treatments for Dependent Personality Disorder

People with dependent personality disorder usually approach therapy passively, conferring all responsibility for their treatment and well-being on the therapist

(Perry, 1989). Getting them to accept responsibility for themselves is consequently a central therapeutic concern. Another difficult therapy issue is what to do about the dependent client's partner (typically a spouse or parent), whose own needs and behaviors may feed into the client's symptoms. Some clinicians propose that separate therapy for the partner may also be needed if the client's disorder is to be fully addressed (Liebowitz et al., 1986).

A variety of treatment strategies have been used for persons with dependent personality disorder, and they have apparently been modestly to moderately helpful. Psychodynamic therapy for these clients focuses on many of the same issues as therapy with depressed persons. In particular, the patient's almost inevitable transference of dependency onto the therapist typically becomes a major treatment focus (Perry, 1989). Cognitive therapists try to help dependent clients challenge and change their assumptions of incompetence and helplessness (Beck & Freeman, 1990). And behavioral therapists often provide assertiveness training to help clients better express their own needs and wishes in relationships.

Finally, as with avoidant personality disorder, a group therapy format seems to be relatively beneficial for persons with this disorder, because it provides them with support from numerous peers rather than from a single, dominant person (Azima, 1993), and offers peer-modeling and practice opportunities for expressing feelings and solving problems (Beck & Freeman, 1990).

## Obsessive-Compulsive Personality Disorder

People with an obsessive-compulsive personality disorder are so intent on doing everything "right" that their efforts impair their productivity, as in the case of Wayne:

> Wayne was advised to seek assistance from a therapist following several months of relatively sleepless nights and a growing immobility and indecisiveness at his job. When first seen, he reported feelings of extreme self-doubt and guilt and prolonged periods of tension and diffuse anxiety. It was established early in therapy that he always had experienced these symptoms. They were now merely more pronounced than before.
>
> The precipitant for this sudden increase in discomfort was a forthcoming change in his academic post. New administrative officers had assumed authority at the college, and he was asked to resign his deanship to return to regular departmental

instruction. In the early sessions, Wayne spoke largely of his fear of facing classroom students again, wondered if he could organize his material well, and doubted that he could keep classes disciplined and interested in his lectures. It was his preoccupation with these matters that he believed was preventing him from concentrating and completing his present responsibilities.

At no time did Wayne express anger toward the new college officials for the "demotion" he was asked to accept. He repeatedly voiced his "complete confidence" in the "rationality of their decision." Yet, when face-to-face with them, he observed that he stuttered and was extremely tremulous.

Wayne was the second of two sons. . . . His father was a successful engineer, and his mother a high school teacher. Both were "efficient, orderly and strict" parents. Life at home was "extremely well planned," with "daily and weekly schedules of responsibilities posted" and "vacations arranged a year or two in advance." Nothing apparently was left to chance. . . . Wayne adopted the "good boy" image. Unable to challenge his brother either physically, intellectually or socially, he became a "paragon of virtue." By being punctilious, scrupulous, methodical and orderly, he could avoid antagonizing his perfectionistic parents, and would, at times, obtain preferred treatment from them. He obeyed their advice, took their guidance as gospel and hesitated making any decision before gaining their approval.

*(Millon, 1969, pp. 278–279)*

People with *obsessive-compulsive personality disorder* display a pattern of preoccupation with orderliness, perfectionism, and mental and interpersonal control, at the expense of flexibility, openness, and efficiency. In their preoccupation with rules and orderliness they lose sight of the larger picture. When confronted with a task, for example, they often become so fixated on organization and details that they fail to grasp the overall point of the activity. As a result, their work is often finished behind schedule or incomplete.

People with this personality disorder set such unreasonably high standards for themselves that they can never be satisfied with their performance. At the same time, they generally refuse to delegate responsibility or to work with a team, convinced that others are too careless or incompetent to do the job right. Their excessive fears of making mistakes may result in indecisiveness and frequent avoidance or postponement of decisions. Furthermore, in devoting all their time to meeting their high standards of performance, they of-

---

*Obsessive-compulsive personality disorder*    A personality disorder in which an individual displays a pattern of preoccupation with orderliness, perfectionism, and mental and interpersonal control.

ten neglect to develop genuine leisure activities and friendships.

People with this personality disorder also display an inflexibility about morals, ethics, and values. Often regarded as closed-minded, they scrupulously adhere to their own personal code and use it as a yardstick by which to measure others. Their rigidity may be reflected in an equally restricted expression of affection. Their relationships are often stilted and superficial.

Obsessive-compulsive persons are rarely generous with their time or money. They are miserly not only in their spending habits but in their inability to throw away anything worn-out or useless, even though they have only the vaguest sentimental or monetary reasons for keeping it (APA, 1994; Warren & Ostrom, 1988).

Obsessive-compulsive personality disorder has a 1.0 to 1.7 percent prevalence in the general population (APA, 1994; Nestadt et al., 1991). Men are twice as likely as women to receive this diagnosis (APA, 1994).

People often believe that obsessive-compulsive personality disorder and obsessive-compulsive disorder (the anxiety disorder) are closely related. Some patients do qualify for both diagnoses, and the two disorders do share some features, although functioning tends to be much more impaired in cases of obsessive-compulsive anxiety disorder (APA, 1994; Pollack, 1987). It is important to note, however, that no empirical support has been found for the notion of a specific link between the personality disorder and the anxiety disorder (Mavissakalian et al., 1990). Moreover, depression, social phobias, and Type A personality patterns are at least as prevalent as obsessive-compulsive anxiety disorder among people with obsessive-compulsive personality disorder (Turner et al., 1991).

## Explanations of Obsessive-Compulsive Personality Disorder

Many explanations of obsessive-compulsive personality disorder borrow heavily from those of obsessive-compulsive anxiety disorder—a dubious practice, given the imperfect links between the two disorders. As with so many of the personality disorders, psychodynamic explanations dominate, and again empirical evidence is limited at best.

Freudian theorists suggest that people with obsessive-compulsive personality disorder are *anal regressive*. That is, because of overly rigid and punitive toilet training during the anal stage, they become very angry and they remain fixated at this stage; they try always to resist their feelings of anger and their instincts to mess, which later leads to the persistent expression of

such traits as orderliness, inhibition, and a passion for collecting things. More contemporary psychodynamic theorists suggest that early struggles with parents over control and independence in any realm may set in motion such angry reactions and personality patterns (Kuriansky, 1988; Mollinger, 1980).

Cognitive theorists have had little to say about the origins of obsessive-compulsive personality disorder, but they do propose that illogical thinking processes help *maintain* the disorder. They point, for example, to black-or-white dichotomous thinking in individuals with this disorder, which may produce rigidity, perfectionism, and procrastination, as well as to their exaggeration of potential consequences of mistakes or errors. Cognitive theorists also consider some people with this personality disorder to be deficient in the cognitive capacity to reflect on life and the world (Miller, 1988).

## Treatments for Obsessive-Compulsive Personality Disorder

Whereas drug therapy and behavior therapy have been highly effective for patients with obsessive-compulsive anxiety disorder (see pp. 162–167), clinical case reports suggest that patients with obsessive-compulsive personality disorder often respond better to psychodynamic or cognitive psychotherapy (Primac, 1993; Jenike, 1991, 1990). Therapists who take these approaches typically try to help the patients become more aware of, directly experience, and accept their real feelings; overcome their insecurities; take risks; and accept their personal limitations (Salzman, 1989). Over time, the therapists also address the clients' tendency to overintellectualize and try to help them "loosen up" and learn to have fun (Liebowitz et al., 1986). Cognitive therapists further work on helping the clients to correct their dichotomous thinking, perfectionism, indecisiveness, and procrastination, and to cope better with their chronic worrying and rumination.

# *Categorizing the Personality Disorders*

The inclusion of personality disorders in recent editions of the DSM reflects their growing diagnostic importance. It appears, however, that more misdiagnoses are made in this area of pathology than in most other DSM categories, an indication of some serious problems in validity and reliability (Zimmerman, 1994).

The diagnostic difficulties are partly due to the nature of the DSM criteria used to identify personality disorders. Many of the criteria consist of inferred traits rather than specific observable behaviors. In other words, each of the diagnoses relies rather heavily on the impressions of the individual clinician. And clinicians tend to vary widely in their beliefs about when a normal personality style crosses the line and warrants classification as a disorder (Widiger & Costa, 1994).

The similarity of various personality disorders within the same cluster presents yet another diagnostic complication. There is so much overlap between the diagnostic criteria for the "anxious" cluster's avoidant personality disorder and dependent personality disorder, for example—feelings of inadequacy, fear of disapproval, and the like—that many clinicians consider it unreasonable to define them as two independent disorders. Thus some theorists view the personality disorders within each cluster as variations on a single deviant mode of personality organization (Livesley et al., 1994; Siever & Davis, 1991).

There is even a troublesome overlap of criteria *between* the three clusters, so that many people seem to qualify for diagnoses in more than one cluster (Dolan et al. 1995; Flick et al., 1993). The prevalence of borderline traits ("dramatic" cluster) among some people with dependent personality disorder ("anxious" cluster), for instance, may suggest that these two disorders in fact represent different degrees of the same behavioral pattern.

A very different yet equally troubling problem is the range of people included in each personality disorder classification (Widiger, 1993, 1992). An individual must meet a certain number of criteria to receive a given diagnosis, but no single feature or characteristic is an essential criterion for any given personality disorder. Thus people who display very different personality profiles may receive the same diagnosis, each client meeting a different set of criteria for the same disorder.

Clearly, investigations into the characteristics, validity, reliability, and interrelationships of the personality disorder categories are still needed (Widiger & Costa, 1994). The diagnostic criteria for the disorders have undergone revision in each of the recent editions of the DSM. In fact, several of the categories themselves have changed from edition to edition. For example, the past DSM category of *passive-aggressive personality disorder,* a pattern of negativistic attitudes and passive resistance to demands for adequate performance in social and occupational situations, has been dropped in DSM-IV because research has failed thus far to establish that it is a cohesive disorder rather than a single problematic trait. The pattern is, in fact, now being studied and considered for inclusion once again in future editions of the DSM.

### Consider This
Try to develop a new organization and listing of personality disorders that improves upon the present categories. How would the current DSM categories fit into your new organization and categories? What would be the advantages and disadvantages of your new way of listing these disorders?

All of these diagnostic problems have led some theorists to suggest alternative approaches to classifying personality disorders. Some believe, for example, that the disorders differ more in degree than in type of dysfunction, and have proposed differentiating them by the *severity* of certain central traits rather than by the presence or absence of specific traits (Widiger, 1993). It is not yet clear where arguments and suggestions of this kind will lead. However, such activity does indicate that more and more clinicians are finding the personality disorders to be important and relevant categories in their work.

### Summing Up
*The "anxious" personality disorders are characterized by the kinds of symptoms found in Axis I anxiety and depressive disorders, including social inhibition and feelings of inadequacy, in avoidant personality disorder; dependency and fears of separation, in dependent personality disorder; and fears of imperfection and lack of control, in obsessive-compulsive personality disorder. Like the personality disorders in the other clusters, the explanations proposed for these disorders have received only limited research support. Treatments for these disorders appear to be somewhat helpful.*

*Misdiagnosis of the various personality disorders are apparently common, indicating that the DSM categories may have limitations and pose serious problems in validity and reliability.*

---

*Passive-aggressive personality disorder*    A category of personality disorder, listed in past versions of the DSM, characterized by a pattern of negativistic attitudes and passive resistance to demands for adequate performance in social and occupational situations.

# The State of the Field
## *Personality Disorders*

Psychologists' attitudes toward the concept of personality have shifted over the years. During the first half of this century, theorists believed deeply in the legitimacy of the concept and tried to identify stable personality traits that would account for behavior. Then they discovered the importance of situational factors and a backlash developed — "personality" became almost an obscene word in some circles. The category of personality disorders has suffered the same fate. When psychodynamic theorists dominated the clinical field, neurotic *character disorders* (later to be called personality disorders) were considered useful clinical categories; but the popularity of these categories declined as other models gained ascendancy. During the 1960s and 1970s, only antisocial personality disorder received much attention.

The concepts of personality and personality disor-
ders have rebounded during the past decade and have been gaining the attention of practitioners and researchers. In recent years, theorists have tried to develop unifying principles that help define and distinguish the personality disorders, and diagnosticians have developed objective tests and interview protocols for assessing them (Zimmerman, 1994; Perry, 1992; Millon, 1987). Such advances have set in motion a wave of systematic research.

So far, only the antisocial and borderline personality disorders have received much study, but in the current research climate we can expect that the other personality disorders will also attract considerable attention in the coming years. Then clinicians should be better able to answer some pressing questions: What are the most useful ways of categorizing the personality disorders? How prevalent are the various disorders? How do they interrelate? How are they related to other kinds of psychological disorders? And what interventions are most effective? To the many people who are impaired and distressed by these patterns, this change in direction may be most helpful.

# *Chapter Review*

1. *Overview:* A *personality disorder* is a pervasive, enduring, and inflexible pattern of inner experience and outward behavior that deviates markedly from the expectations of one's culture and leads to distress or impairment. It typically begins in adolescence or early adulthood and makes for a lifelong ordeal. Explanations for most of the personality disorders have received only limited research support. DSM-IV distinguishes ten personality disorders and separates them into three clusters.

2. *"Odd" Personality Disorders:* Three of the personality disorders are characterized by the kinds of odd or eccentric behavior often seen in the Axis I disorder schizophrenia.

   A. People with *paranoid personality disorder* display a pattern of pervasive distrust and suspiciousness of others. Those with *schizoid personality disorder* display a pattern of detachment from social relationships and a restricted range of emotional expression. Individuals with *schizotypal personality disorder* display a pattern of interpersonal deficits marked by acute discomfort in close relationships, cognitive or perceptual distortions, and behavioral eccentricities.

   B. People with these disorders usually are resistant
to treatment, and treatment gains tend to be modest at best.

3. *"Dramatic" Personality Disorders:* Four of the personality disorders are marked by highly dramatic, emotional, or erratic symptoms.

   A. Persons with *antisocial personality disorder* display a pervasive pattern of disregard for and violation of the rights of others. No known specific intervention for it is particularly effective.

   B. People with *borderline personality disorder* display a pervasive pattern of instability in interpersonal relationships, self-image, and mood, along with marked impulsivity. Psychotherapy apparently can be effective and lead to sustained, though limited, improvement for some clients with this disorder.

   C. Individuals with *histrionic personality disorder,* once called *hysterical personality disorder,* display a pattern of excessive emotionality and attention seeking. Clinical case reports suggest that treatment is helpful on occasion.

   D. People with *narcissistic personality disorder* display a chronic and pervasive pattern of grandiosity, need for admiration, and lack of empathy. This has been characterized as one of the most difficult disorders to treat.

4. *"Anxious" Personality Disorders:* Three of the personality disorders are marked by the kinds of symptoms found in Axis I's anxiety and depressive disorders.
   A. People with *avoidant personality disorder* display a chronic and pervasive pattern of inhibition in social situations, feelings of inadequacy, and extreme sensitivity to negative evaluation.
   B. People with *dependent personality disorder* display a pattern of submissive and clinging behavior, fears of separation, and a pervasive and excessive need to be taken care of.
   C. Individuals with *obsessive-compulsive personality disorder* display a pattern of preoccupation with orderliness, perfectionism, and mental and interpersonal control, at the expense of flexibility, openness, and efficiency.
   D. A variety of treatment strategies have been used for people with these disorders and apparently have been modestly to moderately helpful.

5. *Misdiagnosis:* It appears that misdiagnoses of personality disorders are common, an indication of some serious problems in the diagnostic categories' validity and reliability.

## Key Terms

| | | | |
|---|---|---|---|
| personality | schizotypal | borderline personality | avoidant personality |
| personality disorder |    personality |    disorder |    disorder |
| schizophrenia-spectrum |    disorder | histrionic personality | dependent personality |
|    disorders | ideas of reference |    disorder |    disorder |
| paranoid personality | antisocial personality | hysterical personality | obsessive-compulsive |
|    disorder |    disorder |    disorder |    personality disorder |
| schizoid personality | psychopathy | narcissistic personality | passive-aggressive |
|    disorder | sociopathy |    disorder |    personality disorder |

## Quick Quiz

1. What is a personality disorder, and why are personality disorders listed on Axis II in DSM-IV?

2. What are the principal features of the "odd" personality disorders? What Axis I disorders are these personality disorders similar to?

3. Describe the symptoms of the paranoid, schizoid, and schizotypal personality disorders. What explanations and treatments have been applied to these disorders?

4. What are the "dramatic" personality disorders, and what are the symptoms of each?

5. How have theorists explained antisocial personality disorder? How effectively have clinicians treated this disorder?

6. What are the leading explanations and treatments for the borderline, histrionic, and narcissistic personality disorders? How strongly does research support these explanations and treatments?

7. What kinds of Axis I disorders are the avoidant, dependent, and obsessive-compulsive personality disorders similar to? Has research uncovered strong ties between these personality disorders and their Axis I counterparts?

8. What are the leading explanations for the avoidant, dependent, and obsessive-compulsive personality disorders, and to what extent are they borne out by research? How are the disorders treated, and how effective are the treatments?

9. Describe the social relationship problems caused by each of the personality disorders.

10. What kinds of problems have clinicians confronted when diagnosing personality disorders? What are the causes of these problems, and what solutions have been proposed?

# 17

# Law, Society, and the Mental Health Profession

## Topic Overview

*Clinical-Legal Focus on Abuse and Victimization*

*Clinical Influences on the Criminal Justice System*
    Insanity during the Commission of a Crime
    Incompetence to Stand Trial

*Legal Influences on the Mental Health System*
    Civil Commitment
    Protecting Patients' Rights

*Mental Health, Business, and Economics*

*The Person within the Profession*

*T*hroughout this book we have seen the importance of the roles clinical scientists and practitioners play in our society: they gather and impart knowledge about psychological dysfunctioning, and they treat people who are experiencing psychological problems. They do not, however, perform these functions in a vacuum. Their relationship with their science, their clients, and the public unfolds within a complex social system. Just as we must understand the social context of abnormal behavior in order to appreciate its nature, so must we understand the social context in which abnormal behavior is studied and treated.

Earlier chapters have highlighted a number of the ways clinical scientists and practitioners interact with the public at large and with specific social agencies. They describe how clinicians have helped carry out the government's policy of deinstitutionalization, how the government has regulated clinicians' use of electroconvulsive therapy, and how clinicians have called to society's attention the psychological ordeal of Vietnam veterans. The institutions that probably have the greatest impact on the mental health profession are the legislative and judicial professions—the institutions of law charged with promoting and protecting both the public good and the rights of individuals.

The mental health and legal fields have had an interesting relationship dating back many years. Sometimes the relationship has been harmonious, and the two fields have worked in concert to address the needs of individuals with psychological problems and of society. At other times one field has imposed its will on the other and overridden its judgments, and the relationship has been stormy. It is a relationship with three distinct facets:

1. Both the mental health and legal professions are enormously interested in the social problems of abuse and victimization, and they have tried, often jointly, to address these problems.
2. Mental health professionals have played an important role in the criminal justice system. Clinicians have, for example, been called upon to evaluate the mental stability of many people accused of crimes and thus to help the courts determine their culpability.
3. The legislative and judicial systems have played a major role in regulating some aspects of mental health care. Legal channels have been established to force some individuals to receive psychological treatment and to guarantee that the rights of patients are protected in the mental health system.

In this chapter, we will first discuss these three important areas of intersection between the mental health and legal fields and then go on to examine economic and other social issues relevant to the practice of the mental health profession.

# Clinical-Legal Focus on Abuse and Victimization

As we observed in Chapter 6, victims of abuse and victimization may suffer serious psychological harm (see pp. 169–171), beyond whatever physical damage they may incur. In such cases, mental health professionals may be called upon to help the individuals return to normal functioning. But abuse and victimization create broad social problems as well, such as how to protect the rights and safety of individuals and the values of society. Four areas of abuse and victimization have drawn considerable attention from both the mental health field and the criminal justice system in recent years: rape, spouse abuse, stalking, and child abuse.

## Rape

*Rape*—sexual intercourse or another sexual act forced upon a nonconsenting person or engaged in with an underage person—is prevalent in our society and leaves the victim psychologically traumatized and vulnerable. More than 100,000 rapes are reported to authorities annually (FBI, 1991), but, in fact, the incidence of rape may be many times greater than the number reported (Koss, 1993, 1992). Many victims are reluctant to report a rape because they are ashamed or because they feel that dealing with police or the courts will compound their trauma.

Most rapists are men and most victims are women. Studies estimate that between 8 and 25 percent of all women are raped or are the victims of some sexual assault at some time during their lives (Koss, 1993). Surveys also suggest that most rape victims are young: 29 percent of all victims are under 11 years old, 32 percent are between the ages of 11 and 17, and 29 percent are between 18 and 29. Approximately 22 percent of the victims are raped by strangers; the rest are raped by acquaintances, friends, neighbors, boyfriends or ex-boyfriends, husbands or ex-husbands, fathers or stepfathers, or other relatives (Koss, 1992; Youngstrom, 1992).

---

*Rape*   Sexual intercourse or another sexual act forced upon a nonconsenting person or engaged in with an underage person.

## Rapists

Although rape does by definition involve a sexual act, the primary motivation for this act is often not sex but aggression or anger. According to some clinical theorists, rapists fall into four categories: *sexual sadists,* who are sexually aroused by seeing a victim suffer; *sexual exploiters,* who impulsively use victims as objects of gratification; *inadequate aggressors,* who believe that no woman would voluntarily have sex with them; and *angry abusers,* who seem to displace their rage against women in general upon the victim (Hall, 1992). There is also a suspicion that some adolescents who commit rape may be grappling with issues that are different from those of adults (Harnett & Misch, 1993).

## Victims

The *psychological impact* of rape on a victim is immediate and may last a long time. Rape victims typically experience enormous distress during the week after the assault. Stress continues to rise for the next three weeks, maintains a peak level for another month or so, and then starts to improve over the next few months (Koss, 1993). Indeed, in one study 94 percent of rape victims fully qualified for a clinical diagnosis of *acute stress disorder* when they were observed an average of twelve days after their assault (Rothbaum et al., 1992). Although the majority of rape victims improve psychologically within three or four months, most continue to experience elevated levels of fear, anxiety, self-esteem problems, and sexual dysfunction—effects that may continue for up to 18 months or longer (Koss, 1993; Resick, 1987). Even years after the assault, women who were raped are more likely to qualify for diagnoses of depression, substance-related disorders, and anxiety disorders than other women (Koss, 1993; Burnam et al., 1988; Kilpatrick et al., 1985).

Victims who have a strong psychological foundation and who are bolstered by a strong support system are more likely to make an adequate psychological recovery (Davis et al., 1991: Sales et al., 1984), but the trauma of the sexual assault and its aftermath (including a harsh legal system and a judgmental society) may overwhelm even the most well adjusted and well supported of women. Victims who can express their fear and rage to believing family members, doctors, and police seem to make the most psychological progress (Sadock, 1989).

Rape victims may also experience *short-term somatic problems* as a result of their assault. Many victims suffer physical trauma during the assault, although only half of those injured receive formal medical care (Beebe, 1991; Koss et al., 1991). Between 4 and 30 percent of victims develop a sexually transmitted disease (Koss, 1993; Murphy, 1990) and 5 percent become pregnant (Beebe, 1991; Koss et al., 1991). Yet a recent broad national survey of women revealed that 60 percent of rape victims received no pregnancy testing or prophylaxis, and 73 percent received no information about or testing for exposure to HIV (National Victims Center, 1992).

Some related recent studies by the psychologist Mary Koss and her colleagues indicate that female victims of rape and other crimes are also much more likely than other women to suffer serious *long-term somatic problems* for years afterward (Golding, 1994; Koss & Heslet, 1992; Koss et al., 1991). Interviews with 390 women revealed that victims of rape or assault had poorer general health as well as poorer mental health for at least five years after the crime, made twice as many visits to physicians, and incurred 2½ times more medical expenses.

## Interventions

For years, the criminal justice system seemed to treat victims of rape as if *they* were guilty of inciting the crime. Many victims met with scepticism on the part of police investigators and were accused of dubious moral character and careless behavior in court. Although problems still exist, police and judicial procedures for dealing with victims of rape have been improved considerably in recent years. Today's procedures tend to be more sensitive to the victim's ordeal and more respectful of her needs and rights.

> ### Consider This
> It has been argued that rape victims need support from the medical and legal systems in order to deal effectively with their trauma and its aftermath. How might physicians, police, the courts, and other such agents better address the needs of rape victims?

Similarly, mental health practitioners have become more aware of the special issues confronted by victims of rape and have developed special treatment interventions that are targeted to their needs. For example, a large number of rape crisis intervention centers and other victim services have been developed across the United States, although recent funding limitations have cut back many of these services (Koss, 1993).

Both individual and group therapies have been helpful for victims of rape, but many clinicians believe that group therapy is the treatment of choice (Koss & Harvey, 1991). It is particularly effective at countering feelings of isolation, providing emotional support, validating feelings, and reducing self-blame.

## Spouse Abuse

In Stamford, Conn., a woman married to a *Fortune* 500 executive locked herself into their Lincoln Continental every Saturday night to escape her husband's kicks and punches. She did not leave him because she mistakenly feared he could sue for divorce on grounds of desertion and she, otherwise penniless, would get no alimony.

Barbara, 30, a middle-class housewife from South Hadley, Mass., was first beaten by her husband when she was pregnant. Last summer Barbara's husband hurled a dinner plate across the kitchen at her. His aim was off. The plate shattered against the wall and a piece of it struck their four-year-old daughter in the face, blinding the child in one eye.

In Miami, Diane, 27, a receptionist, said she married "a real nice guy," a Dr. Jekyll who turned into Mr. Hyde a week after the wedding. "Being married to this man was like being a prisoner of war. I was not allowed to visit my family, I couldn't go out on my own. He wouldn't even let me cry. If I did, it started an 'episode.'"

In a Duluth shelter for battered women, Lola, who married 19 years ago at age 18, said her husband was losing control more frequently: "He gets angry because he's coming home with a bag full of groceries and I didn't open the door fast enough. Because he didn't like the way I washed the clothes. Because the supper's not ready. Because supper's ready too soon."

(Time, *September 5, 1983, p. 23*)

As revealed in these cases, *spouse abuse,* the physical mistreatment or misuse of one spouse by the other, can take various forms, from shoving to battering (Sadock, 1989). Most abused spouses are women, married or cohabiting. In 1992 the American Medical Association declared that physical and sexual abuse against women had reached "epidemic proportions," and suggested that physicians be alert for signs of domestic violence in all female patients (Glazer, 1993; AMA, 1992).

A woman in the United States is more likely to be assaulted by an intimate or acquaintence than by a stranger. It is estimated that spouse abuse occurs in at least 4 million homes in the United States each year and that between a fourth and a third of all U.S. women have been abused at least once by their husbands (AMA, 1992). Similarly, many women are battered by the persons they date. The U.S. Surgeon

*Spouse abuse typically affects all members of the family, as revealed in this famous photograph. Police intervention and arrest are much more likely in cases today than in the past.*

General has ranked spouse abuse as the leading cause of injuries to women between the ages of 15 and 44. Indeed, 1,400 women in the U.S. are killed each year by their husbands or someone with whom they have been intimate, nearly one-fourth of all female homicides (Ingrassia & Beck, 1994).

Spouse abuse cuts across all races, religions, educational levels, and socioeconomic groups (Mollerstrom et al., 1992). Some experts believe that more violent abuse, particularly murder, occurs more often at lower socioeconomic levels (Straus & Gelles, 1986). Others suggest that members of the middle class are simply less likely to report abuse, and point to the wider spacing of middle-class homes, which prevents neighbors from detecting violence and calling the police (Glazer, 1993; Sherman, 1992).

For years this behavior was viewed as a private matter, and even the legal system avoided involvement. Indeed, until 1874 a husband had a legal right to beat his wife in the United States. Even after that time, abusers were rarely arrested or prosecuted. Police were reluctant to do anything other than calm down domestic violence, the number-one source of police fatalities. And the courts rarely prosecuted an abuser.

The emphasis on civil rights in the 1970s and the efforts of women's groups finally revealed the magnitude of the problem, and in the past two decades state legislatures have passed more laws to empower the courts to prosecute abusers and protect victims (100 laws were passed in 1993 alone); police have become more oriented toward intervention; and the clinical profession has increasingly studied and treated the problem. Twenty-five states now have laws that require the police to make an arrest when they are called to a scene where domestic violence has been reported. However, arrests do not necessarily lead to convic-

---

*Spouse abuse*   The physical mistreatment or misuse of one spouse by the other, ranging from shoving to battering.

tions, nor do convictions always result in sentences that deter abusive behavior in the future.

## Abusers and Victims

Studies suggest that abusive husbands are often very emotionally dependent on their wives and on their relationships (Murphy et al., 1994). Many consider their wives to be their private property and are extremely jealous and possessive. In fact, some inflict more abuse when their wives pursue outside friendships or even attend to their childrens' needs before their husbands'. Beyond assault, abusive husbands tend to belittle and isolate their wives, and repeatedly make them feel inept, worthless, and dependent. Although the husband may show genuine remorse for a time after beating his wife, he is likely to repeat the behavior (Walker, 1984, 1979).

Many abusive husbands were themselves beaten as children or saw their mothers beaten (Saunders, 1992; Pagelow, 1981). Often they suffer from low self-esteem and feel generally stressed (Russell & Hulson, 1992). A large percentage of them have alcohol-related or other substance-related problems (Mollerstrom et al., 1992; Saunders, 1992).

Victims of abuse typically feel very dependent on their spouse, unable to function on their own, and even unable to experience an identity separate from their spouse. This sense of dependence and their feeling that they are helpless to change the situation keep them in the relationship despite the obvious physical dangers. The great majority of victims are not masochistic, as many clinical theorists once believed (Walker, 1984; Finkelhor et al., 1983). Many stay with their spouses out of economic need.

About 50 percent of victims grew up in homes where they or their mothers were abused, and most come from families that saw male and female roles in stereotyped ways. Many victims have very low self-esteem (Cornell & Gelles, 1983), blame themselves for the abuse, and agree with their spouse that they did something bad to provoke it. Usually the pattern of abuse does not emerge until after the couple is married.

## Interventions

Initially clinicians proposed couple therapy as the treatment of choice for spouse abuse. But they have learned that as long as a woman continues to be abused at home, such an intervention is but a charade. The steps of treatment now preferred are (1) separating a woman from her abusive husband and situation; (2) therapy for the victim to help her recognize her plight, see her options, and experience a more positive self-image and greater autonomy; (3) therapy for the abuser to help him cope with life more effectively, develop more appropriate attitudes toward his wife, and develop more appropriate avenues for expressing anger and frustration (Saunders, 1982; Ganley, 1981); and (4) couple therapy, if both spouses have made satisfactory progress in their individual therapies. A number of community programs have been set up to help provide these intervention services, including hotlines, emergency shelters or "safe houses" for women, and public organizations and self-help groups to aid abused spouses and provide education about the problem (Sullivan et al., 1992).

Duluth, Minnesota, the first jurisdiction to adopt a mandatory arrest policy in cases of spouse abuse, has been a leader in the battered women's movement. It has a comprehensive spouse abuse program in which a first-time offender is jailed overnight and released into a 26-week batterers' program. If he fails to attend three consecutive classes, he goes back to jail. In the ten-year history of the program, Duluth has not reported one case of domestic homicide. On the one hand, over 60 percent of the men who completed the program were found no longer to be abusing their spouses when studied up to eighteen months later (Edelson & Eiskovitz, 1989). On the other hand, at least 40 percent of the men treated in the program repeated their offense within five years, either against the same woman or against a new partner (Sherman, 1992).

Thus, although progress has been made in the last twenty years, the problem of spouse abuse remains a difficult one. The very fact that treatment programs for spouse abuse now exist is an important development both for victims and for our society, and most clinicians believe that many of these programs are on the right track. Because relatively little empirical evaluation of the programs has been undertaken, however, it is not yet possible to know precisely how helpful the various interventions are or how to improve upon them.

# Stalking

In 1992 Teresa Zeleske met a nice, gentle young man, Virgil. They fell in love. Teresa left her husband four months later, and she and Virgil became engaged. Before long, however, Virgil's darker side began to show itself. He took out his anger at work and was promptly fired. In retaliation, he threatened to blow up the building. Although upset, Teresa decided to stick by the man she had agreed to marry, and soon became his wife. But Virgil's problems seemed to increase. He turned his attention to Teresa, listening in on her phone calls and following her. After seven months she could not take it any longer and had Virgil move out. While they were separated Virgil kept begging for forgiveness and asking to be taken back. Teresa refused, but Virgil was persistent. He began harassing her, calling at all hours and accusing her of being "a whore." During one confrontation, Virgil almost strangled Teresa. Going to the police was of no avail—there were no laws in Wisconsin against the kind of harassment Virgil was using to torment Teresa. Eventually, she was able to get a court hearing on domestic battery charges, during which Virgil vowed to kill her. Sadly, Virgil kept his promise a few months later. Teresa returned to her home late one night with two male friends. Three hours later shots were heard from her apartment. Police found all four dead of gunshots—including Virgil, who died by his own hand.

A spate of cases like the horror that befell Teresa Zeleske has spawned great public interest in the harassing behavior called *stalking.* The number of cases of stalking in the United States has been estimated at 200,000 each year (Corwin, 1993). The actual number may be much higher, but law enforcement does not categorize all cases of harassment or abuse as stalking. Are people who harass and threaten others displaying a mental disorder? Where do we draw the line between legal but inappropriate behavior and illegal acts? Which authorities should deal with the problem and how? The mental health and legal communities have joined the rest of us in asking these questions as society searches for a solution to what seems to be a growing problem.

## Stalkers and Victims

Mental health professionals estimate that 90 percent of stalkers suffer from some kind of mental disorder. Some apparently experience an *erotomanic delusion,* a psychotic belief without any basis whatsoever that one is loved by another person who may actually be a casual acquaintance or even a complete stranger (Anderson, 1993). In this split from reality, the deluded person may become obsessed with someone and may even develop a fantasy in which he or she feels compelled to harm or kill that person. More typically, though, stalking is associated with a host of nonpsychotic disturbances, including borderline, antisocial, and narcissistic personality disorders and depression (Moses-Zirkes, 1992). The multiplicity of possibilities makes it more difficult to identify a given person as being likely to become a stalker.

*Stalking*   The persistent pursuit, harassment, or threatening of one person by another.

*While playing in a professional tournament in 1993, tennis star Monica Seles was stabbed by a 38-year-old unemployed man from Germany. The attacker, apparently obsessed with helping the career of another star, Steffi Graf, was described by his aunt as having been a "quiet, reticent child."*

Overall, little research has been done on the psychological underpinnings or patterns of behavior of people who become stalkers, and studies have failed to reveal much information about how or when a person's delusional or obsessive interest in someone crosses the line into action (Dietz et al., 1991). So far, the main point of agreement among all who look at stalking is that it is a complex and little-understood phenomenon.

Headline cases, as when the actress Rebecca Shaeffer of the television show *My Sister Sam* was killed outside her West Hollywood apartment by an obsessed fan, catch the public's attention and spur interest and action. But most victims of stalking are not celebrities. It has been estimated that many of the women who are murdered by husbands or boyfriends have, in fact, been stalked first (Furio, 1993). The victim may go through months or even years of fear and intimidation, changing phone numbers, moving, or hiding. An endless stream of threatening phone calls and letters, intimidating visits, and physical abuse creates an atmosphere of terror that dominates the lives of both victim and stalker.

## Interventions

Unfortunately, threatening and harassing behavior without actual physical violence typically leaves police officials with their hands tied: one cannot be fully protected against actions that have not yet been taken. This is the dilemma facing not only the victims of stalking, but the legal community that wants to protect them and the mental health and civil liberties communities that want to address the needs and rights of all.

Lately a number of state legislatures across the United States have enacted new laws in response to the public outcry over numerous widely publicized cases (Anderson, 1993). These laws make it easier for a stalking victim to obtain a restraining order, but they also have certain limitations. They are, for example, ineffective against stalkers whose first act of violence is murder. In addition, the enforcement of the new laws may have a negative effect in some cases: sitting in jail could fuel rather than extinguish the stalker's anger. Furthermore, many of the antistalking laws are ambiguous and open to interpretation; with each state formulating its own antistalking legislation, federal authorities find it difficult to intervene in a consistent manner. The new laws are also vulnerable to misuse. Spouses may use them to retaliate against partners who have no thought of committing acts the legislation was intended to forestall. Lastly, some of the new laws may violate the constitutional rights of alleged stalkers and may be struck down by the U.S. Supreme Court. This is a chilling prospect for past and potential victims of stalking, but it is natural for the pendulum to swing toward a more restrained approach as the mental health and legal communities try to find a way to protect the rights both of victims and of those who are accused.

## Child Abuse

*Child abuse* is the intentional use of excessive physical or psychological force by an adult on a child, often aimed at hurting or destroying the child (Gil, 1970). The abuser is usually the child's parent. Girls and boys are abused at approximately the same rate. A recent study done by the National Committee for the Prevention of Child Abuse found that 2.9 million cases of child abuse were reported to child services in 1992, as compared with 1.9 million cases reported in 1985 (McCurdy & Daro, 1993). Around a quarter of these reports cited physical abuse, 17 percent sexual abuse, half neglect, and 7 percent emotional maltreatment (Paget et al., 1993; AAPC, 1992).

Surveys suggest that each year one in ten children is subjected to severe violence, such as being kicked, bitten, hit (often with an object), beaten, threatened with a knife or a gun, or assaulted with a knife or a gun (Gelles & Straus, 1987). Physical injury is more likely to occur during the preschool years and adolescence (AHA, 1986). Moreover, it is estimated that annually between 2,000 and 4,000 instances of child abuse result in a child's death (Green, 1989). In fact, some observers believe that physical child abuse and neglect are the leading causes of death among young children.

> What I remember most about my mother was that she was always beating me. She'd beat me with her high heeled shoes, with my father's belt, with a potato masher. When I was eight, she black and blued my legs so badly, I told her I'd go to the police. She said, "Go, they'll just put you into the darkest prison." So I stayed. When my breasts started growing at 13, she beat me across the chest until I fainted. Then she'd hug me and ask forgiveness. . . . Most kids have nightmares about being taken away from their parents. I would sit on our front porch crooning softly of going far, far away to find another mother.
>
> (Time, *September 5, 1983, p. 20*)

Before the turn of the century, the legal system in the United States tried to avoid intervention in family life, even in instances of child abuse (Garrison, 1987). Medical reports of suspected child abuse did not begin to receive widespread attention until the 1960s (Newberger, 1983), and medical and legal professionals did not become actively involved in detecting and intervening in such cases until 1974, when states adopted laws requiring physicians to report cases of suspected child abuse and the Federal Child Abuse Prevention and Treatment Act was passed (Garrison, 1987). Since then media accounts have kept this staggering social problem in the public eye. Numerous federal and state legislatures and court systems have also sprung into more protective and punitive action; and mental health professionals have contributed by developing numerous research and therapy programs.

Two forms of child abuse have been receiving special attention in recent years: psychological abuse and sexual abuse. *Psychological abuse* may include severe rejection; coercive, punitive, and erratic discipline; scapegoating and ridicule; unrealistic expectations; exploitation and corruption; isolation; and refusal to provide help for a child with psychological problems (Hart & Brassard, 1991, 1987; Hart et al., 1987). It probably accompanies all forms of physical abuse and neglect and may occur by itself in about 200,000 cases each year (McCurdy & Dato, 1993; AAPC, 1992). The legal system has devoted little attention to this form of child abuse, but the mental health field has become increasingly concerned about the effects of and treatment for the problem (Garrison, 1987).

*Child sexual abuse,* the use of a child for gratification of adult sexual desires, causes victims enormous psychological damage, including long-term feelings of mistrust, poor self-image, depression, guilt, social

---

*Child abuse*   The intentional use of excessive physical or psychological force by an adult on a child, often aimed at hurting or destroying the child.

*Honoré Daumier's* Fatherly Discipline *reminds us that the line between acceptable discipline and child abuse may be crossed by many parents.*

withdrawal, poor school performance, and difficulties with sexual intimacy. It may occur outside of or in the home. It is estimated that 50,000 to 200,000 new cases occur each year in the United States.

In surveys of adult women, 20 to 35 percent reported having been forced into sexual contact with an adult male as children, many of them with their father or stepfather (Green, 1989). Although the majority of victims are girls, the fact that boys are also sexually abused has been acknowledged within the past ten years (Bolton et al., 1989).

### *Consider This*

Clearly, the lives and rights of abused children must be protected. At the same time, a number of cases have revealed that the reports and memories of some children may be highly imaginative and suggestible. How might clinicians and lawyers obtain more accurate information from children? How is the mere accusation of child abuse itself damaging to the persons accused? And how can we as a society protect the rights both of children and of those who are accused, perhaps unfairly, of child abuse?

Both legal and mental health professionals have increased their focus on the problem of child sexual abuse during the past decade partly because of several highly publicized cases of alleged sexual abuse in day-care centers around the United States. These cases have raised concerns not only about the prevalence of

child sexual abuse in child-care settings, but also about the validity of children's testimony. There has, in fact, been an increasing awareness of the suggestibility of children and the power of interrogators in such cases. Psychologists are being called upon to investigate just how easily a child's memory of events can be altered by adult suggestions and by the pressure of opinionated interviewers. The findings of research on this topic will inevitably have a great influence on the way abuse charges are pursued.

## Abusers and Victims

Since entering into the study of child abuse, clinical researchers have learned that a variety of factors may interact to produce child abuse, including such parental characteristics as poor impulse control and low self-esteem, such parental background factors as having been abused as children and having had poor role models, such situational stresses as marital disputes or family unemployment, and such immediate precipitants as a child's misbehavior (babies who are fussy and irritable are apparently at particularly high risk of being abused). Research shows that physically abusive families also tend to have lower incomes, younger parents with less education, and more likelihood of alcohol or drug abuse (Gelles, 1992; Whipple et al., 1991; Gil, 1970).

The psychological damage of child abuse has been documented in a number of studies and should be anticipated and addressed in child-focused interventions (Roesler & McKenzie, 1994). Research has revealed, for example, impaired academic and behavioral functioning in school among children who are abused (Eckenrode et al., 1993). Research has also uncovered such long-term effects as lower achievement scores later in school; poorer work and study skills; lower social acceptance; more psychological problems such as anxiety, misbehavior, aggression, defiance, hyperactivity, and distractibility; higher arrest records during adolescence or adulthood; a greater risk of becoming criminally violent; a higher unemployment rate, lower-paying jobs, and less education; and a higher suicide rate (Knutson, 1995; Egeland, 1991; Widom, 1991). Finally, numerous studies have documented that more than one-third of victims grow up to be abusive, neglectful, or seriously inept parents themselves (Oliver, 1993).

## Interventions

A number of interventions have been tried in cases of child abuse. For example, parents may be helped to develop insight about themselves and their behavior, receive training on alternatives to abuse, and learn parenting skills in groups and classes such as those offered by the national organization Parents Anonymous. In groups or in individual treatment, they may be taught how to interact with and manage their children more effectively through such behavioral interventions as modeling, role playing, and feedback (Azar & Siegal, 1990; Barth et al., 1983).

Parents may also receive cognitive therapy to help correct misperceptions about their children or themselves (Azar & Siegal, 1990; Azar et al., 1984). Many parents who abuse their children believe that the children actually intend to upset them, and some have unrealistic expectations in regard to their children's behavior (Azar & Rohrbeck, 1986; Plotkin, 1983). A number of treatments are also aimed at helping parents deal more effectively with the situational stresses that often trigger the abuse, such as unemployment, marital discord, or depressed feelings (Campbell et al., 1983).

Some treatment programs combine the various therapy interventions, in accordance with the needs of a particular family (Wolfe et al., 1981). The effects of all such approaches on the parents' behavior, the child's self-esteem and psychological recovery, and family harmony have yet to be fully determined (Azar & Wolfe, 1989).

> ### Summing Up
> *The interests and actions of the mental health profession and the legal system often intersect. Both, for example, have become very interested in understanding and addressing the social problems of abuse and victimization. The judicial system has increasingly clarified the wide scope of such problems as rape, spouse abuse, stalking, and child abuse and has established legal channels for reporting and responding to them. For its part, the mental health system continues to explore the nature and causes of these forms of abuse and victimization and to develop treatments for victims and perpetrators.*

# Clinical Influences on the Criminal Justice System

Our courts mete out what they consider just and appropriate punishment on the assumption that individuals are *responsible* for their crimes and are *capable* of defending themselves in court. If either of these features is lacking, it is considered inappropriate to find individuals guilty or punish them in the usual manner. The courts have decided that *mental instability* is one mediating factor that can indeed render individuals incapable of being responsible for their actions and of defending themselves in court. Although the courts make the final judgment of mental instability, their decisions are guided to a large degree by the opinions of mental health professionals.

When people accused of crimes are judged to be mentally unstable, they are typically sent to a mental institution for treatment, a process called *criminal commitment*. Actually there are two forms of criminal commitment. In one, individuals are judged *mentally unstable at the time of their crime* and accordingly are found innocent of wrongdoing. Those who plead *not guilty by reason of insanity* are permitted to bring mental health professionals into court to support their claim. If they are found not guilty on this basis, they are committed for treatment until they improve enough to be released.

> ### Consider This
> In some states, the defense must prove that a defendant was insane and therefore not guilty by reason of insanity, while in other states the prosecution must prove that a defendant making this plea was *not* insane. Which burden of proof do you think is more appropriate? Under which burden of proof might a defendant be more likely to be found not guilty by reason of insanity?

In a second form of criminal commitment, individuals are judged *mentally unstable at the time of their trial* and accordingly are considered to be incapable of understanding the procedures and defending themselves in court. They are committed for treatment until they are competent to stand trial. Once again, the testimony of mental health professionals is relied on to help determine the defendant's mental incompetence.

## Criminal Commitment and Insanity during Commission of a Crime

In March 1981 the actress Jodie Foster received the following letter:

> Dear Jodie:
>     There is a definite possibility that I will be killed in my attempt to get Reagan. It is for this very reason that I am writing you this letter now. As you well know by now, I

---

*Not guilty by reason of insanity (NGRI)* A verdict stating that defendants are not guilty of committing a crime because they were insane at the time of the crime.

love you very much. The past seven months I have left you dozens of poems, letters and messages in the faint hope you would develop an interest in me. . . . Jodie, I would abandon this idea of getting Reagan in a second if I could only win your heart and live out the rest of my life with you, whether it be in total obscurity or whatever. I will admit to you that the reason I'm going ahead with this attempt now is because I just cannot wait any longer to impress you. I've got to do something now to make you understand in no uncertain terms that I am doing all of this for your sake. By sacrificing my freedom and possibly my life I hope to change your mind about me. This letter is being written an hour before I leave for the Hilton Hotel. Jodie, I'm asking you please to look into your heart and at least give me the chance with this historical deed to gain your respect and love. I love you forever.

*John Hinckley*

Are these the ravings of an insane man? Or are they the heartfelt emotions of a calculating murderer? Soon after writing this letter, John W. Hinckley stood waiting, pistol ready, outside the Washington Hilton Hotel. Moments later, President Ronald Reagan emerged from the hotel, and the popping of pistol fire was heard. As Secret Service men propelled Reagan into the limousine, a policeman and the president's press secretary fell to the pavement. The president had been shot, and by nightfall most of America had seen the face and heard the name of the young man from Colorado.

*Few courtroom decisions have spurred as much debate or legislative action as the jury's verdict that John Hinckley was not guilty by reason of insanity in his attempt to kill President Ronald Reagan. As a consequence of this verdict, Congress and half of the state legislatures changed their criteria for such a verdict.*

Was John Hinckley insane at the time of the shooting? If insane, should he be held responsible for his actions? On June 21, 1982, a jury pronounced Hinckley not guilty by reason of insanity. Hinckley thus joined the ranks of Richard Lawrence, a house painter who shot at Andrew Jackson in 1835, and John Schrank, a saloonkeeper who shot former president Teddy Roosevelt in 1912. Each of these would-be assassins was found not guilty by reason of insanity.

It is important to recognize that "insanity" is a *legal* term, that the definition of insanity used to help determine criminal responsibility is set by legislators, not by clinicians. Thus, defendants with mental disorders do not necessarily fulfill the criteria of legal insanity. The most important precursor of the modern definition of insanity occurred in 1843 in response to the Daniel M'Naghten murder case. M'Naghten shot and killed Edward Drummond, the secretary to British Prime Minister Robert Peel, while trying to shoot Peel. Because of M'Naghten's apparent delusions of persecution, the jury found him to be not guilty by reason of insanity. The public was appalled by this decision, and their angry outcry forced the British law lords to present a new clarification of the insanity defense.

This clarification came to be known as the *M'Naghten rule,* a test of insanity which held that experiencing a mental disorder at the time of a crime does not by itself constitute insanity; the defendant also had to be unable to know right from wrong while committing the crime. The state and federal courts in the United States adopted this test as well.

In the late nineteenth century some state and federal courts, dissatisfied with the M'Naghten rule, adopted an alternative test—the *irresistible impulse test.* This test, which had first been applied in Ohio in 1834, emphasized inability to control one's actions. A person who committed a crime during a "fit of passion" was considered insane and not guilty under this test.

Until recent years, state and federal courts chose between the M'Naghten test and the irresistible impulse test in determining the sanity of criminal defendants; most courts used the M'Naghten criteria. For a while a third test, called the *Durham test,* was popular, but it was soon replaced in most courts. This test, based on a decision handed down by the Supreme Court in 1954, stated simply that individuals are not criminally responsible if their "unlawful act was the product of mental disease or mental defect." This test was meant to offer more flexibility in decisions regarding insanity,

---

*M'Naghten rule*  A widely used legal criterion for insanity which holds people to be insane at the time of committing a crime if, because of a mental disorder, they did not know the nature of the act or did not know right from wrong.

but the general criterion of "mental disease" or "mental defect" proved too broad. It could refer to such problems as alcoholism, drug dependence, and conceivably even headaches or ulcers, which were listed as psychophysiological disorders in DSM-I.

In 1955 the American Law Institute (ALI) formulated a test that combined elements of the M'Naghten, irresistible impulse, and Durham tests. The new test indicated that people are not criminally responsible if they had a mental disease or defect at the time of a crime that rendered them unable to know right from wrong *or* unable to conform their behavior to the requirements of law. For a time the *American Law Institute test* became the most widely accepted legal test of insanity. After the Hinckley verdict, however, there was a public uproar over the "liberal" ALI guidelines, and a movement to toughen the standards gained momentum. In 1983 the American Psychiatric Association recommended removal of the provision that absolved people of responsibility for criminal acts if they were unable to conform their behavior to the requirements of law, and advised retention only of the wrongfulness criterion—essentially a return to the M'Naghten standard.

This revised criminal insanity test, with its renewed emphasis on defendants' inability to know right from wrong, now applies to all cases tried in federal courts and about half of the state courts (Steadman et al., 1993). The broader ALI standard is still used in the remaining state courts, except those in Idaho, Montana, and Utah, which have abolished the insanity plea altogether. Research has not found, however, that the reform criteria actually diminish the likelihood of "not guilty by reason of insanity" verdicts (Ogloff et al., 1992; Finkel 1991, 1989).

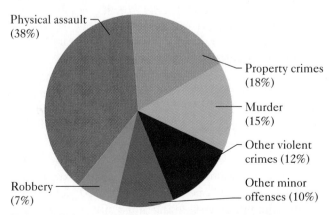

Figure 17-1 *Crimes for which persons are found not guilty by reason of insanity (NGRI). A recent review of NGRI verdicts in eight states revealed that most persons who were acquitted on this basis had been charged with a crime of violence. (Based on Steadman et al., 1993; Callahan et al., 1991.)*

Obviously, severe and confusing mental disorders are more likely than others to impair individuals' judgments of right versus wrong or their ability to control their behavior. Thus it is not surprising that approximately two-thirds of defendants who are acquitted of a crime by reason of insanity qualify for a diagnosis of schizophrenia when they are hospitalized after their acquittal (Steadman et al., 1993). The vast majority have a history of past hospitalization, arrest, or both. In addition, studies reveal that about half of the defendants who successfully plead insanity are white and that 86 percent are male. Their mean age is 32 years.

The crimes for which defendants are found not guilty by reason of insanity vary greatly. Large-scale studies have found, however, that approximately 65 percent of acquittees are charged with a violent crime of some sort (Steadman et al., 1993). Close to 15 percent are accused specifically of murder (see Figure 17-1 and Box 17-1).

## Criticisms of the Insanity Defense

Despite the revisions of the criteria for a finding of insanity, criticism of the insanity defense continues. One concern arises out of the seeming incompatibility between the goals of law and the science of human behavior. Since "insanity" is a legal and moral judgment and not a scientific one, critics argue that the goals and philosophy of law are incompatible with those of behavioral science (Winslade, 1983).

A second criticism questions the validity of current scientific knowledge of abnormal behavior. During a typical insanity defense trial, the testimony of defense clinicians conflicts with the testimony of clinicians hired by the prosecution (Otto, 1989). The jury can be faced with a situation in which no two "experts" altogether agree on their diagnostic assessments. Some people see this lack of professional consensus as evidence that the clinical field is still too primitive to be influencing the outcome of important legal proceedings (Szasz, 1963). Others counter, however, that the field has made great strides; and indeed, some standardized scales have been developed, such as the Rogers Criminal Responsibility Assessment Scales, that help assessors to discriminate the sane from the insane according to the M'Naghten standard and to apply the standard to people of different genders, races, and ages (Rogers & Ewing, 1992; Rogers, 1987).

Perhaps the most widespread criticism of the insanity defense is that it systematically allows dangerous criminals to escape punishment. It is true that some people who successfully plead insanity are in fact released from treatment facilities within months of their

## Box 17-1

# *Famous Cases Involving the Insanity Defense*

**1977** In Michigan, Francine Hughes poured gasoline around the bed where her husband, Mickey, lay in a drunken stupor, then lit a match and set him on fire. At her trial she explained that he had beaten her repeatedly for fourteen years, and that he had threatened to kill her if she tried to leave him. The jury found her not guilty by reason of temporary insanity, transforming her into a national symbol for many abused women. Some people saw the decision as confirmation of a woman's right to self-defense in her own home.

**1978** David "Son of Sam" Berkowitz, serial killer in New York City, was assessed as psychotic by two psychiatrists after he explained that barking dogs had sent him demonic messages to kill. Nevertheless, he was found guilty of his crimes. Long after his trial, he claimed that he had actually made up the delusions.

**1979** Kenneth Bianchi, one of the pair known as the "Hillside Stranglers," entered a plea of not guilty by reason of insanity but along with his cousin was found guilty of sexually assaulting and murdering women in the Los Angeles area in late 1977 and early 1978. Among other claims, Bianchi argued that he had a multiple personality disorder.

**1980** In December the rock music legend John Lennon was murdered by Mark David Chapman. Chapman later explained that he had killed Lennon because he believed Lennon to be a "sell-out." He also described hearing the voice of God, considered himself his generation's "catcher in the rye" (after the J. D. Salinger novel), and compared his role to that of Moses. Despite clinical testimony that supported Chapman's plea of not guilty by reason of insanity, he himself refused to claim that schizophrenia was at the root of his crime. He was judged competent to stand trial and was ultimately convicted of murder.

**1981** In an attempt to prove his love for the actress Jodie Foster, John Hinckley, Jr., tried to assassinate President Ronald Reagan. Hinckley was found not guilty by reason of insanity and was committed to St. Elizabeths Hospital for the criminally insane in Washington, where he remains today.

**1991** Julio Gonzales stood trial for starting a fire that killed eighty-seven people at a social club in New York. A psychologist testified that Gonzales had suffered from a wide range of personality disorders and "long-standing psychological defects" that led him to break with reality, suffer a brief psychotic

episode, and start the fire after having a fight with his girlfriend and being evicted from the club. The jury did not agree with the clinician, however, and Gonzales was convicted and sentenced to prison.

**1992** The 31-year-old Milwaukee mass murderer Jeffrey Dahmer was tried for the killings of fifteen young men. Dahmer apparently drugged some of his victims and performed crude lobotomies on them in an attempt to create zombielike companions for himself. He also dismembered his victims' bodies and stored their parts to be eaten. Although his defense attorney argued that Dahmer was not guilty by reason of insanity, the jury found him guilty as charged.

**1994** On June 23, 1993, 24-year-old Lorena Bobbitt cut off her husband's penis with a twelve-inch kitchen knife while he slept. During her trial, defense attorneys argued that following years of abuse by John Bobbitt, his wife suffered a brief psychotic episode and was seized by an "irresistible impulse" to cut off his penis after he came home drunk and raped her. On January 23, 1994, the jury acquitted her of the charge of malicious wounding by reason of temporary insanity. She was committed to a state mental hospital for further assessment and treatment and released a few months later.

acquittal. Yet it is important to keep in mind that the number of such cases is quite small. Surveys show that the public dramatically overestimates the percentage of defendants who plead insanity, guessing it to be 30 to 40 percent, when in fact it is less than 1 percent (Steadman et al., 1993). Moreover, research suggests that only a minority of these defendants fake or exaggerate their psychological symptoms (Grossman &

Wasyliw, 1988), and only a quarter are actually found not guilty by reason of insanity (Callahan et al., 1991). That is, less than one out of every 400 defendants in the United States is found not guilty by reason of insanity.

During most of United States history, the successful insanity plea amounted to the same thing as a long-term prison sentence—indeed, often a longer sentence than a verdict of guilty would have brought (Ogloff et al., 1992). Treatment in a mental hospital wrought little, if any, improvement, and mental health professionals were therefore reluctant to assert that the offender was unlikely to commit a crime again. However, the increasing effectiveness of drug therapy in institutions, the growing bias against extended institutionalization, and greater emphasis on patients' rights have led of late to earlier releases of offenders from mental hospitals (Blackburn, 1993). In 1992, in the case of *Foucha* v. *Louisiana,* the U.S. Supreme court ruled that the only basis for determining the release of such individuals is whether or not they are still "insane"; they cannot be indefinitely detained in state mental hospitals simply because they are dangerous.

> ### Consider This
> After a patient has been criminally committed to an institution, why might a clinician be reluctant to declare that the person is mentally stable and unlikely to commit the same crime again, even if the patient has shown significant improvement?

### Recent Trends

In recent years, twelve states have added the option of a verdict of "guilty but mentally ill" when a jury is determining the guilt or innocence of a defendant who has pleaded insanity (Steadman et al., 1993). Defendants who receive this verdict are found to have had a mental illness at the time of their crimes, but the illness was not sufficiently related to or responsible for the crime to acquit them of the offense. The "guilty but mentally ill" option allows jurors to convict a person they perceive as dangerous while attempting also to ensure that the individual's therapeutic needs will be met. Defendants found to be guilty but mentally ill are given a prison term with the proviso that they will also undergo treatment if necessary.

Advocates of this new option see it as a better means of maintaining and defending our society's standards of behavior. In Georgia, juries given the option of declaring a person guilty but mentally ill have, in fact, delivered insanity acquittals less often (Callahan et al., 1992). Research with mock juries also has found that the verdict of guilty but mentally ill is readily used by jurors as a compromise, resulting in a two-thirds reduction in verdicts of guilty or not guilty by reason of insanity (Poulson, 1990).

Critics of the concept believe that appropriate mental health care should be made available to all prison-

ers anyway, without any special designation (Cohen, 1993), and point out that the prevalence of mental disorders is much higher among prisoners than among the general population (Gunn et al., 1991; Teplin, 1990). They argue that the verdict often differs from a guilty verdict in name only (Tanay, 1992; Petrella et al., 1985). Critics also argue that the new verdict option may only confuse jurors already faced with an enormously complex task (APA, 1983; Morris, 1983).

Some states allow still another kind of defense, "guilty with diminished capacity." Here a defendant's mental instability is viewed as an extenuating circumstance that should help determine precisely which crime the defendant is guilty of (Slovenko, 1992). The defense lawyer argues that mental dysfunctioning prevented the defendant from having the capacity to harbor the mental intent required for a particular crime, and the accused person should therefore be found guilty of a lesser crime, for example, of manslaughter (murder without prior intent) instead of murder in the first degree (planned murder).

### Sex Offender Statutes

Ever since 1937, when Michigan enacted the first "sex psychopath" statute, many states have given a special designation to sex offenders (Monahan & Davis, 1983). These states presume that persons who are repeatedly found guilty of certain sex crimes have a

*Each segment of the clinical field has its own "forensic" specialists who represent it in the courts and houses of legislature. Forensic psychologists, psychiatrists, and social workers typically receive special training in such duties as evaluating the functioning of criminal defendants, making recommendations concerning patients' rights, and assessing the psychological trauma experienced by crime victims.*

mental disorder and categorize them as "mentally disordered sex offenders."

Unlike defendants who have been found not guilty by reason of insanity, people classified as mentally disordered sex offenders have been convicted of a criminal offense and are thus judged to be morally responsible for their actions. Nevertheless, the status of a sex offender, like that of a person found not guilty by reason of insanity, implies that commitment to a mental health facility is a more appropriate sentence than imprisonment (Small, 1992). In part, such statutes reflect society's conception of sex offenders as sick people. On a practical level, the provisions help prevent the physical abuse that sex offenders sometimes face as ostracized members of prison society.

In recent years a growing number of states have modified or abolished these sex offender statutes and programs. There are several reasons for this trend. First, many states have found these statutes difficult to act on. Some state statutes, for example, require that a candidate for sex offender status be found "sexually dangerous beyond a reasonable doubt," a judgment that often goes beyond the clinical field's expertise (Szasz, 1991). Also, there is evidence that racial bias can significantly affect the assignment of sex offender status (Sturgeon & Taylor, 1980). White Americans are twice as likely to be granted sex offender status as African Americans and Hispanic Americans who have been convicted of similar crimes.

## Criminal Commitment and Incompetence to Stand Trial

Regardless of their state of mind at the time of a crime, defendants may be held to be *mentally incompetent* to stand trial. The competence provisions have been established to ensure that defendants understand the charges and proceedings they are facing and have "sufficient present ability to consult with" their counsel in preparing and conducting an adequate defense. This minimum standard of competence was specified by the Supreme Court in the case of *Dusky v. United States* (1960).

Competence issues typically are raised by the defendant's attorney, although prosecutors and arresting police officers may bring the issue before the court as well (Meyer, 1992). All parties (including the presiding judge) are usually careful to recommend a psycho-

logical examination, usually on an inpatient basis, for any defendant who seems to exhibit signs of mental dysfunctioning. They prefer to err on the side of caution because some convictions have been reversed on appeal when a defendant's competence was not initially established. If the court holds that the defendant is incompetent to participate in his or her defense, the individual is assigned to a mental health facility until he or she is competent to stand trial (Bennett & Kish, 1990). It is important to note that many more cases of criminal commitment result from decisions of mental incompetence than from verdicts of not guilty by reason of insanity (Blackburn, 1993).

A risk inherent in competence provisions is that an innocent defendant may spend years in a mental health facility without having the opportunity to disprove accusations of criminal conduct in court. Some defendants have served longer "sentences" in mental health facilities awaiting competence than they would have in prison if they had been convicted (Meyer, 1992). The possibility of such abuses was curbed by an important Supreme Court ruling in the case of *Jackson v. Indiana* (1972). In this case the Court ruled that a chronically disordered defendant cannot be indefinitely committed under criminal status. After a reasonable amount of time, he or she should be either found competent and tried, set free, or transferred to a mental health facility under civil commitment procedures.

Until the early 1970s, most states followed the practice of requiring the commitment of mentally incompetent defendants to maximum security institutions for the "criminally insane" (Winick, 1983). Under current law, the courts have greater flexibility in such matters. In some cases, particularly when the charge is a minor one, the defendant may be treated on an outpatient basis.

---

*Mental incompetence*   A state of mental instability that leaves defendants unable to understand the legal charges and proceedings they are facing and unable to adequately prepare a defense with their lawyer.

---

*Summing Up*
*Clinicians are often called upon to evaluate the mental stability of people accused of crimes. In some cases, their evaluations influence judges or juries to rule that defendants are not guilty because they were insane during the commission of their crimes. Such judgments are made in accordance with a legal definition of insanity, based in some U.S. jurisdictions on the M'Naghten rule and in others on the American Law Institute test. In other cases, the evaluations of mental health professionals may influence judges to rule that defendants are mentally incompetent to stand trial for a crime and should receive treatment until they are competent.*

# Legal Influences on the Mental Health System

The legal system also has had a significant impact on clinical professionals. First, courts and legislatures have developed the process of **civil commitment**, whereby certain individuals can be forced to undergo mental health treatment. Second, the legal system, on behalf of the state, has also taken on the responsibility of specifying and protecting patients' rights during treatment. The protection of patients' rights is obviously important for those individuals with disorders who have been involuntarily committed, but it is also important for those who have voluntarily sought institutionalization or even outpatient therapy.

## Civil Commitment

Every year in the United States large numbers of mentally disturbed persons are involuntarily committed to mental institutions. These commitments have long been a focus of controversy and debate. In some ways the law provides greater protection for the suspected criminal than for people suspected of displaying psychosis (Burton, 1990).

### Why Commit?

Generally our legal system permits involuntary commitment of individuals when they are considered to be *in need of treatment* and *dangerous to themselves or others*. The state's authority to commit disturbed individuals rests on two principles: *parens patriae* and *police power* (Wettstein, 1988). Under the principle of *parens patriae* ("father of the country"), the state can impose decisions, including involuntary hospitalization, that promote the *individual's* best interests and protect him or her from self-harm or self-neglect. Conversely, police power enables the state to protect *society* from the harm that may be inflicted by a person who is homicidal or otherwise violent.

### Current Procedures

Laws governing the civil commitment process vary from state to state. Some basic procedures, however, are common to most of these laws.

Many formal commitment proceedings are initiated by family members. In response to a son's suicide attempt, for example, his parents may try to persuade him to commit himself to a mental institution. If the son refuses, the parents may go to court and seek an involuntary commitment order. If the son is a minor, the process is simple. It need only be demonstrated that a mental health professional considers such commitment warranted. If the son is an adult, however, the process is more elaborate. The court will usually order a mental examination and provide the individual with the opportunity to contest the commitment attempt in court, often with representation by a lawyer (Holstein, 1993).

Although the Supreme Court has offered few guidelines on the procedural aspects of civil commitment, one important decision, rendered in the case of *Addington v. Texas* (1979), has outlined the *minimum standard of proof* necessary for commitment. Here, the Court ruled that before an individual can be committed, there must be "clear and convincing" proof that he or she is mentally ill and has met the state's criteria for involuntary commitment. It is important to note that the ruling does not suggest what criteria should be used. This matter is left to each state. The ruling determines only the minimum standard of proof that should be applied to whatever commitment criteria the state chooses to enforce.

### Emergency Commitment

Many situations require immediate action; no one can wait for formal commitment proceedings when a life is at stake. An emergency room patient who is suicidal may need immediate treatment and round-the-clock supervision. If treatment could not be applied in such situations without the patient's full consent, the consequences could be tragic.

Therefore, many states give attending physicians (not necessarily psychiatrists in certain states) the right to order temporary commitment and medication of a patient who is behaving in a bizarre or violent manner (Holstein, 1993). Usually the states require certification by two physicians that such patients are in a state of mind that makes them dangerous to themselves or others. Such certifications are often referred to as *two-physician certificates,* or "2 PCs." Limitations on the length of such emergency commitments vary from state to state, but three days is often the limit. Should the physicians who provide treatment determine that a longer period of commitment is necessary, formal commitment proceedings may be initiated.

### Who Is Dangerous?

In the past, people with mental disorders were actually less likely to commit violent or dangerous acts than people without such disorders. It now appears that

---

*Civil commitment*    A legal process by which certain individuals can be forced to undergo mental health treatment.

*The criminal justice system's ability to predict dangerousness is often tragically inadequate, as we are reminded by the case of Jeffrey Dahmer. In 1988, Dahmer was imprisoned for sexually molesting a 13-year-old boy. In 1990, despite his own father's stated concerns, Dahmer was released with only limited followup. By his own admission, he proceeded to drug, strangle, and dismember at least fifteen additional victims.*

these low rates of violence were related, at least in part, to the fact that so many such persons resided in institutions. With the advent of deinstitutionalization and the presence of hundreds of thousands of severely disturbed individuals in the community who currently receive little or no treatment, this pattern has shown signs of shifting.

Although approximately 90 percent of people with mental disorders are in no way violent or dangerous (Swanson et al., 1990), recent studies suggest a modest relationship between severe mental disorders and violent behavior. After reviewing a number of studies, the noted law and psychology professor John Monahan (1993, 1992) concluded the following:

Approximately 15 percent of patients in mental hospitals have assaulted another person prior to admission.

Around 25 percent of patients in mental hospitals assault another person during hospitalization.

Approximately 12 percent of community residents with schizophrenia, major depression, or bipolar disorder have assaulted other people, compared to 2 percent of persons without a mental disorder.

Approximately 4 percent of persons who report having been violent during the past year suffer from schizophrenia. One percent of nonviolent persons suffer from schizophrenia.

Monahan cautions that these findings do not suggest that people with mental disorders are generally dangerous. Nor do they justify the "caricature of the mentally disordered" that is often portrayed by the media, the "shunning of former patients by employers and neighbors," or the "lock 'em up" laws proposed by some politicians. On the other hand, they do indicate that a severe psychological disorder may sometimes be more of a risk factor for violence than mental health experts have generally believed.

Because a determination of dangerousness is frequently required for judicial approval of involuntary civil commitment, the reliable and valid determination of who is dangerous is of major importance. But can mental health professionals accurately predict who will commit violent acts? Unfortunately, research suggests that psychiatrists and psychologists are wrong more often than right when they make *long-term* predictions of violence (McNiel & Binder, 1991; Monahan & Walker, 1990). Most frequently they overestimate the likelihood that a patient will eventually engage in violent behavior. Still, studies suggest that *short-term* predictions—predictions of imminent violence—are more accurate than long-term ones (McNiel & Binder, 1991). Moreover, researchers are now working, with some success, on the development of new assessment and prediction techniques that employ statistical approaches and are relatively more accurate (Campbell, 1995; Klassen & O'Conner, 1988).

## Criticisms of Civil Commitment

Civil commitment has been criticized on several grounds. First, the criterion of dangerousness is a bone of contention. If judgments of dangerousness are often inaccurate, why should they be used as grounds to deprive someone of liberty (Ennis & Emery, 1978)? Second, the legal definitions of "mental illness" and "dangerousness" are vague. The terms may be defined so broadly that there is a danger they will be applied to anyone the evaluators view as undesirable or inferior (Wexler, 1983). Third, the therapeutic value of commitment itself has sometimes been called into question. Research suggests that many persons committed involuntarily do not respond well to therapy (Wanck, 1984). Perceptions of choice and control and personal commitment may be important determinants of a successful outcome in a therapeutic setting (Langer, 1983).

On the basis of these and other arguments, some clinicians hold that involuntary commitment should be abolished (Szasz, 1977, 1963). Moreover, many civil libertarians are wary that involuntary commitment may be abused for purposes of coercive control (Morse, 1982; Ennis & Emory, 1978). Indeed, such abuses by the state have been reported frequently in the former Soviet Union and other countries, where mental hospitals have been used routinely to incarcerate political dissidents.

## Trends in Civil Commitment

The acceptance of broad involuntary commitment statutes probably reached its peak in 1962. In the case of *Robinson* v. *California*, the Supreme Court ruled that the sentencing of persons with drug addictions to correctional institutions may violate the Constitution's ban on cruel and unusual punishment, and it recommended involuntary civil commitment to a mental hospital as a more reasonable action. This ruling encouraged the application of civil commitment proceedings against many kinds of "social deviants." In the years immediately following this ruling, civil commitment procedures granted far fewer rights to "defendants" than did criminal courts (Holstein, 1993). It was particularly difficult for involuntarily committed patients to obtain their release.

During the late 1960s and early 1970s, the plight of the committed was increasingly publicized by reporters, novelists, and civil libertarians who were convinced that numerous persons were being committed unjustifiably. As the public became more aware of the problems surrounding involuntary commitment, state legislatures started to enact stricter and more precise standards for commitment (Holstein, 1993). In turn, rates of involuntary commitment declined, release rates increased, and court decisions favored the broadening of patients' rights (Wanck, 1984).

As a result of this trend, fewer people are institutionalized through civil commitment procedures today than in the past. This state of affairs has not led to more criminal behavior or arrests among people who would have been committed under broader criteria (Teplin et al., 1994; Hiday, 1992). Nevertheless, some

states have become concerned that commitment criteria are now too narrow, and they have started to broaden their criteria once again (Beck & Parry, 1992; Belcher & Blank, 1990). Whether this broadening will actually lead to a return to the vague commitment procedures of past years and whether such a trend is in fact advantageous will become clearer in the coming years.

## Protecting Patients' Rights

Over the past two decades the legal rights of patients with mental disorders have been significantly expanded by court decisions and state and federal legislation. The rights that have received the most attention have been the *right to treatment* and the *right to refuse treatment*.

### The Right to Treatment

If people are committed to mental institutions because of a need for treatment and then do not receive treatment there, the mental institutions become mere prisons for the unconvicted. Faced with the inadequacies of large state mental institutions, some patients and their legal representatives began in the 1960s and 1970s to demand the treatment they felt the state was obligated to provide. A suit filed on those grounds on behalf of institutionalized patients in Alabama led to a landmark in the battle for patients' rights. In the 1972 case of *Wyatt* v. *Stickney*, a federal court ruled that the state was constitutionally obligated to provide "adequate treatment" to all persons who had been committed involuntarily, and it ordered Alabama to provide more therapists, better living conditions, more privacy, opportunities for heterosexual interaction and physical exercise, and a more judicious use of physical restraint and medication. Many of these standards have since been adopted in other court jurisdictions.

Another important decision was handed down in 1975 by the Supreme Court in the case of *O'Connor* v. *Donaldson*. After being confined in a Florida mental institution for more than fourteen years, Kenneth Donaldson sued for release. He argued that, although he had repeatedly sought release and had been overruled by the institution's psychiatrists, he and his fellow patients were receiving inadequate treatment, being largely ignored by the staff, and allowed minimal personal freedom. The Supreme Court ruled in favor of Donaldson, fined the hospital's superintendent, and ruled that such institutions must engage in periodic

---

*Right to treatment*   The legal right of persons, particularly those who are involuntarily committed, to receive adequate treatment.

reviews of their patients' cases. The justices also stated unanimously that the state "cannot constitutionally confine . . . a non-dangerous individual who is capable of surviving safely in freedom by himself or with the help of willing and responsible family members or friends." In a later case of importance, *Youngberg v. Romeo* (1982), the Supreme Court further ruled that persons committed involuntarily have a constitutional right to "reasonably nonrestrictive confinement conditions" as well as "reasonable care and safety."

To make sure that patients with psychological disorders do indeed obtain the rights they gained throughout the 1970s, Congress passed the Protection and Advocacy for Mentally Ill Individuals Act in 1986 (Woodside & Legg, 1990). This law established protection and advocacy systems in all states and U.S. territories and gave advocates who worked for patients the power to investigate possible cases of patient abuse and neglect, and to address these problems legally.

In recent years public advocates have argued that the right to treatment should be extended to the tens of thousands of persons with severe mental disorders who are repeatedly released from hospitals after a short stay and are essentially sent to the streets to care for themselves, often winding up homeless or in prisons. Many mental health advocates are now suing federal and state agencies across the country, demanding that they fulfill the promises of the community mental health movement.

## The Right to Refuse Treatment

During the past two decades, the courts have also established that patients, particularly those in institutions, have the right to refuse certain forms of treatment. Most of the "right to refuse treatment" rulings have centered on *biological treatments*—treatments that are easier to impose on patients without their cooperation and that often seem more intrusive, aversive, and hazardous than psychotherapy. For example, state rulings have consistently granted patients the right to refuse psychosurgery, the form of physical treatment considered most clearly irreversible and therefore most dangerous.

As we saw in Chapter 4, some states have also acknowledged a patient's right to refuse electroconvulsive therapy (ECT), the treatment used in many cases of unipolar depression. The right-to-refuse issue is much less clear-cut with regard to ECT than with respect to psychosurgery. ECT is highly effective for many persons with severe depression. On the other hand, ECT is an extremely aversive form of treatment.

*Right to refuse treatment* The legal right of patients to refuse certain forms of treatment.

In the past, patients did not have the right to refuse psychotropic medications. States viewed these drugs as a benign form of treatment that often helped and rarely hurt patients. As we have seen repeatedly, however, many psychotropic drugs, particularly antipsychotic drugs, are indeed exceedingly powerful and sometimes produce unwanted dangerous, effects. As these undesired effects have become more apparent, some states have granted patients the right to refuse medication. Typically, these states require physicians to explain the purpose of the medication in question to patients and obtain their written consent. If the patient's refusal is considered incompetent, dangerous, or irrational, it can be overturned by an independent psychiatrist, medical committee, or local court (Prehn, 1990; Wettstein, 1988). However, the refusing patient is supported in this review process by a lawyer or a patient advocate.

## Other Rights of Patients

Still other patient rights have also been safeguarded by court decisions over the past few decades. In the 1973 case of *Sounder v. Brennan,* for example, a district court ruled that patients who perform work in mental institutions must receive payment in accordance with the Fair Labor Standards Act. Later the Supreme Court ruled that this right applied in private mental institutions but not in state hospitals.

In the 1974 case of *Stoner v. Miller,* a district court ruled that patients released from state mental hospitals have a right to live in community "adult homes." Similarly, other court decisions during the 1970s acknowledged the right of deinstitutionalized individuals to aftercare treatment.

In the 1975 case of *Dixon v. Weinberger,* a district court ruled that individuals whose psychological disorder is not severe enough to require confinement in a mental institution should receive treatment in less restrictive facilities. If an inpatient program at a community mental health center is available, for example, then that is the facility to which such people should be committed, not a mental hospital.

## The "Rights" Debate

Few would argue with the intent of these guaranteed patient rights. However, many clinicians express concern that these guaranteed rights sometimes lead to undesirable outcomes and may even serve to deprive patients of opportunities for effective recovery. Consider the right to refuse medication. Evidence suggests that this right or the procedures needed to safeguard it may deprive some patients of a faster, more complete

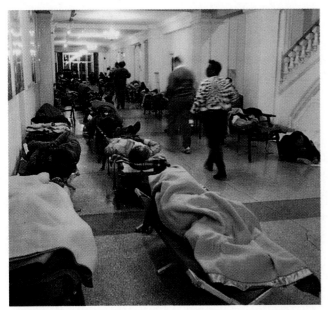

*Although "guaranteed" the right to live in community adult homes, many patients with chronic and severe mental disorders receive no treatment or guidance and wind up on the streets or in public shelters, such as this shelter for the homeless in Washington, D.C.*

recovery (Sheline & Beattie, 1992). If medications can help bring about the recovery of a patient with schizophrenia, does not the patient have the right to that recovery? If confusion causes patients to refuse medication, can clinicians in good conscience go along with that refusal and delay medication while legal channels are cleared? The psychologist Marilyn Whiteside raises concerns of this kind in her description of a 25-year-old patient with mental retardation:

> He was 25 and severely retarded. And after his favorite attendant left, he became self-abusive. He beat his fists against the side of his head until a football helmet had to be ordered for his protection. Then he clawed at his face and gouged out one of his eyes.
>
> The institution psychologists began a behavior program that had mildly aversive consequences: they squirted warm water in his face each time he engaged in self-abuse. When that didn't work, they requested permission to use an electric prod. The Human Rights Committee vetoed this "excessive and inhumane form of correction" because, after all, the young man was retarded, not criminal.
>
> Since nothing effective could be done that abridged the rights and negated the dignity of the developmentally disabled patient, he was verbally reprimanded for his behavior—and allowed to push his thumb through his remaining eye. He is now blind, of course, but he has his rights and presumably his dignity.
>
> *(Whiteside, 1983, p. 13)*

On the other side of the argument, it must be pointed out that the clinical field has not always monitored itself with respect to patients' rights (see Box 17-2). Over the years, for example, many treatment programs have administered medications and other biological treatments carelessly, excessively, or harmfully (Crane, 1973). So the courts and state legislatures have stepped in.

One must also ask whether the field's present state of knowledge justifies allowing clinicians to override patients' rights. That is, can clinicians confidently say that certain treatments will indeed help patients? And can they predict and overcome the potential unwanted effects of certain forms of treatment? Since today's clinicians themselves often are in conflict concerning these issues, it seems appropriate that patients, their advocates, and impartial evaluators continue to play significant roles in the decision-making process.

# *Mental Health, Business, and Economics*

The legislative and judicial systems are not the only social institutions with which mental health professionals interact. Among the others that influence and are influenced by clinical practice and study are the business and economic sectors of society.

## Business and Mental Health

Psychological disorders are among the ten leading work-related diseases and injuries in the United States (Millar, 1984). Moreover, in some states, the number of stress-related worker's compensation claims has risen as much as 700 percent during the past decade (Schut, 1992). The business world has turned to clinical professionals to help develop programs to prevent and remedy such problems (NIOSH, 1988, 1985). Two programs that have gained broad acceptance in the past decade are employee assistance programs and stress-reduction and problem-solving seminars.

***Employee assistance programs*** are run either by mental health professionals who are employed directly by a company or by consulting mental health agencies. Companies publicize the availability of such services in the workplace, educate workers about mental dysfunctioning, and teach supervisors how to identify and refer workers who are in psychological trouble. ***Stress-***

## Box 17-2

# *Ethics and the Mental Health Field*

Discussions of the legal and mental health systems may sometimes give the impression that clinicians are uncaring practitioners who address patients' rights and needs only when they are being monitored by outside forces. This, of course, is not the case. Most clinicians care greatly about their clients and strive to help them and at the same time respect their rights and dignity.

But clinicians do face considerable obstacles in the pursuit of these goals. First, patients' rights and proper care are often complex questions that do not have simple or obvious answers. Second, clinicians, like other kinds of professionals, often have difficulty appreciating the full impact of their actions or altering the system in which they work. Indeed, thousands of conscientious and caring clinicians contributed to the appalling system of institutional care that marked the first half of this century—partly because they did not appreciate how misguided the system was and partly because they felt totally helpless to change the system. A third problem is that, like other professions, the clinical field includes at least a few practitioners who place their own needs and wishes before others'. For the integrity of the profession and the protection of individual clients, such professionals need to be monitored and regulated.

Clinicians do not rely exclusively on the legislative and court systems to address such obstacles to proper and effective clinical practice. They also regulate themselves by continually thinking about, developing, and revising

ethical guidelines for members of the field. Many legal decisions simply place the power of law behind these already-existing professional guidelines.

Each profession within the mental health field has a code of ethics. The code of the American Psychological Association exemplifies the kinds of issues with which the various mental health professions are concerned (APA, 1992). The current code addresses a number of specific points, including the following.

1. *Psychologists are permitted to offer advice* in self-help books, television and radio programs, newspaper and magazine articles, mailed material, and other nontraditional vehicles and settings, provided they do so responsibly and professionally and base their advice on appropriate psychological literature and practices.

2. *Psychologists may not engage in fraudulent research, plagiarizing the work of others or publishing fabricated data or falsified results.* During the past fifteen years, cases of scientific fraud or misconduct have been uncovered in all of the sciences, including psychology. These acts have led to misunderstandings of important issues, taken scientific inquiries in the wrong direction, and undermined public trust. Unfortunately, the effects of research misconduct are hard to undo even after a retraction. The impressions created by false findings may continue to influence the thinking of

both the public and other scientists for years (Pfeifer & Snodgrass, 1990).

3. *Psychologists must acknowledge their limitations with regard to patients who are disabled or whose gender, ethnicity, language, socioeconomic status, or sexual orientation differs from that of the therapist.* This requirement often means that a psychologist should obtain additional training or supervision, consult with an appropriate colleague, or make appropriate referrals in order "to ensure the competence of their services."

4. *Psychologists who make evaluations and testify in legal cases must base their assessments on sufficient information and substantiate their findings appropriately.* If an adequate examination of the individual in question is not possible, psychologists must make clear the limited nature of their testimony.

5. *Psychologists are prohibited from exploiting the trust and dependency of clients and students, sexually or otherwise.* This guideline is meant to address the broad social problem of sexual harassment, as well as the problem of therapists who take sexual advantage of clients in therapy. The current code specifically prohibits psychologists from engaging in sexual intimacies with a present or former therapy client for at least two years after the end of treatment; and even then such

conduct is permissible only in "the most unusual circumstances." Moreover, psychologists may not accept as clients people with whom they have previously engaged in sexual intimacies.

How many therapists actually have a sexual relationship with a client? A 1977 study found that 12.1 percent of male and 2.6 percent of female psychologists admitted having sexual contact with patients (Holroyd & Brodsky, 1977). A 1989 survey of 4,800 therapists revealed that 0.9 percent of male therapists and 0.2 percent of female therapists had had sexual contact with patients (Borys & Pope, 1989). The decline in sexual misconduct by therapists revealed by these studies may indicate that fewer therapists are in fact having sexual relationships with patients (Pope & Bouhoutsos, 1986; Walker & Young, 1986). Alternatively, today's therapists may simply be less willing to admit, even anonymously, the misbehavior that is a felony in a growing number of states.

6. *Psychologists must also adhere to the principle of confidentiality.* The code of ethics affirms that for a client's peace of mind and to facilitate effective therapy, clients must be able to trust that their private exchanges with a therapist will not be disclosed to others. There are times, however, when the principle of complete confidentiality must be compromised. An ex-

ception may arise, for example, in cases of outpatients who are clearly dangerous, even homicidal. In such cases, a therapist may breach confidentiality to initiate involuntary commitment proceedings.

A further qualification of the confidentiality principle has been added as a result of a 1976 ruling by the California Supreme Court in the case of *Tarasoff* v. *Regents of the University of California,* considered one of the most important court decisions affecting client-therapist relationships. The Tarasoff case concerned a mental health outpatient at a University of California hospital who confided to his therapist that he wanted to harm his former girlfriend, Tanya Tarasoff. Several days after terminating therapy, the former patient fulfilled his wish. He stabbed Tanya Tarasoff to death.

Should confidentiality have been breached in this case? The therapist, in fact, felt that it should. Campus police were notified, but the patient was released after some questioning. In their suit against the hospital and therapist, the victim's parents argued that the therapist should have also warned them and their daughter that the patient intended to harm Ms. Tarasoff. The court agreed: "The protective privilege ends where the public peril begins."

In partial concession to the Tarasoff ruling, the current APA code of ethics declares that therapists should reveal confi-

dential information, even without the client's consent, when it is necessary "to protect the patient or client or others from harm." Since the Tarasoff ruling, California's courts have further clarified that therapists are obligated to protect persons who are in close proximity to a client's intended victim (for example, the intended victim's children) and thus in danger. They have also held that the *duty to protect* applies only when the intended victim is identified or readily identifiable, rather than the public at large, and it does not apply when violence is unforeseeable or when the object of a client's intended violence is property rather than a person. A number of other states have either adopted the California courts' rulings or modified them (Pietrofesa et al., 1990). Only a few states have rejected the California principles outright. Moreover, many states have adopted a "Duty to Protect Bill" designed to clarify the standards for confidentiality and action by mental health professionals and protect them from certain civil suits (Monahan, 1993).

Most of today's therapists agree that it is often appropriate to breech confidentiality. Indeed, in one survey almost 80 percent of the therapists reported having broken confidentiality when a client was suicidal, 62 percent when child abuse was occurring, and 58 percent when a client was homicidal (Pope et al., 1987).

## Box 17-3

### *The Itemized Statement in Clinical Psychiatry: A New Concept in Billing*

*(In this article, by Robert S. Hoffman, M.D., which originally appeared in* The Journal of Irreproducible Results, *1980, the psychiatrist's biting wit is equaled only by his sense of outrage over the growing demands made by insurance companies.)*

Due to the rapidly escalating costs of health care delivery, there has been increasing pressure on physicians to document and justify their charges for professional services. This has created a number of serious problems, particularly in the field of psychiatry. Chief among these is the breach of confidentiality that arises when sensitive clinical information is provided to third-party insurance carriers, e.g. the patient's diagnosis or related details about his/her psychiatric disorder. Even when full disclosure of such information is made, insurance carriers frequently deny benefits because the description of the treatment appears imprecise or inadequate. There also has been some criticism of the standard hourly fee-for-service, the argument being that psychiatrists, like other medical specialists, should be required to adjust their fees depending upon the particular treatment offered.

In view of these considerations, a method is required which will bring psychiatric billing in line with accepted medical practice. The procedure illustrated below, which we have successfully employed in our clinic for the past two years, achieves this goal. It requires only a modest investment in time and effort: the tape-recording of all psychotherapy sessions, transcription of tapes, tabulation of therapeutic interventions, and establishment of a relative value scale for the commonly used maneuvers. This can easily be

managed by two full-time medical billing personnel per psychiatrist. The method, in our hands, has been found to increase collections from third-party carriers by 65% and to raise a typical psychiatrist's annual net income almost to the level of a municipal street sweeper or plumber's assistant.

Below is a specimen monthly statement illustrating these principles:

CALVIN L. SKOLNIK, M.D., INC.

A Psychiatry Corporation

Jan. 5, 1978

Mr. Sheldon Rosenberg
492 West Maple Dr.
East Orange, N.J.

Dear Mr. Rosenberg:

In response to the request by your insurer, Great Lakes Casualty and Surety Co., for more precise documentation of professional services rendered, I have prepared the enclosed itemization for the month of December. I trust that this will clarify the situation sufficiently for your benefit payments to be resumed.

Until next Tuesday at 11:00, I remain

Cordially,

CALVIN L. SKOLNIK, M.D.

*reduction* and *problem-solving seminars* are workshops or group sessions in which mental health professionals teach employees coping, problem-solving, and stress-reduction techniques (Kagan et al., 1995). Programs of this kind are just as likely to be organized for higher-level executives as for middle-level managers and assembly-line workers. The expectation of businesses is that these various programs will save money by helping workers develop coping skills that lead to a healthier state of mind, less dysfunctioning on the job, and better job performance.

## Economics and Mental Health

Government-level economic decisions may influence the mental health field's treatment of people with psychological disorders. At first glance, funding for mental health services seems to have risen sharply in the United States over the past two decades. A total of $23 billion was spent on such services in 1988, compared to $3.3 billion in 1969 (Redick et al., 1992). However, if adjustments are made for inflation and funding is stated in 1969 dollars, the 1988 expen-

Charges

| | | | |
|---|---|---|---|
| 140 | clarifications | @ .25 | 35.00 |
| 157 | restatements | @ .25 | 39.25 |
| 17 | broad-focus questions | @ .35 | 5.95 |
| 42 | narrow-focus questions | @ .30 | 12.60 |
| 86 | reflections of dominant emotional theme | @ .35 | 30.10 |
| 38 | resolutions of inconsistencies | @ .45 | 17.10 |
| 22 | pointings out of nonverbal communications | @ .40 | 8.80 |
| 187 | encouragements to say more | @ .15 | 28.05 |
| 371 | sympathetic nods with furrowed brow | @ .10 | 37.10 |
| 517 | acknowledgments of information reception (Uh-huhs, Um-hmmm, etc.) | @ .08 | 41.36 |
| 24 | interpretations of unconscious defense configurations | @ .30 | 7.20 |
| 16 | absolution for evil deeds | @ .50 | 8.00 |
| 2 | pieces of advice | @ .75 | 1.50 |
| 6 | expressions of personal feelings | @ .50 | 3.00 |
| 2 | personal reminiscences | @ .65 | 1.30 |
| 35 | misc. responses (sighs, grunts, belches, etc.) | @ .20 | 7.00 |
| 7 | listening to remarks disparaging therapist's appearance, personal habits, or technique | @ 1.75 | 12.25 |
| 12 | listening to sarcastic remarks about psychiatry | @ 1.00 | 12.00 |
| 3 | listening to psychiatrist jokes | @ .80 | 2.40 |
| 3 | telephone calls to therapist | @ .15 | .45 |
| 1 | telephone call to therapist at especially inopportune moment | @ 10.50 | 10.50 |
| 22 | Kleenex tissues | @ .005 | .11 |
| 1 | ashtray | @ 3.50 | 3.50 |
| 1 | filling and repainting of 1 ashtray-size dent in wall | @ 27.50 | 27.50 |
| 1 | shampooing of soft drink stain on carpet | @ 15.00 | 15.00 |
| 1 | letter of excuse from work | @ 2.50 | 2.50 |
| 2 | surcharges for unusually boring or difficult sessions | @ 35.00 | 70.00 |
| | Subtotal: charges | | $438.52 |

Credits

| | | | |
|---|---|---|---|
| 4 | unusually interesting anecdotes | @ .45 | 1.80 |
| 3 | good jokes | @ .50 | 1.50 |
| 1 | item of gossip about another patient which was found useful in her therapy | @ 3.50 | 3.50 |
| 1 | apology for sarcastic remark | @ 1.00 | 1.00 |
| 1 | use of case history at American Psychiatric Association convention | | 10.00 |
| ½ | chicken salad sandwich on whole wheat c/mayo | @ 1.75 | .88 |
| 7 | bummed cigarettes (65¢/pack) | | .23 |
| 1 | damaged Librium tablet, returned unused | | .10 |
| | Subtotal: credits | | $ 18.99 |
| | Total: PLEASE REMIT— | | $419.53 |

diture is $5.3 billion, a more modest rise from the 1969 total. Thus, although the number of persons in need of or seeking therapy has increased significantly, funding for such services is increasing only modestly. This imbalance inevitably affects the length and frequency of services mental health professionals can supply.

In response to these financial realities, more and more people have to pay for mental health services themselves, and private insurance companies have become a major source of support for such services. Only 56 percent of all mental health services are now government-supported; 44 percent are paid for by direct client fees and private insurance reimbursements (Taube, 1990).

The growing economic role of private insurance companies has a significant effect on the way clinicians go about their work (see Box 17-3). In an effort to reduce their expenditures and to monitor what they are paying for, many of these companies have, for example, developed *managed care systems* in which the insurance company often determines such issues as which therapists clients may choose, the cost of sessions, and the number of sessions a client may be reimbursed for.

Most insurance companies have also instituted a *peer review system* in which a panel of clinicians who essentially work for the insurance companies may periodically review a therapist's report of a client's treatment and recommend that insurance benefits be either continued or terminated. In some cases, insurers require details from the therapist's session notes, often including intimate personal information about the patient in question (Goleman, 1993).

Many therapists and clients dislike peer reviews, claiming that the reports that therapists must make breach confidentiality, even when efforts are made to safeguard anonymity, and that the value of therapy in a given case is sometimes difficult to convey in a brief report. Some also argue that peer review inevitably works to shorten therapy, even if longer-term treatment would be advisable in particular cases.

# The Person within the Profession

The actions and goals of clinical researchers and practitioners not only influence and are influenced by other institutions but are closely tied to their own personal needs and goals. Abnormal psychology is a discipline in which the human strengths, imperfections, wisdom, and clumsiness of its professionals combine to influence the effectiveness of the profession as a whole. We have seen that the needs and preferences of these human beings influence their responses to clients' concerns, their theoretical orientations, and the kinds of clients they choose to work with. And we have also noted that personal leanings sometimes overcome professional standards and lead in extreme cases to instances of research fraud by clinical scientists and sexual misconduct by therapists.

A survey on the mental health of therapists found that 71 percent of 509 psychotherapists reported being in therapy at least once, about a fifth of them three or more times (Norcross et al., 1987). Their reasons for seeking therapy were largely the same as those of other clients: emotional problems, depression, and anxiety topped the list. In related research, a sample of psychotherapists reported being brought up in dysfunctional families, sometimes marked by high rates of physical and sexual abuse, parental alcoholism, insti-

*"Beth, you must learn to recognize Sam's needs, and, Sam, you must learn to recognize Beth's needs, and you both must learn to recognize my needs."*
*(Drawing by Maslin; © 1993 The New Yorker Magazine, Inc.)*

tutionalization of a parent in a mental hospital, or death of a family member (Elliot & Guy, 1993).

The science and profession of abnormal psychology has lofty goals: to understand, predict, and change abnormal functioning. But we must not lose sight of the context in which its activities are conducted. Mental health researchers and clinicians are human beings, living within a society of human beings, working to serve human beings. The mixture of discovery, misdirection, promise, and frustration that we have encountered in these chapters is thus to be expected. When one thinks about it, could the study and treatment of human behavior really proceed in any other way?

*Peer review system*    A system by which clinicians paid by an insurance company may periodically review a therapist's treatment report and recommend the continuation or termination of insurance benefits.

## Summing Up

*The legislative and judicial systems influence and regulate certain aspects of mental health care. First, they have developed the process of civil commitment whereby certain individuals can be forced to undergo mental health treatment, particularly if they are judged to be suffering from a mental disorder that makes them dangerous to themselves or others. Second, the legislative and judicial systems have defined and regulated the rights of patients with mental disorders, particularly their right to adequate treatment when institutionalized and their right to refuse biological and other forms of treatment. Other institutions in society, such as the business and economic sectors, may also influence how mental health services are delivered. Finally, the personal needs and goals of therapists may also have a powerful impact on how they study abnormal behaviors and treat people with mental disorders.*

# The State of the Field
## *Law, Society, and the Mental Health Profession*

Clinical researchers and practitioners once conducted their work in relative isolation. Today, however, their activities are intimately tied to other institutions, such as the legislative, judicial, and economic systems. The main reason for this growing interconnectedness is that the clinical field has achieved a remarkable level of acceptance in and impact on society. When a field achieves such acceptance and impact, it almost inevitably has some influence on the way other institutions are run. It also runs the risk of becoming so influential that other institutions jump in to monitor and restrict its activities.

To an extent, the interrelationship that has evolved between the mental health field and other institutions in our society is a healthy system of checks and bal-ances. It allows the mental health profession to con-tinue providing many useful services, yet helps ensure that its influence does not become excessive or mis-guided. Given the importance of such checks and bal-ances, the close ties between the clinical field and other institutions are likely to continue and even to grow in the coming years.

The enormous growth and impact of the mental health profession make it all the more important that people hold an accurate perception of its strengths *and* weaknesses. As we have seen throughout this book, the field has acquired an impressive body of knowl-edge, especially during the past several decades; how-ever, what mental health professionals do not know and cannot do still outweigh what they do know and can do. Everyone who turns to the field directly or in-directly must recognize this important fact. A society cannot be faulted for being vastly curious about and regularly seeking the input of a field of study—even when the field is young and imperfect—as long as the members of society fully appreciate the actual *state of the field.*

# *Chapter Review*

1. ***Abuse and Victimization:*** The mental health profes-sion interacts with the legislative and judicial sys-tems in various ways. One important area of in-teraction is their attempt to understand and address problems of abuse and victimization.
   A. ***Rape:*** Most rape victims are young (below 29 years of age) and are raped by persons they know. Most qualify for a diagnosis of acute stress disorder in the weeks following the attack and continue to experience lingering psycholog-ical, and in some cases somatic, problems. A strong support system enhances a victim's chances of adequate psychological recovery. Group therapy is particularly helpful.
   B. ***Spouse Abuse:*** Spouse abuse poses a serious threat to many women.
      (1) *Abusers* are often extremely possessive and jealous, tend to belittle and isolate their spouses, suffer from low self-esteem, and feel stressed. *Victims* often feel very depen-dent on their spouse, helpless, and enor-mously needy and have low self-esteem.
      (2) Initially a woman and her abusive husband need to be separated and given therapy sep-arately. Couple therapy may be useful later.
   C. ***Stalking:*** Most stalkers are believed to suffer from the symptoms of a psychological disorder such as erotomanic delusions, personality disor-ders, or depression. State legislatures have en-acted new laws to try to protect victims of stalk-ing, but the laws are limited in effect because of various complications.
   D. ***Child Abuse:*** Child abuse may include physical, sexual, and/or emotional abuse, or neglect. Al-most 3 million cases are reported each year.
      (1) The validity of children's testimony has been debated in *some* sexual abuse cases.
      (2) Child abuse has been tied to such factors as parental inadequacies (e.g., poor impulse control), family stress, poverty, and alcohol or drug abuse. Child abuse may lead to both immediate and long-term negative effects for the child.
      (3) A variety of treatments have been used to change parents' abusive behavior, includ-ing parenting-skill training and cognitive therapy.
2. ***Criminal Commitment:*** Evaluations by clinicians may help judges and juries decide the culpability of defendants, often resulting in criminal commit-ment. There are two forms of criminal commitment:
   A. If defendants are judged to have been mentally unstable at the time they committed a crime, they may be found *not guilty by reason of insan-*

*ity* and placed in a treatment facility rather than a prison.

 (1) In about half the states, insanity is judged in accordance with the *M'Naghten rule*. Other states use the *American Law Institute test*.

 (2) In recent years, twelve states have chosen to also permit a verdict of *guilty but mentally ill*.

 B. Regardless of their state of mind at the time of the crime, defendants may be judged *mentally incompetent* to stand trial, that is, incapable of fully understanding the charges or legal proceedings that confront them. If so, they are typically sent to a mental hospital until they become competent to stand trial.

**3. Civil Commitment:** The legal system also has significant influence on the clinical profession. First, legal channels may be used to commit noncriminals to mental hospitals for treatment, a process called civil commitment. Society allows the involuntary commitment of people considered in need of treatment and dangerous to themselves or others.

**4. Patients' Rights:** Another way that courts and legislatures significantly affect the clinical profession is by specifying a number of legal rights to which mental patients are entitled. The rights that have received the most attention are the *right to treatment* and the *right to refuse treatment*.

**5. Business and Economic Ties:** Clinical practice and study also intersect with business and economic institutions.

 A. Clinicians are often employed to identify and address psychological problems in the workplace.

 B. Increasingly, private insurance companies are setting up reimbursement procedures that may influence the duration and focus of therapy.

**6. Personal Factors:** Mental health activities are affected by the personal needs, values, and goals of the human beings who provide the clinical services.

## Key Terms

| | | | |
|---|---|---|---|
| rape | not guilty by reason of | guilty but mentally ill | right to treatment |
| spouse abuse | insanity (NGRI) | diminished capacity | right to refuse treatment |
| stalking | M'Naghten rule | mental incompetence | employee assistance |
| erotomanic delusion | irresistible impulse | civil commitment | program |
| psychological abuse | test | parens patriae | stress-reduction seminar |
| child abuse | Durham test | police power | problem-solving seminar |
| child sexual abuse | American Law Institute | two-physician certificate | managed care system |
| criminal commitment | (ALI) test | (2 PC) | peer review system |

## Quick Quiz

1. What are the short-term and long-term effects of rape? What factors may help victims of rape make an adequate psychological recovery?

2. How do the criminal justice and legislative systems view and respond to spouse abuse?

3. What personal characteristics, environmental stresses, and childhood experiences are common among men who abuse their spouses and among women who are abused? What treatment procedures are typically applied in cases of spouse abuse?

4. How widespread is the problem of stalking? In what ways are new stalking laws limited?

5. What factors seem often to contribute to child abuse? What are the immediate and long-term effects of child abuse? What interventions have been applied in cases of child abuse?

6. Briefly state the M'Naghten, irresistible impulse, Durham, and ALI tests of insanity. Which tests are used today to determine whether defendants are not guilty by reason of insanity?

7. Explain the "guilty but mentally ill" and "mentally disordered sex offender" verdicts.

8. What are the rationales behind and the procedures for determining whether defendants are mentally incompetent to stand trial?

9. What are the reasons for civil commitment, and how is it carried out? What criticisms have been made of this procedure, and how have they been addressed?

10. What rights have court decisions and legislation guaranteed to patients with psychological disorders?

11. What kinds of programs for the prevention and treatment of psychological problems have been established in business settings?

12. What trends have prevailed in recent years in the funding of mental health care?

# Glossary

**Abnormal psychology**  The scientific study of abnormal behavior in order to describe, predict, explain, and exert some control over abnormal patterns of functioning.

**Acetylcholine**  A neurotransmitter that when present in high levels may be associated with depression.

**Acute stress disorder**  An anxiety disorder in which fear and related symptoms are experienced soon after a traumatic event and last less than a month.

**Addiction**  Physical dependence on a substance, marked by such features as tolerance, withdrawal symptoms during abstinence, or both.

**Affect**  A subjective experience of emotion or mood.

**Affectual awareness**  A technique of sexual therapy in which the client becomes aware of his or her negative emotions regarding sex.

**Aftercare**  A program of posthospitalization care and treatment out in the community.

**Agoraphobia**  A pervasive and complex phobia that makes people avoid public places or situations in which escape might be difficult or help unavailable should they develop incapacitating or upsetting symptoms, such as dizziness or palpitations.

**Agoraphobia without history of panic disorder**  An agoraphobic pattern that does not have its origin in a panic attack.

**Akathisia**  A Parkinsonian symptom consisting of a very high degree of restlessness and agitation and great discomfort in the limbs.

**Alcohol**  Any beverage containing ethyl alcohol, including beer, wine, and liquor.

**Alcohol dehydrogenase**  An enzyme which breaks down alcohol in the stomach before it enters the blood.

**Alcohol withdrawal delirium**  A dramatic reaction experienced by some people who are alcohol-dependent. It occurs within three days of cessation or reduction of drinking and consists of mental confusion, clouded consciousness, and terrifying visual hallucinations. Also known as *delirium tremens* (*DTs*).

**Alcoholics Anonymous (AA)**  A self-help organization that provides support and guidance for persons with alcohol abuse or dependence.

**Alcoholism**  A pattern of behavior in which a person repeatedly abuses or develops a dependence on alcohol.

**Alogia**  A symptom in schizophrenia, characterized by decreased fluency and productivity of speech.

**Alprazolam**  A benzodiazepine drug, also shown to be effective in the treatment of panic disorders. Marketed as Xanax.

**Altruistic suicide**  Suicide committed by people who intentionally sacrifice their lives for the well-being of society.

**Alzheimer's disease**  The most common form of dementia, usually occurring during old age, marked by excessive formations of neurofibrillary tangles and senile plaques in the brain.

**Amenorrhea**  The absence of menstrual cycles.

**Amnesia**  Loss of memory. See also *Anterograde, Dissociative,* and *Retrograde amnesia.*

**Amnestic disorders**  Organically caused disorders in which the primary symptom is memory impairment.

**Amniocentesis**  A prenatal procedure used to rest the amniotic fluid that surrounds the fetus in order to detect the possibility of birth defects.

**Amphetamine**  A stimulant drug that is manufactured in the laboratory.

**Amygdala**  The structure in the brain's limbic system that gives rise to emotional behavior and that may also regulate the link between arousal and memory.

**Anaclitic depression**  A pattern of behavior that includes sadness, withdrawal, weight loss, and trouble sleeping and that is associated with separation from one's mother before the age of 6 years.

**Anal stage**  In psychoanalytic theory, the second 18 months of life, during which the child's focus of pleasure shifts to the anus, and libidinal gratification comes from retaining and passing feces.

**Analogue experiment**  In the context of abnormal psychology, an investigation in which the experimenter induces laboratory subjects to behave in ways that resemble real-life abnormal behavior.

**Anesthesia**  A lessening or loss of sensation for touch or pain.

**Anomic suicides**  Suicide committed by individuals whose social environment fails to provide stability, thus leaving them without a sense of belonging.

**Anorexia nervosa**  A disorder characterized by the relentless pursuit of extreme thinness and by an extreme loss of weight.

**Anoxia**  A complication of birth in which the baby is deprived of oxygen.

**Antabuse (disulfiram)**  A drug that is relatively benign when taken by itself, but causes intense nausea, vomiting, increased heart rate, and dizziness when taken with alcohol. It is often taken by people who are trying to refrain from drinking alcohol.

**Antagonist drug**  Any drug that blocks or changes the effects of another drug.

**Anterograde amnesia**  The inability to remember new information that is acquired after the event that caused amnesia.

**Anthropology**  The study of human cultures and institutions.

**Antianxiety drugs**  Psychotropic drugs that reduce tension and anxiety.

**Antibipolar drugs**  Psychotropic drugs that help stabilize the moods of people suffering from bipolar mood disorder.

**Antibodies**  Bodily chemicals, produced by certain lymphocytes, that seek out and destroy antigens.

**Antidepressant drugs**  Psychotropic drugs that help lift a person's mood.

**Antigens**  Foreign invaders such as bacteria and viruses that stimulate an immune response.

**Antipsychotic drugs**  Psychotropic drugs that help correct grossly confused or distorted thinking characteristic of psychotic disorders.

**Antisocial personality disorder**  A personality disorder characterized by a pervasive pattern of disregard for and violation of other people's rights.

**Anxiety**  Emotional state characterized by fear, apprehension, and physiological arousal.

**Anxiety disorders**  Disorders in which anxiety is a central symptom.

**Anxiety-sensitivity**  According to cognitive-behavioral theorists, the tendency of certain individuals to become preoccupied with their bodily sensations, lose their ability to assess them logically, and interpret them as potentially harmful, leaving some more likely to develop panic attacks.

**Anxiolytics**  See *Antianxiety drugs.*

**Aphasia**  A common symptom in some kinds of dementia, characterized by difficulties in using or understanding language (for example, difficulty producing the names of objects and individuals).

**Aphrodisiac**  A substance that is thought to increase the sex drive.

**Arbitrary inference**  An error in logic in which a person draws negative conclusions on the basis of little or even contrary evidence.

**Assertiveness Training**  A cognitive-behavioral approach to increasing assertive behavior that is socially desirable.

**Assessment**  The process of collecting and interpreting relevant information about a client or subject.

**Asthma**  A medical problem marked by constricting of the trachea and bronchi, which results in shortness of breath, wheezing, coughing, and a choking sensation.

**Asylum**  An early type of mental institution. Initially established to provide care for people with mental disorders, most became virtual prisons in which patients endured degrading conditions.

**Attention-deficit/hyperactivity disorder (ADHD)**  A disorder characterized by the inability to focus attention or by overactive and impulsive behavior or both.

**Attribution**  An explanation of things we see going on around us which points to particular causes.

*Atypical antipsychotic drugs*    A new group of antipsychotic drugs (the most common being clozapine) that have a different mechanism of action than the traditional drugs and appear to cause few extrapyramidal symptoms.

*Auditory hallucination*    A hallucination in which a person hears sounds and voices that are not actually present.

*Augmentative communication systems*    A method for teaching individuals with autism, mental retardation, or cerebral palsy to communicate by pointing to pictures, symbols, letters or words on a communication board or computer.

*Aura*    A warning sensation that frequently precedes a migraine headache.

*Autism*    A pervasive developmental disorder characterized by extreme unresponsiveness to others, poor communication skills, limited skill at imaginative play, and highly restricted and repetitive behavior.

*Autoerotic asphyxia*    A fatal lack of oxygen that people inadvertently self-induce while hanging, suffocating, or strangling themselves during masturbation.

*Automatic thoughts*    According to Aaron Beck, unbidden cognitions that come into the mind, some comforting and some upsetting.

*Autonomic nervous system (ANS)*    The extensive network of nerve fibers that connect the central nervous system to all the other organs of the body.

*Aversion therapy*    A behavioral technique that helps clients acquire anxiety responses to stimuli that they have been finding too attractive.

*Avoidance behavior*    Behavior that removes or avoids anxiety-producing objects or situations.

*Avoidant personality disorder*    A personality disorder in which an individual experiences a chronic and pervasive pattern of inhibition in social situations, feelings of inadequacy, and extreme sensitivity to negative evaluation.

*Avolition*    A symptom in schizophrenia, characterized by apathy, a lack of interest in normal goals, an inability to make decisions, and an inability to initiate or complete a course of action.

*Axon*    The long fiber that extends from the body of the neuron.

*B-cell*    Lymphocyte that produces antibodies.

*Barbiturates*    Addictive sedative-hypnotic drugs used to reduce anxiety or to help persons fall asleep.

*Baroreceptors*    Sensitive nerves in the arteries responsible for alerting the brain when blood pressure becomes too high.

*Baseline data*    An individual's initial response level on a test or scale.

*Basic irrational assumptions*    Inappropriate assumptions guiding the way in which one acts that prejudice a person's chances for happiness and success.

*Battery*    A comprehensive group of tests, each of which targets a specific skill area.

*Behavior*    The response that an organism makes to the stimuli in its environment.

*Behavioral medicine*    A field of study and treatment that combines psychological and physical concepts and interventions to better understand, treat, or prevent medical problems.

*Behavioral model*    A theoretical perspective that emphasizes ingrained behavior and the ways in which it is learned.

*Behavioral self-control training (BSCT)*    An approach to treating alcohol abuse in which clients are taught to monitor their own drinking behavior, set appropriate limits on their drinking, control their rate of drinking, and apply alternative coping behaviors.

*Behavioral therapy (also behavior modification)*    A therapeutic approach that views the goal of therapy as identifying the client's specific problem-causing behaviors and either modifying them or replacing them with more appropriate ones.

*Bender Visual-Motor Gestalt Test*    A neuropsychological test in which a subject is asked to copy a set of nine simple designs and later reproduce the designs from memory.

*Benzodiazepines*    The most common group of antianxiety drugs, which includes Valium, Xanax, and Librium.

*Bereavement*    The process of working through the grief that one feels when a loved one dies.

*Beta-amyloid protein*    A small molecule that forms sphere-shaped deposits called senile plaques. These deposits collect in the spaces between neurons in people with Alzheimer's disease, interfering with memory and learning.

*Beta blocker*    A drug that reduces the physical symptoms of anxiety by binding to B-adrenergic receptors in the brain.

*Bilateral electroconvulsive therapy (ECT)*    A form of electroconvulsive therapy in which two electrodes are used, and electrical current is passed through both sides of the brain.

*Binge*    An episode of uncontrollable eating during which a person consumes a very large quantity of food.

*Binge-eating disorder*    A type of eating disorder in which a person displays a pattern of binge eating without any accompanying compensatory behaviors.

*Binge-eating/purging type anorexia nervosa*    A type of anorexia nervosa in which people engage in eating binges but still lose excessive weight by forcing themselves to vomit after meals or by abusing laxatives or diuretics.

*Biofeedback*    A treatment technique in which the client is given systematic information about key physiological responses as they occur and learns to control the responses voluntarily.

*Biological challenge*    A procedure used to induce panic in subjects or clients by having them exercise vigorously or perform other physical tasks in the presence of a therapist or researcher.

*Biological model*    The theoretical perspective that cites organic processes as the key to human behavior.

*Biological therapy*    The use of physical and chemical procedures to help people overcome psychological difficulties.

*Bipolar disorder*    A disorder marked by alternating or intermixed periods of mania and depression.

*Bipolar I disorder*    A type of bipolar disorder in which a person experiences manic and major depressive episodes.

*Bipolar II disorder*    A type of bipolar disorder in which a person experiences mildly manic (hypomanic) episodes and major depressive episodes.

*Blind design*    An experimental design in which subjects, experimenters, or evaluators do not know which subjects are in the experimental or the control condition.

*Blocking*    A symptom associated with schizophrenia in which thoughts seem to disappear from memory and statements end in silence before they can be completed.

*Blunted affect*    A symptom of schizophrenia in which a person displays less emotion—anger, sadness, joy—than other people.

*Body dysmorphic disorder (dysmorphophobia)*    A somatoform disorder marked by excessive worry that some aspect of one's physical appearance is defective.

*Borderline personality disorder*    A personality disorder in which an individual displays a pervasive pattern of instability in interpersonal relationships, self-image, and mood, and marked impulsivity.

*Brain wave*    The oscillations of electrical potential, as measured by an electroencephalograph, that are created by neurons in the brain.

*Breathing-related sleep disorder*    A sleep disorder in which sleep is frequently disrupted by a breathing problem, causing excessive sleepiness or insomnia.

*Brief psychotic disorder*    Psychotic symptoms that appear suddenly after a very stressful event or a period of emotional turmoil and last anywhere from a few hours to a month.

*Briquet's syndrome*    See *Somatization disorder.*

*Bulimia nervosa*    A disorder characterized by frequent eating binges, during which the person uncontrollably consumes large quantities of food followed by forced vomiting or other extreme compensatory behaviors to avoid gaining weight.

*Caffeine*    A stimulant drug that is commonly consumed in the form of coffee, tea, cola, and chocolate.

*Cannabis drugs*    Drugs produced from the different varieties of the hemp plant, *Cannabis sativa.* They cause a mixture of intoxicating, hallucinogenic, depressant, and stimulant effects.

*Case study*    A detailed account of a person's life and psychological problems.

*Catatonia*    A pattern of extreme psychomotor symptoms found in some forms of schizophrenia, that may include catatonic stupor, rigidity, or posturing.

*Catatonic excitement*    A form of catatonia in which a person moves excitedly, sometimes with wild waving of the arms and legs.

*Catatonic schizophrenia*    Schizophrenia characterized by a severe psychomotor disturbance.

*Catatonic stupor*   A symptom associated with schizophrenia in which a person becomes totally unresponsive to the environment, remaining motionless and silent for long stretches of time.

*Catharsis*   The reliving of past repressed feelings in order to settle internal conflicts and overcome problems.

*Caudate nuclei*   Structures of the basal ganglia that participate in the conversion of sensory input into cognitions and actions.

*Central nervous system*   The brain and spinal cord.

*Cerebral cortex*   The outer layer of the cerebrum, or upper portion of the brain, also known as the gray matter. It is associated with higher cognitive functions.

*Checking compulsion*   A compulsion in which people feel compelled to check the same things over and over.

*Child abuse*   The intentional use of excessive physical or psychological force by an adult on a child, often aimed at hurting or destroying the child.

*Chlorpromazine*   A phenothiazine drug commonly used for treating schizophrenia. Marketed as Thorazine.

*Chromosomal mapping*   A research strategy for studying the DNA of a large extended family in which a particular trait (schizophrenia, for example) is unusually common.

*Chromosomes*   The structures within a cell that contain genes.

*Circadian rhythm sleep disorder*   A sleep disorder in which people experience excessive sleepiness or insomnia as the result of a mismatch between the sleep-wake cycle in their environment and their own circadian sleep-wake cycle.

*Circadian rhythms*   Internal "clocks" consisting of recurrent biological fluctuations.

*Cirrhosis*   An irreversible condition, often caused by excessive drinking, in which the liver becomes scarred and begins to change anatomy and functioning.

*Civil commitment*   A legal process by which certain individuals can be forced to undergo mental health treatment.

*Clang*   A rhyme used by schizophrenic individuals as a guide to formulating thoughts and statements.

*Classical conditioning*   A process of learning by temporal association in which two events that repeatedly occur close together in time become fused in a person's mind and elicit the same response.

*Classification system*   A comprehensive list of categories of mental dysfunctioning, including a description of the symptoms that characterize each category and guidelines for assigning people to the categories.

*Cleaning compulsion*   A common compulsion in which people feel compelled to keep cleaning themselves, their clothing, and their homes.

*Client-centered therapy*   The therapeutic approach developed by Carl Rogers in which therapists try to help clients by being accepting, empathizing accurately and conveying genuineness.

*Clinical psychologist*   A professional who earns a doctorate in clinical psychology by completing four years of graduate training in abnormal functioning and its treatment as well as a one-year internship at a mental hospital or mental health agency.

*Clinical psychology*   The study, assessment, treatment, and prevention of abnormal behavior.

*Clitoris*   The female sex organ located in front of the urinary and vaginal openings. It becomes enlarged during sexual arousal.

*Clomipramine*   An antidepressant drug (brand name Anafranil) that has also proven useful in treating obsessive-compulsive disorder.

*Clozapine (Clozaril)*   The most commonly prescribed atypical antipsychotic drug.

*Cocaine*   A addictive stimulant derived from the coca plant. It is the most powerful natural stimulant known.

*Cognition*   The intellectual capacity to think, remember, and anticipate.

*Cognitive behavior*   Thoughts and beliefs, many of which remain private.

*Cognitive-behavioral model*   A theoretical perspective that attributes psychological problems to cognitive behaviors.

*Cognitive model*   A theoretical perspective that emphasizes the process and content of the thinking that underlies behavior.

*Cognitive therapy*   A therapeutic system developed by Aaron Beck which helps people recognize and change their faulty thinking processes.

*Cognitive triad*   The three forms of negative thinking, encompassing one's view of one's experiences, one's view of oneself, and one's view of the future, that theorist Aaron Beck says lead people to feel depressed.

*Coitus*   Sexual intercourse.

*Community mental health center*   A treatment facility for persons with psychological dysfunctions that provides outpatient psychotherapy and medication and inpatient emergency care.

*Community mental health movement*   A sociopolitical trend emphasizing community care for people with severe psychological disturbances.

*Community mental health treatment*   A therapy format in which therapists try to work with people in settings close to the clients' home, school, and work.

*Compulsion*   A repetitive and rigid behavior or mental act that a person feels compelled to perform in order to prevent or reduce anxiety.

*Compulsive ritual*   A detailed, often elaborate, set of actions that a persons feels compelled to perform at frequent intervals, always in the identical manner.

*Computerized axial tomography (CAT scan)*   A composite image of the brain created by compiling X-ray images taken from many angles.

*Concordance*   A statistical measure of the frequency with which both members of a pair of twins have the same particular trait.

*Conditioned response (CR)*   A response previously associated with an unconditioned stimulus that comes to be elicited by a conditioned stimulus.

*Conditioned stimulus (CS)*   A previously neutral stimulus that comes to be associated with nonneutral stimulus.

*Conditioning*   A simple form of learning in which a given stimulus comes to evoke a given response.

*Conditions of worth*   According to client-centered theorists, the internal standards by which a person judges his or her own lovability and acceptability, determined by the standards (i.e., conditions of worth) to which the person was held as a child.

*Conduct disorder*   A childhood disorder in which the child repeatedly violates the basic rights of others, displaying aggression and sometimes destroying others' property, lying, cheating, or running away from home.

*Confabulation*   A spontaneous fabrication to fill in a gap in one's own memory. Characteristic of people suffering from Korsakoff's syndrome.

*Confederate*   An experimenter's accomplice who plays a role in creating a believable counterfeit situation in an experiment.

*Confidentiality*   The commitment on the part of a professional person not to divulge the information he or she obtains from a client.

*Confound*   A variable other than the independent variable that is also acting on the dependent variable.

*Conjoint family therapy*   A family therapy approach in which the therapist focuses primarily on communication within the family system.

*Contingency management*   A behavioral approach to combat negative, depressive behavior in which the therapist systematically ignores a client's depressive behavior while giving attention and positive reinforcement to constructive statements and behavior.

*Continuous amnesia*   A disturbance of memory in which forgetting continues into the present, and new and ongoing experiences fail to be retained.

*Control group*   In an experiment, a group of subjects who are not exposed to the manipulation of the independent variable.

*Conversion disorder*   A somatoform disorder characterized by one or more physical symptoms or deficits affecting voluntary motor or sensory function.

*Coronary heart disease*   Illness of the heart caused by a blocking of the coronary arteries.

*Correlation*   The degree to which events or characteristics vary in conjunction with each other.

*Correlational method*   A research procedure used to determine the extent to which events or characteristics vary together.

*Correlational coefficient (r)*   A statistical expression of the direction and the magnitude of a correlation, ranging from 21.00 to 11.00.

*Counseling psychology*   A mental health specialty similar to clinical psychology that requires completion of its own graduate training program.

*Couple therapy*   A therapeutic approach in which the therapist works with two people who share a long-term relationship.

*Covert desensitization*   Desensitization training that focuses on imagining confrontations with the frightening objects or situations while in a state of relaxation. See also *In vivo desensitization.*

*Covert sensitization*    A behavioral treatment for eliminating unwanted behavior by pairing the behavior with unpleasant mental images.

*Crack*    A powerful, ready-to-smoke free-base cocaine.

*Creutzfeldt-Jakob disease*    A rare, rapidly progressive dementia caused by a virus, that often includes spasmodic movements.

*Criminal commitment*    A legal process by which individuals accused of crimes are judged to be mentally unstable and are sent to a mental institution for treatment.

*Crisis intervention*    See *Suicide prevention programs.*

*Cross-tolerance*    Tolerance for a drug one has never taken, as a result of using another, similar drug.

*Culture*    A people's common history, values, institutions, habits, skills, technology, and arts.

*Cyclothymic disorder*    A disorder characterized by numerous periods of hypomanic symptoms and mild depressive symptoms.

*Day center (day hospital)*    A treatment center that provides daylong therapeutic activity and care.

*Declarative memory*    Memory for information that is directly accessible to consciousness, such as names, dates, and other learned facts.

*Defense mechanisms*    See *Ego defense mechanisms.*

*Deinstitutionalization*    The practice begun in the mid-twentieth century to release hundreds of thousands of patients from public mental hospitals.

*Delirium*    A rapidly developing clouded state of consciousness in which a person experiences great difficulty concentrating, focusing attention, and maintaining a straightforward stream of thought.

*Delirium tremens (DTs)*    A dramatic withdrawal reaction experienced by some people who are alcohol-dependent. It consists of mental confusion, clouded consciousness, and terrifying visual hallucinations.

*Delusion*    A blatantly false belief firmly held despite evidence to the contrary.

*Delusional disorder*    A disorder consisting of persistent, nonbizarre delusions that are not part of a larger schizophrenic pattern.

*Dementias*    Organically caused syndromes marked by impairments of memory and at least one other cognitive function.

*Demonology*    The belief that abnormal behavior results from supernatural causes such as evil spirits.

*Dendrite*    The extensions, or antennae, located at one end of a neuron that receive impulses from other neurons.

*Denial*    An ego defense mechanism in which a person fails to acknowledge unacceptable thoughts, feelings, or actions.

*Dependent personality disorder*    A personality disorder characterized by a pattern of submissive and clinging behavior, fears of separation, and a pervasive need to be taken care of.

*Dependent variable*    The variable in an experiment that is expected to change as the independent variable is manipulated.

*Depersonalization disorder*    A disorder characterized by a persistent and recurrent feeling of being detached from one's mental processes or body; that is, one feels unreal and alien.

*Depressant*    A substance that slows the activity of the central nervous system and in sufficient dosages causes a reduction of tension and inhibitions.

*Depression*    A low, sad state in which life seems bleak and its challenges overwhelming.

*Derailment (loose associations)*    A common formal thought disorder of schizophrenia, characterized by rapid shifts from one topic of conversation to another.

*Derealization*    The feeling that the external world is unreal and strange.

*Desire phase*    The first phase of the sexual response cycle, characterized by an urge to have sex, sexual fantasies, and feelings of sexual attraction to others.

*Desynchronization*    An imbalance between the body's circadian rhythms and the rhythms of the environment.

*Detoxification*    Systematic and medically supervised withdrawal from a drug.

*Deviance*    Variance from accepted patterns of behavior.

*Diagnosis*    The process of determining whether a person's dysfunction constitutes a particular psychological disorder.

*Diathesis-stress perspective*    The view that a person must first have a biological, psychological, or sociocultural predisposition to a disorder and then be subjected to an immediate form of psychological stress to develop and maintain it.

*Diazepam*    A benzodiazepine drug marketed as Valium.

*Diencephalon*    A brain structure located below the cerebral cortex, consisting of the mammillary bodies, thalamus, and hypothalamus. It plays a key role in memory, among other functions.

*Disorganized schizophrenia*    A type of schizophrenia characterized primarily by confusion, incoherence, and flat or inappropriate affect.

*Displacement*    An ego defense mechanism that channels unacceptable id impulses toward another, safer substitute.

*Disregulation model*    A theory that explains psychophysiological disorders as breakdowns in the body's negative feedback loops, resulting in an interruption of the body's smooth, self-regulating operation.

*Dissociative amnesia*    A dissociative disorder characterized by an inability to recall important personal events and information.

*Dissociative disorders*    Disorders characterized by significant alterations in integrated functioning that are not due to clear physical causes.

*Dissociative fugue*    A dissociative disorder in which a person travels to a new location and may assume a new identity, simultaneously forgetting his or her past.

*Dissociative identify disorder (multiple personality disorder)*    A disorder in which a person displays two or more distinct personalities.

*Dizygotic twins*    Twins who develop from separate eggs.

*Dopamine*    The neurotransmitter whose high activity has been shown to be related to schizophrenia.

*Dopamine hypothesis*    The theory that schizophrenia results from excessive firing of neurons that use the neurotransmitter dopamine.

*Double-bind communication*    Simultaneous messages that are mutually contradictory.

*Double-bind hypothesis*    A family systems theory that says some parents help cause schizophrenic symptoms in their children by repeatedly engaging in communications with them that carry simultaneous contradictory messages.

*Double-blind design*    Experimental procedure in which neither the subject nor the experimenter knows whether the subject has received the experimental treatment or a placebo.

*Down syndrome*    A form of mental retardation related to a abnormality in the twenty-first chromosome.

*Drug abuse*    The excessive intake of a substance that results in emotional, social, occupational, or functional impairment.

*Drug maintenance therapy*    An approach to treating substance abuse in which addicted clients are given legally and medically supervised doses of a substitute drug with which to satisfy their addiction.

*Drug therapy*    The use of psychotropic drugs to alleviate the symptoms of mental disorders.

*DSM-IV (Diagnostic and Statistical Manual-IV)*    The current edition of the classification system developed by the American Psychiatric Association.

*Durham test*    A legal test for determining the responsibility of a person committing a crime. It asks whether the unlawful act is a product of a mental disease or defect. This test was used only for a short period.

*Dyslexia (reading disorder)*    A disorder characterized by a marked impairment in the ability to recognize words and to comprehend what one reads, not caused by visual or hearing defects, poor schooling, or intellectual deficit.

*Dyspareunia*    A disorder in which a person experiences severe pain in the genitals during sexual activity.

*Dyssomnias*    Sleep disorders in which the amount, quality, or timing of sleep is disturbed.

*Dysthymic disorder*    A mood disorder that is similar to but more chronic and less disabling than a major depressive disorder.

*Dystonia*    A Parkinsonian symptom in which involuntary muscle contractions cause bizarre and uncontrollable movements of the face, neck, tongue, and back.

*Echolalia*    A symptom of autism or schizophrenia in which a person responds to being spoken to by repeating some of the other person's words.

*Ego*    One of the three psychological forces proposed by Freud as central to shaping the personality. The ego operates in accordance with the reality principle, employing reason and deliberation.

*Ego defense mechanisms* According to psychoanalytic theory, strategies developed by the ego to control unacceptable id impulses and to avoid or reduce the anxiety they arouse.

*Ego-Dystonic homosexuality* A past DSM category indicating a homosexual preference accompanied by extreme distress.

*Ego psychology* A psychodynamic theory that focuses on the importance of the ego.

*Egoistic suicide* Suicide committed by people over whom society has little or no control, people who are not concerned with the norms or rules of society.

*Ejaculation* Contractions of the muscles at the base of the penis that causes sperm to be ejected.

*Electra complex* According to Freud, the pattern of desires all girls experience in which they develop a sexual attraction for their father, rooted in the fantasy that by seducing him they can have his penis.

*Electroconvulsive therapy (ECT)* A biological treatment for unipolar depression in which electrodes attached to a patient's head send an electric current through the brain, causing a convulsion.

*Electroencephalograph (EEG)* A device that records electrical impulses in the brian.

*Electromyograph (EMG)* A device that provides feedback about the level of muscular tension in the body.

*Emergency commitment* Temporary commitment to a mental hospital of a patient who is behaving in a bizarre or violent way. See also *Two-physician certificates.*

*Employee assistance programs* Mental health programs a company offers its employees.

*Encopresis* A childhood disorder characterized by repeated defecating in inappropriate places.

*Endogenous depression* A depression that develops without apparent antecedents and is assumed to be caused by internal factors.

*Endorphins* Neurotransmitters that help relieve pain and reduce emotional tension. They are sometimes referred to as the body's own opioids.

*Enkephalin* See *Endorphin.*

*Enmeshed family pattern* A family system in which members are overinvolved with each other's affairs and overconcerned about each other's welfare.

*Enuresis* A childhood disorder characterized by repeated bedwetting or wetting of one's clothes.

*Epidemiological study (epidemiology)* An investigation that determines the incidence and prevalence of a disorder in a given population.

*Episodic memory* A person's autobiographical memory of personal experiences and other highly personal material.

*Ergot alkaloid* A naturally occurring compound from which LSD is derived.

*Erogenous zones* Body areas that Freud considered representative of the child's sexual drives and conflicts at each of the normal stages of development.

*Essential hypertension* Chronic high blood pressure brought about by a combination of psychological and physiological factors.

*Estrogen* The primary female sex hormone.

*Ethyl alcohol* The chemical compound in all alcoholic beverages that is rapidly absorbed into the blood and immediately begins to affect the person's functioning.

*Evoked potentials* The brain response patterns recorded on an electroencephalograph while a subject performs a task.

*Excitement phase* The second phase in the sexual response cycle, characterized by general physical arousal, increases in heart rate, muscle tension, blood pressure, and respiration, and specific changes in the pelvic region.

*Exhibitionism* A paraphilia in which persons have recurrent sexually arousing urges to expose or fantasies about exposing their genitals to another person, and may act upon those urges or fantasies.

*Existential anxiety* A universal pervasive fear of the limits and responsibilities of one's existence.

*Existential model* The theoretical perspective that human beings are born with the total freedom to either face up to one's existence and give meaning to one's life or to shrink from that responsibility.

*Existential therapy* Like humanistic therapy, existential therapies emphasize the validity of the individual's phenomenological world and the importance of the here and now, but they also place great emphasis on making choices and on the relationship between therapist and client.

*Exorcism* The practice in early societies of treating abnormality by coaxing evil spirits to leave the person's body.

*Experiment* A scientific procedure in which a variable is manipulated and the effect of the manipulation is observed.

*Experimental group* In an experiment, the group of subjects who are exposed to the independent variable.

*Exposure and response prevention* A treatment for obsessive-compulsive disorder in which clients are exposed to anxiety-arousing thoughts or situations and then prevented from performing their compulsive acts.

*Exposure treatment* Behavioral approaches to treating simple phobias in which clients are exposed to the dreaded object or situation.

*Expressed emotion* The level of criticism, emotional overinvolvement, and hostility displayed in a family. High levels of expressed emotion in family members are thought to be associated with a poorer outcome for recovering individuals with schizophrenia.

*Extinction* The decrease in responding that occurs when an unconditioned stimulus is no longer paired with the conditioned stimulus or when a response is no longer rewarded.

*Extrapyramidal effects* Unwanted movements, such as severe shaking, bizarre-looking contractions of the face and body, and extreme restlessness, sometimes induced by traditional antipsychotic drugs, resulting from the effect of the drugs on the extrapyramidal areas of the brain.

*Facilitated communication* A method for teaching individuals with autism to communicate. The therapist or "facilitator" provides emotional and physical assistance as the individual types or points to letters on a keyboard or communication board.

*Factitious disorder* An illness with no identifiable physical cause, in which the patient is believed to be intentionally producing or feigning symptoms in order to assume a sick role.

*Family pedigree study* The method used by biological researchers to see how many members of a given family have a particular disorder.

*Family systems theory* An approach to human behavior that views the family as a system of interacting parts and proposes that members of a given family interact in consistent ways and operate by implicit rules.

*Family systems therapy* A therapy format in which therapists meet with all members of a family, point out problematic behavior and interactions between the members, and help the whole family to change.

*Family therapy* A therapy format in which therapists meet with all members of a family, point out problematic behavior and interactions between the members, and help the whole family to change.

*Fantasy* An ego defense mechanism in which a person uses imaginary events to satisfy unacceptable impulses.

*Fear* The central nervous system's physiological and emotional response to danger.

*Fear hierarchy* A list of the objects or situations that frighten a person, starting with those which are minimally feared and ending with those which are feared the most. Used in systematic desensitization.

*Female orgasmic disorder* A female dysfunction characterized by a repeated absence of or very long delay in reaching orgasm following normal sexual excitement.

*Female sexual arousal disorder* A female dysfunction characterized by a persistent inability to attain or maintain sexual excitement, including adequate lubrication or genital swelling, during sexual activity.

*Fetal alcohol syndrome* A cluster of problems in a child, including low birth weight, irregularities in the hands and face, and intellectual deficits, caused by excessive alcohol intake by its mother during gestation.

*Fetishism* A paraphilia consisting of recurrent and intense sexual urges, fantasies, or behaviors that involve the use of a nonliving object, often to the exclusion of all other stimuli.

*5-Hydroxyindolcactic acid (5-HIAA)* A component of cerebrospinal fluid that is a metabolite, or by-product, of brain serotonin.

*Fixation* According to Freud, a condition in which the id, ego, and superego do not mature properly and are frozen at an early stage of development.

*Flashback* The recurrence of LSD-induced sensory and emotional changes long after the drug has left the body. (Also called hallucinogen-persisting perception disorder). Or in posttraumatic stress disorder, the re-experiencing of past traumatic events.

*Flat affect*   A symptom of schizophrenia in which the person shows almost no emotions at all.

*Flooding*   A treatment for phobias in which clients are exposed repeatedly and intensively to the feared object and made to see that it is actually quite harmless.

*Folie à deux (shared psychotic disorder)*   A psychotic disorder in which a delusion is shared by two people.

*Forebrain*   The top area of the brain, consisting of the cerebrum, thalamus, and hypothalamus.

*Forensic science*   The study of legal issues relating to medicine or psychology.

*Formal thought disorder*   A disturbance in the production and organization of thought.

*Fragile X syndrome*   A chromosomal disorder characterized by moderate to severe degrees of mental handicap, language impairments, and behavioral problems.

*Free association*   A psychodynamic technique in which the patient describes any thought, feeling, or image that comes to mind, even if it seems unimportant.

*Free-base*   A technique for ingesting cocaine in which the pure cocaine basic alkaloid is chemically separated from processed cocaine, vaporized by heat from a flame, and inhaled with a pipe.

*Free-floating anxiety*   Chronic and persistent feelings of nervousness and agitation that are not clearly attached to a specific, identifiable threat.

*Frontal lobe*   The region of each cerebral hemisphere that governs motor function and abstract thinking.

*Frotteurism*   A paraphilia consisting of recurrent and intense sexual urges, fantasies, or behaviors that involve touching and rubbing against a nonconsenting person.

*Fugue*   See *Dissociative fugue.*

*GABA*   The neurotransmitter gamma aminobutyric acid, whose low activity has been linked to generalized anxiety disorder.

*Galvanic Skin Response (GSR)*   Changes in the electrical resistance of the skin.

*Ganja*   A recreational drug of at least intermediate strength derived from varieties of the hemp plant.

*Gender identity disorder*   A disorder in which a person persistently feels extremely uncomfortable about his or her assigned sex and strongly wishes to be a member of the opposite sex.

*Gene*   A structure within the chromosome that carries a discrete piece of hereditary information.

*General adaptation syndrome*   A three-stage reaction to stress proposed by theorist Hans Selye to describe the relationship between stress and the autonomic nervous system.

*General paresis*   An irreversible, progressive disorder with both physical and mental symptoms, including paralysis and delusions of grandeur.

*Generalized amnesia*   A disorder in which a person forgets both the period beginning with a traumatic event and all other events before the onset of this period.

*Generalized anxiety disorder*   A disorder characterized by persistent and excessive feelings of anxiety and worry about numerous events and activities.

*Genetic linkage study*   A research approach in which extended families with high rates of a disorder over several generations are observed in order to determine whether the disorder closely follows the distribution pattern of other family traits.

*Genital stage*   In Freud's theory, the stage beginning at approximately 12 years old, when the child begins to find sexual pleasure in heterosexual relationships.

*Gerontology*   The study of the physical, emotional, and psychological changes, as well as the disorders, that accompany old age.

*Gestalt therapy*   A humanistic form of therapy developed by Fritz Perls in which therapists try to move their clients toward self-recognition and self-acceptance by frustrating and challenging them.

*Glia*   Brain cells that support the neurons.

*Grief*   The reaction one experiences when a loved one is lost.

*Group home*   Special homes where people with disorders or disabilities are taught self-help, living, and working skills.

*Group therapy*   A therapeutic approach in which a group of people with similar problems meet together with a therapist and discuss the problems or concerns of one or more of the members.

*Guided participation*   A modeling technique in which the therapist and client first construct a fear hierarchy and the client then observes and imitates the therapist, experiencing the least feared item in the hierarchy, a more feared item, and so on.

*Habituation training*   A therapeutic technique in which a therapist tries to evoke a client's obsessive thoughts again and again with the expectation that the thoughts will eventually lose their threatening meaning and generate less anxiety.

*Halcion (triazolam)*   An antianxiety drug which is quickly metabolized in the body.

*Halfway house*   A group home that has a live-in staff to offer support, guidance, and practical advice to residents.

*Hallucination*   The experiencing of imagined sights, sounds, or other sensory experiences as if they were real.

*Hallucinogen*   A substance that primarily causes powerful changes in sensory perception, including intensification of perceptions and the inducement of illusions and hallucinations.

*Hallucinogen persisting perception disorder (flashback)*   The recurrence of drug-induced sensory and emotional changes long after a hallucinogenic drug has left the body.

*Hallucinosis*   A state of perceptual distortion and hallucination.

*Hardiness*   A set of positive attitudes in response to stress that enable a person who has been exposed to life-threatening situations to carry on with a sense of fortitude, control, and commitment.

*Hashish*   The most powerful drug produced from varieties of the hemp plant.

*Hebephrenic schizophrenia*   See *Disorganized schizophrenia.*

*Helper T-cell*   A lymphocyte that identifies antigens and then both multiplies and triggers the production of other kinds of immune cells.

*Helplessness*   See *Learned helplessness.*

*Heroin*   A highly addictive substance derived from opium.

*High*   The pleasant feeling of relaxation and euphoria that follows the rush from certain recreational drugs.

*Hindbrain*   The lower rearward portion of the brain comprised of the medulla, pons, and cerebellum.

*Hippocampus*   Part of the limbic system located below the cerebral cortex that is involved in the memory system. Damage to this area can result in severe memory difficulties.

*Histrionic personality disorder*   A personality disorder, once called hysterical personality disorder, in which an individual displays a pattern of excessive emotionality and attention seeking.

*Homeostasis*   A state in which the parts of a system interact in ways that enable the system to maintain itself and survive.

*Homosexuality*   Sexual preference for a person of one's own gender.

*Humanistic-existential model*   A theoretical point of view that stresses the role of values and choices in determining human individuality and fulfillment.

*Humanistic-existential therapy*   A system of therapy that tries to help clients view themselves and their situations more accurately and acceptingly and move toward actualizing their full potential as human beings.

*Humanistic model*   The theoretical perspective that human beings are born with a natural inclination to be friendly, cooperative, and constructive, and are driven to self-actualize.

*Humanistic therapy*   A system of therapy that tries to help clients look at themselves accurately and acceptingly so that they can fulfill their inborn potential.

*Humors*   From Greek and, later, medieval medical theory, four fluids thought to influence a person's health and temperament.

*Huntington's disease*   An inherited progressive degenerative disease of cognition, emotion, and movement.

*Hydrocephalus*   A disease characterized by an increase in cerebrospinal fluid and resultant head enlargement.

*Hypertension*   Chronic high blood pressure.

*Hypnosis*   A sleeplike, suggestible state during which a person can be directed to act in unusual ways, to experience unusual sensations, to remember seemingly forgotten events, or to forget remembered events.

**Hypnotic amnesia**   A condition in which a person forgets facts, events, and even his or her identity in obedience to an instruction received under hypnosis.

**Hypnotic therapy (hypnotherapy)**   A treatment in which the patient undergoes hypnosis and is then guided to recall forgotten events or perform other therapeutic activities.

**Hypnotism**   The inducing of a trancelike mental state in which a person becomes extremely suggestible.

**Hypoactive sexual desire disorder**   A disorder characterized by a lack of interest in sex and hence a low level of sexual activity.

**Hypochondriasis**   A somatoform disorder in which people mistakenly and incessantly fear that minor fluctuations in their physical functioning indicate a serious disease.

**Hypoxyphilia**   A pattern in which people strangle or smother themselves, or ask their partner to strangle or smother them, to enhance their sexual pleasure.

**Hypomanic pattern**   A pattern in which a person experiences symptoms of mania, but the symptoms are less severe and cause less impairment than a manic episode.

**Hypothalamus**   A part of the brain that helps maintain various bodily functions, including hunger and eating.

**Hypothesis**   A tentative explanation advanced to provide a basis for an investigation.

**Hysteria**   A term once used to describe what is now known as conversion disorder.

**Hysterical disorder**   A disorder, without any organic basis, in which physical functioning is changed or lost.

**Iatrogenic disorder**   A disorder that is unintentionally caused by a practitioner.

**Id**   One of the three psychological forces proposed by Freud as central to shaping personality. The id is the source of instinctual needs, drives, and impulses.

**Identification**   The unconscious incorporation of parental values and feelings and fusing them with one's identity. Also an ego defense mechanism in which persons take on the values and feelings of the person who is causing them anxiety.

**Idiographic understanding**   An understanding of the behavior of a particular individual.

**Illogical thinking**   Habitual illogical ways of thinking that may lead to self-defeating and even pathological conclusions.

**Imipramine**   A tricyclic drug that has been found to be effective in treating unipolar depression.

**Immune system**   The sum of complex bodily systems that detect and destroy antigens.

**Implosive therapy**   A treatment for phobias in which clients are exposed repeatedly to the feared object and made to see that such exposure is harmless. See also *Flooding*.

**Impulse-control disorders**   Disorders in which people fail to resist an impulse, drive, or temptation to perform an act that is harmful to themselves or to others.

**In vivo desensitization**   Desensitization training that makes use of actual physical situations, as opposed to imagined ones. See also *Covert desensitization*.

**Inappropriate affect**   A symptom of schizophrenia in which a person expresses emotions that are unsuited to the situation.

**Incest**   Sexual relations between close relatives.

**Incidence**   The number of new cases of a problem or disorder that occur in a population over a specific period of time.

**Independent variable**   The variable in an experiment that is manipulated to determine whether it has an effect on another variable.

**Individual therapy**   A therapeutic approach in which a therapist sees a client alone for sessions that may last from fifteen minutes to two hours.

**Informed consent**   A person's consent to participate in an experiment or procedure, given with full knowledge of the potential benefits and risks.

**Inhibited power motive style**   A personality style linked to a tendency to develop physical illness and characterized by a strong but inhibited need for power.

**Insanity defense**   A legal defense in which persons charged with a criminal offense claim to be not guilty by reason of insanity at the time of the offense.

**Insight therapy**   Psychotherapeutic approach that helps the patient primarily achieve a greater understanding of his or her problem and key aspects of his or her functioning.

**Insomnia**   The most common dyssomnia, characterized by difficulties initiating and maintaining sleep.

**Instrumental conditioning**   See *Operant conditioning*.

**Integrity test**   A test that seeks to measure whether the test taker is generally honest or dishonest.

**Intelligence quotient (IQ)**   A general score derived from intelligence tests that is considered to represent a person's overall level of intelligence.

**Intelligence test**   A test designed to measure a person's intellectual ability.

**Intermittent explosive disorder**   An impulse-control disorder in which people periodically fail to resist aggressive impulses, leading to the performance of serious assaults on people or destruction of property.

**Interpersonal psychotherapy (IPT)**   A treatment for unipolar patterns of depression. It is based on the premise that because depression occurs in an interpersonal context, clarifying and renegotiating that context is important to a person's recovery.

**Intoxication**   A temporary drug-induced state in which a person exhibits symptoms such as impaired judgment, mood changes, irritability, slurred speech, and loss of coordination.

**Introjection**   The unconscious incorporation of parental values that leads to the development of the superego in the child.

**Irresistible impulse test**   A legal criterion for determining a person's responsibility for committing a crime. This test asks whether the person was unable to control his or her actions.

**Isolation**   An ego defense mechanism in which people unconsciously isolate and disown undesirable and unwanted thoughts, experiencing them as foreign intrusions.

**Juvenile delinquents**   Term used to describe children between the ages of 8 and 18 who break the law.

**Killer T-cell**   A lymphocyte that seeks out and destroys body cells that have been infected by viruses.

**Kleptomania**   An impulse-control disorder characterized by the recurrent failure to resist impulses to steal objects not needed for personal use or monetary value.

**Koro**   A pattern of anxiety found in Southeast Asia in which a man suddenly becomes intensely fearful that his penis will withdraw into his abdomen and that he will die as a result.

**Korsakoff's syndrome**   An alcohol-related disorder marked by extreme confusion, memory impairment, and other neurological symptoms.

**L-dopa**   A precursor of dopamine, given to patients suffering from Parkinson's disease, a disease in which dopamine is low.

**L-glutamate**   A common neurotransmitter that is depleted in the brains of Alzheimer's victims.

**Latency stage**   In psychoanalytic theory, the stage children enter at 6 years of age in which their sexual desires apparently subside and their libidinal energy is devoted to developing new interests, activities, and skills.

**Latent content**   The symbolic meaning of a dream.

**Lateral hypothalamus (LH)**   The region of the hypothalamus that, when activated, produces hunger.

**Learned helplessness**   The perception, based on subjective experience, that one has no control over one's reinforcements.

**Learning disorder**   A developmental disorder marked by impairments in cognitive skills such as reading, mathematics, or language.

**Lesion**   Localized damage to tissue.

**Lethality scale**   A scale used by crisis prevention centers to estimate a caller's potential for suicide.

**Libido**   In Freudian theory, the sexual energy that fuels the id and other forces of personality.

**Life change units (LCUs)**   A system for measuring the stress associated with various life events.

**Light therapy (phototherapy)**   A treatment for seasonal affective disorders in which patients are exposed to intense light for several hours.

**Limbic system**   Region of the brain at the lower part of the cerebrum that controls bodily changes associated with emotions.

*Lithium*   A metallic element that occurs in nature as a mineral salt and is the most effective antibipolar drug.

*Lobotomy*   Psychosurgery that severs the connections between the cortex of the brain's frontal lobes and the lower centers of the brain.

*Localized (circumscribed) amnesia*   In this, the most common form of dissociative amnesia, a person forgets all events that occurred over a limited period of time.

*Locus coeruleus*   A small area in the brainstem that seems to be active in the regulation of emotions.   It is rich in neurons that use norepinephrine.

*Logotherapy*   A treatment that focuses on changing clients' attitudes toward their existence. Developed by Viktor Frankl. See *Paradoxical intention.*

*Long-term memory*   The memory system that contains all the information that we have stored over the years.

*Long term potentiation (LTP)*   A neuron's increased likelihood of responding strongly to future stimulation once it has been stimulated initially.

*Longitudinal study*   An investigation in which the characteristics or behavior of the same subjects is observed on many different occasions over a long period of time.

*Loose associations (derailment)*   A common thought disorder of schizophrenia, characterized by rapid shifts from one topic of conversation to another.

*LSD (lysergic acid diethylamide)*   A hallucinogenic drug derived from ergot alkaloids.

*Luteinizing hormone*   The chemical produced by the pituitary gland that stimulates testosterone production.

*Lycanthropy*   A condition in which a person believes himself or herself to be possessed by wolves or other animals.

*Lymphocytes*   White blood cells that are manufactured in the lymph system and circulate throughout the bloodstream, helping the body overcome antigens.

*M'Naghten rule*   A widely used legal criterion for insanity which holds people to be insane at the time of committing a crime if, because of a mental disorder, they did not know the nature of the act or did not know right from wrong.

*Magnetic resonance imaging (MRI)*   The use of the magnetic property of certain atoms in the brain to create a detailed picture of the brain's structure.

*Mainstreaming*   An approach to educating children with mental retardation in which they are placed in regular classes with children who are not mentally retarded.

*Major depressive disorder*   A severe pattern of unipolar depression that is significantly disabling and is not caused by such factors as drugs or a general medical condition.

*Male erectile disorder*   A male dysfunction characterized by a persistent or recurrent inability to attain an erection or to maintain an erection until completion of sexual activity.

*Male orgasmic disorder*   A male dysfunction characterized by a repeated absence of or very long delay in reaching orgasm following normal sexual excitement.

*Malingering*   Intentionally feigning illness to achieve some external gains, such as financial compensation or military deferment.

*Mania*   A state or episode of euphoria, frenzied activity, or related characteristics.

*Manic-depressive disorder*   See *Bipolar disorder.*

*Manifest content*   The consciously remembered features of a dream.

*Mantra*   A sound, uttered or thought, used to focus one's attention to turn away from ordinary thoughts and concerns during meditation.

*MAO inhibitor*   An antidepressant drug that inhibits the action of the enzyme monoamine oxidase.

*Marijuana*   One of the cannabis drugs, derived from the leaves and flowering tops of the hemp plant, *Cannabis sativa.*

*Marital therapy*   A therapeutic approach in which the therapist works with two people who share a long-term relationship.

*Masochism*   See *Sexual masochism.*

*Masturbation*   Self-stimulation of the genitals to achieve sexual arousal.

*Masturbatory satiation*   A behavioral treatment in which a client masturbates for a prolonged period of time while fantasizing in detail about a paraphiliac object. The procedure is expected to produce a feeling of boredom that in turn becomes associated with the object.

*Mean*   The average of a group of scores.

*Medication-induced movement disorders*   Disturbing movement abnormalities that are sometimes a side effect of antipsychotic drugs. They include Parkinsonian symptoms, neuroleptic malignant syndrome, dystonia, akathisia, and tardive dyskinesia.

*Meditation*   A technique of turning one's concentration inward and achieving a seemingly altered state of consciousness.

*Melancholia*   A condition described by early Greek and Roman philosophers and physicians as consisting of unshakable sadness. Today it is known as depression.

*Melatonin*   A hormone that appears to have a role in regulating mood. Melatonin is secreted when a person's surroundings are dark, but not when they are light.

*Mental incompetence*   A state of mental instability that leaves defendants unable to understand the legal charges and proceedings they are facing and unable to adequately prepare a defense with their lawyer.

*Mental retardation*   A disorder diagnosed when people manifest significant subaverage general intellectual functioning and deficient adaptive behavior.

*Mental status exam*   A set of interview questions and observations designed to reveal the degree and nature of a client's abnormal functioning.

*Mentally ill chemical abuser (MICA)*   A person with a chronic mental disorder who also abuses alcohol or other drugs.

*Mescaline*   A psychedelic drug.

*Mesmerism*   The method employed by Austrian physician F. A. Mesmer to treat hysterical disorder. It was a precursor to hypnotism.

*Metabolism*   The chemical and physical processes that go on in any living organism that break down food and convert it into energy. Also, the biochemical transformation of substances in the cells of living things, as when the liver breaks down alcohol into acetylaldehyde.

*Methadone*   A substitute laboratory-made drug for heroin. See also *Drug maintenance therapy.*

*Microencephaly*   A biological disorder characterized by a small, unusually shaped head, resulting from a combination of hereditary, prenatal, birth, and postnatal factors.

*Midbrain*   The middle region of the brain.

*Migraine headache*   An extremely severe headache that occurs on one side of the head, often preceded by a warning sensation and sometimes accompanied by dizziness, nausea, or vomiting.

*Milieu therapy*   A humanistic approach to institutional treatment based on the premise that institutions can help patients recover by creating a climate conducive to self-respect, individual responsibility, and meaningful activity.

*Mind-body dualism*   The view that the mind is a separate entity from the body, totally unable to affect physical matter or somatic processes.

*Minnesota Multiphasic Personality Inventory (MMPI)*   A widely used personality inventory consisting of a large number of statements which subjects mark as being true or false for them.

*Minor tranquilizers*   See *Antianxiety drugs.*

*Mitral valve prolapse (MVP)*   A cardiac malfunction marked by periodic episodes of heart palpitations.

*Mixed design*   A research design in which correlation analysis is used in concert with other types of analyses. See also *Quasi-experiment.*

*Model*   A set of logically connected assumptions and concepts that help scientists explain and interpret observations.

*Modeling*   A process of learning in which an individual acquires responses by observing and imitating others.

*Monoamine oxidase (MAO)*   A body chemical that destroys the neurotransmitter norepinephrine.

*Monoamine oxidase (MAO) inhibitors*   Antidepressant drugs that lower MAO activity and thus increase the level of norepinephrine activity in the brain.

*Monozygotic twins*   Twins who have developed from a single egg.

*Mood disorder*   Disorder affecting one's emotional state, including depression and bipolar disorder.

*Moral treatment*   A nineteenth century approach to treating people with mental disorders, which emphasized moral guidance, humane and respectful intervention, and kindness.

*Morphine*   A substance derived from opium that is even more effective than opium in relieving pain.

*Multiaxial system*   A classification system in which different "axes," or categories, represent different kinds of diagnostic information. DSM-IV is a multiaxial system.

*Multidimensional risk perspective*  A theory about the causes of a disorder that identifies several different kinds of risk factors which combine to help cause the disorder.

*Multiple personality disorder (dissociative identity disorder)*  A dissociative disorder in which a person displays two or more distinct personalities that repeatedly take control of the person's behavior.

*Munchausen syndrome*  A factitious disorder in which a person travels from hospital to hospital reciting symptoms, gaining admission, and receiving treatment.

*Muscle contraction headache*  A chronic headache caused by the contraction of muscles surrounding the skull.

*Narcissistic personality disorder*  A personality disorder characterized by a chronic and pervasive pattern of grandiosity, need for admiration, and lack of empathy.

*Narcolepsy*  A dyssomnia characterized by sudden onsets of REM sleep during waking hours, generally brought on by strong emotion.

*Narcotic*  Any natural or synthetic derivative of opium.

*Narcotic antagonist*  A substance that counteracts the effects of opioids. See Antagonist drug.

*Natural experiment*  An experiment in which nature, rather than an experimenter, manipulates an independent variable and the experimenter systematically observes the effects.

*Naturalistic observation*  A method for observing behavior in which clinicians or researchers observe clients or subjects in their everyday environments.

*Negative correlation*  A statistical relationship in which the value of one variable increases while the other variable decreases.

*Negative feedback loops*  A physiological process in which the brain receives information about external events from the environment, processes this information, and then stimulates body organs into action. Mechanisms in the organs then provide negative feedback, telling the brain that its stimulation has been sufficient and should now stop.

*Negative symptoms*  Symptoms of schizophrenia that seem to reflect pathological deficits or characteristics that seem to be lacking—flat affect, poverty of speech, and loss of volition.

*Neologism*  A made-up word that has meaning only to the person using it.

*Nerve ending*  The region at the neuron's terminus from which an impulse that has traveled through the neuron is transmitted to a neighboring neuron.

*Neurofibrillary tangles*  Twisted protein fibers found within certain brain cells of people with Alzheimer's disease, interfering with memory and learning.

*Neuroleptic drug*  See *Antipsychotic drugs.*

*Neuroleptic malignant syndrome*  A severe, potentially fatal reaction to antipsychotic drugs, marked by muscle rigidity, fever, altered consciousness, and autonomic dysfunction.

*Neurological*  Relating to the structure or activity of the brain.

*Neuron*  A nerve cell. The brain contains billions of neurons.

*Neuropsychological test*  A test that detects brain impairment by measuring a person's cognitive, perceptual, and motor performances.

*Neurosis*  Freud's term for disorders characterized by intense anxiety, attributed to failure of a person's ego defense mechanisms to cope with his or her unconscious conflicts.

*Neurotransmitter*  A chemical that, released by one neuron, crosses the synaptic space to be received at receptors on the dendrites of adjacent neurons.

*Neutralizing*  A person's attempt to eliminate unwanted, intrusive thoughts by thinking or behaving in ways that put matters right internally or that make amends for unacceptable thoughts.

*Nightmare disorder*  A common parasomnia in which a person experiences chronic distressful, frightening dreams.

*Nocturnal penile tumescence (NPT)*  Erections during sleep.

*Nomothetic understanding*  In the context of abnormal psychology, a general understanding of the nature, causes, and treatments of abnormality.

*Norepinephrine*  A neurotransmitter whose abnormal activity is linked to depression and panic disorder.

*Normalization program*  A treatment program for mentally retarded persons that provides everyday conditions that closely resemble life in the mainstream of society.

*Norms*  A given culture's explicit and implicit rules for appropriate conduct.

*Not guilty by reason of insanity (NGRI)*  A verdict stating that defendants are not guilty of committing a crime because they were insane at the time of the crime.

*Object relations theory*  A psychodynamic theory that views the desire for relatedness with others (objects) as the motivating force in human behavior, focusing on the processes of attachment and separation.

*Observer drift*  The tendency of an observer who is rating subjects in an experiment to gradually and involuntarily change criteria, thus making the data unreliable.

*Obsession*  A persistent thought, impulse, or mental image that is experienced repeatedly, feels intrusive, and causes anxiety.

*Obsessive-compulsive disorder*  A disorder in which a person has recurrent and unwanted thoughts or a need to perform repetitive and ritualistic actions, and an experience of intense anxiety whenever these behaviors are suppressed.

*Obsessive-compulsive personality disorder*  A personality disorder in which an individual displays a pattern of preoccupation with orderliness, perfectionism, and mental and interpersonal control.

*Oedipus complex*  In Freudian theory, the pattern of desires in which boys become attracted to their mother as a sexual object and see their father as a rival they would like to push aside.

*Onychophagia*  Compulsive nail-biting.

*Operant conditioning*  A process of learning in which behavior that leads to satisfying consequences, or rewards, is likely to be repeated.

*Operationalization*  The translating of an abstract variable of interest to an investigator into discrete, observable entities or events.

*Opioid*  Opium or any of the drugs derived from opium, including morphine, heroin, and codeine.

*Opium*  A highly addictive substance made from the sap of the opium poppy seed. It has been widely used for thousands of years to reduce physical and emotional pain.

*Opponent-process theory*  An explanation for drug abuse and dependence based on the interplay of pleasurable emotions that initially come from ingesting the drug and inevitable negative aftereffects that leave a person feeling worse than usual.

*Oppositional defiant disorder*  A childhood disorder in which children argue repeatedly with adults, lose their temper, swear, and feel great anger and resentment.

*Oral stage*  In this earliest development stage in Freud's conceptualization of psychosocial development, the infant's main libidinal gratification comes from feeding and from the body parts involved in it.

*Organic mental disorders*  Mental disorders that have clear physical causes.

*Organicity*  The quality of being caused primarily by damage to the brain or alterations in brain activity.

*Orgasm*  The third stage of the sexual response cycle, consisting of reflexive muscular contractions in the pelvic region.

*Orgasm phase*  The third phase in the sexual response cycle, characterized by reflexive muscular contractions in the pelvic region.

*Orgasmic reorientation*  A procedure for treating certain paraphilias by conditioning clients to respond to new, more appropriate sources of erotic stimulation.

*Outpatient*  A setting for treatment in which persons visit a therapist's office as opposed to remaining in a hospital.

*Overt behavior*  Observable actions or clear verbalizations.

*Pain disorder*  A somatoform disorder characterized by severe and prolonged pain, with psychological factors playing a significant role in the onset, severity, exacerbation, or maintenance of the pain.

*Panic attack*  Periodic, discrete bouts of panic that occur abruptly and reach a peak within 10 minutes.

*Panic disorder*  An anxiety disorder characterized by recurrent and unpredictable panic attacks that occur without apparent provocation.

*Panic disorder with agoraphobia*  A panic disorder in which panic attacks lead to agoraphobic patterns of behavior.

*Panic disorder without agoraphobia*    A panic disorder in which agoraphobia is absent.

*Paradigm*    An implicit theoretical framework that arises out of an explicit set of basic assumptions. A scientist's paradigm affects the way he or she interprets observations and other data.

*Paranoid disorder*    See *Delusional disorder.*

*Paranoid personality disorder*    A personality disorder characterized by a pattern of distrust and suspiciousness of others.

*Paranoid schizophrenia*    A type of schizophrenia characterized primarily by an organized system of delusions and hallucinations.

*Paraphilias*    Disorders characterized by recurrent and intense sexual urges, fantasies, or behaviors involving either nonhuman objects, children, nonconsenting adults, or experiences of suffering or humiliation.

*Paraprofessional*    A person without previous professional training who provides services under the supervision of a mental health professional.

*Parasomnias*    Sleep disorders characterized by the occurrence of abnormal events during sleep.

*Parasuicide*    A person who attempts suicide and lives.

*Parasympathetic nervous system*    The group of nerve fibers of the autonomic nervous system that helps maintain normal organ functioning. It also slows organ functioning after stimulation and returns other body processes to normal.

*Parens patriae*    The principle by which the state can make decisions— such as to hospitalize a person against his or her wishes—that are believed to promote the individual's best interests and protect him or her from self-harm or neglect.

*Parkinson's disease*    A slowly progressive neurological condition marked by tremors, rigidity, unsteadiness, and in many cases dementia.

*Parkinsonian symptom*    Dystonia, akathisia, tardive dyskinesia, and other symptoms similar to those found in Parkinson's disease. Schizophrenic patients taking antipsychotic medication that blocks the activity of dopamine may display one or more of these symptoms.

*Passive-aggressive personality disorder*    A category of personality disorder, listed in past versions of the DSM, characterized by a pattern of negativistic attitudes and passive resistance to demands for adequate performance in social and occupational situations.

*Pathological gambling*    An impulse-control disorder characterized by recurrent and persistent maladaptive gambling behavior that disrupts personal, family, or vocational pursuits.

*PCP*    Phencyclidine, a psychedelic drug.

*Pedophilia*    A paraphilia in which a person has recurrent and intense sexual urges or fantasies about watching, touching, or engaging in sexual acts with prepubescent children, and may carry out these urges or fantasies.

*Peer review system*    A system by which clinicians paid by an insurance company may periodically review a therapist's treatment report and recommend the continuation or termination of insurance benefits.

*Penile prosthesis*    A surgical implantation consisting of a semirigid rod made of rubber and wire that produces an artificial erection.

*Penis envy*    The Freudian theory that girls wish to overcome their feelings of inferiority during the phallic phase by having a penis.

*Performance anxiety*    The fear of performing inadequately and a consequent tension experienced during sex.

*Perseveration*    The persistent repetition of words and statements often seen in schizophrenia or autism.

*Personality*    The unique pattern of behavior, perception, and emotion displayed by each individual.

*Personality assessment*    The gathering of information about the components of someone's personality and any unconscious conflicts he or she may be experiencing.

*Personality disorder*    A pervasive, enduring, and inflexible pattern of inner experience and outward behavior that deviates markedly from the expectations of one's culture and leads to distress or impairment.

*Personality inventory*    A test designed to measure broad personality characteristics, consisting of statements about behaviors, beliefs, and feelings that people are asked to evaluate as characteristic or uncharacteristic of them.

*Personality trait*    An enduring consistency with which a person reacts to and acts upon his or her surroundings.

*Pervasive developmental disorders*    A broad category of disorders beginning in early childhood, characterized by severe and pervasive impairments in reciprocal social interaction skills, communication skills, or the presence of stereotyped behavior, interests, and activities.

*Phallic stage*    In psychoanalytic theory, the period between the third and fourth years when the focus of sexual pleasure shifts to the genitals.

*Phalloplasty*    A procedure used during sex-reassignment surgery to create a functional penis.

*Pharmacotherapist (psychopharmacologist)*    A psychiatrist who primarily prescribes medications.

*Phenomenology*    One's personal experiences and perspectives of the world.

*Phenothiazines*    A group of antihistamine drugs that became the first group of effective antipsychotic medications.

*Phenylketonuria (PKU)*    A metabolic disorder in which the body is unable to metabolize the amino acid phenylalanine into tyrosine. If untreated, the phenylalanine accumulates and is converted into substances that poison the system and cause mental retardation.

*Phobia*    A persistent and irrational fear of a specific object, activity, or situation.

*Phototherapy*    See *Light therapy.*

*Pick's disease*    A degenerative disease of the brain that particularly affects the frontal and temporal lobes.

*Placebo*    A sham treatment that the subject believes to be genuine.

*Play therapy*    An approach to treating childhood disorders that helps children express their conflicts and feelings indirectly by drawing, playing with toys, and making up stories.

*Pleasure principle*    In Freudian theory, the pursuit of gratification that motivates the id.

*Plethysmograph*    A device used to measure sexual arousal.

*Polygraph*    A test that seeks to determine whether or not the test taker is telling the truth by measuring physiological responses such as respiration level, perspiration level, and heart rate.

*Polysubstance use*    The misuse of combinations of drugs to achieve a synergistic effect.

*Polysubstance-related disorder*    A long-term pattern of maladaptive behavior centered around the abuse of or dependence on a combination of drugs.

*Positive correlation*    A statistical relationship in which the values of two variables increase together or decrease together.

*Positive symptoms*    Symptoms of schizophrenia that seem to represent pathological excesses or bizarre additions to a normal repertoire of behavior. They include delusions, hallucinations, disorganized thinking and speech, and inappropriate affect.

*Positron emission tomography (PET scan)*    A computer-produced motion picture showing rates of metabolism throughout the brain.

*Posttraumatic stress disorder*    An anxiety disorder in which fear and related symptoms continue to be experienced long after a traumatic event.

*Poverty of content*    A lack of meaning in spite of high emotion that is often found in the speech of people with schizophrenia who display loose associations.

*Predisposition*    An inborn or acquired vulnerability (or inclination or diathesis) for developing certain symptoms.

*Premature ejaculation*    A dysfunction in which a man reaches orgasm and ejaculates before, on, or shortly after penetration and before the person wishes it.

*Premenstrual dysphoric disorder*    A pattern characterized by markedly depressed mood, anxiety, and marked mood changes, and a decreased interest in activities during the last week of the luteal phase. These symptoms remit within a few days after the onset of menses. This pattern is listed in the appendix of DSM-IV as a category provided for further study.

*Premorbid*    The period prior to the onset of an illness.

*Preparedness*    A predisposition to acquire certain fears.

*Presenile*    Occurring in middle age.

*Presenile dementia*    Dementia occurring in middle age. See also *Dementia.*

*Prevalence*    The total number of cases of a problem or disorder occurring in a population over a specific period of time.

*Prevention*    A key aspect of community mental health programs, which strive to prevent or at least minimize mental disorders.

*Primary gain*    In psychodynamic theory, the gain achieved by hysterical symptoms of keeping internal conflicts out of awareness.

**Primary hypersomnia**  A sleep disorder in which the predominant problem is excessive sleepiness for at least a month, taking the form of prolonged sleep episodes or daytime sleep that occurs almost daily.

**Primary insomnia**  A sleep disorder in which the predominant complaint is an inability to initiate or maintain sleep.

**Primary personality**  The subpersonality that appears more often than the others in individuals with multiple personality disorder.

**Private psychotherapy**  An arrangement by which an individual directly pays a psychologist for counseling services.

**Proband**  The person who is the focus of a genetic study.

**Procedural memory**  Memory of learned physical or cognitive skills we perform without needing to think about them. These memories are not directly accessible to consciousness.

**Prodromal phase**  The period during which symptoms of schizophrenia are not yet prominent, but the person has begun to deteriorate from previous levels of functioning.

**Prognosis**  A prediction on the course and outcome of a disorder.

**Projection**  An ego defense mechanism in which a person attributes to others undesirable characteristics or impulses in himself or herself.

**Projective test**  A test that consists of unstructured or ambiguous material to which people are asked to respond.

**Prolactin**  A pituitary hormone that can interfere with the sex drive.

**Prophylactic drug**  A drug that actually helps prevent symptoms from developing.

**Prospective study**  A study that predicts future changes on the basis of past and present events.

**Protection and advocacy system**  The system by which lawyers and advocates who work for patients may investigate possible cases of patient abuse and neglect and then address any problems they find.

**Prozac (fluoxetine)**  A second-generation antidepressant that appears to have fewer undesired side effects than MAO inhibitors and tricyclics. It also appears to be an effective treatment for eating and obsessive-compulsive disorders.

**Psilocybin**  A psychedelic drug.

**Psychedelic drug**  A substance, such as LSD, that causes profound perceptual changes.

**Psychiatric social worker**  A mental health specialist who is qualified to conduct psychotherapy upon earning a Masters degree or Doctorate in social work.

**Psychiatrist**  A physician who in addition to medical school has completed three to four years of residency training in the treatment of abnormal psychological functioning.

**Psychoanalysis**  The theory or treatment of abnormal psychological functioning, first developed by Sigmund Freud, that emphasizes unconscious conflicts as the cause of psychological dysfunctioning.

**Psychodrama**  A group therapy technique that calls for group members to act out dramatic roles as if they were participating in an improvised play in which they express their feelings and thoughts, explore new behaviors and attitudes, and empathize with the feelings and perspectives of others.

**Psychodynamic model**  The theoretical perspective that sees all human functioning as being shaped by dynamic psychological forces and looks at people's unconscious internal conflicts in order to explain their behavior.

**Psychodynamic therapy**  A system of therapy whose goals are to help clients uncover past traumatic events and the inner conflicts that have resulted from them; resolve, or settle, those conflicts; and resume interrupted personal development.

**Psychogenesis**  The development of abnormal functioning from psychological causes.

**Psychogenic illness**  An illness caused primarily by psychological factors such as worry, family stress, and unconscious needs.

**Psychological autopsy**  A procedure used to analyze information about a deceased person to determine whether the person's death was self inflicted.

**Psychoneuroimmunology**  The study of the connections between stress, illness, and the body's immune system.

**Psychopathology**  Any abnormal pattern of functioning that may be described as deviant, distressful, dysfunctional, or dangerous.

**Psychopathy**  See *Antisocial personality disorder.*

**Psychopharmacologist**  A psychiatrist who primarily prescribes medications.

**Psychophysiological (psychosomatic) disorders**  Illnesses believed to result from an interaction of organic and psychological factors.

**Psychophysiological test**  A test which measures physical responses (such as heart rate and muscle tension) as possible indicators of psychological problems.

**Psychosexual stages**  The developmental stages defined by Freud in which the id, ego, and superego interact. Each stage is marked by a different source of libidinal pleasure.

**Psychosis**  A state in which an individual loses contact with reality in key ways.

**Psychosomatic (psychophysiological) illnesses**  Illnesses that have both psychological and physical causes. DSM-IV labels these illnesses *Psychological factors affecting medical condition.*

**Psychosurgery**  Brain surgery performed as a treatment for mental disorders.

**Psychotherapy**  A treatment procedure in which sufferer and healer employ words, acts, and rituals as a means of overcoming psychological difficulties.

**Psychotropic medications**  Drugs that primarily affect the brain and alleviate many symptoms of mental dysfunctioning.

**Pyromania**  An impulse-control disorder characterized by a pattern of fire setting for pleasure, gratification, or relief from tension.

**Quasi-experiment**  An experiment in which investigators do not randomly assign the subjects to control and experimental groups but instead make use of groups that already exist in the world at large.

**Quinine**  A drug that is often added to heroin to counteract the dangers of infection.

**Random assignment**  A testing condition in which subjects are randomly placed either in the control group or in the experimental group in order to reduce the possibility that preexisting differences between the groups are influencing the results.

**Rap group**  A group that meets to help participants converse about and explore problematic issues in an atmosphere of mutual support.

**Rape**  Sexual intercourse or another sexual act forced upon a nonconsenting person or engaged in with an underage person.

**Rapid eye movement (REM) sleep**  The period of the sleep cycle during which the eyes move quickly, back and forth, indicating that the person is dreaming.

**Rapprochement movement**  An effort to delineate a set of "common therapeutic strategies" that characterize the work of all effective therapists.

**Rational-emotive therapy**  A therapeutic system developed by Albert Ellis that helps clients to discover the irrational assumptions governing their emotional responses and to change those assumptions into constructive ways of viewing the world and themselves.

**Rationalization**  An ego defense mechanism in which one creates acceptable reasons for unwanted or undesirable behavior.

**Reaction formation**  An ego defense mechanism in which a repressed desire is instead expressed by taking on an opposite lifestyle.

**Reactive depression**  A depression that appears to follow on the heels of clear-cut precipitating events.

**Reactivity**  The extent to which the very presence of an observer affects a person's behavior.

**Reality principle**  In Freudian theory, the knowledge we acquire through experience and from the people around us that it can be dangerous or unacceptable to express our id impulses outright.

**Receptor**  A site on a neuron that receives a neurotransmitter.

**Regression**  An ego defense mechanism in which a person returns to a more primitive mode of interacting with the world.

**Reinforcement**  The desirable or undesirable stimuli that follows as a result of an organism's behavior.

**Relapse-prevention training**  A treatment technique in which heavy drinkers are taught to use self-monitoring to identify the situations and emotional changes that place them at high risk for heavy drinking.

**Relaxation training**  A procedure in which clients are taught to release all the tension in their bodies on cue.

**Reliability**  A measure of the consistency of test or research results.

**Repression**  An ego defense mechanism that prevents unacceptable impulses from reaching consciousness.

**Residential treatment center**  A place where people formerly dependent on drugs live, work, and socialize in a drug-free environment.

*Residual schizophrenia*   A condition in which the florid symptoms of schizophrenia have lessened in intensity and number yet remain with the patient in a residual form.

*Resistance*   In psychodynamic therapy, a patient's inclination to stop free associating or to change subjects in order to avoid a potentially painful discussion.

*Resolution phase*   The fourth phase in the sexual response cycle, characterized by relaxation and a decline in arousal following orgasm.

*Response inventories*   Tests designed to measure a person's responses in one specific area of functioning, such as affect, social skills, or cognitive processes.

*Response prevention*   See *Exposure and response prevention.*

*Response set*   A particular way of responding to questions or statements on a test, such as always selecting "true," regardless of the content of the questions.

*Restricting type anorexia nervosa*   A type of anorexia nervosa in which people reduce their weight by restricting their food intake.

*Reticular formation*   The body's arousal center located in the brain.

*Retrograde amnesia*   A lack of memory about events that occurred before the event that caused amnesia.

*Retrospective analysis*   A kind of psychological autopsy in which clinicians and researchers piece together data about a person's suicide from the person's past.

*Retrospective study*   A kind of research study in which subjects are asked to recall past events.

*Reversal design (ABAB)*   An experimental design in which behavior is measured to achieve a baseline (A), then again after the treatment has been applied (B), then again after the conditions during baseline have been reintroduced (A), and then once again after the treatment is reintroduced (B).

*Reward*   A pleasurable stimulus given to an organism to encourage a specific behavior.

*Right to refuse treatment*   The legal right of patients to refuse certain forms of treatment.

*Right to treatment*   The legal right of persons, particularly those who are involuntarily committed, to receive adequate treatment.

*Risk study*   A research method that surveys the biological relatives of a patient who has been diagnosed with a specific abnormality to see which and how many of them have the same disorder.

*Role play*   A therapy technique in which clients are instructed to act out roles assigned to them by the therapist.

*Rorschach test*   A projective test using a subject's reactions to inkblots to help reveal psychological features of the subject.

*Rosenthal effect*   The general finding that the results of any experiment often conform to the expectations of the experimenter. It is attributed to the inescapable effects of bias.

*Rush*   A spasm of warmth and ecstasy that occurs when certain drugs, such as heroin, are ingested.

*Sadism*   Sexual pleasure achieved through inflicting physical or emotional pain.

*Sample*   A group of subjects that is representative of the larger population about which a researcher wishes to make a statement.

*Savant*   A person with a major mental disorder or intellectual handicap who has some extraordinary ability despite his or her handicaps.

*Schizoaffective disorder*   A disorder in which symptoms of both schizophrenia and a mood disorder are prominent.

*Schizoid personality disorder*   A personality disorder in which a person displays a pattern of detachment from social relationships and a restricted range of emotional expression.

*Schizophrenia*   A psychotic disorder in which personal, social, and occupational functioning that were previously adaptive deteriorate as a result of distorted perceptions, disturbed thought processes, deviant emotional states, and motor abnormalities.

*Schizophreniform disorder*   A disorder in which all of the key features of schizophrenia are present but last between one and six months.

*Schizophrenogenic mother*   A type of mother—supposedly cold, domineering, and impervious to the needs of others—who was once thought to cause schizophrenia in the child.

*Schizotypal personality disorder*   A personality disorder in which a person displays a pattern of interpersonal deficits marked by acute discomfort in close relationships, cognitive or perceptual distortions, and behavioral eccentricities.

*School phobia*   A childhood anxiety disorder in which children experience extreme anxiety about attending school and often stay home for an extended period of time.

*School refusal*   See *School phobia.*

*Scientific method*   The process of systematically acquiring and evaluating information through observation to gain an understanding of specific phenomena.

*Seasonal affective disorder (SAD)*   A mood disorder in which mood episodes are related to changes in season. It appears to be related to shifts in the overall amount of light one is exposed to, and correspondingly, to shifts in melatonin secretions.

*Second-generation antidepressants*   New antidepressant drugs that differ structurally from tricyclics and MAO inhibitors.

*Second messengers*   Chemical compound changes within the neuron that are responsible for the cell's response to a neurotransmitter.

*Secondary gain*   In psychodynamic theory, the gain achieved by hysterical symptoms of eliciting kindness or sympathy from others or providing an excuse to avoid unpleasant activities.

*Sedative-hypnotic drug*   A drug used in low doses to reduce anxiety and in higher doses to help people sleep.

*Selective serotonin reuptake inhibitors (SSRI)*   A group of second-generation antidepressant drugs (including fluoxetine, paroxetine, and setraline) that are thought to alter serotonin activity specifically, without affecting other neurotransmitters or biochemical processes.

*Selective amnesia*   A disorder in which the person remembers some but not all events occurring over a circumscribed period of time.

*Self-actualization*   The humanistic process by which people fulfill their potential for goodness and growth.

*Self-efficacy*   The judgment that one can master and perform needed behaviors whenever necessary.

*Self-help group*   A therapy group made up of people who have similar problems and come together to help and support one another without the direct leadership of a professional clinician.

*Self-hypnosis*   The induction by oneself of a hypnotic state.

*Self-instruction training*   A cognitive therapy that teaches people how to make helpful statements to themselves and how to apply such statements in difficult circumstances.

*Self-monitoring*   A technique for monitoring behavior in which clients observe themselves.

*Self psychology*   A variation of psychoanalysis developed by Heinz Kohut that focuses on a person's self-worth.

*Self-statement*   A statement about oneself, sometimes counterproductive, that comes to mind during stressful situations.

*Semantic memory*   A person's memory for abstract, encyclopedic, or categorical information.

*Senile*   Typical of or occurring in people over the age of 65.

*Senile dementia*   See *Dementia.*

*Senile plaques*   Sphere-shaped deposits of beta-amyloid protein that form excessively in the spaces between certain neurons in people with Alzheimer's disease.

*Sensate focus*   A treatment for sexual disorders that instructs couples to take the focus away from intercourse and instead spend time concentrating on mutual massage, kissing, and hugging.

*Separation anxiety disorder*   A childhood disorder characterized by excessive anxiety, even panic, whenever the child is separated from home or a parent.

*Serotonin*   A neurotransmitter whose abnormal activity is linked to depression, eating disorders, and obsessive-compulsive disorder.

*Sex offender statute*   The presumption by legislators that people who are repeatedly found guilty of certain sex crimes are mentally ill and should be categorized as "mentally disordered sex offenders."

*Sexual arousal disorder*   A failure of lubrication or genital swelling in women or an absence of penile erection in men, or the lack of a subjective sense of sexual excitement and pleasure in either men or women.

*Sexual aversion disorder*   A disorder characterized by an aversion to and active avoidance of genital sexual contact with a sexual partner.

*Sexual dysfunction*   A disorder in which a person is unable to function normally in some area of the human sexual response cycle.

*Sexual masochism*   A paraphilia characterized by repeated and intense sexual urges, fantasies, or behaviors that involve being humiliated, beaten, bound, or otherwise made to suffer.

*Sexual pain disorder*    A dysfunction in which a person experiences pain during arousal or intercourse. See also *Dyspareunia* and *Vaginismus*.

*Sexual response cycle*    The generalized sequence of behavior and feelings that occur during sexual intercourse, consisting of desire, arousal, orgasm, and resolution.

*Sexual sadism*    A paraphilia characterized by recurrent and intense sexual urges, fantasies, or behaviors that involve inflicting physical or psychological suffering on others.

*Shaping*    A learning procedure in which successive approximations of the desired behavior are rewarded.

*Shared psychotic disorder (folie à deux)*    A disorder in which a person embraces delusions held by another individual.

*Sheltered workshop*    A protected and supervised workplace that offers clients occupational training.

*Short-term memory*    The memory system that collects new information.

*Shuttle box*    A box partitioned by a barrier that an animal can jump over in order to escape or avoid shock. Used in learned helplessness studies.

*Single-subject experimental design*    A research method in which a single subject is observed and measured both before and after the manipulation of an independent variable.

*Situation (or state) anxiety*    Anxiety experienced in particular situations or environments.

*Sleep apnea*    A disorder in which the person actually stops breathing for up to thirty or more seconds while asleep.

*Sleep terror disorder*    A parasomnia in which persons awaken suddenly during the first third of their major sleep episode, screaming out in extreme fear and agitation.

*Sleepwalking disorder*    A parasomnia in which people repeatedly leave their beds and walk around without being conscious of the episode or remembering it later.

*Social breakdown syndrome*    A pattern of deterioration resulting from institutionalization and characterized by extreme withdrawal, anger, physical aggressiveness, and loss of interest in personal appearance.

*Social phobia*    A severe and persistent fear of social or performance situations in which embarrassment may occur.

*Social skills training*    A therapeutic approach used by behavioral therapists to help people acquire or improve their social skills and assertiveness through the use of role playing and rehearsing of desirable behaviors.

*Social therapy (sociotherapy)*    An approach to therapy in which the therapist makes practical advice and life adjustment a central focus of treatment for schizophrenia.

*Sociocultural model*    The theoretical perspective that emphasizes the effect of society and culture on individual behavior.

*Sociology*    The study of human relationships and social groups.

*Sociopathy*    See *Antisocial personality disorder.*

*Sociotherapy*    See *Social therapy.*

*Sodium amobarbital (amytal)*    A drug used to put people into a near-sleep state during which their inhibitions are lowered, thus helping some persons to recall forgotten events.

*Sodium pentobarbital (pentothal)*    See *Sodium amobarbital.*

*Somatization disorder*    A somatoform disorder characterized by recurring numerous physical ailments without a primary organic basis.

*Somatoform disorder*    A physical illness or ailment that is primarily explained by psychological causes, in which the patient experiences no sense of willing the symptoms or having control over them.

*Somatogenesis*    The development of abnormal functioning from physical causes.

*Somatogenic perspective*    The view that abnormal psychological functioning has physical causes.

*Specific phobia*    A persistent fear of a specific object or situation (excluding social phobia and agoraphobia).

*Spectator role*    A state of mind that some people take during sex, focusing on their sexual performance to such an extent that the performance and their enjoyment are impeded.

*Spouse abuse*    The physical mistreatment or misuse of one spouse by the other, ranging from shoving to battering.

*Stalking*    The persistent pursuit, harassment, or threatening of one person by another.

*Standardization*    The process in which a test is administered to a large group of subjects whose performance then serves as a common standard or norm.

*State-dependent learning*    Learning that is closely linked to a person's state of arousal when the learning first occurred.

*State hospital*    A public mental institution, run by the state.

*Statistical analysis*    The application of principles of probability to the findings of a study in order to learn how likely it is that the findings have occurred by chance.

*Statistical significance*    A measure of the probability that an observed event occurred by chance rather than as the result of a particular relationship or an experimental manipulation.

*Stimulant*    A substance that increases the activity of the central nervous system.

*Stimulus generalization*    A phenomenon in which responses to one stimulus are also elicited by similar stimuli.

*Stress inoculation*    See *Self-instruction training.*

*Stressor*    An event that creates a degree of threat by confronting a person with a demand or opportunity for change of some kind.

*Structural family therapy*    A family systems treatment approach in which the therapist pays particular attention to the family power structure, the role each member plays within the family, and the alliances between family members.

*Structured interview*    An interview format in which the clinician asks prepared questions.

*Structured observation*    A method for observing behavior in which people are monitored in artificial settings created in clinicians' offices or in laboratories.

*Stutter*    A disturbance in the normal fluency and time patterning of speech, characterized by repeating words or sounds, prolonging or interjecting sounds, pausing within a word, or blocking sounds.

*Subintentional death*    A death in which the victim plays an indirect, covert, partial, or unconscious causal role.

*Subject*    An individual chosen to participate in a study.

*Sublimation*    In psychoanalytic theory, the rechanneling of narcissistic impulses into endeavors that are both socially acceptable and personally gratifying. It can also be used as an ego defense mechanism.

*Subpersonalities*    The distinct personalities found in individuals suffering from multiple personality disorder, each with a unique set of memories, behaviors, thoughts, and emotions.

*Substance abuse*    A pattern of behavior in which a person relies on a drug excessively and chronically, allowing it to occupy a central position in his or her life.

*Substance dependence*    A pattern of behavior in which a person relies on a drug excessively and builds a tolerance to it or experiences withdrawal symptoms when he or she abstains from it, or both.

*Substance-related disorder*    A pattern of maladaptive behavior centered around the use of, abuse of, or dependence on certain substances.

*Suicide*    A self-inflicted death in which the person acts intentionally, directly, and consciously.

*Suicide prevention programs*    Programs that try to identify people who are at the point of killing themselves and to help such people perceive their situation more accurately, make better decisions, act more constructively, and overcome their crisis.

*Superego*    One of the three psychological forces proposed by Freud as central to shaping the personality. The superego embodies the values and ideals taught to us by our parents.

*Supportive nursing care*    A treatment, applied to anorexia nervosa in particular, in which well-trained nurses conduct a day-to-day hospital program.

*Symbolic loss*    According to Freudian theory, the loss of a valued object (for example, a loss of employment) which is unconsciously interpreted as the loss of a loved one.

*Sympathetic nervous system*    The nerve fibers of the autonomic nervous system that quicken the heartbeat and produce other changes experienced as fear or anxiety.

*Symptom*    A physical or psychological sign of a disorder.

*Symptom substitution*    The belief held by some psychodynamic therapists that quick symptom reduction is likely to result in the replacement of the old symptoms by new ones.

*Synapse*    The tiny space between the nerve ending of one neuron and the dendrite of another.

*Syndrome*    A cluster of symptoms that usually occur together.

*Synergistic effect*    In pharmacology, an enhancement of effects that occurs when more than one drug is acting on the body at the same time.

*Synesthesia*    A crossing over of sensory perceptions, caused by LSD.

*System of therapy*    A set of treatment principles and techniques employed in accordance with a particular theory of causation and change.

*Systematic desensitization*    A behavioral treatment in which phobic clients learn to react calmly instead of with intense fear to the objects or situations they dread.

*T-group*    A small group guided by a leader and similar to an encounter group in intensity but concerned primarily with educating people.

*Tarantism*    A phenomenon that occurred throughout Europe between A.D. 900 and 1800 in which groups of people would suddenly start to jump around, dance, and go into convulsions.

*Tactrine hydrochloride*    A drug sometimes used to help treat Alzheimer's disease. It prevents the breakdown of the neurotransmitter acetylcholine.

*Tardive dyskinesia*    Extrapyramidal effects, such as involuntary smacking of the lips or wagging of the chin, that appear in some patients after they have taken antipsychotic drugs for an extended period. It is more common in older patients, and it is sometimes difficult or impossible to eliminate. See also *Extrapyramidal effects*.

*Tay-Sachs disease*    A metabolic disorder resulting from a pairing of recessive genes that causes mental deterioration, loss of visual functioning, and death.

*Temporal lobes*    Major regions in the cortex of each hemisphere of the brain that play a key role in memory, among other functions.

*Tension headache*    See *Muscle-contraction headache*.

*Testosterone*    The principal male sex hormone.

*Tetrahydrocannabinol (THC)*    The main active ingredient of cannabis substances.

*Thalamus*    The region of the brain that acts as a relay station for sensory information, sending it to the cerebrum.

*Thanatos*    According to the Freudian view, thanatos is the basic death instinct that functions in opposition to the life instinct.

*Thematic Apperception Test*    A projective test using pictures that depict people in somewhat unclear situations.

*Therapist*    A person who implements a system of therapy to help a person overcome psychological difficulties.

*Therapy*    Special, systematic process for helping people overcome their psychological difficulties. The process may consist primarily of discussion or action (psychotherapy) or of biological intervention.

*Token economy*    A behavioral program in which a person's desirable behaviors are reinforced systematically throughout the day by the awarding of tokens that can be exchanged for goods or privileges.

*Tolerance*    The adjustment the body makes to the habitual presence of certain drugs so that larger and larger doses are required to achieve the initial effect.

*Trait*    A characteristic of an individual that may be observed and measured.

*Trait anxiety*    A person's general level of anxiety.

*Tranquilizer*    A drug that reduces anxiety.

*Transference*    According to psychodynamic theorists, a phenomenon that occurs during psychotherapy, in which patients act toward the therapist as they did or do toward important figures in their lives, particularly parents.

*Transsexualism*    A disorder in which persons feel uncomfortable about their assigned sex and strongly wish to be a member of the opposite sex. They are often preoccupied with getting rid of their primary and secondary sex characteristics and many find their own genitals repugnant.

*Transvestic fetishism*    A paraphilia consisting of recurrent and intense sexual urges, fantasies, or behaviors that involve dressing in clothes of the opposite sex.

*Trephination*    An ancient operation in which a stone instrument was used to cut away a circular section of the skull. It is believed to have been a Stone Age treatment for abnormal behavior.

*Trichotillomania*    An extremely painful and upsetting compulsion in which people repeatedly pull at and even yank out their hair, eyelashes, and eyebrows.

*Tricyclic drug*    An antidepressant drug such as imipramine that has three rings in its molecular structure.

*Trisomy*    Three chromosomes of one kind rather than the usual two.

*Tube and intravenous feeding*    Forced nourishment sometimes provided to sufferers of anorexia nervosa when their condition becomes life-threatening.

*Two-physician certificates (2 PCs)*    A method of emergency involuntary commitment used in some states, marked by certification by two physicians that a person is in such a state of mind as to be dangerous to himself or herself or to others and may be committed involuntarily.

*Type A personality style*    A personality pattern characterized by hostility, cynicism, drivenness, impatience, competitiveness, and ambition.

*Type I schizophrenia*    Schizophrenia that is dominated by positive symptoms, such as delusions, hallucinations, and positive formal thought disorders.

*Type II schizophrenia*    Schizophrenia that is dominated by negative symptoms, such as flat affect, poverty of speech, and loss of volition.

*Tyramine*    A chemical that, if allowed to accumulate, can raise blood pressure dangerously. It is found in many common foods and is broken down by MAO. See also *MAO inhibitor*.

*Ulcer*    A lesion or hole that forms in the wall of the stomach or of the duodenum.

*Unconditional positive regard*    According to humanists, full, warm acceptance of a person regardless of what he or she says, thinks, or feels.

*Unconditioned response (UCR)*    The natural, automatic response elicited by an unconditioned stimulus.

*Unconditioned stimulus (UCS)*    A stimulus that elicits an automatic, natural response.

*Unconscious*    The deeply hidden mass of memories, experiences, and impulses that is viewed in Freudian theory as the wellspring of most behavior.

*Undifferentiated schizophrenia*    A diagnosis assigned to people who are considered schizophrenic but who do not fall neatly into one of the categories of schizophrenia.

*Undoing*    An ego defense mechanism in which a person unconsciously attempts to atone for an unacceptable desire or act by another act.

*Unilateral electroconvulsive therapy (ECT)*    A form of electroconvulsive therapy in which electrodes are attached to only one side of the head and electrical current passes through only one side of the brain. Unilateral ECT causes less confusion and memory loss than bilateral ECT and is equally effective.

*Unipolar depression*    Depression without a history of mania which is followed, upon recovery, by a normal or nearly normal mood.

*Unstructured interview*    An interview format in which the clinician asks questions spontaneously, based on issues that emerge during the interview.

*Vacuum erection device (VED)*    A nonsurgical device that can be used to produce an erection. It consists of a hollow cylinder that is placed over the penis connected to a hand pump.

*Vaginismus*    A condition marked by involuntary contractions of the muscles around the outer third of the vagina, preventing entry of the penis.

*Validity*    The accuracy of a test's or study's results; that is, the extent to which the test or study actually measures or shows what it claims to.

*Valium (diazepam)*    A minor tranquilizer.

*Variable*    Any characteristic or event that can vary, whether from time to time, from place to place, or from person to person.

*Vascular dementia*    A form of dementia caused by cerebrovascular accident or stroke that restricts the blood flow to certain areas of the brain.

*Ventromedial hypothalamus (VMH)*    The region of the hypothalamus that, when activated, depresses hunger.

*Vicarious conditioning*    The process of acquiring fear or other reactions through modeling.

*Visual hallucinations*    Hallucinations in which a person may either experience vague perceptions, perhaps of colors or clouds, or have distinct visions of people, objects, or scenes that are not there.

*Voyeurism*   A paraphilia in which a person has recurrent and intense sexual desires to observe unsuspecting people in secret as they undress or to spy on couples engaged in intercourse, and may act upon these desires.

*Waxy flexibility*   A catatonia in which a person will maintain a posture into which he or she has been placed by someone else.

*Weight set point*   The weight level that a person is predisposed to maintain, set up by a "weight thermostat" that is governed, in part, by the lateral and ventromedial hypothalamus.

*Windigo*   A disorder once common among Algonquin hunters who believed in a supernatural monster that ate human beings and had the power to bewitch them and turn them into cannibals.

*Withdrawal*   Unpleasant, sometimes dangerous reactions that may occur when people who use a drug chronically suddenly stop taking or reduce their dosage of a drug.

*Working through*   The process during psychoanalysis of confronting repressed conflicts, reinterpreting memories and feelings, and overcoming their negative effects.

# References

## Journal Abbreviations

Acta Psychiatr. Scandin. *Acta Psychiatrica Scandinavica*
Addic. Behav. *Addictive Behaviors*
Adol. Psychiat. *Adolescent Psychiatry*
Adv. Behav. Res. Ther. *Advances in Behavior Research and Therapy*
Amer. J. Clin. Hyp. *American Journal of Clinical Hypnosis*
Amer. J. Comm. Psych. *American Journal of Community Psychology*
Amer. J. Ment. Def. *American Journal of Mental Deficiency*
Amer. J. Orthopsychiat. *American Journal of Orthopsychiatry*
Amer. J. Psychiat. *American Journal of Psychiatry*
Amer. J. Psychother. *American Journal of Psychotherapy*
Amer. J. Pub. Hlth. *American Journal of Public Health*
Amer. Psychol. *American Psychologist*
Amer. Sci. *American Scientist*
Ann. Behav. Med. *Annals of Behavioral Medicine*
Ann. Clin. Psychiat. *Annals of Clinical Psychiatry*
Ann. Int. Med. *Annals of Internal Medicine*
Annu. Rev. Neurosci. *Annual Review of Neuroscience*
Annu. Rev. Psychol. *Annual Review of Psychology*
Arch. Fam. Med. *Archives of Family Medicine*
Arch. Gen. Psychiat. *Archives of General Psychiatry*
Arch. Int. Med. *Archives of Internal Medicine*
Austral. New Zeal. J. Psychiat. *Australian and New Zealand Journal of Psychiatry*
Austral. J. Clin. Exp. Hyp. *Australian Journal of Clinical and Experimental Hypnosis*

Behav. Cog. Psychoth. *Behavioral and Cognitive Psycho-Therapy*
Behav. Mod. *Behavior Modification*
Behav. Psychother. *Behavioural Psychotherapy*
Behav. Res. Ther. *Behavior Research and Therapy*
Behav. Sci. *Behavioral Science*
Behav. Ther. *Behavior Therapy*
Biofeed. Self-Reg. *Biofeedback and Self-Regulation*
Bio. Psychiat. *Biological Psychiatry*
Brit. J. Cog. Psychother. *British Journal of Cognitive Psychotherapy*
Brit. J. Psychiat. *British Journal of Psychiatry*
Bull. Menninger Clin. *Bulletin of the Menninger Clinic*
Bull. Psychosom. Soc. *Bulletin of the Psychosomatic Society*

Canad. J. Psychiat. *Canadian J. Psychiatry*
Child Dev. *Child Development*
Clin. Pharm. Ther. *Clinical and Pharmacological Therapy*
Child Psychiat. Human Dev. *Child Psychiatry and Human Development*
Cog. Emot. *Cognitive Emotions*
Cog. Ther. Res. *Cognitive Therapy and Research*
Comprehen. Psychiat. *Comprehensive Psychiatry*

Dis. Nerv. Sys. *Diseases of the Nervous System*
Drug. Alc. Dep. *Drug and Alcohol Dependence*

Eur. Arch. Psychiat. Neurol. Sci. *European Archives of Psychiatry and Neurological Science*

Gen. Hosp. Psychiat. *General Hospital Psychiatry*

Hosp. Comm. Psychiat. *Hospital and Community Psychiatry*

Indiv. Psychol. J. Adlerian Res. Prac. *Individual Psychology: A Journal of Adlerian Theory, Research and Practice*
Integ. Psychiat. *Integrated Psychiatry*
Inter. J. Addic. *International Journal of Addiction*
Inter. J. Clin. Exp. Hyp. *International Journal of Clinical and Experimental Hypnosis*
Inter. J. Eat. Dis. *International Journal of Eating Disorders*
Inter. J. Offend. Ther. Compar. Crimin. *International Journal of Offender Therapy and Comparative Criminology*
Inter. J. Psychoanal. *International Journal of Psychoanalysis*
Inter. J. Psychosom. *International Journal of Psychosomatics*

J. Abnorm. Child Psychol. *Journal of Abnormal Child Psychology*
J. Abnorm. Psychol. *Journal of Abnormal Psychology*

J. Abnorm. Soc. Psychol. *Journal of Abnormal and Social Psychology*
J. Affect. Dis. *Journal of Affective Disorders*
J. Amer. Acad. Child Adol. Psychiat. *Journal of the American Academy of Child and Adolescent Psychiatry*
J. Amer. Acad. Psychoanal. *Journal of the American Academy of Psychoanalysis*
J. Amer. Ger. Soc. *Journal of the American Geriatric Society*
JAMA *Journal of the American Medical Association*
J. Anx. Dis. *Journal of Anxiety Disorders*
J. Appl. Behav. Anal. *Journal of Applied Behavior Analysis*
J. Appl. Behav. Sci. *Journal of Applied Behavioral Sciences*
J. Appl. Soc. Sci. *Journal of Applied Social Sciences*
J. Autism Child. Schizo. *Journal of Autism and Childhood Schizophrenia*
J. Autism Dev. Dis. *Journal of Autism and Developmental Disorders*
J. Behav. Ther. Exp. Psychiat. *Journal of Behavior Therapy and Experimental Psychiatry*
J. Child Psychol. Psychiat. Allied Disc. *Journal of Child Psychology, Psychiatry and Allied Disciplines*
J. Clin. Psychiat. *Journal of Clinical Psychiatry*
J. Cons. Clin. Psychol. *Journal of Consulting and Clinical Psychology*
J. Couns. Psych. *Journal of Counseling Psychology*
J. Exp. Anal. Behav. *Journal of Experimental Analysis of Behavior*
J. Exp. Psychol. *Journal of Experimental Psychology*
J. Gamb. Stud. *Journal of Gambling Studies*
J. Hlth. Soc. Behav. *Journal of Health and Social Behavior*
J. Learn. Dis. *Journal of Learning Disorders*
J. Ment. Hlth. Admin. *Journal of Mental Health Administration*
J. Nerv. Ment. Dis. *Journal of Nervous and Mental Diseases*
J. Neurochem. *Journal of Neurochemistry*
J. Neuropsych. Clin. Neurosci. *Journal of Neuropsychiatry and Clinical Neurosciences*
J. Pers. Assess. *Journal of Personality Assessment*
J. Pers. Dis. *Journal of Personality Disorders*
J. Pers. Soc. Psychol. *Journal of Personality and Social Psychology*
J. Psychiat. Res. *Journal of Psychiatric Research*
J. Psychosom. Med. *Journal of Psychosomatic Medicine*
J. Psychosom. Res. *Journal of Psychosomatic Research*
J. Rehab. *Journal of Rehabilitation*
J. Soc. Behav. Pers. *Journal of Social Behavior and Personality*
J. Soc. Psychol. *Journal of Social Psychology*

Med. Aspects Human Sex. *Mental Aspects of Human Sexuality*

NY St. J. Med. *New York State Journal of Medicine*

Profess. Psychol. *Professional Psychologist*
Prof. Psych. Res. Prac. *Professional Psychology Research and Practice*
Prog. Neuropsychopharm. *Progressive Neuropsychopharmacology*
Psychiat. Ann. *Psychiatric Annals*
Psychiat. Clin. N. Amer. *Psychiatric Clinics of North America*
Psychiat. Hosp. *Psychiatric Hospital*
Psychiat. J. Univ. Ottawa *Psychiatric Journal of the University of Ottawa*
Psychiat. Quart. *Psychiatric Quarterly*
Psychol. Bull. *Psychological Bulletin*
Psychol. Med. *Psychological Medicine*
Psychosom. Med. *Psychosomatic Medicine*
Psych. Rec. *Psychological Record*
Psych. Rep. *Psychological Reports*
Psych. Rev. *Psychological Review*
Psych. Today *Psychology Today*
Psychother. Priv. Prac. *Psychotherapy in Private Practice*
Psychother. Theory Res. Prac. *Psychotherapy: Theory, Research and Practice*

Quart. J. Stud. Alcohol. *Quarterly Journal on the Studies of Alcoholism*

Scientif. Amer. *Scientific American*
Schizo. Bull. *Schizophrenic Bulletin*
Sem. in Neuro. *Seminars in Neurology*
Soc. Behav. Pers. *Social Behavior and Personality*
Soc. Psychiat. *Social Psychiatry*
Soc. Sci. Med. *Social Science and Medicine*
Suic. Life-Threat. Behav. *Suicide and Life-Threatening Behavior*

Abadi, S. (1984). Addiccion: la eterna repeticion de un desencuentro (Acerca de la dependencia humana) [Addiction: The endless repetition of a dis-encounter]. *Revista de Psicoanalisis, 41*(6), 1029–1044.

Abel, G. G. (1989). Paraphilias. In H. I. Kaplan & B. J. Sadock (Eds.), *Comprehensive textbook of psychiatry* (Vol. 1, 5th ed.). Baltimore: Williams & Wilkins.

Abel, G. G., Becker, J. V., & Cunningham-Rathner, J. (1984). Complications, consent, and cognitions in sex between children and adults. *Inter. J. Law Psychiat., 7,* 89–103.

Abel, G. G., & Osborn, C. (1992). The paraphilias: The extent and nature of sexually deviant and criminal behavior. *Psychiat. Clin. N. Amer., 15*(3), 675–687.

Abou-Saleh, M. T. (1992). Lithium. In E. S. Paykel (Ed.), *Handbook of affective disorders.* New York: Guilford.

Abraham, K. (1911). Notes on the psychoanalytic investigation and treatment of manic-depressive insanity and allied conditions. In *Selected papers on psychoanalysis.* New York: Basic Books, 1960, pp. 137–156.

Abraham, K. (1916). The first pregenital stage of the libido. In *Selected papers on psychoanalysis.* New York: Basic Books, 1960, pp. 248–279.

Abraham, S., & Llewellyn-Jones, D. (1984). *Eating disorders: The facts.* New York: Oxford UP.

Abram, K. M., & Teplin, L. A. (1990). Drug disorder, mental illness, and violence. *National Institute on Drug Abuse Research Monograph Series, 103,* 222–238.

Abramson, L. Y., Metalsky, G. I., & Alloy, L. B. (1989). Hopelessness depression: A theory-based subtype of depression. *Psych. Rev., 96*(2), 358–372.

Abramson, L. Y., Seligman, M. E., & Teasdale, J. D. (1978). Learned helplessness in humans: Critique and reformulation. *J. Abnorm. Psychol., 87*(1), 49–74.

Adams, D. M., Overholser, J. C., & Lehnert, K. L. (1994). Perceived family functioning and adolescent suicidal behavior. *J. Amer. Acad. Child Adol. Psychiat., 33*(4), 498–507.

Ader, R., Felten, D. L., & Cohen, N. (Eds.) (1991). *Psychoneuroimmunology.* New York: Academic Press.

Adler, A. (1927). *Individual psychology.* London: Kegan Paul, Trench, Trubner & Co.

Adler, A. (1927). *Understanding human nature.* New York: Premier.

Adler, A. (1931). *What life should mean to you.* New York: Capricorn.

Adler, N. E., Boyce, T., Chesney, M. A., Cohen, S., Folkman, S., Kahn, R. L., & Syme, S. L. (1994). Socioeconomic status and health: The challenge of the gradient. *Amer. Psychol., 49*(1), 15–24.

Adler, T. (1992). Prenatal cocaine exposure has subtle, serious effects. *APA Monitor, 23*(11), 17.

Agras, W. S. (1974). Behavioral approaches to the treatment of essential hypertension. *Inter. J. Obesity, 5*(Suppl. 1), 173–181.

Agras, W. S. (1984). Behavioral medicine: An overview. In A. J. Frances & R. E. Hales (Eds.), *American Psychiatric Association annual review* (Vol. 5). Washington, DC: American Psychiatric Press.

Agras, W. S. (1984). The behavioral treatment of somatic disorders. In W. D. Gentry (Ed.), *Handbook of behavioral medicine.* New York: Guilford.

Agras, W. S. (1985). *Panic: Facing fears, phobias, and anxiety.* New York: W. H. Freeman.

Agras, W. S., Sylvester, D., & Oliveau, D. (1969). The epidemiology of common fears and phobias. *Comprehen. Psychiat., 10*(2), 151–156.

Aguilar, T., & Munson, W. (1992). Leisure education and counseling as intervention components in drug and alcohol treatment for adolescents. *J. Alc. Drug Educ., 37*(3), 23–34.

Aiken, L. R. (1985). *Psychological testing and assessment* (5th ed.). Boston: Allyn & Bacon.

Aiken, L. R. (1994). *Psychological testing and assessment,* (8th edition.). Boston: Allyn and Bacon.

Akhtar, S., Wig, N. H., Verma, V. K., Pershod, D., & Verma, S. K. (1975). A phenomenological analysis of symptoms in obsessive-compulsive neuroses. *Brit. J. Psychiat., 127,* 342–348.

Akiskal, H. S. (1989). The classification of mental disorders. In H. I. Kaplan & B. J. Sadock (Eds.), *Comprehensive textbook of psychiatry* (Vol. 1, 5th ed.). Baltimore: Williams & Wilkins.

Albert, M. S., Butters, N., & Levin, J. (1979). Temporal gradients in the retrograde amnesia of patients with alcoholic Korsakoff's disease. *Arch. Neuro., 36,* 211–216.

Albert, M. S., & Lafleche, G. (1991). Neuropsychological testing of memory disorders. In T. Yanagihara & R. C. Petersen (Eds.), *Memory disorders: Research and clinical practice.* New York: Marcel Dekker, Inc.

Alden, L. (1989). Short-term structured treatment for avoidant personality disorder. *J. Cons. Clin. Psychiat., 57*(6), 756–764.

Alexander, B. (1981). Behavioral approaches to the treatment of bronchial asthma. In C. K. Prokop & L. A. Bradley (Eds.), *Medical psychology: Contributions to behavioral medicine.* New York: Academic Press.

Alexander, J. F., Holtzworth-Munroe, A., & Jameson, P. (1994). The process and outcome of marital and family therapy: Research review and evaluation. In A. E. Bergin & S. L. Garfield (Eds.), *Handbook of psychotherapy and behavior change* (4th ed.). New York: Wiley.

Alldridge, P. (1979). Hospitals, madhouses and asylums: Cycles in the care of the insane. *Brit. J. Psychiat., 134,* 321–334.

Allebeck, P., & Bolund, C. (1991). Suicides and suicide attempts in cancer patients. *Psychol. Med., 21*(4), 979–984.

Allen, J. G. (1993). Dissociative processes: Theoretical underpinnings of a working model for clinician and patient. *Bull. Menninger Clin., 57*(3), 287–308.

Allen, J. G. & Smith, W. H. (1993). Diagnosing dissociative disorders. *Bull. Menninger Clin., 57*(3), 328–343.

Allison, R. B. (1978). A rational psychotherapy plan for multiplicity. *Svensk Tidskrift Hyp., 3,* 9–16.

Alnaes, R., & Torgersen, S. (1989). Clinical differentiation between major depression only, major depression with panic disorder and panic disorder only: Childhood and personality disorder. *Psychiatria Fennica, Suppl.,* 58–64.

Aloni, R., Heller, L., Ofer, O., Mendelson, E., & Davidoff, G. (1992). Noninvasive treatment for erectile dysfunction in the neurogenically disabled population. *J. Sex Marit. Ther., 18*(3), 243–249.

Alpher, V. S. (1992). Introject and identity: Structural-interpersonal analysis and psychological assessment of multiple personality disorder. *J. Pers. Assess., 58*(2), 347–367.

Altemus, M., Pigott, T., L'Heureux, F., Davis, C. L., Rubinow, D. R., Murphy, D. L., & Gold, P. W. (1993). CSF Somatostatin in obsessive-compulsive disorder. *Amer. J. Psychiat., 150*(3), 460–464.

Aman, M. G., & Singh, N. N. (1991). Pharmacological intervention. In J. L. Matson & J. A. Mulick (Eds.), *Handbook of mental retardation.* New York: Pergamon.

American Association for Protecting Children (AAPC). (1992). *Highlights of official child neglect and abuse reporting.* Denver, CO: American Humane Society.

American Assoc. of Retired Persons. (1990). *A profile of older Americans.* Washington, DC.

American Assoc. on Mental Retardation. (1992). *Mental retardation: Definition, classification, and systems of supports* (9th ed.). Washington, DC.

American Humane Assoc. (1986). *Highlights of official child neglect and abuse reporting 1984.* Denver.

American Medical Assoc. (1992). *Diagnostic treatment guidelines on domestic violence.* Washington, DC.

American Psychiatric Assoc. (1983). APA statement on the insanity defense: Insanity defense work group. *Amer. J. Psychiat., 140*(6), 681–688.

American Psychiatric Assoc. (1993). *Practice guideline for major depressive disorder in adults.* Washington, DC.

American Psychiatric Assoc. (1994). *Diagnostic and statistical manual of mental disorders* (4th ed.). Washington, DC.

American Psychological Assoc. (1991, October). *APA-CPA Disaster response project: Interim project report,* Sacramento, CA.

American Psychological Assoc. Ethics Committee. (1992). Ethical Principles of Psychologists and Code of Conduct. *Amer. Psychol., 47*(12), 1597–1611.

Amsterdam, J. D., Brunswick, D. J., & Mendels, J. (1980). The clinical application of tricyclic antidepressant pharmacokinetics and plasma levels. *Amer. J. Psychiat., 137*(6), 653–662.

Amsterdam, J. D., & Hernz, W. J. (1993). Serum antibodies to herpes simplex virus Types I and II in depressed patients. *Bio. Psychiat., 34,* 417–420.

Ananth, J., Djenderdjian, A., Shamasunder, P., Costa, J., et al. (1991). Negative symptoms: Psychopathological models. *J. Psychiat. Neurosci. 16*(1), 12–18.

Anastasi, A. (1982). *Psychological testing* (5th ed.). New York: Macmillan.

Anastopoulos, A. D., & Barkley, R. A. (1992). Attention deficit-hyperactivity disorder. In C. E. Walker & M. C. Roberts (Eds.), *Handbook of clinical child psychology* (2nd ed.). New York: Wiley.

Anderson, A. E. (1985). *Practical comprehensive treatment of anorexia nervosa and bulimia.* Baltimore: Johns Hopkins UP.

Andersen, A. E. (1986). Sexuality and fertility: Women with anorexia nervosa and bulimia. *Med. Aspects of Human Sex., 20,* 138–143.

Andersen, A. E. (1990). Diagnosis and treatment of males with eating disorders. In A. E. Andersen (Ed.), *Males with eating disorders.* New York: Brunner/Mazel Publishers.

Andersen, A. E. (1992). Eating disorders in males: A special case? In K. D. Brownell, J. Rodin, & J. H. Wilmore (Eds.), *Eating, body weight, and performance in athletes: Disorders or modern society.* Philadelphia: Lea & Febiger.

Andersen, B. L., Kiecolt-Glaser, J. K., & Glaser, R. (1994). A biobehavioral model of cancer stress and disease course. *Amer. Psychol., 49*(5), 389–404.

Anderson, J. L., Vasile, R. G., Mooney, J. J. & Bloomingdale, K. L., et al. (1992). Changes in norepinephrine output following light therapy for fall/winter seasonal depression. *Bio. Psychiat., 32*(8), 700–704.

Anderson, N. B., McNeilly, M., & Myers, H. F. (1992). A contextual model for research of race differences in autonomic reactivity. In E. H. Johnson, W. D. Gentry, & S. Julius (Eds.), *Personality, elevated blood pressure, and essential hypertension.* Washington: Hemisphere Publishing Corp.

Anderson, S. C. (1993). Anti-stalking laws: Will they curb the erotomanic's obsessive pursuit? *Law Psychol. Rev., 17,* 171–191.

Andreasen, N. C. (1980). Mania and creativity. In R. H. Belmaker & H. M. van Praag (Eds.), *Mania: An evolving concept.* New York: Spectrum.

Andreasen, N. C., Nasrallah, H. A., Dunn, V. et al. (1986). Structural abnormalities in the frontal system in schizophrenia: A magnetic resonance imaging study. *Arch. Gen. Psychiat., 43,* 136–144.

Andres, R., Muller, C. C., & Sorkin, J. D. (1993). Long-term effects of change in body weight on all-cause mortality: A review. *Ann Int. Med., 113,* 737–743.

Angold, A., & Rutter, M. (1992). Effects of age and pubertal status on depression in a large clinical sample. *Development and Psychopathology, 4*(1), 5–28.

Annas, G. J. (1993). Physician-assisted suicide-Michigan's temporary solution. *New Engl. J. Med. 328*(21), 1573–1574.

Annis, H. M., Davis, C. S., Graham, M. et al. (1989). *A controlled trial of relapse prevention procedures based on self-efficacy theory.* Unpublished manuscript. Toronto: Addiction Research Foundation.

Anslinger, H. J., & Cooper, C. R. (1937). Marijuana: Assassin of youth. *American Magazine, 124,* 19, 153.

Apter, J. T. (1993). Frontiers in biological psychiatry: New drug development. *NJ Med., 90*(2), 144–146.

Arbel, N., & Stravynski, A. (1992). A retrospective study of separation in the development of adult avoidant personality disorder. *Acta Psychiatr. Scandin., 83*(3), 174–178.

Arbiter, N. (1991). Residential programs for women. In *National Conference on Drug Abuse Research and Practice Conference highlights.* Rockville, MD: National Institute on Drug Abuse.

Arieti, S. (1974). *Interpretation of schizophrenia.* New York: Basic Books.

Aring, C. D. (1974). The Gheel experience: Eternal spirit of the chainless mind! *JAMA, 230*(7), 998–1001.

Aring, C. D. (1975). Gheel: The town that cares. *Fam. Hlth., 7*(4), 54–55, 58, 60.

Arlow, J. A. (1989). Psychoanalysis. In R. J. Corsini & D. Wedding (Eds.), *Current psychotherapies.* Itasca, IL: Peacock.

Arndt, W. B., Jr. (1991). *Gender disorders and the paraphilias.* Madison, CT: International Univ.

Arnold, L. E. (1973, October). Is this label necessary? *J. School Hlth., 43,* 510–514.

Arnow, D., & Harrison, R. H. (1991). Affect in early memories of borderline patients. *J. Pers. Assess., 56*(1), 75–83.

Arntz, A., & Lavy, E. (1993). Does stimulus elaboration potentiate exposure in vivo treatment: Two forms of one-session treatment of spider phobia. *Behav. Psychother., 21,* 1–12.

Asarnow, J. R., Asarnow, R. F., Hornstein, N., & Russell, A. (1991). Childhood-onset schizophrenia: Developmental perspectives on schizophrenic disorders. In E. F. Walker (Ed.), *Schizophrenia: A life-course developmental perspective.* San Diego, CA: Academic Press.

Asarnow, J. R., & Horton, A. A. (1990). Coping and stress in families of child psychiatric inpatients: Parents of children with depressive and schizophrenic spectrum disorders. *Child Psychiat. Human Dev., 21*(2), 145–157.

Asberg, M., Traskman, L., & Thoren, P. (1976). 5 HIAA in the cerebrospinal fluid: A biochemical suicide predictor? *Arch. Gen. Psychiat., 33*(10), 1193–1197.

Aserinsky, E., & Kleitman, N. (1953). Eye movements during sleep. *Federal Process, 13,* 6–7.

Ashleigh, E. A., & Fesler, F. A. (1992). Fluoxetine and suicidal preoccupation. *Amer. J. Psychiat., 149*(12), 1750.

Ashton, J. R., & Donnan, S. (1981). Suicide by burning as an epidemic phenomenon: An analysis of 82 deaths and inquests in England and Wales in 1978-9. *Psychol. Med., 11*(4), 735–739.

Asner, J. (1990). Reworking the myth of personal incompetence: Group psychotherapy for bulimia nervosa. *Psychiat. Ann., 20*(7), 395–397.

Auchincloss, E. L., & Weiss, R. W. (1992). Paranoid character and the intolerance of indifference. *J. Amer. Psychoanal. Assoc., 40*(4), 1013–1037.

Auerbach, S. M., & Kilman, P. R. (1977). Crisis intervention: A review of outcome research. *Psychol. Bull., 84,* 1189–1217.

Avery, D. H., Bolte, M. A., Dager, S. R., Wilson, G., et al. (1993). Dawn simu-

lation of winter depression: A controlled study. *Amer. J. Psychiat., 150*(1), 113–117.

Axtell, A., & Newlon, B. J. (1993). An analysis of Adlerian Life Themes of bulimic women. *Indiv. Psychol., 49*(1), 58–67.

Ayd, F. J., Jr. (1956). A clinical evaluation of Frenquel. *J. Nerv. Ment. Dis., 124,* 507–509.

Ayllon, T. (1963). Intensive treatment of psychotic behavior by stimulus satiation and food reinforcement. *Behav. Res. Ther., 1,* 53–62.

Ayllon, T., & Michael, J. (1959). The psychiatric nurse as a behavioral engineer. *J. Exp. Anal. Behav., 2,* 323–334.

Ayllon, T., & Roberts, M. D. (1974). Eliminating discipline problems by strengthening academic performance. *J. Appl. Behav. Anal., 7*(1), 71–76.

Azar, B. (1995). Several genetic traits linked to alcoholism. *APA Monitor, 26* (5), 21–22.

Azar, S. T., Fantuzzo, J. W., & Twentyman, C. T. (1984). An applied behavioral approach to child maltreatment: Back to basics. *Adv. Behav. Res. Ther., 8*(1), 3–11.

Azar, S. T., Robinson, D. R., Hekimian, E. E., & Twentyman, C. T. (1984). Unrealistic expectations and problem solving ability in maltreating and comparison mothers. *J. Cons. Clin. Psychol., 52,* 687–691.

Azar, S. T., & Rohrbeck, C. A. (1986). Child abuse and unrealistic expectations: Further validation of the Parent Opinion Questionnaire. *J. Cons. Clin. Psychol., 54,* 867–868.

Azar, S. T., & Siegal, B. R. (1990). Behavioral treatment of child abuse: A developmental perspective. *Behav. Mod., 14*(3), 279–300.

Azar, S. T., & Wolfe, D. A. (1989). Child abuse and neglect. In E. J. Mash & R. Barkley (Eds.), *Treatment of childhood disorders.* New York: Guilford.

Azima, F. J. C. (1993). Group psychotherapy with personality disorders. In H. I. Kaplan & B. J. Sadock (Eds.), *Comprehensive group psychotherapy* (3rd ed.). Baltimore: Williams & Wilkins.

Baer, L., Platman, S. R., Kassir, S., & Fieve, R. R. (1971). Mechanisms of renal lithium handling and their relationship to mineralcorticoids: A dissociation between sodium and lithium ions. *J. Psychiat. Res., 8*(2), 91–105.

Bagby, E. (1922). The etiology of phobias. *J. Abnorm. Psychol., 17,* 16–18.

Bagley, C. (1991). Poverty and suicide among Native Canadians: A replication. *Psych. Rep., 69*(1), 149–150.

Baker, T., & Brandon, T. H. (1988). Behavioral treatment strategies. In *A report of the Surgeon General: The health consequences of smoking: Nicotine addiction. Rockville, MD:* U.S. Dept. Health and Human Services.

Bailey, J. M., Pillard, R. C., Neale, M. C., et al. (1993). Heritable factors influence sexual orientation in women. *Arch. Gen. Psychiat., 50*(3), 217–223.

Bakken, J., Miltenberger, R. G., & Schauss, S. (1993). Teaching parents with mental retardation: Knowledge versus skills. *Amer. J. Ment. Retard., 97*(4), 405–417.

Baldessarini, R. J. (1983). *Biomedical aspects of depression and its treatment.* Washington, DC: American Psychiatric Association Press, Inc.

Baldwin, S. (1985). Sheep in wolf's clothing: Impact of normalisation teaching on human services and services providers. *Inter. J. Rehab. Res., 8*(2), 131–142.

Ballenger, J. C. (1988). The clinical use of carbamazepine in affective disorders. *J. Clin Psychiat., 49*(Suppl.), 13–19.

Ballenger, J. C., Burrows, G. D., DuPont, R. L., Lesser, I. M. et al. (1988). Alprazolam in panic disorder and agoraphobia: Results from a multicenter trial: I. Efficacy in short-term treatment. *Arch. Gen. Psych., 45*(5), 413–422.

Ballinger, S. E. (1987). Uses and limitations of hypnosis in treating a conversion overlay following somatic trauma. *Austral. J. Clin. Exp. Hyp., 15*(1), 29–37.

Balshem, M., Oxman, G., Van Rooyen, D., & Girod, K. (1992). Syphillis, sex, and crack cocaine: Images of risk and morality. *Soc. Sci. Med., 35*(2), 147–160.

Bancroft, J. (1989). *Human sexuality and its problems.* New York: Churchill-Livingstone.

Bandura, A, (1969). *Principles of behavior modification.* New York: Holt, Rinehart & Winston.

Bandura, A. (1971). Psychotherapy based upon modeling principles. In A. E. Bergin & S. L. Garfield (Eds.), *Handbook of psychotherapy and behavior change.* New York: Wiley.

Bandura, A. (1976). *Social learning theory.* Englewood Cliffs, NJ: Prentice Hall.

Bandura, A. (1977). Self-efficacy: Toward a unifying theory of behavioral change. *Psych. Rev, 84*(2), 191–215.

Bandura, A., & Rosenthal, T. (1966). Vicarious classical conditioning as a function of arousal level. *J. Pers. Soc. Psychol., 3,* 54–62.

Bandura, A., Ross, D., & Ross, S. (1963). Imitation of film-mediated aggressive models. *J. Abnorm. Soc. Psychol., 66,* 3–11.

Bank, L., Marlowe, J. H., Reid, J. B., Patterson, G. R., & Weinrott, M. R.

(1991). A comparative evaluation of parent-training interventions for families of chronic delinquents. *J. Abnorm. Child Psychol., 19,* 15–33.

Baraban, J. M. (1993). The biology of memory. In J. M. Oldham, M. B. Riba, & A. Tasman (Eds.), *Review of Psychiatry,* Vol. 12. Washington, DC: American Psychiatric Press.

Barahal, H. S. (1958). 1000 prefrontal lobotomies: Five to ten year follow-up study. *Psychiat. Quart., 32,* 653–678.

Barber, T. X. (1984). Hypnosis, deep relaxation, and active relaxation: Data, theory and clinical applications. In R. L. Woolfolk & P. M. Lehrer (Eds.), *Principles and practice of stress management.* New York: Guilford.

Barber, T. X. (1993). Hypnosuggestive approaches to stress reduction: Data, theory, and clinical applications. In P. M. Lehrer & R. L. Woolfolk (Eds.), *Principles and practices of stress management* (2nd ed.). New York: Guilford.

Barker, J. G., & Howell, R. J. (1992). The plethysmograph: A review of recent literature. *Bull. Amer. Acad. Psychiat. Law, 20*(1), 13–25.

Barker, P. R., Manderscheid, R. W., Hendershot, G. E., Jack, S. S., Schoenborn, C. A., & Goldstrom, I. (1992). Serious mental illness and disability in the adult household population: United States, 1989. In R. W. Manderscheid & M. A. Sonnenschein (Eds.), *Mental health, United States, 1992.* Washington, DC: U.S. Department of Health and Human Services.

Barlow, D. H. (1986). Causes of sexual dysfunction: The role of anxiety and cognitive interference. *J. Cons. Clin. Psychol., 54,* 140–148.

Barlow, D. H. (1988). Current models of panic disorder and a view from emotion theory. In A. J. Frances & R. E. Hales (Eds.), *American Psychiatric Press review of psychiatry* (Vol. 7). Washington, DC: American Psychiatric Press.

Barlow, D. H., Rapee, R. M., & Brown, T. A. (1992). Behavioral treatment of generalized anxiety disorder. *Behav. Ther., 23,* 551–570.

Barnard, G. W., Fuller, A. K., Robbins, L., & Shaw, T. (1989). *The child molester: An integrated approach to evaluation and treatment.* New York: Brunner/Mazel Publishers.

Barnes, G. E., & Prosen, H. (1985). Parental death and depression. *J. Abnorm. Psychol., 94*(1), 64–69.

Baron, M., Barkai, A., Gruen, R., Peselow, E., et al. (1987). Platelet sup 3H imipramine binding and familial transmission of affective disorders. *Neuropsychobio., 17*(4), 182–186.

Baron-Cohen, S. (1989). Perceptual role taking and protodeclarative pointing in autism. *Brit. J. Dev. Psychol., 7,* 113–127.

Baron-Cohen, S. (1991). Do people with autism understand what causes emotion? *Child Dev., 62,* 385–395.

Barondes, S. H. (1993). *Molecules and mental illness.* New York: Scientific American Library.

Barondes, S. H. (1994, February 25). Thinking about prozac. *Sci., 263,* 1102–1103.

Barraclough, B. M., Jennings, C., & Moss, J. R. (1977). Suicide prevention by the Samaritans: A controlled study of effectiveness. *Lancet, 2,* 237–238.

Barrington, M. R. (1980). Apologia for suicide. In M. P. Battin & D. J. Mayo (Eds.), *Suicide: The philosophical issues.* New York: St. Martin's.

Barry, H., III. (1982). Cultural variations in alcohol abuse. In I. Al-Issa (Ed.), *Culture and psychopathology.* Baltimore: Univ. Park.

Barsky, A. J., & Klerman, G. L. (1983). Overview: Hypochondriasis, bodily complaints and somatic styles. *Amer. J. Psychiat., 140,* 273–283.

Bartels, S., Teague, G., Drake, R., Clark, R., Bush, P., & Noordsy, D. (1993). Substance abuse in schizophrenia: Service utilization and costs. *J. Nerv. Ment. Dis., 181*(4), 227–232.

Barth, R. P., Blythe, B. J., Schinke, S. P., & Schilling, R. F. (1983). Self-control training with maltreating parents. *Child Welfare, 62,* 313–324.

Bartrop, R. W., Lockhurst, E., Lazarus, L., Kiloh, L. G., & Penny, R. (1977). Depressed lymphocyte function after bereavement. *Lancet, 1,* 834–836.

Basoglu, M. (1992). The relationship between panic disorder and agoraphobia. In G. D. Burrows, S. M. Roth, & R. Noyes, Jr., Handbook of anxiety (Vol. 5). Oxford: Elsevier.

Bassett, A. S. (1992). Chromosomal aberrations and schizophrenia: Autosomes. *Brit. J. Psychiat., 161,* 323–334.

Batchelor, W. F. (1988). AIDS 1988. *Amer. Psychol., 43*(11), 853–858.

Bateson, G. (1978, April 21). The double-bind theory-Misunderstood? *Psychiatric News,* p. 40.

Bateson, G., Jackson, D., Haley, J., & Weakland, J. (1956). Toward a theory of schizophrenia. *Behav. Sci., 1,* 251–264.

Batki, S. (1988). Treatment of intravenous drug users with AIDS: The role of methadone maintenance. *J. Psychoac. Drugs, 20,* 213–216.

Battin, M. P. (1980). Manipulated suicide. In M. P. Battin & D. J. Mayo (Eds.), *Suicide: The philosophical issues.* New York: St. Martin's.

Battin, M. P. (1980). Suicide: A fundamental human right? In M. P. Battin & D. J. Mayo (Eds.), *Suicide: The philosophical issues.* New York: St. Martin's.

Battin, M. P. (1982). *Ethical issues in suicide.* Englewood Cliffs, NJ: Prentice Hall.

Battin, M. P. (1993). Suicidology and the right to die. In A. A. Leenaars (Ed.), *Suicidology.* Northvale, NJ: Jason Aronson Inc.

Baum, A., & Fleming, I. (1993). Implications of psychological research on stress and technological accidents. *Amer. Psychol., 48*(6), 665–672.

Baum, A., Gatchel, R. J., & Schaeffer, M. (1983). Emotional, behavioral and physiological effects of chronic stress at Three Mile Island. *J. Cons. Clin. Psychol., 51,* 565–572.

Baxter, L. R., Schwartz, J. M., Bergman, K. S., Szuba, M. P., Guze, B. H., Mazziotta, J. C., Alazraki, A., Selin, C. E., Ferng, H. K., Munford, P., & Phelps, M. E. (1992). Caudate glucose metabolic rate changes with both drug and behavior therapy for obsessive-compulsive disorder. *Arch. Gen. Psychiat., 49,* 681–689.

Baxter, L. R., Schwartz, J. M., Guze, B. H., Bergman, K. et al. (1990). PET imaging in obsessive-compulsive disorder with and without depression. Symposium: Serotonin and its effects on human behavior (1989), Atlanta, GA. *J. Clin. Psychiat., 51*(Suppl.), 61–69.

Beatty, W. B., Salmon, D. P., Butters, N., et al. (1988). Retrograde amnesia in patients with Alzheimer's disease or Huntington's disease. *Neurobio. Aging, 9,* 181–189.

Beaumont, G., & Hetzel, W. (1992). Patients at risk of suicide and overdose. 2nd International Symposium on Moclobemide: RIMA (Reversible Inhibitor of Monoamine Oxidase Type A): A new concept in the treatment of depression. *Psychopharmocol., 106*(Suppl.), 123–126.

Beauvais, F. (1992). The consequences of drug and alcohol use for Indian youth. *Amer. Indian & Alaska Native Ment. Hlth Res., 5*(1), 32–37.

Beck, A. T. (1967). *Depression: Clinical, experimental and theoretical aspects.* New York: Harper & Row.

Beck, A. T. (1976). *Cognitive therapy and the emotional disorders.* New York: International Univ.

Beck, A. T. (1985). Is behavior therapy on course? *Behav. Psychother., 13*(1), 83–84.

Beck, A. T. (1985). Theoretical perspectives on clinical anxiety. In A. H. Tuma & J. D. Maser (Eds.), *Anxiety and the anxiety disorders.* Hillsdale, NJ: Erlbaum.

Beck, A. T. (1988). Cognitive approaches to panic disorder: Theory and therapy. In S. Rachman & J. Maser (Eds.), *Panic: Psychological perspectives.* Hillsdale, NJ: Erlbaum.

Beck, A. T. (1991). Cognitive therapy: A 30-year retrospective. *Amer. Psychol., 46*(4), 368–375.

Beck, A. T. (1993). Cognitive approaches to stress. In P. M. Lehrer & R. L. Woolfolk (Eds.), *Principles and practice of stress management* (2nd ed.). New York: Guilford.

Beck, A. T., & Emery, G., with Greenberg, R. L. (1985). Differentiating anxiety and depression: A test of the cognitive content-specificity hypothesis. *J. Abnorm. Psychol., 96,* 179–183.

Beck, A. T., Freeman, A. & Assoc. (1990). *Cognitive therapy of personality disorders.* New York: Guilford.

Beck, A. T., Laude, R., & Bohnert, M. (1974). Ideational components of anxiety neurosis. *Arch. Gen. Psychiat., 31,* 319–325.

Beck, A. T., Rush, A. J., Shaw, B. F., & Emery, G. (1979). *Cognitive therapy of depression.* New York: Guilford.

Beck, A. T., Ward, C. H., Mendelson, M., Mock, J. E., & Erbaugh, J. (1962). Reliability of psychiatric diagnosis. 2: A study of consistency of clinical judgments and ratings. *Amer. J. Psychiat., 119,* 351–357.

Beck, J. C., & Parry, J. W. (1992). Incompetence, treatment refusal, and hospitalization. *Bull. Amer. Acad. Psychiat. Law, 20*(3), 261–267.

Beck, M., & Cowley, G. (1990, March 26). Beyond lobotomies. *Newsweek,* p. 44.

Becker, J. V. (1989). Impact of sexual abuse on sexual functioning. In S. R. Leiblum & R. C. Rosen (Eds.), *Principles and practice of sex therapy* (2nd ed.). New York: Guilford.

Becker, P., & Comstock, C. (1992, October). *A retrospective look at one MPD/DD group: Recommendations for future MPD/DD groups.* Paper presented at the Ninth International Conference of the International Society for the Study of Multiple Personality and Dissociative Disorders, Chicago.

Bednar, R. L., & Kaul, T. J. (1994). Experimental group research: Can the canon fire? In A. E. Bergin & S. L. Garfield (Eds.), *Handbook of psychotherapy and behavior change* (4th ed.). New York: Wiley.

Beebe, D. K. (1991). Emergency management of the adult female rape victim. *Amer. Fam. Physician, 43,* 2041–2046.

Beers, C. W. (1908). *A mind that found itself.* Garden City, NY: Doubleday.

Begley, S. (1989, August 14). The stuff that dreams are made of. *Newsweek,* p. 40.

Beitchman, J. H., Zucker, K. J., Hood, J. E., DaCosta, G. A., & Cassavia, E. (1992). A review of the long-term effects of childhood sexual abuse. *Child Abuse & Neglect, 16*(1), 101–118.

Beitman, B. D. (1993). Pharmacotherapy and the stages of psychotherapeutic change. In J. M. Oldham, M. B. Riba, & A. Tasman (Eds.), *Rev. Psychiat.* (Vol. 12). Washington, DC: American Psychiatric Press.

Belcher, J. R. (1988). Defining the service needs of homeless mentally ill persons. *Hosp. Comm. Psychiat., 39*(11), 1203–1205.

Belcher, J. R. (1988). The future role of state hospitals. *Psychiat. Hosp., 19*(2), 79–83.

Belcher, J. R., & Blank, H. (1989-90). Protecting the right to involuntary commitment. *J. Appl. Soc. Sci., 14*(1), 95–115.

Belkin, L. (1990, Jun. 6). Doctor tells of first death using his suicide device. *New York Times,* A1, p. 3.

Bellak, L., & Bellak, S. (1952). *Children's apperception test.* New York: Psychology Corp.

Belle, D. (1990). Poverty and women's mental health. *Amer. Psychol., 45*(3), 385–389.

Belli, R. F., Windschitl, P. D., McCarthy, T. T., & Winfrey, S. E. (1992). Detecting memory impairment with a modified test procedure: Manipulating retention interval with centrally presented event items. *J. Exp. Psych. Learning, Memory, and Cognition,* 18, 356–367.

Bellinger, D. L., Felten, S. Y., & Felten, D. L. (1992). Neural-immune interactions. In A. Tasman & B. Riba (Eds.), *Review of psychiatry* (Vol. 11.). Washington, DC: American Psychiatric Press, Inc.

Bender, L. (1938). *A visual motor gestalt test and its clinical use.* New York: American Orthopsychiatric Assoc.

Bennett, G. T., & Kish, G. R. (1990). Incompetency to stand trial: Treatment unaffected by demographic variables. *J. Forensic Sci., 35*(2), 403–412.

Bennett, M. B. (1987). Afro-American women, poverty and mental health: A social essay. *Women and Hlth, 12*(3-4), 213–228.

Bennett, N. A., Spoth, R. L., & Borgen, F. H. (1991). Bulimic symptoms in high school females: Prevalence and relationship with multiple measures of psychological health, *J. Comm. Psychol., 19*(1), 13–28.

Benowitz, N. (1990). Clinical pharmacology of caffeine. *Annual Rev. Med., 41,* 277–288.

Bergler, E. (1951). *Neurotic counterfeit sex.* New York: Grune & Stratton.

Berk, S. N., & Efran, J. S. (1983). Some recent developments in the treatment of neurosis. In C. E. Walker et al. (Eds.), *The handbook of clinical psychology: Theory, research, and practice* (Vol. 2). Homewood, IL: Dow Jones-Irwin.

Berlin, I., Warot, D., Hergueta, T., Molinier, P., Bagot, C., & Puech, A. J. (1993). Comparison of the effects of zolpiden and triazolam on memory functions, psychomotor performances, and postural sway in healthy subjects. *J. Clin. Psychopharmacol., 13*(2), 100–106.

Berlin, I. N. (1987). Suicide among American Indian adolescents: An overview. *Suic. Life-Threat. Behav.,* 17, 218–232.

Berman, A. L. (1986). Helping suicidal adolescents: Needs and responses. In C. A. Corr & J. N. McNeil (Eds.), *Adolescence and death.* New York: Springer.

Berman, S., Delaney, N., Gallagher, D., Atkins, P., & Graeber, M. (1987). Respite care: A partnership between a Veterans Administration nursing home and families to care for frail elders at home. *Gerontologist,* 27, 581–584.

Berney, B. (1993). Round and round it goes: The epidemiology of childhood lead poisoning, 1950-1990. *Milbank Quart., 71*(1), 3–39.

Bernstein, D. A., & Carlson, C. R. (1993). Progressive relaxation: Abbreviated methods. In P. M. Lehrer & R. L. Woolfolk (Eds.), *Principles and practice of stress management* (2nd ed.). New York: Guilford.

Bertelsen, A., Harvald, B., & Hauge, M. (1977). A Danish twin study of manic depressive disorders. *Brit. J. Psychiat., 130,* 330–351.

Beutler, L. E. (1979). Toward specific psychological therapies for specific conditions. *J. Cons. Clin. Psychol.,* 47, 882–892.

Beutler, L. E. (1991). Have all won and must all have prizes? Revisiting Luborsky et al.'s verdict. *J. Cons. Clin. Psychol.,* 59, 226–232.

Beutler, L. E., Machado, P. P. P., & Neufeldt, S. A. (1994). Therapist variables. In A. E. Bergin & S. L. Garfield (Eds.), *Handbook of psychotherapy and behavior change.* New York: Wiley.

Beyer, H. A. (1991). Litigation involving people with mental retardation. In J. L. Matson & J. A. Mulick (Eds.), *Handbook of mental retardation* (2nd ed.). New York: Pergamon Press.

Bickman, L., & Dokecki, P. (1989). Public and private responsibility for mental health services. *Amer. Psychol., 44*(8), 1133–1137.

Bierman, K. L., & Furman, W. (1984). The effects of social skills training and peer involvement on the social adjustment of preadolescents. *Child Dev, 55*(1), 151–162.

Bilder, R. M., Lipschutz-Broch, L., Reiter, G., Geisler, S. H., et al. (1992). Intellectual deficits in first-episode schizophrenia: Evidence for progressive deterioration. *Schizo. Bull., 18*(3), 437–448.

Binet, A., & Simon, T. (1916). *The development of intelligence in children* (The Binet-Simon Scale). Baltimore: Williams & Wilkins.

Birch, H. G., Richardson, S. A., Baird, D. et al. (1970). *Mental subnormality in the community — A clinical and epidemiological study.* Baltimore: Williams & Wilkins.

Bird, H. P., Gould, M. S., Staghezza, B. M. (1993). Patterns of diagnostic comorbidity in a community sample of children aged 9 through 16 years. *J. Amer. Acad. Child Adol. Psychiat., 32*(2), 361–368.

Bird, J. (1979). The behavioral treatment of hysteria. *Brit. J. Psychiat., 134,* 129–137.

Blacher, J., & Baker, B. L. (1994). Family involvement in residential treatment of children with retardation: Is there evidence of detachment? *J. Child Psychol. Psychiat. Allied Disc., 35*(3), 505–520.

Black, D. W., & Winokur, G. (1990). Suicide and psychiatric diagnosis. In S. J. Blumenthal & D. J. Kupfer (Eds.), *Suicide over the life cycle: Risk factors, assessment, and treatment of suicidal patients.* Washington, DC: American Psychiatric Press, Inc.

Black, S. T. (1993). Comparing genuine and simulated suicide notes: A new perspective. *J. Cons. Clin. Psychol., 61*(4), 699–702.

Black, S. T. (1995). Comparing genuine and simulated suicide notes: Response to Diamond et al. (1995). *J. Cons. Clin. Psychol., 63*(1), 49–51.

Blackburn, R. (1993). *The psychology of criminal conduct: Theory, research, and practice.* New York: Wiley.

Blackstein, K. R. (1975). The sensation seeker and anxiety reactivity. Relationship between sensation-seeking scales and the activity preference questionnaire. *J. Clin. Psychol., 31,* 677–681.

Blair, C. D., & Lanyon, R. I. (1981). Exhibitionism: Etiology and treatment. *Psychol. Bull., 89*(3), 439–463.

Blanchard, E. B. (1994). Behavioral medicine and health psychology. In A. E. Bergin & S. L. Garfield (Eds.), *Handbook of psychotherapy and behavior change.* New York: Wiley.

Blanchard, E. B., & Epstein, L. H. (1978). *A biofeedback primer.* Reading, MA: Addison-Wesley.

Blanchard, R., & Hucker, S. J. (1991). Age, transvestism, bondage, and concurrent paraphilic activities in 117 fatal cases of autoerotic asphyxia. *Brit. J. Psychiat., 159,* 371–377.

Bland, R. C., Orn, H., & Newman, S. C. (1988). Lifetime prevalence of psychiatric disorders in Edmonton. *Acta Psychiatr. Scandin.,* 77(Suppl. 338), 24–32.

Blank, A. S. (1982). Apocalypse terminable and interminable: Operation Outreach for Vietnam veterans. *Hosp. Comm. Psychiat., 33*(11), 913–918.

Blatt, S., & Wild, C. (1976). *Schizophrenia: A developmental analysis.* New York: Academic Press.

Blazer, D. (1990). *Emotional problems in later life.* New York: Springer.

Blazer, D. G., George, L. K., & Hughes, D. (1991). The epidemiology of anxiety disorders: An age comparison. In C. Salzman & B. D. Lebowitz (Eds.), *Anxiety in the elderly.* New York: Springer.

Blazer, D. G., Hughes, D., George, L. K., Swartz, M., & Boyer, R. (1991). Generalized anxiety disorder. In. L. N. Robins, & D. A. Regier (Eds.), *Psychiatric disorders in America: The Epidemiologic Catchment Area Study.* New York: Maxwell Macmillan International.

Blehar, M. C., Weissman, M. M., & Gershon, E. S. (1988). Family and genetic studies of affective disorders. National Institute of Mental Health: Family and genetic studies of affective disorders. *Arch. Gen. Psychiat., 45*(3), 288–292.

Bliss, E. L. (1980). Multiple personalities: A report of 14 cases with implications for schizophrenia and hysteria. *Arch. Gen. Psychiat., 37*(12), 1388–1397.

Bliss, E. L. (1980). *Multiple personality, allied disorders and hypnosis.* New York: Oxford UP.

Bliss, E. L. (1985). "How prevalent is multiple personality?": Dr. Bliss replies. *Amer. J. Psychiat., 142*(12), 1527.

Bliss, T., & Gardner, M. A. (1973). Long-lasting potentiation of synaptic transmission in the dentate area of unasesthetized rabbit following stimulation of the prerforant path. *J. Physiol., 232,* 357–374.

Bliwise, N., McCall, M. E., & Swan, S. J. (1987). In E. E. Lurie & J. H. Swan & Assoc. (Eds.), *Serving the mentally ill elderly: Problems and perspectives.* Lexington, MA: Heath.

Bloch, S., Croch, E., & Reibstein, J. (1982). Therapeutic factors in group psychotherapy: A review. *Arch. Gen. Psychiat.,* 27, 216–324.

Block, B., & Pristach, C. A. (1992). Diagnosis and management of the paranoid patient. *Amer. Fam. Physician, 45*(6), 2634, 2640.

Bloom, B. L. (1984). *Community mental health: A general introduction* (2nd ed.). Monterey, CA: Brooks/Cole.

Bloom, F., Lazerson, A., & Hofstadter, L. (1988). *Brain, mind, and behavior.* New York: W. H. Freeman.

Bloomingdale, L., & Bloomingdale, E. (1989). Childhood identification and prophylaxis of antisocial personality disorder. In R. Rosner & H. I. Schwartz (Eds.), *Juvenile psychiatry and the law.* New York: Plenum.

Blum, K., & Noble, E. (1993). Drug dependence and the A1 allele gene. *Drug Alc. Dep., 33*(5).

Blum, K., Noble, E., Sheridan, P., Finley, O., et al. (1991). Association of the

A1 allele of the D2 dopamine receptor gene with severe alcoholism. *Alc.,* 8(5), 409–416.

Bockoven, J. S. (1963). *Moral treatment in American psychiatry.* New York: Springer.

Bogdan, R., & Taylor, S. (1976, Jan.). The judged, not the judges: An insider's view of mental retardation. *Amer. Psychol., 31*(1), 47–52.

Boker, W. (1992). A call for partnership between schizophrenic patients, relatives and professionals. *Brit. J. Psychiat., 161* (suppl. 18), 10–12.

Bolgar, H. (1965). The case study method. In B. B. Wolman (Ed.), *Handbook of clinical psychology.* New York: McGraw-Hill.

Bolton, F., Morris, L., & MacEachron, A. (1989). *Males at risk: The other side of child abuse.* Newbury Park, CA: Sage Publications.

Bolund, C. (1985). Suicide and cancer: II. Medical and care factors in suicides by cancer patients in Sweden, 1973-1976. *J. Psychol. Oncol., 3*(1), 31–52.

Bondi, M. W., & Kaszniak, A. W. (1991). Implicit and explicit memory in Alzheimer's disease and Parkinson's disease. *J. Clin. Exp. Neuropsych., 13,* 339–358.

Bongar, B., Peterson, L. G., Golann, S., & Hardiman, J. J. (1990). Self-mutilation and the chronically suicidal patient: An examination of the frequent visitor to the psychiatric emergency room. *Ann. Clin. Psychiat., 2*(3), 217–222.

Booth, B. M., Blow, F. C., Cook, C. A., et al. (1992). Age and ethnicity among hospitalized alcoholics: a nationwide study. *Alcoholism Clin. Exper. Res., 16*(6), 1029–1034.

Bornstein, P. H., Hamilton, S. B., & Bornstein, M. T. (1986). Self-monitoring procedures. In A. R. Ciminero, K. S. Calhoun, & H. E. Adams (Eds.), *Handbook of behavioral assessment* (2nd ed.). New York: Wiley.

Bornstein, R. A., Schwarzkopf, S. B., Olson, S. C., & Nasrallah, H. A. (1992). Third-ventricle enlargement and neuropsychological deficit in schizophrenia. *Bio. Psychiat., 31*(9), 954–961.

Borys, D. S., & Pope, K. S. (1989). Dual relationships between therapist and client: A national study of psychologists, psychiatrists and social workers. *Profess. Psychol., 20,* 283–293.

Boswell, J. (1933). *The life of Dr. Johnson.* London: J. M. Dent & Sons.

Bott, E. (1928). Teaching of psychology in the medical course. *Bull. Assoc. Amer. Med. Colleges, 3,* 289–304.

Boudewyns, P. A., Tanna, V. L., & Fleischman, D. J. A. (1975). A modified shame aversion therapy for compulsive obscene telephone calling. *Behav. Ther., 6,* 704–707.

Bourgeois, J. A., Hall, M. J., Crosby, R. M., & Drexler, K. G., (1993). An examination of narcissistic personality traits as seen in a military population. *Military Med., 158*(3), 170–174.

Bourgeois, M. (1991). Serotonin, impulsivity and suicide. *Hum. Psychopharmacol. Clin. and Exper., 6*(Suppl.), 31–36.

Bourne, P. G. (1970). *Men, stress & Vietnam.* Boston: Little Brown.

Bower, G. H. (1981). Mood and memory. *Amer. Psychol., 36*(2), 129–148.

Bowlby, J. (1969). *Attachment* (Vol. 1). New York: Basic Books.

Bowlby, J. (1980). By ethology out of psychoanalysis: An experiment in interbreeding. *Animal Behav., 28*(3), 649–656.

Boyd, J. H., Rae, D. S., Thompson, J. W., Burns, B. J., et al. (1990). Phobia: Prevalence and risk factors. *Soc. Psychiat. Psychiat. Epidemiol., 25*(6), 314–323.

Brady, J. P., & Lind, D. L. (1961). Experimental analysis of hysterical blindness: Operant conditioning techniques. *Arch. Gen. Psychiat., 4,* 331–339.

Brady, J. V., Porter, R. W., Conrad, D. G., & Mason, J. W. (1958). Avoidance behavior and the development of gastroduodenal ulcers. *J. Exp. Anal. Behav., 1,* 69–73.

Braun, P., Greenberg, D., Dasberg, H., et al. (1990). Core symptoms of post-traumatic stress disorder unimproved by alprazolam treatment. *J. Clin. Psychiat., 51,* 236–238.

Bray, G. A., Dahms, W. T., Atkinson, R. L. et al. (1980). Factors controlling food intake: A comparison of dieting and intestinal bypass. *Amer. J. Clin. Nutr. 33,* 376–382.

Breier, A., Buchanan, R. W., Kirkpatrick, B., Davis, O. R., et al. (1994). Effects of clozapine on positive and negative symptoms in outpatients with schizophrenia. *Amer. J. Psychiat., 151*(1), 20–26.

Breier, A., Schreiber, J. L., Dyer, L., et al. (1991). NIMH longitudinal study of chronic schizophrenia: Prognosis and predictor of outcome. *Arch. Gen. Psychiat., 48*(7), 642.

Bremner, J. D., Southwick, S. M., Johnson, D. R., Yehuda, R., & Charney, D. S. (1993). Childhood physical abuse and combat-related post-traumatic stress disorder in Vietnam veterans. *Amer. J. Psychiat., 150*(2), 235–239.

Bremner, J. D., Steinberg, M., Southwick, S. M., Johnson, D. R., & Charney, D. S. (1993). Use of the structured clinical interview for DSM-IV dissociative disorders for systematic assessment of dissociative symptoms in post-traumatic stress–disorder. *Amer. J. Psychiat., 150*(7), 1011–1014.

Brende, J. O., & Parson, E. R. (1985). *Vietnam veterans.* New York: Plenum.

Brende, J. O., & Rinsley, D. B. (1981). A case of multiple personality with psychological automatisms. *J. Amer. Acad. Psychoanal., 9*(1), 129–151.

Brent, D. A., Kupfer, D. J., Bromet, E. J., & Dew, M. A. (1988). The assessment and treatment of patients at risk for suicide. In A. J. Frances & R. E. Hales (Eds.), *American Psychiatric Press review of psychiatry* (Vol. 7). Washington, DC: American Psychiatric Press.

Brent, D. A., Perper, J. A., Moritz, G., Allman, C., Friend, A., Roth, C., Schweers, J., Balach, L., & Baugher, M. (1993). Psychiatric risk factors for adolescent suicide: A case-control study. *J. Amer. Acad. Child Adol. Psychiat., 32*(3), 521–529.

Breslin, N. A. (1992). Treatment of schizophrenia: Current practice and future promise. *Hosp. Comm. Psychiat., 43*(9), 877–885.

Breslow, N. (1989). Sources of confusion in the study and treatment of sadomasochism. *J. Soc. Behav. Pers., 4*(3), 263–274.

Brewerton, T. D., Lydiard, R. B., Herzog, D. B., Brotman, A. W., O'Neil, P. M., & Ballenger, J. C. (1995). Comorbidity of Axis I psychiatric disorders in bulimia nervosa. *J. Clin. Psychiat., 56*(2), 77–80.

Briere, J. (1992). Methodological issues in the study of sexual abuse effects. Special section: Adult survivors of childhood sexual abuse. *J. Cons. Clin. Psychol., 60*(2), 196–203.

Britton, A. G. (July/August 1988). Thin is out, fit is in. *American Health,* p. 66–71.

Britton, W. H., & Eaves, R. C. (1986). Relationship between the Vineland Adaptive Behavior Scales-Classroom Edition of the Vineland Social Maturity Scales. *Amer. J. Ment. Def., 91*(1), 105–107.

Brom, D., Kleber, R. J., & Hofman, M. C. (1993). Victims of traffic accidents: Incidence and prevention of post-traumatic stress disorder. *J. Clin Psych., 49*(2), 131–140.

Brooks, G. R., & Richardson, F. C. (1980). Emotional skills training: A treatment program for duodenal ulcer. *Behav. Ther., 11*(2), 198–207.

Brotman, A. W., Herzog, D. B., & Hamburg, P. (1988). Long-term course in 14 bulimic patients treated with psychotherapy. *J. Clin. Psychiat., 49,* 157–160.

Brown, G. L., Goodwin, F. K., Ballenger, J. C., Goyer, P. F., & Major, L. F. (1979). Aggression in humans correlates with cerebrospinal fluid metabolites. *Psychiat. Res., 1,* 131–139.

Brown, G. L., Linnoila, M. I., & Goodwin, F. K. (1992). Impulsivity, aggression, and associated affects: Relationships to self-destructive behavior and suicide. In R. W. Maris, A. L. Berman, J. T. Maltsberger, & R. I. Yufit (Eds.), *Assessment and prediction of suicide.* New York: Guilford.

Brown, J. C., (1983). Paraphilias: Sadomasochism, fetishism, transvestism and transsexuality. *Brit. J. Psychiat., 143,* 227–231.

Brown, L. (1993). Enrollment of drug abusers in HIV clinical trials: A public health imperative for communities of color. *J. Psychoact. Drugs, 25*(1), 45–48.

Brown, T. A., Hertz, R. M., Barlow, D. H. (1992). New developments in cognitive-behavioral treatment of anxiety disorders. In A. Tasman, & M. B. Riba (Eds.), *Review of psychiatry* (Vol. 11). Washington, DC: American Psychiatric Press.

Brown, T. A., Moras, K., Zinbarg, R. E., Barlow, D. H. (1993). Diagnostic and symptom distinguishability of generalized anxiety disorder and obsessive-compulsive disorder. *Behav. Ther., 24,* 227–240.

Browne, A., & Finklehor, D. (1986). Impact of child sexual abuse: A review of the research. *Psychol. Bull., 99*(1), 66–77.

Brownell, K. D., & O'Neil, P. M. (1993). Obesity. In D. H. Barlow (Ed.), *Clinical handbook of psychological disorders: A step-by-step treatment manual* (2nd ed.). New York: Guilford.

Brownell, K. D. & Rodin, J. (1995). Medical, metabolic, and psychological effects of weight–cycling and weight variability. *Arch. Int. Med.*

Brownell, K. D. & Rodin, J. (1994). The dieting maelstrom: Is it possible and advisable to lose weight? *Amer. Psychol., 49*(9), 781–791.

Brownell, K. D., & Wadden, T. A. (1992). Etiology and treatment of obesity: Understanding a serious, prevalent, and refractory disorder. *J. Cons. Clin. Psychol., 60*(4), 505–517.

Bruce, M. L., Leaf, P. J., Rozal, G. P. M., Florio, L., & Hoff, R. A. (1994). Psychiatric status and 9-year mortality data in the New Haven Epidemiological Catchment Area Study. *Amer. J. Psychiat., 151*(5), 716–721.

Bruch, H. (1962). Perceptual and conceptual disturbances in anorexia nervosa. *Psychosom. Med., 24,* 187–194.

Bruch, H. (1973). *Eating disorders: Obesity, anorexia nervosa and the person within.* New York: Basic Books.

Bruch, H. (1973). Psychiatric aspects of obesity. *Psychiat. Ann., 3*(7), 6–10.

Bruch, H. (1974). Anorexia nervosa. In *American handbook of psychiatry* (2nd ed.). New York: Basic Books.

Bruch, H. (1978). *The golden cage: The enigma of anorexia nervosa.* Cambridge, MA: Harvard UP.

Bruch, H. (1981). Developmental considerations of anorexia nervosa and obesity. *Canad. J. Psychiat., 26,* 212–217.

Bruch, H. (1986). Anorexia nervosa: The therapeutic task. In K. D. Brownell & J. P. Foreyt (Eds.), *Handbook of eating disorders: Physiology, psychology and treatment of obesity, anorexia, and bulimia*. New York: Basic Books.

Buchan, H., Johnstone, E. C., McPherson, K., Palmer, R. L., et al. (1992). Who benefits from electroconvulsive therapy? Combined results of the Leicester and Northwick Park trials. *Brit. J. Psychiat., 160,* 355–359.

Buchele, B. J. (1993). Group psychotherapy for persons with multiple personality and dissociative disorders. *Bull. Menninger Clin., 57*(3). 363–370.

Buchsbaum, M. S., & Haier, R. J. (1987). Functional and anatomical brain–imaging: Impact on schizophrenia research. *Schizo. Bull., 13*(1), 115–132.

Buchwald, A. M., & Rudick-Davis, D. (1993). The symptoms of major depression. *J. Abnorm. Psychol., 102*(2), 197–205.

Buckley, P., Thompson, P., Way, L., & Meltzer, H. Y. (1994). Substance abuse among patients with treatment-resistant schizophrenia: Characteristics and implications for clozapine therapy. *Amer. J. Psychiat., 151*(3), 385–389.

Buda, M., & Tsuang, M. T. (1990). The epidemiology of suicide: Implications for clinical practice. In S. J. Blumenthal & D. J. Kupfer (Eds.), *Suicide over the life cycle: Risk factors, assessment, and treatment of suicidal patients*. Washington, DC: American Psychiatric Press.

Buffum, J. (1992). Prescription drugs and sexual function. *Psychiat. Med., 10*(2), 181–198.

Bugental, J. F. (1965). The existential crisis in intensive psychotherapy. *Psychother. Theory Res. Prac., 2*(1), 16–20.

Bujold, A., Ladouceur, R., Sylvain, C., & Boisvert J. M. (1994). Treatment of pathological gamblers: An experimental study. *J. Behav. Ther. Exp. Psychiat., 25*(4), 275–282.

Bukstein, O. G., Brent, D. A., & Kaminer, Y. (1989). Comorbidity of substance abuse and other psychiatric disorders in adolescents. *Amer. J. Psychiat., 146*(9), 1131–1141.

Bullard, D. G. (1988). The treatment of desire disorders in the medically and physically disabled. In R. C. Rosen & S. R. Leiblum (Eds.), *Sexual desire disorders*. New York: Guilford.

Bunney, W. E., & Garland, B. L. (1984). Lithium and its possible modes of actions. In R. M. Post & J. C. Ballenger (Eds.), *Neurobiology of mood disorders* (Vol. I, Frontiers of Clinical Neuroscience). Baltimore: Williams & Wilkins.

Burgess, E., & Haaga, D. A. (1994). The Positive Automatic Thoughts Questionnaire (ATQ-P) and the Automatic Thoughts Questionnaire-Revised (ATQ-RP): Equivalent measures of positive thinking? *Cog. Ther. Res., 18*(1), 15–23.

Burnam, M. A., Stein, J. A., Golding, J. M., Siegel, J. M., Sorenson, S. B., Forsythe, A. B., & Telles, C. A. (1988). Sexual assault and mental disorders in a community population. *J. Cons. Clin. Psychol., 56,* 843–850.

Burns, T. P., & Crisp, A. H. (1985). Factors affecting prognosis in male anorexics. *J. Psychiat. Res., 19*(2-3), 323–328.

Burt, D. D., Loveland, K. A., & Lewis, K. R. (1992). Depression and the onset of dementia in adults with mental retardation. *Amer. J. Ment. Retard., 96*(5), 502–511.

Burton, V. S. (1990). The consequences of official labels: A research note on rights lost by the mentally ill, mentally incompetent, and convicted felons. *Comm. Ment. Hlth. J., 26*(3), 267–276.

Butler, R. N. (1975). Psychiatry and the elderly: An overview. *Amer. J. Psychiat., 132,* 893–900.

Butters, N., & Cermak, L. S. (1980). *Alcoholic Korsakoff's Syndrome*. New York: Academic Press.

Butters, N., Heindel, W. C., & Salmon, D. P. (1990). Dissociation of implicit memory in dementia: Neurological implications. *Bull. Psychonom. Soc., 28*(4), 359–366.

Byrnes, G., & Kelly, I. W. (1992). Crisis calls and lunar cycles: A twenty-year review. *Psych. Rep. 71*(3, Pt. 1), 779–785.

Caddy, G. R. (1985). Cognitive behavior therapy in the treatment of multiple personality. *Behav. Mod., 9*(3), 267–292.

Cadoret, R. J., Yates, W. R., Troughton, E., Woodworth, G., & Stewart, M. A. (1995). Adoption study demonstrating two genetic pathways to drug abuse. *Arch Gen. Psychiat., 52,* 42–52.

Calahan, D., Cisin, I. H., & Crossley, H. M. (1969). *American drinking practices: A national study of drinking behaviors and attitudes*. New Brunswick, NJ: Rutgers Center of Alcohol Studies.

Callahan, L. A., McGreevy, M. A., Cirincione, C., & Steadman, H. J. (1992). Measuring the effects of the GBMI verdict: Georgia's 1982 GBMI reform. *Law and Human Behav., 16*(4), 447–461.

Callahan, L. A., Steadman, H. J., McGreevy, M. A., & Robbins, P. C. (1991). The volume and characteristics of insanity defense pleas: An eight state study. *Bulletin of the American Academy of Psychiatry and the Law, 19*(4), 331–338.

Callner, D. A. (1975). Behavioral treatment approaches to drug abuse: A critical review of the research. *Psychol. Bull., 82*(2), 143–164.

Calorie Control Council. (1991, July 8). Calorie Control Council national survey. *Time Magazine*, p. 51.

Camara, W. J., & Schneider, D. L. (1994). Integrity tests: facts and unresolved issues. *Amer. Psychol., 49*(2), 112–119.

Cameron, D. J., Thomas, R. I., Mulvhill, M., & Bronheim, H. (1987). Delirium: A test of the Diagnostic and Statistical Manual III criteria on medical inpatients. *J. Amer. Ger. Soc., 35,* 1007–1010.

Cameron, N. (1974). Paranoid conditions and paranoia. In S. Arieti & E. Brody (Eds.), *American Handbook of Psychiatry*. New York: Basic Books.

Campbell, J. C. (Ed.) (1995). *Assessing dangerousness: Violence by sexual offenders, batterers, and child abusers*. Thousand Oaks, California: Sage Publications, Inc.

Campbell, J. C. (1995). Prediction of homicide of and by battered women. In J. C. Campbell (Ed.), *Assessing dangerousness: Violence by sexual offenders, batterers, and child abusers*. Thousand Oaks, California: Sage Publications, Inc.

Campbell, R. V., O'Brien, S., Bickett, A. D., & Lutzker, J. R. (1983). In-home parent training of migraine headaches and marital counseling as an ecobehavioral approach to prevent child abuse. *J. Behav. Ther. Exp. Psychiat., 14,* 147–154.

Cannon, T. D., & Marco, E. (1994). Structural brain abnormalities as indicators of vulnerability to schizophrenia. *Schizo. Bull, 20*(1), 89–102.

Cannon, W. (1927). The James-Lange theory of emotions: A critical examination and an alternative. *Amer. J. Psychol., 39,* 106–124.

Cantor, P. (1991). Developmental perspective on prevention and treatment of suicidal youth. In A. A. Leenaars (Ed.), *Life span perspectives of suicide: Time-lines in the suicide process*. New York: Plenum.

Caplan, R., Perdue, S., Tanguay, P. E., & Fish, B. (1990). Formal thought disorder in childhood onset schizophrenia and schizotypal personality disorder. *J. Child Psychol. Psychiat. Allied Disc., 31*(7), 1103–1114.

Carey, G., & DiLalla, D. L. (1994). Personality and psychopathology: Genetic perspectives. *J. Abnorm. Psychol., 103*(1), 32–43.

Carey, G., & Gottesman, I. I., (1981). Twin and family studies of anxiety, phobic, and obsessive disorders. In D. K. Klein & J. Rabkin (Eds.), *Anxiety: New Research and changing concepts*. New York: Raven.

Carey, K. (1989). Emerging treatment guidelines for mentally ill chemical abusers. *Hosp. Comm. Psychiat., 40*(4), 341–342.

Carey, K. (1993). Situational determinants of heavy drinking among college students. *J. Couns. Psych. 40*(2), 217–220.

Carey, M., Carey, K., & Meisler, A, (1991). Psychiatric symptoms in mentally ill chemical abusers. *J. Nerv. Ment. Dis., 179*(3), 136–138.

Carey, M. P., Wincze, J. P., & Meisler, A. W. (1993). Sexual dysfunction: Male erectile disorder. In D. H. Barlow (Ed.), *Clinical handbook of psychological disorders: A step-by-step treatment manual* (2nd ed.). New York: Guilford.

Carlson, G. A., Asarnow, J. R., & Orbach, I. (1994). Developmental aspects of suicidal behavior in children and developmentally delayed adolescents. In G. G. Naom & S. Borst (Eds.), *New directions for child development, no. 64—Children, youth, and suicide: Developmental perspectives*. San Francisco: Jossey-Bass Publishers.

Carlsson, A. (1978). Antipsychotic drugs, neurotransmitters, and schizophrenia. *Amer. J. Psychiat., 135*(2), 104–173.

Carlsson, A. (1978). Does dopamine have a role in schizophrenia? *Bio Psychiat., 13*(1), 3–21.

Carr, A. T., (1979). The psychopathology of fear. In W. Sluckin (Ed.), *Fear in animals and man*. New York: Van Nostrand Reinhold.

Carr, J. (1994). Annotation: Long term outcome for people with Down Syndrome. *J. Child Psychol. Psychiat., 35*(3), 425–439.

Carrington, P. (1978). *Clinically standardized meditation (CSM) instructors kit*. Kendall Park, NJ: Pace Educational Systems.

Carrington, P. (1993). Modern forms of meditation. In P. M. Lehrer & R. L. Woolfolk (Eds.), *Principles and practice of stress management* (2nd ed.). New York: Guilford.

Carroll, K. M., Rounsaville, B. J., & Gawin, F. H. (1991). A comparative trial of psychotherapies for ambulatory cocaine abusers: Relapse prevention and interpersonal psychotherapy. *Amer. J. Drug Alc Abuse, 17,* 229–247.

Carstairs, K. (1992). Paranoid-schizoid or symbiotic? *Inter. J. Psychoanal., 73*(1), 71–85.

Cartwright, R. D., & Lamberg, L. (1992). *Crisis dreaming: Using your dreams to solve your problems*. New York: HarperCollins.

Cash, T. F., Winstead, B. A., & Janda, L. H. (1986, April). The great American shape-up. *Psych. Today,* 30–37.

Caton, C. L. (1982). Effect of length of inpatient treatment for chronic schizophrenia. *Amer. J. Psychiat., 139*(7), 856–861.

Cautela, J. R. (1967). Covert sensitization. *Psych. Rec., 20,* 459–468.

Cauwels, J. M. (1983). *Bulimia: The binge-purge compulsion*. New York: Doubleday.

Cerletti, U., & Bini, L. (1938). L'elettroshock. *Arch. Gen. Neurol. Psychiat. & Psychoanal., 19,* 266–268.

Chait, L. D., Fishman, M. W., & Schuster, C. R. (1985). "Hangover" effects the morning after marijuana smoking. *Drug Alc. Dep., 15*(3), 229–238.

Chamberlain, P. (1985). Increasing the attention span of five mentally handicapped children using their parents as agents of change. *Behav. Psychother., 13*(20), 142–153.

Chambless, D. L., & Gillis, M. M. (1993). Cognitive therapy of anxiety disorders. *J. Cons. Clin. Psychol., 61*(2), 248–260.

Chaney, E. F., Blane, H. T., Abran, H. S., Gotner, J., Lacy, E., McCourt, W. F., Clark, E., & Myers, E. (1978). Skill training with alcoholics. *J. Cons. Clin. Psychol., 46,* 1092–1104.

Char, W. F. (1985). The hysterical spouse. *Med. Aspects Human Sex., 19*(9), 123–133.

Chase, M. (1993, May 28). Psychiatrists declare severe PMS a depressive disorder. *The Wall Street Journal,* p. B1, B6.

Chassin, L., Pillow, D., Curran, P., Molina, B., & Barrera, M. (1993). Relation of parental alcoholism to early adolescent substance use: A test of three mediating mechanisms. *J. Abnorm. Psychol., 102*(1), 3–19.

Chatlos, C. (1987). *Crack: What you should know about the cocaine epidemic.* New York: Perigee Books.

Chemtob, C. M., Bauer, G. B., Neller, G., Hamada, R., et al. (1990). Posttraumatic stress disorder among Special Forces Vietnam veterans. *Military Med., 155*(1), 16–20.

Chengappa, K. N. R., Shelton, M. D., Baker, R. W., Schooler, N. R., Baird, J., & Delaney, J. (1994). The prevalence of akathisia in patients receiving stable doses of clozapine. *J. Clin. Psychiat., 55*(4), 142–145.

Chiavaroli, T. (1992). Rehabilitation from substance abuse in individuals with a history of sexual abuse. *J. Subst. Abuse Treat., 9*(4), 349–354.

Chinner, T. L., & Dalziel, F. R. (1991). An exploratory study on the viability and efficacy of a pet-facilitated therapy project within a hospice. *Journal of Palliative Care, 7*(4), 13–20.

Chiu, L. H. (1971). Manifested anxiety in Chinese and American children. *J. Psychol., 79,* 273–284.

Chodoff, P. (1989). Histrionic personality disorder. In American Psychiatric Association (Eds.), *Treatments of psychiatric disorders: A task force report of the American Psychiatric Association.* Washington, DC: American Psychiatric Press.

Chou, T. (1992). Wake up and smell the coffee: Caffeine, coffee, and the medical consequences. *W. J. Med., 157,* 544–553.

Christensen, A., & Jacobson, N. S. (1994). Who (or what) can do psychotherapy: The status and challenge of nonprofessional therapies. *Psych. Sci., 5*(1), 8–14.

Chynoweth, R. (1977). Significance of suicidal notes. *Austral. New Zeal. J. Psychiat., 11,* 197–200.

Ciompi, L., Dauwalder, H., Maier, C., Aebi, E., Trutsch, K., Kupper, Z., & Rutishauser, C. (1992). The pilot project 'soteria berne': Clinical experiences and results. *Brit. J. Psychiat., 161*(suppl. 18), 145–153.

Clance, P. R., & O'Toole, M. A. (1987). The impostor phenomenon: An integral barrier to empowerment and achievement [Special Issue]. *Women & Ther., 6*(3), 51–64.

Clark, D. A. (1989). *A schema-control model of negative thoughts.* Paper presented at the World Congress of Cognitive Therapy, Oxford, England.

Clark, D. A. (1992). Depressive, anxious and intrusive thoughts in psychiatric inpatients and outpatients. *Behav. Res. Ther., 30,* 93–102.

Clark, D. A., & Purdon, C. (1993). New perspectives for a cognitive theory of obsessions. *Australian Psychologist.*

Clark, D. B., & Sayette, M. A. (1993). Anxiety and the development of alcoholism: Clinical and scientific issues. *Amer. J. Addic., 2,* 59–76.

Clark, D. M. (1993). Cognitive mediation of panic attacks induced by biological challenge tests. *Adv. Behav. Res. Ther., 15,* 75–84.

Clark, L. A., Watson, D., & Mineka, S. (1994). Temperament, personality, and the mood and anxiety disorders. *J. Abnorm. Psychol., 103*(1), 103–116.

Clark, L. A., Watson, D., & Reynolds, S. (1995). Diagnosis and Classification of Psychopathology: Challenges to the Current System and Future Directions. In J. T. Spence, J. M. Darley, & D. J. Foss, (eds.), *Annual Review of Psychology, 46,* 121–151.

Clarkin, J. F., & Kendall, P. C. (1992). Comorbidity and treatment planning: Summary and future directions. *J. Cons. Clin. Psychol., 60*(6), 904–908.

Clarkin, J. F., Glick, I. D., Haas, G. L., Spencer, J. H., et al. (1990). A randomized clinical trial of inpatient family intervention V. Results for affective disorders. *J. Affect. Dis., 18,* 17–28.

Classen, C., Koopman, C., & Spiegel, D. (1993). Trauma and dissociation. *Bull. Menninger Clin., 57*(2), 178–194.

Clavelle, P. R. (1992). Clinicians' perceptions of the comparability of the MMPI and MMPI-2. *Psycholog. Assess., 4*(4), 466–472.

Clinton, D. N., & McKinlay, W. W. (1986). Attitudes to food, eating and

weight in acutely ill and recovered anorectics. *Brit. J. Clin. Psychol., 25*(1), 61–67.

Clozapine Study Group (1993). The safety and efficacy of clozapine in severe treatment-resistant schizophrenic patients in the UK. *Brit. J. Psychiat., 163,* 150–154.

Clum, G. A., Clum, G. A., & Surls, R. (1993). A meta-analysis of treatment for panic disorder. *J. Cons. Clin. Psychol., 61*(2). 317–326.

Coccaro, E. F., & Kavoussi, R. J. (1991). Biological and pharmacological aspects of borderline personality disorder. *Hosp. Comm. Psychiat., 42*(10), 1029–1033.

Coder, T. L., Nelson, R. E., & Aylward, L. K. (1991). Suicide among secondary students. *School Counselor, 38*(5), 358–361.

Coe, C. L., Rosenberg, L. T., Fischer, M., Levine, S. (1987, Dec.). Psychological factors capable of preventing the inhibition of antibody responses in separated infant monkeys. *Child Dev., 58,* 1420–1430.

Coe, W. C. (1989). Posthypnotic amnesia: Theory and research. In N. P. Spanos & J. F. Chaves (Eds.), *Hypnosis: The cognitive-behavioral perspective.* Buffalo, NY: Prometheus Books.

Cogan, J. C., & Rothblum, E. D. (1992). Outcomes of weight-loss programs. *Genetic, Social, and General Psychology Monographs, 118*(4), 385–415.

Cohen, F. (1983). Captives' legal right to mental health care. *Law Psychol. Rev., 17,* 1–39.

Cohen, F. (1993). Stress, emotion, and illness. In L. Temoshok, C. Van Dyke, & L. S. Zegans (Eds.), *Emotions in health and illness: Theoretical and research foundations.* Orlando, FL: Grune & Stratton, Inc.

Cohen, R. (1987). Suddenly, I'm the adult. *Psych. Today,* 70–71.

Cohen, R. M., Semple, W. E., Gross, M., & Nordahl, T. E. (1988). From syndrome to illness: Delineating the pathophysiology of schizophrenia with PET. *Schizo. Bull., 14*(2), 169–176.

Cohen, S., Kaplan, J. R., Cunnick, J. E., Manuck, S. B., et al. (1992). Chronic social stress, affiliation, and cellular immune response in nonhuman primates. *Psych. Sci., 3*(5), 301–304.

Cohen-Sandler, R., Berman, A. L., & King, R. A. (1982). A follow-up study of hospitalized suicidal children. *J. Amer. Acad. Child Psychiat., 214,* 398–403.

Cohen-Sandler, R., Berman, A. L., & King, R. A. (1982). Life stress and symptomatology: Determinants of suicidal behavior in children. *J. Amer. Acad. Child Psychiat., 21,* 178–186.

Colbach, E. M. (1987). Hysteria again and again and again. *Inter. J. Offend. Ther. Compar. Crimin., 31*(1), 41–48.

Cole, D. A., & Turner, J. E., Jr. (1993). Models of cognitive mediation and moderations in child depression. *J. Abnorm. Psychol., 102*(2), 271–281.

Colerick, E. J., & George, L. K. (1986). Predictors of institutionalization among caregivers of patients with Alzheimer's Disease. *J. Amer. Ger. Soc., 34,* 493–498.

Colligan, R. C., & Offord, K. P. (1992). *The MMPI: A contemporary normative study of adolescents.* Norwood, NJ: Alex Publishing Corporation.

Collins, C. S. (February, 1994). Doctor of the soul. *Profiles Magazine,* pp. 39–41.

Comer, R. (1973). *Therapy interviews with a schizophrenic patient.* Unpublished manuscript.

Comptom, W. M., Helzer, J. E., Hwu, H., Yeh, E., McEvoy, L., Tipp, J. E., & Spitznagel, E. L. (1991). New methods in cross-cultural psychiatry: Psychiatric illness in Taiwan and the United States. *Amer. J. Psychiat., 148*(12), 1697–1704.

Conger, J. J. (1951). The effects of alcohol on conflict behavior in the albino rat. *Quart. J. Stud. Alc., 12,* 1–29.

Constantino, G., Malgady, R. G., & Vazquez, C. (1981). A comparison of Murray's TAT and a new thematic apperception test for urban Hispanic children. *Hisp. J. Behav. Sci, 3,* 291–300.

Conway, M., Howell, A., & Glannopoulos, C. (1991). Dysphoria and thought suppression. *Cog. Ther. Res., 15,* 153–166.

Cook, E. W., Melamed, B. G., Cuthbert, B. N., McNeil, D. W., & Land, P. J. (1988). Emotional imagery and the differential diagnosis of anxiety. *J. Cons. Clin. Psychol., 56,* 734–740.

Cooney, N. L., Kadden, R. M., Litt, M. D., & Getter, H. (1991). Matching alcoholics to coping skills or interactional therapies. Two-year follow-up results. *J. Cons. Clin. Psychol., 59,* 598–601.

Coons, P. M. (1980). Multiple personality: Diagnostic considerations. *J. Clin Psychiat., 41*(10), 330–336.

Coons, P. M., Bowman, E. S., & Milstein, V. (1988). Multiple personality disorder: A clinical investigation of 50 cases. *J. Nerv. Ment. Dis., 176*(9), 519–527.

Cooper, A. M. (1981). Narcissism. In S. Arieti & H. K. Brodie (Eds.), *American handbook of psychiatry* (Vol. 7.). New York: Basic Books.

Cooper, A. M., & Ronningstam, E. (1992). Narcissistic personality disorder. In A. Tasman & M. B. Riba (Eds.), *American Psychiatric Press review of psychiatry* (Vol. 11). Washington, DC: American Psychiatric Press.

Cooper, C. L. & Faragher, E. B. (1991). Psychosocial stress and breast cancer.

In N. Plotnikoff, A., Murgo, R. Faith, & J. Wybran (Eds.), *Stress and immunity*. Ann Arbor, MI: CRC Press.

Cooper, J. R., (Ed.). (1977). *Sedative-hypnotic drugs: Risks and benefits.* Washington, DC: GPO.

Copeland, J., & Hall, W. (1992). A comparison of women seeking drug and alcohol treatment in a specialist women's and two traditional mixed-sex treatment services. *Brit. J. Addic., 87*(9), 1293–1302.

Coplan, J. D., Papp, L. A., King, D. L., & Gorman, J. M. (1992). Amelioration of mitral valve prolapse after treatment for panic disorder. *Amer. J. Psychiat., 149*(11), 1587–1588.

Cordova, J. V., & Jacobson, N. S. (1993). Couple distress. In D. H. Barlow (Ed.), *Clinical handbook of psychological disorders: A step-by-step treatment manual* (2nd. ed.). New York: Guilford.

Corkin, S. (1968). Acquisition of motor skill after bilateral medial temporal-lobe excision. *Neuropsychologia, 6,* 255–264.

Corkin, S. (1984). Lasting consequences of bilateral medial temporal lobectomy: Clinical course and experimental findings in H. M. *Sem. in Neuro., 4,* 249–259.

Cornblatt, B. A., & Keilp, J. G. (1994). Impaired attention, genetics, and the pathophysiology of schizophrenia. *Schizo. Bull., 20*(1), 31–46.

Cornelius, J. R., Salloum, I. M., Mezzich, J., Cornelius, M. D., Fabrega, H., Ehler, J. G., Ulrich, R. F., Thase, M. E., & Mann, J. J. (1995). Disproportionate suicidality in patients with comorbid major depression and alcoholism. *Amer. J. Psychiat., 152*(3), 358–364.

Cornell, C. P., & Gelles, R. J. (1983). *Intimate violence in families.* Beverly Hills, CA: Sage.

Corson, S. A., & Corson, E. D. (1978). Pets as mediators of therapy. *Current Psychiat. Ther., 18,* 195–205.

Corwin, M. (1993, May 8). When the law can't protect. *Los Angeles Times,* p. A1.

Coryell, W., & Winokur, G. (1992). Course and outcome. In E. S. Paykel (Ed.), *Handbook of affective disorders.* New York: Guilford.

Costa, E. (1983). Are benzodiazepine recognition sites functional entities for the action of endogenous effectors or merely drug receptors? *Adv. in Biochem. & Psychopharm., 38,* 249–259.

Costa, E. (1985). Benzodiazepine-GABA interactions: A model to investigate the neurobiology of anxiety. In A. H. Tuma & J. Maser (Eds.). *Anxiety and the anxiety disorders.* Hillsdale, NJ: Erlbaum.

Costa, E., Guidotti, A., Mao, C. C., & Suria, A. (1975). New concepts on the mechanism of action of benzodiazepines. *Life Sci., 17*(2), 167–185.

Costa, E., Guidotti, A., & Toffano, G. (1978). Molecular mechanisms mediating the action of benzodiazepines on GABA receptors. *Brit. J. Psychiat., 133,* 239–248.

Counts, D. A. (1990). Abused women and revenge suicide: Anthropological contributions to understanding suicide. In D. Lester (Ed.), *Current concepts of suicide.* Philadelphia: The Charles Press.

Cowen, E. L. (1991). In pursuit of wellness. 98th Annual Convention of the American Psychological Association Distinguished Contributions to Psychology in the Public Interest Award Address (1990, Boston, MA). *Amer. Psychol., 46,* 404–408.

Cowley, G., with Holmes, S., Laueman, J. F., & Gordon, J. (1994, February 7). The culture of Prozac. *Newsweek,* pp. 41–42.

Cox, A., Rutter, M., Newman, S., & Bartak, L. (1975). A comparative study of infantile autism and specific developmental receptive language disorder: II. Parental characteristics. *Brit. J. Psychiat., 126,* 146–159.

Crandall, C. S., Preisler, J. J., & Aussprung, J. (1992). Measuring life events stress in the lives of college students: The Undergraduate Stress Questionnaire (USQ). *J. Behav. Med., 15*(6), 627–662.

Crane, G. E. (1973). Persistent dyskinesia. *Brit. J. Psychiat., 122,* 395–405.

Craske, M. G., & Barlow, D. H. (1993). Panic disorder and agoraphobia. In D. H. Barlow (Ed.), *Clinical handbook of psychological disorders: A step-by-step treatment manual* (2nd ed.). New York: Guilford.

Creed, F., Black, D., & Anthony, P. (1989). Day-hospital and community treatment for acute psychiatric illness: A critical appraisal. *Brit. J. Psychiat., 154,* 300–310.

Creer, C., & Wing, J. K. (1974). *Schizophrenia at home.* London: National Schizophrenia Fellowship.

Creer, T. L. (1994) Asthma: Psychological issues. In R. A. Olson, L. L. Mullins, J. B. Gillman, J. M. Chaney (Eds.). *The sourcebook of pediatric psychotherapy.* Boston: Allyn & Bacon.

Crisp, A. H. (1981). Anorexia nervosa at a normal weight?: The abnormal-normal weight control syndrome. *Inter. J. Psychiat. Med., 11,* 203–233.

Crisp, A. H., Norton, K., Gowers, S., Halek, C., et al. (1991). A controlled study of the effect of therapies aimed at adolescent and family psychopathology in anorexia nervosa. *Brit. J. Psychiat., 159,* 325–333.

Crits-Christoph, P. (1992). The efficacy of brief dynamic psychotherapy: A meta-analysis. *Amer. J. Psychiat., 149,* 151–158.

Crits-Christoph, P., Baranackie, K., Kurcias, J. S., Beck, A. T., Carroll, K., Perry, K., Luborsky, L., McLellan, A. T., Woody, G. E., Thompson, L.,

Gallagher, D., Zitrin, C. (1991). Meta-analysis of therapist effects in psychotherapy outcome studies. *Psychother. Res., 1*(2), 81–91.

Cronbach, L. J., & Meehl, P. E. (1955). Construct validity in psychology tests. *Psychol. Bull., 52,* 281–302.

Cronen, V. E., Johnson, K. M., & Lannamann, J. W. (1983). Paradossi, doppi-legami e circuiti riflessive: Una prospettiva teorica alternativa. *Terapia-Familiare, 14,* 87–120.

Crow, T. J. (1980). Positive and negative schizophrenic symptoms and the role of dopamine: II. *Brit. J. Psychiat., 137,* 383–386.

Crow, T. J. (1982). Positive and negative symptoms and the role of dopamine in schizophrenia. In G. Hemmings (Eds.), *Biological aspects of schizophrenia and addiction.* New York: Wiley.

Crow, T. J. (1985). The two-syndrome concept: Origins and current status. *Schizo. Bull., 11*(3), 471–486.

Cuesta, M. J., Peralta, B., & DeLeon, J. (1994). Schizophrenic syndromes associated with treatment response. *Prog. Neuro-Psychopharmacol. & Biol. Psychiat., 18,* 87–99.

Culver, R., Rotton, J., & Kelly, I. W. (1988). Geophysical variables and behavior: XLIV. Moon mechanisms and myths: A critical appraisal of explanations of purported lunar effects on human behavior. *Psych. Rep., 62*(3), 683–710.

Cummings, E. M., & Davies, P. T. (1994). Maternal depression and child development. *J. Child Psychol. Psychiat., 35*(1), 73–112.

Cummings, J. L. (1993). Amnesia and memory disturbances in neurologic disorders. In J. M. Oldham, M. B. Riba, & A. Tasman, (Eds.), *Rev. Psychiat.* (Vol. 12). Washington, DC: American Psychiatric Press.

Cummings, J. L. & Benson, D. F. (1984). Subcortical dementia: Review of an emerging concept. *Arch. Neuro., 41,* 874–879.

Cunningham, C. E., Benness, B. B., & Siegel, L. S. (1988). Family functioning, time allocation, and parental depression in the families of normal and ADDH children. *J. Clin. Child Psychol., 17*(2), 169–177.

Curtis, J. M., & Cowell, D. R. (1993). Relation of birth order and scores on measures of pathological narcissism. *Psych. Rep., 72*(1), 311–315.

Cutting, J. (1985). *The psychology of schizophrenia.* Edinburgh: Churchill-Livingstone.

Cyr, J. J., & Kalpin, R. A. (1988). Investigating the lunar-lunacy relationship: A reply to Rotton and Kelly. *Psych. Rep., 62*(1), 319–322.

D'Attilio, J. P., Cambell, B. M., Lubold, P., Jacobson, T., et al. (1992). Social support and suicidal potential: Preliminary findings for adolescent populations. *Psych. Rep., 70*(1), 76–78.

Dadds, M. R., Sanders, M. R., Morrison, M., & Rebgetz, M. (1992). Childhood depression and conduct disorder: II. An analysis of family interaction patterns in the home. *J. Abnorm. Psychol., 101*(3), 505–513.

Dahl, A. A. (1993). The personality disorders: A critical review of family, twin, and adoption studies. *J. Pers. Dis.,* Spring (Suppl. 1), 86–99.

Dahlstrom, W. G. (1993). Tests: Small samples, large consequences. *Amer. Psychol., 48*(4), 393–399.

Dare, C., & Eisler, I. (1992). Family therapy for anorexia nervosa. In P. J. Cooper & A. Stein (Eds.), *Feeding problems and eating disorders in children and adolescents.* Philadelphia, PA: Harwood Academic Publishers.

Dashef, S. S. (1984). Active suicide intervention by a campus mental health service: Operation and rationale. *J. Amer. Coll. Hlth., 33*(3), 118–122.

Davanloo, H. (Ed.). (1980). *Short-term dynamic psychotherapy.* New York: Aronson.

Davidson, J. R., Hughes, D., Blazer, D. G., & George, L. K. (1991). Post-traumatic stress disorder in the community: An epidemiological study. *Psychol. Med., 21*(3), 713–721.

Davidson, J. R. T. (1992). Monoamine oxidase inhibitors. In E. S. Paykel (Ed.), *Handbook of affective disorders.* New York: Guilford.

Davidson, K. M. (1995). Diagnosis of depression in alcohol dependence: Changes in prevalence with drinking status. *Brit. J. Psychiat., 166,* 199–204.

Davis, J. D., Kane, J. M., Marder, S. R., Brauzer, B., Gierl, B., Schooler, N., Casey, D. E., & Hassan, M. (1993). Dose response of propheylatic antipsychotics. *J. Clin. Psychiat., 54*(3, suppl.), 24–30.

Davis, J. M. (1980). Antidepressant drugs. In H. I. Kaplan, A. M. Freedman, & B. J. Sadock (Eds.), *Comprehensive textbook of psychiatry III.* Baltimore: Williams & Wilkins.

Davis, J. M., Comaty, J. E., & Janicak, P. G. (1988). The psychological effects of antipsychotic drugs. In C. N. Stefanis & A. D. Rabavilis (Eds.), *Schizophrenia: Recent biosocial developments.* New York: Human Sciences.

Davis, J. M., Klerman, G., & Schildkraut, J. (1967). Drugs used in the treatment of depression. In L. Efron, J. O. Cole, D. Levine, & J. R. Wittenborn (Eds.), *Psychopharmacology: A review of progress.* Washington, DC: U. S. Clearinghouse of Mental Health Information.

Davis, K., Thal, L., Gamzu, E., et al. (1992). A double-blind, placebo-controlled multicenter study of tacrine for Alzheimer's disease. *New Eng. J. Med. 327,* 1253–1259.

Davis, M. (1992). Analysis of aversive memories using the fear potentiated startle paradigm. In N. Butters, & L. R. Squire (Eds.), *The neuropsychology of memory* (2nd ed.). New York: Guilford.

Davis, P. (1989). *In mind of Johnson: A study of Johnson, the Rambler.* London.

Davis, R. C., Brickman, E., & Baker, T. (1991). Supportive and unsupportive responses of others to rape victims: Effects on concurrent victim adjustment. *Amer. J. Comm. Psychol., 19,* 443–451.

Davis, S. F. (1992). Report to the American Psychological Association. Reported in *Psych. Today, 25*(6), 9.

Davison, A. N., & Dobbing, J. (1966). Myelination as a vulnerable period in brain development. *Brit. Med. Bull., 22,* 40–44.

Dawson, G., & Castelloe, P. (1992). Autism. In C. E. Walker (Ed.), *Clinical psychology: Historical and research foundations.* New York: Plenum.

de Wilde, E. J., Kienhorst, I. C. W. M., Diekstra, R. F. W., & Wolters, W. H. G. (1992). The relationship between adolescent suicidal behavior and life events in childhood and adolescence. *Amer. J. Psychiat., 149,* 45–51.

DeAngelis, T. (1992, November). Best psychological treatment for many men: Group therapy. *APA Monitor, 23*(11), p. 31.

DeAngelis, T. (1992, December). Illness linked with repressive style of coping. *APA Monitor,* p. 14.

DeAngelis, T. (1992). Program embodies feminist values to aid women with addictions. *APA Monitor, 23*(11), 29.

DeAngelis, T. (1993, September). Controversial diagnosis is voted into latest DSM. *APA Monitor,* pp. 32–33.

DeAngelis, T. (1994, March). Poor kids are focus of asthma studies, *APA Monitor,* pp. 26–27.

DeAngelis, T. (1994, May). Vets, minorities, single moms mak up homeless population. *APA Monitor, 25*(5), p. 39.

Deering, C. D., Coyne, L., Grame, C. J., Smith, M. J., et al. (1991). Effects of extended hospitalization: A one-year follow-up study. *Bull. Menninger Clin., 55*(4), 444–453.

Deitch, D., & Solit, R. (1993). International training for drug abuse treatment and the issue of cultural relevance. *J. Psychoactive Drugs, 25*(1), 87–92.

Deitz, S. M. (1977). An analysis of programming DRL schedules in educational settings. *Behav. Res. Ther., 15*(1), 103–111.

Dekker, J. (1993). Inhibited male orgasm. In W. O'Donohue and J. Geer (Eds.), *Handbook of sexual dysfunctions.* Boston: Allyn and Bacon.

Delay, J., & Deniker, P. (1952). Le traitement des psychoses par une methode neurolytique derivee h'hibernotherapie: Le 4560 RP utilise seul en cure prolongee et continuee. *Congres des Medicins Alienstes et Neurologistes de France et des Pays du Langue Francaise, 50,* 503–513.

DeLisi, L. E., Crow, T. J., & Hirsch, S. R. (1986). The third biannual winter workshop on schizophrenia. *Arch. Gen. Psychiat., 43*(7), 705–706.

DeLisi, L. E., Hoff, A. L., Kushner, M., Calev. A., et al. (1992). Left ventricular enlargement associated with diagnostic outcome of schizophreniform disorder. *Bio. Psychiat., 32*(2), 199–201.

DeLisi, L. E., Smith, S. B., & Hamovit, J. R. (1986). Herpes simplex virus, cytomegalovirus and Epstein-Barr virus antibody titres in sera from schizophrenic patients. *Psychol. Med., 16*(4), 757–763.

Delisle, J. R. (1986). Death with honors: Suicide among gifted adolescents [Special Issue]. *J. Couns. Dev., 64*(9), 558–560.

Dell, P. F., & Eisenhower, J. W. (1990). Adolescent multiple personality disorder: A preliminary study of eleven cases. *J Amer. Acad. Child Adol. Psychiat., 29*(3), 359–366.

Department of Justice. (1994). Cited in P. Bender, Senate committee praises Delaware Youth Programs. Gannett News Service, April 26, 1994.

DeVeaugh-Geiss, J., Moroz, G., Biederman, J., Cantwell, D. P., et al. (1992). Clomipramine hydrochloride in childhood and adolescent obsessive compulsive disorder: A multicenter trial. *J. Amer. Acad. Child. Adol, Psychiat., 31*(1), 45–49.

Dial, T. H., Pion, G. M., Cooney, B., Kohut, J., Kaplan, K. O., et al. (1992). Training of mental health providers. In R. W. Manderscheid & M. A. Sonnenschein (Eds.), *Mental Health, United States, 1992, DHHS Pub. No. (SMA)92-1942.* Washington, DC: GPO.

Diamond, D. (1987). Psychotherapeutic approaches to the treatment of panic attacks, hypochondriasis and agoraphobia. *Brit. J. Med. Psychol., 60,* 85–90.

Diekstra, R. F. W. (1989). Suicidal behavior in adolescents and young adults: The international picture. *Crisis, 10,* 16–35.

Diekstra, R. F. W. (1989). Suicide and attempted suicide: An international perspective. *Acta Psychiatr. Scandin., 80* (suppl. 354), 1–24.

Diekstra, R. F. W. (1990). An international perspective on the epidemiology and prevention of suicide. In S. J. Blumenthal & D. K. Kupfer (Eds.), *Suicide over the life cycle.* Washington, DC: American Psychiatric Press.

Diekstra, R. F. W. (1990). Suicide, depression and economic conditions. In D. Lester (Ed.), *Current concepts of suicide.* Philadelphia: The Charles Press.

Diener, E. (1984). Subjective well-being. *Psychol. Bull, 95,* 542–575.

Dietz, P. E., Hazelwood, R. R., & Warren, J. (1990). The sexually sadistic criminal and his offenses. *Bull. Amer. Acad. Psychiat. Law, 18*(2), 163–178.

Dietz, P. E., Matthews, D. B., et al. (1991). Threatening and otherwise inappropriate letters to members of the U. S. Congress. *J Forensic Sci., 36*(5), 1445–1468.

DiNardo, P. A., Moras, K., Barlow, D. H., Rapee, R. M., & Brown, T. A. (1993). Reliability of DSM-III-R anxiety disorder categories. *Arch. Gen. Psychiat., 50,* 251–256.

Dircks, P., Grimm, F., Tausch, A., & Wittern, O. (1980). Färoderung der seelischen Lebensqualitat von Krebspatienten durch personenzentrierte Gruppengesprache. *Zeitschrift für Klinische Psychologie, 9,* 241–251.

Doan, B. D. & Bryson, S. E. (1994). Etiological and maintaining factors in multiple personality disorder: A critical review. In R. M. Klein & B. K. Doane (Eds.), *Psychological concepts and dissociative disorders.* Hillsdale, NJ: Lawrence Erlbaum Associates, Publishers.

Dohrenwend, B. P., Levav, I., Shrout, P. E., Schwartz, S., et al. (1992). Socioeconomic status and psychiatric disorders: The causation-selection issue. *Sci, 255*(5047), 946–952.

Dohrmann, R. J., & Laskin, D. M. (1978). An evaluation of electromyographic feedback in the treatment of myofascial pain-dysfunction syndrome. *J. ADA, 96,* 656–662.

Dolan, B., Evans, C., & Norton, K. (1995). Multiple Axis-II diagnoses of personality disorder. *Brit. J. Psychiat., 166,* 107–112.

Dole, V. P., & Nyswander, M. (1965). A medical treatment for heroin addiction. *JAMA, 193,* 646–650.

Dole, V. P., & Nyswander, M. (1967). Heroin addiction, a metabolic disease. *Arch Int. Med., 120,* 19-24.

Domenici, N., & Griffin-Francell, C. (1993). The role of family education. *J. Clin Psychiat. 54*(suppl. 3), 31–34.

Douglas, V. I., Barr, R. G., Amin, K., O'Neill, M. E., & Britton, B. G. (1988). Dosage effects and individual responsivity to methylphenidate in attention deficit disorder. *J. Child Psychol. Psychiat. Allied Disc., 29,* 453–475.

Dowdney, L., & Skuse, D. (1993). Parenting provided by adults with mental retardation. *J. Child Psychol. Psychiat. Allied Disc., 34*(1) 25–47.

Drake, R., Gates, C., & Cotton, P. G. (1984). Suicide among schizophrenics: Who is at risk? *J. Nerv. Ment. Dis., 172*(10), 813–817.

Drake, R. E., Osher, F., & Wallach, M. (1991). Homelessness and dual diagnosis. *Amer. Psychol., 46*(11), 1149–1158.

Drake, R. E., & Wallach, M. A. (1992). Mental patients' attraction to the hospital: Correlates of living preference. *Comm. Ment. Hlth. J., 28*(1), 5–12.

Du Paul, G. J., & Barkley, R. A. (1993). Behavioral contributions to pharmacotherapy: The utility of behavioral methodology in medication treatment of children with attention-deficit hyperactivity disorder. *Behav. Ther., 24,* 47–65.

Dulloo, A., & Girardier, L. (1990). Adaptive changes in energy expenditure during refeeding following low-calorie intake: Evidence for a specific metabolic component favoring fat storage. *Amer. J. Clin. Nutrition, 52,* 415–420.

Dunbar, F. (1948). *Synopsis of psychosomatic diagnosis and treatment.* St. Louis: Mosby.

Durkheim, E. (1951). *Suicide* (J.A. Spaulding & G. Simpson, Trans.). Glencoe, IL: Free Press. (Original work published 1897).

Eaton, W. W., Dryman, A., & Weissman, M. M. (1991). Panic and phobia. In L. N. Robins, & D. A. Reigier (Eds.), *Psychiatric disorders in America: The Epidemiologic Catchment Area Study.* New York: Maxwell Macmillan International.

Eaton, W. W., Kessler, R. C., Wittchen, H. A., & Magee, W. J. (1994). Panic and panic disorder in the United States. *Amer. J. Psychiat., 151*(3), 413–420.

Eckenrode, J., Laird, M., & Doris, J. (1993). School performance and disciplinary problems among abused and neglected children. *Dev. Psych., 29*(1), 54–62.

Eddy, D. M., Wolpert, R. L., & Rosenberg, M. L. (1987). Estimating the effectiveness of interventions to prevent youth suicides. Invitational conference on applications of analytic methods to mental health: Practice, policy, research. *Med. Care, 25*(12), 57–65.

Edelson, J., & Eiskovitz, Z. (1989, September). Intervening with men who batter. *Soc. Serv. Rev.,* pp. 387–414.

Edwin, D. H., & Andersen, A. E. (1990). Psychometric testing in 76 males with eating disorders. In A. E. Andersen (Ed.), *Males with eating disorders.* New York: Brunner/Mazel.

Egan, B. M. (1992). Vascular reactivity, sympathetic tone, and stress. In E. H. Johnson, E. D. Gentry, & S. Julius (Eds.), *Personality, elevated blood pressure, and essential hypertension.* Washington, DC: Hemisphere Publishing Corporation.

Egan, J. (1988). Treatment of borderline conditions in adolescents. *J. Clin. Psychiat., 49*(Suppl. 290), 32–35.

Egeland, B. (1991, Feb.). Presentation. American Association for the Advancement of Science.

Egeland, J. A., Gerhard, D. S., Pauls, D. L., Sussex, J. N. et al. (1987). Bipolar affective disorders linked to DNA markers on chromosome 11. *Nature, 325*(6107), 783–787.

Egeland, J. A. et al. (1984). Amish study: V. Lithium sodium countertransport and catechol methyltransference in pedigrees of bipolar probands. *Amer. J. Psychiat., 141*(9), 1040–1054.

Ehle, G. (1992). Experiences with "planned" dynamic group psychotherapy of patients with anorexia nervosa. *Group Analysis, 25*(1), 43–53.

Ehlers, A. (1993). Interoception and panic disorder. *Adv. Behav. Res. Ther., 15*, 3–21.

Ehlers, A. (1993). Somatic symptoms and panic attacks: A retrospective study of learning experiences. *Behav. Res. Ther., 31*(3), 269–278.

Ehrman, R., Robbins, S., Childress, A., & O'Brien, C. (1992). Conditioned responses to cocaine-related stimuli in cocaine abuse patients. *Psychopharm., 107*(4), 61–70.

Eichler, M., Reisman, A. L., & Borins, E. M. (1992). Gender bias in medical research. *Women and Ther., 12*(4), 523–529.

Eisenthal, S., Koopman, C., & Lazare, A. (1983). Process analysis of two dimensions of the negotiated approach in relation to satisfaction in the initial interview. *J. Nerv. Ment. Dis., 171*, 49–54.

Eitinger, L. (1964). *Concentration camp survivors in Norway and Israel.* New York: Humanities Press.

Eitinger, L. (1969). Psychosomatic problems in concentration camp survivors. *J. Psychosom. Res., 13*, 183–190.

Eitinger, L. (1973). A follow-up study of the Norwegian concentration camp survivors: Mortality and morbidity. *Israel Annals of Psychiatry and Related Disciplines, 11*, 199–210.

Elias, M. (1993, July 15). Poor odds for heroin recovery. USA Today, p. 1D.

Elkin, I. (1994). The NIMH Treatment of Depression Collaborative Research Program: Where we began and where we are. In A. E. Bergin & S. L. Garfiel (Eds.), *Handbook of psychotherapy and behavior change* (4th ed.). New York: Wiley.

Elkins, I. J. & Cromwell, R. L. (1994). Priming effects in schizophrenia: Associative interference and facilitation as a function of visual context. *J. Abnorm. Psychol., 103*(4), 791–800.

Elkins, R. L. (1991). An appraisal of chemical aversion (emetic therapy) approaches to alcoholism treatment. *Behav. Res. Ther., 29*, 387–414.

Ellenberger, H. F. (1970). *The discovery of the unconscious.* New York: Basic Books.

Ellenberger, H. F. (1982). The story of "Anna O"; A critical review with new data. *J. Hist. Behav. Sci., 8*, 267–279.

Elliot, D. M., & Guy, J. D. (1993). Mental health professionals vs. non-mental health professionals: Childhood trauma and adult functioning. *Profess. Psych.: Res. Prac., 24*(1), 83–90.

Ellis, A. (1962). *Reason and emotion in psychotherapy.* Secaucus, NJ: Lyle Stuart.

Ellis, A. (1976). Rational emotive therapy. In V. Binder, A. Binder, & B. Rimland (Eds.), *Modern therapies.* Englewood Cliffs, NJ: Prentice Hall.

Ellis, A. (1976). RET abolishes most of the human ego. *Psychother. Ther. Res. Prac., 13*, 343–348.

Ellis, A. (1976). The rationale-emotive view. *J. Contemp. Psychother., 8*(1), 20–28.

Ellis, A. (1984). Rational-emotive therapy. In R. J. Corsini (Ed.), *Current psychotherapies* (3rd ed.). Itasca, IL: Peacock.

Ellis, A. (1989). Rational Emotive Therapy. In R. J. Corsini & D. Wedding (Eds.). *Current psychotherapies* (4th Ed.). Itasca, IL: Peacock.

Ellis, A. (1991). The revised ABC's of rational-emotive therapy (RET). *J. Rational-Emotive & Cog. Behav. Ther., 9*, 139–172.

Ellis, L. (1987). Relationships of criminality and psychopathy with eight other apparent behavioral manifestations of suboptimal arousal. *Pers. Indiv. Differences, 8*(6), 905–925.

Ellis, T. E., & Ratliff, K. G. (1986). Cognitive characteristics of suicidal and nonsuicidal psychiatric inpatients. *Cog. Ther. Res., 10*(6), 625–634.

Emmelkamp, P. M. (1982). Exposure in vivo treatments. In A. Goldstein & D. Chambles (Eds.), *Agoraphobia: Multiple perspectives on theory and treatment.* New York: Wiley.

Emmelkamp, P. M. (1982). *Phobic and obsessive-compulsive disorders.* New York: Plenum.

Emmelkamp, P. M. (1994). Behavior therapy with adults. In A. E. Bergin & S. L. Garfield (Eds.), *Handbook of psychotherapy and behavior change* (4th ed.). New York: Wiley.

Emmelkamp, P. M., Van Dyck, R., Bitter, M., Heins, R., et al. (1992). Spouse-aided therapy with agoraphobics. *Brit. J. Psychiat., 160*, 51–56.

Emrick, C. D., & Hansen, J. (1983). Assertions regarding effectiveness of treatment for alcoholism: Fact or fantasy? *Amer. Psychol., 38*, 1078–1088.

Ennis, B. J., & Emery, R. D. (1978). *The rights of patients (ACLU Handbook Series).* New York: Avon.

Enns, M. P., Drewnowski, A., & Grinker, J. A. (1987). Body composition, body size estimation, and attitudes towards eating in male college athletes. *Psychosom. Med., 49*(1), 56–64.

Enright, S. J. (1989). Paedophilia: A cognitive/behavioural treatment approach in a single case. *Brit. J. Psychiat., 155*, 399–401.

Epstein, N., Baucom, D. H., & Rankin, L. A. (1993). Treatment of marital conflict: A cognitive-behavioral approach. *Clin Psychol. Rev., 13*(1), 45–57.

Epstein, S. (1983). Hypnotherapeutic control of exhibitionism: A brief communication. *Inter. J. Clin. Exp. Hyp., 31*(2), 63–66.

Erber, R. (1990, Aug.). American Psychological Association Presentation.

Erdelyi, M. H. (1985). *Psychoanalysis: Freud's cognitive psychology.* New York: W. H. Freeman.

Erdelyi, M. H. (1992). Psychodynamics and the unconscious. *Amer. Psychol., 47*(6), 784–787.

Erickson, M. T. (1992). *Behavior disorders of children and adolescents.* Englewood Cliffs, NJ: Prentice Hall.

Erikson, E. (1963). *Childhood and society.* New York: Norton.

Ernst, K. (1985). Die psychische Behandlung Schizophreniekranker in der Klinik [The psychiatric treatment of hospitalized schizophrenics]. Schweizer, *Archiv fur Neurologie, Neurochirurugie und Psychiatrie, 136*(1), 67–74.

Ernst, N. D., & Harlan, W. R. (1991). Obesity and cardiovascular disease in minority populations: Executive summary. Conference highlights, conclusions, and recommendations. *Amer. J. Clin. Nutrit., 53*(Suppl.), 1507–1511.

Eser, A. (1981). "Sanctity" and "quality" of life in a historical comparative view. In S. E. Wallace & A. Eser (Eds.), *Suicide and euthanasia: The rights of personhood.* Knoxville, TN: Univ. Tennessee.

Evans, B. J., & Stanley, R. O. (1991). Hypnoanaesthesia and hypnotic techniques with surgical patients. *Austral. J. Clin. Exp. Hyp., 19*(1), 31–39.

Evans, J. A., & Hamerton, J. L. (1985). Chromosomol anomalies. In A. M. Clarke, A. D. B. Clarke, & J. M. Berg (Eds.), *Mental deficiency: The changing outlook* (4th ed.). London: Methuen.

Fabrega, H., Ulrich, R., Pilkonis, P., & Mezzich, J. (1991). On the homogeneity of personality disorder clusters. *Comprehen. Psychiat., 32*(5), 373–386.

Fackelmann, K. (1993, February 6). Marijuana and the brain: Scientists discover the brain's own THC. *Sci. News, 143*, pp. 88–94.

Faedda, G. L., Tondo, L., Teichner, M. H., Baldessarini, R. J., Gelbard, H. A., & Floris, G. F. (1993). Seasonal mood disorders: Patterns of seasonal recurrence in mania and depression. *Arch. Gen. Psychiat., 50*(1), 17–23.

Fahy, T. A. (1988). The diagnosis of multiple personality disorder. *Brit. J. Psychiat., 153*, 597–606.

Fahy, T. A., Eisler, I., & Russell, G. F. M. (1993). A placebo-controlled trial of d-fenfluramine in bulimia nervosa. *Brit. J. Psychiat., 162*, 597–603.

Fairbank, J. A., & Keane, T. M. (1982). Flooding for combat-related stress disorders: Assessment of anxiety reduction across traumatic memories. *Behav. Ther., 13*, 499–510.

Fairbank, C. G., Kirk, J., O'Connor, M., & Cooper, P. J. (1986). A comparison of two psychological treatments for bulimia nervosa. *Behav. Res. Ther., 24*, 629–643.

Falloon, I. R. H., & Liberman, R. P. (1983). Behavioral family interventions in the management of chronic schizophrenia. In W. R. McFarlane (Ed.), *Family therapy in schizophrenia.* New York: Guilford.

Falloon, I. R. H., Lindley, P., McDonald, R., & Marks, I. M. (1977). Social skills training of outpatient groups: A controlled study of rehearsal and homework. *Brit. J. Psychiat., 131*, 599–609.

Fals, S. W., & Schafer, J. (1992). The treatment of substance abusers diagnosed with obsessive-compulsive disorder: An outcome study. *J. Subst. Abuse Treat., 9*(4), 365–370.

Fals-Steward, W., Marks, A. P., & Schafer, J. (1993). A comparison of behavioral group therapy and individual behavior therapy in treating obsessive-compulsive disorder. *J. Nerv. Ment. Dis., 181*, 189–193.

Farberow, N. L. (1974). *Suicide.* Morristown, NJ: General Learning.

Farberow, N. L. (1991). Adult survivors after suicide: Research problems and needs. In A. A. Leenaars. (Ed.), *Life span perspectives of suicide: Time-lines in the suicide process.* New York: Plenum.

Farberow, N. L. (1993). Bereavement after suicide. In A. A. Leenaars, A. L. Berman, P. Cantor, R. E. Litman, & R. W. Maris (Eds.), *Suicidology.* Northvale, NJ: Jason Aronson, Inc.

Farberow, N. L., & Litman, R. E. (1970). *A comprehensive suicide prevention program.* Los Angeles: Suicide Prevention Center of Los Angeles. Unpublished final report.

Farina, A. (1976). *Abnormal psychology.* Englewood Cliffs, NJ: Prentice Hall.

Farley, C. J. (1994, April 18). The butt stops here. *Time,* pp. 58–64.

Farlow, M., Gracon, S. I., Hershey, L. A., Lewis, K. W., Sadowsky, C. H., Dolan-Ureno, J. (1992). A controlled trial of tacrine in Alzheimer's disease. *JAMA, 268*(18), 2523–2529.

Farrington, D. P. (1991). Psychological contributions to the explanations of offending. *Issues in Criminological & Legal Psychol., 1*(17), 7–19.

Farrugia, D. L. (1992). Recognizing emerging borderline personality disorders. *School Counselor, 39*(3), 195–201.

Fasko, S. N., & Fasko, D. (1991). Suicidal behavior in children. Psychology: A Journal of Human Behavior, 27(4)-28(1), 10-16.

Fauber, R. L., & Long, N. (1992). Parenting in a broader context: A reply to Emery, Finchman, and Cummings. *J. Cons. Clin. Psychol., 60*(6), 913–915.

Fava, G. A., Zielezny, M., Savron, G., & Grandi, S. (1995). Long-term effects of behavioral treatment for panic disorder. *Brit. J. Psychiat., 166,* 87–92.

Fawcett, J., Scheftner, W., Clark, D., Hedeker, D. et al. (1987). Clinical predictors of suicide in patients with major affective disorders: A controlled prospective study. *Amer. J. Psychiat., 144*(1), 35–40.

Fawzy, F. I., Fawzy, N. W., Arndt, L. A., & Pasnau, R. O. (1995). Critical Review of psychosocial interventions in cancer care. *Arch. Gen. Psychiat., 52,* 100–113.

Fedoroff, J. P. (1992). Buspirone hydrochloride in the treatment of an atypical paraphilia. *Arch Sex. Behav., 21*(4), 401–406.

Felten, D. L. (1993). Direct innervation of lymphoid organs: Substrate for neurotransmitter signaling of cells of the immune system. *Neuropsychobio., 28,* 110–112.

Fenichel, O. (1945). *The psychoanalytic theory of neurosis.* New York: Norton.

Fennig, S., Schwartz, J. E., & Bromet, E. J. (1994). Are diagnostic criteria, time of episode and occupational impairment important determinants of the female:male ratio for major depression? *J Affect. Dis., 30,* 147–154.

Fenton, W. S., & McGlashan, T. H. (1994). Antecedents, symptom progression, and long-term outcome of the deficit syndrome in schizophrenia. *Amer. J. Psychiat., 151*(3), 351–356.

Fernandez, F., Levy, J. K. Lachar, B. L., Small, G. W. et al., (1995). The management of depression and anxiety in the elderly. *J. Clin. Psychiat., 56,* [Suppl. 2] 20–29.

Fichter, M. (1990). Psychological therapies in bulimia nervosa. In M. M. Fichter (Ed.), *Bulimia nervosa: Basic research, diagnosis and therapy.* Chichester: Wiley.

Fichtner, C. G., Kuhlman, D. T., Gruenfeld, M. J., & Hughes, J R. (1990). Decreased episodic violence and increased control of dissociation in a carbamazepine-treated case of multiple personality. *Bio Psychiat., 27*(9), 1045–1052.

Field, T. M. (1977). Effects of early separation, interactive deficit, and experimental manipulations on infant-mother face-to-face interaction. *Child. Dev., 48*(3), 763–771.

Fiester, S. J. (1986). Psychotherapeutic management of gastrointestinal disorders. In A. J. Frances & R. E. Hales (Eds.), *Psychiatric update–American Psychiatric Association annual review (Vol. 5).* Washington, DC: American Psychiatric Press.

Fieve, R. R. (1975). *Moodswing.* New York: Morrow.

Figley, C. R. (1978). Symptoms of delayed combat stress among a college sample of Vietnam veterans. *Military Med., 143*(2), 107–110.

Figley, C. R., & Leventman, S. (1990). Introduction: Estrangement and victimization. In C. R. Figley & S. Leventman (Eds.), *Strangers at home: Vietnam veterans since the war.* New York: Praeger.

Fink, D. (1992). The psychotherapy of multiple personality disorder. A case study. *Psychoanal Inquiry, 12*(1), 49–70.

Fink, M. (1992). Electroconvulsive therapy. In E. S. Paykel (Ed.), *Handbook of affective disorders.* New York: Guilford.

Finkel, N. J. (1989). The Insanity Defense Reform Act of 1984: Much ado about nothing. *J. Behav. Sci. Law, 7*(3), 403–419.

Finkel, N. J. (1991). The insanity defense. *Law Hum. Behav., 15*(5), 533–555.

Finkelhor, D., Gelles, R., Hotaling, G., & Straus, M. (Eds.). (1983). *The dark side of families.* Beverly Hills, CA: Sage.

Fischbach, G. D. (1992, September). Mind and brain. *Scientif. Amer.,* p. 48.

Fisher, J. E., & Carstensen, L. L., (1990). Behavior management of the dementias. *Clin Psychol. Rev., 10,* 611–629.

Fitz, A. (1990). Religious and familial factors in the etiology of obsessive-compulsive disorder: A review. *J. Psych. Theo., 18*(2), 141–147.

Flament, M. F. (1990). Epidemiologie du trouble obsessionnel-compulsif chez l'enfant et l'adolescent. [Epidemiology of obsessive-compulsive disorder during childhood and adolescence.] *Encephale, 16,* 311–316.

Flaskerud, J. H. & Hu, L. T. (1992). Racial/ethnic identity and amount and type of psychiatric treatment. *Amer. J. Psychiat., 149*(3), 379–384.

Flavin, D. K., Franklin, J. E., & Frances, R. J. (1990). Substance abuse and suicidal behavior. In S. J. Blumenthal & D. J. Kupfer (Eds.), *Suicide over the life cycle: Risk factors, assessment, and treatment of suicidal patients.* Washington, DC: American Psychiatric Press.

Fleer, J., & Pasewark, R. A. (1982). Prior public health agency contacts of individuals committing suicide. *Psych. Rep., 50*(3, Pt. 2), 1319–1324.

Fleishman, J. A., & Fogel, B. (1994). Coping and depressive symptoms among people with AIDS. *Hlth. Psychol., 13*(2), 156–169.

Flick, S. N., Roy-Byrne, P. P., Cowley, D. S., Shores, M. M., & Dunner, D. L. (1993). DSM-III-R personality disorders in a mood and anxiety disorders clinic: Prevalance, comorbidity, and clinical correlates. *J. Affect. Dis., 27,* 71–79.

Flint, A. J. (1994). Epidemiology and comorbidity of anxiety disorders in the elderly. *Amer. J. Psychiat., 151*(5), 640–649.

Foderaero, L. W. (1993, August 12). Electroshock therapy makes a comeback. *Anchorage Daily News,* p. D3.

Folstein, S., & Rutter, M. L. (1988). Autism: Familial aggregation and genetic implications. *J. Autism Dev. Dis., 18,* 3–11.

Fonagy, P. (1991). Thinking about thinking: Some clinical and theoretical considerations in the treatment of a borderline patient. *Inter. J. Psychoanal., 72*(4), 639–656.

Foster, S. L. & Cone, J. D. (1986). Design and use of direct observation. In A. R. Ciminero, K. S. Calhoun, & H. E. Adams (Eds.), *Handbook of behavioral assessment* (2nd ed.). New York: Wiley.

Foxx, R. M., McMorrow, M. J., Davis, L. A., & Bittle, R. G. (1988). Replacing a chronic schizophrenic man's delusional speech with stimulus appropriate response. *J. Behav. Ther. Exp. Psychiat., 19*(1), 43–50.

Frances, R. J., & Franklin, J. E. (1988). Alcohol and other psychoactive substance use disorders. In J. A. Talbott, R. E. Hales, & S. C. Yudofsky (Eds.), *Textbook of psychiatry.* Washington, DC: American Psychiatric Press.

Francis, M. E., & Pennebaker, J. W. (1992). Putting stress into words: The impact of writing on physiological, absentee, and self-reported emotional well-being measures. *Amer. J. Hlth. Promo., 6*(4), 280–287.

Frank, J. D. (1973). *Persuasion and healing* (Rev. ed.). Baltimore: Johns Hopkins UP.

Frankel, F. H. (1993). Adult reconstruction of childhood events in the multiple personality literature. *Amer. J. Psychiat., 150*(6), 954–958.

Franko, D. L. (1993). The use of a group meal in the brief group therapy of bulimia nervosa. *Inter. J. Group Psychother., 43*(2), 237–242.

Frayn, D. H. (1991). The incidence and significance of perceptual qualities in the reported dreams of patients with anorexia nervosa. *Canad. J. Psychiat., 36*(7), 517–520.

Frederick, C. J. (1969). Suicide notes: A survey and evaluation. *Bull. Suicidology, 8,* 17–26.

Frederiksen, N. (1986). Toward a broader conception of human intelligence. *Amer. Psychol., 41,* 445–452.

Frederiksen, N. (1993). Changing conceptions of intelligence. In G. G. Brannigan & M. R. Merrens (Eds.), *The undaunted psychologist: Adventures in research.* New York: McGraw-Hill.

Freeston, M., Ladouceur, R., Gagnon, F., & Thibodeau, N. (1992). *Beliefs about obsessional thoughts.* Unpublished manuscript. Laval University, Quebec City, Quebec.

Freeston, M., Ladouceur, R., Thibodeau, N., & Gagnon, F. (1992). Cognitive intrusions in a non-clinical population. II. Associations with depressive, anxious, and compulsive symptoms. *Behav. Res. Ther., 30,* 263–271.

Frieberg, P. (1994, April). Gay-rights position takes on significance. *APA Monitor, 25*(4), p. 40.

French, D. J., Nicki, R. M., & Cane, D. B. (1993). Bulimia nervosa: An examination of the anxiety-inhibiting properties of the prospect of vomiting. *Behav. Psychother., 21,* 97–106.

French, O. (1987). More on multiple personality disorder. *Amer. J. Psychiat., 144*(1), 123  124.

Freud, S. (1885). On the general effects of cocaine. *Medicinisch-chirugisches Centralblatt, 20,* 373–375.

Freud, S. (1894). The neuro-psychoses of defense. In J. Strachey (Ed.), *The standard edition of the complete psychological works of Sigmund Freud.* Vol. III. London: Hogarth Press, 1962.

Freud, S. (1900). *The interpretation of dreams.* J. Strachey (Ed. and Trans.). New York: Wiley.

Freud, S. (1909). Analysis of a phobia in a five-year-old boy. In Sigmund Freud: *Collected papers* (Vol. III.). New York: Basic Books.

Freud, S. (1915). A case of paranoia counter to psychoanalytic theory. In *Complete psychological works* (Vol. 14.). London: Hogarth, 1957.

Freud, S. (1917). *A general introduction to psychoanalysis.* Translated by J. Riviere. New York: Liverright, 1963.

Freud, S. (1917). Mourning and melancholia. In *Collected papers* (Vol. 4). London: Hogarth Press and the Institute of Psychoanalysis, 1950, pp. 152–172.

Freud, S. (1924). The loss of reality in neurosis and psychosis. *Collected papers, 2,* 277–282.

Freud, S. (1933). *New introductory lectures on psychoanalysis.* New York: Norton.

Freud, S. (1955). *Notes upon a case of obsessional necrosis.* London: Hogarth Press.

Frick, P. J., Lahley, B. B., Loeber, R., et al. (1992). Familial risk factors to oppositional defiant disorder and conduct disorder: Parental psychopathology and maternal parenting. *J. Cons. Clin. Psychol., 60*(1), 49–55.

Friedberg, J. (1975, August). Electroshock therapy: Let's stop blasting the brain. *Psych. Today,* 18–23, 98–99.

Friedman, H. S., & Booth-Kewley, S. (1987). Personality, type A behavior, and coronary heart disease: The role of emotional expression. *J. Pers. Soc. Psychol., 53*(4), 783–792.

Friedman, H. S., & Booth-Kewley, S. (1987). The "disease-prone personality." *Amer. Psychol., 42,* 534–555.

Friedman, M., & Rosenman, R. (1959). Association of specific overt behavior pattern with blood and cardiovascular findings. *JAMA, 169,* 1286.

Friedman, M., & Rosenman, R. (1974). *Type A behavior and your heart.* New York: Knopf.

Friedman, M., Thoresen, C., Gill, J., et al (1984). Alteration of type A behavior and reduction in cardiac recurrences in postmyocardial infarction patients. *Amer. Heart J., 108*(2).

Friedman, E., et al. (1983). Social interaction and blood pressure: Influence of animal companions. *J. Nerv. Ment. Dis., 171*(8), 461–465.

Friman, P. C., Allen, K. D., Kerwin, M. L. E., & Larzelere, R. (1993). Changes in modern psychology: A citation analysis of the Kuhnian Displacement Thesis. *Amer. Psychol., 48*(6), 658–664.

Friman, P. C., & Warzak, W. J. (1990). Nocturnal enuresis: A prevalent, persistent, yet curable parasomnia. *Pediatrician, 17*(1), 38–45.

Fritz, G. K., Rockney, R. W., & Yeung, A. S. (1994). Plasma levels and efficacy of imipramine treatment for enuresis. *J. Amer. Acad. Child Adol. Psychiat., 33*(1), 60–64.

Fromm, E., & Nash, M. R., eds. (1992). *Contemporary hypnosis research.* New York: Guilford.

Fromm-Reichmann, F. (1948). Notes on the development of treatment of schizophrenia by psychoanalytic psychotherapy. *Psychiat., 11,* 263–273.

Frosch, W. A., Robbins, E. S., & Stern, M. (1965). *Untoward reactions to lysergic acid diethylamide (LSD) resulting in hospitalization.* New Engl. J. Med., 273, 1235–1239.

Fry, R. (1993). Adult physical illness and childhood sexual abuse. *J. Psychosom. Res., 37*(2), 89–103.

Fuller, R. C. (1982, Fall). Carl Rogers, religion, and the role of psychology in American culture. *J. Humanistic Psychol., 22,* 21–32.

Fulwiler, C., & Pope, H. G., Jr. (1987). Depression in personality disorder. In O. G. Cameron (Ed.), *Presentations of depression: Depressive symptoms in medical and other psychiatric disorders.* New York: Wiley.

Funari, D. J., Piekarski, A. M., & Sherwood, R. J. (1991). Treatment outcomes of Vietnam veterans with post–traumatic stress disorder. *Psych. Rep., 68*(2), 571–578.

Furio, J. (1993, January). Can new state laws stop stalkers? *Ms. Magazine.*

Furst, S. S., & Ostow, M. (1979). The psychodynamics of suicide. In L. D. Hankoff & B. Einsidler (Eds.), *Suicide: Theory and clinical aspects.* Littleton, MA: PSG Publishing Company, Inc.


Gabbard, G. O. (1990). *Psychodynamic psychiatry in clinical practice.* Washington, DC: American Psychiatric Press.

Gabbard, G. O., & Coyne, L. (1987). Predictors of response of antisocial patients to hospital treatment. *Hosp. Comm. Psychiat., 38*(11), 1181–1185.

Gacono, C. B., & Meloy, J. R. (1992). The Rorschach and the DSM III-R antisocial personality: A tribute to Robert Linder. *J. Clin. Psychol., 48*(3), 393–406.

Galanter, M. (1993). Network therapy for addiction: A model for office practice. *Amer. J. Psychiat., 150*(1), 28–35.

Gallagher-Thompson, D., Lovett, S., & Rose, J. (1991). Psychotherapeutic interventions for stressed family caregivers. In W. A. Myers (Ed.), *New techniques in the psychotherapy of older patients.* Washington, DC: American Psychiatric Press.

Gallagher-Thompson, D. & Thompson, L. W. (1995). Problems of Aging. In R. J. Comer, *Abnormal Psychology.* W. H. Freeman and Company: New York.

Gammonley, J., & Yates, J. (1991). Pet projects: Animal assisted therapy in nursing homes. *J. Gerontol. Nursing, 17*(1), 12–15.

Ganaway, G. K. (1989). Historical versus narrative truth: Clarifying the role of exogenous trauma in the etiology of MPD and its variants. *Dissoc., 2,* 205–222.

Ganley, A. (1981). *A participant and trainer's manual for working with men who batter.* Washington, DC: Center for Women Policy Studies.

Gannon, L., Luchetta, T., Rhodes, K., Pardie, L., & Segrist, D. (1992). Sex bias in psychological research: Progress or complacency? *Amer. Psychol., 47*(3), 389–396.

Gantz, F., Gallagher-Thompson, D., & Rodman, J. (1991). Cognitive-behavioral facilitation of inhibited grief. In A. Freeman & F. Dattilio (Eds.), *Casebook of cognitive-behavior therapy.* New York: Plenum.

GAP (Group for the Advancement of Psychiatry). (1947, Jan. 22). 18.

Garber, J., Weiss, B., & Shanley, N. (1993). Cognitions, depressive symptoms, and development in adolescents. *J. Abnorm. Psychol., 102*(1), 47–57.

Gardner, D. L., Leibenluft, E., O'Leary, K. M., & Cowdry, R. W. (1991). Self-ratings of anger and hostility in borderline personality disorder. *J. Nerv. Ment. Dis., 179*(3), 157–161.

Gardner, F. L., McGowan, L. P., DiGiuseppe, R., & Sutton-Simon, K. (1980, November). *A comparison of cognitive and behavioral therapies in the reduction of social anxiety.* Paper presented to the American Association of Behavior Therapy, New York.

Gardner, R. (1984, Jul. 12). Full moon lunacy: Fact or fiction. *Trenton Times,* p. B1.

Garety, P. (1991). Reasoning and delusions. *Brit. J. Psychiat., 159*(Suppl. 14), 14–18.

Garfinkel, P. E. (1984). The treatment of anorexia nervosa in Toronto. *J. Psychiat. Res., 19*(2-3), 405–411.

Garfinkel, P. E., & Garner, D. M. (1982). *Anorexia nervosa: A multidimensional perspective.* New York: Brunner/ Mazel.

Garland, A. F., Shaffer, D., & Whittle, B. (1989). A national survey of adolescent suicide prevention programs. *J. Amer. Acad. Child Adol. Psychiat., 28,* 931–934.

Garner, D. M., & Bemis, K. M. (1982). A cognitive-behavioral approach to anorexia nervosa. *Cog. Ther. Res., 6*(2), 123–150.

Garner, D. M., & Bemis, K. M. (1985). Cognitive therapy for anorexia nervosa. In D. M. Garner & P. E. Garfinkel (Eds.), *Handbook of psychotherapy for anorexia nervosa and bulimia.* New York: Guilford.

Garner, D. M., & Garfinkel, P. E. (1980). Sociocultural factors in the development of anorexia nervosa. *Psychol. Med., 10,* 647–656.

Garner, D. M., Garfinkel, P. E., & O'Shaughnessy, M. (1985). The validity of the distinction between bulimia with and without anorexia nervosa. *Amer. J. Psych., 142,* 581–587.

Garner, D. M., Garfinkel, P. E., Schwartz, D., & Thompson, M. (1980). Cultural expectations of thinness in women. *Psych. Rep., 47,* 483–491.

Garner, D. M., Garfinkel, P. E., Stancer, H. C., & Moldofsky, H. (1976). Body image disturbances in anorexia nervosa and obesity. *Psychosom. Med., 38,* 327–336.

Garner, D. M., Olmsted, M. P., Polivy, J. (1984). *The EDI.* Odessa, FL: Psychological Assessment Resources, Inc.

Garner, D. M., Rockert, W., Davis, R., Garner, M. V., Olmsted, M. P., & Eagle, M. (1993). Comparison of cognitive-behavioral and supportive-expressive therapy for bulimia nervosa. *Amer. J. Psychiat., 150*(1), 37–46.

Garner, D. M., Shafer, C., & Rosen, L. (1991). Critical appraisal of the DSM III-R diagnostic criteria for eating disorders. In S. R. Hooper, G. W. Hynd, & R. E. Mattison (Eds.), *Child psychopathology.* Hillsdale, NJ: Lawrence Erlbaum Associates.

Garofalo, G., Ragusa, R. M., Barletta, C., & Spina, E. (1992). Schizophrenia and chromosomal fragile sites. *Amer. J. Psychiat., 149*(8), 1116.

Garrison, C. Z., McKeown, R. E., Valois, R. F., & Vincent, M. L. (1993). Aggression, substance use, and suicidal behaviors in high school students. *Amer. J. Pub. Hlth., 83*(2), 179–184.

Garrison, E. G. (1987). Psychological maltreatment of children: An emerging focus for inquiry and concern. *Amer. Psychol., 42*(2), 157–159.

Gebhard, P. H. (1965). Situational factors affecting human sexual behavior. In F. Beach (Ed.), *Sex and behavior.* New York: Wiley.

Gebhard, P. H., Gagnon, J. H., Pomeroy, W. B., & Christenson, C. V. (1965). *Sex offenders: An analysis of types.* New York: Harper & Row.

Geer, J. H. (1965). The development of a scale to measure fear. *Behav. Res. Ther., 3,* 45–53.

Gelder, M. (1991). Psychological treatment for anxiety disorders: Adjustment disorder with anxious mood, generalized anxiety disorders, panic disorder, agoraphobia, and avoidant personality disorder. In C. Coryell & G. Winokur (Eds.), *The clinical management of anxiety disorders.* New York: Oxford UP.

Gelfand, D. M., Jenson, W. R., & Drew, C. J. (1982). *Understanding child behavior disorders.* New York: Holt, Rinehart & Winston.

Geller, J. L. (1992). A historical perspective on the role of state hospitals viewed from the era of the "revolving door." *Amer. J. Psychiat., 149,* 1526–1533.

Gelles, R. J. (1992). Poverty and violence toward children. *Amer. Behav. Sci., 35*(3), 258–274.

Gelles, R. J., & Straus, M. A. (1987). Is violence toward children increasing? A comparison of 1975 and 1985 national survey rates. *J. Interpersonal Violence, 2,* 212–222.

Gelman, D., & Katel, P. (1993, April 5). The trauma after the storm. *Newsweek.*

Gentry, W. D., & Matarazzo, J. D. (1981). Medical psychology: Three decades of growth and development. In. L. A. Bradley & C. K. Prokop (Eds.), *Medical psychology: A new perspective.* New York: Academic Press.

George, F. R. (1990). Genetic approaches to studying drug abuse: Correlates of drug self-administration. National Institute on Alcohol Abuse and Alcoholism Neuroscience and Behavioral Research Branch Workshop on the Neurochemical Bases on Alcohol-Related Behavior. *Alc., 7*(3), 207–211.

Gerhardt, P., Holmes, D. L., Alessandri, M., Goodman, M. (1991). Social policy on the use of aversive interventions: Empirical, ethical, and legal considerations. *J. Autism Dev. Dis., 21*(3), 265–277.

Gerlach, J., & Hansen, L. (1992). Clozapine and D1/D2 antagonism in extrapyramidal functions. *Brit. J. Psychiat., 160*(suppl), 34–37.

Gerlinghoff, M., & Backmund, H. (1987). Stealing behavior in anorexia nervosa and bulimia nervosa. *Fortschritte-der-Neurologie Psychiatrie, 55*(11), 343–346.

Gershon, E. S. & Rieder, R. O. (1992). Major disorders of mind and brain. *Schientif. Amer.,* pp. 127–133.

Geyer, S. (1992). Artifacts in "limited prospective" designs? Testing confounding effects on response behaviour of women prior to breast surgery. *J. Psychosom. Res., 36*(2), 107–116.

Gheorghiu, V. A., & Orleanu, P. (1982). Dental implant under hypnosis. *Amer. J. Clin. Hyp., 25*(1), 68–70.

Ghubash, R., Hamdi, E., & Bebbington, P. (1992). The Dubai Community Psychiatry Survey: Prevalence and socio-demographic correlates. *Soc. Psychiat. & Psychiatric Epidemiol., 27*(2), 53–61.

Gibbs, M. S. (1989). Factors in the victim that mediate between disaster and psychopathology: A review. *J. of Traumatic Stress, 2,* 489–514.

Giedd, J. N., Castellanos, F. X., Casey, B. J., Kozuch, P., et al. (1994). Quantitative morphology of the corpus callosum in Attention Deficit Hyperactivity Disorder. *Amer. J. Psychiat., 151*(5), 665–669.

Gil, D. (1970). *Violence against children.* Cambridge, MA: Harvard, UP.

Gill, A. D. (1982). Vulnerability to suicide. In E. L. Bassuk, S. C. Schoonover, & A. D. Gill (Eds.), Lifelines: Clinical perspectives on suicide. New York: Plenum.

Gillberg, C. (1992). Subgroups in autism: Are there behavioral phenotypes typical of underlying medical conditions? *J. Intellect. Disabil. Res., 36*(3), 201–214.

Gillberg, C., Ehlers, S., Schaumann, H., Jakobsson, G. et al. (1990). Autism under age 3 years: A clinical study of 28 cases referred for autistic symptoms in infancy. *J. Child Psychol. Psychiat. Allied Disc., 31*(6), 921–934.

Glancy, G. D., & Regehr, C. (1992). The forensic aspects of schizophrenia. *Psychiat. Clin. N. Amer., 15*(3), 575–589.

Glazer, S. (1993, February 26). Violence against women: Is the problem more serious than statistics indicate? *CQ Researcher, 3*(8), 169–192.

Gleaves, D. H., Williamson, D. A., & Barker, S. E. (1993). Confirmatory factor analysis of a multidimensional model of bulimia nervosa. *J. Abnorm. Psychol., 102*(1), 173–176.

Glogower, F. D., Fremouw, W. J., & McCroskey, J. C. (1978). A component analysis of cognitive restructuring. *Cog. Ther. Res., 2*(3), 209–223.

Glynn, S. M. (1990). Token economy approaches for psychiatric patients: Progress and pitfalls of chronic psychiatric illness. *Behav. Mod., 14*(4), 383–407.

Gold, M. S. (1986). *The facts about drugs and alcohol.* New York: Bantam.

Goldberg, J. F., Harrow, M., & Grossman, L. S. (1995). Recurrent affective syndromes in bipolar and unipolar mood disorders at follow-up. *Brit. J. Psychiat., 166,* 382–385.

Goldbloom, D. S., Hicks, L. K., & Garkinkel, P. E. (1990). Platelet serotonin uptake in bulimia nervosa. *Bio. Psychiat., 28*(7), 644–647.

Goldbloom, D. S., & Olmsted, M. P. (1993). Pharmacotherapy of bulimia nervosa with fluoxetine: Assessment of clinically significant attitudinal change. *Amer. J. Psychiat., 150*(5), 770–774.

Golden, M. (1964). Some effects of combining psychological tests on clinical inferences. *J. Cons. Clin. Psychol., 28,* 440–446.

Goldiamond, I. (1965). Self-control procedures in personal behavior problems. *Psych. Rep., 17,* 851–868.

Golding, J. M. (1994). Sexual assault history and physical health in randomly selected Los Angeles women. *Hlth. Psychol., 13*(2), 130–138.

Goldman, M. (1992). Kleptomania: An overview. *Psychiat. Ann., 22*(2), 68–71.

Goldstein, A. (1994). *Addiction: From biology to drug policy.* New York: W. H. Freeman.

Goldstein, G. (1990). Comprehensive Neuropsychological Assessment Batteries. In G. Goldstein & M. Hersen (Eds.), *Handbook of psychological assessment* (2nd ed.). New York: Pergamon.

Goldstein, M. J. (1987). Treatment of families of schizophrenic patients: Theory, practice, and research. *Inter. J. Fam. Psychiat., 8*(2), 99–115.

Goldstein, M. J., (1991). Psychosocial (nonpharmacologic) treatments for schizophrenia. In A. Tasman & S. M. Goldfinger (Eds.), *American Psychiatric Press review of psychiatry* (Vol. 10). Washington, DC: American Psychiatric Press.

Goldstein, M. J., & Palmer, J. O. (1975). *The experience of anxiety: A casebook* (2nd ed.). New York: Oxford UP.

Goleman, D. (1993, April 14). What you reveal to a psychotherapist may go further. *New York Times,* p. C12.

Goleman, D., & Gurin, J. (1993). *Mind/Body Medicine.* Yonkers, NY: Consumers Union of United States, Inc.

Goleman, D., & Gurin, J. (1993). Mind/Body Medicine-At last. *Psych. Today, 26*(2), 16, 80.

Goodman, R. (1990). Technical note: Are perinatal complications causes or consequences of autism? *J. Child Psychol. Psychiat. Allied Disc., 31*(5), 809–812.

Goodman, R., & Ashby, L. (1990). Delayed visual maturation and autism. *Dev. Med. & Child Neurol., 32*(9), 814–819.

Goodman, W. K., McDougle, C., & Price, L. H. (1992). Pharmacotherapy of obsessive–compulsive disorder. *J. Clin. Psychiat., 53*(Suppl. 4), 29–37.

Goodwin, D. W. (1984). Studies of familial alcoholism: A review. *J. Clin. Psychiat., 45*(12, Sect. 2), 14–17.

Goodwin, D. W., Schulsinger, F., Hermansen, L., Guze, S. B., & Winokur, G. A. (1973). Alcohol problems in adoptees raised apart from alcoholic biological parents. *Arch. Gen. Psychiat., 128,* 239–243.

Goodwin, F. K. (1993). Predictors of antidepressant response. *Bull. Menninger Clin., 57*(2), 146–160.

Goodwin, F. K., & Jamison, K. R. (1990). *Manic-depressive illness.* New York: Oxford UP.

Goodwin, G. M. (1992). Tricyclic and newer antidepressants. In E. S. Paykel (Ed.), *Handbook of affective disorders.* New York: Guilford.

Gorman, J. M., Liebowitz, M. R., Fyer, A. J., & Stein, J. (1989). A neuroanatomical hypothesis for panic disorder. *Amer J. Psychiat., 146*(2), 148–161.

Gorman, J. M., Papp, L., & Klein, D. F. (1990). Biological models of panic disorder. In G. D. Burrows, M. Roth, & R. Noyes Jr. (Eds.), *Handbook of anxiety* (Vol. 3). Amsterdam: Elsevier Science Publishers.

Goshen, C. E. (1967). *Documentary history of psychiatry: A source book on historical principles.* New York: Philosophy Library.

Gottesman, I. I. (1991). *Schizophrenia genesis.* New York: W. H. Freeman.

Gottheil, E. (1987). Drug use, misuse and abuse by the elderly. *Med. Aspects of Human Sex., 21*(3), 29–37.

Gottlieb, J. (1981). Mainstreaming: Fulfilling the promise? *Amer. J. Ment. Def., 86*(2), 115–126.

Gottlieb, J., Alter, M., & Gottlieb, B. W. (1991). Litigation involving people with mental retardation. In J. L. Matson & J. A. Mulick (Eds.), *Handbook of mental retardation.* New York: Pergamon.

Gould, M. S., & Shaffer, D. (1986). The impact of suicide in television movies. *New Engl. J. Med., 315,* 690–694.

Gove, W. R. (1982). The current status of the labeling theory of mental illness. In W. R. Gove (Ed.), *Deviance and mental illness.* Beverly Hills, CA: Sage.

Gove, W. R., & Tudor, J. F. (1973). Adult sex roles and mental illness. *Amer. J. Sociol., 78,* 812–835.

Gowers, S., Kadambari, S. R., & Crisp, A. H. (1985). Family structure and order of patients with anorexia nervosa. Conference on Anorexia Nervosa and Related Disorders (1984), Swansea, Wales). *J. Psychiat. Res., 19* (2–3), 247–251.

Graham, J. R. (1977). *The MMPI: A practical guide.* New York: Oxford UP.

Graham, J. R. (1987). *The MMPI: A practical guide* (2nd ed.). New York: Oxford UP.

Graham, J. R. (1993). *MMPI-2: Assessing personality and psychopathology* (2nd ed.). New York: Oxford UP.

Graham, J. R. & Lilly, R. S. (1984). *Psychological testing.* Englewood Cliffs, NJ: Prentice Hall.

Gramzow, R., & Tangney, J. P. (1992). Proneness to shame and the narcissistic personality. *Pers. Soc. Psychol. Bull., 18*(3), 369–376.

Graves, J. S. (1993). Living with mania: a study of outpatient group psychotherapy for bipolar patients. *Amer. J. Psychother., 47*(1), 113–126.

Gray, H. (1959). *Anatomy of the human body* (27th ed.). Philadelphia: Lea & Febiger.

Gray, J. J., & Hoage, C. M. (1990). Bulimia nervosa: Group behavior therapy with exposure plus response prevention. *Psych. Rep., 66*(2), 667–674.

Green, A. H. (1989). Physical and sexual abuse of children. In H. I. Kaplan & B. J. Sadock (Eds.), *Comprehensive textbook of psychiatry/5* (Vol. 2). (5th ed.). Baltimore, MD: Williams & Wilkins.

Green, S. A. (1985). *Mind and body: The psychology of physical illness.* Washington, DC: American Psychiatric Press.

Greenberg, D., & Marks, I. (1982). Behavioral therapy of uncommon referrals. *Brit. J. Psychiat., 141,* 148–153.

Greenberg, E. (1989). Healing the borderline. *Gestalt J.* 12(2), 11–55.

Greenberg, L., Elliott, R., & Lietaer, G. (1994). Research on experimental psychotherapies. In A. E. Bergin & S. L. Garfield (Eds.), *Handbook of psychotherapy and behavior change.* New York: Wiley.

Greenberg, R. P., & Bornstein, R. F. (1988). The dependent personality: II Risk for psychological disorders. *J. Pers. Dis.,* 2(2), 136–143.

Greenfield, S., Swartz, M., Landerman, L., & George, L. (1993). Long-term psychosocial effects of childhood exposure to parental problem drinking. *Amer. J. Psychiat.,* 150(4), 608–619.

Greenhill, L. L. (1992). Pharmacologic treatment of attention deficit hyperactivity disorder. *Psychiat. Clin. N. Amer.,* 15(1), 1–27.

Greist, J. H. (1990). Treatment of obsessive–compulsive disorder: Psychotherapies, drugs, and other somatic treatment. *J. Clin. Psychol.,* 51(Suppl. 8), 44–50.

Greist, J. H. (1992). An integrated approach to treatment of obsessive-compulsive disorder. *J. Clin Psychiat.,* 53(Suppl. 4), 38–41.

Greist, J. H., Jefferson, J. W., Kobak, K. A., Katzelnick, D. J., & Serlin, R. C. (1995). Efficacy and tolerability of serotonin transport inhibitors in obsessive-compulsive disorder. *Arch. Gen. Psychiat.,* 52, 53–60.

Grigg, J. R. (1988). Imitative suicides in an active duty military population. *Military Med.,* 153(2), 79–81.

Grinspoon, L., & Bakalar, J. B. (1986). Can drugs be used to enhance the psychotherapeutic process? *Amer. J. Psychother.,* 40(3), 393–404.

Grinspoon, L., et al. (Eds.) (1986, Oct.) Mental retardation. Part. I. *Ment. Hlth. Letter,* 3(4).

Grisez, G., & Boyle, J. M., Jr. (1979). *Life and death with liberty and justice: A contribution to the euthanasia debate.* Notre Dame, IN: Univ. Notre Dame.

Grizenko, N., Cvejic, H., Vida, S., Sayegh, L. (1991). Behaviour problems of the mentally retarded. *Canad. J. Psychiat.,* 36(10), 712–717.

Grob, G. N. (1966). *State and the mentally ill: A history of Worcester State Hospital in Massachusetts, 1830–1920.* Chapel Hill, NC: Univ. North Carolina.

Grossman, L. S., & Wasyliw, O. (1988). A psychometric study of stereotypes: Assessment of malingering in a criminal forensic group. *J. of Pers. Assess.,* 52(3), 549–563.

Grossman, S. P. (1990> Brain mechanisms concerned with food intake and body-weight regulation. In M. M. Fichter (Ed.), *Bulimia nervosa: Basic research, diagnosis and therapy.* Chichester: Wiley.

Groth, A. N., & Birnbaum, H. J. (1978). Adult sexual orientation and attraction to underage-persons. *Arch. Sex. Behav,* 7, 175–181.

Guillard, P., & Guillard, C. (1987). Suicide and attempted suicide in Martinique. Psychologie Medicale, 19(5), 629–630.

Gunby, P. (1981). Many cancer patients receiving THC as antiemetic. *Med. News.* 245(15), 1515.

Gunderson, J. G., (1988). Personality disorders. In A. M. Nicholi Jr. (Ed.). *The new Harvard guide to psychiatry.* Cambridge, MA: Belknap Press.

Gunn, J., Madel, A., & Swinton, M. (1991). Treatment needs of prisoners with psychiatric disorders. *Brit. Med. J.,* 303, 338–341.

Gupta, R. (1988). Alternative patterns of seasonal affective disorder: Three case reports from North India. *Amer. J. Psychiat.,* 145(4), 515–516.

Gurling, H. M., Sherrington, R. P., Brynjolfsson, J., Read, T., et al. (1989). Recent and future molecular genetic research into schizophrenia. *Schizo. Bull.,* 15(3), 373–382.

Gurman, A., Kniskern, D. P., & Pinsof, W. M. (1986). Research on the process and outcome of marital and family therapy. In S. L. Garfield and A. E. Bergin (Eds.), *Handbook of psychotherapy and behavior change: An evaluative analysis.* (3rd ed.). New York: Wiley.

Gwirtsman, H. E., Guze, B. H., Yager, J., & Gainsley, B. (1990). Fluoxetine treatment of anorexiz nervosa: An open clinical trial. *J. Clin Psychiat.,* 51(9), 378–382.

Haas, G. L., Radomsky, E. D., Glanz, L., Keshavan, M. S., Mann, J. J., & Sweeney, J. A. (1993, May). *Suicidal behavior in schizophrenia: Course-of-illness predictors.* Presented at the Annual Meeting of the Society of Biological Psychiatry, San Francisco, CA.

Hadley, S. W., & Strupp, H. H. (1976). Contemporary views of negative effects in psychotherapy: An integrated account. *Arch. Gen. Psychiat.,* 33(1), 1291–1302.

Haefely, W. (1990). Benzodiazepine receptor and ligands: Structural and functional differences. In I. Hindmarch, G. Beaumont, S. Brandon, & B. E. Leonard (Eds.), *Benzodiazepines: Current concepts (Pt. 1).* Chichester: Wiley.

Haefely, W. (1990). The GABA-benzodiazepine receptor: Biology and pharmacology. In G. Burrows, M. Roth, & R. Noyes (Eds.), *Handbook of Anxiety (Vol. 3).* Amsterdam: Elsevier Science Publishers.

Hafner, H., & an der Heiden, W. (1988). The mental health care system in transition: A study of organization, effectiveness, and costs of complementary care for schizophrenic patients. In C. N. Stefanis, & A. D.

Rabavilis (Eds.), *Schizophrenia: Recent biosocial developments.* New York: Human Sciences.

Hage, J. J., & Bouman, F. G. (1992). Silicone genital prosthesis for female-to-male transsexuals. *Plast. Reconstruct. Surg.,* 90(3), 516–519.

Hahlweg, K., & Markman, H. G. (1988). Effectiveness of behavioral marital therapy: Empirical status of behavioral techniques in preventing and alleviating marital distress. *J. Cons. Clin. Psychol.,* 56(3), 440–447.

Halaas, J. L. Gajiwala, K. F. Maffei, M. Cohen, S. L. et al. (1995). Weight-reducing effects of the plasma protein encoded by the obese gene. *Science,* 269, 543–546.

Hale, C. A., & Borkowski, J. G. (1991). Attention, memory and cognition. In J. L. Matson & J. A. Mulick (Eds.), *Handbook of mental retardation.* New York: Pergamon.

Hall, G. N. (1992). Cited in A round-up of rapists. *Psychol. Today,* 25(6), 12–13.

Hall, L. (with L. Cohn). (1980). *Eat without fear.* Santa Barbara, CA: Gurze.

Hall, S. M., Tunstall, C., Rugg, G., et al. (1985). Nicotine gum and behavioral treatment in smoking cessation. *J. Cons. Clin. Psychol.,* 53, 256–258.

Hallam, R. S., & Rachman, S. (1976). Current status of aversion therapy. In M. Hersen, R. Eisler, & P. Miller (Eds.), *Progress in behavior modification* (Vol. 2). New York: Academic Press.

Halmi, K. A. (1985). Behavioral management for anorexia nervosa. In D. M. Garner & P. E. Garfinkel (Eds.), *Handbook of psychotherapy for anorexia nervosa and bulimia.* New York: Guilford.

Halmi, K. A. (1985). Classification of the eating disorders. *J. Psychiat. Res.,* 19, 113–119.

Halstead, W. C. (1947). *Brain and intelligence: A quantitative study of the frontal lobes.* Chicago: Univ. Chicago.

Hamer, D. H., Hu, S., Magnuson, V. et al. (1993). A linkage between DNA markers on the X chromosome and male sexual orientation. *Sci.,* 261(5119), 321–327.

Hamer, D. H., Hu, S., Magnuson, V. et al. (1993). Genetics and male sexual orientation: [Response]. *Sci.,* 261(5126), 1259.

Hamilton, M. (1976). Electroconvulsive shock on serotonin activity. In S. Malitz & H. A. Sackeim (Eds.), *Electroconvulsive therapy: Clinical and basic research issues.* New York: Ann. NY Acad. Sci.

Hammen, C. L., & Krantz, S. (1976). Effect of success and failure on depressive cognitions. *J. Abnorm. Psychol.,* 85(8), 577–588.

Harding, C. M., Zubin, J., & Strauss, J. S. (1992). Chronicity in schizophrenia: revisited. *Brit. J. Psychiat.,* 161(suppl. 18), 27–37.

Hare, R. D. (1978). Electrodermal and cardiovascular correlates of sociopathy. In R. D. Hare & D. Shalling (Eds.), *Psychopathic behavior: Approaches to research.* New York: Wiley.

Hare, R. D. (1978). Psychopathy and electrodermal responses to nonsignal stimulation. Biological Psychology, 6, 237–246.

Hare, R. D. (1993). *Without conscience: The disturbing world of the psychopaths among us.* New York: Pocket Books.

Harkavy, J. M., & Asnis, G. (1985). Suicide attempts in adolescence: Prevalence and implications. *New Engl. J. Med.,* 313, 1290–1291.

Harlow, H. F., & Harlow, M. K. (1965). The affectional systems. In A. Schrier, H. Harlow, & F. Stollnitz (Eds.), *Behavior of nonhuman primates* (Vol. 2). New York: Academic Press.

Harnett, P. H., & Misch, P. (1993). Developmental issues in the assessment and treatment of adolescent perpetrators of sexual abuse. *J. Adol.,* 16, 396–405.

Haroutunian, V. (1991). Gross anatomy of the brain. In K. Davis, H. Klar, & J. T. Coyle (Eds.), *Foundations of psychiatry.* Philadelphia: Saunders.

Harrell, R. F., Woodyard, E., & Gates, A. I. (1955). *The effects of mothers' diet on the intelligence of the offspring.* New York: Columbia UP.

Harrington, D. L., et al. (1990). Procedural memory in Parkinson's disease: Impaired motor but not visuoperceptual learning. *J. Clin. Exp. Neuropsych.,* 12, 323–339.

Harrington, R. C., Fudge, H., Rutter, M. L., Bredenkamp, D., Groothues, C., & Pridham, J. (1993). Child and adult depression: A test of continuities with data from a family study. *Brit. J. Psychiat.,* 162, 627–633.

Harris, F. C., & Lahey, B. B. (1982). Subject reactivity in direct observation assessment: A review and critical analysis. *Clin. Psychol. Rev.,* 2, 523–538.

Harris, S. L., & Milch, R. E. (1981). Training parents as behavior modifers for their autistic children. *Clin. Psychol. Rev,* 1, 49–63.

Hart, S. N., & Brassard, M. R. (1987). A major threat to children's mental health: Psychological maltreatment. *Amer. Psychol.,* 42(2), 160–165.

Hart, S. N., & Brassard, M. R. (1991). Psychological maltreatment: Progress achieved. *Dev. Psychopath.,* 3(1), 61–70.

Hart, S. N., Germain, R., & Brassard, M. R. (1987). The challenge: To better understand and combat the psychological maltreatment of children and youth. In M. R. Brassard, R. Germain, & S. N. Hart (Eds.), *Psychological maltreatment of children and youth.* New York: Pergamon.

Harter, S., & Marold, D. B. (1994). Psychosocial risk factors contributing to adolescent suicidal ideation. In G. G. Naom & S. Borst (Eds.), *New directions for child development, no. 64—Children, youth, and suicide: Developmental perspectives.* San Francisco: Jossey-Bass Publishers.

Harvey, P. D. (1991). Cognitive and linguistic functions of adolescent children at risk for schizophrenia. In E. F. Walker (Ed.), *Schizophrenia: A lifecourse developmental perspective.* New York: Academic Press.

Hawkins, W. L., French, L. C., Crawford, B. D., & Enzle, M. C. (1988). Depressed affect and time perception. *J. Abnorm. Psychol., 97*(3), 275–280.

Hawton, K. (1986). *Suicide and attempted suicide among children and adolescents.* Beverly Hills, CA: Sage Publications.

Hawton, K., Cole, D., O'Grady, J., & Osborn, M. (1982). Motivational aspects of deliberate self-poisoning in adolescents. *Brit. J. Psychiat., 141,* 286–291.

Hay, L. R., Hay, W. R., & Angle, H. V. (1977). The reactivity of self-recording: A case report of a drug abuser. *Behav. Ther., 8*(5), 1004–1007.

Haynes. S. G., Feinleib, M., & Kannel, W. B. (1980). The relationship of psychosocial factors to coronary heart disease in the Framingham study: III. Eight-year incidence of coronary heart disease. *Amer. J. Epidemiol., 111,* 37–58.

Heather, N., Winton, M., & Rollnick, S. (1982). An empirical test of "a cultural delusion of alcoholics." *Psych. Rep., 50*(2), 379–382.

Heaton, R. K., Baade, L. E., & Johnson, K. L. (1978). Neuropsychological test results associated with psychiatric disorders in adults. *Psychol. Bull., 85,* 141–162.

Heflinger, C. A., Cook, V. J., & Thackrey, M. (1987). Identification of mental retardation by the System of Multiclutural Pluralistic Assessment: Nondiscriminatory or nonexistent? *J. School Psychol., 25*(2), 177–183.

Heikkinen, M., Aro, H., & Lonnqvist, J. (1992). Recent life events and their role in suicide as seen by the spouses. *Acta Psychiatr. Scandin., 86*(6), 489–494.

Heilbrun, A. B., & Witt, N. (1990). Distorted body image as a risk factor in anorexia nervosa: Replication and clarification. *Psych. Rep., 66*(2), 407–416.

Heiman, J. R., Gladue, B. A., Roberts, C. W., & LoPiccolo, J. (1986). Historical and current factors discriminating sexually functional from sexually dysfunctional married couples. *J. of Marital Fam. Ther., 12*(2), 163–174.

Heiman, J. R., & LoPiccolo, J. (1988). *Becoming orgasmic: A personal and sexual growth program for women.* New York: Prentice Hall.

Heimberg, R. G., Salzman, D. G., Holt, C. S., & Blendall, K. (1991). *Cognitive behavioral treatment for social phobia: Effectiveness at five-year follow-up.* Manuscript submitted for publication.

Helms, J. E. (1992). Why is there no study of cultural equivalence in standardized cognitive ability testing? *Amer. Psychol., 47*(9), 1083–1101.

Helzer, J. E., Burnam, A., & McEvoy, L. T. (1991). Alcohol abuse and dependence. In L. N. Robins & D. S. Regier (Eds.), *Psychiatric disorders in America: The Epidemological Catchment Area Study.* New York: Free Press.

Hembree, W. G., Nahas, G. G., & Huang, H. F. S. (1979). Changes in human spermatozoa associated with high dose marihuana-smoking. In G. G. Nahas & W. D. M. Paton (Eds.), *Marijuana: Biological effects.* Elmsford, NY: Pergamon.

Hennager, K. (1993). Flying in dreams. In M. A. Carskadon (Ed.), *Encyclopedia of sleep and dreams.* New York: Macmillan.

Herek, G. M., & Capitanio, J. P. (1993). Public reaction to AIDS in the U.S.: A 2nd generation of stigma. *Amer. J. Pub. Hlth., 83*(4), 574–577.

Herek, G. M., & Glunt, E. K. (1988). An epidemic of stigma: Public reactions to AIDS. *Amer. Psychol., 43* (11), 886–891.

Hermesh, H., Aizenberg, D., Weizman, A., Lapidot, M., Mayor, C., & Munitz, H. (1992). Risk for definite neuroleptic malignant syndrome: A prospective study in 223 consecutive inpatients. *Brit. J. Psychiat., 161,* 254–257.

Hersen, M., Bellack, A. S., Himmelhoch, J. M., & Thase, M. E. (1984). Effects of social skill training, amitriptyline, and psychotherapy in unipolar depressed women. *Behav. Ther., 15,* 21–40.

Herz, M. I. et al. (1971). Day vs. inpatient hospitalization: A controlled study. *Amer. J. Psychiat., 127*(4), 1371–1381.

Herzog, D. B., Keller, M. B., Lavori, P. W., Bradburn, I. S., & Ott, I. L. (1990). Course and outcome of bulimia nervosa. In M. M. Fichter (Ed.), *Bulimia nervosa: Basic research, diagnosis and therapy.* Chichester: Wiley.

Hesselbrock, M. N., & Hesselbrock, V. M. (1992). Relationship of family history, antisocial personality disorder and personality traits in young men at risk for alcoholism. *J. Studies Alc., 53*(6), 619–625.

Heston, L. L. (1992). *Mending minds: A guide to the new psychiatry of depression, anxiety, and other serious mental disorders.* New York: W. H. Freeman.

Hibbert, G. A. (1984). Ideational components of anxiety: Their origin and content. *Brit. J. Psychiat., 144,* 618–624.

Hibma, M., & Griffin, J. F. T. (1994). Brief communication: The influence of

maternal separation on humoral and cellular immunity in farmed deer. *Brain, Behav., and Immunity 8,* 80–85.

Hiday, V. A. (1992). Civil commitment and arrests: An investigation of the criminizalization thesis. *J. Nerv. Ment. Dis., 180*(3), 184–191.

Hiday, V. A. (1992). Coercion in civil commitment: Process, preferences, and outcome. *Inter. J. Law Psychiat. 15*(4), 359–377.

Higuchi, S., Suzuki, K., Yamada, K., Parrish, K., & Kono, H. (1993). Alcoholics with eating disorders: Prevalence and clinical course, A study from Japan. *Brit. J. Psychiat., 162,* 403–406.

Hilgard, E. R. (1977). Controversies over consciousness and the rise of cognitive psychology. *Austral. Psychol., 12*(1), 7–26.

Hilgard, E. R. (1977). Psychology's influence on educational practices: A puzzling history. *Education, 97*(3), 203–219.

Hilgard, E. R. (1987). Research advances in hypnosis: Issues and methods. *Inter. J. Clin. Exper. Hyp., 35,* 248–264.

Hilgard, E. R. (1992). Dissociation and theories of hypnosis. In E. Fromm & M . R. Nash (Eds.), *Contemporary hypnosis research.* New York: Guilford.

Himle, J. A., Himle, D. P., & Thyer, B. A. (1989). Irrational beliefs and anxiety disorders. *J. Rational, Emotive & Cog. Behav. Ther., 7*(3), 155–165.

Hinshaw, S. P. (1991). Stimulant medication and the treatment of aggression in children with attentional deficits. *J. Clin. Child Psychol., 20,* 301–312.

Hiroto, D. S., & Seligman, M. E. (1975). Generality of learned helplessness in man. *J. Pers. Soc. Psychol., 31*(2), 311–327.

Hirsch, S., & Leff, J. (1975). *Abnormalities in parents of schizophrenics.* Oxford: Oxford UP.

Hirschfeld, R. M. (1992). The clinical course of panic disorder and agoraphobia. In G. D. Burrows, S. M. Roth, & R. Noyes, Jr., *Handbook of anxiety* (Vol. 5). Oxford: Elsevier.

Hirschfeld, R. M., & Davidson, L. (1988). Clinical risk factors for suicide. [Special Issue]. *Psychiat. Ann., 18*(11), 628–635.

Hirschfeld, R. M., & Davidson, L. (1988). Risk factors for suicide. In A. J. Frances & R. E. Hales (Eds.), *American Psychiatric Press review of psychiatry* (Vol. 7). Washington, DC: American Psychiatric Press.

Hoberman, H. M., & Garfinkel, B. D. (1988). Completed suicide in children and adolescents. *J. Amer. Acad. Child Adol. Psychiat., 27,* 689–695.

Hobson, J. A., & McCarley, R. W. (1977). The brain as a dream state generator: An activation-synthesis hypothesis of the dream process. *Amer. J. Psychiat., 134*(12), 1335–1348.

Hodgson, R. J., & Rachman, S. (1972). The effects of contamination and washing in obsessional patients. *Behav. Res. Ther., 10,* 111–117.

Hoffman, R. S. (1980). The itemized statement in clinical psychiatry: A new concept in billing. *J. Irreproducible Results, 26*(3), 7–8.

Hogan, R. A. (1968). The implosive technique. *Behav. Res. Ther., 6,* 423–431.

Hogarty, G. E. (1993). Prevention of relapse in chronic schizophrenic patients. *J. Clin. Psychiat., 54*(3, Suppl.), 18–23.

Hogarty, G. E. et al. (1974). Drug and sociotherapy in the aftercare of schizophrenic patients: II. Two-year relapse rates. *Arch. Gen. Psychiat., 31*(5), 609–618.

Hogarty, G. E. et al. (1974). Drug and sociotherapy in the aftercare of schizophrenic patients: III. Adjustment of non-relapsed patients. *Arch. Gen. Psychiat., 31*(5), 609–618.

Hogarty, G. E. et al. (1986). Family psychoeducation, social skills training, and maintenance chemotherapy in the aftercare treatment of schizophrenia: I. One-year effects of a controlled study on relapse and expressed emotion. *Arch. Gen. Psychiat., 43*(7), 633–642.

Hoge, M. A., Farrell, S. P., Munchel, M. E., & Strauss, J. S. (1988). Therapeutic factors in partial hospitalization. *Psychiat., 51*(2), 199–210.

Holden, R. R., Mendonca, J. D., & Mazmanian, D. (1985). Relation of response set to observed suicide intent. *Canad. J. Behav. Sci., 17*(4), 359–368.

Hollinger, P. C., & Offer, D. (1991). Sociodemographic, epidemiologic, and individual attributes. In L. Davidson & M. Linnoila (Ed.), *Risk factors for youth suicide.* New York: Hemisphere.

Hollander, E., Frenkel, M., Decarcia, C., Trungold, S., et al. (1992). Treatment of pathological gambling with clomipramine. *Amer. J. Psychiat., 149*(5), 710–711.

Hollender, M. H. (1988). Hysteria and memory. In H. M. Pettinati (Ed.), Hypnosis and memory. New York: Guilford.

Hollister, L. E. (1986). Health aspects of cannabis. *Pharmacol. Rev., 38*(1), 1–20.

Hollister, L. E., & Csernansky, J. G. (1990). *Clinical pharmacology of psychotherapeutic drugs* (3rd ed.). New York: Churchill-Livingstone.

Hollon, S. D., & Beck, A. T. (1994). Cognitive and cognitive-behavioral therapies. In A. E. Bergin & S. L. Garfiel (Eds.), *Handbook of psychotherapy and behavior change* (4th ed.). New York: Wiley.

Hollon, S. D., DeRubeis, R. J., Evans, M. D., Wiemer, M. J., et al. (1992). Cognitive therapy and pharmacotherapy for depression: Singly or in combination. *Arch. Gen. Psychiat., 49,* 774–781.

Hollon, S. D., Shelton, R. C., & Davis, D. D. (1993). Cognitive therapy for depression: Conceptual issues and clinical efficacy. *J. Cons. Clin. Psychol., 61*(2), 270–275.

Holmes, C. B. (1985). Comment on "Religiosity and U.S. suicide rates, 1972–1978." *J. Clin. Psychol., 41*(4), 580.

Holmes, T. H., & Rahe, R. H. (1967). The social readjustment rating scale. *J. Psychosom. Res., 11,* 213–218.

Holmes, T. H., & Rahe, R. H. (1989). The social readjustment rating scale. In T. H. Holmes & E. M. David (Eds.), *Life, change, life events, and illness: Selected papers.* New York: Praeger.

Holmes, V. F., & Rich, C. L. (1990). Suicide among physicians. In S. J. Blumenthal & D. J. Kupfer (Eds.), *Suicide over the life cycle: Risk factors, assessment, and treatment of suicidal patients.* Washington, DC: American Psychiatric Press.

Holroyd, J. C., & Brodsky, A. M. (1977). Psychologists' attitudes and practices regarding erotic and nonerotic physical contact with patients. *Amer. Psychol., 32,* 843–849.

Holstein, J. A. (1993). *Court-ordered insanity: Interpretive practice and involuntary commitment.* New York: Aldine De Gruyter.

Holt, C. S., Heimberg, R. G., & Hope, D. A. (1992). Avoidant personality disorder and the generalized subtype of social phobia. *J. Abnorm. Psychol., 101*(2), 318–325.

Holzman, P. S., & Matthysse, S. (1990). The genetics of schizophrenia: A review. *Psychol. Sci. 1*(5), 279–286.

Hooker, W. D., & Jones, R. T. (1987). Increased susceptibility to memory intrusions and the Stroop interference effect during acute marijuana intoxication. *Psychopharmaco., 91*(1), 20–24.

Hope, D. A., & Heimberg, R. G. (1993). Social phobia and social anxiety. In D. H. Barlow (Ed.), *Clinical handbook of psychological disorders: A step-by-step treatment manual* (2nd ed.). New York: Guilford.

Hopson, J. L. (1986). The unraveling of insomnia. *Anthropol. Educ. Quart., 20*(6), 42–49.

Horn, M. (1993, November). Memories lost and found. *U. S. News and World Report,* pp. 52–63.

Horner, A. J. (1975). Stages and processes in the development of early object relations and their associated pathologies. *Inter. Rev. Psycho-Anal., 2,* 95–105.

Horner, A. J. (1991). *Psychoanalytic object relations therapy.* Northvale, NJ: Hason Aronson.

Horton, P. C. (1992). A borderline treatment dilemma: To solace or not to solace. In D. Silver & M. Rosenbluth (Eds.), *Handbook of borderline disorders.* Madison, CT: International Universities Press, Inc.

House, J. S., Landis, K. R., & Umberson, D. (1988). Social relationships and health. *Sci., 241*(4865), 540–545.

Howe, A., & Walker, C. E. (1992). Behavioral management of toilet training enuresis, encopresis. *Pediatr. Clin. of N. Amer., 39*(3), 413–432.

Howells, J. G., & Guirguis, W. R. (1985). *The family and schizophrenia.* New York: International Universities Press, Inc.

Hsu, L. K. G. (1980). Outcome of anorexia nervosa: A review of literature (1954–1978). *Arch. Gen. Psychiat., 37,* 1041–1046.

Hsu, L. K. G., Crisp, A. H., & Callender, J. S. (1992). Psychiatric diagnoses in recovered and unrecovered anorectics 22 years after onset of illness: A pilot study. *Comprehen. Psychiat., 33*(2), 123–127.

Hsu, L. K. G., Crisp, A. H., & Harding, B. (1979). Outcome of anorexia nervosa. *Lancet, 1,* 61–65.

Hsu, L. K. G., & Holder, D. (1986). Bulimia nervosa: Treatment and short-term outcome. *Psychol. Med., 16,* 65.

Huang, Y. Y., Colino, A., Selig, D. K., & Malenka, R. D. (1992). The influence of prior synaptic activity on the induction of long-term potentiation. *Science, 255,* 730–733.

Hubbard, R. W., & McIntosh, J. L. (1992). Integrating suicidology into abnormal psychology classes: The revised facts on suicide quiz. *Teaching Psychol., 19*(3), 163–166.

Hughes, C. W. et al. (1984). Cerebral blood flow and cerebrovascular permeability in an inescapable shock (learned helplessness) animal model of depression. *Pharm., Biochem. Behav., 21*(6), 891–894.

Human, J., & Wasem, C. (1991, March). Rural mental health in America. *Amer. Psychol., 46,* 232–239.

Humphreys, K., & Rappaport, J. (1993). From the community mental health movement to the war on drugs: A study in the definition of social problems. *Amer. Psychol., 48*(8), 892–901.

Humphry, D., & Wickett, A. (1986). The right to die: *Understanding euthanasia.* New York: Harper & Row.

Hunt, M. (1974). Sexual behavior in the 1970s. Chicago: Playboy.

Huntington, D. D., & Bender, W. N. (1993). Adolescents with learning disabilities at risk: Emotional well-being, depression, suicide. *J. Learn. Disabil., 26*(3), 159–166.

Hurley, A. D., & Hurley, F. L. (1986). Counseling and psychotherapy with mentally retarded clients: I. The initial interview. *Psych. Aspects of Ment. Retardation Rev., 5*(5), 22–26.

Hurley, J. D., & Meminger, S. R. (1992). A relapse-prevention program: Effects of electromyographic training on high and low levels of state and trait anxiety. *Percep. and Motor Skills, 74*(3, Pt. 1), 699–705.

Hurt, S. W., Reznikoff, M., Clarkin, J. F. (1991). *Psychological assessment, psychiatric diagnosis, and treatment planning.* New York: Brunner/Mazel.

Hutchinson, R. L., & Little, T. J. (1985). A study of alcohol and drug usage by nine- through thirteen-year-old children in Central Indiana. *J. Alc. & Drug Educ., 30*(3), 83–87.

Huws, R. (1991). Cardiac disease and sexual dysfunction. *Sex. Marit. Ther., 6*(2), 119–134.

Hyde, A. P., & Goldman, C. R. (1992). Use of multi-model family group in the comprehensive treatment and rehabilitation of people with schizophrenia. *Psychosoc. Rehab. J., 15*(4), 77–86.

Hyde, J. S. (1990). *Understanding human sexuality* (4th ed.). New York: McGraw-Hill.

Hyler, S. E., & Spitzer, R. T. (1978). Hysteria split asunder. *Amer. J. Psychiat., 135,* 1500–1504.

Ingrassia, M., & Beck, M. (1994, July 4). Patterns of abuse. *Newsweek,* pp. 26–33.

Ironson, G., Taylor, C. B., Boltwood, M., et al. (1992). Effects of anger on left ventricular ejection fraction in coronary artery disease. *Amer. J. Cardiol., 70*(3), 281–285.

Ishii, K. (1991). Measuring mutual causation: Effects of suicide news on suicide in Japan. *Soc. Sci. Res., 20*(2), 188–195.

Iversen, L. L. (1965). *Adv. Drug Res., 2,* 5–23.

Jackson, J. L., Calhoun, K. S., Amick, A. A., Madever, H. M., & Habif, V. L. (1990). Young adult women who report childhood intrafamilial sexual abuse: Subsequent adjustment. *Arch. Sex. Behav., 19*(3), 211–221.

Jacobs, B. L. (Ed.), (1984). *Hallucinogens: neurochemical, behavioral, and clinical perspectives.* New York: Raven Press.

Jacobs, B. L. (1994). Serotonin, motor activity and depression-related disorders. *Amer. Sci., 82,* 456–463.

Jacobs, D., & Klein, M. E. (1993). The expanding role of psychological autopsies. In A. A. Leenaars (Ed.), *Suicidology.* Northvale, NJ: Jason Aronson, Inc.

Jacobs, R. (1993). AIDS communication: College students' AIDS knowledge and information sources. Health Values, The *J. Hlth., Behav., Educ., and Promotion, 17*(3), 32–41.

Jacobsen, L. K., Rabinowitz, I., Popper, M. S., Solomon, R. J., Sokol, M. S., & Pfeffer, C. R. (1994). Interviewing prepubertal children about suicidal ideation and behavior. *J. Amer. Acad. Child Adol. Psychiat., 33*(4), 439–452.

Jacobson, B., & Thurman-Lacey, S. (1992). Effect of caffeine on motor performance by caffeine-naive and -familiar subjects. *Percept. & Motor Skills, 74,* 151–157.

Jacobson, J. W., & Schwartz, A. A. (1991). Evaluating living situations of people with development disabilities. In J. L. Matson & J. A. Mulick (Eds.), *Handbook of mental retardation.* New York: Pergamon.

Jacobson, N. S. (1989). The maintenance of treatment gains following social learning-based marital therapy. *Behav. Ther., 20*(3), 325–336.

Jacobson, N. S., & Addis, M. E. (1993). Research on couple therapy: What do we know? Where are we going? Submitted for publication.

Jacobson, N. S., & Margolin, G. (1979). *Marital therapy: Strategies based on social learning and behavior exchange principles.* New York: Brunner/Mazel.

Jaffe, J. H. (1985). Drug addiction and drug abuse. In Goodman & Gilman (Eds.), *The pharmacological basis of therapeutic behavior.* New York: Macmillan.

James, W. (1890). *Principles of psychology* (Vol. 1). New York: Holt, Rinehart & Winston.

Janowsky, D. S., & Davis, J. M. (1976). Methylphanidate, dextroamphetamine, and levamfetamine: Effects on schizophrenic symptoms. *Arch. Gen. Psychiat., 33*(3), 304–308.

Janowsky, D. S., El-Yousef, M. K., Davis, J. M., & Sekerke, H. J. (1973). Provocation of schizophrenic symptoms by intravenous administration of methylphenidate. *Arch. Gen. Psychiat., 28,* 185–191.

Jefferson, J. W., & Greist, J. H. (1989). Lithium therapy. In H. I. Kaplan & B. J. Sadock (Eds.), *Comprehensive textbook of psychiatry V.* Baltimore: Williams & Wilkins.

Jefferson, L. (1948). These are my sisters. Tulsa, OK: Vickers.

Jemmott, J. B. (1987). Social motives and susceptibility to disease: Stalking individual differences in health risks. *J. Pers., 55*(2), 267–298.

Jenike, M. A. (1991). Approaches to the patient with treatment-refractory obsessive-compulsive disorder. *J. Clin. Psychiat., 51*(Suppl. 2), 15–21.

Jenike, M. A. (1991). Geriatric obsessive-compulsive disorder. *J. Ger. Psychiat. Neuro., 4,* 34–39.

Jenike, M. A. (1991). Management of patients with treatment-resistant obsessive-compulsive disorder. In M. T. Pato & J. Zohar (Eds.), *Current treatments of obsessive-compulsive disorder.* Washington, DC: American Psychiatric Press.

Jenike, M. A. (1991). Obessive-compulsive disorders: A clinical approach. In W. Coryell & G. Winokur (Eds.), *The clinical management of anxiety disorders.* New York: Oxford UP.

Jenike, M. A. (1992). New developments in treatment of obsessive-compulsive disorder. In A. Tasman, & M. B. Riba (Eds.), *Review of psychiatry* (Vol. 11). Washington, DC: American Psychiatric Press.

Jenkins, R. L. (1968). The varieties of children's behavioral problems and family dynamics. *Amer. J. Psychiat., 124*(10), 1440–1445.

Jenkins-Hall, K., & Sacco, W. P. (1991). Effect of client race and depression on evaluations by white therapists. *J. Soc. Clin. Psychol., 10*(3), 322–333.

Johnson, C., & Maddi, K. L. (1986). The etiology of bulimia: Bio-psychosocial perspectives. *Ann. Adol. Psychiat., 13,* 253–273.

Johnson, E. H., Gentry, W. D., & Julius, S. (Eds.) (1992). *Personality, elevated blood pressure, and essential hypertension.* Washington, DC: Hemisphere Publishing Corp.

Johnson, W. D. (1991). Predisposition to emotional distress and psychiatric illness amongst doctors: The role of unconscious and experiential factors. *Brit. J. Med. Psychol., 64*(4), 317–329.

Johnson, W. G., Schlundt, D. G., Barclay, D. R., Carr-Nangle, R. E., Engler, L. B. (1995). A naturalistic functional analysis of binge eating. *Behav. Ther., 26,* 101–118.

Johnson, W. G., Schlundt, D. G., Kelley, M. L., & Ruggiero, L. (1984). Exposure with response prevention and energy regulation in the treatment of bulimia. *Int. J. Eat. Dis., 3,* 37–46.

Johnson-Greene, D., Fatis, M., Sonnek, K., & Shawchuck, C. (1988). A survey of caffeine use and associated side effects in a college population. *J. Drug Educ., 18*(3), 211–219.

Johnston, D. W. (1992). The management of stress in the prevention of coronary heart disease. In S. Maes, H. Leventhal, & M. Johnston (Eds.), *International review of health psychology* (Vol. 1). New York: Wiley.

Johnston, L. D., O'Malley, P. M., & Bachman, J. G. (1993). *National survey results on drug use from the Monitoring the Future Study, 1975–1992.* Rockville, Maryland: National Institute on Drug Abuse.

Jones, M. C. (1971). Personality antecedents and correlates of drinking patterns in women. *J. Cons. Clin. Psychol., 36,* 61–69.

Jones, M. C. (1968). Personality correlates and antecedants of drinking patterns in males. *J. Cons. Clin. Psychol., 32,* 2–12.

Jordan, B. K., Marmar, C. R., Fairbank, J. A., Schlenger, W. E., et al. (1992). Problems in families of male Vietnam veterans with posttraumatic stress disorder. *J. Cons. Clin. Psychol., 60*(6), 916–926.

Joseph, E. (1991). Psychodynamic personality theory. In K. Davis, H. Klar, & J. J. Coyle. (Eds.), *Foundations of psychiatry.* Philadelphia: Saunders.

Joyner, C. D., & Swenson, C. C. (1993). Community-level intervention after a disaster. In C. F. Saylor (Ed.), *Children and disasters.* New York: Plenum.

Juel-Nielsen, N., & Videbech, T. (1970). A twin study of suicide. *Acta Geneticae Medicae et Gemellologiae, 19,* 307–310.

Julien, R. M. (1988). *A primer of drug action* (5th ed.). New York: W. H. Freeman.

Julius, S. (1992). Relationship between the sympathetic tone and cardiovascular responsiveness in the course of hypertension. In E. H. Johnson, E. D. Gentry, & S. Julius (Eds.), *Personality, elevated blood pressure, and essential hypertension.* Washington, DC: Hemisphere Publishing Corp.

Jung, C. G. (1909). *Memories, dreams, and reflections.* New York: Random House.

Jung, C. G. (1967). *The collected works of C. G. Jung.* Princeton, NJ: Princeton UP.

Jungman, J. (1985). De l'agir du toxicomane a l'agir du thérapeute [From the drug addict's acting out to the therapist's action]. *Information Psychiatrique, 61*(3), 383–388.

Kagan, R. (1986). The child behind the mask: Sociopathy as a developmental delay. In W. Reid, D. Dorr, J. Walker, & J. Bonner (Eds.), *Unmasking the psychopath.* New York: Norton.

Kahn, R. S., Wetzler, S., Van Praag, H. A., et al. (1988). Behavioral indication of serotonergic supersensitivity in panic disorder. *Psychiat. Res., 25,* 101–104.

Kahneman, D., & Tversky, A. (1973). On the psychology of prediction. *Psych. Rev., 80*(4), 237–251.

Kaij, L. (1960). Alcoholism in twins: *Studies on the etiology and sequels of abuse of alcohol.* Stockholm: Almquist & Wiksell.

Kail, R. (1992). General slowing of information-processing by persons with mental retardation. *Amer. J. Ment. Retard., 97*(3), 333–341.

Kaminer, Y. (1991). Adolescent substance abuse. In R. J. Frances & S. I. Miller (Eds.), *Clinical textbook of addictive disorders.* New York: Guilford.

Kane, J. M. (1987). Treatment of schizophrenia. *Schizo. Bull., 13*(1), 133–156.

Kane, J. M. (1990). Treatment programme and long-term outcome in chronic schizophrenia. International symposium: Development of a new antipsychotic: Remoxipride (1989, Monte Carlo, Monaco). *Acta Psychiatr. Scandin., 82*(385, Suppl.) 151–157.

Kane, J. M. (1992). Clinical efficacy of clozapine in treatment-refractory schizophrenia: An overview. *Brit. Z. Psychiat., 160*(Suppl. 17), 41–45.

Kane, J. M. & Freeman, H. L. (1994). Towards more effective antipsychotic treatment. *Brit. J. Psychiat., 165* (suppl. 25), 22–31.

Kanner, L. (1943). Autistic disturbances of affective contact. *Nerv. Child. 2,* 217.

Kanner, L. (1954). To what extent is early infantile autism determined by constitutional inadequacies? *Proceedings of the Association for Research in Nervous and Mental Diseases, 33,* 378–385.

Kanof, P. (1991). Neurotransmitter receptor function. In K. Davis, H. Klar, & J. T. Coyle (Eds.), *Foundations of psychiatry.* Philadelphia: Saunders.

Kaplan, H. S. (1974). *The new sex therapy: Active treatment of sexual dysfunction.* New York: Brunner/Mazel.

Kaplan, H. S. (1979). *Disorders of sexual desire.* New York: Brunner/Mazel.

Karasu, T. B. (1992). The worst of times, the best of times. *J. Psychother. Practice Res., 1,* 2–15.

Kardiner, A. (1977). *My analysis with Freud: Reminiscences.* New York: Norton.

Karel, R. (1992, May 1). Hopes of many long-term sufferers dashed as FDA ends medical marijuana program. *Psychiatric News.*

Karon, B. P. (1985). Omission in review of treatment interactions. *Schizo. Bull., 11*(1), 16–17.

Karon, B. P. (1988). Cited in T. De Angelis, "Resistance to therapy seen in therapists, too." *APA Monitor, 19*(11), 21.

Kashani, J. H., Goddard, P., & Reid, J. C. (1989). Correlated of suicidal ideation in a community sample of children and adolescents. *J. Amer. Acad. Child. Adolesc. Psychiat., 28,* 912–917.

Kashden, J., Fremouw, W. J., Callahan, T. S., & Franzen, M. D. (1993). Impulsivity in suicidal and nonsuicidal adolescents. *J. Abnorm. Child Psychol., 21*(3), 339–353.

Kasl, S. V., & Cobb, S. (1970). Blood pressure changes in men undergoing job loss: A preliminary report. *Psychosom. Med., 32*(1), 19–38.

Kato, T., Takahashi, S., Shioiri, T., & Inubushi, T. (1993). Alterations in brain phosphorous metabolism in bipolar disorder detected by in vivo 31 P and 7 Li magnetic resonance spectroscopy. *J. Affect. Dis., 27,* 53–60.

Katz, R. J., Lott, M., Landau, P., & Waldmeier, P. (1993). A clinical test of noradrenergic involvement in the therapeutic mode of action of an experimental antidepressant. *Bio. Psychiat., 33,* 261–266.

Katz, S. E., & Levendusky, P. G. (1990). Cognitive-behavioral approaches to treating borderline and self-mutilating patients. *Bull. Menninger Clin., 54*(3), 398–408.

Kaye, W. H., Weltzin, T. E., Hsu, L. G., & Bulik, C. M. (1991). An open trial of fluoxetine in patients with anorexia nervosa. *J. Clin. Psychiat., 52*(11), 464–471.

Kazdin, A. E. (1989). Childhood depression. In E. J. Mash & R. Barkley (Eds.), *Treatment of childhood disorders.* New York: Guilford.

Kazdin, A. E. (1990). Childhood depression. *J. Child Psychol. Psychiat. Allied Disc., 31,* 121–160.

Kazdin, A. E. (1993). Psychotherapy for children and adolescents: Current progress and future research directions. *Amer. Psychol., 48*(6), 646–657.

Kazdin, A. E. (1994). Methodology, design, and evaluation in psychotherapy research. In A. E. Bergin & S. L. Garfield (Eds.), *Handbook of psychotherapy and behavior change* (4th ed.). New York: Wiley.

Kazdin, A. E. (1994). Psychotherapy for children and adolescents. In A. E. Bergin & S. L. Garfield (Eds.), *Handbook of psychotherapy and behavior change* (4th ed.). New York: Wiley.

Kearney-Cooke, & Steichen-Asch, P. (1990). Men, body image, and eating disorders. In A. E. Andersen (Ed.), *Males with eating disorders.* New York: Brunner/Mazel.

Keen, E. (1970). *Three faces of being: Toward an existential clinical psychology.* By the Meredith Corp. Reprinted by permission of Irvington Publishers.

Keesey, R. E., & Corbett, S. W. (1983). Metabolic defense of the body weight set-point. In A. J. Stunkard & E. Stellar (Eds.), *Eating and its disorders.* New York: Raven Press.

Keith, S. J., Regier, D. A., & Rae, D. S. (1991). Schizophrenic disorders. In L. N. Robins & D. S. Regier (Eds.), *Psychiatric disorders in America: The Epidemiological Catchment Area Study.* New York: Free Press.

Keller, M. B. (1988). Diagnostic issues and clinical course of unipolar illness. In A. J. Frances & R. E. Hales (Eds.), *Review of psychiatry* (Vol. 7). Washington, DC: American Psychiatric Press.

Keller, R., & Shaywitz, B. A. (1986). Amnesia or fugue state: A diagnostic dilemma. *J. Dev. Behav. Pediatrics, 7*(8), 131–132.

Kelley, R. L., & Kodman, F. (1987). A more unified view of the Multiple Personality Disorder. *Soc. Behav. Pers., 15*(2), 165–167.

Kelly, I. W., Laverty, W. H., & Saklofske, D. H. (1990). Geophysical variables and behavior: LXIV. An empirical investigation of the relationship between worldwide automobile traffic disasters and lunar cycles: No relationship. *Psych. Rep., 67*(3, Pt. 1) 987–994.

Kelly, I. W., Saklofske, D. H., & Culver, R. (1990). Aircraft accidents and disasters and full moon: No relationship. *Psychology: A J. of Human Behav., 27*(2), 30–33.

Kelly, J. B. (1982). Divorce: An adult perspective. In B. B. Wolman (Ed.), *Handbook of developmental psychology.* Englewood Cliffs, NJ: Prentice Hall.

Kelly, K. A. (1983). Multiple personality disorders: Treatment coordination in a partial hospital setting. *Bull. Menninger Clin., 57*(3), 390–398.

Kelsoe, J. R., Ginns, E. I., Egeland, J. A., Gerhard, D. S. et al. (1989). Re-evaluation of the linkage relationship between chromosome 11p loci and the gene for bipolar affective disorder in the Old Order Amish. *Nature, 342*(6247), 238–243.

Keltner, B. R. (1992). Caregiving by mothers with mental retardation. *Fam. Comm. Hlth., 15*(2), 10–18.

Kemph, J. P., DeVane, C. L., Levin, G. M., Jarecke, R., & Miller, R. L. (1993). Treatment of aggressive children with clonidine: Results of an open pilot study. *J. Amer. Acad. Child Adol. Psychiat., 32*(3), 577–581.

Kendall, P. C., Chansky, T. E., Friedman, M., Kim, R., Kortlander, E., Sessa, F. M., & Siquelard, L. (1991). Treating anxiety disorders in children and adolescents. In P. C. Kendall (Ed.), *Child and adolescent therapy: Cognitive-behavioral procedures.* New York: Guilford.

Kendall, P. C., Kane, M., Howard, B., & Siqueland, L. (1989). *Cognitive-behavioral therapy for anxious children: Treatment manual.* Philadelphia: Temple Univ.

Kendler, K. S., Heath, A., & Martin, N. G. (1987). A genetic epidemiologic study of self-report suspiciousness. *Comprehen. Psychiat., 28*(3), 187–196.

Kendler, K. S., Heath, A., Neale, M., Kessler, R., & Eaves, L. (1992). A population-based twin study of alcoholism in women. *JAMA, 268*(14), 1877–1882.

Kendler, K. S., McGuire, M., Gruenberg, A. M., O'Hare, A., Spellman, M., & Walsh, D. (1993). The Roscommon Family Study. *Arch. Gen. Psychiat., 50,* 527–540.

Kendler, K. S., McGuire, M., Gruenberg, A. M., & Walsh, D. (1994). An epidemiological, clinical, and family study of simple schizophrenia in County Roscommon, Ireland. *Amer. J. Psychiat., 151*(1), 27–34.

Kendler, K. S., Neale, M. C., Heath, A. C., Kessler, R. C., & Eaves, L. J. (1994). A twin-family study of alcoholism in women. *Amer. J. Psychiat., 151*(5), 707–715.

Kendler, K. S., Ochs, A. L., Gorman, A. M., Hewitt, J. K., Ross, D. E., & Mirsky, A. F. (1991). The structure of schizotypy: A pilot multitrait twin study. *Psychiat. Res., 36*(1), 19–36.

Kennedy, J. L., Giuffra, L. A., Moises, H. W. et al. (1988). Evidence against linkage of schizophrenia to markers on chromosome 5 in a northern Swedish pedigree. *Nature, 336,* 167–168.

Kennedy, L. L. (1992). Partial hospitalization. In A. Tasman & M. B. Riba (Eds.), *Review of psychiatry: Vol. 11.* Washington, DC: American Psychiatric Press.

Kennedy, S. H., Kaplan, A. S., & Garfinkel, P. E. (1992). Intensive hospital treatments for anorexia nervosa and bulimia nervosa. In P. J. Cooper & A. Stein (Eds.), *Feeding problems and eating disorders in children and adolescents.* Philadelphia, PA: Harwood Academic Publishers.

Kernberg, O. F. (1976). *Object-relations theory and clinical psychoanalysis.* New York: Jason Aronson, Inc.

Kernberg, O. F. (1984). *Severe personality disorders.* New Haven, CT: Yale UP.

Kernberg, P. F. (1989). Narcissistic personality disorder in childhood. *Psychiat. Clin. N. Amer., 12*(3), 671–694.

Kessler, R. C., McGonagle, K. A., Zhao, S., Nelson, C. B., Hughes, M., Eshleman, S., Wittchen, H. U., & Kendler, K. S. (1994). Lifetime and 12-month prevalence of DSM-III-R psychiatric disorders in the United States. *Arch. Gen. Psychiat., 51,* 8–19.

Kety, S. (1974). Biochemical and neurochemical effects of electroconvulsive shock. In M. Fink, S. Kety, J. McGaugh, et al. (Eds.), *Psychobiology of convulsive therapy.* Washington, DC: Winston & Sons.

Kety, S. S. (1974). From rationalization to reason. *Amer. J. Psychiat., 131*(9), 957–963.

Kety, S. S. (1988). Schizophrenic illness in the families of schizophrenic adoptees: Findings from the Danish national sample. *Shizo. Bull., 14*(2), 217–222.

Keuthen, N. (1980). *Subjective probability estimation and somatic structures in phobic individuals.* Unpublished manuscript. State University of New York at Stony Brook.

Keys, A., Brozek, J., Henschel, A., Mickelson, O., & Taylor, H. L. (1950). *The biology of human starvation.* Minneapolis: Univ. Minnesota.

Kiecolt-Glaser, J. K., Dura, J. R., Speicher, C. E., Trask, O. J., & Glaser, R. (1991). Spousal caregivers of dementia victims: Longitudintal changes in immunity and health. *Psychosom. Med., 53,* 345–362.

Kiecolt-Glaser, J. K., Garner, W., Speicher, C., Penn, G. M., Holliday, J., & Glaser, R. (1984). Psychosocial modifiers of immunocompetence in medical students. *Psychosom. Med., 46,* 7–14.

Kiecolt-Glaser, J. K., & Glaser, R. (1988). Psychological influences on immunity: Implications for AIDS. *Amer. Psychol., 43*(11), 892–898.

Kiecolt-Glaser, J. K., & Glaser, R. (1992). Psychoneuroimmunology: Can psychological interventions modulate immunity? *J. Cons. Clin. Psychol., 60,* 569–575.

Kiecolt-Glaser, J. K., Ricker, D., Messick, G., Speicher, C. E., Garner, W., & Glaser, R. (1984). Urinary cortisol, cellular immunocompetency and loneliness in psychiatric patients. *Psychosom. Med., 46,* 15–24.

Kienhorst, C. W. M., Wolters, W. H. G., Diekstra, R. F. W., & Otte, E. (1987). A study of the frequency of suicidal behaviour in children aged 5 to 14. *J. Child Psychol. Psychiat. Allied Disc., 28*(1), 151–165.

Kiesler, C. A. (1992). U.S. mental health policy: Doomed to fail. *Amer. Psychol., 47*(9), 1077–1082.

Kiev, A. (1972). *Transcultural psychiatry.* New York: Free Press.

Kiev, A. (1989). Suicide in adults. In J. G. Howells (Ed.), *Modern perspectives in the psychiatry of the affective disorders.* New York: Brunner/Mazel.

Kihlstrom, J. F., Tataryn, D. J., & Hoyt, I. P. (1993). Dissociative disorders, In P. B. Sucker and H. E. Adams (Eds.), *Comprehensive handbook of psychopathology* (2nd ed.). New York: Plenum.

Kilmann, P. R., Sabalis, R. F., Gearing, M. L., Bukstel, L. H., & Scovern, A. W. (1982). The treatment of sexual paraphilias: A review of outcome research. *J. Sex Res., 18,* 193–252.

Kilmann, P. R., Wagner, M. K., & Sotile, W. M. (1977). The differential impact of self-monitoring on smoking behavior: An exploratory study. *J. Clin. Psychol., 33*(3), 912–914.

Kiloh, L. G. (1982). Electroconvulsive therapy. In E. S. Paykel (Ed.), *Handbook of affective disorders.* New York: Guilford.

Kilpatrick, D. G., Best, C. L., Veronen, L. J., Amick, A. E., Vileponteaux, L. A., & Ruff, G. A. (1985). Mental health correlates of criminal victimization: A random community survey. *J. Cons. Clin. Psychol., 53,* 866–873.

Kimball, A. (1993). Nipping and tucking. In skin deep: Our national obsession with looks. *Psych. Today, 26*(3), 96.

Kinard, E. M. (1982). Child abuse and depression: Cause or consequence? *Child Welfare, 61,* 403–413.

Kincel, R. L. (1981). Suicide and its archetypal themes in Rorschach record study of a male attempter. *Brit. J. Projective Psychol. & Pers. Study, 26*(2), 3–11.

King, C., Naylor, M., Hill, E., Shain, B., & Greden, J. (1993). Dysthymia characteristic of heavy alcohol use in depressed adolescents. *Bio. Psychiat., 33,* 210–212.

King, C. A., & Young, R. D. (1981). Peer popularity and peer communication patterns: Hyperactive vs. active but normal boys. *J. Abnorm. Child Psychol., 9*(4), 465–482.

King, G. A., Polivy, J., & Herman, C. P. (1991). Cognitive aspects of dietary restraint: Effects on person memory. *Inter. J. Eat. Dis., 10*(3), 313–321.

King, L. W., Liberman, R. P., & Roberts, J. (1974). *An evaluation of personal effectiveness training (assertive training): A behavior group therapy.* Paper presented at 31st Annual conference of American Group Psychotherapy Association, New York.

King, M. B., & Mezey, G. (1987). Eating behaviour of male racing jockeys. *Psychol. Med., 17,* 249–253.

King, N. J. (1993). Simple and social phobias. In T. H. Ollendick & R. J. Prinz (Eds.), *Advances in clinical child psychology* (Vol. 15). New York: Plenum.

King, N. J., Gullone, E. Tonge, B. J., & Ollendick, T. H. (1993). Self-reports of panic attacks and manifest anxiety in adolescents. *Behav. Res. Ther., 31*(1), 111–116.

King, T. I. (1992). The use of electromyographic biofeedback in treating a client with tension headaches. *Amer. J. Occupat. Ther., 46*(9), 839–842.

Kinsey, A. C., Pomeroy, W. B., & Martin, C. E. (1948). *Sexual behvaior in the human male.* Philadelphia: Saunders.

Kinsey, A. C., Pomeroy, W. B., Martin, C. E., & Gebhard, P. H. (1953). *Sexual behavior in the human female.* Philadelphia: Saunders.

Kinzie, J., Leung, P., Boehnlein, J., Matsunaga, D., et al., (1992). Psychiatric epidemiology of an Indian village: A 19-year replication study. *J. Nerv. Ment. Dis., 180*(1), 33–39.

Kipnis, D. (1987). Psychology and behavioral technology. *Amer. Psychol., 42*(1), 30–36.

Kirk, S. A., & Kutchins, H. (1992). *The selling of DSM: The rhetoric of science in psychiatry.* New York: Aldine De Gruyter.

Kirmayer, L. J., Robbins, J. M., Dworkind, M., & Yaffe, M. J. (1993). Somatization and the recognition of depression and anxiety in primary care. *Amer. J. Psychiat., 150*(5), 734–741.

Kirmayer, L. J., Robbins, J. M., & Paris, J. (1994). Somatoform disorders: Personality and the social matrix of somatic distress. *J. Abnorm. Psychol., 103*(1), 125–136.

Kirsling, R. A. (1986). Review of suicide among elderly persons. *Psych. Rep., 59*(2, Pt. 1), 359–366.

Kivlaham, D. R., Marlatt, G. A., Fromme, K., Coppel, D. B., & Williams E. (1990). Secondary prevention with college drinkers: Evaluation of an alcohol skills training program. *J. Cons. Clin. Psychol., 58*, 805–810.

Klassen, D., & O'Conner, W. (1988). Crime, inpatient admissions and violence among male mental patients. International *J. Psychol. Law & Psychiat., (11)*, 305–312.

Klassen, D., & O'Conner, W. (1988). A prospective study of predictors of violence in adult mental health admissions. *Law and Human Behav., 12*, 143–158.

Klausner, J. D., Sweeney, J. A., Deck, M. D., Haas, G. L., et al. (1992). Clinical correlates of cerebral ventricular enlargement in schizophrenia: Further evidence for frontal lobe disease. *J. Nerv. Ment. Dis., 180*(7), 407–412.

Kleber, H. D., & Gawin, F. H. (1987). "Cocaine withdrawal": In reply. *Arch. Gen. Psychiat., 44*(3), 298.

Kleber, H. D., & Gawin, F. H. (1987). "The physiology of cocaine craving and 'crashing'": In reply. *Arch. Gen. Psychiat., 44*(3), 299–300.

Kleber, H. D. et al. (1985). Clonidine in outpatient detoxification from methadone maintenance. *Arch. Gen. Psychiat., 42*(4), 391–394.

Klein, D. F. (1964). Delineation of two drug-responsive anxiety syndromes. *Psychopharmacologia, 5*, 397–408.

Klein, D. F., & Fink, M. (1962). Psychiatric reaction patterns to imipramine. *Amer. J. Psychiat., 119*, 432–438.

Klein, D. F., Rabkin, J. G., & Gorman, J. M. (1985). Etiological and pathophysiological inferences from the pharmacological treatment of anxiety. In A. H. Tuma & J. Maser (Eds.), *Anxiety and the anxiety disorders*. Hillsdale, NJ: Lawrence Erlbaum Associates.

Klerman, G. L., & Weissman, M. M. (1989). Increasing rates of depression. *JAMA, 261*(15), 2229–2235.

Klerman, G. L., & Weissman, M. M. (1992). Interpersonal psychotherapy. In E. S. Paykel (Ed.), *Handbook of affective disorders*. New York: Guilford.

Klerman, G. L., Weissman, M. M., Markowitz, J., Glick, I., Wilner, P. J., Mason, B., & Shear, M. K. (1994). Medication and psychotherapy. In A. E. Bergin & S. L. Garfiel (Eds.), *Handbook of psychotherapy and behavior change* (4th ed.). New York: Wiley.

Klin, A. (1993). Auditory brainstem responses in autism: Brainstem dysfunction or peripheral hearing loss? *J. Autism Dev. Dis., 23*(1), 15–35.

Kline, N. S. (1958). Clinical experience with iproniazid (Marsilid). *J. Clin. Exp. Psychopath., 19*(1, Suppl.), 72–78.

Kline, P. (1993). *The handbook of psychological testing*. New York: Routledge.

Klingman, A., & Hochdorf, Z. (1993). Coping with distress and self harm: The impact of a primary prevention program among adolescents. *J. Adol. 15*, 121–140.

Kluft, R. P. (1983). Hypnotherapeutic crisis intervention in multiple personality. *Amer. J. Clin. Hyp., 26*(2), 73–83.

Kluft, R. P. (1984). Treatment of multiple personality disorder: A study of 33 cases. *Psychiat. Clin. N. Amer., 7*(1), 9–29.

Kluft, R. P. (Ed.). (1985). *Childhood antecedents of multiple personality*. Washington, DC: American Psychiatric Press.

Kluft, R. P. (1985). Hypnotherapy of childhood multiple personality disorder. *Amer. J. Clin. Hyp., 27*(4), 201–210.

Kluft, R. P. (1987). An update on multiple personality disorder. *J. Hosp. Comm. Psychiat., 38*(4), 363–373.

Kluft, R. P. (1987). The simulation and dissimulation of multiple personality disorder. *Amer. J. Clin. Hyp., 30*(2), 104–118.

Kluft, R. P. (1988). The dissociative disorders. In J. Talbott, R. Hales, & S. Yudofsky (Eds.), *Textbook of psychiatry*. Washington, DC: American Psychiatric Press.

Kluft, R. P. (1991). Multiple personality disorder. In A. Tasman & S. M. Goldfinger (Eds.), *American Psychiatric Press review of psychiatry* (Vol. 10). Washington, DC: American Psychiatric Press.

Kluft, R. P. (1992). Discussion: A specialist's perspective on multiple personality disorder. *Psychoanalytic inquiry, 12*(1), 139–171.

Kluft, R. P. (1994). Multiple personality disorder: Observations on the etiology, natural history, recognition and resolution of a long-neglected condition. In R. M. Klein & B. K. Doane (Eds.), *Psychological concepts and dissociative disorders*. Hillsdale: New Jersey: Lawrence Erlbaum Associates, Publishers.

Knesper, D. J., Pagnucco, D. J., & Wheeler, J. R. (1985). Similarities and differences across mental health services providers and practice settings in the United States. *Amer. Psychol., 40*(12), 1352–1369.

Knutson, J. F. (1995). Psychological characteristics of malteratred children. In J. T. Spence, J. M. Darley, D. J. Foss, (Eds.), *Annual Review of Psychology 46*, 401–431.

Kobasa, S. C. (1979). Stressful life events, personality, and health: An inquiry into hardiness. *J. Pers. Soc. Psychol., 37*(1), 1–11.

Kobasa, S. C. (1982). Commitment and coping in stress resistance among lawyers. *J. Pers. Soc. Psychol., 42*, 707–717.

Kobasa, S. C. (1982). The hardy personality: Towards a social psychology of stress and health. In J. Suls & Sanders (Eds.), *Social psychology of health and illness*. Hillsdale, NJ: Erlbaum.

Kobasa, S. C. (1984). Barriers to work stress: II. The "hardy" personality. In W. D. Gentry, H. Benson, C. J. de Wolff (Eds.), *Behavioral medicine: Work, stress and health*. The Hague: Martinus Nijhoff.

Kobasa, S. C. (1987). Stress responses and personality. In R. C. Barnett, L. Biener, & G. K. Baruch (Eds.), *Gender and stress*. New York: Free Press.

Kobasa, S. C. (1990). Stress resistant personality. In R. E. Ornstein, & C. Swencionis (Eds.), *The healing brain: A scientific reader*. Oxford, England: Pergamon Press.

Koenig, H., & Blazer, D. (1992). Epidemiology of geriatric affective disorders. *Clinics in Ger. Med., 8*, 235–251.

Koenigsberg, H. W. (1993). Combining psychotherapy and pharmacotherapy in the treatment of borderline patients. In J. M. Oldham, M. B. Riba, & A. Tasman (Eds.), *Review of psychiatry*. Washington, DC: American Psychiatric Press.

Kohut, H. (1977). *The restoration of the self*. New York: International Universities Press.

Kolb, L. C. (1992). "Research strategies for decoding the neurochemical basis of resistance to stress": Commentary. *J. Psychopharmacol., 6*(1), 11.

Kolff, C. A., & Doan, R. N. (1985). Victims of torture: Two testimonies. In E. Stover & E. O. Nightingale (Eds.), *The breaking of bodies and minds: Torture, psychiatric abuse, and the health professions*. New York: W. H. Freeman.

Kolodny, R., Masters, W. H., & Johnson, J. (1979). *Textbook of sexual medicine*. Boston: Little, Brown.

Komaroff, A. L., Masuda, M. & Holmes, T. H. (1986). The Social Readjustment Rating Scale: A comparative study of Negro, White, and Mexican Americans. *J. Psychosom. Res., 12*, 121–128.

Komaroff, A. L., Masuda, M. & Holmes, T. H. (1989). The Social Readjustment Rating Scale: A comparative study of Black, White, and Mexican Americans. In T. H. Holmes and E. M. David (Eds.), *Life change, life events, and illness*. New York: Praeger.

Korchin, S. J., & Sands, S. H. (1983). Principles common to all psychotherapies. In C. E. Walker, et al. (Eds.), *The handbook of clinical psychology*. Homewood, IL: Dow Jones-Irwin.

Koson, D. F., & Dvoskin, J. (1982). Arson: A diagnostic study. *Bull. Am. Acad. Psychiat. Law, 10*, 39–49.

Koss, M. P. (1992). The underdetection of rape: Methodological choices influence incidence estimates. *J. Soc. Issues, 48*(1), 61–75.

Koss, M. P. (1993). Rape: Scope, impact, interventions, and public policy responses. *Amer. Psychol., 48*(10), 1062–1069.

Koss, M. P., & Harvey, M. R. (1987). *The rape victim*. Lexington, MA: Stephen Green.

Koss, M. P., & Harvey, M. R. (1991). *The rape victim: Clinical and community interventions*. Newbury Park, CA: Sage.

Koss, M. P. & Heslet, L. (1992). Somatic consequences of violence against women. *Archives of Family Medicine, 1*(1), 53–59.

Koss, M. P., Koss, P., & Woodruff, W. J. (1991). Deleterious effects of criminal victimization on women's health and medical utilization. *Arch. Intern. Med., 151*, 342–357.

Koss, M. P., Woodruff, W. J., & Koss, P. (1991). Criminal victimization among primary care medical patients: Prevalence, incidence, and physician usage. *Behav. Sci. and the Law, 9*, 85–96.

Kosten, T. R. (1988). *The symptomatic and prognostic implications of psychiatric diagnoses in treated substance abusers*. National Institute on Drug Abuse Research Monograph Series, 81, 416–421.

Kraines, S. H., & Thetford, E. S. (1972). *Help for the depressed*. Springfield, IL: Thomas.

Kramer, F. M., Jeffery, R. W., Forster, J. L., & Snell, M. K. (1989). Long-term follow-up of behavioral treatment for obesity: Patterns of weight regain among men and women. *Inter. J. Obesity, 13*, 123–136.

Kramer, M. (1989, August 14). Cited in S. Begley, "The stuff that dreams are made of." *Newsweek*, p. 40.

Kramer, M. (1992). Cited in R. D. Cartwright, & L. Lamberg, "Crisis dreaming: Using your dreams to solve your problems." HarperCollins.

Kramer, P. (1993). *Listening to prozac-A psychiatrist explores mood-altering drugs and the meaning of the self*. New York: Viking.

Kramer, S. & Akhtar, S. (Eds.), (1994). *Mahler and Kohut: Perspectives on development, psychopathology, and technique*. Northvale, New Jersey: Jason Aronson, Inc.

Krantz, L. (1992). *What the odds are.* New York: Harper Perennial.

Kratochwill, T. R. (1992). Single-case research design and analysis: An overview. In T. R. Kratochwill, & J. R. Levin (Eds.), *Single-case research design and analysis: New directions for psychology and education.* Hillsdale, NJ: Lawrence Erlbaum Associates.

Krauss, M. W., Seltzer, M. M., Goodman, S. J. (1992). Social support networks of adults with mental retardation who live at home. *Amer. J. Ment. Retard., 96*(4), 432–441.

Kreisman, D., Blumenthal, R., Borenstein, M., Woerner, M. et al. (1988). Family attitudes and patient social adjustment in a longitudinal study of outpatient schizophrenics receiving low-dose neuroleptics: The family's view. Meeting of the Society for Life History Research on Psychopathology (1984, Baltimore, Maryland). *Psychiat., 51*(1), 3–13.

Kresin, D. (1993). Medical aspects of inhibited sexual desire disorder. In W. O'Donohue and J. Geer (eds.), *Handbook of sexual dysfunctions.* Boston: Allyn and Bacon.

Kuch, K., & Cox, B. J. (1992). Symptoms of PTSD in 124 survivors of the Holocaust. *Amer. J. Psychiat., 149*(3), 337–340.

Kuhn, R. (1958). The treatment of depressive states with G-22355 (imipramine hydrochloride). *Amer. J. Psychiat., 115,* 459–464.

Kuhn, T. S., (1962). *The structure of scientific revolutions.* Chicago: Univ. Chicago.

Kuriansky, J. B. (1988). Personality style and sexuality. In R. A. Brown & J. R. Field (Eds.), *Treatment of sexual problems in individual and couples therapy.* Costa Mesa, CA: PMA Publishing Corp.

Kurlander, H., Miller, W., & Seligman, M. E. P. (1974). *Learned helplessness, depression, and prisoner's dilemma.* Unpublished manuscript.

Kushner, H. L. (1985). Women and suicide and historical perspective. *Signs, 10*(3), 537–552.

Kushner, M. G., Riggs, D. S., Foa, E. B., & Miller, S. M. (1992). Perceived controllability and the development of posttraumatic stress disorder (PTSD) in crime victims. *Behav. Res. Ther., 31*(1), 105–110.

Labbate, L. A., & Snow, M. P. (1992). Post-traumatic stress symptoms among soldiers exposed to combat in the Persian Gulf. *Hosp. & Comm. Psychiat., 43*(8), 831–833.

Lacks, P. (1984). *Bender Gestalt screening for brain dysfunction.* New York: Wiley.

Lader, M. (1992). Hazards of benzodiazepine treatments of anxiety. In G. D. Burrows, S. M. Roth, & R. Noyes, Jr., *Handbook of anxiety* (Vol. 5). Oxford: Elsevier.

Ladouceur, R., Freeston, M. H., Gagnon, F., Thibodeau, N., & Dumont, J. (1995). Cognitive-behavioral treatment of obsessions. *Behav. Mod., 19*(2), 247–257.

Lahey, B. B., Hartdagen, S. E., Frick, P. J., McBurnett, K., et al. (1988). Conduct disorder: Parsing the confounded relation to parental divorce and antisocial personality. *J. Abnorm. Psychol., 97*(3), 334–337.

Lahey, B. B., Piancentini, J. C., McBurnett, K., Stone, P., et al. (1988). Psychopathology in the parents of children with conduct disorder and hyperactivity. *J. Amer. Acad. Child and Adol. Psychiat., 27*(2), 163–170.

Lai, J. Y., & Linden, W. (1992). Gender, anger expression style, and opportunity for anger release determine cardiovascular reaction to and recovery from anger provocation. *Psychosom. Med., 54,* 297–310.

Laing. R. D. (1959). *The divided self: An existential study in sanity and madness.* London: Tavistock Publications.

Laing. R. D. (1964). *The divided self* (2nd ed.) London: Pelican.

Laing. R. D. (1967). *The politics of experience.* New York: Pantheon.

Lam, R. W., Berkowitz, A. L., Berga, S. L., Clark, C. M. et al. (1990). Melatonin suppression in bipolar and unipolar mood disorders. *Psychiat. Res., 33*(2), 129–134.

Lamb, H. R. (1982). *Treating the long-term mentally ill.* San Francisco: Jossey-Bass.

Lamb, H. R. (1988). When the chronically mentally ill need acute hospitalization: Maximizing its benefits: *Psychiat. Ann., 18*(7), 426–430.

Lamb, H. R., & Goertzel, V. (1977). The long-term patient in the era of community treatment. *Arch. Gen. Psychiat., 34*(6), 679–682.

Lambert, M. J., & Bergin, A. E. (1994). The effectiveness of psychotherapy. In A. E. Bergin, & S. L. Garfield (Eds.), *Handbook of psychotherapy and behavioral change* (4th ed.). New York: Wiley.

Lambert, M. J., & Hill, C. E. (1994). Assessing psychotherapy outcomes and processes. In A. E. Bergin & S. L. Garfield (Eds.), *Handbook of psychotherapy and behavioral change* (4th ed.). New York: Wiley.

Lambert, M. J., Shapiro, D. A., & Bergin, A. E. (1986). The effectiveness of psychotherapy. In S. L. Garfield & A. E. Bergin (Eds.), *Handbook of psychotherapy and behavioral change* (3rd ed.). New York: Wiley.

Lambert, M. J., Weber, F. D., & Sykes, J. D. (1993, April). Psychotherapy versus placebo. Poster presented at the annual meetings of the Western Psychological Association, Phoenix.

Lamberti, J. S., & Cummings, S. (1992). Hands-on restraints in the treatment of multiple personality disorder. *Hosp. Comm. Psychiat., 43*(3), 283–284.

Lang, P. J. (1985). The cognitive psychophysiology of emotion: Fear and anxiety. In A. H. Tuma & J. D. Maser (Eds.), *Anxiety and anxiety disorders.* Hillsdale, NJ: Erlbaum.

Langer, E. J. (1983). *The psychology of control.* Beverly Hills, CA: Sage.

Langevin, R., Bain, J., Wortzman, G., Hucker, S., et al. (1988). Sexual sadism: Brain, blood, and behavior. *Ann. NY Acad. Sci., 528,* 163–171.

Langwieler, G., & Linden, M. (1993). Therapist individuality in the diagnosis and treatment of depression. *J. Affect. Dis., 27,* 1–12.

Largo, R. H., Pfister, D., Molinari, L., et al. (1989). Significance of prenatal, perinatal and postnatal factors in the development of AGA preterm infants at five to seven years. *Dev. Med. Child Neurol., 32,* 30–45.

Lawrence, C. (1987). An integrated spiritual and psychological growth model in the treatment of narcissism. *J. Psychol. Theol., 15*(3), 205–213.

Lawrence, G. H. (1986). Using computers for the treatment of psychological problems. *Computers in Human Behav., 2*(1), 43–62.

Lazarus, A. A. (1965). The treatment of a sexually inadequate man. In L. P. Ullman & L. Krasner (Eds.), *Case studies in behavior modification.* New York: Holt, Rinehart, & Winston.

Lazarus, R. S. (1990). Stress, coping, and illness. In H. S. Friedman (Ed.), *Personality and disease.* New York: Wiley.

Lazarus, R. S., & Folkman, S. (1984). *Stress, appraisal, and coping.* New York: Springer.

Leaman, T. L. (1992). *Healing the anxiety diseases.* New York: Plenum.

Lebegue, B. (1991). Paraphilias in U.S. pornography titles: "Pornography made me do it" (Ted Bundy). *Bull. Amer. Acad. Psychiat. Law, 19*(1), 43–48.

Lebell, M. B., Marder, S. R., Mintz, J., Mintz, L. I., Tompson, M., Wirshing, W., Johnston-Cronk, K., McKenzie, J. (1993). Patients' perceptions of family emotional climate and outcome in schizophrenia. *Brit. J. Psychiat., 162,* 751–754.

Ledoux, S. Choquet, M., & Manfredi, R. (1993). Associated factors for self-reported binge eating among male and female adolescents. *J. Adol. 16,* 75–91.

Lee, D. E. (1985). Alternative self-destruction. *Percep. & Motor Skills, 61*(3, Part 2), 1065–1066.

Leenaars, A. A. (1989). *Suicide notes: Predictive clues and patterns.* New York: Human Sciences.

Leenaars, A. A. (1991). Suicide in the young adult. In A. A. Leenaars (Ed.), Life span perspectives of suicide: *Time-lines in the suicide process.* New York: Plenum.

Leenaars, A. A. (1992). Suicide notes, communication, and ideation. In R. W. Maris, A. L. Berman, J. T. Maltsberger, & R. I. Yufit (Eds.), *Assessment and prediction of suicide.* New York: Guilford.

Leenaars, A. A., & Lester, D. (1992). Facts and myths of suicide in Canada and the United States. *J. Soc. Psychol., 132*(6), 787–789.

Leff, J. (1992). Schizophrenia and similar conditions. *Inter. J. Ment. Hlth., 21*(2), 25–40.

Leff, J., & Vaughn, C. (1976, Nov.). Schizophrenia and family life. *Psychol. Today,* 13–18.

Lehman, R. S. (1991). *Statistics and research design in the behavioral sciences.* Belmont, CA: Wadsworth.

Lehmann, H. E. (1967). Psychiatric disorders not in standard nomenclature. In A. M. Freedman, H. I. Kaplan, & H. S. Kaplan (Eds.), *Comprehensive textbook of psychiatry.* Baltimore: Williams & Wilkins.

Lehrer, P. M., Carr, R., Sargunaraj, D., & Woolfolk, R. L. (1993). Differential effects of stress–management therapies in behavioral medicine. In P. M. Lehrer & R. L. Woolfolk (Eds.), *Principles and practice of stress management* (2nd ed.). New York: Guilford.

Leitenberg, H., Rosen, J. C., Wolf, J., Vara, L. S., Detzer, M. J., & Srebnik, D. (1993). Comparison of cognitive-behavior therapy and desipramine in the treatment of bulimia nervosa. *Behav. Res. Ther., 32*(1), 37–45.

Leland, H. (1991). Adaptive behavior scales. In J. L. Matson & J. A. Mulick (Eds.), *Handbook of mental retardation.* New York: Pergamon.

Lenzenweger, M. J., Cornblatt, B. A., & Putnick. (1991). Schizotypy and sustained attention. *J. Abnorm. Psychol., 100*(1), 84–89.

Leon, G. R. (1984). *Case histories of deviant behavior* (3rd ed.). Boston: Allyn & Bacon.

Leonard, B. E. (1992). Effects of pharmacological treatments on neurotransmitter receptors in anxiety disorders. In G. D. Burrows, S. M. Roth, & R. Noyes, Jr., *Handbook of anxiety* (Vol. 5). Oxford: Elsevier.

Lepine, J. P., Chignon, J. M., & Teherani, M. (1993). Suicide attempts in patients with panic disorder. *Arch. Gen. Psychiat., 50,* 144–149.

Lerer, B. Shapira, B., Calev, A., Tubi, N., Drexler, H., Kindler, S., Lidsky, D., Schwartz, J. E. (1995). Antidepressant and cognitive effects of twice- versus three-times-weekly ECT. *Amer. J. Psychiat., 152*(4), 564–570.

Lerner, H. D. (1986). Current developments in the psychoanalytic psychotherapy of anorexia nervosa and bulimia nervosa. *Clin. Psychologist,* 39(2), 39–43.

Lerner, H. D., & Lerner, P. M. (Eds.), (1988). *Primitive mental states and the Rorschach.* Madison, CT: Inter. Univ. Press.

Leroux, J. A. (1986). Suicidal behavior and gifted adolescents. *Roeper Rev.,* 9(2), 77–79.

Leshner, A. I., et al. (1992). Outcasts on the main street: *Report of the Federal Task Force on Homelessness and Severe Mental Illness.* Washington, DC: Interagency Council on the Homeless.

Lester, D. (1972). Myth of suicide prevention. *Comprehen. Psychiat.,* 13(6), 555–560.

Lester, D. (1985). Accidental deaths as disguised suicides. *Psych. Rep.,* 56(2), 626.

Lester, D. (1985). The quality of life in modern America and suicide and homicide rates. *J. Soc. Psychol.,* 125(6), 779–780.

Lester, D. (1989). Can we prevent suicide? New York: AMS Press.

Lester, D. (1991). The etiology of suicide and homicide in urban and rural America. *J. of Rural Comm. Psychol.,* 12(1), 15–27.

Leszcz, M. (1992). Group psychotherapy of the borderline patient. In D. Silver & M. Rosenbluth (Eds.), *Handbook of Borderline Disorders.* Madison, CT: Inter. Univ. Press.

Letourneau, E., & O'Donohue, W. (1993). Sexual desire disorders. In W. O'Donohue & J. Geer (Eds.), *Handbook of sexual dysfunctions.* Boston: Allyn and Bacon.

LeUnes, A. D., Nation, J. R., & Turley, N. M. (1980). Male-female performance in learned helplessness. *J. Psychol.,* 104, 255–258.

LeVay, S. (1991). A difference in hypothalamic structure between heterosexual and homosexual men. *Science,* 253(5023), 1034–1037.

LeVay, S. & Hamer, D. H. (1994, May). Evidence for a biological influence in male homosexuality [Review]. *Sci. Amer.,* 270(5), 44–49.

Levenson, J. L. (1985). Neuroleptic malignant syndrome. *Amer. J Psychiat.,* 142, 1137–1145.

Levenson, M. R. (1992). Rethinking psychopathy. *Theory and Psychol.,* 2(1), 51–71.

Levin, B. L. (1992). Managed health care: A national perspective. In R. W. Manderscheid & M. A. Sonnenschein (Eds.), *Mental health, United States, 1992.* Washington, DC: U.S. Department of Health and Human Services.

Levin, H., Chengappa, K. R., Kambhampati, R. K., Mahdavi, N., et al. (1992). Should chronic treatment-refractory akathisia be an indication for the use of clozapine in schizophrenic patients? *J. Clin. Psychiat.,* 53(7), 248–251.

Levin, H. S., Mattis, S., Ruff, R. M., Eisenberg, H. M., Marshall, L. F., Tabaddor, K., High, W. M. Jr., & Frankowski, R. F. (1987). Neurobehavioral outcome of following minor head injury: A three-center study. *J. of Neurosurgery,* 66, 234–243.

Levine, M. D. (1975). Children with encopresis: A descriptive analysis. *Pediatrics,* 56, 412–416.

Levine, M. D. (1987). How schools can help combat student eating disorders: *Anroexia nervosa and bulimia.* Washington, DC: National Education Assoc.

Levine, M. D. (1988). *Introduction to eating disorders: What the educator, health, and mental health professional need to know.* Presentation at the Seventh National Conference on Eating Disorders of the National Anorexic Aid Society. Columbus, OH.

Levinson, V. R. (1985). The compatibility of the disease concept with a psychodynamic approach in the treatment of alcoholism. Special issue: Psychosocial issues in the treatment of alcoholism. *Alcoholism Treat. Quart.,* 2, 7–24.

Levitan, H. L. (1981). Implications of certain dreams reported by patients in a bulimic phase of anorexia nervosa. *Canad. J. Psychiat.,* 26(4), 228–231.

Levitt, E. E. (1989). *The clinical application of MMPI Special Scales.* Hillsdale, NJ: Erlbaum.

Levor, R. M., Cohen, M. J., Naliboff, B. D., & McArthur, D. (1986). Psychosocial precursors and correlates of migraine headache. *J. Cons. Clin. Psychol.,* 54, 347–353.

Levy, N. B. (1985). Conversion disorder. In. R. C. Simons (Ed.), *Understanding human behavior in health and illness* (3rd ed.). Baltimore: Williams & Wilkins.

Levy, N. B. (1985). The psychophysiological disorders: An overview. In R. C. Simons (Ed.), *Understanding human behavior in health and illness* (3rd ed.). Baltimore: Williams & Wilkins.

Levy, S. M., & Roberts, D. C. (1992). Clinical significance of psychoneuroimmunology: Prediction of cancer outcomes. In N. Schneiderman, P. McCabe, & A. Baum (Eds.), *Perspectives in behavioral medicine: Stress and disease processes.* Hillsdale, NJ: Lawrence Erlbaum Associates.

Lewinsohn, P. M., Antonuccio, D. O., Steinmetz, J. L., & Teri, L. (1984). *The coping with depression course.* Eugene, OR: Castalia.

Lewinsohn, P. M., Biglan, A., & Zeiss, A. M. (1976). Behavioral treatment of depression. In P. O. Davidson (Ed.), *The behavioral management of anxiety, depression and pain.* New York: Brunner/Mazel.

Lewinsohn, P. M., Clarke, G. N., Hops, H., & Andrews, J. (1990). Cognitive-behavioral treatment for depressed adolescents. *Behav. Ther.,* 21, 385–401.

Lewinsohn, P. M., & Graf, M. (1973). Pleasant activities and depression. *J. Cons. Clin. Psychol.,* 41(2), 261–268.

Lewinsohn, P. M., Rohde, P., Teri, L., & Tilson, M. (1990, April). Presentation. Western Psychological Assoc.

Lewinsohn, P. M., Sullivan, J. M., & Grosscup, S. J. (1982). Behavioral therapy: Clinical applications. In A. T. Rush (Ed.), *Short-term psychotherapies for the depressed patient.* New York: Guilford.

Lewinsohn, P. M., Youngren, M. A., & Grosscup, S. J. (1979). Reinforcement and depression. In R. A. Depue (Ed.), *The psychobiology of the depressive disorders.* New York: Academic.

Lewis, C. E., & Bucholz, K. K. (1991). Alcoholism, antisocial behavior and family history. *Brit. J. Addic.,* 86(2), 177–194.

Lewy, A. J., Ahmed, S., Jackson, J. M., & Sack, R. L. (1992). Melatonin shifts human circadian rhythms according to a phase-response curve. *Chronobio. Internatl., 9* (5), 380–392.

Liberman, R. P. (1982). Assessment of social skills. *Schizo. Bull.,* 8(1), 82–84.

Liberman, R. P. (1994). Treatment and rehabilitation of the seriously mentally ill in China: Impressions of a society in transition. *Amer. J. Orthopsychiat.,* 64(1), 68–76.

Liberman, R. P., & Corrigan, P. W. (1993). Designing new psychosocial treatments for schizophrenia. *Psychiat.,* 56, 238–253.

Lichtenstein, E. (1980). *Psychotherapy: Approaches and applications.* Monterey, CA: Brooks/Cole.

Lickey, M. E., & Gordon, B. (1991). *Medicine and mental illness: The use of drugs in psychiatry.* New York: W. H. Freeman.

Lie, N. (1992). Follow-ups of children with attention deficit hyperactivity disorder. *Acta Psychiatr. Scandin.,* 85, 40.

Liebowitz, M. Stone, M. & Turkat, I. D. (1986). Treatment of personality disorders. In A. Frances & R. Hales (Eds.), *American Psychiatric Association annual review* (Vol. 5). Washington, DC: American Psychiatric Press.

Liebowitz, M. R., Schneider, F. R., Hollander, E., & Welkowitz, L. A., et al. (1991). Treatment of social phobia with drugs other than benzodiazepines. *J. Clin Psychiat.,* 52(Suppl), 10–15.

Lifton, R. J. (1973). *Home from the war: Vietnam veterans, neither victims nor executioners.* New York: Simon & Schuster.

Lindholm, C., & Lindholm C. (1981, July.). World's strangest mental illnesses. *Science Digest.*

Lindner, M. (1968). *Hereditary and environmental influences upon resistance to stress.* Unpublished doctoral dissertation, University of Pennsylvania.

Lindsay, D. S., & Read, J. D. (1994). Psychotherapy and memories of childhood sexual abuse: A cognitive perspective. *J. of Applied Cog.. Psychol., 8,* 281–338.

Lindstrom, E. M., Ohlund, L. S., Lindstrom, L. H., & Ohman, A. (1992). Symptomatology and electrodermal activity as predictors of neuroleptic response in young male schizophrenic inpatients. *Psychiat. Res.,* 42(2), 145–158.

Linehan, M. M., & Kehrer, C. A. (1993). Borderline personality disorder. In D. H. Barlow (Ed.)., *Clinical handbook of psychological disorders: A step-by-step treatment manual* (2nd ed.). New York: Guilford.

Linehan, M. M., & Nielsen, S. L. (1981). Assessment of suicide ideation and parasuicide: Hopelessness and social desirability. *J. Cons. Clin. Psychol.,* 49(5), 773–775.

Lingswiler, V. M., Crowther, J. H., & Stephens, N. A. (1989). Affective and cognitive antecedents to eating episodes in bulimia and binge eating. *Inter. J. Eat. Dis.,* 8(5), 533–539.

Linsky, A. S., Strauss, M. A., & Colby, J. P. (1985). Stressful events, stressful conditions and alcohol problems in the United States: A partial test of Bale's theory. *J. Stud. Alc.,* 46(1), 72–80.

Linz, T. D., Hooper, S. R., Hynd, G. W., Isaac, W. et al. (1990). Frontal lobe functioning in conduct disordered juveniles: Preliminary findings. *Arch Clin. Neuropsychol.,* 5(4), 411–416.

Lipowski, Z. J. (1987). Somatization: Medicine's unsolved problem. *Psychosom.,* 28(6), 294–297.

Lipsky, M. J., Kassinove, H., & Miller, N. J. (1980). Effects of rational-emotive therapy, rational role reversal, and rational-emotive imagery on the emotional adjustment of community mental health center patients. *J. Cons. Clin. Psychol.,* 48(3), 366–374.

Lipton, H. L. (1988). A prescription for change. *Generations,* 12(4), 74–79.

Lisansky-Gomberg, E. (1993). Women and alcohol: Use and abuse. *J. Nerv. Ment. Dis., 181*(4), 211–216.

Lissner, L., Odell, P. M., D'Agostino, R. B., Stokes, J, Kreger, B. E., Belanger, A. J., & Brownell, K. D. (1991). Variability of body weight and health outcomes in the Farmingham population. *New Engl. J. Med.,* 324, 1839–1844.

Little, K. B., & Shneidman, E. S. (1959). Congruences among interpretations of psychological test and amamnestic data. *Psychol. Monographs, 73* (476).

Livesley, W. J., Schroeder, M. L., Jackson, D. N., & Jang, K. L. (1994). Categorical distinctions in the study of personality disorder: Implications for classification. *J. Abnorm. Psychol., 103*(1), 6–17.

Lloyd, G. K., Fletcher, A, & Minchin, M. C. W. (1992). GABA agonists as potential anxiolytics. (1992). In G. D. Burrows, S. M. Roth, & R. Noyes, Jr., *Handbood of anxiety* (Vol. 5). Oxford: Elsevier.

Loebel, J. P., Loebel, J. S., Dager, S. R., Centerwall, B. S., et al (1991). Anticipation of nursing home placement may be a precipitant of suicide among the elderly. *J. Amer. Ger. Soc., 39*(4), 407–408.

Loeber, R. (1991). Antisocial behavior: More enduring than changeable? *J. Amer. Acad. Child Adol. Psychiat., 30*, 393–397.

Loewenstein, R. J. (1991). Psychogenic amnesia and psychogenic fugue: A comprehensive review. In A. Tasman & S. M. Goldfinger (Eds.), *American Psychiatric Press review of psychiatry* (Vol. 10). Washington, DC: American Psychiatric Press.

Loftus, E. F. (1993). The reality of repressed memories. *Amer. Psychol., 48*, 518–537.

Logue, A. W. (1991). *The psychology of eating and drinking.* New York: W. H. Freeman.

Long. G. C., & Cordle, C. J. (1982). Psychological treatment of binge eating and self-induced vomiting. *Brit. J. Med. Psychol., 55*, 139–145.

Long, P., Forehand, R., Wierson, M., & Morgan, A. (1994). Does parent training with young noncompliant children have effects? *Behav. Res. Ther., 21*(1), 101–107.

Longshore, D., Hsieh, S. C., Anglin, M. D., et al. (1992). Ethnic patterns in drug abuse treatment utilization. Special issue: multicultural mental health and substance abuse services. *J. Ment. Hlth. Admin., 19*(3), 268–277.

Loomer, H. P., Saunders, J. C., & Kline, N. S. (1957). A clinical and pharmacodynamic evaluation of iproniazid as a psychic energizer. *Amer. Psychiat. Assoc. Res. Rep., 8*, 129.

LoPiccolo, J. (1985). Advances in diagnosis and treatment of male sexual dysfunction. *J. Sex Marital Ther., 11*(4), 215–232.

LoPiccolo, J. (1990). Treatment of sexual dysfunction. In A. S. Bellak, M. Hersen, & A. E. Kazdin (Eds.), *Inter. handbook of behavior modification and therapy* (2nd ed.). New York: Plenum.

LoPiccolo, J. (1991). Post-modern sex therapy for erectile failure. In R. C. Rosen & S. R. Leiblum (Eds.), *Erectile failure: Diagnosis and treatment.* New York: Guilford.

LoPiccolo, J. (1992). Paraphilias. *Nordisk Sexologi, 10*(1), 1-14.

LoPiccolo, J. (1995). Sexual disorders and gender identity disorders. In R. J. Comer. *Abnormal psychology.* W. H. Freeman and Company: New York.

LoPiccolo, J., & Friedman, J. R. (1988). Broad spectrum treatment of low sexual desire: Integration of cognitive, behavioral, and systemic treatment. In S. Leiblum & R. Rosen (Eds.), *Sexual desire disorders.* New York: Guilford.

LoPiccolo, J., & Stock, W. E. (1987). Sexual function, dysfunction, and counseling in gynecological practice. In Z. Rosenwaks, F. Benjamin, & M. L. Stone (Eds.), *Gynecol.* New York: Macmillan.

Lorand, S. (1968). Dynamics and therapy of depressive states. In W. Gaylin (Ed.), *The meaning of despair.* New York: Aronson.

Lovaas, O. I. (1987). Behavioral treatment and normal educational/intellectual functioning in young autistic children. *J. Cons. Clin. Psychol., 55*, 3–9.

Love, S. R., Matson, J. L., & West, D. (1990). Mothers as effective therapists for autistic children's phobias. *J. Appl. Behav. Anal., 23*(3), 379–385.

Lovejoy, M. (1982). Expectations and the recovery process. *Schizo. Bull., 8*(4), 605–609.

Lowenstein, L. F. (1989). The etiology, diagnosis and treatment of the fire-setting behavior of children. *Child Psychiat. Human Dev., 19*(3), 186–194.

Lubetsky, M. J. (1986). The psychiatrist's role in the assessment and treatment of the mentally retarded child. *Child Psychiat. Human Dev., 16*(4), 261–273.

Lubin, B. (1983). Group therapy. In I. B. Weiner (Ed.), *Clinical methods in psychology* (2nd ed.). New York: Wiley.

Luborsky, L. (1973). Forgetting and remembering (momentary forgetting) during psychotherapy. In M. Mayman (Ed.), *Psychoanalytic research and psychological issues* (Monograph 30). New York: International Univ.

Luborsky, L., Singer, B., & Luborsky, L. (1975). Comparative studies of psychotherapies. *Arch. Gen. Psychiat., 32*, 995–1008.

Ludolph, P. S., Westen, D., Misle, B., Jackson, A., et al. (1990). The borderline diagnosis in adolescents: Symptoms and developmental history. *Amer. J. Psychiat., 147*(4), 470–476.

Luntz, B. K., & Widom, C. S. (1994). Antisocial personality disorder in abused and neglected children grown up. *Amer. J. Psychiat., 151*(5), 670–674.

Lutgendorf, S. K., Antoni, M. H., Kumar, M., & Schneiderman, N. (1994). Changes in cognitive coping strategies predict EBV-Antibody titre change following a stressor disclosure induction. *J. Psychosom. Res., 38*(1), 63–68.

Lykken, D. T. (1957). A study of anxiety in the sociopathic personality. *J. Abnorm. Soc. Psychol., 55*, 6–10.

Lynch, G. & Baudry, M. (1984). The biochemistry of memory: A new and specific hypothesis. *Science, 224*, 1057–1063.

Lyness, J. M., Conwell, Y., & Nelson, J. C. (1992). Suicide attempts in elderly psychiatric inpatients. *J. Amer. Ger. Soc., 40*(4), 320–324.

Lyons, K. A., (1992). Shattered mirror: A fragment of the treatment of a patient with multiple personality disorder. *Psychoanal. Quart., 12*(1), 71–94.

Lyon, L. S. (1985). Facilitating telephone number recall in a case of psychogenic amnesia. *J. Behav. Ther. Exp. Psychiat., 16*(2), 147–149.

Lyons, L. C., & Woods, P. J. (1991). The efficacy of rational-emotive therapy: A quantitative review of the outcome research. *Clin. Psychol. Rev., 11*, 357–369.

Macciardi, G., Kennedy, J. L., Ruocco, L., Guiffra, L., et al. (1992). A genetic-linkage study of schizophrenia to chromosome 5 markers in a northern Italian population. *Bio. Psychiat., 31*(7), 720–728.

MacDonald, M. L., & Schnur, R. E. (1987). Anxieties and American elders: Proposals for assessment and treatment. In L. Michelson & L. M. Ascher (Eds.), *Anxiety and stress disorders: Cognitive behavioral assessment and treatment.* New York: Guilford.

Mace, N., & Rabins, P. (1991). *The 36-hour day* (2nd ed.). Baltimore: Johns Hopkins Univ.

MacHovek, F. J. (1981). Hypnosis to facilitate recall in psychogenic amnesia and fugue states: Treatment variables. *Amer. J. Clin. Hyp., 24*(1), 7–13.

Machover, K. (1949). *Personality projection in the drawing of the human figure.* Springfield, IL: Thomas.

Maddi, S. R. (1990). Issues and interventions in stress mastery. In H. S. Friedman (Ed.), *Personality and disease.* New York: Wiley.

Maddox, G. L. (1988). Aging, drinking and alcohol abuse. *Generations, 12*(4), 14–16.

Madianos, M. G., & Madianou, D. (1992). The effects of long-term community care on relapse and adjustment of persons with chronic schizophrenia. *Inter. J. Ment. Hlth., 21*(1), 37–49.

Maher, B. A. (1974). Delusional thinking and perceptual disorder. *J. Indiv. Psychol., 30*(1), 98–113.

Maher, B. A., & Maher, W. B. (1994). Personality and psychopathology: A historical perspective. *J. Abnorm. Psychol., 103*(1), 72–77.

Maher, W. B., & Maher, B. A. (1985). Psychopathology: I. From ancient times to the eighteenth century. In G. A. Kimble & K. Schlesinger (Eds.), *Topics in the history of psychology* (Vol. 2). Hillsdale, NJ: Erlbaum.

Mahler, M. (1974). Symbiosis and individuation: The psychological birth of the human infant. *Psychoanal. Study Child, 29*, 89–106.

Mahler, M. (1979). On the first three subphases of the separation-individuation process. In *Selected papers of Margaret Mahler, Vol. 2.* New York: Jason Aronson.

Mahoney, G., Glover, A., & Finger, I. (1981). Relationship between language and sensorimotor development of Down syndrome and nonretarded children. *Amer. J. Ment. Def., 86*(1), 21–27.

Maier, S. F., Laudenslager, M. L., & Ryan, S. M. (1985). Stressor controllability, immune function, and endogenous opiates. In F. R. Brush & J. B. Overmier (Eds.), *Affect, conditioning and cognition: Essays on the determinants of behavior.* Hillsdale, NJ: Erlbaum.

Mainer, S. F., Watkins, L. R., & Fleshner, M. (1994). Psychoneuroimmunology: The interface between behavior, brain and immunity. *Amer. Psychol., 49*(12), 1004–1017.

Main, M. (1989). Adult attachment classification system. In M. Main (Ed.), *Behavior and the development of representational models of attachment: Five methods of assessment.* New York: Cambridge UP.

Maj, M., Satz, P., Janssen, R., Zaudig, M., et al. (1994). WHO neuropsychiatric AIDS study, Cross-sectional Phase II. *Arch. Gen. Psychiat., 51*, 51–61.

Malamud, B. (1979). Dublin's lives. New York: Farrar Straus Giroux.

Malcolm, A. H. (1990, Jun. 9). Giving death a hand. *New York Times,* A6.

Maletzky, B. M. (1980). Assisted covert sensitization. In D. J. Cox & R. J. Daitzman (Eds.), *Exhibitionism: Description, assessment, and treatment.* New York: Garland STPM.

Maller, R. G., & Reiss, S. (1992). Anxiety sensitivity in 1984 and panic attacks in 1987. *J. Anx. Dis., 6*(3), 241–247.

Maltsberger, J. T. (1991). The prevention of suicide in adults. In A. A. Leenaars (Ed.), The prevention of suicide in adults. In A. A. Leenaars

(Ed.), *Life span perspectives of suicide: Time-lines in the suicide process.* New York: Plenum.

Manderscheid, R., & Rosenstein, M. (1992). Homeless persons with mental illness and alcohol or other drug abuse: Current research, policy, and prospects. *Curr. Opinion in Psychiat., 5,* 273–278.

Manderscheid, R. W., & Sonnenschein, M. A. (1992). *Mental health, United States, 1992.* Rockville, MD: U.S. Department of Health and Human Services.

Mannuzza, S., Klein, R. G., Bessler, A., Malloy, P., & LaPadula, M. (1993). Adult outcome of hyperactive boys. *Arch. Gen. Psychiat., 50,* 565–576.

Mannuzza, S., Schneier, F. R., Chapman, T. F., Liebowitz, M. R., Klein, D. F., Fyer, A. J. (1995). Generalized social phobia. *Arch. Gen. Psychiat., 52,* 230–237.

Manschreck, T. C. (1985). Delusional (paranoid) disorders. In H. I. Kaplan & B. J. Sadock (Eds.), *Comprehensive textbook of psychiatry* (4th ed.). Baltimore: Williams & Wilkins.

Marcus, B. F. (1989). Incest and the borderline syndrome: The mediating role of identity. *Psychoanal. Psychol., 6*(2), 199–215.

Marfo, K., & Kysela, G. M. (1985). Early intervention with mentally handicapped children: A critical appraisal of applied research. *J. of Pediatric Psychol., 10,* 305–324.

Margo, G. M., & Newman, J. S. (1989). Venesection as a rare form of self-multilation. *Amer. J. Psychother., 43*(3), 427–432.

Margraf, J. (1993). Hyperventilation and panic disorder: A psychophysiological connection. *Adv. Behav. Res. Ther., 15,* 49–74.

Margraf, J., Barlow, D. H., Clark, D. M., & Telch, M. J. (1993). Psychological treatment of panic: Work in progress on outcome, active ingredients, and follow-up. *Behav. Res. Ther., 31*(1), 1–8.

Margraf, J., Ehlers, A., Roth, W. T., Clark, D. B., et al. (1991). How "blind" are double-blind studies? *J. Cons. Clin. Psychol., 59*(1), 184–187.

Maris, R. W. (Ed.), (1986). *Biology of suicide.* New York: Guilford.

Maris, R. W. (1992). Methods of suicide. In R. W. Maris, A. L. Berman, J. T. Maltsberger, & R. I. Yufit (Eds.), *Assessment and prediction of suicide.* New York: Guilford.

Maris, R. W. (1992). Overview of the study of suicide assessment and prediction. In R. W. Maris, A. L. Berman, J. T. Maltsberger, & R. I. Yufit (Eds.), *Assessment and prediction of suicide.* New York: Guilford.

Marks, I. M. (1986). Genetics of fear and anxiety disorders. *Brit. J. Psychiat., 149,* 406–418.

Marks, I. M. (1987). Comment on S. Lloyd Williams' "On anxiety and phobia." *J. Anx. Dis., 1*(2), 181–196.

Marks, I. M. (1987). Fears, phobias and rituals: Panic, anxiety and their disorders. New York: Oxford UP.

Marks, I. M., & Gelder, M. G. (1967). Transvestism and fetishism: Clinical and psychological changes during faradic aversion. *Brit. J. Psychiat., 113,* 711–730.

Marks, I. M., & Swinson, R. (1992). Behavioral and/or drug therapy. In G. D. Burrows, S. M. Roth, & R. Noyes, Jr., *Handbook of anxiety* (Vol. 5). Oxford: Elsevier.

Marlatt, G. A. (1985). Controlled drinking: The controversy rages on. *Amer. Psychol., 40*(3), 374–375.

Marlatt, G. A., & Gordon, J. (Eds.), (1980). Determinants of relapse: Implications for the maintenance of behavior change. In P. Davidson & S. Davidson (Eds.), *Behavioral medicine.* New York: Brunner/Mazel.

Marlatt, G. A., & Gordon, J. R. (1985). *Relapse prevention: Maintenance strategies in the treatment of addictive behaviors.* New York: Guilford.

Marlatt, G. A., Kosturn, C. F., & Lang, A. R. (1975). Provocation to anger and opportunity for retaliation as determinants of alcohol consumption in social drinkers. *J. Abnorm. Psychol., 84*(6), 652–659.

Marmar, C. R., Foy, C., Kagan, B., & Pynoos, R. S. (1993). An integrated approach for treating post–traumatic stress. In J. M. Oldman, M. B. Riba, & A. Tasman (Eds.), *Review of psychiatry, Vol. 12.* Washington, DC: American Psychiatric Press.

Marmor, J. (1987). The psychotherapeutic process: Common denominators in diverse approaches. In J. K. Zeig, (Ed.), *The evolution of psychotherapy.* New York: Brunner/Mazel.

Marquis, J. N., & Morgan, W. G. (1969). *A guidebook for systematic desensitization.* Palo Alto, CA: Veterans Admin. Hospital.

Marshall, W. L., & Lippens, K. (1977). The clinical value of boredom: A procedure for reducing inappropriate sexual interests. *J. Nerv. Ment. Dis., 165,* 283–287.

Marston, W. M. (1917). Systolic blood pressure changes in deception. *J. Exp. Phsyiol., 2,* 117–163.

Martin, G., & Pear, J. (1988). *Behavior modification* (3rd ed.). Englewood Cliffs, NJ: Prentice Hall.

Martin, F. E. (1985). The treatment and outcome of anorexia nervosa in adolescents: A prospective study and five year follow-up. *J. Psychiat. Res., 19*(2-3), 509–514.

Martin, F. E. (1985). Anorexia nervosa: A review of the theoretical per-

spectives and treatment approaches. *Brit. J. Occupat. Ther., 48*(8), 236–240.

Martin, F. E. (1990). The relevance of a systemic model for the study and treatment of anorexia nervosa in adolescents [Special Issue]. *Canad. J. Psychiat., 35*(6), 496–500.

Martin, W. T. (1984). Religiosity and U.S. suicide rates, 1972–1978. *J. Clin. Psychol., 40*(5), 1166–1169.

Martineau, J., Barthelemy, C., Jouve, J., Muh, J. P. (1992). Monoamines (serotonin and catecholamines) and their derivatives in infantile autism. Age-related changes and drug effects. *Dev. Med. Child Neuro., 34*(7), 593–603.

Marzuk, P. M., Tardiff, K., Leon, A. C., Stajic, M., Morgan, E. B., & Mann, J. J. (1992). Prevalence of cocaine use among residents of New York City who committed suicide during a one-year period. *Amer. J. Psychiat., 149*(3), 371–375.

Mason, M. A., & Gibbs, J. T. (1992). Patterns of adolescent psychiatric hospitalization: Implications for social policy. *Amer. J. Orthopsychiat., 62*(3), 447–457.

Masters, W. H., & Johnson, V. E. (1966). *Human sexual response.* Boston: Little, Brown.

Masters, W. H., & Johnson, V. E. (1970). *Human sexual inadequacy.* Boston: Little, Brown.

Masterson, J. F. (1990). Psychotherapy of borderline and narcissistic disorders: Establishing a therapeutic alliance. *J. Pers. Dis., 4*(2), 182–191.

Matarazzo, J. D. (1984). Behavioral health: A 1990 challenge for the health sciences professions. In J. D. Matarazzo, S. M. Weiss, J. A. Herd, N. E. Miller, & S. M. Weiss (Eds.), *Behavioral health: A handbook of health enhancement and disease prevention.* New York: Wiley.

Matarazzo, J. D. (1992). Psychological testing and assessment in the 21st century. *Amer. Psychol., 47*(8), 1007–1018.

Mathew, N. T. (1990). Advances in cluster headache. *Neurologic Clinics, 8*(4), 867–890.

Mathew, R., Wilson, W., Blazer, D., & George, L. (1993). Psychiatric disorders in adult children of alcoholics: Data from the Epidemiologic Catchment Area Project. *Amer. J. Psychiat., 150*(5), 793–796.

Mathew, R., Wilson, W., Humphreys, D., Lowe, J., & Weithe, K. (1993). Depersonalization after marijuana smoking. *Bio. Psychiat., 33,* 431–441.

Mathews, A., Mogg, K., Kentish, J. & Eysenck, M. (1995). Effect of psychological treatment on cognitive bias in generalized anxiety disorder. *Behav. Res. Ther., 33*(3), 293–303.

Matson, J. L., & Gorman-Smith, D. (1986). A review of treatment research for aggressive and disruptive behavior in the mentally retarded. *Appl. Res. in Ment. Retardation, 7*(1), 95–103.

Matsuyama, S. S., Jarvik, L. F., & Kumar, V. (1985). Dementia: Genetics. In T. Arie (Ed.), *Recent advances in psychogeriatrics.* London: Churchill-Livingstone.

Mattick, R. P., & Newman, C. R. (1991). Social phobia and avoidant personality disorder. *Inter. Rev. Psychiat., 3*(2), 163–173.

Mavissakalian, M. R. (1990). Sequential combination of imipramine and self-directed exposure in the treatment of panic disorder with agoraphobia. *J. Clin. Psychiat., 51*(5), 184–188.

Mavissakalian, M. R. (1993). Combined behavioral and pharmacological treatment of anxiety disorders. In A. A. Leenaars (Ed.), *Suicidology.* Northvale, NJ: Jason Aronson.

Mavreas, V. G., Tomaras, V., Karydi, V., Economous, M. (1992). Expressed emotion in families of chronic schizophrenics and its association with clinical measures. *Soc. Psychiat. and Psychiat., Epidemiol., 27*(1), 4–9.

May, P. R. A., & Tuma, A. H. (1964). Choice of criteria for the assessment of treatment outcome. *J. Psychiat. Res., 2*(3), 16–527.

May, P. R. A., Tuma, A. H., & Dixon, W. J. (1981). Schizophrenia: A follow-up study of the results of five forms of treatment. *Arch. Gen. Psychiat., 38,* 776–784.

May, R. (1967). *Psychology and the human dilemma.* New York: Van Nostrand Reinhold.

May, R. (1987). Therapy in our day. In J. K. Zeig (Ed.), *The evolution of psychotherapy.* New York: Brunner/Mazel.

May, R., Angel, E., & Ellenberger, H. F. (1958). *Existence: A new dimension in psychiatry and psychology.* New York: Basic Books.

May, R., & Yalom, I. (1989). Existential psychotherapy. In R. J. Corsini & D. Wedding (Eds.), *Current psychotherapies.* Itasca, IL: Peacock.

Mays, D., & Franks, C. M. (1985). *Negative outcome in psychotherapy and what to do about it.* New York: Springer.

McCarthy, P. R., Katz, I. R., & Foa, E. B. (1991). Cognitive-behavioral treatment of anxiety in the elderly: A proposed model. In C. Salzman & B. D. Leibowitz (Eds.), *Anxiety in the elderly.* New York: Springer.

McClelland, D. C. (1985). The social mandate of health psychology. *Amer. Behav. Scientist, 28*(4), 451–467.

McClelland, D. C. (1993). Motives and health. In G. G. Brannigan & M. R. Merrens (Eds.), *The undaunted psychologist.* New York: McGraw-Hill.

McCord, W., & McCord, J. (1960). *Origins of alcoholism*. Stanford, CA: Stanford UP.

McCormack, A., Rokous, F. E., Hazelwood, R. R., & Burgess, A. W. (1992). An exploration of incest in the childhood development of serial rapists. *J. Fam. Violence, 7*(3), 219–228.

McCormick, R. A. (1994). The importance of coping skill enhancement in the treatment of the pathological gambler. Special issue: Pathological gambling: Clinical issues: I. *J. of Gamb. Stud., 10*(1), 77–86.

McCoy, S. A. (1976). Clinical judgments of normal childhood behavior. *J. Cons. Clin. Psychol., 44*(5), 710–714.

McCurdy, & Daro, D. (1993). *Current trends: A fifty state survey*. National Committee for the Prevention of Child Abuse. Washington, DC: Authors.

McEachin, J. J., Smith, T., & Lovaas, O. I. (1993). Long-term outcome for children with autism who received early intensive behavioral treatment. *Amer. J. Ment. Retard., 97*(4), 359–372.

McElroy, L. P. (1992). Early indicators of pathological dissociation in sexually abused children. *Child Abuse and Neglect, 16*(6), 833–846.

McElroy, S. L., Hudson, J. L., Pope H. G., & Keck, P. E. (1991). Kleptomania: Clinical characteristics and associated psychopathology. *Psychol. Med., 21*(1), 93–108.

McElroy, S. L., Hudson, J. I., Pope, H. G., Keck, P. E., et al. (1992). The DSM-III-R impulse control disorders not elsewhere classified: Clinical characteristics and relationship to other psychiatric disorders. *Amer. J. Psychiat., 149*(3), 318–327.

McElroy, S. L., Keck, P. E., & Friedman, L. M. (1995). Minimizing and managing antidepressant side effects. *J. Clin. Psychiat., 56*(Suppl. 2), 49–55.

McElroy, S. L., Phillips, K. A., & Keck, P. E. Jr. (1994). Obsessive compulsive spectrum disorder. *J. Clin. Psychiat., 33*–53.

McEvoy, J. (1992). Fragile X syndrome: A brief overview. *Educ. Psychol. in Practice, 8*(3), 146–149.

McFarlane, A. C. (1991). Post–traumatic stress disorder. *Inter. Rev. Psychiat., 3*(2), 203–213.

McGhie, A., & Chapman, J. S. (1961). Disorders of attention and perception in early schizophrenia. *Brit. J. Med. Psychol., 34*, 103–116.

McGlashan, T. H. (1986). Schizotypal personality disorder: Chestnut Lodge follow-up study: VI. Long-term follow-up perspectives. *Arch. Gen. Psychiat., 43*(4), 329–334.

McGlashan, T. H. (1988). A selective review of recent North American long-term follow-up studies of schizophrenia. *Schizo. Bull., 14*(4), 515–542.

McGrath, P. J., Stewart, J. W., Nunes, E. V., Ocepek-Welikson, K., et al., (1993). A double-blind crossover trial of imipramine and phenelzine for outpatients with treatment-refractory depression. *Amer. J. Psychiat., 150*(1), 118–123.

McGuffin, P., & Thapar, A. (1992). The genetics of personality disorder. *Brit. J. Psychiat., 160*, 12–23.

McGuire, D. (1982). The problem of children's suicide: Ages 5–14. *Inter. J. Offend. Ther. Compar. Crimin., 26*(1), 10–17.

McIntosh, J. L. (1987). Suicide: Training and education needs with an emphasis on the elderly. *Gerontol. & Ger. Educ., 7*, 125–139.

McIntosh, J. L. (1991). Epidemiology of suicide in the U.S. In A. A. Leenaars (Ed.), *Life span perspectives of suicide*. New York: Plenum.

McIntosh, J. L. (1992). Epidemiology of suicide in the elderly. *Suic. Life-Threat. Behav., 22*(1), 15–35.

McIntosh, J. L. (1992). Methods of suicide. In R. W. Maris, A. L. Berman, J. T. Maltsberger, & R. I. Yufit (Eds.), *Assessment and prediction of suicide*. New York: Guilford.

McIntosh, J. L., Hubbard, R. W., & Santos, J. F. (1985). Suicide facts and myths: A study of prevalence. *Death Stud., 9*, 267–281.

McIntosh, J. L., & Santos, J. F. (1982). Changing patterns in methods of suicide by race and sex. *Suic. Life-Threat. Behav., 12*, 221–233.

McKay, J. R., Alterman, A. I., McLellan, A. T., Snider, E. C., & O'Brien, C. P. (1995). Effect of random versus nonrandom assignment in a comparison of inpatient and day hospital rehabilitation for male alcoholics. *J. Cons. Clin. Psychol., 63*(1), 70–78.

McLean, A., Temkin, N. R., Dikmen, S., & Wyler, A. R. (1983). The behavioral sequelae of head injury. *J. Clin. Neuropsych., 5*, 361–376.

McMahon, R. J., & Wells, K. C. (1989). Conduct disorders. In E. J. Mash & R. Barkley (Eds.), *Treatment of childhood disorders*. New York: Guilford.

McNally, R. J., & Lukach, B. M. (1991). Behavioral treatment of zoophilic exhibitionism. *J. Behav. Ther. Exp. Psychiat., 22*(4), 281–284.

McNeal, E. T., & Cimbolic, P. (1986). Antidepressants and biochemical theories of depression. *Psychol. Bull., 99*(3), 361–374.

McNeil, E. B. (1967). *The quiet furies*. Englewood Cliffs, NJ: Prentice Hall.

McNiel, D. E., & Binder, R. L. (1991). Clinical assessment of the risk of violence among psychiatric inpatients. *Amer. J. Psychiat., 148*(10), 1317–1321.

McQuiston, J. T. (1993, February 23). Suffolk mother's illness imperils son, judge rules. *The New York Times*, pp. B1, B2.

McShane, W., & Redoutey, L. J. (1987). Community hospitals and community mental health agenices: Partners in service delivery. Annual Meeting of the Association of Mental Health Administrators (1986, San Francisco, California). *J. Ment. Hlth. Admin., 14*(2), 1–6.

Mednick, S. A. (1971). Birth defects and schizophrenia. *Psych. Today, 4*, 48–50.

Meehl, P. E. (1951). *Research results for counselors*. St. Paul, MN: State Dept. Education.

Meehl, P. E. (1960). The cognitive activity of the clinician. *Amer. Psychol., 15*, 19–27.

Mehta, M. (1990). A comparative study of family-based and patient-based behavioural management in obsessive-compulsive disorder. *Brit. J. Psychiat., 157*, 133–135.

Meichenbaum, D. H. (1972). Cognitive modification of test-anxious college studens. *J. Cons. Clin. Psychol., 39*, 370–380.

Meichenbaum, D. H. (1972). Examination of model characteristics in reducing avoidance behavior. *J. Behav. Ther. Exp. Psychiat., 3*, 225–227.

Meichenbaum, D. H. (1974). *Cognitive behavior modification*. Morristown, NJ: General Learning.

Meichenbaum, D. H. (1974). Self–instruction methods. In F. H. Kanfer & A. P. Goldstein (Eds.), *Helping people change*. New York: Pergamon.

Meichenbaum, D. H. (1975). A self-instructional approach to stress management: A proposal for stress inoculation training. In I. Sarason & C. D. Spielberger (Eds.), *Stress and anxiety* (Vol. 2). New York: Wiley.

Meichenbaum, D. H. (1975). Enhancing creativity by modifying what subjects say to themselves. *Amer. Educ. Res. J., 12*(2), 129–145.

Meichenbaum, D. H. (1975). Theoretical and treatment implications of development research on verbal control of behavior. *Canad. Psychol. Rev., 16*(1), 22–27.

Meichenbaum, D. H. (1975). Toward a cognitive of self–control. In G. Schwartz & D. Shapiro (Eds.), *Consciousness and self–regulation: Advances in research*. New York: Plenum.

Meichenbaum, D. H. (1977). Cognitive behavior modification: An integrative approach. New York: Plenum.

Meichenbaum, D. H. (1977). Dr. Ellis, please stand up. *Couns. Psychologist, 7*(1), 43–44.

Meichenbaum, D. H. (1993). Stress inoculation training: A 20-year update. In P. M. Lehrer & R. L. Woolfolk (Eds.), *Principles and practice of stress management* (2nd ed.). New York: Guilford.

Meichenbaum, D. H. (1993). The personal journey of a psychotherapist and his mother. In G. G. Brannigan & M. R. Merrens (Eds.), *The undaunted psychologist: Adventures in research*. New York: McGraw-Hill.

Melges, F. T., & Swartz, M. S. (1989). Oscillations of attachment in borderline personality disorder. *Amer. J. Psychiat., 146*(9), 1115–1120.

Melick, M., Logue, J., & Frederick, C. (1992). Stress and disaster. In L. Goldberger & S. Breznitz (Eds.), *Handbook of stress*. New York: Free Press.

Meltzer, H. L. (1991). Is there a specific membrane defect in bipolar disorders? *Bio. Psychiat., 30*, 1071–1074.

Meltzer, H. Y. (1987). Biological studies in schizophrenia. *Schizo. Bull., 13*(1), 77–111.

Meltzer, H. Y. (1991). The mechanism of action in novel antipsychotic drugs. *Schizo. Bull. 17*(2), 263–287.

Meltzer, H. Y. (1992). Dimensions of outcome with clozapine. *Brit. J. Psychiat., 160*(suppl. 17), 46–53.

Meltzer, H. Y. (1992). Treatment of the neuroleptic-nonresponsive schizophrenic patient. *Schizo. Bull., 18*(3), 515–542.

Meltzer, H. Y. (1993). Clozapine: A major advance in the treatment of schizophrenia. *The Harvard Ment. Hlth. Letter, 19*(2), 4–6.

Melville, J. (1978). *Phobias and obsessions*. New York: Penguin.

Mendes-de-Leon, C. F. (1992). Anger and impatience/irritability in patients of low socioeconomic status with acute coronary heart disease. *J. Behav. Med., 15*(3), 273–284.

Mendlewicz, J., Simon, P., Sevy, S., Charon, F., Brocas, H., Legros, S., & Vassart, G. (1987). Polymorphic DNA marker on X chromosome and manic depression. *Lancet 1*, 1230–1232.

Menke, J. A., McClead, R. E., & Hansen, N. B. (1991). Perspectives on perinatal complications associated with mental retardation. In J. L. Matson & J. A. Mulick (Eds.), *Handbook of mental retardation*. New York: Pergamon.

Menzies, R. G., & Clarke, J. C. (1993). A comparison of in vivo and vicarious exposure in the treatment of childhood water phobia. *Behav. Res. Ther., 31*(1), 9–15.

Merrill, J., Milner, G., Owens, J., & Vale, A. (1992). Alcohol and attempted suicide. *Brit. J. Addic., 87*(1), 83–89.

Mersch, P. P. (1995). The treatment of social phobia: The differential effectiveness of exposure *in vivo* and an integration of exposure *in vivo*, rational emotive therapy and social skills training. *Behav. Res. Ther., 33*(3), 259–269.

Mersch, P. P., Emmelkamp, P. M., & Lips, C. (1991). Social phobia: Individual response patterns and the long-term effects of behavioural and cognitive interventions. A follow-up study. *Behav. Res. Ther., 29*(4), 357–362.

Merskey, H. (1986). Classification of chronic pain: Descriptions of chronic pain syndromes and definitions of pain terms. *Pain, 3,* 226.

Merskey, H. (1992). The manufacture of personalities: The production of multiple personality disorder. *Brit. J. Psychiat., 160,* 327–340.

Messer, A. A. (1985). Narcissistic people. *Med. Aspects Human Sex., 19*(9), 169–184.

Messer, S. B., Tishby, O., & Spillman, A. (1992). Taking context seriously in psychotherapy research: Relating therapist interventions to patient progress in brief psychodynamic therapy. *J. Cons. Clin. Psychol., 60*(5), 678–688.

Metalsky, G. I., Joiner, T. E. Jr., Hardin, T. S., & Abramson, L. Y. (1993). Depressive reactions to failure in a naturalistic setting: A test of the hopelessness and self-esteem theories of depression. *J. Abnorm. Psychol., 102*(1), 101–109.

Meyer, R. E., Murray, R. F., Jr., Thomas, F. B., et al. (1989). *Prevention and treatment of alcohol problems: Research opportunities.* Washington, DC: National Academy.

Meyer, R. G. (1992). *Abnormal behavior and the criminal justice system.* New York: Lexington Books.

Meyer, V. (1966). Modification of expectations in cases with obsessional rituals. *Behav. Res. Ther., 4,* 273–280.

Michaelson, R. (1993). Flood volunteers build emotional levees. *APA Monitor, 24*(10), p. 30.

Michels, R. (1992). The borderline patient: Shifts in theoretical emphasis and implications for treatment. In D. Silver & M. Rosenbluth (Eds.), *Handbook of borderline disorders.* Madison, CT: International Universities Press.

Michelson, L. K., & Marchione, K. (1991). Behavioral, cognitive and pharmacological treatments of panic disorder with agoraphobia: Critique and synthesis. *J. Cons. Clin. Psychol., 59*(1), 100–114.

Mickalide, A. D. (1990). Sociocultural factors influencing weight among males. In A. E. Andersen (Ed.), *Males with eating disorders.* New York: Brunner/Mazel.

Miesel, A. (1989). *The right to die.* New York: Wiley.

Miklowitz, D. J. (1994). Family risk indicators in schizophrenia. *Schizo. Bull., 20*(1), 137–149.

Miklowitz, D. J., Goldstein, M. J., Nuechterlein, K. H., Synder, K. S., et al. (1988). Family factors and the course of bipolar affective disorder. *Arch. Gen. Psychiat., 45*(3), 225–231.

Millar, J. D. (1984). The NIOSH-suggested list of the ten leading work-related diseases and injuries. *J. Occupat. Med., 26,* 340–341.

Miller, H. L., Coombs, D. W., Leeper, J. D., et al. (1984). An analysis of the effects of suicide prevention facilities on suicide rates in the United States. *Amer. J. Pub. Hlth., 74,* 340–343.

Miller, L. (1988). Neurocognitive aspects of remorse: Impulsivity-compulsivity-reflectivity. *Psychother. Patient, 5,* 63–76.

Miller, N. E. (1948). Studies of fear as an acquirable drive. I. Fear as a motivation and fear-reduction as reinforcement in the learning of new responses. *J. Exp. Psychol., 38,* 89–101.

Miller, N. S., & Gold, M. S. (1990). Benzodiazepines: Tolerance, dependence, abuse, and addiction. *J. Psychoact. Drugs, 22*(1), 23–33.

Miller, N. S., Klahr, A. L., Gold, M. S., Sweeney, K, et al. (1990). The prevalence of marijuana (cannabis) use and dependence in cocaine dependence. *N.Y. St. J. Med., 90*(10), 491–492.

Miller, P. M., Ingham, J. G., & Davidson, S. (1976). Life events, symptoms, and social support. *J. Psychiat., Res., 20*(6), 514–522.

Miller, W. R. (1982). Treating problem drinkers: What works? *Behav. Ther., 5,* 15–18.

Miller, W. R. (1983). Controlled drinking, *Quart. J. Stud. Alc., 44,* 68–83.

Miller, W. R., & Hester, R. K. (1980). Treating the problem drinker: Modern approaches: In W. R. Miller (Ed.), *The addictive behaviors: Treatment of alcoholism, drug abuse, smoking, and obesity.* Elmsford: NY: Pergamon.

Miller, W. R., & Hester, R. K. (1986). Inpatient alcoholism treatment: Who benefits? *Amer. Psychol., 41,* 794–805.

Miller, W. R., Leckman, A. L., Delaney, H. D., & Tinchom, M. (1992). Long-term follow-up of behavioral self-control training. *J. of Stud. on Alc., 51,* 108–115.

Miller, W. R., & Seligman, M. E. (1975). Depression and learned helplessness in man. *J. Abnorm. Psychol., 84*(3), 228–238.

Millon, T. (1969). *Modern psychopathology: A biosocial approach to maladaptive learning and functioning.* Philadelphia: Saunders.

Millon, T. (1987). *Manual for the MCMI-II* (2nd ed.). Minneapolis, MN: National Computer Systems.

Millon, T. (1987). Millon Clinical Multiaxial Inventory-II: *Manual for the MCMI-II* (2nd ed.). Minneapolis, MN: National Computer Systems.

Millon, T. (1990). The disorders of personality. In L. A. Pervin (Ed.), *Handbook of personality theory and practice.* New York: Guilford.

Millon, T. (1990). *Toward a new personology.* New York: Wiley.

Milner, B. (1971). Interhemispheric difference in the loalization of psychological processes in man. *Brit. Med. Bull., 27,* 272–277.

Mineka, S., & Sutton, S. K. (1992). Cognitive biases and the emotional disorders. *Psychol. Sci., 3*(1), 65–69.

Minuchin, S. (1974). *Families and family therapy.* Cambridge, MA: Harvard UP.

Minuchin, S. (1987). My many voices. In J. K. Zeig (Ed.), *The evolution of psychotherapy.* New York: Brunner/Mazel.

Minuchin, S. (1992). *Family healing.* New York: Free Press.

Minuchin, S., Rosman, B. L., & Baker, L. (1978). *Psychosomatic families: Anorexia nervosa in context.* Cambridge, MA: Harvard UP.

Mirin, S. M., & Weiss, R. D. (1991). Substance abuse and mental illness. In R. J. Frances & S. I. Miller (Eds.), *Clinical textbook of addictive disorders.* New York: Guilford.

M.I.T. (1993, Dec. 3). Cited in "Mental depression costs $43.7 billion, study shows." *The Daily News.*

Mitchell, J. E., & de Zwaan, M. (1993). Pharmacological treatments of binge eating. In C. G. Fairburn & G. T. Wilson (Eds.), *Binge eating: Nature, assessment, and treatment.* New York: Guilford.

Mitchell, J. E., Hatsukami, D., Goff, G., Pyle, R. L., Eckert, E. D., & Davis, L. E. (1985). Intensive outpatient group treatment for bulimia. In D. M. Garner & P. E. Garfinkel (Eds.), *Handbook of psychotherapy for anorexia nervosa and bulimia.* New York: Guilford.

Mitchell, J. E., Pyle, R. L., Eckert, E. D., Hatsukami, D. et al. (1990). Bulimia nervosa in overweight individuals. *J. Nerv. Ment. Dis., 178*(5), 324–327.

Mitchell, J. E., Pyle, R. L., & Fletcher, L. (1991). The topography of binge eating, vomiting and laxative abuse. *Inter. J. Eat. Dis., 10*(1), 43–48.

Modestin, J., & Villiger, C. (1989). Follow-up study on borderline versus nonborderline personality disorders. *Comprehen. Psychiat., 30*(3), 236–244.

Modrow, J. (1992). *How to become a schizophrenic: The case against biological psychiatry.* Everett, Washington, DC: Apollyon Press.

Mohler, H., & Okada, T. (1977). Benzodiazepine receptor: Demonstration in the central nervous system. *Sci. 198*(4319), 849–851.

Mohler, H., Richards, J. G., & Wu, J.-Y. (1981). *Autoradiographic localization of benzodiazepine receptors in immunocytochemically identified Y-aminobutryic synapses.* Proceedings of the National Academy of Sciences, U.S.A., 78, 1935–1938.

Mohr, D. C., & Beutler, L. E. (1990). Erectile dysfunction: A review of diagnostic and treatment procedures. *Clin. Psychol. Rev., 10*(1), 123–150.

Mohr, J. W., Turner, R. E., & Jerry, M. B. (1964). *Pedophilia and exhibiionism.* Toronto: Univ. Toronto.

Moller, H. J. (1990). Suicide risk and treatment problems in patients who have attempted suicide. In D. Lester (Ed.), *Current concepts of suicide.* Philadelphia: The Charles Press.

Mollerstrom, W. W., Patchner, M. A., & Milner, J. S. (1992). Family violence in the Air Force: A look at offenders and the role of the Family Advocacy Program. *Military Med., 157*(7), 371–374.

Mollinger, R. N. (1980). Antithesis and the obsessive-compulsive. *Psychoanal. Rev., 67*(4), 465–477.

Monahan, J. (1992). Mental disorder and violent behavior: Perceptions and evidence. *Amer. Psychol., 47*(4), 511–521.

Monahan, J. (1993). Limiting therapist exposure to Tarasoff liability: Guidelines for risk containment. *Amer. Psychol., 48*(3), 242–250.

Monahan, J. (1993). Mental disorders and violence: Another look. In S. Hodgins (Ed.), *Mental disorder and crime.* Newbury Park: Sage Publications.

Monahan, J., & Davis, S. K. (1983). Mentally disordered sex offenders. In J. Monahan & H. J. Steadman (Eds.), *Mentally disordered offenders.* New York: Plenum.

Monahan, J., & Walker, L. (Eds.). (1990). *Social science in law: Cases and materials* (2nd ed.). Westbury, NJ: Foundation Press.

Moneymaker, J. M., & Strimple, E. O. (1991). Animals and inmates: A sharing companionship behind bars. *J. Offend. Rehab., 16*(3-4), 133–152.

Montagu, J. D., & Coles, E. M. (1966). Mechanism and measurement of the galvanic skin response. *Psychol. Bull., 65,* 261–279.

Montgomery, S. A., Bebbington, P., Cowen, P., Deakin, W., et al. (1993). Guidelines for treating depressive illness with antidepressants. *J. Psychopharmacol., 7*(1), 19–23.

Moore, D. R., & Arthur, J. L. (1983). Juvenile delinquency. In T. Ollendick & M. Hersen (Eds.), *Handbook of child psychopathology.* New York: Plenum.

Morales, A., Condra, M., Heaton, J. P. W., & Varrin, S. (1991). Impotence: Organic factors and management approach. *Sex. Marit. Ther., 6*(2), 97–106.

Moreno, I., Saiz, R. J., & Lopez, I. J. J. (1991). Serotonin and gambling dependence. *Human Psychopharmacol.-Clin.-and-Exper., 6*(Suppl), 9–12.

Morgan, C. D., & Murray, H. A. (1935). A method of investigating fantasies: The Thematic Apperception Test. *Arch. Neurol. Psychiat., 34,* 289–306.

Morokoff, P. J. (1978). Determinants of female orgasm. In J. LoPiccolo & L. LoPiccolo (Eds.), *Handbook of sex therapy.* New York: Plenum.

Morokoff, P. J. (1988). Sexuality in premenopausal and postmenopausal women. *Psychol. of Women Quart., 12,* 489–511.

Morokoff, P. J. (1993). Female sexual arousal disorder. In W. O'Donohue and J. Geer (Eds.), *Handbook of sexual dysfunctions.* Boston: Allyn and Bacon.

Morokoff, P. J., & Gillilland, R. (1993). Stress, sexual functioning, and marital satisfaction. *J. Sex Res., 30*(1), 43–53.

Morris, G. (1983). Acquittal by reason of insanity: Developments in the law. In J. Monahan & H. J. Steadman (Eds.), *Mentally disordered offenders.* New York: Plenum.

Morris, R. G., & Baddeley, A. D. (1988). Primary and working memory functioning in Alzheimer-type dementia. *J. of Clin. Exper. Neuropsycho., 10,* 279–296.

Morrison, J. (1989). Histrionic personality disorder in women with somatization disorder. *Psychosom., 30*(4), 433–437.

Morrissette, D. L., Skinner, M. H., Hoffman, B. B., Levine, R. E., & Davison, J. M. (1993). Effects of antihypertensive drugs Atenolol and Nifedipine on sexual function in older men: A placebo-controlled, crossover study. *Arch. Sex. Behav., 22*(2), 99–109.

Morse, S. J. (1982). A preference for liberty: The case against involuntary commitment of the mentally disordered. *Calif. Law Rev., 70,* 55–106.

Moses-Zirkes, S. (1992, October 10). Psychologists question anti-stalking laws' utility. *APA Monitor, 23,* p. 53.

Motto, J. (1967). Suicide and suggestibility: The role of the press. *Amer. J. Psychiat., 124,* 252–256.

Motto, J. (1980). The right to suicide: A psychiatrist's view. In M. P. Battin & D. J. Mayo (Eds.), *Suicide: The philosophical issues.* New York: St. Martin's.

Mowrer, O. H. (1939). A stimulus-response analysis of anxiety and its role as a reinforcing agent. *Psychol. Rev., 46,* 553–566.

Mowrer, O. H. (1939). *An experimentally produced "social problem" in rats* [Film]. Bethlehem, PA: Psychological Cinema Register, Lehigh Univ.

Mowrer, O. H. (1947). On the dual nature of learning: A reinterpretation of "conditioning" and "problem-solving." *Harvard Educ. Rev., 17,* 102–148.

Mowrer, O. H., & Mowrer, W. M. (1938). Enuresis: A method for its study and treatment. *Amer. J. Orthopsychiat., 8,* 436–459.

Mueser, K. T., Bellack, A. S., & Brady, E. U. (1990). Hallucinations in schizophrenia. *Acta Psychiatr. Scandin., 82*(1), 29–36.

Mueser, K. T., & Glynn, S. M. (1990). Behavioral family therapy for schizophrenia. In M. Hersen, R. M. Eisler, & P. M. Miller (Eds.), *Progress in behavior modification, Vol. 26.* Newbury Park, CA: Sage Publications.

Mulkern, V. M., & Manderscheid, R. W. (1989). Characteristics of community support program clients in 1980 and 1984. *Hosp. Comm. Psychiat., 40*(2), 165–172.

Mullan, M., Crawford, F., Axelman, K., Houlden, H., Lilius L., Winblad, B., & Lannfelt, L., (1992). A pathogenic mutation for probable Alzheimer's disease in APP gene at the N-terminus of Beta-amyloid. *Nature Genet., 1,* 345–347.

Mullins, L. L., Olson, R. A., & Chaney, J. M. (1992). A social learning/family systems approach to the treatment of somatoform disorders in children and adolescents. *Fam. Systems Med., 10*(2), 201–212.

Munk, J. P., & Mortensen, P. B. (1992). Social outcome in schizophrenia: A 13-year follow-up. *Social Psychiatry and Psychiat. Epidemiol., 27*(3), 129–134.

Murphy, C. M., Meyer, S. L., & O'Leary, K. D. (1994). Dependency characteristics of partner–assaultive men. *J. Abnorm. Psychol., 103*(4), 729–735.

Murphy, J. B., & Lipshultz, L. I. (1988). Infertility in the paraplegic male. In E. A. Tanagho, T. F. Lue, & R. D. McClure (Eds.), *Contemporary management of impotence and infertility.* Baltimore: Williams & Wilkins.

Murphy, J. M. (1976, March). Psychiatric labeling in cross-cultural perspective: Similar kinds of disturbed behavior appear to be labeled abnormal in diverse cultures. *Sci., 101*(4231), 1019–1028.

Murphy, S. M. (1990). Rape, sexually transmitted diseases and human immunodeficiency virus infection. *Inter. J. of STD and AIDS, 1,* 79–82.

Murphy, S. M., Owen, R. T., & Tyrer, P. J. (1984). Withdrawal symptoms after six weeks' treatment with diazepam. *Lancet, 2,* 1389.

Murray, B. (1993). Human Nature: Attitudes and Age. *Psych. Today, 26*(2), 96.

Murray, H. A. (1938). *Explorations in personality.* Fairlawn, NJ: Oxford UP.

Murray, J. B. (1986). Psychological aspects of anorexia nervosa. *Gen. Soc. & Gen. Psychol. Monographs, 112*(1), 5–40.

Murray, J. D., & Keller, P. A. (1991, March), Psychology and rural America: Current status and future directions. *Amer. Psychol., 46,* 220–231.

Murrell, J., Farlow, M., Bernardino, G., & Benson, M. D. (1991). A mutation in the amyloid precursor protein associated with hereditary Alzheimer's disease. *Sci., 254,* 97–99.

Murstein, B. I., & Fontaine, P. A. (1993). The public's knowledge about psychologists and other mental health professionals. *Amer. Psychol., 48*(7), 839–845.

Murtagh, D. R. & Greenwood, K. M. (1995). Identifying effective psychological treatments for insomnia. A meta-analysis. *J. Cons. Clin. Psychol., 63*(1), 79–89.

Muuss, R. E. (1986). Adolescent eating disorder: Bulimia. *Adol., 21*(82), 257–267.

Myatt, R. J., & Greenblatt, M. (1993). Adolescent suicidal behavior. In A. A. Leenaars. (Ed.), *Suicidology.* Northvale, NJ: Jason Aronson.

Nace, E. P. (1992). Alcoholism and the borderline patient. In D. Silver & M. Rosenbluth (Eds.), *Handbook of borderline disorders.* Madison, CT: International Universities Press.

Nagy, J., & Szatmari, P. (1986). A chart review of schizotypal personality disorders in children. *J. Autism Dev. Dis., 16*(3), 351–367.

Nagy, L. M., Krystal, J. H., Charney, D. S., Merikangas, K. R., & Woods, S. W. (1993). Long-term outcome of panic disorder after short-term imipramine and behavioral group treatment: 2.9-year naturalistic follow-up study. *J. Clin. Psychopharmacol., 13*(1), 16–24.

Nagy, L. M., Morgan, C. A., III, Southwick, S. M., & Charney, D. S. (1993). Open prospective trial of fluoxetine for post–traumatic stress disorder. *J. Clin Psychopharmacol, 13*(2), 107–113.

Nahas, G. G. (1984). Toxicology and pharmacology. In G. G. Nahas (Ed.), *Marijuana in science and medicine.* New York: Raven Press.

Narrow, W. E., Regier, D. A., Rae, D. S., Manderscheid, R. W., & Locke, B. Z. (1993). Use of services by persons with mental and addictive disorders: Findings from the National Institute of Mental Health Epidemiologic Catchment Area Program. *Arch. Gen. Psychiat., 50,* 95–107.

Nash, M. R., Hulsey, T. L., Sexton, M. C., Harralson, T. L., & Lambert, W. (1993). Long-term sequelae of childhood sexual abuse: Perceived family environment, psycho-pathology, and dissociation. *J. Cons. Clin. Psychol., 61,* 276–283.

National Alliance for the Mentally Ill (NAMI). (1994). *Personal communication.*

National Center for Health Statistics. (1988). Vital statistics of the United States, 1985, Vol. 2. *Mortality.* Washington, DC: Government Printing Office.

National Center for Health Statistics. (1988). Vital statistics of the United States, 1986, Vol. 2. *Mortality.* Washington: DC: Government Printing Office.

National Center for Health Statistics. (1990). Vital statistics of the United States, 1987, Vol. 2. *Mortality.* Washington, DC: Government Printing Office.

National Center for Health Statistics (1991). Vital statistics of the United States (Vol. 2): *Mortality - Part A* [for the years 1966-1988]. Washington, DC: U. S. Government Printing Office.

National Center for Health Statistics. (1993). Advance report of final mortality statistics, 1991. *Monthly Vital Statistics Report, Vol 42*(2), Hyattsville, MD: U.S. Public Health Service.

National Commission on Children (1991). *Speaking of kids: A national survey of children and parents.* Washington, DC.

National Institute for Occupational Safety & Health. (1985). *Proposed national strategies for the prevention of leading work-related diseases and injuries.* (Pt. 1, NTIS No. PB87-114740). Cincinnati: Assoc. of Schools of Public Health/NIOSH.

National Institute for Occupational Safety & Health. (1988). *Proposed national strategies for the prevention of leading work-related diseases and injuries.* (Pt. 2, NTIS No. PB89-130348). Cincinnati: Assoc. of Schools of Public Health/NIOSH.

National Institute of Mental Health (NIMH) (1992). Statistical Research Branch. Unpublished estimate.

National Institute on Alcohol Abuse and Alcoholism (1991). Alcohol Alert #11. *Estimating the economic cost of alcohol abuse.* Rockville, MD.

National Institute on Alcohol Abuse and Alcoholism (1991). Alcohol Alert #14. *Alcoholism and co-occurring disorders.* Rockville, MD.

National Institute on Alcohol Abuse and Alcoholism (1992). Alcohol Alert #15. *Alcohol and AIDA.* Rockville, MD.

National Inssitute on Alcohol Abuse and Alcoholism (1992). Alcohol Alert #16. *Moderate drinking.* Rockville, MD.

National Institute on Drug Abuse (1990). *Substance abuse among blacks in the U.S.* Rockville, MD.

National Institute on Drug Abuse (1990). *Substance abuse among Hispanic Americans.* Rockville, MD.

National Institute on Drug Abuse (1991). *Annual Emergency Room Data, 1991.* Rockville, MD.

National Institute on Drug Abuse (1992). *Annual Medical Examiner Data, 1991.* Rockville, MD.

National Institute on Drug Abuse (1991). *Third triennial report to Congress on drug abuse and drug abuse research.* Rockville, MD.

National Institute on Drug Abuse (1992). National Household *Survey on Drug Abuse: Population Estimates 1991.* Rockville, MD.

National Institute on Drug Abuse (1993). National Household *Survey on Drug Abuse: Highlights 1991.* Rockville, MD.

National Institute on Drug Abuse (1993). *National survey results on drug use from monitoring the future study, 1975–1992.* Rockville, MD.

National Institute on Drug Abuse (1993). *National survey results on drug use from monitoring the future study, 1975–1992, Vol. II.* Rockville, MD.

National Victims Center. (1992, April). *Rape in America: A report to the nation.* Arlington, VA.

Nelson, R. O. (1977). Assessment and therapeutic functions of self-monitoring. In. M. Hersen. R. M. Eisler, & P. M. Miller (Eds.), *Progress in behavior modification.* New York: Academic Press.

Nelson, R. O., (1981). Realistic dependent measures for clinical use. *J. Cons. Clin. Psychol., 49,* 168–182.

Nemiah, J. C. (1984). In T. R. Insel (Ed.), *New findings in obsessive–compulsive disorder.* Washington, DC: American Psychiatric Press. [7-6].

Nestadt, G., Romanoski, A. J., Brown, C. H., Chahal, R., et al. (1991). DSM-III compulsive personality disorder: An epidemiological survey. *Psychol. Med., 21*(2), 461–471.

Nestadt, G., Romanoski, A. J., Chahal, R., Merchant, A., Folstein, M. F., Gruenberg, E. M., & McHugh, P. R. (1990). An epidemiological study of histrionic personality disorder. *Psychol. Med., 29,* 413–422.

Neuman, P. A., & Halvorson, P. A. (1983). *Anorexia nervosa and bulimia: A handbook for counselors and therapists.* New York: Van Nostrand Reinhold.

Newberger, E. H. (1983). The helping hand strikes again: Unintended consequences of child abuse reporting. *J. Clin. Child. Psychol., 12,* 307–311.

Newman, J. P., & Kosson, D. S. (1986). Passive avoidance learning in psychopathic and nonpsychopathic offenders. *J. Abnorm. Psychol., 95,* 257–263.

Newman, J. P. & Kosson, D. S., & Patterson, C. M. (1987). Response perseveration in psychopaths. *J. Abnorm. Psychol., 96,* 145–149.

Newman, J. P., Kosson, D. S., & Patterson, C. M. (1992). Delay of gratification in psychopathic and nonpsychopathic offenders. *J. Abnorm. Psychol., 101*(4), 630–636.

Nichols, M. P. (1984). *Family therapy: Concepts and methods.* New York: Gardner Press.

Nichols, M. P. (1992). *The power of family therapy.* New York: Gardner Press.

Nides, M. A., Rakos, R. F., Gonzales, D., Murray, R. P., Tashkin, D. P., Bjornson-Benson, W. M., Lindgren, P., & Connett, J. E. (1995). *J. Cons. Clin. Psychol., 63*(1), 60–69.

Nielsen, S. (1990). Epidemiology of anorexia nervosa in Denmark from 1973 to 1987: A nationwide register study of psychiatric admission. *Acta Psychiatr. Scandin., 81*(6), 507–514.

Nieto, E., Vieta, E., Lázaro, L., Gastó, C., et al. (1992). Serious suicide attempts in the elderly. *Psychopath. 25*(4), 183–188.

Nitenson, N. C., & Cole, J. O. (1993). Psychotropic-induced sexual dysfunction. In D. L. Dunner (ed.), *Current psychiatric therapy.* Philadelphia: Saunders.

Nolen-Hoeksema, S. (1987). Sex differences in unipolar depression: Evidence and theory. *Psychol. Bull., 101*(2), 259–282.

Nolen-Hoeksema, S. (1990). *Sex differences in depression.* Stanford, CA: Stanford UP.

Nolen-Hoeksema, S., Girgus, J. S., & Seligman, M. E. (1992). Predictors and consequences of childhood depressive symptoms: A 5-year long longitudinal study. *J. Abnorm. Psychol., 101*(3), 405–422.

Noonan, J. R. (1971). An obsessive-compulsive reaction treated by induced anxiety. *Amer. J. Psychother., 25*(2), 293–299.

Norcross, J. C., & Prochaska, J. O. (1984). Where do behavior (and other) therapists take their troubles? II. *Behav. Therapist, 7*(2), 26–27.

Norcross, J. C., & Prochaska, J. O. (1986). Psychotherapist heal thyself: I. The psychological distress and self-change of psychologists, counselors, and laypersons. *Psychother. 23,* 102–114.

Norcross, J. C., Prochaska, J. O., & Farber, J. A. (1993). Psychologists conducting psychotherapy: New findings and historical comparisons on the psychotherapy division membership. *Psychother., 30*(4), 692–697.

Norcross, J. C., Strausser, D. J., & Missar, C. D. (1988). The process and outcomes of psychotherapists' personal treatment experiences. *Psychother., 25,* 36–43.

Norcross, J. C., et al., (1987). Presentation. Eastern Psychological Assoc.

Norden, M. J. (1994). Clinical case study: Buspirone treatment of sexual dysfunction associated with selective serotonin re-uptake inhibitors. *Depression, 2,* 109–112.

Nordstrom, P., & Asberg, M. (1992). Suicide risk and serotonin. *Inter. Clin. Psychopharmcol., 6*(Suppl 6), 12–21.

Norris, P. A., & Fahrion, S. L. (1993). Autogenic biofeedback in psychophysiological therapy and stress management. In P. M. Lehrer & R. L. Woolfolk (Eds.), *Principles and practice of stress management* (2nd ed.). New York: Guilford.

Norton, G. R., Rockman, G. E., Luy, B., & Marion, T. (1993). Suicide, chemical abuse, and panic attacks: A preliminary report. *Behav. Res. Ther., 31*(1), 37–40.

Nurnberger, J. I., Jr., & Gershon, E. S. (1984). Genetics of affective disorders. In R. M. Post & J. C. Ballenger (Eds.), *Neurobiology of mood disorders* (Vol. I. Frontiers of Clinical Neuroscience). Baltimore: Williams & Wilkins.

Nurnberger, J. I., Jr. & Gershon, E. S. (1992). Genetics. In E. S. Paykel (Ed.), *Handbook of affective disorders.* New York: Guilford.

Nutzinger, D. O., & de Zwaan, M. (1990). Behavioral treatment of bulimia (nervosa). In M. M. Fichter (Ed.), *Bulimia nervosa: Basic research, diagnosis and therapy.* Chichester: Wiley.

O'Brien, C. P., O'Brien, T. J., Mintz, J., & Brady, J. P. (1975). Conditioning of narcotic abstinence symptoms in human subjects. *Drug. Alc. Dep., 1,* 115–123.

O'Connell, D. S. (1983) The placebo effect and psychotherapy. *Psychother. Theory Res. Prac., 20*(3), 337–345.

O'Hare, T. (1992). The substance-abusing chronically mentally ill client: Prevalance, assessment, treatment and policy concerns. *Soc. Work, 37*(2), 185–187.

O'Leary, K. D., & Kent, R. (1973). Behavior modification for social action: Research tactics and problems. In L. A. Hamerlynck, L. C. Handy, & E. J. Mash (Eds.), *Behavior change: Methodology, concepts, and practice.* Champaign, IL: Research Press.

O'Leary, K. D., & Wilson, G. T. (1987). *Behavior therapy: Application and outcome.* (2nd ed.). Englewood Cliffs, NJ: Prentice Hall.

O'Leary, K. M., Brouwers, P., Gardner, D. L., Cowdry, R. W. (1991). Neuropsychological testing of patients with borderline personality disorder. *Amer. J. Psychiat., 148*(1), 106–111.

O'Leary, K. M., Turner, E. R., Gardner, D., & Cowdry, R. W. (1991). Homogeneous group therapy of borderline personality disorder. *Group, 15*(1), 56–64.

O'Malley, S., Jaffe, A., Chang, G., Schottenfeld, R., Meyer, R., & Rounsaville, B. (1992). Naltrexone and coping skills therapy for alcohol dependence. *Arch. Gen. Psychiat., 49,* 881–888.

O'Sullivan, G., & Marks, I. (1991). Follow-up studies of behavioral treatment of phobias and obsessive–compulsive neuroses. *Psychiat. Ann., 21*(6), 368–373.

O'Sullivan, G., & Marks, I. M. (1991). Long-term outcome of phobic and obsessive-compulsive disorders after treatment. In R. Noyes, G. D. Burrows, & M. Roth (Eds.), *Handbook of Anxiety* (Vol. 4). Amsterdam: Elsevier Science Publishers.

O'Sullivan, G., Noshirvani, H., Marks, I., Monteiro, W., et al. (1991). Six-year follow-up after exposure and clomipramine therapy for obsessive–compulsive disorder. *J. Clin. Psychiat., 52*(4), 150–155.

O'Sullivan, M. J., Peterson, P. D., Cox, G. B., & Kirkeby, J. (1989). Ethnic populations: Community mental health services ten years later. *Amer. J. Comm. Psychol., 17,* 17–30.

Oakley-Browne, M. A. (1991). The epidemiology of anxiety disorders. *Inter. Rev. Psychiat., 3,*(2) 243–252.

Oberlander, E. L., Schneier, F. R., & Liebowitz, M. R. (1994). Physical disability and social phobia. *J. Clin. Psychopharm, 14*(2), 136–143.

Oei, T. P., Lim, B., & Hennessy, B. (1990). Psychological dysfunction in battle: Combat stress reactions and post–traumatic stress disorder. *Clin Psychol. Rev., 10*(3), 355–388.

Office for Substance Abuse Prevention (1991). *Children of alcoholics: Alcoholism tends to run in families.* Rockville, MD.

Office for Substance Abuse Prevention (1991). *College youth.* Rockville, MD.

Office for Substance Abuse Prevention (1991). *Crack cocaine: A challenge for prevention.* (Ed. R. Dupone). Rockville, MD: OSAP.

Office for Substance Abuse Prevention (1991). *Impaired driving.* Rockville, MD.

Ogden, J. A. & Corkin, S. (1991). Memories of H. M. In W. C. Abraham, M. C. Corballis, & K. G. White (Eds.), *Memory mechanisms: A tribute to G. V. Goddard.* Hillsdale, New Jersey: Lawrence Erlbaum Associates, Publishers.

Ogloff, J. R. P., Schweighofer, A., Turnball, S. D., & Whittemore, K. (1992). Empirical research regarding the insanity defense: How much do we really know? In J. R. P. Ogloff (Ed.), *Law and psychology: The broadening of the discipline.*

Ohman, A. (1993). Stimulus prepotency and fear learning: Data and theory. In N. Birbaumer, & A. Öhman (Eds.), *The Organization of Emotion: Cognitive, clinical, and psychophysiological perspectives.* Göttingen, FRG: Hogrefe & Huber.

Ohman, A., Erixon, G., & Lofberg, I. (1975). Phobias and preparedness:

Phobic versus neutral pictures as continued stimuli for human autonomic responses. *J. Abnorm. Psychol., 84,* 41–45.

Ohman, A., & Soares, J. J. F. (1993). On the automatic nature of phobic fear: Conditioned electrodermal responses to masked fear-relevant stimuli. *J. Abnorm. Psychol., 102*(1), 121–132.

Olfson, M., Pincus, H. A., & Dial, T. H. (1994). Professional practice patterns of U. S. Psychiatrists. *Amer. J. Psychiat., 151*(1), 89–95.

Oliver, J. E. (1993). Intergenerational transmission of child abuse: Rates, research and clinical implications. *Amer. J. Psychiat., 150*(9).

Olmos de Paz, T. (1990). Working-through and insight in child psychoanalysis. *Melanie Klein & Obj. Relations, 8*(1), 99–112.

Olmsted, M. P., Kaplan, A. S., & Rockert, W. (1994). Rate and prediction of relapse in bulimia nervosa. *Amer. J. Psychiat., 151*(5), 738–743.

Opler, L. A., Caton, C. L. M., Shrout, P., Dominguez, B., & Kass, F. I. (1994). Symptom profiles and homelessness in schizophrenia. *J. Nerv. Ment. Dis., 182*(3), 174–178.

Orlebeke, J. F., Boomsma, D. I., Goren, L. J. G., Verschoor, A. M., Van Den Bree, M. J. M. (1992). Elevated sinistrality in transsexuals. *Neuropsych., 6*(4), 351–355.

Orloff, L. M., Battle, M. A., Baer, L., Ivanjack, L., Pettit, A., R., Buttolph, M. L., & Jenike, M. A. (1994). Long-term follow-up of 85 patients with obsessive-compulsive disorder. *Amer. J. Psychiat., 151*(3), 441–442.

Osgood, M. J. (1987). Suicide and the elderly. *Generations, 11,*(3), 47–51.

Ost, L. G., (1991). Acquisition of blood and injection phobia and anxiety response patterns in clinical patients. *Behav. Res. Ther., 29*(4), 323–332.

Otto, R. K. (1989). Bias and expert testimony of mental health professionals in adversarial proceedings: A preliminary investigation. *Behav. Sci. Law, 7*(2), 267–273.

Ottosson, J. O. (1985). Use and misuse of electroconvulsive treatment. *Bio Psychiat., 20*(9), 933–946.

Overholser, J. C. (1992). Interpersonal dependency and social loss. *Pers. Indiv. Differences, 13*(1), 17–23.

Overstreet, D. H. (1993). The Flinders sensitive line rats: A genetic animal model of depression. *Neurosci. Biobehav. Rev., 17,* 51–68.

Overton, D. (1964). State-dependent or "dissociated" learning produced with pentobarbital. *J. Compar. Physiol. Psychol., 57,* 3–12.

Overton, D. (1966). State-dependent learning produced by depressant and atropine-like drugs. *Psychopharmacologia, 10,* 6–31.

Owen, M. K., Lancee, W. J., & Freeman, S. J. (1986). Psychological factors and depressive symptoms. *J. Nerv. Ment. Dis., 174*(1), 15–23.

Oyemade, U. J. (1989). Parents and children getting a head start against drugs. *Fact Sheet 1989.* Alexandria, VA: National Head Start Association.

Pace, T. M., & Dixon, D. N. (1993). Changes in depressive self-schemata and depressive symptoms following cognitive therapy. *J. Couns. Psychol., 40*(3), 288–294.

Pagelow, M. D. (1981). *Family violence.* New York: CBS Education.

Paget, K. D., Philp, J. D., & Abramczyk, L. W. (1993). Recent developments in child neglect. In T. H. Ollendick, & R. J. Prinz (Eds.), *Advances in clinical child psychology* (Vol. 15). New York: Plenum.

Painter, K. (1992, March 25). Drunken-driving casualties aren't the only victims of alcohol abuse. *USA Today,* p. 5D.

Pajer, K. (1995). New strategies in the treatment of depression in women. *J. Clin. Psychiat., 56* (Suppl. 2), 30–37.

Papp, L. A., Coplan, J., & Gorman, J. M. (1992). Neurobiology of anxiety. In A. Tasman, & M. B. Riba (Eds.), *Review of psychiatry* (Vol 11). Washington, DC: American Psychiatric Press.

Papp, L. A., & Gorman, J. M. (1993). Pharmacological approach to the management of stress and anxiety disorders. In P. M. Lehrer & R. L. Woolfolk (Eds.), *Principles and practice of stress management* (2nd ed.). New York: Guilford.

Paris, J. (1990). Completed suicide in borderline personality disorder. *Psychiat. Ann., 20*(1), 19–21.

Paris, J. (1991) Personality disorders, parasuicide, and culture. *Transcult. Psychiat. Res. Rev., 28*(1), 25–39.

Paris, J., Nowlis, D., Brown, R. (1988). Developmental factors in the outcome of borderline personality disorder. *Comprehen. Psychiat., 29*(2), 147–150.

Parker, G. (1992). Early environment. In E. S. Paykel (Ed.), *Handbook of affective disorders.* New York: Guilford.

Parker, G., Hadzi-Pavlovic, D., Brodaty, H., Boyce, P., Mitchell, P., Wilhelm, K., Hickie, I., & Eyers, K. (1993). Psychomotor disturbance in depression: Defining the constructs. *J. Affect. Dis., 27,* 255–265.

Parker, N. (1991). The Gary David case. *Austral. New Zeal. J. Psychiat., 25*(3), 371–374.

Parker, P. E. (1993). A case report of Munchausen Syndrome with mixed psychological features. *Psychosom., 34*(4), 360–364.

Parnas, J. (1988). Assortative mating in schizophrenia: Results from Copenhagen high-risk study. *Psychiat, 51*(1), 58–64.

Parnas, J., Cannon, T. D., Jacobsen, B., Schulsinger, H., Schulsinger, F., & Mednick, S. A. (1993). Lifetime DSM-III-R diagnostic outcomes in the offspring of schizophrenic mothers. *Arch. Gen. Psychiat., 50,* 707–714.

Parnas, J., Jorgensen, A., et al. (1989). Pre-morbid psychopathology in schizophrenia spectrum. *Brit. J. Psychiat., 155,* 623–627.

Parnas, J., Schulsinger, F., Schulsinger, H., Mednick, S. A., & Teasdale, T. W. (1982). Behavioral precursors of schizophrenia spectrum: A prospective study. *Arch. Gen. Psychiat., 39,* 658–664.

Parnas, J. et al. (1982). Behavioral precursors of schizophrenia spectrum: A prospective study. *Arch. Gen. Psychiat., 39*(6), 858–884.

Patrick, C. J., Bradley, M. M., & Land, P. J. (1993). Emotion in the criminal psychopath: Startle reflex modulation. *J. Abnorm. Psychol., 102*(1), 82–92.

Patrick, C. J., Cuthbert, B. N., & Land, P. J. (1990). Emotion in the criminal psychopath: Fear imagery. *Psychophys. 27*(Suppl.), 55.

Patterson, G. R. (1982). *Coercive family process.* Eugene, OR: Castalia.

Patterson, G. R. (1986). Performance models for antisocial boys. *Amer. Psychol., 41,* 432–444.

Patton, G. C., Johnson-Sabine, E., Wood, K., Mann, A. H. et al. (1990). Abnormal eating attitudes in London schoolgirls: A prospective epidemiological study: Outcome at twelve–month follow-up. *Psychol. Med., 20*(2), 383–394.

Paul, G. L. (1967). The strategy of outcome research in psychotherapy. *J. Cons. Psych., 31,* 109–118.

Paul, G. L., & Lentz, R. (1977). *Psychosocial treatment of the chronic mental patient.* Cambridge, MA: Harvard UP.

Paurohit, N., Dowd, E. T., & Cottingham, H. F. (1982). The role of verbal and nonverbal cues in the formation of first impressions of black and white counselors. *J. Couns. Psychol., 4,* 371–378.

Paykel, E. S. (1991). Stress and life events. In L. Davidson & M. Linnoila (Eds.), *Risk factors for youth suicide.* New York: Hemisphere.

Paykel, E. S., & Cooper, Z. (1992). Life events and social stress. In E. S. Paykel (Ed.), *Handbook of affective disorders.* New York: Guilford.

Payne, A. F. (1928). *Sentence completion.* New York: New York Guidance Clinics.

Payte, T. J. (1989). Combined treatment modalities: The need for innovative approaches. Third National Forum on AIDS and Chemical Dependency of the American Society of Addiction Medicine. *J. Psychoact. Drugs, 21*(4), 431–434.

Peachey, J. E., & Franklin, T. (1985). Methadone treatment of opiate dependence in Canada. *Brit. J. Addic., 80*(3), 291–299.

Peck, M. (1982). Youth suicide. *Death Educ., 6*(1), 27–47.

Peele, S. (1989). *Diseasing of America: Addiction treatment out of control.* Lexington, MA: Lexington Books/D.C. Heath & Company.

Peele, S. (1992). Alcoholism, politics, and bureaucracy: The consensus against controlled-drinking therapy in America. *Addic. Behav. 17,* 49–62.

Pendery, M. L., Maltzman, I. M., & West, L. J. (1982). Controlled drinking by alcoholics? New findings and a reevaluation of a major affirmative study. *Sci., 217*(4555), 169–175.

Pendleton, L., Tisdale, M., & Marler, M. (1991). Personality pathology in bulimics versus controls. *Comprehen. Psychiat., 32*(6), 516–520.

Pericak-Vance, M. A., Bebout, J. L., Gaskell, P. C., Yamaoka, L. H., Hung, W. Y., Alberts, M. J., Walker, A. P., Bartlett, J., Haynes, C. A., & Welsh, K. A. (1991). Linkage studies in familial Alzheimer Disease: Evidence for chromosome 19 linkage. *Amer. J. Human Genet., 48,* 1034–1050.

Perkins, D. O., Leserman, J., Gilmore, J. H., Petitto, J. M., & Evans, D. L. (1991). Stress, depression and immunity: Research findings and clinical implications. In N. Plotnikoff, A. Murgo, R. Faith, & J. Wybran (Eds.), *Stress and immunity.* Boca Raton: CRC Press.

Perls, F. S. (1973). *The Gestalt approach.* Palo Alto: Science Behav.

Perris, C. (1988). Decentralization, sectorization, and the development of alternatives to institutional care in a northern county in Sweden. In C. N. Stefanis & A. D. Rabavilis (Eds.), *Schizophrenia: Recent biosocial developments.* New York: Human Sci.

Perry, J. C. (1989). Dependent personality disorder. In American Psychiatric Association (Eds.), *Treatments of psychiatric disorders: A task force report of the American Psychiatric Association.* Washington, DC: American Psychiatric Press.

Perry, J. C. (1992). Problems and considerations in the valid assessment of personality disorders. *Amer. J. Psychiat., 149,* 1645–1653.

Perry, J. C., Herman, J. L., & Van der Kolk, B. A. (1990). Psychotherapy and psychological trauma in borderline personality disorder. *Psychiat. Ann., 20*(1), 33–43.

Perry, J. C., & Jacobs, D. (1982). Overview: Clinical applications of the amytal interview in psychiatric emergency settings. *Amer. J. Psychiat., 139*(5), 552–559.

Perry, S., Difede, J., Musngi, G., Frances, A. J., et al. (1992). Predictors of post–traumatic stress disorder after burn injury. *Amer. J. Psychiat., 149*(7), 931–935.

Perry, W., & Braff, D. L., (1994). Information-processing deficits and thought disorder in schizophrenia. *Amer. J. Psychiat., 151*(3), 363–367.

Persons, J. B. (1991). Psychotherapy outcome studies do not accurately represent current models of psychotherapy: A proposed remedy. *Amer. Psychol., 46*(2), 99–106.

Petersen, A. C., Compas, B., & Brooks-Gunn, J. (1991). *Depression in adolescence: Implications of current research for programs and policy.* Report prepared for the Carnegie Council on Adolescent Development, Washington, DC.

Petersen, A. C., Compas, B. E., Brooks-Gunn, J., Ey, S., & Grant, K. E. (1993). Depression in adolescence. *Amer. Psychol., 48*(2), 155–168.

Peterson, C. (1993). Helpless behavior. *Behav. Res. Ther., 31*(3), 289–295.

Peterson, C., Colvin, D., & Lin, E. H. (1992). Explanatory style and helplessness. *Soc. Behav. Pers. 20*(1), 1–13.

Petrella, R. C., Benedek, E. P., Bank, S. C., & Packer, I. K. (1985). Examining the application of the guilty but mentally ill verdict in Michigan. *Hosp. Comm. Psychiat., 36*(3), 254–259.

Pfeffer, C. R. (1986). *The suicidal child.* New York: Guilford.

Pfeffer, C. R. (1988). Risk factors associated with youth suicide: A clinical perspective. *Psychiat. Ann., 18*(11), 652–656.

Pfeffer, C. R. (1990). Clinical perspectives on treatment of suicidal behavior among children and adolescents. *Psychiat. Ann., 20*(3), 143–150.

Pfeffer, C. R. (1993). Suicidal children. In A. A. Leenaars (Ed.), *Suicidology.* Northvale, NJ: Jason Aronson.

Pfeifer, M. P., & Snodgrass, G. L. (1990). The continued use of retractable invalid scientific literature. *JAMA, 263*(10), 1420–1427.

Pfeifer, S. I., & Nelson, D. D. (1992). The cutting edge in services for people with autism. *J. Autism Dev. Dis., 22*(1), 95–105.

Phares, E. J. (1979). *Clinical psychology: Concepts, methods, and profession.* Homewood, IL: Dorsey.

Phelan, J. (1976). *Howard Hughes: The hidden years.* New York: Random House.

Phelps, L., & Grabowski, J. (1993). Fetal Alcohol Syndrome: Diagnostic features and psychoeducational risk factors. *School Psychol. Quart., 7*(2), 112–128.

Philipp, E., Willershausen-Zonnchen, B., Hamm, G., & Pirke, K. M. (1991). Oral and dental characteristics in bulimic and anorectic patients. *Inter. J. Eat. Dis., 10*(4), 423–431.

Phillips, D. P. (1983). The impact of mass media violence on U.S. homicides. *Amer. Sociol. Rev., 48,* 560–568.

Phillips, D. P., Lesyna, K., P. Paight, D. J. (1992). Suicide and the media. In R. W. Maris, A. L. Berman, J. T. Maltsberger, & R. I. Yufit (Eds.), *Assessment and prediction of suicide.* New York: Guilford.

Phillips, D. P., & Ruth, T. E. (1993). Adequacy of official suicide statistics for scientific research and public policy. *Suic, Life-Threat. Behav., 23*(4), 307–319.

Phillips, K. A., McElroy, S. L., Keck, P. E., Pope, H. G., et al. (1993). Body dysmorphic disorder: 30 cases of imagined ugliness. *Amer. J. Psychiat., 150*(2), 302–308.

Philpott, R. M. (1990). Affective disorder and physical illness in old age. *Inter. Clin. Psychopharm., 5*(3), 7–20.

Physicians' Desk Reference (48th ed.). (1994). Montvalle, NJ: Medical Economic Data Production Company.

Pickar, D., Owen, R. R., & Litman, R. E. (1991). New developments in pharmacotherapy of schizophrenia. In A. Tasman & S. M. Goldfinger (Eds.), *American Psychiatric Press review of psychiatry* (Volume 10). Washington, DC: American Psychiatric Press.

Pickens, R., & Fletcher, B. (1991). Overview of treatment issues. In R. Pickens, C. Leukefeld & C. Schuster (Eds.), *Improving drug abuse treatment.* Rockville, MD: National Institute on Drug Abuse.

Pietrofesa, J. J. et al. (1990). The mental health counselor and "duty to warn." *J. Mental Hlth. Couns., 12*(2), 129–137.

Pine, C. J. (1981). Suicide in American Indian and Alaskan native tradition. *White Cloud J., 2*(3), 3–8.

Pinkston, E. M., & Linsk, N. L. (1984). Behavioral family intervention with the impaired elderly. *Gerontologist, 24,* 576–583.

Pithers, W. D. (1990). Relapse prevention with sexual aggressors. In W. L. Marshall, D. R. Laws, & H. E. Barbaree (Eds.), *Handbook of sexual assault.* New York: Plenum.

Pithers, W. D., & Cumming, G. F. (1989). Can relapses be prevented? Initial outcome data for the Vermont Treatment Program for Sexual Aggressors. In D. R. Laws (Ed.), *Relapse prevention with sex offenders.* New York: Guilford.

Plakun, E. M. (1991). Prediction of outcome in borderline personality disorder. *J. Pers. Dis., 5*(2), 93–101.

Plasse, T. F. et al. (1991). Recent clinical experience with dronabinol. *Pharm. Biochem. Beh., 40,* 695.

Plotkin, R. (1983). *Cognitive mediation in disciplinary action among mothers who have absued or neglected their children: Dispositional and environmental factors.* Unpublished doctoral dissertation. Univ. Rochester.

Pogue-Geile, M. F. (1989). The prognostic significance of negative symptoms in schizophrenia. Symposium: Negative symptoms in schizophrenia (1987, London, England). *Brit. J. Psychiat., 155*(7, Suppl.), 123–127.

Polcin, D. (1992). Issues in the treatment of dual diagnosis clients who have chronic mental illness. *Profess. Psychol. Res. Pract., 23*(1), 30–37.

Polivy, J., & Herman, C. P. (1985). Dieting and bingeing: A causal analysis. *Amer. Psychol., 40,* 193–201.

Polk, W. M. (1983). Treatment of exhibitionism in a 38-year-old male by hypnotically assisted covert sensitization. *Inter. J. Clin. Exp. Hyp., 31,* 132–138.

Pollack, J. M. (1987). Relationship of obsessive-compulsive personality to obsessive-compulsive disorder: A review of the literature. *J. Psychol., 121*(2), 137–148.

Pollack, W. (1989). Schizophrenia and the self: Contributions of psychoanalytic self-psychology. *Schizo. Bull., 15*(2), 311–322.

Pomara, N., Deptula, D., Singh, R., & Monroy, C. (1991). Cognitive toxicity of benzodiazepines in the elderly. In C. Salzman & B. D. Lebowitz (Eds.), *Anxiety in the elderly.* New York: Springer.

Pope, H. G., Hudson, J. I., & Jonas, J. M. (1983). Antidepressant treatment of bulimia: Preliminary experience and practical recommendations. *J. Psychiat., 140,* 554–558.

Pope, H. G., Hudson, J. I., & Jonas, J. M. (1983). Bulimia treated with imipramine: A placebo-controlled, double-blind study. *Amer. J. Psychiat., 140*(5), 554–558.

Pope, K. S., & Bouhoutsos, J. (1986). *Sexual intimacy between therapists and patients.* New York: Praeger.

Pope, K. S., Tabachnick, B. G., & Keith-Spiegel, P. (1987). Ethics of practice: The beliefs and behaviors of psychologists as therapists. *Amer. Psychol., 42*(11), 993–1166.

Popper, C. W. (1988). Disorders usually first evident in infancy, childhood, or adolescence, In J. Talbott, R. S. Hales, & S. C. Yudofsky (Eds.), *Textbook of psychiatry.* American Psychiatric Press.

Poretz, M., & Sinrod, B. (1991). *Do you do it with the lights on?* New York: Ballantine Books.

Portegies, P., Enting, R. H., de Gans, J., Algra, P. R., Derix, M. M., Lange, J. M., & Goudsmit, J. (1993). Presentation and coures of AIDS dementia complex: 10 years of following in Amsterdam & The Netherlands. *AIDS, 7*(5), 669–675.

Porter, S., Kelly, K. A., & Grame, C. J. (1993). Family treatment of spouses and children of patients with multiple personality disorder. *Bull. Menninger Clin., 57*(3), 371–379.

Post, R. M., Ballanger, J. C., & Goodwin, F. K. (1980). Cerebrospinal fluid studies of neurotransmitter function in manic and depressive illness. In J. H. Wood (Ed.), *The neurobiology of cerebrospinal fluid, Volume 1.* New York: Plenum.

Post, R. M. et al. (1978). Cerebrospinal fluid norepinephrine in affective illness. *Amer. J. Psychiat., 135*(8), 907–912.

Poulson, R. L. (1990). Mock juror attribution of criminal responsibility: Effects of race and the guilty but mentally ill (GBMI) option: *J. Appl. Soc. Psychol,. 20*(19), 1596–1611.

Powers, P. S., Schocken, D. D., Feld, J., Holloway, J. D., et al. (1991). Cardiac function during weight restoration in anorexia nervosa. *Inter. J. Eat. Dis., 10*(5), 521–530.

Prehn, R. A. (1990). Medication refusal: Suggestions for intervention. *Psychiat. Hosp., 21*(1), 37–40.

Price, J. (1988). How to stabilize families: A therapist's guide to maintaining the status quo. *J. Strategic & Systemic Ther., 7*(4), 21–27.

Price, R. W., Brew, B., Sidtis, J., Rosenblum, M., Scheck, A. C., & Cleary, P. (1988). The brain in AIDS: Central nervous system HIV-1 infection and AIDS dementia complex. *Sci. 239,* 586–592.

Prien, R. F. (1992). Maintenance treatment. In E. S. Paykel (Ed.), *Handbook of affective disorders.* New York: Guilford.

Prien, R. F., Caffey, E. M., Jr., & Klett, C. J. (1974). Factors associated with treatment success in lithium carbonate prophylaxis. *Arch. Gen. Psychiat., 31,* 189–192.

Primac, D. W. (1993). Measuring change in a brief therapy of a compulsive personality. *Psych. Rep., 72*(1), 309–310.

Prochaska, J. O. (1984). *Systems of psychotherapy.* Chicago: Dorsey.

Prochaska, J. O., DiClemente, C. C., & Norcross, J. C. (1992). In search of how people change. *Amer. Psychol., 47*(9), 1102–1114.

Prochaska, J. O., & Norcross, J. C. (1994). *Systems of psychotherapy: A transtheoretical analysis* (3rd ed.). Pacific Grove, CA: Brooks/Cole.

Prusiner, S. B. (1991). Molecular biology of prion diseases. *Sci. 252,* 1515–1522.

Prussin, R. A., & Harvey, P. D. (1991). Depression, dietary restraint, and binge eating in female runners. *Addic. Behav., 16*(5), 295–301.

Puente, A. E. (1990). Psychological assessment of minority group members. In G. Goldstein & M. Hersen (Eds.), *Handbook of psychological assessment* (2nd ed.). *Pergamon general psychology series, Vol. 131.* New York: Pergamon.

Pueschel, S. M., & Thuline, H. C. (1991). Chromosome disorders. In J. L. Matson & J. A. Mulick (Eds.), *Handbook of mental retardation.* New York: Pergamon.

Puri, B. K., Baxter, R., Cordess, C. C. (1995). Characteristics of fire-setters: A study and proposed multiaxial psychiatric classification, *Brit. J. Psychiat., 166,* 393–396.

Putnam, F. W. (1984). The psychophysiologic investigation of multiple personality disorder. *Psychiat. Clin. N. Amer., 7,* 31–40.

Putnam, F. W. (1985). Dissociation as a response to extreme trauma. In R. P. Kluft, *Childhood antecedents of multiple personality.* Washington, DC: American Psychiatric Press.

Putnam, F. W. (1985). Multiple personality disorder. *Med. Aspects Human Sex., 19*(6), 59–74.

Putnam, F. W. (1988). The switch process in multiple personality disorder and other state-change disorders. *Dissoc., 1,* 24–32.

Putnam, F. W. (1992). Are alter personalities fragments of figments? *Psychoanalytic Inquiry, 12*(1), 95–111.

Putnam, F. W., Guroff, J. J., Silberman, E. K., Barban, L., et al. (1986). The clinical phenomenology of multiple personality disorder: Review of 100 recent cases. *J. Clin. Psych., 47*(6), 285–293.

Putnam, F. W., Zahn, T. P., & Post, R. M. (1990). Differential autonomic nervous system activity in multiple personality disorder. *Psychiat. Res., 31*(3), 251–260.

Quality Assurance Project. (1990). Treatment outlines for paranoid, schizotypal and schizoid personality disorders. *Austral. New Zeal. J. Psychiat., 24,* 339–350.

Quality Assurance Project. (1991). Treatment outlines for antisocial personality disorder. *Austral. New Zeal. J. Psychiat., 25,* 541–547.

Quevillon, R. P. (1993). Vaginismus. In W. O'Donohue & J. Geer (Eds.), *Handbook of sexual dysfunctions.* Boston: Allyn and Bacon.

Quinsey, V. L., & Earls, G. M. (1990). The modificator of sexual preferences. In W. L. Marshall, D. R. Laws, & H. E. Barbaree (Eds.), *Handbook of sexual assault.* New York: Plenum.

Rabins, P. V. & Folstein, M. F. (1982). Delirium and dementia: Diagnostic criteria and fatality rates. *Brit. J. Psychiat., 140,* 149–153.

Raboch, J., & Raboch, J. (1992). Infrequent orgasm in women. *J. Sex and Marit. Ther., 18*(2), 114–120.

Rachman, S. (1966). Sexual fetishism: An experimental analog. *Psych. Rec., 18,* 25–27.

Rachman, S. (1985). A note on the conditioning theory of fear acquisition. *Behav. Ther., 16*(4), 426–428.

Rachman, S. (1985). Obsessional-compulsive disorders. In B. P. Bradley & C. T. Thompson (Eds.), *Psychological applications in psychiatry.* Chichester, England: Wiley.

Rachman, S. (1985). The treatment of anxiety disorders: A critique of the implications of psychopathology. In A. Tuma and J. Maser (Eds.), *Anxiety and the anxiety disorders.* Hillsdale, NJ: Erlbaum.

Rachman, S. (1993). Obsessions, responsibility and guilt. *Behav. Res. Ther., 31*(2), 149–154.

Rachman, S., & Hodgson, R. (1980). *Obsessions and compulsions.* Englewood Cliffs, NJ: Prentice Hall.

Rachman, S., Hodgson, R., & Marzillier, J. (1970). Treatment of an obsessional-compulsive disorder by modelling. *Behav. Res. Ther., 8,* 385–392.

Ragin, A. B., Pogue-Geile, M. F., & Oltmanns, T. F. (1989). Poverty of speech in schizophrenia and depression during inpatient and post-hospital periods. *Brit. J. Psychiat., 154,* 52–57.

Ragland, J. D., & Berman, A. L. (1991). Farm crisis and suicide: Dying on the vine? *Omega J. of Death and Dying, 22*(3), 173–185.

Rahe, R. H. (1968). *Life-change measurement as a predictor of illness.* Proceedings of the Royal Society of Medicine, 61, 1124–1126.

Raine, A. (1989). Evoked potentials and psychopathy. *Int. J. Psychophysiol., 8*(1), 1–16.

Raine, A., Lencz, T., Reynolds, G. P., Harrison, G., et al. (1992). An evaluation of structural and functional prefrontal deficits in schizophrenia: MRI and neuropsychological measures. *Psychiat. Res. Neuroimaging, 45*(2), 123–137.

Raine, A., Sheard, C., Reynolds, G. P., & Lencz, T. (1992). Prefrontal structural and functional deficits associated with individual differences in schizotypal personality. *Schiz. Res., 7*(3), 237–247.

Ramm, E., Marks, I. M., Yuksel, S., & Stern, R. S. (1981). Anxiety management training for anxiety states: Positive compared with negative self-statements. *Brit. J. Psychiat., 140,* 367–373.

Rand, C. S., & Kuldau, J. M. (1991). Restrained eating (weight concerns) in the general population and among students. *Inter. J. Eat. Dis., 10*(6), 699–708.

Rapee, R. M. (1993). Psychological factors in panic disorder. *Adv. Behav. Res. Ther., 15*(1), 85–102.

Rapee, R. M. (1995). Psychological factors influencing the affective response to biological challenge procedures in panic disorder. *Journal of Anxiety Disorders, 9*(1), 59–74.

Raphling, D. L. (1989). Fetishism in a woman. *J. Amer. Psychoanal. Assoc., 37*(2), 465–491.

Rapoport, J. L. (1989, March). The biology of obsessions and compulsions. *Scientif. Amer.,* 82–89.

Rapoport, J. L. (1991). Recent advances in obsessive-compulsive disorder. *Neuropsychopharm., 5*(1), 1–10.

Raskin, D. C. (1982). The scientific basis of polygraph techniques and their uses in the judicial process. In A. Trankell (Ed.), *Reconstructing the past: The role of psychologists in criminal trials.* Stockholm: Norstedt & Soners.

Raskin, M., Peeke, H. V. S., Dickman, W., & Pinkster, H. (1982). Panic and generalized anxiety disorders: Developmental antecedents and precipitants. *Arch. Gen. Psychiat., 39,* 687–689.

Raskin, N. H., Hobobuchi, Y., & Lamb, S. A. (1987). Headaches may arise from perturbation of the brain. *Headache, 27,* 416–420.

Raskin, N. J., & Rogers, C. R. (1989). Person-centered therapy. In R. J. Corsini & D. Wedding (Eds.), *Current psychotherapies.* Itasca, IL: Peacock.

Rathner, G., Bönsch, C., Maurer, G., Walter, M. H., & Säollner, W. (1993). The impact of a 'guided self-help group' on bulimic women: A prospective 15-month study of attenders and non-attenders. *J. Psychosom. Res., 37*(4), 389–396.

Ray, O., & Ksir, C. (1993). Drugs, society, & human behavior. St. Louis: Mosby.

Rebert, W. M., Stanton, A. L., Schwarz, R. M. (1991). Influence of personality attributes and daily moods on bulimic eating patterns. *Addict. Behav., 16*(6), 497–505.

Redefer, L. A., & Goodman, J. F. (1989). Pet-facilitated therapy with autistic children. *J. Autism Dev. Dis., 19*(3), 461–467.

Redick, R. W., Witkin, M. J., Atay, J. E., & Manderscheid, R. W. (1992). Specialty mental health system characteristics. In R. W. Manderscheid & M. A. Sonnenschein (Eds.), *Mental health, United States, 1992.* Washington, DC: U.S. Department of Health and Human Services.

Redmond, D. E. (1977). Alterations in the function of the nucleus locus coeruleus: A possible model for studies of anxiety. In I. Hanin & E. Usdin (Eds.), *Animal models in psychiatry and neurology.* New York: Pergamon.

Redmond, D. E. (1979). New and old evidence for the involvement of a brain norepinephrine system in anxiety. In W. E. Fann, I. Karacan, A. D. Pokorny, & R. L. Williams (Eds.), *Phenomenology and treatment of anxiety.* New York: Spectrum.

Redmond, D. E. (1981). Clonidine and the primate locus coeruleus: Evidence suggesting anxiolytic and anti-withdrawal effects. In H. Lal & S. Fielding, *Psychopharmacology of clonidine.* New York: Alan R. Liss.

Rees, L. (1964). The importance of psychological, allergic and infective factors in childhood asthma. *J. Psychosom. Res., 7*(4), 253–262.

Regier, D. A., Narrow, W. E., Rae, D. S., Manderscheid, R. W., Locke, B. Z., & Goodwin, F. K. (1993). The de facto U.S. Mental and Addictive Disorders Service System: Epidemiologic Catchment Area prospective 1-year prevalence rates of disorders in services. *Arch. Gen. Psychiat., 50,* 85–94.

Reich, J. H. (1987). Sex distribution of DSM-III personality disorders in psychiatric outpatients. *Amer. J. Psychiat., 144*(4), 485–488.

Reich, J. H. (1990). Comparisons of males and females with DSM-III dependent personality disorder. *Psychiat. Res., 33*(2), 207–214.

Reid, R., & Lininger, T. (1993). Sexual pain disorders in the female. In W. O'Donohue and J. Geer (Eds.), *Handbook of sexual dysfunctions.* Boston: Allyn and Bacon.

Reid, W. H., & Burke, W. J. (1989). Antisocial personality disorder. In American Psychiatric Association (Eds.), *Treatments of psychiatric disorders: A task force report of the American Psychiatric Association.* Washington, DC: American Psychiatric Press.

Reik, T. (1989). The characteristics of masochism. *Amer. Imago, 46*(2-3), 161–195.

Reis, B. E. (1993). Toward a psychoanalytic understanding of multiple personality disorder. *Bull. Menninger Clin., 57*(3), 309–318.

Reisman, J. M. (1991). *A history of clinical psychology* (2nd ed.). New York: Hemisphere Pub. Corp.

Reiss, S. (1985). The mentally retarded, emotionally disturbed adult. In M. Sigman (Ed.), *Children with emotional disorders and developmental disabilities.* New York: Grune & Stratton.

Reitan, R. M., & Wolfson, D. (1985). *The Halstead-Reitan Neuropsychological Test Battery: Theory and clinical interpretation*. Tucson, AZ: Neuropsychology.

Remington, G., Pollock, B., Voineskos, G., Reed, K., & Coulter, K. (1993). Acutely psychotic patients receiving high-dose Haloperidol therapy. *J. Clin. Psychopharmacol., 13*(1), 41–45.

Renneberg, G., Goldstein, A. J., Phillips, D., Chambless, D. L. (1990). Intensive behavioral group treatment of avoidant personality disorder. *Behav. Ther., 21*(3), 363–377.

Repp, A. C., Barton, L. E., & Brulle, A. R. (1986). Assessing a least restrictive educational environment transfer through social comparison. *Educ. & Training of the Ment. Retarded, 21*(1), 54–61.

Resick, P. A. (1987). Psychological effects of victimization: Implications for the criminal justice system. *Crime & Delinquency, 22*, 468–478.

Restak, R. M. (1979). The sex-change conspiracy. *Psych. Today, 20*, 20–25.

Rice, K. M., & Blanchard, E. B. (1982). Biofeedback in the treatment of anxiety disorder. *Clin. Psychol. Rev., 2*, 557–577.

Richman, J. (1991). Suicide and the elderly. In A. A. Leenaars (Ed.), *Life span perspectives of suicide: Time-lines in the suicide process*. New York: Plenum.

Richman, N. E., & Sokolove, R. L. (1992). The experience of aloneness, object representation, and evocative memory in borderline and neurotic patients. *Psychoanal. Psychiat., 9*(1), 77–91.

Rickels, K., & Schweizer, E. (1990). The clinical course and long-term management of generalized anxiety disorder. *J. Clin. Psychopharm., 10*(Suppl. 3), 101–110.

Rickels, K., Schweizer, E., Weiss, S., & Zavodnick, S. (1993). Maintenance drug treatment for panic disorder II. Short- and long-term outcome after drug taper. *Arch. Gen. Psychiat., 50*, 61–68.

Rietvald, W. J. (1992). Neurotransmitters and the pharmacology of the suprachiasmatic nuclei. *Pharmacol. Therapy, 56*(1), 119–130.

Riggs, D. S., & Foa, E. B. (1993). Obsessive–compulsive disorder. In D. H. Barlow (Ed.), *Clinical handbook of psychological disorders: A step-by-step treatment manual* (2nd ed.). New York: Guilford.

Rimland, B. (1992). *Form letter regarding high–dosage vitamin B6 and magnesium therapy for autism and related disorders*. Autism Research Institute, publication 39E.

Rimland, B. (1992). *Leominster: Is pollution a cause of autism?* Autism Research Review International, 6(2), 1.

Ringuette, E., & Kennedy, T. (1966). An experimental study of the double bind hypothesis. *J. Abnorm. Psychol., 71*, 136–141.

Ritchie, E. C. (1992). Treatment of gas mask phobia. *Military Med., 157*(2), 104–106.

Roache, J. D., Cherek, D. R., Bennett, R. H., Schenkler, J. C., & Cowan, K. A. (1993). Differential effects of triazolam and ethanol on awareness, memory, and psychomotor performance. *J. Clin. Psychopharmacol., 13*(1), 3–15.

Roazen, P. (1992). The rise and fall of Bruno Bettelheim. *Psychohist. Rev., 20*(3), 221–250.

Robbins, D. R., & Alessi, N. C. (1985). Depressive symptoms and suicidal behavior in adolescents. *Amer. J. Psychiat., 142*(5), 588–592.

Roberts, A. R. (1979). Organization of suicide prevention agencies. In L. D. Hankoff & B. Einsidler (Eds.), *Suicide: Theory and clinical aspects*. Littleton, MA: PSG Publishing Company.

Roberts, A. R. (1990). *Crisis intervention handbook: Assessment, intervention, and research*. Belmont, CA: Wadsworth.

Roberts, G. W., Gentleman, S. M., Lynch, A., & Graham, D. I. (1991). Beta-A4 amyloid protein deposition in brain after head trauma. *Lancet, 338*, 1422–1423.

Robertson, M. (1992). *Starving in the silence: An exploration of anorexia nervosa*. New York: New York University Press.

Robertson, E. (1992). The challenge of dual diagnosis. *J. Hlth. Care for the Poor and Underserved, 3*(1), 198–207.

Robins, L. N., Locke, B. Z., & Regier, D. A. (1991). An overview of psychiatric disorders in America. In L. N. Robins, & D. A. Regier (Eds.), *Psychiatric disorders in America: The Epidemiological Catchment Area Study*. New York: Free Press.

Rodin, J. (1992). Sick of worrying about the way you look? Read this. *Psych. Today, 25*(1), 56–60.

Rodriguez, O. (1986). Overcoming barriers to services among chronically mentally ill Hispanics: Lessons from the Project COPA evaluation: *Research Bulletin, 9*(1), Hispanic Research Center, Fordham University, Bronx, New York: .

Roehrich, L. & Kinder, B. N. (1991). Alcohol expectancies and male sexuality: Review and implications for sex therapy. *J. Sex and Marit. Ther., 17*(1), 45–54.

Roesler, T. A., & McKenzie, N. (1994). Effects of childhood trauma on psychological functioning adults sexually abused as children. *J. Nerv. Ment. Dis., 182*(3), 145–150.

Rogers, C. R. (1951). *Client-centered therapy*. Boston: Houghton Mifflin.

Rogers, C. R. (1961). *On becoming a person*. Boston: Houghton Mifflin.

Rogers, C. R. (Ed.), (1967). *The therapeutic relationship and its impact: A study of psychotherapy with schizophrenics*. Madison, WI: Univ. Wisconsin.

Rogers, C. R. (1987). Rogers, Kohut, and Erickson: A personal perspective on some similarities and differences. In J. K. Zeig (Ed.), *The evolution of psychotherapy*. New York: Brunner/Mazel.

Rogers, C. R., & Dymond, R. (1954). *Psychotherapy and personality change*. Chicago: Univ. Chicago.

Rogers, C. R., & Sanford, R. C. (1989). Client-centered psychotherapy. In H. I. Kaplan & B. J. Sadock (Eds.), *Comprehensive textbook of psychiatry* (Vol. 1, 5th ed.). Baltimore: Williams & Wilkins.

Rogers, J. C., & Holloway, R. L. (1990). Assessing threats to the validity of experimental and observational designs. *Fam. Prac. Res. J., 10*(2), 81–95.

Rogers, R. (1987). Assessment of criminal responsibility: Empirical advances and unanswered questions. *J. Psychiat. & Law, 51*(1), 73–82.

Rogers, R., & Ewing, C. P. (1992). The measurement of insanity: Debating the merits of the R-CRAS and its alternatives. *Inter. J. Law Psychiat., 15*, 113–123.

Rogler, L. H., Malgady, R. G., & Rodriguez, O. (1989). *Hispanics and mental health: A framework for research*. Malabar, FL: Krieger Publishing Company.

Rohsenow, D. J., Smith, R. E., & Johnson, S. (1985). Stress–management training as a prevention program for heavy social drinkers: Cognition, affect, drinking, and individual differences. *Addic. Behav., 10*(1), 45–54.

Roll, M., & Theorell, T. (1987). Acute chest pain without obvious organic cause before age 40: Personality and recent life events. *J. Psychosom. Res., 31*(2), 215–221.

Rolls, B. J., Fedroff, I. C., & Guthrie, J. F. (1991). Gender differences in eating behavior and body weight regulation. *Hlth. Psychol., 10*(2), 133–142.

Ronen, T. (1993). Intervention package for treating encopresis in a 6-year-old boy: A case study. *Behav. Psychother., 21*, 127–135.

Ronen, T., Wozner, Y., & Rahav, G. (1992). Cognitive intervention in enuresis. *Child Fam. Beh. Ther., 14*(2), 1–14.

Roper, G., Rachman, S., & Hodgson, R. (1973). An experiment on obsessional checking. *Behav. Res. Ther., 11*, 271–277.

Roper, M. (1992). Reaching the babies through the mothers: The effects of prosecution on pregnant substance abusers. *Law Psychol. Rev., 16*, 171–188.

Roscoe, B., Martin, G. L., & Pear, J. J. (1980). Systematic self–desensitization of fear of flying: A case study. In G. L. Martin and J. G. Osborne (Eds.), *Helping in the community: Behavioral applications*. New York: Plenum.

Rosen, J. C., & Gross, J. (1987). Prevalence of weight reducing and weight gaining in adolescent girls and boys. *Hlth. Psychol., 6*, 131–147.

Rosen, J. C., & Leitenberg, H. (1982). Bulimia nervosa: Treatment with exposure and response prevention. *Behav. Ther., 13*(1), 117–124.

Rosen, J. C., & Leitenberg, H. (1985). Exposure plus response prevention treatment of bulimia. In D. M. Garner & P. E. Garfinkel (Eds.), *Handbook of psychotherapy for anorexia nervosa and bulimia*. New York: Guilford.

Rosen, J. C., Orosan, P., & Reiter, J. (1995). Cognitive behavior therapy for negative body image in obese women. *Behav. Ther., 26*, 25–42.

Rosenbaum, M. (1980). The role of the term schizophrenia in the decline of diagnoses of multiple personality. *Arch. Gen. Psychiat., 37*(12), 1383–1385.

Rosenbaum, M., & Berger, M. (Eds.), (1963). *Group psychotherapy and group function*. New York: Basic Books.

Rosenberg, H. (1993). Prediction of controlled drinking by alcoholics and problem drinkers. *Psychol. Bull., 113*(1), 129–139.

Rosenhan, D. L. (1973). On being sane in insane places. *Sci., 179*(4070), 250–258.

Rosenman, R. H. (1990). Type A behavior pattern: A personal overview. *J. Soc. Behav. Pers., 5*, 1–24.

Rosenstein, M. J., Milazzo-Sayre, L. J., & Manderscheid, R. W. (1989). Care of persons with schizophrenia: A statisical profile. *Schizo. Bull., 15*(1), 45–58.

Rosenstein, M. J., Milazzo-Sayre, L. J., & Manderscheid, R. W. (1990). Characteristics of persons using specialty inpatient, outpatient, and partial care programs in 1986. In R. W. Manderscheid & M. A. Sonnenschein (Eds.), *Mental health, United States, 1990*. DHHS Pub. No. (ADM)90-1708. Washington, DC: GPO.

Rosenthal, N. E., & Blehar, M. C. (Eds.), (1989). *Seasonal affective disorders and phototherapy*. New York: Guilford.

Rosenthal, R. (1966). *Experimenter effects in behavioral research*. New York: Appleton-Century-Crofts.

Rosenthal, R. J. (1992). Pathological gambling. *Psychiat. Ann., 22*(2), 72–78.

Roskies, E., Seraganian, P., Oseasohn, R., Hanley, J. A., Collu, R., Martin, N.,

& Smigla, C. (1986). The Montreal Type A Intervention Project: Major findings. *Hlth. Psychol., 5,* 45–69.

Ross, A. O. (1981). *Child behavior therapy: Principles, procedures and empirical basis.* New York: Wiley.

Ross, C. A., & Gahan, P. (1988). Techniques in the treatment of multiple personality disorder. *Amer. J. Psychother., 42*(1), 40–52.

Ross, C. A., Miller, S. D., Bjornson, L., Reagor, P., Fraser, G. A., & Anderson G. (1991). Abuse histories in 102 cases of multiple personality disorder. *Canad. J. Psychiat., 36,* 97–101.

Ross, C. A., Miller, S. D., Reagor, P., & Bjornson, L., et al. (1990). Structured interview data on 102 cases of multiple personality disorder from four centers. *Amer. J. Psychiat., 147*(5), 596–601.

Ross, C. A., Norton, G. R., & Wozney, K. (1989). Multiple personality disorder: An analysis of 236 cases. *Canad. J. Psychiat., 34*(5), 413–418.

Ross, S. B. (1983). The therapeutic use of animals with the handicapped. *Inter. Child Welfare Rev., 56,* 26–39.

Ross, S. M., Gottfredson, D. K., Christensen, P., & Weaver, R. (1986). Cognitive self statements in depression: Findings across clinical populations. *Cog. Ther. Res., 10*(2), 159–165.

Rothbaum, B. O., Foa, E. B., Riggs, D. S., Murdock, T., & Walsh, W. (1992). A prospective examination of post–traumatic stress disorder in rape victims. *J. of Traumatic Stress, 5*(3), 455–475.

Rothblum, E. D. (1992). The stigma of women's weight: Social and economic realities. *Fem. and Psychol., 2*(1), 61–73.

Rotheram-Borus, M. J., Piacentini, J., Miller, S., Graae, F., & Castro-Blanco, D. (1994). Brief cognitive-behavioral treatment for adolescent suicide attempters and their families. *J. Amer. Acad. Child Adol. Psychiat., 33*(4), 508–517.

Rothman, D. (1985). *ECT: The historical, social and professional sources of the controversy.* In NIH Consensus Development Conference: Electroconvulsive therapy. Bethesda, MD: NIH & NIMH.

Rotter, M., Kalus, O., Losonczy, M., Guo, L., et al. (1991). Lateral ventricular enlargement in schizotypal personality disorder. *Bio. Psychiat., 29,* 182–185.

Rovner, S. (1993, April 6). Anxiety disorders are real and expensive. *Washington Post,* p. WH5.

Roy, A. (1982). Suicide in chronic schizophrenics. *Brit. J. Psychiat., 141,* 171–177.

Roy, A. (1992). Genetics, biology, and suicide in the family. In R. W. Maris, A. L. Berman, J. T. Maltsberger, & R. I. Yufit (Eds.), *Assessment and prediction of suicide.* New York: Guilford.

Roy, A. (1992). Suicide in schizophrenia. *Inter. Rev. Psychiat., 4*(2), 205–209.

Roy-Byrne, P. P., & Wingerson, D. (1992). Pharmacotherapy of anxiety disorders. In A. Tasman, & M. B. Riba (Eds.), *Review of psychiatry* (Vol. 11). Washington, DC: American Psychiatric Press.

Rozin, P., & Stoess, C. (1993). Is there a general tendency to become addicted? *Addic. Behav., 18,* 81–87.

Rozynko, V., & Dondershine, H. E. (1991). Trauma focus group therapy for Vietnam veterans with PTSD. *Psychother., 28*(1), 157–161.

Rubonis, A. V., & Bickman, L. (1991). Psychological impairment in the wake of disaster: The disaster-psychopathology relationship. *Psychol. Bull., 109,* 384–399.

Rudolph, J., Langer, I., & Tausch, R. (1980). An investigation of the psychological affects and conditions of person-centered individual psychotherapy. *Zeitschrift für Klinische Psychologie: Forschung und Praxis, 9,* 23–33.

Ruedrich, S. L., Chu, C., & Wadle, C. V. (1985). The amytal interview in the treatment of psychogenic amnesia [Speical Issue]. *Hosp. Comm. Psychiat., 36*(10), 1045–1046.

Russell, G. (1981). The current treatment of anorexia nervosa. *Brit. J. Psychiat., 138,* 164–166.

Russell, R. J., & Hulson, B. (1992). Physical and psychological abuse of heterosexual partners. *Personality and Indiv. Differences, 13*(4), 457–473.

Rutter, M. (1966). Prognosis: Psychotic children in adolescence and early adult life. In J. K. Wing (Ed.), *Childhood autism: Clinical, educational, and social aspects.* Elmsford, NY: Pergamon.

Rutter, M. (1968). Concepts of autism: A review of research. *J. Child Psychol. Psychiat. Allied Disc., 9,* 1–25.

Rutter, M. (1971). The description and classification of infantile autism. In D. Churchill, D. Alpern, & M. DeMeyer, *Infantile autism.* Springfield, IL: Thomas.

Rutter, M., & Bartak, L. (1971). Causes of infantile autism: Some considerations from recent research. *J. Autism Child. Schizo., 1,* 20–32.

Sachs, R. G. (1986). The adjunctive role of social support systems. In B. G. Braun (Ed.), *The treatment of multiple personality disorder.* Washington, DC: American Psychiatric Press.

Sadock, B. J. (1989). Group psychotherapy, combined individual and group psychotherapy, and psychodrama. In H. I. Kaplan & B. J. Sadock (Eds.), *Comprehensive textbook of psychiatry* (Vol. 1, 5th ed.). Baltimore: Williams & Wilkins.

Sadock, V. A. (1989). Rape, spouse abuse, and incest. In H. J. Kaplan & B. J. Sadock (Eds.), *Comprehensive textbook of psychiatry* (Vol. 1, 5th ed.). Baltimore: Williams & Wilkins.

Safferman, A. Z., Lieberman, J. A., Kane, J. M., Szymanski, S., & Kinon, B. (1991). Update on the clinical efficacy and side effects of clozapine. *Schizo. Bull., 17*(2), 247–261.

Sakheim, D. K., Hess, E. P., & Chivas, A. (1988). General principles for short-term inpatient work with multiple personality-disorder patients. *Psychother., 24,* 117–124.

Salama, A. A. (1988). The antisocial personality (the sociopathic personality). *Psychiat., J. Univ. Ottawa, 13*(3), 149–151.

Sales, E., Baum, M., & Shore, B. (1984). Victim readjustment following assault. *J. Soc. Issues, 40*(1), 117–136.

Salisbury, J. J., & Mitchell, J. E. (1991). Bone mineral density and anorexia nervosa in women. *Amer. J. Psychiat., 148*(6), 768–774.

Salkovskis, P. M. (1985). Obsessional-compulsive problems: A cognitive-behavioural analysis. *Behav. Res. Ther., 23,* 571–584.

Salkovskis, P. M. (1989). Cognitive-behavioural factors and the persistence of intrusive thoughts in obsessional problems. *Behav. Res. Ther., 27,* 677–682.

Salkovskis, P. M., & Westbrook, D. (1989). Behaviour therapy and obsessional ruminations: Can failure be turned into success? *Behav. Res. Ther., 27,* 149–160.

Salzman, C. (1995). Medication compliance in the elderly. *J. Clin. Psychiat., 56,*[Suppl. 1] 18–22.

Salzman, L. (1968). *The obsessive personality.* New York: Science House.

Salzman, L. (1980). *Psychotherapy of the obsessive personality.* New York: Aronson.

Salzman, L. (1985). Psychotherapeutic management of obsessive-compulsive patients. *Amer. J. Psychother., 39*(3), 323–330.

Salzman, L. (1989). Compulsive personality disorder. In *Treatments of Psychiatric Disorders.* Washington, DC: American Psychiatric Press.

Sameroff, A. J., & Seifer, R. (1990). Early contributors to developmental risk. In J. E. Rolf, A. S. Masten, D. Cicchetti, K. H. Neuchterlein, & S. Weintraub (Eds.), *Risk and protective factors in the development of psychopathology.* New York: Cambridge UP.

Sanchez-Canovas, J., Botella-Arbona, C., Ballestin, G. P., & Soriano-Pastor, J. (1991). Intervencion comportamental y analisis ipsativo normativo en un trastorno de ansiedad. [Behavioral intervention and ipsative-normative analysis in an anxiety disorder]. *Analisis y Modificacion de Conducta, 17*(51), 115–151.

Sander, F. M., & Feldman, L. B. (1993). Integrating individual, marital, and family therapy. In J. M. Oldham, M. B. Riba, & A. Tasman (Eds.), *Review of psychiatry* (Vol. 12). Washington, DC: American Psychiatric Press.

Sanderman, R., & Ormel, J. (1992). De Utrechtse Coping Lijst (UCL): Validiteit en betrouwbaarheid [The Utrecht Coping List (UCL): Validity and reliability. *Gedrag and Gezondheid Tijdschrift voor Psychologie and Gezondheid, 20*(1), 32–37.

Sanderson, W. C., DiNardo, P. A., Rapee, R. M., & Barlow, D. H. (1990). Syndrome comorbidity in patients diagnosed with a DSM-III-R anxiety disorder. *J. Abnorm. Psychol., 99*(3), 308–312.

Sandoval, J., Davis, J. M., & Wilson, M. P. (1987). An overview of the school-based prevention of adolescent suicide. *Spec. Serv. in the Schools, 3*(3–4), 103–120.

Sanford, R. C. (1987). An inquiry into the evolution of the client-centered approach to psychotherapy. In J. K. Zeig (Ed.), *The evolution of psychotherapy.* New York: Brunner/Mazel.

Sarrel, P. M., & Sarrel, L. J. (1989). Dyspareunia and vaginismus. In American Psychiatric Association, *Treatments for psychiatric disorders: A task force report of the American Psychiatric Association.* Vol. 3, pp. 2291–2299. Washington, DC: American Psychiatric Association.

Satir, V. (1964). *Conjoint family therapy: A guide to therapy and technique.* Palo Alto, CA: Science & Behavior Books.

Satir, V. (1967). *Conjoint family therapy* (Rev. Ed.) Palo Alto, CA: Science and Behavior Books.

Satir, V. (1987). Going behind the obvious: The psychotherapeutic journey. In J. K. Zeig (Ed.), *The evolution of psychotherapy.* New York: Brunner/Mazel.

Saunders, D. G. (1992). A typology of men who batter: Three types derived from cluster analysis. *Amer. J. Orthopsychiat., 62*(2), 264–275.

Saunders, D. G. (1982). Counseling the violent husband. In P. A. Keller & L. G. Ritt (Eds.), *Innovations in clinical practice: A source book* (Vol. 1). Sarasota, FL: Professional Resource Exchange.

Saunders, R. (1985). Bulimia: An expanded definition. *Soc. Casework, 66*(10), 603–610.

Savishinsky, J. S. (1992). Intimacy, domesticity and pet therapy with the elderly: Expectation and experience among nursing home volunteers. *Soc. Sci. Med., 34*(12), 1325–1334.

Saxe, G. N., van der Kolk, B. A., Berkowitz, R., Chinman, G., Hall, K., Lieberg, G., & Schwartz, J. (1993). Dissociative disorders in psychiatric inpatients. *Amer. J. Psychiat., 150*(7), 1037–1042.

Saxe, L., Dougherty, D., & Cross, T. P. (1985). The validity of polygraph testing: Scientific analysis and public controversy. *Amer. Psychol., 40*(3), 355–366.

Schachter, D. L. (1989). Autobiographical memory in a case of multiple personality disorder. *J. Abnorm. Psychol., 98*(4), 508–514.

Schachter, D. L., Glisky, E. L., & McGlynn, S. M. (1990). Impact of memory disorder on everyday life: Awareness of deficits and return to work. In D. Tupper & K. Cicerone (Eds.), *The Neuropsychology of everyday life* (Vol. 1): Theories and basic competencies. Boston: Kluwer Academic Publishers.

Scheff, T. J. (1966). *Being mentally ill: A sociological theroy.* Chicago: Aldine.

Scheff, T. J. (1975). *Labeling madness.* Englewood Cliffs, NJ: Prentice Hall.

Schellenberg, G. D., Bird, T., Wijsman, E. M., et al. (1992). Genetic linkage evidence for a familiar Alzheimer's disease locus on chromosome 14. *Sci. 258,* 668–671.

Scherling, D. (1994). Prenatal cocaine exposure and childhood psychopathology: A developmental analysis. *Amer. J. Orthopsychiat., 64*(1), 9–19.

Schiavi, R. C., White, D., Mandeli, J., & Schreiner-Engel, P. (1993). Hormones and nocturnal penile tumescence in healthy aging men. *Arch. Sex. Behav., 22*(2), 207–216.

Schiele, B. C., & Brozek, J. (1948). Experimental neurosis resulting from semistarvation in man. *Psychosom. Med., 10,* 31–50.

Schiff, S. M. (1988). Treatment approaches for older alcoholics. *Generations, 12*(4), 41–45.

Schildkraut, J. J. (1965). The catecholamine hypothesis of affective disorders: A review of supporting evidence. *Amer. J. Psychiat., 122*(5), 509–522.

Schlichter, K. J., & Horan, J. J. (1981). Effects of stress inoculation on the anger and aggression management skills of institutionalized juvenile delinquents. *Cog. Ther. Res., 5*(4), 359–365.

Schloss, P. J., & Smith, M. A. (1994). *Applied Behavior analysis in the classroom.* Boston: Allyn & Bacon.

Schmauk, F. J. (1970). Punishment, arousal, and avoidance learning in sociopaths. *J. Abnorm. Psychol., 76*(3, Pt. 1), 325–335.

Schmidt, F. L. (1992). What do data really mean? Research findings, meta-analysis, and cumulative knowledge in psychology. *Amer. Psychol., 47*(10), 1173–1181.

Schneider, R. H., Alexander, C. N., & Wallace, R. K. (1992). In search of an optimal behavioral treatment for hypertension: A review and focus on transcendental meditation. In E. H. Johnson, W. D. Gentry, & S. Julius (Eds.), *Personality, elevated blood pressure, and essential hypertension.* Washington, DC: Hemisphere Pub. Corp.

Schneiderman, L., & Baum, A. (1992). Acute and chronic stress and the immune system. In N. Schneiderman, P. McCabe, & A. Baum (Eds.), *Perspectives in behavioral medicine: Stress and disease processes.* Hillsdale, NJ: Lawrence Erlbaum Associates.

Schneier, F. R., Spitzer, R. L., Gibbon, M., Fyer, A. J., et al. (1991). The relationship of social phobia subtypes and avoidant personality. *Comprehen. Psychiat., 32*(6), 496–502.

Schnurr, P. P., Friedman, M. J., & Rosenberg, S. D. (1993). Premilitary MMPI scores as predictors of combat-related PTSD symptoms. *Amer. J. Psychiat., 150*(3), 479–483.

Scholing, A., & Emmelkamp, P. M. G. (1993). Cognitive and behavioral treatments of fear of blushing, sweating or trembling. *Behav. Res. Ther., 31,* 155–170.

Scholing, A., & Emmelkamp, P. M. G. (1993). Exposure with and without cognitive therapy for generalized social phobia: Effects of individual and group treatment. *Behav. Res. Ther.*

Schover, L. R., & LoPiccolo, J. (1992). Treatment effectiveness for dysfunctions of sexual desires. *J. Sex Marit. Ther., 8*(3), 179–197.

Schreiber, F. R. (1973). *Sybil.* Chicago: Regnery.

Schuckit, M. A., & Schuckit, J. J. (1991). In L. Davidson & M. Linnoila (Eds.), *Risk factors for youth suicide.* New York: Hemisphere.

Schuldberg, D., French, C., Stone, B. L., & Heberle, J. (1988). Creativity and schizotypal traits: Creativity test scores and perceptual aberration, magical ideation, and impulsive nonconformity. *J. Nerv. Ment. Dis., 176*(11), 648–57.

Schulz, R. (1994). Report. Psychosomatic Society.

Schut, J. (1992). From the folks who brought you the hot-tub. *Institutional Investor, 26,* p. 171.

Schwartz, G. E. (1977). Psychosomatic disorders and biofeedback: A psychobiological model of disregulation. In J. D. Maser and M. E. P. Selig-

man (Eds.), *Psychopathology: Experimental models.* San Francisco: W. H. Freeman.

Schwartz, G. E. (1982). Testing the biopsychosocial model: The ultimate challenge facing behavioral medicine? *J. Cons. Clin. Psychol., 50*(6), 1040–1053.

Schwartz, S., & Johnson, J. J. (1985). *Psychopathology of childhood.* New York: Pergamon.

Schwarz, J., & Lindner, A. (1992). Inpatient treatment of male pathological gamblers in Germany. *J. Gamb. Stud., 8*(1), 93–109.

Schwarz, K., Harding, R., Harrington, D., & Farr, B. (1993). Hospital management of a patient with intractable factitious disorder. *Psychosom., 34*(3), 265–267.

Scola, P. S. (1991). Classification and social status. In J. L. Maston & J. A. Mulick (Eds.), *Handbook of mental retardation.* New York: Pergamon.

Searleman, A. & Herrmann, D. (1994). *Memory from a broader perspective.* New York: McGraw-Hill, Inc.

Sederer, L. I. (1992). Brief hospitalization. In A. Tasman & M. B. Riba (Eds.), *Review of psychiatry: Vol. 11.* Washington, DC: American Psychiatric Press.

Sedvall, G. (1990). Monoamines and schizophrenia. International symposium: Development of a new antipsy-chotic: *Remoxipride. Acta Psychiatr. Scandin., 82*(358, Suppl.). 7–13.

Sedvall, G. (1990). PET imaging of dopamine receptors in human basal ganglia: Relevance to mental illness. *Trends in Neurosci., 13*(7), 302–308.

Segal, B. M. (1988). A borderline style of functioning: The role of family, society, and heredity: An overview. *Child Psychiat., Human Dev., 18*(4), 219–238.

Segraves, R. T. (1988). Drugs and desire. In R. C. Rosen & S. R. Leiblum (Eds.), *Sexual desire disorders.* New York: Guilford.

Segraves, R. T. (1988). Hormones and libido. In R. C. Rosen & S. R. Lieblum (Eds.), *Sexual desire disorders.* New York: Guilford.

Seiden, R. H. (1981). Mellowing with age: Factors influencing the nonwhite suicide rate. *Inter. J. Aging and Human Devel., 13,* 265–284.

Seidman, J. (1990). The neuropsychology of schizophrenia: A neurodevelopmental and case study approach. *J. Neuropsychiat. & Clin. Neurosci., 2*(3), 301–312.

Seligman, M. E. P. (1971). Phobias and preparedness. *Behav. Ther., 2,* 307–320.

Seligman, M. E. P. (1975). *Helplessness.* San Francisco: W. H. Freeman.

Seligman, M. E. P. (1992). Wednesday's children. *Psych. Today, 25*(1), 61.

Seligman, M. E. P., Castellon, C., Cacciola, J., Schulman P., et al. (1988). Explanatory style change during cognitive therapy for unipolar depression. *J. Abnorm. Psychol., 97*(1), 13–18.

Seligmann, J., Rogers, P., & Annin, P. (1994, May 2). The pressure to lose. *Newsweek,* pp. 60–61.

Selkoe, D. J. (1992). Alzheimer's disease: New insights into an emerging epidemic. *J. Ger. Psychiat., 25*(2), 211–227.

Selling, L. S. (1940). Men against madness. New York: Greenberg.

Selye, H. (1976). *Stress in health and disease.* Woburn, MA: Butterworth.

Semans, J. H. (1956). Premature ejaculation: A new approach. *Southern Med. J., 49,* 353–357.

Senter, N. W., Winslade, W. J., Liston, E. H. et al., (1984). *Electroconvulsive therapy.* Bethesda, MD: NIH and NIMH.

Settlage, C. F. (1994). On the contribution of separation-individuation theory to psychoanalysis: Developmental process, pathogenesis, therapeutic process, and technique. In S. Kramer & S. Akhtar (Eds.), *Mahler and Kohut: Perspectives on development, psychopathology, and technique.* Northvale, New Jersey: Jason Aronson, Inc.

Shader, R. I., & Greenblatt, D. J. (1993, May 13). Use of benzodiazepines in anxiety disorders. *New. Engl. J. Med.,* pp. 1398–1405.

Shadish, W. R., Montgomery, L. M., Wilson, P., Wilson, M. R., Bright, I., & Okwumakua, T. (1993). The effects of family and marital psychotherapies: A meta-analysis. *J. Cons. Clin. Psychol., 61,* 61.

Shah, A. V., Parulkar, G. B., Mattoo, B., Bowalekdar, S. K., et al. (1991). Clinical evaluation of buspirone and diazepam in generalized anxiety disorders. *Curr. Therapeutic Res., 50*(6), 827–834.

Shaner, A., Khalsa, M., Roberts, L., Wilkins, J., Anglin, D., & Hsieh, S. (1993). Unrecognized cocaine use among schizophrenic patients. *Amer. J. Psychiat., 150*(5), 758–762.

Shapiro, A. K., & Morris, L. A. (1978). The placebo effect in medical and psychological therapies. In S. L. Garfield & A. E. Bergin (Eds.), *Handbook of psychotherapy and behavior change* (2nd ed.). New York: Wiley.

Shapiro, D. A. (1982). Overview: Clinical and physiological comparison of meditation with other self-control strategies. *Amer. J. Psychiat., 139*(3), 267–274.

Sharp, C. W., & Freeman, C. P. L. (1993). The medical complications of anorexia nervosa. *Brit. J. Psychiat., 162,* 452–462.

Shaunesey, K., Cohen, J. L., Plummer, B., & Berman, A. (1993). Suicidality in hospitalized adolescents: Relationship to prior abuse. *Amer. J. Orthopsychiat., 63*(1), 113–119.

Shedler, J., & Block, J. (1990). Adolescent drug use and psychological health: A longitudinal inquiry. *Amer. Psychol., 45*(5), 612–630.

Shedler, J., Mayman, M., & Manis, M. (1993). The illusion of mental health. *Amer. Psychol., 48*(11), 1117–1131.

Sheline, Y., & Beattie, M. (1992). Effects of the right to refuse treatment medication in an emergency psychiatric service. *Hosp. Comm. Psychiat., 43*(6), 640–642.

Sher, K. J., & Trull, T. J. (1994). Personality and disinhibitry psychopathology: Alcoholism and antisocial personality disorder. *J. Abnorm. Psychol., 103*(1), 92–102.

Sheras, P., & Worchel, S. (1979). *Clinical psychology: A social psychological approach.* New York: Van Nostrand.

Sherlock, R. (1983). Suicide and public policy: A critique of the "New Consensus." *J. Bioethics, 4,* 58–70.

Sherman, L. W. (1992). *Policing domestic violence.* New York: Free Press.

Sherman, R., & Thompson, R. (1990). *Bulimia: A guide for family and friends.* Lexington, MA: Lexington.

Sherrington, R., Rogaev, E. I., Liang, Y., Rogaeva, E. A. et al. (1995). Cloning of a gene bearing missense mutations in early-onset familial Alzheimer's disease. *Nature, 375,* 754–760.

Shi, J., Benowitz, N., Denaro, C., & Sheiner, L. (1993). Pharmacokinetic-pharmacodynamic modeling of caffeine: Tolerance to pressor effects. *Clin. Pharm. Ther., 53*(1), 6–15.

Shneidman, E. S. (1963). Orientations toward death: Subintentioned death and indirect suicide. In R. W. White (Ed.), *The study of lives.* New York: Atherton.

Shneidman, E. S. (1973). Suicide notes reconsidered. *Psychiat., 36,* 379–394.

Shneidman, E. S. (1979). An overview: Personality, motivation, and behavior theories. In L. D. Hankoff & B. Einsidler (Eds.), *Suicide: Theory and clinical aspects.* Littleton, MA: PSG Pub. Co.

Shneidman, E. S. (1981). Suicide. *Suic. Life-Threat. Behav., 11*(4), 198–220.

Shneidman, E. S. (1985). *Definition of suicide.* New York: Wiley.

Shneidman, E. S. (1987, Mar.). At the point of no return. *Psychol. Today.*

Shneidman, E. S. (1993). *Suicide as psychache: A clinical approach to self-destructive behavior.* Northvale, NJ: Jason Aronson.

Shneidman, E. S., & Farberow, N. (1968). The Suicide Prevention Center of Los Angeles. In H. L. P. Resnick (Ed.), *Suicidal behaviors: Diagnosis and management.* Boston: Little, Brown.

Shuller, D. Y., & McNamara, J. R. (1980). The use of information derived from norms and from a credible source to counter expectancy effects in behavioral assessment. *Behav. Assess., 2,* 183–196.

Siegel, K. (1988). Rational suicide. In S. Lesse (Ed.), *What we know about suicidal behavior and how to treat it.* Northvale, NJ: Jason Aronson.

Siever, L. J. (1981). Schizoid and schizotypal personality disorders. In J. R. Lion (Ed.), *Personality disorders-diagnosis and management.* Malibu, FL: R. E. Krieger.

Siever, L. J. (1992). Schizophrenia spectrum personality disorders. In A. Tasman & M. B. Riba (Eds.), *American Psychiatric Press review of psychiatry* (Vol. 11). Washington, DC: American Psychiatric Press.

Siever, L. J., & Davis, K. L. (1991). A psychobiological perspective on the personality disorders. *Amer. J. Psychiat., 148*(12), 1647–1658.

Siever, L. J., Davis, K. L. & Gorman, L. K. (1991). Pathogenesis of mood disorders. In K. Davis, H. Klar, & J. T. Coyle, *Foundations of psychiatry.* Philadelphia: Saunders.

Siever, L. J., Keefe, R., & Bernstein, D. (1990). Eye–tracking impairment in clinically-identified patients with schizotypal personality disorder. *Amer. J. Psychiat., 147,* 740–745.

Siever, L. J., Silverman, J. M., Horvath, T. B., et al. (1990). Increased morbid risk for schizophrenia-related disorders in relatives of schizotypal personality disordered patients. *Arch. Gen. Psychiat., 47*(7), 634–640.

Sifneos, P. E. (1987). *Short-term dynamic psychotherapy evaluation and technique* (2nd ed.). New York: Plenum.

Sifneos, P. E. (1992). *Short-term anxiety-provoking psychotherapy: A treatment manual.* New York: Basic Books.

Sigerist, H. E. (1943). *Civilization and disease.* Ithaca, NY: Cornell UP.

Silver, J. M., & Yudofsky, S. C. (1988). Psychopharmacology and electroconvulsive therapy. In J. A. Talbotto, R. E. Hales, & S. C. Yudofsky (Eds.), *The American Psychiatric Press textbook of psychiatry.* Washington, DC: American Psychiatric Press.

Silverman, K., Evans, S. M., Strain, E. C., & Griffiths, R. R. (1992). Withdrawal syndrome after the double-blind cessation of caffeine consumption. *New Engl. J. Med., 327*(16), 1109–1114.

Silverman, P. (1992). An introduction to self-help groups. In B. J. White & E. J. Madara (Eds.), *The self-help sourcebook: Finding & forming mutual aid self-help groups.* Denville, NJ: St. Clares-Riverside Medical Center.

Silverstein, B., Perdue, L., Peterson, B., & Kelly, E. (1986). The role of mass media in promoting a thin standard of bodily attractiveness for women. *Sex Roles, 14,* 519–532.

Silverstone, P. H. (1990). Low self-esteem in eating disordered patients in the absence of depression. *Psych. Rep., 67*(1), 276–278.

Silverstone, T., & Hunt, N. (1992). Symptoms and assessment of mania. In E. S. Paykel (Ed.), *Handbook of affective disorders.* New York: Guilford.

Simhandl, C., & Meszaros, K. (1992). The use of carbamazepine in the treatment of schizophrenia and schizoaffective psychoses: A review. *J. Psychiat. Neurosci., 17*(1), 1–14.

Simmon (1990). Media and Market Study. In Skin deep: Our national obsession with looks. *Psych. Today, 26*(3), 96.

Simon, R. (1987, January). Interview in Turkington, C., Treatment of depressed elderly could prevent silent suicides. *APA Monitor,* p. 13.

Simon, Y., Bellisle, F., Monneuse, M. O., Samuel-Lajeunesse, B., & Drewnowski, A. (1993). Taste responsiveness in anorexia nervosa. *Brit. J. Psychiat., 162,* 244–246.

Simons, L. S. (1989). Privatization and the mental health system: A private sector view. *Amer. Psychol., 44*(8), 1138–1141.

Simons, R. C. (1981). Contemporary problems of psychoanalytic technique. *J. Amer. Psychoanal. Assoc., 29*(3), 643–658.

Simpson, C. J., Hyde, C. E., & Faragher, E. B. (1989). The chronically mentally ill in community facilities: A study of quality of life. *Brit. J. Psychiat., 154,* 77–82.

Simpson, R. L., & Sasso, G. M. (1992). Full inclusion of students with autism in general education settings: Values versus science. *Focus on Autistic Behav., 7*(3), 1–13.

Simpson, R. O., & Halpin, G. (1986). Agreement between parents and teachers in using the Revised Behavior Problem Checklist to identify deviant behavior in children. *Behav. Dis., 12*(1), 54–58.

Sines, L. K. (1959). The relative contribution of four kinds of data to accuracy in personality assessment. *J. Cons. Psychol., 23,* 483–495.

Singh, A., & Lucki, I. (1993). Antidepressant-like activity of compounds with varying efficacy at 5-HT receptors. *Neuropharm., 32*(4), 331–340.

Singh, G. (1981). The malignant neuroleptic syndrome (a review with report of three cases). *Indian J. Psychiat., 23,* 179–183.

Siomopoulos, V. (1988). Narcissistic personality disorder: Clinical features. *Amer. J. Psychother., 42*(2), 240–253.

Sipprelle, R. C. (1992). A Vet Center experience: Multievent trauma, delayed treatment type. In D. W. Foy (Ed.), Treating PTSD: Cognitive-behavioral strategies. *Treatment Manuals for Practitioners.* New York: Guilford.

Sizemore, C. C., & Huber, R. J. (1988). The twenty-two faces of Eve. *Individ. Psychol. J. Adlerian Theory Res. Prac., 44*(1), 53–62.

Skinner, B. F. (1948). Superstition in the pigeon. *J. Exp. Psychol., 38,* 168–172.

Slater, E., & Shields, J. (1969). Genetical aspects of anxiety. Special Publication No. 3. M. H. Lader (Ed.), *Brit. J. Psychiat.,* 62–71.

Sleek, S. (1995). Unlocking the restriction on drinking. *APA Monitor, 26*(6), 23.

Slovenko, R. (1992). Is diminished capacity really dead? *Psychiat. Ann., 22*(11), 566–570.

Small, M. A. (1992). The legal context of mentally disordered sex offender (MDSO) treatment programs. *Crimin. Justice and Behav., 19*(2), 127–142.

Smith, A. C. (1982). *Schizophrenia and madness.* London: Allen & Unwin.

Smith, A. L., & Weissman, M. M. (1992). Epidemiology. In E. S. Paykel (Ed.), *Handbook of affective disorders.* New York: Guilford.

Smith, E., North, C., & Spitznagel, E. (1993). Alcohol, drugs, and psychiatric comorbidity among homeless women: An epidemiologic study. *J. Clin. Psychiat., 54*(3), 82–87.

Smith, J. E., Waldorf, A., & Trembath, D. L. (1990). "Single white male looking for thin, very attractive. . . " *Sex Roles, 23*(11), 675–685.

Smith, K. (1991). Comments on "Teen suicide and changing cause-of-death certification, 1953–1987." *Suic. Life-Threat. Behav., 21*(3), 260–262.

Smith, M. L., & Glass G. V. (1977). Meta-analysis of psychotherapy outcome studies. *Amer. Psychol., 32*(9), 752–760.

Smith, M. L., Glass, G. V., & Miller, T. I. (1980). *The benefits of psychotherapy.* Baltimore: Johns Hopkins Univ.

Smith, R. E. (1988). The logic and design of case study research. *Sports Psychologist, 2*(1), 1–12.

Smith, T. C., & Smith, B. L. (1986). The relationship between the WISC-R and WRAT-R for a sample of rural referred children. *Psychol. Schools, 23*(3), 252–254.

Smith, W. H. (1993). Incorporating hypnosis into the psychotherapy of patients with multiple personality disorder. *Bull. Menninger Clin., 57*(3), 344–354.

Smoller, J. W. (1986). The etiology and treatment of childhood. In G. C. Ellenbogen (Ed.), *Oral sadism and the vegetarian personality.* New York: Brunner/Mazel.

Smyer, M. A. (1989). Nursing homes as a setting for psychological practice: Public policy perspectives. *Amer. Psychol., 44*(10), 1307–1314.

Snow, E. (1976, Dec.). In the snow. *Texas Monthly Magazine.*

Snyder, D. K., Wills, R. M., & Grady-Fletcher, A. (1991). Long-term effectiveness of behavioral versus insight-oriented marital therapy: A 4-year follow-up study. *J. Cons. Clin. Psychol., 59*(1), 138–141.

Snyder, D. K., Wills, R. M., & Grady-Fletcher, A. (1991). Risks and challenges of long-term psychotherapy outcome research: Reply to Jacobson. *J. Cons. Clin. Psychol., 59*(1), 146–149.

Snyder, F. (1970). The phenomenology of dreaming. In L. Madlow & L. Snow (Eds.), *The psychodynamic implications of the physiological studies on dreams.* Springfield, IL: C. C. Thomas.

Snyder, M. L. (1992). Unemployment and suicide in Northern Ireland. *Psych. Rep., 70*(3, Pt. 2), 1116–1118.

Snyder, S. (1976). Dopamine and schizophrenia. *Psychiat., Ann., 8*(1), 53–84.

Snyder, S. (1976). The dopamine hypotheses of schizophrenia: Focus on the dopamine receptor. *Amer. J. Psychiat., 133*(2), 197–202.

Snyder, S. (1977, Mar.). Opiate receptors and internal opiates. *Scientif. Amer.,* 44–56.

Snyder, S. (1977). Opiate receptors in the brain. *New Engl. J. Med., 296,* 266–271.

Snyder, S. (1986). *Drugs and the brain.* New York: Scientific American Library.

Snyder, S. (1991). Drugs, neurotransmitters, and the brain. In P. Corsi (Ed.), *The enchanted loom: Chapters in the history of neuroscience.* New York: Oxford UP.

Snyder, W. V. (1947). *Casebook of non-directive counseling.* Boston: Houghton Mifflin.

Sobell, M. B., & Sobell, L. C. (1973). Alcoholics treated by individualized behavior therapy: One year treatment outcome. *Behav. Res. Ther., 11*(4), 599–618.

Sobell, M. B., & Sobell, L. C. (1973). Individualized behavior therapy for alcoholics. *Behav. Ther., 4*(1), 49–72.

Sobell, M. B., & Sobell, L. C. (1976). Second year treatment outcome of alcoholics treated by individualized behavior therapy: Results. *Behav. Res. Ther., 14*(3), 195–215.

Sobell, M. B., & Sobell, L. C. (1984). The aftermath of heresy: A response to Pendery et al.'s (1982) critique of "Individualized Behavior Therapy for Alcoholics." *Behav. Res. Ther., 22*(4), 413–440.

Sobell, M. B., & Sobell, L. C. (1984). Under the microscope yet again: A commentary on Walker and Roach's critique of the Dickens Committee's enquiry into our research. *Brit. J. Addic., 79*(2), 157–168.

Sohlberg, S., & Norring, C. (1992). A three-year prospective study of life events and course for adults with anorexia nervosa/bulimia nervosa. *Psychosom. Med., 54*(1), 59–70.

Sokol-Kessler, L., & Becker, A. T. (1987). *Cognitive treatment of panic disorders.* Paper presented at the 140th Annual Meeting of the American Psychiatric Assoc. Chicago.

Solomon, D. A., Keitner, G. I., Miller, I. W., Shea, M. T., & Keller, M. B. (1995). Course of illness and maintenance treatments for patients with bipolar disorder. *J. Clin. Psychiat., 56,* 5–13.

Solomon, R. L. (1980). The opponent-process theory of acquired motivation: The costs of pleasure and the benefits of pain. *Amer. Psychol., 35,* 691–712.

Soltys, S. M. (1992). Pyromania and firesetting behaviors. *Psychiat. Ann., 22*(2), 79–83.

Solyom, L., Freeman, R. J., & Miles, J. E. (1982). A comparative psychometric study of anorexia nervosa and obsessive neurosis. *Canad. J. Psychiat., 27*(4), 282–286.

Spalter, A. R., Gwirtsman, H. E., Demitrack, M. A., & Gold, P. W. (1993). Thyroid function in bulimia nervosa. *Bio. Psychiat., 33,* 100–414.

Spanos, N. P., & Coe, W. C. (1992). A social-psychologist approach to hypnosis. In E. Fromm & M. R. Nash (Eds.), *Contemporary hypnosis research.* New York: Guilford.

Sparr, L. F., Boehnlein, J. K., & Cooney, T. G. (1986). The medical management of the paranoid patient. *Gen. Hosp. Psychiat., 8*(1), 49–55.

Spear, N. E. (1973). Retrieval of memory in animals. *Psych. Rev., 80,* 163–194.

Spector, I. P., & Carey, M. P. (1990). Incidence and prevalence of sexual dysfunctions: A critical review of the empirical literature. *Arch. Sex. Behav., 19*(4), 389–408.

Spielberger, C. D. (1966). Theory and research on anxiety. In C. D. Spielberger (Ed.), *Anxiety and behavior.* New York: Academic Press.

Spielberger, C. D. (1985). Anxiety, cognition, and affect: A state-trait perspective. In A. H. Tuma & J. Maser (Eds.), *Anxiety and the anxiety disorders.* Hillsdale, NJ: Erlbaum.

Spirito, A., Brown, L., Overholser, J., & Fritz, G. (1989). Attempted suicide in adolescence: A review and critique of the literature. *Clin. Psychol. Rev., 9,* 335–363.

Spitz, R. A. (1945). Hospitalization: An inquiry into the genesis of psychiatric conditions of early childhood. In R. S. Eissler, A. Freud, H. Hartman, & E. Kris (Eds.), *The psychoanalytic study of the child* (Vol. 1). New York: International Universities Press.

Spitz, R. A. (1946). Anaclitic depression. *The psychoanalytic study of the child* (Vol. 2). New York: International Universities Press.

Spitzer, J. (1990). On treating patients diagnosed with narcissistic personality disorder: The induction phase. *Issues in Ego Psychol., 13*(1), 54–65.

Spitzer, R. L., Skodol, A., Gibbon, M., & Williams, J. B. W. (1981). DSM-III case book (1st ed.). Washington, DC: *Amer. Psychiat. Press.*

Spitzer, R. L., Skodol, A., Gibbon, M., & Williams, J. B. W. (1983). Psychopathology: A case book. New York: McGraw-Hill.

Squire, L. R. (1977). ECT and memory loss. *Amer. J. Psychiat., 134,* 997–1001.

Squire, L. R., Knowlton, B., & Musen, G. (1993). The structure and organization of memory. In L. W. Porter & M. R. Rosenzweig (Eds.), *Annu. Rev. Psychology, 44,* 453–495.

Squire, L. R., & Slater, P. C. (1983). Electroconvulsive therapy and complaints of memory dysfunction: A prospective three-year follow-up study. *Brit. J. Psychiat., 142,* 1–8.

Squires, R. F., & Braestrup, C. (1977). Benzodiazepine receptors in rat brain. *Nature, 266*(5604), 732–734.

Stack, S. (1981). Comparative analysis of immigration and suicide. *Psych. Rep., 49*(2), 509–510.

Stack, S. (1987). Celebrities and suicide: A taxonomy and analysis, 1948–1983. *Amer. Sociological Rev., 52,* 401–412.

Stahmer, A. C., & Schreibman, L. (1992). Teaching children with autism appropriate play in unsupervised environments using a self-management treatment package. *J. Appl. Behav. Anal., 25*(2), 447–459.

Stampfl, T. G. (1975). Implosive therapy: Staring down your nightmares. *Psych. Today, 8*(9), 66–68; 72–73.

Stanford, S. C., & Salmon, P. (1993). *Stress: From synapse to syndrome.* London: Academic Press.

Stanley, M., Stanley, B., Traskman-Bendz, L., Mann, J. J., & Meyendorff, E. (1986). Neurochemical findings in suicide completers and suicide attempters. In R. W. Maris (Ed.), *Biology of suicide.* New York: Guilford.

Stark, K. D., Rouse, L. W., & Livingston, R. (1991). Treatment of depression during childhood and adolescence: Cognitive-behavioral procedures for the individual and family. In P. C. Kendall (Ed.), *Child and adolescent therapy: Cognitive behavioral procedures.* New York: Guilford.

Stark-Adamek, C. (1992). Sexism in research: The limits of academic freedom. *Women and ther., 12*(4), 103–111.

Steadman, H. J., Monahan, J., Robbins, P. C., Appelbaum, P., Grisso, T., Klassen, D., Mulvey, E. P., & Roth, L. (1993). From dangerousness to risk assessment: Implications for appropriate research strategies. In S. Hodgins (Ed.), *Mental disorder and crime.* New York: Sage Publications.

Steen, S. N., Oppliger, R. A., & Brownell K. D. (1988). Metabolic effects of repeated weight loss and regain in adolescent wrestlers. *JAMA, 260,* 47–50.

Stefansson, C. G., & Wicks, S. (1991). Health care occupations and suicide in Sweden 1961–1985. *Soc. Psychiat. Psychiat. Epidemiol., 26*(6), 259–264.

Stein, D. J., Hollander, E., Anthony, D. T., Schneier, F. R., et al. (1992). Serotonergic medications for sexual obsessions, sexual addictions, and paraphilias. *J. Clin. Psychiat., 53*(8), 267–271.

Stein, D. J., Hollander, E., & Liebowitz, M. R. (1993). Neurobiology of impulsivity and the impulse control disorders. *J. Neuropsychiat. Clin. Neurosci, 5*(1), 9–17.

Stein, M. B., Walker, J. R., & Forde, D. R. (1994). Setting diagnostic thresholds for social phobia: Considerations from a community survey of social anxiety. *Amer. J. Psychiat., 151*(3), 408–412.

Stein, Z., Susser, M., Saenger, G., & Marolla, F. (1972). Nutrition and mental performance. *Sci., 178,* 708–713.

Steinberg, M. (1993). *Interviewer's guide to the Structured Clinical Interview for DSM-IV dissociative disorders.* Washington, DC: American Psychiatric Press.

Steinbrook, R. (1992). The polygraph test: A flawed diagnostic method. *New Engl. J. Med., 327*(2), 122–123.

Steiner, H., Smith, C., Rosenkranz, R. T., & Litt, I. (1991). The early care and feeding of anorexics. *Child Psychiat. Human Dev., 21*(3), 163–167.

Steinglass, P., Tislenko, L., & Reiss, D. (1985). Stability/instability in the alcoholic marriage: The interrelationships between course of alcoholism, family process, and marital outcome. *Fam. Process, 24*(3), 365–376.

Steketee, G., & Foa, E. B. (1987). Rape victims: Post–traumatic stress responses and their treatment. *J. Anx. Dis., 1,* 69–86.

Stillion, J. M. (1985). *Death and the sexes: An examination of differential longevity, attitudes, behaviors, and coping skills.* Washington, DC: Hemisphere.

Stock, W. (1993). Inhibited female orgasm. In W. O'Donohue & J. Geer (Eds.), *Handbook of sexual dysfunctions*. Boston: Allyn and Bacon.

Stokes, T. E., & Osnes, P. G. (1989). An operant pursuit of generalization. *Behav. Ther., 20*(3), 337–355.

Stone, M. H. (1989). Schizoid personality disorder. In American Psychiatric Association (Eds.), *Treatments of psychiatric disorders: A task force report of the American Psychiatric Association*. Washington, DC: American Psychiatric Press.

Stonier, P. D. (1992). "Are double-blind controlled trials always necessary?": Response. *Human Psychopharmacol. Clin. Exper., 7*(1), 57–60.

Stoyva, J. M., & Budzynski, T. H. (1993). Biofeedback methods in the treatment of anxiety and stress disorders. In P. M. Lehrer & R. L. Woolfolk (Eds.), *Principles and practice of stress management* (2nd ed.). New York: Guilford.

Strakowski, S. M., Lonczak, H. S., Sax, K. W., West, S. A., Crist, R. M., & Thienhaus, O. J. (1995). The effects of race on diagnosis and disposition from a psychiatric emergency service. *J. Clin. Psychiat., 56*(3), 101–107.

Strange, P. G. (1992). *Brain biochemistry and brain disorders*. New York: Oxford UP.

Strassberg, D. S., Kelly, M. P., Carroll, C., & Kircher, J. C. (1987). The psychophysiological nature of premature ejaculation. *Arch. Sex. Beh., 16*(4), 327–336.

Strassberg, D. S., Mahoney, J. M., Schaugaard, M., & Hale, V. E. (1990). The role of anxiety in premature ejaculation: A psychophysiological model. *Arch. Sex. Behav., 15*(4), 251–257.

Strauss, J., & Ryan, R. (1987). Autonomy disturbances in subtypes of anorexia nervosa. *J. Abnorm. Psychol., 96*(3), 254–258.

Strickland, B. R., Hale, W. D., & Anderson, L. K. (1975). Effect of induced mood states on activity and self-reported affect. *J. Cons. Clin. Psychol., 43*(4), 587.

Striegel-Moore, R. H., Silberstein, L. R., & Rodin, J. (1986). Toward an understanding of risk factors for bulimia. *Amer. Psychol., 41*(3), 246–263.

Striegel-Moore, R. H., Silberstein, L. R., & Rodin, J. (1993). The social self in bulimia nervosa: Public self-consciousness, social anxiety, and perceived fraudulence. *J. Abnorm. Psychol., 102*(2), 297–303.

Strober, M. (1992). Family factors in adolescent eating disorders. In P. J. Cooper & A. Stein (Eds.), *Feeding problems and eating disorders in children and adolescents*. Philadelphia: Harwood Academic Publishers.

Strober, M., & Yager, J. (1985). A development perspective on the treatment of anorexia nervosa in adolescents. In D. M. Garner & P. E. Garfinkel (Eds.), *Handbook of psychotherapy for anorexia nervosa and bulimia*. New York: Guilford.

Stroebe, M., Gergen, M. M., Gergen, K. J., & Stroebe, W. (1992). Broken hearts or broken bonds: Love and death in historical perspectives. *Amer. Psychol., 47*(10), 1205–1212.

Strupp, H. H. (1989). Psychotherapy: Can the practitioner learn from the researcher? *Amer. Psychol., 44*, 717–724.

Stuhr, U., & Meyer, A. E. (1991). Hamburg Short Psychotherapy Comparison Experiment. In M. Crago & L. Beutler (Eds.), *Psychotherapy research: An international review of programmatic studies*. American Psychological Association.

Stunkard, A. J., Sorenson, T. I. A., Hanis, C., Teasdale, T. W., et al. (1986). An adoption study of human obesity. *New Engl. J. Med., 314*, 193–198.

Stunkard, A. J. & Wadden T. A. (1992). Psychological aspects of severe obesity. *Amer. J. Clin. Nutrition, 55*(Suppl.), 524–532.

Sturgeon, V., & Taylor, J. (1980). Report of a five-year follow-up study of mentally disordered sex offenders released from Atascadero State Hospital in 1973. *Crimin. Justice J. Western State Univ., San Diego, 4*, 31–64.

Suddath, R. L., Christison, G. W., & Torrey, E. F. (1990). Anatomical abnormalities in the brains of monozygotic twins discordant for schizophrenia. *New Engl. J. Med., 322*(12), 789–794.

Sudhalter, V., Cohen, I. L., Silverman, W., & Wolf-Schein, E. G. (1990). Conversational analyses of males with fragile X, Down syndrome, and autism: Comparison of the emergence of deviant language. *Amer. J. Ment. Retard., 94*, 431–441.

Sue, S. (1977). Community mental health services to minority groups: Some optimism, some pessimism. *Amer. Psychol., 32*(8), 616–624.

Sue, S. (1991). Ethnicity and culture in psychological research and practice. In L. Garnets, J. M. Jones, D. Kimmel, S. Sue, & C. Tavris (Eds.), *Psychological perspectives on human diversity in America*. Washington, DC: American Psychological Association.

Sue, S., Zane, N., & Young, K. (1994). Research on psychotherapy with culturally diverse populations. In A. E. Bergin & S. L. Garfield (Eds.), *Handbook of psychotherapy and behavior change*. New York: Wiley.

Sullivan, C. M., Tan, C., Basta, J., Rumptz, M., et al. (1992). An advocacy intervention program for women with abusive partners: Initial evaluation. *Amer. J. Comm. Psychol., 20*(3), 309–332.

Suokas, J., & Lonnqvist, J. (1991). Selection of patients who attempted suicide for psychiatric consultation. *Acta Psychiatr. Scandin., 83*(3), 179–182.

Suppes, T., Baldessarini, R. J., Faedda, G. L., & Tohen, M. (1991). Risk of recurrence following discontinuation of lithium treatment in bipolar disorder. *Arch. Gen. Psychiat., 48*(12), 1082–1088.

Suter, S. (1986). *Health psychophysiology: Mind-body interactions in wellness and illness*. Hillsdale, NJ: Erlbaum.

Sutker, P. B., Allain, A. N., & Winstead, D. K. (1993). Psychopathology and psychiatric diagnoses of World War II Pacific Theater prisoner of war survivors and combat veterans. *Amer. J. Psychiat., 150*(2), 240–245.

Svartberg, M., & Stiles, T. C. (1991). Comparative effects of short-term psychodynamic psychotherapy: A meta-analysis. *J. Cons. Clin. Psychol., 59*, 704–714.

Svrakic, D. M. (1990). Pessimism and depression: Clinical and phenomenological distinction. *Eur. J. Psychiat., 4*(3), 139–145.

Svrakic, D. M. (1990). The functional dynamics of the narcissistic personality. *Amer. J. Psychother., 44*(2), 189–203.

Swanson, J., Holzer, C., Ganju, V., & Jono, R. (1990). Violence and psychiatric disorder in the community: Evidence from the Epidemiological Catchment Area Surveys. *Hosp. Comm. Psychiat., 41*, 761–770.

Swayze, V. W. (1995). Frontal leukotomy and related psychosurgical procedures in the era before antipsychotics (1935–1954): A historical overview. *Amer. J. Psychiat., 152*(4), 505–515.

Swedo, S. E., Pietrini, P., Leonard, H. L., Schapiro, M. B., et al. (1992). Cerebral glucose metabolism in childhood-onset obsessive-compulsive disorder: Revisualization during pharmacotherapy. *Arch. Gen. Psychiat., 49*(9), 690–694.

Swonger, A. K., & Constantine, L. L. (1983). *Drugs and therapy: A handbook of psychotropic drugs* (2nd ed.). Boston: Little, Brown.

Szasz, T. S. (1961). *The myth of mental illness: Foundations of a theory of personal conduct*. New York: Hoeber-Harper.

Szasz, T. S. (1963). *Law, liberty, and psychiatry*. Englewood Cliffs, NJ: Prentice Hall.

Szasz, T. S. (1963). *The manufacture of madness*. New York: Harper & Row.

Szasz, T. S. (1977). *Psychiatric slavery*. New York: Free Press.

Szasz, T. S. (1987). Justifying coercion through theology and therapy. In J. K. Zeig (Ed.), *The evolution of psychotherapy*. New York: Brunner/Mazel.

Szasz, T. S. (1991). The medicalization of sex. *J. Humanistic Psychol., 31*(3), 34–42.

Tanagho, E. A., Lue, T. F., & McClure, R. D. (1988). *Contemporary management of impotence and infertility*. Baltimore: Williams & Wilkins.

Tanay, E. (1992). The verdict with two names. *Psychiat. Ann., 22*(11), 571–573.

Tanzi, R. C., St. George Hyslop, P. H., & Gusella, J. T. (1989). Molecular genetic approaches to Alzheimer's disease. *Trends Neurosci., 12*(4), 152–158.

Tanzi, R. E. (1991). Gene mutations in inherited amyloidopathies of the nervous system. *Amer. J. Human Genetics, 49*, 507–510.

Taube, C. A. (1990). Funding and expenditures for mental illness. In R. W. Manderscheid & M. A. Sonnenschein (Eds.), *Mental health U.S., 1990*. DHHS #(ADM) 90-1708. Washington, DC: GOP.

Tavris, C. (1993). *Beware the incest-survivor machine*. New York Times Review of Books.

Taylor, J. R., & Carroll, J. L. (1987). Current issues in electroconvulsive therapy. *Psych. Rep., 60*(3, Pt. 1).

Teicher, M. H., Glod, C., & Cole, J. O. (1990). Emergence of intense suicidal preoccupation during fluoxetine treatment. *Amer. J. Psychiat., 147*(2), 207–210.

Tenenbaum, J. (1983). ECT regulation reconsidered. *Ment. Dis. Law Reporter, 7*, 148–157.

Tennant, C. (1988). Psychological causes of duodenal ulcer. *Austral. N. Zeal. J. Psychiat., 22*(2), 195–202.

Teplin, L. A. (1990). The prevalence of severe mental disorder among male urban jail detainees: Comparison with the Epidemiologic Catchment Area Program. *Amer. J. Pub. Hlth., 80*, 663–669.

Teplin, L. A., Abram, K. M., & McClelland, G. M. (1994). Does psychiatric disorder predict violent crime among released jail detainees? *Amer. Psychol., 49*(4), 335–342.

Teri, L., & Lewinsohn, P. M. (1986). Individual and group treatment of unipolar depression: Comparison of treatment outcome and identification of predictors of successful treatment outcome. *Behav. Ther., 17*(3), 215–228.

Terr, L. (1988). What happens to early memories of trauma? A study of twenty children under age five at the time of documented traumatic events. Annual Meeting of the American Psychiatry Association. *J. Amer. Academy Child Adol. Psychiat., 27*(1), 96–104.

Thapar, A., Davies, G., Jones, T., & Rivett, M. (1992). Treatment of childhood encopresis: A review. *Child Care, Hlth. Dev., 18*(6), 343–353.

Theander, S. (1970). Anorexia nervosa. *Acta Psychiatr. Scandin.,* (Suppl.), 1–194.

Thelen, M. H. & Cormier, J. F. (1995). Desire to be thinner and weight control among children and their parents. *Behav. Ther., 26,* 85–99.

Thigpen, C. H., & Cleckley, H. M. (1957). *The three faces of Eve.* New York: McGraw-Hill.

Thompson, R. A., & Sherman, R. T. (1993). *Helping athletes with eating disorders.* Champaign, IL: Human Kinetics Publishers.

Tice, D. (1990, Aug.). Presentation. Washington, DC: American Psychological Assoc.

Tiller, J., Schmidt, U., Treasure, J. (1993). Compulsory treatment for anorexia nervosa: Compassion or coercion? *Brit. J. Psychiat., 162,* 679–680.

Tillich, P. (1952, Dec.). Anxiety, religion, and medicine. *Pastoral Psychol., 3,* 11–17.

Tishler, D. L., McKenry, P. C., & Morgan, K. C. (1981). Adolescent suicide attempts: Some significant factors. *Suic. Life-Threat. Behav., 11*(2), 86–92.

Tobin, D. L., & Johnson, C. L. (1991). The integration of psychodynamic and behavior therapy in the treatment of eating disorders: Clinical issue versus theoretical mystique. In C. L. Johnson (Ed.), *Psychodynamic treatment of anorexia nervosa and bulimia.* New York: Guilford.

Todd, T. C., & Stanton, M. D. (1983). Research on marital and family therapy: Answeres, issues, and recommendations for the future. In B. B. Wolman & G. Stricker (Eds.), *Handbook of family and marital therapy.* New York: Plenum.

Tolstrup, K. et al. (1985). Long-term outcome of 151 cases of anorexia nervosa: The Copenhagen anorexia nervosa follow-up study. *Acta Psychiatr., Scandin., 71*(4), 380–387.

Tomchek, L. B., Gordon, R., Arnold, M., Handleman, J. (1992). Teaching preschool children with autism and their normally developing peers: Meeting the challenges of integrated education. *Focus Autistic Behav., 7*(2), 1–17.

Torrey, E. F. (1988). *Nowhere to go: The tragic odyssey of the homeless mentally ill.* New York: Harper & Row.

Torrey, E. F. (1991). A viral-anatomical explanation of schizophrenia. *Schizo. Bull., 17*(1), 15–18.

Torrey, E. F., Wolfe, S. M., & Flynn, L. M. (1988). *Care of the seriously mentally ill: A rating of state programs* (2nd ed.). Washington, DC: Public Citizen Health Research Group and National Alliance for the Mentally Ill.

Torrey, E. F., Bowler, A. E., Rawlings, R., & Terrazas, A. (1993). Seasonality of schizophrenia and stillbirths. *Schizo. Bull., 19*(3), 557–562.

Toufexis, A. (1993). The personality pill. *Time,* Oct 11, pp. 61–62.

Treaster, J. B. (1992, September 20). After hurricane, Floridians show symptoms seen in war. *New York Times.*

Tross, S., & Hirsch D. A. (1988). Psychological distress and neuropsychological complications of HIV infection and AIDS. *Amer. Psychol., 43*(11), 929–934.

Trovato, F. (1987). A longitudinal analysis of divorce and suicide in Canada. *J. Marriage Fam. 49,* 193–203.

Tsoi, W. F. (1992). Male and female transsexuals: A comparison. *Singapore Med. J. 33*(2), 182–185.

Turkat, I. D., Keane, S. P., Thompson-Pope, S. K. (1990). Social processing errors among paranoid personalities. *J. Psychopath. Behav. Assess., 12*(3), 263–269.

Turkington, C. (1987). Treatment of depressed elderly could prevent "silent suicides." *APA Monitor, 18,*(1), p. 13.

Turkington, C. (1992). Social variables tied to heart attack deaths. *APA Monitor, 23*(5), 44.

Turner, L. A., Althof, S. E., Levin, S. B., Bodner, D. R., Kursh, E. D., & Resnick, M. I. (1991). External vacuum devices in the treatment of erectile dysfunction: A one-year study of sexual and psychosocial impact. *J. Sex Marit. Ther., 17*(2), 81–93.

Turner, S. M., Beidel, D. C., Borden, J. W., Stanley, M. A., et al. (1991). Social phobia: Axis I and II corrlates. *J. Abnorm. Psychol., 100*(1), 102–106.

Turner, S. M., Beidel, D. C., Dancu, C. V., & Keys, D. J. (1986). Psychopathology of social phobia comparison to avoidant personality disorder. *J. Abnorm. Psychol., 95*(4), 389–394.

Twain, M. (1885). *The adventures of Huckleberry Finn.*

Tweed, J. L., Schoenbach, V. J., & George, L. K. (1989). The effects of childhood parental death and divorce on six-month history of anxiety disorders. *Brit. J. Psychiat., 154,* 823–828.

Tyor, P. L., & Bell, L. V. (1984). *Caring for the retarded in America: A history.* Westport, CT: Greenwood.

U.S. Bureau of the Census. (1990, 1988, 1968, 1947). *Statistical abstract of the United States.* Washington, DC: GPO.

Ullmann, L. P., & Krasner, L. (1975). *A psychological approach to abnormal behavior* (2nd ed.). Englewood Cliffs, NJ: Prentice Hall.

Ursano, R. J., Boydstun, J. A., & Wheatley, R. D. (1981). Pyschiatric illness in U. S. Air Force Vietnam prisoners of war: A five-year follow-up. *Amer. J. Psychiat., 138*(3), 310–314.

Vaillant, G. E. (1983). Natural history of male alcoholism: V. Is alcoholism the cart or the horse to sociopathy? *Brit. J. Addic., 78*(3), 317–326.

Vaillant, G. E. (1994). Ego mechanisms of defense and personality psychopathology. *J. Abnorm. Psychol., 103*(1) 44–50.

Vaillant, G. E., & Milofsky, E. S. (1982). Natural history of male alcoholism: IV. Paths to recovery. *Arch. Gen. Psychiat., 39,* 127–133.

Vaillant, G. E., & Milofsky, E. S. (1982). The etiology of alcoholism: A prospective viewpoint. *Amer. Psychol., 37,* 494–503.

Vaillant, G. E., & Perry, J. C. (1985). Personality disorders. In H. I. Kaplan & B. J. Sadock (Eds.), *Comprehensive textbook of psychiatry* (4th ed.). Baltimore: Williams & Wilkins.

Vaillant, P. M., & Antonowicz, D. H. (1992). Rapists, incest offenders, and child molesters in treatment: Cognitive and social skills training. *Inter. J. Offend. Ther. Compar. Crimin., 36*(3), 221–230.

Valenstein, E. S. (1986). *Great and desperate cures.* New York: Basic Books.

Valenti-Hein, D. C., Yarnold, P. R., & Mueser, K. T. (1994). Evaluation of the dating skills program for improving heterosocial interactions in people with mental retardation. *Behav. Mod., 18*(1), 32–46.

Van Bourgondien, M. E., & Schopler, E. (1990). Critical issues in the residential care of people with autism. *J. Autism Dev. Dis., 20*(3), 391–399.

Van de Castle, R. (1993). Content of dreams. In M. A. Carskadon (Ed.), *Encyclopedia of sleep and dreams.* New York: Macmillan.

van den Berg, J. H. (1971). What is psychotherapy? *Humanitas, 7*(3), 321–370.

Van Hasselt, V., Null, J., Kempton, T., & Buckstein, O. ((1993). Social skills and depression in adolescent substance abusers. *Addic. Behav., 18,* 9–18.

Van Praag, H. M. (1983). CSF 5-HIAA and suicide in non-depressed schizophrenics. *Lancet, ii,* 977–978.

Van Praag, H. M. (1983). In search of the action mechanism of antidepressants. 5-HTP/tyrosine mixtures in depression. *Neuropharmacol., 22,* 433–440.

Van-Gent, E. M., & Zwart, F. M. (1991). Psychoeducation of partners of bipolar-manic patients. *J. Affect. Dis., 21*(1), 15–18.

Vanderlinden, J. & Vandereycken, W. (1991). Guidelines for the family therapeutic approach to eating disorders. *Psychother. Psychosom., 56,* 36–42.

Varis, K. (1987). Psychosomatic factors in gastrointestinal disorders. *Ann. Clin. Res., 19*(2), 135–142.

Vatz, R., & Weinberg, L. (1993, January 10). Keno krazy? *Washington Post,* p. C5.

Vaughan, K., Doyle, M., McConaghy, N., Blaszcznski, A. (1992). The relationship between relative's expressed emotion and schizophrenic relapse: An Australian replication. *Soc. Psychiat. Psychiat. Epidemiol, 27*(1), 10–15.

Velamoor, V. R., Norman, R. M., Caroff, S. N., et al (1994). Progression of symptoms in neuroleptic malignant syndrome. *J. Nerv. Ment. Dis., 182,* 168–173.

Velleman, R., & Orford, J. (1993). The adult adjustment of offspring of parents with drinking problems. *Brit. J. Psychiat., 162,* 503–516.

Vellucci, S. V. (1989). Anxiety. In R. A. Webster & C. C. Jordan (Eds.), *Neurotransmitters, drugs and disease.* Oxford: Blackwell Scientific Publications.

Verfaellie, M., Cermak, L. S., Blackford, S. P., et al. (1990). Strategic and automatic priming of semantic memory in alcoholic Korsakoff patients. *Brain and Cognition, 13*(2), 178–192.

Vieira, C. (1993). Nudity in dreams. In M. A. Carskadon (Ed.), *Encyclopedia of Sleep and Dreams.* New York: Macmillan.

Viken R. J. (1992). Therapy evaluation: Using an absurd pseudotreatment to demonstrate research issues. *Teaching of Psychol., 19*(2), 108–110.

Vitousek, K., & Manke, F. (1994). Personality variables and disorders in anorexia nervosa and bulimia nervosa. *J. Abnorm. Psychol., 103*(1), 137–147.

Vogele, C., & Steptoe, A. (1993). Anger inhibition and family history as modulators of cardiovascular responses to mental stress in adolescent boys. *J. Psychosom. Res., 37*(5), 503–514.

Volkmar, F. R., Carter, A., Sparrow, S. S., & Cicchetti, D. V. (1993). Quantifying social development in autism. *J. Amer. Acad. Child Adol. Psychiat., 32*(3), 627–632.

Volpicelli, J., Alterman, A., Hayashida, M., & O'Brien, C. (1992). Naltrexone in the treatment of alcohol dependence. *Arch. Gen. Psychiat., 49,* 876–880.

Von Korff, M., Nestadt, G., Romanoski, A. et al. (1985). Prevalence of treated and untreated DSM-III schizophrenia. *J. Nerv. Ment. Dis., 173,* 577–581.

Vredenbrug, K., Flett, G. L., & Krames, L. (1993). Analogue versus clinical depression: A critical reappraisal. *Psychol. Bull., 113*(2), 327–344.

Wadden, T. A., & Anderton C. H. (1982). The clinical use of hypnosis. *Psychol. Bull., 91*(2), 215–243.

Wadden, T. A., Stunkard, A. J., & Liebschutz, J. (1988). Three-year follow-up of the treatment of obesity by very low calorie diet, behavior therapy, and their combination. *J. Cons. Clin. Psychol., 56*(6), 925–928.

Wagner, G., & Kaplan, H. S. (1993). *The new injection treatment for impotence.* New York: Brunner/Mazel.

Wahl, O. F., & Hunter, J. (1992). Are gender effects being neglected in schizophrenia research? *Schizo. Bull., 18*(2), 313–318.

Walker, E., & Young, T. D. (1986). *A killing cure.* New York: Henry Holt.

Walker, L. E. (1979). The battered woman. New York: Harper & Row.

Walker, L. E. (1984). Battered women, psychology, and public policy. *Amer. Psychol., 39*(10), 1178–1182.

Walker, L. E. (1984). *The battered woman syndrome.* New York: Springer.

Wallace, B. (1993). Cross-cultural counseling with the chemically dependent: Preparing for service delivery within a culture of violence. *J. Psychoact. Drugs, 25*(1), 9–12.

Wallen, J. (1992). A comparison of male and female clients in substance abuse treatment. *J. Subst. Abuse Treat., 9*(3), 243–248.

Walsh, J. (1990). Assessment and treatment of the schizotypal personality disorder. *J. Independ. Soc. Work, 4*(3), 41–59.

Walsh, J., & Engelhardt, C. L. (1993). Myths about dreaming. In M. A. Carskadon (Ed.), *Encyclopedia of sleep and dreams.* New York: Macmillan.

Wanck, B. (1984). Two decades of involuntary hospitalization legislation. *Amer. J. Psychiat., 41*, 33–38.

Ware, J. E., et al. (1984). Health and the use of outpatient mental health services. *Amer. Psychol., 39*(10), 1090–1100.

Warren, L. W., & Ostrom, J. C. (1988). Pack rats: World-class savers. *Psych. Today, 22*(2), 58–62.

Wartenberg, A. A., Nirenberg, T. D., Liepman, M. R., Silvia, L. Y. et al. (1990). Detoxification of alcoholics: Improving care by symptom-triggered sedation. *Alcoholism: Clin. Exp. Res., 14*(1), 71–75.

Washton, A. M. (1987). Cocaine: Drug epidemic of the 80's. In D. Allen (Ed.), *The cocaine crisis.* New York: Pergamon.

Washton, A. M., & Stone-Washton, N. (1990). Abstinence and relapse in outpatient cocaine addicts. *J. Psychoact. Drugs, 22*(2), 135–147.

Wasserman, I. M. (1992). The impact of epidemic, war, prohibition and media on suicide: United States, 1910–1920. *Suic. Life-Threat. Behav., 22*(2), 240–254.

Wasylenki, D. (1992). Psychotherapy of schizophrenia revisited. *Hosp. Comm. Psychiat., 43*(2), 123–128.

Waters, L. (1990). Reinforcing the empty fortress: An examination of recent research into the treatment of autism. *Educ. Stud., 16*(1), 3–16.

Watkins-Duncan, B. A. (1992). Principles for formulating treatment with Black patients. *Psychother., 29*(3), 452–457.

Watson, C. G. (1987). Recidivism in "controlled drinker" alcoholics: A longitudinal study. *J. Clin. Psychol., 43*(3), 404–412.

Watson, J. B. (1930). *Behaviorism* (Rev. ed.). Chicago: The University of Chicago Press.

Watson, J. B., & Rayner, R. (1920). Conditioned emotional reaction. *J. Exp. Psychol., 3*, 1–14.

Webster, R. L. (1991). Fluency enhancement in stutterers advances in self-regulation through sensory augmentation. In J. G. Carlson, & A. R. Seifert (Eds.), *International perspectives on self-regulation and health.* New York: Plenum.

Wechsler, H., Grosser, G. H., & Greenblatt, M. (1965). Research evaluating antidepressant medications on hospitalized mental patients: A survey of published reports during a five-year period. *J. Nerv. Ment. Dis., 141*, 231–239.

Wechsler, J. A. (1972). *In a darkness.* New York: Norton.

Wehmeyer, M. L. (1992). Self-determination and the education of students with mental retardation. *Educ. Training Ment. Retard., 27*(4), 302–314.

Weidman, A. A. (1985). Engaging the families or substance abusing adolescents in family therapy. *J. Substance Abuse Treatment, 2*(2), 97–105.

Weinberger, D. R. (1991). Schizophrenia (Forward to Section I). In A. Tasman & S. M. Goldfinger (Eds.), *American Psychiatric Press review of psychiatry* (Vol. 10). Washington, DC: American Psychiatric Press.

Weinberger, D. R., & Kleinman, J. E. (1986). Observations of the brain in schizophrenia. In A. J. Frances & R. E. Hales (Eds.), *Psychiatry update* (Vol. 5). Washington, DC: American Psychiatric Press.

Weiner, H., Thaler, M., Reiser, M. F., & Mirsky, I. A. (1957). Etiology of duodenal ulcer: I. Relation of specific psychological characteristics to rate of gastric secretion (serum pepsinogen). *Psychosom. Med., 19*, 1–10.

Weiner, R. D. (1984). Does electroconvulsive therapy cause brain damage? *Behav. Brain Sci., 7*, 1–54.

Weingartner, H., et al. (1984). Cognitive impairments in Parkinson's disease distinguishing between effort-demanding and automatic cognitive processes. *Psychiatry Res., 11*, 223–235.

Weir, R. F. (1992). The morality of physician-assisted suicide. *Law, Med., Hlth. Care, 20*(1-2), 116–126.

Weishaar, M. E., & Beck, A. T. (1992). Clinical and cognitive predictors of suicide. In R. W. Maris, A. L. Berman, J. T. Maltsberger, & R. I. Yufit (Eds.), *Assessment and prediction of suicide.* New York: Guilford.

Weisheit, R. A. (1990). Domestic marijuana growers: Mainstreaming deviance. *Deviant Behav., 11*(2), 107–129.

Weiss, D. E. (1991). *The great divide.* New York: Poseidon Press/Simon & Schuster.

Weiss, D. S., & Marmar, C. R. (1993). Teaching time-limited dynamic psychotherapy for post–traumatic stress disorder and pathological grief. *Psychotherapy.*

Weiss, D. S., Marmar, C. R., Schlenger, W. E., & Fairback, J. A., et al., (1992). The prevalence of lifetime and partial post–traumatic stress disorder in Vietnam theater veterans. *J. Traumatic Stress, 5*(3), 365–376.

Weiss, J. M. (1977). Ulcers. In J. D. Maser & M. E. P. Seligman (Eds.), *Psychopathology: Experimental models.* San Francisco: W. H. Freeman.

Weissman, M. M., Bruce, M. L., Leaf, P. J., Florio, L. P., & Holzer, C. (1991). Affective disorders. In L. N. Robins & D. A. Regier (Eds.), *Psychiatric disorders in America: The Epidemiologic Catchment Area Study.* New York: Free Press.

Weissman, M. M., Myeres, J. K., & Harding, P. S. (1978). Psychiatric disorders in a U. S. urban community. *Amer. J. Psychiat., 135*, 459–462.

Weissman, M. M., et al. (The cross-national collaborative group) (1992). The changing rate of major depression: Cross-national comparisons. *JAMA, 268*(21), 3098–3105.

Weizman, R., & Hart, J. (1987). Sexual behavior in healthy married elderly men. *Arch. Sex. Behav., 16*(1), 39–44.

Wells, M. E., & Hinkle, J. S. (1990). Elimination of childhood encopresis: A family systems approach. *J. Ment. Hlth. Couns., 12*(4), 520–526.

Wender, P. H., Kety, S. S., Rosenthal, D., Schulsinger, F., Ortmann, J., & Lunde, I. (1986). Psychiatric disorders in the biological and adoptive families of adopted and individuals with affective disorders. *Arch. Gen. Psychiat., 43*, 923–929.

Wertheim, E. H., & Poulakis, Z. (1992). The relationship among the General Attitude and Belief Scale, other dysfunctional cognition measures, and depressive of bulimic tendencies. *J. Rational Emot. Cog.-Behav. Ther., 10*(4), 219–233.

West, L. J. (1993). Reflections of the right to die. In A. A. Leenaars (Ed.), *Suicidology.* Northvale, NJ: Jason Aronson.

Westen, D. (1991). Cognitive-behavioral interventions in the psychoanalytic psychotherapy of borderline personality disorders. *Clin. Psychol. Rev., 11*(3), 211–230.

Weston, S. C., & Siever, L. J. (1993). Biological correlates of personality disorders. *J. Pers. Dis.,* Spring (Suppl.), 129–148.

Wettstein, R. M. (1988). Psychiatry and the law. In J. A. Talbotto, R. E. Hales & S. C. Yudofsky (Eds.), *American Psychiatric Press textbook of psychiatry.* Washington, DC: American Psychiatric Press.

Wexler, D. B. (1983). The structure of civil commitment. *Law & Human Behav., 7*, 1–18.

Weyerer, S., & Hafner, H. (1992). Epidemiologie psychischer Storungen [Epidemiology of mental disorders]. *Zeitschrift fur Klinische Psychologie, 21*(1), 106–120.

Whelan, J. P., & Houts, A. C. (1990). Effects of a waking schedule on primary enuretic children treated with full-spectrum home training. *Hlth. Psychol., 9*, 164–176.

Wherry, J. N., McMillan, S. L., & Hutchison, H. T. (1991). Differential diagnosis and treatment of conversion disorder and Guillain-Barre Syndrome. *Clin. Pediatrics, 30*(10), 578–585.

Whipple, E. E., Webster, S. C., & Stratton, C. (1991). The role of parental stress in physically abusive families. Child Abuse and Neglect: *Inter. J., 15*(3), 279.

White, B. J., & Madara, E. J. (Eds.), (1992). *The self-help sourcebook: Finding & forming mutual aid self-help groups.* Denville, NJ: St. Clares-Riverside Medical Center.

Whitehead, W. E. (1992). Biofeedback treatment of gastrointestinal disorders. *Biofeed. Self-Reg., 17*(1), 59–76.

Whitehorn, J. C., & Betz, B. J. (1975). *Effective psychotherapy with the schizophrenic patient.* New York: Jason Aronson.

Whiteside, M. (1983, Sep. 12). A bedeviling new hysteria. *Newsweek.*

Whiting, J. W. et al. (1966). *Six cultures series: I. Field guide for a study of socialization.* New York: Wiley.

Whittaker, S., & Bry, B. H. (1992). Overt and covert parental conflict and adolescent problems: Observed marital interaction in clinical and non-clinical families. *Fam. Ther., 19*(1), 43–54.

Widiger, T. A. (1992). Categorical versus dimensional classification: Implications from and for research. *J. Pers., Dis., 6*, 287–300.

Widiger, T. A. (1993). The DSM-III-R categorical personality disorder diagnoses: A critique and an alternative. *Psychological Inquiry, 4,* 75–90.

Widiger, T. A., Corbitt, E. M., & Millon, T. (1992). Antisocial personality disorder. In A. Tasman & M. B. Riba (Eds.), *American Psychiatric Press review of psychiatry* (Vol. 11). Washington, DC: American Psychiatric Press.

Widiger, T. A., & Costa, P. T. (1994). Personality and personality disorders. *J. Abnorm. Psychol., 103*(1), 78–91.

Widom, C. S. (1991, Feb.). Presentation. American Assoc. for the Advancement of Science.

Wiens, A. N. (1990). Structured clinical interviews for adults. In G. Goldstein & M. Hersen (Eds.), *Handbook of psychological assessment* (2nd ed.). New York: Pergamon.

Wierzbicki, M. & Pekarik, G. (1993). A meta-analysis of psychotherapy dropout. *Professional Psychology Research and Practice, 24*(2), 190–195.

Wilbur, C. B. (1984). Treatment of multiple personality. *Psychiat. Ann., 14,* 27–31.

Wilcox, J. A. (1990). Fluoxetine and bulimia. *J. Psychoact. Drugs, 22*(1), 81–82.

Wilfley, D. E., Agras, W. S., Telch, C. F., Rossiter, E. M., Schenider, J. A., Cole, A. G., Sifford, L., & Raeburn, S. D. (1993). Group cognitive-behavioral therapy and group interpersonal psychotherapy for the nonpurging bulimic individual: A controlled comparison. *J. Cons. Clin. Psychol., 61*(2), 296–305.

Williams, C. C. (1983). The mental foxhole: The Vietnam veterans' search for meaning. *Amer. J. Orthopsychiat., 53*(1), 4–17.

Williams, R. B., Barefoot, J. C., Califf, R. M., Haney, T. L., et al. (1992). Prognostic importance of social and economic resources among medically treated patients with angiographically documented coronary artery disease. *JAMA, 268*(19), 2652.

Williamson, D. A., Cubic, B. A., & Gleaves, D. H. (1993). Equivalence of body image disturbances in anorexia and bulimia nervosa. *J. Abnorm. Psychol., 102*(1), 177–180.

Willner, P. (1984). Cognitive functioning in depression: A review of theory and research. *Psychol. Med., 14*(4), 807–823.

Wilson, G. T. (1994). Behavioral treatment of obesity: Thirty years and counting. *Adv. Behav. Res. Therr, 16,* 31–75.

Wilson, G. T., & Fairburn, C. G. (1993). Cognitive treatments for eating disorders. *J. Cons. Clin. Psychol., 61*(2), 261–269.

Wilson, G. T., & Pike, K. M. (1993). Eating disorders. In D. H. Barlow (Ed.), *Clinical handbook of Psychological Disorders: A step-by-step treatment manual* (2nd ed.). New York: Guilford.

Wilson, G. T., Rossiter, E., Kleifield, E. I., & Lindholm, L. (1986). Cognitive-behavioral treatment of bulimia nervosa: A controlled evaluation. *Behav. Res. Ther., 24*(3), 277–288.

Wilson, W. M. (1992). The Stanford-Binet: Fourth edition and form L-M in assessment of young children with mental retardation. *Men. Retard., 30*(2), 81–84.

Wing, L. (1976). *Early childhood autism.* Oxford: Pergamon.

Wing, L., & Wing, J. K. (1971). Multiple impairments in early childhood autism. *J. Autism Child. Schizo., 1,* 256–266.

Winick, B. J. (1983). Incompetency to stand trial: Developments in the law. In J. Monahan & H. J. Steadman (Eds.), *Mentally disordered offenders.* New York: Plenum.

Winick, M., Meyer, K., & Harris, R. C. (1975). Malnutrition and environmental enrichment by early adoption. *Sci.,* 1173–1175.

Winokur, A. et al. (1980). Withdrawal reaction from long-term low-dosage administration of diazepam: A double-blind placebo-controlled case study. *Arch. Gen. Psych., 37*(1), 101–105.

Winslade, W. J. (1983). *The insanity plea.* New York: Scribner.

Winslade, W. J. (1988). Electroconvulsive therapy: Legal regulations and ethical concerns. In A. J. Frances & R. E. Hales (Eds.), *American Psychiatric Press review of psychiatry* (Vol. 7). Washington, DC: American Psychiatric Press.

Winslade, W. J., Liston, E. H., Ross, J. W., et al. (1984). Medical, judicial, and statutory regulation of ECT in the United States. *Amer. J. Psychiat., 141,* 1349–1355.

Winson, J. (1990, Nov.). The meaning of dreams. *Scientif. Amer.,* 86–96.

Winston, A., & Pollack, J. (1991). Brief adaptive psychotherapy. *Psychiat. Ann., 21*(7), 415–418.

Winters, K. C., Stinchfield, R., & Fulkerson, J. (1993). Patterns and characteristics of adolescent gambling. *J. Gamb. Stud., 9*(4), 371–386.

Wise, T. N., Fagan, P. J., Schmidt, C. W., Ponticas, Y., et al. (1991). Personality and sexual functioning of transvestitic fetishists and other paraphilics. *J. Nerv. Ment. Dis., 179*(1), 694–698.

Wiseman, C. V., Gray, J. J., Mosimann, J. E., & Ahrens, A. H. (1992). Cultural expectations of thinness in women: An update. *Inter. J. Eat. Dis., 11*(1), 85–89.

Witkin, M. J., Atay, J. E., Fell, A. S., & Manderscheid, R. W. (1990). Specialty mental health system characteristics. In R. W. Manderscheid & M. A. Sonnenschein (Eds.), *Mental health, United States* (DHHS Pub. No. ADM 90-1708). Washington, DC: GPO.

Wittchen, H. U., Essau, C., & vonZerssen, D. (1992). Lifetime and six-month prevalence of mental disorders in the Munich Follow-up Study. *Eur. Arch. Psychiat. Clin. Neurosci., 241*(4), 247–258.

Wittrock, D. A., & Blanchard, E. B. (1992). Thermal biofeedback treatment of mild hypertension: A comparison of effects on conventional and ambulatory blood pressure measures. *Behav. Mod., 16*(3), 283–304.

Wixted, J. T., Morrison, R. L., & Bellack, A. S. (1988). Social skills training in the treatment of negative symptoms [Special Issue]. *Inter. J. Ment. Hlth., 17*(1), 3–21.

Wlazlo, Z., Schroeder-Hartwig, K., Hand, I., Kaiser, G., & Munchau, N. (1990). Exposure in vivo vs. social skills training for social phobia: Long-term outcome and differential effects. *Behav. Res. Ther., 28,* 181–193.

Wolberg, L. R. (1967). *The technique of psychotherapy.* New York: Grune & Stratton.

Wolfe, D. A., Kaufman, D., Aragona, J., & Sandler, J. (1981). *The child management program for abusive parents.* Winter Park, FL: Anna.

Wolfe, S. M., Fugate, L., Hulstrand, E. P., Kamimoto, L. E. (1988). *Worst pills best pills: The older adult's guide to avoiding drug-induced death or illness.* Washington, DC: Public Citizen Health Research Group.

Wolff, S. (1991). Schizoid personality in childhood and adult life I: The vagaries of diagnostic labeling. *Brit. J. Psychiat., 159,* 615–620.

Wolpe, J. (1958). *Psychotherapy by reciprocal inhibition.* Stanford, CA: Stanford UP.

Wolpe, J. (1987). The promotion of scientific psychotherapy: A long voyage. In J. K. Zeig (Ed.), *The evolution of psychotherapy.* New York: Brunner/Mazel.

Wolpe, J. (1990). *The practice of behavior therapy* (4th ed.). Elmsford, NY: Pergamon.

Wood, D., Del Nuovo, A., Bucky, S. F., Schein, S. F., & Michalik, M. (1981). Psychodrama with an alcohol abuser population. *U. S. Navy Med., 72,* 22–30.

Woodbury, M. M., DeMaso, D. R., & Goldman, S. J. (1992). An integrated medical psychiatric approach to conversion symptoms in a four-year-old. *J. Amer. Acad. Child Adol. Psychiat., 31*(6), 1095–1097.

Woodruff, R. A., Goodwin, D. W., & Guze, S. B. (1973). *Psychiatric diagnosis.* New York: Oxford UP.

Woodside, M. R., & Legg, B. H. (1990). Patient advocacy: A mental health perspective. *J. Ment. Hlth. Couns., 12*(1), 38–50.

Woodward, B., Duckworth, K. S., & Gutheil, T. G. (1993). The pharmacotherapist-psychotherapist collaboration. In J. M. Oldham, M. B. Riba, & A. Tasman (Eds.), *Review of psychiatry* (Vol. 12). Washington, DC: American Psychiatric Press.

Woody, R. H., & Robertson, M. (1988). *Becoming a clinical psychologist.* Madison, CT: International Universities Press.

Wooley, S. C., & Wooley, O. W. (1979). Obesity and women—I. A closer look at the facts. *Women's Stud. Inter. Quart., 2,* 67–79.

Wooley, S. C., & Wooley, O. W. (1982). The Beverly Hills eating disorder: The mass marketing of anorexia nervosa. *Inter. J. Eat. Dis., 1,* 57–69.

Wooley, S. C., & Wooley, O. W. (1985). Intensive outpatient and residential treatment for bulimia. In D. M. Garner & P. E. Garfinkel (Eds.), *Handbook of psychotherapy for anorexia nervosa and bulimia.* New York: Guilford.

Woolfolk, R. L., Carr-Kaffashan, L., McNulty, T. F., & Lehrer, P. M. (1976). Meditation training as a treatment for insomnia. *Behav. Ther. 7*(3), 359–365.

Workman, E. A., & Short, D. D. (1993). Atypical antidepressants versus imipramine in the treatment of major depression: A meta-analysis. *J. Clin. Psychiat., 54*(1), 5–12.

World Health Organization (WHO). (1988, July 1). *Correlates of youth suicide.* Geneva: World Health Organization, Division of Mental Health.

Worth, D. (1991). A service delivery system model for AIDS prevention for women. In *National Conference on Drug Abuse Research and Practice Conference Highlights.* Rockville, MD: National Institute on Drug Abuse.

Wright, L. S. (1985). High school polydrug users and abusers. *Adolescence, 20*(80), 852–861.

Wright, L. S. (1985). Suicidal thoughts and their relationship to family stress and personal problems among high school seniors and college undergraduates. *Adolescence, 20*(79), 575–580.

Wulsin, L., Bachop, M., & Hoffman, D. (1988). Group therapy in manic-depressive illness. *Amer. J. Psychother., 42,* 263–271.

Wurtman, J. J., & Wurtman, R. J. (1982). Studies on the appetite for carbohydrates in rates and humans. *J. Psychiat. Res., 17*(2), 213–221.

Wurtman, R. J. (1983). Behavioural effects of nutrients. *Lancet, i,* 1145–1147.

Wurtman, R. J., & Wurtman, J. J. (1984). Nutritional control of central neurotransmitters. In K. M. Pirke & D. Ploog (Eds.), *The psychobiology of anorexia nervosa*. Berlin: Springer-Verlag.

Yabe, K., Tsukahar, R., Mita, K., & Aoki, H. (1985). Developmental trends of jumping reaction time by means of EMG in mentally retarded children. *J. Ment. Def. Res., 29*(2), 137–145.

Yager, J. (1985). The outpatient treatment of bulimia. *Bull. Menninger Clin., 49*(3), 203–226.

Yager, J., Rorty, M., & Rossotto, E. (1995). Coping styles differ between recovered and nonrecovered women with bulimia nervosa, but not between recovered women and non-eating disordered control subjects. *J. Nerv. Ment. Dis., 183*(2), 86–94.

Yalom, I. D. (1985). *The theory and practice of group psychotherapy* (3rd ed.). New York: Basic Books.

Yama, M., Fogas, B., Teegarden, L., & Hastings. B. (1993). Childhood sexual abuse and parental alcoholism: Interactive effects in adult women. *Amer. J. Orthopsychiat., 63*(2), 300–305.

Yang, B., Stack, S., & Lester, D. (1992). Suicide and unemployment: Predicting the smoothed trend and yearly fluctuations. *J. Socioec., 21*(1), 39–41.

Yank, G. R., Bentley, K. J., & Hargrove, D. S. (1993). The vulnerability-stress model of schizophrenia: Advances in psychosocial treatment. *Amer. J. Orthopsychiat., 63*(1), 55–69.

Yap, P. M. (1951). Mental diseases peculiar to certain cultures: a survey of comparative psychiatry. *J. Ment. Sci., 97*, 313–327.

Yates, A. (1989). Current perspectives of the eating disorders: I. History, psychological and biological aspects. *J. Amer. Acad. Child Adol. Psychiat., 28*(6), 813–828.

Yazici, O., Aricioglu, F., Gurvit, G., Ucok, A., Tastaban, Y., Canberk, O., Ozguroglu, M., Durat, T., Sahin, D. (1993). Noradrenergic and serotoninergic depression? *J. Affect. Dis., 27*, 123–129.

Yontef, G. M., & Simkin, J. F. (1989). Gestalt therapy. In R. J. Corsini & D. Wedding (Eds.), *Current psychotherapies*. Itasca, IL: Peacock.

Young, A. M., & Herling, S. (1986). Drugs as reinforcers: Studies in laboratory animals. In S. R. Goldberg & I. P. Stolerman (Eds.), *Behavioral analysis of drug dependence*. Orlando, FL: Academic Press.

Young, G. A. (1994). Asthma: Medical issues. In R. A. Olson, L. L. Mullins, J. B. Gillman, & J. M. Chaney (Eds.), *The sourcebook of pediatric psychology*. Boston: Allyn and Bacon. Wilbur, C. B. (1984). Treatment of multiple personality. *Psychiat. Ann., 14*, 27–31.

Young, J. E., Beck, A. T., & Weinberger, A. (1993). Depression. In D. H. Barlow (Ed.), *Clinical handbook of psychological disorders: A step-by-step treatment manual* (2nd ed.). New York: Guilford.

Young, T. J. (1991). Suicide and homicide among Native Americans: Anomie or social learning? *Psych. Rep., 68*(3, Pt. 2), 1137–1138.

Youngstrom, N. (1992). Grim news from national study of rape. *APA Monitor, 23*(7), p.38.

Youngstrom, N. (1992). Psychology helps a shattered L.A. *APA Monitor, 23*(7), p. 1, 12.

Yudofsky, S., Silver, J., & Hales, R. (1993). Cocaine and aggressive behavior:

Neurobiological and clinical perspectives. *Bull. Menninger Clin., 57*(2), 218–226.

Yuwiler, A., Shih, J. C., Chen, C., Ritvo, E. R. (1992). Hyperserotoninemia and antiserotonin antibodies in autism and other disorders. *J. Autism Dev. Dis., 22*(1), 33–45.

Zastowny, T. R., Lehman, A. F., Cole, R. E., & Kane C. (1992). Family management of schizophrenia: A comparison of behavioral and supportive family treatment. *Psychiat. Quart., 63*(2), 159–186.

Zax, M., & Cowen, E. L. (1969). Research on early detection and prevention of emotional dysfunction in young school children. In C. D. Speilberger (Ed.), *Current topics in clinical and community psychology* (Vol. 1). New York: Academic.

Zax, M., & Cowen, E. L. (1976). *Abnormal psychology: Changing conceptions*. New York: Holt, Rinehart & Winston.

Zerbe, K. J. (1990). Through the storm: Psychoanalytic theory in the psychotherapy of the anxiety disorders. *Bull. Menninger Clin., 54*(2), 171–183.

Zerbe, K. J. (1993). Selves that starve and suffocate: The continuum of eating disorders and dissociative phenomena. *Bull. Menninger Clin., 57*(3), 319–327.

Zerbe, K. J. (1993). Whose body is it anyway? Understanding and treating psychosomatic aspects of eating disorders. *Bull. Menninger Clin., 57*(2), 161–177.

Zetin, M. (1990). Obsessive-compulsive disorder. *Stress Med., 6*(4), 311–321.

Zettle, R. D., Haflich, J. L., & Reynolds, R. A. (1992). Responsivity of cognitive therapy as a function of treatment format and client personality dimensions. *J. Clin. Psychol., 48*(6), 787–797.

Zigler, E., & Hodapp, R. M. (1991). Behavioral functioning in individuals with mental retardation. *Annu. Rev. Psychol., 42*, 29–50.

Zigler, E., Taussig, C., & Black, K. (1992). Early childhood intervention: A promising preventative for juvenile delinquency. *Amer. Psychol., 47*(8), 997–1006.

Zilbergeld, B. (1978). Male sexuality. Boston: Little, Brown.

Zilboorg, G., & Henry, G. W. (1941). *A history of medical psychology*. New York: Norton.

Zill, N., & Schoenborn, C. A. (1990, November). *Developmental, learning, and emotional problems: Health of our nation's children, United States, 1988*. Advance Data: National Center for Health Statistics, Number 190.

Zimmerman, M. (1994). Diagnosing personality disorders: A review of issues and research methods. *Arch. Gen. Psychiat., 51*, 225–245.

Zimmerman, M., & Coryell, W. (1989). DSM-III personality disorder diagnoses in a nonpatient sample: Demographic correlates and comorbidity. *Arch. Gen. Psychiat., 46*(8), 682–689.

Zuckerman, M. (1978). Sensation seeking and psychopathy. In R. D. Hare & D. Schalling (Eds.), *Psychopathic behavior: Approaches to research*. New York: Wiley.

Zuger, A. (1993, July). The Baron strikes again. *Discover*, pp. 28–30.

# Photo Credits

CHAPTER 1, 1: Scala/Art Resource, NY; 3: Carol Beckwith; 4: Catherine Allemand/Gamma-Liason; 5: *Ripley's Believe it or not!*, © 1994 Ripley Entertainment Inc., Registered Trademark of Ripley Entertainment Inc., 6: John W. Verano; 7: Zentralbibliothek, Zurich; 8: Bettmann Archives; 10ul: Girolamo Di Benvenuto, *St. Catherine Exorcising a Possessed Woman* (15th c.), Denver Art Museum, Kress Collection; 10br: NYPL Rare Book Room; 11ur: Sir John Soanne's Museum, London; 11br: The Library Company of Philadelphia; 13: National Library of Medicine; 15: Bettmann Archives; 19: Jerry Cooke/Photo Researchers; 19: Rhoda M. Karp; CHAPTER 2, 31: Will & Deni McIntyre/Science Source/Photo Researchers; 33: Gary Larson, Chronicle Features; 38: Reprinted by permission of the publishers from Henry A. Murray, *Thematic Apperception Test*, Cambridge, Mass.: Harvard University Press, © 1943 by the President and Fellows of Harvard College, © 1971 by Henry A. Murray; 39: Rick Friedman/Black Star; 43bl: Joe McNally/Sygma; 43ur: Hans Breiter, Mark S. Cohen, Bruce Rosen, University of California, Los Angeles; 45: Travis Amos; 46: Louis Wain; 47: Fogg Art Museum, Harvard University; 52: © 1984 by Doug Milman and Gerald Mayerhofer, *Are You Normal*, New York: Quill; 55: Jim Wilson/Woodfin Camp & Associates; 58: Ruth Westheimer; CHAPTER 3, 62: *The Quiet Room*, Oskar Schlemmer, 1926; 67: Laura Dwight; 68: Mary Evans Picture Library/Sigmund Freud Copyrights; 70: Catherine Karnow/Woodfin Camp & Associates; 72: Ursula Edelmann, Frankfurt; 77: Joseph Wolpe; 79: The National Broadcasting Company, Inc.; 80: Grant Wood, American, 1891–1942, *American Gothic,* oil on beaver board, 1930, 76 × 63.3 cm, Friends of American Art Collection, 1930.934. photograph © 1994, The Art Institute of Chicago. All Rights Reserved; 81: Albert Bandura; 82: Gary Larson, Universal Press Syndicate; 83: Leif Skoogfors/Woodfin Camp & Associates; 87: Joel Gordon; 89: Leif Skoogfors/Woodfin Camp & Associates; 90: Jimi Lott, *Spokane* (Wash.) *Review & Chronicle*; 92: Jánod Kalmár; CHAPTER 4, 96: Nancy Kedersha/Immunogen; 98: From Zola Morgan et al., 1986; 99: Centre National de Recherches Iconographiques; 100: Washington University School of Medicine; 102: Ohio Historical Society; 103: James D. Wilson; 107: Peter Turnley/Black Star; 108: Alon Reininger/Woodfin Camp & Associates; 110: Marc Geller; 113bl: Liz Mangelsdorf/*San Francisco Examiner;* 116: Carol Guzy/*Washington Post;* CHAPTER 5, 121: *Voice II,* George Tooker, 1970. National Academy of Design, NY; 123: Tom Sanders/Photri; 126: Museum of Modern Art Film Stills Archive; 129: Callahan; 130: RUBES by Leigh Rubin by permission of Leigh Rubin and Creators Syndicate; 131: Kobal Collection; 133: Julie Newdoll, Computer Graphics Laboratory, UCSF. © Regents University of California; 135: © 1991, *Newsweek*, Inc. All rights reserved. Reprinted by permission. (Artist: Coco Masuda); 136: Dan McCoy/Rainbow; 139: George Tooker, *The Subway*, 1950, Whitney Museum of American Art, Juliana Force Purchase 50.23.; 143: Museum of Modern Art Film Stills Archive; 144: USAir; 146: Andrew Sacks/Black Star; CHAPTER 6, 151: Henri Matisse. Girandon/Art Resource, NY; 156: Nick Didlick/Reuters—Bettmann Archives; 159: Gary Larson, Universal Press Syndicate; 161: Smithsonian Institution/National Air and Space Museum; 168: Christopher Morris/Black Star; 170: National Archives; 171: Alain Keler/Sygma; 174: J. P. Laffont/Sygma; CHAPTER 7, 178: Paul Dance/Tony Stone Images; 179: George P. A. Healy, 1887, The National Portrait Gallery, Smithsonian Institution; 181: Manfred Kreiner/Black Star; 182: Edvard Munch, *Melancholia, Laura,* 1899, Oslo kommunes kunstsamlinger Munch-Museet; 184: The Dorthea Lange Collection, Oakland Museum; 186: Homer Sykes/Woodfin Camp & Associates; 187: Harlow Primate Laboratory, University of Wisconsin; 193: PEANUTS by Charles Schulz, © 1956 United Features Syndicate, Inc.; 195: Chuck Fishman/Woodfin Camp & Associates; 197: Will McIntyre/Photo Researchers; 201: Gerd Ludwig/Woodfin Camp & Associates; 202: Travis Amos; 205: Lilly Library; 208: A. Knudsen/Sygma; CHAPTER 8, 212: Boehringer Ingelheim International GmbH, photo Lennart Nilsson, *The Body Victorious,* Dell Publishing; 219: Mary Evans Picture Library/Sigmund Freud Copyrights; 222: J. James, Science

Photo Library/Photo Researchers; 223: Lester Sloan/Woodfin Camp & Associates; 225: Lionel Cihes/Associated Press; 228: Boehringer Ingelheim International GmbH, photo Lennart Nilsson; 232: Ted Spiegel/Black Star; 233: Louis Psihoyos/Matrix; 234: Sidney Harris; 236: Ted Spagna; 238: Frank Fournier/Woodfin Camp & Associates; CHAPTER 9, 240: *Two Figures,* John Carroll, 1929. Collection of the Newark Museum. Gift of Mr. and Mrs. Lesley G. Sheafer, 1954; 245: Joseph LoPiccolo; 250: Catherine Karnow/Woodfin Camp & Associates; 251: Gilbert Dupuy/Black Star; 252: The Kobal Collection; 257: Peter Yates/Picture Group; 260: Joel Gordon; 261: The Bettmann Archive; 262: Marc Geller; CHAPTER 10, 267: Oscar Burriel/Latin Stock/ Science Source/Photo Researchers; 268: B. Schiffman/Gamma-Liaison; 270: Wallace Kirkland/*Life,* © Time Warner Inc.; 271: David Garner; 274: James Wilson/Woodfin Camp & Associates; 276: Pierre August Renoir, *Seated Bather,* 1903–1906, Detroit Institute of the Arts bequest of Robert H. Tannahill; 276: Donna Terek, Michigan Magazine (*The Detroit News/Free Press);* 279: Historical Research Center, Houston Academy of Medicine, Texas Medical Center Library; 282: Richard Howard, © 1991 *Discover;* 284: Patt Blue; 287: Michelle Bogre; CHAPTER 11, 290: *Das Schweigen,* Heinrich Füssli, 1799–1802. Kunsthaus, Zurich; 292: National Cancer Society; 297: John Chiasson/Gamma-Liaison; 299: Tony O'Brian/Picture Group; 300: Bettmann Archives; 304: Charlie Steiner/JB Pictures; 305: E.T. Archives; 308: Vaughan Fleming/Science Photo Library/Photo Researchers; 310l: Richard E. Aaron/Sygma; 310r: Stephen Ellison/Shooting Star; 312: James Aronovski/Picture Group; 313: George Steinmetz; 316: Steve Raymer/National Geographic Society; 320: Phil Huber/Black Star; CHAPTER 12, 321: Joly/Publiphoto; 322: Grant Haller, *Seattle Post Intelligencer*/Sygma; 324: Pressenbild/Adventure Photo; 327: Ralf-Finn Hestoft/SABA; 330: Steve Nickerson/Black Star; 332: Karsh/Woodfin Camp & Associates; 335: John Kaplan/Media Alliance; 337: H. Yamaguchi/Gamma-Liaison; 339: Lawrence Migdale; 340: Greg Smith/SABA; CHAPTER 13, 343: Prinzehorn Collection, Heidelberg; 346: David Graham/Black Star; 348: NYPL Performing Arts Research Center; 349: Oskar Diethelm Historical Library, Cornell Medical College, New York Hospital; 350: Antoine Wiertz, *Hunger, Madness, Crime,* 1864, Royal Museum, Belgium; 353: Kobal Collection; 355: Courtesy of the artist, Gerald Scarfe and Tin Blue Ltd.; 357: Julie Newdoll, Computer Graphics Laboratory, UCSF. © Regents University of California; 359: National Institute of Mental Health; 360l: Francisco Jose de Goya, *The Madhouse,* Prado, Madrid/Art Resource New York; 360r: Museum of Modern Art Film Stills Archive; 362: Bettmann Archives; 364: Museum of Modern Art Film Stills Archive; 365: Lynn Johnson/Black Star; 369: Christopher Morris/Black Star; 369: Christopher Morris/Black Star; 370: Andrew Savulich/New York Times Pictures; 372: Andrew Holbrooke/Black Star; CHAPTER 14, 376: *Schlemihl in the Loneliness of His Room,* Ernst Kirchner, 1915. Ingeborg & Dr. Wolfgang Henze-Ketterer, Wichtrach/Bern; 379: Associated Press/Wide World Photos; 382: Kobal Collection; 383: *People,* © 1989 Debra Lex; 385: Thorensen; 387: Ernest Hilgard, Stanford University; 393: Richard Falco/Black Star; 394: Christopher Little/Outline; CHAPTER 15, 399: *Pavois d'Oreilles,* Jean Dubuffet, 1961. Victoria & Albert Museum, London/Art Resource, NY; 402: Arthur Pollock, *Boston Herald; 403:* Janet Kelly/*Eagle-Times,* Reading, Pennsylvania; 404: Paul Chesley/Tony Stone Worldwide; 405: April Saul, *The Philadelphia Inquirer;* 406: Michael Amendolia/*The News Limited,* Sydney; 408: Michael Heron/ Woodfin Camp & Associates; 413l: Susan Young; 413r: *Newsweek,* E. Lee White; 416: Frank Varney; 417: Photofest; 418: Joel Gordon; 423: Lloyd Fox, *The Philadelphia Inquirer;* 424: B. Leonard Holman and Thomas C. Hill, Harvard Medical School; 427: Lynn Johnson/Black Star; CHAPTER 16, 431: Jurgen Reisch/Tony Stone Images; 436: Joel Gordon; 437: Kobal Collection; 441: Michael S. Yamashita/Woodfin Camp & Associates; 442: Associated Press/Wide World Photos; 443: Rob Nelson/Black Star; 443: Sipa Press; 446: Kobal Collection; 449: GARFIELD, Jim Davis © 1985 United Features Syndicate, Inc.; 452:

# Name Index

# Subject Index